Ethiopia

PUBLISHER'S FOREWORD

When people ask me which is my favourite Bradt guide, I answer unhesitatingly: *Ethiopia* by Philip Briggs. Even if they don't ask I tell them, because this is an exceptional book. It receives more fan letters than any other, and one reader who was robbed of the contents of his tent spent two adventurous days retrieving the only possession he couldn't manage without – Philip's guide. Here are some extracts from recent letters:

> 'Briggs's travel guide for Ethiopia is absolutely fantastic and indispensable. I am currently a volunteer living in Ethiopia and it truly has been as important as my lariam and sunscreen.'

> 'I have just returned from Ethiopia where your book proved invaluable; God knows what I should have done without it…'

> 'Honestly, I've hardly ever enjoyed reading a guidebook as much as this time. Usually, guidebooks don't have all this useful and detailed information for individual travellers.'

> 'Your guide…was a real pleasure for me. Not many travel guides are so very readable.'

> 'I greatly enjoyed reading your book, which you have written in a personal style which reflects your great liking for the country and its people. Congratulations!'

And finally, another robbery…

> 'I left the safety of my overland tour in Kenya to travel Ethiopia independently in April 2004. I found myself being shot at by bandits with AK47s in northern Kenya about 50km south of the border with Ethiopia. We were treated OK but all I was left with was the clothes I was wearing and my invaluable Bradt guide to Ethiopia. Due to my determination not to let the bandits win I then spent seven weeks travelling around Ethiopia. Your guide is the best I have used as it really does tell you how to get from tiny villages, to ancient sites, to cities, and to meet the ordinary people. Despite such a stressful start to my adventure, and the difficulties with bus travel in Ethiopia, I will never forget what wonderful people Ethiopians are. Without your guide I would have turned back.'

Hilary Bradt

23 High Street, Chalfont St Peter, Bucks SL9 9QE, England
☏ 01753 893444 f 01753 892333
e info@bradtguides.com www.bradtguides.com

Ethiopia

THE BRADT TRAVEL GUIDE

Fourth Edition

Philip Briggs

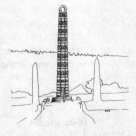

Bradt Travel Guides Ltd, UK
The Globe Pequot Press Inc, USA

Fourth edition October 2005
First published 1995

Bradt Travel Guides Ltd
23 High Street, Chalfont St Peter, Bucks SL9 9QE, England
www.bradtguides.com
Published in the USA by The Globe Pequot Press Inc, 246 Goose Lane,
PO Box 480, Guilford, Connecticut 06437-0480

British Library Cataloguing in Publication Data
A catalogue record for this book is available from the British Library

ISBN-10: 1 84162 128 5
ISBN-13: 978 1 84162 128 9

Photographs
Front cover: Oromo girl, Harar (Ariadne Van Zandbergen)
Text: Ariadne Van Zandbergen (AVZ), James Calder (JC)

Illustrations Roger Barnes, Annabel Milne, Mike Unwin,
Carole Vincer
Maps Alan Whitaker

Typeset from the author's disc by Wakewing, High Wycombe
Printed and bound in Italy by Legoprint SpA, Lavis (TN)

Author

Philip Briggs (philari@hixnet.co.za) is a travel writer and tour leader specialising in east and southern Africa. Born in Britain and raised in South Africa, Philip started travelling in east Africa in 1986 and has since spent half of his time exploring the highways and back roads of the subcontinent. In 1991, Bradt published his first book *Guide to South Africa* and he has since authored or co-authored Bradt guidebooks to Tanzania, Uganda, Rwanda, Ethiopia, Malawi, Mozambique, Ghana and east & southern Africa. He has also contributed to guidebooks published by the AA and Insight Discovery, and writes regularly for several leading British and South African periodicals.

CONTRIBUTORS
John Graham, whose lively writings about Ethiopia for the *Addis Tribune* form the basis of several boxes in this guide, grew up in Canada and obtained his BA in African History at the University of Calgary. Since volunteering with OXFAM for the 1984 famine in Ethiopia, John has lived in and visited much of Africa working with OXFAM and Save the Children. A resident of Ethiopia since 1997, he has travelled throughout the country, and regularly contributes travel articles to the *Addis Tribune* and *Entrepreneur* newspapers and the Ethiopian Airlines' magazine *Selamta*. His first book of travel essays, *Ethiopia Off the Beaten Trail*, has recently been published by Shama Books.

Ariadne Van Zandbergen (ariadne@hixnet.co.za, www.africaimagelibrary.co.za) is the main photographic contributor to this book, and she also supplied all update information for sections on the Simien Mountains, Arba Minch, the Konso Highlands, South Omo, and the Danakil Desert. A freelance photographer and tour guide, Ariadne was born and raised in Belgium, before travelling through Africa from Morocco to South Africa in 1994–95. Now married to Philip Briggs and resident in South Africa, she has visited more than 25 African countries and her photographs have appeared in numerous books, maps, periodicals and pamphlets. Her first photographic book *Africa: Continent of Contrasts*, a collaboration with Philip Briggs and photographer Martin Harvey, was published in 2005.

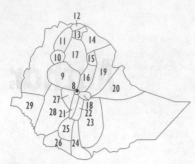

Contents

LIST OF MAPS

For key to map symbols see page 136.

Acknowledgements

As ever, I'm indebted to my wife Ariadne Van Zandbergen for her company and support in Ethiopia and at home, as well as for collecting update material for several key parts of Ethiopia, and to Tricia Hayne of Bradt Travel Guides for her immense support in preparing this fourth edition.

Both Ariadne and I would like to express our warmest gratitude to the following for co-operation and assistance in getting us to and around Ethiopia to research this fourth edition: Sisay Getachew of the Ethiopian Tourist Commission; Blen Dessalegn and Tesfaye Wolde Maryam of Ethiopian Airlines; Yared Belete and Birhan Abesha of Grant Express Tours & Travel Services; Mekonnen Mengasha and Hassan Abduiwassie of Galaxy Express Travel; Heidi Normann & Bisrat Weldu of Ethio Travel & Tours; Dario Morello of Greenland Tours; Tewodros Getnet of Sterling Travel & Tours; Mizan Kassa of Wabe Shebelle Hotels; Dawit Mulugeta and the staff of the Plaza Hotel in Addis Ababa and Tewebe Fanta of Lal Hotels.

Others who contributed important information include Tony Hickey of Village Ethiopia, Susan & Nassos Russous of ERVS, Stuart Williams of the Protected Areas Project, Yirmid Demeke of the Institute of Biodiversity Conservation, Nesru Shikur and Frank Riskin in Addis Ababa, Haile Selassie Berhe in Axum, Tesfaye Mekonnen in Gorgora, Habte Yitbare in Lalibela, Tewodros Firew in Bahir Dar, Fasil Mesfin of Galaxy Express in Gonder, and the tourist offices in Dilla, Mekele, Assaita and Harar.

Continued thanks to Commissioner of Tourism Yusuf Abdullahi Sukkar for advice and help in obtaining maps for the previous edition; to the late Dr Stuart Munro-Hay for historical corrections; to Nelson Jonnes for permission to use his plan of the churches at Lalibela as a source; to Dr Richard Pankhurst and Dr Alula Pankhurst for permission to extract relevant material from their published writings; to Jan Vermeulen for permission to extract birding information from his online trip report; and to the prolific John Graham and Shama Publishers for permission to base boxes about several aspects of Ethiopia on John's writing.

Finally, I'm immensely grateful to the many readers of the third edition who wrote in with useful tips and information, and whose diverse experiences and opinions have helped shape this fourth edition. Thanks to you all: Marjan Dik, Sally Still, Mary Kakefuda, Margery Nzerem, Yvonne Stokman, Dirk Singer, Dawit Shifaw, Annie De Ruyck, Anna Hammernik, Gilly Prentis, Steve Rooke, Jan Tromp, Laurent Fobe, John Ellis, Tesfayesus Yimenu, Nora Wakim, Jenny Gold, Teresa Levonian Cole, Frank Riskin, Sandip Patel, Hisako Tajima, Wendy Flanagan, Kevin McBriarty, Sally Von Holdt, Petrus Trottestam, Wouter Prakken, Owen Barder, Grethe Petersen, Bert Reubens, Dan Reece, Lukasz Mazur, Juliet Martinez, Philippe Moseley, Chris Husbands and Giulio Cibrario.

Introduction

My first contact with things Ethiopian came by chance, when a friend suggested a meal at a Nairobi restaurant run by Ethiopian refugees. The food alone was extraordinary – a delicious fiery orange stew called *kai wat*, splattered on what looked like a piece of foam rubber with the lateral dimensions of a bicycle tyre, and was apparently called *injera* – but even that didn't prepare me for what was to follow.

A troupe of white-robed musicians approached our table and erupted into smirking discord. Then, signalled by an alarming vibrato shriek, all hell burst loose in the form of a solitary Ethiopian dancer. Her mouth was contorted into the sort of psychotically rapturous grimace you'd expect from Jack Nicholson at his most hammy. Her eyes glowed. Her shoulders jerked and twitched to build up a manic, dislocating rhythm. Beneath her robe – driven, presumably, by her metronomic shoulders – a pair of diminutive breasts somehow contrived to flap up and down with an agitated regularity suggestive of a sparrow trapped behind a closed window. I left that room with one overwhelming impression: Ethiopians are completely bonkers. I knew, too, that I had to visit their country.

A year later, back in July 1994, I found myself flying to Addis Ababa to research the first edition of this guide. In the months that followed, I discovered Ethiopia to be every bit as fantastic as I had hoped: culturally, historically and scenically, it is the most extraordinary country I have ever visited. And since returning home, infatuated to the point of obsession, I have discovered that it is impossible to talk about Ethiopia without first saying what it is not. Ethiopia has become practically synonymous with famine and desert, to the extent that the sales manager of Ethiopian Airlines' Johannesburg office regularly receives tactful enquiries about what, if any, food is served on their flights.

That, in a continent plagued by drought and erratic rainfall, one particular famine has left the world with the misconception that Ethiopia is nothing but a desert says much about the workings of the mass media. It says rather less about Ethiopia.

Contrary to Western myth, the elevated central plateau that covers half of Ethiopia's surface area, and supports the vast majority of its population, is quite possibly the most extensive contiguous area of fertile land in the eastern side of Africa. The deserts do exist, stretching from the base of the plateau to the Kenyan border and the Red Sea and Somali coast, but they are, as you might expect, thinly populated; they have little impact on the life of most Ethiopians – and they are most unlikely to be visited by tourists. To all intents and purposes, the fertile highland plateau is Ethiopia.

Ethiopia's fledgling tourist industry revolves around the richest historical heritage in sub-Saharan Africa. The town of Axum was, from the 1st to 7th centuries AD, the centre of an empire which stretched from the Nile River across the Red Sea to Yemen. The medieval capital of Lalibela boasts a cluster of monolithic rock-hewn churches regarded by many as the unofficial eighth wonder of the world. There is also Gonder, the site of five 17th-century castles built by King Fasil and his successors. And all around the country are little-visited monasteries and rock-hewn churches, many of them over 1,000 years old and still in active use.

Historical sites are the focal point of tourism in Ethiopia, but they threaten at times to be swamped by the breathtaking scenery. Every bus trip in the Ethiopian Highlands is a visual treat, whether you are snaking into the 1km-deep Blue Nile Gorge, rolling past the sculpted sandstone cliffs and valleys of Tigrai, undulating over the grassy moorland and cultivated fields of the central highlands, winding through the lush forests of the west and south, or belting across the Rift Valley floor, its acacia scrub dotted by extinct volcanoes, crumbling lava flows and beautiful lakes, and hemmed in by the sheer walls of the Rift Escarpment. Mere words cannot do justice to Ethiopia's scenery.

Isolated from similar habitats by the fringing deserts, the Ethiopian Highlands have a remarkably high level of biological endemicity. Large mammals such as the Simien fox, mountain nyala, Walia ibex and gelada baboon are found nowhere but the highlands, as are 30 of the 800-plus species of birds which have been recorded in the country. This makes national parks like Bale and Simien a paradise for natural history enthusiasts, as well as for the hikers and mule trekkers who visit them for their scenery. Over a period of time, Ethiopia's recognised tourist attractions become incidental to the thrill of just being in this most extraordinary country. The people of the highlands have assimilated a variety of African, Judaic and even Egyptian influences to form one of the most unusual and self-contained cultures on this planet. Dervla Murphy said in 1968 that 'travelling in Ethiopia gives one the Orlando-like illusion of living through different centuries'. This remains the case: the independence of spirit which made Ethiopia the one country to emerge uncolonised from the 19th-century scramble for Africa is still its most compelling attraction; even today, there is a sense of otherness to Ethiopia that is as intoxicating as it is elusive. Practically every tangible facet of Ethiopian culture is unique. Obscured by the media-refracted glare of the surrounding deserts, Ethiopia feels like the archetypal forgotten land.

Ethiopia confounds every expectation. You arrive expecting a vast featureless desert and instead find yourself overwhelmed by majestic landscapes and climatic abundance. You expect a land ravaged to the point of ruin by years of civil war, and instead you find close to the best civil amenities in Africa and almost no obvious signs that a war ever took place. You arrive expecting to see human degradation and abject poverty, and instead find yourself immersed in a culture besotted with itself and its history, and marked by a sense of unforced pride that is positively infectious.

Ethiopia is a true revelation. It is the most welcoming, enjoyable and uplifting country I have ever visited. For independent travellers, the combination of good, inexpensive facilities and practically limitless opportunities for off-the-beaten-track diversions makes Ethiopia among the most rewarding and attractive countries in Africa. When the world taps its feet, Ethiopia, I suspect, will always breakdance with its shoulders.

And, in case you're wondering, there's really no need to pack sandwiches for the flight.

TRANSCRIPTION OF ETHIOPIAN NAMES

Ethiopians use a unique script to transcribe Amharigna and several other languages. This has led to a wide divergence in English transcriptions of Ethiopian place names and other Amharigna words, and also inconsistent use of double characters. Even a straightforward place name like Matu is spelt variously as Metu, Mattuu etc, while names like Zikwala can become virtually unrecognisable (Zouquela). When consulting different books and maps, it's advisable to keep an eye open for varied spellings and to use your imagination. My policy in this book has been to go for the simplest spelling, or the one that to me sounds closest to the local pronunciation. I have stuck with Ethiopic versions of names; for instance Tewodros (Theodore), Yohannis (John), Maryam (Mary) and Giyorgis (George). The exception is that if hotels or restaurants are signposted in English, then I have normally (but not infallibly) followed the signposted spelling exactly.

Part One

General Information

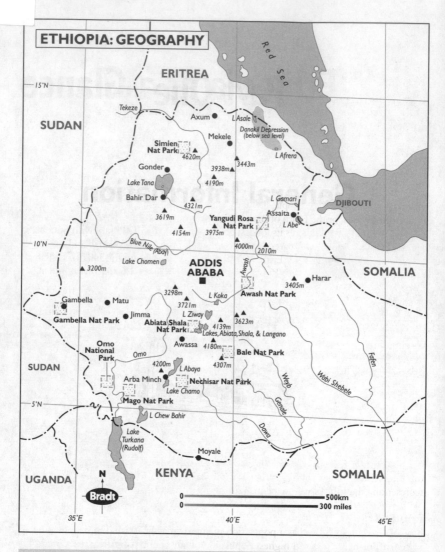

ETHIOPIA: GEOGRAPHY

Red Sea

ERITREA

15°N

SUDAN

Tekeze

Axum

L Asale

Danakil Depression
(below sea level)

Mekele

Simien
Nat Park
▲ 4620m

3938m ▲ ▲ 3443m

L Afrera

4190m

Gonder

Lake Tana

Bahir Dar

4321m

L Gamari

Yangudi Rosa
Nat Park
▲ 3975m

Assaita

L Abe

DJIBOUTI

3619m

4154m

4000m ▲ 2010m

Blue Nile (Abay)

10°N

Lake Chomen

ADDIS
ABABA
■

Awash

SOMALIA

▲ 3200m

3298m ▲

L Koka

3405m ▲ ● Harar

Gambella

● Matu

3721m ▲

Awash Nat Park

Gambella Nat Park

● Jimma

L Ziway

Abiata Shala
Nat Park

3623m
▲ ▲

Omo
National
Park

Awassa

4139m ▲
Lakes, Abiata, Shala, & Langano

Omo

4180m ▲ ▲

Bale Nat Park

SUDAN

4200m ▲

L Abaya

4307m

Arba Minch

Lake Chamo

Nechisar Nat Park

Weyb

Wabi Shebele

Fafen

Mago Nat Park

Gende

Dawa

5°N

L Chew Bahir

Lake
Turkana
(Rudolf)

Moyale

UGANDA

N

KENYA

SOMALIA

Bradt

0 ━━━━━━━ 500km
0 ━━━━━━━ 300 miles

35°E

40°E

45°E

Ethiopia at a Glance

FACTS AND FIGURES

Location

The Federal Republic of Ethiopia, formerly known as Abyssinia, is a land-locked republic in northeast Africa, or the Horn of Africa, lying between 3.5 to 15 degrees north and 33 to 48 degrees east. Ethiopia shares its longest border, of more than 1,600km, with Somalia to the east (this border includes part of the as yet unrecognised state of Somaliland). Ethiopia is bounded to the northeast by Eritrea for 910km, and by Djibouti for 340km. It shares a southern border of 830km with Kenya, and a western border of 1,600km with Sudan.

Size

Ethiopia covers an area of 1,104,300km², making it the tenth largest country in Africa. For the sake of comparison, Ethiopia covers approximately twice the area of Kenya or the state of Texas and five times the area of the United Kingdom or New Zealand. Of other African countries, it is closest in size to South Africa. Roughly 7,500km² of Ethiopia's surface area is water.

Capital

The capital of Ethiopia is Addis Ababa, which lies at the heart of the country in the central highlands at an altitude of 2,300m. It is the third highest capital city in the world.

Flag

The national flag consists of the so-called Pan-African colours: vertical bands of green at the top, yellow in the centre, and red at the base. In the middle of this is a symbol representing the sun – a yellow pentagram from which emanate several yellow rays.

Population

Ethiopia currently (2005) has a population of approximately 70 million people. This is, rather surprisingly, the third highest population of any country in Africa, exceeded only by Egypt and Nigeria. The major ethnic/linguistic groups are the Oromo (40%), Amhara (22%), Tigrai (10%), Sidamo (9%) and Somali (6%).

The 1987 population of Addis Ababa was approximately 1.6 million, but by 1994 it had swelled to 2.3 million and today it probably stands at around the three million mark. Reliable population figures for other large towns do not exist, and the available estimates are evidently not entirely reliable (different sources place the population of Gambella, for instance, as far apart as 24,000 and 72,000) but other towns whose population probably exceeds the 100,000 mark are Dire Dawa (265,000), Adama (190,000), Gonder (151,000), Bahir Dar (146,000), Mekele (142,000), Dessie (131,000), Jimma (125,000), Awassa (116,000), Bishoftu (102,000) and Harar (100,000). Other towns with a population of greater than 50,000, in approximate descending order of size, are Kombolcha, Shashemene, Adigrat, Arba Minch, Nekemte, Debre Markos, Asela, Hosaina, Sodo, Debre Birhan, Gambella, Ziway and Dilla.

More than half of the population of Ethiopia is aged 16 or under, and the population growth rate stands at roughly 2.75% per annum. As some measure of the effect of this rapid growth, the population was estimated at 24.2 million (excluding Eritrea) as recently as 1968. Then, only 19 towns outside of Eritrea harboured more than 10,000 people, as opposed to approximately 125 such towns today. As a point of reference, the ten largest towns in Ethiopia back in 1968 were Addis Ababa (645,000), Dire Dawa (50,700), Harar (42,700), Dessie (40,600), Gonder (30,700), Jimma (30,580), Adama (27,800), Mekele (23,100), Bishoftu (22,000) and Debre Markos (21,500). Other towns whose populations then stood at greater than 10,000 were Axum, Adwa, Asela, Nekemte, Bahir Dar, Dilla, Akaki, Sodo and Yirga Alem.

Government

Prior to 1974, Ethiopia was an empire with a feudal system of government, headed from 1930 onwards by His Imperial Majesty Haile Selassie. The emperor was deposed and killed in the 1974 revolution, after which a 'provisional' military dictatorship, known as the Derg (literally 'Committee'), was installed. In 1984, Mengistu Haile Maryam, leader of the Derg, established the so-called Workers' Party as the sole legal party in Ethiopia. A new constitution, making Ethiopia a one-party republic with a formal president, was enacted in 1987. President Mengistu was ousted in 1991 by two rebel movements, the Ethiopian People's Revolutionary Democratic Front (EPRDF) and Eritrean People's Liberation Front (EPLF).

In 1991, a transitional government was installed by the EPRDF, which was a coalition party comprising the Tigraian People's Liberation Front (TPLF), the Ethiopian People's Democratic Movement (EPDM) and the Oromo People's Democratic Organisation (OPDO). The transitional government, made up of an 87-seat Council of Representatives led by TPLF chairman Meles Zenawi, was charged with drawing up a new constitution to replace the dictatorial systems of the past with a more democratic and federal form of government.

In December 1994, Ethiopia adopted a new federal constitution that decentralised many aspects of government. The country has subsequently been divided into a revised set of eight regions and three city-states, with borders delineated along ethno-linguistic lines. The regions are constitutionally guaranteed political autonomy in most aspects of internal government, although central government remains responsible for national and international affairs and policies.

The new constitution also enforced for the first time in Ethiopian history a democratic parliamentarian government, based around two representative bodies: the Council of the People's Representatives and The Federal Council.

The head of state is the State President, currently Girmay Wolde Giyorgis, who is elected by a two-thirds majority in a joint session of both councils and can sit for a maximum of two terms. Executive power is vested in the Prime Minister and Council of Ministers, who are elected from members of the Council of the People's Representatives. Ethiopia's first democratic election was held in May 1995. On 22 August of that year, the newly elected federal government embarked on its first five-year term under the EPRDF and Prime Minister Meles Zenawi and President Nagasso Gidada. A second democratic election held in May 2000 returned Zenawi and the EPRDF to power, as did the May 2005 election, albeit with a vastly reduced majority.

Economy

Ethiopia is one of the world's poorest nations. In the late 1980s, the per capita income was US$120 per annum, and it is unlikely to have increased since that time. The average life expectancy has dropped from 47 to 45 in recent years, primarily due to AIDS-related deaths – roughly 2.5 million Ethiopians are estimated to be HIV positive. The birth rate is 45 per 1,000 people, with an infant mortality rate of 10%. Adult literacy stands at 35%.

The Ethiopian economy is dominated by subsistence agriculture. The Ethiopian Highlands are very fertile, and are criss-crossed by large rivers with enormous untapped potential for irrigation projects, but many parts of the country, particularly in the east and northeast, are prone to periodic rain failures and locust plagues, so there is a constant threat of local famines. The growing of coffee occupies 25% of the population and coffee accounts for 55% of Ethiopia's exports. The main crop grown for local consumption is *tef*, the grain used to make *injera* (a kind of pancake widely available throughout the country).

Ethiopia is rich in mineral deposits and ores such as gold and iron have been mined since ancient times. There has, however, been little commercial exploitation of Ethiopia's minerals, largely due to inaccessibility. The main product mined is salt. Manufacture in Ethiopia is limited almost entirely to the processing of agricultural products.

The recent war with Eritrea forced the government to throw a large proportion of their scarce reserves at military investment, and to increase taxes. Development of services and the infrastructure suffered as a result of the war, which also precipitated a sharp decline in foreign investment.

Geography

The Ethiopian landscape is dominated by the volcanically formed Ethiopian or Abyssinian Highlands, a region often but somewhat misleadingly referred to as a plateau, since it is in fact dramatically mountainous. The central plateau, isolated on three sides by low-lying semi-desert or desert, has an average altitude of above 2,000m and includes 20 peaks of 4,000m or higher. The Ethiopian Highlands are bisected by the Rift Valley, which starts at the Red Sea, then continues through the Danakil Depression (a desert area that contains one of the lowest points on the earth's surface) and through southern Ethiopia to Mozambique in southern Africa. The part of the Rift Valley south of Addis Ababa is notable for its string of eight lakes.

The most extensive mountain ranges on the highlands are the Simiens, which lie directly north of Gonder and rise to the fourth highest peak in Africa, Ras Dashen, whose height is normally given as 4,620m. Another significant range is the Bale Mountains, which lie in the southern highlands to the east of the Rift Valley. The Ethiopian Highlands form the source of four major river systems. The best known of these is the Blue Nile, or Abay, which rises near Lake Tana in the northwest, and supplies most of the water that flows into Egypt's Nile Valley. The Baro and Tekaze (or Shire) rivers feed the White Nile, the river that flows out of Lake Victoria in Uganda to join the Blue Nile at Khartoum in Sudan. Within Ethiopia, the Blue Nile arcs through the highlands south of Lake Tana to form a vast gorge comparable in size and depth to Namibia's Fish River Canyon and the Grand Canyon in the USA.

Several other major river systems run through Ethiopia. The Wabe Shebelle rises in the Bale area and courses through the southeast of the country into Somalia. The Omo River rises in the western highlands around Kaffa to drain into Lake Turkana on the Kenyan border. The Awash rises in Showa and then follows the course of the Rift Valley northwards before disappearing into a series of desert lakes near the Djibouti border.

Climate

Ethiopia shows a wide climatic variation, ranging from the peaks of Bale, which receive periodic snowfall, to regular daytime temperatures of over 50°C in the Danakil Desert (see *Climate chart*, page 6). As a rule, the central highlands have a temperate climate and average daytime temperature of 16°C, belying their proximity to the equator. The eastern lowlands and the far south are dry and hot. The western lowlands are moist and hot, making them the one part of the country that feels truly tropical. The southern Rift Valley, much of which lies at the relatively high altitude of 1,500m, is temperate to hot and seasonally moist.

The precipitation pattern in the northern and central highlands is that the bulk of the rain falls between mid June and early October. This pattern changes as you head further south: the rainy season in the Rift Valley generally starts and ends a few weeks earlier than in the highlands, while in South Omo most of the rain falls in March, April and May, and other parts of the south have two rainy seasons, falling either side of the highlands' rainy season of July to September. Contrary to popular perceptions, most highland parts of Ethiopia receive a healthy average annual rainfall figure, with the far west being

CLIMATE CHART

The local climate charts listed below have been selected to reflect the enormous regional variation in temperature, rainfall and seasons noted throughout the country.

Addis Ababa (2,400m)

	Jan	Feb	Mar	Apr	May	Jun	Jul	Aug	Sep	Oct	Nov	Dec
Ave Temp (°C)	16	17	18	18	18	17	16	16	15	15	15	15
Rainfall (mm)	30	40	45	70	90	110	210	280	160	30	10	15

Adama (1,130m)

	Jan	Feb	Mar	Apr	May	Jun	Jul	Aug	Sep	Oct	Nov	Dec
Ave Temp (°C)	19	21	22	23	22	21	20	20	19	19	18	18
Rainfall (mm)	10	15	60	55	45	60	180	220	100	30	10	20

Dire Dawa (1,200m)

	Jan	Feb	Mar	Apr	May	Jun	Jul	Aug	Sep	Oct	Nov	Dec
Ave Temp (°C)	21	23	25	27	28	27	25	25	25	23	22	21
Rainfall (mm)	0	30	45	60	40	30	100	130	60	30	5	5

Gambella (400m)

	Jan	Feb	Mar	Apr	May	Jun	Jul	Aug	Sep	Oct	Nov	Dec
Ave Temp (°C)	28	30	31	29	27	25	25	26	26	26	27	27
Rainfall (mm)	5	10	25	50	160	175	220	230	180	100	50	10

Goba (2,750m)

	Jan	Feb	Mar	Apr	May	Jun	Jul	Aug	Sep	Oct	Nov	Dec
Ave Temp (°C)	12	13	14	14	14	15	14	13	13	12	11	12
Rainfall (mm)	25	30	75	125	100	50	90	115	120	130	60	15

Gonder (2,120m)

	Jan	Feb	Mar	Apr	May	Jun	Jul	Aug	Sep	Oct	Nov	Dec
Ave Temp (°C)	19	20	21	22	21	19	18	18	19	19	18	18
Rainfall (mm)	10	10	25	40	90	170	310	300	160	30	20	15

Harar (1,850m)

	Jan	Feb	Mar	Apr	May	Jun	Jul	Aug	Sep	Oct	Nov	Dec
Ave Temp (°C)	18	20	20	20	19	18	18	18	18	19	18	18
Rainfall (mm)	10	20	30	100	50	50	80	150	75	30	10	10

particularly moist – indeed much of the southwest receives an average annual rainfall in excess of 2,000mm.

The northeast highlands are much drier, and have a less reliable rainy season, than other highland parts of Ethiopia. Tigrai and parts of Amhara are prone to complete rainfall failure; this tends to happen about once every decade. It was such a rainfall failure that, exacerbated by tactics of the Mengistu government, led to the notorious famine of 1985. In normal years, however, the highlands become something of a mud bath during the rains, with an average of 1,000mm falling over two or three months. Fortunately, from a tourist's point of view, rain tends to fall in dramatic storms that end as suddenly as they start, a situation that is infinitely more conducive to travel than days of protracted drizzle.

Jimma (2,300m)

	Jan	Feb	Mar	Apr	May	Jun	Jul	Aug	Sep	Oct	Nov	Dec
Ave Temp (°C)	18	19	20	20	19	19	18	18	19	18	18	17
Rainfall (mm)	40	50	85	160	150	210	195	175	160	90	20	30

Kelafo (typical eastern desert 'Bereha' climate – 400m)

	Jan	Feb	Mar	Apr	May	Jun	Jul	Aug	Sep	Oct	Nov	Dec
Ave Temp (°C)	28	30	32	33	30	28	28	29	30	30	29	30
Rainfall (mm)	0	0	25	50	40	0	0	5	10	30	40	5

Matu (1,800m)

	Jan	Feb	Mar	Apr	May	Jun	Jul	Aug	Sep	Oct	Nov	Dec
Ave Temp (°C)	18	20	21	21	20	18	18	19	19	18	17	17
Rainfall (mm)	40	45	90	80	210	240	300	290	285	140	45	50

Mekele (2,500m)

	Jan	Feb	Mar	Apr	May	Jun	Jul	Aug	Sep	Oct	Nov	Dec
Ave Temp (°C)	17	18	18	19	20	18	18	18	18	17	17	16
Rainfall (mm)	0	10	25	30	25	35	200	210	60	10	10	5

Moyale (1,200m)

	Jan	Feb	Mar	Apr	May	Jun	Jul	Aug	Sep	Oct	Nov	Dec
Ave Temp (°C)	24	24	23	22	21	20	20	21	21	22	23	23
Rainfall (mm)	10	15	50	210	90	20	15	20	20	200	110	50

Negele Borena (1,450m)

	Jan	Feb	Mar	Apr	May	Jun	Jul	Aug	Sep	Oct	Nov	Dec
Ave Temp (°C)	19	21	20	19	18	18	17	18	19	18	18	19
Rainfall (mm)	15	30	40	185	155	15	10	10	30	180	30	15

Nekemte (2,000m)

	Jan	Feb	Mar	Apr	May	Jun	Jul	Aug	Sep	Oct	Nov	Dec
Ave Temp (°C)	19	20	21	20	18	17	16	18	18	19	19	18
Rainfall (mm)	15	20	50	80	260	380	400	375	260	90	75	30

Sodo (2,000m)

	Jan	Feb	Mar	Apr	May	Jun	Jul	Aug	Sep	Oct	Nov	Dec
Ave Temp (°C)	23	23	22	21	20	18	16	18	20	23	23	22
Rainfall (mm)	25	20	90	130	140	130	210	260	120	130	45	30

ETHIOPIAN CLIMATIC ZONES

Ethiopians traditionally recognise five climatic zones, each of which has distinctive features linked to altitude, rainfall and temperature. These are as follows:

Bereha Hot and arid desert lowlands that typically lie below 500m and receive significantly less than 500mm of precipitation annually, not generally cultivatable so mostly inhabited by pastoralists, eg: most of the Somali border area and the Rift Valley north of Addis Ababa

Kolla Warm to hot mid-altitude locations that receive sufficient rainfall for cultivation without relying on irrigation, eg: the Rift Valley between Addis Ababa and Awassa, or Gambella region

Weyna Dega Warm to cool medium- to high-altitude locations typically receiving more than 1,500mm of rainfall annually, often naturally forested though much of this has been cleared over the centuries, excellent for cultivation of grains (especially *tef*) and coffee, eg: Addis Ababa, Gonder, Asela, Goba, Jimma, Matu and most other highlands below the 2,600m contour

Dega Cool to cold, medium-to-high rainfall, high-altitude locations that would naturally support grassland or coniferous forest and now are mostly used to cultivate grains such as barley and wheat, eg: Dinsho, Debre Birhan, Mehal Meda, Ankober and other highland areas with an altitude in the range 2,600–3,200m

Worch Chilly, medium-to-low rainfall Afro-alpine regions supporting a cover of heath-like vegetation that isn't generally conducive to cultivation, eg: Sanetti Plateau (Bale National Park), the eastern peaks of the Simiens, Guassa Plateau and other plateaus or peaks above 3,200–3,500m

FEDERAL REGIONS

Ethiopia has been subject to several regional reshuffles in recent decades. It was divided into 15 regions prior to 1987, reorganised into 29 regions in the 1987 constitution, and then returned to more or less where it had started in 1991, when the transitional government divided the country into 14 administrative regions. These were based precisely on 13 of the original regions, with Addis Ababa administered separately, and Assab and Eritrea by then part of independent Eritrea. In 1994, Ethiopia became a federal republic and the regional map was redrawn from scratch, this time along widely accepted ethno-linguistic lines. The result was eight regional states (*astedader akabibi*) and three city-states, all of which had far stronger federal powers than the old regions. Each region is divided into a few zones and a larger number of districts or *Woredas*. On the whole, these district names are of no interest to tourists, but a few are of historical significance, or are regularly referred to in casual use, or function as 'Special *Woredas*' devoted to a particular small ethnic group and with a higher degree of autonomy that normal *Woredas*.

The modern regions of Ethiopia are described below in alphabetical order:

Addis Ababa

Located more or less at the dead centre of Ethiopia, and surrounded by the state of Oromia, the capital city of Ethiopia is governed as a 540km² city-state of which less than 5% is rural. According to the 1994 census, the population of Addis Ababa is 2.3 million of which 51.6% are female. Almost half of Addis Ababa's cosmopolitan population is Amhara, with Oromo, Gurage and Tigraian residents respectively making up 19%, 17% and 7.6% of the remainder. More than 80% of its residents are Orthodox Christians. The

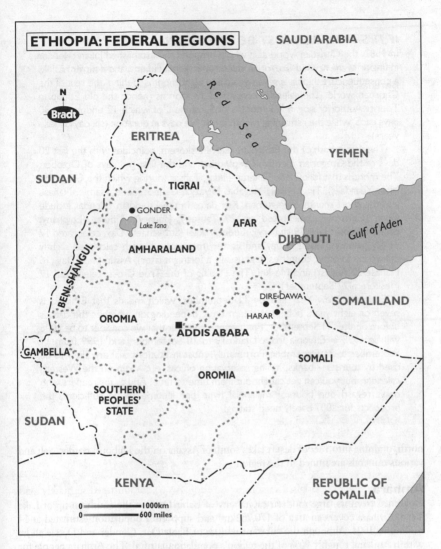

ETHIOPIA: FEDERAL REGIONS

capital city is subdivided into six zones and 28 *Woredas*. Amharic is the working language, but English is widely spoken.

Afar

Although it covers a vast area of 270,000km² running up the border with Djibouti and Eritrea, Afar region is arid, thinly populated and almost bereft of large towns. According to the 1994 census, the total population of Afar is 1.1 million, of which less than 10% live in urban areas. The tiny capital of Assaita will be replaced by the purpose-built capital of Semere in the near future. Afar region is named for the pastoral people who comprise roughly 92% of its population (the remainder consists mostly of people from elsewhere in Ethiopia who have settled in the region). Geographically, Afar forms the most northerly part of the Rift Valley, and it is characterised by low-lying plains which receive less than 200mm of rainfall annually. The Awash River runs through Afar from south to

IF IT'S 1999, WE MUST BE IN ETHIOPIA...

In 1582, the Christian world as a whole dropped the established Julian calendar in favour of the revised Gregorian calendar. Ethiopia did not, and it never has! As a consequence, Ethiopia is seven years and eight months 'behind' the rest of the Christian world. The calendar consists of 13 months (hence the old Ethiopian Tourist Authority slogan '13 months of Sunshine'), of which 12 endure for 30 days each, while the remaining month is just five days in duration (six days in leap years).

The first month of the Ethiopian year, Meskerem, coincides with the last 20 days of the Gregorian month of September and the first ten days of October. The months that follow are Tekemt, Hidar, Tahsas (during which the Gregorian New Year falls), Tir, Yekatit, Megabit, Miyazya, Genbot, Sene, Hamle, Nahase and the short month of Pagumen. Key dates in the Ethiopian calendar include Gena (Christmas, celebrated on 29 Tahsas/7 January), Timkat (Epiphany, celebrated on 11 Tir/19 January), Kiddist Mikael (St Michael's Day, celebrated 12 Tir/29 January), Good Friday and Easter (moveable, though calculated slightly differently to other countries, and usually a fortnight later), Assumption Day (16 Nahase/22 August) and Meskel (The Finding of the True Cross, celebrated 17 Meskerem/27 September).

Ethiopian New Year falls on 11 September, which means that Ethiopia is seven or eight years behind Western time, depending on whether the date is before or after 11 September. For instance, the year that we consider to be 2006 will be 1998 in Ethiopia from 1 January to 10 September, and 1999 from 11 September to 31 December. Fortunately, most institutions that are likely to be used by tourists – banks, airline reservation offices, etc – run on the Western calendar, but you can get caught out from time to time. And as for readers who don't regard one bout of millennial hype per lifetime to be sufficient, the prospects for 2007 barely need stating!

north, draining into a set of desert lakes south of Assaita on the Djibouti border. Salt and various minerals are mined in the region.

Amhara

Governed from its large modern capital city of Bahir Dar, on the southern tip of Lake Tana, Amhara covers an area of 170,752km² and supports a population estimated at 14 million in 1994. Although the substantial cities of Bahir Dar, Gonder and Dessie all lie within Amhara, roughly 90% of the region's population is rural. The Amhara people for whom the state is named comprise more than 90% of the population, and Orthodox Christians outnumber Muslims by a ratio of 4:1. Several of Ethiopia's most popular tourist sites lie in Amhara, most notably the former imperial capitals of Lalibela and Gonder. The Simien Mountains to the north of Gonder include Ethiopia's highest peak, the 4,620m Mount Ras Dashen, and harbour the country's main concentrations of the endemic gelada baboon and Walia ibex. Lake Tana, Ethiopia's largest body of water and source of the Blue Nile, also falls within Amhara, as does the Blue Nile Falls.

Benishangul-Gumuz

The most obscure of Ethiopia's regions, practically never visited by tourists, is Benishangul-Gumuz, which runs for about 2,000km along the Sudanese border to the east of Amhara, but is on average no more than 200km wide. Relatively low-lying but with an annual rainfall in excess of 1,000mm, this remote and poorly developed area is characterised by a hot, humid climate. The regional population of about 500,000 is governed from the small capital town of Asosa in the south.

Dire Dawa

Governed as a city-state, Dire Dawa is Ethiopia's second largest city, with a population exceeding 150,000. The administrative boundaries of the city cover an area of around 130km², and are surrounded on all sides by the region of Oromia. The dominant ethnic group of this cosmopolitan city is the Oromo (48%), but there are also substantial Amhara, Somali and Gurage populations. Amhara is the official language of Dire Dawa, and Muslims outnumber Christians by a ratio of 2:1. The Ethio-Djibouti railway, which runs through Dire Dawa, has played an important role in the growth of this city, and continues to lie at the heart of its trade economy.

Gambella

The small state, which covers an area of 25,274km² along the southern Sudanese border, essentially comprises lush, humid lowland draining into the Baro River, an important tributary of the Nile. Relatively remote and undeveloped, Gambella region supports a predominantly rural population of roughly 200,000 ethnically varied people. The main nationalities represented in the vicinity of the regional capital, the small river port of Gambella, are the Nuer and Anuwak, who respectively account for 40% and 27% of the regional population. Minority groups include the Mezhenger, Apana, Komo and various recent migrants from the highlands. Although the state is predominantly Christian, more than half the population subscribes to a recently introduced Western denomination, with the remainder adhering to Orthodox Christianity, Muslim, or traditional animism. A fair amount of wildlife – lion, elephant and buffalo as well as various monkeys and antelope – persists in Gambella region.

Harari

Consisting of the walled city of Harar and its immediate environs, Harari is essentially a modern revival of the autonomous city-state of Harar, which was one of the most powerful regional political entities from the 16th until the late 19th century, when it was co-opted into Abyssinia by Menelik II. The state covers an area of roughly 350km² and supports a population estimated at 140,000, of which some 80,000 are city dwellers. Roughly half of the population is Oromo, with the Amhara accounting for another 33% and the Harari only 7%. Despite Harar's reputation as the home of Islamic Ethiopia, roughly 40% of its population is Christian. The lush farmland around Harar is known for its chat and coffee plantations, but other major crops include sorghum, maize and oranges.

Oromia

The vast region of Oromia covers an area of more than 350,000km² (almost one-third of the country) and supports a correspondingly large population of almost 20 million people. Roughly 85% of the regional population is Oromo, and another 10% Amhara. Aside from the 5% who still practise animist or other traditional religions, the regional split between Christian and Muslim is as good as even. The official language of Oromifa is inscribed with Latin script rather than the Arabic characters used elsewhere in the country. With its mostly fertile soils, Oromia is the breadbasket of Ethiopia, producing more than half of the nation's agricultural crop, and it is also home to almost half of its large livestock. Geographically and climatically diverse, Oromia hosts many of Ethiopia's more alluring natural attractions, notably Bale and Awash national parks and the lakes of the Rift Valley and Bishoftu. It is rich in minerals, ranging from gold and platinum to iron ore and limestone. Oromia encircles and is currently governed from Addis Ababa

ETHIOPIAN TIME

Ethiopians, like the Swahili of neighbouring Kenya and Tanzania, measure time in 12-hour cycles starting at 06.00 and 18.00. In other words, their seven o'clock is our one o'clock, and vice versa. To ask the time in Amharigna, you say *sa'at sintno?* Times are *and sa'at* (hour one) through to *asir hulet sa'at* (hour 12). When talking Amharigna, you can be confident all times will be Ethiopian. When talking English, people may or may not give you European time, so check. If they say am or pm, it will definitely be European time. Otherwise, ask if it is Europe (pronounced like Orop) time or *habbishat* time; or else convert to Ethiopian time – for instance, if someone says a bus leaves at one, ask if they mean *and sa'at* or *sabat sa'at*. After a month in the country, I decided it was simplest to change my watch to Ethiopian time.

With typical Ethiopian perversity, kids who speak no other English love asking you the time. Of course, they don't understand the answer. It is worth getting to know how to give times in Amharigna purely for the astonishment of kids' faces when you whammy them with the reply they're not expecting. This is quite simple because Ethiopians only worry about gradations of five minutes – so four minutes past five becomes five minutes past five, etc. Note, however, that I was once quite sternly ticked off for giving seven minutes past as five minutes past – seven minutes past is, or so I was informed, ten minutes past!

So here, assuming you've pushed your watch six hours forward, is the full list of times from *and sa'at* to *hulet sa'at*:

13.00	and	13.35	lehulet hamist guda
13.05	and kemist	13.40	lehulet haya guda
13.10	and kesir	13.45	lehulet rub guda
13.15	and kerub	13.50	lehulet asir guda
13.20	and kehaya	13.55	lehulet amist guda
13.25	and kahayamst	14.00	hulet
13.30	and tekul		

(known as Finfine in Oromifa and sometimes signposted as such within the state) but the administration is likely to relocate to Adama (Nazret) within the lifespan of this fourth edition.

Somalia

Named for the distinctive Somali people, who comprise 95% of its population, this is the second largest of Ethiopia's regions, covering an area of 250,000km² along the Somali border. Much of the region is desert or semi-desert, and despite its vast area, the total population is less than four million. The capital is Jijiga, to the east of Harar. Almost 99% of the population is Muslim, and most of its residents are pastoralists. The important Wabe Shebelle River runs through the region.

Southern Nations, Nationalities and Peoples' State

Although it smells like the handiwork of an uninspired committee, the name of this 112,323km² region does provide an accurate reflection of its incredible cultural diversity. The regional population of roughly 11 million represents some 45 different ethnolinguistic groups, of which none comprises 20% of the regional population, and only the Sidamo, Gurage and Walaita make up more than 10% each. The regional capital is the modern city of Awassa, set on the shore of the eponymous lake, and much of the region lies in the relatively low-lying Rift Valley and Kenyan border area. The most important crop is coffee. Aside from the Rift Valley lakes, the most popular tourist attraction is the remote cultural tribes of South Omo zone.

Tigrai

Ethiopia's most northerly region is Tigrai, which covers 80,000km² and is administered from its capital city of Mekele. The population totals 3.5 million, of which 95% are Orthodox Christian and the remainder Muslim. The Tigraian people, the dominant ethnic group, are agriculturists who also herd cattle and other livestock. Tigrai is drier than other parts of highland Ethiopia, and prone to periodic droughts, but the region is intensively cultivated and in some areas terraced. Tigrai has been central to many of the more important events in Ethiopian history, from the adoption of Christianity by the Axumite Emperor in the 4th century, to the defeat of Italy outside Adwa 1,500 years later. The city of Axum and associated archaeological sites are the main tourist attractions, but the 120 rock-hewn churches scattered throughout the east of the country are also well worth exploring.

Emperor Haile Selassie

THE **ENCHANTED** WORLD OF ETHIOPIA

Ethiopia is... old beyond imagination, dating back to the very beginnings of mankind. It is also the land of the Queen of Sheba, a place of legendary rulers, fabulous kingdoms and ancient mysteries. Mother nature was in a playful mood when she created Ethiopia, the result is a land that varies greatly from one region to the next. With more than 80 languages and some 200 dialects, each ethnic group, preserves its own unique customs, traditions, and costumes.

You'll find all the major religions of the world in Ethiopia. But for all this exotic variety, the people of Ethiopia are as one in their friendliness and hospitality. Come fly with Ethiopian Airlines and discover a land of fascinating people and culture.

Ethiopian
የኢትዮጵያ

AFRICA'S WORLD CLASS AIRLINE

VISIT US AT WWW.ETHIOPIANAIRLINES.COM FOR CONVENIENT ONLINE BOOKING. CONTACT YOUR TRAVEL AGENT, THE NEAREST ETHIOPIAN AIRLINES OFFICE OR THE ETHIOPIAN AIRLINES CENTRAL RESERVATIONS OFFICE: TEL (251-11) 6616666 FAX (251-11) 6611474

Culture and History

Ethiopia has a cultural, historical and linguistic identity quite distinct from that of the rest of Africa, largely because it has spent long periods of its history in virtual isolation. It is fair, if rather simplistic, to say that Ethiopia is where the Ancient World and Africa meet. Northern Ethiopia, or more specifically the ancient Axumite Kingdom, which centred on the modern province of Tigrai, had strong links with Ancient Egypt, the Judaic civilisations of the Middle East, and Greece, evidenced by much of the ancient art and architecture that has been unearthed in the region. Pre-Christian civilisation in Tigrai is divided by historians into several eras, but stripping away the technicalities it can be said that Axum was an urbanised culture of blended classical and African influences from at least 600BC and quite possibly earlier.

Modern Ethiopia is heavily influenced by Judaism. The Ethiopian Orthodox Church, founded in Axum in the 4th century AD, has multifarious Jewish influences, which – along with the presence of an ancient Jewish community in the former provinces of Gojjam and Wolo – suggests a large pre-Christian Judaic influence in Ethiopia. Islam, too, arrived in Ethiopia in its formative years, and it is the dominant religious group in eastern Ethiopia south of Tigrai. In this torrent of well-attested Judaic influences, it is often forgotten that much of what is now southern Ethiopia has few ancient links to the Judaic world. The Oromo (referred to as the Galla prior to the 20th century) are Ethiopia's largest linguistic group. They were pagan when they first swept up the Rift Valley into Ethiopia in the 15th century, but are now predominantly Christian, with imported Catholic and Protestant denominations more influential than they are in northern Ethiopia. The society and culture of southern Ethiopia are more typically African in nature than those of the north. In the Omo Valley and the far western lowlands near Sudan is a variety of peoples whose modern lifestyle is still deeply African in every sense – in fact, you would struggle to find people anywhere in east Africa so cut off from the mainstream of modern life.

Before plunging into further religious and historical discussion, it should be noted that the term Ethiopia, as used historically, need not refer to Ethiopia as we know it now. The term Ethiopic arose in Ancient Greece (it means burnt-faced) and was one of two used to describe the dark-skinned people of sub-Saharan Africa. The other term, Nubian, referred to the almost black-skinned people of the Nile Valley in what is now Sudan. Ethiopians, in biblical or classical terms, are in essence Axumites, or more broadly the people who lived in the Ethiopian Highlands roughly north of the Blue Nile. In medieval times and during the Renaissance, nobody in Europe knew quite where Africa began or ended – medieval literature often uses the terms India and Ethiopia interchangeably – but there was a strong association of Ethiopia with the wealthy and isolated Christian kingdom of a person who Europeans called Prester John. Once again, then, medieval Ethiopia is best thought of as the Christian empire of the highlands which, judging by the distribution of churches from this time, extended from Tigrai to Showa province just south of modern-day Addis Ababa. As Europeans gradually came to explore Ethiopia, the terms Ethiopia and Abyssinia (the latter deriving from the Arabic word *habbishat*) became interchangeable.

Again, the Abyssinians or Ethiopians would generally be seen as the subjects of the Christian empire, who were often at war with the Muslim empires of the eastern highlands and the Galla. Modern Ethiopia is a by-product of the 19th-century scramble for Africa, and it incorporates the old Muslim empire based around Harar, vast tracts of thinly inhabited Somali, Afar and Borena territory, the lands occupied by the Oromo and, in the far west, areas that the Greeks would have considered to be Nubian. In my opinion – and in the context of what follows – Ethiopia, Abyssinia and *habbishat* are approximately synonymous terms relating to the Christian empire of the highlands, at least until the great unifying leaders of the late 19th century – Tewodros, Yohannis IV and Menelik II – laid the groundwork for the modern Ethiopian state. None of which means for a moment that, in a modern sense, a Muslim from Harar is any less Ethiopian than a Christian from Axum.

The present chapter dwells mainly on the old Christian cultures of the highlands, and their Muslim counterparts. Background details for other Ethiopian cultures are to be found in appropriate chapters of the regional part of this guide.

LANGUAGE

Ethiopia supports a diverse mix of linguistic groups. Some 70 languages are spoken in Ethiopia, most of them belonging to the Semetic or Cushitic branches of the Afro-Asiatic family. The most important Semetic languages are Amharigna (Amharic) and Tigrigna of northern Ethiopia, both of which descend from Ge'ez, the language of ancient Axum which is still used by the Ethiopian Orthodox Church today. The Gurage and Zay of southern Ethiopia also speak Semetic languages, as do the people of Harar in the east. Amharigna was the official language of Ethiopia under Mengistu and it remains the *lingua franca* in most parts of the country that are likely to be visited by tourists. Ethiopia's Semetic languages are transcribed in a script that is unique to the country. This consists of over 200 characters, each of which denotes a syllable as opposed to a letter.

Cushitic languages are dominant in southern and eastern Ethiopia. The most significant of these is Oromifa (Oromigna), the language of the Oromo (or Galla), Ethiopia's largest ethnic group. The Somali language also belongs to the Cushitic group. Cushitic speakers transcribe their language using the same Roman alphabet that we do: you may well be told that the Oromo 'speak' Roman. In the Omo River Valley, a localised group of languages of Afro-Asiatic origin is spoken. These are known as Omotic languages, and are quite closely affiliated to the Cushitic group. Along the western border with Sudan, languages are mostly of the unrelated Nilotic group.

It should be noted that linguistic terms need not imply anything about ethnicity. Many British people with a purely Celtic genealogy, or Afro-Americans for that matter, speak only English, which is a language of the west Germanic branch of the Indo-European group. Linguistic patterns are the best means available to scientists for tracing the broad sweep of prehistoric population movements, and in some instances – for instance the Oromifa-speaking Oromo – there is a strong association between language and a cohesive ethnic identity. Nevertheless, the exclusive use of a Semetic language in Tigrai need not mean that all Tigraian people are of Semetic origin. Just as one would not refer to an English-speaking American as English, it is more accurate to speak of Cushitic- or Semetic-speakers, rather than Cushites or Semites. A semantic point, but one which is often misunderstood, particularly in the African context, and which has (I use the past tense optimistically) fuelled more than its share of racist pontificating.

English is the most widely spoken European language as it is used for secondary education. French is heard on occasion in some parts of the country, particularly in the southeastern highlands near Djibouti. Some elderly Ethiopians speak Italian, most commonly in Tigrai and around Addis Ababa. (See also *Appendix 3*.)

RELIGION

The main religions in Ethiopia are Christianity and Islam. Until recently, a population of indigenous Ethiopian Jews, known as the Bet Israel (House of Israel) or Falasha, was concentrated in the part of Amhara region formerly administered as Gojjam and Wolo Provinces. In medieval times, the Falasha were a major force in Ethiopia's internal politics, but several centuries of warfare and persecution had reduced their numbers greatly by the late 20th century, and the 30,000 individuals who survived were airlifted to Israel in the last decade of the Derg's rule. A few isolated Falasha communities reputedly inhabit the remote mountains of Lasta district in eastern Amhara.

It is difficult to find reliable figures for the relative distribution and proportion of Muslims and Christians in Ethiopia. Some sources suggest that 50–60% of Ethiopia is Muslim. Geographically, this could well be the case, as the thinly populated eastern lowlands are strongly Muslim, but I find this an incredible figure in population terms. I'm told that the recent census suggests that 25% of Ethiopians are Muslim, which is at least plausible, though it still sounds a little high. The main concentrations of Muslims are in the eastern part of the country, especially in the regions of Harari, Somali and Afar, as well as in the far east of Tigrai, Amhara and Oromia. Whatever the statistics say, Ethiopia feels like a predominantly Christian country.

The majority of Ethiopian Christians belong to the Ethiopian Orthodox Church, which is often, but erroneously, referred to by outsiders as the Coptic Church. The Coptic Church is an Egyptian Church (*Coptic* is an Ancient Greek word meaning Egyptian) which took shape in Alexandria in the 2nd and 3rd centuries AD, and broke away from Rome and Constantinople in AD451 following its adoption of the Monophysitic doctrine. (This contentious doctrine, which asserts the single and primarily divine nature of Christ, was considered heretical by Rome and Constantinople, whose Dualistic philosophy held that Christ had discrete human and divine personalities.) The Ethiopian Orthodox Church was founded in Axum in the 4th century AD and its first bishop, Frumentius, was consecrated in Alexandria. Strong ties have always existed between the Churches of Ethiopia and Alexandria, and until 1955 the Ethiopian Church *technically* fell under Alexandria's governance. Within Ethiopia, however, it was the Abbot of Debre Libanos and not the archbishop sent from Alexandria who assumed the role of church primate. Since 1955, the Ethiopian Orthodox Church has been self-governing, with its own seat on the World Council of Churches. Not once have I heard an Ethiopian Christian call his church Coptic, nor did the word meet with any recognition when I used it in Ethiopia. The Church of Ethiopia is, like the much less numerically significant Coptic Church, a Monophysitic Church; more importantly, to Ethiopians it is *the* Ethiopian Orthodox Church, and bracketing it with the Coptic Church is a typical example of a Western refusal to recognise any institution that is unique to sub-Saharan Africa.

Am I being too harsh? I recently laid my hands on a history of religion (in its favour, almost the only source which confirmed my growing suspicion that the Coptic Church of Ethiopia was a Western label) which describes Ethiopian Christians as 'ignorant', their religious notions as 'almost entirely superstitious' and the Church itself as 'one of the most degraded forms into which Christianity has degenerated'.

Even the most casual familiarity with the customs of the Ethiopian Orthodox Church is proof that it is a most singular institution, further removed from the Coptic Church than most Western denominations are from each other. Apart from the odd emissary from Alexandria, Ethiopian Christianity developed in virtual isolation until the arrival of the Portuguese Jesuits in the 15th century and, although its fundamentals are indisputably Christian, the rituals are infused with all sorts of archaic Jewish influences, acquired, one imagines, from the Falasha and other ancient Jewish sects that lived in pre-Christian Ethiopia. Orthodox Ethiopians practise male circumcision a few days after birth, they hold regular fasting days, and the women are governed by a variety of menstruation taboos. They recognise both the Christian Sabbath of Sunday *and* the Jewish Sabbath of Saturday; and they indulge in celebratory religious dances that would be considered blasphemous by other Christian denominations.

At the heart of Ethiopian mysticism lies an unfathomable, and I think rather fascinating, relationship between Christianity and the Ark of the Covenant, the very core of Judaism until its apparent disappearance from Jerusalem led to the reforms of Josiah in around 650BC. Ethiopians believe that the original Ark was brought to Axum in the 1st millennium BC, and that it rests there to this day. What's more, the most holy item in every Ethiopian church is the *tabot* – a replica of the Ark (or, more accurately, a replica of one of the Tablets of the Law which were placed in the Ark by Moses). The *tabot* is only removed from the Holy of Holies on important religious days, and it is at all times obscured from view by a cover of draped sheets.

While the north of Ethiopia is predominantly Orthodox, other exotic denominations such as Catholicism and Protestantism have found their way to the country, and they are practised widely in the south, most numerously among Oromifa-speakers, whose conversion to Christianity is a relatively recent thing.

HISTORY

Much of Ethiopia's fascination lies in its myriad historical sites. This is the only country in sub-Saharan Africa with tangible historical remnants stretching back to the ancient Mediterranean civilisations. One might reasonably expect there to be a huge body of writing on Ethiopian history and its relationship to other civilisations. There isn't. To quote Philip Marsden-Smedley's *A Far Country*: 'Ethiopia crept up on me... Often, where I'd expected a chapter, in general histories of the Christian Church, books of African Art, there was a single reference – or nothing at all. And soon I found the same facts recurring and realised that Ethiopian scholarship was, like its subject, cut off from the mainstream. The only general history of the country I could find was published in 1935.'

In 1994, when I tried to get a general grasp of Ethiopian history before visiting the country, I had a similar experience. I was startled to discover that Oliver and Fage's *Short History of Africa* contains not one reference to Axum. In the end, my limited knowledge stemmed from a French history translated into English in 1959, unearthed for me by a friend who works in South Africa's largest library, and a 1992 book called *The Sign and the Seal* which attempts to substantiate the Ethiopian claim that the Ark of the Covenant resides in Axum. The situation improved when I arrived in Ethiopia to find a fair number of locally published books of a historical nature. But, even then, armed with all I could find on Ethiopian history, I felt a strong sense of dissatisfaction with my booty. What was lacking was a centre from which a layperson could explore more esoteric or specific writings. This situation has improved since 1994, with the publication of a couple of useful and concise general histories (see *Further Reading*), though both of these are primarily concerned with modern rather than ancient Ethiopia.

A basic grasp of ancient Ethiopian history is integral to getting the most from the country. Tourism to Ethiopia revolves around historical sites; no less important, Ethiopians identify strongly with their history, and they generally enjoy speaking to visitors who share their enthusiasm. I only wish there was a balanced general history I could recommend to readers. To produce something that will suffice, I have to work from a plethora of sources that are consistent only in their divergence. The traditional beliefs held by most Ethiopians and the orthodoxies of Western historians might as well be parallel universes. Even 'proper' historical writing is riddled with contradictory dates and ideas, and many of the oft-repeated orthodoxies are refuted by more recent and mostly unpublished archaeological research taking place in the country right now.

Fortunately, it is not my job to resolve the apparent contradictions of Ethiopian history, but to attempt to transmit its fascination and my enthusiasm to tourists. Bearing this in mind, what follows draws equally on the fantastic speculation of folklore and the necessarily conservative speculation of historians; in order to provide some balance, I have not been averse to a little speculation myself. Ethiopian history is too absorbing to be treated as blandly as sticking to the 'facts' would require. Determining the facts before about AD1600 is in any case full of open questions. To me, it matters less that the Queen of Sheba was really Ethiopian or Haile Selassie was really descended from the Jewish King Solomon than it does that most Ethiopians believe it to be true. It is such beliefs that have shaped Ethiopian culture; through repetition, they have attained a vicarious truth.

In the section on pre-Christian history, I am indebted to Graham Hancock's *The Sign and the Seal*; a book that is certainly not without flaws, but which does have the virtues of ignoring the orthodoxies where the evidence points elsewhere, and of probing the past with enthusiasm, imagination and an apparent lack of preconceptions. I also owe a great debt to Bahru Zewde's excellent and commendably plainly written *A History of Modern Ethiopia 1855–1974*; were it not for this book, the relevant period in this section would be considerably less cohesive than it is.

The cradle of humankind?

The east African Rift Valley is almost certainly where modern human beings and their hominid ancestors evolved, and Ethiopia has as strong claims as any African country in this respect. Hominids are generally divided into two genera, *Australopithecus* and *Homo*, the former extinct for at least a million years, and the latter now represented by only one species – *Homo sapiens* (modern man). The paucity of hominid fossils collected before the 1960s meant that for many years it was assumed the most common australopithecine fossil, *A. africanus*, had evolved directly into the genus *Homo* and was thus man's oldest identifiable ancestor.

This linear theory of human evolution blurred when the Leakeys' discoveries at Olduvai Gorge in Tanzania suggested that at least two types of australopithecine had existed, and that the later species *A. robustus* had less in common with modern man than its more lightly built ancestor *A. africanus*. Then, in 1972, the discovery of a two-million-year-old skull of a previously undescribed species, *Homo habilis*, at Lake Turkana in Kenya, provided the first conclusive evidence that some *Australopithecus* and *Homo* species had lived alongside each other for at least one million years. As more fossils came to light, including older examples of *Homo erectus* (the direct ancestor of modern humans), it became clear that several different hominid species had existed alongside each other in the Rift Valley until perhaps half a million years ago. Increasingly, it looked as if all known members of *Australopithecus* and *Homo* belonged to two discrete evolutionary lines, presumably with a yet-to-be-discovered common ancestor. The only flaw in this theory was the time scale involved: it didn't seem possible that there had been adequate time for the oldest-known australopithecine to have evolved into *Homo habilis*.

In 1974, an almost complete hominid skeleton was discovered by Donald Johanson in Hadar, in the Danakil region of northern Ethiopia. The skeleton, named Lucy (the song *Lucy in the Sky with Diamonds* was playing in camp shortly after the discovery), turned out to be that of a 3.5-million-year-old australopithecine of an entirely new species dubbed *A. afarensis*. The discovery of Lucy not only demonstrated that bipedal (or semi-bipedal – the length of *afarensis*'s arms suggest it was as comfortable swinging through the trees as it was on its morning jog) hominids had evolved much earlier than previously assumed, but it also created a likely candidate for the common ancestry of later australopithecine species and the human chain of evolution. As more *A. afarensis* fragments came to light in the Danakil, many palaeontologists argued that the wide divergence in their skull and body sizes indicated that not one but several australopithecine species lived in the Danakil at this time, and that any one of them – or none of them, for that matter – might be ancestral to modern humans. This discrepancy was clarified in 1994, when the first complete male *afarensis* skull was uncovered less than 10km from where Lucy had lain. It is now clear that the difference in size is because *afarensis* males were almost twice the weight of females. And if all the Danakil australopithecine fossils are of one species, then that species was remarkably successful, as the known specimens span a period of almost one million years. The history of palaeontology is littered with fossils that rewrote the human evolutionary tree overnight but, until another such fossil is unearthed, it is difficult to escape the conclusion that Lucy and her kin were the common ancestor of the genus *Homo* and later australopithecine species. Incidentally, Lucy is now on display in the National Museum in Addis Ababa.

In the 1960s it was widely thought that humans and apes diverged around 20 million years ago, but recent DNA evidence has shown modern man and chimpanzees to be far more closely related than previously assumed – in fact, many biologists feel that less biased observers would place us in the same genus as chimpanzees, who are more closely related to humans than they are to any other living creature. It is now thought that the hominid and chimpanzee evolutionary lines diverged from a common ancestor between four and six million years ago. A recent fossil discovery in the Danakil is being mooted widely as the so-called missing link, the most recent common ancestor of modern African apes and modern humans. The fossils consist of the incomplete bones and the dentition of 17 hominids that lived in a forested habitat about 4.4 million years ago. The few bones discovered to date don't include specimens of legs or hips, which makes precise classification impossible, but the dentition is closer to that of chimpanzees than to any known hominid species, yet it has several hominid features. The species has been classified provisionally as a form of australopithecine, dubbed *A. ramidus*, but it may well belong to an entirely new genus that provides the final link in tracing the broad sweep of human evolution.

So, is Ethiopia the cradle of humankind? Well, the specifics of human evolution remain controversial, and are likely to do so for some time, largely because it is impossible to gauge how complete or representative the known fossil record is. The discovery of large numbers of hominid fossils in one area may indicate simply that conditions at the time were suitable for fossilisation, that current conditions are suitable for recovering those fossils and, crucially, that palaeontologists are looking there. If a vital link in the evolutionary chain was once distributed in an area not yet explored by palaeontologists, it will remain unknown to science.

What does seem certain is that the entire history of human evolution was played out in Africa, including the evolution of *Homo sapiens* from *Homo erectus*. The fact that most crucial

BEFORE LUCY

In 2001 it was announced that the northern Ethiopian Rift Valley had yielded yet another hominid fossil find of shattering significance. The jawbone and other parts of a 5.8-million-year-old hominid were unearthed in 1997 by Yohannis Haile Selassie, an Ethiopian graduate student. The fossils have been assigned to a new genus *Arpipithecus*, which shows clear affiliations with both chimpanzees and humans, and almost certainly forms the so-called missing link between hominids and their apelike ancestors. Furthermore, while it remains the case that tracing the line of human ancestry based on the existing fossil evidence is akin to guessing the subject of a 1,000-piece jigsaw based on a random 20 pieces, this new finding, in an area that was densely forested six million years ago, does cast some doubt on the accepted notion that the first hominids started to walk upright as an evolutionary adaptation to a savanna environment.

discoveries have taken place in the Rift Valley makes Kenya, Tanzania and Ethiopia the most likely candidates for the cradle of humankind, but it should be noted that the Rift is where palaeontologists have tended to focus their attentions in the search for our ancestry.

Pre-history

The first known inhabitants of the Ethiopian Highlands were Stone-Age hunter-gatherers who were closely related to the Khoisan of southern Africa. Stone-Age rock paintings have survived in places like Dire Dawa and Cascase in Eritrea, and tools have been unearthed at several sites, most notably Melka Kunture near Addis Ababa.

The most researched part of Ethiopia in prehistoric terms is what is now the northern province of Tigrai and the newly independent country of Eritrea. The nature of the society in this region prior to about 1000BC is open to speculation. It can be assumed that pastoralism was practised before 4000BC. Conclusive evidence of millet cultivation dating from around 3000BC has been found at Gobedra near Axum, as has indigenous pottery of a similar vintage.

There is reason to think that the northern Ethiopian society of this time had links with Ancient Egypt. The ethnic origin of the Ancient Egyptians is an unsettled question, but some academics think they came to the area from elsewhere in Africa. Several Greek historians of the 1st millennium BC considered the Egyptians and Ethiopians to be of the same race, and one goes so far as to claim it was Ethiopians, led to the country by the Greek god Osiris in around 3000BC, who founded the Egyptian civilisation. Rather less questionable is that the Ancient Egyptians, from around 2500BC, made some naval explorations south to a land they called Punt, which they believed to be their ancestral home. That Punt lay somewhere along the African coast is beyond dispute, but precisely where it lay is anybody's guess. Most current thinking places Punt in modern-day Somalia, while other sources suggest the Axumite port of Adulis in Eritrea or even somewhere on the Tanzanian coast. It is worth noting, as well, that the so-called Ethiopian Dynasty founded in Egypt in 720BC was definitely of Nubian origin. There is, at present, no conclusive evidence one way or the other on links between Egypt and any part of Africa south of Meroe (in Nubia) prior to the 1st millennium BC.

Archaeological and written sources leave no room for doubt that, by 1000BC, northern Ethiopia supported an agricultural and probably quite urbanised civilisation of some magnitude. It was this so-called pre-Axumite society as much as any external influence which laid the foundation for the Axumite Empire that was to follow. The pre-Axumite period is commonly divided into two phases: the South Arabian or Sabaean period between 1000BC and 400BC, and an intermediary period that preceded the founding of Axum in around the 1st century AD. Several archaeologists currently working in Ethiopia feel these divisions are rather arbitrary, especially now it has been ascertained that Axum was occupied as early as 500BC.

One of the major pre-Axumite sites in northern Ethiopia is Yeha, where there is a large, well-preserved stone temple estimated to be at least 2,500 years old. There are also the remains of stone dwellings and catacomb-like tombs. Smaller temples have been found at other sites, as have large and impressive sculptures (many of which are on display in the Addis Ababa National Museum) and a variety of different free-standing altars. Strong religious and cultural links with the Sabaean Kingdom in modern-day Yemen have been noted at Yeha and sites of a similar vintage. It is clear from isolated discoveries of Egyptian and other foreign artefacts that this civilisation was in contact and probably traded with the other major civilisations of the time. Much of the indigenous pottery suggests Greek influences. At this stage, a mere handful of pre-Axumite sites have undergone more than cursory investigation; a 1988 paper by J W Michels lists at least 40 yet-to-be-excavated sites in Tigrai and Eritrea. It is likely that a great deal more will emerge about pre-Axumite society in the course of time.

Traditional history

Ethiopians themselves are in little doubt about their early history. According to oral tradition, Ethiopia was settled by Ethiopic, the great-grandson of Noah. Ethiopic's son, Aksumai, founded the capital of Axum and also a dynasty of rulers that lasted for between 52 and 97 generations. The last, and many say the greatest, of these monarchs was Queen Makeda who, in the 11th and 10th centuries BC, owned a fleet of 73 ships and a caravan of 520 camels which traded with places as far afield as Palestine and India. Makeda ruled Ethiopia and Yemen for 31 years from her capital a few kilometres outside modern-day Axum, which, according to Ethiopians, was known as Sabea.

Early in her rule, it is claimed, the Queen of Sabea (better known to Westerners as the Queen of Sheba) travelled to Jerusalem to visit King Solomon. She brought with her gifts of gold, ivory and spices, and in return she was invited to stay in the royal palace. The two monarchs apparently developed a healthy friendship, the result of which was that Makeda returned home not only converted to Judaism but also carrying the foetal Ibn-al-Malik (Son of the King), whose name later became bastardised to Menelik. At the age of 22, Menelik returned to Jerusalem to visit his father. He was greeted by a joyous reception and stayed in Jerusalem for three years, learning the law of Moses. When he decided to return home, he was, as Solomon's oldest son, offered heirship of the throne, which he declined. Solomon allowed Menelik to return to Ethiopia, but he also ordered all his high commissioners to send their oldest sons with Menelik and each of the 12 tribes of Israel to send along 1,000 of their people.

Accompanying Menelik on his journey home was Azariah, the first-born son of the high priest of the temple of Jerusalem. Azariah was told in a dream that he should take with him the holiest of all Judaic artefacts, the Ark of the Covenant. When Menelik was first told about this, he was angry, but then he dreamt that it was God's will. King Solomon discovered the Ark's absence and led his soldiers after Menelik's enormous entourage, but he too dreamt that it was right for his son to have the Ark, though he insisted on keeping its disappearance a secret. The Ark has remained in Ethiopia ever since, and is now locked away in the Church of St Mary Zion in Axum. On Menelik's return, his mother abdicated in his favour. The Solomonic Dynasty founded by Menelik ruled Ethiopia almost unbroken until 1974, when the 237th Solomonic monarch, Haile Selassie, was overthrown in the revolution.

Most Ethiopians accept this version of events unquestioningly, but it has never been taken very seriously by Western historians. The oldest written version of the Makeda legend is found in a highly fanciful 14th-century Ge'ez volume known as the *Kebre Negest*. This book claims to be a translation of a lost Coptic document dating to the 4th century or earlier; an unlikely claim, especially as the book was written at a time when the so-called Solomonic Dynasty had reasserted its power after several centuries of Zagwe rule. Much of the *Kebre Negest* is undoubtedly medieval fabrication and royal myth-making woven from Sabaean legends around holes in the relevant biblical passages. Nevertheless, there is a significant grain of truth behind the elaboration. To disregard the *Kebre Negest* entirely is to ignore not just the many biblical references to Ethiopia, but also the considerable Jewish influences that permeate Ethiopian culture.

There are more than 30 Old Testament references to Ethiopia (or Cush, as it was known to the Hebrews). Moses, the founder of the Hebrew faith, is known to have married an Ethiopian woman (Numbers 12:1); while Genesis contains a reference to the Ghion River which, it claims, 'compasseth the whole land of Ethiopia'. Even if you take into account the fact that Ethiopia and Cush were once vague geographical terms referring to Africa south of the Sahara, the parts of Africa which are most likely to have been visited by Hebrews are those which were the most accessible. Moreover, the Ghion River is plainly what we now call the Blue Nile, which forms a sweeping arc beneath the part of Ethiopia most influenced by Judaism and the source of which is still referred to in Ethiopia as Ghion.

In the book of Isaiah, we hear of the 'country ... beyond the rivers of Cush, who send ambassadors by sea, in papyrus skiffs over the waters ... a people tall and bronzed'; while in the 7th-century BC book of Zephaniah, the Lord speaks the following words: 'from beyond the rivers of Ethiopia my suppliants, even the daughter of my dispersed, shall bring mine offering', which surely suggests some sort of Jewish dispersal to Ethiopia.

As has been noted elsewhere, the Ethiopian Orthodox Church is unique in its Jewish influence and the emphasis placed on the Book of Jubilees (Genesis and the first part of Exodus). But the purest Jewish influence in Ethiopia is found among the Falasha people, whose tradition relating to Makeda and Solomon is broadly similar to the Christian version. Current Western opinion tends to favour the view that the Falasha are relatively recent arrivals to the area, descendants of a Jewish community established in Yemen in around AD70, but this theory disregards the archaic nature of Falasha rituals which appear to date from before Josiah's reforms of around 640BC. There is no evidence to oppose the possibility that the Falasha's ancestors couldn't have arrived in Ethiopia directly from Jerusalem via the Nile and Tekaze rivers; in fact, this seems rather likely, as the Falasha homeland, as far as it can be established, has always been the area between the Tekaze and Lake Tana.

One reason why the Falasha may have been disregarded in the calculations of modern historians is that their numbers and importance have dwindled greatly in the last few centuries (the last few thousand individuals were airlifted to Israel in 1991) and there have been few modern studies on their traditions. But early travellers such as James Bruce, who spent a long time among the Falasha at a time when they had far more numerical and political importance, recorded their traditions clearly, and it has to be significant that, in 1973, the Chief Rabbi of Jerusalem recognised the Falasha as true Jews, excusing many of their outdated practices on the basis that they must have been severed from the main body of Jewry at a time when these practices were current.

Another serious objection to the traditional account is that pre-Axumite civilisations in Tigrai appear to have been predominantly pagan, worshipping the sun and moon, with later traces of Hellenistic (Greek) influences. Carvings of ibex suggest these animals had a special significance to pre-Axumites, as they did to Sabaeans, and the large statues of women found at many sites suggest a female fertility cult at odds with monotheistic Judaic traditions. But if the Falasha arrived from the west, and their homeland was roughly the same as in historical times (southwest of Tigrai), an absence of Jewish artefacts in Tigrai doesn't preclude the possibility of Jewish and pagan cultures existing side by side in Ethiopia prior to the arrival of Christianity. Perhaps the Jewish faith spread into Tigrai long after it had been established around Lake Tana. Possibly the Axumites were not Jewish at all, but their version of Christianity was influenced by neighbouring Jewish practices, or by Jews who converted at the same time. Either way, most objections to the traditional beliefs rest on the assumption that they originated in Axum. If the traditional account *does* relate to a real event, then the arrival of the Falasha seems the most likely candidate. I find it strange that I have nowhere encountered the suggestion that the *Kebre Negest* account was a Falasha tradition which was later adopted by the Axumites, who would in all probability have distorted it and merged it with their own legends.

The identity of the biblical Queen of Sheba is central to the Ethiopian legends. Although her origin is an open question, most scholars believe that she was Queen Bilkis of Sabea (in modern-day Yemen), on which basis they disregard the Ethiopian legend about Queen Makeda of Axum and suggest that the account in the *Kebre Negest* has borrowed cleverly from Arabian legends about Queen Bilkis. It strikes me, however, that a Sabaean origin for the Queen of Sheba does not preclude the possibility that one of her sons may have formed a dynasty in Ethiopia, especially as some pre-Axumite inscriptions from Ethiopia mention a ruler of Sabea, confirming that there was a place called Saba (Sheba) in Ethiopia in 500BC. In fact, given that the Sabaean civilisation appears to have had close links with pre-Axumite Ethiopia, and that the Ethiopian legends claim that Queen Makeda ruled over Yemen as well as Ethiopia, it seems rather likely. Ignore the more obvious mythologising around the Makeda legend (it does seem a little unlikely that her feet turned into asses' hooves when she stepped in the blood of a dragon as a child, a disfigurement which only Solomon was able to cure) and the traditional account is difficult to disregard entirely, if only as an allegory of a real Sabaean or Jewish migration to Ethiopia.

THE ARK OF THE COVENANT

In Axum's Maryam Tsion Church lies an artefact which, were it proved to be genuine, would add immense substance to Ethiopian legendeering. Unfortunately only one person alive has ever seen this artefact. The Ark of the Covenant is, according to Ethiopian Christians, kept under lock and key in Maryam Tsion, and only the official guardian is allowed to enter. There is no doubting the importance the legend of the Ark plays in Ethiopian Christianity and few people would question the sincerity of the Ethiopian claim. But, superficially at least, its presence in Axum does seem rather far-fetched.

For those unfamiliar with the Old Testament, the Ark of the Covenant was built by the Children of Israel to hold the Tablets of Law given to Moses by God on Mount Sinai. According to the Bible, God gave Moses precise instructions on its design and embellishments. It was thus vested with a deadly power which was particularly devastating in time of battle. After the Jews settled in Jerusalem, the Ark was enshrined in a temple built by Solomon in the 10th century BC, where it remained until the temple was destroyed by the Babylonians in 587BC. While it resided in Jerusalem, the Ark was the most treasured artefact of the Jewish faith, virtually the personification of God, and in many biblical passages it is referred to simply as Jehovah. After the destruction of Solomon's temple, it disappeared. Despite several attempts over the centuries, the Ark has never been recovered.

Graham Hancock, in his book *The Sign and the Seal*, investigated the Ethiopian claim to the Ark and constructed a plausible sequence of events to support it. Hancock points out, and he is not the first person to have done so, that there is strong reason to believe the Ark vanished from Jerusalem long before 587BC. Nowhere in the Bible is it stated that the Ark was taken by the Babylonians, which seems decidedly strange, considering its religious importance; books written during the reign of Josiah (640BC) hint that it had probably disappeared by then. Hancock suggests the Ark was removed during the reign of Manasseh (687–642BC), a king who horrified religious leaders by desecrating Solomon's temple with an idol they considered to be sacrilegious. He suggests that the Ark was removed from the temple by angry priests and taken out of the kingdom, and that the loss of the Ark, when it was discovered by Josiah, was kept a secret from the laity.

Hancock circumvents the major historical loophole in the Ethiopian Ark theory, namely that the evidence currently available suggests that Axum was founded several centuries after Solomon's time, by dating the Ark's arrival in Axum to King Ezana's well-documented conversion to Christianity in the 4th century AD. He discovered that the priests on the Lake Tana island monastery of Tana Kirkos claim to have records stating that the Ark was kept on the island for 800 years prior to its removal to Axum. This claim is given some admittedly rather scant support by the presence of several sacrificial stones of probable Jewish origin on Tana Kirkos.

The Axumite Empire

The roots of modern Ethiopia lie in the Axumite Empire. The origins of this empire and the age of the town of Axum remain obscure, and much of the information I have seems contradictory, but there are few who would query that Axum was one of the most important and technologically advanced civilisations of its time, or that it was a major force in world trade between the 1st and 7th centuries AD.

Most written sources will tell you the Axumite Kingdom became a trade centre of note in the 1st century AD. This assertion is based on the rather negative evidence that Axum is first mentioned by name in a 1st-century Greek document *The Periplus of the Ancient Sea*,

Hancock then discovered that a large Jewish settlement and a temple modelled on Solomon's original had been built on Elephantine Island near Aswan on the Nile River. It is generally accepted this temple was founded in or around the reign of Manasseh, and the fact that the priests at the Elephantine corresponded with priests in Jerusalem is well documented. It appears that the priests here retained sacrificial rites similar to those of the Falasha, confirming that they diverged from the Jewish mainstream before the rule of Josiah. What's more, the temple was destroyed by the Egyptians in around 410BC. The Jewish community on Elephantine is thought to have escaped from the island, but nobody knows where they fled. To all intents and purposes, they vanished. Hancock, naturally enough, suggests they went to Ethiopia. He also claims that this theory accords closely with the legend told to him by an old Falasha priest he met in Israel, who rejected the Makeda story, but claimed that his ancestors had lived in Egypt for several centuries en route from Israel, and that the Ark which they brought with them resided in the Lake Tana region for even longer before being stolen by the Axumite Christians.

As a non-historian, I am unsure how seriously to take Hancock's book, but I do find it difficult not to cock an eyebrow at any theory that contrives to incorporate both the Freemasons *and* the lost city of Atlantis. That said, the central thrust of the book – the ideas summarised and simplified above – seems soundly plausible, even if, by Hancock's own admission, it is purely circumstantial. My conclusion is that, if his facts are correct, Hancock has certainly proved it *possible* that the Ark is in Axum. He has also provided a strong case for the Falasha having arrived in Ethiopia from the northwest, and he has put a slant on Ethiopian history which makes sense of traditional accounts while explaining many of their more implausible aspects – the reasons why I have devoted so much space to his ideas here. But I am no better equipped than the average layperson to judge the accuracy of his facts. I hope the Ark is in Ethiopia; come to the crunch, I don't think I'd put money on it, but I'd rather never know than have my suspicions confirmed. If nothing else, *The Sign and the Seal* is a wonderful exercise in windmill-tilting. It is also a most readable book, and its subject matter is fascinating. I suggest you locate a copy and decide for yourself.

Persuasive as Hancock's arguments might be, Stuart Munro-Hay points out that the story about the Ark of the Covenant is mentioned in none of the tales about Ezana's conversion, in none of the stories about the Nine Saints or about King Kaleb's conquest of Yemen (against a Jewish king, moreover), nor even in the Ethiopian accounts of the end of the monarchy when Queen Gudit attacked the country, or when the Zagwe rose to power. In fact, the first reference to the Ark being in Ethiopia is by Abu Salib, during the reign of Lalibela in around 1210. I can only agree with Munro-Hay that this is 'odd, to say the least, if the Ethiopians then believed that the most powerful symbol of God was in their capital city'. Certainly, I look forward to reading his new book on the subject (see *Further Reading*, page 560), which was published in 2005.

and by the absence of any concrete evidence to date the city from an earlier period. In fact, Adulis, the main port of Axum, is probably older than Axum town. Furthermore, the Axumite Empire as described in the *Periplus* stretched along the coast from modern-day Port Sudan south to Berbera, and into the interior almost as far as the Nile. It seems unlikely such a vast kingdom sprang up in a matter of a few years. The long absence of any archaeological evidence dating Axum to before the 1st century AD is mainly because, prior to Neville Chittick's 1972–74 excavations, a minute percentage of Axum had been excavated, and no major archaeological work on Axum had been published since 1913! As it happens, Munro-Hay's full report on Chittick's excavations, published in 1989, pushes the date of foundation back to the 1st century BC. Furthermore, an archaeologist who worked on a 1992 excavation of a hill outside the modern town told me the team had found rock-hewn catacombs dating to around the 5th century BC. At the time of writing, only a fraction of Axum has been excavated and dozens of other sites in Tigrai await exploration. The simple truth is that nobody knows when Axum and its empire were founded; any date that is based only on formative excavations must in its very nature be conservative.

Adulis lay 50km from modern-day Massawa in Eritrea. According to the *Periplus*, it took three days to travel from Adulis to the main trading centre of Koloe and a further five days to the capital, Axum. The Axumites traded with India, Arabia, Persia and Rome, and the King of Axum was familiar with Greek literature. From other written sources, it is clear that in the 2nd century AD, under King Gadarat, Axum expanded its empire to include parts of modern-day Yemen. Some idea of Axum's contemporary importance is given by the 3rd-century Persian writer, Manni, who listed it as one of the four great kingdoms in the world, along with Persia, China and Rome.

The Axumites were a literate people who developed a unique language called Ge'ez and used a unique script that was based on the Sabaean alphabet. That they were skilled masons is apparent from the impressive free-masonry of the subterranean tombs in Axum town. But the most impressive technological achievement of the Axumites was the erection of several solid granite stelae, the largest of which, now collapsed, was 33m high, taller even than the similar granite obelisks of Egypt. Nobody knows how such heavy slabs of rock were erected; the tradition in Axum is that it was with the aid of the Ark of the Covenant.

The most powerful and influential of the Axumite kings was Ezana, who ruled in the early part of the 4th century along with his twin brother Saizana. Ezana was influenced by two Syrian Christians, Frumentius and Aedissius, and in AD337–40 he made Christianity the official religion of his empire. For once, scholars and Ethiopians are in agreement on this point, though some Ethiopians insist on the slightly earlier date of AD320. Ezana's conversion is documented by the Roman writer Rufinus, and on Axumite coins minted after AD341 the older sun and moon symbols are replaced by a cross. Ezana was a good military leader who led the campaign to conquer Yemen, and also led an expedition to secure control of the territory as far west as the confluence of the Nile and Atbara rivers, where he left a stele. Many inscribed stelae listing Ezana's exploits and recording his gratitude to God have been unearthed around Axum, most of them carved in Ge'ez, Greek and Sabaean.

The most influential of Ezana's actions was undoubtedly his conversion to Christianity. There is a traditional belief that an Ethiopian emissary brought news of the Christian faith to Axum in the time of Queen Candice (around AD50) but there is no suggestion that this led to any changes in Axumite beliefs. Ezana is reliably credited with building the first church in Axum, in which the artefact believed by Ethiopians to be the Ark of the Covenant was later placed. His mentor, Frumentius, was consecrated as the first bishop of Axum, Abba Salama. Ezana and his brother, who for many years ruled Ethiopia in tandem, were almost certainly the Abreha and Atsbeha who are, rather optimistically, claimed locally to have initiated the carving of many rock-hewn churches throughout Tigrai and as far afield as modern-day Addis Ababa.

It is probable that Christianity only made serious inroads into the Axumite Empire in the mid 5th century, when nine so-called Syrian monks (the monks were in fact from a variety of parts of the Roman Empire) fled to Ethiopia. The nine monks preached widely throughout the empire, and they built many churches including the one still in use at Debre Damo monastery. They have been canonised by the Ethiopian Church and each of them has a special holy day dedicated to his memory. Many churches bear one or other of their names – Abba (saint) Aregawi or Mikael, Abba Alef, Abba Tsama, Abba Aftse, Abba Gerima, Abba Liqanos, Abba Guba, Abba Yemata and Abba Panteleon.

Another important Axumite king was Kaleb, who took the throne in the early 6th century and ruled for at least 30 years. It is probable that the empire's prosperity peaked under Kaleb, who campaigned against a Jewish leader who had usurped Yemen and won the territory back for Axum, albeit at a heavy cost. Kaleb's palace, on a hill above the town, was reportedly most beautiful; a Byzantine traveller called Cosmos who visited Axum in AD525 marvelled at the statues of unicorns on its corners, and the tame elephant and giraffe enclosed in the palace grounds. Kaleb's son, Gebre Meskel, appears to have ruled from the same palace. Gebre Meskel is remembered not so much for his military prowess as for his contribution to Ethiopian Christianity. He was the patron of St Yared, who is credited with inventing the notation and form of Ethiopian religious music, and also with writing many songs, poems and chants which are still in use today.

Axum has to this day retained its position as the centre of Ethiopian Christianity. In every other sense, it appears to have fallen into decline soon after Kaleb's rule ended. Many reasons for this have been put forward – local environmental factors such as deforestation and erosion, internal unrest, and the increasing wealth in the east of the empire – but the main factors were almost certainly those linked to a more general decline in Axumite fortunes: the rise of Islam and consequent Arab usurpation of Axum's Red Sea trade routes in AD640, and the increasing importance of Persian-founded routes between the Persian Gulf and the Swahili coast south of Mogadishu. By AD750, Adulis had become a ghost town, and the Kingdom of Axum sank thereafter into global obscurity. From that time on, the country was known as Abyssinia, until the 20th century when it became Ethiopia.

Ethiopia's dark age

It is arguably only from a Western perspective that the collapse of Axum's maritime trade routes signalled the end of Axumite importance. More accurate to say that Axum turned its attention elsewhere by expanding its influence over the Jewish communities of Lasta (near Lalibela) and the Lake Tana region and further south into modern-day Showa. The period between AD750 and 1270 thus saw the Axumite Kingdom (based in what are now Tigrai and Ethiopia) transformed into the precursor of the Ethiopia we know: a Christian empire which covers most of the Ethiopian Highlands. It is also probably true that this extended period of isolation allowed the Ethiopian Church to become the cohesive and idiosyncratic institution it is today. Indicative of a renewed religious energy is the fact that most of Ethiopia's 300 rock-hewn churches date from this period.

Nevertheless, Ethiopia's increasing isolation during this period means that little detail is known of its internal politics, a situation paralleling that of, say, Britain for several centuries after the withdrawal and collapse of the Roman Empire. It is uncertain, for instance, whether the Axumite kings continued to rule from Axum after AD750, or whether they adopted a series of floating capitals. Arab writings suggest that a permanent capital called Kubar was used in the 9th and 10th centuries. The site of this capital has never been found, and it is likely that it was abandoned in the late 10th century, but it was probably south of Axum.

Ethiopian traditions relating to the end of the 1st millennium AD are dominated by the memory of one Queen Yodit (Judith), also known by the alternative names of *Esat* or *Gudit*, both of which mean 'the monster'. Yodit is said to have been born in Lasta, the daughter of a Falasha king called Gideon. She was born at a time of great religious tension. The Christian expansion southwards led to the repression of the Falasha Jews, who refused to pay taxes to the Axumite monarchy and suffered regular punitive raids as a result. Yodit is credited with uniting the Falasha into a cohesive unit, and with leading a march on Axum with the intention of removing Christianity from Ethiopia altogether. The holy city was reduced to rubble and dozens of other churches and Christian settlements were burnt to the ground. Yodit is reputed to have ruled Ethiopia until her death 40 years later, during which time she destroyed many of the finest achievements of the Axumite civilisation and had thousands of Christians put to death.

I have not encountered serious suggestion that Yodit was anything but a genuine historical figure. Exactly when she lived is another matter. Ethiopian tradition dates her rise to AD852, and claims that her onslaught precipitated the move of the Axumite monarchy to Showa. This seems unlikely. Arab writings suggest that Yemenic and Axumite rulers kept sporadic contact well into the 10th century. Furthermore, correspondence between the Nubian and Ethiopian monarchs in around AD980 states unambiguously that the area was plagued by a hostile queen at this time. It seems more likely, then, that Yodit's reign of terror was in the late 10th century which, given her legendary destructiveness, might explain why the site of the capital of Kubar (if it ever existed) has never been found.

The Zagwe Dynasty

Tradition has it that Yodit died in AD892 when a whirlwind swept her up near Wukro, and that she was buried at nearby Adi Kaweh, her grave marked by a pile of stones. Once news of her death filtered to Showa, the Solomonic heir Anbessa Wudim returned to Axum and defeated the Falasha in battle to reclaim his right to the throne. Axum remained unstable, however, and in AD922, King D'il Nead was overthrown by one of his generals, Tekle Haymanot, who took the regal name of Zagwe and founded the dynasty of the same name. This tradition doesn't tally with the most likely dates of Yodit's rule. It has been suggested that the Zagwe Dynasty followed directly from Yodit, and was founded by Jews who later converted to Christianity. This idea is circumstantially supported by the fact that the Zagwe based themselves in Lasta, which at the time was a strongly Jewish region and was almost certainly the birthplace of Yodit.

However, the dating of the Zagwe Dynasty is itself rather obscure. Various sources date their usurpation of the throne from as far apart as AD922 and 1150, with the latter date favoured by more credible sources. Several traditional lists of Zagwe rulers are in existence, but only seven kings appear on all versions and, rather improbably, all but the last are said to have ruled for exactly 40 years. Despite the uncertainty surrounding dates, the Zagwe leaders appear to have introduced a new stability and unity in Ethiopia. It was under the most renowned Zagwe king, Lalibela, that Ethiopian Christianity reached the pinnacle of its physical expression in the form of the cluster of rock-hewn churches carved at the Zagwe capital of Roha (which later became known as Lalibela in honour of the king). It is widely agreed that the Zagwe period of rule ended when a Solomonic descendant called Yekuno Amlak took the throne in 1270. Even here, however, some sources claim that the last Zagwe monarch abdicated of his own free will, others that he was killed in battle by the supporters of his Solomonic successor. Either way, the new king granted land and various other hereditary concessions to the Zagwe line, and these have been upheld into modern times.

It was almost certainly under the Solomonic rulers of the 13th to 15th centuries that much of the mythologising that surrounds Ethiopian history took place. The *Kebre Negest*, the book containing the first record of the Sheba legend and Solomonic claims, was written shortly after the line was reinstated, probably to lend credibility to the new rulers by responding to Zagwe claims of descent from Moses. In many respects, the period after 1270 can be seen as the Ethiopian renaissance. Ethiopian history after 1270 can be discussed on much firmer ground than anything that preceded it; writing and religious art apparently flourished, most particularly under Zara Yaqob (1434–68), who is regarded as having been one of Ethiopia's greatest and most influential kings. The empire continued to expand southward into Showa, and it was ruled from a succession of floating capitals in Showa and later the Lake Tana area. This slow expansion and relative stasis was accompanied by growing tension between the Christian empire and the Muslims who lived beyond its eastern fringes, and it was rocked by spasmodic conflict, including several generally unsuccessful incursions to capture the Red Sea ports which had once formed a part of Axum.

The land of Prester John

It was probably during Zagwe rule that the legend of Prester John took root in Europe. The origin of this legend is now rather obscure, but it seems to have taken hold in the 12th century and impressed the European clergy to such an extent that in 1177 Pope Alexander III sent a message to Prester John (the messenger apparently never returned). The essence of the legend, elaborated on by explorers such as Marco Polo, was that a vast and wealthy Christian kingdom existed somewhere in the 'Indies' (at the time a vague term which covered practically anywhere in the world that was unknown to Europeans) and that it was ruled over by Prester John, who was both king and high priest, and a descendant of the Magi (a group of Persian magicians, three of whom were probably the wise men who attended Jesus shortly after his birth).

As with so many aspects of Ethiopian history, the substance behind the Prester John legend is rather elusive. It is widely thought that the legend had its roots in Ethiopia, but

THE SOLOMONIC DYNASTY

The so-called Solomonic Dynasty, referred to both in this chapter and elsewhere in the book, is said to have ruled Ethiopia for 3,000 years, a practically unbroken lineage of 237 emperors stretching from Menelik I, son of King Solomon and the Queen of Sheba, to Haile Selassie. Like so much else that passes for Ethiopian history, it is also something of a myth. First of all, even the most imperialist of Ethiopians will accept that the Solomonic chain was broken by several centuries of Zagwe rule prior to the late 13th century, when it was supposedly restored by Emperor Yakuno Amlak. Furthermore, there is no historical base for Yakuno Amlak's claim to Solomonic ancestry. On the contrary, academic opinion is that the legendary foundation of Axum by Menelik, son of King Solomon and the Queen of Sheba, was invented (or adapted from a similar Yemeni legend) in the time of Yakuno Amlak to substantiate the new emperor's claim to the throne.

Academic opinion is, of course, only opinion: well founded, but nevertheless an educated guess, based on the lack of any concrete evidence to suggest that the Solomonic legend was in circulation prior to the 13th century. The traditional assertion that Yakuno Amlak was a distant descendant of Solomon has to be regarded as improbable in the extreme, but it is difficult to disprove. Oddly enough, however, one does not need to delve deep into Ethiopia's past to debunk the Solomonic myth. As reader Harry Atkins correctly points out: 'Even in the 19th century, the last ruler of Gonder was not related to Tewodros I, who was not related to Yohannis IV, who was not related to Menelik II. There is no way that Haile Selassie was the 237th Solomonic Emperor.'

precisely how knowledge of a Christian kingdom in Africa reached Europe is an open question. One Ethiopian legend is that Lalibela visited Jerusalem prior to becoming the King of Ethiopia. A few modern sources suggest that the Prester John story was founded on a letter sent to Europe by an Ethiopian king called Yohannis, and it was this letter to which the Pope responded. And as far as I am aware, the Ethiopian Church has maintained links with Alexandria throughout its history, so news could have infiltrated to Europe through Egypt. Or perhaps the legend of Prester John and the reality of a Christian kingdom in Ethiopia is mere coincidence. Whatever truth lay behind the legend, Prester John was a shadowy fringe presence in medieval lore. References to him are scattered through religious and other mystical writing of the period, and it seems probable that the lure of his wealthy kingdom and desire to communicate with a fellow Christian empire was part of the reason behind the Portuguese explorations of Africa which resulted in their arrival in Ethiopia in 1520.

The Muslim–Christian War (1528–60)

Islamic presence in Ethiopia dates back to the time of Mohammed. In AD615, several of Mohammed's followers, his wife among them, fled to Axum where they were offered protection by the king and allowed to settle at Negash. Mohammed himself held Ethiopians in great esteem and warned his followers never to harm them. For several centuries, an uneasy peace existed between Christian Ethiopia and the Islamic world, even as an increasing amount of Islamic settlement took place along the eastern fringes of the Christian kingdom. By the end of the Zagwe era, the Muslim faith had spread throughout Somali and Afar territories and to the southern highlands around Harar, Bale and Arsi, while small bands of Muslims had dispersed into areas that were traditionally part of the Christian empire. Sensing a threat to their sovereignty, and to trade routes to the Red Sea, the Ethiopian Christians launched an attack against the Muslims of Adal in around 1290, which led to a series of skirmishes and wars, and, ultimately, in the mid 14th century, to the expansion of the Christian empire deep into southern Ethiopia. In its attempts to retain its sovereignty, Ethiopia made great efforts to convert pagan highlanders and Falasha to the Christian faith, and also sent abroad envoys to strengthen its links with Christian communities in the Sudan, Egypt, Alexandria and Armenia.

In 1528 a Muslim leader known as Ahmed Gragn (Ahmed the left-handed) took control of the Muslim city of Harar in the eastern highlands. From Harar, Gragn led his army of Afar and Somali Muslims on an annual raid on the Christian Highlands, timed every year to exploit the weakness of Christians during the Lent fast. Gragn's destructiveness can be compared to that of Yodit several centuries before. Many rock-hewn churches throughout Ethiopia still bear the scars of his campaign; of less permanent structures, such as the church at Axum, which was rebuilt after Yodit's reign, no trace remains. The Ethiopian emperor of the time, Lebna Dengal, was chased around his kingdom by Gragn, eventually to die a fugitive in 1540. By 1535, Gragn held Showa, Lasta, Amhara and Tigrai – in other words most of Christian Ethiopia.

Gragn's campaign more or less coincided with the first contact between Europe and Ethiopia, which occurred in 1493, the second-last year of the reign of the youthful Emperor Iskinder, with the arrival – via Egypt, India and the Persian Gulf – of Pero de Covilhão, a 'spy' sent by the Portuguese King John in search of the legendary Land of Prester John. Instead of fulfilling the second part of his mission by returning home, however, Covilhão stayed on in Ethiopia to serve as an advisor to a succession of emperors and regents. He was still there in 1520, when the first full Portuguese expedition to Ethiopia, as documented by the priest Francisco Alvares in the classic book *A True Relation of the Land of Prester John*, was received at the Monastery of Debre Libanos by Emperor Lebna Dengal. Shortly before his death in exile, Lebna Dengal wrote to Portugal asking for help in restoring his kingdom. Were it not for the intervention of the

Portuguese, it is quite likely that Ethiopian Christianity would have been buried under the Muslim onslaught.

In 1543, Emperor Galawdewos's army, propped up by the Portuguese, killed Gragn and defeated his army in a battle near Lake Tana. Galawdewos's attempts to rebuild the shattered Christian empire were frequently frustrated by raids led by Gragn's wife and nephew. In 1559 the emperor was killed and his severed head displayed in Harar. But the long years of war had drained the resources of Christians and Muslims alike; the real winners were the pagan Galla (now known as the Oromo) who expanded out of the Rift Valley into areas laid waste by the fighting. By 1560, the Galla had virtually surrounded Harar and had overrun much of Showa, providing not only a buffer zone between the exhausted Christians and Muslims, but also a new threat to both of the established groups.

The Gonder period (1635–1855)

The Christians were faced with a new disaster as Portuguese ex-soldiers settled around the temporary capital on Lake Tana. In 1622, Emperor Susneyos made a full conversion to Catholicism under the influence of his close friend and regular travelling companion, the Spanish-born Jesuit priest Pero Pais, and he outlawed the Orthodox Church and suspended traditional church officials. This move was naturally very unpopular with Ethiopian Christians, thousands upon thousands of whom were persecuted to death for pursuing their centuries-old faith. Increasingly isolated from his subjects, the emperor was forced to abdicate in favour of his son Fasil in 1632. The new emperor reinstated the Orthodox Church and banned foreigners from his empire. From the 1640s until James Bruce's journey in 1770, only one European, a French doctor, was permitted to enter Ethiopia.

Ethiopia had lacked a permanent capital since 1270. In order to help re-unite Church and State, Fasil broke with this tradition by settling at the small town of Gonder, north of Lake Tana. Gonder was named the permanent capital of Ethiopia in 1636, a title it kept for more than 200 years. This move to Gonder signalled an era of relative peace under a succession of strong, popular emperors, most notably Fasil himself and Iyasu I. Then, under Iyasu II (1730–55), the throne was gradually undermined by Ras (Prince) Mikael of Tigrai, who assumed an increasing backstage importance, twice assassinating emperors and replacing them with others of his choice. For much of the Gonder period, the war between Christians and Galla had been a problem, as had priestly fears about contact between the court and exotic Christian denominations. King Ioas (1755–69) lost almost all support by marrying a Galla woman and insisting on Galla being spoken in court. By 1779, when Takla Giyorgis took power, the king's role was little more than ornamental. The period between 1784 and 1855 is generally referred to as the 'era of the princes'; the Gonder-based rulers of this period are remembered as the shadow emperors.

Ethiopia under Emperor Tewodros II (1855–69)

In 1855, Ethiopia was not so much a unified state as a loose alliance of squabbling fiefdoms run by wealthy local dynasties, who were in turn reigned over by an ineffectual emperor. The empire was threatened not merely by internal power struggles, but also by the external threat posed by Egypt, who wanted to control the Nile from its source in Lake Tana. Were it not for the vision of one Kasa Hayla, Ethiopia could well have collapsed altogether.

Kasa Hayla grew up in the home of Kenfu Haylu, a man who played a major role in campaigns against Egypt and who ruled a minor fief in western Ethiopia. When Kenfu died in 1839, Kasa was denied the heirdom of the fief he had hoped for, and instead became a *shifta* (bandit), though reportedly not an ignoble one, as he developed a Robin Hood-like obsession with wealth redistribution, and also led several private campaigns against Egyptian intruders. By 1850, he ruled the fiefdom he believed to be his by default. He then led a series of campaigns against other princes. In 1855 he defeated the heir to the throne outside Gonder, and had himself crowned Emperor Tewodros II.

History has cast Tewodros as the instigator of Ethiopian unity, and he is now among the country's most revered historical figures. That he never achieved sustained popularity in his lifetime is due to the brutality and ruthless fanaticism with which he pursued his goals of Ethiopian unity and independence. He attempted, with a fair degree of success, to re-unite the fiefdoms under a strong central government; and, less successfully, to modernise the national army. He established an arms factory near his capital of Debre Tabor and gradually accumulated a large arsenal on Makdala Hill near Dessie. Tewodros had strong anti-feudal instincts which led to his abolition of the slave trade and his expropriation of large tracts of fallow church-owned land for the use of peasant farmers. These socialist efforts won him few friends among the clergy and the nobility and, at any given time during his reign, one or other of the old fiefdoms was in rebellion. The strict discipline he imposed on his army led to a high rate of desertion and the continual internal strife cost many of his soldiers their lives: by 1866, his army had dwindled from 60,000 men to 10,000.

Amid growing unpopularity at home, Tewodros's sense of frustration was cemented by his failure to enlist European, and more specifically British, support for his modernising efforts and quest for absolute Ethiopian sovereignty. In 1867, Tewodros retreated embittered to the top of Makdala Hill. With him, he took several British prisoners in a final desperate bid to lever European support: a fatal misjudgement. In 1869, Britain sent a force of 32,000 men led by Sir Robert Napier to capture Tewodros. Makdala was encircled. Instead of fighting, Tewodros wrote a long letter to Napier listing his failed ambitions and castigating his countrymen for their backwardness. Then he took his own life.

Ethiopia under Emperor Yohannis IV (1872–89)

The struggle for succession after Tewodros's suicide took a military form, culminating in the Battle of Assam in 1871, wherein the incumbent emperor Takla Giyorgis was defeated by his brother-in-law and the ruler of Tigrai, Kasa Mercha, whose superior weaponry had been acquired in exchange for supporting Britain in the march to Makdala. Kasa crowned himself Emperor Yohannis IV and ruled from 1872 to 1889. Yohannis was a deeply religious man, a proud nationalist, and a skilled military tactician who nevertheless initiated a more diplomatic form of rule than had Tewodros.

Yohannis's ambition of creating national unity through diplomatic rather than military means was undermined by British duplicity, Egyptian ambitions to control the source of the Nile at Lake Tana, and, not least, the actions of his main rival for the throne, the Showan prince Menelik, who consistently played internal politics while Yohannis fought external powers. Yohannis returned Menelik to his regional seat after ten years of imprisonment under Tewodros. Menelik repaid the favour by seizing Wolo and inserting his ally, Mohammed Ali, as governor while Yohannis was employed in leading successful campaigns against Egypt at Gundat and Gura in 1875–76. When Yohannis returned from his campaigning, Menelik was unwilling to take on the emperor's superior and more experienced army, and Yohannis preferred to settle things diplomatically: a compromise was reached under the Leche Agreement of 1878, which formalised the relationship between the emperor and regional leaders.

Yohannis then turned his attention to negotiating with Europe and Egypt for official recognition of Ethiopian sovereignty. His cause was helped greatly when the Mahdist War broke out in Sudan in 1882, and Britain, who that very year had unilaterally occupied Egypt, realised it needed Ethiopia's assistance to rescue its troops from Sudan. The Treaty of Adwa, signed by Yohannis and a British negotiator in 1884, met most of Yohannis's demands: most significantly the return of Bogos, a part of Ethiopia occupied by Egypt, and the right to the free import of goods including arms and ammunition. The treaty also allowed Britain dominion over the port of Massawa. While Yohannis faithfully kept his part of the bargain by rescuing British troops from Mahdist Sudan, and eventually gave his life in this cause, Britain broke the spirit of the agreement barely a year after it was signed by handing Massawa to Italy.

Italy was a newcomer to Africa. Nevertheless, with the tacit support of Britain, who had little interest in Ethiopia other than ensuring the source of the Nile was kept out of French hands, Italy proved a major threat to Ethiopian sovereignty. The Italian army occupied several Red Sea ports in 1886. Anticipating a march inland, Yohannis attacked their fort at the port at Saati in January 1887. The Ethiopians were repulsed at Saati, but the next day they attacked and destroyed a force of 500 Italians at Dogali. In March 1888, Yohannis led 80,000 men in an attack on Saati, but the Italians refused to leave their fort and fight, and the news of a successful Mahdist attack on Gonder, still the official capital of Ethiopia, and also of Menelik's plans to rise against the emperor, forced Yohannis to turn his troops on these more immediate problems. On 9 March 1889, Yohannis led his troops against the Mahdist stronghold at Matema. Ethiopia won the battle, effectively ending the Mahdist threat, but not before Yohannis was fatally wounded. Menelik was crowned emperor of Ethiopia.

Emperor Menelik II (1889–1913)

From his base in Showa, Menelik had done much to unite Ethiopia during Yohannis's reign, even if his major motives were entirely cynical: the expansion of Showan territory, the opening up of trade routes blocked by hostile fiefdoms, and a demonstration of his own leadership and military prowess. Between 1882 and 1888, Harar, Arsi, most of the fiefdoms of the southwest, and large tracts of Galla land were captured by Menelik. It was also while Yohannis was in power that Menelik moved the Showan capital to the Intoto Hills, a range that was rich in Solomonic associations and which boasted two ancient rock-hewn churches. In 1886, Menelik moved his capital into the valley below Intoto, to the site of what was to become Addis Ababa.

Menelik came to national power during the most severe famine in Ethiopia's recorded history. The *Kefu Qan* (Evil Days) of 1888–92 was a direct result of a rinderpest epidemic triggered by the importation of cattle by the Italians, and the crisis was exacerbated by drought and locust plagues. This famine cannot be seen in isolation from the ongoing wars of the 19th century, nor can it be dissociated from the greed of the feuding princes. Peasant resources had been stretched to the limit long before the advent of rinderpest.

During Yohannis's time, Menelik had been in friendly contact with the Italians at Massawa, trading promises of peace for weapons to expand his own empire and to challenge the emperor. In May 1889, he signed the Treaty of Wechale, granting Italy the part of Ethiopia which was to become Eritrea in exchange for recognition of Ethiopian sovereignty over the rest of the country. What Menelik didn't realise was that the Italians had inserted a clause in the Italian version of the document, but not in the Amharigna equivalent, which demanded that Ethiopia make all her foreign contacts through Italy, in effect reducing Ethiopia to an Italian protectorate. Italy further undermined the spirit of the treaty when, in 1891, it successfully courted several Tigraian princes into alliance with Eritrea. When the princes revolted against the prospective colonisers in 1894, Italy was left with one course open to attain its goal of colonising Ethiopia: military confrontation.

In October 1895, Italy occupied Adigrat on the Tigraian side of the border, and also established a fort at the Tigraian capital of Mekele. Menelik led a force of 100,000 men to Tigrai and, after a couple of inconsequential skirmishes, the two armies met in the hills around Adwa. The memory of the Battle of Adwa, which took place on 1 March 1896, remains one of the proudest moments in Ethiopian history. Through their own faulty map-reading as much as anything, the Italian troops were humiliatingly routed, the first time ever that a European power was defeated by Africans in a battle of consequence. In Rome, nearly 100,000 people signed a petition demanding Italian withdrawal from Ethiopia and, although Italy retained Eritrea, the borders of which were formalised in 1900, it was to be almost 40 years before they again crossed the Ethiopian border in anger. Ethiopia was the only part of Africa to survive as an independent state following the European scramble.

In many senses, Menelik completed the process of unification and modernisation that had been started by Tewodros and Yohannis. His period of rule saw the introduction of electricity, telephones, schools and hospitals, and also the building of the Addis Ababa–Djibouti railway. It also saw a re-intensification of the slave trade which, although it had been present in Ethiopia since time immemorial, had been curbed if not halted by Tewodros. Slavery was the pretext used by Europe to block Ethiopia's entry to the League of Nations and to sanction against the import of arms and ammunition to Ethiopia. The slave raids, in which many thousands of Ethiopians died, were the major blemish on a period of rule that was one of the longest periods of sustained peace Ethiopia had known for a long time.

The rise of Haile Selassie (1913–36)

Menelik died of old age in 1913. His chosen successor, Iyasu, is remembered as much for his good looks and raffish lifestyle as anything he achieved. In fact, had he ever been given the chance, Iyasu could well have been the relatively progressive leader that Ethiopia needed to drag it out of feudalism. Iyasu tried to curb the slave trade; he did much to incorporate Ethiopia's often-neglected Muslim population (several of his wives were Muslim and he financed the building of many mosques); and he showed little regard for the ageing and self-serving Showan government which he inherited from Menelik. Or to put it another way, Iyasu succeeded in annoying the slave-owning nobility, the clergy of the Orthodox Church, and the political status quo. In 1916, while visiting Jijiga in an attempt to improve relations with Ethiopia's Somali population, Iyasu was overthrown. He was eventually captured in 1921 and imprisoned in Fiche in north Showa.

The two main rivals to succeed Iyasu were Zawditu Menelik, the sheltered daughter of the dead emperor, and Ras Tefari Mekonnen, the ambitious son of the Harari governor Ras Mekonnen and grandson of an earlier Showan monarch. The Showan nobility, who had called most of the shots as the ailing Menelik reached the end of his reign, favoured Zawditu for her political naïvety and evident potential for ineffectuality. A compromise was reached wherein Zawditu became empress, and Tefari the official heir to the throne. In actuality, the younger, more worldly and better-educated Ras Tefari assumed a regent-like role and the two governed in tandem, a situation that became increasingly tense as Tefari's dominance grew. This ambiguous relationship was resolved in 1930, when the empress's husband was killed in rather murky circumstances in a civil battle. Two days later, Zawditu herself succumbed, apparently to that most Victorian of maladies, heartbreak. Ras Tefari was crowned under the name Haile Selassie in November 1930.

Haile Selassie set to work on drafting a new constitution with the claimed intent of doing away with feudalism and limiting the powers of the regional princes. Consciously or not, the effect of the constitution was further to entrench the regional nobility in a ministerial system based more on heredity than on merit. The first parliament, which assembled in November 1931, consisted of a senate whose members were appointed directly by the emperor, and a chamber of deputies whose members were elected by the landed gentry. The only regional leader to challenge the constitution was Ras Haylu of Gojjam. After attempting to free Iyasu from his confinement in Fiche, Haylu was sentenced to life imprisonment in 1932 and Gojjam was placed under the administration of one of the emperor's allies. Haile Selassie can be credited with creating the first unambiguously unified Ethiopian state. Equally unambiguous was the fact that this state gave no meaningful constitutional protection or power to the overwhelming majority of its citizens.

The Italian occupation (1936–41)

The first serious challenge to Haile Selassie's rule came not from within the country but from Italy. The immediate effect of the Battle of Adwa had been the abandonment of Italian colonial aspirations south of the Eritrean border, but the humiliation afforded to the Italian army at Adwa still rankled, particularly in the nationalistic fervour that accompanied the rise to power of Mussolini's fascists in 1922. Mussolini's initial attempts to gain economic control of Ethiopia were disguised behind diplomacy but, by the time Haile Selassie had gained absolute power over Ethiopia, the Italians had more or less abandoned this approach in favour of subterfuge and force. The former tactic was most effective in Tigrai, an outlying region of northern Ethiopia with close historical and cultural links to neighbouring Eritrea. Italy charmed the Tigraian nobility, whose response when war broke out in 1935 varied from lukewarm resistance to taking the Italian side against Ethiopia.

The first harbinger of war was the Walwal Incident of December 1934, wherein a remote Ethiopian military post on the disputed Italian Somaliland border region was attacked by Italian troops. The skirmish was initiated by Italy, and Italy suffered considerably less loss of life than did Ethiopia. Nevertheless, the political climate in Europe was such that countries like Britain and France were more than willing to sacrifice Ethiopian interests to the cause of frustrating an alliance between Mussolini and Hitler. Italy made absurd demands for reparations. Ethiopia took these to the League of Nations (it had become a member state in 1925) for arbitration, but its perfectly valid arguments were ignored; Italy was in effect given a free hand in Ethiopia.

The Italian army crossed from Eritrea to Tigrai in October 1935. By 8 November, Italy had occupied Adigrat, Mekele and, to its immense satisfaction, Adwa. The Ethiopian army entered Tigrai in January 1936. After a couple of minor Ethiopian victories, most notably at the first Battle of Tembien, Italy's superior air power and its use of prohibited mustard gas proved decisive. The Battle of Maychew, which took place on 31 March 1936, is generally regarded as the last concerted Ethiopian resistance to Italian occupation. Although several minor skirmishes distracted the Italians as they marched from Maychew to Addis Ababa, it was when news of Italy's victory at Maychew reached the capital that the emperor went into exile and the streets erupted into anarchic and unfocused mass violence.

Italy incorporated Ethiopia, Eritrea and Italian Somaliland into one large territory which they named Italian East Africa. Addis Ababa was made the colonial capital, while Jimma, Gonder, Harar, Asmara and Mogadishu became regional administrative centres. The Italian influence on all these cities is still evident today, as it is on several smaller towns. More lasting was the Italian influence on the internal transport infrastructure, particularly in the north, where they cut roads through seemingly impossible territory. This positive legacy must, however, be set against their successful bid to cripple indigenous businesses and replace them with parastatal organisations. This state interventionism proved to be particularly damaging in the agricultural sector: the importation of grain, almost unknown before 1935, became a feature of the Italian and post-Italian eras. Ultimately, though, the high level of internal resistance to the exotic regime, and its eventual collapse in 1941, meant that it was too ineffectual and short-lived to have many lasting effects on Ethiopia.

Throughout the Italian occupation, the Ethiopian nobility combined time-buying diplomacy and well-organised guerrilla warfare to undermine the regime. The fascists' response was characteristically brutal. When, in 1937, an unsuccessful attempt was made on the life of the Italian viceroy, the Italian Blackshirts ran riot in the capital, burning down houses and decapitating and disembowelling Ethiopians, mostly at random, though the intelligentsia was particularly targeted and few survived the rampage. The Ethiopian resistance won few battles of note, but its role in demoralising the occupiers laid the foundation for the easy British victory over the Italian troops in the Allied liberation campaign of January 1941.

Post-war Ethiopia under Haile Selassie (1941–74)

Haile Selassie was returned to his throne immediately the Allied troops drove Italy back into Eritrea. Eritrea and Italian Somaliland were placed under the rule of the British Military Administration. When war ended, the UN was left to determine the status of the three countries which had been co-administrated under Italy. Haile Selassie naturally wanted all the territories to be integrated under his imperial government. When it was decided that Italian Somaliland should be governed under a ten-year trusteeship then granted full independence, Ethiopia's demands for Eritrea and the access to the Red Sea it offered became more concerted. To its aid came the USA and Britain, both of which had a good relationship with Haile Selassie and a vested interest in keeping at least one Red Sea territory in friendly hands. With more than a touch of cynicism on the part of certain of its member states, and after no meaningful consultation with the Eritreans, the UN forced Eritrea into a highly ambiguous federation with Ethiopia.

The US intervention over Eritrea led to a decreasing European role in determining Ethiopian affairs and much stronger links being forged with the other side of the Atlantic. As the oil-rich Middle East came to play an increasingly important role in international affairs, so too did Ethiopia and its Red Sea harbours in US foreign policy. In exchange for using Asmara as their Red Sea base, the US developed a military training and armoury programme for Ethiopia which, by 1970, absorbed more than half the US budget for military aid to Africa. Little wonder, then, that the world barely noticed when, using the pretext of a minor skirmish the preceding year, Eritrean federation became colonisation. In 1962, Ethiopia formally annexed Eritrea, dissolved the Eritrean Assembly, and placed the federated territory under what was practically military rule. The terms of federation gave Eritrea no recourse to argue its case before the UN. So began a war for self-determination which lasted almost 30 years, cost the lives of more than 100,000 Eritreans, and never once figured on the UN's agenda.

Few modern leaders have become so deeply associated with a country's image for so long a time as did Emperor Haile Selassie. As Ras Tefari, he wielded much of the power behind the throne between 1916 and 1930; as emperor he ruled almost unchallenged, except for the brief Italian interlude, between 1930 and 1974. Despite the mystique that surrounded him, however, Haile Selassie did very little to develop his country. The 1931 constitution created a united empire by entrenching the rights of the nobility; it had done little to improve the lot of ordinary Ethiopians. The revised constitution of 1955 introduced universal suffrage, but the absence of any cohesive political parties and the high salaries offered to parliamentarians attracted self-seeking careerists rather than politicians of substance. The low turnouts at elections suggest that political education was non-existent and most Ethiopians saw the constitutional revision for the window dressing it undoubtedly was. In essence, the Ethiopia of 1960 or 1970 was no less feudal than had been the Ethiopia of 1930. The economy remained as subsistence-based as ever, with trade and industry accounting for a mere 10% of the GDP. In many respects, and despite its proud independence, Ethiopia lacked an infrastructure comparable even to those of the underdeveloped colonies that surrounded it.

Little wonder, then, that the wave of colonial resistance which swept through Africa after World War II, and which resulted in the independence of most of the former African colonies in the early 1960s, was mirrored by a rising tide of imperial resistance in post-occupation Ethiopia. Underground opposition to the emperor started almost immediately the Italian occupation ended. The most persistent of the dissidents, Takala Walda-Hawaryat, had supported the emperor before the occupation but, like many ex-resistance leaders, he strongly opposed Haile Selassie's return to power after having sat out the occupation in exile. Takala attempted to install one of Iyasu's sons in place of Haile Selassie and was detained. In 1946 he became involved in another anti-imperial plot, and was detained for another eight years. Takala was killed in a police shoot-out in 1969. By this time, however, a more concerted anti-imperialist movement had emerged, its objections not so much to Haile Selassie himself as to the outmoded feudal system he represented.

The first serious threat to imperial power came in the form of an attempted military coup initiated by the left-wing intellectual Garmame Naway and implemented by his brother Brigadier-General Mengistu Naway, leader of the Imperial Bodyguard. On 14 December 1960, while Haile Selassie was away in Brazil, the Imperial Bodyguard effectively imprisoned his cabinet at the Imperial Palace, having lured them there by claiming that the empress was terminally ill, then announced that a new government would be formed to combat the country's backwardness and poverty. Haile Selassie flew back to Asmara and from there instructed the military – whose tottering loyalty was secured by the promise of a substantial pay rise – to storm the palace. Garmame Naway was killed in the shoot-out, along with several cabinet members, while his brother Mengistu was captured in the act of fleeing and hanged for treason.

Haile Selassie returned to his palace, but it wasn't quite business as usual from thereon, although the last person to recognise this was arguably the emperor himself. Indeed, on the Pan-African front, as a spate of former European colonial possessions were transformed into independent self-governing nations during the early 1960s, the figurehead status of Ethiopia's septuagenarian head of state was entrenched by the selection of Addis Ababa as capital of the newly formed Organisation of African Unity (OAU) in 1963. On the domestic front, by contrast, the attempted coup sparked a more widespread cry for reform and greater recognition that imperial rule was open to challenge. Between 1963 and 1970, Bale was in a permanent state of revolt, while a successful local coup was staged in Gojjam in 1968. There were also revolts in parts of Sidamo (1960) and Wolo (1970), while Addis Ababa witnessed regular student demonstrations from 1965 onwards, and the military became increasingly divided into imperial loyalist and liberationist factions. From 1967 onwards, the Eritrean Liberation Front (ELF) and Eritrean People's Liberation Front (EPLF) became highly militarised in their bid to achieve full independence for their province.

The ageing Haile Selassie responded to the atmosphere of dissent and loud cries for land reform – most Ethiopian peasants were still subject to the whims of local landlords – with increasingly repressive measures. Matters came to a head over the tragic 1973 famine in Wolo and Tigrai. As the BBC aired heartbreaking footage of starving Ethiopians, the imperial government first refused to acknowledge the famine's existence, and then – having retracted its initial denials – failed to respond to the crisis with any action meaningful enough to prevent the estimated 200,000 deaths that ensued. The disgraced cabinet resigned in February 1974 and a new prime minister was appointed shortly thereafter. Too little, too late: at around the same time the armed forces and police had established a co-ordinating committee called the Derg, which – guided by the slogan *Ethiopia Tidkem* (Ethiopia First) – gradually insinuated itself into a position of effective power by arresting officials it regarded to be incompetent and/or self-serving, and replacing the recently installed prime minister with a stooge in July of the same year.

On 12 September 1974, following seven months of ceaseless strikes, demonstrations, local peasant revolts and military mutinies, what little power the octogenarian (and possibly semi-senile) Haile Selassie still wielded was finally curtailed. The military arrested the emperor in his palace, and – in mockery of a grandiose imperial motorcade – drove him to a prison cell in the back of a Volkswagen Beetle, while his embittered subjects yelled out 'Leba!' (Thief!). Details of the imperial imprisonment are unclear and only started to emerge many years later. Certainly, Haile Selassie was still alive when the Derg officially abolished the monarchy in March 1975, and he even made one last (unofficial) public appearance three months later prior to being hospitalised for an operation. It would appear, however, that 3,000 years of supposed Solomonic rule ended in the imperial palace on 27 August 1975, with the ailing and deposed emperor succumbing not to a heart attack, as the official line had it at the time, but to a smothering pillow held in place by his effective successor Colonel Mengistu Haile Maryam. Ethiopia's last emperor was buried next to a latrine outside the palace, only for his remains to be exhumed in the early 1990s and stored for several years in the Menelik Mausoleum in Addis Ababa. Haile Selassie was finally accorded a formal burial at Trinity Cathedral in November 2000.

The Derg (1974–91)

Immediately after the arrest of the emperor, power was handed to the socialist-inspired Military Co-ordinating Committee known as the Derg. Lofty socialist ideals or not, the Derg soon proved to be even more ruthless and duplicitous in achieving its goals than was its predecessor. Despite the ELF and EPLF having helped them get to power, the Derg wanted to retain Eritrea and determined that this should be done through force. In September 1974, they asked the prominent General Aman to lead them and to be their spokesperson; when Aman resigned two months later in protest at the Derg policy on Eritrea, he was placed under house arrest and killed. Fifty-seven important officials were executed without trial, including two previous prime ministers.

A provisional military government was formed by the Derg in November under the leadership of General Tefari Benti. A series of radical policies was implemented, most crucially the Land Reform Bill of March 1975, which outlawed private land ownership and allowed for the formation of collective land use under local *kebele* councils. Disenchantment with US support for the previous government and the persistence of a feudalistic economy into the 1970s made Ethiopia a fertile ground for socialism. Most of the Derg's attempts at collectivisation, villagisation and resettlement were met neither with popular support nor with significant success. Agricultural productivity showed less growth than population figures throughout Derg rule.

The number of local and national opposition groups mushroomed in 1975–76. One of the most important was the Tigraian People's Liberation Front (TPLF), which received training from the EPLF and allied itself to the cause of Eritrean self-determination while demanding a truly democratic Ethiopian government rather than a ruthless military dictatorship. The Derg responded to this outbreak of dissent with mass arrests and executions. The situation was exploited mercilessly by Vice-Chairman Mengistu Haile Maryam, who used it to justify an internal purge of the Derg, a self-serving process which culminated in February 1977 with the execution of seven party leaders including General Tefari. Mengistu thus became the unopposed leader of the provisional government; those who opposed him didn't do so for long.

By 1977, large parts of Eritrea were under rebel rule. There were rumblings from the newly founded Oromo Liberation Front (OLF), the organisation that represented Ethiopia's largest ethnic group. Somali-populated parts of eastern Ethiopia rose against the government army, aided by troops from Somalia, precipitating Russian and Cuban withdrawal from Somalia and support for Ethiopia. The result was a low-scale but occasionally very bloody war (10,000 troops died on each side in 1978) between Somalia and Ethiopia which closed the Djibouti railway line for several years and was only fully resolved in 1988. The unrest spread to the capital, where street conflict resulted in several hundreds of deaths. Furthermore, in early 1979, an estimated one million Ethiopians were affected by a famine in Tigrai, Wolo and Eritrea, and at least 10,000 people died.

Mengistu contrived to pull the country back into some sort of order in 1980, as much as anything by arresting and killing opposition leaders, and driving those who survived his purges into exile. Thousands upon thousands of Ethiopians were killed by the army; it is evidence of the cruelty of his regime that when a family wanted to collect a body for burial, it was required to pay the cost of the fatal bullet. Despite the semblance of peace, much of Somali-populated Ethiopia was practically autonomous, and the EPLF and TPLF continued to engage the regime in sporadic conflict.

Ethiopia leapt into the world spotlight in 1985. The latest famine was the worst in living memory. Its roots lay in three successive rainfall failures in Tigrai, Wolo, the eastern lowlands and even parts of Gonder and Gojjam, but it was exacerbated by politics: at first a Western refusal to send aid to a socialist country, and then, when aid finally arrived, by Mengistu's unwillingness to help food get to the troublesome province of Tigrai. One in five Ethiopians were affected by the famine; one million died, most of them in the northeast. It was a natural phenomenon, but the tragic scale it reached was entirely preventable.

In September 1987, Ethiopia was proclaimed a 'People's Democratic Republic' and technically returned to civilian rule, on the basis of a contrived election in which all candidates were nominated by the Derg. Mengistu was returned to power. In the same year, the Ethiopian People's Revolutionary Democratic Movement (EPRDM), allied to the TPLF and apparently supported by the EPLF, was formed with the major aim of initiating a true national democracy as opposed to regional secession. In May 1988, the government declared a state of emergency in Tigrai and Eritrea as an increasing number of major towns, even some as far south as Wolo, fell under rebel rule. Attempted peace talks in April 1989 met with dismal failure. By the turn of the decade, Mengistu remained in control of most of Ethiopia, but his regime's days were numbered.

Ethiopia post-1990

The final nail was driven into the Derg by the collapse of European socialism in 1990. This resulted in a cutback in military aid to Mengistu, and his weakened army was finally driven completely from Tigrai and Eritrea. In May 1991, the EPRDM captured Addis Ababa and Mengistu jetted to safety in Zimbabwe. The new transitional government established by the EPRDM and headed up by President Meles Zenawi abandoned Mengistu's failed socialist policies, and allowed the EPLF to set up a transitional government in Eritrea. After a referendum in which Eritreans voted overwhelmingly in favour of secession, Eritrea was granted full independence in April 1993.

Ethiopia may have been the only African country that avoided long-term colonialism, but equally it was also one of the last to enjoy any semblance of democratic rule. The first move to correct this was taken in December 1994, when the transitional government implemented a federal constitution that divided the country into 11 electoral regions, each of which was guaranteed political autonomy on regional matters and proportional representation in a central government. This move paved the way for the country's first democratic election in May 1995, which saw Zenawi voted in as Prime Minster alongside President Nagasso Gidada (a coupling that was returned to power in the election of 2000). Ethiopia, in late 1995, seemed set to put its troubled past behind it, under a democratically elected government that is by far the most egalitarian and least repressive the country has ever known.

Ethiopia's first years of democratic rule were tainted, however, by a gradual deterioration in its relationship with neighbouring Eritrea. The first outward sign of the two countries' growing economic antagonism was the relatively innocuous Eritrean

ETHIOPIAN NAMES

Ethiopians have a different system of naming to most Western countries, one that resembles the Islamic system. As is customary in the West, the first name of any Ethiopian is their given name. The difference is that the second name of any Ethiopian is not an inherited family name, but simply the father's given name. In other words, an Ethiopian man called Belai Tadese is not Belai of the Tadese family, but Belai the son of Tadese, and he would be addressed as Belai. It is polite to address people older than you, or whom you respect, as Ato (Mister) or Waziro (Mrs). Again, you would use the person's own name, not their father's name – Belai Tadese would be addressed not as Ato Tadese but as Ato Belai. If Ato Belai has a daughter who is named Guenet, she will be known as Guenet Belai. If she marries somebody called Bekele Haile, her name won't change to Guenet Haile but will stay Guenet Belai. She would be addressed as Waziro Guenet and her husband as Ato Bekele. If they have a child they name Yohannis, he will be known as Yohannis Bekele.

It is worth noting that Ethiopians will not ask for your surname but for your father's name. When dealing with officials, you should obviously give the parental name on your passport – your surname. You will also find that, even in the most formal of situations, Ethiopians address Westerners according to their custom rather than ours – I am often addressed as Ato or Mister Philip, never by my surname.

decision, in November 1997, to replace the common currency of the birr with a new currency called the nacfa. The growing estrangement between the two governments – which only ten years earlier had been fighting alongside each other against the Derg – took more concrete expression in May 1998. Up until this point, the EPLF and EPRDM had tacitly agreed that the international boundary between Eritrea and Ethiopia would adhere to the regional border under the Derg. On 6 May, however, Eritrean soldiers approached Badme, the principal town of Ethiopia's 400km² Yirga Triangle, provoking a police shoot-out in which both sides suffered fatalities. The joint Ethiopian–Eritrean commission that met in Addis Ababa two days later was unable to defuse the situation, and a second military skirmish followed on 12 May. Ethiopia demanded the immediate withdrawal of Eritrean troops from the Yirga Triangle. Eritrea responded by claiming that the Yirga Triangle historically belonged to Eritrea and had been effectively occupied by Ethiopia prior to the Eritrean attack.

The abrupt transformation from free border to open hostility – which surprised most outside observers and locals alike – seemed initially to be unlikely to amount to more than a few border skirmishes over what was, and remains, a relatively insignificant patch of barely arable earth. On 5 June, however, the stakes were raised when Eritrean planes cluster-bombed residential parts of Mekele, including an elementary school, leaving 55 civilians dead and 136 wounded. Ethiopia retaliated swiftly by launching two air strikes on Eritrean military installations outside Asmara. In the following week, Eritrea launched a second cluster-bomb attack on Ethiopian civilians, targeting the border town of Adigrat, and expelled an estimated 30,000 Ethiopian residents from Eritrea. Despite growing international pressure for a negotiated settlement, both parties set about amassing troops at the border – some estimates place the number as high as 200,000 on each side. Border tension erupted into a full-scale military conflict in the first week of February 1999. By the end of that month, it is estimated that at least 20,000 Eritreans had been killed in the conflict, with a similar number of casualties on the Ethiopian side. The total tally of dead and wounded over the ensuing months remains a matter for conjecture; the humanitarian and economic cost of the enforced conscription, mass expulsions of each other's citizens and displacement of thousands of civilians on both sides are impossible to measure.

In part due to Ethiopia's superior diplomacy, and in part because the disputed territory had clearly been under Ethiopian jurisdiction since Eritrean independence, the OAU called for Eritrea to withdraw from all occupied Ethiopian territories on 21 June. Eritrea refused, and another bout of fighting broke out over the next week, leaving thousands more dead on both sides. Eritrea did little to help its increasingly indefensible position when its president refused to attend an OAU peace summit in Libya on 10 July. The pattern of failed attempts at diplomacy, generally initiated by Ethiopia, followed by a fresh outburst of border fighting, persisted for the remainder of 1999. One of the most pointless wars in living memory had by now taken on a significance that extended far beyond the patch of land that had provoked it, and many observers queried whether either side would ever be prepared to back down. By early 2000, a tense virtual ceasefire hung over the border, but the Eritrean government publicly announced that it would not withdraw, and was ready for further conflict. The first diplomatic breakthrough occurred in late February 2000, when the US envoy Anthony Lake and OAU special envoy Ahmed Ouyahia shuttled between Asmara and Addis Ababa in an attempt to secure a negotiated solution. Renewed conflict broke out over May and June, but by this time the Yirga Triangle was firmly back under Ethiopian control, and this final Eritrean attack resulted in an outright victory for Ethiopia, presumably the spur that drove Eritrea to the negotiating table. The ensuing Algiers conference resulted in an immediate ceasefire under the supervision of a UN peacekeeping force. On 12 December 2000 a peace agreement was signed, and the Yirga Triangle was formally restored to Ethiopian territory.

Cliché it might be, but it is difficult to see either side as a victor of an episode that resulted in such large-scale loss of life, and in the wholesale economic and social disruption of two closely affiliated countries that must rank as among the poorest in the

DANGER: TOURISTS

Tourism need not be a destructive force for tribal people but unfortunately it frequently is. We at Bradt Travel Guides Ltd totally support the initiative of the charity Survival in protecting the rights of tribal peoples:

Recognise land rights
Obtain permission to enter
Pay properly
Behave as if on private property

Respect tribal peoples
Don't demean, degrade, insult or patronise

Don't bring in disease
Diseases such as colds can kill tribal peoples
AIDS is a killer

Survival (11–15 Emerald Street, London WC1N 3QL, England; ☎ 020 7242 1441; f 020 7242 1771; e survival@gn.apc.org) is a worldwide organisation supporting tribal peoples. It stands for their right to decide their own future and helps them protect their lives, lands and human rights.

world. As this book goes to print, it remains the case that many thousands of Ethiopians formerly resident in Eritrea, or Eritreans formerly resident in Ethiopia, remain in 'exile' in their nominal 'home country'. The financial toll – money that could so easily have been pumped into the road infrastructure, education, you name it really – is immeasurable, as was the loss of economic momentum and growing international confidence that characterised Ethiopia's immediate post-Derg years.

That momentum has been regained since the war ended, though the continued closure of the border with Eritrea and occasional war-mongering outburst from the Ethiopian government is cause for long-term unease. And, partially because of this, Ethiopia's third general election, held in May 2005, demonstrated a mass retraction of urban support for Zenawi and the EPRDF.

The final poll results, which were announced almost four months later following repeat elections in 32 controversial constituencies, saw the EPRDF win the third term it sought with 327 of the possible 547 seats as compared to the opposition Coalition for Unity and Democracy's 170. But this represented a dramatic swing from the 2000 election, when all but 12 seats had been held by the EPRDF. Furthermore, the opposition took all 23 seats in Addis Ababa, leaving the government without much credibility in the country's most sophisticated voting block.

Where this leaves Ethiopia is unclear, but – despite the violent clashes between protesters and armed forced that left 38 civilians in June, and a more recent EU report questioning how free and fair the election actually was – it feels like an exciting and positive development, one with few precedents anywhere in Africa. As one friend in Addis Ababa wrote in a recent email: 'Ethiopia will never be the same again; the democratic trend is now irreversible'.

Wildlife

Ethiopia is a land of dramatic natural contrasts. Altitudes span the lowest point on the African continent as well as the fourth highest peak, while climatic conditions range from the scorching arid badlands of the Somali–Kenyan border region to the drenched slopes of the fertile southwest. The vegetation is no less diverse than the topography and climate, embracing parched desert, drenched rainforest, brittle heath-like Afro-alpine moorland, and pretty much everything in between.

Far from being the monotonous thirstland of Western myth, the southern and western highlands of Ethiopia boast the most extensive indigenous rainforest to be found anywhere in the eastern half of Africa. The central highlands, though more openly vegetated, are green, fertile and densely cultivated. Towards the end of the rains, in September and early October, the wild flowers that blanket the highlands are second only to those of Namaqualand in South Africa, in number if not variety. The northeast highlands of Tigrai are drier and generally quite thinly vegetated except during the rains. The Rift Valley south of Addis Ababa has a characteristically African appearance, with vegetation dominated by grasses and flat-topped acacia trees. The western lowlands around Gambella have lushly tropical vegetation. Only the vast but rarely visited eastern and southern lowlands conform to the image of Ethiopia as a featureless desert.

It is probably fair to say that Ethiopia's greatest natural attraction to the average tourist will be the wonderful and ever-changing scenery. Wildlife, though once prolific, has been hunted out in most areas, and even those savanna national parks – Nechisar, Mago, Omo and Awash – which do protect typical African savanna environments support low volumes of game by comparison with their counterparts in most eastern and southern African countries. Balanced against this, Ethiopia's fauna and flora, though essentially typical of sub-Saharan Africa, also displays some strong links to lands north of the Sahara, ie: north Africa, Europe and the Middle East. One manifestation of this is the presence of several species that are endemic (unique) to Ethiopia because of their isolation from similar habitats, including the Ethiopian wolf, gelada baboon, mountain nyala, Walia ibex and Somali wild ass.

Whatever it may lack in terms of mammalian abundance, Ethiopia is one of Africa's key birdwatching destinations. A rapidly growing national checklist of more than 800 bird species includes 16 endemics, as well as a similar number of near-endemics whose range extends into a small part of neighbouring Eritrea or into Somalia. For birdwatchers based in Africa, Ethiopia is also of great interest for a number of Palaearctic migrants and residents that are rare or absent further south. For birdwatchers based elsewhere, Ethiopia offers as good an introduction to African birds as any country. True enough that Kenya, Uganda and Tanzania all have significantly longer checklists, but specialist ornithological tours to Ethiopia often pick up in excess of 450 species over two weeks, a total that would be difficult to beat anywhere in Africa.

MAMMALS
The number of large mammal species present in Ethiopia is comparable with countries like Kenya and Tanzania, but populations are generally low and many species'

OVERVIEW OF ETHIOPIA'S PROTECTED AREAS

There are nine national parks in Ethiopia, most of which were demarcated in the 1960s or 1970s but have yet to be formally gazetted. In the highlands, the **Simien Mountains National Park** (page 235) and **Bale Mountains National Park** (page 459) protect Ethiopia's two highest mountain ranges. The primary attractions of these parks are scenic and they are most popular with hikers, though Bale is accessible to non-hikers by the highest all-weather road in Africa. Neither park protects large volumes of game, but they do form the last remaining strongholds of Ethiopia's endemic large mammals. Bale is the better park for wildlife viewing: the endemic Ethiopian wolf and mountain nyala are common, as is a variety of more widespread mammal species and 16 endemic birds. Simien is the more scenic reserve and the best for trekking. Three endemic mammals – Walia ibex, Ethiopian wolf and gelada baboon – are present in the Simien range, but only the baboon is common enough to be seen by most hikers.

Four national parks lie in the Rift Valley. The northernmost of these is **Yangudi Rassa National Park** (page 383), set in the very dry Somali border region. The park has been set aside to protect the Somali wild ass, the ancestor of the domestic donkey. It is reasonably accessible, as the main Assab road runs right through it, but is of marginal interest to most tourists, especially as the odds of seeing the ass are negligible. The more accessible **Awash National Park** (page 375), which lies a few hours' drive east of Addis Ababa and protects a varied though somewhat depleted mammalian fauna, is a dry-country reserve abutting the Awash River below the impressive Fantelle Volcano. In the southern Rift, **Abiata-Shala National Park** (page 438) and **Nechisar National Park** (page 490) protect respectively lakes Abiata and Shala, and lakes Chamo and Abaya. Both parks are scenically attractive and provide wonderful birding, but only Nechisar supports significant herds of game, most visibly common zebra and various antelope.

The most important reserves for large game are **Omo National Park** (page 518) and **Mago National Park** (page 518), which adjoin each other in the Omo Valley near the Kenyan border. These national parks still support thin but substantial populations of elephant, buffalo, lion and a large variety of antelopes and primates. Finally, **Gambella National Park** (page 551) lies in the remote, marshy west close to the town of Gambella, and as with Mago and Omo it still supports significant though

distribution is restricted to remnant pockets in remote areas. Because game viewing is not a major feature of tourism in Ethiopia, detailed descriptions of appearance and behaviour are restricted to those species that are of special interest to visitors to Ethiopia. For species that can be seen more readily in other parts of Africa, I have limited my comments to pocket descriptions and details of known or probable distribution and status within Ethiopia. This section should thus be seen as an Ethiopia-specific supplement to any of the continental field guides recommended at the end of this book.

Predators

The large predator most likely to be seen in Ethiopia is the **spotted hyena**, which is present in the most thinly populated parts of the country, especially at lower altitudes, and is reasonably visible in most national parks and reserves. Scavenging spotted hyena commonly frequent the outskirts of towns. The most reliable place to see hyenas is Harar, where a so-called hyena

Spotted hyena

diminishing herds of elephant and buffalo, as well as the localised white-eared kob and Nile lechwe, and predators such as lion and leopard.

Several important sanctuaries have not yet been awarded national park status. The most accessible of these is **Senkele Wildlife Sanctuary** (page 445) near Shashemene, which despite its small size forms the main stronghold of the endemic Swayne's hartebeest. Further south, **Yabello Wildlife Sanctuary** (page 481) near the town of the same name supports a variety of dry country antelope, large herds of Burchell's zebra, and endemic Streseman's bush crow and white-tailed swallow. The **Babile Elephant Sanctuary** (page 410) near Harar is home to a small but seasonally accessible population of small-tusked desert elephants. The recently founded **Entoto Natural Park** (page 172) on the outskirts of Addis Ababa supports some large game, but is mainly of interest to birders, as is the underrated **Menegasha Forest Reserve** (page 481) to its west. A newly developed area of great interest to hikers, trekkers and wildlife enthusiasts is the trail through the **Dodola–Adaba Forest Reserve** (page 454), where five cabins offer access to highland species similar to those in Bale National Park. Then there is the little-known **Guassa Plateau** (page 329) near Debre Sina, a 300-year-old community reserve protecting the country's third largest population of Ethiopian wolves, as well as most of the endemic highland birds.

Many unprotected parts of Ethiopia offer good but limited wildlife viewing; the following list is far from comprehensive, and several other interesting spots are covered in the main body of this guide. The forests of the western highlands still support a high density of monkeys, often to be seen from the roadside, as well as a rich selection of forest birds. The Rift Valley lakes all offer superb birding, particularly the unprotected Ziway and Awassa, the latter also home to troops of guereza monkey. Also in the Rift Valley, the forests around Wondo Genet are known for their excellent forest birding and prolific monkeys. Hippos and crocodiles survive in many unprotected areas, of which Lake Boyo outside Jimma and the Koko Dam near Adama are very accessible. Gelada baboons are often seen outside national parks in certain parts of the northern highlands, notably Ankober and Mugar Gorge. Another great birding spot in the north is Lake Tana, and the nearby Blue Nile Falls. Due to the conservationist ethics of the Ethiopian Orthodox Church, many old monasteries and churches lie in isolated patches of indigenous woodland, which often support a few monkeys and forest bird species.

man lures them every evening with raw meat. Other hyena species occur in Ethiopia but they are secretive and nocturnal and most unlikely to be seen.

Africa's three large feline species – lion, leopard and cheetah – are all present in Ethiopia. The **leopard** is probably the most numerous large feline, because its favoured habitats of forest and rocky areas are well represented. Leopards have been recorded in most national parks and can be assumed to inhabit the forests of the south and west, but they are notoriously secretive (which is why they are still common outside of reserves throughout Africa) and you would be lucky to see one. Ethiopians often refer to the leopard as a tiger, because the Amharigna word 'Nebir' is used to describe both cat species.

The Abyssinian race of **lion**, distinguished by its below-average size and the male's impressive black mane, still appears to be widespread,

Leopard

particularly in the savanna and dry thorn bush of the Rift Valley and the Somali and Kenyan border regions, but it is very thinly distributed. Lions have been recorded in recent times in such unlikely habitats as the Afro-alpine moorland and forests of Bale, and they are heard from time to time at Nechisar. Lions are often heard at night, and occasionally seen by day, in parts of Awash, Nechisar, Bale, Omo and Mago national parks, but sightings cannot be counted on as they can in many east African reserves. The one place you can be certain of seeing the Abyssinian lion is at Siddist Kilo in Addis Ababa – where they are kept in cages!

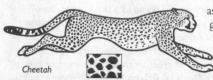

Cheetah

The **cheetah** is the large feline most associated with open country and it is generally found in drier climates than lions and leopards. Cheetahs are occasionally seen in Awash and Nechisar national parks, but with a low frequency that suggests they are vagrants. It is reasonable to assume that cheetahs survive in small numbers throughout the dry plains of the southeast and in thinly populated parts of the Rift Valley, and that they occasionally wander into national parks and reserves in these areas.

The **African hunting dog** has been recorded in several national parks, most recently Bale, but it is now very rare in Ethiopia and, as elsewhere in Africa, considered to be an endangered species. A variety of smaller and mostly nocturnal predators occur in Ethiopia, of which the most notable is the Ethiopian wolf (see box below). All three African **jackal** species are present, most visibly the black-backed jackal, a fairly common

THE ETHIOPIAN WOLF

The one predator that every wildlife enthusiast will want to see is the Ethiopian wolf *Canis simensis*, the most rare of the world's 37 canid species, and listed as critically endangered on the 2000 IUCN Red List. The genetic affinities of this unusual predator puzzled scientists for several decades, as reflected in several misleading common names – until recently, outsiders most often called it the Simien fox, while Ethiopians still know it as the red jackal (*kai kebero* in Amharigna). But recent DNA tests have determined that despite appearances to the contrary, it is neither fox nor jackal, but a closer genetic ally of the European grey wolf than any other African canid. It probably evolved from an extinct wolf species that colonised the area in the late Pleistocene era. Two distinct races are recognised, distinguished by slight differences in coloration and skull shape, with the Rift Valley forming the natural divide between these populations.

The Ethiopian wolf stands about 60cm high, making it significantly larger than any jackal, and has a long muzzle similar to that of a coyote. It has a predominantly rufous coat, broken up by white throat and flank markings, and a black tail. It is a diurnal hunter of Afro-alpine moorland and short grassland, where it feeds mostly on rodents, including the endemic giant mole rat. Unlike most canids, it is essentially a courser rather than a hunter, though packs have been observed to bring down small antelope, and it will often eat carrion.

As recently as the mid 19th century, the Ethiopian wolf was widespread and common in the Ethiopian Highlands. Its numbers have since dwindled dramatically, for reasons that are not understood precisely but which are probably more related to introduced diseases such as canine distemper and rabies (the culprits, incidentally, for the drastic reduction in continent-wide African hunting dog populations in the last few decades) than to deliberate hunting. The wolf is now practically confined to high-

resident in most national parks and other thinly populated parts of the country. The common or Asiatic jackal is more common in the north, and sometimes seen from the road in more remote parts of Tigrai. Bat-eared fox, civet, serval, caracal and the insectivorous aardvark are widespread but very rarely seen nocturnal predators, mostly associated with dry country

African hunting dog

and savanna. We did, however, see bat-eared fox a few times on the road between Omorate and Murelle in South Omo.

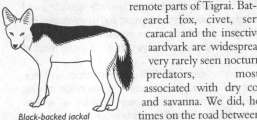

Black-backed jackal

Primates

It is not a little ironic, given Ethiopia's international image, that the large mammal most frequently seen from the roadside in the south and west is the forest-dwelling **guereza** or **black-and-white colobus monkey**. This beautiful monkey is easily distinguished from other primates by its white beard and flowing white tail and is commonly seen in family groups. Its major habitat is

Guereza monkey

altitude moorland in national parks and on other high mountains.

Fewer than 600 Ethiopian wolves are left in the wild, spread across about ten isolated populations, of which only four are thought to number more than 20 individuals, and can be considered viable breeding populations. The southern race is by far the more numerous and more concentrated of the two. Its main stronghold is Bale National Park, where an estimated population of perhaps 200 represents a major decline from Chris Hillman's estimate of 700 in 1976. Another 80–150 Ethiopian wolves live in scattered pockets in the Arsi Highlands, which lie to the immediate east of Bale. It is not known to what extent the different populations in Arsi and Bale interbreed with each other, and thus whether they form one reasonably large gene pool or several smaller ones.

The northern race of Ethiopian wolf may number fewer than 100 in the wild. Its long-term prospects are forlorn indeed. The wolf population in the Simien Mountains has never recovered from a rabies epidemic several years ago, and it now stands at no more than 40 individuals, and probably fewer. A more important stronghold for the northern race is the Guassa Plateau, where at least 50 individuals are thought to remain. One or two packs probably survive in a few other remote moorland localities, such as Mount Guna and Mount Abuna Josef, but in such small numbers, and so far from other populations, that even their short-term prospects are bleak.

Rare they might be, but Ethiopian wolves are not difficult to see, at least not in Bale National Park. On the road through the open Sanetti Plateau, sightings are virtually guaranteed, even from public transport. Hikers, or people who drive up for the day, might encounter wolves a dozen times!

The IUCN-published *The Ethiopian Wolf: Status Survey and Conservation Action Plan* compiled by Claudio Sillero-Zuburi and David Macdonald is highly recommended to those with a special interest in this unique canid and its conservation.

GELADAS

The striking and unmistakable gelada *Thercopithecus gelada* is the most common of Ethiopia's endemic large mammal species, with the population estimated by some to be as high as 500,000. The male gelada is a spectacularly handsome and unmistakable beast, possessed of an imposing golden mane and heart-shaped red chest patch. This patch is thought to serve the same purpose as the colourful buttocks or testicles found on those African monkeys that don't spend most of their lives sitting on their bums!

The gelada is the only mammal endemic to Ethiopia that cannot to some extent be regarded as endangered. This singular primate is unique in that it feeds predominantly on grasses, and it is probably the most sociable of African monkeys, with conglomerations of 500 or more regularly recorded in one field. It has a harem-based social structure that is regarded to be the most complex of any animal other than humans.

In evolutionary terms, the gelada is something of a relic, the only surviving representative of a genus of grazing monkeys that once ranged far more broadly across Africa. The gelada stock is ancestral not only to the modern baboons that have largely displaced them in savanna and other open habitats, but also to the baboon-like drills of west Africa, and to the smaller and more arboreal mangabeys, both of which have re-adapted to rainforest habitats.

The gelada is distributed throughout the northern highlands, where it is generally associated with cliffs and ravines. You're bound to see them if you visit the Simien Mountains, which form the species' main stronghold, and they are also numerous on the Guassa Plateau. They are often seen in the vicinity of Ankober, Debre Sina and Debre Libanos, and at the Muger River Gorge near Addis Ababa.

forest canopies so it is abundant in the western and southeastern highlands, but it is also found in smaller stands of moist woodland throughout the south, most notably on the shore of Lake Awasa, in the forests of Nechisar, at Wondo Genet and on Mount Zikwala.

The other common small primate of Ethiopia is the **grivet monkey**, a species that is more generally associated with wooded savanna than it is with true forest, though in Ethiopia its choice of habitat seems more eclectic than elsewhere – it is likely to be seen wherever there are indigenous trees. The Ethiopian race of the widespread vervet (or grivet) monkey is quite distinct from other east African races; it is a darker grey in general colour and has white cheek-marks. The first time I saw an Ethiopian vervet its markings were so misleading that I mistook it for a form of samango monkey, which is the common monkey of evergreen forests from Kenya all the way to South Africa. A little curiously, samango monkeys appear to be absent from Ethiopia's forests, which perhaps explains why vervet monkeys are found in much denser vegetation here than they are elsewhere in Africa. The very localised and secretive **Bale monkey**, thought by some authorities to be a race of vervet and by others a distinct species, is confined to bamboo stands in Harenna and other forest south of the Bale Massif.

Disregarding the endemic gelada (see box above), two true **baboon** species are found in Ethiopia. The most common is the olive or **Anubis baboon** – regarded by some to be a race of the common or savanna baboon, Africa's most widespread primate. This dark olive-brown baboon has a wide habitat tolerance and is common in most of the national parks, as well as in

Common baboon

rocky areas and cliffs throughout the south and west of the country. The more lightly built – and lightly coloured – **Hamadryas baboon** is found in Awash National Park and more northerly parts of the Rift Valley and its escarpment.

Antelope

A large number of antelope species are present in Ethiopia, many of them with limited distribution, largely because so many different habitats converge around the Ethiopian Highlands.

The *tragelaphus* family, a group of antelopes that is notable for its spiralled horns and striking markings, is the best represented antelope genus in Ethiopia, comprising six of the nine species present, including the endemic **mountain nyala** (see box page 53). The most widespread of these is the **bushbuck**, a slightly hunchbacked inhabitant of all types of forest and riverine woodland – including exotic eucalyptus stands. The commoner race in Ethiopia, **Powell's bushbuck**, is found in relatively low-lying habitats such as the forest at Wondo Genet and in Nechisar National Park. It has a typical bushbuck appearance: the handsome male, chestnut-brown in general colour with white striping or spotting and relatively small horns, and the smaller, hornless female, reddish-brown with white spotting reminiscent of certain northern-hemisphere deer. Even more handsome is **Menelik's bushbuck**, the male of which is almost black in colour, with white throat and leg markings and light spotting on its flanks. This is a highland race, endemic to Ethiopia, and most commonly seen around Dinsho at Bale National Park and in the Entoto Hills and other forests near Addis Ababa.

Bushbuck

The greater and lesser **kudu** are both widespread in southern Ethiopia. Both species are dark grey in general colour and have white vertical stripes on their sides (the lesser kudu normally has ten or more stripes, the greater kudu fewer than ten). The greater kudu is the second tallest of all African antelopes and the male, when fully grown, has magnificent spiralling horns up to 1.5m in length. Both species live in woodland; they are often found alongside each other, though the lesser kudu has a greater tolerance of dry conditions. The greater kudu is

Greater
and
lesser kudu

very common in Nechisar National Park and a viable population is present in Abiata-Shala. Both kudu species are found in Awash National Park, and they may be seen outside reserves in the dry acacia woodland of the far south and east.

The only African antelope that is larger than the greater kudu is the **eland**, the least characteristic *tragelaphus* species. It has a rather bovine appearance, with twisted horns that seem absurdly small for an animal of its size, and a light tan coat with faint stripes. As far as I am aware, elands are found only in the Omo Valley, where they are seasonally abundant.

Eland

The **gazelle** family comprises a dozen similar-looking species, most of which inhabit arid habitats and half of which are thought to occur somewhere in Ethiopia. Gazelles are medium-sized antelopes with gently curved small-to-medium-sized horns, a tan coat

AFRICAN WILD ASS

Yangudi Rassa National Park, bisected by the Assaita road to the north of Awash National Park, is the home of the African wild ass, the ancestor of the domestic donkey. The wild ass is not a true Ethiopian endemic; it still occurs in parts of India, and was once a lot more widespread in Africa, where Nubian, Somali and Algerian races were recognised. The Nubian and Algerian races are probably extinct now – occasional reports of wild asses are thought to be misidentified feral donkeys. Neither is any wild ass left in Somalia, which had a population of 10,000 at the turn of the 20th century. The 300 to 500 wild asses that live in Yangudi Rassa are therefore the only confirmed population left in Africa.

I've not seen a wild ass – few have! – but a former warden of Yangudi Rassa told me they are very beautiful in their wild state. They are seen with reasonable frequency in the park, but are difficult to distinguish from the more common feral donkeys with which they co-inhabit. Reportedly, you can tell the wild ass from the donkey by its sleeker, plainer coat – a rather subtle difference in the field, I would imagine.

with white underparts and in some species a black side-stripe. **Grant's gazelle**, a long-horned species without a side-stripe, will be familiar to anybody who has visited east Africa's reserves. It reaches the northern extent of its range in the southern Rift Valley of Ethiopia, and is often seen in Nechisar National Park and along the Moyale road south of Dilla. The total Ethiopian population is estimated at about 6,000.

The gazelle most likely to be seen by tourists to Ethiopia is **Soemmering's gazelle**, which like Grant's gazelle has no side-stripe, but is easily distinguished by its black face with white cheek-stripes and relatively small, backward-facing horns. Both species have a white rump, but that of Grant's is less extensive and is bordered by black stripes. Soemmering's gazelle is quite common on the plains around Awash National Park and is often seen along the roads to Harar and Assab. This gazelle, though listed as present in six countries, is now extirpated or very rare in most of them. The nucleus population of about 6,500 in the northern Ethiopian Rift Valley is by far the most significant one left.

Thomson's gazelle

Thomson's gazelle is the most common east African species, easily recognised by its heavy black side-stripe and, in the case of the Ethiopian and Sudanese race (called the **Mongalla**), a white eye-circle. In Ethiopia, the 'Tommy' is historically restricted to the far southwest, where it might well be extirpated. Similar in size and general appearance to Thomson's gazelle, but darker and with a less defined side-stripe, **Speke's gazelle** is endemic to Somalia, bar one old record for the Ogaden area of southeast Ethiopia. The much paler and very plain **Dorcas gazelle** is a Saharan species that occurs in the Djibouti border area of Ethiopia, where it is quite common. **Heuglin's gazelle**, red in colour with a thin black side-stripe, is a race of the Sahelian red-fronted gazelle that occurs locally in the Sudanese–Ethiopian border area to the east of the Nile River.

The **gerenuk** is an atypical and unmistakable gazelle with a red-brown coat and a very long neck. Its range extends from east Africa into the drier parts of southern Ethiopia, where it may be seen stretched up on its hind legs browsing on the higher branches of acacia trees. The gerenuk is the most commonly seen large antelope in the South Omo region. Similar in appearance, the **dibatag** is a rare antelope whose range has always been confined to a specific type of evergreen bush in Somalia and the Ogaden region of southeast Ethiopia. The population has decreased dramatically in recent years, and protection of the remaining dibatag is made difficult by the ongoing unrest and high level of banditry in the Somali–Ethiopian border area. Should you happen to come across a dibatag, the combination of white eye-ring extending down the nose and elongated neck will be diagnostic.

Two virtually indistinguishable **reedbuck** species are found in Ethiopia. These are medium-sized antelopes with a plain light tan coat, generally found in high grass and moorland. The **Bohor reedbuck** is common in Bale National Park. The **mountain reedbuck** occurs throughout the country and is regularly seen at Fantelle Volcano in Awash National Park. Related to the reedbuck is the **waterbuck**, a large antelope with a shaggy brown coat and sizeable lyre-shaped horns; the Defassa race of waterbuck has a pale rump while the common race has an upside-down white U on its rump. Waterbuck are most often seen grazing in relatively open vegetation near water; they are found at a few scattered localities in southern Ethiopia.

Reedbuck

Common (left) and Defassa waterbuck

The related **Nile lechwe** is an exceptionally handsome antelope associated with marshy ground and floodplains in the border area of Sudan and Ethiopia. Its main range is in Sudan, where it is still thought to be present in herds of a thousand or more. In Ethiopia, it is practically restricted to Gambella National Park, where it is increasingly scarce and vulnerable – recent estimates suggest the Ethiopian population may be fewer than 100. Also restricted to the Gambella area, the **white-eared kob** is a localised and possibly endangered race of the widespread kob antelope. Its current status in Ethiopia is uncertain, but numbers are thought to be very low.

WALIA IBEX

Ethiopia's rarest endemic is the Walia ibex, formerly widespread in the mountains of the north, but now restricted to the Simien Mountains, where it is uncommon but quite often seen by hikers. The Walia ibex is a type of goat that lives on narrow mountain ledges, and can easily be recognised by the large decurved horns of adults of both sexes. The males' horns are larger than the females', and may measure in excess of 1m. The presence of carved ibex on many pre-Christian religious shrines in Axum indicates that it was once considerably more widespread than it is today.

By the 19th century, the Walia ibex's range was restricted to the Simiens, but the population is thought to have numbered several thousand before the Italian occupation. By 1963, it had dropped to below 200, largely as a result of hunting. The population is currently estimated at about 300, but it is hoped that this will be boosted by more stringent enforcement of the ban on hunting. The ibex has no natural enemies, and the park could probably support up to 3,000 individuals.

The **common hartebeest** is a large, tan, and rather awkward-looking plains antelope, related to the famous wildebeest or gnu (which, despite its abundance in east Africa, doesn't occur in Ethiopia). Several races of hartebeest are recognised, of which three occur in Ethiopia, including one endemic. The non-endemics are the **Lelwel hartebeest**, which is quite common in parts of South Omo, and the **tora hartebeest**, which is present in unknown numbers in the northwest lowlands. The endangered **Swayne's hartebeest** is now extinct in Somalia, and thus effectively endemic to Ethiopia, where it occurs in and near the southern Rift Valley. The most significant protected population occurs in Senkele Game Reserve, where numbers plummeted from 2,400 in 1989 to fewer than 200 after the fighting that took place in the area in 1991. The Senkele population has subsequently increased slightly, but even together with the small population found in Nechisar National Park, it is probable that fewer than 500 Swayne's hartebeest remain in the wild. The closely related **tiang**, a race of the east African topi, is similar in gait and shape to the hartebeest, but the much darker coat precludes confusion. The tiang occurs widely in the Omo Valley and the Gambella region.

Hartebeest

The unmistakable **Beisa oryx** is a large, handsome dry-country antelope, easily recognised by its distinctive scimitar-like horns. The main centre of population within Ethiopia is in and around Awash National Park, where more than 1,000 oryx are present, often to be observed from the main road towards Harar. Large herds also migrate seasonally within the South Omo region. Thin and increasingly vulnerable populations survive in most other arid parts of Ethiopia.

Dik-diks are small, brown antelopes with tan legs and distinctive extended snouts. Four species are recognised, two of which are found in Ethiopia. All dik-dik species are browsers that live independently of water, and they are generally seen singly or in pairs in dry acacia scrub. **Guenther's dik-dik** is found throughout the lowlands of southern Ethiopia and is often seen from the roadside, particularly in South Omo and Nechisar National Park. **Salt's dik-dik**, endemic to the Horn of Africa, is widespread in the dry east, and frequently seen from the Harar road. Some field guides indicate incorrectly the occurrence in eastern Ethiopia of a Somali endemic, the silver dik-dik.

Klipspringer

The **klipspringer** is a slightly built antelope with a stiff-looking grey-brown coat. It is associated with rocky hills and cliffs and may be seen in suitable habitats anywhere in Ethiopia. It is common in Bale National Park.

The **duiker** family is a group of over 15 small antelope species, most of which live in forest undergrowth. Until recently, it was assumed that the **common duiker**, the only member of the family to inhabit open country, was also the only duiker found in Ethiopia. In 1986, however, a small red duiker was reliably observed in the Harenna Forest within Bale National Park, while in 1996 a similar duiker was observed in Omo National Park. The geographical probability is that the former is **Harvey's red duiker** and the latter **Weyn's red duiker**, but this is far from certain, and an endemic race or species is not out of the question.

Common duiker

MOUNTAIN NYALA

Ethiopia's one fully endemic antelope species is the mountain nyala *Tragelaphus buxtoni* – not, as its name might suggest, a particularly close relative of the nyala of southern Africa, but more probably evolved from a race of greater kudu. The mountain nyala is similar in size and shape to the greater kudu but it has smaller (though by no means insignificant) horns with only one twist as opposed to the greater kudu's two or three. The shaggy coat of the mountain nyala is brownish rather than plain grey, and the striping is indistinct. Mountain nyala live in herds of five to ten animals in juniper and hagenia forests in the southeast highlands.

The mountain nyala has the distinction of being the last discovered of all African antelopes; the first documented specimen was shot by one Major Buxton in 1908, and described formally two years later. The extent to which mountain nyala numbers declined in the 20th century is undocumented. The antelope probably has always had a somewhat restricted range, but numbers outside of national parks appear to be in decline, and the species is listed as endangered on the IUCN Red List.

The main protected population is found in the north of Bale National Park, around Dinsho and Mount Gaysay. Numbers here soared from about 1,000 in the 1960s to 4,000 in the late 1980s, but plummeted back to 150 in 1991 as the antelope were shot in revenge for forced removals undertaken by the Mengistu regime. Fortunately, the population quickly recovered to about 1,000, according to transect counts undertaken in 1997. Outside of Bale, a small population of mountain nyala is protected in the Kuni Muktar Sanctuary, which lies in the highlands southeast of Awash National Park. Substantial populations still cling on in forested parts of the Arsi Highlands such as Dodola, though numbers are unknown. The global population is estimated to stand between 2,000 and 4,000 individuals.

Other large mammals

Within Ethiopia, many of Africa's most distinctive large mammals are practically restricted to South Omo, among them **elephant**, **giraffe**, **buffalo** and **black rhinoceros**, the last almost certainly now exterminated. Another small elephant population occurs in Babile Elephant Sanctuary to the south of Harar, and small numbers of giraffe and buffalo occur elsewhere in the little-visited Kenyan and Sudanese border areas.

Hippopotami are widely but patchily distributed in Ethiopia, because they are always associated with lakes or large rivers. They occur in Lake Tana and in most of the Rift Valley lakes, though current details of status are not available – they are certainly not as easily seen in Ethiopia as they are in Kenya's lakes. The best places to see hippos are Nechisar National Park, at the source

Cape buffalo

of the Nile near Bahir Dar on Lake Tana, at Lake Boye near Jimma, and at Koko Dam near Adama.

Two swine species are found in Ethiopia. The **warthog** is found in wooded savanna and frequently seen near water. It is found in most national parks and is especially common around Dinsho in Bale. The **bushpig** is a larger, darker and hairier beast found in forests or dense woodland. It is probably common in all Ethiopian forests but its nocturnal habits and chosen habitats make it difficult to see. I was very lucky to see a pair in the Harenna Forest in Bale.

Warthog

Burchell's zebra – also called the common or plains zebra – is the common equine of sub-Saharan Africa. It is found throughout the south of Ethiopia and is the most numerous large mammal species in Nechisar National Park. The much larger and more densely striped **Grevy's zebra** is restricted to southern Ethiopia and northern Kenya. In Ethiopia, it is thinly distributed in the Kenyan border area east of the Omo Valley, and in the Rift Valley north of Awash National Park.

REPTILES
Nile crocodile

The order *Crocodilia* dates back at least 150 million years, and fossil forms that lived contemporaneously with dinosaurs are remarkably unchanged from their modern descendants, of which the Nile crocodile is the largest living reptile, regularly growing to lengths of up to 6m. Widespread throughout Africa, the Nile crocodile was once common in most large rivers and lakes, but it has been exterminated in many areas in the past century – hunted professionally for its skin as well as by vengeful local villagers. Contrary to popular legend, Nile crocodiles generally feed mostly on fish, at least where densities are sufficient. They will also prey on drinking or swimming mammals where the opportunity presents itself, dragging their victim underwater until it drowns, then storing it under a submerged log or tree until it has decomposed sufficiently for them to eat. A large crocodile is capable of killing a lion or wildebeest, or an adult human for that matter, and in certain areas such as the Mara or Grumeti rivers in the Serengeti, large mammals do form their main prey. Today, large crocodiles are mostly confined to protected areas. The gargantuan specimens that lurk around the so-called Crocodile Market in Nechisar National Park are a truly primeval sight. Other possible sites for croc sightings are the southern Omo River, the Baro River downstream of Gambella, the Awash River near Awash National Park and Nazret, and other large bodies of water at lower to medium altitudes.

Snakes

A wide variety of snakes are found in Ethiopia, though – fortunately, most would agree – they are typically very shy and unlikely to be seen unless actively sought. One of the snakes most likely to be seen on safari is Africa's largest, the **rock python**, which has a gold-on-black mottled skin and regularly grows to lengths exceeding 5m. Non-venomous, pythons kill their prey by strangulation, wrapping their muscular bodies around it until it cannot breathe, then swallowing it whole and dozing off for a couple of months while it is digested. Pythons feed mainly on small antelopes, large rodents and similar. They are harmless to adult humans, but could conceivably kill a small child, and might be encountered almost anywhere when slumbering.

Of the venomous snakes, one of the most commonly encountered is the **puff adder**, a large, thick resident of savanna and rocky habitats. Although it feeds mainly on rodents, the puff adder will strike when threatened, and it is rightly considered the most dangerous of African snakes, not because it is especially venomous or aggressive, but because its notoriously sluggish disposition means it is more often disturbed than other snakes. The related **Gabon viper** is possibly the largest African viper, growing up to 2m long, very heavily built, and with a beautiful cryptic geometric gold, black and brown skin pattern that blends perfectly into the rainforest litter it inhabits. Although highly venomous, it is more placid and less likely to be encountered than the puff adder.

Several **cobra** species, including the spitting cobra, are present in Ethiopia, most with characteristic hoods that they raise when about to strike, though they are all very seldom seen. Another widespread family is the **mambas**, of which the black mamba – which will only attack when cornered, despite an unfounded reputation for unprovoked aggression – is the largest venomous snake in Africa, measuring up to 3.5m long. Theoretically, the most toxic of Africa's snakes is said to be the **boomslang**, a variably coloured and, as its name – literally tree-snake – suggests, largely arboreal snake that is reputed not to have accounted for one known human fatality, as it is back-fanged and very non-aggressive.

Most snakes are in fact non-venomous and not even potentially harmful to any other living creature much bigger than a rat. One of the more non-venomous snakes in the region is the **green tree snake** (sometimes mistaken for a boomslang, though the latter is never as green and more often brown), which feeds mostly on amphibians. The **mole snake** is a common and widespread grey-brown savanna resident that grows up to 2m long, and feeds on moles and other rodents. The remarkable **egg-eating snakes** live exclusively on bird eggs, dislocating their jaws to swallow the egg whole, then eventually regurgitating the crushed shell in a neat little package. Many snakes will take eggs opportunistically, for which reason large-scale agitation among birds in a tree is often a good indication that a snake (or small bird of prey) is around.

Lizards

All African lizards are harmless to humans, with the arguable exception of the **giant monitor lizards**, which could in theory inflict a nasty bite if cornered. Two species of monitor occur in east Africa, the water and savanna monitor, the latter growing up to 2.2m long and occasionally seen in the vicinity of termite mounds, the former slightly smaller but far more regularly observed by tourists. Their size alone might make it possible for one to fleetingly mistake a monitor for a small crocodile, but the more colourful yellow-dappled skin precludes sustained confusion. Both species are predators, feeding on anything from bird eggs to smaller reptiles and mammals, but will also eat carrion opportunistically.

Visitors to tropical Africa will soon become familiar with the **common house gecko**, an endearing bug-eyed, translucent white lizard, which as its name suggests reliably inhabits most houses as well as lodge rooms, scampering up walls and upside-down on the ceiling in pursuit of pesky insects attracted to the lights. Also very common in some lodge grounds are various **agama** species, distinguished from other common lizards by their relatively large size of around 20–25cm, basking habits, and almost plastic-looking scaling – depending on the species, a combination of blue, purple, orange or red, with the flattened head generally a different colour to the torso. Another common family is the **skinks**: small, long-tailed lizards, most of which are quite dark and have a few thin black stripes running from head to tail.

Tortoises and terrapins

These peculiar reptiles are unique in being protected by a prototypal suit of armour formed by their heavy exoskeleton. The most common of the terrestrial tortoises in the region is the **leopard tortoise**, which is named after its gold-and-black mottled shell, can weigh up to 30kg, and has been known to live for more than 50 years in captivity. It is often seen motoring along in the slow lane of game reserve roads. Four species of terrapin

CHAMELEONS

Common and widespread in parts of Ethiopia, but not easily seen unless they are actively searched for, chameleons are arguably the most intriguing of African reptiles. True chameleons of the family *Chamaeleontidae* are confined to the Old World, with the most important centre of speciation being the island of Madagascar, to which about half of the world's 120 recognised species are endemic. Aside from two species of chameleon apiece in Asia and Europe, the remainder is distributed across mainland Africa.

Chameleons are best known for their capacity to change colour, a trait that has often been exaggerated in popular literature, and which is generally influenced by mood more than the colour of the background. Some chameleons are more adept at changing colour than others, with the most variable being the common chameleon *Chamaeleo chamaeleon* of the Mediterranean region, with more than 100 colour and pattern variations recorded. Many African chameleons are typically green in colour but will gradually take on a browner hue when they descend from the foliage in more exposed terrain, for instance while crossing a road. Several change colour and pattern far more dramatically when they feel threatened or are confronted by a rival of the same species. Different chameleon species also vary greatly in size, with the largest being Oustalet's chameleon of Madagascar, known to reach a length of almost 80cm.

A remarkable physiological feature common to all true chameleons is their protuberant round eyes, which offer a potential 180° vision on both sides and are able to swivel around independently of each other. Only when one of them isolates a suitably juicy-looking insect will the two eyes focus in the same direction as the chameleon stalks slowly forward until it is close enough to use the other unique weapon in its armoury. This is its sticky-tipped tongue, which is typically about the same length as its body and remains coiled up within its mouth most of the time, to be unleashed in a sudden, blink-and-you'll-miss-it lunge to zap a selected item of prey.

– essentially the freshwater equivalent of turtles – are resident in east Africa, all somewhat flatter in shape than the tortoises, and generally with a plainer brown shell. They might be seen sunning on rocks close to water or peering out from roadside puddles. The largest is the Nile soft-shelled terrapin, which has a wide, flat shell and in rare instances might reach a length of almost 1m.

BIRDS

Ethiopia's proximity to the equator and great habitat diversity means its avifauna is one of the richest in Africa. Urban and Brown's *Checklist of the Birds of Ethiopia*, published in 1971, lists 827 species, of which 665 are resident or presumed resident, and the remainder are Palaearctic or intra-African migrants. The checklist was compiled at a time when Eritrea was a part of Ethiopia, so about 20 of the species listed – including several oceanic gulls and terns – can no longer be considered to be Ethiopian. Taking into account birds that were first recorded in Ethiopia after 1971, or have only been described since then, a total count of around 850 species of birds is a realistic estimate. It is quite possible that further species await discovery in the little-known forests of the south and west, or elsewhere – a new and presumably endemic species of nightjar was discovered as recently as 1992 in the very accessible Nechisar National Park.

I read recently that 40% of Ethiopia's tourism comes from birdwatchers. While this figure does feel like gross overstatement, it nevertheless underscores the growing popularity of the pastime, as well as Ethiopia's significance as a birding destination. One major reason for Ethiopia's high profile among birdwatchers is the large number

In addition to their unique eyes and tongues, many chameleons are adorned with an array of facial casques, flaps, horns and crests that enhance their already somewhat fearsome prehistoric appearance.

In Ethiopia, you're most likely to come across a chameleon by chance when it is crossing a road, in which case it should be easy to take a closer look at it, since most move slowly and deliberately. Chameleons are also often seen on night game drives, when their ghostly nocturnal colouring shows up clearly under a spotlight – as well as making it pretty clear why these strange creatures are regarded with both fear and awe in many local African cultures. More actively, you could ask your guide if they know where to find a chameleon – a few individuals will be resident in most lodge grounds.

The flap-necked chameleon *Chamaeleo delepis* is probably the most regularly observed species of savanna and woodland habitats in east Africa. Often observed crossing roads, it is generally around 15cm long and bright green in colour with few distinctive markings, but individuals might be up to 30cm in length and will turn tan or brown under the right conditions. Another closely related and widespread savanna and woodland species is the similarly sized graceful chameleon *Chamaeleo gracilis*, which is generally yellow-green in colour and often has a white horizontal stripe along its flanks.

Characteristic of east African montane forests, three-horned chameleons form a closely allied species cluster of some taxonomic uncertainty. Typically darker than the savanna chameleons and around 20cm in length, the males of all taxa within this cluster are distinguished by a trio of long nasal horns that project forward from their faces. Perhaps the most alluring of east Africa's chameleons is the giant chameleon *Chamaeleo melleri*, a bulky dark-green creature with yellow stripes and a small solitary horn, mainly associated with the Eastern Arc forests, where it feeds on small reptiles (including snakes) as well as insects.

of species that are endemic or near-endemic – in Africa, comparable only to South Africa and Tanzania. Another is that, while the total species count is not as high as some other African countries, it is probably easier to amass a trip list of 400 species over a normal-length holiday in Ethiopia than it is in any African country other than perhaps Kenya.

It is always difficult to know where to pitch the birding section in a general travel guide. Essentially, this is because the birds most likely to capture the interest of the casual visitor are generally not the same species most significant to a serious ornithologist. For a first-time visitor to Africa with a passing interest in birds – an interest that often tends to develop as one travels amidst its avian abundance – it will be the most colourful and largest birds that tend to capture the eye: rollers, bee-eaters, cranes, storks, hornbills and such. The truly dedicated, by contrast, will be more than willing to make a two-day side trip to tick a range-restricted endemic lark which, when all's said and done, looks and behaves pretty much like any of a dozen other drab lark species found in Ethiopia. And there will be many visitors who fall between these poles, who have a genuine and strong interest in birding, but not to the extent that they'd forsake a visit to the rock-hewn churches of Lalibela in order to tick a localised endemic. Furthermore, even among reasonably serious birders, the significance of any given sighting might be influenced by which parts of Africa – or elsewhere in the world – they have visited before. And finally, it is often the case that a good locality for a bird with a very limited distribution within any given country might be of great interest to resident birders, but rather less so to visitors who have been to a country where the same bird is more common. Put simply,

WEAVERS

Placed by some authorities in the same family as the closely related sparrows, the weavers of the family Ploceidae are a quintessential part of Africa's natural landscape, common and highly visible in virtually every habitat from rainforest to desert. The name of the family derives from the intricate and elaborate nests – typically (but not always) a roughly oval ball of dried grass, reeds and twigs – that are built by the dextrous males of most species.

It can be fascinating to watch a male weaver at work. First, a nest site is chosen, usually at the end of a thin hanging branch or frond, which is immediately stripped of leaves to protect against snakes. The weaver then flies back and forth to the site, carrying the building material blade by blade in its heavy beak, first using a few thick strands to hang a skeletal nest from the end of a branch, then gradually completing the structure by interweaving numerous thinner blades of grass into the main frame. Once completed, the nest is subjected to the attention of his chosen partner, who will tear it apart if the result is less than satisfactory, and so the process starts all over again.

All but 12 of the 113 described weaver species are resident on the African mainland or associated islands, with some 26 represented within Ethiopia alone. About 28 of the Ethiopian species are placed in the genus Ploceus (true weavers), which is surely the most characteristic of all African bird genera. Most of the Ploceus weavers are slightly larger than a sparrow, and display a strong sexual dimorphism. Females are with few exceptions drab buff- or olive-brown birds, with some streaking on the back, and perhaps a hint of yellow on the belly.

Most male Ploceus weavers conform to the basic colour pattern of the 'masked weaver' – predominantly yellow, with streaky back and wings, and a distinct black facial mask, often bordered orange. Eight Ethiopian weaver species fit this masked weaver prototype more or less absolutely, and another five approximate to it rather less exactly, for instance by having a chestnut-brown mask, or a full black head, or a black back, or being more chestnut than yellow on the belly. Identification of the masked weavers can be tricky without experience – useful clues are the exact shape of the mask, the presence and extent of the fringing orange, and the colour of the eye and the back.

The golden weavers, of which no species are present in Ethiopia, are also brilliant yellow and/or light orange with some light streaking on the back, but they lack a mask or any other strong distinguishing features. The handful of forest-associated Ploceus weavers, by contrast, tends to have quite different and very striking colour patterns, and although sexually dimorphic, the female is often as boldly marked as the male. The

an entire book could – and hopefully one day will – be dedicated to Ethiopia's best birding sites. This is not that book.

Given the above, I have chosen to direct this section primarily towards reasonably serious birders. The first heading below focuses on endemic and other species that are likely to be of high interest to all visiting birders. The second heading outlines the established itinerary used by most birding tours. For more information about bird-related books and websites, check the *Further Reading* section on page 569–70.

Endemics and other 'specials'

For any dedicated birdwatcher planning a once-in-a-lifetime trip to Ethiopia, particularly those with experience of birding elsewhere in Africa, a primary goal will be to identify those species whose range is actually – or practically – confined to Ethiopia. Indeed, many

most aberrant among these are Vieillot's and Maxwell's black weavers, the males of which are totally black except for their eyes, while the black-billed weaver reverses the prototype by being all black with a yellow facemask.

The most extensive weaver colonies are often found in reed beds and waterside vegetation, generally with several species present. Most weavers don't have a distinctive song, but they compensate with a rowdy jumble of harsh swizzles, rattles and nasal notes that can reach deafening proportions near large colonies. One more cohesive song you will often hear seasonally around weaver colonies is a cyclic 'dee-dee-dee-Diederik', often accelerating to a hysterical crescendo when several birds call at once. This is the call of the Diederik cuckoo, a handsome green-and-white cuckoo that lays its eggs in weaver nests.

Oddly, while most east African *Ploceus* weavers are common, even abundant, in suitable habitats, seven highly localised species are listed as range-restricted, and three of these – one Kenyan endemic and two Tanzanian endemics – are regarded to be of global conservation concern. The only highly localised weaver whose territory nudges onto Ethiopian soil is the Juba weaver, a Somali-biome species that can be seen in a few specific locations in the southeast. Another species whose range centres on Ethiopia is Rüppell's weaver, which occurs throughout the highlands.

Most of the colonial weavers, perhaps relying on safety in numbers, build relatively plain nests with a roughly oval shape and an unadorned entrance hole. The nests of certain more solitary weavers, by contrast, are far more elaborate. Several weavers, for instance, protect their nests from egg-eating invaders by attaching tubular entrance tunnels to the base – in the case of the spectacled weaver, sometimes twice as long as the nest itself. The Grosbeak weaver (a peculiar larger-than-average brown-and-white weaver of reed-beds, distinguished by its outsized bill and placed in the monospecific genus *Amblyospiza*) constructs a large and distinctive domed nest, which is supported by a pair of reeds, and woven as precisely as the finest basketwork, with a neat raised entrance hole at the front. By contrast, the scruffiest nests are built by the various species of sparrow- and buffalo-weaver, relatively drab but highly gregarious dry-country birds that are common in the acacia scrub of the Ethiopian Rift Valley.

ornithological tours are structured almost entirely around this consideration, forsaking time in more generally rewarding and accessible birding areas for trips to remote parts of the country that host one particular endemic.

Ethiopia's 'must-see' birds fall into several categories, the most important of which are the true endemics, species not known to occur outside of Ethiopia. The taxonomic status of some such birds awaits clarification, and new species have been discovered with remarkable regularity in recent decades, making it impossible to say precisely how many birds fall into this category. The most conservative estimate is 16 species, but the spate of recent (and in some cases controversial) splits of what were formerly considered races into full species brings that figure to around 24.

A similar number of bird species might be described as former Ethiopian endemics, since their range extends into Eritrea, which became an independent state in 1993. For a variety of reasons – not least the practical consideration that very few visiting birders would be likely to undertake a separate trip to Eritrea at a later stage – these former endemics are treated as full endemics in the main body of this guide.

A third category of birds that any dedicated birder to Ethiopia would hope to encounter constitutes about half a dozen species that are more or less confined to Ethiopia and war-torn Somalia. There is, too, a considerable number of bird species whose range extends throughout the contiguous arid country of northern Kenya, Somalia and southern Ethiopia. In many instances, such birds are easily seen in parts of Ethiopia that are routinely visited by birders for their endemics, whereas their range within Kenya falls into areas infrequently included in birding itineraries. Finally, there is a miscellaneous group of birds that fit into none of the above categories, but which for one or other reason are likely to be sought eagerly by any visiting birder.

An annotated list covering most of the endemics, near-endemics, and other 'key' bird species follows. Names and sequence follow the plates in Sinclair & Ryan's *Birds of Africa South of the Sahara*, which is probably now the most useful single volume field guide for Ethiopia. The plate number in Sinclair & Ryan (SR) follows the Latin name, followed in turn by the plate number for Van Perlo's more established *Illustrated Checklist* (VP). A single asterisk (*) indicates a species endemic to Ethiopia, a double asterisk (**) one endemic to Ethiopia and Eritrea, a triple asterisk (***) a near-endemic or a 'Horn of Africa endemic' whose range might extend into Somalia, Sudan, Eritrea and/or the far north of Kenya, but which for all practical purposes is likely to be seen only in Ethiopia.

** **Wattled ibis** *Bostrychia carunculata* (SR 56.3, VP 9.1) Common, widespread and vociferous highland resident. Might be confused with the superficially similar hadeda ibis.

Waldrapp *Gerontimus eremita* (SR -, VP 9.5) North African endemic. Formerly bred on cliffs in northern Ethiopian Highlands. Not observed in Ethiopia for several years. Probably exterminated.

* **Blue-winged goose** *Cyanochen cyanopterus* (SR 64.1, VP 10.6) Associated with water in the highlands. Reliable sites include Gefersa Reservoir near Addis Ababa, and Sanetti Plateau, Bale Mountains.

Ruddy shelduck *Tadorna ferruginea* (SR 64.4, VP 10.4) Only sub-Saharan breeding population on Sanetti Plateau, where commonly observed near water. A host of other Palaearctic waterfowl are regular winter migrants, likely to be seen on any of the Ethiopian Rift Valley lakes, but are vagrant or localised elsewhere in east Africa ie: garganey, tufted duck, ferruginous duck, common pochard, Eurasian wigeon, gadwall and mallard.

Lammergeyer (Bearded vulture) *Gypaetus barbatus* (SR 74.4, VP 13.4) Associated with cliffs and mountains, this magnificent vulture is widespread in suitable Old World habitats, but increasingly rare except in Ethiopian Highlands, which form its major stronghold globally.

Golden eagle *Aquila chrysaetos* (SR 102.2, VP -) The only population in sub-Saharan Africa was first identified at Bale Mountains in 1988 and confirmed to breed there in 1993. May occur elsewhere in Ethiopia. Requires experience to distinguish from other, more numerous brown *Aquila* eagles.

Vulturine guineafowl *Acryllium vulturinum* (SR 118.7, VP 25.17) Large, distinctive fowl with brilliant cobalt chest. Confined to arid parts of east Africa and the Horn. Very common in suitable habitats in southern Ethiopia.

*** **Archer's Francolin** *Scleroptila lorti* (SR 122.5, VP -) Recently 'split' from Orange River Francolin, this has a range centred on Ethiopia's Rift Valley, nudging into Somalia and northern Kenya, with a second subpopulation confined to the far northwest of Ethiopia.

Moorland francolin *Scleroptila psilolaemus* (SR 122.6, VP 24.4) Highland fowl, very common in Bale and some other Ethiopian moorland habitats, elsewhere occurs only on four less accessible moorland areas in Kenya, where it is relatively uncommon.

* **Harwood's spurfowl (francolin)** *Pternistes harwoodi* (SR 126.4, VP 24.13) Range practically restricted to Jemma Valley north of Addis Ababa, where it is quite common. Requires special visit to Jemma Valley to see it.

*** **Erckell's spurfowl (francolin)** *Pternistes erckelii* (SR 130.1, VP 24.18) Large, dark-faced game bird more or less restricted to northern highlands of Ethiopia, nudging into Eritrea, with an isolated subpopulation in eastern Sudan.

*** **Chestnut-naped francolin** *Francolinus castaneicollis* (SR 130.3, VP 24.16) Near-endemic. Recorded once in Kenya; isolated population in northern Somalia. Forest-fringe species common in Bale Mountains and other relatively moist parts of the Ethiopian Highlands.

White-winged flufftail *Sarothrura ayresii* (SR 134.2, VP 25.7) Rare and elusive marsh bird, global population fewer than 1,000, restricted to a few specific localities in South Africa, Zimbabwe and Ethiopia. The main stronghold is Ethiopia's Sultata Plain, 100km north of Addis Ababa. Unlikely to be seen by casual visitors.

** **Rouget's rail** *Rougetius rougetii* (SR 136.5, VP 26.5) Associated with marshes and vegetation fringing water. Widespread in the highlands, but most easily seen in Bale Mountains, where it is common and confiding.

Wattled crane *Bugeranus carunculatus* (SR 144.5, VP 27.1) Endangered and localised resident of grassy or marshy highlands with discontinuous distribution from South Africa to Ethiopia. Sanetti Plateau in Bale Mountains one of a handful of sites in Africa where it is reliably observed. The Eurasian and Demoiselle cranes are Palaearctic migrants whose sub-Saharan African range is centred on Sudan and Ethiopia.

*** **Heuglin's bustard** *Neotis heuglinii* (SR 146.3, VP 27.8) Dry-country species likely to be seen only in Somali border region and South Omo.

Arabian bustard *Ardeotis arabs* (SR 146.5, VP 27.11) Localised dry-country bird of north Africa and Arabia; resident in Awash National Park and northern Rift Valley.

* **Spot-breasted lapwing (plover)** *Vanellus melanocephalus* (SR 168.5, VP 31.3) Locally common in highlands, particularly Bale area, and usually associated with water.

** **White-collared pigeon** *Columba albitorques* (SR 202.3, VP 38.8) Common to abundant in most highland habitats, including Addis Ababa.

*** **African white-winged (turtle) dove** *Streptopelia semitorquata* (SR 206.7, VP 39.15) Restricted-range species of Somalia, Ethiopia and Kenyan border region. Associated with riverine woodland, regularly observed near the Dawa River Bridge between Negele Borena and Yabello.

* **Yellow-fronted parrot** *Poicephalus flavifrons* (SR 212.6, VP 40.14) Localised forest inhabitant, often seen flying quickly and noisily between tree canopies at Wondo Genet, Menegasha Forest, Dinsho (Bale) and similar habitats.

** **Black-winged lovebird** *Agapornis swinderiana* (SR 216.3, VP 40.5) Common in most wooded highland habitats. Often observed in the isolated forest patches that tend to surround churches.

* White-cheeked turaco *Tauraco leucolophus* (SR 220.5, VP 41.12) Striking and vociferous woodland endemic often seen in suitable highland habitats, including hotel gardens.

* (Prince) Ruspoli's turaco *Tauraco ruspolii* (SR 220.6, VP 41.13) Highly sought but elusive endemic of southern forests, known from only a handful of localities, of which the most accessible is Genale near Negele Borena.

*** (Abyssinian) long-eared owl *Asio (otus) abyssinicus* (SR 236.6, VP 43.14) Classified as race of Eurasian long-eared owl by many authorities. Only confirmed non-Ethiopian record is one specimen taken on Mount Kenya in 1961. Uncommon, shy and seldom seen unless the location of its daytime roost is known.

* Nechisar nightjar *Caprimulgus solala* (SR 252.5, VP -) Recently described species known only from one wing found in Nechisar National Park. The absence of reliable field sightings must cast some doubt on its taxonomic validity.

*** Black-billed wood-hoopoe *Phoeniculus somaliensis* (SR 268.3, VP 49.15) The most widespread Ethiopian wood-hoopoe, associated with dry-ish acacia habitats, with range extending into significant portions of Eritrea and Somalia.

Hemprich's hornbill *Tockus hemprichii* (SR 292.6, VP 50.18) Large, striking, cliff-associated hornbill whose range centres on Ethiopia, extending into portions of Somalia and Eritrea, and down the Kenyan Rift as far as Baringo.

** Banded barbet *Lybius undatus* (SR 302.5, VP 52.6) Widespread and quite common resident of woodland. Often seen in southern Rift Valley, but might be seen almost anywhere.

** Abyssinian (golden-backed) woodpecker *Dendropicus abyssinicus* (SR 322.4, VP 55.6) Widespread resident of woodland and forest, but nowhere common.

* Degodi lark *Mirafra degodiensis* (SR 336.4, VP 57.1) First collected 1971 in the Bogol Manyo area, still the only known locality, and a day's drive either way from Negele Borena. Sympatric with several other larks, and requires careful identification.

* Sidamo (long-clawed) lark *Heteromirafra sidamoensis* (SR 338.3, VP 57.18) First collected 1968 near Arero junction, 15km from Negele Borena, which remains the best locality. Sympatric with several other larks, and requires careful identification.

* Erlanger's lark *Calandrella erlangeri* (SR 346.3, VP -) A recent controversial split from *C. cinerea*, which it strongly resembles, this is among the more common and conspicuous larks of the Ethiopian Highlands.

* Brown saw-wing (swallow) *Psalidoprocne antinorii* Confined to forests in the southern highlands and Rift Valley, where it is the only saw-wing present, and reasonably common. Generally regarded as a race of *P. pristoptera* (SR 354.3, VP 59.12), but may warrant specific status.

*** Ethiopian saw-wing (swallow) *Psalidoprocne oleagina* Confined to southwest Ethiopia and southern Sudan, where it is the only saw-wing present and quite likely to be seen around Yabello. Generally regarded as a race of the black saw-wing *P. pristoptera* (SR 354.3, VP 59.12), but may warrant specific status.

* White-tailed swallow *Hirundo megaensis* (SR 358.5, VP 58.8) Endemic to Ethiopia. Restricted to arid acacia woodland around Yabello and Mega. Small parties often seen flying in the vicinity of termite hills. Distinguished from all other swallows by conspicuous white tail.

* **Ethiopian cliff swallow** *Hirundo* (SR -, VP 59.8) Recently discovered and as yet uncollected and undescribed species, known from Awash River Gorge and Lake Langano. May be more widespread than current knowledge suggests, possibly synonymous with Red Sea cliff swallow, known from one specimen collected near Port Sudan.

* **Abyssinian longclaw** *Macronyx flavicollis* (SR 366.5, VP 60.19) Widespread resident of high-altitude grassland, particularly common in the Bale area.

* **Ethiopian (Black-headed forest) oriole** *Oriolus monacha* (SR 384.4, VP 82.5) Similar to black-headed oriole, but inhabits true forest rather than woodland, and has an equally distinct but different call. Fairly common and active in forested habitats.

(Red-billed) chough *Pyrrhocorax pyrrhocorax* (SR 386.4, VP 85.10) Eurasian species with isolated Ethiopian population of perhaps 1,200 birds centred on Bale Mountains and northern highlands.

* **Streseman's (Abyssinian/Ethiopian) bush crow** *Zavattariornis stresemanni* (SR 386.5, VP 85.8) The proverbial odd bird, loosely affiliated to the crow family, but quite unlike most crows in behaviour and appearance. Confined to a small area of dry thornbush centred on Yabello, where parties of five or so birds are regularly seen from the roadside.

*** **Dwarf raven** *Corvus edithae* (SR 388.3, VP -) Recent, controversial split from larger *C. ruficollis* (VP 85.11), range more or less confined to Somalia and the eastern half of Ethiopia.

** **Thick-billed raven** *Corvus crassirostris* (SR 388.6, VP 85.15) Common and widespread throughout the highlands.

** **White-backed (black) tit** *Parus leuconotus* (SR 394.5, VP 78.8) Widespread but uncommon resident of forested habitats on both sides of the Rift. Often seen moving restlessly through mid-stratum in Dinsho (Bale), Wondo Genet, and developed hotel gardens in Addis Ababa.

*** **White-rumped babbler** *Turdoides leucopygia* (SR 402.6, VP 77.17) Common and conspicuous resident of wooded highlands and rivers, with range extending into small portions of Eritrea and Somalia.

*** **Somali bulbul** *Pycnonotus somaliensis* (SR 410.5) Recent split from common bulbul (VP 62.11) ranging between northern Somalia and eastern Ethiopia.

*** **Sombre rock chat** *Cercomela dubia* (SR 462.6, VP 65.13) Excluded from Ethiopian endemic status on the basis of one old record from Somalia, this is broadly confined to arid, rocky habitats in the northern Rift Valley, for instance Mount Fantelle in Awash National Park.

** **Rüppell's (black) chat** *Myrmecocichla melaena* (SR 466.1, VP 64.19) Common resident of rocky highlands north of Addis Ababa. Often tame around churches in Tigrai and Lalibela.

*** **Somali wheatear** *Oenanthe phillipsi* (SR 472.1, VP 64.12) Rare and localised Somali species with range extended into southeast Ethiopia. Not known from any Ethiopian locality regularly visited by birders. Note that the black-eared wheatear, desert wheatear and red-tailed wheatear all regularly overwinter in Ethiopia but not further south.

** **White-winged cliff-chat** *Myrmecocichla semirufa* (SR 472.6, VP 64.18) Occupies similar habitats to *M. melaena*, and also most common in the north. Could be mistaken for the very similar mocking cliff-chat, which often occurs alongside it in similar habitats.

* **Bale parisoma** *Parisoma griseaventris* (SR 494.3, VP -) Often lumped with practically indistinguishable brown parisoma, but confined to juniper and hagenia woodland and bracken thickets above 3,500m on the northern slopes of Bale Mountains.

* **Abyssinian catbird** *Parophasma galinieri* (SR 494.6, VP 77.7) Unusual species of undetermined affiliations, notable for its striking, melodic call. Common but elusive resident of juniper and other indigenous highland forest. Often observed at Dinsho (Bale) and in developed hotel grounds in Addis Ababa.

** **Ethiopian cisticola** *cistocola lugubris* (SR 506.7, VP -) Recent split from *C. marginatus*, this is a nondescript but vocal and conspicuous resident of moist areas and rank grass in the Ethiopian Highlands.

* **Abyssinian slaty flycatcher** *Melaenornis chocolatina* (SR 546.6, VP 74.20) Common resident of highland wood and forest both sides of the Rift. The white iris, similar to that of allied white-eyed slaty flycatcher (though less prominent), is misleadingly omitted from the illustration in Van Perlo.

*** **Somali (chestnut-winged) starling** *Onychognathus blythii* (SR 608.6, VP 86.8) Within Ethiopia, formerly thought to be restricted to arid northeast, but has recently been recorded by reliable observers at sites as diverse as Ankober, Bale Mountains and Mount Fantelle. Could be confused with other chestnut-winged starlings, though the long, tapering tail is unique.

** **White-billed starling** *Onychognathus albirostris* (SR 610.4, VP 86.11) Only chestnut-winged starling with white bill. Associated with cliffs and dwellings. Often seen around churches at Lalibela.

*** **Shining sunbird** *Cinnyrus hebessinica* (SR 630.6, VP 79.5) Brilliantly coloured sunbird common in Ethiopian Rift Valley but with range extending into parts of northern Kenya, Somalia and Eritrea.

*** **Swainson's sparrow** *Passer swainsonii* (SR 650.4, VP -) Recent split from grey-headed sparrow, range centred on Ethiopia, where it is common throughout, but extending into Eritrea, Somalia and far northeast of Sudan.

*** **Pale (petronia) rock finch** *Carpospiza brachydactyla* (SR 652.4) Nondescript sparrow-like dry-country bird confined to northern Ethiopia and bordering parts of Eritrea and Sudan.

*** **Rüppell's weaver** *Ploceus galbula* (SR 660.3, VP 89.20) Restricted to the Horn of Africa and Yemen. Common, sociable resident of savanna and light woodland.

*** **Juba (Salvadori's) weaver** *Ploceus dischrocephalus* (SR 672.4, VP 89.13) Endemic to Horn of Africa. In Ethiopia, restricted to southeast, regular at Dawa River Bridge between Negele Borena and Yabello.

* **Abyssinian yellow-rumped (white-throated) seedeater (serin)** *Serinus xanthopygius* (SR 716.3, VP 96.7) Confined to northern highlands, where it is uncommon to rare, and most likely to be seen at Tis Isat or the Ankober area.

* **Yellow-throated seedeater (serin)** *Serinus flavigula* (SR 716.5, VP 96.12) Uncommon and localised dry-country species, formerly regarded by some authorities to be a hybrid rather than a discrete genetic form. Confined to northern Rift, where it is regularly seen on Mount Fantelle and at Aliyu Amba near Ankober.

* **Salvadori's serin** *Serinus xantholaemus* (SR 716.6, VP 96.13) Distinctive and very localised dry-country serin discovered in 1980, and until recently known only from two locations: Arero and Sof Omar. Recent sightings on the Bogol Manyo road and south of Negele Borena would suggest the bird is more widespread than previously assumed.

★ Ethiopian (black-headed) siskin (serin) *Serinus nigriceps* (SR 718.2, VP 96.2) Common, widespread and distinctive species of high-altitude grassland and heather. Abundant around Bale Highlands.

★★★ African citril *Serinus citrinelloides* (SR 720.1, VP 96.3) Recently split from western and southern specific forms, of which the former nominate race is essentially a bird of the Ethiopian Highlands, with a discrete population confined to southern Sudan.

★★★ Brown-rumped seedeater (serin) *Serinus tristriatis* (SR 724.5, VP 96.18) Endemic to Horn of Africa. Common and confiding in Addis Ababa and other highland towns, where it seems to occupy a house sparrow-like niche.

★ Ankober serin *Serinus ankobernis* (SR 724.7, VP 96.10) Endemic to Ethiopia. Discovered in 1976 and until recently thought to be confined to a small area of steep escarpment near Ankober, but recent sightings in the Simien Mountains and elsewhere suggest it is actually quite widespread in the highlands.

Ornithological itineraries
While any ornithological itinerary will depend greatly on available time, level of interest, and budget, Ethiopia does boast a defined birding itinerary which, with minor variations, is followed by most organised tours. Unlike the standard 'historical circuit', this itinerary is focused on areas south of Addis Ababa, which is where most of the more localised endemics are to be found, and it can only be covered thoroughly in a private vehicle. Most of the sites mentioned below are covered in detail in the main body of this guide, so what follows is an outline itinerary only.

Southern circuit
The main birding circuit through the south requires an absolute minimum of ten days, though two weeks would be more realistic, and the extra four days would effectively double your birding time. With reasonable levels of dedication, luck and skill – or a skilled local bird guide – a total bird list of 350–400 species should be achievable over two weeks on this circuit. About 20 of the endemics are all but certain if you follow this route in its entirety over two weeks, though there are a couple (Salvadori's serin, Degodi lark, Abyssinian woodpecker) that are occasionally missed by visiting birders – and you'd be extraordinarily lucky to see a Nechisar nightjar. If possible, there would be much to be said for keeping the day-to-day itinerary reasonably flexible, particularly with regard to sites associated with one specific endemic, so that you can stay on or push ahead depending on how quickly you locate the desired bird. Only six of the endemics are more or less confined to areas north of Addis Ababa, and so are unlikely to be seen on this southern circuit (see *Northern excursions* on page 68).

Addis Ababa and Rift Valley (2 + nights)
A typical birding itinerary might start with a night in Addis Ababa, visiting the Entoto Natural Park or Menegasha Forest (both good for highland forest endemics) or the Gefersa Reservoir (good for water-associated and grassland endemics). This can be followed by a night or two in the Rift Valley, where one should stop at as many of the lakes as possible. Ziway is probably the best of the lakes for birds associated with open water and marsh, the Abiata-Shala complex for shorebirds, and Awassa for a mix of good water and acacia woodland species. Another important site in the Rift Valley is Wondo Genet, which is excellent for forest birds including several endemics. Depending on your

BUTTERFLIES

Ethiopia's immense wealth of invertebrate life is largely overlooked by visitors, but is perhaps most easily appreciated in the form of butterflies and moths of the order *Lepidoptera*. Several forests in Ethiopia harbour hundreds of different butterfly species, and one might easily see a greater selection in the course of a day than one could in a lifetime of exploring the English countryside.

The *Lepidoptera* are placed in the class *Insecta*, which includes ants, beetles and locusts among others. All insects are distinguished from other invertebrates, such as arachnids (spiders) and crustaceans, by their combination of six legs, a pair of frontal antennae, and a body divided into a distinct head, thorax and abdomen. Insects are the only flying invertebrates, and although some primitive orders have never evolved wings, and other more recently evolved orders have discarded them, most flying insects have two pairs of wings, one of which, as in the case of flies, might have been modified beyond immediate recognition. The butterflies and moths of the order *Lepidoptera* have two sets of wings and are distinguished from all other insect orders by the tiny ridged wing-scales that create their characteristic bright colours.

The most spectacular of all butterflies are the swallowtails of the family *Papilionidae*, of which roughly 100 species have been identified in Africa. Named for the streamers that trail from the base of their wings, swallowtails are typically large and colourful, and relatively easy to observe when they feed on mammal dung deposited on forest trails and roads. The west African giant swallowtail, a black, orange and green gem with a wingspan of up to 20cm, is probably the largest butterfly in the world, but it's seldom seem as it tends to stick to the forest canopy.

The *Pieridae* is a family of medium-sized butterflies, generally smaller than the swallowtails and with wider wings, of which many species are present in Ethiopia, several as seasonal intra-African migrants. Most species are predominantly white in

time limitations, anything from one night to a week could be spent in the Rift Valley at various lakes and at Wondo Genet.

Bale Highlands (2–3 nights)

From the Rift Valley, one can cut up the escarpment from Shashemene via Dodola towards Bale National Park. A village near Kofele, on the road between Shashemene and Dodola, is often mentioned in birding literature as the most reliable place to see the endemic Abyssinian long-eared owl, but recent reports are that the individual resident in this village is dead. The forest around the Bale park headquarters at Dinsho warrants a long session of birding, as the most reliable place in Ethiopia to see several localised and endemic forest birds. It is advisable to spend two nights in the Bale area, so you can allow a full day for birding on the Sanetti Plateau, which is the best place in Ethiopia to see endemics associated with grassland as well as a number of other notable species. With reasonable levels of luck, dedication and skill (or at least a skilled guide), a list of well over 200 species, including about half of the birds endemic to Ethiopia (or to Ethiopia and Eritrea), could be expected after two nights each in the Rift Valley and Bale areas. With a third night at Bale, it would be possible to head out for a day trip to the Sof Omar Caves, which is the best place to seek out the very localised Salvadori's serin.

Negele Borena and surrounds (2–3 nights)

From Bale, it is normal to head south to Negele Borena through the Sanetti Plateau, Harenna Forest and Dola Mena. This road may be impassable after heavy rain, when the Genale River presents an insurmountable obstacle, so check road conditions first. This is

colour, with some yellow, orange, black or even red and blue markings on the wings.

The most diverse family of butterflies in Africa is the *Lycaenidae*, which accounts for almost 500 of the 1,500 species recorded continent-wide. Known also as Gossamer Wings, this varied family consists mostly of small- to medium-sized butterflies, with a wingspan of 1–5cm, dull underwings, and brilliant violet blue, copper or rufous-orange upper wings. The larvae of many *Lycaenidae* species have a symbiotic relationship with ants – they secrete a fluid that is milked by the ants and are thus permitted to shelter in their nests.

Another well-represented family is the *Nymphalidae*, a diversely coloured group of small to large butterflies, generally associated with forest edges or interiors. The *Nymphalidae* are also known as brush-footed butterflies, because their forelegs have evolved into non-functional brush-like structures. One of the more common and distinctive species is the African blue tiger *Tirumala petiverana*, a large black butterfly with about two-dozen blue-white wing spots, often observed in forest paths near puddles or feeding from animal droppings.

The family *Charaxidae*, regarded by some authorities to be a subfamily of the *Nymphalidae*, is represented in Africa by roughly 200 species. Typically large, robust, strong fliers with one or two short tails on each wing, the butterflies in this family vary greatly in coloration, and several species appear to be scarce and localised since they inhabit forest canopies and are seldom observed.

Rather less spectacular are the grass-skipper species of the family *Hersperiidae*, most of which are small and rather drably coloured, though some are more attractively marked in black, white and/or yellow. The grass-skippers are regarded to form the evolutionary link between butterflies and the generally more nocturnal moths, represented in Ethiopia by several families of which the most impressive are the boldly patterned giant silk-moths of the family *Saturniidae*.

a long drive, so there won't be too much birding time along the way, especially if you want to stop at Genale, the best place to seek out the endemic Prince Ruspoli's turaco. The junction of the Bogol Manyo and Arero roads, 15km from Negele Borena, is the only known site for the endemic Sidamo lark. Depending on your dedication, an overnight excursion from Negele Borena to Bogol Manyo takes you to the only known locality for the endemic Degodi lark, and an area where Salvadori's serin has recently been observed. Both of these larks can be difficult to locate and identify, so give yourself a bit of time to search for them.

Yabello and surrounds (1–3 nights)
The road from Negele Borena to Yabello offers good dry-country birding in general, and is home to several of the species associated with the arid country shared with Somalia and northern Kenya. There are a couple of specific sites along this road where all birding tours stop. The first is the aforementioned junction with the Bogol Manyo road. The next is the Dawa River Bridge, a reliable place to pick up the very localised Juba weaver and white-winged turtle dove. Finally, the forests around Arero are home to Prince Ruspoli's turaco, and the surrounding area is also one of the few known localities for Salvadori's serin. Also at Arero, you should start looking out for Streseman's bush crow and white-tailed swallow, the two endemics whose restricted range is centred on Yabello. Both of these birds are generally easy to locate and identify, and the odds are you'll have seen them even before you arrive at Yabello. From Yabello, it is possible to drive to Addis Ababa or Awash National Park over a long day, provided you don't stop more often than is necessary. Less frenetic would be to break up the drive with a night at Wondo Genet

or at one of the Rift Valley lakes – you could choose where to stay depending on the gaps in your list of birds identified to date. A third option (see below) would be to cut through via Konso to Arba Minch and Nechisar National Park.

Nechisar National Park (2–3 nights)

Arguably something of a fool's errand, the diversion through Arba Minch allows you to spend time in Nechisar National Park, the only known locality for the Nechisar nightjar. In common with other nightjars, this species is (presumably) nocturnal, so you'd be most likely to see it on the road after dusk. Several other nightjar species are present in Nechisar, so careful identification would be required if you aim to be the first person to see this bird alive. A photograph would probably be required for the record to be accepted; it's often very easy to sneak up on foot to within photographic range of nightjars caught in the headlights! The elusive nightjar aside, Nechisar's most interesting birding habitat is the groundwater forest near the entrance gate. From Nechisar, you can drive directly to Addis Ababa or Awash National Park in a day.

Awash National Park (2–3 nights)

The two most important specials for this park are the sombre rock chat and yellow-throated serin, both of which are regular on Mount Fantelle. The best part of a day should be allocated to seeking out these birds. The Ethiopian cliff swallow is most easily seen in the Awash Gorge at the southern end of the park. Awash is also one of the best general bird sites in Ethiopia, for which reason a second full day is strongly recommended.

Northern excursions

On the whole, northern Ethiopia is of less interest to birders than the south, though any birdwatcher hoping to see all of Ethiopia's endemics would need to undertake two specific trips north, both of which are covered in detail in the regional part of this guide. The first trip is to Ankober, the best place to see the localised Ankober serin and the springboard for a short side trip to Aliyu Amba, a recently discovered site for the yellow-throated serin. This trip could be extended to include the Guassa Plateau near Mehal Meda, a moorland area supporting similar species to the Sanetti Plateau. The second trip leads to the Jemma Valley, the only reliable spot for the endemic Harwood's francolin. On either trip, one would stand a good chance of encountering some of the other four endemics whose range is more or less restricted to the north, ie: white-winged cliff-chat, Rüppell's black chat, white-billed starling, and white-throated serin. At a serious push, either trip would form a viable day excursion from the capital, though in both cases it would be better to allow for two days and a full night.

Planning and Preparation

This chapter covers most practical aspects of preparing for a trip to Ethiopia, from visas and other paperwork to planning an itinerary. Health-related preparation is covered in *Chapter 7*. You will also be better equipped to think through your style of travel and what you want to pack if you read the chapter *Travelling in Ethiopia*.

WHEN TO VISIT

Ethiopia can be visited at any time of year. People are often advised against travelling during the rainy season, which normally runs from June until early October, but with Lalibela being accessible all year through, this is less of an issue that it used to be. Indeed, having travelled in Ethiopia at most times of year myself, I actually feel the rainy season is my favourite period, partially because there are fewer other tourists at sites such as Lalibela, but above all because the scenery is so much more impressive when the countryside is green and well watered. A lovely time of year is September through to early October, when the whole country is a riot of wild Meskel flowers.

The most popular time to visit Ethiopia is between October and January, when the rains are over but the countryside is still quite green. Many travellers try to schedule their trip to coincide with important festivals such as Ethiopian New Year, Ethiopian Christmas, Timkat or Meskel. The European winter is also the best time for birds, as resident species are supplemented by large numbers of Palaearctic migrants.

One area where travel options are restricted during the rains is South Omo. The rains here typically fall in April and May, but they may run earlier or later, for which reason March and June are also probably best avoided, as are the short rains in October.

TOURIST INFORMATION

Very little information about Ethiopia is available outside the country. Ethiopian Airlines offices and Ethiopian embassies will be able to give you information about internal flight schedules and current visa and entry requirements. Details of tourist information services within Ethiopia are given in *Chapter 5*. It is also worth consulting the websites run by the UK and US governments, respectively www.fco.gov.uk and http://travel.state.gov/travel_warnings, and other websites listed in *Appendix 2, Further Reading*.

GETTING TO ETHIOPIA
By air

Ethiopian Airlines is Africa's oldest airline. Contrary to many people's prejudices, it is a highly regarded carrier, and it offers the most extensive network of intra-African flights of any airline in the world. Ethiopian Airlines flies either directly or in conjunction with another carrier between Addis Ababa and 24 African cities, most major Middle Eastern, European and North American cities, and Bombay, Delhi, Bangkok, Tokyo and Beijing in Asia. Bookings can be made online at www.flyethiopian.com, or by emailing reservation@ethiopianairlines.com, or through Ethiopian Airlines offices or agencies in your country of departure. The contact phone number for Ethiopian Airlines throughout the USA is +1 877 389 6753 (+1 877 ET-WORLD) – physical offices are present in Dallas, Denver, Los Angeles, New York, San Francisco, Seattle and Washington DC. Elsewhere, the offices most likely to be of interest to readers are:

Amsterdam ☊ +31 20 642 9190; e ETHIOPIAN.AIRLINES@worldonline.nl
Beijing ☊ +86 10 6505 0314/5
Cairo ☊ +20 2 574 0603/0852; e calam@ethiopianairlines.com
Dar es Salaam ☊ +255 22 211 7063/4/5; e daram@ethiopianairlines.com
Delhi ☊ +91 11 2331 2302/3/4; e sthdel@ndb.vsnl.net.in
Djibouti ☊ +253 351007/4235; e JIBAM@ethiopianairlines.com
Frankfurt ☊ +49 69 274 0070; e ethiopian.fra@t-online.de
Geneva ☊ +41 22 716 1750; e Geneva@ethiopianairlines.com
Harare ☊ +263 4 790705/6; e ethhre@icon.cp.zw
Johannesburg ☊ +27 11 616 7624/5/6/8; e jnbam@ethiopianairlines.com
Khartoum ☊ +249 83 762062/3; e ETAIR@sudanmail.net.sd
London ☊ +44 20 8987 7000/9086
Milan ☊ +39 2 805 6562; e Ethiopian-mil@mclink.it
Nairobi ☊ +254 2 337211/822236; e nboet@nbi.ispkenya.om
New York ☊ +1 212 867 0095, toll-free: +1 800 445 2733
Paris ☊ +33 1 53 76 05 38
Rome ☊ +39 6 4201 1199; e ethiopian-ROM@mclink.it
Stockholm ☊ +46 8 440 2900; e res-ethiopianm@telia.com
Tokyo ☊ +81 3 3281 1990
Toronto ☊ +1 905 678 7335

LONG-HAUL FLIGHTS, CLOTS AND DVT
Dr Jane Wilson-Howarth

Long-haul air travel increases the risk of deep vein thrombosis. Although recent research has suggested that many of us develop clots when immobilised, most resolve without us ever having been aware of them. In certain susceptible individuals, though, large clots form and these can break away and lodge in the lungs. This is dangerous but happens in a tiny minority of passengers.

Studies have shown that flights of over five-and-a-half-hours are significant, and that people who take lots of shorter flights over a short space of time form clots. People at highest risk are:

• Those who have had a clot before – unless they are now taking warfarin
• People over 80 years of age
• Those who have recently had a major operation or surgery for varicose veins
• Someone who has had a hip or knee replacement in the last three months
• Cancer sufferers
• Those who have ever had a stroke
• People with heart disease
• Those with a close blood relative who has had a clot

Those with a slightly increased risk:

• People over 40
• Women who are pregnant or have had a baby in the last couple of weeks
• People taking female hormones or other oestrogen therapy
• Heavy smokers
• Those who have very severe varicose veins
• The very obese or the very tall (over 6ft/1.8m) or short (under 5ft/1.5m)

Other major airlines that fly to Addis Ababa are Air France, Alitalia, British Airways, SAS, KLM, Lufthansa and Kenya Airways. There are dozens upon dozens of travel agents in London offering cheap flights to Africa, and it's worth checking out the ads in magazines like *Time Out* and *TNT* and phoning around before you book anything.

An established London operator, well worth contacting, is **Africa Travel Centre** (*4 Medway Court, Leigh Street, London WC1H 9OX;* ℡ *020 7387 1211;* f *020 7383 7512*). Two reputable agents specialising in cheap round-the-world-type tickets rather than Africa specifically are **Trailfinders** (*42–48 Earls Court Road, London W8 6EJ;* ℡ *020 7938 3366;* f *020 7937 9294*) and **STA** (*117 Euston Road, London NW1 2SX;* ℡ *020 7361 6262;* f *020 7937 9570*). There are STA branches in Bristol, Cambridge, Oxford and Manchester.

An **airport tax** of US$20 is levied when you fly out of Ethiopia. This must be paid in hard currency, and preferably cash since an extra commission is taken for travellers' cheques.

Overland

The main overland route south from Europe, often referred to as the Nile Route, goes through Egypt and Sudan, entering Ethiopia west of Gonder. This route was closed for many years due to political instability in Sudan, and it remains potentially volatile, but travellers have been getting through with relative ease for two or three years prior to publication of this fourth edition (for further details, see box *Crossing between Ethiopia and Sudan*, page 232). If you opt to head this way, do keep your ears to the ground, and be prepared to fly over troubled areas, for instance between Cairo and Khartoum or Khartoum and Addis Ababa. It is no longer possible to cross between Ethiopia and Sudan

A deep vein thrombosis (DVT) is a blood clot that forms in the deep leg veins. This is very different from irritating but harmless superficial phlebitis. DVT causes swelling and redness of one leg, usually with heat and pain in one calf and sometimes the thigh. A DVT is only dangerous if a clot breaks away and travels to the lungs (pulmonary embolus). Symptoms of a pulmonary embolus (PE) include chest pain that is worse on breathing in deeply, shortness of breath, and sometimes coughing up small amounts of blood. The symptoms commonly start three to ten days after a long flight. Anyone who thinks that they might have a DVT needs to see a doctor immediately who will arrange a scan. Warfarin tablets (to thin the blood) are then taken for at least six months.

Prevention of DVT

Several conditions make the problem more likely. Immobility is the key, and factors like reduced oxygen in cabin air and dehydration may also contribute. To reduce the risk of thrombosis on a long journey:

* Exercise before and after the flight
* Keep mobile before and during the flight; move around every couple of hours
* During the flight drink plenty of water or juices
* Avoid taking sleeping pills and excessive tea, coffee and alcohol
* Perform exercises that mimic walking and tense the calf muscles
* Consider wearing flight socks or support stockings (see www.legshealth.com)
* Taking a meal of oily fish (mackerel, trout, salmon, sardines, etc) in the 24 hours before departure reduces blood clotability and thus DVT risk
* The jury is still out on whether it is worth taking an aspirin before flying, but this can be discussed with your GP.

If you think you are at increased risk of a clot, ask your doctor if it is safe to travel.

via Eritrea, as the border between Eritrea and Ethiopia has been closed for some years and looks set to remain that way.

Travellers heading up to Ethiopia from more southerly parts of Africa have a more straightforward ride. In terms of safety, the route from South Africa to Kenya via Zimbabwe, Zambia and Tanzania has been good for over a decade. The most volatile part of this route is the Kenyan/Ethiopian border area, as northern Kenya is prone to spasmodic outbreaks of Somali-related banditry. Plenty of people get through from Kenya without a problem, but the situation is subject to frequent change. As always, your best source of information is travellers coming in the opposite direction.

PAPERWORK

A valid **passport** is required to enter Ethiopia. Check well in advance that it hasn't expired and will not do so for a while, since you may be refused entry on a passport that's due to expire within six months of your intended departure date. Many African countries impose a similar ruling, so if you are undertaking an open-ended trip in Africa and your passport is due to expire in a year or so, it would be sensible to organise a fresh one before you leave home.

All visitors to Ethiopia require a **visa**, though as of early 2002, citizens of the USA, Canada, Mexico, Brazil, New Zealand, Australia, South Africa, China, Japan, Korea, Israel, Russia, the UK and all other European Union nations can buy a three-month visa upon arrival at Bole International Airport for around US$30. Other passport holders will need to arrange a visa in advance – if you live in a country where there is no Ethiopian Embassy, and travel with Ethiopian Airways, you can apply for a visa through the airline office. Should you need to spend longer in the country than is stamped into your passport, you should be aware that the only place where extensions can be granted is the Immigration office on Churchill Avenue in Addis Ababa. Visa extensions cost the birr equivalent of US$20, regardless of the length of the extension, and they take 24 hours to be processed.

It is, in theory, compulsory to have a valid **yellow fever vaccination** to enter Ethiopia, though we've never been asked for one in the past, and cannot say what would happen were you to be asked to produce a certificate you don't have.

Should there be any possibility you'll want to drive or hire a vehicle while you're in the country, do organise an **international driving licence** (any AA office in a country in which you're licensed to drive will do this for a nominal fee).

For **security** reasons, it's advisable to detail all your important information on one sheet of paper, photocopy it, and distribute a few copies in your luggage, your money-belt, and amongst relatives or friends at home. The sort of things you want to include on this are your travellers' cheque numbers and refund information, travel insurance policy details and 24-hour emergency contact number, passport number, details of relatives or friends to be contacted in an emergency, bank and credit card details, camera and lens serial numbers etc.

Should your passport be lost or stolen, it will generally be easier to get a replacement if you have a photocopy of the important pages.

Ethiopian embassies and honorary consulates

Australia Honorary Consulate, PO Box 2088, Fitzroy Mail Centre, Victoria, Melbourne 3065; ✆ +61 39417 3419; f +61 39417 3219

Austria Ethiopian Embassy, Freidrich Schmidt Platz 3/3, 1080 Vienna; ✆ +431 710 2168; f +431 710 2171

Belgium Ethiopian Embassy, Av de Tervueren 231, 1150 Brussels; ✆ +322 771 3294; f +322 771 4914

Canada Ethiopian Embassy, 151 Slater St, Suite 210, Ottawa, Ontario K1P 5H3; ✆ +613 235 6637; f +613 235 4638

Côte d'Ivoire Ethiopian Embassy, Immeuble Nour-Al-Hayat, 8e Etage, Abidjan; ☎ +225 213365; f +225 213709
Egypt Ethiopian Embassy, 6 Abdrahman Sussin St, Gumhuria Sq, Dokki, Cairo; ☎ +202 335 3696; f +202 335 3699
Eritrea Ethiopian Embassy, Franklin D Roosevelt St, Asmara; ☎ +04 116365; f +04 116144
France Ethiopian Embassy, 35 av Charles Floquet, Paris; ☎ +33 147 83 83 95; f +33 143 06 52 14
Germany Ethiopian Embassy, IMHON Str 31, Bonn; ☎ +49 22 823 3041; f +49 22 823 3045
Ghana Ethiopian Embassy, 2 Milne Close, Airport Residential Area, Accra; ☎ +233 21 775928; f +233 21 776807
Greece Honorary Consulate, 253 Sigrou Av, Athens; ☎ +930 3483; f +942 6050
Italy Ethiopian Embassy, Via Andrea Vesalio 16–18, 00161 Rome; ☎ +39 6 440 2602; f +39 6 440 3676
Japan Ethiopian Embassy, 1-14-15 Midorigaoka, Meguro-ku, Tokyo 152; ☎ +81 3 3718 1003; f +81 3 3718 0978
Kenya Ethiopian Embassy, State House Av, Nairobi; ☎ +254 2 723035; f +254 2 723401
Malaysia Honorary Consulate, 23 Chin Bee Av, Singapore 619943; ☎ +65 262 1233; f +65 261 2800
Norway Honorary Consulate, Torjusbakken 19, 0378 Oslo; ☎ +47 2214 3318
Senegal Ethiopian Embassy, 18 Bd de la Republique, Dakar; ☎ +221 821 9890; f +221 821 0805
South Africa Ethiopian Embassy, 47 Charles St, Baileys Mucklenenuk, Pretoria; ☎ +27 12 346 3542; f +27 12 346 3867
Spain Honorary Consulate, C/Gran Via 55–6b, Madrid 28013; ☎ +433 7982; f +551 2276
Sudan Ethiopian Embassy, Khartoum South, Plot No 4, Block 384BC; ☎ +249 11 451156; f +249 11 471141
Sweden Ethiopian Embassy, Erik Dahlbergsallen 15–1, Stockholm; ☎ +46 8 665 6030; f +46 8 660 9561
Switzerland Ethiopian Embassy, 56 Rue de Miollebiau, 1209 Geneva; ☎ +41 22 733 0750; f +41 22 740 1129
Thailand Honorary Consulate, 962/14 Prannok Rd, Bangkok 10700; ☎ +662 412 1066; f +662 412 1068
Uganda Ethiopian Embassy, Plot No 51B, Lumumba Av, Nakasero, Kampala; ☎ +256 4123 1010; f +256 4123 1782
UK Ethiopian Embassy, 17 Princes Gate, London SW7 1PZ; ☎ +44 020 7589 7212; f +44 020 7584 7054
USA Ethiopian Embassy, 2134 Kalorama Rd, NW Washington DC 20008; ☎ +1 202 234 2281; f +1 202 328 7950
Zimbabwe Ethiopian Embassy, 14 Lanark Rd, Belgravia, Harare; ☎ +2634 725822; f +2634 720259

Immigration and customs

Arriving by air

Provided you have an onward ticket and a valid passport and visa, you should whiz through the formalities without complication. I've never spoken to anybody who arrived in Ethiopia with a one-way air ticket, which can lead to complications in some African countries, but equally I've certainly had no reader feedback to indicate that arriving on a one-way ticket is a problem. Nevertheless, it might be worth pre-empting any possible complication. What most countries fear is that one-way arrivals will be stranded in their country without funds enough to leave, so a ticket out of another African country should be as good as a ticket out of Ethiopia. The more money you are carrying, the less likely it is your finances will be queried (a credit card can be useful as it implies unlimited access to funds). Assuming that arriving on a one-way ticket means you intend to travel to other countries, it is definitely worth underlining this intent by arriving in Ethiopia with a visa or visitor's pass for the next country you plan to visit.

Arriving overland

The most common overland entry point is Moyale on the Kenyan border. This has a reputation as a very relaxed crossing – though the border does close from time to time and the situation seems to be fluid. The major complication arriving at this border from Kenya is that the Ethiopian Embassy in Nairobi sometimes only issues visas on production of an air ticket to Addis Ababa. If you're heading this way, it's advisable to speak to travellers coming the other way for current advice (places like the New Kenya Lodge, Mrs Roche's and Iqbal Hotel in Nairobi are good for meeting overland travellers). Details of the crossing are included in the box *Moyale to Nairobi* on page 485.

At the time of writing, travelling between Ethiopia and Eritrea is impossible, and it may be some time before the borders reopen. In the past, however, the crossing was straightforward, provided you had the appropriate visa, which could be obtained at the Eritrean Embassy in Addis Ababa. If you were returning to Ethiopia from Eritrea, you needed a multiple-entry visa for Ethiopia.

Overland travel between Ethiopia and Somalia is also difficult at the time of writing, and the situation with Sudan changes all the time. The appropriate embassies will be able to tell you whether overland travel is currently permitted. Travellers coming the other way are your best source of practical advice.

It is also possible to travel overland between Djibouti and Ethiopia, though few people do so. The best way to cross between the countries is by using the rail service that connects Addis Ababa and Djibouti via Dire Dawa (see box *The Djibouti Railway*, page 394). It is also possible to travel there along the surfaced road through the northern Rift Valley covered in *Chapter 19*.

MONEY MATTERS
Organising your finances

The safest way to take money to Ethiopia is in the form of travellers' cheques, which can be refunded if they are stolen. Most major currencies are accepted in Ethiopian banks, but unless you have a strong reason for not doing so, it is probably a good idea to carry US dollar travellers' cheques (though the recent strength of the euro is starting to undermine the long-standing status of the US dollar). More obscure currencies may cause confusion at banks outside Addis Ababa or if you try to pay for government hotels or other services in hard currency.

It is advisable to carry a portion of your funds in hard currency banknotes, which are easier to exchange outside of the capital. If you are thinking of using the black market, it is essential to have US dollars cash; high denomination bills are preferable, but US$100 notes issued after the year 2000 may be refused. Banks can also be unwilling to accept older US dollar banknotes because of the number of forgeries in circulation. There seems to be less of an issue with smaller banknotes, so unless you can locate spanking new US$100 bills, then denominations of US$50 are probably the best overall compromise.

No matter how long you intend to spend in Ethiopia, I would advise that you bring whatever money you will need with you. Rather return home with unused travellers' cheques than get into the complications of having money sent to you. This is a hassle in most African countries – I've heard of people taking up to four weeks to receive a bank draft – and in Ethiopia, as in most other countries, you will have to accept your money in local currency and then change it back to hard currency on departure. I have no reason to suppose that Addis Ababa is particularly bad where bank drafts and the like are concerned – in fact, my gut feeling is that it would be better than most African capitals – but I really wouldn't want to put it to the test.

Credit cards are of limited use in Ethiopia. The major cards will be accepted to settle room and restaurant bills at the Addis Ababa Hilton and Sheraton, and a few other hotels in the capital, but nowhere else in the country. There are ATMs in the capital and other large cities, but these are for the exclusive use of local cardholders and will not accept international credit or debit cards. The *only* place where you can draw cash against a credit card is at the Sheraton and Bole Road branches of the Dashen Bank in Addis Ababa, and this transaction will attract a 6% charge. If you do bring a credit card, it should be as a fallback in case of an emergency, not as a primary source of funds.

Planning a budget

Budgeting is a personal thing, dependent on how much time you are spending in the country, what you are doing while you are there and how much money you can afford to spend.

Short-stay budgets

Short-stay tourists will find Ethiopia undemanding on their wallets. You can expect to pay an average of around US$30–40 per night for a room in a government hotel and, except perhaps in Addis Ababa, you'd struggle to top US$10 per day on food and drink. Most visitors with time restraints will want to fly between major places of interest, for which they can expect to pay around US$50 per leg. Add to that about US$10 per day on guide and entrance fees, and a daily budget of US$100 for one person or US$150 for two looks very generous. If you were prepared to stay in the sort of mid-range private hotels that exist in most major towns, around US$70/100 for one/two people would still look generous.

Where Ethiopia does get expensive is when you take organised driving tours and safaris. The low volume of tourists means that arrangements tend to be personalised, and thus a safari to somewhere like South Omo will be far more expensive than an equivalent safari in Kenya or Tanzania.

There is nothing preventing short-stay visitors from operating on the sort of budget that you would normally associate with long-stay visitors, except that the distances between major attractions make flying virtually essential if you are to see much of the country in a short space of time.

Long-stay budgets

If you use facilities that are mainly geared to locals, Ethiopia is a very inexpensive country, even by African standards. You can always find a basic room in a local hotel for around US$2–3 and a meal for less than US$1.50. Buses are cheap, as are drinks. Rigidly budget-conscious travellers could probably keep costs down to US$10 per day per person, but US$15 would give you considerably more flexibility. At US$20 per day, you could, within reason, do what you like.

If you are on a restricted budget, it is often a useful device to separate your daily budget from one-off expenses. This is less the case in Ethiopia than most African countries, because few travellers will be doing expensive one-off activities such as safaris, gorilla tracking, or climbing Kilimanjaro. Nevertheless, there are always going to be days that a variety of factors (historical site and guide fees, air tickets) conspire to make expensive. At current prices, a daily budget of around US$10 with a few hundred dollars spare for one-off expenses would be very comfortable for most travellers.

PACKING

There are two simple rules to bear in mind when you decide what to take with you to Ethiopia. The first is to bring with you *everything* that you could possibly need and that might not be readily available when you need it. The second is to carry as little as possible. Somewhat contradictory rules, you might think, and you'd be right – so the key is finding the right balance, something that probably depends on personal experience as much as anything. Worth stressing is that most genuine necessities are surprisingly easy to get hold of in Ethiopia, and that most of the ingenious gadgets you can buy in camping shops are likely to amount to dead weight on the road. If it came to it, you could easily travel in Ethiopia with little more than a change of clothes, a few basic toiletries and a medical kit.

Carrying luggage

Assuming that you'll be using public transport, you'll want to carry your luggage on your back, either in a backpack or in a suitcase that converts into one, since you'll tend to spend a lot of time walking between bus stations and hotels. Which of these you choose depends mainly on your style of travel. If you intend doing a lot of hiking you definitely want a proper backpack. On the other hand, if you'll be doing things where it might be a good idea to shake off the negative image attached to backpackers, then there would be obvious advantages in being able to convert your backpack into a conventional suitcase.

My preference before I started travelling in the company of an equipment-laden photographer was a robust 35 litre daypack. The advantages of keeping luggage as light and compact as possible are manifold. For starters, you can rest it on your lap on bus trips, avoiding complications such as extra charges for luggage, arguments about where your bag should be stored, and the slight but real risk of theft if your luggage ends up on the roof. A compact bag also makes for greater mobility, whether you're hiking or looking for a hotel in town. The sacrifice? Leave behind camping equipment and a sleeping bag. Do this, and it's quite possible to fit everything you truly need into a daypack, and possibly even a few luxuries – I've always travelled with binoculars, a bird field guide and at least five novels, and still used to keep my weight down to around 8kg. Frankly, it puzzles me what the many backpackers who wander around with an enormous pack and absolutely no camping equipment actually carry!

If your luggage won't squeeze into a daypack, a sensible compromise is to carry a large daypack in your rucksack. That way, you can carry a tent and other camping equipment when you need it, but at other times reduce your luggage to fit into a daypack and leave what you're not using in storage.

Travellers carrying a lot of valuable items should look for a pack that can easily be padlocked. A locked bag can, of course, be slashed open, but in Ethiopia you are still most likely to encounter casual theft of the sort to which a lock would be a real deterrent.

Clothes

Clothes may be light but they are also bulky, so it's advisable to take the minimum. You can easily and cheaply replace worn items in Ethiopia. In my opinion, what you need is one or possibly two pairs of trousers and/or skirts, one pair of shorts, three shirts or T-shirts, a couple of sweaters, a light waterproof windbreaker during the rainy season, enough socks and underwear to last five to seven days, one solid pair of shoes or boots for walking, and one pair of sandals, thongs or other light shoes.

When you select your clothes, remember that jeans are heavy to carry, hot to wear, and slow to dry. Far better to bring light cotton trousers and, if you intend spending a while in montane regions, tracksuit bottoms for extra cover on chilly nights. Skirts are best made of a light natural fabric such as cotton. T-shirts are lighter and less bulky than proper shirts, though the top pocket of a shirt (particularly if it buttons up) is a good place to carry spending money in markets and bus stations, since it's easier to keep an eye on than trouser pockets. Despite its equatorial location, much of Ethiopia is decidedly chilly, especially at night, so a couple of sweaters or sweatshirts are essential. There is a massive used clothing industry in Ethiopia, and at most markets you'll find stalls selling jumpers of dubious aesthetic but impeccable functional value for next to nothing – you might consider buying such clothing on the spot and giving it away afterwards.

Ethiopians are modest dressers and the country has a significant Muslim population – you should select your clothing with this in mind. Women should never expose their knees or shoulders in public, so shorts and sleeveless tops are out. It isn't entirely acceptable for women to wear trousers in Muslim areas, but neither will it cause serious offence. Men should always wear a shirt in public places. Trousers are generally more acceptable than shorts, though again this isn't rigid. Sensitivity about dress is more of a factor in the predominantly Muslim eastern regions than it is elsewhere in Ethiopia.

Socks and underwear must be made from natural fabrics. Bear in mind that re-using sweaty undergarments will encourage fungal infections such as athlete's foot, as well as prickly heat in the groin region. Socks and underpants are light and compact enough that it's worth bringing a week's supply. As for footwear, genuine hiking boots are worth considering only if you're a serious off-road hiker, since they are very heavy whether on your feet or in your pack. A good pair of walking shoes, preferably made of leather and with good ankle support, is a good compromise. It's also useful to carry sandals, thongs or other light shoes. Flip-flops are useful as protection from the floors of communal showers, and they are very light to carry. Just watch out for irregular pavements!

Once in Ethiopia, every town has a market selling secondhand clothing at dirt-cheap prices, where you can replace tired clothing with something fresh. Getting clothes made from local fabrics is also quick and relatively inexpensive.

Camping equipment

The case for bringing camping equipment to Ethiopia is compelling only if you intend to hike in remote areas. In most other situations, rooms are cheap and campsites few and far between, so this isn't a country where camping will save huge sums of cash. The main argument against carrying camping equipment is that it will increase the weight and bulk of your luggage by up to 5kg, all of which is dead weight except for when you camp. One area where a tent is a definite asset is South Omo, though if you travel to this region with a tour operator, they will normally supply camping gear on request.

If you decide to carry camping equipment, the key is to look for the lightest available gear. It is now possible to buy a lightweight tent weighing little more than 2kg, but make sure that the one you buy is mosquito proof. Other essentials for camping include a sleeping bag and a roll-mat, which will serve as both insulation and padding. You might want to carry a stove for occasions when no firewood is available. If you do carry a stove, it's worth knowing that Camping Gaz cylinders are not available in Ethiopia. A box of firelighter blocks will get a fire going in the most unpromising conditions. It would also be advisable to carry a pot, plate, cup and cutlery.

Other useful items

Most backpackers, even those with no intention of camping, carry a **sleeping bag**. A lightweight sleeping bag will be more than adequate in Ethiopia; better still in this climate would be to carry a sheet sleeping bag, something you can easily make yourself. You might meet travellers who, when they stay in local lodgings, habitually place their own sleeping bag on top of the bedding provided. Nutters, in my opinion, and I'd imagine that a sleeping bag would be less likely to protect against fleas than to be infested by the things.

I wouldn't leave home without **binoculars**, which some might say makes me the nutter. Seriously, though, if you're interested in natural history, it's difficult to imagine anything that will give you such value-for-weight entertainment as a pair of light compact binoculars, which these days needn't be much heavier or bulkier than a pack of cards. Binoculars are essential if you want to get a good look at birds (Africa boasts a remarkably

PHOTOGRAPHIC TIPS
Ariadne Van Zandbergen
Equipment
Although with some thought and an eye for composition you can take reasonable photos with a 'point and shoot' camera, you need an SLR camera with one or more lenses if you are at all serious about photography. If you carry only one lens in Ethiopia, a 28–70mm or similar zoom should be ideal. For a second lens, a 80–200mm or 70–300mm or similar will be excellent for candid shots, for wildlife, and for varying your composition.

Film
Print film is the preference of most casual photographers, slide film of professionals and some dedicated amateurs. Slide film is more expensive than print film, but this is broadly compensated for by cheaper development costs. Most photographers working outdoors in Africa favour Fujichrome slide film, in particular Sensia 100, Provia 100 (the professional equivalent to Sensia) or Velvia 50. Slow films (ie: those with a low ASA (ISO) rating) produce less grainy and sharper images than fast films, but can be tricky without a tripod in low light. Velvia 50 is extremely fine-grained and shows stunning colour saturation; it is the film I normally use in soft, even light or overcast weather. Sensia or Provia may be preferable in low light, since 100 ASA allows you to work at a faster shutter speed than 50 ASA. Because 100 ASA is more tolerant of contrast, it is also preferable in harsh light.

For print photography, a combination of 100 or 200 ASA film should be ideal. For the best results it is advisable to stick to recognised brands. Fujicolor produces excellent print films, with the Superia 100 and 200 recommended.

Some basics
The automatic programmes provided with many cameras are limited in the sense that the camera cannot think, but only makes calculations. A better investment than any amount of electronic wizardry would be to read a photographic manual for beginners and get to grips with such basics as the relationship between aperture and shutter speed.

Beginners should also note that a low shutter speed can result in camera shake and therefore a blurred image. For hand-held photographs of static subjects using a low-magnification lens (eg: 28–70), select a shutter speed of at least 1/60th of a second. For lenses of higher magnification, the rule of thumb is that the shutter speed should be at least the inverse of the magnification (for instance, a speed of 1/300 or faster on a 300 magnification lens). You can use lower shutter speeds with a tripod.

Most modern cameras include a built-in light meter, and give users the choice of three types of metering: matrix, centre-weighted or spot metering. You will need to understand how these different systems work to make proper use of them. Built-in light meters are reliable in most circumstances, but in uneven light, or where there is a lot of sky, you may want to take your metering selectively, for instance by taking a spot reading on the main subject. The meter will tend to under or overexpose when pointed at an almost white or black subject. This can be countered by taking a reading

colourful avifauna even if you've no desire to put a name to everything that flaps) or to watch distant mammals in game reserves. For most purposes, 7x21 compact binoculars will be fine, though some might prefer 7x35 traditional binoculars for their larger field of vision. Serious birdwatchers will find a 10x magnification more useful.

against an 18% grey card, or a substitute such as grass or light grey rocks – basically anything that isn't almost black, almost white or highly reflective.

Dust and heat
Dust and heat are often a problem in Africa. Keep your equipment in a sealed bag, stow films in an airtight container (such as a small cooler bag), leave used films in your hotel room, and avoid changing film in dusty conditions. On rough roads, I always carry my camera equipment on my lap to protect against vibration and bumps. Never stow camera equipment or film in a car boot (it will bake), or let it stand in direct sunlight.

Light
The light in Africa is much harsher than in Europe or North America, for which reason the most striking outdoor photographs are often taken during the hour or two of 'golden light' after dawn and before sunset. Shooting in low light may enforce the use of very low shutter speeds, in which case a tripod (ideally) or monopod (lighter) will be required to avoid camera shake. Be alert to the long shadows cast by a low sun; these show up more on photographs than to the naked eye.

With careful handling, side lighting and back lighting can produce stunning effects, especially in soft light and at sunrise or sunset. Generally, however, it is best to shoot with the sun behind you. Because of this, most buildings and landscapes are essentially a 'morning shot' or 'afternoon shot', depending on the direction in which they face. When you spend a couple of nights in one place, you'll improve your results by planning the best time to take pictures of static subjects (a compass can come in handy).

When photographing people or animals in the harsh midday sun, images taken in light but even shade are likely to look nicer than those taken in direct sunlight or patchy shade, since the latter conditions create too much contrast. Fill-in flash is almost essential if you want to capture facial detail of dark-skinned people in harsh or contrasting light.

Protocol
Ethiopia is on the whole very relaxed about photography. Apart from a few museums and sensitive government or military installations, you can photograph virtually everything, including 800-year-old bibles and paintings in the old churches. However tempting it may be, I would suggest you don't use flash on these treasures, since this will damage them in the long run. If you want to photograph inside the churches and you have an SLR camera it pays to bring a tripod and work with slow exposures without flash. Aside from your responsibility not to damage the artefacts you'll get much nicer photos of these subjects without flash.

Except in general street or market scenes, it is unacceptable to photograph people without permission. Some people will refuse, but most will agree – for a small payment. In most parts of Ethiopia, birr 1–5 is an accepted 'fee', depending on the area and situation. Even the most willing subject will often pose stiffly when a camera is pointed at them; relax them by making a joke, and take a few shots in quick succession to improve the odds of capturing a natural pose.

Some travellers like to carry their own **padlock**: not a bad idea in Ethiopia, particularly if you intend to stay mostly in shoestring hotels or travel to small towns, where not all hotels will supply padlocks. A combination lock might be the best idea, since potential thieves in Ethiopia are far more likely to have experience of picking locks with keys.

Your **toilet bag** should at the very minimum include soap (secured in a plastic bag or soap holder unless you enjoy a soapy toothbrush!), shampoo, toothbrush and toothpaste. This sort of stuff is easy to replace as you go along, so there's no need to bring family-sized packs. Men will probably want a **razor**. Women should carry enough **tampons** and/or **sanitary pads** to see them through, since these items may not always be immediately available. If you wear **contact lenses**, be aware that the various cleansing and storing fluids are not readily available in Ethiopia and, since many people find the intense sun and dust irritates their eyes, you might consider reverting to glasses. Nobody should forget to bring a **towel**, or to keep handy a roll of **loo paper**, which although widely available at shops and kiosks cannot always be relied upon to be present where it's most urgently needed.

A **torch** will be useful not only if you are camping or staying in towns where there is no electricity, but also for visiting old churches, which tend to be very gloomy inside. Also worth bringing are a **universal plug**, a **penknife**, a **travel washing line** and a compact **alarm clock** for those early morning starts. Increasingly important as more and more travellers carry electronic camera equipment is a **universal electric socket adaptor** for charging your batteries in hotel rooms. Also very useful is **a few metres of wraparound cloth**, which might serve as a towel, a bed sheet, something to cover up with after a trip to a common shower or a night-time loo excursion, a shoulder cover if local custom requires, a curtain in a bus, and better sun protection if you burn easily than any amount of sun cream. Some travellers carry **games** – most commonly a **pack of cards**, less often chess or draughts or travel Scrabble – to while away the hours between bus trips.

English-language **reading material** of any description is difficult to locate outside of Addis Ababa, and even there you'll find the range limited. Bring a good stock of reading matter with you. Bearing in mind that English-language newspapers are impossible to locate outside of the capital, you might think about carrying a **short-wave radio**, though the growing ubiquity of satellite television and CNN has made this less important than it was a few years ago.

You should carry a small **medical kit**, the contents of which are discussed in *Chapter 7*, as are **mosquito nets**. Two items of tropical toiletry that are surprisingly difficult to get hold of in Ethiopia are **mosquito repellent** for skin application, and **sun block**. In both cases, you are advised to bring all you need with you, though aerial repellents can be bought almost anywhere. A medically qualified reader writes: 'Thinking about *injera* and Ethiopian eating habits, I would advise all travellers to carry with them some sort of **anti-bacterial disinfectant hand-wash solution** which makes eating with your hands (as Ethiopians do) so much healthier.'

PLANNING AN ITINERARY

Itineraries are subjective things, dependent on how much time you have, your chosen or enforced style of travel, and your interests. The simplistic itineraries included in many travel guides annoy me for several reasons. Firstly, they tend to assume we all have the same interests. Secondly, they are packaged into periods that may not suit everyone (what use is a three-week itinerary if you're spending 16 days in the country?). Thirdly, they encourage an inflexible approach to travel, and discourage initiative and adventurousness. Finally, in countries that I know well, they always seem to be ridiculously crammed – fine on paper, but in reality they would involve spending most of your time in the country whizzing about in a car or bus.

Rather than prescribe a few itineraries, this section attempts to give you an idea of what is and isn't possible – to allow you to think through what *you* want to do in Ethiopia, and how long you would need to do it. In that sense, it is an overview of the regional part of the guide.

If there is a single piece of advice I would give any visitor to Ethiopia (or to any other country for that matter), it is to allocate your time realistically. You can, for instance, easily cover the main attractions of the historical circuit by air in nine or ten days. You could, at a push, do it in seven days, but my advice to somebody with only a week in the country would be to drop one of the places off your itinerary. You will enjoy yourself more, and get far more from the places you visit, if you are not constantly operating behind the clock. Much the same can be said for visitors bussing around the historical circuit. If you really wanted to, you could cover the main attractions in two weeks, but anything from eight to ten of those 14 days would be dominated by long bus trips. In African terms, Ethiopian buses are fine as these things go – but believe me, there is a limit to the number of trips you can handle in rapid succession.

The historical circuit

Ethiopia's main tourist focus is the well-defined historical circuit in the north. This is covered in the nine chapters of Section Three of this book as a clockwise loop from Addis Ababa, passing through the four established tourist centres of Bahir Dar (the base for visiting Lake Tana's monasteries and Tis Abay Waterfall on the Blue Nile), Gonder, Axum and Lalibela. In this book, coverage of these major centres is supplemented by information on other towns and tourist attractions along the loop; this may be distracting to tourists who are flying. Basically, if you only want to read up on the 'big four', Bahir Dar is in *Chapter 10*, Gonder in *Chapter 11*, Axum in *Chapter 12* and Lalibela in *Chapter 17*.

By road, this loop covers a distance of around 3,000km. Roads in the region are in fair repair, but they are not conducive to speed because of the mountainous terrain as much as anything. In other words, travelling by bus or private vehicle is not realistic where time is a factor. Fortunately, Ethiopian Airlines cover all the main towns on the historical circuit. Although internal flights are reasonably efficient, they will not necessarily run at times that allow you to do any significant sightseeing on the day you fly, and you can probably expect some degree of mucking around (you must, for instance, confirm each leg from where it flies as soon as you arrive there). On this basis, I would recommend you give yourself a clear day between flights in every place you visit. This means that to visit all four major centres you need eight nights out of Addis. If you don't have this sort of time, I would cut Bahir Dar out of the itinerary. On the other hand, if you have longer, you could easily devote a second day to Axum or Bahir Dar, and any number of days to visiting rock-hewn churches in the Lalibela region (by mule or on foot from town).

Two other attractions on the historical loop that might be of interest to short-stay visitors are Simien Mountains National Park and the rock-hewn churches of Tigrai. The Simiens (covered in *Chapter 11*) are visited from Gonder – you can reach the park headquarters at Debark in a morning by bus or taxi. The prime attractions here are spectacular scenery and the opportunity to see three of Ethiopia's four endemic large mammal species. Access is by foot or mule. It would be unrealistic to set aside fewer than four days to see the Simiens (including travel to or from Gonder); six days – or even longer – would be better. The rock-hewn churches of Tigrai lie north of the regional capital of Mekele. The possibilities in this area are practically endless, ranging from visiting some of the more accessible churches over a day or two on public transport through to seven-day hikes or driving trips in the Gheralta area (see *Chapter 13*). All that need be said here is that Ethiopian Airlines fly to Mekele.

Touring the historical circuit by public transport is relatively straightforward. If you have more time than money, travelling by bus is much cheaper than flying on a day-by-day basis. But, because it will take much longer, the overall cost will be much the same. Advantages of bus travel are that it allows you to soak up the magnificent scenery and to visit more obscure places of interest. To do a full tour of the historical circuit would use up ten or 11 days on buses alone (two days less if you bypassed

Lalibela at Woldia). Allowing for at least one full day at each of the major tourist attractions, and a few days' rest here and there, anything much less than three weeks – four weeks if you have thoughts of hiking in the Simiens or exploring Tigrai in depth – would be heavy going.

If you don't have this sort of time, two compromise options exist. One is to skip Axum and cut across from Gonder to Woldia which, if you wanted to see Lalibela, would still require eight or nine days' pure travel and a very tight minimum of two weeks overall. A more sensible compromise might be to go as far as Axum by bus, then to fly back to Addis via Lalibela; this would involve only five days of pure bus travel. Even if you allow for two days interrupted by flights, you could do this reasonably comfortably over two weeks.

The south and east

The southern Rift Valley lake region is the most popular in Ethiopia after the historical circuit. There is, however, no single obvious circuit through the region – but there is no desperate need to think through your timing. Shashemene, the transport hub of the south, is only five or six hours from Addis by bus, and even from more dispersed spots like Harar, Arba Minch, Negele Borena or Goba, you are within a comfortable two days'

TOUR OPERATORS IN ETHIOPIA

All of Ethiopia's better tour operators are based in Addis Ababa, though many also have satellite operations at the major tourist centres of the north. The following list is selective rather than exhaustive:

Dinknesh Ethiopia Tour ☎ +251 11 1567837; e mulugenet@ethionet.et; www.ethiopiatravel.com. A wide range of quality tours with an emphasis on excellent service.
Ethio Travel & Tours ☎ +251 11 5526644 or +251 91 1213177; f +251 11 1567151; e info@ethiotravelandtours.com; www.ethiotravelandtours.com. This new joint Danish–Ethiopian venture offers a good range of tours around Ethiopia, and has its own base at the Ghion Hotel in Bahir Dar.
Ethiopian Rift Valley Safaris ☎ +251 11 1552128/8591/1127; f +251 11 1550298; e ervs@ethionet.et; www.ethiopianriftvalleysafaris.com. This highly regarded company owns the only permanent lodge in South Omo, and specialises in upmarket safaris to this region, inclusive of game drives, game walks and river rafting. Not for the impecunious, but otherwise highly recommended.
Experience Ethiopia Travel ☎ +251 11 5519291/5152336/5530809/5153712; f +251 11 5529982; e eet@ethionet.et; www.telecom.net.et/~eet. One of the leading tour operators in the country offering a wide variety of tailor-made tours from historic sightseeing in the north to bird watching in the Rift Valley and Bale Mountains.
Galaxy Express Travel ☎ +251 11 5510355/5517646; f +251 11 5511236; e galaxyexpress@ethionet.et; www.galaxyexpressethiopia.com. One of the best-equipped tour operators in Ethiopia, with efficient and responsive management, a large fleet of well-maintained vehicles, and branch offices in Gonder, Axum and Bahir Dar manned by articulate, energetic and flexible young guides. Rates are competitive and service is excellent – a recommended first contact. The office is next to the Ras Hotel in Addis Ababa.
Grant Express Travel and Tours Services (GETTS) ☎ +251 11 5534678/5534379/5554680; m +251 91 1233289; f +251 11 5534395; e grandexpress@ethionet.et or getts@ethionet.et; www.getts.com.et. This dynamic, responsive and competitively priced new company benefits greatly from the hands-on management style of the vastly experienced former guide Yared Belete – another good first contact for bespoke travels almost anywhere in Ethiopia.

reach of the capital. In other words, travel in most of this region can be as organised or as whimsical as your temperament dictates.

If you veer towards organised travel, the best way to see a fair amount of the south is to join a tour or hire a vehicle and driver (in Ethiopia, tours and car hire generally amount to the same thing) through an Addis Ababa operator. Tours can be arranged to cater for most tastes, but generally you would be looking at two or three days to see a few Rift Valley lakes, and you could extend this by a day or two by appending either Awash or Nechisar National Park to your itinerary. To see South Omo properly, eight days is the absolute minimum duration for a round road trip from Addis Ababa.

A more whimsical approach is just that. You could spend weeks exploring the south and east and it would be silly to try to suggest a specific public transport itinerary. The one place in the south that should be singled out here is Bale National Park. Not only is this the one place in southern Ethiopia geared towards hiking, but it also offers the most important concentration of Ethiopia's endemic animals. Unlike at Simien, you can see Bale's endemic mammals easily without having to hike. Bale is also home to about half of Ethiopia's endemic bird species, and most of these are easy to see in the area. The NTO (National Tourist Organisation) organises five-day trips to Bale. Independent travellers should allow two days in each direction between Addis and Bale.

Green Land Tours \ +251 11 6185875/6510339; m +251 91 1203614/1215722; f +251 11 6632595; e greenplc@yahoo.com or dario@greenlandethiopia.com; www.greenland-ethiopia.com. One of the fastest-growing and most prominent new operators in Ethiopia, Italian-owned-and-managed Green Land Tours covers all parts of the country but specialises in 4x4 expeditions to the Rift Valley and far southwest, where it has lodges in Turmi, Arba Minch and Langano.

Hess Travel \ +251 11 5515820; f +251 11 5512675; e hesstravel@ethionet.et. This is a highly regarded and experienced company with efficient German–Ethiopian management. It is recommended in particular to German and French speakers, and special-interest groups.

Jacaranda Tours \ +251 1 6628625; f +251 11 6627954; e jacarandatours@ethionet.et; info@jacarandatours.net; www.jacarandatours.net. Offers packages to breathtaking scenery and ancient civilisations.

Jenman African Safaris \ +27 21 6837826; UK \ 08717 202011; e info@jenmansafaris.com; www.jenmansafaris.com. Leaders in tailor-made and scheduled safaris and tours in Ethiopia.

Sterling Travels \ +251 11 5514666/5511333/5518705; m +251 91 1692494/1201397/1209300; f 011 5512944; e sterling@ethionet.et; www.sterlingtravels.net. This established and highly regarded outbound operator has recently branched into inbound tours countrywide, with a strong emphasis on the burgeoning Asian market.

Travel Ethiopia \ +251 11 5525479/5523165/5508870/5515166; f +251 11 5551276/5510200; e travelethiopia@ethionet.et; www.travelethiopia.net. This reputable company, affiliated with Village Ethiopia, offers the usual packages, as well as specialist excursions to the remote tribes and Omo National Park on the west of the Omo River.

Village Ethiopia \ +251 11 5523497/5508869/5515166 ext 220; f +251 11 5551276; e village.ethiopia@ethionet.et; www.village-ethiopia.com. Owned and managed by long-time resident Tony Hickey, this small and responsive company offers reasonable rates and reliable travel advice based on years of travel experience in Ethiopia. In addition to the usual historical circuit packages, Village Ethiopia specialises in the Awash and Afar regions (with one permanent lodge built and another being developed in the area), the rock-hewn churches of Tigrai, and trekking, ornithological and adventure tours. It also deals regularly with film crews and other specialist requirement groups.

Special interests

Ethiopia is not a country I would associate with special-interest holidays. The combination of wonderful scenery, unusual and reasonably prolific wildlife, and fascinating historical sites makes it a wonderfully rewarding and constantly stimulating country for the generalist. But it would take an abnormally obsessive specialist to visit Ethiopia and not have their agenda overwhelmed to some extent by the sheer, well, *Ethiopianess* of the country. To put it another way, it is easy to say for a country like Kenya or Tanzania that historians should visit such and such, birdwatchers should visit here, scuba divers should visit there etc, but Ethiopia is so much more than the sum of its parts that such an approach seems unfair and limiting. Ethiopia itself is a special interest. It may well be the sort of country you either love or hate, but it would be difficult to treat it as just another African country. If you visit Ethiopia, the best reason to do so is to see Ethiopia for itself.

Which is not to say Ethiopia doesn't cater for special-interest groups; it most certainly does. History, I think, we can take for granted. Only the most focused of specialists would visit Ethiopia and ignore the major historical treasures of the north. But if historical sites are a passion, there are hundreds of more obscure sites you could visit – they are littered throughout this guide and it is impossible to highlight individual places.

For hikers and natural history enthusiasts, the two national parks of the highlands – Bale and Simien – are the most obvious points of interest. But it's fair to say that a keen and experienced hiker will see potential hikes on an almost daily basis in Ethiopia. This is a fantastically scenic country, and throughout this guide I point out places I passed which looked to have a high level of hiking or walking potential. More general game viewing is best in the south of the country, at national parks like Awash, Nechisar, Omo and Mago. But, really, if it's a straightforward safari you are after, countries like Kenya, Tanzania, Zimbabwe or South Africa have infinitely better game viewing than Ethiopia. A special-interest group that is exceptionally well catered for in Ethiopia is birdwatchers; with over 800 species recorded, including more than 30 endemics, this is one of Africa's finest birdwatching countries, with the lakes and national parks in the south being particularly productive.

But I have to come back to my first point: Ethiopia is too singular and overwhelming to compartmentalise into special-interest activities. It is a country that will excite and enthral on a daily basis, one that will leave you pondering with puzzlement and frothing with excitement for months after you return home. To be honest, I find myself completely stuck trying to think in terms of special-interest holidays to Ethiopia – just visit the country with an open mind and agenda, and prepare to Ethiopiate.

Off-the-beaten-track travel

Ethiopia's main tourist sites could hardly be described as crawling with tourists, certainly not by comparison with similarly compelling sites elsewhere in the world. Nevertheless, visiting the obvious tourist attractions is not the only way to explore a country – nor does it necessarily give you the most accurate picture of a country. A rambling bar room conversation will tell you infinitely more about the realities of modern Ethiopia than will any number of endemic birds or crumbling ruins. I should say very quickly that I am *not* about to enter the traveller versus tourist debate – snobbery is tedious in whichever direction it faces – and I know that, when I was working as a computer programmer in London, a week or two in Cornwall would have fitted the bill far better than a similar period in a rural African village. Nor am I recommending that you bypass places like Lalibela (to visit Ethiopia and *not* see Lalibela would be sheer madness). Nevertheless, it is a fact that in every country where I have travelled, even one as scenic and rich in history as Ethiopia, my dearest and most lasting memories are of people, of the magic moments when cultural gaps dissolved into the

Previous page Deacon at the yearly Meskal ceremony (Finding of the True Cross), Addis Ababa (AVZ)

Above Malachite kingfisher, Lake Ziway (AVZ)

Right Village weaver building nest (AVZ)

Below Gelada baboon, *Theropithecus gelada*, Simien Mountains National Park (AVZ)

ether (or the bottle!) and I found myself goodness knows where with goodness knows who – and having a wild time.

If you have only a short time in Ethiopia, common sense dictates that you should focus your attention on the places you really want to see. But if you have the luxury of a longer period of time, it is worth exploring some of Ethiopia's less-visited areas. You need not actually head 'off the beaten track' to do this – stopping along the beaten track can amount to the same thing. Ideas of this sort are scattered throughout this guide, but Tigrai and its rock-hewn churches offer particularly rich pickings for travellers who want to take things slowly.

A couple of relatively quick off-the-beaten-track trips suggest themselves. One, if you are visiting Bale, is to return to Shashemene via Dola Mena and Negele Borena. A good overnight trip from Addis is to the wonderful but little-visited cluster of historical sites around Melka Awash. And then there is the mother of off-the-beaten-track routes, the loop west through the forested mountains around Nekemte and Jimma to the remote river port at Gambella, a 10–14 day round bus trip which fills an entire chapter of this guide (see *Chapter 28*).

Throughout the guide I mention off-the-beaten-track possibilities that I didn't explore, and I have no doubt that imaginative map-gazing will reveal a few more. When I first travelled, I allowed travel guides to be my limitation; I assumed that if it wasn't 'in the book' it either couldn't be visited or else wasn't worth visiting. Early into researching my first 'difficult' guide (on Tanzania), I realised that when it comes down to it, all you really need to know about a given place is that there is transport to get you there and somewhere to stay when you arrive. To me, there is no bigger kick than hopping on a bus and driving into the unknown. For this reason, I would encourage any adventurous traveller to see this book not as a bible but as a springboard. In the book or not, if there's a bus, it sounds interesting, and you have no specific reason to think there's any danger attached – then go for it. Reckless advice? Perhaps, but it is a philosophy without which this book could never have been researched.

Organised tours
UK
Aardvark Safaris RBL House, Ordnance Rd, Tidworth, Hants SP9 7QD; ✆ 01980 849160; f 01980 849161; e mail@aardvarksafaris.com; www.aardvarksafaris.com. Arrange cultural trips led by anthropologists.

Art of Travel The Travel House, 51 Castle St, Cirencester, Glos GL7 1QD; ✆ 01285 650011; f 01285 885888; e safari@artoftravel.co.uk; www.artoftravel.co.uk. Organise group trips to the religious festivals, as well as tailor-made tours.

Footloose Adventure Travel 3 Springs Pavement, Ilkley, West Yorks LS29 8HD; ✆ 01943 604030; f 01943 604070; e info@footloose.co.uk; www.footlooseadventure.co.uk. Trekking and tailor-made tours.

Gane & Marshall International ✆ 020 8441 9592; f 020 8441 7376; e holidays@ganeandmarshall.co.uk; www.ganeandmarshall.co.uk . Tailor-made itineraries; historical and cultural tours.

Journeys by Design 11 Eaton Pl, Brighton BN2 1EH; ✆ 01273 623790; f 01273 621766; e will@journeysbydesign.co.uk; www.journeysbydesign.co.uk. Tour operator specialising in east and southern Africa.

Rainbow Tours 305 Upper St, London N1 2TU; ✆ 0207 266 1004; e info@rainbowtours.com; www.rainbowtours.co.uk. Tailor-made itineraries for individuals or small groups, yearly trip to the Timket festivals in January.

Silk Steps Deep Meadow, Edington, Bridgwater TA7 9JH; ✆ 01278 722460; f 01278 723617; e info@silksteps.co.uk; www.silksteps.co.uk. Quality tailor-made and group travel arrangements.

Steppes Travel 51 Castle St, Cirencester, Glos GL7 1QD; ☎ 01285 650011;
e africa@steppestravel.co.uk; www.steppesafrica.co.uk. Specialists in tailor-made and small group departures.
The Ultimate Travel Company 25–27 Vanston Pl, London SW6 1AZ; ☎ 020 7386 4646; f 020 7381 0836; e enquiry@theultimatetravelcompany.co.uk; www.theultimatetravelcompany.co.uk. Offer group treks and tailor-made trips.
Tim Best Travel 68 Old Brompton Rd, London SW3 3LQ; ☎ 020 7591 0300; f 020 7591 0301; e info@timbesttravel.com; www.timbesttravel.com. Tailor-made itineraries to the north and south of the country.
Wildlife Worldwide Chameleon House, 162 Selsdon Rd, South Croydon, Surrey CR2 6PJ; ☎ 020 8667 9158; f 020 8667 1960; e jo@wildlifeworldwide.com; www.wildlifeworldwide.com. Specialise in tailor-made wildlife holidays.
Yumo 7 Hanson St, London W1W 6TE; ☎/f 020 7631 5337; e info@yumo.net. Specialists in customised tours in Ethiopia.

South Africa
South African tour operators with specialist experience in Ethiopia:

Unusual Destinations ☎ 11 706 1991; f 11 463 1469; e info@unusualdestinations.com; www.unusualdestinations.com
WildLife Adventures ☎ 21 702 0643; f 21 702 0644; e wildladv@mweb.co.za; www.wildlifeadventures.co.za. Branches in South Africa and Zimbabwe. Offer two group tours, including a trekking option, as well as tailor-made variations.

Travelling in Ethiopia

TOURIST INFORMATION

The main tourist office of the state-run Ethiopian Tourist Commission (ETC) is on Meskel Square in Addis Ababa. It is worth visiting to pick up informative and illustrated free booklets about Bale, Simien and Lalibela, which are usually in stock (but sometimes absent between reprints). The tourist office also stocks a range of less useful pamphlets on other tourist attractions, but it is weak when it comes to current practical advice. The general spirit seems to be to hand over the freebies and get you back out on the street as quickly as possible. The ETC should not be confused with the NTO (National Tourist Organisation), the formerly ubiquitous but now increasingly low profile state-run travel agency.

There is a regional tourist office in every regional capital, as well as at some major tourist attractions. The best of these is the Tigrai tourist office in Mekele, which stocks some great booklets about the rock-hewn churches and other regional attractions, and can also give very detailed advice about more obscure churches. Otherwise, regional and local offices vary greatly in their usefulness, ranging from the well-informed offices at Dilla and Gonder, through the helpful if slightly disorganised offices in Bahir Dar and Awassa, down to the apparently pointless exercises in job creation to be found in Harar and Gambella.

In towns where there is no official tourist office, the Ministry of Sport and Culture is often worth a visit, though your luck will depend on the enthusiasm of the individual to whom you speak – in places that don't receive much tourism, this enthusiasm can be considerable.

PUBLIC HOLIDAYS

In any country you should be aware of public holidays, as many shops will be closed. The most significant practical consequence of public holidays in Ethiopia is that banks close, something you should plan around when you change money, especially if you travel between March and May, when most of the holidays are concentrated. Public holidays that are also religious festivals generally involve colourful celebrations and processions, so it is worth trying to get to one of the main religious sites – Lalibela, Gonder or Axum – for the occasion. Check the movable dates before you travel.

7 January	Ethiopian Christmas	1 May	International Labour Day
19 January	Ethiopian Epiphany	5 May	Patriots' Victory Day
2 March	Adwa Day	28 May	Downfall of the Derg
Movable	Ramadan	Movable	Moulid
6 April	Patriots' Victory Day	11 September	Ethiopian New Year
Movable	Ethiopian Good Friday	27 September	Meskel
Movable	Ethiopian Easter		

MONEY

The unit of currency is the birr, also referred to as the dux or, a little confusingly, the dollar. Notes are printed in denominations of birr 100, 50, 10, 5 and 1; and 50, 25, 10, 5 and 1 cent coins are minted. The birr is one of the strongest currencies in Africa, with exchange rates in mid 2005 at roughly US$1 = birr 8.50. E1 = birr 10 and £1 = birr 16, a pleasant change from the decimal shifts required to calculate prices in many African countries. For quick mental conversion of the birr prices quoted in this guide, the euro and US dollar rates are both close enough to 10:1 that lopping off a zero will give a good enough idea of costs in a more familiar own currency.

Foreign exchange

You can exchange money at most branches of the Commercial Bank of Ethiopia (CBE) or Dashen Bank. In Addis Ababa, this is a straightforward procedure taking anything from ten to 20 minutes, though neither bank is as efficient as the branches of the NIB and United Banks in the Hilton Hotel. In other large cities, bank procedures are much faster than they used to be, comparable to Addis Ababa really, but in small towns it can take ages to change money at a bank. Banking hours in Addis Ababa are from 09.00 to 16.00 weekdays, with a lunch break between noon and 14.00. The CBE branch at Bole Airport is open every day of the week. There are also a few private banks that offer foreign-exchange services, but in our experience the rates are often worse than at the CBE.

It is worth noting that many smaller towns have no bank, or a bank not equipped to deal with foreign-exchange transactions, or one that can handle cash but not travellers' cheques. Common sense dictates that you try to plan ahead to avoid getting into a situation where you need to change money in a small town (even if facilities do exist, they will be slow). I would certainly try to do any required transactions in one of the following towns: Addis Ababa, Bahir Dar, Gonder, Axum, Adigrat, Mekele, Dessie, Adama, Awassa, Moyale, Arba Minch, Jimma, Dire Dawa and Harar. Note that no reliable foreign-exchange facilities are available in Lalibela, or between Awassa and Moyale, or on Konso and South Omo, and that the CBE in Ziway can deal with cash only.

The only other place where money can sometimes be changed officially is at government hotels. This facility is open only to hotel residents and rates are rather poor compared with those of the CBE. Should you get stuck in Lalibela, the Roha Hotel offers a fair rate and will deal with non-residents.

Since the devaluation of the birr in October 1992, the difference between the black market and official rates has been negligible – about 5% at best – but the black market can come in useful in Addis Ababa when you need to change money outside of banking hours. Travellers' cheques are not accepted on the black market, nor are any currencies other than US dollars.

Many people consider using the black market to be immoral. There are, of course, countries where using the black market is practically essential because the gulf between official and unofficial rates is too great to ignore, and prices reflect black-market rates. This is not the case in Ethiopia; the official rate is very favourable to visitors. The moral argument against using the black market is that you are robbing government coffers of valuable hard currency in order to make your cheap holiday even cheaper. I was for several years an advocate of this argument. Now, I'm not so sure. I don't have a great deal of faith in how any government spends its money and you could argue that exchanging privately is more likely to stimulate the economy because it puts hard currency directly into the hands of traders and businessmen. Moral concerns aside, travellers who use the black market are open to being cheated. This is not a big problem in Ethiopia, but I would advise against changing money on the street – rather speak to somebody at your hotel or at a restaurant or curio shop to set something up in a controlled environment.

Prices quoted in this guide

It is always difficult to decide whether to quote prices in local currency or in US dollars. The main argument for sticking with local currency is that it makes the book easier to work with in the country, and doesn't lead to absurd figures. The argument against is that most African currencies are subject to sudden downward spirals in exchange rates, which tend to drag local prices with them. My opinion generally in Africa is that US dollar prices are more useful in the medium term than prices in local currency, since they are less likely to be rendered meaningless by sudden changes in exchange rates. However, Ethiopia's currency has remained quite stable, and prices in local currency have not changed dramatically over the decade that I've been associated with the country. For this reason, this time around I've decided to quote prices in birr, except where the hotel itself quotes a US dollar price.

I'm aware that birr prices are less useful than hard currency prices at the planning stage of your trip. As mentioned above, at least for anybody used to thinking in terms of US dollars or euro, lopping a zero off the end of the birr price will give you a working estimate of any given cost in American or British terms.

The prices quoted in this book were collected in early to mid 2005. Any changes to exchange rates and local prices after that are beyond my control, but you will find that prices in Ethiopia are reasonably consistent countrywide. Whatever happens, the rates quoted in this book will be a useful relative guideline once you have a feel for current prices.

GETTING AROUND
By air
If your time in Ethiopia is limited, flying is far and away the most efficient way to get around. Even travellers who wouldn't normally do so might think about using a couple of flights in Ethiopia. For starters, the full spectacle of Ethiopia's ravine-ravaged landscape is best seen from the air (the leg between Gonder and Lalibela is particularly recommended). You could also save a lot of time by flying out to a far-flung destination – for instance Axum, Jinka or Gambella – and working your way back overland, rather than repeating a similar bus trip out and back.

Ethiopian Airlines runs a good network of domestic flights connecting Addis Ababa to most major tourist destinations. The best connections are in the north, where at least one flight daily goes in either direction between any combination of Addis Ababa, Bahir Dar, Gonder, Lalibela and Axum (flights to Mekele are slightly less numerous). There are also flights to other parts of the country, such as Arba Minch, Jinka, Gambella, Jimma and Dire Dawa. The internal flights are generally efficient and they normally leave to schedule, but last-minute schedule changes are commonplace and you can probably expect on average one serious hold-up when you fly around the historical circuit. The soundest advice I can give in this regard is always to allow one non-travel day between flights, which eliminates the possibility of missing something important.

It is advisable to book domestic flights *before* you travel to Ethiopia, particularly if your inbound flight is with Ethiopian Airlines. Booked in conjunction with an Ethiopian Airlines international ticket, the fare for three or more domestic legs in northern Ethiopia works out at US$50 per leg, and substantial discounts are available for other domestic flights. Booked in isolation of an international ticket, fares are not as cheap as they used to be, and recent letters from travellers indicate they are also quite variable. For the full northern circuit, you should be looking at about US$350 (Ethiopian residents get the same tickets at about half that price). Individual legs in the north go for between US$75 and US$100, and those to the south and east are even pricier. International Ethiopian Airlines offices generally accept credit cards, as does the main office in Addis Ababa, but cards cannot be used at their offices elsewhere in the country.

Having booked domestic flights, Ethiopian Airlines is famously flexible about changes of date. It is never a problem to change a flight date with a day or two's notice, provided seats are available for the day on which you want to fly. The converse of this flexible policy is that every individual leg of your ticket *must* be confirmed at the point of departure the day before you fly.

The baggage limit on most domestic flights has been increased to 20kg following the modernisation of several airports and subsequent replacement of light 17-seat planes to small jets carrying upwards of 50 passengers. Flights to more remote areas, such as Jinka and Gambella, may still impose a 10kg limit, depending on the plane being used. A nominal airport departure tax of birr 10, payable in local currency, is charged on all domestic flights. Luggage and body searches are part of the Ethiopian Airlines experience; they are generally very thorough but done with a reasonable level of politeness. If you are carrying anything that could possibly be perceived to be an antiquity, it will be confiscated at Axum Airport.

By bus

Ethiopian road transport compares well to that in many other parts of Africa. Because Ethiopia is one of only two African countries where it is illegal for passengers to stand in the aisle, buses are rarely crowded. The driving is as sober as it gets in Africa and, because buses rarely indulge in the African custom of stopping every 100m to pick up another passenger, you can generally expect to cover 30km in an hour on dirt and 40–50km on surfaced roads. Best of all, and quite unique in my African experience, there are organised breakfast and/or lunch stops on longer runs. The conductor will let everyone off the bus for 20 minutes or so for a meal, a drink, and the use of a toilet.

In fact, there is only one real problem with bus transport in Ethiopia: the size of the country. The northern historical circuit requires around 3,000km of road travel – at an average progress rate of 30km/h this means 100 hours or the bulk of ten waking days must be spent on buses. If you try to do a circuit like this in two or three weeks you're going to get very fed up with being on buses. It should be emphasised that if time is a factor, you would be sensible to cut the number of bus rides you need to do by using a few flights.

The best buses where they are available (which includes the main loop through the historical circuit, from Bahir Dar to Gonder to Axum to Adigrat, as well as Adama to Dire Dawa) are the recently introduced Iveco/Cacciamla ones known by everybody in Ethiopia as Katchamale. On other routes, there are government buses and private buses. Where there is a choice, private buses are preferable for short runs (say up to 150km) and government buses are better for long runs. The reasoning behind this is that government buses are faster and better maintained, which is an advantage over a long distance (see box *Bus Ceremony*, page 92), but private buses get going more quickly.

On some runs buses leave throughout the morning; on other runs buses leave at a specific time, which will normally be at 05.30 or 06.00. By leave, I mean you have to be at the bus station to buy a ticket; an actual departure before 07.00 is something to write home about. In some cases, you may be required to buy a ticket the day before departure, but you will still be told to be at the bus station at 05.30, and there's still very little chance of anything rolling much before 07.00. But it can happen! As far as possible, I've indicated local departure patterns throughout the regional section of this guide, but this sort of thing is subject to change. It is always advisable to check the current situation on the afternoon before you want to travel – and remember you'll generally, but not always, be quoted departure times in the Ethiopian clock (see box *Ethiopian Time*, page 12).

Think about your approach to using buses. All-day trips are tiring and boring – even with the scheduled breaks – and on most long runs it is possible to break up the trip with an overnight stop en route. Where this is the case, I try to avoid covering more than 200km in a day, though obviously this is a matter of personal preference. On very long trips, such as Addis Ababa to Arba Minch or Bahir Dar, direct buses take two days with an overnight stop on the way. On this sort of trip drivers tend to bypass large, well-equipped towns in favour of smaller places where they happen to have an arrangement

THE JOYS OF PUBLIC TRANSPORT
Edited from a letter by Arthur Gerfers

In Ziway, I realised that I was low on money and would have to head to the bank before catching a bus to Shashemene and on to Awassa. I hailed a *gari* in the main road and requested to go to the bank. The driver was an idiot and kept trying to take me to the bus station. At last, after much drama over the 50 cents I paid him (standard rate), he deposited me at the Development Bank, which does not change travellers' cheques. They sent me to Commercial Bank. The *gari* driver gave me the same tired drama over the fare and dumped me grudgingly at the Commercial Bank. There they told me to go to Shashemene...

I hail another *gari* and head to the bus station. Only this one insists on dropping me at the main road where buses are clustered willy-nilly around a large hotel. I ask around for Shashemene and am told to wait. At some point, after I shoo all the beggars and shoeshine boys away, a bus arrives with no windscreen, just a plastic sheet with holes. The thing seems dodgy, but I board anyway, anxious to arrive in Awassa at a decent hour. The bus makes it about 500m before a cop stops it and we turn into the police station. The driver, of course, says nothing to the passengers about what to do next, but instead disembarks and starts chewing the fat with the police. I seize the initiative and move. The poor Ethiopians on board decide belatedly to follow suit, their raggedy towels on their heads making them all the more pathetic in their indecision.

I insist to the next *gari* driver that he take me to the 'autobus terra' and he does so. After stubbornly extracting my change from the *gari* driver, I make my way over the dusty pitch that serves as a bus station. Buses line the back fence and people stand round idly. At my behest, it seems one bus decides it is destined for Shashemene. An hour ensues before the thing finally fills and we're off! But no – we end up stopping at the same hotel where the windshield-less bus picked me up before. We wait around with no luck. Then we hit the road. But wait. We are headed in the wrong direction. We are driving back to the bus station! There we stop again and the guys try to shove a few more people into the already full enough bus. After a lengthy pause we make a move. You guessed it, right back to the bus hotel. Once we finally hit the road we stop for just about every shepherd. In addition, the bus is terribly slow and every vehicle on the road passes us with amazing velocity. At least my seat is comfortable and I only have a sleeping guy's elbow in my back to contend with. (Easy, I am way used to it by now.)

My ride to Awassa is your basic minibus. I push in after lodging my bag into someone's cramped crotch. We set off and I think to myself, 'great – just 20km to go!' Only no! We are turning around to pick up even more passengers. After doing this twice, the driver and ticket guy finally agree we are packed in enough to go now. The trip is longer than I expected with plenty of holes in the road, extra stunt-like swerving and even a police check! We arrive in Awassa just in time to learn that the bank is closed.

with a hotel owner. If you are in a rush you will probably get where you want quicker on a direct bus, but you might prefer to take things stage by stage and choose for yourself where you stay overnight.

Light vehicles such as pick-up trucks and minibuses are less widely used in Ethiopia than in many other African countries. You can, however, rely on there being some form of regular light transport between large towns that are close together (for instance, Adwa and Axum, Goba and Robe or Dire Dawa and Harar). It is also possible to town-hop on

BUS CEREMONY

You've heard about Ethiopian coffee ceremonies and *chat* ceremonies? Rather less well publicised is the ancient bus-boarding ceremony as practised on many government buses. This typically starts at about 05.30 and it involves a set of complicated rituals that take up to two hours to complete.

To participate in this venerable ceremony, you must first buy a ticket for a long-haul government bus. Then, rain or shine, you will be permitted to join the queue that forms outside the bus, and to watch men dressed in the traditional luggage-loaders' uniform of trousers and a T-shirt as they load luggage onto the roof. This entertaining ritual may take up to one hour, and once it is over, all ticket-holders are led around the bus by the conductor in a full circle. The completion of this mysterious ritual loop signifies that it is time for tickets to be checked, ensuring that only passengers with tickets board the bus. Once this is done, the queue breaks ranks and a scrum develops around the doors with pickpockets and anybody else who feels so inclined entering the fray. Eventually, you literally pop out of the throng and into the bus, to discover that any available seats are hidden behind an impenetrable mass of passengers' relatives and dithering cigarette sellers and the like.

As the aisles thin out, and you find a seat, you might well think that the ritual is over. With luck, however, it will now enter its final and most exciting phase. There are too many passengers on the bus. Somebody has sneaked on without a ticket! Panic! Shout! Argue! Everybody's ticket is checked again, the offender is found, and a ten-minute altercation ensues before he or she is thrown off the bus or, more likely, issued with a ticket.

In yet another tragic example of ancient custom being sacrificed at the altar of commercialism and efficiency, most private buses in Ethiopia have dispensed with the elaborate and enigmatic bus-boarding ritual practised by their forefathers. Instead, people simply board the bus until it is full, at which point the bus sets off, and the conductor marches up the aisle selling tickets. Some would argue, of course, that dispensing with the old ceremony does speed things up somewhat. And they would have a point ...

light vehicles on some major routes (between Axum, Adigrat and Mekele; Addis Ababa and Adama; and Mojo and Awassa). The other situation where light vehicles come into play is on routes where there are no buses, for instance between Goba and Negele Borena or Arba Minch and Jinka. Generally, these light vehicles are privately owned, are more crowded than buses, and fares are higher.

Buses are cheap. Typically you are looking at around US$1 per 100km, though road conditions and travel time will also affect the fare. If you use light vehicles on routes where there are no buses, expect to pay considerably more than you would for a comparable distance on a bus route. As an example, Goba to Dola Mena costs around US$5 whereas a similar distance by bus might be around US$2. Another quirk is that on some routes you may be expected to pay full price for covering only part of the distance (for instance, if you ask a bus going from Shashemene to Ziway to drop you at Langano, you'll probably have to pay the full fare to Ziway). To avert potential paranoia, I should stress that in neither case is this because you are a foreigner. I cannot recall being overcharged on a bus in Ethiopia.

It is worth noting that Ethiopians are entirely irrational about opening bus windows. Immediately after the bus departs, all the windows are closed and your fellow passengers will be very reluctant to open them again. Even if half the passengers are graphically suffering from motion sickness, merely cracking open your window will cause pandemonium in the rows behind you. And do you want to know why? Health. *Health!* It's beyond me why a nation that cheerfully tolerates pissing and shitting in the middle of the street should be terrified of a bit of fresh air, but that's Ethiopia!

By rail
The only rail service in Ethiopia is the French-built line between Addis and Djibouti, which stops en route at Awash and Dire Dawa. See *Chapter 20* for details.

By ferry
Two ferry services run on Lake Tana: a daily service between Bahir Dar and Zege, and a weekly overnight service between Bahir Dar and Gorgora. The former service is closed to foreigners but hopefully this will change. See *Chapter 10* for details.

BICYCLES
Edited from a letter by Arthur Gerfers

Bicycle rental is very cheap in Ethiopia, and I personally prefer it to any other form of transport. I rented a bicycle in almost every place where one was available. I found it more pleasant to cover distances on a bicycle, not least of all because it enabled me to dodge the beggars and manoeuvre through crowds of yelling children with greater ease – though it is amazing how far some of those little chaps will run!

The price of a bike for the day shouldn't be more than US$2. Bikes rented for a few days cost about US$1 per day. If the bike guy doesn't accept this price, then just walk away. Either he will eventually come running or some other kid, who has been watching you test out the first bike, will offer you his bike… and the whole thing starts all over again!

Always TEST DRIVE the bike before renting it. You can't get the feel of a bike if the seat is too high or too low. Often the seat is also too loose. Have the seat adjusted to suit you. Perseverance is the key here. The bike guy doesn't have anything else better to do anyway. Once you have taken the bike for a spin, and it catches your fancy, pay attention to a few other factors:

- Bent handlebars gripped such that the knuckles line up parallel to the legs are going to wear on your wrists more quickly than straight handlebars gripped such that the knuckles line up parallel to the handlebars. If you have a choice (and if you are in no hurry, you probably do) straight handlebars are recommended.
- Pedals are a must. Without pedals your feet will cramp up quick. If the pedals are broken, missing or do not adjust properly with the turning of the cranks, do not take the bicycle.
- Brakes are important. Make sure they work at least somewhat. Though most Ethiopian cyclists on the road get by without them, and some trips (like flat overland ones) don't require them, brakes are usually necessary in some form.
- Insist on a pump. The bike guy or his brother or cousin, is bound to have one. And, should you have a flat tyre, you will be glad to have one too. Again, perseverance is the key here.

A final note on the day after: it is not unusual to have an especially sore bum on the day after a trying bike ride. The best way to overcome this mild irritation is to ride the bike again as often as possible. The pain will subside in another day or two. These few rules of thumb should ensure a more enjoyable biking holiday!

By bicycle

Anybody thinking about cycling around Ethiopia should refer to the detailed online report www.owen.org/cycling/ethiopia, written by Owen Barder and Grethe Petersen, who undertook a cycling holiday there in 2002. See also the box *Bicycles*, page 93.

Taxis and *garis*

Taxis can be found in many larger towns. Except in Addis and towns with a high tourist turnover (for instance Gonder), they are very cheap but foreigners are frequently asked higher prices and you should expect to bargain. When I was in Ethiopia, birr 1 was the standard fare for a short trip in towns like Adama and Dire Dawa. Taxis in Addis are far more expensive (though still cheap by international standards) and often drivers will refuse to drop their prices for foreigners. In towns with a cool climate, the horse-drawn cart or *gari* replaces taxis. These are even cheaper than taxis and very useful for reaching places a few kilometres out of town.

Hitching

Hitching is not impossible on main roads. The prime advantage of finding a lift in a private vehicle is not so much that it will save money – you will generally be expected to pay for lifts with Ethiopians, sometimes more than you might have paid for the equivalent trip on a bus – but the speed at which you travel and the relative comfort. My

ROAD MAP CODES

Road conditions in Ethiopia, as elsewhere in Africa, are extremely variable, which can make it difficult to predict driving times based purely on the distance involved – there are some (admittedly not many) stretches of Ethiopian asphalt so good that you could cover 100km in an hour without undue risk, while at the other extreme are rutted dirt tracks where it would be difficult to achieve an average driving speed of 20km/h, and nigh impossible after heavy rain. For this region, all regional maps in this guide show not only the distance between two points, but also rate the road quality using the following grading system:

A = Good asphalt road, not too many curves or steep gradients, should be able to average 80–100km/h without driving recklessly.

B = Asphalt, but the combination of potholes and/or steep gradients and/or sharp curves and/or other impediments will restrict you to a realistic average driving speed of 60–70km/h.

C = Good dirt road, not too many curves or steep gradients, should be able to average 50–60km/h without driving recklessly.

D = Adequate dirt road, but the combination of rutted stretches and/or steep gradients and/or sharp curves and/or other impediments will restrict you to a realistic average driving speed of around 30–50km/h.

E = Poor dirt road, more or less passable all year through, but need high clearance, ideally 4x4, cannot expect to average more than 20–30km/h.

F = Poor dirt road or track, 4x4 required, driving speed low but variable, dependent on weather, may be impassable during the rains.

Note that the accuracy of this grading system will of course be linked to the power and quality of your vehicle, and the skill of the driver. Furthermore, not all roads are consistent – even the best asphalt road might have the odd poor stretch, or curving ascent, and detours created by roadworks are often highly disruptive.

DRIVING IN ETHIOPIA

Extracted from an article by John Graham, the full text of which can be viewed online at www.addistribune.com

The countryside is full of quirky pedestrians. The children have devised a number of games to play with drivers. One of the more charming is 'let's stand in the road defiantly and see if the car stops before we lose our nerve and run to the side'. This is only slightly more popular than 'let me see if I can push my friend in front of a car'.

Shepherd boys have a pleasant way of passing their sometimes boring hours – making a line of sharp rocks across the road! Then there is the good old pastime of throwing rocks at cars, something that was not entirely unknown amongst the urchins where I grew up. One local official, trying to demonstrate to me the gratitude of the people for some good work we were doing, said that our organisation was so good that the children in his *Woreda* didn't even throw stones at our cars! As we were driving out, sure enough, one did!

On the adult side, there is the curious criss-cross tradition. This stems from a rural belief that if a person crosses in front of a moving vehicle it will lengthen their life. Of course, if they fail to cross successfully, their life is considerably shortened. On almost every trip, we've had to brake abruptly at least a few times as some pedestrian suddenly hears us from behind and launches him or herself across the road metres in front of us. The loud skidding, honking, and occasionally shouting which accompanies this event is usually greeted by the pedestrian with a big smile. I found this galling and irritating, until some kind and patient Ethiopian assured me that the smile was to show embarrassment, not amusement at the chaos they had caused.

The maze of obstacles that one has to negotiate to drive in rural Ethiopia used to leave me breathless in admiration of our drivers. Knowing me too well, my wife pointedly said on our first trip out of town that she felt that local drivers were essential for long trips and I shouldn't consider driving. At the time I sympathised. After a while the psychology of the people and animals at the side of the road, not to mention the manic drivers in the middle, became clearer. Now that I've driven myself all over rural Ethiopia, I recognise a sixth sense that tells me that this donkey is not going to launch itself in front of me, while that other one just might. There is nothing that can protect even the most experienced driver from the full-fledged unexpected dash onto the road by a pedestrian or animal – but the rest becomes relatively straightforward.

attitude to hitching was that it wasn't worth the bother when trying to travel between towns, largely because most vehicles that go past will be local traffic. That said, if you are hopping between small towns, or find yourself stuck on the side of the road between towns (at Lake Langano for instance), you might as well wave down anything that moves. Most of the lifts I was offered were not directly hitched but came from people I had met in bars or hotels the night before, or else were organised for me through friendly hotel or shop owners; the message being that the best way to get lifts in private vehicles is to make friends and put the word around.

Car hire

It is straightforward enough to hire a vehicle in Addis Ababa, but as a rule a driver will be supplied so in essence you are really organising a tailored tour or safari. Car hire in Ethiopia is expensive by any standards – the lowest rate you'll get will be about US$100 per day, and US$150 or higher is likely from a reputable tour company. Avis is represented in Ethiopia by Galaxy Express, but most other operators in Addis Ababa can arrange car hire (see box *Tour Operators in Ethiopia*, page 82). If you are thinking of driving yourself, be warned that Ethiopian roads are not what you are used to at home. Many Ethiopian roads are in poor condition, and the pedestrians and livestock share a quality of indifference I've encountered nowhere else in Africa when it comes to dawdling in the middle of the road while a hooting vehicle hurtles towards them at full tilt. See also the box *Driving in Ethiopia*, page 95.

ACCOMMODATION

If you are not particularly fussy, finding a room in Ethiopia is rarely a problem, though genuine tourist-class hotels are limited to major tourist centres. Accommodation at all levels is inexpensive, even by African standards. Few Ethiopian hotels distinguish between double and single occupancy. Almost without exception, rooms in private hotels will have a bed made to sleep two, and the price of the rooms is the same whether it is occupied by one or two – or for that matter half-a-dozen – people. Even the most basic

ACCOMMODATION CATEGORIES

In order to guide readers of this fourth edition through the immense number of hotels in many Ethiopian towns, accommodation entries have been divided into five categories. The purpose of the categorisation is twofold: to break up long hotel listings that span a wide price range, and to help readers isolate the range of hotels in any given town that best suits their budget and taste. The application of categories is not rigid, and an element of subjectivity is inevitable, since it is based first and foremost on the feel of any given hotel rather than the absolute price (prices are quoted for all entries anyway) and does depend on what other accommodation is available in any given town. It should also be noted that assessments relating to the value for money represented by any given hotel are to be read in the context of the stated category, as well as the individual town.

A brief explanation of each category follows:

International

This category includes top-of-the-range hotels that would be considered reasonably upmarket – two stars or above – anywhere in Africa. No more than three hotels in Ethiopia fall into this bracket, and they are all in the capital. Prices are upwards of US$100.

Upmarket

This category lists hotels – often government owned – that are essentially aimed at tourists, and regularly used by package tours and such. Hotels in this category typically have motel-standard rooms, and facilities such as hot water, satellite television, and restaurants serving Western food. While upmarket hotels in Ethiopia are generally very comfortable and quite efficiently run, one should not approach them with unreasonable expectations – most would struggle to get a one-star rating anywhere else in the world. Room rates are generally very reasonable for what you get – US$20–50 – and often quoted in US dollars. This is the first category to look at if you simply want the best available accommodation irrespective of price.

Moderate

This category consists of superior local hotels, mainly but not exclusively privately owned. You can expect any hotel in this category to have clean and quite smart en-

hotels in Ethiopia generally have electric sockets for charging mobile phones, digital cameras and similar devices in every room, though you might want to confirm this before taking a room in the shoestring range.

Tourist-class hotels

Most tourist-class hotels are run by one of four government chains, all of which have at least one hotel in Addis Ababa. The Ghion Hotel Group runs all government hotels in the north and has units in Bahir Dar, Gonder, Axum, Mekele, Lalibela, Dessie and Kombolcha. The Ras Hotel Group is represented in the southeast, with units in Bishoftu, Adama, Dire Dawa, Harar, Awash National Park, Asela and Goba. The Wabe Shebelle Group runs hotels in the south, with units at Lake Langano, Awassa and Wondo Genet. The Ethiopia Hotel Group dominates in the west, and has units in Ambo, Nekemte, Gambella, Jimma and Weliso. Hotels in these chains can be booked through any tour operator, or through the chain's flagship hotel in Addis Ababa.

Outside of Addis, few government hotels cost more than US$50 per room, and many – especially those in the south and west – are little more than US$20. Most will have rooms

suite rooms with hot water and possibly television. Most will also have a decent restaurant and English-speaking staff. In most cases, moderate hotels are significantly cheaper than upmarket hotels – birr 80–120 (less than US$15) is typical outside of Addis Ababa. This is the category to look at if your first priority is a reasonable level of comfort, but you also want to keep down accommodation costs.

Budget

Hotels in this category are aimed largely at the local market and definitely don't approach international standards, but are still reasonably comfortable and in many cases have en-suite facilities. In other words, they are a cut above the shoestring dumps that proliferate in most towns. Budget hotels generally have clean rooms with cold and sometimes hot running water. In some cases, hotels without en-suite rooms are listed in this category, either because they are unusually clean and pleasant, or because accommodation in that town tends to be expensive. Prices in this category generally work out at less than birr 80 (US$10), but there is a lot of regional variation. In the south, and even in parts of the north where tourists are still irregular, you might pay as little as birr 30 for a decent en-suite budget room. This is the category to look at if you are on a limited budget, but want to avoid total squalor!

Shoestring

Shoestring accommodation consists of the cheapest rooms around, usually unpretentious local guesthouses that double as brothels and have common showers (or no shower at all). I've personally stayed at plenty of shoestring hotels in Ethiopia, and in many cases they are perfectly pleasant taken on their own terms. Just as often, they are flea-ridden dumps. It is obviously difficult for a travel writer to assess every one of the dozens of shoestring hotels that are found in most Ethiopian towns, so recommendations in this range should be seen as pointers rather than absolute. This is the category for budget travellers who want to keep accommodation to US$2 per night or below, irrespective of what discomfort that might involve. Shoestring accommodation cannot generally be recommended to single female travellers.

with private hot showers and bowl toilets. By international standards, few government hotels would scrape much more than a one-star rating; they could generally be described as comfortable but tatty. Until recently, most government hotels insisted on payment in hard currency, but this has fallen away in recent years and you will now generally be quoted a price in birr. I have even heard of people asking to pay in US dollars and being refused. Bookings can be made through the National Tourist Organisation or through the head office of the individual hotel group, which in all instances is the hotel in Addis after which the group is named (see *Chapter 8*). Note that most (but not all) government hotels will call a room with a double bed a single room, and a room with two singles a double.

The Bekele Mola Hotel Group has several hotels in southern Ethiopia. This is a private hotel group but several of its units – most notably those at Arba Minch, Lake Langano and Robe – are similar in standard to government hotels and considerably less expensive. There are also Bekele Mola hotels in Bishoftu, Mojo, Adama, Meki, Ziway, Shashemene and Moyale, all of which have good rooms with private showers and bowl toilets for around US$3–5. Outside of Addis, there are no more than a handful of other private hotels that edge into the tourist-class category.

Local hotels

The vast majority of budget hotels in Ethiopia are straightforward local places with Spartan furnishing, cell-like rooms, communal toilets, and either communal showers or else no showers at all. Hotels like this are dubbed shoestring hotels in this book.

In larger towns, there are generally one or two budget hotels of superior standard. These are distinguished from the mass of shoestring places by having en-suite rooms

'FARANJI' PRICES

It is common practice for government hotels, national parks and museums in Ethiopia (and many other African countries) to charge higher rates to foreigners than to Ethiopians. Although this practice antagonises many tourists, it is not so unreasonable as it might seem. Westerners generally earn a lot more than Ethiopians do – an Ethiopian secretary or high-school teacher might earn the equivalent of US$50 per month. If a blanket entrance fee were to be charged for all places that are part of the Ethiopian heritage, it would either be so low that foreigners were practically being allowed in for free, or so high that none but the wealthiest Ethiopians could afford to visit. Fair enough, in my opinion, that rates are tiered.

With government hotels that cater primarily to tourists, it is more realistic to see the local rate as discounted than to see the foreigner rate as inflated. The only issue is whether the foreigner rate is a fair reflection of a hotel's quality. In Ethiopia, the answer generally is yes. Government hotels in Ethiopia are basic by international standards, but by the same standards they are very cheap.

Since first researching this book, inflated *faranji* prices have become prevalent even at the grimmest of private hotels. I became quite irritated at this when I researched this fourth edition. It smacks of opportunism: such hotels are not offering a discounted rate to locals, but are instead overcharging the very occasional tourist who pitches up on their doorstep.

All of this would be less annoying were hotel owners more open to negotiation, but most would rather see a tourist walk away than compromise on the price. This arrogance seems to stem from two fundamentals. The first is that government hotels charge even more, the second that *faranjis* are all so rich (or stupid) that they will pay any rate asked of them. What a lot of hotel owners don't get is that their rooms aren't up to government hotel standards, and that travellers who favour private hotels over

(rooms with private showers and toilets, often referred to as self-contained in Ethiopia and elsewhere in east Africa), and also by being slightly more expensive. These hotels appear to be geared primarily to relatively well-heeled Ethiopians, so that the standard room prices reflect the local economy, though it is increasingly the case that tourists will be charged a special *faranji* price of around twice the local rate. Except for in a handful of major tourist centres, you can expect to pay around US$3–5 for a room in a superior budget hotel, which is exceptional value for money by any standards. Travellers on a very tight budget should be aware that, although it will often be assumed that *faranji* prefer self-contained rooms, almost all superior budget hotels also have cheaper rooms using communal showers, and that these are generally similar in price but of a higher standard than rooms in true shoestring hotels.

The shoestring category embraces a good 95% of hotels in Ethiopia. In larger towns, there may be 30 or 40 such establishments. In the sort of small town where elsewhere in Africa you might expect at best one hotel, there may be half-a-dozen in Ethiopia. Hotels in this category can range from dirty, noisy, showerless brothels with flaking paint and sagging, flea-ridden beds, to bright and cheery family-run establishments with good communal showers and clean, comfortable rooms.

Rooms in this range generally cost from birr 10–20, dependent more on the town you are in than the quality of the hotel. In other words, in most towns there will be a standard price for hotels in this category, regardless of quality (in fact, I have often been asked more for a room in a dump than for a far nicer room a few doors down). It is difficult to imagine that many travellers, even those on the tightest budget, will worry too much about whether they're paying a birr or three or less, so in the regional part of the guide I

government hotels do so to save money. The silliest thing about wildly inflated *faranji* prices (up to five times the local rate) is that everybody loses out. On several occasions on our most recent trip, we ended up using an inferior hotel when we would have happily paid the non-*faranji* rate – or any reasonable price – to sleep at a better one. The hotel lost the custom, we lost out on a more comfortable room, yet both could have gained were the hotel owner not so inflexible.

Another frustration associated with *faranji* prices at hotels that see few tourists is that they are not market-driven in the way that rates for locals are, which means that prices are often thoroughly arbitrary. In Sodo, for instance, half-a-dozen hotels offer roughly similar en-suite accommodation at a uniform birr 25 to locals, yet the same batch of hotels charges anything from birr 30 to birr 50 to the odd *faranji* who might pitch up on their doorstep. Clearly the hotel that charges birr 30 is the best value, but it may not be the best hotel per se, and it could gratuitously raise its rates to birr 50 at any point, so that it might represent relatively poor value overnight – especially as the best hotel of the lot currently charges birr 35. Likewise, in a town where one or two hotels opt not to charge an inflated *faranji* price, these anomalies can make all the other hotels in that town look like poor value. And yet again, this could change overnight.

I don't have a major objection to being asked a higher rate than locals when the standard of the room is commensurate. I do resent being asked – nay, being expected to hand over without quibble – a rate that both the hotel owner and I know is plain silly. And I very much resent being quoted a normal rate by the receptionist, taking a room, and then having the owner demand that I pay three times what I was originally asked because some underling 'forgot' about the *faranji* price – something that happened to me on half-a-dozen occasions on my most recent trip. It's lousy business practice, lousy PR, and only furthers the impression one sometimes has that many Ethiopians are xenophobic to a point that borders on racism.

have often not quoted individual prices for hotels in this category, but have instead listed the better places.

Bearing in mind that many large towns have dozens of shoestring hotels, and that prices are relatively uniform, it is worth choosing your hotel with care. The hotels mentioned in this guide were the best when I visited, but this sort of thing is apt to change. Ethiopian hotel owners tend to devote little time to maintenance, so that the newest hotels are often the cleanest and brightest. As a rule, I found that the exterior of a hotel was generally a fair reflection of the interior, and that – sexist or not – hotels with female owners, or a strong female presence, were cleaner and friendlier than those run only by men. Always ask to see the shower and toilet before you take a room.

Most cheap hotels in Ethiopia to some extent double as brothels, but this does vary. There are hotels in Addis Ababa that only offer rooms on an hourly basis, whereas many family-run places would actively discourage open prostitution. If you're unused to African travel conditions, it might be mildly disconcerting to wake in the night to the sound of quadraphonic orgasms and creaking beds, but there is no real reason why this should affect you. From a male perspective, the so-called bar girls that hang out in most hotels, bars and restaurants are, in pure numerical terms, the most prolific I've come across in Africa, but generally they are not as persistent or brash as their Kenyan counterparts. Men travelling alone and couples needn't assume that just because a place encourages prostitution it is dirtier or less secure than a place that doesn't. All things considered, I'd rather sleep in a clean room and risk being woken by graphic squelchy noises from the room next door than I would spend the entire night fending off insects. The priorities of women travelling alone might be a bit different here.

Particularly in the northern provinces of Tigrai and Wolo, many shoestring hotels don't have a shower, or when they do there is an additional charge for using it. In many cases it will be cheaper in the long run to take a room with a private shower than it will to take a room using communal showers. In Debre Birhan, for example, most shoestring hotels cost birr 6 or 8 per room and charge an extra birr 2 per shower (so a couple who shower in the evening and the morning will pay an additional birr 8), yet there are a few hotels with self-contained rooms for between birr 10 and birr 15. In the south, east and west, most shoestring hotels *do* have showers (though it is best to check before taking a room) and use of them is almost always included in the price of the room. It should be noted that, where it applies, the additional charge for showering is for Ethiopians as well as *faranji* – you are *not* being ripped off.

Camping
The opportunities for organised camping in Ethiopia are limited to a few facility-free campsites in various national parks, the Wabe Shebelle Hotel at Wondo Genet, and the Bekele Mola hotels at Lake Langano and in Arba Minch. You can sometimes camp in the grounds of government hotels, but this will generally be more expensive than finding a room. The only area where campsites are widely used by travellers is South Omo.

Camping wild is reputedly safe in most parts of the country, and motorised travellers in particular may find it more attractive to set up camp discreetly in a remote area than to overnight in towns. On the whole, though, unless you are coming to Ethiopia from parts of Africa where camping facilities are more widespread, or you intend hiking in off-the-beaten-track areas, the additional weight and hassle involved in carrying camping equipment is difficult to justify in Ethiopia (see *Camping equipment*, page 77).

EATING AND DRINKING
To anyone who has travelled elsewhere in Africa, Ethiopian food comes as a welcome revelation. Instead of the bland gristle and starch that is the standard restaurant fare in most African small towns, Ethiopian food is deliciously spicy and you can eat well

virtually anywhere in the country. Contrary to many people's expectations, most of Ethiopia is fertile, food is easy to find, and portions are generous and very cheap. If you are travelling in tandem you'll often find that one plate of food – which costs no more than a dollar – will be adequate to feed two.

Ethiopian dishes

A wide variety of different dishes is available in Ethiopia. Most of them are unique to the country, so it is worth familiarising yourself with their names as soon as you arrive.

The staple source of carbohydrates in Ethiopia is *injera*, a large, pancake-shaped substance made from *tef*, a nutty-tasting grain that is unique to Ethiopia and comes in three varieties: white, brown and red. The *tef* dough is fermented for up to three days before it is cooked, the result of which is a foam-rubber texture and a slightly sour taste reminiscent of sherbet. *Injera* is normally served with a bowl of *wat* stew. The ritual is to take a piece of *injera* in your hand and use it to scoop the accompaniment into your mouth. If you dine with Ethiopians, it is normal for everyone to eat off the same plate.

Ethiopians will often tell you that *injera* is of little nutritional value. This is not the case at all. Gram for gram, *tef* supplies more fibre-rich bran and nutritious germ than any other grain, containing 15% protein, 3% fat and 82% complex carbohydrates. This is partly as a result of it being smaller than any other edible grain and having a proportionately larger husk, which is where most of the nutrients in any grain are stored. *Tef* contains almost 20 times more calcium than wheat or barley, it has two to three times the iron content of other grains, and it is the only grain to contain symbiotic yeast – which means that no yeast needs to be added during the preparation of *injera*.

There are two types of *wat* sauce: *kai wat* is red in colour (*kai* literally means red) and very hot, and flavoured with *beriberi* (peppers), onions and garlic; *alicha wat* has a yellowish colour and is generally quite bland. There is a widely held belief among Ethiopians that they are the only people in the world who can tolerate spicy food, so unless you specify what you want you will generally be served with *alicha wat*. To my taste, *alicha wat* is pretty horrible, though in part this is because it is too bland to offset the sourness of the *injera*. If you're not overly fond of spicy food, order *wat misto*, which consists of half-portions of *kai* and *alicha wat*, sometimes served in separate bowls and sometimes mixed together.

Most *wat* is made from meat (*siga*). The most common meat in the highlands is lamb (*bege*), while in drier areas you will most often be served with goat (*figel*). Beef (*bure*) is also eaten, mostly in large towns. In towns near lakes, fish (*asa*) predominates. I have also come across *tripe wat* – which is the same as our tripe but pronounced *trippy*. The official national dish of Ethiopia is *doro wat*, made of chicken, but this is to be avoided if you are hungry, as it is traditional to serve only a lonely drumstick or wing in a bowl of sauce. Normally *kai wat* consists of meat boiled in the *kai* sauce, but you may also come across *tibs kai wat*, which means the meat was fried before the sauce was added. If the meat is minced prior to cooking, then the dish is known as *minje tabish*.

Vegetarian *wats* are served mainly on Wednesday and Friday, the Orthodox fasting days, and can be made from puréed beans (*shiro wat*), halved beans (*kik wat*) and lentils (*misr wat*). The normal dish on fasting days is *atkilt bayinetu*, which consists of dollops of various vegetarian *wats*, as well as piles of spinach (*gomon*), beetroot (*kai iser*) and vegetable stew (*atkilt alicha*) heaped discretely in a circle on the *injera*.

Fried meat (*siga tibs*) is also very popular in Ethiopia, as is boiled meat (*siga kekel*). Other dishes, found mainly in large towns, are crumbed meat or fish cutlet (*siga* or *asa kutilet*), roast meat (*siga arosto*), steak (*stek*) and a mildly spicy brown stew (*gulash*). Then there is *kitfo*, a very bland form of fried mince, and *kitfo special*, the same dish but uncooked, which should be avoided purely for health reasons.

A popular breakfast dish, and a useful fallback in the evening if you don't fancy anything else that's on offer, is *inkolala tibs* – literally fried eggs, but more like scrambled eggs, cooked on request with slices of onion (*shinkuts*), green pepper (*karia*) and tomato (*tamatim*). Another common breakfast dish is *yinjera firfir*, which consists of pieces of *injera* soaked in *kai wat* sauce and eaten with – you guessed it – *injera*. Note that *firfir* literally means torn-up: *inkolala firfir* is exactly the same as *inkolala tibs*, but hacked at a bit before it is served. Also popular at breakfast is *ful*, a spicy bean dish made with lots of garlic.

Menus are normally printed in Amharigna script so you will have to ask what's available (*magi min ale?*). As a rule, you won't understand a word of the rushed reply, so you'll probably have to suggest a few possibilities yourself. The way to phrase this is to start with the type of meat, or vegetable (prefaced with *ye*), then the type of dish. In other words, fried goat is *yefigel tibs*, fish cutlet is *yasa kutilet*, *kai wat* made with lentils is *yemisr kai wat*, and *alicha wat* made with beef is *yebure alicha wat*. If all else fails, ask for *sekondo misto*, which consists of small portions of everything on the menu.

The variety of food at local restaurants decreases during the fasting weeks of Ethiopian Lent, a period that generally occupies most of March and April, since Orthodox Christians will only eat vegetarian dishes during this period. Most non-vegetarians travelling in off-the-beaten-track areas get a bit frustrated by this, whereas vegetarians will find it a good time to travel. It doesn't affect travellers so much in Muslim areas, nor will it alter the variety of food on offer at tourist-oriented restaurants.

Chat

I don't know where else to put this, and you *do* eat it! *Chat* is a mildly stimulating leaf that is traditionally popular with Muslims (who are forbidden from drinking alcohol) and is now chewed throughout Ethiopia. For readers who have visited Kenya, it is pretty similar to *miraa*, though I gather not exactly the same plant (and you see few Ethiopians with the manically glazed eyes I've come to associate with *miraa*-ed out Kenyans).

Chat ceremony is generally a social thing. The idea is for a few people to gather in a room, where you each grab a few branches, pick off the greenest leaves, pop them into your mouth one by one, mush it all up into a cud, chew for a few hours and then, with whatever strength is left in your jaw, spit out the remaining pulp. Ideally, you devote the afternoon to group mastication, then go for a few beers to neutralise the sleeplessness that the leaves induce. The leaves taste very bitter so a spoonful of sugar helps it all go down. Now, I must admit that to me the effort involved in spending the afternoon chewing myself into foul-tasting oblivion holds little appeal – especially when all sorts of cheap, pleasant-tasting, no-effort-required alcoholic substances are available in Ethiopia – but *chat* has its devotees among travellers. It must be said that not everybody will spend their spare Ethiopian afternoons dashing about towns, plotting maps and checking out hotel rooms. As an Ethiopian friend says: '*chat* ceremony is good for killing time.'

The centre of *chat* cultivation and chewing is the Muslim town of Harar – at the end of a bus ride in this area it looks as if the vehicle has been overrun by psycho-caterpillars – but you can get the stuff at markets all over the country. It's not expensive, but it's worth taking along an Ethiopian friend to ensure you locate the best-quality *chat* – prices do reflect quality and the youngest leaves are the best.

Sticking with leaves green and mind-altering, it should be clarified somewhere in this book that the link between Rastafarianism and Ethiopians is by and large a one-way thing. Smoking marijuana is illegal in Ethiopia and, generally speaking, it is less socially acceptable than in most Western countries. You should certainly not assume that an Ethiopian male with plaited hair is adorned for anything but religious reasons. Basically, if you must smoke dope in Ethiopia be as discreet as you would be at home, if not more so – not only to keep yourself out of jail, but also to maintain the good name of travellers.

Western food

If you feel like a break from *injera* (and you will), many restaurants serve pasta (look out for variant spellings such as *spiggttii* or *makarronni*) skimpily topped with a spicy sauce. Even in the smallest villages you can usually find fresh, crusty bread (*dabo*) as an alternative accompaniment.

Many hotels in Addis, and government hotels throughout the country, serve standard Western food such as roast chicken, fish kebabs, roast meat and steaks. Generally this is a couple of birr more expensive than eating at local restaurants, but nowhere outside of Addis are you likely to pay more than US$1.50 for a meal.

An attractive feature of Ethiopia is the numerous pastry shops in Addis and other medium-to-large towns. These generally serve a selection of freshly baked iced and plain cakes, wonderful biscuits and good bread, along with coffee, tea and puréed fruit juice. Pastry shops are great for sweet-toothed breakfasts and snacks, and you'll walk away with plenty of change from a dollar. Also on the snack front, look out for *ashet* (roasted maize cobs); the cry of the kids who sell it, which sounds remarkably like *shit*, should attract your attention. *Kolo* is a delicious snack of roasted grains or pulses, sometimes covered in spice, and sold by the handful for a few cents.

Drinks

The Kaffa Province of Ethiopia is thought to be where coffee originated, and the coffee bean accounts for more than half of Ethiopia's exports. Nevertheless, having visited other African coffee-growing countries where hotel coffee is invariably insipid, I expected the worst in Ethiopia. I was wrong. Ethiopians are coffee-mad and their espresso-style coffee (*buna*), served with two spoons of sugar, is rich, sweet and thoroughly addictive. Coffee with milk is *buna watat*. In small towns, sweet tea (*shai*) is more widely available than coffee.

You'll often be invited to join a traditional coffee ceremony, in which the grains are roasted over charcoal, ground while the water is boiled, then used to make three successive pots of coffee. It's not advisable to accept if you're in a rush or want to get any sleep (it is rude to leave before the third round has been drunk), but you should certainly experience it at least once in your trip. Despite the pomp you might associate with the word ceremony, it's really just a social thing... in the words of the same Ethiopian friend who demystified *chat* ceremony, the main purpose of the ceremony is often 'just for killing time'. Instant coffee holds little appeal in a country where few people have jobs – or even television.

The usual soft drinks – Coca-Cola, Pepsi, Fanta – are widely available and very cheap. The generic name for soft drinks is *leslasa*. Ethiopians apparently consider it quite sensible to order a *leslasa*, see what comes, then send the waiter back if it isn't the brand they want. If thirst is a greater factor than the need to conform to what I can only assume is yet another Ethiopian time-killer – *leslasa* ceremony? – you might want to ask in advance what drinks are available (*leslasa min aleh?*) and settle on a brand at this formative stage of the transaction.

A little more surprisingly, carbonated mineral water is bottled locally and is widely available for around birr 2 per 750ml bottle. It is best to ask for mineral water by brand name, which is *Ambo* in central, south and western Ethiopia, and *Babile* (pronounced Bubbily – I'm not sure if this is coincidence) in the east. In Tigrai, you can only get inferior mineral water imported from Eritrea. Worth noting, for those who for instance use contact lenses, is that still mineral water is difficult to locate outside of Addis Ababa.

Ethiopia's prime soft drink is fruit juice, which is really puréed fruit. What is available depends somewhat on season and location, but the most common juices are banana, avocado, papaya, orange and guava. If in doubt, ask for *espris*, which consists of layers of all available juices. The result is thick, creamy, healthy and absolutely delicious. A glass of juice generally costs around birr 2.

The most popular local tipple is *tej*, a mead-like drink made from honey (*mar*) or sugar (*isukalama*). *Mar tej* is a considerable improvement on most African home-brews, and very alcoholic, but personally I couldn't get into it on a daily basis. *Isukalama tej* is entirely avoidable. *Tej* is not served in normal bars; you will have to go to a *tej abet* to drink it. A 750ml bottle of *tej* costs around birr 4. Locally brewed beer, made from millet or maize, is called *tella*. This is similar to the local brew of east and southern Africa, and no less foul in Ethiopia than it is elsewhere in the region.

Acceptable bottled lager is sold throughout Ethiopia. There are several brands, among them *Castel*, *Bati*, *Bedele*, *St George*, *Harar* and *Dashen*. A 350ml bottle of beer costs around birr 4 (US$0.50), with prices varying slightly, depending on where you buy it. Draught lager is available in Addis and a few other large towns in central and eastern Ethiopia (from memory, these are Harar, Dire Dawa, Adama, Bishoftu, Debre Birhan and Weliso) and it is very cheap. A beer journalist writes: 'Ethiopia now has a licensed *Guinness Foreign Extra Stout*, something beer geeks always seek, and it says 'Guinness is Good for You' in Amharic on the neck label! Hakim Stout, from the Harare Brewery, isn't bad, although it's not really a stout.' Wine is brewed locally; the result is indifferent but affordable, especially if bought directly from a shop. Imported spirits are served in most bars at very cheap prices for generous tots.

SHOPPING

Shops in Ethiopia are generally well stocked by African standards, though readers who are unfamiliar with African conditions should realise that this is a very relative statement. Basic goods are widely available; luxuries are not. Most medium-to-large towns have stationery shops, good pharmacies, music shops and general stores. Even in small towns you'll find kiosks that sell most things you're likely to want – batteries, pens, paper, soap, washing powder, dry biscuits, boiled sweets, bottled drinks, toilet rolls (which Ethiopians rather endearingly call *soft*), mosquito spray and incense (useful for rooms with drifting toilet smells).

Most towns and villages have markets. In larger towns these will be open every day but the main market day throughout the country is Saturday. In some towns, especially small towns that serve large rural areas, there is an additional market day. Market days are usually the best days to visit off-the-beaten-track areas, as there will be far more transport. Buying from markets rather than shops actively puts money into the hands of a local community.

Exporting souvenirs and antiques

Many of Ethiopia's ancient treasures have been stolen or removed from the country in recent years, most infamously the 5–7kg gold Lalibela Cross that was stolen from the Church of Medhane Alem in Lalibela in March 1997 and returned two years later. But many smaller items have gone, too, and the Ethiopian authorities are understandably cracking down on what tourists can take out of the country. Indeed, individual tourists should think twice before they buy antiquities – aside from the fact that such behaviour is gradually depleting the country of its cultural resources, many genuine old items will have been stolen from their real owner for resale to tourists.

In this light, and with slight artistic licence, I'm quoting in full the advice of Tony Howard and Di Taylor on the subject:

> Buying things to take out of the country can be a bit of a hassle. Anything
> that can be considered old or antique reportedly needs a permit whether it
> is silver, wood, cotton or whatever. Ivory is illegal (as, we were told, are
> three-legged wooden stools!). Old silver crosses and religious items are
> also a problem. Whatever you buy, first ask the shopkeeper if it's a
> permitted item (he may not know) and make sure you get a receipt.

Take the goods and receipts and then get hold of plenty of thick wrapping paper and good sellotape (both available at the stationery shop down the road from the museum just before reaching the Arat Kilo roundabout, or at the British Council). Then go to the National Museum, where the office to the left of the main museum will approve your purchases or not, as the case may be. You must then wrap your purchases, and the museum staff will stamp the wrapping paper and for less than birr 1 per item give you an export permit. This permit must be shown at the airport with the goods still wrapped and the paper intact, and you should be out with no further problem.

Or don't bother with the permit and just hope that you won't be stopped at the airport. If you are, you may lose the lot – it's up to you. Conversely, we went to all that trouble and nobody at the airport stopped us or asked to see what we had in our bags – such is life!

I can add to this by saying that a similar thing applies on a local level, particularly at Axum, where the museum opposite the stelae field can reputedly do the same. The officers at Axum search luggage thoroughly, and they will confiscate any item they view to be suspect. You can dismiss this as bureaucracy but, before you do, you might allow for the fact that tourists have stolen several items right out of the Axum Museum in the recent past, and the customs officials are not archaeologists.

NIGHTLIFE, MUSIC AND DANCING

Most Ethiopian towns can be relied upon to have a handful of lively bars. I have not, as a rule, pointed to individual bars in the regional part of this book – my impression was that the action moves from night to night, and it's easy enough to follow your nose. The atmosphere in Ethiopian bars is generally easy, inclusive and rather dissolute – it is not uncommon for bar girls to outnumber paying drinkers. Ethiopians who speak a bit of English will go out of their way to chat to you. I found that the genuine friendliness I encountered in bars often neutralised the 'plonkers' and shouters who plagued me during daylight hours.

Bars are also the best place to hear Ethiopian music, which, like most aspects of Ethiopian culture, is pretty unusual and self-contained – though increasingly the hi-fi is subservient to the television when football is being broadcast live. You do hear the odd bit of Western music, but mostly it's local stuff. The most widely played Ethiopian 'pop' is broadly Western in influence, but the melodies are decidedly Arabic. In the hands of female vocalists like Aster Aweke (the grande dame of Ethiopian pop, now recording from the USA), Hana Shenkute and Gigi, the eerie, quavering pitch of voice cuts right through the saccharine backing to moving and addictive effect – not, I might add, an observation of which I've managed to convince many people outside of Ethiopia.

Traditional and regional music also receives a fair amount of play, though far less than it did a decade back. Music from the southwest has much in common with west African music – propulsive rhythms, chiming guitars, and lots of ebullient shouting. Somebody to listen out for is Kaisha Seta, who plays music sung in Walaitigna and occasionally the Dorze language of Chencha. Music from the north and east is steeped more in Arabic rhythms. I was particularly taken by a brand of Tigraian music, which is characterised by earthy, hypnotic chord sequences not unlike some types of rural blues, and a wryly grumbling vocal quality (not that I understood a word) that reminded me of a style of South African accordion 'blues' from the 1970s.

Cassettes of Ethiopian music can be bought very cheaply everywhere in the country. In Addis and other large cities, you can also buy Ethiopian music on CDs, which cost around birr 25 if printed locally, an excellent deal, but rather more if they are imported. If you want some mementoes (and why not remember a country with the music that you drank to, rather than a few meaningless knick-knacks?), other musicians worth giving a listen to are Tilahun Gasese, Kiros Alamayu, Hirot Bekele, Efram Tamaru, Kenedi Mangasha, Bizunesh Bekele and Marta Ashagne (all names garnered by the 'who is this music? – *museeka yeman?*' – method, which is something you shouldn't be afraid to try in bars).

If Ethiopian music is refreshingly self-contained, the dancing is plain bizarre, particularly the styles that originate in the north but which are now practised in most of the country. In some parts of Ethiopia people traditionally leap up and down like the Maasai of east Africa, or do the more standard hip wriggling of east Africa. But it is the women of Amhara and Tigrai that stick in the mind – fixed grins, hot-coal eyes and madly flapping breasts all held together by shuddering shoulder movements, creating a whirling demonic whole that manages to be robotic and erotic at the same time. Several government hotels in Addis have resident bands and dancers – well worth visiting as they'll demonstrate a wide variety of styles, and any thoughts of touristiness will be quelled by the fact you'll likely as not be the only *faranji* in the audience. But there is no need to be just an observer – this isn't a frigid culture thing, it's how Ethiopians dance, and spontaneous raves occur at bars throughout the country. You'll always be welcome to join in, and be expected to provide some amusement by attempting to emulate the moves. It's great fun.

MEDIA AND COMMUNICATIONS
Newspapers
Except in Addis, where a couple of indifferent locally published English-language papers can be bought, as can magazines such as *Time* and *Newsweek*, you are unlikely ever to see a newspaper you can read in Ethiopia.

Television
Ethiopia's domestic television service isn't much to get excited about. The nightly news service is in Amharigna, though you may catch the odd bit of international news in English. A recent development is the spread of satellite television in Ethiopia, especially the South African-based multi-channel service DSTV. This is something of a mixed blessing – it's great when you want some news from home, or to watch live sport, but there are times when it seems impossible to find a bar or restaurant whose atmosphere isn't dominated by a television shouting at the clientele.

Post
Ethiopia has a good internal and international post service, which celebrated its centenary in 1994. Mail between most parts of Europe and Addis Ababa takes around a week, but it can take longer from elsewhere in the world (my mail from South Africa took up to a month). Local and international airletters are available. If you can't locate international airletters, ask for local ones and extra stamps. International mail sent from Ethiopia is the cheapest I have come across in Africa. Postage rates are very cheap.

Telephone
Ethiopia has a remarkably good telephone service when compared with most parts of Africa. There are telecommunications centres in most towns, and even functional phone booths. It is generally easiest to make international calls from the telecommunications centre on Churchill Avenue in Addis Ababa. Expect to wait anything between ten minutes and an hour for your call to be placed. International phone rates are very cheap.

Internet and email
The only server that currently operates in Ethiopia is the state-run Ethionet, which is effectively a monopoly protected by law, though there is some talk of private servers

being permitted and introduced in the near future. This means that all locally hosted Ethiopian email addresses have the same suffix, which changed from @telecom.net.et to @ethionet.et in 2005, with a six-month window period (after which addresses ending @telecom.net.et will be rejected, so if you come across any address like this, change it to @ethionet.et).

Reliable internet cafés are dotted all around Addis Ababa, and cost a very reasonable birr 0.20 to 0.30 per minute (around US$1.50–2 per hour). Elsewhere, internet usage and access lags far behind that of many neighbouring countries, though most large towns offer some sort of service, ranging from almost as good as Addis Ababa (Bahir Dar, Awassa, Harar, Dire Dawa, Jimma, Gonder) to very slow and costly (Lalibela, Axum). As things stand, short-stay travellers could waste a lot of time at a PC if they depend on having internet access or receiving email outside of Addis Ababa.

Almost every internet café in Ethiopia has its home page set to Yahoo!, and most Ethiopians seem to have a Yahoo! (as opposed to a hotmail) address. The downside of this is that getting on to the Yahoo! home page can be a slow process when half of Ethiopia's internet population is trying to do the same. If you have a Yahoo! ID or email address it will in fact work on any of the Yahoo! country sites and you will find it easier to check your mail via yahoo.co.uk, yahoo.ca, yahoo.de or yahoo.fr.

CRIME

Ethiopia is generally a very safe country. Casual theft and pickpocketing are fairly commonplace in parts of the country, notably Addis Ababa and to some extent in larger towns such as Dire Dawa, Gonder and Bahir Dar. Fortunately, this sort of thing is almost never accompanied by violence. In Addis Ababa, pickpockets might operate anywhere, but favoured areas are the Mercato, and in the vicinity of government hotels in the city centre. Violent crimes aren't a cause for serious concern, but as in any large city one should not wander around at night with a large amount of money or important documents.

In other parts of Ethiopia, the risk of being pickpocketed is more or less confined to bus stations and markets, and even then only in larger towns. At bus stations, this is most likely to be a loner operating in the surge of people getting on to a bus. In the streets, a favoured trick is for one person to distract you by bumping into you or grabbing your arm, while a second person slips his fingers in your pocket from the other side. It's advisable to leave valuables and any money you don't need in a hotel room, to carry the money you do need in a relatively inaccessible place, and to always turn quickly in the other direction if somebody does bump into you or grab you. A useful ruse is to stuff something bulky but valueless (a bit of scrunched-up tissue or an empty cigarette pack) as a decoy in a more accessible pocket. If you need to go out with important documents or foreign currency, carry it in a concealed money-belt, and carry some cash separately so that you need not reveal your money-belt in public.

Thieves often pick up on uncertainty and home in on what they perceive to be an easy victim. In Addis Ababa, where there are plenty of experienced thieves and con artists, always walk quickly and decisively. When you arrive in a new town by bus, stroll out of the bus station quickly and confidently as if you know exactly where you're going (even if you don't). Avoid letting the kids who often hang around bus stations latch on to you. Once through the crowds, you can sit down somewhere and check your map, or ask for directions.

One area of risk that is difficult to quantify is that of armed bandits – *shifta* – holding up a bus. This was quite commonplace a few years ago, but is no longer serious cause for concern, except perhaps in eastern areas near the Somali border.

It is easy enough to let warnings about theft induce an element of paranoia into your thinking. There is no cause for this sort of overreaction. If you are moderately careful and sensible, the chance of hitting anything more serious than pickpocketing is very small. Far more remarkable than the odd bit of theft, especially when you consider how much poverty there is in the country, is the overwhelming honesty that is the norm in Ethiopia.

HASSLES

In my experience, and that of many readers, the level of day-to-day hassle in Ethiopia is higher than in most African countries. I am not talking about serious problems like bribery, overt hostility or life-threatening crimes, but rather that it can start to feel like your every move is accompanied by comment, staring and by screaming children. This phenomenon is not unique to Ethiopia, but it can take on proportions that I have experienced nowhere else in Africa (though, admittedly, far less often on my 2005 research trip than on all previous ones).

The degree to which your trip will be accompanied by this sort of hassle will be directly related to your manner of travel. If you fly or are driven around on a short-stay holiday, stay mainly at upmarket hotels, and generally walk around in the company of a professional guide, you'll be almost entirely buffered from this aspect of Ethiopia. Not so travellers who spend longer in the country, make extensive use of buses, stay mainly in local hotels, and have no travel companion.

The most persistent irritant in Ethiopia is the phenomenon I have dubbed *faranji* **hysteria**: groups of screaming children who follow travellers around yelling '*faranji*, *faranji*' or 'you, you, you' ad nauseam. Although inherently inoffensive, being trailed by a mob of 20 kids yelling out 'you' for hours on end does tend to wear on one's reserves of good humour after a time! *Faranji* hysteria does occasionally extend to throwing stones – when this happened to me, the behaviour reminded me of Western children teasing a dog, half aware it might bite them, but also wanting to see how far they can go.

The best response to *faranji* hysteria is to poke gentle fun at the kids. If a kid shouts 'you', yell 'you' back, or if they shout '*faranji*', respond with '*habbishat*' (Ethiopian). Responses in Amharigna generally amuse Ethiopians, who are not used to it from tourists. When a child asks you for money, smile, ask how much, and haggle the 'price' up until everybody around realises you are joking; or ask *lemin?* (why). It would be cruel to do something like this to a genuine beggar, but most of the kids who ask for money are chancing it, and they invariably respond to this sort of thing with laughter – or a bemused expression gets everybody else laughing. Humour may not always defuse the mob, but it is generally a more successful ploy than showing anger or irritation!

Another regular problem is the youngish lads – dubbed '**plonkers**' in earlier editions of this guide – who will latch on to you, accompany you uninvited to your hotel or wherever you are going, then demand money, ask to be your guide, expect you to marry their sister, or something equally inappropriate. 'Plonkers' are a very identifiable type, so much so that after a while in Ethiopia you can pick one out walking towards you 100m away! They are always male, and generally deadly earnest (and equally banal), relatively educated, and out of work. Nine times out of ten, the worst a 'plonker' will do is bore you for a couple of hours and then expect to be paid for it; sometimes they might also expect you to send them to university in your home country, or to find them a job. A telltale sign of plonkerdom is the irritating habit of prefacing every question with 'I think' and then, after having plonked through a repertoire of five English sentences, starting all over again. Another is pointing out the obvious – 'that is a cow', 'that is a river'... Conversational gambits along the lines of 'Ethiopia is a poor country' or 'work is difficult to find' are reliable pointers to where, sooner or later, a new acquaintance will lead more directly. 'Plonkers' are not a threat: they are just quite appalling company and entirely immune to subtle dissuasion.

My best advice regarding 'plonkers' is to shake them off swiftly. For that matter, shake off anybody who befriends you when you first arrive in a town. If that sounds harsh, the fact is that you're not in Ethiopia to perform the social function of entertaining bores (I honestly wonder if the reason some of these types approach foreigners is because everybody they know runs a mile the moment they open their mouths). And, let's face it, when you arrive in an unfamiliar town carrying a heavy pack after a ten-hour bus trip, your first priority is not to make idle chit-chat with a stranger or to organise the stranger's further education. The sort of person who approaches you under these circumstances has to have a deficiency in the imagination department. And if they don't lack imagination, then they almost certainly have an ulterior motive. If you need help or directions on arriving in a town, far better approach somebody yourself than allow yourself to become obliged to somebody who approaches you, quite possibly with the intent of creating that sense of obligation.

Specifics aside, many travellers find it rather trying to travel in an environment where they have no privacy, and where every move seems to attract comment or attention. This manifests itself in many small ways: beggars cross the street to catch your attention, complete bores feel they have the right to monopolise your company, and even the most straightforward situations such as catching a bus or ordering a meal can become surrounded by fuss and complication. There is no real way around this. If you are travelling rough and for a long period, it will genuinely help to take the odd break – an afternoon with a book in the garden of a smart hotel can be tremendously therapeutic, as can the reading room of the British Council in Addis Ababa.

Women travellers

The overwhelming majority of feedback from female travellers suggests that Ethiopia is a relatively safe country for single women travellers. The risk of rape or seriously threatening harassment is probably lower than in many Westernised countries. A recent letter from Hisako Tajima is representative: 'As a solo female traveller, I found Ethiopia to be a very easy and friendly country, refreshingly free of amorous male advances that make countries like Egypt and Turkey such a chore.'

The most regular complaint from female travellers is teenage boys yelling out 'Fuck you' from across the street, something to which male travellers are also subjected. Yelling out obscenities at tourists is not an everyday occurrence (unless you decide to live in Shashemene), and it is unlikely to happen when you are in the company of a respected guide or another local person. Although unpleasant, it is ultimately a less innocuous variation on the sort of verbal crap that all single travellers have to put up with from time to time in Ethiopia.

One place that several female travellers have found threatening is the Mercato in Addis Ababa. Fran Gohd, who found the country safe and friendly in general, writes: 'We went to the market. We were the only women and were given hostile looks and hissed at repeatedly. I was told 'Fuck you' several times after I didn't give the men asking me money. I was asked by a 12-year-old boy if I wanted to have sex. This got worse as we approached the part of the market where they sold *chat*. I felt like I could've been dragged off the street and disappeared without trace.'

Women travellers are urged to avoid staying at hotels at the brothel-cum-bar-room end of the price scale. Outside of Addis Ababa, no respectable Ethiopian woman would dream of going to a bar, since Ethiopian men assume that any woman they see in a bar is a prostitute. While they might recognise that this isn't the case with a female traveller, hanging about in the lowest shoestring hotels does place you in an environment where motives might be misinterpreted.

On the subject of dress, Ethiopia has a substantial Muslim population, and in rural areas particularly both Muslims and Christians tend to dress modestly. Anna Rank has this to say: 'If I wear sleeveless clothes then I tend to get a constant stream of comments and stares, although this does not particularly bother me in Addis. I would not dress in this manner in smaller towns where *faranjis* are few and far between.' Fran Gohd again: 'We came prepared with skirts and headscarves, but there was no need to wear them. We wore pants and that was acceptable. I saw some women travellers wearing shorts, but I'm not sure that I'd feel comfortable with that unless they extended below the knee and even then I'd think twice.'

A couple of recent encounters have made me newly aware of the problems specifically facing black female travellers in Africa. In most African societies, Ethiopia included, women are placed in a subservient role that seems positively medieval by Western standards. European women are not expected to fit the mould, but nobody seems quite certain on which side of the chasm to place black Western women. Black women who travel alone in Ethiopia are in for a strange time, and they will often experience African sexual attitudes at first hand. The obvious area of solution is to dress and carry yourself in a manner that precludes confusion: don't come with a rucksack full of flowing African dresses and bright blouses, but rather wear jeans or preppy clothes, things that would rarely be seen on an Ethiopian woman.

One final point is that you should be aware that when Ethiopians ask you to play with them, they are not suggesting a quick grope but that you make conversation – the Amharic *techawot* means both to talk and to play.

Bureaucracy and bribery

To read many African travel guides, you would think that the average tourist to Africa is ploughing through a minefield of bribery and bureaucracy. This is not the case. To put things in some perspective, I have yet to be asked for a bribe in more than a decade of African travel. Neither can I think of more than a handful of incidents of unbridled bureaucratic stupidity, against which I must balance perhaps ten times as many incidents where bureaucrats have gone out of their way to help me. You might encounter the odd surly bureaucrat in Ethiopia, and you can expect to run up against a certain amount of inefficiency, but more often than not you will encounter a level of friendliness and helpfulness from government employees that few Africans visiting Europe will ever know.

Some travellers seem to hit interminable problems with bureaucrats. I suspect many such problems stem not from the bureaucrat but from the attitude of the traveller. It is normal in Ethiopia to ask strangers their name, their home country, where they have come from and where they are going. If Ethiopian officials do this, it is more likely they are making small talk or practising their English than that they have any professional interest in the answers. But it is not difficult to see how small talk of this sort, if misinterpreted by a traveller and responded to argumentatively, might lead to problems.

Many Africans are understandably sensitive to what they perceive (I think correctly) as Western arrogance towards Africa. If you approach an official encounter aggressively, over-assertively, or with an air of exasperation, you risk pressing exactly the wrong buttons. Far better to be friendly but formal, indulge in whatever small talk comes your way, and to treat officials with respect. If things do get peculiar, keep your sense of humour, and explain your problem slowly using words that the official will be familiar with (not all Ethiopian officials speak much English and shouting the same sentence 20 times can only antagonise).

Whatever your fears about bribery and bureaucracy, the humbling reality is that as a visitor to Ethiopia – or almost any other African country – you will generally be pushed to the front of every queue and treated with the utmost courtesy by officials. Now when British post offices start saying 'hey, that chap at the back of the queue looks like a foreigner, we'd better serve him first', then perhaps we can start complaining about African officials.

Bridging the Cultural Gap

This chapter examines the relationship between tourism and the host country. It is a subject that should be of concern to all tourists, and particularly independent travellers, who will continually interact with Ethiopians on a one-to-one basis and thus play an ambassadorial role for both their country and travellers in general.

In a section that dwells extensively on matters of culture, it seems relevant to state that I grew up in South Africa and, since 1986, have spent about half of my time travelling independently in various parts of Africa. I am not so arrogant that I claim to understand African cultures or to be able to speak for all Africans. On the contrary, a major motivation behind writing a section of this sort is that moving regularly between African and Western cultures has made me acutely conscious of how difficult it is for anybody of a Western upbringing (and that includes myself) to form unprejudiced opinions on matters African. Nevertheless, my mental and practical involvement with Africa over the years has allowed me to think through most travel-related issues as they relate to Africa from a less culture-bound perspective than could a one-off visitor – no less so because I grew up in a culture notable for its overtly racist and Afrophobic propaganda. If apartheid bequeathed me one thing, it is a vicious distrust of dogma and any other received wisdom.

In an age of buzzwords like eco-tourism and responsible tourism, it is to be assumed that a large proportion of tourists are concerned about their effect on the countries they visit, and with how best to bridge the gap between their own and local cultures. But I do feel that it is sometimes promoted in a rather idealised, artificial manner. Media focus on tourist-related issues may create a greater awareness in the West of the potentially negative effects of tourism, but is it reaching the people who count most: those who are actually travelling?

No matter how much prospective travellers read on the subject of responsible tourism prior to their trip, neat ideological certainties will not prepare them for the muddy realities of semi-Westernised urban societies that include among their members thieves, con artists, beggars, prostitutes and a plethora of other arguably unsavoury characters. Most developing countries are overwhelming to first-time visitors; many travellers' ideals vanish beneath the culture shock. And when they turn to their guidebook, or talk to other travellers, the chances are that the only guidance they will receive will be how to spend as little money as possible, or the sort of vague generalisations about theft and bureaucracy which are less a guide than they are an inducement to paranoia.

I do not think it is realistic to promote responsible tourism without also giving serious thought to the stresses facing visitors to developing countries. The most effective way to do this is not through the mass media, but through the guidebooks that accompany most travellers on their journey. When I talk to other travellers, I sense that many are flipping between two non-convergent ideologies: the perfectly genuine concern of the liberalised West they have left behind, and the entirely self-absorbed creeds of budget travel. I think it is vital that we reconcile these divergent ideals, and that guidebooks provide their users with a realistic framework within which they can think through tourist-related issues.

That is what this section attempts to do. My aim is not to lay down the law, but to stimulate debate and to look honestly and holistically at aspects of tourism that concern not only me, but many other travellers to whom I have spoken. If this sounds arrogant or self-righteous, I should add that I am not asking that anybody agree with any of my conclusions – I return from every African trip with revised views and fresh opinions – and that I have no doubt that the person who has learnt the most from writing this section is myself.

Before you read any further, I would like to put forward one important and easily missed perspective on tourism. There is one question we almost invariably ask visitors to our own country; it is the same question I am asked most frequently when I travel in Africa. And it is not 'Do you understand our country?' It is not 'Are you behaving responsibly in our country?' It is 'Do you *like* our country?' Like us, Ethiopians are proud of their country, and want to know that visitors feel the same way. Is it not our first responsibility as visitors to do our damnedest to *enjoy* the country we visit – to ensure that we can answer the one question we will always be asked with an honest and enthusiastic 'Yes'?

RESPONSIBLE TOURISM

On the face of it, the current trend towards promoting responsible and sustainable tourism is a long-overdue and positive shift in emphasis. For too long, unscrupulous travel writers, tour operators and resort owners have encouraged tourism without really concerning themselves with the environmental or social consequences. Unchecked, I have no doubt they will continue to do so, and within this framework I actively encourage tourists to Ethiopia or elsewhere to act responsibly.

Sounds good, but what do we mean by acting responsibly? In the UK a body called Tourism Concern (☏ *020 8944 0464*) is at the forefront of promoting responsible tourism. It has produced a most useful set of guidelines, reproduced here in abbreviated form:

1 Be a considerate guest – your resort is someone else's home.
2 Save precious natural resources. Try not to waste water. Switch off lights and air conditioning when you go out.
3 Be kind to wildlife. Loud music, bonfires, litter and off-road driving can disturb or destroy animals and plants.
4 Be adventurous! Get out and meet the local people by walking and cycling, and eating in local restaurants.
5 Always ask before taking photographs or video recordings of people.
6 Support traditional skills and businesses by buying crafts made in the area ... but do safeguard nature by avoiding souvenirs made from wildlife products.

I agree entirely with these guidelines. In fact, I could add several more to the list:

7 Always dress and behave in a manner that is in keeping with local sensibilities.
8 Respect and obey the laws of the country you visit.
9 Do not let the occasional need to bargain over prices blind you to the fact that, where uncertainty exists, it is always better to be generous than stingy when dealing with people less wealthy than yourself.
10 Do not draw cultural inferences from the behaviour of individuals.
11 Put your money directly into the local economy, for instance by eating and sleeping at local and privately owned establishments rather than government or foreign-owned concerns.
12 Humour is almost always a better way to deal with minor irritations than assertiveness or aggression.

Within the context of a book like this, I think it important that responsible tourism is stressed. I do, however, think there are dangers inherent in promoting tourist-related issues through the mass media, where all information about Africa tends to be presented selectively and in isolation from other related issues. My experience, when I lived in London, is that a sudden media focus on one or other aspect of Africa often left the general public with more misapprehensions than balanced information. And, if what I have seen of the promotion of responsible tourism is representative, I fear it is creating the impression that tourism is inherently damaging to developing countries.

This idea should be firmly quashed, at least in the context of Ethiopia and Africa as a whole. Africa is a desperately poor continent. Its most pressing need is not the preservation of a few pristine environments or cultures, but to meld its traditions with the exotic and often inappropriate economic and political systems which were imposed on it from the late 19th century onwards, to the end of creating a meaningful role for it in the global economy. Tourism is the world's largest industry: some 15% of jobs worldwide are tourism-related. At present, less than 3% of the global revenue raised by tourism goes to African countries. In this context, tourism is not a problem; it is the one thing that might help kick-start Africa out of its present predicaments, by creating employment and raising foreign revenue through more honest means than aid.

One of the major problems facing African countries, most of which are desperate for more tourism, is that the continent has gained such a negative media image as a whole. In this context, the responsible tourism lobby may ultimately do more harm than good, by furthering the 'bad news out of Africa' syndrome, and the impression that tourism is intrinsically negative. So, yes, responsible tourism has its place; it is emphatically better than irresponsible tourism. But the issues it addresses should be subservient to the greater issue of how to attract more tourism to Africa.

GUILT

We in the West take many things for granted – food, water, electricity and the right to housing, education and information. We are used to democratic societies where we are free to live more or less as we choose; we can, with a modicum of intelligence, education and good fortune, pick and choose the work we want to do; in many countries, we can even choose not to work but to receive state support. I am not for a moment saying that nobody in the West is a victim of circumstance or ill fortune. Nevertheless, most people in a Western society are shielded by the state from destitution, starvation, poor sanitation and all the other maladies of genuine poverty.

To someone raised in the West, first exposure to the developing world is always something of a shock. However concerned you may be about the inequality of global wealth distribution, and however much you may have read and thought about the issues, confronting the reality is something entirely different from dealing with it in the abstract. And most of us, to some extent, respond with a feeling of guilt. Now, guilt is an unfashionable emotion. Pop psychologists and magazines tell us it is entirely useless, and they are probably right. Nevertheless, guilt is real. Where it exists, it is better admitted to and confronted than denied. On a global level, the developing world *has* suffered greatly at the hands of the West, and it continues to do so. We should expect to experience some level of guilt when confronting the realities of a country like Ethiopia – it would take an overdeveloped sense of self-righteousness not to – and accept that this guilt *will* influence our thoughts and actions. In this light, it is best we consciously confront the question of guilt and decide to what degree and in what manner we should respond to it.

A common response to a country like Ethiopia is to feel that it is wrong to enjoy ourselves amid such suffering; that tourism is frivolously out of context in such a poor country; that we are exploiting Ethiopia by taking advantage of its poverty to have a cheap holiday. To resolve this sort of misgiving, we must recognise that what is making us feel guilty has nothing to do with tourism. Tourism is not responsible for the inequalities of the world. Your presence in a country like Ethiopia in no way exacerbates any local suffering. On the contrary, Ethiopia, like most developing countries, is desperate to encourage tourism because it brings in foreign revenue and creates business opportunities and jobs. If you want to do something for a country like Ethiopia, spending your money there is asserting your consumer power in the most positive manner possible. It strikes me as a far more appropriate response than to travel only in developed countries and pretend the inequality doesn't exist.

Guilt, in this context, is not merely useless, but counterproductive. It can lead us to take purgative or defensive actions where rational thought would be more appropriate. In this light, I suspect that an element of guilt is responsible for many of our knee-jerk responses to African dilemmas. This is natural and normal enough; but the important thing, if we are to try and draw conclusions about tourism in Ethiopia, is that we are alert to the possibility that guilt is clouding our judgement, and that we aim for an understanding that is motivated primarily by the needs of Ethiopians and not by our own need to alleviate our guilt.

I have long held doubts about my work. I have been torn between the feeling that it is useful and constructive to be writing books that might encourage tourism to little-visited countries, the fear that tourism might in some way damage the country, and an anger at the way that some tourists, most especially budget travellers, ride roughshod over Africa. By chance, I happened across a James Baldwin quote the other day: 'The price one pays for pursuing any profession or calling is an intimate knowledge of its ugly side.' This hit home: tourism has its ugly sides, but we should not allow them to obscure its far greater potential for good.

CULTURAL PERSPECTIVES

If I have learnt one thing from my African travels, it is the impenetrability of other cultures. There is much to be said for the cosmopolitan openness to other cultures which, in somewhere like London, allows you to flit from Indian to Cantonese to Italian restaurants, to hear music and read books from all over the world, and to visit museums and art galleries which celebrate the diversity of human cultural evolution. But it does, I suspect, mislead many Westerners into the feeling that other cultures are more accessible and easily assimilated than is really the case. This can often lead to misunderstanding, confusion and disappointment when they are confronted with a country as culturally self-contained and unfamiliar as Ethiopia.

A culture, according to Victorian anthropologist Sir Edward Tyler, is 'that complex whole which includes knowledge, belief, art, morals, law, custom, and any other habits and capabilities acquired by man as a member of society'. Most of us are, of course, aware of this on some level; nevertheless, travelling amid an unfamiliar culture brings the truth of it home more than any textbook can.

It is easy, when confronted by an unfamiliar culture, to attribute everything you see to culture and ignore the role of individuality. Ethiopians are no less individuals than we are; all human behaviour is found there. Like many points relating to culture, I suspect this is more readily grasped on an intellectual level than it is incorporated into our gut thinking. Or, to put it more bluntly, when confronted by a bore in Ethiopia, it helps to retain the perspective that you are dealing first and foremost with a bore, and that it is merely the manifestation of their tediousness which is cultural. In Ethiopia, as anywhere else, most people are polite and decent. Unfortunately, the small proportion of loudmouths tends to make a stronger impression than the silent majority. The truth is that the drunk who rambles inanely at you does so not because he is Ethiopian, but because he is drunk. The children who yell and perform do so not because they are Ethiopian but because they are children. The beggar who crosses the street to catch your attention does so not because he is Ethiopian but because he is desperate. By the same logic, the fellow bus passenger who buys you lunch does so not because he is Ethiopian but because he's a friendly guy; and people who grab you by the arm and pull you on to the dance floor do so not because they are Ethiopian, but because they are having a good time and they want you to join in. Travellers to Ethiopia are interacting with individuals as much as they are interacting with an alien culture.

A common response when confronted with an entirely unfamiliar culture is a kind of intellectual straw clutching. All too often, I hear tourists expounding on a country's culture or politics on the basis of what their tour guide told them or the wit and wisdom of some bloke they met on a bus. I'm as guilty as anybody of reaching sweeping conclusions on the basis of one person's comments – I merely draw attention to it.

It is also a Western tendency to romanticise 'ethnic' cultures, to see in them an antidote to the commercialism of our own society, and to see any cultural change in non-Western societies as negative. But cultures are not static. A few years ago, in an interview in *Wanderlust* magazine, Dervla Murphy, author of *In Ethiopia with a Mule*, said she would hate to return to Ethiopia and see the changes that have occurred in the last 30 years. I can empathise with her – perhaps I'll feel the same about 'my' Ethiopia a couple of decades from now – but it is ultimately a selfish concern. I doubt that Ethiopian society has changed any more in the last 30 years than has English or American society. And if it has, so what? We accept the organic nature of our own culture. Why do we find it so difficult to accept the same thing in other societies?

Concerned Westerners shake their heads at the sad spectacle of Africans asking for payment to allow their photograph to be taken or performing traditional dances for cash. Tourism is corrupting them, they have become commercialised. Rubbish! The destruction of traditional African cultures started over a century ago and it is virtually complete; for many modern Africans tourism is a lifeline. What, apart from their relative income, is the difference between a semi-professional Maasai poser and Kate Moss walking the catwalk, or a bunch of Africans dancing for tourists and Robbie Williams wriggling his bum in a pop video? In a cash-based economy, we are all driven by commercial needs, and many of us spend a significant proportion of our time employed in activities that we would certainly not undertake were they not generating income. Within the law, it is up to individuals to determine their own morality. To say that tourists are 'spoiling' a local culture is to say that local people are incapable of making moral decisions for themselves, and also to say that the preservation of a pristine culture is a greater issue than the individual welfare of the people concerned. We live in an increasingly homogenous world, very few corners of which have not been sucked into a cash economy, and, just as we enjoy visiting different countries and trying different foods, so should we accept that people from other countries have the right to want to opt for aspects of Western culture.

There is a certain amount of unconscious hypocrisy in Western attitudes to ethnic cultures. For instance, most of us would be happy to see the abolition of the tradition of so-called female circumcision, a common practice in many parts of Africa. By the same token, I expect that most Westerners would have little problem with Ethiopian monasteries opening their doors to females, or the Afar people of the Danakil Desert dropping their tradition of lopping off the testicles of any male intruder. It strikes me that, on the one hand, we want to liberalise and change those aspects of ethnic cultures we find morally repugnant, but on the other hand we want to preserve the rest of the culture in a pristine form. This is simply silly. It is perhaps the danger of multi-cultural societies that they treat cultures as commodities: keep the bits you like and chuck the rest.

To me, much of the fascination of modern Africa is the interaction between indigenous and exotic cultures, the emergence of a dynamic something that might be described as an Afro-Western society. It is right that we respect African traditions; far better that we romanticise them than do as previous generations did and ridicule them. Best of all, though, is that we accept Africa as it is; we look for the reality, not for what we want to see. I ask readers not to fall into the trap of thinking that the culture of traditional villages is more valid than that of the urbanite. In my experience, an evening in a local bar will tell you infinitely more about the realities of modern Africa than any number of camera-based exchanges with 'ethnic' Africans.

My experience is that it is practically impossible to understand another culture. You can learn about Ethiopians, you can learn from Ethiopians, but this knowledge will all be assimilated within the framework of your own cultural background. In fact, what you really learn from immersing yourself in another culture is to place the parochial concerns of your own culture in perspective. It is for this reason that travel is so mentally liberating and refreshing. Cultural gaps are not an obstacle to individual communication or enjoyment, but they will taint your perceptions of a country like Ethiopia. It is our most deeply seated cultural assumptions that we are most blind to and least able to overcome; that is why we should always be wary of making unconsidered judgements about African situations.

GIVING

Africans perceive Westerners to be far wealthier than they are. In general, it is difficult to quibble with this article of faith. In many instances, however, Africans have difficulty in distinguishing between the budgets and aims of individual tourists, and of their governments and aid organisations. Which is a nice way of saying that tourists are made to feel as though everybody wants something from them. For most of us, this poses daily dilemmas. It would take a hard-hearted person not to feel some unease at the gulf between the wealth and opportunities in the West and the desperate poverty of many Ethiopians. It is, nevertheless, irritating, dehumanising and tiring continually to be treated like a walking bank.

What follows are some thoughts and guidelines on various aspects of giving and how to deal with them. The thread that runs through my opinions is that you should *never* give things to people who ask just because you are a foreigner. The give-me, give-me, give-me attitude is prevalent enough already in Ethiopia; responding to it will only reinforce it.

Gifts

I must discourage the practice of indiscriminately handing out sweets, pens or trinkets to children. The motive for doing this *is* selfish – to make yourself feel better. It has, also, a rather paternalistic air, which I personally feel uncomfortable with. An entirely selfish concern, but one that anybody will understand if they spend a while travelling independently in Ethiopia, is that in some Ethiopian towns I had children ask me for money or sweets or a pen perhaps 100 times in an hour. There are plenty of Ethiopian towns where the children are genuinely friendly and never ask you for things. I am convinced it would need only one naive tourist and a bag of sweets to change that.

A less clear-cut issue is that of giving gifts to those who go out of their way to help you. The people who approach you in a country such as Ethiopia collectively possess such a mixed bag of motives that it is often difficult to decide who is genuinely friendly and who is mercenary. In Ethiopia, the extremes are greater than in any other country I've visited. In no other country have I so often been bought a drink by a stranger in a bar, or offered to share a meal by a fellow bus passenger; but neither have I ever had to put up with so many chancers.

The simple solution to all this is not to carry gifts. If someone buys you a drink, buy the next round. If someone buys you a meal, offer them a drink, or just accept their generosity with visible gratitude. It is very wrong to make a policy of cadging off the locals, but it is also unfair to let your guilt rob people of their individuality and dignity.

Just because the Ethiopian economy is poor, this doesn't mean we cannot accept the hospitality of individual Ethiopians – such people are tremendous ambassadors for their country, and in many instances they *want* to signal their hospitality to you. Treat them with the same give-and-take that you would expect from a fellow traveller; treat them like an equal and not a 'poor Ethiopian'.

The one exception would be if you were to end up staying with an Ethiopian family. That sort of generosity should always be responded to – just as you would respond to a Western person with whom you stayed. But there are all sorts of informal responses. Why not buy a crate of beer (assuming they drink), take them out for a meal, or ask them if there is something that *they* would like from your country and remember to send it to them when you get home. I find it difficult to disassociate the idea of carrying an assortment of gifts from the general paternalism of the West towards Africa. There are less formulaic and more individual ways of responding to generosity. For that matter, polite gratitude is sometimes the most appropriate response. Take things as they come.

Begging

There are beggars everywhere in Ethiopia, especially in Addis Ababa, and most of them make a beeline for foreigners. Ethiopians themselves often give loose change to genuine beggars, and I tended to follow suit. If I had a spare coin when I passed a beggar, I generally gave it to them. How did I decide which beggars to give it to? Quite simple – under no circumstances would I give money to a beggar, even if they were genuine, who approached me individually because of my skin colour. Needless to say, blind beggars did very well out of me.

Tipping and guide fees

The qualified guides who work in Ethiopia's main historical centres usually charge a fixed rate of birr 100–200 per party per day. They will sometimes be open to negotiation out of season. Elsewhere, for a knowledgeable professional guide, birr 20 for up to two hours and birr 10 for every hour thereafter is a fair-to-generous guideline. In both cases it is best to agree a price upfront. If you want to arrange informal guides in other areas, you should also discuss a fee in advance. It is difficult to generalise, but birr 10–15 for a youngster and twice that amount for an adult feels about right, depending on how long you are out, and whether you are in an expensive town or in a rural area where money goes further.

There are some tiresome guides (mostly non-professional) who will routinely go into a sulk after you have paid them in the hope they can manipulate a bit of extra cash out of you, often spoiling what might otherwise have been a good day out in the process. Never give in to this sort of crap! And if any guide happens to pull the old stunt of thrusting your payment back into your hands in feigned disgust at its paltriness, my advice is to call his bluff – take the money, walk off, and you'll be amazed how quickly he decides that he actually would like the money after all.

Sometimes you may find a couple of kids offer to show you the way somewhere in or near a town. If the kids are really obliging you may want to give them a little something. At the other extreme, they might demand birr 20 for five minutes' exertion, and the only thing you'd willingly give them is a swift kick in the posterior. The problem, of course, is that by giving something to the first type, you may be Frankenstein to the second. In Ethiopian society, children are expected to do as adults tell them, and this includes running small errands, even for strangers. If an adult instructs a child to show you the way to the post office or wherever, giving the kid money may go to undermining the social fabric of the country. It's a difficult one but, whatever you do, bear in mind that in a country where many working people draw a monthly wage of US$50 or less, anything more than birr 1–2 would be disproportionate for a child who has run a small errand or walked with you for a few hundred metres.

Tipping waiters is not the established custom in Ethiopia, but it is acceptable and greatly appreciated by the recipient, who might well earn less than birr 200 per month in actual salary. At upmarket restaurants such as those in government hotels, the 10% tip that is customary in many Western countries is a fair-to-generous guideline (in fact, a service charge is levied at most such restaurants, but the odds of this ending up in the hands of the waiters and waitresses is negligible). In private restaurants and bars, it's entirely at your discretion: tipping is not expected, but leaving behind a coin or two in a coffee or pastry shop or local restaurant would be appreciated, while birr 1-2 would be a decent tip in a proper restaurant.

Tipping guides and waiters is fine because that's their job. There are, however, times when somebody helps you and you are unsure whether that person might expect a tip. In this situation, I prefer a more unambiguously friendly gesture than giving money, such as inviting the person for a coffee and pastry, or buying them a beer or cold drink, or offering them a cigarette. It really is a matter of judgement, perhaps even intuition. A major factor is whether the person is employed: in our eyes, somebody who earns US$50 a month is poor, but in their own country they are relatively well-off and they would be helping you through kindness, not for money. In fact, to treat them as needy, or anything less than a peer, would be demeaning. Far better to make the sort of social gesture that you might make to a fellow traveller.

OVERCHARGING AND BARGAINING

Overcharging tourists is relatively uncommon in Ethiopia, but it happens, especially in Addis and at certain major tourist centres (Bahir Dar is the worst). Once again, it is one of those things that needs to be put in some perspective. For most of us the small amount we are overcharged from time to time is inconsequential in itself; it is the simple fact we are being overcharged that irks. I expect this is because it is a manifestation of the wider feeling that you are being treated as different because you are foreign. Being overcharged should annoy you no more than, say, having somebody offer their seat on a bus. The difference is that it is rather unfair to show your annoyance to somebody whose intention is to be polite.

You should assume that bargaining is the norm with taxi and *gari* drivers, particularly in Addis, and at curio stalls anywhere in the country. It is, at the time of writing, unlikely you will be overcharged for restaurant meals or other foodstuffs. Overcharging is not a normal practice on buses and on other public transport (even in Addis, I was asked above the going rate only two or three times in around 100 minibus rides). Again, bearing in mind that I spent four months in the country and in the course of my job I frequently looked at ten or 20 hotels in a day, I feel it is unusual for hotels to ask seriously high prices of tourists. There are exceptions – most of which fall along the blurred line of what are apparently standard *faranji* prices – but you'll soon get a feel for hotel prices and be able to smell a ridiculous rate. It is, of course, possible that overcharging will become a more widespread practice as tourism in Ethiopia increases.

When you think you are being overcharged, it is tempting to fall back on aggressive posturing and accusing the person of ripping you off. This is rarely necessary. Rather query the price gently, or simply say it is too expensive for you. This gives the person the opportunity to lower the price while retaining their honour – to appear to be generous.

Where you are unsure of the acceptable price, and make gentle queries, I would assume that, if the person appears to be unwilling to lower the price, the very real likelihood is that this is because the price is fair. Remember that bargaining is quite acceptable in Ethiopia, and that there *is* a difference between blatant overcharging and asking a flexible price. It is not true that because somebody drops the price, they were initially trying to cheat you. It *may* even be that they are being more generous than normal because you are a foreigner. Once again, you are dealing with individuals, not 'Ethiopians'.

You can also pre-empt overcharging and the resultant arguments by asking prices in advance or observing what others pay. Be conscious of the room for misunderstanding. For instance, the reason that you might be charged more than neighbouring passengers on a bus is that they are not going as far as you.

There is a school of traveller that claims every price can be bargained down; that a birr 6 hotel room can be reduced to birr 5, or that a bunch of bananas for birr 1 can be bargained down by a few cents. Perhaps they are right. I still don't like their attitude, nor would I try to emulate them. Look at it from the sellers' perspective – how would you feel if you ran a small business and the average man in the street accepted your not-unfair prices but the obviously rich customers haggled every time? You would correctly identify them as mean. I suspect too that travellers like this contribute to the overcharging mentality just as much as travellers who unthinkingly accept every price they are asked. Certainly, if every traveller who came to my hotel argued the toss over price, my response after a few incidents would be to raise the *faranji* price so we could argue back down to what I would have asked in the first place. Ultimately, if the price being asked appears to be reasonable, if you can easily afford it, and if the person with whom you are haggling obviously needs the money more than you, then the sensible and correct response is generosity. Which brings me to my pet subject...

BUDGET TRAVEL AND MEANNESS

Travelling for a long time in cheap countries does strange things to your mind. After a time, you become so used to local prices that it is easy to lose sight of how inexpensive things actually are. We all lose perspective at times – find ourselves eating unpalatable food to save a sum of money that wouldn't buy us an uncooked potato at home – and some travellers become so wrapped up in squeezing every last cent out of their budget that you wonder if they think about anything but how to save money. Implicit in the almost competitive attitude of many travellers is the maxim that the best traveller is the one who spends the least. This is a sad attitude, and one that few of us would *rationally* adhere to. Unfortunately, however, it is also terribly infectious. Most travellers – and I am no exception – get caught up in the cheapskate mentality at times. For this reason, it is worth giving some honest thought to your attitude to budgeting *before* you visit Ethiopia.

Wherever the cheap-is-best mentality stems from, it is impossible to argue against the fact that it is a reaction to the materialism of *our* society. It always annoys me to hear travellers explain how poor they are (the old 'we travellers are not like the rich tourists' routine) to Africans. Do we really expect the average African to give credence to the notion that somebody who can fly to their country and spend more daily than they earn in a month is *poor*? By global standards, anybody who can afford to travel is wealthy – if not in actual cash-in-hand, then in that they will be returning to a society where an income of some form can virtually be taken for granted. The option of travelling is a privilege, and one that is denied to the overwhelming majority of people who live in the developing world.

Certain attitudes that prevail among hard-core budget travellers are unambiguously despicable. I have a fundamental problem with actions such as using bogus student cards to get discounts for museums or train tickets, or trying to enter national parks and archaeological sites without paying fees. This sort of thing deservedly earns travellers a bad name. It is immoral, not to say parasitic, to try to get a reduced fee to visit a museum which, in all probability, is being subsidised by the government of a poor country. Most Western countries rightly object to foreigners abusing *their* social benefit systems... and no, two wrongs don't make a right. I think that anybody from a more financially advantaged society should at least be prepared to pay their way in Ethiopia, and also have some respect for the laws of the country.

IMPRESSIONS OF ETHIOPIA
1: From a letter by Dr Oliver Zoellner

I found the Ethiopians a very welcoming, friendly, kind and loveable people. Even the poorest, most miserable people always seemed to be happy to greet me and talk to me, if only with sign language. I was often very touched by this. Although I do not feel 'guilty' about my relative wealth compared to their absolute poverty and terrible living conditions (Western Europe and Ethiopia are just not comparable – they are truly worlds apart), I would suggest to every traveller to come psychologically prepared for some harrowing sights. It's endurable as long as you just let the images flow by like in a 3D movie – but the moment you start thinking about the people and their situation, you're lost. I think I was in shock for two weeks, something I have never experienced in other poor countries (and I'm not easily shocked, believe me). My personal view of the world has changed, and although I don't think I will travel to Ethiopia again, I am glad I was there.

2: From a letter by Dirk Singer

Here is the thing about Ethiopia: From what we could see the overwhelming majority of tourists are older and the sort who like flush toilets and don't like getting ill. Internal tours in Ethiopia are expensive – the amount we paid could have got us a much more stress-free break in (say) the Gulf States. And unfortunately the tourist infrastructure just isn't up to it yet. We found it much more basic than for example Madagascar where we were a year and a half ago. Ethiopians make life needlessly difficult for tourists, where one or two better hotels on the Northern Historical Circuit could make all the difference. Really, this country desperately needs a little bit of investment if any tourist boom is to come about. Unfortunately, no travel guide prepared me beforehand how basic things would actually be: what the hotels are really like, where you can stop for a loo break on some of the main roads, getting ill etc. Your average reader is not likely to be some backpacker who gets a perverse pleasure about roughing it. However, despite all the frustrations of Ethiopia, it was a rewarding experience. You meet some unique people and see some amazing things. Being in Lalibela for example was almost like being transported to another planet! You also see the best and the worst of people. The worst: kids pretending to have deformities in Addis in trying to get money off you, Western tourists staying at the Sheraton arguing with museum staff over the extra birr 20 charge for foreigners. The best: an old man offering my wife his stick in Lalibela when he saw she had trouble walking, foreigners who have given up a much better lifestyle abroad to try and help in Ethiopia.

Otherwise, I don't think that penny-pinching has a major impact on the host country, except where it leads to aggressive bargaining or accusing everyone of ripping you off, subjects covered elsewhere in this book. Having said that, in my opinion it is truly arrogant to think that spending less money somehow makes you a better traveller or more like an Ethiopian. It is undeniable that travelling on public transport and staying in non-government hotels does bring you closer to the local culture than if you travel as part of an organised tour, but whether you spend US$10 a day or US$15 is pretty meaningless. If anything, the less you spend, the less you justify your presence in a developing country – the reason why countries like Ethiopia want to encourage tourism is to help stimulate their national economy. And even if you ignore this side of things, the person most affected by penny-pinching will be yourself. To use a simplistic example, the difference between spending US$2 or US$4 on a room is financially immaterial in a Western context, yet I am constantly amazed at how many travellers would as a point of pride take the cheaper option – and then moan about the bedbugs and fleas that ruined their night's sleep. Likewise, there are travellers who won't visit major museums or archaeological sites, because the fee – which wouldn't buy them a hamburger at home – is a 'rip-off'.

In my view, the sensible approach to budgeting is to decide in advance how much you can spend daily, and work backwards from there. In other words, if you can comfortably afford up to US$10 per night for a room, then why not look for value for money within that price band, not for the cheapest room you can find? Why not enjoy the fact that in a local Ethiopian hotel a good meal and three or four beers will leave you change from US$5, instead of hiding in your room gloating over the fact that you've had another virtually expense-free day? If you feel like a drink at a government hotel, why not just have one and forget the fact that beers are fractionally more expensive than in private bars? In my experience, travellers who obsess over every penny they spend tend to become paranoid about being overcharged and aggressive in their dealing with locals, and they frequently miss out on opportunities by placing expenditure above everything else. In that sense, their attitude is no less isolating than that of the package tourists at whom they sneer. At home, we would rightly call such behaviour mean. Is meanness an admirable trait just because you are travelling in a developing country? I think not.

Most long-term travellers are on a relatively tight budget. I'm not saying that you need to go crazy with money, only that you should keep things in perspective. In Ethiopia, I could have scrimped and saved to keep my expenses down to around US$8 a day. Instead, I had a wonderful time on around US$12 a day. This is not a great difference. When you come across the sort of traveller that looks down on anybody who spends more than they do, for goodness sake don't try to emulate them. Obsessive penny-pinching is the most unhealthy, joyless and limiting attitude a traveller can have; in a country as cheap as Ethiopia it is completely unnecessary – and it's certainly nothing to feel superior about. If we are to get competitive about travel, then I'd give top marks not to the traveller who spends the least money but to the one who learns the most from the trip or who has the most fun.

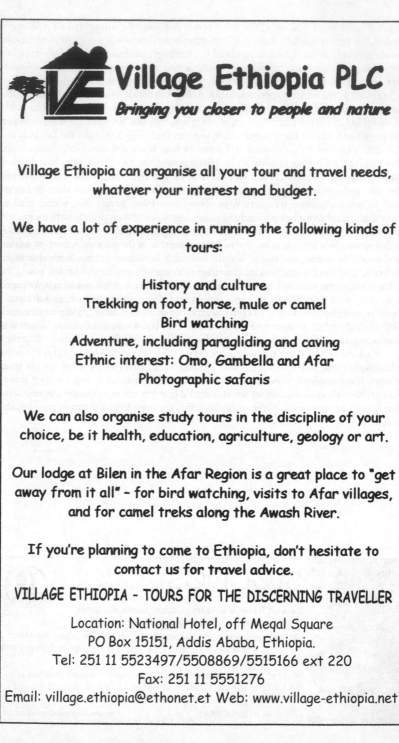

Health and Safety

Ethiopia boasts an impressive array of tropical diseases, but with some sensible precautions the chance of catching anything very serious is not great. Most travellers who spend a while in the country will become ill at some point in their trip, but this is most likely to be straightforward travellers' diarrhoea or a cold. There appears to be a greater risk of travellers contracting more serious sanitation-related diseases (typhoid, hepatitis A and E) in Ethiopia than in other parts of east Africa, but the risk is decreased by having the appropriate immunisations before you leave home and by avoiding high-risk foods once you are in the country. This prevalence of sanitation-related diseases has to be balanced against the fact that there is far less likelihood of contracting malaria in Ethiopia than there is in most other parts of tropical Africa. Before you travel to Ethiopia, ensure you receive the necessary immunisations and, if you plan on entering a malarial area, seek advice on which tablets are currently most effective and also consider how to prevent mosquitoes from biting you – subjects that are covered below.

PREPARATIONS
Travel insurance
Don't think about visiting Ethiopia without comprehensive medical travel insurance: one that will fly you home in an emergency. The ISIS policy, available in Britain through STA (✆ *020 7361 6262*), is inexpensive and has a good reputation.

Immunisations
Several weeks before departing for Ethiopia British readers should visit one of the 36 British Airways Travel Clinics (✆ *01276 685040 for the nearest location*) or another of the many clinics which now have daily updated computer links with centres for tropical medicine. These will tell you what you risk in a particular season and region.

You will need a yellow fever immunisation unless this is contraindicated for medical reasons, and may be required to show an international immunisation certificate as proof of this. To be fully effective this vaccine should be taken at least ten days prior to travel and lasts for ten years. It is also strongly advisable to be immunised against typhoid, polio, diphtheria and tetanus. Travellers should also be advised to have immunisation against hepatitis A with hepatitis A vaccine (eg: Havrix Monodose, Avaxim). One dose of vaccine lasts for one year and can be boosted to give protection for up to 20 years. The course of two injections costs about £100, but don't let the price dissuade you from having it. Acquiring hepatitis A could effectively end your travels and leave you ill for several months, and according to local doctors, it is often caught by visitors to Ethiopia.

If you intend travelling more than 24 hours away from medical facilities, consider rabies immunisation. Ideally three doses of vaccine should be taken and can be given over a minimum period of 21 days. However, if time is short even two or one dose of vaccine is better than nothing at all.

Hepatitis B vaccination should be considered for longer trips or for those working in situations where the likelihood of contact with blood is increased or when working closely with local children. Three injections are ideal, given over a minimum period of three weeks before travel. If more time is available then the doses can be spread over eight weeks or longer.

Medical kit

Take a small medical kit with you. This should contain malaria tablets, soluble aspirin or paracetamol (good for gargling when you have a sore throat and for reducing fever and pains), plasters (band-aids), potassium permanganate crystals or another favoured drying antiseptic, iodine for sterilising water and cleaning wounds, sunblock, and condoms or femidoms. Some travel clinics in Britain will try to persuade you to buy a variety of antibiotics as a precaution. This is not necessary as most antibiotics are widely available in Ethiopia, and you should be hesitant about taking them without medical advice. Depending on your travel plans, it is a good idea to carry a course of tablets as a cure for malaria – Malarone is now considered to be the best treatment, with quinine and fansidar or quinine and doxycycline a close second. Seek up-to-date advice from a travel clinic.

Travel clinics

UK

British Airways Travel Clinic and Immunisation Service 156 Regent St, London W1; ☎ 020 7439 9584. This place also sells travellers' supplies and has a branch of Stanford's travel book and map shop. There are now BA clinics all around Britain and three in South Africa. To find your nearest one, phone 01276 685040.

Fleet Street Travel Clinic 29 Fleet St, London EC4Y 1AA; ☎ 020 7353 5678

MASTA (Medical Advisory Service for Travellers Abroad) Keppel St, London WC1 7HT; ☎ 09068 224100. This is a premium-line number, charged at 50p per minute.

NHS travel website www.fitfortravel.scot.nhs.uk, provides country-by-country advice on immunisation and malaria, plus details of recent developments, and a list of relevant health organisations.

Nomad Travel Pharmacy and Vaccination Centre 3–4 Wellington Terrace, Turnpike Lane, London N8 0PX; ☎ 020 8889 7014

Thames Medical 157 Waterloo Rd, London SE1 8US; ☎ 020 7902 9000. Competitively priced, one-stop travel health service. All profits go to its affiliated company InterHealth which provides healthcare for overseas workers on Christian projects.

Trailfinders Immunisation Clinic 194 Kensington High St, London W8 7RG; ☎ 020 7938 3999. Non-profit-making private clinic with a one-stop shop for health advice, vaccines and travel goods, visas and passport services.

Irish Republic

Tropical Medical Bureau Grafton Street Medical Centre, Grafton Buildings, 34 Grafton St, Dublin 2; ☎ 353 1 671 9200. This organisation has a useful website specific to tropical destinations: http://www.tmb.ie.

USA

Centers for Disease Control 1600 Clifton Rd, Atlanta, GA 30333; ☎ 877 FYI TRIP; 800 311 3435; web: www.cdc.gov/travel. This organisation is the central source of travel information in the USA. Each summer they publish the invaluable Health Information for International Travel which is available from the Division of Quarantine at the above address.

Connaught Laboratories PO Box 187, Swiftwater, PA 18370; ☎ 800 822 2463. They will send a free list of specialist tropical-medicine physicians in your state.

IAMAT (International Association for Medical Assistance to Travelers) 736 Center St, Lewiston, NY 14092. A non-profit organisation which provides lists of English-speaking doctors abroad.

Canada
IAMAT (International Association for Medical Assistance to Travelers) Suite 1, 1287 St Clair Av West, Toronto, Ontario M6E 1B8; ↘ 416 652 0137
TMVC (Travel Doctors Group) Sulphur Springs Rd, Ancaster, Ontario; ↘ 905 648 1112; web: www.tmvc.com.au

Australia and New Zealand
TMVC ↘ 1300 65 88 44; www.tmvc.com.au. TMVC has 20 clinics in Australia, New Zealand and Thailand, including: *Auckland* Canterbury Arcade, 170 Queen St, Auckland City; ↘ 373 3531; *Brisbane* Dr Deborah Mills, Qantas Domestic Building, 6th floor, 247 Adelaide St, Brisbane, QLD 4000; ↘ 7 3221 9066; f 7 3321 7076; *Melbourne* Dr Sonny Lau, 393 Little Bourke St, 2nd floor, Melbourne, VIC 3000; ↘ 3 9602 5788; f 3 9670 8394; *Sydney* Dr Mandy Hu, Dymocks Building, 7th floor, 428 George St, Sydney, NSW 2000; ↘ 2 221 7133; f 2 221 8401

South Africa
There are six British Airways travel clinics in South Africa, including *Johannesburg* ↘ 011 807 3132; *Cape Town* ↘ 021 419 3172; *Durban* ↘ 031 303 2423; *Knysna* ↘ 044 382 6366; *East London* ↘ 043 743 7471; *Port Elizabeth* ↘ 041 374 7471
TMVC (Travel Doctor Group) 113 DF Malan Dr, Roosevelt Park, Johannesburg; ↘ 011 888 7488. Consult www.tmvc.com.au for addresses of other clinics in South Africa.

Switzerland
IAMAT (International Association for Medical Assistance to Travellers) 57 Voirets, 1212 Grand Lancy, Geneva; web: www.sentex.net/~iamat

DISEASES
Diarrhoea and related illnesses
Diarrhoea affects at least half of those who travel in the tropics. The best solution is to rest up for a day, and to stop eating your normal diet, avoid alcohol, and take lots of clear fluids. If you are hungry take bland light food such as plain biscuits, boiled rice or boiled potatoes. The bacteria responsible for most diarrhoea and related symptoms (such as the abdominal pains caused by the stomach trying to expel bad food) will normally die within 36 hours if deprived of food.

Blockers such as Imodium, Lomotil and codeine phosphate should only be taken if you have no access to sanitation, for instance if you have to travel by bus. This is because blockers generally keep the poisons in your system, and so make you feel unwell for longer. They are sometimes useful if bowel cramps persist for more than 48 hours, as can be the case with salmonella poisoning. On the other hand, it is dangerous to take blockers with dysentery (evidenced by blood, slime or fever with the diarrhoea). Really, if diarrhoea or related symptoms persist much beyond 36 hours, the sensible thing to do is consult a doctor or pharmacist. The chances are you have nothing serious, but you could well have something like giardia, which can persist until it is treated (see below).

When you have diarrhoea, it is important you drink a lot. Oral rehydration salts (ORS) such as Dioralyte, Electrolade and Rehidrat are excellent, or you can make your own salt and sugar rehydration fluid. If you are vomiting you can still absorb sipped fluids, and ORS is better than most. Sip the drink slowly and avoid anything that is very hot or cold. Try to drink a glass of rehydration fluid every time your bowels open. If you are not eating, you need to drink around three litres of fluid daily in a temperate climate; more if it is hot, you are at a high altitude, or you have a fever or diarrhoea. If you are vomiting, do not worry about the quantity you produce – it is never as much as it looks. Dehydration is the only serious complication of diarrhoea and vomiting; provided you keep sipping slowly you will replace sufficient lost fluids, even if you have cholera.

In Ethiopia, diarrhoea that persists beyond 48 hours could be giardia, a protozoan infection that, in addition to diarrhoea, often causes severe flatulence, abdominal distension and sulphurous belching. Giardia is common in Ethiopia and, although it is not a serious illness, it is unpleasant enough that you will want treatment as quickly as possible. Visit a laboratory for a stool test. Giardia is usually rapidly cured, and appropriate medication is readily available in Ethiopia. You shouldn't touch alcohol while on medication for giardia.

If you have diarrhoea with blood or you have a fever, see a doctor for a stool test. You should seek medical advice as soon as possible as it is very likely that you will need antibiotics and the sooner they are started the better. Chronic diarrhoea will make it practically impossible to travel anywhere, and if nothing else, seeing a doctor will ease your mind.

How to avoid diarrhoea and other food- and water-borne diseases

There are a great many myths about how diarrhoea is acquired, but most travellers become sick from contaminated food. Salads, especially lettuce, are always a likely source of diarrhoea. Food which is freshly cooked or thoroughly reheated should be safe, and sizzling hot street foods are invariably safer than those served at buffets at expensive hotels. Ice cream is an ideal medium for bacterial cultures and it is often not kept adequately frozen due to power cuts. Ice may be made with unboiled water, and it could have been deposited on the roadside on its journey from the ice factory.

In any Third World country, you'll hear all sorts of contradictory information about the safety of drinking tap water. In Ethiopia, I would tend to assume that all tap water is unsafe to drink, except perhaps in Addis Ababa. The best way to purify water is by boiling it: simply bringing it to the boil kills 99% of bugs, and keeping it on the boil for a further minute kills everything at altitudes of below roughly 4,500m (which is everywhere in Ethiopia). Boiling water is more effective than using iodine, which is in turn more effective than any chlorine-based water purification tablet. Cheap bottled mineral water is available throughout Ethiopia, and as far as I am aware it is perfectly safe to drink. In my opinion, you're best sticking to bottled mineral water and avoiding tap water altogether.

Malaria

Malaria kills about a million Africans every year. Of the travellers who return to Britain with malaria, 92% have caught it in Africa. You are 100 times more likely to catch malaria in Africa than you are in Asia. In most African countries, visitors are urged to take malaria tablets as a matter of course. The situation in Ethiopia is less clear-cut, and is dependent on which parts of the country you intend to visit, and at what time of year you will be there. Malaria is present in most parts of tropical Africa below around 2,000m, and the *Anopheles* mosquito which transmits the malaria parasite is most abundant near the marshes and still water in which it breeds. In other words, malaria is most prevalent in low-lying areas where there is water, and especially after rain.

Malaria is absent from most parts of the Ethiopian Plateau, for instance the Bale Highlands, the central highlands around Addis Ababa, and the western highlands around Jimma. It is not prevalent at most points along the northern historical circuit, the one notable exception being Bahir Dar and elsewhere on the shore of Lake Tana, which lies at 1,830m and is increasingly subject to outbreaks of the disease, particularly during the rainy season – though the risk of contracting it is slight by comparison with many popular safari destinations in east and southern Africa.

In the Rift Valley, malaria is generally seasonal, with spasmodic and localised outbreaks taking place during the rainy season. The severity of these outbreaks varies greatly from year to year and place to place, and usually they are well publicised by word of mouth because most residents of the Ethiopian Highlands have as little resistance to malaria as do Europeans. Nevertheless, it is safest to assume that an element of risk exists throughout the Rift Valley (which includes Dire Dawa, Awash National Park, Adama, the Rift Valley Lakes, Arba Minch and Moyale) during the rains, even though the incidence of malaria is rarely comparable to that in many parts of east Africa. The same applies to other relatively dry low-lying areas, such as those east and south of the Bale Mountains. The two areas of Ethiopia that are most likely to be visited by tourists and where malaria is a definite year-round threat are the Omo Valley (Omo and Mago national parks) and the western lowlands around Gambella.

So do you take malaria pills or not? Definitely, if you are visiting a high-risk area like the Omo Valley or Gambella at any time of year, or if you are travelling in the Rift Valley during the wet season. On the other hand, if your travels will be restricted to highland areas, or you visit in the dry season and avoid high-risk areas, there is a case for not taking them. Having said that, it can be argued that even the slight risk present in some parts of the country is justification for taking all possible precautions. A visitor to Ethiopia who does not regularly visit the tropics would probably be wiser to err on the side of caution and to take malaria tablets. If you opt not to take tablets, you should be doubly aware of any symptoms that might be malarial, and take extra care to avoiding being bitten by mosquitoes (see pages 129–30).

Mefloquine (Lariam) is the most effective prophylactic agent for Ethiopia but is not suitable for everyone, so should only be taken on a doctor's recommendation. If this drug is suggested, then start two and a half weeks before departure to check it suits you. Stop immediately if it seems to cause depression or anxiety, visual or hearing disturbances, severe headaches or changes in heart rhythm. Anyone who is pregnant, has been treated for depression or psychiatric problems, has diabetes controlled by oral therapy, who is epileptic (or who has suffered fits in the past), or has a close blood relative who is epileptic, should not take Mefloquine. Malarone (paudrine and atovaquone) is now considered to be as effective as Lariam. It has the advantage of having relatively few side effects and need only be started one to two days before entering a malarial area, whilst you are there and for seven days after. Although expensive, it is ideal for short stays, as you are more likely to complete the course. Paediatric Malarone is also available and is based on body weight (in kgs). If your child is below 40kg then they will need this formulation. In the UK Malarone has been licensed for use for up to three months.

Doxycycline (100mg daily) is a good alternative if Mefloquine is unsuitable or Malarone is too expensive and need only be started one to two days before arrival in a malarial region. Like Lariam and Malarone it can only be obtained from a doctor. There is a possibility of allergic skin reactions developing in sunlight in approximately 1-3% of people. If this happens the drug should be stopped. Women using the oral contraceptive should use additional protection for the first four weeks.

Chloroquine (Nivaquine or Avloclor) two-weekly and proguanil (Paludrine) two-daily are now considered to be the least effective. They should only be used if there is no suitable alternative.

All prophylactic agents should be taken after or with the evening meal, washed down with plenty of fluids and, with the exception of Malarone, continued for four weeks after leaving the last malarial area. Be aware, however, that resistance patterns and thus the effectiveness of particular drugs are prone to change. Your GP may not be aware of new developments, so you are advised to consult a travel clinic for current advice, or phone 020 7636 7921 for recorded information.

Equally important as taking malaria pills is making every reasonable effort not to be bitten by mosquitoes. Many travellers assume that simply taking pills gives them full protection against malaria. It doesn't. It stuns me how many travellers and even expatriates wander around at night in shorts and flip-flops in parts of Africa where malaria is endemic. The fact is that drug resistance is widespread in Africa, and the most certain way to avoid malaria is to not be bitten by mosquitoes. This doesn't mean that avoiding bites is an alternative to taking pills – nobody will be able to prevent every potential bite – but that you should do both.

Even if you take your malaria tablets meticulously and are careful to avoid being bitten, you might still contract malaria. If you experience headaches, or even a general sense of disorientation or flu-like aches and pains, you may have malaria. However, the only consistent symptom is a high temperature (38° or more). It is vital you seek medical advice immediately. Local doctors see malaria all the time; they will know it in all its guises and know the best treatment for local resistance patterns. Untreated malaria can rapidly be fatal, but even prophylactic-resistant strains normally respond well to treatment, provided that you do not leave it too late.

If you are unable to reach a doctor, you may have to treat yourself. For this reason, it is advisable to carry a cure in your medical kit. Malarone is considered the safest and most effective treatment for malaria in Africa. Once again, this could change, so seek advice from a travel clinic before you leave for Ethiopia.

Malaria typically takes from one week to three months to develop but it can take as long as a year if you are taking prophylactic medication. This means that you may only display symptoms after you leave Ethiopia; you are advised to continue with prophylactics for at least four weeks after returning home (except for Malarone, which need only be continued for seven days). It is all too easy to forget your pills once you are in the everyday routine of life at home, but you should make every effort to remember. If you display symptoms which could possibly be malarial, even if this happens a year after you return home, get to a doctor and be sure to mention that you have been exposed to malaria.

Finally, if you have a fever and the malaria test is negative (though this does not exclude malaria), you may have typhoid, which should also receive immediate treatment. Where typhoid testing is unavailable, a routine blood test can give a strong indication of this disease.

Bilharzia or schistosomiasis

This is carried by a worm which spends part of its life inside freshwater snails, and infects people when they swim or paddle in still or slow-moving, well-oxygenated, well-vegetated fresh water. The first symptom of infection is an itchy patch where the worm entered your skin, then perhaps, a fortnight later, fever and other vague symptoms of being unwell. Much later, you may notice blood in the urine or motions if you have a heavy infestation. Although there is a very good cure for bilharzia, drug resistance is emerging. It is wise to avoid infection. A blood test performed six weeks or more after leaving an area of risk will establish whether you have been infected.

As a rule, a fast-flowing mountain stream is very low risk, while a sluggish river or lake is high risk. If you dry off promptly after spending ten minutes or less in the water, the parasite does not have time to penetrate your skin and so cannot infect you.

AIDS and venereal disease

HIV and other venereal diseases are widespread in Ethiopia, and the high level of prostitution suggests this pattern will continue. The risks involved in having unprotected sex, particularly with a prostitute, barely need stating. Condoms and femidoms offer a high level of protection against HIV and other venereal diseases, and spermicides and spermicidal pessaries also reduce the risk of transmission.

Hospital workers in Ethiopia deal with AIDS victims on a regular basis. Contrary to Western prejudices, they do realise the danger involved in using non-sterilised needles, and the likelihood of being confronted with one in a town hospital or clinic is low. If, however, you need treatment in a really remote area, where supplies might be a problem, you may be glad to be carrying a needle in your medical kit. Blood transfusions can also transmit the disease.

Meningitis

This is a particularly nasty disease as it can kill within hours of the first symptoms appearing. The telltale symptom is the combination of a blinding headache and usually a fever. A vaccination protects against the common and serious bacterial form in Africa, but not against all of the many kinds of meningitis. Local papers normally report localised outbreaks. If you show symptoms, get to a doctor immediately.

Rabies and animal bites

Rabies is carried by all mammals – beware the village dogs and small monkeys that are used to being fed in the parks – and is passed on to humans through a bite, a scratch, or a lick of an open wound. You must always assume any animal is rabid (unless personally known to you) and seek medical help as soon as possible. In the interim, scrub the wound with soap and bottled or boiled water, then pour on a strong iodine or alcohol solution. This helps stop the rabies virus entering the body and will guard against wound infections, including tetanus. If you intend to have contact with animals and/or are likely to be more than 24 hours away from medical help, then vaccination is advised. Ideally, three pre-exposure doses should be taken over three weeks. If you are bitten by any animal, treatment should be given as soon as possible, but it is never too late to seek help as the incubation period for rabies can be very long. Tell the doctors if you have had pre-exposure vaccine. Remember, if you contract rabies the mortality rate is 100% and death from rabies is probably one of the worst ways to go!

Tetanus

Tetanus is caught through deep, dirty wounds, so ensure that any wounds are thoroughly cleaned. Immunisation gives good protection for ten years, provided you do not have an overwhelming number of tetanus bacteria on board. Keep immunised and be sensible about first-aid.

MEDICAL FACILITIES

Most doctors speak good English and are very helpful. In larger towns there are hospitals where outpatients can be treated and there are basic laboratory facilities for blood and stool tests. Where there is no hospital or clinic, or you can't find a doctor, pharmacists generally speak good English and are often experienced diagnosticians (most Ethiopians consult pharmacists rather than doctors), and they will be able to tell you where laboratory facilities can be found. In Addis, the clinic opposite the Gandhi Hospital has an excellent laboratory.

Medication, consultations and tests are all very cheap when compared with Western countries – outside of Addis Ababa, a consultation, blood or stool test and medication are unlikely to set you back more than US$5 - so for goodness' sake don't let your budget put you off visiting a doctor.

INSECTS

Even if you are taking malaria tablets, you should take steps to avoid being bitten by insects and by mosquitoes in particular. The most imperative reason for doing so is the increasing levels of resistance to preventative drugs. Whatever pills you take, there remains a significant risk of being infected by malaria in areas below 1,800m. Of much less concern, but still a risk, are several other mosquito-borne viral fevers which either are, or else might be, present in low- and medium-altitude parts of Ethiopia. Dengue, the only one of these diseases that is anything close to being common, is very nasty with symptoms that include severe muscle cramps, high fever and a measles-like rash; fatalities are exceptional but medical help should be sought. The other diseases in this category are too rare to be a cause for serious concern; nevertheless, they are difficult to treat, and some of them are potentially fatal. It is not only mosquitoes that might carry nasty diseases; leishmania, another difficult-to-treat disease, is spread by sandfly bites. Before you panic, it should be stressed that all these diseases, other than malaria, are most unlikely to be caught by travellers. I mention them mainly to illustrate that malaria pills on their own do not guarantee your safety against serious insect-borne diseases.

The *Anopheles* mosquito which spreads malaria emerges at dusk, as do sandflies and most other disease-carrying mosquitoes. The exception to this is the Aedes mosquito carrying dengue fever, which flies during the day, so use insect repellents (see below) during the day time if you see any mosquitoes around. After dusk you will greatly reduce your chances of being bitten and contracting other insect-borne diseases if you wear long trousers and socks in the evening and cover exposed parts of your body with insect repellent, preferably a DEET-based preparation such as Repel. Sprays of this sort are not available in Ethiopia; bring one with you.

The *Anopheles* mosquito hunts mostly at ground level and it can bite through thin socks, so it is worth putting repellent on your ankles, even if they are covered. DEET-impregnated ankle-bands (marketed by MASTA at the London School of Hygiene and Tropical Medicine) are also quite effective, though they may get you some funny looks. When walking in scrub and forest areas, you should cover and spray yourself by day as well; the *Aedes* mosquito which spreads dengue is a day-biter. Solid shoes, socks and trousers will, in any case, protect you against snakes, sharp thorns, ticks, and harmless but irritating biters like midges.

Like many insects, mosquitoes are drawn to direct light. If you are camping, never put a lamp near the opening of your tent, or you will have a swarm of mosquitoes and other insects waiting to join you when you retire. In hotel rooms, be aware that the longer you leave on your light, the greater the number of insects with which you are likely to share your accommodation.

Once you are in bed, the most effective form of protection against mosquitoes is an impregnated net. Basically though, once you're in Ethiopia, your only option is Mobil Insecticide Spray, which is for spraying rooms (not your body) and is available throughout the country. Far better, though, is to carry your own permethrin-impregnated net, which will protect you against everything (these are available in BA Travel Clinics, Trailfinders, MASTA and from good camping shops such as Blacks).

To balance the warnings, a reminder that in most parts of the Ethiopian Highlands you are unlikely to even encounter a mosquito, and that disease-carrying sandflies are only really likely to be found in rural villages. It should be stressed, too, that the overwhelming majority of insects don't bite people, and of those that do, most are entirely harmless – rather fortunate, as cheap hotels in Ethiopia tend to approach menagerie status on the insect front. Mattresses quite often contain bedbugs and fleas, which drive some people crazy, but they are both essentially harmless.

As much to guarantee a good night's sleep as anything, it's worth getting into the habit of spraying your room with insecticide before you retire. If bedbugs become a nuisance, a sleeping mat will insulate you from them. Best of all, bring an enclosed sleeping net, such as the ones put out by Long Road in the USA ($510 450 4763$), which will eliminate all nocturnal insect problems.

Flies are locally abundant in Ethiopia, particularly during and immediately after the rains, and Lalibela deserves some sort of award in this direction! Ultimately, there's not a lot you can do about flies – though I noticed they liked me most when I was sweaty, and least when I was freshly showered. You get used to them.

OUTDOOR HEALTH
Sun and heat
The equatorial sun is vicious. Although it is impossible to avoid some exposure to the sun, it would be foolish to sunbathe needlessly. Tanning ages your skin and it can cause skin cancer. If you are coming to Ethiopia from a less harsh climate, let your body get used to the sunlight gradually or you will end up with sunburn. Take things too far, and sunstroke – a potentially fatal condition – may be the result. Wear sunscreen and build up your exposure gradually, starting with no more than 20 minutes a day. Avoid exposing yourself for more than two hours in any day, and stay out of the sun between noon and 15.00.

Always wear clothes made from natural fabrics such as 100% cotton. These help prevent fungal infections and other rashes. Athletes' foot is prevalent, so wear thongs in communal showers.

Even small cuts are inclined to go septic in the tropics. Clean any lesion with a dilute solution of potassium permanganate or iodine two to three times daily. Antiseptic creams are not suitable for the tropics; wounds must be kept dry and covered.

Dangerous animals
There are very few parts of Ethiopia where you are likely to come into contact with potentially dangerous large mammals. Elephant, buffalo and black rhinoceros – the most dangerous of Africa's terrestrial herbivores – are practically restricted to the Omo Valley and remote border areas.

The large mammal that you need most concern yourself with is the hippopotamus, which is reportedly responsible for more human deaths than any other African mammal. This is not because it is especially aggressive, but because its response to any disturbance while it is grazing is to head directly for the safety of water, and it will trample anything that gets in its way. You should be cautious around any lake or large river unless you know for a fact that hippos are not present. Hippos are most likely to be out grazing towards dusk, in the early morning, and in overcast weather. The danger is getting between a hippo and the water – it would be most unlikely to attack you if it perceived a clear path to safety – so the risk is greater the closer you are to the shore. You should never walk in reed-beds unless you are certain that no hippos are present. On the other hand, you have little to fear on land by approaching a hippo that is already in the water.

Another animal you should watch out for near water is the crocodile, though only a very large croc is likely to attack a person, and then only if you are actually in the water or standing right on the shore. Anywhere near a town or village, you can be fairly sure that potential man-eaters will have been disposed of by their potential prey, so the risk is greatest in water away from human habitation.

There are campsites in Africa where vervet monkeys and baboons have become dangerous pests. We are not aware of any such place in Ethiopia, but it could happen. It is worth mentioning that feeding these animals is highly irresponsible; not only does it encourage them to scavenge, but – if the animals become bold to the point where they are potentially dangerous – it may lead to their being shot. If you join a guided tour where the driver or guide feeds baboons for your amusement, I would ask him not to. Finally, while vervet monkeys are too small to progress much beyond being a nuisance, baboons are very dangerous and have often killed children and maimed adults with their vicious teeth. Do not tease or underestimate them. If primates are hanging around a campsite, and you wander off leaving fruit in your tent, don't expect it still to be standing when you return.

The dangers associated with large predators are often exaggerated. Most large predators will stay well clear of humans, and they are more likely to kill through accident or self-defence than design. Lions are arguably the one exception, but it is still very rare

DUST!
From a letter by Arthur Gerfers

I found it interesting that in a land as dry and dusty as Ethiopia, you make no mention of the one thing that made me sick during my seven weeks in the country: dust!

The houses in Ethiopia are made of dust, the roads are made of dust, the churches are full of dust, and the air is heavily charged with millions of particles. I don't think the hazards of dust can be overemphasised. Mine is a case in point. I paid no attention to the layers of red dust building up on my trousers during endless days of travel on Ethiopian buses. If it doesn't disturb the locals, why should it disturb me? I was careful to avoid getting that gritty feeling in my teeth, but it never occurred to me to cover my nose and mouth. On the three-day journey from Lalibela to Gonder the dust began to weigh heavily in my lungs. It was especially unfortunate that the seat we had chosen on the third day was positioned over a very porous wheel well. Dust flew in through the cracks in the floor, through the open windows, through the door and the air vent in the roof. Beams of sunlight caught the small red granules in the air darting about like as many atoms. It became difficult to breathe, as I began to register the state of my dust-clogged lungs after a good week of dusty travel.

I had great trouble breathing by the time we reached Gonder and my wheezing was worrying my travelling companion. Keen to indulge ourselves for a few bus-free, dust-free days, we set off in search of a place offering suitable comfort. The Fogera Hotel seemed the best option. Now you know it is a bit of a hike from the bus station and then there's the uphill bit before you reach that cul-de-sac where the hotel is. About halfway through I felt like my lungs would burst my ribcage under the strain of my backpack! Being someone who has never had asthma or any other respiratory illnesses I was feeling quite a bit panicky. My snot came out reddish brown when I blew my nose and I couldn't stop coughing once I started. Four solid days I spent convalescing in Fogera's gardens. Though I was very glad to be away from the 'you' contingents and the 'faranji' choirs, I felt lame and cheated by this pesky airborne soil. Even afterward, while strolling through town, the smell of dust made me sick to my stomach. It took a couple of weeks before I felt normal again.

From then on, I was very careful to tie a bandana around my nose and mouth during long dusty journeys. And though I may have looked like some Wild West train robber to the average European, my example was followed by a surprising number of locals; plus, most important of all, I never got sick again. Dust, especially on long, cramped bus rides, deserves attention, just as much as diarrhoea or dangerous animals any day!

for a lion to attack a person without cause and, in Ethiopia, lions are too thinly distributed to be a cause for concern, except perhaps in the Omo region. Leopards are more widespread but they are only likely to attack people if they are cornered. Cheetahs never attack people. Spotted hyenas are common in Ethiopia, they are frequently associated with human settlements and they are potentially very dangerous. Fortunately, they are also cowardly in their dealings with humans. A slight but real danger if you sleep in the bush without a tent is that a passing hyena might investigate a hairy object sticking out of a sleeping bag and decapitate you through predatory curiosity. If you are in an area where large predators are still reasonably common, sleeping in a sealed tent practically guarantees your safety – unless you do something daft like put meat in your tent.

Above Sanetti Plateau, Bale
Mountains National Park (AVZ)

Left Simien wolf (AVZ)

Below Flamingos, Lake Abiata,
Abiata-Shala National Park (AVZ)

Above Traditional fishing, Gambella (AVZ)

Left Priest at Pantaleon Monastery on outskirts of Axum (JC)

Below Debre Birhan Selassie Church, Gonder (AVZ)

Snakebites

Although poisonous snakes are present throughout Ethiopia, they pose little real threat to humans. The reason for this is that most snakes are very shy and secretive, and will move off at the slightest sign of human activity. The one place where you should be conscious of the possible presence of snakes is on rocky slopes and cliffs, particularly where you are scrambling up or down using your hands. This is because snakes respond to seismic vibrations – in most habitats they will sense your footsteps and slither away long before you get near them, but they may not on a rocky slope. You also have a greater danger of cornering a snake, or being unable to get away yourself, in a steep rocky habitat. Finally, rocky areas are the favoured dwelling place of Africa's most dangerous snake, the puff adder. The danger with puff adders is that they are unusually slothful, and the one species of venomous snake that doesn't generally move off in response to human foot-treads.

As a general rule, you should wear trousers, socks and solid boots when you walk in the bush. Good boots will protect against the 50% of snake bites that occur below the ankle; trousers will help to deflect bites higher up on the leg. If you see a snake, wait to let it pass. If it rises to strike, the common advice is to stand dead still – snakes strike in response to movement. All well and good, but on the one occasion where a snake reared at this author, and twice when he has been with someone whom this happened to, instinct won over logic and the person concerned retreated as quickly as possible in the opposite direction. This tactic worked perfectly well.

If the worst should happen, don't panic. Most snakes are non-venomous; venom is only dispensed in about 50% of bites by venomous snakes, and it is uncommon for a bite to contain enough venom to kill an adult. The chances are that the person will not come to any harm. Keep the victim still and calm; wash the wound with soap then wipe it gently away from the bite with a clean cloth to remove any venom from the skin surface. Remove rings, bangles or watches in anticipation of swelling. If possible, splint the bitten limb – movement quickens the rate of venom absorption. The victim should then be taken to a doctor or hospital. If it is possible to catch the snake *without risk*, do so and take it with you, ever conscious of the fact that a decapitated head can still envenomate. The victim will then be kept under observation. Antivenin should only be administered by someone who knows what they are doing if and when signs of envenomation occur. Meanwhile:

DO NOT give alcohol or aspirin. Paracetamol is safe.
DO NOT cut, incise or suck the wound.
DO NOT apply potassium permanganate.
DO keep the bitten part *below* heart height.

DISABLED TRAVEL

Bradt Travel Guides holds extensive notes by Gordon Rattray offering advice for wheelchair travellers in Ethiopia. If you would like a copy, please contact Bradt on info@bradtguides.com.

KEY TO STANDARD SYMBOLS — Bradt

—·—·—	International boundary	✚	Hospital/clinic
------	Province/region	✚	Health centre/pharmacy
■	Capital city	⌂	Hotel/inn etc
●	Main town/city	▲	Campsite
○	Small town/village	▲	Hut, shelter etc
✈	Airport (international)	ℹ	Tourist information
✈	Airport (other)	✝	Cathedral/church
═══	Railway	ℭ	Mosque
☐	Railway station	☗	Museum/art gallery
═══	Main road (paved)	⊞	Historic building
═══	Main road (dual)	⛫	Castle/fortress
═══	Main road	╲	City wall etc
═══	Other road	♪	Telecommunication centre
======	Track (4x4)	☺	Theatre/cinema
🚐	Bus station etc	🏃	Stadium
⛴	Ferry	✗	Restaurant
-------	Ferry route	♀	Bar/pub
⊶⊷	Road distance pins	☆	Night club/casino
⊶12.C-D⊷	Distance (km between pins) Road categories (A–F)	@	Internet access
1 km	Distance between interrupted road cases	$	Bank
National park	National park	❀	Botanical garden/site
	Urban park (town plans)	●	Other place of interest
	Swamp/marsh	▲	Summit (height in metres)
	Market area (town plans)	☀	Scenic viewpoint
	Bridge	∴	Ancient/archaeological site
	River (town plans)	○	Hot spring/spring
	Normally dry watercourse (town plans)	⌇	Waterfall
Ⓟ	Car park	♧	Specific woodland feature
⛽	Petrol station/garage	◉	Outpost
✉	Post office	-------	Featured walk/hike/trek
Ⓔ	Embassy	-------	Other walk/hike/trek

The size of some symbols may vary to suit an individual context.
Other map symbols may be shown. These may be explained in key boxes on individual maps.

Part Two

Addis Ababa

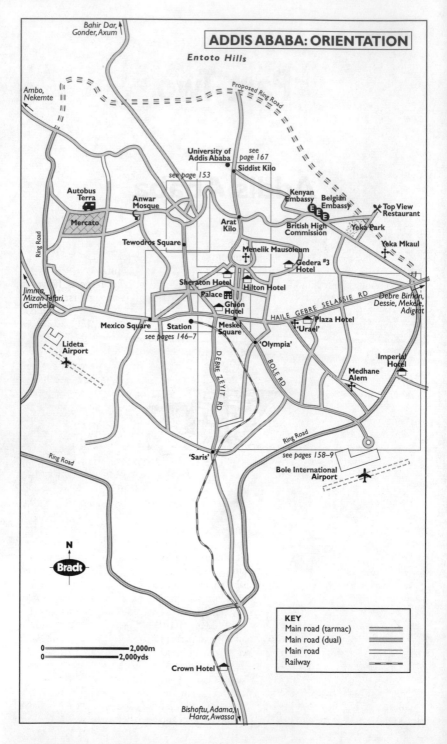

ADDIS ABABA: ORIENTATION

Entoto Hills

Bahir Dar,
Gonder, Axum

Proposed Ring Road

Ambo,
Nekemte

University of
Addis Ababa

*see
page 167*

Siddist Kilo

see page 153

Autobus
Terra

Anwar
Mosque

Kenyan
Embassy

Belgian
Embassy

Top View
Restaurant

Mercato

British High
Commission

Yeka Park

Arat
Kilo

Tewodros Square

Yeka Mkaul

Ring Road

Menelik Mausoleum

Gedera #3
Hotel

Sheraton Hotel

Hilton Hotel

Jimma,
Mizan Tefari,
Gambella

Palace

Debre Birhan,
Dessie, Mekele,
Adigrat

Ghion
Hotel

HAILE GEBRE SELASSIE RD

Mexico Square

Station

Meskel
Square

Plaza Hotel

see pages 146–7

'Urael'

Lideta
Airport

'Olympia'

Imperial
Hotel

DEBRE ZEYIT RD

BOLE RD

Medhane
Alem

Ring Road

'Saris'

see pages 158–9

Ring Road

Bole International
Airport

N

Bradt

0 ———— 2,000m
0 ———— 2,000yds

Crown Hotel

KEY
Main road (tarmac)
Main road (dual)
Main road
Railway

Bishoftu, Adama,
Harar, Awassa

Addis Ababa 8

The world's third highest capital city, Addis Ababa (which somewhat improbably means 'New Flower', and is often shortened to plain 'Addis') lies in the central highlands of Ethiopia at an altitude of 2,400m. Climatically, this large city is a highly encouraging introduction to Ethiopia: characterised, throughout the year, both day and night, by comfortable temperate weather, interrupted by the occasional torrential downpour, Addis Ababa will swiftly dispel any lingering preconceptions about Ethiopia being a searing desert. In most other respects, however, Addis Ababa and its three million residents can be rather overwhelming on first exposure, with beggars, cripples, taxi drivers and hawkers clamouring for your attention, and con artists and pickpockets doing their utmost to divert it. Visitors on organised tours will be reasonably sheltered from Addis's more bombastic elements, but independent travellers who haven't visited a large Third World city before – and, indeed, many who have – are likely to end their first day in Addis Ababa feeling somewhat besieged. A not unreasonable response to Addis Ababa would be to move on as swiftly as possible. Certainly, those who touchdown at Bole Airport in the morning or early afternoon could easily bus straight on to somewhere like Bishoftu or Adama, and save prolonged confrontation with the capital for a later date.

Like most African cities, Addis does tend to grow on you. When I researched the first edition of this guide, I found it difficult to reconcile the notes I made after my first day in Addis with the city I eventually came to know and, if not exactly love, then certainly like and enjoy. It's difficult to pinpoint any single reason for this. One factor, particularly for those who travel rough, is that the capital's relatively Westernised facilities look a lot more inviting after a week or two bussing through the sticks than they do coming directly from Europe or wherever. Another is that Addis Ababa's less savoury elements – the pickpockets, con artists and bogus students – are far more easily handled and deflected once one has become attuned to Ethiopia more generally. Eventually, sadly, the visitor will even become somewhat if not entirely numbed to Addis's shocking parade of polio cripples, amputee war veterans, ragged street children, naked beggars and ranting loonies. More than anything, though, Addis Ababa grows on the visitor because it is all bark and very little bite. For all the hustlers and opportunistic thieves, the show-off teenagers who gratuitously yell 'Fuck off' at travellers and make lewd propositions to single females, the actual threat to one's personal safety is negligible. I'd feel safer spending a month in downtown Addis Ababa than I would an hour in parts of Nairobi or Johannesburg – or parts of many Western capitals. And beneath the grotesquery and poverty there lies the infectious spirit that is characteristic of Ethiopia. Addis Ababa is a busy, bustling, exciting city; the hassle that one might occasionally receive comes from only a tiny fraction of its predominantly friendly population – don't let first impressions put you off.

Short-stay visitors to Ethiopia often see little more of the capital than a few blurred street scenes as they are whisked from airport to hotel and back before flying to the more noteworthy historical sights of the north. But travellers with more time on their hands will find it worth making the effort to like Addis Ababa. This is a city with a real buzz, one possessed of a sense of self-definition and place lacking entirely from the many African capitals whose governments have attempted – and largely failed – to create misplaced pockets of Western urbanity in otherwise under-developed nations. Perhaps the highest praise one can direct at this chaotic, contradictory and compelling city is this: Addis Ababa *does* feel exactly as the Ethiopian capital *should* feel – singularly and unmistakably Ethiopian.

Moreover, Addis Ababa is also one of the few African cities whose environs offer a wide variety of exceptional sightseeing. Although it is a relatively modern city, founded by Emperor Menelik II in 1887, the surrounding Entoto Hills have long been a major centre of Showan politics. Unconfirmed legend has it that the rulers of Axum fled to Entoto during the purgative reign of Queen Yodit, while the presence of two disused rock-hewn churches within 10km of the modern city centre highlights the strong medieval links between Entoto and the Zagwe capital of Lalibela. In addition to the above, there are several interesting museums in Addis, most notably the Ethnographic and National museums, respectively ranking with the best of their type in Africa. Further afield, but still within day-tripping distance of the capital, there is wonderful birdwatching and rambling in the Akaki Wetlands, lush highland forest rattling with birds and monkeys in the Menegasha, a field of seven crater lakes at Bishoftu, the atmospheric and historic monastery of Debre Libanos, and an extant rock-hewn church, fascinating prehistoric site, and field of medieval engraved stelae clustered along the Butajira road. Addis Ababa offers more than enough in the way of sightseeing and outings to keep a curious traveller going for a week, something you could not say of too many African capitals.

ORIENTATION

Addis Ababa is a large city, most of its streets are unsignposted, and many of its main roads and other landmarks have long gone by two or even three names, with the name shown on most maps differing from the one in common use. This confusing situation is further exacerbated by the recent decision to name 52 of the city's roads after each of the non-Ethiopian member states of the Organisation of African Unity (OAU), in response to a recent threat to relocate the OAU headquarters in Addis Ababa to another African city. All in all, then, Addis Ababa can be a bit confusing – so read through this with a map in hand before you start exploring. The names used in this guide mostly follow popular usage, not the official maps.

The **city centre** is more or less rectangular, defined by **Mexico Square** in the southwest, **Meskel Square** (also called Abiot and less often Revolution Square) in the southeast, the **Hilton Hotel** in the northeast and **Tewodros Square** in the northwest. The main thoroughfare through the city centre is **Churchill Avenue** (the southern end of which was recently renamed Gambia Road). This wide road runs downhill from north to south, starting at the area known as the Piazza and passing the immigration office, post office, main branch of the Commercial Bank of Ethiopia, National Theatre, Ras Hotel and telecommunications building, to terminate at the square in front of the **railway station**. The main thoroughfare from west to east is **Ras Mekonnen Avenue**, which runs from Mexico Square past the Adama bus station and railway station, where it intersects with Gambia Road. It then continues east past the stadium and Meskel Square to become **Haile Gebre Selassie Road** (until recently called the Asmara road), which leads east out of the city centre via Adwa Square (more commonly known as **Megenagna**) towards Debre Birhan, Mekele and Asmara.

Two important roads run south from Ras Mekonnen Avenue. The first lies immediately west of Meskel Square and leads out of town to most destinations in the south and west. Somewhat confusingly, it is marked on maps as Ras Baru Avenue but is more commonly referred to as the **Debre Zeyit Road**, the name that I will use in this chapter, even though the town formerly known as Debre Zeyit has now reverted to its original name of Bishoftu. Immediately east of Meskel Square, the road marked on most maps as Africa Avenue but more commonly referred to as **Bole Road** terminates at Bole International Airport, 5km out of town.

The area known as the **Piazza** lies immediately north of the city centre, from where it can be reached by heading uphill along Churchill Avenue with the City Hall clear in your sights. The Piazza is a loosely defined area, centred on **De Gaulle Square**, bounded by Adwa Avenue and the Taitu Hotel to the east, and by Kidus Giyorgis Church and the City Hall to the west. The Piazza is a busy shopping area, with a great many budget hotels and restaurants concentrated in the vicinity of **Adwa Avenue**.

Adwa Avenue arcs east of the Piazza to **Megabit Square**, a major four-way junction most commonly referred to as **Arat Kilo**. The road that runs north from Arat Kilo heads into the Entoto Hills via the National Museum, the University campus at Yekatit 12 Square (**Siddist Kilo**), and the US Embassy. The road running east from Arat Kilo, often referred to as the **Yeka road**, passes the British Embassy and Yeka Park before joining **Haile Gebre Selassie Road** at Adwa Square. The road running south from Arat Kilo passes the Menelik II Mausoleum, the mapping authority, the Hilton Hotel, the Palace and the UN building before it intersects with Ras Mekonnen Avenue at Meskel Square.

About 1km west of the Piazza, Addis Ketema or **Mercato** is a tight grid of streets centred on what is reputedly the largest market in Africa. On Habte Giyorgis Street, the main road that runs along the north of Mercato, is the **main bus station**, known as the Autobus Terra.

In mid 2005, the southern three-quarters of the new freeway-like **Ring Road** encircling Addis Ababa was operational, and generally very quick to get around, but it is not clear when the remainder of this road will be completed. For now, the Ring Road starts at Adwa Square (where the **Yeka road** and **Haile Gebre Selassie Road** intersect), then runs southward past the Imperial Hotel to Bole International Airport, before veering west towards the Debre Zeyit Road, and then cutting through the Kidus Yosef Cemetery as it runs southward parallel to the Debre Zeyit Road for about 3.5km. After crossing the Debre Zeyit Road, it then veers northwest to Ayer Tena on the Jimma road, before cutting northeast to an intersection with the Ambo road.

GETTING AROUND
An efficient network of minibuses services Addis Ababa's roads. Public transport starts running at around 05.00, and peters out at around 20.00–21.00. The minibuses are never crowded and there is no significant risk of theft. They are also very cheap (even a long ride, for instance from the Piazza to Bole Airport, costs around birr 2–3). Overcharging foreigners is not the custom – it has happened to me twice in hundreds of minibus rides.

The **main minibus stops** are opposite De Gaulle Square on the Piazza; at Arat Kilo; opposite the Autobus Terra near the Mercato; in front of the railway station; in front of and opposite the stadium on Ras Mekonnen Avenue; and on Churchill Avenue opposite the post office. There will generally be minibuses heading in every conceivable direction from any such stop, so it's worth knowing the calls for various destinations as well as landmarks that the conductors will recognise. If you spend only a day or two in Addis Ababa, familiarising yourself with this network may not be worth the effort, given that taxis are so cheap, but it's easy enough to figure out if you have the time.

One of the most useful **minibus routes** to travellers, described using landmarks favoured by conductors, runs between Bole Airport and the Piazza via Olympia, Meskel Square, the Ambassador Theatre and the post office. Other significant routes emanating from the Piazza run to the Mercato and the Autobus Terra, to Mexico Square via the post

MENELIK II'S 'NEW FLOWER'

Addis Ababa, officially founded in 1887, is not the only African city to have sprung up from nothing little more than a century ago, to grow into a modern metropolis of several million people. However, it owes its modern status as one of the five largest cities in sub-Saharan Africa to the unlikely combination of a grandfather's prophecy, an empress's whim, and the timely intervention of an Australian tree!

In the early 1880s, the King of Showa, the future Emperor Menelik II, abandoned his capital at Ankober in favour of the Entoto Hills. What inspired this is unclear, but the Entoto area had great historical significance to the Showan aristocracy before being occupied by the Oromo after the religious wars of the 16th century. It was Menelik's expansionist grandfather, King Sahle Selassie, who reclaimed the area for Showa, prophesying that his grandson would build a large house in the valley below Entoto, from which would grow a great city.

At the end of the cold rainy season of 1886, Menelik II and his royal entourage moved down from the chilly hilltops of Entoto, to set up camp around the hot springs known as Filwoha. The emperor's wife Taitu fell in love with natural hot baths and the abundance of mimosa trees, and suggested that her husband build her a house there. Menelik concurred, recognising this to be the site described in his grandfather's prophecy. The royal party soon retreated to the hilltop capital, but a house was built at Filwoha, and the emperor and his entourage returned to the site the Empress Taitu would christen Addis Ababa – New Flower – after the rains of 1887.

Although posterity has settled on 1887 as the year in which Addis Ababa became the capital if not of Ethiopia then of its future emperor, the shift to Filwoha was more gradual. Most of Menelik's correspondence prior to 1891 was despatched from Entoto, and it was 1889, months before his formal coronation as emperor, when he set about building a proper palace in the valley. Outsiders seem to have regarded the move from Entoto as folly. A French visitor in 1887 described the suggestion this site might one day house a great city as 'fantasy'. A decade later, European visitors felt the growing lack of firewood – now transported 20km from Menegasha – would force the new flower to die before reaching full bloom. Indeed, Menelik made tentative plans to relocate his capital some 50km west to a forested site he christened Addis Alem – New World – and have a palace constructed there. Bizarrely, it was a stand of eucalyptus trees planted by a foreign resident in 1894 that would save Addis Ababa. Spurred by his Swiss advisor Alfred Ilg, Menelik II noticed how rapidly these trees grew, and instead of shifting the capital he decided to import vast quantities of eucalyptus seedlings. The residents of the nascent city were initially unimpressed, above all by the smell of the exotic trees, but their phenomenal growth rate soon swept such delicacies aside.

The Addis Ababa of Menelik's time bore scant resemblance to the city it has become. The palace was impressive and well organised: a 3km² compound that enclosed 50 buildings, employed and housed some 8,000 people, and – courtesy of Ilg's engineering prowess – had piped water by 1894 and electricity by 1905. As early as 1894, Menelik II and Ilg were discussing plans to construct a railway to the French port of Djibouti. By 1897, the Saturday market – situated on the site of an older Oromo market not far from the modern Piazza below the recently completed Church of St George – attracted up to 50,000 people from the surrounding countryside.

For all that, Menelik's capital was essentially a compacted rural sprawl. Few modern buildings existed outside of the royal compound, and the population, according to one French visitor, stood at a mere 100,000 settled over an area of about 55km²! The account of Herbert Vivian, who arrived in the Ethiopian capital in 1900, is typical:

> I happened to turn around and ask one of my men, 'When on earth are we ever going to reach Addis Ababa?'
> 'But sah'b, here it is.'
> 'Where?'
> 'Here, we have already arrived.'
> I looked around incredulously, and saw nothing but a few summer huts and an occasional white tent, all very far from each other, scattered over a rough hilly basin at the foot of steep hills. I would scarcely believe that I was approaching a village. That this could be the capital of a great empire, the residence of the King of Kings, seemed monstrous and out of the question. 'Then, pray, where is Menelik's palace?' I asked with a sneer. The men pointed to the horizon, and I could just make out what seemed to be a fairly large homestead with a number of trees and huts crouching on the top of a hill.
> The capital is a camp rather than a town… To appreciate Addis Ababa it is necessary to realise that this strange capital covers some fifty square miles, and contains a very large population, which has never been counted. Streets there are none, and to go from one point of the town to the other you must simply bestride your mule and prepare to ride across country. Three quarters of an hour at least are necessary for a pilgrimage from the British Agency to the Palace, and as much again to the market. On either of these journeys you must cross three or four ravines with stony, precipitous banks and a torrent-bed full of slippery boulders.

Fifteen years later Menelik II was dead, but his capital had become, in the words of one contemporary visitor, a 'mushroom city'. Another 15 years on, Haile Selassie was enthroned as emperor, and Addis Ababa entered the modern era as the most populous settlement in Africa between Cairo and Johannesburg – some maintain it still is today.

And yet the city's rustic roots are evident to any visitor. In 1969, a Ministry of Information handbook to Ethiopia described the capital as

> a surprising mixture of the Near East, the Mediterranean and the Wild West. Donkeys jostle with diplomatic Cadillacs; camels loaded with charcoal plod up the hills behind 14-ton Italian diesel lorries; dignified country gentlemen in jodhpurs, topi and fly whisk have to stand on traffic crossings waiting for buses loaded with schoolchildren to pass. Young Ethiopian executives dash from meeting to meeting in cars against a backdrop of modern office blocks and corrugated iron roof huts. Shop girls wear national costume and out of small cafés comes the smell of frankincense and the twang of the masenko, one of Ethiopia's most ancient instruments.

True, Cadillacs and jodhpurs may have gone the way of Rubik's cube and bell-bottoms, and Addis Ababa's post-war office blocks aren't quite the gleaming icons of modernist architecture they might have been a few years after they were built. But, otherwise, it sounds an awful lot like Addis Ababa today.

office and Ras Hotel, and to Arat Kilo (where you can change minibus for Siddist Kilo or for Urael Junction on Haile Gebre Selassie Road) via Adwa Avenue. There are also minibuses between Bole Road and Mercato via Olympia, Meskel Square and Mexico Square; Ras Mekonnen Avenue opposite the stadium and Arat Kilo via Meskel Square and the Hilton Hotel; Ras Mekonnen Avenue and Saris (on the Debre Zeyit Road); Ras Mekonnen Road and Adwa Square (Meganagna) via Haile Gebre Selassie Road; and Arat Kilo and Siddist Kilo. People hop on and off minibuses the whole time; you'll rarely wait more than five minutes for a ride along any of these routes.

Buses also trundle around Addis. They are even cheaper than minibuses, but slower, less frequent, and often overcrowded. Buses also have a bad reputation for pickpockets and snatch thieves. You are strongly advised against using them.

Private **taxis** can be found at ranks in front of all the main government hotels, as well as at the airport, on Ras Mekonnen Avenue in front of the stadium, and at De Gaulle Square on the Piazza. Taxis are very inexpensive by international standards, even at the inflated rates generally asked of foreigners, and are even cheaper if you are prepared to bargain.

GETTING THERE AND AWAY
By air
Most visitors will first arrive in Addis by air. **Bole International Airport** is only 5km from the city centre and **taxis** can be hired at a kiosk in the airport building. Fares are fixed and very reasonable – around birr 30–40 depending on which part of the city you are heading for. Private taxis can be hired outside the airport, and will be cheaper provided you negotiate, but this saving should be balanced against the added exposure of your luggage to theft. The risk is minimal, but perhaps not worth it at this early point in your holiday! If your flight arrives very late at night, it is advisable to book a hotel room in advance or failing that to stay at the airport until sunrise.

Minibuses do run between the airport and city centre at a fare of around birr 2 (US$0.25). These will generally follow Bole Road to Meskel Square, and then veer up Ras Desta Damtew Road past the Ambassador Theatre to the post office, from where they will follow Churchill Avenue to De Gaulle Square on the Piazza. In most African cities I would advise against using public transport as soon as you arrive. In Addis, however, it is difficult to see a real objection to doing this; no significant risk of theft is attached to using minibuses and usually there will be room for your luggage. Having said that, you're unlikely to be very alert after a long flight, for which reason I would consider using a minibus only if you are heading to a hotel along the route described above. You really don't want to be plonked down in the city centre and have to take another minibus or walk to your hotel, and quite possibly get lost, all just to save a few dollars.

Ethiopian Airlines' **domestic flights** also leave from Bole International Airport.

By bus
The two main bus stations in Addis are the Autobus Terra near Mercato and the smaller terminal near the railway station on Ras Mekonnen Avenue. Buses to Adama and Bishoftu leave from Ras Mekonnen Avenue; all other buses leave from the main Autobus Terra. There are minibuses between the Piazza and the city centre and the Autobus Terra, and between the Ras Mekonnen bus station and the Piazza. I never had a problem taking my luggage on minibuses – they're not crowded.

Note that there is some talk of closing down the central Autobus Terra and replacing it with five smaller bus stations, situated along each of the main exit routes from Addis Ababa. In other words, there would be one bus station on Haile Gebre Selassie Road for Debre Birhan, Dessie, Mekele and other destinations in the northeast; one along the Debre Zeyit Road for Adama, Awash, Harar, Dire Dawa, Awassa and other destinations in the Rift Valley; one along the Jimma road for Welkite, Jimma and other destinations southwest of the city; one along the Ambo road for Ambo, Nekemte and other western destinations; and one near Sheger Park for Fiche, Bahir Dar, Gonder and other destinations in the northwest. When this will happen is an open question, as is the exact location of the proposed new bus stations.

By rail
The railway station serves the line to Djibouti, which is mainly of interest if you are heading to Dire Dawa or Harar in the east of the country. For details of the rail service to Addis Ababa and Djibouti via Dire Dawa, see the box *The Djibouti Railway* on page 394.

WHERE TO STAY
One thing you don't need to worry about is finding a hotel room in Addis Ababa. There must be a thousand hotels scattered around the city. True, the vast majority of these are dollar-a-night dumps ill-suited to even the most cockroach-hardened of backpackers, but at every level above this the choices are manifold, and prices, as a rule, are a very reasonable reflection of quality. The world-class Addis Ababa Sheraton tops any list in terms of both price and quality, followed at a distant second by the more down-to-earth and affordable, but nevertheless international standard, Addis Ababa Hilton. Perhaps 50 hotels fall into the upmarket or moderate bracket, offering accommodation adequate to most tourists at prices ranging from US$20–100. Lower on the comfort rung is an even greater choice of decent budget hotels falling in the birr 80–160 (US$10–20) range, and shoestring hotels coming in at under birr 80 (US$10). The following listings are as exhaustive as time, space and common sense allows (most readers will, after all, stay in only one or at most two hotels in the capital), but there are doubtless further gems awaiting discovery.

International hotels (US$100+)
Addis Ababa Sheraton (290 rooms) Taitu St; ☎ 011 5171717; f 011 5172727; e reservationsaddisababa@luxurycollection.com. The top hotel in Addis Ababa, indeed anywhere in Ethiopia, is the plush and architecturally inspired Sheraton, which opened with a flourish in 1998 after long years of construction. Praised as one of the finest city hotels anywhere in Africa – a not unreasonable assessment in my opinion – the Sheraton is a world-class hostelry, and the feeling upon entering the lavish reception area is rather like stepping out of downtown Addis Ababa into a European capital. Several excellent restaurants can be found within the hotel, ranging from the relatively affordable Breezes Restaurant by the pool (fantastic light show at the fountain in the evening) to the wonderful but pricey East Indian Shaheen Restaurant. There is a nice piano bar near the entrance, a high-priced nightclub (birr 75 entrance), and a row of well-stocked shops, banks and travel agents. Rooms and service are immaculate. Prices reflect this high standard, ranging from US$240 for a straight en-suite dbl to US$2,800 for a chalet suite.
Addis Ababa Hilton (400 rooms) ☎ 011 5518400; f 011 5510064; e hilton.addis@ethionet.et. The only other international-quality hotel is the long standing and highly regarded Hilton, which lies in 15 acres of landscaped grounds close to the UN headquarters. The Hilton has all the facilities you would expect of an international-class hotel, including closed-circuit television, AC and minibars in the rooms, a thermal swimming pool, tennis courts, jacuzzi, sauna, and several highly rated restaurants. Full business services are available, as are conference facilities, and most of the rooms have undergone recent renovations. Room rates start at US$150 for an en-suite dbl.

Upmarket (approximately US$50–80)
Queen of Sheba Hotel (40 rooms) ☎ 011 6615400/6188282/6180000; f 011 6613174; e QueenShebaHotel@ethionet.et. Far better than either of the above is this newer hotel on Haile Gebre Selassie Road, about 1km from the city centre. Combining elements of traditional décor

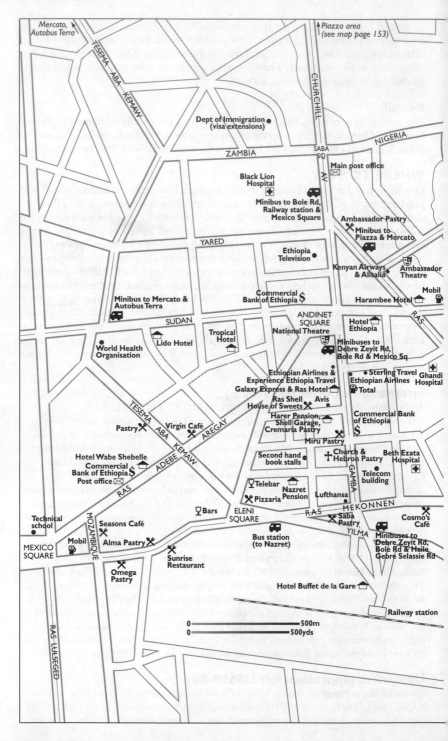

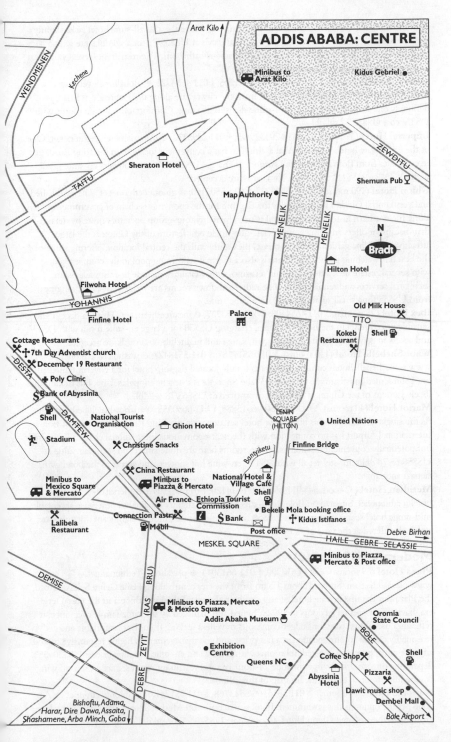

ADDIS ABABA: CENTRE

with international-standard facilities and a rare aura of efficiency, this all-suite hotel lacks slightly for atmosphere, but is very good value by any standards at US$69/79 for a sgl/dbl suite with a large bedroom, lounge with DSTV and fridge, and spacious bathroom. The restaurant serves good local and international dishes. Visa cards are accepted.

Global Hotel (52 rooms) ↘ 011 4664766/4663906; f 011 4664723; e globalhotel@ethionet.et. This plush new hotel, situated about 1km from the city centre along the Debre Zeyit Road, is definitely one of the smartest and best-value deals in its range. Comfortable en-suite rooms with DSTV cost US$52/57 sgl/dbl.

Imperial Hotel (64 rooms) ↘ 011 6293329/95; f 011 6293332; e imperialhotel@ethionet.et. One of the top private hotels in Addis Ababa, this also has a convenient location on the Ring Road, just five minutes from Bole International Airport. It charges US$66/84 for a compact en-suite sgl/dbl with DSTV, or US$114 for a suite. Visa cards are accepted.

Ghion Hotel (190 rooms) ↘ 011 5513222; f 011 5505150; e ghion@ethionet.et. The established and very central Ghion Hotel serves as the flagship for the eponymous chain of government hotels along the northern historical circuit, and is used by many tour-group operators more by default than because it offers anything very special. The single best feature of the Ghion is the large, attractive, rambling garden, which contrasts pleasantly with the central location, offering some of the best birdwatching in the city. There is also a thermal swimming pool in the complex, along with several restaurants, a nightclub and a casino. Other facilities include in-room television, secretarial services and tennis courts. The rather rundown rooms are indifferent value, ranging from US$55 for a small sgl to US$112 for a large suite.

Ibex Hotel (25 rooms) ↘ 011 4654400; f 011 4653737; e ibex@ethionet.et. This is a decent and sensibly priced hotel in the Bole Road area, charging US$50 for a large en-suite room with DSTV and access to good facilities including a gym, sauna and nightclub. Visa cards are accepted.

Wabe Shebelle Hotel (110 rooms) ↘ 011 5517187; f 011 5518477; e washo.et@ethionet.et; www.wabeshebellehotels.com.et. Another centrally located flagship hotel for a government chain, one represented mostly in the south, the Wabe Shebelle is a decent enough set-up, but lacking the lovely gardens of the Ghion, it feels a bit overpriced at US$65/78 sgl/dbl.

Mariot Hotel (40 rooms) ↘ 011 6630500/6615889; f 011 6630555; e mariot-hotel@ethionet.et. As the single 'r' confirms, this bland new hotel set alongside the Ring Road within view of Bole International Airport has no connection with the near-eponymous international chain. Uninspired but potentially convenient location aside, the rooms here are quite smart and seem fair value at US$58/68/78 dbl/semi-ste/ste, all with DSTV, en-suite hot shower, and access to the hotel gym, jacuzzi and sauna.

Meridian Hotel (32 rooms) ↘ 011 6615050/6614120; f 011 6615092; e meridian-hotel@ethionet.et. Situated on Bole Road, this bland and slightly fraying but otherwise acceptable mid-range hotel seems overpriced at US$58 for an en-suite dbl, though significant discounts are routinely offered at the raise of an eyebrow.

Moderate (US$25–40)

Plaza Hotel (39 rooms) ↘ 011 6612200; f 011 6613044; e plazahotel@ethionet.net. www.plazaaddis.com. Situated about 1.5km from the city centre along Haile Gebre Selassie Road, the Plaza was the first private hotel of any quality to be established in Ethiopia in the post-Derg era, having first opened its doors in 1992. Owned and managed by the same family ever since, it remains a useful first base for budget-conscious travellers seeking friendly, comfortable and reasonably central accommodation at a fair price, and the management is highly responsive to advance email queries. Carpeted dbl rooms with DSTV and en-suite hot shower cost US$30–35 depending on size, and facilities include 24-hour bar and restaurant room service. A second wing is scheduled to open during the lifespan of this edition.

National Hotel (34 rooms) ↘ 011 5515166/5513768; f 011 5512417; e Ghion@ethionet.et. A good central option is this government hotel situated just off Meskel Square overlooking the large grounds of the affiliated Ghion Hotel. Rooms cost US$20/24 for sgl/dbl occupancy, or US$29 for large suites, and have DSTV and hot water. Guests can make free use of the swimming pool and other facilities at the smarter Ghion Hotel next door.

Crown Hotel (32 rooms) ☎ 011 4341444/4391046; f 011 4341428; e crownhotel@ethionet.et. Situated about 10km out of town on the Debre Zeyit Road, not far from the Ring Road off-ramp, this comfortable hotel is favoured by a number of tour operators, and the large en-suite rooms are good value at US$23/28/32 sgl/dbl/ste. The biggest plus is the award-winning traditional restaurant, where you can eat like an emperor for birr 20 per head while watching one of the best dancing displays in Addis. The biggest minus for independent travellers is the distance from the city centre, though plenty of minibuses stream past throughout the day.

Axum Hotel (40 rooms) ☎ 011 6613916; f 011 6614265; e axum.d@ethionet.et. Situated alongside Haile Gebre Selassie Road about 2km east of Meskel Square, this rather plush hotel combines comfortable modern rooms with traditionally decorated common areas, and seems fair value at US$30/34/36 for a sgl/dbl/twin with DSTV and en-suite hot shower.

Ras Amba Hotel (25 rooms) ☎ 011 1228080/1233221; e rahot@ethionet.et; www.rasambahotel.com. The new hotel has a rather out-of-the-way location about 1km east of Arat Kilo, but it is popular with business travellers and seems reasonable value at US$36/48/60 for a spacious en-suite sgl/dbl/twin with DSTV, hot shower and a private balcony offering a great view over the city centre.

Yordanis Hotel (36 rooms) ☎ 011 5515711; f 011 5516655. Situated off Haile Gebre Selassie Road about 1km east of Meskel Square, this place has been recommended by many tour operators and readers for its bright, compact en-suite rooms with video, television and hot water, which cost US$25/30/35 sgl/dbl/ste.

Extreme Hotel (45 rooms) ☎ 011 1553777; f 011 1551077. Centrally located, roughly midway between the city centre and the Piazza, this oddly named hotel is about as extreme as a buttered muffin, but it has friendly management and seems good value at birr 150–220 for cramped but clean en-suite doubles.

Budget (approximately US$10–25)

Itegue Taitu Hotel (73 rooms) ☎ 011 1560787. The first hotel to be established in Addis Ababa was constructed for the Empress Taitu (wife of Menelik II) in 1907 to a design by the locally celebrated Armenian architect Minas Kherbekian. Situated 500m from what was then the main market area and is now the Piazza, the Taitu was privatised in 1999 but retains much of its original character, with an exterior instantly recognisable from a photograph taken in 1909 and a spacious interior of high ceilings, creaky wooden floors and period furnishing. The rooms in the main building are steeped in period character and seem excellent value at birr 138/166 for a dbl without/with en-suite hot shower. It's difficult to quibble about the birr 115 charged for the en-suite rooms in a less atmospheric outbuilding or the similarly remote budget dbl rooms (using common hot shower) at birr 46. The restaurant, which serves Ethiopian cuisine in traditional décor, is also recommended.

Finfine Hotel (44 rooms) ☎ 011 5514711. Another old, reasonably central and creakily atmospheric budget choice, the Finfine Hotel was constructed as the Hotel d'Europe in the early years of Haile Selassie's reign, and was renamed the Duke Hotel during the Derg era. Its present-day Oromifa name derives from that of the adjacent hot springs complex, whose therapeutic waters formed a primary factor in persuading Emperor Menelik to relocate his capital from the Entoto Hills to the valley below. Large en-suite rooms with hot shower, dbl bed and telephone cost birr 167. There are worse places for a drink than the green courtyard behind the reception area, and the traditionally decorated restaurant is highly recommended for Ethiopian food.

Hawi Hotel (24 rooms) ☎ 011 4654499. Offering consistently good value since the first edition of this guide was researched, this unpretentious and comfortable hotel on the Debre Zeyit Road charges a very reasonable birr 100 for a clean room with a large dbl bed, en-suite hot shower and well-maintained furnishings. It also has a pleasant restaurant, bar and coffee lounge, and lies right on a minibus route.

Gedera Hotel #3 (25 rooms) ✆ 011 5521905; e gedera3@yahoo.com. Popular with price-conscious tour operators and business visitors to Ethiopia, this small, friendly hotel lies to the northeast of the city centre towards Arat Kilo. The smart rooms are very good value at around birr 126/137/262 sgl/dbl/ste, and come with DSTV, hot water and continental breakfast. The location, off any minibus route, is a drawback for those who are dependent on public transport, though a few taxis are normally to be found sitting outside the hotel. The food isn't up to much, but fortunately the excellent Canapé Restaurant lies just around the corner.

Concorde Hotel (22 rooms) ✆ 011 4654959; f 011 4653193; e hotelconcorde@ethionet.et. Situated about 2km from the city centre along the Debre Zeyit Road, the Concorde is best known perhaps for the nightclub in its basement, but it also offers very acceptable accommodation. The carpeted rooms with a dbl bed, TV and en-suite hot shower costing US$22 are fair value, but far better are the large suites with wooden floors for US$29.

Filwoha Hotel (20 rooms) ✆ 011 5519000. Situated opposite the Finfine Hotel, this more modern high-rise block also forms part of the hot springs complex (Filwoha means 'hot water') but the characterless and rather rundown en-suite doubles seem like poor value at birr 250.

Central Showa Hotel (32 rooms) ✆ 011 6615001/6632554; f 011 6610063. One of several decent hotels strung along Haile Gebre Selassie Road, this popular high-rise charges birr 165/196 for a dbl/twin with a fridge, telephone, DSTV and hot shower. A decent restaurant serves local and foreign dishes.

Hotel Buffet de la Gare (8 rooms) ✆ 011 5517888. This pleasantly timeworn small hotel is tucked away in green grounds in front of the central railway station, and charges birr 90/160 for a sgl/dbl room with en-suite hot showers.

Ras Hotel (100 rooms) ✆ 011 5517060; f 011 5517533. With a superb central location on Churchill Avenue, this rather rundown government hotel doesn't lack for character and seems decent value at birr 80/120 for a sgl/dbl with en-suite hot shower. The patio bar and restaurant is a popular central spot for a rendezvous.

Shoestring (under US$10)

Wutma Hotel (15 rooms) ✆ 011 1562878; e wutma@yahoo.com. This is my marginal favourite of two evergreen budget traveller hangouts that face each other on Muniyem Street below the Piazza. The odd dissenter notwithstanding, reader feedback about the Wutma is as uniformly positive as could be hoped for, and this hotel remains my first port of call in Addis Ababa. Small but clean en-suite rooms with a dbl bed and temperamental hot-water boilers cost birr 60 for a single person or couple, or birr 70 for two people of the same sex. The restaurant is reasonably good, there's an on-site internet café, and the staff is helpful and experienced when it comes to sorting out things like 4x4 rental, changing money and such.

Baro Hotel (26 rooms) ✆ 011 1574157; f 011 1559846; e barohotel@ethionet.et. Facing the Wutma, this similarly priced and even longer serving backpackers' favourite is a useful fallback when the Wutma is full. The rooms vary far more in standard than in price, so that while some travellers feel they have had a good deal, others are less charitable (rooms 8–13 are the best). What is almost beyond dispute is that the Baro is a safe, friendly and affordable place to adjust to Addis Ababa, a good place to meet other travellers, and well equipped to deal with such practicalities as changing money, telephone calls, internet access, safe luggage storage and 4x4 rental. If you are looking for travel companions, the Wutma is perhaps *the* place in Addis to meet other travellers. It's not bad value, either, at birr 65/75/85/105 for a clean sgl/dbl/twin/triple with hot water.

Wanza Hotel (16 rooms) ✆ 011 5156177. A long-standing favourite, this friendly small hotel off Bole Road has a convenient location within easy walking distance of the city centre, and it lies within 500m of several bars and restaurants, as well as a strategic minibus route. The clean tiled rooms, all of which are en suite with hot water and have a proper dbl bed, cost birr 70–80 depending on size.

Abyssinia Hotel Tucked away in the back roads behind the Addis Ababa Museum, this is another established favourite, charging birr 40 for a clean dbl room with a hot shower. There is some noise from the pub, but the staff are friendly and the food is good.

Debre Damo Hotel (24 rooms) ⟍ 011 6612630/6622921; f 011 6622920; e debredamo@ethionet.et. Not quite the bargain it was a few years ago, this double-storey hotel about 2km from the city centre on Haile Gebre Selassie Road still seems pretty good value at birr 68/96 for a sgl/dbl using the common shower or birr 115/120 for a sgl/dbl with en-suite hot showers and TV. The attached restaurant serves Indian, Ethiopian and Western dishes for around birr 20.

National Hotel Not to be confused with the government hotel of the same name near the UN headquarters, this is the pick of the cluster of cheaper hotels that lies along the short road between the Taitu Hotel and De Gaulle Square. It charges birr 35 for a basic but large room with a dbl bed using strong common hot showers.

Belair Hotel ⟍ 011 1114655. Popular with overland truck companies, this old standby is situated beside the Indian Chancery, where it is signposted from the main road between Arat Kilo and the British High Commission. Large and clean en-suite rooms cost birr 60 (with dbl bed and hot shower), while similar rooms using the common shower cost birr 30.

WHERE TO EAT AND DRINK

If finding a room in Addis is straightforward, then locating a decent meal is even easier. Top-quality restaurants specialising in most recognised international cuisines are to be found dotted around the city, with main courses typically costing from birr 25–40. Several of the government hotels have reasonable restaurants serving inexpensive Western dishes such as roast meat and steak, and there are also several private budget restaurants specialising in Italian-influenced dishes or else local cuisine. For snacks, there are dozens of pastry shops, many of which serve savoury mini-pizzas and spicy hamburgers in addition to the usual cakes and biscuits.

Given that few restaurants in Addis Ababa are seriously expensive, and that it is often convenient to eat near your hotel or in a part of town you're visiting for another reason, I've grouped restaurants by area rather than price or the type of cuisine. A selective shortlist of highlights, for those who simply want to catch a taxi to the best restaurants irrespective of price or location, are Castelli's (Italian), Cottage and Canapé (European), Agelgil and Habesha (Ethiopian) and Sangham (Indian). The collection of restaurants in both the Sheraton and Hilton Hotels is also world class. Booking is not normally necessary.

City centre

The city centre is surprisingly thin on good restaurants, at least by comparison with the Bole Road area, but travellers will end up taking lunch here, and it's also easy to reach in the evening on public transport, wherever you are based. One of the best and oldest of the central places is the **Cottage Restaurant** (⟍ 011 5516359), on Ras Desta Damtew Street between the Harambee and Ghion Hotels, which serves excellent Swiss and other continental food in the birr 30–40 range. On the same road, further towards the Ghion Hotel, excellent pizzas are to be had at the **Pizza Romano** for around birr 25 apiece, along with burgers, steaks and a limited selection of pasta dishes. The **Christine Snack Bar**, practically next to the entrance of the Ghion Hotel, is a cheap and cheerful local eatery, very popular for lunch, and good value at around birr 10–12 for steaks, burgers, fried fish or local dishes. Just past the Ghion, the **China Bar and Restaurant** (⟍ 011 5513772) is a decent if unexceptional Chinese restaurant where you can expect to pay around birr 30–40 per head for a main course with rice.

On Ras Mekonnen Road, close to the tourist office, the **Garden Court Restaurant** (⟍ 011 6620918) is a very pleasant place to sit, with a patio on the street, and it serves the usual pastries and coffee along with pasta dishes, burgers and sandwiches. A few hundred metres further west, the **Lalibela Restaurant** serves good steaks for around birr 15. There is a house band here on most nights, at no cover charge, though drinks are double

> **YOHANNIS KITFO**
> *From a letter by Des Blonyal*
> I became very partial to the Ethiopian *kitfo* dish while I lived in Addis Ababa. Typically, it's served raw (*terea*) or partially cooked (*lublub*). I prefer it to be fully cooked (*yebesela*). The best *kitfo* house by far is Yohannis *kitfo*, located somewhere off Haile Gebre Selassie Road (you'll have to take a taxi, it's difficult for the average tourist to find). The special *kitfo* dish comes with *gomen* (a type of cabbage, almost like spinach), *eib* (cottage cheese) and roasted *kocho* (bread-like rubbery stuff made from the stem of the enset or false banana tree). I recommend the special *kitfo*. There are also other good *kitfo* houses in town but this is the best and probably most expensive at birr 20 for the special *kitfo*. The butter used is of the special pure Gurage variety, not mixed with oil. If you don't ask for *yebesela kitfo*, you will more than likely get *terea* or *lublub kitfo*. Beware though, it can be very spicy – it's wise to order a couple of cold beers with it!

the normal price. The **Ras Hotel** on Churchill Avenue serves standard government hotel fare at very reasonable prices, and the patio is a good place to watch Addis Ababa go by. The restaurant at the **Hotel Buffet de la Gare** is pretty good, with occasional live music on Fridays and Saturdays, while excellent traditional and international food can be enjoyed at the **Sunrise Restaurant** (✆ *011 5516280*), which is situated in an old house along on Ras Mekonnen Road in the direction of Mexico Square. Somewhat less central, the **Old Milk House** on Tito Road, around the corner from the Hilton Hotel, is a popular hangout with both expatriates and trendy locals, and serves pizzas and other international cuisine in or out of doors.

Pastry shops are dotted all over the city centre. Two of the best are the **Betel** and **Miru** pastries, which are situated a few doors apart on Churchill Avenue, and concoct irresistible delicacies that wouldn't look, or taste, out of place in a European capital – prices are slightly above the odds, but worth it! On the same road, the **Shell House of Sweets** stands out not only for its delicious cakes but also for its savoury mini-pizzas, milkshakes and ice cream cones. Similar in standard and price, and with a more spacious seating arrangement, the trendy **Hotline Pastry & Restaurant** close to the National Hotel is a great place for breakfast – croissants, fresh orange juice and superlative coffee – but also serves top-notch pastries and cakes, as well as pasta dishes and burgers. The nearby **Village Café** has been recommended as similar. The **Connection Pastry**, between the Ghion Hotel and tourist office, is more typically Ethiopian in standards, but the pastries, juice and fruit salad are all excellent and inexpensive.

Piazza and surrounds

The options for eating out around the Piazza are relatively limited, but the area does host Addis Ababa's oldest restaurant, and arguably its best. Owned and managed by the same Italian family for more than 50 years, **Castelli's** (✆ *011 1571757/1563580*) specialises in pasta dishes, grills and seafood, with most dishes falling in the birr 40–60 range. If that seems dauntingly expensive, very good pizzas are to be had for around birr 15 at **The Pizzeria** on Mahatma Gandhi Road, just below the Piazza, The **GK Restaurant** next door to this serves everything from lamb cutlets and *kai wat* to pasta and pizzas; the food is nothing extraordinary, but portions are large and most items on the menu cost little more than birr 10. Around the corner, the **Oroscopo Restaurant** is another top-notch budget eatery specialising in Italian dishes for around birr 15.

On Adwa Avenue, the **InterLangano Restaurant**, housed in an Italian-era double-storey building, serves good roast meat and Ethiopian standards for up to birr 15 per main

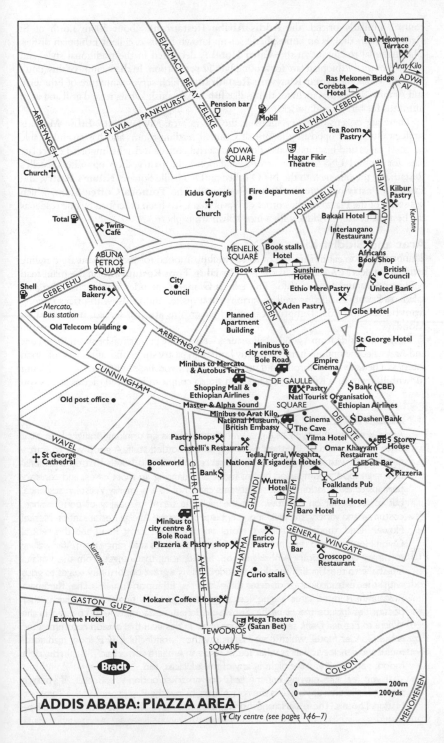

ADDIS ABABA: PIAZZA AREA

↓ City centre (see pages 146–7)

course. Similarly priced, the **Addis Ababa Restaurant**, about 500m north of St George's Cathedral, is an atmospheric set-up known for its excellent Ethiopian dishes. The 'national restaurant' at the **Taitu Hotel** is decorated in the traditional style, and serves the usual Ethiopian fare for around birr 12 per portion. In the vicinity of this, don't miss the venerable **Omar Khayyam Restaurant**, which serves a mixture of Ethiopian and Arabian dishes that includes things like fish kebab, shish kebab, mixed grill and even hummus for birr 10 and under.

There are dozens of pastry shops in the Piazza area. My favourite, **Ethio Mere**, is strategically placed opposite the British Council reading room, and has an unbeatable range of cakes and biscuits. It also does wonderful coffee, and sells imported chocolate bars for around US$2. Other recommendations: the pastry shop opposite Castelli's Restaurant, the one next to the NTO office on De Gaulle Square, **Kibur's Pastry**, and **Enrico's Pastry** opposite the Birhan Restaurant. The **Tomoca Coffee Shop**, which lies south of the Piazza on the corner of Wavel Road, has been described by one reader as the best coffee bar in Addis, with a nice Italian atmosphere.

Arat and Siddist Kilo

The best place to eat in this part of town, well positioned for lunch if you are trawling around the nearby museums, is the popular **Blue Tops Restaurant** on the main road between Arat and Siddist Kilo. The extensive menu includes sandwiches, burgers, salads and other snacks, as well as various pasta dishes and grills, with prices ranging from birr 20 upwards. Tempting cakes and ice creams are also served. It is closed on Mondays.

Otherwise, aside from a good – but seatless – take-away pizza shop between Blue Tops and Arat Kilo, the options here are mostly limited to pastry shops and unremarkable local eateries. The truly adventurous, and unabashedly carnivorous, might want to head south (downhill) from Arat Kilo, where a left turn after a couple of hundred metres brings you

ADDIS ABABA BY NIGHT

Addis is remarkably lively at night, with the emphasis on drinking draught beer till it dries up at around 22.00, then switching to the bottled stuff. A good way to start a night out is with a meal at one of several restaurants and hotels that do traditional Ethiopian food accompanied by live music and dancing. In most cases, and contrary perhaps to expectations, such restaurants cater not to a primarily Western audience, but to locals out on the town for the night. In terms of quality of performance, costumes and variety, the pick at present is probably the Agelgil Restaurant on Meskel Flower Road, though the Crown Hotel on the Debre Zeyit Road and the central Ghion Hotel are also recommended. With musical styles that range from Afar wailing to meaty contemporary Amharigna pop, and dancing that ranges from the Walaita hip-shake to the Tigraian shoulder-shudder, this is a great opportunity to get to grips with the extraordinarily diverse thing that is Ethiopian music. The Karamara Restaurant is in the same league, less staged and generally busier and livelier. Other possibilities include the Habesha, Showa or Banatu restaurants – all covered in the *Where to Eat and Drink* section. Another place in this vein that's been recommended is the Gonder Hotel, which Kate Harris says has 'wonderful fasting food, traditional music and dancing as well as what seems to be an Amhara comedian... (?)'. In the right mood, you might end the night at any of these places, too...

If you feel like moving on, the best downmarket option – especially if you are staying in the area anyway – is the row of bars below the Piazza around the Taitu and National hotels. There's a strong Tigraian element here, plenty of dancing – you'll be

to a famous line of butcher-cum-restaurant shops specialising in *tessema tsegur* – raw beef! Here, for birr 10 or so, you can select a huge chunk of prime steak straight from the carcass, and eat it as it comes, or cooked, as you please!

An excellent and unusual restaurant in this part of town is the **Armenian Club**, which lies on a back road just north of Ras Mekonnen Bridge, and serves an excellent range of seriously inexpensive meat and vegetarian dishes. The **Ras Mekonnen Terrace** (❧ *011 1570909*) above the same bridge serves excellent traditional food.

Bole Road

Bole Road is undoubtedly the best part of Addis Ababa for eating out, with more than enough restaurants to keep you busy for a fortnight without eating at the same place twice. A recommended starting point, and a good introduction to Ethiopian food, is the renowned **Karamara Restaurant** (❧ *011 5158013*), which despite its touristy appearance – done up like a traditional *tukul* (round thatched house) – still predominantly caters to well-to-do locals. The food is very good and affordable, and the atmosphere is great, with traditional music and dancing on most evenings. In the same vein, the **Habesha Restaurant** (❧ *011 5518358*) serves good traditional Ethiopian dishes at around birr 15 in an attractive setting. It has a beautiful outdoor seating area, and a non-stop coffee ceremony in a *tukul*, with live music after 20.00.

More upmarket recommendations along Bole Road, most with meals in the birr 30–40 range, include the **Sangham Restaurant** (*Indian,* ❧ *011 5518976*), **Al Baraka Restaurant** (*Lebanese,* ❧ *011 5155903*), **Rainbow** (*Korean and Japanese,* ❧ *011 6631318/6637964*), **Pizza Deli Roma** (*Italian,* ❧ *011 5511202*) and **Little Italy/My Flavour** (*Continental,* ❧ *011 5150414*). For cheaper eats, the **Peacock Hotel** is resoundingly popular with local professionals, serving a variety of local and Western dishes in the birr 12–20 range, while the **Randa Fast Food** does respectable *schwarmas*, burgers and meat sandwiches for birr 10–12. To the right of Bole Road just before the

urged to join in and you'll make a lot of friends if you do – and a surprising amount of English spoken. The activity seems to shuffle from pub to pub as the night progresses, and more than once I have found myself emerging from the last drinking hole at sunrise. I never sensed any threat of theft along this road, but as always it would be sensible to carry only the money you need.

Bars in the city centre tend to be more subdued, as most of them are in hotels. One exception is the Seven Eleven Bar, which seems to be a popular drinking hole with Ethiopian businessmen. Any place that can break from Ethiopian music for a tape that segues between Chicken Shack (I kid you not), Randy Crawford and some best-forgotten country-and-western dirge from the 1970s gets my seal of approval! More upmarket is My Pub on Haile Gebre Selassie Road near the Plaza Hotel. This is a good place to play pool, drink beer and make friends in the international community. The food is good, too, and the price right. Altogether more pretentious is the chilled-out La Gazelle Piano Bar on Bole Road near the Meridian Hotel.

For African as opposed to Ethiopian music – and a similar clientele – try the Unity 2000 Club on the Debre Zeyit Road (coming from town, turn left at the Greece Embassy/Burundi Embassy signpost). For Ethiopian music, the Aroz Hotel on the road to Entoto Mountain (near the Italian Cultural Institute) has been recommended, along with the Concorde Club on the Debre Zeyit Road and the expensive Gaslight Night Club in the Sheraton. A good live band sometimes plays at the lively Hotel Buffet de la Gare on weekends after about 20.00. There is live jazz every Thursday at The Coffee House, which stands in front of the Egyptian Embassy near Siddist Kilo.

airport roundabout, the excellent **Il Caminetto** serves a justifiably popular four-course Italian lunch for around birr 27, which is very popular with Ethiopian businesspeople.

You won't walk far on Bole Road without stumbling over a decent pastry shop. One of the best is **Saay Pastry**, where excellent cakes are supplemented by cappuccino, ice cream and other yummy odds and ends. Nearby, the busy **Pelican Pastry** is very good value, not only for cakes, but also for mini-pizzas, burgers and other snacks. Closer to the town centre, the **Purple Café** and **Pastaleria Geletalia** are both very good. Top marks, however, must go to **La Parisienne**, around the corner from the Purple Café, which serves marvellous cakes and the best croissants in town, as well as toasted sandwiches, snacks, and an array of coffees.

Suburban restaurants

Recommended as much for its locale as for the food, the popular **Top View Restaurant** (⟋ 011 6627350) lies on the footslopes of the Entoto Mountains, from where it has a grandstand view towards the city centre. Italian-influenced cuisine falls into the birr 35–50 bracket.

For French cuisine, particularly if you are staying around the corner at the Gedera Hotel #3, the **Canapé Restaurant** is excellent and most main courses are in the birr 30–40 range. Another recommended French restaurant is **La Petite Paris**, located in southwest Addis Ababa near the Canadian Embassy.

Arguably the best traditional eatery at the moment is the **Agelgil Restaurant** (⟋ 011 4653288), which is situated in the old Villa Verde building on Meskel Flower Road near the junction with the Debre Zeyit Road about 3km northwest of the Olympia intersection with Bole Road. The restaurant has a live five-man band playing traditional instruments at a sensible sound level, two good singers and an excellent cultural dance group who dance every evening except Wednesday. The food is very good at birr 20–35, as is the *tej*, and for *injera*-phobes they will do excellent fish and salad dishes with bread. There is no entrance fee but drinks do cost birr 10. Also highly recommended in the traditional food, music and dancing at the **Crown Hotel**.

THEFT AND SAFETY

A bit of bad-news-and-good-news scenario this! The bad news is that Addis Ababa is one of the worst cities in sub-Saharan Africa when it comes to casual theft and con tricks. The good news is that violent crime of the sort you get in Nairobi or Johannesburg is very unusual. People who have travelled in north Africa reckon that Addis Ababa is relatively sedate by comparison with large cities in Morocco and Egypt. Pickpockets are the major threat to travellers, and few people will spend long in Addis without having an attempt made on them.

Pickpockets and con artists like to prey on Ethiopian Airlines transit passengers and other newcomers, so they tend to congregate where there are plenty of tourists and in other crowded places. Those who specialise in fleecing tourists often hang out in the open area in front of the ETC office and at the entrances of government hotels, especially the Ghion, Ras, Harambee and Ethiopia hotels. There are also plenty of less discriminating pickpockets around the railway station, any crowded minibus stand, the Mercato area, and on the buses that operate within the city (but not the minibuses). My experience was that pickpockets and con artists are less prolific in the Piazza than in the city centre, but recent reports suggest this may no longer be the case.

The modus operandi of Addis's pickpockets is a twin-pronged attack wherein the first person bumps into you, grabs your legs, clings on to your arm, or distracts you in some other way while a second person fishes in your pocket. So, if somebody distracts you on one side, you should not respond directly but instead immediately check out what is happening on your other side. It's not a bad idea to stuff your trouser pocket with

FRIENDLY STUDENTS

The scam most frequently tried on newcomers to Addis involves being accosted by a friendly 'student' who invites you a traditional ceremony – coffee or *tej* – at the end of which you are presented with a bill totalling as much as US$100 or more. I've had more than a dozen letters from readers who fell victim to this trick, so it seems worth repeating one encounter in full:

> After checking into the Wutma Hotel, we went for a walk around the city. We were approached by a pleasant young student, who offered to show us around. Having said he worked at the Wutma, we thought this may not be a bad idea, and so the next day we took him as an escort to the Mercato Market, where one needs to be on guard against pickpockets. At the end of this trip, he invited us to a coffee making ceremony that evening. BEWARE all travellers, do not go to one of these in Addis Ababa! I should have known better, having done a considerable amount of travelling, but against my better judgement we went to a house where we met 'local' girls in national dress, performing Ethiopian dances and serving Ethiopian food. Unfortunately they were also drinking imported brandy! After a couple of hours we decided to leave and were presented with a large bill of $100! Not a good start! We met other travellers who had also been conned similarly in Addis, so it is becoming quite a scam in the city.

The moral is quite simple. Don't trust any supposed student you meet in Addis Ababa. Assume that anybody who says they work at your hotel, or who remembers meeting you yesterday, is a liar. Don't be lured to a coffee or any other ceremony. And remember always that plausibility is the con artist's most valuable asset!

something useless such as a wad of tissue or an empty cigarette box, which serves nicely as a decoy. And note that the kids who sell cigarettes and newspapers around Churchill Avenue are not above playing the distracting role, so rather buy such odds and ends from shops. Bag slashing is also a bit of a problem, so if you're carrying anything important (passport or travellers' cheques) keep it in your money-belt. Carrying a daypack in Addis definitely marks you out as a tourist.

The chancers who hang out near the places like the ETC, Churchill Avenue, and in front of the Ghion Hotel are relatively harmless; their basic agenda is to get you talking, sucker you into feeling sorry for them, then ask you for something. Typical approaches include standard 'how do you like Ethiopia?' questioning, or claiming to be the waiter or gardener at your hotel, or asking 'Do you remember me?'. Sometimes the approaches verge on pure 'plonker' territory: 'In Ethiopia we celebrate New Year every year!' Once hooked, you may be in for a straightforward request for money, or something more insidious. A common trick is to ask you for a drink at a private bar, then to present you with a bill for US$50 or something equally comic (see box *Friendly Students* above). Another ploy is to tell you about some one-off happening that you can only see today. Con artists in Addis excel when it comes to manipulating foreigners' emotions, and the longer you indulge them the more difficult they become to shake off. If you live in any large city, you know that when a stranger approaches you in the street they are almost always lost, irritatingly drunk, or a beggar with a sob-story. Addis is no different – except that no resident of the city is going to stop to ask a tourist directions.

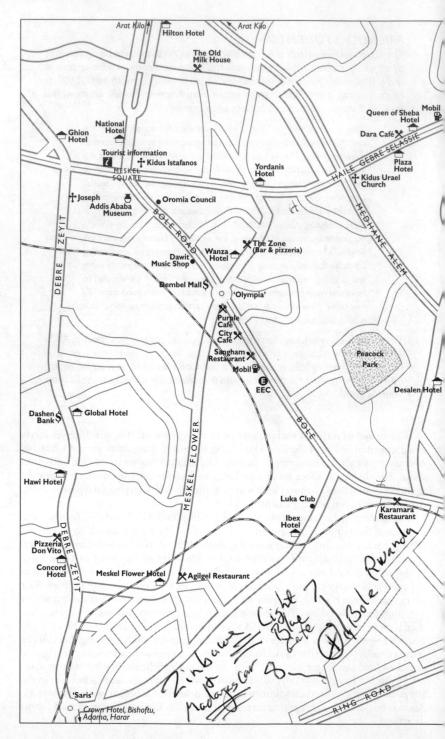

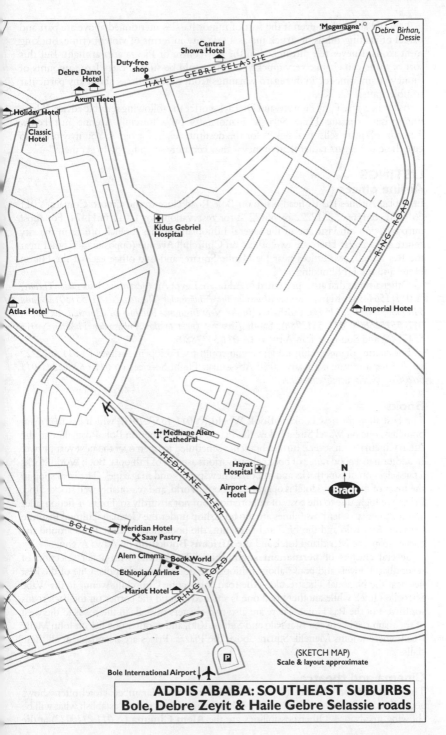

ADDIS ABABA: SOUTHEAST SUBURBS
Bole, Debre Zeyit & Haile Gebre Selassie roads

I should stress that, even if the sort of minor hassles mentioned above are part and parcel of visiting Addis, it struck me as a safe city in terms of violent crime. Sticking to lit roads, I never felt threatened in the city centre or Piazza area at night. But this sort of thing can change very quickly, and it would be silly to carry large amounts of money at any time, or to disregard warnings from other sources about any particular trouble spots.

As for beggars, Tony Howard and Di Taylor offer the following sensible advice: 'Hope Enterprises opposite Haile Selassie Handicrafts on Churchill Avenue just below Tewodros Square sells meal tickets for the destitute: eight for birr 4. You may prefer to give these to beggars rather than money – they certainly seem happy to get them!'

LISTINGS
Airline offices
Ethiopian Airlines has its head office on Bole Road close to the airport. Contact ⏦ 011 6616161, 6616666, 5512222 or 6612222 for reservations, or f 011 6611474. For most purposes, you can visit one of the several Ethiopian Airlines' branch offices in the city centre and Piazza. There are two offices on Churchill Avenue (opposite each other near the Ras Hotel), two offices near De Gaulle Square, and one office each at the Hilton Hotel and the UN building.

Other airlines that are represented in Addis are Egypt Air (*next to the Ambassador Theatre;* ⏦ *011 1564494*), Kenya Airways (*next to the Ambassador Theatre;* ⏦ *011 5513018/9 and 5153339;* f *011 5511543*), Lufthansa (*in the New Insurance building on Churchill Avenue;* ⏦ *011 5515666;* f *011 5512988*), Saudi Airways (*next to the Ambassador Theatre;* ⏦ *011 5517746*) and South African Airways (⏦ *011 5537880*).

For charter flights within Ethiopia, you could try Ethiopian Airlines (⏦ *011 6612222 ext 403*) or a private company called Abyssinian Flight Services (⏦ *011 6620622;* f *011 6620620;* e *solo.flight@ethionet.et*).

Books
The best shop for new books is **Book World** (⏦ *011 1559010/3*), which has two main branches, one on Wavel Street below the Piazza and the other on Bole Road close to the Alem Cinema, with several further branches scheduled to open over the next year or two. In addition to a good range of books about various aspects of Ethiopia, Book World stocks a fair selection of paperbacks and imported newspapers and magazines. The bookshop in the foyer of the Hilton Hotel is operated by Book World, and reasonably well stocked too. Prices are high, due to the costs of importation, but not absurdly so. For non-fiction titles about Ethiopia, other possibilities are the bookshop under the German Cultural Institute between Arat Kilo and the National Museum, the bookshop on Bole Road around the corner from the Meridian Hotel, and the **Africans Bookshop** on Adwa Avenue.

Several clusters of **permanent secondhand bookstalls** with a fair selection of secondhand novels and books about Ethiopia are dotted around Addis. One of the best lies near the National Theatre, along the road connecting Churchill Avenue to the Wabe Shebelle Hotel, while another good one is situated around the corner on the back roads southwest of the Ras Hotel. There are also two clusters of stalls in the roads to the west of the main road between Arat Kilo and Siddist Kilo, and another one lies on John Melly Road where it joins Menelik Square above the Piazza. Prices are negotiable at all these stalls.

Cinema and theatre
The **Ambassador Theatre** (⏦ *011 5537637*) near the Harambee Hotel often shows good films, and tickets cost a mere birr 4, but it isn't always easy to establish what will be showing in advance. Other possibilities are the **Alem Cinema** (⏦ *011 2130022*) at the

airport end of Bole Road and the **Empire Cinema** (✆ *011 1579467*) and **Ethiopia Cinema** (✆ *011 1116690*) on the Piazza. Every Wednesday evening at 19.00 a film is shown at the US Embassy; it's open to all but you need to bring your passport.

Unlike the cinemas in Addis Ababa, the theatres generally stage productions in Amharigna, which can make them rather heavy going for foreigners who don't speak the language. The Mega Theatre (✆ *011 1118084/1553577*) on Tewodros Square is the oldest in town, built circa 1920, while other possibilities include the National Theatre (✆ *011 5158225/5154147*) further south along Churchill Avenue and the Hagar Fikre Theatre (✆ *011 1119820/1124158*) near the Piazza.

Also worth checking out is the Alliance Ethio-Français on Wavel Road south of the Piazza, which regularly hosts plays, art exhibitions, local musical evenings, and other cultural activities. For a current programme, contact ✆ 011 1550213 or check the website www.allianceaddis.org.

Embassies

Travellers heading south from Ethiopia to Kenya might want to note that the Kenya High Commission in Addis Ababa is reportedly very unco-operative, and that Kenyan visas are available at Moyale (as they are at all overland borders into Kenya) with no hassles or additional charges. Other embassies and high commissions in Addis Ababa include the following:

Austria PO Box 1219; ✆ 011 3712144; f 011 3712140
Belgium PO Box 1239; ✆ 011 6611813; f 011 6613636
Canada PO Box 1130; ✆ 011 3713022; f 011 3710333
Djibouti PO Box 1022; ✆ 011 6613200; f 011 6612504
Egypt PO Box 1611; ✆ 011 1553077; f 011 1552722
France PO Box 1464; ✆ 011 1550066; f 011 5511180
Germany PO Box 660; ✆ 011 1550433; f 011 1551311
Ireland PO Box 9585; ✆ 011 3710835
Israel PO Box 1266; ✆ 011 6460999; f 011 6610608
Italy PO Box 1105; ✆ 011 1553044; f 011 1550218
Kenya PO Box 3301; ✆ 011 6610033; f 011 6611433
Netherlands PO Box 1241; ✆ 011 3711100; f 011 3711577
Russia PO Box 1500; ✆ 011 6611828; f 011 6613795
Sudan PO Box 1110; ✆ 011 5516477; f 011 5518141
Sweden PO Box 1029; ✆ 011 5516699; f 011 5515830
Switzerland PO Box 1106; ✆ 011 3710577; f 011 3712805
UK PO Box 858; ✆ 011 6612354; f 011 6610588
USA PO Box 1041; ✆ 011 1551002; f 011 1551166

Internet and email

Internet cafés are dotted all around Addis Ababa. The standard charge is birr 20–25 per minute, which works out at around US$1.50 per hour, though it is worth noting that many upmarket hotels charge double or triple that rate. Particularly popular with travellers are the inexpensive internet cafés attached to the Baro and Wutma hotels, but there are numerous other cafés concentrated along Bole Road (try MKTV Business Centre opposite the Angola Chancery), the Piazza, the city centre and the Arat and Siddist Kilo areas.

Maps

The 1:2,000,000 map of Ethiopia produced by the Ethiopian Tourist Commission (ETC) is available from the curio kiosks in several of the government hotels in Addis. There is a fairly useful albeit very dated map of Addis on the back. There are useful maps of the Bale and Simien mountains in the give-away booklets distributed at the ETC office on Meskel Square. Basic but usable maps of Nechisar, Abiata-Shala, Bale and Awash national parks are available from the Department of Natural Resources on Bole Road.

The Ethiopian Mapping Authority (EMA) office opposite the Hilton Hotel is open from 08.30 to 16.30 Monday to Friday, closing for lunch from 12.30 (11.30 on Friday) to 13.30. They normally sell a useful 1:25,000 map of greater Addis Ababa for around US$1.50, though it is often out of stock. The EMA 1:2,000,000 map of Ethiopia, which sells for around US$2, is more accurate than the ETC map but doesn't show distances between towns.

The EMA stocks good 1:50,000 maps covering most of the southern, central and western highlands, but not all areas north of Gonder or east of Awash National Park. They also sell useful 1:250,000 maps covering the whole country. These are now sold to casual tourists without complication, though the procedure is quite bureaucratic and they will probably refuse to sell any maps that touch on border areas. They might also refuse to sell you more than ten different maps in one batch, for 'security' reasons – a ploy so fiendishly cunning that it would be bound to foil any major international crime ring for a good ten seconds before its evil mastermind hatched the ingenious scheme of sending in a second person to buy the rest of the maps. Note, too, that if the cashier is off on a jaunt or at home feeling poorly, then no maps whatsoever can be sold.

If it is vital that you have certain maps, then you should contact the EMA well in advance. The address is PO Box 597, Addis Ababa; ☎ 011 5518445; f 011 5515189.

Medical and emergencies
There are plenty of GPs in the city centre and the Piazza area. All doctors speak passable English and most have in-house laboratories able to perform most straightforward blood, stool or urine tests. For an emergency, contact the Panorama Clinic at ☎ 011 4651666 or 24-hour callout ☎ 091 1223700. For any tests that an ordinary GP is unable to do, visit the excellent Ras Desta Damtew Laboratory (☎ *011 1553399*), which lies on the road of the same name opposite the Gandhi Hospital, or else the Black Lion Hospital (☎ *011 5511211*) near the Immigration Department. Other recommended clinics and hospitals include the Africa Higher Clinic (☎ *011 2766817/8*), Bethezata Higher Clinic (☎ *011 5514470 or 091 1201279*) and St Gebriel Hospital (☎ *011 6614400/6617622*). To contact the Red Cross, dial 92 or 907. For other emergencies dial 91.

Pharmacists in Addis are generally well stocked and helpful. I can recommend the pharmacist on Churchill Avenue between the National Theatre and Ras Hotel, the one on Ras Desta Damtew Road roughly opposite the Ambassador Theatre, and the one on Mahatma Gandhi Road roughly opposite the GK Restaurant.

Newspapers
A couple of local English-language papers of indifferent quality can be bought from street vendors in Addis. Imported newspapers in English and French can usually be bought in the foyers of the Hilton Hotel and UN building a couple of days after publication, while *Time* and *Newsweek* are available in most government hotels in the city centre. The public reading room in the British Council on Adwa Avenue has ten-day-old copies of most of the British broadsheets.

Post
The main post office is on Churchill Avenue. There are several branch post offices dotted around the city, and the queues are rarely daunting. Sending freight out of Addis Ababa is very cheap, but best arranged with your airline.

Shopping

Shops in Addis are well stocked and they compare favourably with those of most African cities. There are loads of different shops along the lower half of Churchill Avenue, and along Adwa Avenue in the Piazza area.

For curio shopping, try the dozen or so well-stocked stalls and shops that lie near Tewodros Square on Churchill Avenue and Mahatma Gandhi Road. There are also curio kiosks in most of the smarter tourist-class hotels. Prices at the stalls on Churchill Avenue are highly negotiable, but are generally fixed at hotels and more upmarket shops in the city centre. Most shops and offices close up for an hour or two sometime between 12.00 and 14.00 – there is little point in trying to get anything done during these hours.

If you want to take home some Ethiopian music, the 'Ethiopiques' series and other imported Ethiopian CDs are normally available at the book kiosk in the foyer of the Hilton for birr 120-plus. For a good section of locally manufactured CDs (which cost birr 25–30) try Alpha Sound or Master Sound on the Piazza, Elektra Music near Anwar Mosque between the Piazza and the Mercato, or Dawit Music Shop on Bole Road near the Purple Café.

Swimming pools

Addis Ababa is not often so torrid that making a beeline for the nearest swimming pool is likely to be a high priority. But, should the urge strike, the thermal swimming pool at the Ghion Hotel (with 10m diving platform) is a reliable bet, and charges a reasonable entrance fee of birr 14. Also realistically priced at birr 10 per person – more for a sauna or massage – is the Filwoha Hotel's pool, fed by hot springs. The swimming pools at the Hilton and Sheraton hotels are fabulous (the latter complete with views of the surrounding shanties), and very popular with wealthy Ethiopians and expatriates. It's probably fair to say that any visitor who's prepared to fork out the equivalent of US$10 for a quick splash will be ensconced at one of these hotels anyway!

Tour operators and booking agencies

Several tour operators are based in Addis Ababa. For details see pages 82–3.

Tourist information

The **Ethiopian Tourist Commission (ETC)** headquarters on Meskel Square sporadically stocks very useful free booklets on Lalibela and Simien and Bale national parks, as well as more superficial pamphlets on other parts of the country. The staff at the National Museum is a good source of practical information relating to obscure historical and archaeological sites. ℩ 011 5512310 or (airport) 6184290.

Visa extensions

These can be obtained at the **Department of Immigration** on Churchill Avenue. This is normally a straightforward procedure, but note that a passport-sized photograph is required (there's a photo kiosk outside) and a fee of approximately US$20 must be paid (in local currency). Visa extensions normally take 24 hours, but they can be done on the same day by special request, provided you make the application in the morning.

SIGHTSEEING IN AND AROUND ADDIS ABABA

An excellent companion to any pedestrian exploration of the capital is Milena Batistoni and Gian Paolo Chiari's revelatory book *Old Tracks in the New Flower: A Historical Guide to Addis Ababa*, which describes more than 130 of its more interesting buildings along a series of different day walks. Rich in historical detail with regard to the city's formative years, this book was published by Arada Books in 2004 and can be bought at any bookshop in Addis Ababa for birr 100.

City centre walking tour

Addis Ababa's relatively modern city centre started to take shape following the arrival of the railway at the south end of what is now Churchill Avenue in 1917, and its present-day street plan was finalised during the Italian occupation. The city centre is arguably of interest more for its cafés, restaurants and shops than for a plethora of riveting sightseeing. All the same, one could easily spend a day exploring the various small museums and other landmarks that dot central Addis Ababa. A suggested walking itinerary, taking in most such landmarks, might start at Tewodros Square, continuing south along Churchill Avenue past Saba Square to the junction with Ras Mekonnen Avenue, and following this eastward past the stadium to Meskel Square and the nearby Addis Ababa Museum. From Meskel Square, you could continue northwards up the shady Menelik II Avenue, then head along Taitu Street, passing the Sheraton Hotel and possibly the Filwoha Hot Springs en route back to your starting point at Churchill Avenue.

For the sake of coherency, the major sites in the city centre are described following the above route, but one could pick up this loop at another point, or visit any one place of interest by taxi or minibus. Travellers exploring the city centre on foot are urged to carry no more money than they will need for the day, and to leave other valuables and important documents behind in their hotel – pickpockets are rife in several areas. Note, too, that we've had recent reports of travellers being stopped by the police for taking photographs of the 'very secret area' looking uphill along Churchill Avenue towards the Town Hall – one person reports having had their film destroyed by the police.

One of the most interesting buildings in this part of town is the **Mega Theatre**, a rectangular double-storey stone construction that dates to the 1920s and was originally named the Club de l'Union. A combined cinema, bar, dancing hall and casino, the French-owned club acquired a rather seedy reputation that earned it the soubriquet of **Satan Bet** – Devil's House – from suspicious Ethiopians, a name that is still in casual use today.

Heading downhill, about 100m south of Saba Square, the **Postal Museum** next to the main post office will be of great interest to philatelists, since it displays examples of every stamp ever issued in Ethiopia since the postal service was founded over a century ago. The nearby **National Library**, reached along Yared Road, houses the country's largest collection of ancient church manuscripts – 355 at the last count. Most of these have been recovered from old churches and monasteries; the oldest manuscript is a 15th-century document retrieved from the monastery of Hayk Istafanos. The National Library also claims to possess a copy of every book ever written about Ethiopia.

Back on Churchill Avenue, following it southwards, you'll pass a small public area to your right, dominated by the **Tiglachin Memorial**, a tall, geometric statue of a lion, erected in 1978 and dedicated to the men and women who gave their lives in the cross-border war with Somalia. Immediately south of the monument, the **National Theatre** is of little architectural merit, but it does stage Amharigna plays in the evenings, and marks the beginning of a row of good curio shops and inviting cafés – a regular haunt for pickpockets. Opposite the junction with Ras Mekonnen Avenue stands the bombastic but rundown neo-colonial style **Railway Station**, which was built by the Parisian architect Paul Barria over 1928–29 and inaugurated by the Empress Zawditu months before her premature death.

Heading eastward along Ras Mekonnen Avenue, you pass to your left the large **Addis Ababa Stadium**, built in the mid 1960s, and the site of most international football matches – including Ethiopia's fondly remembered home victory in the third Africa Nations Cup. A few hundred metres further, you arrive at **Meskel Square**, an important landmark, and notable among other things for one of the scariest pedestrian road crossings you're ever likely to navigate. The **Tourist Office** is situated on the northern side of Meskel Square, below the podium used by Mengistu to address the masses in the days when it was known as Revolution Square, as is the excellent Garden Court Restaurant and a couple of great pastry shops.

Off Bole Road, housed in a former royal residence five minutes' walk south of Meskel Square, the **Addis Ababa Museum** (*wkday 08.30–12.30 and 13.30–17.30; wkend 08.30–12.30; entrance birr 2*) is well worth a couple of hours' investigation. Besides a collection of old ceremonial and official clothes, the museum displays a marvellous collection of photographs from the early days of Addis Ababa, providing an interesting contrast to the more modern images that are also on display.

Rising uphill to the northeast of Meskel Square, the shady Menelik II Avenue, bisected by a green traffic island, is lined by a number of historic buildings. On the east of the avenue, the modern **Church of Kidus Istafanos** stands in an attractive green garden overlooking Meskel Square. Built during the Haile Selassie era, this church is notable for the mosaic above the main entrance, depicting the martyrdom of its namesake Saint Stephen. On festival days and Sundays, white-robed worshippers congregate in the large grounds, a scene characteristic of rural Ethiopia, but transplanted to the big city. Next to the church, the imposing **Africa Hall** was also constructed by Haile Selassie, to serve as the headquarters of the Organisation of African Unity. The Italian architecture of Africa Hall seems somewhat divorced from its Ethiopian setting, but the immense stained-glass mural, created by the lauded local artist Afewerk Tekle, more than justifies a look inside. Further uphill, to the left, a pair of steel gates guards the verdant grounds of the **Imperial Palace**, built in 1955 to mark the occasion of Haile Selassie's 25-year jubilee. The palace is closed to the public, and pulling out a camera in the vicinity of the gates is emphatically forbidden.

At the junction immediately north of the palace, you have three onward options. The first is to follow Atse Yohannis Avenue back towards the city centre, passing en route the attractively time-warped **Finfine Hotel** and nearby **Filwoha Hot Springs** (in the hotel of the same name), the presence of which first encouraged Menelik to move his capital down from the Entoto Hills. The second option is to continue north up Menelik II Avenue, passing the **Hilton Hotel** to your right and the **Ethiopia Mapping Authority** amid a row of other government buildings to your left. After 200m or so, turn left into the improbably named Development Through Co-operation Avenue at the T-junction, then after another 100m or so turn left into Taitu Road, passing the **Sheraton Hotel** en route back to the city centre. A third option, assuming that you want to move on to the museums near the University, or to the Piazza area, is to pick up one of the regular minibuses to Arat Kilo or Siddist Kilo at the T-junction. Between this T-junction and Arat Kilo lie a number of historic churches, described under the heading below.

The churches of Kiddist Maryam, Kidane Mihret and Kiddist Selassie

This trio of historical churches is situated to the north of Menelik II Avenue, tucked away in a substantial forested area that also hides the former Palace of Menelik II, today the seat of government and closed to casual visitors. The church complex is reached from around the back, by following a little road that circles the back of the hill towards Arat Kilo, then passing through the guarded entrance gate, past the uninteresting modern church of St Gabriel. Once inside the complex, head towards the tacky statue of St Mary and the disciples that was donated by the Italians during the occupation, and the tall bell tower which is shaped like an Axumite obelisk – looking out for squawking flocks of the endemic black-winged lovebird on the way.

Near this statue stands the oldest of the churches, **Kiddist Maryam**, built by Empress Zawditu in 1911. This attractive square stone church has four Axumite-style colonnaded arches on each of its exterior walls and carved lions guarding the entrance, and it is topped by a large central dome and one smaller dome on each corner. Below the church, reached via a low staircase, the eerie subterranean **Menelik II Mausoleum** encloses the carved marble tombs of Emperor Menelik II, his wife Empress Taitu, and their daughter Empress Zawditu. Also buried here is Abuna Matthias, the Patriarch of the Ethiopian Orthodox Church who presided over the coronation of Menelik II, and a daughter of Haile Selassie who died at the age of 22. The remains of Haile Selassie were held in this church prior to his formal burial in November 2000, 25 years after his death. Church treasures include an illuminated Bible that belonged to Emperor Yohannis IV. In the main part of the church, a series of murals depicts several important events in Ethiopian history. To the left of Kiddist Maryam, **Kidane Mihret** is a circular church noted for its interior paintings and nearby sacred springs, which produce holy water used for baptism ceremonies.

From Kiddist Maryam, a short walk along Development Through Co-operation Avenue leads to the **Kiddist Selassie (Holy Trinity) Cathedral**, the cornerstone of which was laid by Haile Selassie in 1933. This very large church has a rather Arabic façade, while the interior is lavishly decorated by ecclesiastical paintings in both the modern and medieval Ethiopian style. Within the grounds lie stone monuments dedicated to the first victims of the Derg regime, to the soldiers who died while resisting the Italian occupation, and to the British officers who died during the Allied campaign that ended the occupation. Several members of the Ethiopian aristocracy are buried here, as is the famous suffragette and Ethiopian sympathiser Sylvia Pankhurst.

The Holy Trinity Cathedral's biggest and most recent claim to fame is as **the final resting place of Emperor Haile Selassie**, who was reburied in the church grounds on 5 November 2000, 25 years after his death. Originally buried by his killers next to a toilet, the Emperor's exhumed remains were later housed for several years in a small coffin within the Menelik II Mausoleum. The colourful reburial procession, which ran uphill from Meskel Square, was attended by a substantial international Rastafarian contingent, headed by Rita Marley (the widow of Bob Marley), who said: 'Rasta people will be all loving his Imperial Majesty, Emperor Haile Selassie I. There is no end of his reign.' In early 2001, Haile Selassie's granite tomb – which stands next to an identical tomb holding the remains of his wife – was not yet open to the public, but this is likely to change in the near future.

Arat Kilo and Siddist Kilo

These two major traffic roundabouts are respectively situated – as their Amharigna names suggest – about 4km and 6km from the city centre, and are easily reached by minibus from the city centre or the Piazza area. Two of Ethiopia's best museums lie in this area, which also forms a major centre of student activity, with various departments of the University of Addis Ababa lining the road between the two roundabouts.

Coming from the city centre or Piazza, you'll first hit **Arat Kilo**, a large roundabout surrounded by chaotic minibus termini, shops and small local cafés. Next to the terminus on the road heading south to the city centre, the **Women Fuel Wood Carriers Project** shop is an interesting place to browse for curios, and it is clustered with a few other shops selling traditional Ethiopian clothes. To the east of the roundabout, the **Museum of Natural History** contains a collection of stuffed animals that struck me as pretty uninspired by comparison with similar museums in other African capitals, which doesn't mean it won't be of passing interest to some first-time visitors to Africa.

A ten-minute walk uphill from Arat Kilo towards Siddist Kilo leads to the **National Museum of Ethiopia**, housed in green grounds on the left-hand side of the road. This is one of the best museums of its type I've seen in Africa, not only for the quality and diversity of the exhibits, but also for the knowledgeable guides who work there. Archaeological exhibits include a realistic replica of the 3.5 million-year-old skull of Lucy (or Dinquinesh – 'thou art wonderful' – to Ethiopians), a hominid woman of the species *Australopithecus afarensis*. The discovery of this skull in 1974 forced a complete rethink of

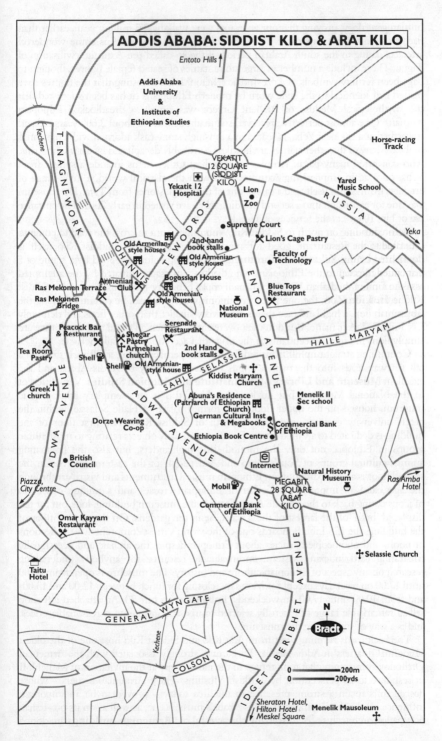

ADDIS ABABA: SIDDIST KILO & ARAT KILO

Entoto Hills ↑

Addis Ababa
University
&
Institute of
Ethiopian Studies

Horse-racing
Track

Kechene

TENAGNEWORK

VEKATIT
12 SQUARE
(SIDDIST
KILO)

Yekatit 12
Hospital

Lion
Zoo

Yared
Music School

RUSSIA

Yeka

YOHANNIS

TEWODROS

Supreme Court

Lion's Cage Pastry

2nd-hand
book stalls

Old Armenian-
style houses

Old Armenian-
style house

Faculty of
Technology

ENTOTO AVENUE

Ras Mekonen Terrace

Armenian
Club

Bogossian House

Blue Tops
Restaurant

HAILE MARYAM

Ras Mekonen
Bridge

Old Armenian-
style houses

National
Museum

Peacock Bar
& Restaurant

Serenade
Restaurant

Tea Room
Pastry

Shegar
Pastry

2nd Hand
book stalls

Shell

Armenian church

SAHLE SELASSIE

ADWA AVENUE

Shell

Old Armenian-
style house

Kiddist Maryam
Church

Menelik II
Sec school

Greek
church

Abuna's Residence
(Patriarch of Ethiopian
Church)

Dorze Weaving
Co-op

ADWA AVENUE

German Cultural Inst
& Megabooks

Commercial Bank
of Ethiopia

Ethiopia Book Centre

British
Council

Internet

Natural History
Museum

Ras Amba
Hotel

Piazza,
City Centre

Mobil

MEGABIT
28 SQUARE
(ARAT
KILO)

Omar Kayyam
Restaurant

Commercial Bank
of Ethiopia

IDGET BERIBHET AVENUE

Selassie Church

Taitu
Hotel

N

Bradt

GENERAL WYNGATE

Kechene

COLSON

0 ————— 200m
0 ————— 200yds

Sheraton Hotel,
Hilton Hotel
Meskel Square

Menelik Mausoleum

human genealogy, proving that our ancestors were walking 2.5 million years earlier than had previously been supposed. The national museum also contains some wonderful artefacts dating to the south Arabian period of the so-called pre-Axumite civilisation of Tigrai. These include a number of large stone statues of seated female figures, thought to have been fertility symbols of a pre-Judaic religion. It is interesting that the figures have plaited hair identical to the style worn by modern Ethiopians (it has been suggested that the mythological Medusa of Ancient Greece was simply a dreadlocked Ethiopian woman). One almost perfectly preserved statue, thought to be about 2,600 years old and unearthed at a site near Yeha, is seated in a 2m-high stone cask adorned with engravings of ibex. Many of the other statues are headless – probably decapitated by early Christians, who converted many pagan temples to churches. Other items include a sphinx from Yeha, once again emphasising Axumite links with the classical world, a huge range of artefacts from Axum itself, and a cast of one of the Gragn stones from Tiya. The museum was due for expansion into a second building when we visited in early 2001. The entrance fee of birr 10 covers the services of a guide.

Before heading on north to Siddist Kilo, you might want to cross the road to pop into the Blue Tops Restaurant, good for meals, snacks, or pastries. Siddist Kilo itself is dominated by the **Yekatit 12 Monument**, a towering column topped by a statue of a lion and dedicated to the Ethiopians who died in a massacre initiated by the attempted assassination of the Italian Viceroy Graziani on 19 February 1937. Also situated at Siddist Kilo is the **Lion Zoo**, the one place in Ethiopia where you can be certain of seeing the Abyssinian lion, a highland race that is reportedly smaller than other lions and definitely has a much darker mane. But don't get overexcited – when all's said and done, they are simply lions in cages, descendants of the pride that accompanied Haile Selassie.

Continuing straight uphill from Siddist Kilo for perhaps 500m, a left turn through a tall gateway leads into the main campus of the University of Addis Ababa and the excellent **Museum and Library of the Institute of Ethiopian Studies**. Very different to the National Museum, but no less absorbing, this is an exemplary ethnographic museum, housed on the upper floors of a former palace of Haile Selassie, within the green university grounds immediately north of Siddist Kilo. The first floor of the building is dedicated to a varied array of artefacts and daily objects relating to most ethnic groups in Ethiopia, not only the monotheistic highlanders, but also the fascinating animist cultural groups of South Omo and Afar people of the eastern deserts. On the second floor is a new exhibition on Ethiopian musical instruments and visual art through the ages, and an impressive selection of Ethiopian crosses and a unique collection of icons dating back to the Middle Ages. Outside the museum building, look out for the displaced 'head' of the largest of the Tiya stelae in the gardens. On the ground floor of the building, the IES Library hoards one of the world's most comprehensive collections of books and photocopied articles about Ethiopia; despite the archaic and occasionally frustrating card indexing system, an invaluable resource for anybody undertaking research on any aspect of Ethiopian culture and history. The museum is open from 08.00 until 17.00 on weekdays except for Mondays (closing for lunch between 12.00 and 13.00) and from 10.00 until 17.00 on weekends. Entrance costs birr 20. An attached gift shop sells a remarkable range of carefully selected tourist and gift items at reasonable prices, and is a way of supporting the museum.

The back roads running west from Arat Kilo and Siddist Kilo host one of the oldest residential quarters in Addis Ababa. This area is strongly associated with the Armenian Orthodox community that took refuge in the nascent city at the invitation of Menelik II in response to its persecution by Turkish Muslims. These Armenian settlers – whose descendants retain a strong presence in the area today – proved to be an important influence on the development of Addis Ababa's music scene, as well as on its pre-Italian occupation architecture. A great many characterful old **Armenian buildings** are dotted around this quiet suburb, many close to the junction of Tewodros and Welete Yohannis streets. Possibly the oldest extant house in Addis Ababa, dating to around 1886, the thatched one-storey residence built by **Krikorios Bogossion** on Welete Yohannis Street is still owned by the Bogossion family, and interested visitors may be invited to take a look around the period-furnished interior.

The Piazza

Prior to the 1938 Italian construction of a 'Grand Mercato Indegeno' (the present-day Mercato) and simultaneous expansion of the modern city centre, the Piazza – or more correctly Arada – was the economic pulse of Addis Ababa and site of the city's most important bank, market, hotel and shops. Arada Market, described as one European visitor as 'picturesque chaos', was held around a sprawling sycamore fig on what is today De Gaulle Square, peaking in activity on Saturdays, which is also when public executions were held right through until the early years of Haile Selassie's rule.

Today, the Piazza, though dominated by post-Italian occupation constructions, is also studded with Armenian-influenced relics of the Menelik era. Most of the older buildings are in poor repair, a situation that wasn't improved by the extensive damage caused during a riot in April 2001 – though the area as a whole seems to have undergone a striking facelift of late. One of the few buildings that does remain in pristine condition is the **Itegue Taitu Hotel**, which is the oldest hostelry in the city, practically unchanged in appearance since 1907, and definitely worth a look in for the spacious architecture, period furnishings, and excellent national restaurant.

Other interesting buildings in the area include the stone **Bank of Abyssinia**, which dates to 1905 and lies on the south side of General Wingate Street behind the Taitu, and the **Foalklands Bar** next door, which has gone somewhat downhill since it was consecrated as a Greek Orthodox church to accommodate the Greek manager of the Taitu circa 1915. Around the corner, next to the Omar Khayyam Restaurant, a fabulously sprawling five-storey house designed by Minas Kherbekian (the Armenian architect who also designed the Taitu) stood as the tallest in the city prior to the Italian occupation.

Another important landmark in the Piazza area is **St George's Cathedral**, founded by Menelik in 1896 to commemorate the victory over Italy in the Battle of Adwa, though the church itself dates to 1905–11. Subsequent emperors of Ethiopia were crowned in this, the oldest of Addis Ababa's churches. The walls of the church are graced by some fine paintings and tile murals by Afewerk Tekle, commissioned during post-World War II restoration work initiated by Haile Selassie. The interesting museum, open from 08.30–17.30 daily except for Monday, stands in the church grounds, as does the engraved tomb of the popular singer Mary Armide.

Mercato

This is the biggest shopping area in Addis – and I'm told the largest market on the African continent. Mercato is wistfully described elsewhere as having 'pungent aromas of incense and spices... [that]... make a stunning impact on the senses'. On the pungency front, I must admit that I was more impacted upon by rotting vegetables and human excreta. Perhaps it was just a hot day.

Whiffy or not, Mercato *is* the real commercial hub of Addis, a vast grid of roads lined with stalls, kiosks and small shops, where you can buy just about anything you might want: the latest local cassettes; traditional crosses, clothes and other curios; vegetables, spices and pulses; custom-made silver and gold jewellery – there is even an entire street devoted to selling *chat*! Needless to say, prices are generally negotiable, and pickpocketing and bag-snatching are rife – it might be advisable to visit Mercato first time round without much money and, after you've browsed, to return another day to buy what you want.

Washa Mikael Church

Given that there is so much interest in the rock-hewn churches of Lalibela and Tigrai, you might expect that a rock-hewn church lying within easy walking distance of the capital would be a major tourist attraction. In fact, there are two such churches, of which the easiest to walk to is **Washa Mikael**, and both go unvisited by the vast majority of visitors to Addis Ababa. I considered Washa Mikael to be a fine church and well worth the walk when I visited it a few years ago, a reaction that might well have been influenced by the fact I had no idea what to expect from it. Reader consensus appears to be that it's a disappointment. Either way, subsequent to my visit, several tourists have been mugged along the road up, some of them by 'guides' they picked up at the base to avoid such a fate. For this reason, unless you have a 4x4 to drive up in, it would be advisable either to take a guide from town, or to carry nothing worth stealing with you.

According to the priests at nearby **Tekle Haymanot Church**, Washa Mikael was excavated by Abreha and Atsbeha in the 4th century. The 12th or 13th centuries seem more likely, especially as it is far closer in execution to the 12th-century churches at Lalibela than to older churches in Tigrai. Washa Mikael is a semi-monolith – freed from the surrounding rock on three sides. It is excavated entirely from below the ground, and its enclosure is reached via a short tunnel through the rock. Locals may tell you that the church was used as a hideout during the Italian occupation, when it lost its roof to an Italian bomb and fell into disuse, to be replaced by Tekle Haymanot Church. Academic opinion is that the roof collapsed more than a century ago, while another story has it that it was de-sanctified in 1897 by Emperor Menelik II, who sent the *tabot* to Yeka Mikael Church down the road.

Paradoxically, this roofless condition of the church allows you to get a far better idea of the layout than is normally possible. The pillars and walls are still standing, and you can scramble over the rocks into what used to be the Holy of Holies where the *tabot* was stored. There are several windows and candle niches along the walls, and there is a holy pool fed by underground springs. Overgrown it may be, but Washa Mikael is in my opinion a very impressive excavation – though take heed that one reader has accused me of being over-imaginative in this description.

To get to the church, take a minibus from Arat Kilo to Yeka Park, about 1km past the British Embassy. A side road to your left immediately east of the park leads uphill to a track through the cemetery of Kidus Mikael Church. When you hit a T-junction with an unsurfaced road, turn right. You should follow this road for about ten minutes, across a bridge, then climb steeply before you reach a left fork immediately before another bridge. From here, there are two options; on the way out I would advise you to take the longer but more straightforward route, which means ignoring the left fork and continuing straight along a road that climbs a eucalyptus-clad hill. After about 500m, the road descends towards a tin-roofed village. At the base of the hill, just before you enter the village, the road crosses a small watercourse where there is a distinctive small hill to your right. Immediately after the watercourse, take the road to your left, and follow it for about 300m till you reach a T-junction, where you need to turn left. From here it's a straightforward 1–2km slog along a road that curls steeply uphill through eucalyptus forest. At the top of the hill, you come out in a meadow. The road turns sharply left, and after about 200m there is a small rocky peak to your left. The church is here, in a fenced enclosure near the road but not visible from it. If in doubt, you'll see plenty of locals along the walk out – just keep asking for directions (better to ask for Tekle Haymanot than Washa Mikael). People have recently been asked an entrance fee of birr 20–30.

Once you're at the church, it will be evident that you can reduce the return distance by as much as 50% by cutting downhill through the forest behind Tekle Haymanot back to the road, and then, about 500m further, at the sharp left turn that marks the end of the steepest part of the descent, by crossing through the light forest back to the fork near the bridge. You could, of course, try to go out to the church by using these short cuts, but you risk getting lost – the short cuts are only obvious once you have your bearings.

Entoto Maryam

The Entoto Hills were the site of Menelik's capital before Addis Ababa was founded in 1887. The only obvious relic of this era, the still-functional **Entoto Maryam Church**, is an octagonal building with a traditionally painted interior, where Menelik was crowned in 1882. The interior can only be seen during and immediately after the church services, which are held every morning ending at around 09.00. In the church compound, the **Entoto Saint Mary, Emperor Menelik and Empress Taitu Memorial Museum**, which opened in 1987, houses an interesting collection of religious items and ceremonial clothing dating from Menelik's time. Entrance costs birr 10, and the museum is closed on Mondays.

Entoto Maryam can be reached by private taxi, or else by catching a bus from Arat Kilo northwards past Siddist Kilo to the terminus at the footslopes of the Entoto Hills. About 100m and signposted from this terminus, the local women (under the auspices of the **Women Fuel Wood Carriers Project**, supported by the ILO) have established a souvenir and gift shop selling hand-woven cotton shawls, traditional *gabbis* and *netelas*, and sisal hats, baskets and much more. From here, you can follow the main road uphill on foot for about 2–3km, a tough slog that will take at least an hour. The alternatives are to wait at the terminus for one of the occasional minibuses

THE ASNI GALLERY

PO Box 1896, Addis Ababa, Ethiopia; ℡ 011 1117360; f 011 5515691; e asnigallery@hotmail.com

Established as recently as 1996, the Asni Gallery is already entrenched as an essential fixture on the itinerary of any tourist with a passing interest in contemporary Ethiopian art. The gallery is housed in an attractive early 20th-century residence, built by Indian masons for Afanegus Telahun, who served as Minister of Justice under the ill-fated Emperor Iyasu. It lies on the footslopes of the Entoto Hills, about five minutes' drive from the university campus on Siddist Kilo: follow the Entoto road out of town past the French Embassy, then take the first right turn after passing a Total petrol station.

The Asni Gallery displays a wide variety of contemporary Ethiopian art, which generally combines elements of traditional painting with contemporary international influences. The upper floor of the building hosts a permanent display of works by artists who have had training at the Addis Ababa Fine Arts School since its establishment in 1959. This includes the gallery's own collection, as well as works on loan from local collectors, the Addis Ababa School of Fine Arts and Design, and from individual artists. The ground floor is reserved for temporary exhibitions, up to six of which are hosted annually.

The gallery is open on Tuesday and Wednesday from 14.30 to 17.30, and on Thursday, Friday and Saturday from 10.00 until 17.30. Appointments can be made for other times. A popular time to visit is at around 13.00 Thursday and Saturday, when an excellent vegetarian buffet deriving from a combination of Ethiopian fasting food and international cuisine is served in the balcony. In addition to selling art, the gift shop stocks customised printed posters, bookmarks, postcards and T-shirts. Entrance costs birr 10 or birr 5 for students.

ENTOTO NATURAL PARK

Were it not for the eucalyptus forests that cover the Entoto Hills, Addis Ababa's tenure as the Ethiopian capital might have been rather short-lived. The area around Addis is not naturally rich in firewood, and it was largely due to the arrival of these fast-growing exotics from Australia that Menelik abandoned a plan to move west to Addis Alem. In this light, it is understandable that much is made of Ethiopia's eucalyptus forests – a British television documentary made in the Haile Selassie era goes so far as to suggest that Addis be renamed Eucalyptropolis or something equally catchy.

I find it difficult to get terribly excited about Antipodean exotics, especially in a country that has so much indigenous forest. Planting eucalyptus trees in already deforested areas might ultimately save indigenous forests from being felled, so it is arguably an ecologically valid move. That doesn't change the fact that the eucalyptus is a most unattractive tree, or that eucalyptus plantations, wherever they occur in Africa, are generally void of birds and mammals, and often adversely affect the water table and local drainage patterns.

The recent foundation of the Entoto Natural Park, the entrance to which lies a short distance past the church of Entoto Maryam, is thus of great significance to the conservation of Addis Ababa's few remaining natural assets. This 13,000ha park consists of a part of the mountain range that was leased to the Ethiopian Heritage Trust in 1995. Though still embryonic so far as tourist facilities are concerned, the natural park spans altitudes of 2,600m to 3,200m, and offers spectacular views in all directions. Some large mammals persist in the area, including spotted hyena, common jackal, leopard, vervet monkey, and various small antelopes – populations may well rise with long-term protection.

The new park is of particular interest to birdwatchers, with some 200 species recorded in the mixed habitats of forest, woodland, cultivation, grassy meadows, rocky slopes, cliffs, streams and marshes. Among the more interesting birds that are regularly recorded by visitors are the Abyssinian woodpecker, Abyssinian catbird, wattled ibis, moorland francolin, white-collared pigeon, black-winged lovebird, white-cheeked turaco, mountain nightjar, banded barbet, white-winged cliff-chat, Abyssinian ground thrush, brown parisoma, white-backed black tit, Ethiopian oriole and white-billed starling. The park also provides great viewing for vultures, including lammergeyer, as well as various eagles and hawks.

Funding is currently being sought to establish an infrastructure for visitors, but as things stand facilities are non-existent at the time of writing. As one reader notes: 'Trying to find the Entoto Hills Nature Park proved fruitless – neither the tour guides that I asked nor the locals could put me on the right path. A local did walk me about the area, but it was fairly desolate, no birds apart from ravens and brown-rumped serin.'

that go all the way up to the church (as, I'm told, do number 17 buses), or to catch a private taxi. About 2km past Entoto Maryam, there is a disused 13th-century rock-hewn church called **Kidus Raguel** which, like Washa Mikael, was partially destroyed during the Italian occupation. Marie Hogervost writes: 'One of my friends went to an **exorcism** at Entoto Maryam. These take place on Sundays at 05.00, and last for about an hour. People that are suspected of being possessed by the devil are cured with holy water, and many other diseases like AIDS are cured. You are supposed to become religious as soon as you have seen this, according to many Ethiopian friends, but even if you don't it is an interesting spectacle.'

Short trips further afield

Unusually for an African capital, Addis Ababa lies at the centre of an area rich in places of interest, most of which can be visited either as a day trip from the capital or else as a preliminary to travels further afield. Many such places of interest are overlooked by tourists in their rush to get to Ethiopia's more renowned attractions. They are also, for the most part, highly accessible, and offer what amounts to some excellent off-the-beaten-track travel with a minimum of effort. These places are described along routes covered elsewhere in this book, but it is worth giving a quick overview here.

The main string of attractions lies on the road to Adama, a large town about 100km southeast of the capital and a useful springboard to most parts of east and southern Ethiopia. Attractions along the Adama road include the Akaki River Wetlands, the crater-lake field at Bishoftu, and Mounts Yerer and Zikwala. From Adama, you can also visit the popular hot springs resort at Sodore.

A second cluster of attractions, mostly with a historical bent, lies around Melka Awash and Tiya on the Butajira road. From Melka Awash you could, at a push, visit in a day an ancient rock-hewn church, a field of mysterious engraved tomb-markers which date to the 14th century or thereabouts, and the prehistoric Stone-Age site at Melka Kunture.

North of Addis, the Durba Waterfall is one of the highest in the country, and the surrounding area offers wonderful views across the Muger Valley Gorge, as well as a good chance of close-up views of the endemic gelada baboon. The monastery of Debre Libanos is also a feasible site for a day trip.

To the west, Ambo is a hot-spring resort mostly of interest to Addis weekenders. On the way there you pass Gefersa Reservoir and Menelik's turn-of-the-century proposed capital at Addis Alem. Ambo is also the base from which you can visit forested Lake Wenchi. Another excellent day or overnight goal to the west of the city is the Menegasha Forest.

The monthly excursions run by the Ethiopian Wildlife Society go to most of the places mentioned above. Tourists are welcome to join these excursions by contacting Elizabeth Asfaw on ☎ 011 5517200 (room 235), or on 011 4164045 after hours.

Part Three

Northern Ethiopia

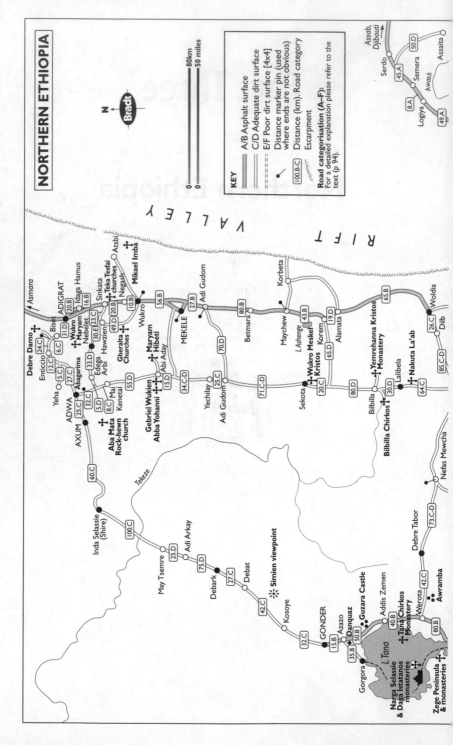

NORTHERN ETHIOPIA

N · Bradt

0 _____ 80km
0 _____ 50 miles

KEY

—— A/B Asphalt surface
—— C/D Adequate dirt surface
·········· E/F Poor dirt surface [4x4]
•—— Distance marker pin (used
      where ends are not obvious)
100.B-C Distance (km). Road category
✓✓✓✓ Escarpment

Road categorisation (A–F):
For a detailed explanation please refer to the
text (p 94).

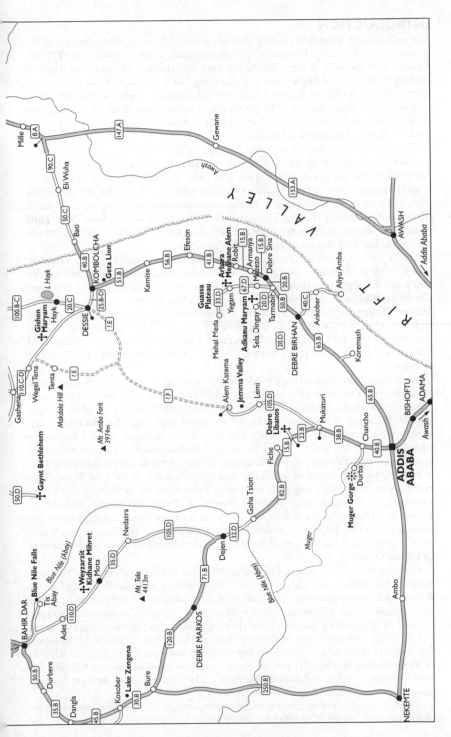

INTRODUCTION

The well-defined 'historical circuit' through northern Ethiopia forms the core of the country's tourist industry. It is probably no exaggeration to say that 98% of travellers to Ethiopia base the bulk of their itinerary around this circuit, and rightly so. There is nothing in sub-Saharan Africa – in a sense, nothing else in the world – that prepares the visitor for the wealth of historical and cultural treasures, both ancient and living, contained in northern Ethiopia. The circuit pivots around **four cities**, all very different to the others, and followed in this section in the **clockwise direction** favoured by most tour operators and independent travellers.

The standard **first stop** in northern Ethiopia is the modern city of **Bahir Dar**, a bustling commercial centre set on the southern shore of Lake Tana, the largest body of water in Ethiopia and official source of the Blue Nile. In addition to hosting a fascinating traditional daily market and rich birdlife, Bahir Dar forms the obvious base for several day trips: to the multitude of atmospheric medieval **monasteries** dotted around the forested islands and peninsulas of Lake Tana, as well as to the sensational **Blue Nile Falls** (sensational, that is, on the increasingly rare occasions when the Nile's water hasn't been diverted to fuel a neighbouring hydro-electric generator).

To the north of Lake Tana, a popular **second stop** on the northern circuit is **Gonder**, which served as Ethiopia's capital for almost 300 years from 1635 onwards, and is today noted for its impressive **16th-century castles** as well as the beautifully decorated **Church of Debre Birhan Selassie**. To the north of Gonder, lies the staggeringly scenic **Simien Mountains National Park**, home to the country's main concentrations of the endemic gelada baboon and Walia ibex. Following the recent construction of a rough road into the Simien Mountains, this lovely range – traditionally the preserve of hardened trekkers and hikers – also forms a feasible goal for a day or overnight 4x4 trip out of Gonder.

A common **third stop** on the historical circuit is the ancient capital of **Axum**, which lies close to the Eritrean border at the heart of the former Axumite Empire, the dominant economic and political force in the region for about a millennium prior to its collapse circa AD700. Axum is best known today for the **giant engraved obelisks** (stelae) that tower over the northeast of the town. But the entire city stands above a fascinating miscellany of ancient relics – dingy catacombs, ruined palaces, rock engravings and inscribed tablets – that pay collective testament to the enterprise and complexity of what is perhaps the most enigmatic of all the ancient civilisations of the Old World. This enigma is amplified when one visits the nearby **Yeha Temple**, estimated to have been constructed 2,500 years ago. Axum's **Church of Tsion Maryam** – claimed by Ethiopians to house the Ark of the Covenant – has for more than 1,600 years lain at the spiritual heart of the Ethiopian Orthodox Church; the Axumite architectural legacy lives on in several ancient churches, notably the male-only clifftop gem that is the **Monastery of Debre Damo**.

For most visitors to Ethiopia, the **highlight** of the northern circuit is the medieval capital of **Lalibela**, where high in the chilly mountains of Wolo stands a complex of a **dozen rock-hewn churches** often and justifiably ranked as the eighth wonder of the ancient world. Reachable only on foot or by mule until a couple of decades back, but now serviced by daily buses and flights, these churches stand as an inspirational active shrine to a Christian civilisation that predates its northern European equivalent by centuries. And around Lalibela lie several more ecclesiastic gems: the beautiful Axumite cave church of **Yemrehanna Kristos**, the isolated monasteries and churches around **Bilbilla**, the remote montane retreat of **Asheton Maryam**... all set amid some of the most fantastic mountain scenery on the African continent.

The majority of travellers take one of three approaches to exploring the 'big four' cities of the northern circuit. The first, and less strenuous, approach is to **fly** between the aforementioned stops, exploring the towns, and sometimes arranging day excursions to nearby places of interest. One could, in theory, see the best of the northern circuit over five days, since flights generally take only an hour or so, leaving one with plenty of time to explore in between. In practice, however, the combination of sudden schedule changes, occasional delays, and the need to reconfirm all domestic flights at the point of departure, makes it advisable to dedicate about eight days to a flying excursion around the northern circuit. This will allow for a full day between flights to explore each of the major towns at leisure.

A more demanding option is to **drive** around the historical circuit in a rented 4x4 with a driver and/or guide, or – tougher still – to do the whole circuit using **buses** and other public transport. The disadvantage of road travel is that it is time consuming and sometimes exhausting – recent improvements in several trunk roads notwithstanding, a realistic minimum of 12–14 days is required to cover this circuit by road, and three weeks or longer would be better, especially if you are using public transport. The main advantages of driving over flying are firstly that you get to see far more of the beautiful mountain scenery, and secondly that you have the opportunity of escaping the relatively well-trodden tourist trail to visit areas where tourists remain an infrequent sight. As a thorough read through this section will make abundantly clear, there is infinitely more to northern Ethiopia than its four established historical cities. The list of off-the-beaten-track possibilities is practically endless; to name one example, the vastly underrated rock-hewn churches of Tigrai alone could keep an interested traveller busy for weeks.

SECTION STRUCTURE

So far as is realistically possible, this section is designed to be as user-friendly to travellers who fly between the major highlights as it is to those who travel by road. The section consists of nine chapters in all. Each of the 'big four' towns on the historical circuit forms the subject of one dedicated chapter, which covers not only the town itself, but also any other places of interest that are regularly or easily visited from it. As such, each of these four chapters – respectively entitled *Bahir Dar and Lake Tana*; *Gonder and the Simien Mountains*; *Axum and the Adigrat Road* and *Lalibela and Surrounds* – functions as a stand-alone guide to the town and its environs, whether one arrives there by air, bus, or in a private vehicle.

Few tourists who fly around northern Ethiopia will have much need to look beyond the aforementioned four chapters. But for those who travel by road, there remain the bits in between, the journeys as well as the destinations – journeys, it must be said, that are often brimming with latent possibilities for off-the-beaten-track exploration. It is the in-between bits that form the subject of the remaining five chapters, which are entitled *Addis Ababa to Lake Tana by Road*; *Rock-hewn Churches of Northeast Tigrai*; *Mekele and the Danakil*; *Dessie, Woldia and Surrounds* and *Dessie to Addis Ababa*. These chapters explore not only the main roads that connect the 'big four' towns, but investigate enough diversions and stops along the way to keep one busy for months.

The chapters in this section stick with previous editions of this guide by following the northern circuit in a broadly clockwise direction, starting and ending in Addis Ababa. Whilst this may cause minor inconvenience to travellers who work in the opposite direction, the reality – for whatever reason – is that most travellers do follow the northern circuit in a clockwise loop. It strikes me that a more random structure would be significantly less useful than a directional one to travellers heading 'forwards' while having few benefits to travellers working 'backwards'.

One structural quirk, at least from the point of view of those bussing or driving between sites, is that Lalibela does not lie on the main road circuit through the north, and can be reached by road from several different directions. The most popular approach road leads westward from Woldia (on the main road between Mekele and Addis Ababa), while alternative routes lead from Werota (between Bahir Dar and Gonder) via Debre Tabor, from Axum via Adwa, Abi Aday and Sekota, and from Mekele via Korem and Sekota. A new road connecting Lalibela directly to Addis Ababa via Alem Katema and Tenta has been under intermittent construction for several years and may already be a viable option at the end of the dry season. These options are discussed more fully within the chapter *Lalibela and Surrounds*.

Addis Ababa to Lake Tana by Road

This chapter follows the two road routes between Addis Ababa and Bahir Dar, the latter being the principal town on Lake Tana and a popular first stop along the historical circuit. The main 560km road between these cities – via Dejen and Debre Markos – is now sealed with asphalt for all but the steep 30km stretch that passes through the Blue Nile Gorge between Goha Tsion and Dejen. The road can easily be driven in a private vehicle in one day, or covered by any of several direct bus services (most of which currently entail an overnight stop en route, though this is changing), but for those who prefer to dawdle, the route is also endowed with a number of little-visited potential diversions.

The most significant geographical landmark between Addis Ababa and Bahir Dar is the Blue Nile Gorge, which can, at a push, be visited as a round day trip from the capital in a private vehicle. Between Addis Ababa and the Blue Nile Gorge, the main sites of interest are the spectacular and underrated Muger River Gorge (a potential day trip from Addis even on public transport) and the famous medieval monastery of Debre Libanos.

Roughly 230km north of Addis Ababa, shortly after passing through Dejen on the northern rim of the Blue Nile Gorge, there is a major fork in the road. Both routes north from here lead to Bahir Dar. The eastern route, via Mota, is the less interesting of the two, and the road is unsealed, but is shorter at around 240km. The western route, about 90km longer, passes through Debre Markos, the largest town covered in this chapter and former capital of the defunct Gojjam region, and offers some interesting yet accessible off-the-beaten-track possibilities in the vicinity of Kosober, including montane forests, crater lakes, waterfalls, and the 'true' source of the Nile as identified by James Bruce.

FROM ADDIS ABABA TO DEJEN
Chancho and the Muger Gorge
On leaving Addis Ababa, the Bahir Dar road climbs the eucalyptus-clad Entoto Hills into high moorland. The first stop, **Chancho**, lies 40km from the capital in an area of rolling grassland and babbling streams. Chancho is of little interest in itself, but it's a reasonably large town in attractive surrounds and, more significantly, the springboard for visits to the immense Muger River Gorge – a good day trip from the capital, or first stop along the historic route. Public transport between the Autobus Terra in Addis and Chancho runs all day through, taking about one hour in either direction. If you're looking to overnight in Chancho before heading further north, there is no shortage of shoestring accommodation, with the most promising option being the Chancho Motel on the Addis Ababa side of town just before the turn-off to Durba.

Access to **Muger Gorge** is from the village of Durba, where there is a waterfall, which, although it carries a low volume of water, makes a dramatic plunge of around 100m into a side gorge. Just past the village, the Durba Cement Factory stands on a rock promontory with wonderful views in three directions. The Durba area is at its best in

September and October, when the water is high and the countryside is a patchwork of colourful flowers, mostly the yellow Meskel flower but also several other varieties coloured blue, pink, white and purple. An incentive for visiting the region at any time of year is the presence of gelada baboons, which are often seen just outside the village. There is also good birdwatching: a pair of lammergeyers breeds on the cliffs near the waterfall, while other birds worth looking out for include black eagle, gymnogene, Hemprich's hornbill, and the endemic white-billed starling. **Durba** is a peaceful, leafy village, with at least one shoestring hotel. It only takes a glance at the surrounding area to see it has enormous potential for walking and hiking – a footpath leads from the cement factory to the base of the gorge, or you could follow the rim north of Durba for several kilometres. If you are looking for some off-the-beaten-track hiking in the Addis area, the Muger Gorge feels like an excellent option. Take some food along, as there's not much available in Durba.

Durba lies about 20km west of the Bahir Dar road, and can be reached via a turn-off at the southern end of Chancho. The light vehicles that serve as erratic public transport between Durba and Chancho can usually be located at the junction, and are most prolific on Saturday (market day). On other days, the earliest possible start is recommended, or you could get stuck in Durba. In fact, with an early enough start, you could think about walking back: it's a 20km hike but the slopes are gentle, the scenery is good, and you cross several babbling streams. If you are on foot, or are driving yourself, do stop at the Sibale River about 2km out of Chancho, as it has a reputation for attracting unusual migrant birds alongside endemics such as black-headed siskin, wattled ibis and Abyssinian longclaw.

Jemma Valley

Lying to the east of the Debre Libanos road, the pretty Jemma Valley is named for the river that formed it, a tributary of the Blue Nile. The area is of great interest to birders as the most accessible place to tick Harwood's francolin, an Ethiopian endemic restricted to a handful of sites in the Blue Nile watershed region. Lying at an altitude of between 1,300m and 2,000m, the valley is dominated by acacia woodland, and also supports other interesting birds including the endemic Rüppell's cliff-chat, white-billed starling and white-throated seedeater, as well as vinaceous dove, foxy cisticola, speckle-fronted weaver, black-faced firefinch and stone partridge.

The valley is reached by turning right from the main road to Lake Tana at Mukaturi, which lies roughly 40km north of Chancho and 20km south of the junction for Debre Libanos, and can be reached from Addis Ababa by direct buses. From the junction at Mukaturi, a 105km road descends via Lemi to the small town of Alem Katema, which lies at the base of the valley next to a stretch of the Jemma River where the range-restricted francolin is very common. Two buses daily run along this road, leaving Mukaturi at about 05.30 and 08.00 and arriving at Alem Katema about four hours later. Basic accommodation is available in Mukaturi, Lemi, and Alem Katema. As things stand, Alem Katema is something of a dead end, but a new road northward to Tenta and Lalibela is reputedly under construction.

Debre Libanos and Ras Darge's Bridge

Past Chancho, the Bahir Dar road continues through high moorland swathed in unusual heather-like vegetation and, particularly after Debre Tegist, offering some impressive views across rugged montane scenery. After some 57km, you'll pass a viewpoint to the right and a parking lot to the left, the latter adorned by a plaque erected in 2005 to commemorate Ethio-Japanese co-operation in the construction of this (excellent) new 200km asphalt road between Addis Ababa and Goha Tsion. Another 3km further, precisely 100km out of Addis Ababa, a rough side road leads eastward to the renowned medieval monastery of Debre Libanos, which stands at the base of a magnificent 700m-high canyon known (for reasons that are unclear) as Wusha Gadel (Dog Valley).

A reliable tradition states that Debre Libanos was founded in 1284 by Abuna Tekle Haymanot, the priest who was instrumental to the contemporaneous spread of Christianity through Showa. Tekle Haymanot spent roughly a decade studying the scriptures at each of two of northern Ethiopia's most important monasteries, Hayk Istafanos and Debre Damo, and his influence is widely associated with the reinstatement of the so-called Solomonic dynasty after centuries of Zagwe rule. One of the many bizarre legends associated with this important figure, who is usually depicted as having one leg and six wings, is that he spent seven years standing on one leg praying, and subsisted on one seed a year (fed to him by a bird), before eventually his spare leg withered away and fell off!

Originally known as Debre Asbo, Debre Libanos was given its present name by Emperor Zara Yaqob in 1445. At around the same time, Debre Libanos usurped Hayk Istafanos as the political centre of the Ethiopian Church, a position it consolidated under the powerful leadership of Abbot Marha Kristos from 1463 to 1497. It was here, in 1520, that Emperor Lebna Dengal formally received the first Portuguese mission to Ethiopia; here, too, that the priest Francisco Alvares, a member of that mission, made contact with Pero de Covilhão, the 'spy' who had been sent overland by King John of Portugal to explore the land of Prester John three decades earlier. Debre Libanos retained its political significance until as recently as the Italian occupation, when – as a perceived hotbed of patriotic anti-Italian sentiment – both the monastery and its inhabitants were destroyed by the fascist troops (see box *Graziani's Revenge*, page 184). It remains an important pilgrimage site for Orthodox Christians.

The modern church, built in the 1950s by Haile Selassie to replace the one destroyed by the fascists, is tucked away in a small wooded gorge that feels intimate and secluded next to the surrounding canyon. The rather bombastic exterior is typical of latter-day Ethiopian churches, but the attractive marble interior, decorated with stained-glass windows of various saints, compensates. Entrance costs a rather steep birr 50, with an additional birr 50 charge levied for use of a video camera. A signpost stipulates that entry to the church is forbidden to menstruating women and to anybody who has had sexual intercourse within the previous 48 hours.

The church aside, there is a definite aura about Debre Libanos, especially if you follow the footpaths along the stream – boosted by several waterfalls tumbling over the gorge's edge – that runs past the new church to its derelict predecessor. There is a small woody village about 1km towards the main road from the church. It's all very beautiful and serene; in the right frame of mind one could spend several days wandering around the valley. On the opposite side of the stream to the main church, the cave where Tekle Haymanot prayed until his death (aged 98, according to tradition) is now maintained as a shrine. The caretaker priest here will gladly bless visitors with holy water from the cave, provided that they haven't eaten anything yet that day. Some of the monks and nuns live in nearby caves.

Little more than 100m north of the turn-off to Debre Libanos, a 500m footpath leads east from the Bahir Dar road to a lichen- and moss-stained stone bridge that spans the Gur River before it plunges for several hundred metres over a cliff edge to eventually flow into the Jemma, a tributary of the Nile. Presumably as a result of confusion with the two 17th-century bridges that span the Nile below the Blue Nile Falls, this is now widely referred to as the 'Portuguese Bridge'. Despite a convincingly timeworn appearance, however, it was actually built at the cusp of the 19th and 20th centuries by Ras Darge, a relation of Menelik II, using the traditional sealant of limestone and crushed ostrich shell instead of cement. Not only is Ras Darge's Bridge of some historical interest, but the view from the lip of the gorge is fantastic. Cross the bridge and follow the cliff edge to your

GRAZIANI'S REVENGE

During the Italian occupation, Debre Libanos was the target of one of the most heinous atrocities committed by the fascists, who believed some of its monks to have been involved in a failed attempt on Viceroy Graziani's life. On 20 May 1937, the fascist troops descended on a Tekle Haymanot Day celebration close to Fiche, seized 297 monks, and shot them. A few days later, more than 100 young deacons attached to the monastery were slaughtered, and Graziani telegraphed Mussolini in Rome to say that: 'Of the monastery nothing remains.'

In 1998, an article by Ian Campbell and Degife Gabre-Tsadik revealed that a second, related massacre took place about a week later. At least 400 lay people who had attended the celebration for the saint were detained by the Italians, separated from the monks, tied together, and transported by truck to the village of Engecha on the old Ankober road. According to two eyewitnesses interviewed by Campbell, the prisoners were lined up along the edge of two 10m-long trenches, and then mowed down with machine-gun fire. The lay victims of this massacre were buried, without ceremony, where they fell. The bones of the martyred monks and deacons can still be seen at the monastery.

Debre Libanos had served as the head of the Ethiopian Church for four centuries prior to this massacre, but as John Graham points out: 'Graziani not only killed the priests, he also killed Debre Libanos as the centre of the Church. It never recovered from the loss of the priests and teachers. Although it was resurrected, and a new and wonderful church was built there in the 1950s, it could never become the centre of learning it had previously been.'

right for a view back to the waterfall and the *Washa Gelada* – Gelada Cave – where a troop of these striking primates sleeps most nights. Keep an eye open, too, for highland birds such as lammergeyer, auger buzzard, Abyssinian ground hornbill and the endemic banded barbet, Abyssinian woodpecker, Rüppell's black chat and white-winged cliff-chat.

Getting there and away

The junction to Debre Libanos lies on the main road between Addis Ababa and Bahir Dar some 60km north of Chancho and 15km south of Fiche, the closest town. The church lies 4km along the junction along a partially surfaced road from where several troops of relatively habituated gelada baboons are regularly observed. With your own vehicle, the monastery is a perfectly feasible day trip from either of these towns, or from Addis Ababa – the drive from the capital would take about 90 minutes to two hours each way – and it could also be visited en route between Addis and points further north.

Using public transport, the easiest base from which to visit is Fiche: at least one pick-up truck leaves here for Debre Libanos at around 08.00. If you are staying at the junction town in Fiche, you should be able to catch a lift with the pick-up, though it's just possible it will be full – the owner of the Alem Hotel might be able to phone through to Fiche to reserve a seat. Alternatively, any transport heading between Chancho and Fiche can drop you at the junction, from where it's a beautiful 60-minute walk to the church.

When you're ready to leave Debre Libanos, you'll probably have to walk out as far as the main Addis road – vehicles from Fiche appear to turn around immediately they arrive. This is only a 4km walk but it is *very* steep. Still, you'll have the whole afternoon to do it, and there are great views over the sandstone canyon and terraced cultivation of the slopes. Once at the main road, you should have little difficulty finding a ride in either direction.

Debre Libanos can be visited from Addis Ababa as a day trip using public transport. Henk Klaassen provides details: 'I made the trip to Debre Libanos in one day. The morning bus from Addis Ababa drops you off direct in front of the church by 10.00. I walked the area until 13.00, and was fortunate to get a hitch all the way back to Chancho. I caught a pick-up from there, and was back in Addis by 16.00.'

The short footpath to Ras Darge's Bridge is clearly signposted 'Portuguese Bridge' about 100m past the junction. A few curio-seller-cum-aspirant-guides hang around the signpost but the bridge is easy to find without assistance (the footpath is clear enough) and most locals speak insufficient English to make any contribution beyond stating the blatantly obvious. If you take a guide – or let one tag along – he will expect a tip of birr 10 to 20.

Accommodation
Hotel Haile Maryam Situated alongside the main Bahir Dar road immediately south of the junction to Debre Libanos, this basic but not unpleasant hotel charges birr 10 for a clean room with a ¾ bed. Food, refrigerated drinks and bucket showers are available, and the surrounding countryside is densely populated with geladas, highland birds and curio sellers. The only alternative is a small, unsignposted, showerless, and even more basic hotel in the village 1km from the church – the Pepsi and Mirinda signs on the outside wall render it difficult to miss.

Fiche
Fiche lies 3km off the main Gonder road about 75km north of Chancho and 15km north of Debre Libanos. Despite a pleasant, welcoming atmosphere and cool, breezy climate, Fiche is unremittingly ordinary, and really only of interest to travellers as the closest town to Debre Libanos. The town's main claim to notoriety is as the site of Ras Kassa's house, where Emperor Iyasu was imprisoned for most of the 1920s, after being overthrown at the hand of the future Emperor Haile Selassie. Ras Kassa's house, sadly, is long gone, though locals will show you the hilltop site where it stood.

Getting there and away
A few buses run daily between Addis and Fiche. These appear to leave throughout the morning and take around four hours. Instead of going right through to Fiche, ask to be dropped at the junction, where there is a separate town with better accommodation. Regular pick-up trucks cover the 3km between the junction town and Fiche.

No transport leaves from Fiche to any points further north, so if you're heading on to Debre Markos or Bahir Dar, you'll be reliant on finding vehicles coming from Addis. These generally pass through the junction town without detouring to Fiche, with activity peaking between 10.00 and 12.00.

Note that transport from Fiche to Addis Ababa or Debre Libanos generally fills up in the town centre, so you may not be able to embark at the junction.

Accommodation
Alem Hotel (34 rooms) ☏ 011 1350003. One of several lodgings situated alongside the Debre Markos road immediately north of the junction to the town centre, this has been the hotel of choice in Fiche for a full decade. Options include rooms using common shower for birr 16, small en-suite rooms with a shower dangling over the toilet for birr 20, and larger rooms with the shower discrete from the toilet for birr 30 – all reasonably clean and with a ¾ bed. The restaurant serves good *yebege kai wat*. The obliging owner speaks enough English to give current information on Debre Libanos and can usually help with lifts northward.

Blue Nile Gorge
This truly magnificent gorge, which spans altitudes of around 2,500m to 1,200m, is comparable in scale with America's Grand Canyon, and – quite how one measures these things I don't know – is often cited to be the largest canyon in Africa, a title also

frequently bestowed on Namibia's Fish River Canyon. The gorge follows the course of the Blue Nile as it arcs south of Lake Tana before it gushes out of Ethiopia into Sudan. Travelling between Fiche and Debre Markos, you will cross the gorge on one of the most chilling roads I have ever seen. Built by the Italians, and supported by viaducts in several places, it is an awesome feat of engineering; there are places where you can barely see the road's edge from a bus window, only a sheer plunge of perhaps 100m.

Most traffic slows to a crawl as it crosses the gorge – the 30km of dirt road between Goha Tsion and Dejen typically takes an hour to cover in a private vehicle and up to three hours in a bus – which gives you plenty of time to admire the expansive views over terraced slopes and euphorbia-studded cliffs to the opposite wall. As the bus descends, there is a corresponding rise in temperature and humidity, and the slow progress makes for a sweaty couple of hours, particularly if your fellow passengers decide to play greenhouse and freak at the merest hint of a cracked-open window! Immediately after you cross the bridge across the Nile, you'll see a small waterfall surrounded by stalactite-like rock formations and ficus trees on the left side of the road – potentially an attractive picnic spot, though marred somewhat by the rather overwhelming toilet smell!

The first stop after crossing the gorge is Dejen, which lies at an altitude of around 2,400m, yet is still close enough to the gorge to make a viable base for further exploration on foot. There is plenty of shoestring accommodation: the double-storey Alem Hotel behind the town's only filling station looks comfortably the most attractive option. A few kilometres north of Dejen, the main road splits into the direct route to Bahir Dar and a longer route to the same destination via the regional capital of Debre Markos. Whichever way you go, the pretty rolling countryside seems rather pedestrian after the gorge, though the highland cool comes as a major relief.

DEJEN TO BAHIR DAR VIA MOTA

This is the shorter of the two routes between Addis Ababa and Bahir Dar, but also the less popular one, since the road is unsurfaced and generally in mediocre condition. Some buses between the cities do, however, head this way, presumably because it saves on fuel, overnighting either at Mota, a small town situated some 110km south of Bahir Dar, or at else at whichever other village takes the driver's fancy. The most notable tourist attractions along this road are in the vicinity of Mota, at the southern end of an area that was an important royal fiefdom during the early Gonderine period.

Several significant but seldom-visited churches lie along the road between Dejen and Mota, or within striking distance of it. The disused church of Weyname Kidane Mihret, situated no more than 5km north of Bichena, was renowned for the superb 200-year-old cloth paintings that decorated its every wall, as described in an *Ethiopian Observer* article by Walter Krafft, who in 1971 had been the church's first European visitor. Sadly, just three years later, thieves tore every last painting from the church walls, and the cloth was cut into fragments that later turned up as curios in Addis Ababa.

Also of interest is the medieval monastery of Dima Giyorgis, which stands on the rim of the Blue Nile Gorge some 14km along a track that branches to the east 15km north of Bichena. The hilltop Monastery of Debre Work Maryam, which lies some 30km north of Bichena, and was reputedly founded in Axumite times, hold several important treasures including an icon said to have belonged to Saint Luke. Another 20km northwest of this, Dingayama Maryam (literally 'Mary on the Rocks') is an elaborately decorated hilltop church built in the time of Emperor Susneyos, a painting of whom graces the walls. Set on the rim of the Blue Nile Gorge about 25km east of the main road near Wofit, the remote but palatial stone church of Mertule Maryam, site of Emperor Susneyos's coronation, is probably the oldest European-influenced building in Ethiopia

– it was constructed in the dying years of the 16th century by Empress Eleni, the long-lived and highly influential wife of Zara Yaqob, with assistance from the Portuguese spy Pero de Covilhão. All these churches are described in some detail in Paul Henze's *Ethiopian Journeys* (see *Further Reading*, page 565)

Mota itself is the closest town to Sebara Dildi, the 17th-century footbridge over the Nile built during the rule of Emperor Fasilidas, and the subject of an aborted search by Thomas Pakenham, described in his book *The Mountains of Rasselas*. All things considered, four hours in either direction by mule or foot does seem a long, long way to go to see a broken bridge, but for those in pursuit of the truly esoteric it might be an irresistible option!

More alluring is the little-visited church of Weyzazirt Kidhane Mihret, which lies about 5km east of the Bahir Dar road some 15km past Mota. Constructed by Princess Seble-Wengiel, daughter of Emperor Fasilidas, this church is adorned with some superb 17th-century paintings – including a series depicting the twelve apostles on the colonnades – and also houses the mummified remains of its founder and her husband.

Gonji Tewodros is another interesting Gonderine church, built on the rim of the Blue Nile Gorge by one of the sons of Emperor Fasilidas, and reached by continuing along the main Bahir Dar road for 8km past the turn-off to Weyzazirt, then following a side road to the east for 9km.

Near Debre Mai, some 30km before you reach Bahir Dar, stand the ruins of the 17th-century Gimbe Maryam and Yebada palaces, constructed respectively by Emperors Susneyos and Fasilidas. The former palace lies about 5km west of the town and the latter 3km from town; both are accessible on foot or by mule only.

DEJEN TO BAHIR DAR VIA DEBRE MARKOS
Debre Markos
Assuming that urban facilities feature highly in your priorities, the former capital of the defunct province of Gojjam, set at an altitude of 2,410m in the moist highlands north of the Blue Nile Gorge, is the obvious place to break up the long bus trip from the capital to Bahir Dar. With a breezy highland ambience – the town was formerly known as Mankorar (cold place) – and a neatly laid-out town centre supporting a population of around 65,000, Debre Markos is an attractive enough stopover, albeit one with few compelling sights and more than its fair share of pubescent yelling at any passing foreigner.

Historically, Debre Markos's main claim to fame is as the site of the surrender of some 14,000 Italian troops to a mere 300 members of the combined Ethiopian–Allied army in April 1941, a key event in the collapse of the Italian occupation. The closest thing to a must-see in Debre Markos is the impressively decorated church for which the town is named, which was constructed in the last years of the 19th century by a local prince. Set in an attractive wooded compound, the church and its outbuildings lie about ten minutes' walk along the dirt road that slopes uphill in a southerly direction between the Total Garage and the Adahu Recreation Centre on the central traffic roundabout.

Getting there and away
Debre Markos lies 300km northwest of Addis Ababa along a road that is surfaced in its entirety except for the 30km stretch through the Blue Nile Gorge. The drive should take around five to six hours in a private vehicle, though you ought to allow another hour or two for stops. Direct buses to Debre Markos leave Addis Ababa at around 05.30 daily. There is no direct transport if you are coming to Debre Markos from somewhere like Fiche or Dejen, so you will be reliant on finding an empty seat on a bus coming from Addis. If this proves to be difficult, hitching is a reasonably feasible option along this route. In the opposite direction, buses to Addis Ababa also leave at around 05.30, and finding a seat appears to be straightforward.

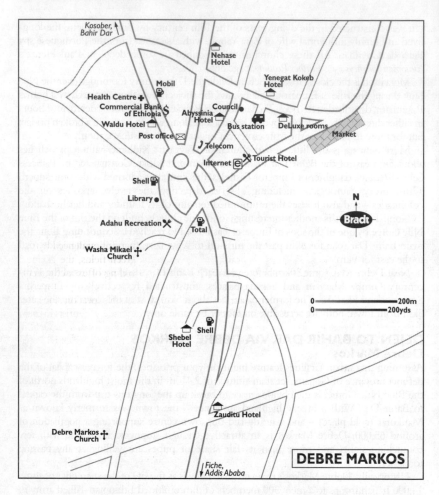

Heading on to Bahir Dar, you will need to be at the bus station at 05.30 to stand much chance of getting a ticket on the council bus, though the complicated and chaotic booking procedure means you'll be lucky if you depart much before 08.00. If you fail to get a ticket straight through to Bahir Dar, a bus or two leaves Debre Markos for Dangla via Kosober at 09.00, and there is plenty of transport from Dangla to Bahir Dar. Overall, this is a better option than the council bus, and there is plenty of budget accommodation in Dangla in the unlikely event you were to get stuck there overnight – the Hahu Hotel on the Addis Ababa side of town looks the best bet.

Where to stay and eat
Shebel Hotel (31 rooms) ✆ 058 7711410. Tucked away behind a Shell Garage on the Addis Ababa road perhaps 200m from the main traffic roundabout, this smart multi-storey hotel charges birr 50 for a sgl (with a proper dbl bed) or birr 80 for a dbl (one single bed and one ¾ bed), all carpeted and en suite with hot water. The ground-floor bar has DSTV and the restaurant serves a selection of local and Western dishes in the birr 8–16 range.

Yenegat Kobeb Hotel The pick of a meagre crop of shoestring hotels dotted around the bus station, this two-storey hotel charges birr 30 for a large en-suite room (cold shower only) with a ¾ bed.

Tourist Hotel Once the premier hotel in Debre Markos, the long-serving Tourist Hotel no longer has any rooms, but it's a good spot for a drink or meal, and the town's only internet café is right next door.

Kosober and Awi zone

The autonomous administrative zone of Awi, home to the Agaw people since Axumite times, lies to the northwest of Debre Markos, where it is bisected by the main asphalt road to Bahir Dar. The Agaw, whose neatly fenced compounds and circular homesteads – tall thatched roofs bound tightly by entwined bamboo sticks – form such a prominent feature of the countryside, are also known for their ecologically sustainable and highly productive traditional agricultural practices. Indeed, thanks to the communal monitoring of resources such as water and forests in Awi over several centuries, few if any other comparably cultivated parts of Ethiopia retain such a significant cover of indigenous woodland.

Blessed with a bountiful rainfall (more than 2,000mm per annum at higher altitudes) and fertile red soil, the landscape of Awi, though geologically subdued today, is – like that of Bishoftu closer to Addis Ababa – overtly volcanic in origin. Indeed, the area has experienced extensive eruptive activity within the last million years, as evidenced by the black basaltic rocks strewn like porous cannonballs across its green fields, the gigantic plugs that jut skywards from the surrounding hills, and a sprinkling of extinct craters, several of which support perennial or seasonal lakes.

Despite its wealth of low-key natural attractions and highly accessible location along the main road between Addis Ababa and Bahir Dar, Awi is generally bypassed by tourists in their haste to reach Lake Tana and the other big guns of the northern circuit. And fair enough, if your time is limited and your tolerance of basic conditions low, then Awi probably doesn't warrant your attention. Equally, the area is rich in potential for birdwatchers, ramblers and other nature lovers, and it will provide a refreshing rustic break from 'touristy' Ethiopia to those for whom travel is about the journey as much as the destination.

The obvious base from which to explore Awi is the small junction town of Kosober, which straddles the asphalt Bahir Dar road some 5km south of a magnificent volcanic plug called Mount Zivixi. Often referred to (and signposted as) Injibara, the name of the surrounding district, Kosober boasts good public transport connections in most directions, and is well endowed with small hotels and eateries, albeit none that comes close to conforming to tourist-class standards. Other significant settlements include Kesa, Tilili and Bure, which respectively lie 8km, 15km and 30km southeast of Kosober along the main road towards Debre Markos – all three towns boast a few basic hotels, while Bure is of minor logistical note as the northern terminus of a 250km unsurfaced road to Nekemte.

Getting there and around

Kosober lies exactly 150km northeast of Debre Markos along the road to Bahir Dar. Coming from the south, buses from Debre Markos to Dangla leave at around 09.00 and stop in Kosober. Buses from Debre Markos to Bahir Dar also stop at Kosober, and will also drop travellers at the other towns mentioned above, but it would be customary to pay the full fare even if you hop off halfway. There is also quite a bit of local public transport connecting Kosober to other small towns in the area, as well as to Dangla 35km further north, from where there is plenty of transport on to Bahir Dar.

Where to stay and eat

Yordanis Pension This quiet, clean and pleasant little guesthouse is clearly signposted on the right side of the road towards Bahir Dar about 500m past the central junction in Kosober. It charges birr 15 for a large room with ¾ bed using powerful common showers. No food or drink is available.

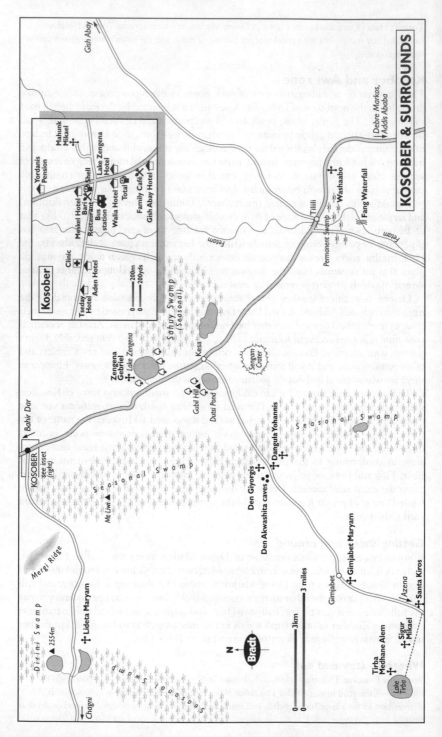

Aden Hotel Situated about 400m along the Chagni road, this offers adequate but not-so-clean rooms with ¾ bed for birr 12 en suite or birr 10 using a common shower. Potentially noisy bar and restaurant attached.

Tseday Hotel Similar in standard to the Aden next door, this charges birr 10 for a clean room with ¾ bed using common showers.

Family Café Fresh bread, doughnuts, coffee and other snacks served next to the Total Garage on the Debre Markos road.

Excursions
Fang Waterfall
Situated on the Fetam River some 3km south of Tilili, this attractive waterfall is most notable perhaps for the striking rock formations it has exposed – a grid of shiny black hexagonal basalt columns whose crystalline shape is associated with lava that has cooled unusually quickly. The waterfall itself stands about 15m high, and can be very impressive after heavy rain, while in less torrential circumstances the pool at its base looks safe for a chilly dip. To get there, follow the road towards Kosober out of Tilili for about 500m after crossing the Fetam River, then turn left into a motorable track at the faded orange signpost that reads 'Stay at Interesting Fang Waterfall'. About 2km along this track, a marshy area to the right looks promising for endemics such as Rouget's rail and blue-winged goose, then after another 1km, you should hear the waterfall – and see the outline of the tree-lined gorge into which it tumbles – some 300m to your left. A couple of basic lodges can be found in Tilili.

Gish Abay
The most geographically poignant landmark in Agaw country is an inherently unremarkable freshwater spring protected within the grounds of Gish Mikael Monastery some 30km due east of Kosober as the crow flies. Known as Gish Abay or Abay Minch, this is the starting point of the Gilgil Abay (literally, Calf Nile), which, as the most voluminous of the 60-odd rivers that flow into Lake Tana, is generally accepted to be the ultimate source of the Blue Nile. The sacred spring is also believed to have strong healing powers, and it has been regarded as geographically significant by Ethiopians for many centuries – the Spanish priest Pero Pais was taken there by Emperor Susneyos in 1613, and it was also visited by James Bruce in 1770.

The closest town to Gish Mikael is Sekala (also sometimes referred to as Gish Abay), which lies 35km along a side road that branches northeast from the main Debre Markos road at Tilili. There are a few basic hotels in Sekala, should you wish to spend the night before heading out to Gish Mikael, which lies about 90 minutes' walk further south. Because the water is regarded to be holy you will not be permitted to see the spring if you have eaten anything that day – it's worth getting there early, as travellers who arrive in the afternoon might be turned away on suspicion of having eaten.

Close to Gish Abay, a trio of holy springs known locally as the Father, Son and Holy Spirit emerges from a hole above a cave into a warm natural pool where it is possible to swim. Further afield, some 15km northwest of Sekala, a small field of obelisks, only one of which is still standing, is known locally as Dingay Yegragn (Gragn's Rocks) in reference to the Islamic warlord Ahmed Gragn, who caused so much havoc in the Lake Tana hinterland in the 16th century.

Lake Dutsi and Gubil Forest
The small and seasonal Lake Dutsi lies at the base of the domed Gubil Hill on the western outskirts of Kesa, a small junction town that flanks the Debre Markos road some 2km south of Lake Zengena. The lake supports large numbers of water-associated birds during the rains, while the small and readily accessible evergreen forest that swathes

Gubil is noted for its highland forest birds. Two other points of natural interest lie within easy walking distance of Kesa: the Sahuy Floodplain and associated seasonal lake northeast of the main road, and the imposing Mount Sengem, whose wooded slopes, which rise from the southern outskirts of town to an altitude of above 2,500m, hide an impressive 1,000m-deep volcanic crater. At least one basic hotel is to be found in Kesa.

Gimjabet, Den Akwashita and Lake Tirba

Given the Ethiopian gift for mythologising, you'd expect a decent tall story to be attached to a town with the name Gimjabet – literally 'Treasury'. But evidently not – the residents we interrogated about the town's name came up with nothing more illuminating than a blank 'it's always been called that'. Most likely the name derives from the church of Gimjabet Maryam, which lies on the southern outskirts of town and must once have secured some important church treasures. But who knows: perhaps it is simply a waggish reference to the incongruously large and plush Commercial Bank of Ethiopia edifice that rises assertively above every other building in the decidedly low-rise town centre?

Roughly halfway along the serviceable 10km dirt road that runs southeast to Gimjabet from Kesa, immediately outside the stone compound enclosing the Church of Den Giyorgis, the Den Akwashita Caves consists of a series of four overgrown sinkhole-like entrances that open into a large natural tunnel said locally to run for several kilometres underground. In times of war, the cave system has often served as a refuge (perhaps treasure was stored there too?), and the subterranean river that passes within 50m of the last entrance is regarded as holy by the local clergy, though you need a torch to see it.

The other attraction in the Gimjabet area is the pretty Tirba Crater Lake, which fills the floor of a 1km² caldera some 4km west of the town as the crow flies. To get there, you must first follow the road to Azena southwest for 3km until you see the Church of Sahta Kiros to the left. From here, it's a roughly 30-minute walk northwest to the lakeshore Tirba Medhane Alem, following a footpath that starts opposite Sahta Kiros and passes the Church of Sigur Mikael on the way.

Lake Zengena

Foremost among Awi's beauty spots, situated just 6km south of Kosober practically alongside the Debre Markos road, is the spectacular freshwater Zengena Crater Lake. The forested rim of this near-perfect crater is set at an altitude of 2,500m, and the lakeshore lies perhaps 30m below this, but the crater itself – and thus the lake – is rumoured to be almost 1,000m deep. The northern slopes of the crater support an artificial cypress plantation as well as the recently constructed church of Zengena Gebriel, but the southern slopes retain a cover of lush indigenous acacia woodland. Grivet monkeys are much in evidence, and there is plenty of birdlife too.

To get to Zengena from Kosober, follow the Debre Markos road south for 6km until you see a cypress-covered slope to your left, then follow the rough dirt track that leads through the plantation for about 200m to a shady parking area. Coming from the south, the track lies to the right about 2km after you pass through Kesa. Either way, the lake itself is invisible from the main road – and, for that matter, from the parking area, from where a steep 50m footpath leads downhill to the shore. Local authorities hope eventually to build a tourist lodge on the crater rim – until such time as that happens, the lake would make for an idyllic picnic spot en route to Bahir Dar, assuming that the local children leave you in peace.

Dirini Swamp

Situated within a collapsed caldera opposite the Church of Lideta Maryam, exactly 9.5km from Kosober along the unsealed road to Chagni, the perennial Dirini Swamp is of interest primarily for a varied selection of water-associated birds, including Rouget's rail, black-crowned crane, blue-winged goose and other waterfowl, as well as various herons, ibises and waders. Although the swamp lies no more than 500m north of the Chagni road, its existence is obscured by the crater walls during the dry season, so you could easily drive right past! During the wet season, the swamp often spills out from the crater to fill a second (non-volcanic) depression south of the road, in which case it can't be missed. An impressive volcanic plug juts skyward from a thicket of indigenous woodland on the north shore of the swamp – it looks eminently climbable and the views from the top should be excellent! Chagni, incidentally, is the largest town in Awi, supporting a population of around 25,000, and there is plenty of public transport there from Kosober – the only potential attraction I'm aware of in its immediate vicinity, however, is the seldom-visited Dondar Waterfall.

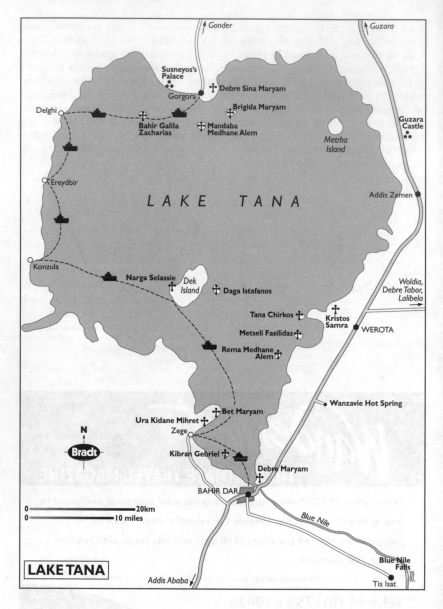

LAKE TANA

Bahir Dar and Lake Tana

Set at an altitude of 1,830m, Lake Tana is the largest lake in Ethiopia, with a surface area of 3,673km², and it is also the source of the Blue Nile, a connection that explains many of Ethiopia's links with the ancient world. Tana was known to the Ancient Greeks as Pseboe, and to the Ancient Egyptians as Coloe; it was described by a 5th-century Greek dramatist as the 'copper-tinted lake... that is the jewel of Ethiopia'. Even today, the papyrus *tankwa* that sail the lake bear a striking resemblance to the boats of Ancient Egypt.

Aside from the southern spur from which the Nile flows, and on which Bahir Dar is situated, Tana has a broadly circular shape measuring some 65km in diameter. It was formed at least 20 million years ago, by an ancient lava extrusion that effectively functions as a natural dam. Averaging some 14m in depth, and dotted with more than three-dozen islands, many of which are inhabited, Tana harbours at least 26 different fish species, of which 17 are endemic to the lake. Tana is also renowned for its varied birdlife – flotillas of white pelican being a particularly common sight – while the shallows support small pods of hippos.

The Tana area is the traditional home of the Amhara, a Christian people whose language was for many years the national language of Ethiopia. Tana was also the homeland of the Falasha who, although they are ethnically identical to the Amhara and speak the same language, practise a form of Judaism that appears to have been severed from the Jewish mainstream before 650BC. There are now very few Falasha people left in the Tana region; after centuries of persecution, most of them were airlifted to Israel in 1991.

Between the collapse of the Zagwe dynasty in the late 13th century and the establishment of Gonder as a permanent capital in the early 17th century, Tana was the political and spiritual focus of the Christian empire. Several temporary capitals were established on or near the lake's shore, and it is here where the Portuguese force led by Christopher Da Gama spent most of its time in Ethiopia. Many of the island monasteries which dot Lake Tana date to this time, though some are older – the monastery at Tana Chirkos, for one, appears to have served as a spiritual retreat long before Christianity was established in the region.

The largest city and most important tourist centre in the Tana region is Bahir Dar, which lies on the southern lakeshore close to the Nile outlet, and is connected by regular flights to Addis Ababa and the other major tourist centres of northern Ethiopia. In addition to being an attractive city in its own right, Bahir Dar serves as the obvious base from which to explore the region's other main attractions: the Blue Nile Falls and myriad monasteries dotted around the lake. Bahir Dar aside, the only significant lakeshore settlement is Gorgora, which lies on the northern shore 60km from the city of Gonder, and is connected to Bahir Dar by a weekly ferry service.

BAHIR DAR

This large town on the southern shore of Lake Tana has a sticky tropical ambience unusual for northern Ethiopia and more similar to somewhere like Awassa in the southern Rift Valley. Palm-lined avenues and pretty lakeside vistas make Bahir Dar a decidedly attractive town, and it is also the base for visits to the Blue Nile Falls and Lake Tana's many monasteries. With tourist amenities that are among the best in the country, Bahir Dar is an excellent place to settle into for a few days.

As recently as the early 1950s, Bahir Dar was little more than a sleepy lakeshore village, overshadowed politically and economically by Gonder to the north and Debre Markos to the south. The initial stimulus for its subsequent rapid growth was the decision to build a hydro-electric plant at nearby Tis Abay. Subsequent to this, Bahir Dar has become one of Ethiopia's most important industrial centres and the country's fifth largest town, with a population approaching the 150,000 mark – and western outskirts that have visibly expanded since 1994, when the first edition of this guide was researched. In 1995, Bahir Dar leapfrogged ahead of Gonder, Dessie and Debre Markos – the respective former administrative capitals of the defunct provinces of Gonder, Wolo and Gojjam – when a capital was selected for the redrawn Federal Region of Amhara.

Although the town itself is modern, the waterfront church of Bahir Dar Giyorgis, situated near the main traffic roundabout, was founded at least 400 years ago. The original church was knocked down to make way for a larger and more modern but not unattractive edifice in the Haile Selassie era, but the compound also houses a disused two-storey stone tower, architecturally reminiscent of the Gonderine palaces, and whose construction is attributed to the Jesuit priest Pero Pais during the reign of Susneyos.

As with so many large Ethiopian towns, the juxtaposition between urban modernity and rustic traditionalism is a striking feature of Bahir Dar, no more so than in the bustling daily central market, which ranks as one of the finest in the country and well worth a couple of hours. The goatskin *injera*-holder called an *agelgil*, traditionally used by herdsmen as a 'picnic basket', makes for an unusual and inexpensive souvenir, as does the locally produced white *shama* cloth. Only 500m west of the Ghion Hotel, a footpath leads to the lakeshore, where there is a fish market, a great many papyrus *tankwa* boats, and often large numbers of pelicans.

Many travellers love Bahir Dar without reservation, but others reckon that their time there was marred by the histrionics of various guides, fixers and compulsive yellers. The 'hassle factor' does seem to have died down considerably in recent years, but it remains the case that initial impressions tend to be influenced by whether you arrive by air or by bus. The reception committee at the bus station is notorious for latching on to travellers and trying to set up their accommodation in the hope of a commission from the hotel, which the traveller will cover by paying more than they would have otherwise – and be warned that such touts often claim any hotel that doesn't give commissions is full. Staying at a slightly more expensive hotel, or away from the town centre, will definitely help protect you from unwanted attention. So, too, will exploring the town in the company of a local guide.

Getting there and away
By air
At least two and sometimes more Ethiopian Airlines' flights connect Bahir Dar and Addis Ababa in either direction daily. The flight takes about one hour. There is also at least one flight daily in either direction between Bahir Dar and Gonder, Axum and Lalibela. Onward tickets *must* be reconfirmed a day ahead of schedule at Ethiopian Airlines' city office, which keeps normal business hours seven days a week, and lies between the main roundabout and the Ghion Hotel.

The airport lies about 3km west of the town centre, and unless you are booked into a hotel with a shuttle service, or being met by a tour operator, you'll have to get a taxi into town, which shouldn't cost more than birr 20 per group. Worth noting here that the Ghion Hotel, which offers good rates to budget travellers, also includes a free airport transfer in its services.

By road

Bahir Dar lies 560km from Addis Ababa along the surfaced (but for 30km unsurfaced) road through Debre Markos and Kosober. A significantly shorter route through Mota also connects Addis Ababa and Bahir Dar, and offers more in the way of sightseeing for aficionados of arcane churches, but this road is unsurfaced north of Goha Tsion, so it takes longer to drive than the Debre Markos route. In a private vehicle, the drive from Addis Ababa to Bahir Dar via Debre Markos can be undertaken in one long day, even allowing for the popular diversion to Debre Libanos, but two days would allow for a more relaxed drive as well as further sightseeing.

The most efficient way to get between Addis Ababa and Bahir Dar using public transport is a recently introduced minibus service, which costs birr 120 per person and reliably completes the journey in one full day. Minibuses leave Addis Ababa at around 06.00 from the Shell garage near Habte Giyorgis Bridge, which lies about 200m past Abuna Petros Square in the direction of the Mercato Tickets, and they leave Bahir Dar at the same time from in front of the Ghion Hotel. The cheaper but slower alternative is direct buses between Addis Ababa and Bahir Dar, which leave in either direction at around 06.00, and cost birr 60–70 (buses via Debre Markos being slightly more expensive than those travelling through Mota). The Walia bus is reportedly the most comfortable and reliable service at the time of writing. Whatever bus you use, the journey nearly always involves an overnight stop along the way. If the prospect of sleeping in a village fleapit doesn't grab you, and you don't want to pay extra for a minibus, it is possible to split the trip into two separate day-long bus rides, stopping at Debre Markos, Kosober or Mota. Potential stops on the road between Addis Ababa and Bahir Dar are discussed more fully in *Chapter 9*.

Bahir Dar and Gonder lie 180km apart via a road that is now surfaced almost in its entirety. The drive takes about three hours in a private vehicle, not allowing for possible diversions to Awramba or Guzara Castle. Buses leave in either direction at 06.00, 08.00 and 16.00, cost birr 23, and take around four hours. Slightly quicker and roughly double the price is the new minibus service that will leave Bahir Dar from in front of the Ghion Hotel. You can also charter a private minibus for around birr 700 one-way, which would work out quite reasonably for a group of five or more. To get to Lalibela on public transport, you need to catch the 06.00 bus to Dessie, disembark at Gashena, and hope for a lift from there.

THE NILE OUTLET AND BEZAWIT HILL

A worthwhile short excursion if you have a few hours to spare in Bahir Dar is to the Blue Nile, which exits Lake Tana on the eastern outskirts of town. To reach the outlet, you can walk, cycle or catch a charter taxi or local minibus to about 1km past the Blue Nile Springs Hotel, where a large bridge crosses the river. The wide river here provides ideal conditions for hippos and crocodiles, both of which are occasionally seen from the bridge, and the monastery of Debre Maryam can be reached easily and affordably (see page 208).

A popular onward option from here involves taking the first right turn after the bridge and following it for about 2.5km to the top of Bezawit Hill, which is dominated by an ostentatious split-level palace built for Haile Selassie in 1967 and used by him on only two occasions during the remaining seven years of his rule. Entrance to the disused palace is forbidden, as is photography of the exterior, but the hill does provide an excellent vantage point over the town and Lake Tana, especially at dusk, and there's a chance of seeing hippos in the river below.

By boat

Rather absurdly, tourists are not permitted to make use of the daily ferry between Bahir Dar and the Zege Peninsula. The inexpensive weekly ferry across Lake Tana to Gorgora, a short bus ride away from Gonder, was opened to tourists a few years back (see box *The Lake Tana Ferry*, pages 202–3). Possibilities for exploring the Lake Tana monasteries as a day trip are discussed elsewhere in this chapter, but it is worth mentioning here that one could extend such a trip to terminate at Gorgora – not a cheap option at birr 2,000 or so, but reasonably affordable if it is divided between a large group.

Where to stay
Upmarket

Tana Hotel (64 rooms) ↘ 058 1110603; e ghion@ethionet.et; www.ghionhotel.com.et. Part of the government-owned Ghion chain, the Tana is Bahir Dar's most expensive and probably its most alluring hotel, situated a couple of kilometres out of town along the Gonder road. The first choice of most tour operators, the Tana boasts one overwhelming selling point: the large, thickly wooded lakeshore grounds, which offer genuine respite from the nearby city and host a rich variety of birds ranging from giant kingfisher and various herons to colourful woodland dwellers such as double-toothed and banded barbet, Bruce's green pigeon and white-cheeked turaco. The food is nothing to write home about – standard government hotel fare – though if you're staying a couple of nights you might want to spice things up by asking the kitchen to prepare a traditional buffet. Unlike most of its smarter competitors, which have 24-hour hot water, the Tana has hot water for a few hours in the morning and evening only. En-suite rooms cost US$36/48/60 sgl/dbl/ste.

Bahir Dar Resort Hotel Situated on the western outskirts of town, this hotel has been under development for seven years now, and rumours that it will open soon under a new buyer – offering accommodation comparable with or better than the Tana Hotel at a similar price – may or may not have some substance.

Moderate

Summerland Hotel (40 rooms) ↘ 058 2206566. The newest of several high-rise hotels dotted around the city centre, the five-storey Summerland Hotel opened in early 2005 and has a great waterfront location – or rather, would have were the lake view not compromised by the decidedly eye-distracting presence of the new Amhara Development Building looming in the foreground. It would be churlish to criticise the rooms, which are as plush as it gets in northern Ethiopia – clean tiled floor, DSTV, 24-hour hot water – without being in any respect memorable. The restaurant, by contrast, has an unusually ambitious menu, and looks well worth a try at around birr 16–20 for a main course. En-suite rooms cost birr 189/289/300 sgl/dbl/twin.

Papyrus Hotel (100 rooms) ↘ 058 2205100; f 058 2205047; e sattyr@ethionet.et. Situated at the tail end of the city centre, with a less-than-captivating view of a Shell garage, this blandly functional and relatively modern multi-storey building lies some distance from the lake, but arguably compensates by being centred on a large, clean – and in this sweaty climate rather welcome – swimming pool. It's not the bargain it was a few years ago, but the comfortable en-suite rooms remain acceptable value for money at birr 214/268 sgle/dble with DSTV or birr 322–536 for a suite.

Dib Anbessa Hotel (30 rooms) ↘ 058 2201436; f 058 2201818. Older and not quite so slick as the hotels listed above, this pleasant hotel – a popular option with many tour operators and regular visitors – is correspondingly cheaper, and it has a reasonably attractive location on the city-centre side of the main waterfront road. It charges birr 165/185 for a comfortable en-suite sgl/dbl with hot water and TV.

Ethio Star Hotel (44 rooms) ↘ 058 2202026. The cheapest hotel in this range, the Ethio Star seems reasonable value at birr 100/150 (negotiable) for a large, clean albeit rather rundown en-suite sgl/dbl with nets, hot water and a balcony facing the lake.

To Charlie Borden

c/o Clinton Foundation

Thanks so much for the
look! We had a royal
blast.
See you soon —
Martha & Betsy

Budget

Ghion Hotel (30 rooms) ☎ 058 2200111/740; f 058 2200303; e ghionbd@ethionet.et or bisratwel@yahoo.com. Formerly part of the Ghion chain, this privatised hotel is both centrally and scenically located, with the lake lapping its gracious lawns, pelicans huddling on the waterfront, and white-cheeked turaco, paradise flycatcher and spotted eagle owl resident in the giant *ficus* trees. Lakeshore bungalows cost birr 100–200, and while the official price of a slightly rundown en-suite dbl depends on whom you ask, the owner is sympathetic to the needs of budget travellers, and it's an open secret that the rooms at the back go for birr 50 on demand – which, with hot water on tap and the best location in town, easily ranks as the best deal in Bahir Dar. The food is good, there's an on-site internet café, hotel residents get a free airport transfer, and it's as good a place as any to set up reliable boat trips to the islands.

Bahir Dar Pension This pleasant new hotel, situated around the corner from the tourist office and the Ghion Hotel, charges birr 40 for a clean room with a ³/₄ bed using a common cold shower or birr 60 for a similar room with en-suite hot shower. The traditional food is regarded to be among the best in town – most dishes are in the birr 10–15 range – but the popular campfire party held in the courtyard on Saturday and Sunday nights should probably be viewed as a deterrent if you're planning an early night.

Enkutatash Hotel Situated on the south side of the Addis Ababa road a short distance past the Ghion Hotel, this relatively new place – an offshoot of the perennially popular eponymous restaurant behind Telecommunications – charges a very reasonable birr 40/50 for a compact but clean en-suite sgl/dbl.

Tsegaye Pension ☎ 058 2221550. This central new hotel is good value at birr 50 for a clean room with a ³/₄ bed, a private balcony, netting, and en-suite cold shower.

Shoestring

Tana Pension ☎ 058 2201302. The best cheapie in town, simply because it declines to charge a discriminatory *faranji* price, this friendly pension is situated on the main north–south road through town, close to the bus station, and right above a good pastry shop and restaurant. The clean sgl rooms (³/₄ bed) with a balcony and access to common hot showers cost birr 20. This hotel has adhered to a one-price-for-all policy for years, and it deserves our support so long as this remains the case!

Axum Hotel ☎ 058 2204849. By far the best of a cluster of cheap hotels behind the bus station, this charges birr 30 for a small but clean en-suite room with a ³/₄ bed and a cold shower. The other hotels on this road, as marked on the map, generally charge the same price for an inferior room using common showers.

Where to eat and drink

The upmarket and moderate hotels listed above all have decent restaurants serving local and foreign dishes in the birr 15–20 range. The restaurants at the **Dib Anbessa** and **Papyrus** hotels have good reputations, the new **Summerland Hotel** has a more interesting menu, and the out-of-town **Tana Hotel** is slightly pricier but comes with a far more attractive setting. The food at the relatively inexpensive **Ghion Hotel** is also pretty good, with a menu as varied as any, and you can eat on the shady veranda or in the atmospheric grounds.

Tucked away in the back roads behind Telecommunications, the **Enkutatash Restaurant** is a popular local eatery (house speciality fish cutlet) that has for some years been entrenched as one of Bahir Dar's top tourist spots – unfortunately it appears to have responded to the ubiquitous guidebook recommendations by charging discriminatory *faranji* prices of up to birr 10–20. The **Enkutatash Hotel #2**, under the same ownership and similar in standard and price, offers the option of eating on the patio or first-floor balcony.

Another good local restaurant serving a variety of local and Western dishes in the birr 6–10 range is the **Ethio-Espaniolito** behind the Dib Anbessa Hotel. For good Ethiopian

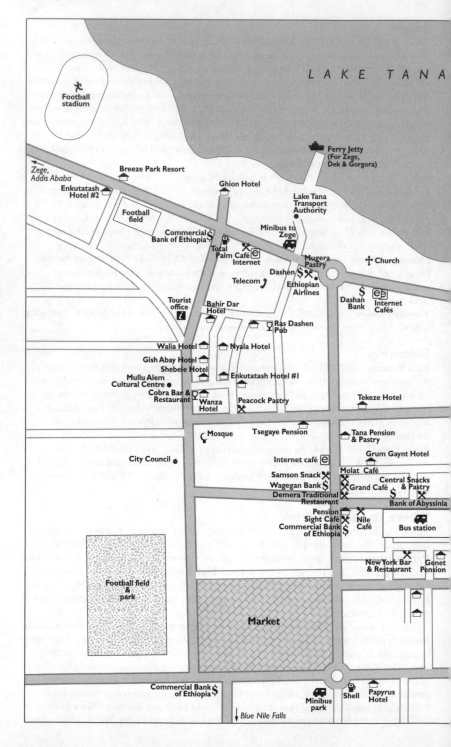

LAKE TANA

Football stadium

Zege, Addis Ababa

Breeze Park Resort

Enkutatash Hotel #2

Football field

Ghion Hotel

Ferry Jetty (For Zege, Dek & Gorgora)

Lake Tana Transport Authority

Commercial Bank of Ethiopia

Total

Palm Café
Internet

Minibus to Zege

Mugera Pastry

✝ Church

Dashen

Telecom

Ethiopian Airlines

Dashan Bank

Internet Cafés

Tourist office

Bahir Dar Hotel

Ras Dashen Pub

Walia Hotel

Nyala Hotel

Gish Abay Hotel

Shebele Hotel

Mullu Alem Cultural Centre ●

Enkutatash Hotel #1

Cobra Bar & Restaurant

Wanza Hotel

Peacock Pastry

Tekeze Hotel

ᘓ Mosque

Tsegaye Pension

Tana Pension & Pastry

City Council ●

Internet café

Grum Gaynt Hotel

Molat Café

Samson Snack

Wagegan Bank

Demera Traditional Restaurant

Grand Café

Central Snacks & Pastry

Bank of Abyssinia

Pension

Sight Café

Commercial Bank of Ethiopia

Nile Café

Bus station

New York Bar & Restaurant

Genet Pension

Football field & park

Market

Commercial Bank of Ethiopia

Minibus park

Shell

Papyrus Hotel

↓ Blue Nile Falls

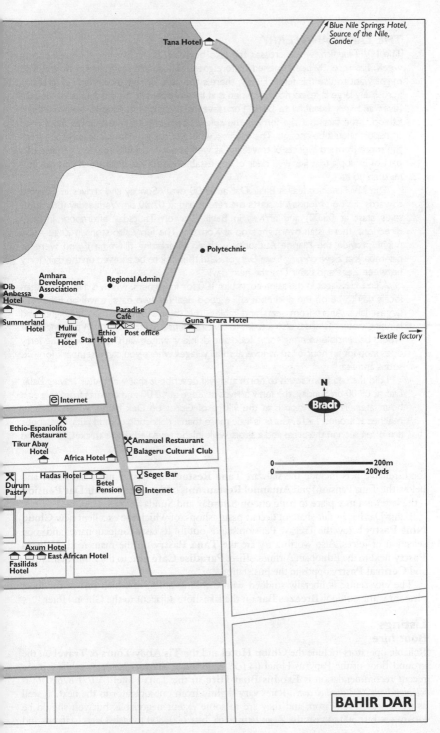

Blue Nile Springs Hotel,
Source of the Nile,
Gonder

Tana Hotel

Polytechnic

Amhara
Development
Association

Regional Admin

Dib
Anbessa
Hotel

Paradise
Café

Summerland
Hotel

Mullu
Enyew
Hotel

Ethio
Star Hotel

Post office

Guna Terara Hotel

Textile factory

N

Bradt

Internet

Ethio-Espaniolito
Restaurant

Tikur Abay
Hotel

Africa Hotel

Amanuel Restaurant
Balageru Cultural Club

Seget Bar

Durum
Pastry

Hadas Hotel

Betel
Pension

Internet

0 ————————— 200m
0 ————————— 200yds

Axum Hotel

East African Hotel

Fasilidas
Hotel

BAHIR DAR

THE LAKE TANA FERRY

The MV *Tananich*, which crosses the lake between Bahir Dar and Gorgora once a week, has recently been opened to foreigners. There are several reasons why you might want to use this ferry. Firstly, there's the aura of romance attached to sailing across any large lake, particularly when that lake happens to be the source of the Nile River and very beautiful to boot. For travellers who are bussing through northern Ethiopia, the fact that the ferry is the sole opportunity to take a break from road transport should be enough. The trip as a whole offers a mellow, cheap respite from the more frenzied aspects of travelling, as well as a wonderfully low-key glimpse of a part of Ethiopia that lies well clear of any established tourist itinerary. If you can fit it in, then do it.

The MV *Tananich* leaves Bahir Dar at 09.00 every Sunday and arrives in Gorgora towards dusk on Monday. It starts the return trip at 07.30 on Wednesday (but ticket sales start at 06.00) and arrives in Bahir Dar on Thursday afternoon. In both directions, there is an overnight stop at Konzula. The ferry also stops in Zege – you might provide the Marine Authority with an interesting dilemma if you were to disembark at Zege coming from Gorgora and then ask to be allowed on the daily ferry between Zege and Bahir Dar the next day!

A first-class seat in the salon costs birr 100 for foreigners, which is a lot more than locals pay to be on the deck, but still a good deal for two days' travel on Ethiopia's largest lake. Apart from seats and tables, the salon's only facilities are lights and running water. There is also a toilet for exclusive use of staff and salon passengers. It would be sensible to bring some food and drinking water with you, though the ferry does stop for an hour or so at several small villages where you can disembark for *wat*, sodas and tea.

I did the trip from south to north and will describe it that way. After leaving Bahir Dar at 09.00 on Sunday, the ferry arrives at Zege at 10.00 and departs from there an hour later. The next stop is at the village of Gurer on Dek Island, which the boat reaches at around 15.15. Gurer is little more than a collection of mud huts, but hippos are often seen in the area, and a short walk inland revealed dense thicket, forest and

food, reliable bets include the stalwart **Tana Restaurant** (above the Tana Pastry and below the Tana Pension) and **Amanuel Restaurant**, or the upstart **Bahir Dar Pension** – the latter is a nice place to hang out on Saturday and Sunday nights.

Bahir Dar has its fair share of decent pastry shops, of which the excellent new **Cloud Nine Pastry** below the Tsegaye Pension stands out for its tasty confectionaries and good selection of juices. Also worth a try are the **Tana Pastry** on the main road, **Mugera Pastry** next to the Ethiopian Airlines office, **Paradise Café** next to the Ethio Star Hotel, and **Central Pastry** opposite the bus station.

The city centre is liberally studded with drinking holes, of which one of the most pleasant is the outdoor **Breezes Bar** on the lakeshore adjacent to the Ghion Hotel.

Listings
Boat hire

Reliable operators include the **Ghion Hotel** and the **Tis Abay Tours & Travel** on the ground floor of the Papyrus Hotel (✆ *058 2208541;* e *sattyr@ethionet.et*), while a more recent recommendation is **Exodus Boat Hire** in the Tana Hotel (✆ *091 8760056;* e *solomonchane2003@yahoo.com*). Rates vary slightly from one operator to the next, as well as from season to season, and they are to some extent negotiable, but you should be looking at birr 300 to visit the Zege Peninsula, birr 600–800 to visit Dago Istafanos and swamp. There are several other islands in this group, including the one housing Daga Istafanos monastery. There is no hotel in Gurer, but with a tent, some food, and – ideally – a map, it could be an interesting place to explore, secure in the knowledge that the boat will return in three days' time.

When the boat arrives in Konzula at around 18.00, your first priority should be a mad dash to find a room at the only hotel. The village gets visitors only twice a week, and it's not braced for the influx. There's no need to panic, just get to the village quickly – plenty of rooms were available when I arrived, but they had run out ten minutes later. It's a fairly steep ten-minute walk from the pier to the village, so it might speed things up to lock your luggage in the salon and collect it later (for that matter, I would have few qualms about locking it there overnight and just taking up a daypack). Once there, the hotel is predictably basic, predictably overpriced – at least for *faranjis*, who pay birr 20 a room that wouldn't fetch half that price were there any choice in the matter – and lacking any running water. The attached restaurant serves fried eggs and tasty *asa wat*.

There's not anything compelling to do or see in Konzula, aside from the small church with its attractively wooded grounds, and if you arrive at dusk you're unlikely to be in much of a mood to explore. Even if you are, the mass of children that will follow your every step might be a little daunting. I've never seen anything like the kids here: I must have had a pack of 100 trailing behind me. To be fair, there wasn't any request for money or anything like that. Konzula seems a friendly place, but it doesn't see too many *faranji* visitors.

The ferry departs from Konzula at 09.00 on Monday and arrives at Eseydbir two hours later. This is a pretty if unremarkable town, where you should be able to locate a soda and something to eat. The next stop, at around 14.30, is at Delghi, a larger town on a rather bland stretch of shore. Delghi has a restaurant, and even a hotel. From Delghi, the ferry takes about three hours to reach Gorgora (see page 217).

Note that this is Ethiopia, not Switzerland, and while the ferry schedule is reasonably reliable, exact timings may vary according to the amount of cargo to be loaded, mechanical problems, or the captain's whim.

Narga Selassie, and birr 1,000 if you want to include Tana Chirkos in that itinerary. A boat to Gorgora on the northern lakeshore costs around birr 2,000. Note that prices are per boat rather than per person (most boats will seat four to six passengers comfortably) but they exclude church entrance fees.

Entertainment
The **Balageru Cultural Club** (\ *058 2202448*) next to the Amanuel Restaurant stands out for its lively traditional music and dancing from all over Ethiopia. Nightly performances start at 20.00 and carry on for about three hours: the atmosphere is very informal, the clientele predominantly local, and you can come and go as you please. Instead of charging an entrance fee, a small levy is charged on beers and sodas, which cost birr 6 apiece. It is customary to tip the dancers at the end of the show.

Situated close to the tourist office, the more ostentatious municipal **Mullu Alem Cultural Centre**, despite the fancy name, serves as little other than a cinema, showing foreign films on Saturday and Sunday only.

Foreign exchange
During normal banking hours, US dollar and other major denomination travellers' cheques and cash can be exchanged into local currency at the Dashen Bank or (rather less efficiently)

at Commercial Bank of Ethiopia branches opposite the Ghion Hotel and a block up from the Papyrus Hotel. At other times, your only option is to try to exchange US dollars cash with one of the smarter hotels – a service generally offered to hotel residents only.

Getting about
Minibuses run from the main roundabout along the Gonder road past the Blue Nile Springs Hotel. There is also a taxi rank on the main roundabout, and one on the same roundabout as the Papyrus Hotel. Bicycles can be hired at the Ghion Hotel or along the road between the main roundabout and the market; expect to pay around birr 3–5 per hour. Details of organising boat trips to the various Lake Tana monasteries, and of reaching the Blue Nile Falls, are included under the sections on these excursions.

Guides
Travellers on pre-booked packages will generally be allocated local guides working for the company they have booked with. For independent travellers, there is little inherent need to take on a guide in town or to visit the Blue Nile Falls (though it can be argued that a good local guide will deflect a lot of hassle). A guide isn't far short of necessary if you want to set up a trip to the lake monasteries, if only to negotiate church fees on your behalf. Although no shortage of 'guides' wander the streets of Bahir Dar offering their services to independent travellers, it's worth asking around for a reputable, experienced guide at the Ghion or Tana Hotel – the official guides who work for Galaxy, the NTO and other tour operators will often take independent travellers around when they are not busy.

Internet and email
Numerous internet cafés are now dotted all around Bahir Dar and charge a fairly uniform birr 0.30 per minute. The two cafés on the main waterfront road next to Ethiopian Airlines are recommended, as is the one in the Ghion Hotel.

Tourist information
The **Amhara Regional Tourist Office** (✆ 058 2201686/2650; e amhtour@ethionet.et) was formerly set in the grounds of the Tana Hotel, but it now boasts an altogether more convenient location along a back road behind the Commercial Bank of Ethiopia. It stocks a couple of useful brochures covering local tourist attractions, though for practical local travel advice, you would be better off picking the brains of one of the private tour operators in the Tana or Ghion hotels.

THE BLUE NILE FALLS
About 30km after it exits Lake Tana, the Blue Nile plunges over a 45m-high rock face to form one of Africa's most spectacular waterfalls, known locally as Tis Abay ('Smoke of the Nile') or Tis Isat ('Water that Smokes'). Tis Abay consists of four separate streams and is most impressive for the sheer volume of water that pours over it, particularly during the rainy season. The Nile is 400m wide above the waterfall; in the gorge below, it follows a much narrower course estimated to be 37m deep!

The 18th-century Scottish traveller James Bruce, who is often credited as the first European to see Tis Abay (in fact, the waterfall was known to the Portuguese at least a century before Bruce's visit), described the waterfall as 'a magnificent sight, that ages, added to the greatest length of human life, would not efface or eradicate from my memory; it struck me with a kind of stupor, and a total oblivion of where I was, and of every other sublunary concern'. After reading this, I was a little disappointed by the actuality when I first saw Tis Abay in 1994 – it isn't in the same league as Victoria Falls, to which it is often compared – but with less fanciful expectations, Ethiopia's premier waterfall in full flow has to be classed as a sight not to be missed.

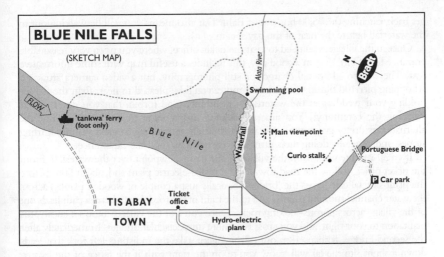

Whatever mild disappointment I experienced back then cannot be compared to that of more recent visitors to Tis Abay. In the words of Steve Rooke, a tour leader who visits Ethiopia annually: 'The Blue Nile Falls are no more! Gone are the thundering waters and clouds of spray with their attendant rainbows. All that is left is a small narrow trickle across a vast expanse of bare rock – frankly, the waterfall at Awash is more impressive!' The reason for the falls' demise is the recent completion of a hydro-electric plant that diverts something like 95% of the water when it is operating. Various rumours are doing the rounds about the long-term status of the waterfall – among them that the hydro-electric plant will cease operating by day once a new plant is built on a proposed dam on the Tekaze River, or that the plant will be turned off on Sunday mornings for the benefit of the tourist industry. Either way, as Steve Rooke points out: 'Reducing the Blue Nile Falls to a Disneyland-type attraction that is turned on and off at will detracts from the whole experience; more important perhaps is that the lack of water is devastating a spray-soaked ecosystem that has taken thousands of years to evolve.'

As things stand, the unfortunate reality is that so long as the plant keeps running, the Cliff Formerly Known as the Blue Nile Falls is not worth making a special effort to see – with devastating consequences for Bahir Dar's nascent tourist industry. Full details of visiting the falls are retained below, in the hope that the water will come back online during the lifespan of this edition, but this is far from certain. Note, too, that while most official guides in Bahir Dar are forthright about the situation at Tis Abay, we have had reports of unscrupulous unofficial guides not mentioning the problem to potential clients, or claiming untruthfully that the waterfall will be running at a specific time.

To the west of Tis Abay, in the Yagume Escarpment some 7km off the road, stands Dengai Debelo, an impressive rock-hewn church said to have been carved by King Lalibela before his coronation.

Getting there and away

The most straightforward way of visiting the waterfall is to organise a half-day excursion from Bahir Dar with a reputable tour operator. It's also very easy to visit the waterfall independently. There are four buses daily between Bahir Dar and the village of Tis Abay. These leave the main bus station at roughly 06.00, 09.00, 12.00 and 13.00. The trip takes an hour and, upon arriving in Tis Abay, the buses fill up immediately and return to Bahir Dar. The last bus out of Tis Abay will leave at around 15.00, and it's possible to pay a child to keep a seat for you. Aside from the obvious advantage of allowing you more time to get back, catching the 06.00 bus out of Bahir Dar also means you will be walking out to the waterfall before the heat of the day sets in.

Once at the village, you need to visit the ticket office, where you pay a very reasonable entrance fee of birr 15 – on a good day, this includes a useful map with some informative text. There is no additional charge for still photography, but a video camera attracts a whopping birr 100 filming fee (birr 25 more, you'll be pleased to hear, than the fee for holding your wedding at the waterfall – assuming, God forbid, that you don't intend videoing the ceremony!) You are not obliged to pay extra to hire a guide, but the alternative is pretty gruesome – a train of children demanding money, yelling, hurling stones, and generally doing their utmost to ensure they spoil the experience.

It's a 30-minute walk from the village to the main viewpoint over the waterfall. From the ticket office, follow the road towards the hydro-electric plant and, about 50m before the plant's metal gate, cross the 'bridge' (basically just a couple of wooden planks) across the water channel running parallel and to the right of the road. From here, a path leads out of the village across porous-looking rocks. Once you exit the village, there's a eucalyptus plantation to your right, and you cross two more unspectacular bridges. Immediately after the second bridge, perhaps 1km out of the village, take the indistinct left fork that leads down a slight slope. You will know you're on the right path if the fence of the hydro-electric plant lies to your left and a church is briefly visible through the trees to your right.

This slope leads down to the Nile. You will cross the river on a large stone bridge called Agam Dildi, built by the Portuguese in around 1620 during the reign of Emperor Susneyos. There's some dense riverine woodland here, and enough birds to delay enthusiasts for a good hour – African thrush, white-headed babbler, blue-breasted bee-eater, northern crowned crane and the endemic wattled ibis, white-cheeked turaco, white-billed starling, black-winged lovebird and yellow-fronted parrot. Once across the bridge, the path curves uphill to the right then immediately veers back to the left past a few huts, from where you can more or less follow the contour to the viewpoint opposite the falls – if your ears aren't an adequate guide, then the hydro-electric plant, visible to your left on the opposite bank of the river, surely will be. The series of viewpoints here is directly opposite the waterfall and offers dramatic views. From the second viewpoint you can often see a rainbow in the spray.

Those with the energy can continue along a footpath that runs downhill parallel to the waterfall. After about 15 minutes you need to turn left to wade across a large stream known as the Alata, and must then turn back following the stream's course to the base of the waterfall. It is actually possible to shower in a waist-height pool below a small slipstream on the side of the waterfall – a breathtaking sensation as the water plunges on you from 40m above – but this is safe only during the dry season, and you should be very careful not to go any further towards the main fall as the currents are deadly. From here, you can return the way you came, or follow the Nile for about 20 minutes to where (during the dry season only) a papyrus *tankwa* or motorboat will be waiting to carry you across the river for birr 10 per person.

Where to stay

Most people visit Tis Abay as a day trip from Bahir Dar, but there are a couple of basic hotels in the village should you want to spend a night there. A more attractive option, perhaps, is to camp near the waterfall. You can camp freely anywhere in the area, though you are advised to bring all your food with you from Bahir Dar, and might want to organise a guard from the police station, which costs birr 40.

THE LAKE TANA MONASTERIES

The islands and peninsulas of Lake Tana collectively house more than 20 monastic churches, many of which were founded during the 14th-century rule of Amda Tsion, though some are possibly older, and at least two (Narga Selassie and Metseli Fasilidas) date to the Gonderine period. A popular local legend has it that seven of the most important 14th-century monasteries were founded by a loosely allied group of monks known as the seven stars. These are Daga Istafanos (founded by Hirute Amlak), Kibran Gebriel (Abuna Yohannis), Ura Kidane Mihret (Abuna Betre Maryam), Bahir Galila Zacharias (Abuna Zacharias), Mandaba Medhane Alem (Ras Asai), Gugubie (Afkrene Egzi) and Debre Maryam (Tadewos Tselalesh).

Many of the Lake Tana monasteries remained practically unknown to outsiders prior to Major Robert Cheesman's pioneering 1930s expedition during which he became the first European to visit all the islands on Lake Tana, as documented in his definitive (but out of print and maddeningly difficult to locate) book *Lake Tana And the Blue Nile: An Abyssinian Quest*. Architecturally, none stands comparison to the rock-hewn and Axumite churches of Tigrai and Lasta, but several are beautifully decorated, none more so than the relatively accessible Ura Kidane Mihret on the Zege Peninsula, covered from top to bottom with paintings that collectively serve as a visual encyclopaedia of Ethiopian ecclesiastical concerns. Also highly impressive in this regard is the more remote, and modern, Gonderine-era church of Narga Selassie.

Many of Lake Tana's monasteries have fascinating treasure houses. For bibliophiles, Kibran Gebriel, the closest true island monastery to Bahir Dar, is of particular interest for its library of almost 200 old books. At Daga Istafanos, visitors can be taken to see the mummified remains of five former emperors of Ethiopia, notably Fasilidas (the founder of Gonder), while on Tana Chirkos there stand three Judaic sacrificial pillars, claimed by the author Graham Hancock to support a legend that this island was for 800 years used to store the Ark of the Covenant.

Steeped in mystery and legend, the old churches of Lake Tana form peaceful retreats for their monastic residents and visiting tourists alike. As in so many parts of Ethiopia, the strong conservationist element in Orthodox Christianity has ensured that the monasteries practically double as nature sanctuaries. The Zege Peninsula, which supports by far the largest remaining tract of natural forest on Lake Tana, still harbours monkeys and various forest birds, while most of the monastic islands, considering their dense population, remain remarkably undisturbed in environmental terms. Combined with the romance attached to being afloat in a beautiful tropical lake that is not only the largest in Ethiopia, but also the source of the world's longest river, a day trip to at least one of these monasteries will be a highlight of any stay in Bahir Dar.

Arranging a trip

Monastery-hopping on Lake Tana used to be dauntingly expensive, largely because private operators were prohibited from chartering out boats, thus enforcing on foreign tourists the use of the Marine Authority's 'tourist boat' at an extortionate rate of around US$30 per hour. All this has changed for the better in recent years: several private operators now offer much more realistic deals, ranging from around birr 300 per group for a half-day trip to the southern monasteries, and birr 700–1,000 for a full-day trip to the central monasteries. The only monasteries which can be visited more cheaply by independent travellers are Debre Maryam, a short walk and ten-minute ride by *tankwa* from Bahir Dar, and those on the Zege Peninsula, which is now accessible from Bahir Dar by road public transport.

In addition to the boat charter fee, all the monasteries charge an entrance fee. The most expensive to visit is Daga Istafanos, which has charged birr 50 per person for some years now, and the cheapest is budget-friendly Debre Maryam at birr 15 per person. The rest, in theory, charge birr 20 per person too. In practice, however, you might be asked a starting price of birr 30–50, one that can be reduced by firm negotiation.

It should be noted that women are not and have never been permitted to enter most of the monasteries – a nugget of information that local tour operators have been known to divulge only once a trip is paid up and in progress! Many female travellers find this ruling offensive, but it does date back several centuries and, as a well-meaning brochure produced by the monks of Daga Istafanos notes, 'it is not meant to belittle women'. To elaborate: 'The reason why women and all domestic animals are not allowed is the thinking that creatures of the opposite sex could be bad examples for the monks, especially those young at age. These young virgin hermits should subdue their body to the service of their God, and the devil should not attack them with the spear of adultery, like the Apostle Saint Paul said: "Younger widows may not be placed on the roll."' The exceptions to the men-only rule are the less isolated monasteries that lie on peninsulas or islands where the monks routinely interact with secular communities, ie: Debre Maryam, Narga Selassie and the monasteries on the Zege Peninsula.

Southern monasteries

The most accessible monasteries from Bahir Dar are those on the southern part of the lake. All of the monasteries mentioned below could be visited over the course of a long half-day by boat, though generally speaking Debre Maryam is visited only by independent travellers with limited time or money, while package tours tend to aim for Ura Kidane Mihret on the Zege Peninsula. If you are setting up your own boat trip to the southern monasteries, a good combination is Kibran Gebriel, Ura Kidane Mihret and possibly Azwa Maryam, for which you should expect to pay birr 200–300 per group for the boat charter, as well as the usual church entrance fees.

Debre Maryam

Founded by Abuna Tadewos Tselalesh near the Nile Outlet during the 14th-century reign of Amda Tsion, Debre Maryam is the only monastery that can easily be visited independently without significant effort or expense. The temple is reputedly very ancient; the rest of the church – rather plain in appearance – is little more than a century old, having been rebuilt during the rule of Emperor Tewodros. In terms of treasures, the church is also relatively impoverished, though there are at least three ancient Ge'ez goatskin manuscripts stored inside. It is said that the monastery grounds are inhabited by many invisible saints. The priest here is very friendly, used to budget travellers, and evidently enjoys modelling for photographs – while by no means the finest of the monasteries, Debre Maryam is agreed by all to be a good day outing!

The cheapest way to visit Debre Maryam is to follow the Gonder road out of town for about 20 minutes, turning left on to a clear track just before the bridge across the Nile. From here, it's a five-to-ten-minute walk to a stretch of shore where you'll find a few boatmen and their papyrus *tankwa* boats ready and willing to take you across the water to the monastery – a five-to-ten-minute boat ride which should cost no more than birr 10 for the return trip. It's advisable to head out early in the day, before the wind starts up, or the water might be too choppy for a *tankwa* to cross.

Debre Maryam can also be visited relatively cheaply from town by motorboat, in conjunction with a spot close to the outlet of the Nile where hippopotami are resident. The round trip takes two to three hours and should cost around birr 100.

Kibran Gebriel

The closest monastery to Bahir Dar, and visible from the town, Kibran Gebriel lies on a tiny, forested crescent – presumably part of the rim of an extinct volcano – which, somewhat incredibly, provides sanctuary to as many as 40 monks. It was founded in the 13th century by a hermit called Abuna Yohannis, who named it after the married couple – Gebriel and Kibran – who rowed him out to the island and later returned there to check on his health. The church, on the highest point of the island, was rebuilt in the 17th century by King Dawit II to a similar design to the better-known Ura Kidane Mihret on Zege. Kibran Gebriel boasts no paintings of note, but it houses the largest library of ancient books of any church in the region – almost 200 volumes in total including a beautifully illustrated 15th-century Life of Christ.

The island can easily be visited in conjunction with the monasteries on the Zege Peninsula, and is no more than 30 minutes by boat from Bahir Dar. Women are forbidden from setting foot on the island, though a legend that Empress Mentewab once visited it, but declined to enter the church when she realised she was menstruating, would suggest that this has not always been the case. The smaller forested island of Entons immediately south of Kibran used to be a nunnery but was abandoned some years ago – however a recent report from a traveller who was offered to be shown the 'women's monastery' adjacent to Kibran Gebriel suggests that the disused church might still be worth a look.

Ura Kidane Mihret and the Zege Peninsula
The forested Zege Peninsula is studded with medieval churches, of which Ura Kidane Mihret ranks not only as the most impressive of the southern monasteries, but also possibly the most beautiful church anywhere in the Tana region. This, combined with its relative proximity to Bahir Dar, has made it the most frequently visited church on the lake. Set within bleak stone walls, the monastery was founded in the 14th century by a Saint called Betre Maryam, who hailed from the Muger River in Showa and started training as a priest after being visited by two angels at the age of seven (Betre Maryam literally means 'Rod of Mary', and is a reference to the saint's steeliness when it came to beating off the devil and other demons).

The circular church was built in the 16th century. The walls are covered in an incredible jumble of murals, painted between 100 and 250 years ago (the most recent were executed by an artist called Engida during the dying years of the reign of Menelik II, and many of which have been restored in the last few decades. These paintings are positively Chaucerian in their physicality, ribaldry and gore, and it is no hyperbole to say that they offer a genuinely revealing glimpse into medieval Ethiopia – so do give yourself time to look at them closely. There are also some intriguing line drawings on one of the doors, and the museum has a few old crowns of Ethiopian kings, leather-bound Bibles and other ancient treasures.

Reachable from Ura Kidane Mihret by boat, or by following a 2km footpath through thick forest, stand the disused churches of **Mehal Giyorgis** and **Bet Maryam**. Mehal Giyorgis is little more than a shell but there are some 18th-century murals on the standing walls. There are several antiquities locked away in Bet Maryam. Another interesting church on the peninsula is **Azuwa Maryam**, which lies closer to Ura Kidane Mihret, and also boasts several animated 18th-century paintings.

The most normal way to visit Ura Kidane Mihret is by charter boat direct from Bahir Dar, which takes about an hour, terminating at a jetty five-to-ten-minutes' easy walk from the monastery itself. It is also now quite easy to visit the peninsula by a recently renovated road from Bahir Dar, whether by private vehicle or public transport. It would also be possible to visit the monastery using the daily public ferry between Bahir Dar and Zege village were it not that the Marine Authority forbids tourists from using the service. For more details see box *The Zege Peninsula* on page 210.

Central monasteries
Although less easily accessible from Bahir Dar than the Zege Peninsula, the string of monasteries that runs from east to west across the centre of Lake Tana is arguably more intriguing. These monasteries fall into two main clusters: one close to the eastern

THE ZEGE PENINSULA

The forested peninsula of Zege, together with the eponymous village, is one of the most accessible points on the Lake Tana shore using public transport. Until recently, however, ease of access was restricted to locals, since the Lake Tana Transport Authority's daily ferry connecting Bahir Dar to Zege was off-limits to tourists through the continued application of a law dating to the Mengistu era, when interaction between Ethiopians and foreigners was discouraged. In three previous editions of this guide, I have stated that I doubt this situation will persist indefinitely. So far, I have been wrong in my assumption that the relevant authorities might one day be overcome by a bout of common sense, but the good news for this fourth edition is that the recent upgrading of the 22km track to Zege means there is now reliable public transport from Bahir Dar.

The main attraction of Zege is of course the monasteries that dot the peninsula (see *Ura Kidane Mihret and the Zege Peninsula*, page 209), which would collectively take the best part of a day to check out on foot from Zege village. The most interesting and popular of these monasteries, Ura Kidane Mihret, lies only 3km from the village, and could therefore be visited as a round trip in two to three hours. To get there, follow the steep footpath out from the central market to the top of the peninsula, from where you take a left fork to enter the forest and head west towards the churches. You can't really go wrong from here: there are a couple of small side paths, but the main track is wide and clear – indeed, with a private vehicle you can drive to within 200m of the church – and there are plenty of people to direct you along the way. You'll find plenty of hysterical youngsters hanging around the compound offering their services as a guide – you can safely ignore them, as the monks will show you everything anyway.

The forest itself is worth taking slowly. It's one of the few large indigenous forests in this part of Ethiopia, and it makes an appealing change from the characteristic open grassland of the region. Wild coffee dominates the undergrowth, vervet monkeys shake the canopy, parrots screech and hornbills explode into cacophony, and colourful butterflies flutter at your feet. With glimpses of the lake to your right, this is a lovely walk, even if you elect not to visit the monasteries.

lakeshore, of which Tana Chirkos with its mysterious sacrificial stones is without doubt the most important; and the other dead central, of which the beautifully decorated Narga Selassie on Dek Island, and Daga Istafanos – housing the mummified remains of five former emperors – are the highlights.

With a very early start from Bahir Dar, it is possible to visit the three monasteries mentioned above (but no others) in one long day; expect to pay up to birr 1,000 for the boat charter. A more popular option, however, is to head for one or other cluster, which allows for a slightly later start, and will cost around birr 700 for the boat. Church entrance fees are extra, and you are advised to bring plenty of mineral water and food. Unless the boat is covered, you'll also want some sunblock and a hat. Women travellers should be reminded that, with the exception of Narga Selassie, all the central monasteries permit male visitors only.

Tana Chirkos

This small island monastery, separated from the eastern shore by a narrow marshy corridor, is dominated by a striking spine of rock perhaps 30m high, and fringed by riparian forest supporting several pairs of fish eagle. It has acquired something approaching cult status since the publication of Graham Hancock's book *The Sign and the Seal*, which attempts to substantiate an ancient tradition that the Ark of the Covenant was

On first impressions, Zege village isn't much of a place: a couple of roads lined with mud houses radiating from a large central marketplace. The surrounding forest gives it some ambience, especially at night when it's all bobbing candles and chirping cicadas – there's no electricity or cars. If idling is on the agenda, no better place to do so than on the attractive pier, with the lake stretching in front of you and the forested peninsula to your left. More acquisitively, you can buy goatskin *injera* baskets on Zege for about half of what you would pay in town.

Minibuses to Zege cost birr 5 one-way, and leave Bahir Dar a few times daily (ironically) from in front of the Lake Tana Transport Authority compound. If you want to check the situation with the ferry, it normally leaves Bahir Dar at 07.30 daily and passengers need to be at the compound 30 minutes earlier – there is only one class and tickets are very cheap. Whether by land or by water, the trip to Zege takes about one hour. If you want to overnight in Zege, the pick of the lodges is the Abay Hotel, which charges birr 5 for a very basic room using a common shower and serves acceptable food and drink, followed by the Yebiste Erko Hotel, an even more basic, family-run lodge charging birr 6 for a cramped room (bucket showers only). The other hotels in town are no better and charge silly *faranji* prices.

The road between Bahir Dar and Zege is now passable all year through, so it is possible to drive there in a private vehicle from Bahir Dar, as well as to cycle there, which takes two to three hours in either direction. Bicycles can easily be hired in Bahir Dar for birr 2–3 per hour or birr 20–30 per day, but try to get reasonably sturdy ones, and insist on a pump and tyre repair kit. To get to Zege, take the surfaced main road west out of town, past the Ghion Hotel, and climb the slightly hilly road towards the airport for 4.5km until you see a water tower to your right and a small hill to your left. Turn right here, then after another 4.5km you'll reach a Y-junction where you must turn right again, in the direction of the lake. About 2km further, turn right at a T-junction, then after another 2.5km cross the recently constructed bridge across the Efransi River. After the river crossing, you need to keep going for another 8–9km – the small tracks through the area sometimes cross each other, but if you stick to what appears to be the main track, then you can't really go wrong.

stowed on the island for some 600 years before it was transferred to Axum in the 4th century AD by King Ezana.

One tradition has it that the Christian monastery was founded on the site of an older temple during the 6th-century reign of Gebre Meskel by Saint Yared and Abuna Aregawi. Another tradition holds that the monastery was founded two centuries earlier by Frumentius, the first Bishop of Axum, who was buried there. Other sources suggest that the island converted to Christianity a mere 540 years ago. Whenever the monastery was founded, the architecturally undistinguished church, which was built about 100 years ago with funding from Ras Gugsa of Debre Tabor, looks more timeworn than it does ancient, and none of the paintings that adorn it looks significantly more than a decade old.

Far more interesting than the monastery itself is a trio of hollowed-out sacrificial pillars that stand alongside it, testifying to the island's importance as a Judaic religious shrine in pre-Christian times. The local priests say that the pillars date from King Solomon's time and were used to make dyes. Given the Ethiopian predilection for mythologising – one local tradition has it that the Virgin Mary rested here on her (presumably somewhat circuitous) return from Egypt to Israel, and a 'footprint' on one of the island's rocks is claimed to be that of none other than her immaculately conceived firstborn son – it is stretching a point to conclude, as Hancock does, that these pillars provide circumstantial support for the Ark once having resided on the island.

Tana Chirkos lies some three hours from Bahir Dar by boat; the walk from the jetty to the monastery takes no more than five minutes. On the way to the island (or coming back), it is possible to look at two further monasteries, both on small forested islands about 30 minutes from Tana Chirkos. These are Rema Medhane Alem, a recently rebuilt church in which are stored a few interesting old paintings, and Mitseli Fasilidas, founded during the rule of the emperor after whom it is named, and architecturally undistinguished – though the surrounding forest is rich in birdlife.

With a private vehicle, and ideally a local guide, Tana Chirkos can also be visited by taking the main road to Gonder from Bahir Dar for about 70km, then following rough tracks for about 5km east to the mainland church of Kristos Samra, itself an important pilgrimage site in honour of the nun after whom it is named. From the mainland, a papyrus *tankwa* can easily be arranged to Tana Chirkos, a ten-minute trip which shouldn't cost more than birr 20 return.

Daga Istafanos

The largest monastery on the lake, home to as many as 200 monks, Daga Istafanos lies on a small wedge-shaped island immediately east of the much larger Dek Island. A reliable (and for once apparently uncontested) tradition states that the monastery was founded in the late 13th century by Hiruta Amlak, a nephew of Emperor Yekuno Amlak who served his apprenticeship under Iyasu Moa at Hayk Istafanos at the same time as the future Archbishop Tekle Haymanot. A somewhat less probable tradition has it that Hiruta Amlak was guided to the shores of Lake Tana by Istafanos from Hayk, and was then ferried from mainland to island on a pair of divine stones that can still be seen in the grounds of the monastery he founded. The church on the island's conical peak is relatively uninteresting and not especially old – it was rebuilt after the original burnt to the ground in the 19th century – although there is a rather unusual monochrome painting of an angel on one of the inner doors. Tradition has it that Daga Istafanos is where the Ark of the Covenant was hidden during Ahmed Gragn's 16th-century occupation of Axum.

The main point of interest at Daga Istafanos today is the mausoleum, which contains the mummified remains of at least five Ethiopian emperors: Yakuno Amlak (1268–93), Dawit I (1428–30), Zara Yaqob (1434–68), Susneyos (1607–32) and Fasilidas (1632–76). The glass coffins in which the mummies now lie are recent acquisitions, donated by Haile Selassie after he visited the monastery in 1951. The mummy of Fasilidas is the best preserved of the five, and his facial features are still eerily discernible. A tiny skeleton next to this is said to be the remains of Fasilidas's favourite son, who was crowned as his father's successor but collapsed and died under the weight of the crown.

It is something of a mystery as to when, why and how the mummies ended up on this remote island: some say during the Mahdist invasion of Gonder in the late 19th century, others during the Italian occupation, but there also seems to be good reason to believe that the dead kings were brought here for mummification shortly after they died. Certainly, Daga Istafanos was a popular retreat for several of the abovementioned kings, and its tranquillity was reputedly also favoured by Tewodros II, who took communion there on several occasions. Several other treasures associated with these kings are stored in the mausoleum: old crowns, a goatskin book with some line drawings dating from the 14th century, and two immaculately preserved 15th-century paintings of the Madonna with uncharacteristically detailed and non-stylised facial features.

Daga Istafanos lies about three hours by boat from Bahir Dar, 90 minutes from Tana Chirkos, and an hour from Narga Selassie. The walk from the jetty to the church is quite steep, and takes about 15 minutes, with a chance of encountering the odd monkey along the way. It can be visited in conjunction with the nearby monastery of Metseli Fasilidas, which was founded by Emperor Fasilidas of Gonder and reputedly contains an interesting collection of old books and manuscripts.

Narga Selassie

Situated on the western shore of Dek, the largest island on Lake Tana, Narga Selassie is, with the possible exception of the much older Ura Kidane Mihret, the most ornately decorated of all the lake monasteries. Built in the 18th century for Princess Mentewab (regent for Emperor Iyasu II), the stone walls surrounding the compound, with their domed turrets, are typically Gonderine, and not dissimilar in appearance to the walls surrounding the church next to Mentewab's palace at Kuskuam outside Gonder. The compound, its 'old grey towers, forgotten on this lonely island' looked somewhat neglected when Cheesman visited it in the 1930s, but the church was restored with funding by Haile Selassie in 1951 and the roof was renovated again in 2001.

The main church is circular in shape and surrounded by stone pillars (one of which is decorated by an etching of the pipe-puffing explorer James Bruce, a close associate of Mentewab). As with Ura Kidane Mihret, the inner walls are covered from top to bottom with a riotous and absorbing collection of paintings, most thought to date from the 18th century. In addition to the usual pictures of saints and their exploits, there is a painting of the church's founder lying prostrate before Mary and the Baby Jesus, probably the only contemporaneous portrait of Mentewab to survive. Another interesting one shows a church on a fish, the latter about to be speared by an angel – evidently relating to a legend about a town on Lake Tana that was being harassed by a big fish until the angel intervened.

Narga Selassie lies some three hours from Bahir Dar by boat, and an hour from Daga Istafanos. The monastery is practically next to the jetty. There are two other monasteries on Dek Island, Arsema Semaetat and Mota Maryam, but neither is regularly visited by tourists.

Northern monasteries

Four ancient but seldom-visited monasteries dot the islands off the northern shore of Lake Tana, all of them somewhat remote from Bahir Dar – a boat charter from there would cost the best part of birr 2,000 – but situated within easy striking distance of the northern ferry terminal of Gorgora. The best way to explore these monasteries is to charter a boat from Gorgora, which can organised through the Lake Tana Transport Authority for birr 250–500 for up to five people, depending on which churches you opt to visit, or for about two-thirds that price through one of a handful of private boat owners. The monasteries, which can be visited in conjunction with the port of Old Gorgora, generally ask for a donation of birr 20 per person apiece, but do note that women are not allowed on any of the islands. A good contact for making arrangements in the Gorgora area is the locally based guide Tesfaye Mekonnen (✆ 058 1115679).

Probably the most venerated of the northern monasteries is **Mandaba Medhane Alem**, which lies about 30 minutes from Gorgora by motorboat. The monastery was founded in the 14th century by Ras Asai, the ascetic son of Emperor Amda Tsion, and its monks, among the most devout and virtuous in Ethiopia, are considered to be angels made flesh. The church is of greatest interest for its superb collection of old manuscripts, paintings and other antiquated treasures. The church itself underwent major reconstruction in the 1950s, but parts of the interior, including the painted door frame, are very old.

Much the same goes for **Brigida Maryam**: built by Amda Tsion in the 14th century but reconstructed three times since owing to fire damage, the church is of limited architectural interest, but it does host some genuine treasures, most notably perhaps a superb 16th-century painting of Mary. Nearby **Angara Tekle Haymanot** has few treasures and the present-day church dates to the Haile Selassie era.

Somewhat further afield, about an hour by boat from Gorgora, **Bahir Galila Zacharias** has the oldest church of the northern island monasteries, possibly dating to the 14th century, though it is currently under scaffolding. Bahir Galila is Amharic for 'Sea of Galilee', and it was founded in the 14th century by a monk called Zacharias, who could reputedly walk on water. The monastery is remembered for the massacre of most of its monks by Ahmed Gragn in the 16th century.

BAHIR DAR TO GONDER BY ROAD

With the recent surfacing of the 185km road that runs east of Lake Tana between Bahir Dar and Gonder, even tourists who fly between all other points of interest in northern Ethiopia might regard driving between these two cities to be an attractive prospect. The drive is not particularly time consuming – you're looking at about four hours on public transport, no more than three (excluding breaks) in a decent private vehicle – and you don't risk losing the best part of a day to inconvenient midday flight schedules and unexpected delays. Furthermore, tackling this one domestic journey by road offers short-stay visitors to Ethiopia an experience of the countryside away from the towns and historical sites.

If time is a factor, you could easily leave Bahir Dar after breakfast and be in Gonder for lunch, or vice versa. But if you're not in a rush, there are a few worthwhile minor diversions en route. First among these, set in a thickly wooded grove to the east of the main road some 50km from Bahir Dar, is the **Wanzaye Hot Springs**, which bubble from beneath the earth at temperatures in excess of 42°C to feed a series of pools that empty into the Gumara River. Regarded as holy by Ethiopians, and popular for its therapeutic qualities, Wanzaye is also of interest for the colourful birds and monkeys that inhabit the surrounding riparian vegetation. It is unclear whether the former government hotel and campsite at the springs is still operational.

Altogether different in nature is the weaving co-operative of **Awramba** (✆ 058 2206276), which can be reached by turning right onto the Woldia road about 60km from Bahir Dar (and less than 1km north of Werota). Follow the Woldia road for 8km until you reach a (poorly) signposted junction to the right, and then follow this rough road for another 2km to the village. Awramba was founded in 1985 by a group of 20 people to demonstrate to its members and to other Ethiopians that the best escape route from poverty and hunger is not religion or prayer but education and plain hard work. Remarkable simply for being the only overtly atheistic society I've come across *anywhere* in Africa (pride of place is given not to a mosque or a church but to a surprisingly well-stocked school library), this isolated community, which now consists of about 100 families totalling 400 individuals, also prides itself on an egalitarian non-sexist, non-racist policy (the weaving work is shared between men and women), on the formal healthcare and support it provides to the elderly, and on a pre-school aimed primarily at children under the age of seven, but also attended by older people seeking to attain a basic level of literacy.

Better known to Ethiopians than to tourists thanks to a recent TV appearance in which the village chairman unveiled his unorthodox religious views to a somewhat startled nation, Awramba welcomes foreign visitors, though it's rather quiet on Wednesdays and Saturdays when most inhabitants are at the market. Ask to be shown the school, the library, the dormitories for aged members of the community, the innovative *injera* cookers in the adobe houses (whose curvaceous design rather reminds me of Mali's Dogon country), and the communal weaving area with its 20 handmade looms.

No entrance fee is charged at Awramba, and begging is actively frowned upon, so the most appropriate way to contribute would be to buy some of the handspun cotton and wool items in the warehouse – a range of *shamas*, scarves, shirts and blankets costs half what you'd pay in most other parts of the country. It is worth

GORGORA

The little-visited town of Gorgora, situated on the northern shore of Lake Tana, is today dominated by the large, leafy Lake Tana Transport Authority compound, an attractive

noting that this must be the only place we've been in Ethiopia where not one child yelled at us or approached us asking for money or a pen or sweets – an utterly refreshing experience, so please, please, please can those who follow in our footsteps help keep it that way by resisting the temptation to hand out trinkets indiscriminately.

Back on the surfaced road, **Addis Zemen**, about 40km north of Werota, is the most substantial town between Bahir Dar and Gonder – which isn't saying a great deal, but does make it the best place to stop for a meal, a cold drink, or a bed for the night. North of Addis Zemen, the road ascends into hillier territory, passing a striking isolated rock formation known as the Devil's Nose after about 4km.

Some 25km further, past the small village of Emfraz, a short but rough track to the right leads uphill to **Guzara Castle**, which is generally regarded to have been built for Emperor Sarsa Dengal in 1571–72. Easily visible from the main road, and offering grand views across to Lake Tana, this imposing building, evidently built with a strong Portuguese input, comes across as a clear stylistic precursor of the more famous castles built half a century later by Sarsa Dengal's grandson Fasilidas and his successors at Gonder. Indeed, Guzara's architectural resemblance to the Gonderine castle has led to recent expert speculation that it was built by Susneyos or Fasilidas rather than Sarsa Dengal. Despite years of neglect, the castle is still in fair shape, and it was in the process of being restored to its full former glory with US funding in 2005.

About 30km further north, easily visible from the main road about 5km past the village of **Maksegno Gebeya** (which translates somewhat prosaically but thoroughly accurately as 'Tuesday Market'), **Bet Bahari Mikael** is an impressive fortress-like stone church built during the early 16th century (more than 100 years before the Gonderine castles) by Emperor Lebna Dengal with some architectural input from his Portuguese advisor Pero de Covilhão. The church boasts two domes – one as originally constructed by Lebna Dengal, one added in the 1960s by Haile Selassie – and parts are in urgent need of maintenance after having been bombarded during fighting between government and rebel forces in 1990.

Crowned as a child, Lebna Dengal's was an eventful rule – it started under the regency of the former Empress Eleni in 1508, was punctuated by the reception of the first Portuguese envoy to Ethiopia in 1520, and ended in 1540 at the Tigraian monastery of Debre Damo, where the emperor died of illness and exhaustion following 12 years of bitter war with the Islamic army of Ahmed Gragn. Three years after Lebna Dengal's death, on 11 February 1543, Gragn himself was killed in the Battle of Weyna Daga, to be buried, somewhat fittingly, a mere 20km from Bet Bahari Mikael at a place called Sentara.

Some say that the fatal blow to Gragn was struck by a Portuguese musket ball fired by the army of Lebna Dengal's son Galawdewos, others that he was stung to death by one of those bee swarms that turn up habitually during critical junctures in Ethiopian history. Either way, the **Tomb of Ahmed Gragn** still stands at Sentara today, and can be reached along a 20km side road east from the Bahir Dar–Gonder road between Maksegno Gebeya and Bet Bahari Mikael. Many Ethiopian Muslims make the pilgrimage to the tomb on the anniversary of Gragn's death, although this being a predominantly Christian area, shrines erected at the site have a habit of vanishing before the next anniversary comes around! Some 4km before reaching the tomb, the road passes an extant tree stump where Gragn is said to have rested whilst mortally wounded.

spot that will prove highly rewarding to birdwatchers. Founded in medieval times, when it served as one of the many temporary capitals of the period, Gorgora has strong historical associations with Gonder 60km to its north, and even today it doesn't really seem to belong in the standard Lake Tana tourist circuit, but feels more like a lakeshore satellite to Fasilidas's former capital (to which it is linked by regular road transport). Gorgora was an important port during the Italian occupation, the most obvious relic of which is the so-called Mussolini Pillar – so far as I can ascertain, a lighthouse-like construction that helped guide ships towards the harbour – that stands on a hill above the town and is clearly visible on the road in from Gonder.

A highlight of any visit to Gorgora will be a visit to the **Monastery of Debre Sina Maryam**, which lies along a motorable track five minutes' walk from the town centre, and permits women visitors – entrance costs birr 25 per person. As is so often the case, the history of this church varies with the telling, but most likely it was founded circa 1334 by a monk called Hesterus who hailed from the town of Debre Sina further southeast. The present building, a fine example of a thatched circular church, probably dates to the 16th century, though the carved Axumite windows and frames might well have been lifted from an earlier building.

The murals on Debre Sina Maryam rank with the most complex and vivid to be seen in the Tana region. Local tradition claims them to be medieval in origin, but the greater probability is that they were executed in the early Gonderine Period under the patronage of the noblewoman Melako Tawit, who is depicted on one mural. According to the priests, the woman in question was the elder sister of Emperor Fasilidas, but more likely perhaps she was the wife of Iyasu I – evidently both women had the same name. Either way, the most recent murals were painted at least 300 years ago, making them significantly older than their counterparts at Ura Kidane Mihret or Narga Selassie. What's more, the lowest row of paintings does look significantly older than the one that includes the portrait of Melako Tawit, and it's also very different stylistically – compare the facial detail of the lower and higher portraits of Mary on the wall as you enter – so it could be that some paintings are older than others.

Two of the church's most striking wall panels depict the devil rolling about in laughter as Adam and Eve sample the forbidden fruit, and a decidedly smug-looking King Herod and cronies making bloodthirsty work of the newly born children of Israel. The church's greatest treasure is a glass-covered portrait known as the 'Egyptian Saint Mary': an utterly implausible legend has it that this painting was made when Mary was exiled to Egypt, and the local priests claim that it lights up spontaneously from time to time, and has the capacity to revive dead children.

Also of interest in the Gorgora area is the Portuguese cathedral built during Susneyos's day but abandoned after Fasilidas booted out the Catholic settlers. To reach the cathedral, you can either walk east along the lakeshore for several hours, or head out of Gorgora for 8km along the Gonder road, then turn left at a small village and follow a track back towards the lake for about 15km – the track isn't very clear so keep asking directions. The cathedral is now an overgrown ruin, but what does remain – tall walls, pillars and archways engraved with flowers and crosses – is sufficient to hint at its former grandeur. There is talk of restoring the church with UNESCO help.

On a peninsula roughly 10km west of Gorgora stands 'Old Gorgora' and the ruined palace constructed by Emperor Susneyos between 1625 and 1630 with Portuguese assistance. The building isn't in the greatest shape, but it is of some interest architecturally as an immediate precursor to the more renowned palaces of Gonder. Old Gorgora can only be visited by boat – these can be chartered through the Lake Tana Transport Authority for around birr 500, or more cheaply through a private operator – and the excursion can be combined with stops en route at some of northern monasteries described on page 213.

Getting there and away

Gorgora is the northern terminus of the weekly ferry to and from Bahir Dar (see box *The Lake Tana Ferry,* pages 202–3). It is also possible to charter a private boat from Bahir Dar for around birr 2,000 for up to six people. The port lies 60km south of Gonder along a reasonable dirt road and the drive takes slightly longer than one hour. Two buses ply the Gonder road every morning, the first leaving at 06.00 and the second at around 10.00, and there are also regular minibuses – the trip takes two hours and tickets cost birr 10. Coming from Gonder, minibuses to Gorgora leave from the bus station near the Axum Hotel.

Where to stay and eat

The government-owned **Gorgora Hotel**, run by the Marine Authority and set within their compound, has a good position on the lakeshore. The spacious and attractive rooms have private showers and toilets, and seem fair value at birr 110/165 for a double/twin. Camping in the attractive grounds costs birr 28 per tent. The restaurant is excellent and affordable.

The selection of cheaper hotels in Gorgora is restricted to an unsignposted place immediately outside the gate to the Marine Authority compound. The rooms here would be perfectly acceptable for a dollar-a-night hotel, but they're overpriced at the *faranji* rate of birr 20 – especially as there is no shower.

218

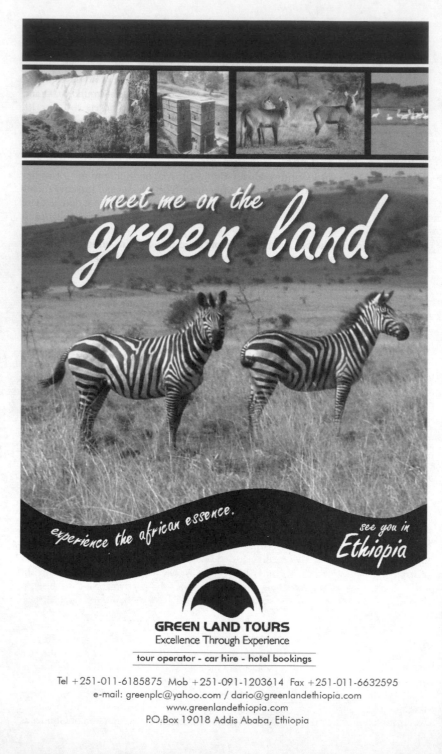

GREEN LAND TOURS
Excellence Through Experience

tour operator - car hire - hotel bookings

Tel +251-011-6185875 Mob +251-091-1203614 Fax +251-011-6632595
e-mail: greenplc@yahoo.com / dario@greenlandethiopia.com
www.greenlandethiopia.com
P.O.Box 19018 Addis Ababa, Ethiopia

Gonder and the Simien Mountains

The city of Gonder was, until 1994, capital and principal town of an eponymous province that was subsequently absorbed into the Federal Region of Amhara. Founded by King Fasilidas in 1635, the city served as the imperial capital for 250 years prior to the rise of King Tewodros and associated power shift southward to Showa. Gonder is one of the main tourist attractions on the northern historical circuit, best known for its 17th-century castles and palaces, but studded with several other points of interest, most notably the fantastically decorated church of Debre Birhan Selassie ten minutes' walk from the town centre. Gonder is also the obvious base from which to stage day trips or longer treks into the scenic Simien Mountains National Park, Ethiopia's most popular hiking destination.

The city of Gonder is the main travel gateway to the region, serviced by daily Ethiopian Airlines flights, a few buses daily from Bahir Dar, and less regular buses northwards towards Axum. The region can also be approached through Gorgora, the northern terminus of the Lake Tana Ferry, and linked to Gonder by regular public transport (see previous chapter).

GONDER

Gonder is probably the most immediately impressive of Ethiopia's major ex-capitals, but its antiquities are for the most part less enduringly memorable than those at the more ancient towns of Axum or Lalibela. The city was founded in 1635 by Emperor Fasilidas (often abbreviated to Fasil) in the aftermath of a tumultuous century during which the Abyssinian Empire had virtually collapsed under the onslaught of the Muslim leader Ahmed Gragn, and was then torn apart by internal religious conflict after Emperor Susneyos converted to Catholicism in 1622. Influenced by the Portuguese Jesuits, who had settled around his temporary court on the shores of Lake Tana, Susneyos imposed Catholicism on his subjects by declaring it the state religion and attempting to close down the Orthodox Church. The result of this unpopular policy was a period of violent instability during which an estimated 32,000 peasants were killed by the royal army. In 1632, Susneyos partially redeemed himself when he abdicated in favour of his son Fasilidas, who immediately reinstated the traditional state religion and expelled the Portuguese from the empire.

After a period of several centuries during which Ethiopia was ruled from a succession of temporary capitals, the last of which, Danquaz, lay some 20km from Gonder, Fasilidas recognised that a permanent capital might help provide greater internal stability. He settled on the small village of Gonder, with its strategic hilltop location at an altitude of 2,120m in the southern foothills of the Simien Mountains. One oft-repeated story has it that Fasilidas selected Gonder because it fulfilled an ancient tradition by having the initial letter of G (some historians maintain that this 'tradition' was manufactured by the royal myth-machine subsequent to the adoption of Gonder as capital). By the time of Fasilidas's death in 1667, Gonder had become the largest and most important city in the empire, with a population in excess of 60,000. It retained its position as the capital of Ethiopia for 250 years, though this status was increasingly nominal from the late 18th century onwards as the central monarchy gradually lost importance to powerful regional rulers.

Having enjoyed something of a revival during and subsequent to the Italian occupation, Gonder is today the fourth largest city in Ethiopia, with a population though to exceed 150,000. It is also a very pleasant city, with a friendly, laidback, almost countrified mood by comparison with Addis Ababa or even Bahir Dar. The walled Royal Enclosure that dominates the city centre contains several well-preserved castles and other buildings, and definitely warrants a half-day's exploration. Also of interest in Gonder are Fasilidas's Bathing Pool, the elaborately decorated Debre Birhan Selassie Church, and out-of-town palaces built by Princess Mentewab and Emperor Susneyos. Juxtaposed against this distinctive Gonderine architecture, much of the modern town centre dates from the Italian occupation of 1936–41, and hints of Art Deco and other pre-war European styles can be detected in many of the rundown buildings that line the central Piazza.

Getting there and away
By air
Ethiopian Airlines flies daily between Gonder and Addis Ababa, Bahir Dar, Axum and Lalibela. The airport is about 20km out of town, just off the main Bahir Dar road, so you'll have to catch a taxi or try to make an arrangement with one of the tour buses that meet most flights. Fares are negotiable as always, but should not exceed birr 30 for a taxi charter.

Air tickets out of Gonder can and should be reconfirmed at the Ethiopian Airlines office on the Piazza below the Royal Compound.

By boat
For details of the ferry connecting Bahir Dar to Gorgora, 60km south of Gonder, see the previous chapter. There is regular road transport between Gorgora and Gonder.

By road
Coming from the south, direct buses between Addis Ababa and Gonder leave at around 06.00 in either direction and take two days, stopping overnight at Debre Markos or one of the smaller towns on the way. These buses are not used by many tourists, since it would mean passing straight through Bahir Dar. More normal therefore is to catch one bus to Bahir Dar, spend a night or two there, and then bus on to Gonder, which costs birr 23 and takes about four hours on what is now a good asphalt road. A little surprisingly, all buses between Bahir Dar and Gonder leave in the early morning, but minibuses – about double the price – leave Bahir Dar throughout the day from in front of the Ghion Hotel. The 185km trip takes about three hours without breaks in a private vehicle – see also the box *Bahir Dar to Gonder by Road*, page 214.

Heading north from Gonder, a couple of buses leave at around 05.30 daily for Debark (the base for hiking in the Simien Mountains) and take around four hours to get there. If you are heading directly to Axum, then your best bet is to catch the 06.30 bus to Shire (Inda Selassie). (See box *Gonder to Axum by Road*, page 236.) There is plenty of accommodation in Shire, and regular transport on to Axum.

Details of travelling directly from Gonder to Lalibela by road are included under Lalibela in the *Getting there and away* section (page 337).

Buses out of Gonder generally need to be booked the afternoon before departure.

Where to stay

It can safely be said, at the time of writing, that any sentence including the words 'Gonder', 'clean', 'cheap' and 'hotel' will almost always include the word 'not'. Gonder has long suffered from a shortage of decent hotels, and a tendency for its more basic hotels to charge what come across as absurdly inflated *faranji* prices by comparison with, say, Axum or Bahir Dar. As a result, the accommodation listings below should be read in the understanding that no hotel in Gonder (other than the upmarket Goha and Fogera) would rank as good value for money anywhere else in Ethiopia except perhaps Lalibela. Some of the cheaper places will offer off-season discounts if you look convincingly disgruntled. By contrast, most hotels charge an even more inflated rate over the week building up to Timkat (20 January).

Upmarket

Goha Hotel (64 rooms) ☎ 058 1110634; f 058 1111920; e ghion@ethionet.et; www.ghionhotel.com.et. Rated by many as the best hotel in the government Ghion chain, the Goha is perched attractively on a hill about 1.5km from the town centre. The great view over town and the above-average service make this one of the best hotels in northern Ethiopia. Rooms cost US$36/48/60 sgl/dbl/ste. For those who are staying in the town centre, and who don't mind the stiff 30-minute walk or are prepared to pay for a taxi, the Goha is a nice place to head to watch the sunset and enjoy a smart dinner – the three-course set menu costs around birr 25.

Fogera Hotel (16 rooms) ☎ 058 1110405. The pick of Gonder's private hotels is this rehabilitated former government establishment, which lies in a compact green garden about five minutes' walk from the town centre. Originally built as a villa by one of Mussolini's fascists, the Fogera is still possessed of the rather dishevelled and musty time-warped aura common to many former (and extant) government hotels. That said, the hotel does boast some real character, and the well-maintained semi-detached bungalows with twin beds and en-suite hot showers seem reasonable value at birr 225 – better value still if you can arrange an 'out of season' discount. The restaurant, one of the best in town, serves predictable government hotel fare at birr 15–20 for a main course.

Moderate

Circle Hotel (26 rooms) ☎ 058 1111991. This unmistakable circular high-rise building, set just off the Piazza, stands out comfortably as the best deal in this range. The large, carpeted rooms with en-suite hot shower and DSTV cost birr 80 for a sgl with a large dbl bed or birr 100 for a twin. Some rooms are rather more frayed than others, so ask to check your room before you register. The first-floor restaurant receives mixed reports, and there's a breezy rooftop bar.

Quara Hotel (16 rooms) ☎ 058 1110040. One of the better deals in Gonder, this tolerably rundown government hotel boasts a great location on the Piazza, and – despite the less than encouraging exterior – it almost feels realistically priced at birr 75/88 sgl/dbl occupancy of an en-suite room with a proper dbl bed and hot shower.

Merkuriaw Alemaya Hotel (24 rooms) Boasting a convenient (albeit potentially noisy) location between the bus station and the Royal Ghebbi, this reasonably smart and characterless new five-storey hotel is indifferent value at birr 80/120 for a small but spotless en-suite sgl/dbl.

Humera Pension ☎ 058 1110787. Situated within easy walking distance of the town centre on the right side of the road to the Goha Hotel, this new three-storey hotel offers adequate accommodation in small tiled en-suite rooms with hot water for an overpriced birr 100/130 sgl/dbl.

Nile Gonder Hotel (36 rooms) ☎ 058 1111600; f 058 1111800. This once-popular high-rise hotel next to the Circle is looking very rundown of late, and the cramped, musty rooms are overpriced, even by Gonder's standards, at birr 80 for a sgl with a ¾ bed or birr 135 for a twin. The nominal group discount offered to large parties doesn't compensate for the silly starting price.

Terara Hotel (38 rooms) ☎ 058 1110153. The finest hostelry in Gonder during the late Imperial era, when it went by the name Itegue Menen, this has suffered badly from neglect

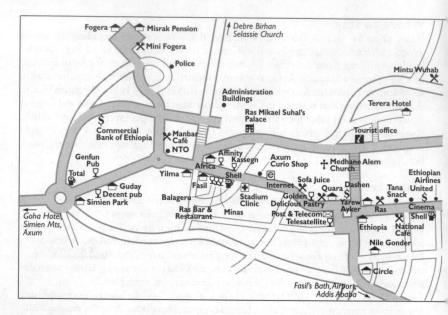

over subsequent decades – the only hint of its former heyday comes in the form of delusional *faranji* prices of birr 75 for a small, dingy dbl using common showers or birr 112 for a similarly gloomy room with en-suite facilities. Redeeming features? Well, the manager is worth meeting if you've ever wondered what an Ethiopian Basil Fawlty might be like, and the garden bar is actually quite nice! Camping is permitted at birr 60 per tent with a vehicle, or birr 40 without.

Simien Park Hotel ☎ 058 1113481. This dingy multi-storey hotel, no relation to its popular namesake in Debark, is elevated into the moderate bracket by virtue of its price alone – a contender for this edition's 'All Ethiopia Silly Faranji Price Award' at birr 80/120 for a sgl/dbl room inferior to what's on offer at most of the hotels listed in the budget category!

Budget

Fanna Recreation Hotel ☎ 058 1115184. If you can live with the non-central location, this is probably the best-value accommodation in Gonder, charging birr 50 for a clean, carpeted semi-detached room with a ¾ bed and en-suite hot shower. The hotel is set in spacious green grounds adjacent to Fasilidas's Pool, and a popular bar/restaurant is attached.

Fasil Hotel ☎ 058 1110221. One of the longest-serving hotels in Gonder, this centrally located and recently refurbished gem may lack for en-suite rooms, but it has plenty of character and seems about as good value as you'll find in the town centre at birr 50/60 for a bright, spacious and airy high-ceilinged sgl/dbl with sink and common hot shower.

Belegez Pension ☎ 058 1114356; f 058 1114347. This small pension in the back roads behind the Royal Ghebbi isn't exactly a bargain, but it's one of the better deals in town at birr 80 for a small room with a ¾ bed and en-suite hot shower. The rooms using common showers seem rather dear at birr 60.

Misrak Pension ☎ 058 1110069. Set in a quiet green compound next to the Fogera Hotel, this once popular pension is a textbook example of a place that's responded to ubiquitous guidebook recommendations by screwing over the books' readerships. It remains adequately clean and friendly, but the small en-suite rooms with ¾ bed and cold shower are poor value at the inflated (albeit seasonally negotiable) *faranji* price of birr 100. The smaller rooms using common showers are a joke at birr 60.

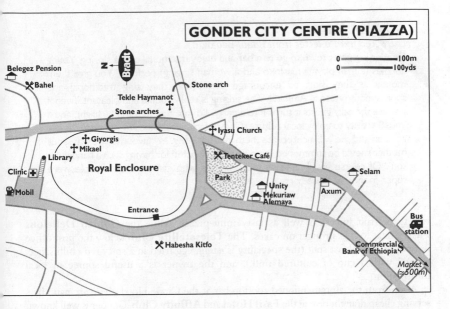

GONDER CITY CENTRE (PIAZZA)

Belegez Pension
Bahel
Bradt
Stone arch
Tekle Haymanot
Stone arches
Iyasu Church
Giyorgis
Mikael
Library
Clinic
Mobil
Royal Enclosure
Tenteker Café
Park
Selam
Unity
Mekuriaw
Alemaya
Axum
Entrance
Bus station
Habesha Kitfo
Commercial Bank of Ethiopia
Market (≈500m)

Shoestring

Selam Hotel (20 rooms) Situated a block away from the bus station, this new double-storey hotel, popular with locals, charges birr 20 for a clean sgl (with ³/₄ bed) using common cold showers.

Ethiopia Hotel (21 rooms) This is the established shoestring favourite by virtue of its central location on the Piazza, and the paucity of notable alternatives. It no longer charges the same rate to all comers, but still seems quite reasonable at birr 15 for a no-frills sgl (³/₄ bed) or birr 25 for a twin, and access to sporadically functioning common showers.

Unity Hotel The egalitarian spirit implied in the name of this multi-storey hotel doesn't extend to the discriminatory pricing structure – it's adequate but rather grubby at the *faranji* price of birr 40 for a small room with a ³/₄ bed and common cold showers.

Where to eat and drink

Gonder boasts a pretty decent selection of eateries. Of the government hotels past and present, the **Goha Hotel** tops the list with its three-course set dinners and lunches at birr 25 per head, but it's not madly convenient unless you are sleeping there. More centrally, the restaurants at the **Fogera Hotel** and **Quara Hotel** have picked up of late, and are regarded by tour guides to serve the best *faranji* food in town – expect to pay birr 15–20 at the former and birr 10–15 at the latter. As for the **Terara Hotel**, the garden bar is as a good a place as any to knock back a pre- or post-dinner tipple, but you'd have to pay me to try the food!

If you adhere to the maxim of following the locals, the **Circle Hotel** used to be the place to head for, and the rooftop bar still affords a pleasant view over the Piazza and the roofs of the Royal Compound, but we've heard several complaints about the food of late. For local food, **Habesha Kitfo** opposite the entrance to the Royal Compound is recommended for its attractive traditional décor and good *kitfo* and other Ethiopian dishes. Less attractive to look at but just as good when it comes to Ethiopian cuisine is the **Mini Fogera Restaurant** on the same square as the Fogera Hotel.

The pick of the pastry shops is the **Manbar Café**, where you'll find a good selection of pastries, as well as fresh juice and coffee. **Sofa Juice** serves the widest

GONDER'S BARS
Extracted from a letter from Raoul Boulakia

Gonder is a great town to go to a bar and enjoy traditional praise singing. Young couples (a man playing masinko and a woman singing) perform. You give them money as they sing, to encourage them, and they sing traditional and spontaneous praise in Amharic. The singing is really soulful and pleasant. Even if you are the only guests it turns into a party. I'd rate that as a trip highlight, and a 'must' activity to enjoy local culture. Guests can suggest lines to the singer as she goes on and she will incorporate them into her song. My favourite line was 'your mother should be summoned to court and convicted for having such a handsome son'. Of course you'll need to make friends who can translate. People were super-friendly at these bars.

variety of fruit juices, as well as tasty mini-pizzas, while the **Golden Delicious Pastry** next to it is stronger on cakes. The **Telesatellite Club** below the post office is a popular breakfast spot (the speciality is *nashif*, egg fried in a spicy red chilli sauce, topped with a cup of cultured milk), and the owner is a useful source of local information.

Aside from the aforementioned rooftop bar at the Circle Hotel, there are patio bars serving cheap draught beer at the **Fasil Hotel** and **Affinity Club**. Gonder is well known for its nightlife, with the greatest density of seedy and seedier bars clustered in the back streets behind the NTO office. Traditional music and dancing can be enjoyed on most nights at the **Balageru Bar** next to the Fasil Hotel and the **Minas Bar & Nightclub** next to the Shell garage some 30m closer to the town centre.

Listings
Foreign exchange
Both branches of the Commercial Bank of Ethiopia (see map) offer a foreign-exchange service, as does the generally more efficient Dashen Bank next to the Quara Hotel. Cash and travellers' cheques in most major currencies are accepted. The service is quicker than in most other parts of Ethiopia.

Getting around
Cheap minibuses cover most main roads between central and suburban Gonder. Charter taxis are readily available – you should pay about birr 5–10 within the city centre and up to birr 15 for suburban destinations such as Fasil's Bath or Debre Birhan Selassie Church, but will invariably be asked a lot more.

Guides
Although Gonder has the usual crew of freelance guides who hang around the Piazza, they are not, in our experience, at all pushy. There is no need to take a guide to visit the Royal Compound, as guide services are offered free with the entry ticket. Nor is it essential to take a guide to the better-known historical sites around town, though it may simplify things linguistically. Most guides can organise day trips to the Simien Mountains, but do check prices against those offered by the tourist office and private tour operators before agreeing to anything.

Internet and email
Gonder seems to suffer from a paucity of internet cafés by comparison with nearby Bahir Dar.

Meal tickets

In Gonder (just like in Addis Ababa) it is possible to buy meal tickets for beggars. They are available from Habesha Kitfo opposite the entrance to the Royal Enclosure. A bundle of nine meal tickets costs birr 5. For each ticket somebody can get two small loaves of bread at any participating bakery.

Tourist information

A knowledgeable and helpful former guide runs the recently opened tourist office above the Piazza. The office stocks a fair selection of brochures about Gonder and places further afield. The prices quoted for motorised day trips out of Gonder are far cheaper than those offered by most private guides and tour companies. The office is open weekdays only from 08.30 to 12.30 and 13.30 to 17.30.

Tour operators

If you want to organise your Simien hike through a proper tour operator, four local specialists can be recommended: the Galaxy Express branch office based in the Goha Hotel (✆ 058 1111546 or 091 8770347); Explore Simien Tours in the Quara Hotel (✆ 058 1110040 or 091 8770280; e fasilm_675@yahoo.com); Explore Abyssinia Travel at the base of the Circle Hotel (✆ 058 1111917, f 058 1110620; e seyoumyigzaw@yahoo.com) and Bedassa Jote Tours & Trekking (✆ 058 1115073; e bejgobena@yahoo.com). Typical all-inclusive rates for a five-day hike out of Gonder with any of these companies will be around birr 2,000 per head for four people or birr 2,800 per head for two people.

Activities and excursions

Gonder's most important tourist attraction is the Fasil Ghebbi or Royal Enclosure, a walled compound of 17th-century castles and buildings lying in the city centre at the southern end of the Piazza. Similar in vintage and architectural style is Fasilidas's Pool, a couple of kilometres from the city centre. The entrance ticket to the Royal Enclosure, which costs birr 50, is valid for the day of purchase only. If you have a couple of days in town, it's worth planning your sightseeing around the fact that this ticket also covers entrance to Fasilidas's Pool, but not to other historical sites.

Of several old churches dotted around Gonder, the most beautiful is the lavishly decorated Debre Birhan Selassie, 1km from the city centre, and regarded by some experts to contain the finest art of its period anywhere in Ethiopia. Also well worth a visit is Kuskuam Maryam, set on a hill 5km from the city centre: the church itself is modern and undistinguished, but the adjoining residence of the Empress Mentewab is both architecturally interesting and atmospheric, as well as offering a great view over the city centre. Of minor interest are the central church of Medhane Alem and suburban church of Kidus Yohannis. Probably of greater interest to scholars than to tourists is the former capital of Danquaz, established by Emperor Susneyos but abandoned by his son Fasilidas in favour of Gonder.

Although the ideal way to explore the Simien Mountains is over several days hiking or trekking, the new road into the national park makes a full-day trip from Gonder a realistic and increasingly popular excursion. A more affordable alternative is the half-day trip to Kosoye viewpoint 32km from town along the Simien road. In order that fly-in visitors to Gonder don't overlook these options, they are briefly covered below as excursions from the city, rather than under the full section on the Simien Mountains later in the chapter.

Fasil Ghebbi (Royal Enclosure) and the city centre

The Fasil Ghebbi lies at the heart of modern Gonder and gives the city much of its character. Surrounded by high stone walls, the enclosure covers an area of 70,000m^2 and

A ROYAL BANQUET AT GONDER

When James Bruce published the five-volume account of his Ethiopian journey under the title *Travels to Discover the Source of the Nile* in 1790, its contents seemed so outrageous to polite European society that they were widely dismissed as fabrication. Of all the passages in the book, none proved to be as controversial as an account of a banquet held at the Royal Ghebbi in Gonder, from which the following edited extracts are drawn:

A long table is set in the middle of a large room, and benches beside it for the guests. A cow or bull, one or more, is brought close to the door and carved up alive. The prodigious noise the animal makes is the signal for the company to sit down to table.

There are then laid out before every guest – instead of plates – pancakes, and something thicker and tougher. It is unleavened bread of a sourish taste, far from being disagreeable, and very easily digested, made of a grain called tef. Three or four of these cakes are put uppermost, for the food of the person opposite to whose seat they are placed. Beneath these are four of five of ordinary bread, which serve the master to wipe his fingers on, and afterwards the servant for bread to his dinner.

Three or four servants then come, each with a square piece of beef in their bare hands, laying it upon the cakes of tef, without cloth or anything else beneath them. By this time all the guests have knives in their hands. The company are so ranged that one man sits between two women. The man with his knife cuts a thin piece, which would be thought a good beefsteak in England, while you see the motion of the fibres yet perfectly distinct, and alive in the flesh. No man in Abyssinia, of any fashion whatever, feeds himself or touches his own meat. The women take the steak and cut it lengthwise like strings, about the thickness of your little finger, then crossways into square pieces, something smaller than dice. This they lay upon a piece of tef-bread, strongly powdered with black pepper and salt; they then wrap it up in the tef-bread like a cartridge.

contains six castles, a complex of connecting tunnels and raised walkways, and several smaller buildings. It's a fascinating place to explore, and the guides who work there are generally quite knowledgeable; it is recommended that you first walk around under their tuition, then return on your own later to soak up some of the atmosphere. The entrance fee of birr 50, valid only for the day of purchase, includes the services of an official guide (who will expect a tip), and still photography. A video camera attracts an additional fee of birr 75.

The most impressive castle within the enclosure is the original built by Fasilidas, which was built circa 1640, partially restored in the mid 20th century, and more fully restored, using the original construction methods, with UNESCO funding between 1999 and 2002. **Fasilidas's Castle** is made of stone and shows a unique combination of Portuguese, Axumite and even Indian influences. The ground floor consists of reception and dining areas. The walls are decorated with a symbol similar to the Star of David, which became the emblem of the Ethiopian royal family after the Solomonic dynasty reclaimed the throne in the 13th century. The first-floor roof of the castle was used for prayer and religious ceremonies, and it is also where Fasilidas addressed the townsfolk. Fasilidas's prayer room, also on the first floor, has four windows, every one of which faces a church. Stairs lead from the roof to the small second-floor room that Fasilidas used as

In the meantime the man, having put up his knife, with each hand resting upon his neighbour's knee, his body stooping, his head low and forward, and mouth open very like an idiot, turns to the one whose cartridge is first ready, who stuffs the whole of it into his mouth, which is so full that he is constant danger of being choked. This is a mark of grandeur. The greater the man would seem to be, the larger the piece he takes into his mouth; the more noise he makes in chewing it, the more polite he is thought to be. They indeed have a proverb that says: 'Beggars and thieves only eat small pieces, or without making a noise.'

Having dispatched this morsel, which he does very expeditiously, his next female neighbour holds forth another cartridge, which goes the same way, and so forth, until he is satisfied. He never drinks before he has finished eating, and before he begins drinking, in gratitude to the two fair ones that feed him, he rolls up two small cartridges of the same shape and form, and each of his neighbours opens her mouth at the same time, while with each hand he puts the portions into their mouths. He then falls to drinking out of a handsome horn; the ladies eat until they are satisfied, and they all drink together. A great deal of joy and mirth goes around, very seldom with any mixture of acrimony or ill humour.

Those within are very much elevated: love lights all its fires, and everything is permitted with absolute freedom. There is no coyness, no delays, no need of appointments or retirement to gratify their wishes. There are no rooms but one, in which they sacrifice both to Bacchus and to Venus. The two men nearest the vacuum a pair have made on the bench by leaving their seats, hold their upper garments like a screen before the two that have left the bench; and, if we may judge by sound, they seem to think it as great a shame to make love in silence as to eat.

Replaced in their seats again, the company drink the happy couple's health, and their example is followed at different ends of the table, as each couple is disposed. All this passes without remark or scandal, not a licentious word is uttered, nor the most distant joke made upon the transaction.

his sleeping quarters. Above this is an open balcony, which was probably the watchtower. This third-floor platform, 32m above the ground, offers views in all directions; on a clear day, you can even see Lake Tana on the horizon, emphasising the strategic advantage of choosing Gonder as a capital.

The other major relic of Fasilidas's reign is the **Royal Archive building**. This was partially destroyed during World War II when Britain bombed the Italian headquarters, which lay within the compound. There are also several crumbling buildings behind the castle, and a bathing pool, all of which are thought to have been built by Fasilidas. Near to Fasilidas's castle, the tiny castle built by Fasilidas's successor Emperor Yohannis I (1667–82) is the least interesting building in the compound.

Yohannis I was succeeded by Emperor Iyasu (1682–1706), who is regarded as the greatest ruler of the Gonder period. Iyasu was a popular and peace-loving emperor, who nevertheless spent much of his rule at war with the Oromo of southern Ethiopia. **Iyasu's Castle** is one of the largest in the compound, and the most ornately constructed. In its prime it was extremely beautiful, decorated with ivory, gold leaf, precious stones and paintings. Unfortunately it was partially damaged by an earthquake in 1704, and the ground-floor ceiling collapsed under the British bombardment in World War II. It is now little more than a shell. In rather better condition is the three-room sauna that was constructed by Iyasu alongside his castle. The guide will demonstrate how the various chambers were used to create steam. Iyasu is also credited with the construction of the raised walkways that connect Gonder's three oldest castles.

In 1699 Iyasu was visited by a French doctor called Poncet, who described the emperor as a 'lively and sagacious genius' and also left an account of a ceremony that gives some flavour of 17th-century Gonder. According to Poncet, an assembly of 12,000 soldiers in battle dress attended the ceremony, and the emperor arrived with 'two princes of the blood in splendid dresses... holding a magnificent canopy under which the emperor walked, preceded by his trumpets, kettledrums, fifes, harps and other instruments'. Poncet's visit led indirectly to greater contact between Iyasu and European Catholics, a cause of great concern to the Orthodox clergy coming less than a century after the religious strife under Emperor Susneyos. In 1706, the emperor was ousted by his son Tekle Haymanot with the support of the clergy, setting the scene for another phase of Catholic–Orthodox tension.

Four kings were crowned and then assassinated in the 15 years after Iyasu was ousted. Only one of them, Dawit III (1716–21), another of Iyasu's sons, left his mark on the Royal Enclosure in the form of a **lion cage**. The black-maned Abyssinian lion was an important royal symbol right through to Haile Selassie's rule in the 20th century, and I'm told that this cage held live lions until the last one died in 1992. Dawit III also built a large **concert hall**, which is still standing today.

Emperor Dawit III was poisoned in 1721, to be succeeded by his brother Bakafa, who ruled Ethiopia for nine years, and left his mark on the Royal Enclosure by building **Bakafa's Castle**, some **stables**, and an immense **banquet hall**. This hall was the victim of a British or Italian raid, depending on whom you believe (and has since been rendered unrecognisable by a feeble attempt at restoration using concrete!). Bakafa was a powerful but heavy-handed ruler, and his attempts to restore the strength of the monarchy, which had been badly affected by 15 years of intrigue and ineffective rule, alienated his most powerful subjects.

Bakafa's son, Iyasu II (1730–55), ascended the throne under the regency of his mother Mentewab, who proved to be the last of Gonder's castle-builders. **Mentewab's Castle** is a fine building, decorated with Gonder crosses, and in such good condition that it is now used as the public library. Mentewab's Catholic leanings only furthered the religious divisions in the empire, and her artistically inclined son proved an ineffective ruler. After 1755, the monarchy decreased in importance as it became a puppet of powerful regional princes, and no further building took place in the Royal Enclosure.

Three churches lie within separate compounds within the main walls of the Royal Enclosure. The oldest, **Gemjabet Maryam**, was founded by Fasilidas, who was buried there in 1767. The modern church building is of limited interest, though it is the site of the grave of Walter Plowden, a close associate of Emperor Tewodros, and its treasury holds some excellent 19th-century paintings. The churches of **Elfin Giyorgis** and **Asasame Kidus Mikael** are also modern, built over destroyed churches respectively attributed to Emperors Dawit II and Fasilidas.

Also in the city centre, but outside of the Royal Enclosure, there are a few other historical sites worth looking at. One such building is **Ras Ghimb**, the palace built by Ras Mikael Suhul in the late 18th century, and subsequently used as a holiday residence by Emperor Haile Selassie and as an interrogation hall under the Mengistu regime. Judging by outward appearances, this impressive building is still in reasonable shape, and it now houses the offices of a UN Project for Forest Plantation and Integrated Development. It has been closed to visitors for as long as anybody can remember.

Close to Ras Ghimb, but obscured behind a swathe of tall juniper trees, the **Church of Medhane Alem** is the seat of the Bishop of Gonder, and one of the few churches in the city to have survived the Mahdist invasion more or less untouched. Founded by

THE EMPEROR'S HORSE

Outside the enclosure of Fasilidas's Pool stands a small domed pavilion that is supported by six pillars and not unlike a disused bandstand in appearance. Local tradition has it that this was the mausoleum built by Emperor Iyasu I for a horse called Suviel. According to legend, the injured Suviel was captured by Muslim foes after its owner Emperor Yohannis I was killed in battle in the Sudan. The horse was healed by a disguised 'stranger' – in fact, Yohannis's son, the future Emperor Iyasu I, who tricked the Muslims into letting him ride Suviel, then fled away on horseback. When the Muslims gave chase, Suviel leapt across a gorge too wide for a lesser horse to cross, and both he and the future emperor returned safely to Gonder. This story seems wildly far-fetched, given that no evidence exists to suggest Yohannis died in the Sudan. It is more likely the little pavilion is where the early emperors of Gonder stood during ceremonies held at the pool.

Fasilidas, and originally part of the imperial palace, the restored church is faithful to the original design, but the extensive paintings on the outer wall of the sanctuary probably date to the late 19th century but may well replicate much older paintings that preceded them.

Fasilidas's Pool and surrounds

About 2km out of the town centre, along the Bahir Dar road, lies the 2,800m² sunken bathing pool generally attributed to Emperor Fasilidas. Enclosed by a tall stone wall with six turrets, the pool is overlooked by a two-storey building widely said to have been Fasilidas's second residence. Some sources attribute the pool to the later reign of Emperor Iyasu I, while others suggest it may in fact be the earliest of Fasilidas's constructions, predating his famous castle. You can walk out to the pool from the town centre, or else take a local minibus. Entrance to the pool is included in the price for visiting the Royal Enclosure, so take your ticket with you (tickets cannot be bought at the pool itself).

Often referred to as a swimming pool, the sunken construction – which is dry most of the year through – has probably always been used ceremonially rather than for royal leisure pursuits. The pool is the central stage on which the Timkat or Epiphany Festival is celebrated in Gonder. This takes place on the 11th day of Tir (variably between 18 and 20 January) and – should you be around at the time – is a sight not to be missed. Led by colourfully attired priests carrying *tabots* and crosses, thousands of white-robed worshippers converge around the pool in the afternoon, where they are blessed and sprinkled with its holy water.

Another low-key stone building close to the pool is popularly known as the **House of Chickens**. Local legend somewhat improbably claims that this served as a royal chicken run under Fasilidas; a pre-Mengistu ETC brochure suggests, more plausibly, that it might have housed a 'sweating house isolated for the cure of contagious diseases'.

A short walk away from Fasil's Pool, the church of **Kidus Yohannis** was founded under Iyasu II and destroyed by the Dervish in 1888. The outer walls are still standing, however, and a well-preserved vestry in one of the turrets now serves as the sanctuary of what is otherwise in effect an open-air church!

Kuskuam

Set at an altitude of 2,234m on Debre Tsehai (Mountain of Sun), which overlooks the city of Gonder, the palatial stone complex known as Kuskuam – after a Coptic convent

THE BEAUTIFUL EMPRESS

Paul Henze has described the Empress Mentewab as 'a subject awaiting a biographer'. And certainly the fondly remembered builder of Kuskuam and Narga Selassie must rank among the most charismatic figures of the Gonderine Era – as well, folklore has it, as a queen of great generosity, wit, comeliness and political savvy.

Two contradictory stories relate to Mentewab's union with Bakafa. One legend has it that Mentewab was raised in humble circumstances in a district called Quara to the west of Lake Tana. In the early 1720s, Bakafa happened to be travelling through this district when he fell seriously ill. The ailing emperor was taken in by a local farmer, and was nursed back to health by the farmer's beautiful daughter Birhan Mogasa ('Splendour of Light'). And Bakafa was so enamoured with his saviour that he married her as soon as he was fit enough to return to Gonder.

The other version, as told by Mentewab's official chronicler, is that she was the daughter of a princess called Yolyana, who dressed her up in the finest cloths and golden jewellery and arranged for her to be introduced to the king. 'When Bakafa saw her he was very happy because she was so completely beautiful, and he said to her "You have no fault at all!"', recalls the chronicler: 'Then he made her sit beside him and had delicious foods brought, and they ate and drank together. That day he knew her as Adam knew Eve, and she conceived immediately.'

Whichever story is true, there is no doubting Bakafa's appreciation of the wife who would outlive both him and their eldest son, the Emperor Iyasu – it was he who bestowed upon her the exclamatory throne name Mentewab, which translates as 'How Beautiful Though Art!'

in Egypt – was constructed as the residence of the Empress Mentewab after the death of her husband Emperor Bakafa in 1730. Mentewab served for many years as regent for her young son Iyasu II, so that her out-of-town residence took over from the old Royal Enclosure as the centre of imperial affairs in the mid 18th century. It is here, at Kuskuam, that the Scots explorer James Bruce spent several sociable months waiting for permission to visit the source of the Nile at Gish Abay, in the process becoming a close friend and confidant of Mentewab. (It has also been claimed that Bruce had an affair with one of the Empress's married daughters, who bore him a child at Kuskuam, though it died before it could be christened.)

Although in a state of partial ruin, Kuskuam makes for a fascinating excursion from central Gonder. The overall shape of the main palace is clearly discernible, with most of the first-floor walls still intact, as is one staircase and part of the first floor. An ornate Gonderine cross is carved over the door to Mentewab's bedroom. Little remains of the queen's personal chapel, which was once adorned with paintings as impressive as those at Debre Birhan Selassie, representing every saint venerated by the Ethiopian Church. A round building ingeniously designed to get around the prohibition on menstruating women entering a church, the chapel has 12 alcoves, which the queen would visit in turn every hour to pray when 'unclean', while a priest stood outside praying and swinging incense. Better preserved is the impressive banquet hall, which must be at least 10m high. Engravings of animals and crosses decorate the outer wall of the banquet hall; there is also an etching of Abuna Yohannis, Patriarch of the Ethiopian Church during Mentewab's regency. The almost cartoon-like style of some of these etchings is similar to those (including one of James Bruce) at the Lake Tana monastery of Narga Selassie, also built by Mentewab.

The church of Kuskuam Maryam, set alongside the royal residence, suffered the same fate as most Gonderine churches during the Mahdist War. Rebuilt during the Italian occupation, it is elaborately decorated, though none of the paintings dates to before 1970. The bones of Mentewab and Iyasu II were retrieved from the ground during the church's reconstruction, and are now housed in a glass coffin within the anterooms. There is a big celebration at the church every 15 November.

Entrance to Kuskuam costs birr 15. The complex lies about 5km from the city centre. To get there, drive or catch a shared minibus from the Piazza to the Medical College, from where a road signposted to the right leads uphill for about 1.5km to the church and ruined palace. If you don't fancy walking the last, rather steep stretch, a taxi from the Piazza should cost around birr 15 one-way. There are great views over the city centre on the way up, and the juniper and olive trees around the ruined palace host a variety of colourful birds.

Debre Birhan Selassie

There are said to be 44 churches in Gonder, at least seven of which date from Fasilidas's rule, but most of the original buildings were destroyed in 1888 when Gonder was attacked by the Dervish or Mahdist of Sudan. The only Gonderine church that escaped entirely untouched was Debre Birhan Selassie ('Mountain of the Enlightened Trinity'), saved from the Dervish by the intervention of a swarm of bees... or so they say in Gonder.

Founded by Iyasu I in the 1690s, Debre Birhan Selassie was the most important church in 18th-century Gonder, when it was the site of several royal burials. The dating of the modern building is open to question: the original church was almost certainly circular in shape, and remained so after it was restored following a fire in 1707. It is likely that the modern rectangular building was constructed in the late 18th century, following the destruction of the original building by lightning. Whenever it was built, this beautiful church, along with the much more imposing one built by Fasilidas in Axum, which it resembles, offers some idea of what other treasures might be in Gonder today had it not been for the Mahdist War.

While Debre Birhan Selassie is not without architectural merit, it is of greatest interest for the prolific paintings inside. The much-photographed ceiling, decorated with

SYMBOLIC ARCHITECTURE OF DEBRE BIRHAN SELASSIE
Extracted from a letter from John Moore

Debre Birhan Selassie is certainly one of the, if not the, most beautiful of the Ethiopian churches. Perhaps the reason it's so special and that such care and effort was put into it is that the emperor intended to move the Ark of the Covenant there from Axum. As a result, it is not round like all the other churches in the Gonder region but rectangular and you can still see clearly the foundations of the round church previously on the site. It was built roughly to the same directions as Solomon's Temple in Jerusalem, where the Ark came from. The perimeter wall has 12 equidistant round towers representing the 12 Apostles, one of which is larger than the rest and was intended to house relics associated with the Ark. The gateway is the '13th tower' and represents Christ. The gateway's superstructure is built to look like a royal lion couchant, which it does more or less, and the tail of the lion, which looks like a comma, is carved on the key-stone of the arch in the wall to the west of the church, signifying the omnipresence of Christ. Near the top of the south end of the roof are seven niches supporting a seven-pronged medallion, with an ostrich egg on each prong. Seven signifies the seven days of creation and eggs represent the power of the creative spirit.

CROSSING BETWEEN ETHIOPIA AND SUDAN
By Paul Clammer
Here are my experiences travelling from Gonder to Khartoum. Sudanese visas are straightforward to obtain in Addis. A form, photo and US$61 are all that is needed along with a letter of introduction from your embassy (as a British citizen, I had to pay a huge birr 455 for that sheet of headed note paper!). I picked up my visa in 72 hours, although some travellers with US passports have recently reported long delays.

Once in Gonder, check into a decent hotel – the trip takes several days, so spoil yourself with hot showers while you can. The border on the Ethiopian side is at Metemma, but because there's no accommodation there, buses from Gonder only go as far as Shihedi, 40km away, which takes around seven hours. This was one of the bumpiest and most uncomfortable bus rides I took in Ethiopia (there was some healthy competition!) – bad roads, dust, no curtains on the sunny side of the bus, and the obligatory shut windows. The road should be better now, however, thanks to a new trade agreement between Ethiopia and Sudan that depends on upgrading the road link between Addis and Port Sudan.

There are streetlights in Shihedi, which shows that the town at least aspires to an electricity supply, but there was no other evidence of one when I passed through. There are two hotels, one on each side of the bus station. Both cost birr 15; neither has a reliable flow of running water. Shihedi feels like the end of Ethiopia, and having come down from the highlands, the temperature is higher and you really start to sweat.

The next day is a sad one as you are leaving Ethiopia, but a joyous one too as you kiss goodbye to those pre-dawn starts to catch a bus. The 06.00 bus to Metemma potters around town for a while looking for passengers before the 90-minute hop to the border. Metemma is a mess: *tukuls*, goats, plastic bags and the rest. Don't assume that you should just walk to the end of the street to find the border – in fact you have to dodge through a maze of thatch to find immigration and get stamped out. You'll almost certainly have to ask to be shown the way, but there it is: a neat painted sign and a man at a desk, trying to look official while ignoring the tick infestation. With your stamp in your passport, head for the border – it's obvious where to go. Underneath an Ethiopian flag by the crossing, two men lying on rope beds insisted that they were customs, but they could hardly be bothered to look in my rucksack.

As you walk 10m into Sudan, you notice the difference immediately. Where have all the kids shouting 'Faranji' gone? Proceedings are pretty straightforward – a brief customs check then immigration, although you need to change money to pay 4,000 Sudanese Dinar for 'security registration' when you get stamped in (US$1=260SD). The guy at customs was quite happy to let me wander about having left my rucksack with him, but I had a bit of a job trying to hunt down a moneychanger. Registering at the border (effectively a second stamp in your passport) means that you no longer have to register at the Ministry of the Interior on arrival in Khartoum.

The border at Gallabat is a dusty one-horse outpost that once played an important role in Ethio-Sudanese history. It was here in March 1889 that the Mahdist army

paintings of 80 cherubic faces, is probably the most famous single example of ecclesiastical art in Ethiopia. The walls are also painted with dozens of separate scenes: the southern wall concentrates on the life of Christ, while the northern wall depicts various saints. One of the most striking individual paintings is an unusually fearsome depiction of the devil surrounded by flames, to be found on the wall to the left of the main door, while next to this door is a striking image of a captive Mohammed being led by the devil.

fought and beat the Ethiopian forces of Yohannis IV. Over 15,000 men died, and so many captives were taken back to the markets of Omdurman it caused the price of slaves to collapse. It was a pyrrhic victory – the Ethiopian king was killed, but the cream of the Mahdist army was destroyed and the battle essentially marked the end of the expansionist dreams of the Khalifa.

From Gallabat, take whatever transport is going to Gedaref, which is on the tarmac road to Khartoum. This generally means a truck. I wound up in the back of a Land Rover having paid 2,000SD (around US$8) for the privilege of being squeezed in with 20 others. Foreigners pay more than Sudanese, and that included Ethiopians. If it hasn't already been taken, pay a premium to sit in the cab with the driver – luxury indeed. Take plenty of water and wrap up against the sun and the dust. There's no real road to speak of, and the trip usually takes around six hours, but breakdowns and delays can double this. Vehicles may sometimes break the journey halfway at the village of Doka. From Gallabat to Gedaref is very difficult in the rainy season, as there is plenty of thick black cotton soil to bog down any unwary vehicle that contemplates such an unwise and muddy venture. The terrain is so flat and the tracks are relatively free of bone-crunching bumps, but I still wouldn't recommend the drive on purely recreational grounds.

Pulling in to Gedaref you'd be forgiven a lump in the throat and a tear in the eye at the sight of a sealed road and a town lit with electricity. Gedaref is large enough but lacking in interest, so you'll want to push on to Khartoum as soon as possible. There are several shoestring options. The Amir Hotel is fair value at 2,000SD for a room, or you can revel in a hot shower at the plusher El Motwakil Hotel (rooms from 8,000SD). From here it couldn't be easier – 400km to Khartoum breezes by in a modern coach on a tarmac road, and you didn't even have to fight for your seat.

For those travelling from Sudan to Ethiopia the deal is much the same, although I'd caution about timings. Just as there is no accommodation at Metemma, neither is there at Gallabat. As a result, anyone heading in this direction would be strongly advised to leave Gedaref at the crack of dawn to get across the border and on to Shihedi in one day. Border transport leaves from near the Greek Orthodox church. If you do run late, it would be easy enough to arrange some sort of place to sleep in Gallabat, as Sudanese hospitality is such that no-one would ever leave a stranger in the lurch. After crossing the border, all will end up spending a night in Shihedi anyway, as the daily Gonder bus leaves at the usual early hour, way before the border opens.

Whichever way you are travelling it is essential to obtain a visa in advance. Until recently the Ethiopian Embassy in Khartoum had a frustrating rule that they would only issue visas for travel by air, but this has thankfully been abolished. For entering Sudan, Addis Ababa is one of the most agreeable places to get a Sudanese visa, with the necessary stamp usually issued without hassle in less than 48 hours. A yellow fever certificate is also mandatory.

Paul Clammer is the author of the pioneering Sudan: The Bradt Travel Guide, *which was first published in 2005 and is available online at www.bradtguides.com.*

The paintings are traditionally held to be the work of the 17th-century artist Haile Meskel, but it is more likely that several artists were involved and that the majority were painted during the rule of Egwala Tsion (1801–17), who is depicted prostrating himself before the cross on one of the murals.

The church lies about 1km out of town, a ten-minute walk from the stairs below the administrative offices. After climbing the stairs, simply continue straight ahead along a rolling country road with views back to the Royal Enclosure. You can't miss the church – it's enclosed by a high stone wall and surrounded by juniper trees. An entrance fee of birr 15 is charged. The caretaker of several years' standing is very helpful and not at all pushy; a small tip will be appreciated but is not expected. Flash photography is forbidden; to photograph the famous roof without tripods you'll have to use a table as support. A good time to visit the church is around 30 minutes before sunset, when the sun's rays penetrate the interior to enhance the spiritual atmosphere.

Danquaz

Situated some 20km south of modern Gonder, Danquaz was the last of several semi-permanent capitals established by Emperor Susneyos in the early 17th century, and it was also used by Emperor Fasilidas for the first three years of his reign, after which he relocated his capital to Gonder. Contemporary accounts and archaeological research indicate that Danquaz was an impressive and well-built complex – in many senses the precursor to the foundation of a permanent capital at Gonder.

Sadly, little of the former capital remains today. Susneyos founded the Church of Azusa Tekle Haymanot, perched atop a small hill, but as with so many Gonderine churches the original building was destroyed during the Mahdist War. Rebuilt in the 1950s, it is of limited historical interest, though the original stone walls enclosing the compound do survive intact. There are a couple of engraved crosses with 16 arms each on the outer wall to the right of the main gate, while a small house built into the wall and reputedly lived in by Susneyos stands on the other side of the gate.

A five-minute walk downhill from the church is the pool (ask for *Atse Mawegna* – the King's Pool) built by Susneyos and believed to be the model on which Fasil's Pool in Gonder was based. Now dry and somewhat overgrown, the sunken walls of the pool are still clearly discernible. Recent excavations suggest that the pool was filled via a subterranean channel leading from the nearby river.

Historically important as this site may be, there isn't much left to capture the imagination of the casual visitor. It is, however, accessible enough, and would make an easy side trip in a vehicle on the way to or from the airport. Azazo lies on the junction of the airport and Bahir Dar roads. To get to the church, follow the Bahir Dar road from the junction for about 1km, then take a right turn along a clear side road, which after another 1km or so leads uphill to the church. There is regular public transport between Gonder and Azazo.

Wolleka (Falasha village)

Situated roughly 5km from Gonder along the Axum road, this formerly famous Falasha village is the only accessible place where you can check out something of the tradition of Ethiopian Judaism. Even so, it has to be classed as something of a letdown. Wolleka was vacated by its original occupants between 1985 and 1992, when most of Ethiopia's 'Black Jews' were airlifted to Jerusalem by the Israeli government to liberate them from the repressive Mengistu regime. All that remains today is the old synagogue, the design of which mimics a typical circular Ethiopian church, but with a Star of David rather than a cross on its roof. In order to satisfy (or should that be exploit?) the passing tourist traffic, the Christian inhabitants of Wolleka have started to make pottery in the Falasha tradition, but the product is of limited aesthetic merit and the standard of workmanship is low.

Kosoye

It is said that this viewpoint, 32km from Gonder, so appealed to Queen Elizabeth II that she instructed her driver to stop there for tea whilst travelling between Gonder and Axum in 1965. Legend or not, it is a great spot, with a sweeping view across the lowlands to the Simien Mountains, and a recommended half-day excursion for those who don't have time to get to the Simiens proper. The one-hour walk along the cliff offers a good chance of seeing gelada and guereza monkeys, as well as birds of prey such as lammergeyer. Transport can be arranged through the tourist office or private tour operators for around birr 300 per group. You can also get there easily by taking the bus going to Debark.

DEBARK

This sprawling town of 20,000 straddles the main Gonder–Axum road 100km north of Gonder and 250km southwest of Axum at a chilly altitude of around 2,800m on the western base of the awesome Simien Mountains National Park. Debark is the traditional trailhead for Simien hikes and treks, and – although many hikers now drive deeper into the park to start their hike – all prospective visitors must stop in at the park headquarters on the Gonder side of Debark to buy the necessary permits. Despite its proximity to Ethiopia's most popular trekking destination, the town itself is rather nondescript and lacking in scenic qualities. Facilities include a couple of decent budget hotels, what must surely be the world's most persistent shoeshine boys, and a decent market and bakery where 'helpful' youngsters try to insinuate themselves into any and every transaction with a *faranji* in the hope of bolstering the price to gain a commission.

Getting there and away

If you are making your way to Debark independently, two buses daily head there from Gonder, leaving at around 06.00 and 10.30 and taking three to four hours. Alternatively, you can hire a taxi in Gonder for about birr 500 – the journey to Debark takes two hours in a private vehicle – though you will have to arrange a pick-up date with the driver if you want to return the same way. Another option is to organise your whole trek with a tour operator, including private transport to and from Debark – or, for that matter, directly to and from one of the national park campsites.

In a private vehicle, the drive between Debark and Axum takes about six hours, longer if you stop along the way. Coming from Axum on public transport, catch a minibus to Shire (Inda Selassie), which costs around birr 20 and takes about 90 minutes, and spend the night there before catching the early-morning bus to Gonder, which will drop you in Debark. Heading northwards from Debark to Axum, the first bus from Gonder to Inda Selassie arrives in Debark at around 09.00 and it is often full. To be certain of a seat, you could ask somebody to go to Gonder the day before and buy your ticket. The bus usually arrives in Shire in the mid afternoon, leaving you time to catch a minibus on to Axum the same day.

Where to stay and eat

Simien Park Hotel (13 rooms) ✆ 058 1113481. This long-serving lodge on the main road through Debark charges birr 30/40/50 for a basic but clean sgl/dbl/twin using the common cold shower, or birr 70 for a dbl with en-suite cold shower. It has a decent restaurant serving excellent roast lamb (except during fasting periods) as well as other Ethiopian and Western dishes in the birr 10–15 range. Camping is permitted in the back garden, and the hotel can rent out most of the camping gear required for a Simien hike. The owner-manager is a very helpful soul.

Red Fox Hotel This new hotel is to a similar standard as Simien Park, and it stands just five minutes' walk from the bus station in Debark. Rooms using a common shower cost birr 25/45 sgl/dbl. The bar/restaurant serves decent local food and has DSTV. The management is friendly and helpful.

SIMIEN MOUNTAINS NATIONAL PARK

Expanded from text originally written by David Else and Ariadne Van Zandbergen

Situated about 100km north of Gonder to the east side of the Axum road, the Simien Mountains is one of Africa's largest ranges, studded with at least a dozen peaks topping the 4,000m mark. These include Ras Dashen (also spelt Ras Dejen), the highest point in Ethiopia and possibly the fourth highest peak in Africa (see box *On Top of the World*, page 246). The western side of the range, excluding Ras Dashen, was designated as the Simien

GONDER TO AXUM BY ROAD

The drive between Gonder and Axum takes around eight hours in a good private vehicle, not allowing for breaks. There is no direct bus service between the cities, but there are direct buses between Gonder and Shire (Inda Selassie), leaving at 06.30 in either direction, taking around ten hours, and stopping at Debark (the base for climbing the Simien Mountains). Minibuses between Shire and Axum leave throughout the day and take about 90 minutes. So it is easy enough to bus between Gonder and Axum in a day, but for those who would prefer to dawdle along this scenic route rather than spend a full day cooped up in a bus, I'm retaining an edited and updated version of the section on travelling between Gonder and Axum that appeared in the first edition.

Buses between Gonder and Adi Arkay leave at around 06.00 to 06.30 in either direction and take about eight hours, stopping at Debark en route to drop off and pick up passengers. The road between Gonder and Debark climbs through a typically pretty highland landscape of rolling hills, brightened in September by profuse wild flowers. Immediately after Debark, you plunge into the Simien foothills along a road that I would rate as the most dramatic I've seen in Africa (a title, incidentally, that I had awarded to the descent into the Blue Nile Gorge only a few days before), and perhaps the most scary as well. The Italian-built road clings giddily to the slopes, and the drama is increased by the presence of the jaggedly evocative spines of the Simiens towering to your left. The altitude drop between Debark and Adi Arkay is close on 2,000m, and the 70km drive takes up to three hours of endless switchbacks!

Adi Arkay is a pleasant enough town, stunningly situated, reasonably free of *faranji* hysteria, blessed with a striking little stone church, and with a higher fly count than most. A possible off-the-beaten-track excursion from here is to Waldiba Monastery towards the remote Tekaze Valley. One of the oldest monastic schools in Ethiopia, Waldiba was established at a site which, legend has it, was visited by Joseph, Mary and Jesus during their time in Egypt. While at Waldiba, they received a divine message to

Mountains National Park in 1969, and the entire range was listed as a UNESCO World Heritage Site in 1979.

A single dirt road runs through the park, branching eastward from Debark, and then passing through Sankaber and Chennek camps en route to the Bwahit Pass, where it branches southward to terminate some 10km outside of the park boundary at the small town of Mekane Birhan. This road is open to tourist vehicles, and it provides the opportunity to see most of the park's key habitats in a short space of time (even as a day trip from Gonder), as well as offering almost certain sightings of gelada. For further details, see the box *The Simiens by Road* on page 240.

A less efficient but more satisfactory way to explore the Simiens is on foot or by mule, following an extensive network of tracks used by local people to travel between the villages on the lower slopes or to reach the high pastures for grazing animals. These tracks are ideal walking routes and, combined with the range's impressive scenery, make the Simiens an excellent area for trekking. Most trekking routes take you through small villages and terraced fields in the lower valleys, before reaching a series of dramatic cliffs and escarpments. Beyond the escarpments you reach the beautiful alpine meadows and the rugged wilderness of the high peak areas.

Geography

The Simien range consists of several major plateaux divided by large river valleys. The western plateau is bounded on the north and east by a massive escarpment, many

return to Jerusalem, which they did by taking a subterranean passage via Eritrea or Yemen. The monastery cannot be reached in a vehicle, and makes for a long day trip on muleback. Several other interesting monasteries lie in the area, and can be visited over a few days from the village of Sekwar Maryam, which has accommodation and lies close to Waldiba.

You have a few rather basic hotels to choose from in Adi Arkay. The pick is the Ras Dashen Hotel, but it is madly overpriced at birr 30 for a basic room using a common shower. If you don't feel like paying this inflated *faranji* price, a few other hotels charge birr 10 for an even scruffier room. The Tekaze Hotel has no rooms but serves reasonably good local food. Remarkably, one letter mentions seeing a lammergeyer perched on a tree right outside the Ras Dashen Hotel.

Bus tickets between Adi Arkay and May Tsemre can be hard to come by, so it might be worth asking around at the overnight truck stop when you arrive for a lift the next day. If this doesn't work, beg the driver of the Axum bus to take you as far as May Tsemre the next morning. This is only 25km further down the road, and he may give you standing room on the basis that there are no police checks on the way. From May Tsemre, you should quickly enough find transport to Shire, but if not there are a few very basic hotels lining the main road.

Shire – marked on most maps as Inda Selassie – is a sizeable place, and reasonably attractive, but there's little to hold you and plenty of transport through to Axum, 60km (90 minutes by minibus) to the east. If you do get stuck, there are several hotels to choose from and most represent good value for money. The Lalibela Hotel (☎ 034 4442633) on the Debark side of town (turn left next to the Commercial Bank of Ethiopia building) charges birr 40 for a clean tiled room with a ³/₄ bed and en-suite hot showers or birr 20 for a smaller room with cold water only. Better value still is the Hanan Hotel next door (☎ 057 4442080), where clean rooms with a ³/₄ bed and en-suite hot shower cost birr 22. Other reader recommendations are the Africa Hotel, Tewelde Hotel, and the National Hotel behind the bus station.

kilometres long and over 1,000m high in places, and cut along its length by steep gorges. The views from the top of the escarpment look north over the vast plains towards Eritrea. At their foot are the remains of ancient hills, now eroded into hundreds of pinnacles and buttresses that were described so eloquently by Rosita Forbes, the formidable traveller who first reached this region in the 1920s:

> The most marvellous of all Abyssinian landscapes opened before us, as we looked across a gorge of clouded amethyst... A thousand years ago, when the old gods reigned in Ethiopia, they must have played chess with these stupendous crags, for we saw bishops' mitres cut in lapis lazuli, castles with the ruby of approaching sunset on their turrets, an emerald knight where the forest crept up on the rock, and far away a king, crowned with sapphire, and guarded by a row of pawns. When the gods exchanged their games for shield and bucklers to fight the new men clamouring at their gates, they turned the pieces of their chessboard into mountains. In Simien they stand enchanted, till once again the world is pagan and the titans and the earth gods lean down from the monstrous cloud banks to wager a star or two on their sport.

Rosita Forbes, *From Red Sea to Blue Nile – A Thousand Miles of Ethiopia*, 1925

Much of this escarpment area is contained within the Simien Mountains National Park, which covers the western side of the range, running east as far as the 4,430m Mount

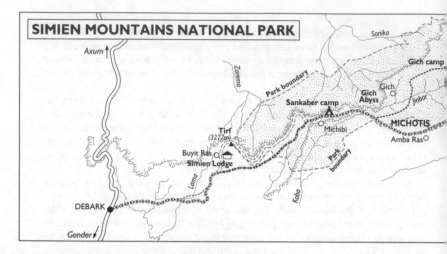

Bwahit, and includes some of the most dramatic sections of trekking along the edge of the escarpment. Ras Dashen, the highest point in the range, lies about 10km east of the national park, and is separated from it by the massive gorge carved by the Masheha River.

Wildlife

Three of Ethiopia's endemic large mammals are resident in the Simiens. The gelada baboon is the most common of these, with an estimated population of at least 7,000 often to be seen congregating in grazing herds of up to 400 individuals, especially in the vicinity of Sankaber. By contrast, the Ethiopian wolf is now very rare in the mountains, with a population of no more than 50 individuals concentrated mostly in the Afro-alpine moorland on the upper slopes of Bwahit, Ras Dashen and Kidus Yared.

The Walia ibex, whose range is now restricted entirely to the Simiens, was poached close to extinction in the late 1960s, when just 150 animals survived. The estimated number of ibex had increased to 400 by 1989, but it declined to 250 in the aftermath of the collapse of the Derg. The population is once again on the rise, however, with some recent estimates as high as 550–600 individuals. Hikers quite often see ibex from the trail running along the ridge between Gich and Chennek via Imet Gogo.

Of the non-endemic mammals, klipspringer and bushbuck are present, but seldom seen. Nor are you likely to see spotted hyena, even though their droppings are often scattered around the camps. You're more likely to see common jackal, which also haunts the camps.

The number of birds recorded in the Simiens is not high – about 180 species to date, if one includes the lower slopes – and endemics are not as well represented as they are at Bale. The mountains are noted for cliff-nesting birds of prey, in particular the large and powerful lammergeyer, which can often be seen soaring above the escarpments on the north side of the national park, and is also a regular sight at Sankaber and Gich camps.

Where to stay
Upmarket

Simien Lodge (20 rooms) ☎ 011 6189398; m 091 1203937; European bookings +33 4 76 64 30 78; e simiens@simiens.com; www.simiens.com. Filling a long-vacant niche for genuine international accommodation in the Simien Mountains, this eco-friendly new lodge at Buyit Ras, on the right side of the road between Debark and Sankaber, is scheduled to open towards the end of 2005. It will combine traditional *tukul*-style exteriors with international-quality interiors, and appropriate high-

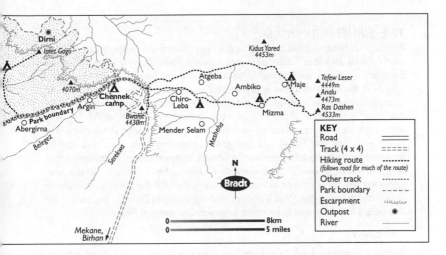

altitude features such as solar-powered underfloor heating and hot water. A restaurant serving international cuisine will seat 50 people, with day visitors welcome to drop in for a meal. The surrounding area is populated by habituated geladas, and the lodge will organise foot and horse treks in the surrounding mountains. Visitors will be invited to participate in community projects (school, hospital, park), and there will be evening entertainment in the bar. The management will probably only allow tour companies who comply with the tourist charter currently being prepared by the tourist commission to stay. Rates will be US$100 per person, inclusive of breakfast and dinner. Cheaper backpacker accommodation will also be available for US$20 per person (bed only) in a dormitory *tukul* with basic bunk beds (sleeping bag required) and hot showers.

Huts and camping

The hutted national park camps at Sankaber, Gich and Chennek were destroyed during the fighting in the 1980s. The huts have been rebuilt, but are now for the exclusive use of park employees, with the exception of Sankaber, where two nine-bed lodges offering basic dormitory accommodation cost birr 40 per person per night.

Elsewhere, this leaves you two options: either you must be completely self-contained with tent and camping equipment, including sleeping bag, stove and cooking gear; or else you can lodge with local people in the villages. Most local people are happy to make space in their hut for a visitor, as it provides a bit of extra income (you should pay birr 10 or less per night). Be warned that conditions are basic: you'll sleep on the floor or maybe on a bed (a wooden platform with goats or cows underneath to provide warmth), and you're in for a rough time if you're sensitive to flea bites. Your guide will find you a hut to stay in, if you take this option.

If you camp, it's usual to pitch near a village, so that your guide and scout have somewhere to sleep. When the park is busy, the guides tend to plonk their clients village-style in the closest possible proximity to each other – do feel free to point out that the campsites are large and it's not necessary to trip over your neighbour's guy ropes every time you leave your tent. There is a shower at each of the camps, but no running water. The toilets are filthy.

Getting organised

Debark is the obvious place to organise a hike, and the people here set up treks all the time, so things normally fall into place very smoothly. The chances are you'll quickly be approached by one of the official guides when you arrive in town, but if not, just head to

THE SIMIENS BY ROAD

Although trekking remains the best way to see the Simiens properly, a good 4x4 road runs via Sankaber, Chennek and the Bwahit Pass, allowing more sedentary travellers, or those with limited time, to get a good feel for the scenery and wildlife in the space of a few hours. Indeed, with an early start, it is possible to cover this road as far as Bwahit as a day trip out of Gonder, though this is hardly the most satisfactory approach, and the rushed timeframe might arguably encourage the driver to speed in what is a fragile environment. A full-day trip in a 4x4 will cost birr 900–1,200 per group excluding park fees, and can be arranged through any tour operator in Gonder at short notice. If you have more time, however, it would be preferable to overnight in Debark, at the new upmarket Simien Lodge, or at one of the camps within the park, and to return to Gonder the next day. With a one- or two-night stop in Debark, the park could also be explored by vehicle en route between Gonder and Axum.

the efficient national park office, which lies along the Gonder road about ten minutes' walk from the Simien Park Hotel. Although Debark is well organised, nothing happens that quickly, so if you are making independent arrangements, you should ideally leave yourself enough time to complete formalities on the afternoon you arrive, spend the night there, and then set off into the mountains the following morning.

The entrance gate to the park lies near Buyit Ras, some 15km from Debark along the road to Sankaber, but all park fees must be paid at the national park office in Debark (\ *058 1113482;* e *walia.smnp@ethionet.et*). Receipts are checked at the entrance gate. The national park office in Debark is open 08.30–12.30 and 13.30–17.30 Monday to Thursday, 08.30–11.30 and 13.30–17.30 Friday, and 08.30–12.00 and 14.00–17.00 Saturday and Sunday. These include an entrance fee of birr 50 per person per 48 hours (payable even if you hike outside the national park boundaries), a one-off vehicle fee of birr 10, a camping fee of birr 20 per night (or lodge fee of birr 40 per night for Sankaber), and a mandatory scout fee of birr 30 per day. The optional fee for a guide is birr 70 per day, while muleteers cost birr 20 each per day.

Many travellers now make their initial trekking arrangements in Gonder. The basic set-up is that somebody in Gonder will approach you offering to organise a hike. He will check what, if any, extra equipment you need and advise you about routes, stocking up on food, and all other aspects of a hike. He will then ring your requirements through to Debark, and arrange for somebody to meet your bus. By all accounts, this is a very smooth procedure, and because you pay nothing until you get to Debark, no risk is attached. Depending on group size, a five-day hike organised in Debark or Gonder will typically work out at around birr 1,000–1,500 per person exclusive of transport between Gonder and Debark, but inclusive of park fees, scout, guide, mules, and mule-drivers. You can cut the cost by omitting some of the above. A cook, stove, tent and sleeping bag can be arranged if required.

Several tour operators in Gonder (see *Listings* on page 225) offer more expensive packages inclusive of a cook, good food, and private transport between Gonder and Debark in one or both directions. If you opt for such a package, you might as well arrange to be driven as far as Sankaber on the first day of your trip, and to be picked up at Sankaber or Chennek on the last day – this will cut the duration of the trip by two or three days. A five-day trip of this sort, taking in Sankaber, Gich, Imet Gogo, Chennek and Bwahit Pass, is likely to cost upwards of birr 2,000 per head.

Even if you don't have a private vehicle, it is increasingly easy to pick up transport along the road from Debark to Sankaber and Chennek, and while nothing is certain, you can plan on this basis with a reasonably secure mind. At least one bus daily runs between Debark and Mekane Birhan via the two camps, and there is also occasional truck transport – expect to pay birr 10–15 per person, plus extra for luggage. Heading out to the mountains, you can ask around at the market in Debark or wait for a lift at the clearly signposted junction to the national park. Heading back to Debark, you can assume that any vehicle heading west along the road through the Simiens is bound for Debark. Another possibility is a lift with other tourists, which you can ask about at the Simien Park or Red Fox hotels.

Whether you arrange things in Gonder or Debark, it is all pretty straightforward and readers' feedback has been consistently positive about the guides and national park office.

Equipment and supplies

Debark has a few shops and stalls where you can buy basic items such as rice, lentils, bread, biscuits, rope, candles, soap and plastic water containers. Rather than buying food in Debark, however, small groups who plan on staying in or near villages seem to have little difficulty arranging basic meals and things like eggs and *injera* as they go along, though I'd be hesitant about relying on this completely. Better to stock up in Gonder, where several shops stock pasta, salt, sugar, tea, coffee and biscuits, plus tins of fish, meat

DERESGE MARYAM
Edited from an email by Petrus Trottestam

A wonderful off-the-beaten-track site I discovered on a recent trip to Ethiopia is the Church of Deresge Maryam on the Janna Mora plains south of Simien National Park. It was here in the early 1850s that Ras Wube of Tigrai, with the architectural assistance of the German botanists Wilhelm Schimper and Eduard Zander as architects and craftsmen, had a small Byzantine castle with two adjoining churches erected for his anticipated coronation as Emperor of Ethiopia. On 9 February 1855, however, just two days before the coronation was scheduled, Ras Wube was defeated at Deresge by his upstart enemy Ras Kasa at the Battle of Deresge. The coronation ceremony at Deresge Maryam went ahead all the same, with the one critical difference that Ras Wube was imprisoned for the event, and Ras Kasa had himself crowned as Emperor by Abuna Salama under the throne name Tewodros II.

Deresge Maryam is beautifully set on a podocarpus-covered hill about 2km north of the town of Mekane Birhan. Surrounded by three stone walls, the impressive and mostly intact castle is topped by an 11m-high belfry, which the local clergy still rings for mass. The skull and bones of the defeated Tigraian prince, who died in prison in 1868, is reputedly still held within the main church.

To get there, use the gravel road through the Simien National Park across the Bwahit Pass, and then follow it south for another 30km to the unsignposted turn-off to Deresge. From the junction you can walk to the church, a ten minute stroll up the green hill to the right. Using this route does of course mean paying the park entrance fees, but the scenery along the way justifies the expense. I suppose there is also a possibility of getting to Deresge on muleback from Dabat (some 27km south of Debark on the Gonder–Axum road), which would spare you the park entrance fees but would also take a great deal longer.

Just north of Mekane Birhan there is also a ruined military stronghold of Ras Wube from the 1850s, set on a rather steep hill on the left side of the road (entering the town).

CULTURAL INTERCHANGE IN THE SIMIENS

Edited from an email from Jozef Serneels and Katrien Holvoet

Based on our experience, it seems that the situation regarding lodging with local people in the villages has deteriorated in recent years. Our wish to do this was discussed with and agreed upon by the co-ordinator of the guides, but having made arrangements our 'official guide' wasn't keen about the whole idea and wanted to renege. There was, he said, no food in the villages. When we pointed out it was harvest season, he said that *faranji* could not eat barley *injera* and local beds were full of fleas. After some one-way discussions on the evening before we set off, we split up.

The next morning, our 'official guide' more or less complied. On our first night he brought us to Sankaber ranger post and he cooked us spaghetti. He found us a bed in the house of the family of a ranger (where we found out how cold the mountains are in December). On our second night we slept on the floor in Gich village in a small hut. Again our guide cooked us food: this time a chicken and some eggs. The third night we slept again in Sankaber in an empty hut where the guide put up some straw mattresses and prepared us spaghetti. So much for 'lodging with local people in the villages'!

From our experience, sleeping with local people is quite possible, but you will need to be firm and clear that this is your intention. Eating with local people seems to be more problematic. Perhaps this is because the guides have been burnt before, by tourists who couldn't cope with local farmers' food, or perhaps there are bad feelings or conflicts between the official guides and the villagers.

Our broader impression was that the tourists/guides/rangers on the one hand, and villagers on the other, do not interact (except in the sale of *tella*). This seems unhealthy. We feel that with a little negotiation between the park office, the guides and the rural village communities or individual families a proper 'system of lodging with local people in the villages' can be organised. All it requires is some discussion about what villagers expect, what can be reasonably provided to tourists, agreement on places to sleep, what food can be prepared, who prepares it, the use of firewood, and prices. This would enrich the experience of tourists who seek cultural interaction rather than isolation, while also being of benefit to local farmers. Could a guidebook promote such an idea?

and chicken. If your tastes are more elaborate, you can buy imported goods like chocolate, porridge oats, cheese, jam and custard creams in Addis Ababa.

If you don't have all the equipment you need, you can rent most obvious items of trekking gear at the Simien Park Hotel in Debark. This includes tents, sleeping bags, roll mattresses, simple kerosene stoves and aluminium cooking pots. Expect to pay around birr 50 per day for the full kit. Deforestation is a real problem in Ethiopia generally and in the Simien Mountains specifically. Travellers are therefore urged to rent a stove rather than depend on fires for cooking, and are certainly discouraged from making large wasteful bonfires to keep themselves warm at night. Note that it is forbidden to light fires outside the designated campsites.

A good sleeping bag and warm clothing is essential in the chilly peaks of the Simiens. A thick windbreaker or other heavy waterproof jacket will be ideal, but many travellers won't be willing to carry something like this all the way around Ethiopia for just a few days' use. Secondhand clothes are available very cheaply in markets throughout Ethiopia: one option would be to buy a couple of thick jumpers before you set off, and to leave them with a local when you are through with them. Waterproof gear is necessary between May and October.

We've received several reports of people becoming ill through drinking untreated water in the mountains, and I'm told that the cooks may not be aware of the importance of boiling rather than just warming drinking water. You should thus personally ensure this is done properly. Given that water takes some time to boil at this altitude, it might be worth carrying some purifying tablets – inferior though they are to boiling water – as a fallback.

Guides and scouts

The park rules stipulate that an armed scout must accompany all visitors. This costs birr 30 per day. In theory, the scout should be self-sufficient for food. In practice, he'll probably run out of food after a few days, if he brings any food at all, so consider buying extra rice and salt. If you go all the way to Ras Dashen, the park officials will suggest you take two scouts for extra safety, so that one can guard your camp while the other comes with you to the summit. This is recommended but not obligatory.

The Simien guides are not park employees, but they are officially organised into a co-operative, and take tourists into the park on a rotational basis. The official guides are all trained by the tourist office in Gonder, speak good English, and charge a standard birr 70–100 per day. It is not compulsory to trek with a local guide, and the scouts know all the paths. Most readers have showered their Simien guides with praise, but others have complained that the guides do little but state the blindingly obvious – one dissenter asks 'why would you want to *pay* somebody to babble in your ear incessantly?'

Mules

Unlike on most other mountains in east Africa, porters are not available for the Simiens, so it is conventional to take mules as pack animals. Carrying all your own gear and food is not recommended (unless you're used to backpacking), as distances are long and routes undulating. The scout and guide will expect you to hire at least one mule to carry their food and blankets. With the mule you have to hire a driver (horseman), who loads them up, makes sure they're fed and watered, and chases after them when they run away. Each mule will cost birr 20 per day, as will each driver.

You can also hire a mule to ride. If your time is limited and you want to do a long trek this is recommended. Even if you ride for only a few short stretches during the day, it makes the trek much more enjoyable and increases the distance you can cover. It's also good fun. Before hiring a mule check that it's in good condition. Make the driver lead it up and down; if there's a hint of a limp, don't hire it. Local saddles are basic and often used without a blanket underneath. Lift up the saddle and check the mule's back; if there are cuts or sores, don't hire it. And insist that any mule you hire for riding or carrying gear has a blanket under the saddle for padding.

Trekking routes

You have several route options, depending on the time you have, the distance you want to cover, and whether or not you drive part way into the park. Your route is also determined by the places where you can sleep the night and find water. Most visitors stay at or near the national park camps (even though the huts have been destroyed) as the water supply is reliable and the positions good (spaced a day's walk apart). The park camps are at Sankaber, Gich and Chennek. Distances between camps can be long and most days require between four and eight hours of walking. You need to be reasonably fit. However, as the trekking route described here follows paths and tracks for most of the distance, conditions underfoot are not too hard. It is worth planning your hike in conjunction with the excellent 1:100,000 Simien Mountains map published by the University of Bern in 2003 – it can easily be bought in Debark at the time of writing and all names used in the trail descriptions below conform to this map.

You should not underestimate the effects of altitude when planning your route, especially if you have flown in direct from Europe and have had little time to acclimatise. This is particularly important if you are going all the way to the summit of Ras Dashen. Although severe altitude-related illnesses (of the type suffered by trekkers on Mount Kenya and Kilimanjaro) are unlikely, you may experience headaches, shortness of breath, loss of appetite and general lethargy at higher altitudes. The best way to avoid these symptoms is to acclimatise properly by making a steady ascent. Do not try and rush to conquer Ras Dashen in four days: spend an extra night at one of the high camps (such as Chennek or Gich) and take a rest day. This will make your trek much more rewarding and enjoyable.

Some people are happy to visit the park for just two days, doing a short walk and staying one night at Sankaber. Other people spend ten days or more in the mountains, doing a long trek all the way to Ras Dashen, and diverting to several of the smaller peaks. In between these two extremes are several other options.

Here are some suggestions:

Four days (three nights) – sleeping at Sankaber, Gich, and then at Sankaber again;
Five days (four nights) – sleeping at Sankaber, Chennek (for two nights, going to the summit of Bwahit or the viewpoint on the way to Ras Dashen, on the day in between), then at Sankaber again;
Seven days (six nights) – sleeping at Sankaber, Chennek, Ambiko (for two nights, going up Ras Dashen in between), then back to Chennek and Sankaber again.

Route stages
In this section the various trekking routes have been broken into stages. Each is one day long. You can combine all of them to create a major trek, or combine just a few of them for a shorter trek. Times given are walking times only; you should allow extra time for lunch stops, photos, rests or simply looking at the view. Times will also be shorter if you ride your mule a lot.

Stage one: Debark to Sankaber (5–7 hours)
Leave Debark (2,800m) on the dirt road that leads through the market and then heads in an easterly direction through the outskirts of the town. The dirt road passes through fields, then crosses the Lama River and climbs steeply on to the western plateau. You reach the plateau's northern escarpment near Chinkwanit and follow this to reach the village of Michibi and Sankaber Camp (3,250m). You may cross or follow the road during this stage, but don't let your guide follow it all the way as you'll miss the views between Chinkwanit and Michibi. Worth noting, if you don't want to do this hike in one day, that there is a camp called Buyit Ras (3,230m) about halfway between Debark and Sankaber, close to the site of the tourist lodge that was under construction in 2005.

Stage two: Sankaber to Gich (5–7 hours)
Follow the track eastward along a narrow ridge, with the escarpment to the north and the Koba River Valley to the south. Drop into the Koba, and then climb steeply up through an area called Michotis. To your left is the Gich Abyss, as well as a large waterfall where the Jinbar River plunges into the abyss. About three to four hours from Sankaber, the paths divide. Keep left and drop into the valley, across the Jinbar River, then steeply up through Gich village to reach Gich Camp (3,600m). From Gich Camp it's one to two hours to the summit of Imet Gogo (3,925m), a large peak to the east of the camp, with spectacular views north and east across the foothills and plains.

Stage three: Gich to Chennek (5–7 hours)
Assuming that you use the track running south along the western escarpment via Imet Gogo rather than the main road marked on most maps, this is possibly the most

spectacular stage anywhere in the Simiens, offering superb views to the valleys below. Other major peaks you pass on the way are Shayno Sefer (3,962m) and Inatye (4,070m). It's also a good area to look for gelada, lammergeyer, and the rare Walia ibex. Alternatively, you can miss Gich and go direct from Sankaber to Chennek (3,620m), as described in stage four.

Stage four: Sankaber to Chennek (6–8 hours)

Follow the directions in stage two above to pass through Michotis. Where the routes divide (left goes to Gich), keep right and up, and follow the track along the crest of a broad ridge. This area is called Abergirna. About four to six hours from Sankaber the track starts to descend into the huge Belegez River Valley. The track zigzags steeply down, crossing several streams, then climbs up again slightly, passing on the left a U-shaped gap in the escarpment wall (through which you get splendid views), to reach Chennek Camp. Chennek is one of the most spectacular spots on this trekking route through the Simiens, and the surrounding slopes are thick with giant lobelias and other Afro-alpine scrub. The views are stunning in all directions, out from the escarpment edge, across the foothills, up to the surrounding peaks of Imet Gogo and Bwahit (4,430m), and westwards down the Belegez Valley. It's also a good place to observe wildlife; the surrounding cliffs are a favoured haunt of lammergeyers and gelada baboons. If you stay two nights at Chennek and then return towards Debark, a good destination for the day in between is the viewpoint overlooking the Mesheha River described below.

Stage five: Chennek to Ambiko (6–8 hours)

Heading east from Chennek, you leave the national park. The track climbs up a valley to the left (north) of Bwahit Peak, which overlooks the camp. About one-and-a-half hours from Chennek, after crossing the Bwahit Pass (4,200m), you reach a viewpoint. To the east, across the vast valley of the Mesheha River and its tributaries, you get your first sighting of Ras Dashen (4,533m) – the highest point in a wall of cliffs and peaks on the skyline on the far side of the valley. From the viewpoint the path drops steeply down, passing through the village of Chiro-Leba (3,300m; the tin-roofed school is a good landmark), and continues down through tributary valleys to reach the Mesheha River (2,800m; five to seven hours from Chennek). The path goes steeply up again to reach the village of Ambiko (3,200m) after another hour.

Stage six: Ambiko to Ras Dashen summit and return (7–9 hours)

It's usual to stay two nights at Ambiko, going up to the summit of Ras Dashen on the day in between. A dawn start is advised. From Ambiko, continue up the valley to reach the small village of Mizma (3,500m), where the path swings left and climbs steeply to reach a ridge crest overlooking a larger valley. Keeping this larger valley down to your left, follow the path eastwards, and head towards Ras Dashen's rocky west face, visible at the head of the valley. About three to four hours from Ambiko you pass through a gap in an old stone wall, then swing left up a broad ridge to enter a wide semi-circular corrie, surrounded by three major buttresses with steep sides of exposed rock. From this point it's impossible to see which buttress is the highest. The summit of Ras Dashen is on the top of the buttress on the left. To reach it, scramble up a gully through the cliffs to reach the cairn (pile of rocks) marking the summit (about four to five hours from Ambiko). Return to Ambiko by the same route (allow three to four hours).

Stages six to eight

From Ambiko it's usual to return to Debark by the same route: stage six – Ambiko to Chennek (six to eight hours); stage seven – Chennek to Sankaber (five to six hours); stage eight – Sankaber to Debark (six to seven hours) – though nine days out of ten you should

ON TOP OF THE WORLD?

Rowland and Ann Bowker set the cat among the pigeons with the following observation: 'Ras Dashen is NOT on the top of the buttress on the left. This is the top to which guides take trekkers and tell them that is the highest point. From this 'top' there is an obviously higher top quite close (which looks as if it requires rock-climbing) and probably even a higher one in the distance (the rightmost top as you stand in the corrie). This is very unfortunate for the climber who wishes to stand on the very highest point in Ethiopia. Unfortunately one is under the control of the guide and scout. There may be technical problems on the true summit, but perhaps one could have a go at it. This would mean making it clear to the guide that you wanted to aim for the rightmost top and insisting on a pre-dawn start from Ambiko.'

A more recent letter from another reader concurs: 'When we reached the summit, a few peaks on the same crest looked a little higher to me, and I'm not sure whether this was just a question of perspective. Of course I asked our scout a few times whether we were on the highest point in Ethiopia, and he gave the predictable answer – I don't know who knows the truth!'

The plot thickened during the course of updating this fourth edition, when I noticed that the new 1:100,000 map of the Simiens gives the height of Ras Dashen as 4,533m rather than the 4,620m quoted in previous editions of this guide. Initially I assumed this to be a blip on my part, but this is not the case: almost every official source I can locate, including various EMA maps, the National Atlas of Ethiopia, government handbooks dating back to the 1960s, and the official website of the Federal Region of Amhara, also gives the altitude of Ras Dashen as 4,620m! A quick online search also came down slightly in favour of the higher figure, with a few deviants settling on 4,543m.

Frankly, I don't know who knows the truth either! But my best guess – based on the credibility of the various sources – is that 4,533m is most probably the correct altitude. And if that is the case, then Ras Dashen is not, as is often claimed, the fourth highest mountain in Africa, but the fifth, falling one place behind Tanzania's Mount Meru. Furthermore, the queries raised by the Bowkers most probably can be explained by a trick of perspective: the peaks to which they are presumably referring, Analu and Tefew Leser, just 1km and 2km further north respectively, both rise to within 60m of Ras Dashen itself.

have no problem hitching a lift with a truck from Chennek to Debark if you want to cut out the last two days.

After the trek to Debark, you can return either to the park office or to the Simien Hotel to unload your mules and pay off the guide. It is polite to buy your 'crew' some tea and bread, while sorting out these final matters. If service has been good, a small tip to the guide, horseman and scout is appropriate and always appreciated. As a rule of thumb, a tip should be an extra one to two days' wages per every five to seven days of work.

Axum and the Adigrat Road

The present chapter covers the far north of the Federal Region of Tigrai, starting with the ancient city of Axum in the west, then following the main road east through Adwa as far as the junction town of Adigrat. Together with neighbouring Eritrea, it is an area that might be regarded as the fulcrum of Ethiopian culture. Axum (also spelt Aksum) was in existence at least three centuries before the birth of Christ, when it emerged as the imperial capital of the mighty Axumite Empire. The ancient city is also the site of Ethiopia's oldest Christian sanctuary, the Cathedral of Tsion Maryam, founded in the 4th century and still regarded to be the spiritual home of Ethiopian Orthodox Christianity.

Tigrai has a distinctly different character from the rest of Ethiopia. Historically and culturally, it shares strong links, both ancient and modern, with neighbouring Eritrea, which together with Tigrai formed the core of the ancient Axumite Empire. The mountainous sandstone rockscapes of Tigrai have an angular, wild quality quite distinct from the more curvaceous green hills seen elsewhere in the Ethiopian Highlands. A memorable feature of this harsh and dry landscape is the prolific stone terracing which is used to cultivate the slopes, though it is rather ineffective in years of drought, which generally occur once every decade. Tigraian houses, too, are built of stone, and they give the towns and villages a sense of orderly permanence that is rare in Africa.

The Tigraian people were persecuted under the Mengistu government, which, by frustrating all attempts at food distribution, must take a large share of the blame for the notorious famine of 1985. It is largely through Tigraian resistance that Mengistu was toppled in 1991, and that Eritrea was granted the independence for which it had fought for over two decades. Historical and cultural links notwithstanding, relationships between the two regions have yet to recover from the bloody border war of 1998–2000, which pitched the predominantly Tigraian leadership of Ethiopia against its former comrades in Eritrea.

AXUM

My initial response upon arriving at Axum in the course of researching the first edition of this guidebook was how small and inauspicious the town appeared to be given its estimable pedigree. And so has it been since the mid 16th century, when Ahmed Gragn led a destructive attack on the former capital of the Axumite Empire and razed its premier church. Francisco Alvares, who visited Axum perhaps a decade before Gragn's arrival, described it as 'a large town of very good houses, such that there are none like them in the whole of Ethiopia, and very good wells of water, and worked masonry, and also in most of the houses ancient figures of lions, dogs and birds, all well made in stone'. A century later, according to Manuel de Almeida, Axum had been reduced to 'a place of about a hundred inhabitants [where] everywhere there are ruins to be seen'.

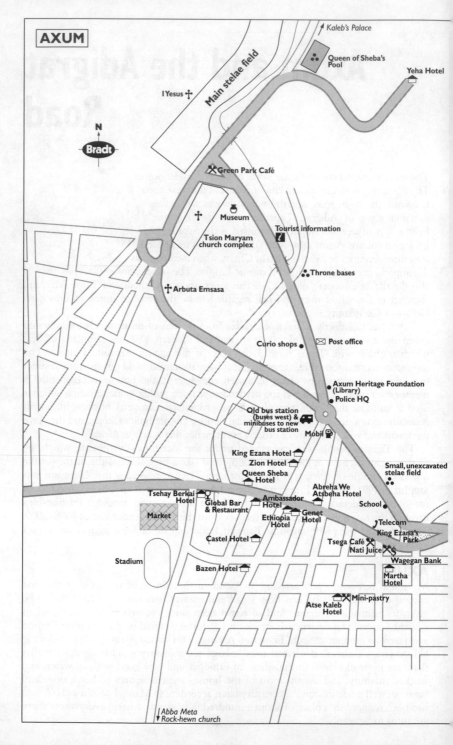

AXUM

↖ Kaleb's Palace

Queen of Sheba's Pool

Yeha Hotel

Main stelae field

I Yesus †

N

Bradt

Green Park Café

Museum

Tsion Maryam church complex

Tourist information

Throne bases

† Arbuta Emsasa

Curio shops

Post office

Axum Heritage Foundation (Library)

Police HQ

Old bus station (buses west) & minibuses to new bus station

Mobil

King Ezana Hotel

Zion Hotel

Queen Sheba Hotel

Small, unexcavated stelae field

Tsehay Berkai Hotel

Global Bar & Restaurant

Ambassador Hotel

Abreha We Atsbeha Hotel

School

Genet Hotel

Market

Ethiopia Hotel

Telecom

Castel Hotel

Tsega Café

King Ezana's Park

Nati Juice

Stadium

Bazen Hotel

Wagegan Bank

Martha Hotel

Mini-pastry

Atse Kaleb Hotel

↓ Abba Meta
Rock-hewn church

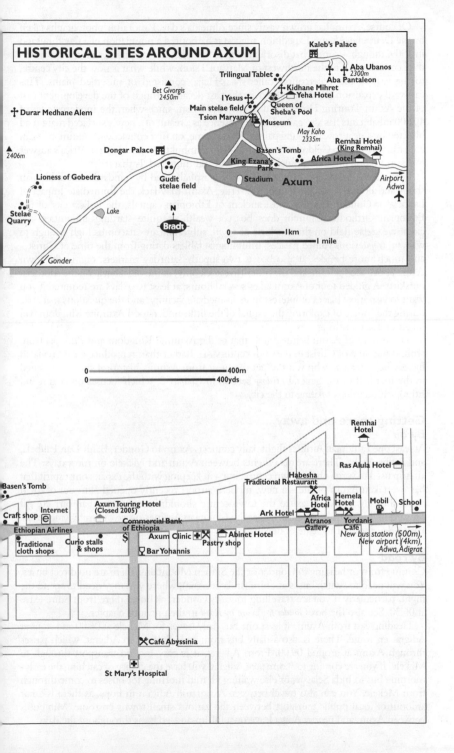

HISTORICAL SITES AROUND AXUM

Kaleb's Palace

Aba Ubanos
2300m
Aba Pantaleon

Trilingual Tablet

Kidhane Mihret
Yeha Hotel

Bet Givorgis
2450m

I Yesus
Main stelae field
Tsion Maryam

Queen of
Sheba's Pool

Museum

Durar Medhane Alem

May Koho
2335m

Remhai Hotel
(King Remhai)

2406m

Dongar Palace

Basen's Tomb

King Ezana's
Park

Africa Hotel

Lioness of Gobedra

Gudit
stelae field

Stadium

Axum

Airport,
Adwa

Lake

N

Stelae
Quarry

Bradt

Gonder

0 ———— 1km
0 ———— 1 mile

0 ———————— 400m
0 ———————— 400yds

Remhai
Hotel

Basen's Tomb

Ras Alula Hotel

Habesha
Traditional Restaurant

Africa
Hotel

Hemela
Hotel

Mobil

School

Craft shop

Internet

Axum Touring Hotel
(Closed 2005)

Ark Hotel

Atranos
Gallery

Yordanis
Café

Ethiopian Airlines

Commercial Bank
of Ethiopia

Axum Clinic

Abinet Hotel

New bus station (500m),
New airport (4km),
Adwa, Adigrat

Traditional
cloth shops

Curio stalls
& shops

Pastry shop

Bar Yohannis

Café Abyssinia

St Mary's Hospital

Of course, Axum has grown vastly since Almeida's day. Panoramic photographs taken by the Deutsche-Aksum Expedition suggest it harboured a population of a few thousand in 1909, though – somewhat disorientating at first glance – it appears that the town was then concentrated to the northwest of Maryam Tsion, while what is now the city centre, to the east of the watercourse called Mai Hejja, consisted of unsettled plains. This eastward expansion has continued over the past decade – much of the development east of the Axum Touring Hotel postdates my 1994 visit, since when the modern town of 40,000 inhabitants has also gained some presence as a result of a newly surfaced main road bisected by a neat row of young palms. All the same, on first contact with Axum, one can empathise with Bob Geldof, who on landing in Timbuktu (arguably west Africa's answer to Axum) reputedly took a quick look around and muttered 'Is that it?'

Fortunately, in Axum's case, a strip of fresh asphalt lined by standard-issue Ethiopian shops and houses is decidedly not 'it'. True, Axum may lack the immediate impact of Lalibela or Gonder, but this most ancient of Ethiopian capitals, the holiest city of the Ethiopian Orthodox Church, does boast a wealth of quite startling antiquities: the extensive stelae field on the outskirts of town, subterranean catacombs high enough to walk in, mysterious ruined palaces, multilingual tablets dating from the time of Christ – and much more besides. It also boasts two superb Saturday markets: one in the town centre above the stadium, and the other (livestock only) at the old airstrip on the southern outskirts. A guided tour of Axum takes several hours; at least two days are required if you want to visit most places of interest in its immediate vicinity, and the questions that arise during the course of exploring the capital of the little-understood Axumite Kingdom will linger on for months...

The history of Axum is integral to that of the Axumite Kingdom and Ethiopia from around the time of Christ to the 10th century AD. Rather than reproduce an abbreviated history here, readers who want to get the most from Axum's historical sites are pointed to the first half of the general *History* section in *Chapter 2*, which focuses on Axum and Ethiopian traditions relating to the city.

Getting there and away
By air
At least one Ethiopian Airlines flight daily connects Axum to Gonder, Bahir Dar, Lalibela, and Addis Ababa. There are also flights between Axum and Mekele on most days. The airstrip used to verge on the town centre, but – in keeping with the expansionist spirit that has overtaken Axum of late – a new, modern airport recently opened 5km out of town along the Adwa road. A taxi to the town centre shouldn't cost more than birr 20. All onward flights must be reconfirmed at the Ethiopian Airlines office opposite King Ezana Park a day ahead of the date of departure.

By road
Coming from or heading to Gonder or the Simien Mountains, there are no direct buses. You will need to switch buses at Shire (Inda Selassie), where you may need to spend the night, particularly if you are travelling towards Gonder, as buses there from Shire leave at 06.30. See also the box *Gonder to Axum by Road* in the previous chapter.

Heading east from Axum, at least one bus daily leaves for Mekele at 06.00 and stops at Adigrat en route. There is also a daily bus from Inda Selassie to Adigrat, which passes through Axum at around 09.00. From Adigrat, it is easy to find transport through to Mekele. If you are coming to Axum *from* Adigrat, you have the choice of catching the early-morning bus to Inda Selassie, or else waiting till mid morning for buses to come through from Mekele. You can also travel between Axum and Adigrat in hops, as there is a fair amount of local public transport between the various small towns en route. Minibuses between Axum and nearby Adwa leave on a fill-up-and-go basis throughout the day.

Note that buses heading west from Axum towards Shire depart from the old central bus station, essentially a patch of open ground on the traffic roundabout immediately north of the King Ezana Hotel. All buses to easterly destinations such as Adwa, Adigrat and Mekele now depart from the smart new bus station, which has a rather inconvenient location about 1.5km out of town along the Adwa road. Regular minibuses run between the old and new bus stations for the princely fare of birr 1.

Before the border war between Ethiopia and Eritrea, daily buses ran directly between Axum and Asmara, leaving in the early morning, while one bus between Shire and Asmara passed through Axum at around 09.00. These services will presumably resume if and when the border between the two countries reopens.

Most visitors who travel by road arrive at Axum from Gonder and depart in the direction of Adigrat (or vice versa). Two other little-known but potentially interesting onward options exist, however, both of which initially involve heading south at Adwa along the road towards Adi Arkay. The first option is to continue southward from Adi Arkay to Sekota and Lalibela – with an early start and a private vehicle, the full trip from Axum to Lalibela can be covered in one long dusty day (the drive would take about eight hours not allowing for breaks – or breakdowns!), but there is enough to see on the way to justify an overnight stop at Abi Aday (for more information, see box *To Lalibela via Sekota*, page 338). Alternatively, if you are heading on to the rock-hewn churches of Gheralta, the little-used route to Hawzien via Adwa and Nebelet, the closest town to the remote rock-hewn church of Maryam Wukro, can be covered in four to five hours from Axum without breaks or diversions (see box *Hawzien to Axum via Maryam Wukro*, page 283).

Where to stay

Axum boasts a good variety of accommodation by Ethiopian standards, and – certainly after Gonder or Lalibela – it seems particularly well equipped with attractive and sensibly priced budget hotels.

Upmarket

Yeha Hotel (63 rooms) ☏ 034 7750605; e ghion@ethionet.et; www.ghionhotel.com.et. Part of the government Ghion chain, this rather time-warped but well-managed hotel is most notable for its wonderful situation on a wooded hilltop that overlooks the town centre. A good tar road leads to the hotel, or you can walk there from the stelae field in ten (steep) minutes, passing the Queen of Sheba's Pool en route. The restaurant has traditional décor and fair Western food, while the patio is a classic spot for sundowners with the stelae field below and plenty of birds rattling around in the fig trees above. The Galaxy Express office is in this hotel. Functional rooms with en-suite showers (hot water morning and evening only) cost US$36/48/60 sgl/dbl/ste.

Remhai Hotel (65 rooms) ☏ 034 7751501/7752168 or 011 4669991/2; f 034 7752894; e remhot@ethionet.et; www.remhai-hotel.com. Providing the Yeha with some genuine competition, this new hotel on the eastern fringe of the town centre is a relatively smart and stylish multi-storey affair that easily ranks as the best in town in terms of facilities and services, but comes a poor second to the Yeha in terms of location and atmosphere. The rooms, indisputably better than the ones at the Yeha, are good value by any standards at birr 225 for a sgl, birr 340 for a twin or dbl, or US$54/70 for a semi-ste/ste – all with DSTV, fridge, and telephone. Smaller rooms without a telephone cost birr 127/170 sgl/dbl. Facilities include an internet café, 24-hour electricity and water, a good curio shop, and a free airport shuttle. The bland concrete courtyard I was rude about in the last edition has now been supplemented by an altogether more inviting swimming pool area, and a gym and sauna are also under construction. A good Western restaurant in the main building serves meals in the birr 20–25 range, while a traditional *tukul* next to the swimming pool serves local food accompanied by traditional music and dancing from 18.30 onwards on Tuesday, Thursday, Saturday and Sunday.

Moderate

Axum Touring Hotel ⑁ 034 7750205/78. Closed for renovations in mid 2005 following a change of ownership, this stalwart of the Imperial era was once the best – indeed only – hotel in Axum. Last time I looked in, it still retained the slightly moribund institutional aura characteristic of so many former government hotels, though the flowering grounds went a long way towards compensating. Expect en-suite rooms to cost around birr 100 when it reopens.

Ark Hotel (20 rooms) ⑁ 034 7752676. This new hotel on the eastern side of the town centre charges birr 80/100 for spacious clean sgl/dbl rooms with en-suite hot showers. There is a decent restaurant, an internet café on the ground floor, and the management is very friendly. Room rates are usually negotiable out of season.

Abunet Hotel (30 rooms) ⑁ 034 7753857. Another friendly new hotel on the eastern side of town, the Abunet charges birr 70/100 for a clean and spacious sgl/dbl with tiled floor and en-suite hot showers. Airport transfers can be arranged for birr 10. The first-floor restaurant is one of the best and busiest in town.

Budget

Africa Hotel (48 rooms) ⑁ 034 7753700/01; e africaho@ethionet.com. Consistently popular with travellers since it opened in the mid 1990s thanks to a high standard of cleanliness, reasonable prices and a helpful hands-on owner-manager, the Africa Hotel ranks among my favourite budget lodgings anywhere in Ethiopia. It also boasts good facilities in the form of a free airport shuttle (just phone when you land), DSTV in the bar, an internet café, and a good restaurant and juice bar, and the staff can hook you up with reliable local guides for a city tour. A double-storey building enclosing an attractive green courtyard, it charges birr 50/70 for a large, clean dbl/twin with en-suite hot shower, or birr 10 extra for a room with DSTV, while rooms using a common shower cost birr 25.

Atse Kaleb Hotel (20 rooms) ⑁ 034 7752222. Another long-serving favourite (indeed, it's been owned and managed by the same family for 30 years), this friendly hotel, set around a large green courtyard in the back roads east of the market, charges birr 50 for a large dbl room with en-suite hot shower, or birr 30 for a sgl using the common hot shower. Food and drinks are available, but it serves primarily as a pension.

Shoestring

Most of Axum's cheap-if-you're-Ethiopian hotels charge such high *faranji* prices that they are only slightly less expensive than the ones listed in the budget category, and a lot less attractive. Aside from the exceptions listed below, the **Huri**, **Abreha we Atsbeha**, **Queen Sheba** and **Genet** hotels form part of a cluster of perhaps a dozen basic lodgings running south from the old bus station – and if cheap and grotty is what you want, then cheap and grotty they most certainly are.

Hermela Hotel ⑁ 034 7751106. A definite notch down from any of the places listed above, this new double-storey hotel, situated a block up from the Africa, is already looking rather rundown and musty. The en-suite rooms with a ¾ bed and hot shower are indifferent value at the asking rate of birr 50, and the rooms using a common shower are a joke at birr 40, but the management seems very willing to negotiate – knock birr 10–15 off the asking price and it would represent decent value for money.

Ras Alula Hotel ⑁ 034 7753622. The closest hotel to the new bus station, this new place charges birr 50 for a clean en-suite room with a ¾ bed and a hot shower. A bar and restaurant is attached.

Bazen Hotel ⑁ 034 7752298. A notable exception is the friendly three-storey Bazen Hotel, where for birr 30 you get a very clean room with a dbl bed and access to a common hot shower.

Where to eat

Several of the hotels listed above have decent restaurants. Top of the range is probably the **Remhai Hotel**, though – as with accommodation – it's tempting to recommend the Yeha

Hotel as first choice purely on the basis of the superb view from the patio. Either way, you're looking at around birr 30 for a meal inclusive of taxes. The restaurant at the **Africa Hotel** is pretty good, too, combining Western dishes with local fare in the birr 10–15 range, and it also serves excellent fruit juice. The **Ark** and **Abunet** hotels are comparable in standard, though the former doesn't prepare meat dishes during fasting times.

For Ethiopian fare, the **Habesha Traditional Restaurant** in the back roads close to the Remhai Hotel is well worth a try: most meals are in the birr 10–16 range, it will prepare meat dishes even during fasting times, and traditional music and dancing can be arranged with a few hours' notice. Similar in standard, but with more overtly traditional décor, the **Café Abyssinia** next to the hospital serves good local and *faranji* dishes in the birr 10–12 range, and the adjacent pastry shop offers some of the best confectionaries and juices in town. Another good spot for breakfast, pastries and coffee is the **Tela Café**, while **Nati Fruit Juice** on the opposite side of the road serves inexpensive and wholesome juices.

Listings
Craft and souvenir shops
Axum is particularly well endowed with shops selling Ethiopian handicrafts, ranging from religious icons and other old artefacts to modern carvings and cotton shama cloth. Situated between the Ark and the Africa Hotels, the modern Atranos Gallery comes highly recommended, but there are several other good shops running along the road towards Maryam Tsion and the road between Ethiopian Airlines and Africa Hotel.

Internet and email
Internet facilities in Axum exist only at a handful of hotels catering primarily to tourists, ie: the Remhai, the Ark and the Africa. Rates in Axum are uniformly high at around birr 1 per minute, but this is likely to change very soon, which should also prompt the opening of more internet cafés.

Library
Situated in a former palace between the main traffic roundabout and the Cathedral of Maryam Tsion, the **Axum Heritage Foundation** (❱ 034 7752871) houses an excellent library including a collection of several hundred titles about Ethiopia, many of which are rare or out of print. Casual visitors are welcome to browse through the collection during the opening hours of 08.30 to 17.30 Monday to Friday.

Minibus rental
The Abunet Hotel has a modern minibus it rents out for day excursions from Axum. Rates are to some extent negotiable, but expect to pay around birr 500 per groups of up to four people to visit Yeha, or birr 950 to visit Debre Damo and Yeha. Minibuses can also be arranged through local tourist guides.

Swimming
Axum is tangibly warmer than most other places of interest in Ethiopia, for which reason an afternoon at the swimming pool at the Remhai Hotel might be tempting – it costs birr 15 to swim, whether or not you are resident at the hotel.

Tourist information
The Tigrai Tourist Commission (❱ 034 7753924) office is clearly signposted near the Axum Museum along the road towards the stelae field. It is a good source of local information and is also where you pay the birr 50 entrance fee that covers the various secular historical sites dotted around town.

Sightseeing in Axum

To see Axum's main cluster of antiquities, walk out past the old bus station towards the stelae field on the northwestern outskirts of town. En route, you need to stop at the Tigrai Tourist Commission office to locate the (sometimes elusive) man who sells tickets that allow access to all the secular historical sites within walking distance of the town. These tickets cost birr 50 per person, with a 50% reduction in price on presentation of a student card, and a rather less significant discount for groups of six or more people. Knowledgeable guides are provided on request and ask around birr 100 per day per group. The unofficial guides are best avoided. Don't forget to bring along your torch. Note that there is a separate charge to visit the church compound.

The notes here will be better understood if read in conjunction with the *History* section in *Chapter 2* of this book.

Axum Museum

If you can rein in your eagerness to explore the stelae field, it can be instructive to poke around the museum first. Exploring the stelae field conveys something of the majesty of ancient Axum, but it is the tour through the marvellous site museum that illustrates just how cosmopolitan and technologically advanced the city was. This is an exemplary museum and it deserves thorough investigation.

The first display is a selection of ancient rock tablets, which are inscribed in a variety of languages including a form of Sabaean that preceded the Ge'ez of Christian Axum. This early Sabaean writing consisted of consonants only, but it is similar enough to the modern Amharigna script that the letters (though obviously not the meaning of the words) are intelligible to Ethiopians today.

The museum also contains an array of Axumite household artefacts, ranging from a water filter to a set of drinking glasses that were imported from Egypt. There is a collection of Axumite crosses and coins, the latter minted up until the 6th century AD. A more recent artefact is a 700-year-old leather Bible, written in Ge'ez and decorated with illuminations.

Some new explanatory posters have been added recently, funded by an American–Italian archaeological research project. They give an overview of the history of Axum, its major archaeological sites and the various artefacts found. This will help you to get a broader and better picture of what is of archaeological relevance in Axum and the surrounding area, in a context that contrasts with the more outlandish myths and legends that are recounted by guides in Axum as if they were accepted fact.

The stelae field

A tour normally starts at the main stelae field opposite the Church of Tsion Maryam, which consists of some 75 or more stelae of various shapes and sizes, concentrated within an area of less than 1,000m². Do note that while most of the larger stelae are linked by local tradition to a specific king, and these traditions are referred to in the text that follows, these associations have little scholarly basis.

The modern view of the stelae field is dominated by the stele accredited to King Ezana, the third largest ever erected at Axum. This engraved block of solid granite, which stands some 23m high, was transported from a quarry 4km distant, most probably by elephants. No satisfactory explanation has been postulated for how such a massive block of stone was erected – one Axumite tradition has it that it was the work of the mysterious powers of the Ark of the Covenant. The stele is carved with a door and nine windows, which are thought to symbolise the door and nine chambers of Ezana's tomb, and the nine palaces built by the king. Ezana's stele is slightly tilted, and at one point there were fears it might eventually topple over, but recent measurements compared with those taken 100 years ago suggest it was erected at this angle.

UNCOVERING AXUM

The earliest excavations at Axum were conducted during the first three months of 1906 by the Deutsche-Aksum Expedition (DAE), led by Dr Enno Litmann and funded by the German Kaiser. The massively detailed report of this expedition, which includes extensive notes on the two main stelae fields, Kaleb's Palace, and several churches, was published in German in 1913. It had long been out of print when an English translation, edited and annotated by leading archaeologist and Axum expert Dr David Phillipson, and lavishly illustrated with line drawings and photographs taken in 1906, was published as *The Monuments of Aksum* by the Addis Ababa University Press in 1997. While aspects of the DAE report are inevitably dated, it remains a marvellously detailed and informative introduction to the main historical sites dotted around the modern town; it costs around birr 80 and is more easily obtained in Addis Ababa than in Axum.

Between 1906 and 1992, only two significant series of excavations took place at Axum, both of which were terminated after the assassination of Haile Selassie in 1974. The French excavations at Dongar Palace and several other sites, initiated in 1952 and supervised by Francis Anfrey, resulted in several sketchy preliminary accounts but have as yet yielded no detailed report. Stuart Munro-Hay published a full account of the excavations at the main stelae field undertaken by Neville Chittick for the British Institute in east Africa in the early 1970s after Chittick's death. In 1991, Munro-Hay published the most detailed and readable existing account of Axumite society, a book entitled *Aksum: An African Civilisation of Late Antiquity*. Although not widely accessible in printed form, the full text of this book can be accessed online at www.users.vnet.net/alight/aksum.

In this book, Munro-Hay writes: 'Of all the important ancient civilisations of the past, that of the ancient Ethiopian kingdom of Aksum still remains perhaps the least known… Its history and civilisation has been largely ignored, or at most accorded only brief mention, in the majority of recent books purporting to deal at large with ancient African civilisations, or with the world of late antiquity… When this book was in preparation, I wrote to the archaeology editor of one of Britain's most prominent history and archaeology publishers about its prospects. He replied that, although he had a degree in archaeology, he had never heard of Aksum.'

The subsequent decade has seen a number of important new excavations undertaken in and around Axum, the results of which generally remain unpublished. Only a tiny fraction of known sites around Axum have been excavated, and new sites are being discovered at a faster pace than the established ones are being investigated. It is thus safe to say that almost anything written about Axum today is based on relatively sketchy archaeological foundations. One can only guess at what further excavation of this mysterious city might yet reveal.

The largest of Axum's stelae, credited by tradition to the 3rd-century King Remhai, now lies shattered on the ground. Its collapse is linked by tradition to Queen Yodit, who destroyed many of Axum's finest buildings, but scholarly opinion is that it toppled over either while it was being erected or soon afterwards, probably because the base of the stele was too small to support it. Remhai's stele still lies where it fell. It weighs 500 tons and would be over 33m high were it standing. It is decorated with a door and 12 windows.

Not far from this stele, Remhai's tomb consists of 12 underground vaults that are high enough to walk through. The most striking thing about this tomb is the precision of its masonry, which consists of large blocks of granite held together by metal pins. In the back vault, Remhai's sealed stone coffin lies where it was abandoned after Neville Chittick's excavations were aborted following the 1974 revolution.

During the Italian occupation, the second largest Axumite stele, which stands 26m high and whose builder is unknown, was carved into three blocks for ease of transportation and reassembled on the Piazza in Rome. Several years of negotiation between the Ethiopian and Italian governments have culminated with the recent return of the looted stele to its rightful home. The first block arrived in Axum to scenes of public jubilation on 19 April 2005, and the other two blocks followed shortly afterwards. The stele will only be re-erected once archaeologists have determined how the heavy cranes that will be used in the process might affect the tunnels in a recently discovered necropolis below the car park in front of the stelae field.

Ezana was the first Christian ruler of Axum, and the last one to build a stele. The stelae of Axum are not, however, thought to have any religious significance, but to have demonstrated the power and importance of the ruler who built them. It is not surprising, then, that Ezana, the conqueror of Yemen and parts of modern-day Sudan, is credited with building such an impressive monument. There are many smaller stelae scattered around the site, and a few other places in town where a few smaller and in most cases collapsed stelae can be seen, for instance on the opposite side of the road to the school next to King Ezana's Park.

Mai Shum

Often referred to as the **Queen of Sheba's Swimming Pool**, Mai Shum is a small reservoir situated alongside the northern end of the stelae field at the junction of the tracks that lead to the Yeha Hotel and to the Tomb of Kaleb. Traditions regarding the excavation of the pool are, even by Ethiopian standards, somewhat divergent. At one end of the timescale is the popular legend that Mai Shum was created some 3,000 years ago as a bathing place for the Queen of Sheba. At the other is the more credible story that it was dug by Abuna Samuel, Bishop of Axum during the early 15th-century reign of Emperor Yishak. The notion that the Queen of Sheba ever unrobed and took a dip in Mai Shum has to be classified as fanciful, but there is reason to think that the pool was excavated in Axumite times, as were the stone steps leading down to it, and that Abuna Samuel's contribution consisted of clearing and possibly enlarging the existing basin. Suggestively, the name Axum is thought to derive from the phrase 'Ak Shum', which consists of a Cushitic word meaning water and a Semitic word for chief, while 'Mai' is the Tigrigna equivalent to 'Ak' – so that both Mai Shum and Axum translate as 'Water of the Chief', leaving open the possibility that the town is named after the pool alongside which it was founded.

Cathedral of Tsion Maryam

From the museum, you'll probably move on to the compound of the Cathedral of Tsion Maryam (St Mary of Zion), where a church of that name was constructed above an old pagan shrine by King Ezana in the 4th century. Ethiopia's first church, the original Maryam Tsion church, which consisted of 12 temples, has been destroyed, most probably by the 16th-century Muslim leader Ahmed Gragn, though one version of events is that it was a victim of the rampages of Queen Yodit, and that Gragn destroyed a later replacement church.

Francisco Alvares, who visited Axum in 1520, penned what is, so far as I'm aware, the most detailed surviving description of the church destroyed by Gragn. It was, the Portuguese priest wrote, 'a very noble church, the first there was in Ethiopia... named Saint Mary of Zion... because the apostles sent [its altar stone] from Mount Zion. This church is very large. It has five aisles of good width and of great length, vaulted above, and all the vaults closed; the ceilings and sides are painted. Below, the body of the church is well worked with handsome cut stones; it has seven chapels, all with their backs to the east, and their altars well ornamented.

'This church has a large enclosure, and it is also surrounded by another larger enclosure, like the enclosing wall of a large town or city. Within the enclosure are handsome groups of one-storey buildings, and all spout out water by strong figures of lions and dogs of stone. Inside this large enclosure there are two mansions... which belong to two rectors of the church; and the other houses are of canons and monks. In the large enclosure, at the gate nearest the church, there is a large ruin, built in a square, which in other time was a house, and it has at each corner a big stone pillar, squared and worked. This house is called Ambacabete, which means house of lions. They say that in this house were the captive lions, and there are still some always travelling, and there go before the Prester John four captive lions.'

The oldest-functioning church in the compound today resembles the castles of Gonder – not surprising, as Gonder's founder, Emperor Fasilidas, built it. There are some good paintings and musical instruments inside the church, but entrance is forbidden to women. The foundations of one of the original 12 temples have been left undisturbed as a mark of respect, and there is some talk of archaeological excavation taking place below it in the near future. As for the rather overblown piece of 20th-century architecture that now forms the largest church in the compound, this was built in the 1960s under Haile Selassie – sadly, its ugly spire competes with the ancient stelae for horizon space. Haile Selassie's wife built the museum next to the old church, which is worth visiting for its collection of ancient crowns, crosses and other church relics. Behind the old church stands the so-called Throne of David, which is where the Axumite emperors were crowned, as well as the Thrones of the Judges, a row of a dozen old throne bases that suffered some damage at the hands of Gragn's army.

Axum's most famous religious artefact, the Tabot or supposed Ark of the Covenant, is kept in a sanctified outbuilding within the compound, but there's not much chance of being allowed to see it – indeed, only two westerners claim to have had the privilege! Yohannis Tomacean, who viewed it in 1764, described it as 'a piece of stone with a few incomplete letters on it'. A century later, RP Dimotheos, was shown 'a tablet of pinkish marble of the type one normally finds in Egypt... quadrangular, 24cm long by 22cm wide [on which] the Ten Commandments, five on one side, five on the other [were] written obliquely in Turkish fashion'. Dimotheos thought the 'nearly intact' tablet to be perhaps 600 years old, and quite clearly he was shown a different artefact to the one seen by Tomacean – almost certainly, both men were allowed to view *a* tabot, but not *the* Tabot.

Entrance to the church compound costs birr 60, a somewhat steep fee by comparison with that charged for the other historical sites, especially for female visitors (women have been banned from entering the most interesting church in the compound since its predecessor was attacked by Queen Yodit in the 10th century). There is no charge for visiting the nearby Church of Arbuta Insesa (Four Animals), a circular church constructed in the 17th century by Iyasu I and rebuilt in its present rectangular style in 1962, when several ancient tombs were found underneath it. Refreshingly low-key by comparison to the contemporaneous eyesore built by Haile Selassie next door, Arbuta Insesa is worth visiting for the interesting modern paintings that adorn its walls.

King Ezana's Park and King Basen's Tomb

There are two major historical sites within the modern town centre. In King Ezana's Park, a tablet inscribed in Sabaean, Ge'ez and Greek stands where it was originally placed in the 4th century AD. Other relics in the park include standing pillars from what was presumably Ezana's palace, a stele, what looks like a tomb, and an innocuous-looking slab of stone that could be mistaken for a park bench but was in fact used for cleaning corpses. This site, like several others that have been fenced off around the town, has never been excavated.

Not far from the park, marked by the customary stele, is King Basen's Tomb. According to the chronology of Axumite kings, Basen would have been ruling over Axum at the time of Christ's birth. His tomb lies underground and is entered via a man-high tunnel, but it differs from the tombs in the main stelae field in that it is hewn out of rock as opposed to being built from stone blocks. The graves chiselled into the side of the entry tunnel are probably where Basen's family was laid to rest. At the end of the tunnel are two much larger vaults in which the king and his wife are thought to have been entombed. Discrete from the king's tomb is a series of graves carved into the rock, reminiscent of the similar but much more recent graves carved into the surrounding walls of the churches at Lalibela.

Excursions further afield

Several important sites lie within a 5km radius of the city centre, and most can be visited on foot if you so choose, or in a rented vehicle or taxi.

The Tombs of Kaleb and Gebre Meskel

On a hilltop some 2km north of the town centre stand the 'two houses under the ground, into which men do not enter without a lamp' as mentioned in the writings of Francisco Alvares. Local tradition has it that these tombs, whose entrances lie just 23m apart, were excavated below the palaces of the powerful 6th-century Emperor Kaleb and his son and successor Gebre Meskel, and the two emperors were entombed within them. While these assertions are difficult to verify, there is no strong reason to doubt them either (except perhaps that contradictory legends claim Kaleb was buried at Pantaleon Monastery and Gebre Meskel at Debre Damo) and the set of raised stone crosses on one tomb, together with the absence of any stelae, implies it dates to the Christian era.

Dr Littman excavated the site in 1898, at which time the whole construction was buried. Little remains of the palace itself, but the burial vaults underneath it are in excellent condition, though grave robbers have cleared out their contents – all that remains are the stone sarcophagi referred to by Alvares as 'the treasure chests of the Queen of Sheba'! The subterranean architecture is similar to that of Remhai's Tomb, which was constructed below the stelae field some 300 years earlier. The most obvious difference lies in the masonry: whereas Remhai's Tomb was constructed by riveting together cubed stone blocks, this one is made of freely interlocking blocks of irregular shape. Legend has it that a secret tunnel goes all the way from the tombs to Eritrea and/or Yemen.

To get to the twin tombs, start from the square in front of the stelae field, and (assuming that you are facing the stelae) follow the asphalt road to your right. After no more than five minutes, after passing the rightward fork to the Yeha Hotel, you will pass the pool known as Mai Shum on your right. From here, it's a fairly straightforward 20-minute hike to the ruined palace, following a motorable track that offers some fine views over the stelae field, dwarfed though it is by the singularly ugly spire of the 20th-century Tsion Maryam Church.

About halfway up the hill is a reminder of just what may lie undiscovered beneath the soil around Axum. In the 1980s, a farmer discovered a **trilingual tablet** that had been inscribed under King Ezana. The tablet praises God for his help in the conquest of Yemen. It also warns that anybody who dares move the tablet will meet an untimely death. The tablet lies exactly where it was found, but is easy to miss because it is protected in a makeshift hut. As with Kaleb's tomb, the entrance fee for the museum and stelae field covers the tablet too.

Debre Liqanos Monastery

From Kaleb's Palace, a clear path to your right leads after 20–30 minutes to a hilltop monastery founded by Abba Liqanos, a Constantinople-born member of the Nine Saints who evangelised in the vicinity of present-day Adwa in the 6th century. The original Axumite church, thought to have been converted by Abba Liqanos and his followers from an older non-Christian temple, was replaced several centuries ago, but fragments such as the pillar next to the baptismal font can still be seen. Women may enter the monastery compound and look at the various holy crosses and books, but the church interior is accessible to men only. Many people feel this walk is worthwhile just for the scenery and the opportunity to escape the yelling kids and wannabe guides. Instead of returning to Axum the way you came, a steep shortcut leads down the hill to bring you out on the road between Basen's Tomb and Maryam Tsion. Entrance costs birr 20.

Pantaleon Monastery

This attractive monastery, situated 5km out of town on a euphorbia-clad pinnacle known as Debre Katin, boasts one of the oldest and most historically important churches in the country. Pantaleon was founded in the early 6th century by Abba Pantaleon, a son of a Byzantine nobleman who entered the monastic life as a child and later became one of the 'Nine Saints' who fled to Ethiopia when the Monophysitic doctrine was proclaimed to be heretical. Local tradition has it that Pantaleon spent the last 45 years of his life praying and healing the sick from the confines of a tall, narrow monastic cell in which he was forced to spend 24 hours a day in a standing position. Pantaleon was an advisor to King Kaleb, who joined the monastery after he abdicated in favour of his son Gebre Meskel in roughly AD550. Another plausible local tradition claims that Abba Yared, the contemporary of Gebre Meskel who invented the notation of Ethiopian ecclesiastical music and compiled the Mazgaba Degwa (Treasury of Hymns), spent much of his life at Pantaleon.

As with its counterpart at Debre Libanos, the hilltop church at Pantaleon is thought to have been built on the site of an older non-Christian temple and is open to men only. According to the priests, the church's sanctuary – which is off-limits to the laity – stands atop a stone staircase leading to a subterranean rock-hewn pit that formed part of the original temple. Visitors can be taken to the stone pit where Abba Pantaleon endured his hermitage, and to the nearby rock where King Kaleb sat when he sought the priest's blessing or counsel. Both men are said to have been buried in the stone cemetery in the church compound. Women may enter the brightly painted modern church that stands below the original.

Pantaleon can be reached on foot from the monastery of Debre Liqanos, a roughly 45-minute walk through lovely countryside. A quicker way back to town is to descend the southern slope of the hill via a footpath that leads to a motorable track which emerges on the Adwa road roughly 100m past the Africa Hotel. You can, of course, visit the monastery as a standalone excursion by using this second track, either on foot or by vehicle – the monastery is clearly visible and signposted from the Adwa road.

Dongar and the Gudit Stelae Field

Another important site that lies outside of the modern town is Dongar, popularly known as the Queen of Sheba's Palace, which was discovered as recently as 1950. As with so many sites in Axum, many questions surround the construction of this palace, but it is unlikely to have anything to do with the Queen of Sheba. The French archaeologist Francis Antrey, who excavated the site in 1952 but never published the bulk of his findings, concluded that the palace was most probably built in the 7th century AD. I'm told that more recent excavations and carbon-dating tests, the results of which are not yet published, indicate that the palace may in fact date to the pre-Christian era.

Whenever it was built, the intact floor plan and entrance stairs are sufficient to confirm that it was probably the most impressive palace ever built in Axum, consisting of more than 50 rooms, and boasting an elaborate drainage system. It is also where many of the more unusual relics now housed in Axum's museum were found. The palace stands 20–30 minutes' walk from the town centre on the northern edge of the Gonder road. You will need your ticket from the tourist office to enter the site.

On the opposite side of the road to the palace is a field of hundreds of relatively small and unadorned stelae, which aside from one 22.5m stele and another 7.5m stele are generally not much more than 2m high. This is referred to locally as the Gudit Stelae Field, Gudit being an alternative rendition of Yodit, the Falasha queen traditionally said to have razed much of ancient Axum. The traditional link between Gudit and these stelae has yet to be explained to me, but one popular tradition does maintain that the largest stele within the field marks the grave of Makeda, the Queen of Sheba. Based on limited archaeological exploration in 1974 and 1994–96, these stelae have been confirmed to mark graves of some sort. One tomb contained several artefacts that appear to date from the 3rd century AD, suggesting that this field was broadly contemporaneous with the main stelae field in town. A likely explanation is that it was a burial ground for dignitaries considered less important than those buried at the main stelae field.

Ad Hankara and the Gobedra Lioness

Also along the Gonder road, reached via a 1km side road running to the north opposite the electrical substation at Ad Hankara, some 2–3km or so past Dongar, is the hillside quarry from whence came the stelae that stand outside Axum. Amongst the broken rock that litters the hill can clearly be seen rocks from where some of the larger stelae were cut, and there is also one partially carved stele that lies in situ.

A short walk further uphill, etched into a flat rockface with a southwest orientation, there is a 3.27m-long outline figure of a crouching lion known as the Gobedra Lioness. The story behind this isolated and singular carving has long been a source of speculation. Tradition asserts that the Archangel Mikael was attacked by a lion here, and that he repelled the lion with such force it left an outline in the rock. The presence of a carved cross alongside the carving was for some time thought to indicate a post-Christian date, but it is more likely that the lioness was carved in pre-Christian times and the cross was carved next to it later. In *The Sign and the Seal*, Graham Hancock suggests it was the work of the Knights Templar who he believed visited the area in medieval times, but it was more probably carved during the reign of Gebre Meskel. Whether the carving has any deep significance or was merely decorative is anybody's guess.

There is a small lake on the way between Dongar and Ad Hankara where pelicans and a variety of storks and wintering ducks and waders are seasonally abundant.

Dereka Abba Meta

Axum, with its elevated ecclesiastical status, ancient tomb-carving tradition, and local abundance of suitable sandstone outcrops, might reasonably be expected to lie at the epicentre of a cluster of rock-hewn churches similar to those that surround Wukro or Lalibela. Oddly, however, the opposite is the case. Aside from the subterranean chamber rumoured to lie beneath the sanctuary of Pantaleon Monastery, the only rock-hewn church I'm aware of within day-tripping distance of Axum is the little-known Abba Meta, carved into the eastern wall of a wooded gorge near Dereka, some 9km south of the town centre.

Abba Meta is named after its Roman-born excavator, a rather shadowy 6th-century figure who (like the church itself) is also sometimes referred to as Abba Libanos (not to be confused with Abba Liqanos) and whose name replaces that of Abba Aregawi in some lists of the 'Nine Saints'. Tradition has it that Abba Meta was exiled to Dereka after he accused the Patriarch of the Ethiopian Church of corrupt practices, and spent several years there secluded in a monastic cell – quite possibly one of the artificial caves carved into the cliff above the church that today bears his name. Eventually, the Patriarch received a divine message instructing him to accept Abba Meta's criticisms, and the pardoned priest left Dereka for Gunda Gundo, where he founded a monastery with the support of Emperor Gebre Meskel.

As with many other Tigraian rock churches, Dereka Abba Meta is not as straightforward to visit as it could be. I failed to gain entry on two separate attempts, mainly because no key was available – I'm told that the caretaker priest lives some distance away, is normally absent on Saturdays (market day in Axum), and is a reliable presence only before 09.00 on Sundays and special mass days. Even when he is available to unlock the church, entry is forbidden to women. I have no reliable information about the church interior, but one deacon told me that it consists of a single chamber large enough to seat 100 people, and contains two engraved rock columns but no paintings. According to the same deacon, the artificial caves in the nearby cliff represent failed early attempts to excavate a church into unyielding rock, but to me they look more like disused monastic cells. Even if you fail to enter the church, the surrounding euphorbia-studded rockscapes are quite magnificent, and the lush forest in the gorge – fed by a holy spring – supports plenty of monkeys and birds.

Dereka Abba Meta can be approached to within a few hundred metres by 4x4. From central Axum, follow the Gonder road as far as the Tsehai Berki Hotel, then turn left immediately afterwards, following a dirt road that runs slightly downhill past the stadium and market (both to your right) before it curves through a shallow watercourse to cross the old airstrip after about 700m. About 800m after crossing the airstrip, the road forks, and you need to take the rather rough-looking track to your right. Follow this track for another 5.5km (passing an electric pylon some 2km past the junction), then turn right again at another fork. About 500m further, watch out for the marshy patch in the road – you could easily get bogged down in it, so consider walking – then after another 1km, there is a spot where you can park your car before walking the last stretch to the top of the gorge, from where a short but steep path runs through the base of the gorge to the prominent blue-and-white church door.

FROM AXUM TO ADIGRAT

If you want, the 122km trip between Axum and Adigrat, Tigrai's second largest town, can be done as a straightforward three-to-four-hour drive or bus ride. There are, however, several places of interest along the way, most notably the ruins at Yeha, the ancient clifftop monastery of Debre Damo, and the town of Adwa. Light vehicles run throughout the day between Axum and Adwa, Adwa and Enticcio, Enticcio and Biset, and Biset and Adigrat, so hopping between places of interest is reasonably easy, provided that you're not in a rush!

The road between Axum and Adigrat passes through rugged sandstone terrain. This is most spectacular between Biset and Adigrat, where it climbs to above 3,000m, offering terrific views over terraced slopes and the cliffs of the Hista River Gorge, and then snakes down a mountain pass to Adigrat 600m below.

Adwa

Slightly larger than Axum, and a more important centre of industrial and population growth, the neat little town of Adwa has an attractive setting amid the stark granite hills so typical of Tigrai. Adwa is of limited interest to tourists, but of tremendous significance to Ethiopians: it was in the surrounding hills that Emperor Menelik II defeated the Italian army on 1 March 1896, thereby ensuring that his empire would be the only African state to enter the 20th century as a fully independent entity.

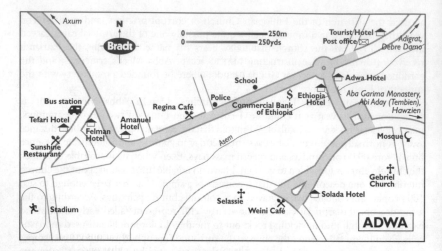

The most likely reason why an independent traveller might want to overnight in Adwa is to get a head start visiting the Yeha ruins the next morning or to pick up early-morning transport southward to Abi Aday. If you do need to spend a night, it is a pleasant enough place, and remarkably unaffected by tourism considering its close proximity to Axum. The main point of interest in the town centre is the Church of Adwa Inda Selassie, which was built by Emperor Yohannis IV and is decorated with some superb late 19th-century murals.

Getting there and away
Adwa lies 22km east of Axum along a good road that is asphalted as far as Axum Airport but unsurfaced thereafter. The drive takes about 20 minutes in a private vehicle, and about 30 minutes in one of the regular minibuses that nip backwards and forwards between the two towns throughout the day. There is plenty of transport from Adwa east through to Adigrat, Mekele and points along the main road in between. One bus daily connects Adwa to Mekele via Abi Aday, leaving Adwa at around 06.00 and passing through Abi Aday about five hours later (see also the boxes *To Lalibela via Sekota* and *Axum to Hawzien via Maryam Wukro* on pages 338 and 283 respectively).

Where to stay and eat
Tefari Hotel ☎ 034 7710828. Situated on the outskirts of town next to the bus station, this is ostensibly the best hotel in Adwa, charging birr 50 for a slightly rundown en-suite room with a ¾ bed and hot shower, or birr 25 for a room using the common shower. No food is served, but the Sunshine Restaurant next door serves the usual local dishes, while snacks and pastries are available at the Regina Café, 300m back towards the town centre.
Tourist Hotel About the best of the more central lodgings, this place charges birr 20 for a clean room with a ¾ bed and common cold shower.
Weini Café Situated in the town centre below Inda Selassie Church, this small café serves decent pastries, juice and coffee.

Madera Abba Garima
The monastery of Abba Garima at Madera, 5km east of Adwa as the crow flies, was founded during the 6th century by the eponymous number of the 'Nine Saints'. According to legend, Abba Garima was of royal Byzantine birth, and he served as the reluctant king of his homeland for seven years before Abba Pantaleon summoned him to

evangelise in Axum. There he arrived three hours later, on the back of the Archangel Gabriel. The monastery of Abba Garima was reputedly built by the Emperor Gebre Meskel, and its namesake lived there for about 20 years, performing miracles and healing the sick, until one day he ascended to the sky and was never seen again. A holy spring on the hill above the monastery is said to have started life when Abba Garima spat on the spot from where it emerges.

More recently, it was from Abba Garima that Menelik II observed the Italian troops as they approached Adwa prior to Ethiopia's decisive victory over the aspirant colonists in 1896. A year later, Ras Alula, the Governor of Hamasien and accomplished military tactician who famously defeated a contingent of 500 Italian troops at Dogali in present-day Eritrea in January 1887, died at Abba Garima of wounds sustained at the Battle of Adwa. Ras Alula's modest tomb still stands outside the rear entrance of the church, and several of his possessions are now held in the treasury.

The church at Abba Garima is said to be 1,500 years old. It looks far newer than that, but the twin stelae and bowl-like rocks that stand in front of its main door might well date to Axumite times. Abba Garima is today best known for its treasury, which contains a fantastic collection of ancient crowns, crosses and other artefacts donated by various emperors and nobles over the centuries, including a silver cross with gold inlays that once belonged to Gebre Meskel, and the crown of Zara Yaqob. The extensive library includes an illuminated gospel supposedly written and illustrated in one day by Abba Garima himself (it's probably not *quite* that ancient, but some experts reckon it dates to the 8th century, which would make it the oldest-known manuscript in Ethiopia), as well as an equally antiquated history of the monastery's early days written by a priest called Hawi. Stored somewhat perversely in the midst of these treasures is a modern wall clock of the sort you'd find in any suburban Western kitchen – when I asked what it was doing there, I received the deadpan answer that it was yet another precious item the church had received as a gift!

Abba Garima lies about 10km from Adwa by road. To get there, follow the Adi Abay road southeast from Adwa for 7km, and then take the rough 3km track signposted to your left. Women are not permitted to enter the church or the treasury, but the priests will sometimes take the most important treasures outside to show female visitors. Equally, sometimes they won't. Male visitors are sometimes welcome to look around the church and treasury, but on other occasions they may be refused entry to one or the other – or to both – unless they can produce a letter of authority. It could well be that your willingness to pay more than the official church entry fee of birr 20 is the determining factor – you may be asked as much as birr 100 to see the Gospel of Abba Garima, which is stored in a glass container to protect from further wear and tear! But the set-up does come across as rather whimsical, so as one reader notes: 'Be warned – you could be in for a lot of fuss for a very meagre result!'

Yeha

Not so much a village today as a small cluster of rustic stone houses, Yeha was once the most important city in Tigrai. Situated about 50km northeast of Axum, the ruined city was founded at least 2,800 years ago, and it served as the capital of a pre-Axumite empire called Damot for centuries prior to being usurped by Axum circa 100BC. The relationship between the two ancient Tigraian capitals is little understood. Rock-hewn tombs similar to those of King Basen in Axum demonstrate that Yeha had its own dignitaries and rulers. But it is a matter for conjecture whether Yeha and Axum were always independent political entities, or whether one town ruled over the other. What is clear is that by the time the Axumite Empire entered its most influential period, Yeha was a town of little political significance.

Yeha's single most remarkable antiquity is a well-preserved stone temple that stands 12m high, consists of up to 52 layers of masonry, and was built at least 2,500 years ago.

Nobody knows what religion was originally practised in the temple, but appearances suggest links with the pagan faith of the Sabaean civilisation of south Arabia and inscriptions refer to a deity called Ilmukah. The large statues of plump, dreadlocked women found at Yeha and other contemporary sites (now mostly housed in the National Museum in Addis Ababa) indicate a fertility cult of sorts, and the abundant engravings of ibex suggest this animal was of some religious significance.

One of the reasons why the temple at Yeha is in such good condition is that it became the centre of a monastic Christian community in the early 6th century. This church was founded by Abba Afse, one of the 'Nine Saints', who was guided there by an angel after having spent 12 years living at the monastery of Abba Garima. It seems entirely credible that the high stone monastery surrounding the ancient temple dates to this era; certainly it boasts one of the most remarkable treasure houses of any Ethiopian church, containing many ancient illuminated manuscripts and crowns. In addition to the temple and church treasures, Yeha is attractive for its scenic surrounds and characteristically Tigraian sandstone homesteads.

The turn-off to Yeha is clearly signposted on the left side of the Adigrat road some 27km past Adwa. Yeha lies 5km north of the main road. Light vehicles travelling between Adwa and Enticcio will be able to drop you at the turn-off, and to pick you up later in the day. There is no public transport to Yeha itself, but there's enough tourist traffic that you'd be unlucky not to get a lift in at least one direction – if the worst comes to the worst, it takes about 90 minutes to reach the site on foot. An early start is recommended to ensure you don't get stuck along the roadside, and be warned that it can get very hot, so you ought to carry some water if you are thinking of walking. There is no restriction on women visiting the church, and an entrance fee of birr 20 coves both this and the old temple. A small 'resort' next to the church car park serves basic meals and cold drinks – and if you are really desperate for somewhere to crash, it also offers very basic accommodation for birr 5.

Enticcio

This small town on the Inguya River lies on the Adigrat road about 12km east of the Yeha turn-off. If you end up spending the night, your best bet is the Debre Damo Hotel, a friendly double-storey lodge whose owner speaks good English and charges birr 15 for a basic but clean room with a ¾ bed and common showers. Food and drinks are also available at the hotel. Transport out of Enticcio is easy to find in either direction.

Debre Damo Monastery

The monastery of Debre Damo is notable for its 6th-century Axumite stone church, as well as for its impregnable clifftop position. The isolated monastery lies on a 3,000m-high *amba* (flat-topped hill) covering an area of 0.5km² and surrounded by sheer cliffs. It is something of a mystery how the founder of the monastery, Abba Aregawi, reached the top, and also how the monks carried up the stones with which the church was built. One tradition has it that a flying serpent carried the founding monk to the top. It is also said that Abba Aregawi's disciple, Tekle Haymanot, sprouted wings to escape when the Devil cut the rope on which he was climbing up – after which he was able to make regular flying trips to Jerusalem! Today, the only way to reach Debre Damo – unless you happen to have a helicopter or flying serpent to hand – is by ascending a 15m-high cliff with the aid of a leather rope.

The double-storey main church, named after Abba Aregawi, is widely regarded to be the oldest extant non-rock-hewn church in Ethiopia. Legend has it that it was built by Aregawi himself, but much of it probably dates to the 10th and 11th centuries, and it was refurbished in the 1950s under the direction of David Buxton, a leading expert on Axumite architecture. The architecture shows strong Axumite influences, built up with layers of thick wood and whitewashed stone, and the wooden ceiling is decorated with animal engravings. Note that only the portal and narthex are open to the public.

Other ancient buildings include a secondary church, built on the spot where Abuna Aregawi is said to have vanished into thin air at the end of his mortal existence. Near this church is a number of rock-hewn tombs. On the main cliff there are several cramped hermit caves, the inhabitants of which subsist on bread and water lowered from the monastery by rope. In 1540, the Emperor Lebna Dengal, in exile after his defeat by Ahmed Gragn, died at Debre Damo. It is also said that the 6th-century Axumite ruler Gebre Meskel is buried at the monastery. Debre Damo, like Gishen Maryam after it, served for some centuries as a place of imprisonment for princes with a claim to the imperial throne. When Queen Yodit overthrew Axum, she reputedly massacred all the princes at Debre Damo – up to 400 of them according to some accounts.

Debre Damo lies 11km north of the Adigrat road, along a poorly signposted turn-off some 24km east of Enticcio, 6km west of Biset, and 37km from Adigrat. In a private vehicle, the monastery can easily be visited as a day trip out of Axum, Adwa or Adigrat, or en route between Axum and Adigrat. If you are renting a vehicle for the express purpose of visiting Debre Damo, Adigrat is likely to be the cheapest option – expect to pay around birr 300 for a 4x4 or minibus as compared to around birr 900 from Axum or Adwa.

There is no formal public transport along the road to Debre Damo, so most backpackers catch a bus between Adigrat and Adwa, ask to be dropped at the turn-off, and improvise from there. You could also visit the monastery out of Biset, where there are a few hotels, all fairly basic – the first hotel to the left as you enter town from the direction of Adwa has been recommended as clean and friendly, and the attached restaurant serves good *tibs*. Once at the junction, hitching or otherwise finding a lift certainly isn't out of the question, indeed many travellers get lucky in both directions, but nor can it be guaranteed. So be prepared for a long, hot 11km walk in either direction, take plenty of water, sunblock and a hat, and also maybe some food. If you need to, you can sleep at the monastery, but no food is available, the drinking water is dubious, and the insects are prolific.

Before ascending to Debre Damo, you will need to pay a fee to the priest who pulls the strings – birr 50 is the official non-negotiable rate, and a tip may also be expected. Women are forbidden from visiting Debre Damo, and prospective male visitors should expect to be interrogated about their faith before being allowed to visit.

ADIGRAT

Adigrat is the second largest town in Tigrai, with a population of around 70,000, and it stands at the pivotal junction of the roads to Axum, Mekele and Asmara, the capital of Eritrea. It's a bustling, friendly, rather cosmopolitan town, where plenty of English is spoken, and it has strong historical and cultural links to Eritrea. Since the recent war with Eritrea, in which Adigrat played a frontline role, it might be expected to have suffered economically through the loss of cross-border trade, but business appeared to be booming in 2005 and the town had visibly expanded since my previous visit four years earlier. Economically buoyant though it might be, Adigrat offers little in the way of sightseeing, but its distinctively Tigraian character and wonderful mountain setting make it an easy place to settle into for a night or two.

The busy market is definitely worth visiting. It's a good place to buy Tigraian coffeepots and local cloths as well as the nationally renowned honey that comes from Alitena. Just behind the market lies Adigrat Chirkos Church, covered in fine 19th-century paintings depicting angels and with a balcony offering a great view over the town. There is also a large Catholic church which bears a strong resemblance to a church in Florence. Equally unusual is the new Medhane Alem Church, a rectangular sandstone

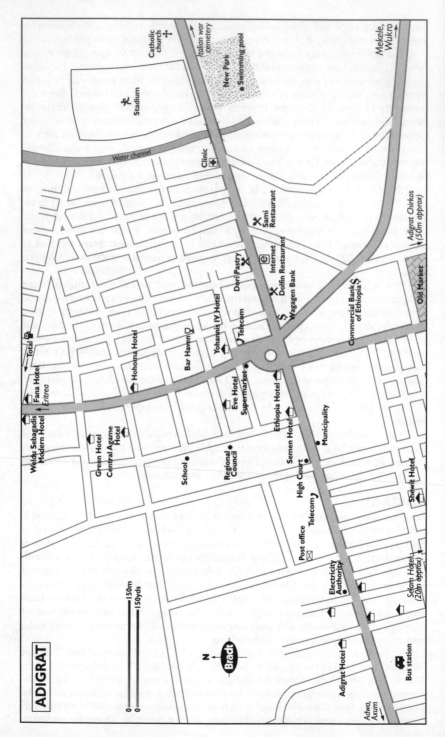

building that more closely resembles a fort than any other church I've seen in Ethiopia. The park between the main roundabout and the Catholic Church has been developed as a recreational centre with a swimming pool, albeit one predictably bereft of water when I last dropped in! Coming from Axum, Adigrat also boasts relatively good internet facilities – the café on the ground floor of the Green Hotel is recommended.

Adigrat would serve as a good base for exploring some of the rock-hewn churches described in the next chapter. It is closer to most of these churches than is Mekele, and even without a private vehicle, it could be used as a base from which to visit churches along the main Mekele road as far south as Wukro. Aside from the rock churches covered in the next chapter, there are a couple more that lie very near to Adigrat. The closest, **Mayaba Samuel**, was badly burnt at some unspecified time in the past and has since fallen into disuse. It is basically an extended cavern, about 2.5m high but with a very low entrance. A few paintings survived the fire, including an orange painting of Christ. The church is in a rock face in the hills west of the Mekele road, and takes less than an hour to walk to from the town centre. You will probably need a guide to find it.

In the village of Kirsaba, about 7km along the Asmara road, **Mikael Kirsaba** is rather unusual in that it consists of a modern church with an older four-chambered rock-hewn church built underneath it. The story goes that the original church (excavated in the 5th century by the horns of an agitated bull, if the local priests are to be believed) was doused with petrol by the Italians on their way to Adwa in 1896, but that the petrol miraculously turned to water before the church could be set aflame. The waterlogged church was not drained because the water was regarded as holy, so a new church was built above it by Menelik II. Any vehicle heading towards Asmara will be able to drop you at Kirsaba, but be aware that women are forbidden from entering the church, the priest with the key is often difficult to locate, he may well demand you produce one of those letters of authority deemed redundant by the Tigrai Tourist Commission – and even if you surmount all these obstacles, there is really very little to see other than a gloomy, waterlogged pit and some attractive 20th-century paintings.

Getting there and away
There are good bus connections between Adigrat, Axum and Mekele. (The Asmara bus service is curtailed in the aftermath of the border war, but should resume as and when the border reopens.) In addition to buses which start their trip in Adigrat, buses between Mekele and Axum or Asmara pass through Adigrat en route, generally in the mid morning, so there is less pressure than normal to get an early start.

A variety of light vehicles run throughout the day between Adigrat and more local destinations such as Sinkata, Wukro and Biset.

Where to stay
Moderate
Hohama Hotel (20 rooms) ☎ 034 4452469. This new hotel is comfortably the smartest option in Adigrat, and also the best value since it doesn't seem to charge a discriminatory *faranji* price at the time of writing (though this might change). A neat compact motel-style room with a proper dbl bed, television, and en-suite hot shower costs birr 50, while larger mini-suites cost birr 60. The ground-floor restaurant has a good range of local and Western dishes in the birr 10–15 range, and is one of the few places in town to serve meat during fasting periods.

Budget
Weldu Sebagadis Modern Hotel (24 rooms) ☎ 034 4450275; e helenzz2002@yahoo.com. This long-serving and friendly travellers' favourite charges birr 60 for a large, clean room with ¾ bed and en-suite hot shower, or birr 30 for similar rooms using a common shower. The restaurant serves *faranji* and local dishes in the birr 8–12 range. It is a good place to try *tholoh*, a dish specific to

IROB COUNTRY

Extracts from a letter from Dr Ann Waters-Bayer

As my work is in agricultural development and as the vast majority of Ethiopians live from agriculture, I feel that too little attention was paid to this subject in your book. Ethiopia is a centre of genetic diversity and domestication of plants and animals, and it has a great wealth of indigenous knowledge and expertise in soil and water management, as well as a long history of animal traction, something that is quite unusual for sub-Saharan Africa. Last year I travelled on foot in northeastern Tigrai, in the vicinity of Alitena near the Eritrean border on the rugged escarpment leading down from the highlands to the Red Sea, and marvelled at the way that the local Saho-speaking Irob people are capturing soil with dry-stone walls and creating agricultural land where there was none before, in the midst of bare rock. The Irob are benefiting from erosion on the high plateau, and doing their best to capture soil before it disappears into the Red Sea.

During my wanderings in this area, I came across Catholic churches in Alitena, Aiga, Weratle and Magauma. They are fine stone buildings and like Catholic churches everywhere they seem disproportionately large for the surrounding population. But on the occasion of major holidays, it is amazing how full the churches become. The services are seemingly interminable. When I was there, a new stone church was being built by villagers in Ado Burra, just below Mount Asimba, a wild and forested area that had served as the secret natural fortress of the Tigraian People's Liberation Front. On the other side of Mount Asimba is the ancient Ethiopian Orthodox church of Gunda Gundo, which for travellers who have not already got as far as Mount Asimba is most easily approached from the south via Adigrat, Edaga Hamus and Suba Sa'essi.

It is possible to get to Alitena by 4x4 along a road built 30 years ago by local people with their bare hands. It leads from Salembessa on the surfaced road from Adigrat to Asmara (the capital of Eritrea). Besides the huge Catholic church in Alitena, it is interesting to see the small chapel built by the French missionaries when they started their work in Tigrai in 1846. It is situated in the mission overlooking the town. On the opposite side of town, beside the church, is the sisters' convent and a beautiful Montessori kindergarten. In the area around Alitena and other parts of the Adigrat diocese, the local people have done impressive work in building footpaths – laying down stone, building up stone along cliff faces, or cutting the path directly into the cliff using only hammer and chisel. For anybody wanting to walk for several days through a spectacular landscape, perhaps with a donkey or mule to carry the load, these footpaths make the going much easier. In Alitena there are several young men and women with 12 years of schooling who speak English and would gladly serve as guides for walking tours. Indeed, I hope this is one income-generating activity that they will be able to build up over time.

We ate fondue-like *tholoh* when we stayed in Irob farmers' homes during our visits to mountain hamlets. Another local delicacy is the pure white honey from Alitena, which can be bought in Adigrat market and is well known throughout Ethiopia.

Note from PB – Subsequent to Ann's time in the area, Irob country was one of the parts of Ethiopia most affected by the war with Eritrea.

this part of Ethiopia which is eaten like Swiss fondue – small balls of cooked barley are taken on the tip of a forked stick and dunked into a spicy sauce thick with butter and yoghurt!

Central Agame Hotel ☏ 034 4452466. This decent new hotel seems relatively overpriced at birr 80 for a clean and quite spacious room with ¾ bed, television and en-suite hot shower. The restaurant is good.

Shewit Hotel ☏ 034 4453028. This rather scruffy hotel is in the same price range as all the above and has the solitary advantage over them of lying much closer to the bus station. Otherwise, the basic rooms with ¾ bed cost birr 60 with en-suite shower or birr 40 without – put it this way, in terms of value for money, remove the two middle letters and you've hit the nail on the head!

Eve Hotel ☏ 034 4451933. The neat en-suite rooms with hot water and TV cost birr 40–50/80–100 sgl/dbl occupancy – quite good value for lone travellers but not much of a bargain for couples.

Shoestring

Selam Hotel ☏ 034 4450385. Conveniently located a block or two from the bus station, this three-storey hotel is clean, friendly and decent value at birr 25 (negotiable) for a room with ¾ bed using spotless common showers.

Ethiopia Hotel This stalwart cheapie is still the pick in its price range – true, a few readers have compared it unfavourably to the hotels above, but this seems unfair when it charges a quarter of the price. An adequate room with a ¾ bed and en-suite cold shower costs birr 15, while one using lukewarm common showers cost birr 10. The restaurant no longer functions.

Yohannis IV Hotel ☏ 034 4450284. Situated opposite the Ethiopia Hotel, this charges birr 15 for a room with a ¾ bed and common shower.

Semen Hotel Amongst the usual giddying selection of knock-shop-cum-budget-dives, this merits recognition for its unintentional honesty!

Where to eat

The smarter hotels listed above all serve good food, though only the Hohama serves meat during fasting periods. The **Sami Restaurant** is the best standalone eatery, serving a variety of local meat, fish and vegetarian dishes. Between meals, the **Dori Pastry and Bakery** was for some years the only pastry shop in Adigrat, but it has recently been joined by the **Yohannis IV Café** on the ground floor of the eponymous hotel – both places serve cakes, bread, juice and coffee. The **Hwalti Hotel** has been recommended for good vegetarian and meat *tholoh*.

St Mary of Zion Cathedral

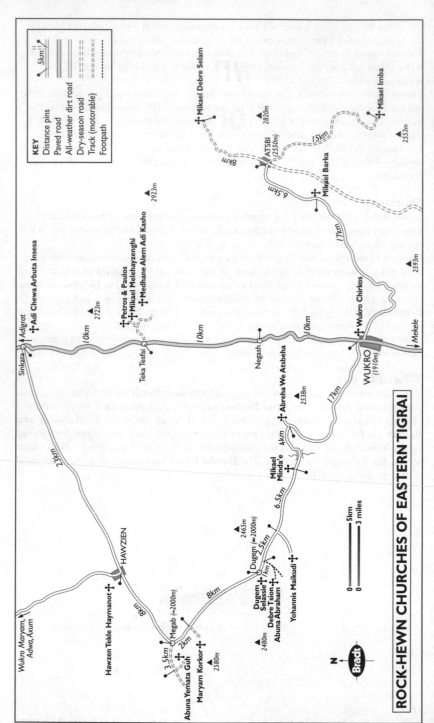

ROCK-HEWN CHURCHES OF EASTERN TIGRAI

Rock-hewn Churches of Northeast Tigrai

The epithet of 'best-kept secret' has been applied to so many modern mediocrities that it seems ludicrously inadequate when confronted by religious sanctuaries as magnificently obscure as the churches carved into the sandstone cliffs of Tigrai. Practically unknown to other Ethiopians – let alone the outside world – before 1966, the rock-hewn churches of Tigrai have been described by the British academic Ivy Pearce as 'the greatest of the historical-cultural heritages of the Ethiopian people'. Most of these architectural gems remain in active use today, several house paintings and other sacred medieval artefacts, and every one of them is imbued with an aura of spirituality that seeps from the very rock into which they are carved.

The rock-hewn churches of Tigrai do not function primarily as tourist attractions. A select crop of about 20 churches is described in brochures compiled by the Tigrai Tourist Commission (TTC). The most popular and accessible of these churches might be visited by outsiders once or twice a week, the rest perhaps every two or three months. As for the rest – well, it would not surprise me to learn that half of the rock-hewn churches in Tigrai have gone unseen by foreigners since the 1974 revolution. Visits by foreigners are generally tolerated, sometimes welcomed, and occasionally met with visible distrust. Fortunately, because the Tigraian churches are more scattered and less accessible than their counterparts at Lalibela, it's difficult to envisage their spiritual integrity ever being threatened by coaches full of prying tourists.

Sensitivity towards an older way of life is a prerequisite for exploring the Tigraian churches. So, too, is patience and humour. Many of the priests are rigidly bureaucratic, and refuse to entertain visitors without written authority from the tourist office (easily obtained!). Others will not allow foreigners into their churches during mass, nor, as is customary in Ethiopia, will they open up the church if a mass has already been held on that day. At more inaccessible churches, the priests are understandably loath to undertake the long trek up from the plains unless a large pre-agreed tip is added to the official entrance fee. Then there is the small matter of locating the priest who keeps the key, an obstacle we failed to surmount on first attempt at perhaps half of the churches we visited.

With sufficient time, and a philosophical frame of mind, exploring these churches is likely to be a highlight of any trip through Ethiopia. True, none of the individual churches compares in architecture or impact to the complex at Lalibela. But, balanced against this, these remote churches do retain an aura of isolation and mystery that many people – I am not one of them – feel Lalibela has sacrificed as it has grown in accessibility and popularity. Furthermore, it is in Tigrai, more than anywhere else, that one is confronted by the radical nature of Ethiopian Christianity. During mass, or at festivals, these remarkable rock edifices witness scenes straight out of the Bible: white-robed worshippers chanting and swaying in prayer, prostrating themselves before the altar, or standing outside the church sharing thick, rough *injera* and beakers of alcoholic *t'ella*. This, one senses, is Christianity much as it would have been practised before the Vatican was built, before Martin Luther or Henry VIII, before Billy Graham – an almost surreal reminder that the religion we associate with American televangelism and quaint European country churches is at root every bit as Middle Eastern as Islam or Judaism. It is utterly fantastic!

Many of the Tigraian rock churches lie along the main road between Adigrat and Mekele, or can be visited from it. Four main clusters are covered in this chapter, of which the churches that lie along the main road between Sinkata and Wukro are the most accessible to those without private transport or limited time. The pick of these churches is undoubtedly Adi Kasho Medhane Alem, part of the highly accessible Teka Tesfai cluster 10km south of Sinkata. A second rather loose cluster consists of Wukro Chirkos – the most accessible of all the Tigraian churches, as it lies 500m from the main road in the town of Wukro – and the magnificent Abreha we Atsbeha church along the Hawzien road. The most extensive cluster is found in the Gheralta region, which lies to the south of Hawzien and includes some of the most stunningly situated churches anywhere in Ethiopia. Gheralta can easily be explored out of Hawzien with a vehicle, or over a few days of hiking, bearing in mind that the region's finest churches are reached by long, steep walks that require a fair level of fitness. A fourth and more dispersed cluster lies in the Atsbi area, to the east of Wukro. With one exception, the Atsbi churches can be explored only with a vehicle.

Note that churches may be referred to either by their church name or else by the name of the place where they are situated. Medhane Alem Church at Adi Kasho, for instance, is sometimes referred to as Medhane Alem and sometimes as Adi Kasho. To ease confusion – and it can become very confusing – I've always strung the two names together.

BACKGROUND

It is anybody's guess as to why the rock-hewn churches of Tigrai were so often carved into relatively inaccessible cliff faces – was it for security, or for spiritual isolation, or simply because cliff faces are inherently good places to carve churches, and cliff faces are inherently inaccessible? Certainly, if keeping away outsiders *was* the objective, then the excavators of these churches did an admirable job, judging by the obscurity in which many of these churches languished throughout the first century of regular European presence in Ethiopia. Several 19th-century visitors to Tigrai – for instance Henry Salt, Nathaniel Pierce and Frances Harrison Smith – must have passed within a kilometre of some of these churches without ever suspecting that they existed.

In 1868, the British expedition led by Napier passed through the small Tigraian village of Wukro where they were shown an astonishing church carved into a rocky outcrop. For six full decades after this, it was assumed by the outside world that this church was the only one of its type in Tigrai. In 1928, Dr Enza Parona visited the monastery of Abba Yohanni in the Tembien, and four further churches were 'discovered' and described by Antonio Mordini during the Italian occupation, among them Maryam and Giyorgis Wukro to the southeast of Adwa. The list was added to in 1948, when Beatrice Playne visited several rock-hewn churches in Tigrai, including the formerly undescribed Mikael Imba near Atsbi and Tekle Haymanot in Hawzien. Nevertheless when Sauter published an exhaustive list of all known Ethiopian rock-hewn churches in 1963, fewer than ten were listed for Tigrai.

All of which provides context to the veritable buzz that followed the 1966 Conference of Ethiopian Studies, during which Dr Abba Tewelde Medhin Josief, a Catholic priest from Adigrat, announced the existence of at least 123 rock-hewn churches in Tigrai, more than three-quarters of which were still in active use. Dr Josief died soon afterwards, but his findings were pursued by the Swiss photographer Georg Gerster, who travelled to eight churches (including Petros and Paulos Melehayzenghi, which was apparently overlooked by Josief) to produce a fantastic photographic essay entitled *Rocks of Faith* for the British *Sunday Times*. Over the next three years, the British academics David Buxton, Ivy Pearce and Ruth Plant collectively visited 75 Tigraian rock-hewn churches and published several papers based on their formative research. The most useful of these first appeared in a 1971 issue of the *Ethiopian Observer* (Vol XIII, No 3), which was devoted exclusively to the Tigraian churches and described more than 70 individual churches in full. By 1973, when Ivy Pearce published a supplementary list describing another 17 churches in the *Ethiopian Observer* (Vol XVI, No 1), the full list of confirmed rock-hewn church in Tigrai had been extended to 153, of which all but 26 were still in active use, and several other churches were known of by word of mouth only. The 1974 revolution put paid to any further research in the region, and nothing of consequence has been published about the Tigraian churches since that time. Nor, so far as I'm aware, has any further research been undertaken into the comparative or absolute dating of these fascinating edifices. These pre-revolution publications mentioned above, now long out of print, have all been used extensively in compiling this chapter.

The churches of Tigrai were generally excavated using a very different method to that favoured at Lalibela. The most impressive churches in and around Lalibela were generally created in two phases: first of all a moat-like subterranean trench would be excavated deep into a horizontal rock, then the church itself would be chiselled into the monolithic block of rock created at the centre of the trench. More characteristic of the Tigrai region, however, are churches carved into a vertical cliff face or from an outcrop, the former sometimes expanding onto a ledge where a false entrance has been added. So far as I'm aware, not one monolithic church is to be found in Tigrai, and the only major church that qualifies as a three-quarter monolith (where three full walls have been carved free of the original rock) is Mikael Imba.

The antiquity of most of the Tigraian rock-hewn churches remains largely a matter of conjecture. Every church has its own oral tradition regarding its excavation; in many cases, the church is dated to the rule of Abreha and Atsbeha, the twin emperors of Axum who converted to Christianity in the middle of the 4th century AD. Often, these anecdotal claims are riddled with apparent inconsistencies. In some instances, I was told that a church had been hewn by a specific emperor, but at a date centuries before or after that emperor ruled. At several churches, the traditions related to me personally were very different to those mentioned in the TTC publication about the same church. There seems also to be a competitive element in the traditional accounts. At several of the churches ascribed to Abreha and Atsbeha, the priest told us that the church we were visiting was the first carved by the twin emperors, and mentioned by name other churches that make similar but – according to him – erroneous claims. To anybody who has travelled extensively in Ethiopia, and read widely about the country, such inconsistencies will not be unfamiliar terrain. Nevertheless, it makes it difficult to treat the local traditions very seriously.

It can be said with confidence that the overwhelming majority of the Tigraian churches were excavated prior to the 16th century. Subsequent to his own exploration of the area, David Buxton recognised that many churches in Wukro, Tembien and Gheralta had been accurately located in the writings of the Jesuit priest, Manuel Barradas, who lived in Ethiopia in 1624–40. And, as Ruth Plant points out, it can reasonably be assumed that Christian Ethiopia in the 16th century was too preoccupied with the immediate survival of the empire against the onslaught of Ahmed Gragn to have expended much energy in excavating houses of worship. Beyond this, however, the dating of the churches is open to speculation.

David Buxton, a leading authority on Axumite architecture, has thus far produced the only coherent attempt to place the churches within a formal chronological framework. In a 70-page essay, published in the Italian periodical *Archologia* in 1971, Buxton divides the churches into five broad chronological styles. The earliest style, which he calls Archaic

Ethiopian Basilica and which he ascribes to the 10th and 11th centuries, consists of relatively crude attempts to reproduce the classic built-up Axumite church style in rock. In Buxton's view, the only church that can be placed unambiguously in this prototypical category, based on such archaic features as its colonnaded portico, is Adi Kasho Medhane Alem. He does describe several other superficially similar churches, notably Maryam Hibeti in the Tembien, but reckons that all of them display anachronistic features suggesting they are later imitations.

The next chronological architectural style as identified by Buxton is the Inscribed Cross Church, which peaked in popularity in the 11th and 12th centuries. The layout of all churches in this category consists of a cruciform plan within a larger square, a distinctively Tigraian style that seems to have no obvious precursor in built-up churches. Several of the best-known churches in Tigrai fall clearly into this category, for instance Wukro Chirkos, Mikael Imba and Abreha we Atsbeha (the last described by Buxton as 'the most perfect example of the cross-in-square layout'). Buxton believes that these churches clearly predate the excavations at Lalibela, and raises the intriguing possibility that the Bet Giyorgis in Lalibela, with its uniquely cruciform exterior, is the product of a conscious attempt to externalise the form of an Inscribed Cross Church.

Buxton goes on to describe three further styles, of which the Classic Ethiopia Basilica, a direct architectural progression from the Archaic Ethiopian Basilica, is probably roughly contemporaneous with the churches at Lalibela. The churches in what he refers to as the earlier series of the Tigraian Basilica style, which includes many of those in the Gheralta region, probably date to the 13th and 14th centuries, and thus post-date Lalibela. The later series of Tigraian Basilica includes several churches in the Tembien, the one area where oral tradition and academic opinion are in broad agreement, dating most of the excavations to the 14th- and 15th-century reigns of Emperors Dawit and Zara Yaqob.

An interesting pattern that seems to emerge from Buxton's relative chronology is a broad westward movement in the excavation of Tigraian churches, with those lying to the east of what is now the main Adigrat–Mekele road generally predating the Gheralta churches, which in turn predate those in the Tembien. If that is the case, might not the absolute dating of these churches be linked to the as yet poorly understood shifts of imperial power bases between the collapse of Axum and the rise of Lalibela four centuries later? For that matter, could it not be that some apparent chronological differences are also a reflection of regional variations in style? In this context, it's worth noting that the travelling time between, say, Abi Aday and Atsbi was far greater in previous centuries than it is today, and that many of the churches in question were practically invisible from the outside prior to the recent addition of built-up exteriors. Buxton himself notes that 'both the monolithic church and the elaborated exterior were specialities of Lalibela, and neither the one nor the other was ever adopted as an ideal by the Tigraian rock-hewers'. Much the same might be said for the cross-in-square style which seems to have its epicentre in Wukro, and the various Basilica styles that are predominant farther west.

Another potential stumbling block in dating the churches is that many might have been extended or redecorated one or more times in their history, thereby resulting in apparently anachronistic architectural features. It is clearly the case that many church paintings, though very old, are far more modern than the edifices that house them, while the southern third of Mikael Melehayzenghi is accepted to be a relatively recent addition to a much older church. It is possible, too, that some churches might have started life as partially hewn cave temples in pre-Christian times – a tradition of this sort is attributed locally to the church of Tekle Haymanot in Hawzien. A further circumstantial argument for supposing that some of the rock-hewn churches of Tigrai might have roots in the earliest Christian or even pre-Christian times is the presence of similar, albeit more primitive, rock-hewn tombs in Axum. It seems reasonable to start from the basis that some sort of architectural continuum links Ethiopia's various rock-hewn edifices.

The dates of excavation suggested by Buxton, like those ascribed to the churches by oral tradition, are often quoted as immutable fact. It should be noted, therefore, that Buxton himself takes great pains to emphasise that his chronological scheme is no better than provisional, and he frequently phrases his opinions in the guise of educated guesses. How the churches were excavated is not in question. The broad reason why they were carved will be clear to anybody who visits one of these active shrines of Christian worship today. But as for when, who knows? The temptation to look for reasons why some Tigraian churches might be as old as the traditions claim is irresistible. Yet it is interesting to note that while no suggestion has ever been made that any Ethiopian rock-hewn church dates to the post-Gragn era, at least two such churches (the 'new' Petros and Paulos in Tigrai and a church near Debre Tabor in Amhara) were excavated over the last 20 years. The work of latter-day glory hunters, or evidence that the rock-hewing tradition is not as frozen in the past as people tend to think, who knows? As Ruth Plant wrote in the introduction to the most exhaustive inventory of Tigraian rock-hewn churches yet published, 'it is vital to keep an open mind as to dates'.

BUREAUCRACY

One of the things that makes the rock-hewn churches of Tigrai so absorbing is that they are not primarily tourist attractions, but active sites of worship. The more accessible and publicised churches might go for weeks without being visited by a tourist; there are probably many churches that haven't been seen by as many as a dozen foreigners ever. But, if the remote and often parochial character of the churches enhances the sense of privilege experienced by the occasional visitor, it can also lie at the root of several areas of bureaucratic frustration. Absent priests, silly attempts at overcharging and unnecessary requests for permits are all part and parcel of the Tigraian church experience. All this will be simplified if you are travelling with a vehicle and an Ethiopian (preferably Tigrigna-speaking) guide, though even they may not always be able to locate a priest who's gone walkabout. If you are travelling independently it's probably fair to say that there are no hard and fast rules when it comes to dealing with the issues addressed below – a degree of flexibility and forbearance is a prerequisite!

Finding the priest

At any given church, there is generally only one priest who carries a key for the front door. If that priest isn't around, nobody can get into the church, and that's that. In our experience, the worst time to visit any church is on the local market day (Saturday in Atsbi and the Tembien; Wednesday in Gheralta), when the priest will reliably be off on a shopping spree. It is also the case that while some priests live close to their church, others live some way away, and will almost always never be around except during services. Another factor is that some priests will visit a church dedicated to a particular saint on the day dedicated to that saint, the implication of which is that visiting a church dedicated to St Maryam on St Maryam's Day is a good idea, but any church dedicated to another saint might just be one priest short of an open door.

This isn't complicated enough? Well most priests will not allow tourists into their church during any special mass (which generally runs from about 10.00 to 15.00), and it is customary to lock up the church for the rest of the day after a special mass has been held. In other words, if you want to visit a church on a mass day, then you need to be there before 10.00 to be reasonably certain of gaining entrance.

The net result of all this, based on our visits to the area, is that you've about a 50% chance of getting into any given church on any given day. With a vehicle, you can at least establish when the priest is likely to be around and return later. Without one, your best bet is to try to establish in advance whether there is any reason why the priest is likely not to be at the church that you intend to visit. This, I'm afraid, is far from foolproof.

Permits

Assuming key availability, all rock-hewn and other historically significant churches in Tigrai are officially open to any foreigner on a payment of the set fee of birr 20 per person. The only officially sanctioned exceptions to this ruling are Axum's Maryam Tsion and Debre Damo, which charge birr 60 and 50 respectively, and those (mostly monastic) churches that are off-limits to all women. Unfortunately, however, many priests in Tigrai will still refuse entry to foreigners who don't arrive in the company of a badge-wearing guide employed by the Tigrai Tourist Commission (TTC) or bearing an official letter of introduction from the same organisation. Until recently, the TTC would issue such a letter on demand, but they will no longer do so, on the basis that it is not officially required. Unfortunately, however, it is the opinion of the individual priest which carries most weight on the ground. And it remains the case that some priests *will* ask for a letter of introduction, and will either refuse entry to visitors without one, or will treat their lack of official TTC sanction as justification to ask more than the official TTC entrance fee.

It's a classic numbskull bureaucratic stand-off, and unfortunately the biggest loser is any traveller who undertakes a substantial drive and/or hike to a remote church unaccompanied by a TTC guide, only to be refused entry or to be forced to endure the sort of protracted argument about payment that can ruin an outing. There are no hard and fast rules with regard to this, but based on my experience, you may well require official TTC sanction (in the form of a badge-wearing guide or a letter) to enter any church to the west of the main Adigrat–Mekele road (which includes all the Gheralta and Tembien churches), but are unlikely to do so at churches lying to the east of this road (which includes the Teka Tesfai and Atsbi churches, as well as Wukro Chirkos and Adi Chewa). Exceptions to this rule include Gebriel Tsilalmao, where a permit may be required, and Hawzien Tekle Haymanot and Abreha Atsbeha, to the west of the road, where it may not. It goes without saying that our experience may not be definitive, and that this situation could change – for better or for worse – at any time. It is also the case that travellers accompanied by a non-TTC guide who speaks Tigrigna (or better still hails from Tigrai) are more likely to gain the co-operation of the mostly Tigraian priests than those who don't.

Fees

The official fee for entering any church is birr 20. The reality is not quite so straightforward. Many of the churches now ask a starting fee of birr 30–50. We were successfully able to negotiate this down to birr 20 in all cases, but the bad humour with which some of these negotiations were conducted cast a shadow over the experience. In addition to the entrance fee, for which you should in theory be given a receipt, the priest who shows you around will normally expect a tip of birr 10–20, and he may ask for this before you go into the church. At churches where the priest has to walk with you for 30 minutes or longer before actually reaching the church, the tip is thoroughly deserved. A couple of the priests we encountered were grumpy and obstructive, and we refused to tip them.

Worth noting here that in addition to tipping the priest himself, you will be expected to slip a note to the person who locates the priest, and in the direction of anybody you photograph in or around the churches. Local kids who offer to carry your daypack or any other luggage will also expect a tip. So, too, come to think of it, may anybody else who accompanies you to the church, whether or not they actually contributed to the expedition.

Guides

The churches at Wukro, Sinkata, Hawzien and Teka Tesfai can easily be visited using public or private transport, with no strenuous legwork involved. A guide will be helpful to visit some of these churches, but it is not necessary to take one, and casual arrangements can be made locally. The other churches in the region require greater effort and/or expense to visit. Even if you generally prefer to travel independently, there are several reasons why you might think about arranging for a knowledgeable guide to accompany you. Firstly, there are no reliable maps of the region. Secondly, it can be very time consuming finding the priest who keeps the key unless you speak Amharigna (or better Tigrigna). Finally, assuming you take an official TTC guide, you are unlikely to be refused entrance to any churches, or to be pressured into paying an exorbitant unofficial entrance fee. For the Gheralta, Atsbi or Abi Aday churches, it is possible to arrange a guide locally, but you can be more certain of an experienced, knowledgeable guide by hiring one through the TTC office in Mekele or Wukro at a fixed cost of birr 100 per day.

Most churches can be approached in a 4x4 vehicle (though as they tend to be on cliffs, you will always have to walk the final stretch). You can hire a vehicle in advance out of Addis Ababa, or else fly or bus to Mekele and arrange to have a vehicle meet you there. Alternatively, the TTC office in Wukro can arrange minibus or 4x4 hire to visit Gheralta or Atsbi for around birr 500 per day.

In order to see the interior of any of these churches properly, you need a torch or a candle. Don't forget to bring a torch, some food and water, and a stash of change for tips and church entrance fees! Readers are urged to resist the temptation to use flash photography on old paintings, as repeated exposure to a flash can damage them – in any event, the combination of ambient light and a tripod will generally produce far richer colours and more atmospheric results.

Further information

For further information, particularly regarding less frequently visited churches, the TTC offices in Mekele and Wukro are usually knowledgeable, enthusiastic and helpful. For contact details, see the *Wukro* and *Mekele* listings on pages 287 and 297 respectively. The TTC also stocks a detailed series of pamphlets about the churches, one dedicated to each of the main clusters. Note, however, that the 1:50,000 maps of the region compiled by the Ethiopian Map Authority are notoriously unreliable. The map in this book, though not definitive, is the most reliable in print.

THE ADIGRAT–WUKRO ROAD

The most accessible rock-hewn churches in Tigrai are the seven that lie within easy walking distance of the main road between Adigrat and Mekele. With a private vehicle, it would be possible to check out most of these churches over the course of a long day driving between Adigrat and Mekele. Even on public transport you could probably see most of them over two days, spending a night en route at Sinkata, Negash or Wukro, the main towns along this road.

Four of the churches along this road are clustered within about 2km of each other east of Teka Tesfai: the 'new' and 'old' Petros and Paulos Melehayzenghi, Mikael Melehayzenghi, and Medhane Alem Adi Kasho. The last of these churches is regarded to be the oldest and one of the finest churches in Tigrai by some authorities, and the whole cluster makes for such a rewarding half-day walking excursion that it is worth looking at even if you visit no other church in the region. Two further churches, Gebriel Tsilalmao and Adi Chewa, lie to the north of Teka Tesfai, about 20 minutes' walk from the main road. Both are isolated from other rock-hewn churches, and are less attractive to travellers with limited time than the Teka Tesfai cluster. The last of the seven churches is Wukro Chirkos, which lies on the outskirts of the town of Wukro, and is covered under *Wukro* on page 287.

Idaga Hamus

This is an unremarkable small town straddling the main Mekele road roughly 20km south of Adigrat. About 1km south of town, 100m east of the main road and visible from it, is what appears to be an abandoned and partially collapsed rock-hewn church. It's not the most riveting example of the architectural style, it has to be said, but on the other hand there is no charge for taking a quick poke around. The Behre Negash Hotel on the main junction in Idaga Hamus looks a more appealing prospect than any other hotel between Adigrat and Wukro. Note, too, that the 6th-century monastery of Gunda Gundo Maryam, signposted blithely to the left as you enter town from the Adigrat side, is actually the best part of half a day's travelling distance away in either direction, first by road, then by muleback or on foot!

Gebriel Tsilalmao

The most northerly extant church close to the main Adigrat–Mekele road is Gebriel Tsilalmao, which lies about 3km north of the small village of Mai Megelta. It is a reasonably large church of unknown antiquity, supported by unusually thick cruciform columns with double-bracket capitals covered in recent-looking paintings – when I asked the priest whether the artwork was new or restored, the priest said simply that it had always been there! Other notable features include the neatly cut arches, the engraved roofs of the six bays, two windows cut in Axumite style, an entrance with a built-up porch, and a large room in the back bisected by a column. A pair of evidently disused hermit cells is carved into the outer wall.

To reach Gebriel Tsilalmao, look out for the clearly signposted turn-off to the east roughly 8km south of Idaga Hamus or 8km north of Sinkata. Follow this track eastward for 2km, crossing a seasonal area of marsh, into a narrow gorge ringed by steep wooded hills. The church lies immediately to your right, less than five minutes' walk up a staircase. The priest lives about 30 minutes' walk away, and if he isn't around when you arrive, you might have to wait for somebody to fetch him. You can distract yourself by exploring the riparian woodland around the church and permanent marsh patch on the opposite side of the gorge; the trees harbour grivet monkeys, squirrels and numerous birds (look out for the gorgeous white-cheeked turaco), while Rouget's rail appears to be resident in the marsh. Be warned that when we last visited this church in 2001, we were asked to show a permit.

Sinkata and Adi Chewa Arbuta Insesa

Situated 36km south of Adigrat at the junction of the Mekele road and the side road to Hawzien (see *Hawzien and the Gheralta Churches*, page 281), Sinkata is a quietly attractive village of stone houses, looked over by sandstone cliffs to the east, and offering stunning views over the Gheralta plains. There's plenty of transport through Sinkata along the main road, but transport to Hawzien is erratic and might leave at any time – or not at all! There are a few basic hotels in Sinkata charging a standard birr 6 for a room. The **Ma'ereb Hotel** on the main road looks about the best, and has a common shower and friendly atmosphere. The **Walwalo Hotel**, one block from the main road, also looks OK.

Immediately east of Sinkata, the rock-hewn church of **Arbuta Insesa** (The Four Animals) at **Adi Chewa** can easily be reached on foot or by vehicle from the village. This is a large church with several unusual features, most notably a domed ceiling almost 5m in height (the deepest of its kind in any Tigraian church) and strange red-and-yellow stencil-like figures on the thick columns. There are also more typical paintings in the church. To get to the Arbuta Insesa by road, follow the Mekele road south of town for about 500m, then turn left on to a side road directly opposite the signpost for 'World Vision Ethiopia'. After 800m, you'll hit a T-junction where you need to turn right, from where it's another 1km to the base of the cliff. The church lies about 20m up the cliff face, and it can be reached in less than five minutes along a moderately steep footpath. If you are walking from Sinkata, you could cut through the village and walk directly across the fields to the church in 20 minutes – the whitewashed exterior and bright-green door will be clearly visible as soon as you've crossed the first rise at the edge of the village.

The Teka Tesfai cluster

Also known as Tsaeda Imba, this is the most accessible cluster of churches in Tigrai, sited only 2km east of the main Adigrat–Mekele road. There is no accommodation in the immediate vicinity, though rooms are available in nearby Sinkata and Negash. The cluster is easily visited as a day trip from either Adigrat or Wukro on public transport, and could be covered as a day trip from Mekele in a private vehicle. It consists of three old churches and one new one, each very different and all within 2km of each other.

The finest of the Teka Tesfai churches is **Medhane Alem Adi Kasho**, described by Ruth Plant as 'one of the truly great churches of the Tigrai'. It is, I think, most impressive for its size and complex architecture. The imposing exterior is cut free from the rock behind, with four columns in front and two large doors, and it is covered in recent but very attractive paintings. The interior has a cathedral-like atmosphere, and the magnificent roof is dense with patterned etchings. Although experts regard Medhane Alem to be less perfectly executed than the churches of Wukro Chirkos and Abreha and Atsbeha, I felt that, along with Mikael Imba, it is the most atmospheric of the Tigraian churches east of Gheralta. For photographers, the airy front cloister offers excellent possibilities for moody interior shots, while the west-facing exterior is ideal for late-afternoon light. Note that the priest here usually asks an entrance fee of birr 30, and is not open to amiable negotiation.

Medhane Alem is quite possibly the oldest rock-hewn church in Tigrai, or anywhere in Ethiopia. Writing in the late 1960s, David Buxton noted that Medhane Alem is 'the only church I know that can be placed with confidence in the earliest category of rock-churches'. Buxton regarded it to combine 'all the features to be expected in a very early Ethiopian church and not a single one that could point to a later date'. Unsurprisingly, one local tradition links the excavation of the church to the time of Abreha and Atsbeha. Rather less expected is a tradition claiming it to be the work of Jesus Christ himself – echoing (or pre-empting) a tradition at Lalibela's Beta Giyorgis, it is said that the holes in the rock path leading to the church were made by Christ's horse. On somewhat firmer academic ground, Buxton regarded Medhane Alem to most likely date to the late 10th or early 11th century, and thought that it formed the Zagwe dynasty's 'earliest-known attempt to copy a Debra-Damo-type church in solid rock'.

Very different in style, **Petros and Paulos Melehayzenghi** lies halfway up a cliff, and it is visible from the main road. Petros and Paulos isn't truly rock-hewn, as only the sanctuary lies within the rock – the rest of the church has been built out on to a ledge. It does, however, boast some fascinatingly primitive paintings of angels and saints, which can be seen clearly because the church has fallen into disuse and the damaged roof lets in a fair amount of light. Reaching the church involves a vertiginous ascent up footholds; this rather tested my not-too-good head for heights, but it is not really dangerous if taken slowly and carefully. The view from the ledge, deep into the heart of Gheralta, is superb. Entrance to the church used to be free, and should really still be since it is disused, but the family which lives at the base of the cliff appears to have taken on the weighty responsibility of collecting a birr 20 fee. It is to be hoped that some of this money will be used to help preserve the paintings, which have faded dramatically as a result of exposure over the past decade.

The original church of Petros and Paulos Melehayzenghi was evidently still in use in the late 1960s, when Ivy Pearce met the priests and was shown 'a large number of very interesting books and manuscripts', as it was a few years later when Paul Henze visited. At some point in the interim, the *tabot* has been moved to the **new Church of Petros and Paulos**, which is carved into the base of the ledge. This church, carved between 1982 and 1996, is the work of Halefom Retta, who claimed to have received instruction from the Archangel Gabriel (when I asked him what motivated him to build the new church, he said that the old one was too difficult for women to reach!). Sadly, the

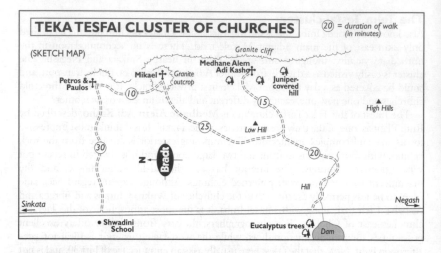

The last of the Teka Tesfai churches is **Mikael Melehayzenghi**, which lies within a domed rock outcrop between Medhane Alem and Petros and Paulos. Very different in execution to any other rock-hewn church I've seen in Ethiopia, Mikael Melehayzenghi is entered via a low doorway, which gives way to a surprisingly large interior with a finely carved dome almost 3m in height. This church is said locally to date to the 8th century, though the southern third was added in the 19th century. A notable decoration is a vivid painting of unknown antiquity that depicts Christ saving Adam and Eve from (or possibly abandoning them to) a pair of ferocious dragon-like creatures at the Last Judgement. The usual birr 20 entrance fee is charged.

Getting there and away

The Teka Tesfai cluster is signposted to the east of the main Adigrat–Wukro road, roughly 10km south of Sinkata and a similar distance north of Negash. To visit it on public transport, ask to be dropped at Shwadini School, where you shouldn't have any difficulty finding somebody to point you in the right direction. You can head out to the churches independently, but it's worth taking a local guide, if only to help locate the priests who keep the church keys, and to avoid getting more involved than necessary with the rather avaricious family that lives at the base of Petros and Paulos. Birr 20–30 seems to be the going rate for one of the youthful guides who will find you before you find them.

From the signpost, you can follow any of several footpaths across the fields towards the cliffs to the east of the road. You'll soon see Petros and Paulos Melehayzenghi halfway up the cliff, and can walk there from the road in 20–30 minutes. From Petros and Paulos, it's a 20-minute walk southward across relatively flat fields to the prominent euphorbia-studded rock outcrop that houses Mikael Melehayzenghi. To reach Medhane Alem from Mikael, continue southwards towards a low rocky hill until you come to a rough semi-motorable track, where you want to cut to your left, over the low hill, to a second, larger hill covered in olive and juniper trees. The track takes you to the base of the second hill. From there, it's a steepish hike along a clear footpath to the top of the hill. The church lies just below the rise, in a grove of olive trees.

Once you've seen Medhane Alem you can return the way you came, but you might prefer to take a short cut (about 40 minutes as opposed to one hour). This involves following the motorable track back to the low hill, where you should take the left fork, and basically follow it straight ahead for ten to 15 minutes until you come to a marshy area and stream. Follow the footpath that runs roughly parallel to the stream until, after about ten minutes, you cross a rocky ridge. The main road is clearly visible from here, as is the dam on the opposite side of it. You shouldn't have a problem picking up a lift from here to Wukro or Sinkata.

With private transport, you can drive right to the base of Petros and Paulos, and to within about 300m of Mikael Melehayzenghi. The motorable track to Adi Kasho has deteriorated in recent years, so that even with a private vehicle, you'll need to walk there from the base of Mikael Melehayzenghi. This takes about 30 minutes, and is reasonably flat except for a final scramble up a 45° rock face.

Negash

Something of an anomaly in the heart of Ethiopia's main concentration of rock-hewn churches is the small hilltop village of Negash, which straddles the main Adigrat–Mekele road about 10km south of Teka Tesfai and 10km north of Wukro. Negash was the site of the first Muslim settlement in Ethiopia, granted to more than 100 early Islamic refugees (including Mohammed's daughter Rukiya and his future wives Uma Habiba and Uma Salama) by the Axumite Emperor Asihima in AD615. The name of the town is an Arabic corruption of the Ethiopian *Negus* (Emperor or King), and may simply have been chosen as a token of thanks by the Muslim refugees. There is, however, an obscure, probably untrue, but nevertheless persistent Muslim tradition that Negus Asihima converted to Islam under the influence of Mohammed, and there is some reason to think he was buried at Negash after his death in AD630.

Ancient Negash may be, and sacred too – some Ethiopian Muslims regard it to be the most holy Islamic town after Mecca – but the town has little to show for it today. The large modern mosque, reputedly built on the site of the 7th-century original, is the target of an annual pilgrimage and festival, but it's nothing to look at. More interesting, assuming that you can find it, is the elusive 7th-century Muslim graveyard that was recently discovered in the town.

You can easily visit Negash as a day trip from Wukro, in tandem with the churches at Teka Tesfai. There are two basic hotels facing each other on the main road about 100m from the mosque.

HAWZIEN AND THE GHERALTA

Looping to the west of the main Adigrat–Mekele road, between Sinkata and Wukro, a well-maintained secondary road runs through the small town of Hawzien, the villages of Megab and Dugem, and the church of Abreha we Atsbeha. More than twice as long as the direct route between Sinkata and Wukro (72km as opposed to 30km), this road passes through a fantastic spaghetti-western landscape of flat dry plains and towering rock outcrops known as the Gheralta. Although it is scenically spectacular, the Gheralta region is most famous for its 35-odd rock-hewn churches, the largest concentration anywhere in Ethiopia. These churches aren't generally regarded to be the oldest or the most architecturally impressive in Tigrai, but they are probably the most captivating to the casual visitor, due to their magnificent setting, atmospheric interiors, and wealth of old paintings and church treasures.

Exploring the Gheralta region is not quite as straightforward as visiting the churches along the main Adigrat–Mekele road. For a start, the region's finest churches are situated in high isolation on the outcrops of the Gheralta ridge. This means that a relatively strenuous ascent is involved in getting to see any given church, and that only the fittest of travellers will be in a position to consider visiting more than two such churches in the course of one day. Another obstacle, unless you travel with a TTC guide, is that some churches might still refuse entry to strangers unless they can produce a letter of authority. That said, with a private vehicle, a Tigrigna-speaking guide, and a reasonable level of fitness, the Gheralta churches are as accessible as anywhere else in Ethiopia.

Independent travel in Gheralta is to some extent restricted by the limited amount of public transport and poor accommodation. These problems, by no means insurmountable, are addressed in further detail below, but it's worth noting upfront that Gheralta will almost certainly prove frustrating to independent travellers who expect something better than shoestring accommodation, or who aren't prepared to approach transportation with a degree of flexibility. On the other hand, Gheralta is practically custom-made for any traveller who is attracted to the prospect of heading off the beaten track into an area as rich scenically as it is culturally.

Getting around

Hawzien is most easily reached along a well-maintained 23km-long side road that branches west from the main Adigrat–Mekele road at Sinkata. The roughly 50km-long road between Hawzien and Wukro through Gheralta is also in a good state of repair, and since all the major Gheralta churches lie within 20km of Hawzien by road, they can easily be explored in a private vehicle using Hawzien as a base. Another possible base for exploring Gheralta with a private vehicle is Wukro, which lies about 30km from Dugem and 40km from Megab, the two villages closest to the best churches. Any one church in the Gheralta could be driven to as a day trip from Adigrat or Mekele, or even en route between these towns. Given that the walk to most of the more important churches takes 30–60 minutes in either direction, it would be unrealistic to attempt to see more than one or maybe two churches in this way.

For travellers dependent on public transport, a few light vehicles and trucks run along the Sinkata–Hawzien road daily. Traffic is heaviest on a Wednesday, the main market day both in Hawzien and in the villages of Gheralta, but this is also when the priests are most likely to be on walkabout. A daily bus service connecting Hawzien to Mekele via Megab, Dugem and Wukro departs at around 06.00 in either direction and will drop you off anywhere en route, though you may have to pay full fare. With a few days available, it would be more than possible to walk from Hawzien to Megab and Dugem, the closest villages to the more interesting churches. Megab lies only 8km from Hawzien by road, and Dugem another 10km towards Wukro; basic rooms are available in both villages, and camping is permitted. If walking doesn't appeal, you could explore the possibility of hiring a bicycle, mule or horse-drawn *gari* out of Hawzien. If you are thinking of hiring a 4x4 vehicle to visit one or two of the Gheralta churches as a day trip, expect to pay around birr 500 for a full day. A vehicle is more easily hired in Wukro than in Hawzien, with the advantage that you could stop at Abreha we Atsbeha church en route (see page 290).

A little-used alternative route to Hawzien and the Gheralta leads from Adwa via Nebelet, the closest town to the remote rock-hewn church of Maryam Wukro. Although the road is rough in parts and requires a 4x4, especially the stretch between Hawzien and Nebelet, you could probably drive between Axum and Hawzien in about five to six hours using this route, adding another two hours for the excursion to Maryam Wukro.

Hawzien

The small town of Hawzien lies 23km from the Adigrat–Mekele road, and is reached by a side road that branches westward at Sinkata. Hawzien is of greatest interest as the gateway to the Gheralta region, but it is also of some historical interest in its own right. The town, which appears on the oldest-known maps of Tigrai, was reputedly founded by the Sadqan – 'the Righteous Ones' – a group of zealous Christian exiles said to have been as numerous 'as the army of a king' and to have subsisted on grass only. The Sadqan fled

HAWZIEN TO AXUM VIA MARYAM WUKRO

The little-used 110km back route that connects Hawzien to Adwa via the hamlets of Nebelet and Edaga Arbi is of potential interest to travellers for two reasons. The first is as a rough but relatively direct route to the Gheralta churches from Axum, one that can be covered in about half the time it takes to traverse the more normal (and less bumpy) road via Adigrat. The second is to visit what must rank as one of the most remote of the major Tigraian churches, namely Maryam Wukro, which is situated to the north of Nebelet, some 37km from Hawzien (about two hours' drive in either direction if you are thinking of doing it as a round trip).

Starting from Hawzien, the hilly 30km road to Nebelet is in rather poor shape, with some stretches that are rough and rocky, others that are deep with sand, so you are unlikely to get through in less than 90 minutes, longer after rain, though this might well change once proposed roadworks have been completed. Nebelet itself is a typical small Tigraian village of neat sandstone houses, set in spectacular isolation below a tall rock outcrop reminiscent of Gheralta. There's no accommodation in town that I'm aware of, nor does there seem to be any public transport in either direction, but a few small shops sell basic local food and water-cooled drinks.

The 7km track from Nebelet to Maryam Wukro is unambiguously 4x4 territory and not always easy to follow. It takes the best part of 30 minutes to traverse, ideally having picked up somebody in Nebelet to act as a guide. On the plus side, you can drive to within 10m of the church compound, the priest with the key lives very nearby, and there is no longer any bureaucracy attached to entering the church, nor even a fixed fee – you'll be asked to donate whatever you are comfortable with!

It is odd to think that this remote church, with its unflattering exterior, was one of the first Tigraian rock-hewn edifices be visited by a foreigner (Professor Mordini in 1939). Maryam Wukro was subsequently described by Ruth Plant as 'a great example of Tigraian architecture' and by David Buxton as 'the most elaborate and even fantastic cliff church I know'. As with Mikael Debre Selam near Atsbi, Maryam Wukro combines elements of rock-hewn and built-up Axumite architecture, though the rock-hewn part of the church is much larger and airier, with a 10m-high interior in parts, and comprising three aisles and bays. Notable features include an unsupported double arch, several thick pillars, ancient rock etchings, and more modern paintings. The church is said to have been excavated by angels during the reign of Abreha and Atsbeha, who were regular visitors, and there is also a niche in the back where Maryam herself sometimes comes to pray and weep. Reached via a wooden ladder, a more crudely hewn chapel, Wukro Giyorgis, is carved into the cliff face above Maryam and has a few floor-level openings looking into the larger church. David Buxton indicated that this church might have been modelled on the Axumite church at Debre Damo, and had some influence on the architecture of the cliff churches in Lalibela.

If you are continuing on towards Axum, it's 33km by road from Nebelet to Edaga Arbi, an undistinguished small town set below the ancient hilltop monastery of Abuna Tsama. A little-known site of interest in this area, only 15km from town but so far as I can ascertain inaccessible by road, is a field of some 140 Axumite stelae at Henzat. There is plenty of public transport from Edaga Arbi through to Adwa, then on to Axum, following a good 12km dirt road that intersects with the Abi Aday road some 32km south of Adwa and 8km north of Mai Kenetal. In a private vehicle, expect the drive from Edaga Arbi to Axum to take about 90 minutes.

the worldly Roman Church in the late 5th century to preach their ascetic 'heresies' to Ethiopians. Legend has it that the Sadqan were persecuted by local animist tribes and, despite the protective efforts of King Kaleb of Axum, they were eventually massacred. Heaps of bones believed to date from this genocide are preserved at several sites associated with the Sadqan.

More recently, in 1988, Hawzien was the target of one of the most vicious public excesses of the Mengistu regime, when its marketplace was bombed from the air. An estimated 2,500 people died in this tragic and apparently unprovoked civilian massacre. The walls of several buildings destroyed in the bombing still stand on the outskirts of town, along the footpath to Tekle Haymanot church. In the marketplace, four ancient stelae – judging by appearance, of similar vintage to the so-called Gudit stelae outside Axum – were knocked over by the bombing. The stelae are still intact, however, and a couple of them have been re-erected.

Also of interest in Hawzien is the church of **Hawzien Tekle Haymanot**, which lies about five minutes' walk from the town centre in a wooded grove next to a river. The modern built-up church encloses a small rock-hewn church, thought to be one of the oldest in Tigrai based on the finely carved capital and column, which according to Ruth Plant, bears a strong resemblance to the original throne in Axum. If local traditions are to be believed, this church might well have started life as a partially hewn temple in pre-Christian times. Unfortunately, the rock-hewn section now forms the sanctuary, and is thus off-limits to lay visitors. I was allowed to peek into the sanctuary through the door, and the priest was kind enough to light it up for my benefit, but on the whole the experience seemed a relatively underwhelming return for the birr 20 investment.

Details of reaching Hawzien are given under the heading *Getting around*, page 282. The best place to stay is the 30-room **Central Tigrai Hotel**, which is cleaner and more comfortable than anything in Wukro, though not exactly a bargain at birr 40 for an adequate first-floor room with ¾ bed, or birr 30 for a scruffier ground-floor room, all using common showers. The large, green central courtyard doesn't quite offset this hotel's long-standing construction-site atmosphere. The restaurant serves decent local meals, beers, and other cold drinks.

Megab and nearby churches

The small village of Megab lies at the base of the northern tip of the Gheralta Mountains, precisely 8km from Hawzien along a gently undulating dirt road. The drive from Hawzien takes 15–20 minutes, and you could walk in less than two hours, with the only significant slopes occurring over the 1–2km after you leave Hawzien. In addition to having a superlative setting below a row of dramatic rock outcrops, Megab lies within easy walking distance of a clutch of wonderful rock-hewn churches, described below. The Werkanash family runs a small informal and unsignposted guesthouse on the west side of the road next to the junction for Abuna Yemata Guh; it has four basic single rooms at birr 8 apiece, bucket showers are available, and the attached restaurant can prepare local dishes and pasta. The less said about the children at Megab the better – but I strongly urge visitors to resist the persistent demands for money, sweets, biscuits, bic pens et al.

Abuna Yemata Guh

The most compelling church in the Megab area – indeed, probably the most spectacularly situated rock-hewn church anywhere in Ethiopia – is Abuna Yemata Guh. This small but very beautiful church has been carved into the top of one of the tall perpendicular rock pillars that dominate Megab's southwestern horizon. The interior of the church, reached via a small crack in the rock, is notable for its extensive and perfectly preserved wall and roof murals, thought to date from the 15th century and regarded by Ruth Plant as 'the most sophisticated paintings found so far in Tigrai'. Nine of the apostles are depicted in a circle in one of the roof domes, while the nine Syrian monks are depicted in the other. The wall paintings include one of the remaining three apostles, as well as a large frieze of the church's namesake, Abuna Yemata, on horseback. There are stunning views from the narrow ledge that leads to the church, looking over a sheer drop of roughly 200m. To get to Abuna Yemata Guh from Megab, you must first follow the signposted track that forks southwest from the Dugem road next to the Fitsum Bar. The footpath to the church lies about 3.5km along this track; a flat 45 minutes for pedestrians, or ten minutes in a vehicle. Having located the priest, the hike up to the church takes 40–60 minutes, climbing roughly 500m in altitude.

The last part of the ascent to Abuna Yemata Guh involves clambering up a sheer cliff face using handgrips and footholds. It is probably not dangerous provided that you are reasonably fit and agile, and have a good head for heights. But it should emphatically not be attempted by anybody who has doubts about their agility, or who has even the mildest tendency towards vertigo – were you to panic or freeze on this face, you would be in serious trouble indeed. And if you do decide to abstain, you will be in good company. Ivy Pearce, the first *faranji* to visit several of the Tigraian rock-hewn churches, wrote of the ascent to Guh that: 'I came face to face with a cliff face with only footholds and handgrips at irregular intervals. The climb I could not manage as my arms were not long enough [and] the handgrips too wide to grasp firmly. I didn't want to take risks, so gave it up and sat on a small ledge below.'

Abuna Gebre Mikael
Situated on the Koraro Escarpment about 15km southwest of Guh, the little-visited church of Abuna Gebre Mikael, reputedly carved by its namesake in the 4th century, is regarded to be one of the finest in the Gheralta. Set in the base of a 20m-high cliff, the church has an unusually ornate carved exterior, and a large cruciform interior supported by eight columns. Both the columns and the neatly hewn ceiling cupolas are decorated with brightly coloured paintings lit by four windows and an imposing wooden doorway. The steep walk to the church takes about 45 minutes and involves some clambering and jumping between rocks, though nothing as dodgy as the ascent of Abuna Yemata Guh.

Debre Maryam Korkor
This monastic church is set on a small plateau atop a sheer-sided 2,480m-high mountain a short distance southeast of Guh. The built-up façade, recently painted bright green, is rather off-putting, but the interior is very atmospheric and large, almost 10m wide, 17m deep and 6m high. Architectural features include 12 cruciform pillars with bracket capitals, and seven arches stylistically reminiscent of those at Abreha we Atsbeha. Predictably, local tradition links the excavation of Debre Maryam Korkor with the twin emperors (Buxton placed it in the early series of Tigraian Basilica churches, carved after those at Lalibela). The fine artwork on the walls and columns is said locally to date from the 13th century. Ivy Pearce and Ruth Plant both felt that it was probably painted in the 17th century, citing a painting of the Virgin Mary with a circle around her abdomen (indicating the development of the foetal Jesus Christ) as typical of that era.

On the way up to Debre Maryam Korkor, the footpath passes a disused and partially collapsed rock-hewn church that said to have served as a nunnery before the monastery attached to the church was founded, probably during the reign of Zara Yaqob. Two or three minutes' walk from Debre Maryam Korkor, another rock-hewn church called Abba Daniel Korkor is set above a sheer precipice with stunning views over the surrounding plains. This church, which consists of only two small rooms, has also fallen into disuse. Lay visitors can therefore enter the former sanctuary, the walls of which are covered in old paintings. The entrance fee of birr 20 covers both the extant church and the two disused ones.

The track to Debre Maryam Korkor is clearly signposted 2km from Megab on the southwest side of the Dugem road. The first 1km of this track, bordered by a hedge of euphorbia shrubs, is motorable. The priest with the key lives in the village at the end of the motorable track. Having located him, the hike to the church takes the best part of an hour. After crossing the fields to the base of the mountain, the footpath rises steeply through a natural rock passage (watch out for loose rocks underfoot), coming out at the abandoned nunnery. From here, you can use the shorter 'men's route', which involves scrambling up footholds and handgrips on a 60° rock face, or the slightly longer but less vertiginous 'women's route'.

Dugem and nearby churches

The village of Dugem straddles the road between Hawzien and Wukro, precisely 10km from Megab (two hours by foot along a very flat stretch of road), and a more undulating 14km from the church of Abreha we Atsbeha. Like Megab, Dugem has a scenic location at the base of the Gheralta Mountains. In addition to being the springboard for hikes to a number of interesting churches, Dugem boasts a small rock-hewn church of its own called Dugem Selassie, unusual in that it is situated on the plain rather than high in the mountains. Dugem Selassie is carved into a granite outcrop within the compound of the eponymous modern church, and there is a bath of holy water at its entrance. The small size of this church, together with features that Ruth Plant found reminiscent of King Kaleb's tomb in Axum, has led some experts to think it was originally carved as a tomb. It is possible to camp within the compound of Dugem Selassie. Otherwise, no formal accommodation exists in Dugem, though the friendly folk at the Andinet Snack Bar can roll out a mattress or two for a few birr if required.

Abuna Abraham Debre Tsion

Few who visit Debre Tsion will disagree with Ruth Plant's estimation that it is 'one of the great churches of the Tigrai, both from the architectural and devotional aspect'. Debre Tsion is a monastic cliff church, carved into a rusty sandstone face high above the village of Dugem; it has an impressive and unusually ornate exterior, currently despoiled by the corrugated-iron shelters, designed to limit seepage, that cover the doors. Debre Tsion must have the largest ground plan of any rock-hewn church in the region. The main body of the church is itself fairly large, and consists of four bays with decorated domed roofs, supported by pillars and walls covered in murals of various Old Testament figures. Arcing behind the main church is a tall deep rock-hewn passage, which leads to a decorated cell said to have been the personal prayer room of Abuna Abraham. Amongst the church's treasures is a beautiful 15th-century ceremonial fan, one metre in diameter, and comprising 34 individual panels, each painted with a figure of a saint. Although the priests will open it up for a small additional payment, the fan is starting to fray and tear in places, and it seems unlikely to survive much longer if it is regularly opened and closed.

Debre Tsion is named for Abuna Abraham, the monk who is said to have founded and excavated the church in the time of Abreha and Atsbeha. Experts believe the church to date from the 14th century or thereabouts. On the way up, the priest can show you a much smaller church that was hewn into an existing cave. Now disused, this is said to have been Abuna Abraham's first attempt at carving a church in the area. As with many other Ethiopian saints, Abraham was partial to demonstrating his faith through self-abuse: close to the old church lies a natural bed of jagged rocks on which the saint would writhe around while he prayed! Abuna Abraham is reputedly buried beneath the floor of Debre Tsion. There is a festival here on 21 Hidar (normally 30 November).

A motorable track to Debre Tsion is signposted to the southwest of the Wukro road 3.5km southeast of Dugem. You can drive the first 1km or so. From there you need to walk for about 20 minutes across flat fields to the back of the mountain. A steep but otherwise quite easy 30–40-minute hike brings you to the summit and the church – pausing, as is the convention, at the spot where Abuna Abraham is said to have stopped to pray whenever he climbed up. As with other churches that involve a long hike, it's important to locate the priest at the base. The standard birr 20 entrance fee is charged.

Yohannis Maikudi

Situated 2km southeast of Debre Tsion as the crow flies, Yohannis Maikudi has been described by David Buxton as 'the most interesting [church dedicated to Yohannis] I have seen, and memorable, too, for its means of access, which is a narrow cleft between bulging walls of bare, glaring sandstone'. Ivy Pearce felt that Yohannis Maikudi had a more 'reverent and holy atmosphere' than any other church she visited in the Tigrai. The 130m² rectangular church is notable architecturally for its Axumite doors, one of which is reserved for male worshippers, the other for females. The walls and roof are densely covered in primitive but evocative paintings of Old and New Testament scenes. These exceptionally well-preserved murals are thought to be at least 300 years old, and are very different in style to any other church paintings found in Gheralta – Dale Otto, a member of Ivy Pearce's expedition to Tigrai, thought that they displayed both Byzantine and Nubian influences.

Yohannis Maikudi can be visited on its own or in conjunction with nearby Debre Tsion. The walk, whether from Debre Tsion or from the end of the motorable track used to reach Debre Tsion, takes about one hour.

WUKRO AND SURROUNDS

The only sizeable town between Adigrat and Mekele, Wukro supports a permanent population of around 22,000, as well as a more transient military quota associated with its strategic importance in the wake of the border war with Eritrea – soldiers are to be seen everywhere. With its relaxed if rather nondescript character, Wukro forms a convenient base from which to explore a number of rock-hewn churches. There is a major rock-hewn church on the outskirts of town, and the town is situated a mere 20km by road from the fine Teka Tesfai churches described above. It also stands at the pivotal junction of the main Adigrat–Mekele road, the branch road east to the Atsbi churches and the Danakil Desert, and the branch road west to Hawzien via Abreha we Atsbeha and the Gheralta churches.

A significant recent development in Wukro is the inauguration of a well-run branch of the Tigrai Tourist Commission (*opening hours 08.00 to 17.00;* ⟍ *034 4430340*), which is clearly signposted on the Mekele side of town, on the opposite side of the main road to the bus station. The office stocks a good range of brochures and the guides who staff it are very knowledgeable about local attractions and helpful when it comes to arranging car hire and other activities. Sadly, Wukro's enormous potential as a tourist focus is not otherwise reflected by its amenities – particularly disappointing is a selection of hotels that are uniformly dire even by small-town Ethiopian standards, and in most cases exist purely to service a by-the-hour market amplified by the recent heightened military presence. Market day is Thursday.

Getting there and away

Wukro is an important junction town, connected by regular transport to Adigrat, Mekele and intermediate points. With an early start, you could easily stop off in Wukro just to see the church and still get between Adigrat and Mekele in a day. Heading east, a few 4x4 vehicles daily ply up and down the road between Wukro and Atsbi. Public transport between Wukro and Hawzien (via Abreha we Atsbeha, Megab and Dugem) is rather less frequent, but at least one bus daily passes through at around 09.00 en route from Mekele to Hawzien. There may be additional buses on Wednesday (market day in Gheralta).

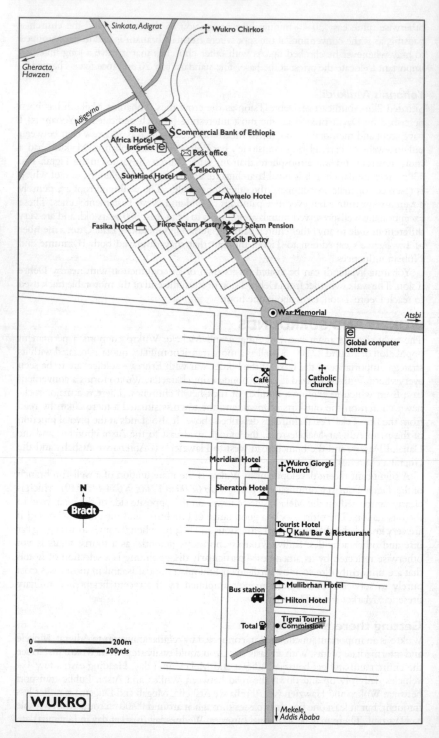

Sinkata, Adigrat

✝ Wukro Chirkos

Gheracta,
Hawzen

Adigeyno

Shell

$ Commercial Bank of Ethiopia

Africa Hotel
Internet

✉ Post office

Sunshine Hotel

Telecom

Awlaelo Hotel

Fasika Hotel

Fikre Selam Pastry

Selam Pension

Zebib Pastry

War Memorial

Atsbi

Global computer
centre

Café

Catholic
church

Meridian Hotel

✝ Wukro Giorgis
Church

Sheraton Hotel

Tourist Hotel

Kalu Bar & Restaurant

N

Bradt

Mullibrhan Hotel

Bus station

Hilton Hotel

Total

Tigrai Tourist
Commission

0 ——— 200m
0 ——— 200yds

WUKRO

Mekele,
Addis Ababa

Where to stay

Sheraton Hotel (10 rooms) ⚲ 034 4430779. Situated a couple of blocks down from the bus station, and on the same side of the road, this really is nothing special (presumptuous name aside), but it does at least seem clean, friendly and relatively wholesome. The small rooms with ¾ bed cost birr 20, and use a common shower.

Fasika Hotel Situated along a back street but signposted from the main road, this is the established standout in Wukro, charging birr 15 for a reasonably clean first-floor room using common hot showers. A few readers have balked at its recommendation in previous editions of this guide, but all is relative – it is well above par for Wukro, but would be unlikely to be listed at all were it located in any town with higher overall standards!

Mullibrhan Hotel Situated opposite the new bus station, this isn't the Hilton (that, believe it or not, is right next door, and it's a serious dump) but the dingy rooms with cold shower and large dbl beds are fair value at birr 15. One minor quibble is that some idiot plumber decided to place the shower right over the toilet in lieu of a genuine flushing device; the solution is to use the common toilet and reserve the en-suite facilities for showering only.

Selam Pension This somewhat puritanical establishment, once popular with travellers, now seems intent on proving an inverse relationship between chastity and poor hygiene. Unmarried couples are emphatically not welcomed by the unfriendly management, married couples may struggle to gain the benefit of the doubt, soldiers with bar-girl in tow presumably get pretty short shrift, and sgl rooms (almost uniquely in Ethiopia) have genuine single beds rather than the standard ¾ or dbl! If the management dedicated this much attention to cleanliness, the rooms (using common showers) might be good value at birr 10/20 sgl/twin. But they don't. And they're not!

Where to eat

Awlaelo Hotel Formerly the Ecolate Hotel, this has a few scruffy rooms for birr 10, but they could get a bit noisy because they are situated right next to the courtyard *tukuls* and pool table. It is, however, one of the best places to eat in Wukro, with a clientele dominated by local businessmen rather than soldiers, and a reasonably varied menu including *doro wat* and pasta. It is also one restaurant where the Ethiopian belief that their food is too hot for *faranji* palates has some substance.

Fikre Selam Pastry Shop Situated on the main street, this serves a thoroughly welcome selection of pastries, cakes, coffee and fruit juices, as well as tasty fried eggs and mini-pizzas. A second anonymous pastry shop, a door or three up, is also good.

Kalu Bar & Restaurant This relatively smart new eatery on the Mekele side of town serves tasty *tibs*, *kai wat* and other dishes – meat is available even during fasting periods.

Churches around Wukro

In addition to Wukro Chirkos, which lies on the outskirts of town and is described below, Wukro makes a good base for day trips to any of the churches situated back along the Adigrat road, whether on public transport or in a private vehicle. Also described below is the important church of Abreha we Atsbeha, which lies about 17km from Wukro along the road to Gheralta and Hawzien, as well as Minda'e Mikael 4km further along the same road. All the churches listed under the heading *Churches around Atsbi* (page 292) form realistic goals for a day trip out of Wukro: Mikael Barka on public transport, the rest with a private vehicle only. With a private vehicle, the churches of Gheralta can also be explored from Wukro, though Hawzien is closer to these churches and boasts a hotel far nicer than anything that's available in Wukro.

Wukro Chirkos

Jutting out from a low cliff in mock-monolithic style, **Wukro Chirkos** lies about 500m out of town on a low hill east of the main road. The church is regarded by locals to date from the 4th-century rule of Abreha and Atsbeha, but is thought by David Buxton to have been excavated at a later date than Adi Kasho Medhane Alem and perhaps a century before the churches of Lalibela. The lovely line drawings on the ceiling must date to the 15th century or earlier, since they were partially destroyed when the Muslim leader Ahmed Gragn burned the church. The external roof and raised porch were added in 1958 due to seepage. The inside consists of a large domed reception area and three 'rooms'. My reactions to Chirkos when I first saw it back in 1994 must be tempered against the fact it was the first rock-hewn church I visited, but I was awe-struck by its size, and by the realisation that each flake of its interior had been removed by human effort. Nevertheless, Wukro Chirkos is the single most accessible rock-hewn church in Tigrai, and travellers bussing through to anywhere north of Mekele are strongly recommended to pop in for a look, even if they have no time to visit another church. The standard entrance fee of birr 20 is charged without fuss. Because the church is attached to a large town, it is nearly always open and travellers are likely to be made welcome even during services.

Abreha we Atsbeha

Regarded by many experts to be the finest rock-hewn church in Tigrai, **Abreha we Atsbeha** lies halfway along the new road between Dugem and Wukro. The imposing front of the church, reached via a flight of stone stairs, is partially free-cut from the cliff and was reputedly added after Queen Yodit burnt the original exterior. It lies behind a more recently added Italian portico. The interior is very large – 16m wide, 13m deep, and 6m high – and cruciform in shape, with a beautifully carved roof supported by 13 large pillars and several decorated arches. There are three sanctuaries, with *tabots* respectively dedicated to Gebriel, Mikael and Maryam. The well-preserved and beautifully executed murals are relatively recent, many dating from the reign of Yohannis IV, and depict a complete history of the Ethiopian Church. The church's claims to antiquity are emphasised by its many treasures, among them a prayer cross that is said to have belonged to Abba Salama, the first Bishop of Ethiopia, who was appointed by none other than King Abreha.

Local tradition has it that this church was excavated in AD335–40 by the twin kings for whom it is named, and whose mother reputedly came from the area. It is also said that the kings' mummified bodies are preserved in the church, stored in a box that is kept in the Holy of Holies. The last priest who tried to open this box, some years back, was severely burnt on his hands, and nobody has given it a go since! How true these claims are is anybody's guess. Buxton believed the church was carved in the 10th century AD, but it could be that the church in its present incarnation is an extension of an earlier, smaller rock-hewn church. Dr Josief indicated that Abreha we Atsbeha might have been abandoned for some time before being reoccupied and redecorated in medieval times.

Local tradition has it that the Falasha Queen Yodit attacked Abreha we Atsbeha, burnt part of it, and destroyed a pillar. The queen became ill while she was inside the church, and ran off with some sacred rocks that gave off a supernatural light. She was killed hours later by a heavenly gale that swept her to a spot outside Wukro, where she is buried beneath a plain stone cairn – anybody in Wukro can take you to the spot. The links with Abreha and Atsbeha make this one of the few Tigraian rock-hewn churches that has long been known beyond its parish. It is the target of a major pilgrimage on 4 Tekemt (normally 14 October) and it is one of the nine churches known to Westerners before 1966.

Abreha we Atsbeha lies 17km from Wukro along a good but mountainous dirt road and can easily be visited as a self-standing excursion from the town. The drive takes about 45 minutes in either direction, passing through some magnificent scenery, and there is a good chance of encountering salt caravans fresh from the Danakil along the first 10km or so. Coming from Wukro, the junction to Abreha we Atsbeha is signposted to the left roughly 500m along the Adigrat road. There is little or no public transport along this road. I've heard from readers who hired a bicycle to get to Abreha we Atsbeha, though the serious slopes mean this is not a trip for all but the fittest of travellers. It should also be possible to hire one of the 4x4s that hang about Wukro bus station waiting for passengers to Atsbi – bank on a three-hour round trip and expect to pay birr 100 or upwards.

Abreha we Atsbeha can also be visited as an extension of the Gheralta circuit, since it is situated only 14km from the village of Dugem. The Wukro–Dugem road runs almost past Abreha we Atsbeha, along a 500m side road leading through a small village which is apparently named for the church. Vehicles can be parked in an open area, from where a three-minute walk up a short but steep staircase leads to the church itself. There is no accommodation in the area.

Mikael Minda'e

This relatively unknown church, perched on a low cliff about 200m north of the Wukro–Dugem road roughly 4km past Abreha we Atsbeha, is easily picked out owing to the whitewashed built-up exterior added in the year 2000. Architecturally, Mikael Minda'e isn't a particularly interesting representative of the genre – the interior is rather small, with large pillars but no noteworthy paintings or etchings – but it's an atmospheric church. We enjoyed our visit as much as anything for the priests, who were so unused to tourists that we actually had to explain to them about the entrance fee. The priests were in an amiable post-mass state of inebriation, and bounced around the church telling us tall stories in slurred Tigrigna, leaping in front of the camera at inappropriate moments, and offering us glasses of *tella*.

One of the priests – admittedly not the most sober among them – told us an interesting tradition relating to Mikael Minda'e. If I understood him correctly (he really was sloshed), the church was partially excavated by Abreha and Atsbeha before they went off to fight a war in which Abreha was killed. Atsbeha returned to the unfinished church carrying Abreha's body, with the intention of burying his brother there when it was completed. While Atsbeha was busy chiselling, however, a bird picked up Abreha's body and took it to a nearby cliff face. Atsbeha took this as a sign to start excavating a new church in which to bury his brother, at the place selected by the bird – now the church of Abreha we Atsbeha, 4km from Mikael Minda'e.

ATSBI AND SURROUNDS

The town of Atsbi consists of a characteristically attractive Tigraian assemblage of traditional stone houses situated at an altitude of around 2,500m on a plateau some 25km east of Wukro. In addition to lying along the ancient salt caravan route and modern road between Wukro and the Danakil Desert, Atsbi lies at the epicentre of a loose cluster of important rock-hewn and Axumite churches. Marked on some maps as Inda Selassie, Atsbi is connected to Wukro by a good unsurfaced road (and reasonably regular public transport) offering some magnificent views as it ascends the plateau. Should you elect to spend the night in Atsbi, there are at least two indifferent dollar-a-night hotels to choose from. Realistically, however, motorised travellers who intend visiting some of the churches around Atsbi can easily do so using Wukro as a base, while travellers without a vehicle will need to be prepared for some serious hiking or trekking to see the more interesting churches in the area. The town is at its most colourful on market day, which is Saturday, and this is also when transport from Wukro is most regular. Unfortunately, however, Saturday is a bad day to visit churches in the Atsbi area, as the priests will in all probability be at the market. We were not asked for a permit at any of the Atsbi churches.

Churches around Atsbi

Mikael Barka

The most accessible of the churches in this area is Mikael Barka, visible from the main road between Atsbi and Wukro. An uninspiring built-up portico, built in the 1960s and painted luminous green, gives little indication of what lies inside. Mikael Barka is a cavernously gloomy but very atmospheric rock-hewn church, excavated in a cruciform shape, and decorated with numerous murals on the domed roof, and a large etched cross on one of the 12 columns. The priest told me that the church was founded during the 9th-century reign of Emperor Dil Ne'ad; other oral traditions associate Mikael Barka with Abuna Abraham, who was active in the 6th century, while David Buxton felt it probably post-dated the Lalibela churches. So no ambiguity about that, then! The scorching over the roof is linked by tradition with an attack by Queen Yodit in the 10th century.

Mikael Barka is signposted at the base of a small isolated hill precisely 18.5km from Wukro and 6km from Atsbi. The footpath that leads to the church is fairly steep, but not arduous, and the walk up takes no more than 15 minutes. This is one church that independent travellers can reach quite easily, using public transport between Wukro and Atsbi, though an early start is advised to be certain of finding transport back. It would also be possible to overnight in Atsbi and walk to and from the church. The family that lives in a stone house opposite the signpost to the church should know whether the priest is around. The standard birr 20 entrance fee is charged.

Mikael Imba

This superb three-quarter monolith, first reported to the outside world by Beatrice Payne in 1948, boasts what is probably the most impressive exterior of any rock-hewn church in Tigrai. Outwardly, the west-facing façade of Mikael Imba looks more like a transplant from Lalibela than it resembles any other Tigraian church (photographers should visit the church in the afternoon when the façade catches the sun). The monks here predictably claim that Mikael Imba dates from the rule of Abreha and Atsbeha, while David Buxton regarded it to be an 11th- or 12th-century excavation. Either way, Mikael Imba must have been the closest thing to a true monolith in existence at the time it was excavated, and it seems likely to have served as a model for the style of rock-hewn church now associated with Lalibela and surrounds. The vast interior is magnificent, and unusually well lit owing to the large frontal windows. A total of 25 pillars support the 6m-high ceiling, and although modestly decorated by comparison with the Gheralta churches, the precision of the workmanship is such that it looks as if it was excavated yesterday. Notable features include a large Greek cross hewn into the ceiling, the decorated wooden doors, and a treasure house containing an ancient metal cross and several old manuscripts. There is a pool containing holy water outside the church.

Mikael Imba is situated at an altitude of 2,329m on an *amba* (flat-topped hill) some 15km south of Atsbi along a rough and occasionally unclear dirt track (a local guide might be useful). The last 1km of the track is very rough, so even with a 4x4 it would be advisable to walk this stretch, which passes through a memorable landscape of glowing sandstone cliffs, patches of juniper and euphorbia trees, and layered mountains receding to the horizon. From the base of the hill, the steep ascent takes about ten minutes, and involves using safe footholds on one short stretch, as well as climbing up an old but solid wooden ladder to the summit. When we visited, the 'treasurer' charged us the standard birr 20 fee, and did not ask to see a permit, but he was neither co-operative nor friendly, and admitted that he didn't like tourists visiting the monastery. Whether this attitude extends to the normal priest, I cannot say, but it marred what was otherwise a highlight of our time in the region.

Mikael Debre Selam

Photographed in 1966 by Georg Gerster, the first *faranji* to visit it, Mikael Debre Selam is unusual if not unique in combining a fine rock-hewn church with the Axumite sandwich architectural style associated with the monastery of Yemrehanna Kristos near Lalibela. Described by Ivy Pearce as an 'extraordinary… church within a church', Debre Selam outwardly consists of a built-up cave church, protected within a relatively modern whitewashed portico. The church was built using alternating layers of whitewashed stone and wood, the latter decorated with geometric patterns, while one of the wooden window shutters is decorated with a very old cloth painting of the Virgin Mary and Child. The rock-hewn part of the church, which includes the sanctuary, is small and rather gloomy due to a lack of exterior windows, but the precise execution of the carved arches and pillars echoes the skilled workmanship of Mikael Imba. A sealed cave in the cliff above the church is said locally to be the tomb of the 6th-century Emperor Gebre Meskel, during whose reign the church was reputedly constructed. While certain archaic features superficially support this local tradition, academic opinion is that Debre Selam post-dates the Lalibela churches.

Mikael Debre Selam is situated at an altitude of 2,670m, high on a cliff face about 7km north of Atsbi town as the crow flies. To get there, follow the main road north out of town, which soon deteriorates to become an occasionally unclear track suitable for 4x4 only. After about 5km, a signpost to the left points along the track to the church. This track is motorable until you reach the Hidar River, after another 3km. The white portico of the church is clearly visible for some distance before you reach the river. Although there is a potentially fordable track across the Hidar, it should probably only be attempted when the water is very low. A safer bet is to leave your car here and wade through the chilly river on foot. Having crossed the river, the walk to the church takes about 30 minutes along a steepish footpath offering great views over the valley below.

THE TEMBIEN

The Tembien was until recently regarded as one of the remote parts of Tigrai, and it probably still should be, the recent construction of an all-weather dirt road connecting Mekele and Adwa to its major town Abi Aday notwithstanding. Historically, the region is remembered as the birthplace of Emperors Yohannis IV and Ras Alula, while other Tigraians know it for its delicious honey and hyperactive Awri dancing. In addition, the Tembien probably houses the highest concentration of rock-hewn churches outside of Lalibela and Gheralta.

Access to Abi Aday itself is now relatively straightforward. Good roads connect it to Mekele, Adwa, Sekota and Lalibela, and there are regular public transport connections with the first three towns. The more interesting churches around Atsbi are, however, only readily accessible to travellers with private transport, for whom the Tembien – in theory – makes a worthwhile excursion from Mekele or Adwa, and can also be explored from either town en route to or from the new road to Lalibela. In practice, you may battle to gain entrance to some churches without an official TTC guide in tow, which basically rules out any option that doesn't see you arriving here *after* having passed through Wukro or Mekele.

Abi Aday

Abi Aday literally means 'Big Town', and although not quite the metropolis this might suggest, it is a reasonably substantial and seemingly quite rapidly expanding settlement, set in a dusty valley below an impressive cliff. The town is divided into two parts by a small bridge across the Tsechi River. The lower part of town is where the better hotels are, and where buses stop. The upper part of town is where you'll find the marketplace, Elsa's Hotel, and the seedier bars in which you're most likely to see Awri dancing as the *tej* hits the mark. This aside, Abi Aday holds little of interest except as a base from which to explore the nearby churches.

Getting there and away

Abi Aday is connected to Mekele by a good 95km unsurfaced road, which passes through the bustling highland market centre of Hagare Selam, before descending along a spectacular mountain pass to the junction with the roads north towards Adwa and south towards Sekota and Lalibela. If you are driving yourself, you need to head right – towards Adwa – at this junction. At least two buses run between Mekele and Abi Aday daily.

The main road between Adwa and Abi Aday via Mai Kinetel is also 95km long and takes no more than two hours to cover in a private vehicle (add on another 20–30 minutes coming to or from Axum). Regular minibuses to Abi Aday leave Adwa from a junction about 200m west of the main square and take around four hours.

For details of the road south to Sekota and Lalibela, see the box *To Lalibela via Sekota* on page 338.

Where to stay
Budget

Ras Alula Hotel (20 rooms) ✆ 034 4460621. Situated on the outskirts of town opposite the hospital about 1km along the Adwa road, this new and unexpectedly comfortable three-storey hotel charges birr 40 for a clean room with en-suite hot shower and a ³/₄ bed. There is a ground-floor bar, but no food is available at the time of writing, though this might change in the future.

Shoestring

Debre Selam Pension This friendly family-run place in the town centre, just 200m from the bus station, has recently elevated itself from a standard one-floor lodge centred on an open courtyard by the addition of a smarter two-storey annex. Simple but clean rooms with a ³/₄ bed cost birr 15 using a common shower, or birr 20 with an en-suite cold shower.

Birhan Reda Pension This adequate local lodging in the town centre charges an inflated *faranji* price of birr 15/30 sgl/dbl occupancy, and has an attitude to match.

Where to eat

The best place for a full meal is **Elsa's Hotel**. Unexpectedly, there is a rather good juice shop on the main junction more or less opposite the Debre Selam; the English-speaking owner is articulate and helpful, and video shows are sometimes held here at night.

Churches around Abi Aday
Abba Yohanni

This remote but fantastically situated monastery, visited by Dr Enzo Parona in 1928, lies midway up a tall west-facing sandstone cliff on a mountain called Debre Ansa. The façade, partially built after the original rock collapsed during excavation, is visible for miles before you arrive at the cliff base. It is one of the more photogenic exteriors, set high on a golden cliff, but does require afternoon light. The main church is reached via an atmospheric labyrinth of tunnels and nooks, incorporating the de-sanctified rock-hewn church of Kidane Mihret, and opening on to a series of ledges offering great views to the plains below. The rock-hewn church itself is very large, consisting of four domed bays standing up to 9m high and 14 carved columns, and is named after its founder Abba Yohanni, who is believed to have excavated it in the 14th century. Because the church is monastic, women are forbidden from entering the main building. Based on our experience, however, women are permitted to wander through the tunnel complex that leads up to the church.

To reach Abba Yohanni from Abi Aday, follow the Adwa road for 8km, then turn left on to a side road signposted for the church. After roughly 7km, you should park at the village of Menji at the base of the cliff. It's an easy 10–15-minute walk from the road to the monastery. There is no public transport to Menji.

Gebriel Wukien

The most accessible of the Tembien churches, Gebriel Wukien lies within easy walking distance of the main road between Abi Aday and Adwa. It appears to me to be a subterranean monolith, sunk within an excavated trench in a manner similar to several churches at Lalibela, although it is difficult to be sure of this because of the 20th-century stone roofing and mortar walls that cover and enclose the trench. Ruth Plant regarded Gebriel Wukien to be 'undoubtedly the most remarkable church' of the 15 she visited in the Tembien, and thought the quality of the carving of the four bays and several arches to be comparable with Adi Kasho Medhane Alem. Carved into a cliff behind the church are several monastic cells, as well as a kitchen and eating room where we were invited to drink *tella* with the friendly monks.

David Buxton placed Gebriel Wukien in the later series of Tigraian Basilica churches, which ties in with the oft-quoted tradition that this church was excavated during the 15th-century reign of Emperor Zara Yaqob. Undermining this rare instance of apparent academic and traditional concord, the priest who showed us around Gebriel Wukien told us that the cloth in front of the altar was a gift from Zara Yaqob, but the church itself was excavated during the 6th-century reign of Emperor Gebre Meskel. Accurate or not, this would appear to be a firmly established tradition, since we were shown the tomb of the church's purported founder, Abba Daniel, as well as a magnificent gold-plated diamond cross which reputedly belonged to him. The cloth paintings on the main door are also, and somewhat improbably, said to date to the time of Gebre Meskel.

To reach Gebriel Wukien from Abi Aday, follow the main Adwa road north for 16km, then turn left along a side road signposted for the church. After about 1km, you will reach a stand of fig trees and a water pump, where you can park your car in the shade. From the water pump, a footpath leads to the church, which despite its proximity to the road is very well hidden in a thicket of euphorbia and other scrubs. The walk takes no more than ten minutes, and the gradient is among the gentlest of any approach to a rock-hewn church in Tigrai. We were told that a fee of birr 30 was charged to visitors with a TTC guide and birr 100 to those without one.

Maryam Hibeti

This little-visited and rather lovely church, a close structural relative of Medhane Alem in Adi Kasho, is regarded by David Buxton to be a 15th-century replica of that prototypal church, a date which ties in with the local tradition ascribing it to the reign of Emperor Zara Yaqob. Maryam Hibeti translates as 'the hidden Maryam', an apt name for an excavation that lies in a wooded enclave on the side of a gorge, invisible until you are within metres of the imposing façade. The interior, though large, is gloomy and unadorned, dominated by six arched columns, and a natural pool of therapeutic holy water immediately inside the main door. The well-lit and partially sunken cloister, by contrast, is atmospherically earthy because of the lack of adornment, and very photogenic.

To get to Maryam Hibeti from Abi Aday, follow the Adwa road north for roughly 18km, then take a right turn, which after 2km leads to Werkamba. This is a small characteristically Tigraian town of stone houses, centred around a large marketplace and boasting a few shops and local restaurants but, so far as we could establish, no accommodation of any description. Continue along the main road through Werkamba for 4km until you reach another small village dominated by a war memorial. Turn left at the fork immediately past this village, following an occasionally unclear 4x4 track along a fertile plain for about 10km to the sizeable village of Adeha, where you can park your car. You'll need to find a guide here to help you locate the priest, who lives some distance from the village. Using a rather circuitous route past the priest's house, it took us a good 90 minutes to reach the church, and about an hour to walk back to Adeha. The footpath, much of which runs through the flat base of the gorge, is rough in places, but it doesn't involve any serious clambering except arguably along the short final ascent to the actual church. The area is, however, relatively low-lying and hot, and we regretted not taking any water with us.

A written permit or TTC guide is evidently essential in order to visit Maryam Hibeti – or at least to enjoy such a visit. We were asked to produce our permit (by soldiers and farmers) on four separate occasions en route to the church. It is worth noting, too, that although the church's name is more normally written as Maryam Hibito, locals definitely know it as Maryam Hibeti.

Emanuel Maibaha

Situated on the slopes of Mount Zala, Emanuel Maibaha lies close to the old road between Hagere Selam and Abi Aday, for which reason it was one of the more accessible churches in the Tembien prior to the construction of the new road. The church is reputedly where Maibaha's most famous son, the Emperor Yohannis IV, was baptised as a child. Hidden within a prominent whitewashed built exterior, the rock-hewn church measures 9m wide and 10m deep, is supported by four large pillars, and is notable for the Croix Pauttée on the domed ceiling. We were told that Emanuel Maibaha can be reached by following the same directions to Maryam Hibeti, but turning left instead of right at the fork after the village with the prominent war memorial 4km past Werkamba. So far as we could see, however, this road petered out after about 2km. Another, more reliable possibility would be to follow the old Abi Aday road out of Hagere Selam for 13km; Emanuel Maibaha lies on the side of this road and its bold white exterior would be difficult to miss.

Mekele and the Danakil

This chapter covers the Tigraian capital city of Mekele, together
with the remote Danakil Depression to its east, and various
minor points of interest along the 230km road that connects
Mekele to Woldia on the junction of the main road between
Addis Ababa and Asmara and the China Road to Lalibela.
Mekele is of limited interest to tourists, though, as the most
modern city in northeast Ethiopia, it is a great place for
backpackers to take a break between long bus rides. Mekele is the only
city with genuine tourist-class accommodation and amenities to lie within striking
distance of the rock-hewn churches described in the previous chapter.

MEKELE

In 1944, David Buxton dismissed the Tigraian capital as 'a dreary place set in a featureless
landscape'. Three decades later, Paul Henze wrote that it was 'a scattered town which, in
spite of its solid stone houses, has a chronically unfinished look' and 'small, even in
comparison to most Ethiopian provincial capitals' but also 'lively and developing rapidly'.
Today, it is those last four prophetic words that most aptly describe Mekele as it sprawls
energetically across a hill-ringed basin at an altitude of roughly 2,200m in the rocky
Tigraian Highlands.

Mekele today is a large, burgeoning city whose contradictions seem to encapsulate
those of Ethiopia as it enters the 21st century – flash modern high-rise buildings tower
above rows of rustic stone homesteads, while neatly suited, cell-phone clasping
businessmen hurry past rural Tigraians as they amble towards the market in their
traditional attire. Yet, paradoxically perhaps, Mekele is also possessed of a satisfying sense
of cohesion unusual for urban Ethiopia – clean, orderly, vibrant, overwhelmingly
Tigraian, largely unaffected by tourism, and refreshingly free of chanting children and
self-appointed guides. True, the city boasts few compelling tourist attractions, but a great
selection of affordable accommodation, decent restaurants and tempting pastry shops
makes it an attractive place to rest up between bus trips or from which to explore the
rock-hewn churches around Wukro in a hired vehicle.

Mekele is of little historical importance by comparison with many smaller Tigraian
towns. Unlike Adwa, or even Wukro and Hawzien, it doesn't appear on early maps of the
area, nor is it referred to in any document written before the 1830s. The modern city
owes its pre-eminence to Emperor Yohannis IV (1871–89), who believed he had been
conceived in the area, and treated it as his *de facto* capital. During the early years of his
reign, when he was based at Tewodros's former capital of Debre Birhan, Yohannis IV
founded a number of churches in Mekele. He relocated to Mekele in 1881, and the palace
he constructed there over 1882–84, now a museum, served as the main imperial
residence during the latter part of his reign.

Mekele has served as capital of Tigrai ever since, but even as recently as 1970 it was a
rustic small town with a population of less than 20,000. Mekele didn't feature among

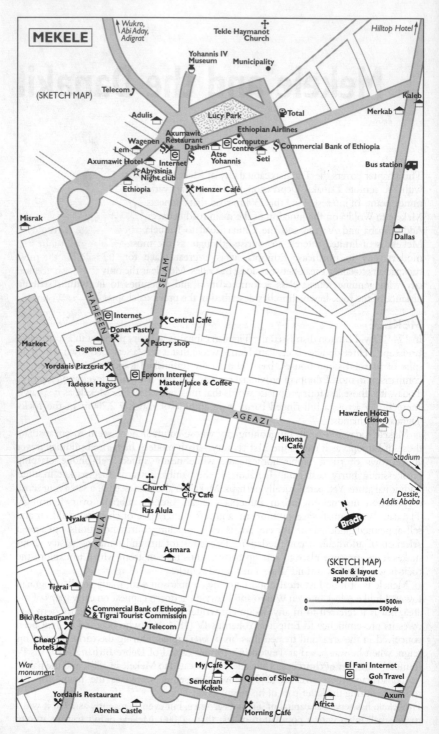

MEKELE

(SKETCH MAP)

Wukro,
Abi Aday,
Adigrat

Hilltop Hotel

Tekle Haymanot
Church

Yohannis IV
Museum

Municipality

Telecom

Kaleb

Adulis

Lucy Park

Total

Merkab

Axumawit
Restaurant

Ethiopian Airlines

Wagenen

Dashen

Computer
centre

Commercial Bank of Ethiopia

Lem

Internet

Atse
Yohannis

Seti

Axumawit Hotel

Bus station

Abyssinia
Night club

Ethiopia

Mienzer Café

Misrak

Dallas

SELAM

HAHEFEN

Internet

Central Café

Donat Pastry

Market

Segenet

Pastry shop

Yordanis Pizzeria

Tadesse Hagos

Eprom Internet

Master Juice & Coffee

Hawzien Hotel
(closed)

AGEAZI

Stadium

Mikona
Café

Dessie,
Addis Ababa

Church

City Café

Ras Alula

N

Bradt

Nyala

ALULA

Asmara

(SKETCH MAP)
Scale & layout
approximate

0 ——————— 500m
0 ——————— 500yds

Tigrai

Biki Restaurant

Commercial Bank of Ethiopia
& Tigrai Tourist Commission

Cheap
hotels

Telecom

War
monument

My Café

El Fani Internet

Semenani
Kokeb

Queen of Sheba

Goh Travel

Axum

Yordanis Restaurant

Africa

Abreha Castle

Morning Café

Ethiopia's ten largest towns in the 1984 census, but – in large part because of its favoured status with the (largely Tigraian) post-Derg national government – it is now the fifth-largest city in Ethiopia, with a population estimated at 140,000 and rising.

Getting there and away
By air
Daily flights with Ethiopian Airlines connect Mekele to Addis Ababa. There are also flights most days to Axum, Bahir Dar, Gonder and Lalibela. The airport, which lies about 5km from the city centre, is a corrugated-iron building, but scheduled for reconstruction along the same lines as those at Lalibela and Axum. Taxis to the airport are available from the city centre. All outward flights should be confirmed a day in advance at the Ethiopian Airlines office on the main roundabout opposite the museum.

By road
Mekele lies 780km from Addis Ababa along a mostly asphalt road through Debre Birhan, Dessie and Woldia. It is feasible, with a very early start, to drive between the two cities in one day, but it would certainly be preferable to break up the trip with an overnight stop at Dessie or elsewhere. Several road routes exist between Mekele and Lalibela: the most direct option, via Abi Aday and Sekota, could be covered in a day at a push (better, however, to take a night's break at Abi Aday and check out some of the Tembien churches), but most tourist vehicles prefer the longer but smoother route via Woldia.

The road northward from Mekele to Adigrat takes about 90 minutes to two hours to cover in a private vehicle without breaks, but most tourists opt to stop at Wukro Chirkos and/or some of the other rock-hewn churches in the vicinity. It is possible to drive between Mekele and Axum in one long day, either via Adigrat or Hawzien, routes covered in the previous two chapters, but in both cases it would be a long slog without any opportunities for sightseeing.

Mekele's main bus station was recently relocated from the city centre to the east end of Ageazi Street next to the (currently closed) Hawzien Hotel. Early-morning buses run daily in both directions between Mekele and Hawzien, Adwa, Axum and Asmara to the north (though the latter service is suspended due to the closure of the Eritrean border), and Woldia and Dessie to the south. There is transport between Mekele and Wukro or Adigrat throughout the day. Heading south, there is a 09.00 bus to Adi Gudem, from where you shouldn't have to wait too long for a lift through to Maychew (see *Mekele to Woldia by Road* on page 307). There are also a few vehicles daily between Mekele and Abi Aday on the new Axum–Lalibela road.

Where to stay
Moderate
Axum Hotel (40 rooms) ↘ 034 4405155/6/7 or 011 6613916; f 034 4406115. Under the same ownership as its namesake in Addis Ababa, this modern high-rise hotel is probably the best overall bet in Mekele, with a reasonably central location, an excellent traditionally decorated restaurant and reception area, and large carpeted rooms with DSTV and en-suite hot shower for birr 180/210/360 sgl/dbl/ste.

Abreha Castle Hotel (22 rooms) ↘ 034 4400288. Set in a 19th-century stone castle built by a nobleman called Abreha Aria, this prominent local landmark was restored and converted to a hotel in the 1960s by a grandson of Yohannis IV. It's an attractive hotel, with plenty of character and a winning setting in green gardens overlooking the town centre, all of which compensates for the slightly superior facilities and more modern feel of its competitors. Large, comfortable rooms with en-suite hot bath and TV cost birr 150/250 sgl/dbl.

Hilltop Hotel (32 rooms) ↘ 034 4405683/4. Formerly the Bubu Hills Hotel, the Hilltop is – as its name suggests – perched on a suburban rise about 1km from the town centre, and it offers what would be an attractive view were it not for the factories that loom in the foreground. The large semi-detached rooms, which cost birr 120/180 for sgl/dbl occupancy, are comfortable and clean, albeit a touch frayed at the seams, and they all have a proper dbl bed, a fridge, DSTV, and an en-suite hot bath. The restaurant serves decent meals.

Hawzien Hotel ✆ 034 4406955–8 or 011 5155052; f 034 4404349. Prior to its closure due to bankruptcy in 2004, this was similar in standard and price to the Axum. Its future status is uncertain.

Budget

Seti Hotel ✆ 034 4400608. The best value in its price range for some years, the Seti Hotel has a useful location on the main square opposite the museum, and it charges birr 52/77 for a cavernous sgl/dbl with hot bath, or birr 30/60 for a sgl/dbl using common shower. The ground-floor restaurant isn't up to much.

Atse Yohannis Hotel (30 rooms) ✆ 034 4406760/2; f 034 4406761. Situated around the corner from the Seti in a high-rise building above the Nyala Insurance Company, this pleasant hotel seems mildly overpriced at birr 103/138 for a carpeted sgl/dbl room with DSTV, en-suite hot shower and private balcony. It has a good restaurant and lively patio bar on the first floor.

Axumawit Hotel ✆ 034 4403671; f 034 4403670. Comparable in standard with the above, and very close to them, this charges birr 128 for a first-class dbl with en-suite hot shower and TV, or birr 40/52 for a sgl/dbl using common showers.

Ras Aiula Hotel The large, clean rooms at this central hotel also seem overpriced at birr 120–130 for a clean dbl with en-suite hot shower.

Shoestring

Merkeb Hotel ✆ 034 4410360. This new hotel situated on the opposite side of the road to the bus station is very good value at birr 30–35 for a compact but clean tiled room with en-suite hot shower and a ¾ bed.

Dallas Hotel ✆ 034 4414100. Another new hotel located alongside the bus station, this charges birr 25 for a very clean room with ¾ bed, using common cold showers.

Tadesse Hagos Hotel The best of several cheapies clustered along Alula Road around what used to be the bus station, between the Abreha Castle Hotel and the Commercial Bank of Ethiopia. Adequately clean dbl rooms cost birr 30 using a common shower, or birr 50 with a private hot shower.

Queen of Sheba Hotel ✆ 034 4401718. This simple but clean hotel has unfortunately responded to its popularity with budget travellers by hiking *faranji* prices up to a somewhat unrealistic birr 40/60 for a sgl/dbl using common cold showers.

Adulis Hotel Deceptively smart-looking hotel on the main square with scruffy rooms using a common shower for birr 30.

Where to eat

All of the hotels listed in the moderate and budget category have restaurants serving local and Western dishes at reasonable prices. Of the more central places, the **Atse Yohannis** and **Axumawit** hotels are both worth trying, and are excellent value at around birr 15 for a substantial main course. A notch up from these is the smart restaurant at the **Axum Hotel**, where main courses cost around birr 20 and a three-course set menu birr 30. The **Abreha Castle Hotel** has the most attractive location and view if you feel like eating outdoors.

The **Yordanis Restaurant** at the southern end of Alula Road has a great atmosphere, with several small *tukuls* in the courtyard and a smart indoor area. It serves a variety of Ethiopian and Italian dishes, including pizzas and grills, most of which cost birr 10–20. We weren't very impressed by the pizzas, but the other dishes are pretty good. Ice cream and fruit salad are also available.

At least a dozen pastry shops are dotted along and around Alula and Selam roads – for what it's worth, the **Dehab Pastry** and **Lateria Café** are both very good.

Supermarkets in Mekele are unusually well stocked with sweets, biscuits, tinned foods and the like, making it a good place to stock up if you plan to hike around Gheralta or head into the Danakil.

Listings
Foreign exchange
Cash and travellers' cheques in US dollars and other major currencies can be converted to local currency at any major bank. The branch of the Commercial Bank of Ethiopia on the junction of Alula and Ageazi streets is unusually efficient, but the Dashen Bank on the main square is better.

Internet
Browsing facilities are available for around birr 0.30 per minute at several internet cafés. The Eprom Business Centre and Computer Centre next to the Atse Yohannis Hotel are both good.

Tourist information
The organised and helpful Tigrai Tourist Commission (TTC) stocks a series of useful illustrated brochures covering the major rock-hewn churches in the province. It can also supply advice about visiting less-known historical sites in Tigrai, and will provide travellers with a local guide for birr 100 per day as required. The TTC has relocated its office at least three times in the past decade, but for the time being it is on the fifth floor of the Commercial Bank of Ethiopia Building on the southwest end of Alula Street (\ *034 4409360;* f *034 4401032*).

Tour operators
Situated a couple of doors up from the Axum Hotel, **GK Ahadu Tours** (\ *034 5508662;* e *gkahadu@ethionet.et*) can organise 4x4 excursions to the rock-hewn churches around Wukro as well as to the Danakil. You could also try the new and untested **Horn Africa Travel Agency** (\ *034 4409200/4402397;* e *arayatilah@ethionet.et* or *arayatilahun@yahoo.com*).

Activities and excursions
City centre
The premier attraction is the **Yohannis IV Museum**, sited in the palace built for the emperor by a European architect, and described by the British Envoy Francis Harrison Smith, who visited Mekele in 1886 as being 'like an old-fashioned English church'. Still architecturally impressive, the rather esoteric displays of royal paraphernalia justify the nominal entrance fee, and there is a great view from the palace roof, one that Yohannis, who had a phobia about climbing stairs, may never have enjoyed personally. The museum is open from 08.30 to 12.30 and 13.30 to 17.30 daily except Mondays and Fridays. Photography is forbidden inside or outside. Other relics of the Yohannis era in Mekele are the churches of Tekle Haymanot, Medhane Alem and Kidane Mihret, all of which were built by the emperor in the 1870s.

Mekele's legendary **market**, situated a couple of blocks west of the city centre, is the urban terminus of the traditional salt caravan route from the Danakil Desert. Slabs of salt are mined in the Arho region of this inhospitable area, and carried on camelback by caravans through Atsbi to Mekele. The journey between Arho and Mekele takes longer than a week, during which time the *Arhotai* (the name given to the Afar and Raya people who make the journey) subsist on a type of dry bread called *bircutta*. With luck, you can see these caravans arriving – the main market day is Monday, but the salt traders might arrive on other days.

AYDER SCHOOL
Based on a column by John Graham, the full text of which can be read online at www.addistribune.com

The unprovoked aerial bombardment of a civilian part of Mekele on 5 June 1998 was a major factor in the escalation of the border war between Ethiopia and Eritrea. The Ayder School, situated in a poor residential suburb opposite a modern hospital, was worst hit by the bombing. Eleven students, two adults and a baby were killed, and several rescuers were injured as the plane circled back to drop a second bomb. The school is still in use, but the holes where the bombs fell remain. Preserved as a museum, one of the classrooms that was hit still has a gaping hole in its roof, and the desks stand as they were on the day, gouged with shrapnel marks. Other crude mementoes of the attack are lined up starkly on the tables, while pictures of the blood-spattered bodies line the walls. A row of trees has been planted in the school grounds to remember each of the victims.

The Tigraian People's Liberation Front Monument, 15 minutes' walk and easily visible from the Abreha Castle Hotel, is inspiring and well worth making the effort to see.

Chelekot
The small village of Chelekot (aka Celicut), set on a green hill 17km south of Mekele, was a far more important settlement than the modern capital in the early 19th century. Chelekot housed the court of the Tigraian Prince Ras Wolde Selassie, who, prior to his death in 1816, was probably the most powerful regional ruler in Ethiopia at a time when the imperial court at Gonder had little influence beyond its immediate vicinity. A staunch supporter of Solomonic rule, Wolde Selassie was notable among other things for having been served as aide by Nathaniel Pearce, a young Englishman who found his way to the Tigraian court in 1810, married an Ethiopian woman, and stayed on there for three years after the Ras's death.

Henry Salt, the first European to write about the Ethiopian interior since James Bruce's day, visited the court of Wolde Selassie in 1805 and 1810. Built between Salt's visits, the main point of interest in the village today is the church of Chelekot Selassie. This architecturally impressive example of the circular *tukul* style of churches is covered in beautiful 19th-century paintings, and it houses several treasures dating to the rule of Wolde Selassie.

There's no public transport to Chelekot, but it's a recommended excursion if you have your own vehicle or can afford a taxi.

Chele Anka Waterfall
This tall, narrow waterfall on the Chele Anka (aka Chelanqua) River tumbles for around 60m into a gorge 8km southwest of Mekele, and is particularly dramatic during the rainy season. The waterfall is located about 1.5km from Debir, itself a rather interesting and picturesque village of traditional Tigraian stone houses. To get there, follow the main road west of Mekele, past the war memorial and new University for Business and Economy, and as you reach the outskirts of town follow the tracks south asking for Debir. Once at the village, anybody will lead you to a viewpoint over the gorge and waterfall next to the attractive old church of Debir Maryam. A steep footpath leads from the lip of the gorge to the base of the waterfall, where there is a pool said by locals to be safe for swimming. There is no public transport to Debir, nor would the track be passable in an ordinary saloon car, so the best way to get there is in a private 4x4 or by horse-drawn *gari*.

THE DANAKIL DEPRESSION

Written in collaboration with Ariadne Van Zandbergen

The Danakil (or Dallol) Depression, which straddles the Eritrean border to the east of the Tigraian Highlands, is officially listed as the hottest place on earth, with an average temperature of 34–35°C. Much of this vast and practically unpopulated region lies below sea level, dipping to a frazzled nadir of –116m at Dallol, near Lake Asale, the lowest spot of *terra firma* on the African continent. One of the driest and most tectonically active areas on the planet, the Danakil is an area of singular geological fascination: a strange lunar landscape studded with active volcanoes, malodorous sulphur-caked hot springs, solidified black lava flows, and vast salt-encrusted basins.

The Danakil is effectively a southerly terrestrial extension of the rifting process that formed the Red Sea, set at the juncture of the African, Arabian and Somali tectonic plates, and its low-lying surface was once fully submerged by saline water. Relics of those distant days include Lakes Asale and Afrera, both of which lie at the centre of an ancient salt-extraction industry linking the somewhat restricted economy of the Danakil to the more naturally bountiful Tigraian Highlands around Mekele.

It is some measure of the Danakil's geological activity that more than 30 active or dormant volcanoes – roughly one-quarter of the African total as listed by the Smithsonian Institute Global Volcanism Program – are shared between its Ethiopian and Eritrean components. Following a series of fault lines running in a north-to-northwesterly direction, these volcanoes are all geological infants, having formed over the past million years, and a great many took their present shape within the last 10,000 years.

The most substantial volcanic range is the so-called Danakil Alps, whose highest peak, the 2,219m Mount Nabro, lies within Eritrea some 8km northeast of Mallahle (1,875m) on the Ethiopian border. Other notable volcanoes include the spectacular peaks of Borale (812m) and Afrera (1,295m), both of which rise in magnificent isolation from the sunken (–103m) shoreline of Lake Afrera, and the more westerly Alayita, a vast massif that rises to 1,501m and last erupted in 1901 and 1915.

The most regularly visited volcanic range in the Danakil is Erta Ale (sometimes spelt Ertale or Irta'ale), which consists of seven active peaks extending over an area of 2,350km² between Kebit Ale (287m, on the west shore of Lake Asale) to Haile Gubbi (521m, about 20km north of Lake Afrera). Of the three peaks that top the 600m mark, most remarkable is Erta Ale itself, which is listed as the most active volcano in Africa, having hosted a permanent lava lake for longer than 120 years, and which has been in a state of continuous eruption since 1967.

The Danakil's climatic inhospitality is mirrored by the reputation of its nomadic Afar inhabitants (see box *The Afar* on page 382), who as recently as the Italian occupation had the somewhat discouraging custom of welcoming strangers by lopping off their testicles. While scrotal intactness is no longer a cause for concern, the Danakil remains a challenging travel destination: daytime temperatures frequently soar above 50°C, there's no shade worth talking about as alleviation, the heat is often exacerbated by the fierce gale known as the Gara (Fire Wind), and creature comforts are limited to what you bring in yourself. The best time to visit is the relatively cool season between November and March.

Short of joining one of the salt caravans that connect Lake Asale to Mekele, as the occasional adventurous soul does, access to the Danakil is practically impossible without private transport. Even then, it would be akin to madness to stray from the handful of reasonably well-travelled tracks without a knowledgeable local guide and ideally a backup vehicle – or, failing that, a full range of spares and a high level of mechanical competence. Visitors should be self-sufficient in food and water (bank on a minimum of five litres of drinking water per person per day, and carry enough excess in jerry cans to last a few days extra), and will also need to take camping and cooking gear, since no accommodation or firewood is available. The desert nights can be refreshingly chilly, so bring a light jumper or a sweatshirt.

There are two main access points to the Danakil. The first, situated about 120km from Mekele along the salt caravan route to Lake Asale, is the small town of Berahile, which offers good access to Dallol, Lake Asale and Erta Ale. The second leads to the small junction town of Serdo on the Assab road (see page 381), which lies a full day's drive from Lake Afrera and two days' drive from Erta Ale. The more southerly route out of Serdo is longer and very remote, whereas the route through Berahile attracts a stream of salt caravans (an estimated one million camels pass through annually), a reassuring thought in the event of an irreparable vehicle breakdown. It would be perfectly possible to do the trip as a loop, starting in Mekele then continuing to Berahile, Hamed Ale, Dallol, Lake Asale, Erta Ale, Lake Afrera and finally Serdo – or vice versa. However you go about it, you would ideally be looking at a minimum of three nights' camping in the desert.

Coming from the south, permission to travel to the Danakil must be obtained from the tourist office at Semera, which lies 48km before Serdo coming from Addis. Coming from Mekele, you can obtain advance permission from the Afar Tourism Commission (\ 033 6660181; f 033 6660488) or else visit the helpful Tigrai Tourist Commission office in Mekele for directions to the relevant authority. Either way, you will also need to check into the regional tourist office 1km before Berahile on the Mekele road, which is also where you can arrange a local Afar guide for birr 100 per day. In theory the guide should bring all his own food and water, but in practice he will probably plan on scavenging both resources from friends along the way – or, failing that, from his clients. If you are thinking of heading out further on camelback or foot, the regional tourist office can also arrange a camel for birr 50 per day and a goatskin to carry water.

For further information about the geology of Danakil, as well as some tantalising pictures of its volcanoes and other landscapes, check out the following websites: www.dankalia.com and www.swisseduc.ch/stromboli/perm/erta/index-en.html.

Berahile

Situated at an altitude of around 1,000m, this unexpectedly large and attractive town, set in a valley below stark twin peaks, is neither truly of the highlands nor truly of the desert. Nevertheless, with its combination of typically Tigraian stone houses and more austere Afar huts, it is an agreeable point of transition between the two natural realms. The town also serves as an important stop on the salt caravan trail between Danakil and Mekele: if you spend the night here, it's worth checking out the encampment on the outskirts of town where the traders unload their camels for the night and feed them fresh fodder transported from the highlands.

If you arrive at Berahile in a private vehicle, you're unlikely to stick around much longer than it takes to organise your guide and permits at the tourist office 1km from town, perhaps grab a bite to eat, and knock back the last cold (water-cooled, that is) drink you'll see for a while. Beers are sold at a bar on the hill – something of a military hangout, as the genuine locals are mostly Islamic and don't drink. Arriving by bus – at least one covers the road from Mekele every three days, but you'll need to check when it next departs at the bus station in Mekele – your only viable next move would be to try to hook up with a camel caravan heading towards the salt lakes.

The drive from Mekele to Berahile shouldn't take longer than four hours. To get there, head north out of Mekele for 15km, joining the main Adigrat road at Mai Mekdan, then continue northwards for another 15km to Agulae, where you need to turn right onto a dirt road signposted for the rock-hewn churches around Atsbi. A few kilometres later, turn right again, at a village that may (or may not) be called Birki Birki, from where it's a straightforward run of about 80km to Berahile, passing some attractive aloe-strewn slopes (and usually a caravan or three) along the way. There is no formal accommodation in

Berahile, but you should be able to make a plan to camp or to sleep in a local family compound.

Hamed Ela, Dallol and Lake Asale

The small village of Hamed Ela, which lies 48km east of Berahile along a rough caravan track, is the usual springboard for visits to Dallol and Lake Asale, whether you are a tourist or a caravan trader. It is a pleasant, relaxed place, bordered by a pair of deep wells where you can watch the industrious local Afar draw up a meagre catch of muddy water in a goatskin container. There is no accommodation – most visitors set up camp on the edge of town – but lukewarm soft drinks and basic food are normally available if you don't have your own.

The 48km track from Berahile to Hamed Ela is very rough and rocky, and the drive takes about three hours in a good 4x4. The same track is used by the camel caravans, which usually overnight at an encampment known as Asa Bolo – basically a few makeshift Afar huts set near a permanent pool. The track follows a seasonal river gorge for much of its length, and passes some impressive rock formations along the way. About 3km before Hamed Ela, there stands a small rock formation that locals claim marks the sea-level point, but my map reading would suggest that you are already well below sea level at this point.

It's worth spending two nights at Hamed Ela to give yourself time to visit the lowest point of the Danakil, which lies about 20km further north of Hamed Ela along a rough but flat track to an eerie abandoned American phosphate-mining encampment marked on many maps as a village called Dallol. The main attraction of this area – indeed, a highlight of any Danakil adventure – is a surreal multihued field of sulphurous hot springs studded with steaming conical vents, strange ripple-like rock formations, and sprinkled with a rather adhesive coarse orange deposit that looks rather like dyed icing sugar. Try to get here in the early morning, when the light is fantastic and the temperature not too unbearable.

You can return via Lake Asale, the shore of which lies about 13km from Dallol and 8km from Hamed Ela, and is sometimes referred to as Regut by the salt traders. The salt-mining activity moves seasonally, but your guide should be able to locate it – though it cannot always be approached too closely in a vehicle, as it might sink! The site consists of literally hundreds of Afar cameleers chipping at the salty crust to extract neat 30x40cm rectangular tablets. One bar costs birr 1.25 at source, but in Mekele it will fetch birr 12 and more again in more distant parts of the highlands. Each bar weighs about 6.5kg; one camel can carry up to 200kg, or about 30 bars. The saltpans are supposed to be haunted at night by a devil or evil spirit called Abo Lalu.

Before heading on anywhere from Hamed Ela, you will need to pick up one or maybe two armed guards or police. Given half the chance, however, the local Afar will attempt to swell your party further with additional guides, police and 'secret guards'. If you are travelling with a decent company, it shouldn't get out of hand and if it does it shouldn't become your problem. On the other hand, if you are personally paying the guide fees etc, then expect every effort to be made to fill every available seat (and quite possibly the roof too). Space permitting, you could be looking at half-a-dozen Kalashnikov-toting freeloaders expecting to be paid birr 100 apiece per day to weigh down your vehicle, drink your water, chatter incessantly, stop the vehicle to greet their pals at every roadside settlement, and collaborate with the driver and guide in dreaming up obstacles to anything you might want to do that interferes with their party.

Erta Ale

Earmarked by the Afar Regional Government as the centrepiece of a forthcoming 'crater national park', Erta Ale ranks as one of the most alluring – and physically challenging – natural attractions anywhere in Ethiopia. Rising from below sea level to an altitude of 613m, Erta Ale is a shield volcano with a base diameter of 30km and a 1km^2 caldera at its summit. Nestled within the caldera are two pit craters: the larger, more northerly one, though currently inactive, held a lava lake in 1968 and 1973, while the smaller ellipsoid central pit contains the world's only permanent lava lake, which measures about 60m across and is 100m long.

Scientists think the lake must have a continuous link to a shallow magma chamber, which is itself fed on a regular basis by magma associated with the formation of the Rift. Significant changes in activity were noted at Erta Ale over 2004–05, including high levels of degassing, fissure eruptions on the northern flank, and a fresh breach on the southern crater that has caused the lava to overflow its terrace and rise up to within 20m of the crater rim. Several earthquakes have also been recorded in the vicinity of Erta Ale in recent years, suggesting that a major eruption may be imminent.

To reach Erta Ale from Hamed Ela, follow the rough and sometimes indistinguishable track that heads almost directly due south towards Lake Afrera, running roughly parallel to the Erta Ale range, whose peaks – Allu (429m), Dala Filla (613m), Borale Ale (668m), Erta Ale itself and Ale Bugu (1,031m) – stand 10–20km away on the eastern horizon. There are several small Afar settlements along the track, which passes through an ever-changing landscape of sand, rocks, scrubland and even the occasional palm-lined oasis. Depending on the strength of your 4x4, the skill of your driver, the competence of your guide, and the number of friends your guards need to visit, this drive might take anything from five hours to a full day. After about 60km, the track brings you to a small village that lies almost directly due west of the prominent peak of Ale Bugu, and goes by several different names, among them Gadala, Jelibahi and Durubu.

From here you need to veer east for 20km, across solidified lava flows and passing the northern base of Ale Bugu, to the village of El Dom at the base of Erta Ale. The volcano can be ascended by foot or on camelback from El Dom over three to four hours. No actual climbing is involved, and the slopes are generally quite gentle, but it's a tough hike all the same, due to the hard underfoot conditions, blistering heat, and lack of shade. For this reason, it's a good idea to ascend in the dark, leaving El Dom at around 03.00 so that your arrival at the peak more or less coincides with the sunrise. It is possible to camp on the top of Erta Ale, but you would have to bring everything with you, including shade, food and water.

Lake Afrera

Lake Afrera, which extends over almost 100km² some 30km southeast of Erta Ale as the crow flies, is a highly saline body of water fed by the abundant thermal springs that rise on its northeastern and southeastern shores. It is also known as Lake Giulietti, in honour of the Italian explorer Giuseppe Maria Giulietti, whose pioneering 1881 expedition to the Danakil was curtailed when his entire party was slaughtered by Afar tribesmen in present-day Eritrea. Afrera lies at an altitude of 103m below sea level, and the solitary island in the southern half of the lake (which goes by the rather apt name of Deset) is listed as the lowest lying in the world.

Lake Afrera is a stunning apparition, with its emerald-green waters overshadowed by the looming black basalt of Mounts Borale and Afrera, the dormant volcanoes that respectively rise to 812m and 1,295m above its eastern and southern shores. As with Lake Asale, Afrera is an important source of coarse salt, which is extracted for transportation to the highlands from the extensive crusts that divide its southernmost shore from Mount Afrera.

The western shore of Afrera can be reached from El Dom (at the base of Erta Ale) along a rough road that involves retracing your tracks in a westerly direction for some 20km, passing Ale Bugu to your left, and then heading southeast for 60km. This track is rough and difficult to follow in parts, and it can take anything from five to ten hours to cover, so the earliest possible start is recommended. Lake Afrera is also a full day's drive (about 150km) northwards from Serdo, a small junction town on the Assab road some 40km northeast of the regional capital Semera.

MEKELE TO WOLDIA BY ROAD

Most travellers will probably want to travel directly between Mekele and Woldia, a straightforward 230km run on a recently asphalted road that takes about four hours in a private vehicle and up to six hours by bus. Buses to Woldia leave Mekele at around 06.00. If you can't find a bus specifically going to Woldia, take one that is heading on to Dessie or Addis Ababa. Buses coming from Adigrat may pass through Mekele later in the day – your chances of getting a seat are good, but cannot be relied upon fully. Travelling in the opposite direction, you should be able to find a seat on a bus running from Dessie to Mekele; these generally pass through Woldia in the mid morning.

It is equally possible to do the Mekele–Woldia run in hops and dribbles over two or more days. The most convincing reasons to break up this trip would be to stop at Lake Ashenge, or – somewhat more esoterically – to visit the town of Maychew, the site of the decisive battle that led to the Italian occupation of Ethiopia in 1936. Travelling in stages also allows for a later start, breaks a very scenic route into comfortable travel bites, and adds an element of chance to your itinerary – never a bad thing if you have the time. Many of the small towns and other sites described below might be of interest to motorised travellers.

ADI GUDEM AND BETMARA

Adi Gudem is the first town south of Mekele, situated some 35km from the regional capital. A small bus runs back and forth along the connecting road throughout the day (there is generally a departure at around 09.00), taking just over an hour in either direction. Adi Gudem is a typically Tigraian small town of sandstone houses and puzzled stares. A couple of small hotels can be relied upon for a friendly reception and a cup of hot tea, if not much else. Early-morning buses aside, there's something of a public transport vacuum between Adi Gudem and Maychew, 80km further down the road, but there are plenty of trucks and it's easy to organise a lift.

The small, breezy town of **Betmara**, about halfway between Adi Gudem and Maychew, is where the buses generally stop for a tea break. If you've been in Tigrai for some time, the road south of Betmara climbs into the greenest hills you'll have seen in a while. Betmara marks the beginning of a stretch of road as awesome as any in Ethiopia, a 100km succession of dizzying hairpin climbs and descents through Maychew and Korem, culminating in a breathtaking drop of perhaps 1,000m to Alamata – thrilling stuff in dry weather, terrifyingly slippery when the road is wet. Technically, you will still be in Tigrai until you head south of Alamata, but scenically you leave it behind at Betmara.

MAYCHEW

Maychew – pronounced *macho* – is atypical of Tigraian towns in that there are few sandstone buildings, and it lacks an identifiable shape or centre. Before I arrived, Maychew was described to me as a one-street town – a little unfair, as the street stretches for a good 2km – but nevertheless it has an untidy, dusty feel that reminded me of similarly amorphous towns in southern Ethiopia, such as Robe and Dodola.

On 31 March 1936, the hills around Maychew were the scene of the final, decisive battle in Mussolini's bid to conquer Ethiopia, a 13-hour confrontation whose outcome was virtually predetermined by Italy's overwhelming dominance of the air. The Battle of Maychew is remembered as the start of the Italian occupation of 1936–41, the one period in its 3,000-year history when outsiders ruled Ethiopia.

The Maychew area is wonderfully green and hilly, and it strikes me as having enormous potential for off-the-beaten-track hiking and rambling. If you feel like exploring, there is no shortage of affordable accommodation. An anonymous hotel in front of the petrol station charges birr 30 for a very clean room with en-suite cold shower and toilet. The Yekatit Hotel, situated at the Korem end of town opposite the post office, is another decent place, with clean rooms and common showers – look out for the black-and-white checked wall and green signpost that reads 'Hotel'.

TO ALAMATA VIA LAKE ASHENGE

Two roads connect Maychew to Alamata. The new road via Mehoni is no shorter than the old road via Korem, but it is flatter, better maintained, and therefore faster and safer – you'll whiz through in an hour in a private vehicle, and public transport doesn't take much longer. Unfortunately, the new road is also far less scenic than the 62km old road to Alamata. If you opt for the old road, light vehicles trot back and forth throughout the day, stopping at Korem – Maychew revisited, but scruffier, and with plenty of gaudy hotels along the main street – about two-thirds of the way to Alamata. A very new and spanking clean hotel on the roundabout when coming from the Adigrat road immediately on entering the village charges birr 12 for a room.

A more alluring attraction than Korem, Lake Ashenge achieved some historical notoriety as the site of the Battle of Afla, which resulted in the capture and eventual grisly execution of the Portuguese commander Christofe da Gama by Ahmed Gragn in 1542. Situated at an altitude of 2,400m about halfway between Maychew and Korem, and clearly visible from the roadside, Ashenge is a beautiful mountain-ringed stretch of slightly saline water that covers an area of 14,000ha in an old volcanic crater, and is fed by several small streams but has no known outlet. The lake forms an excellent target for birders, particularly during the European winter when more than 20,000 waterbirds congregate around it, including ferruginous and maccoa duck, northern shoveler, southern pochard and great-crested grebe. At all times of year, endemics such as wattled ibis, Rouget's rail and black-headed siskin are likely to be seen alongside other resident grassland species. Several footpaths lead from the road to the lakeshore.

Practically bordering Lake Ashenge, the Hashengu Forest Reserve (aka Hugumburda State Forest) is the highest portion of an extensive area of indigenous coniferous forest spanning the Alamata Escarpment from an altitude of 1,600m to 2,600m. It is one of the few substantial forests left in Tigrai, notable among other things for harbouring the rare endemic plant *Delosperma abyssinica* and more than a dozen forest birds not normally associated with Tigrai, for instance the Abyssinian catbird. An all-weather road runs through part of the forest – ask for the turn-off about 2km north of the lake – and camping is permitted at the guard's encampment.

ALAMATA

The descent from Korem to Alamata is simply spectacular, and the sharp drop in altitude brings you to a hot plain that couldn't be more different from the green highlands you've just passed through. Alamata is calmer than either Maychew or Korem, and it feels smaller – or at least more compact – with a dusty frontier atmosphere, enhanced by the towering presence of the wildly majestic escarpment to the north.

Not least among Alamata's assets is the **Tewodros Belai Hotel**, which offers clean self-contained rooms with hot shower and double bed for birr 20, similar rooms with a smaller bed and cold shower for birr 15, and rooms using common shower for birr 11. The owner is friendly and speaks English, and there's a pleasant courtyard bar. The restaurant is the only place in Ethiopia where I had *shiro tagamino*, which is a delicious spicy dish made from crushed beans cooked with oil. The **Raya Hotel**, directly facing the Tewodros Belai, is arguably a bit smarter and unquestionably a great deal pricier at birr 40/50 for a self-contained double with cold/hot shower, and rooms using a common shower at birr 25.

Dessie, Woldia and Surrounds

Situated in the northeastern highlands some 400km from Addis Ababa by road, Dessie is the former capital of the defunct Wolo region, and serves today as capital of the South Wolo zone of the Amhara Nations region. Dessie, though probably the least interesting of Ethiopia's major cities, is nevertheless of significance to travellers dependent on public transport as a logical point to break the long trip between Woldia (at the junction to Lalibela) or Mekele and Addis Ababa. Situated only 25km east of Dessie, and linked to it by a zippy asphalt road and regular minibuses, the smaller but by no means insubstantial town of Kombolcha is the site of Dessie's airport, and is also used as an overnight stop by many travellers. Viewed purely as an overnight stop, there is not much to choose between the two: Dessie boasts a few smarter hotels, while Kombolcha has the better selection of budget options. The decisive factor should probably be which way you'll be headed the next day, with Dessie lying closer to Woldia and Mekele, and Kombolcha closer to Addis Ababa.

Although infrequently explored by tourists, the Dessie area boasts several interesting possibilities for excursions. The most accessible of these, certainly on public transport, is the scenic Lake Hayk, noted for its prolific birdlife and the historic male-only monastery of Hayk Istafanos, and situated practically alongside the Woldia road less than 30km north of Dessie. Of interest to the historically minded traveller is the renowned monastery at Gishen Maryam and Emperor Tewodros's former capital at Makdala Hill, both of which lie along side roads west of Dessie and are something of an expedition to reach, even with private transport. More accessible from the Kombolcha side is the vibrant mixed Afar and Oromo market held every Monday at Bati (on the road towards Mille and Assaita), and the ancient and mysterious lion carved into a rock at Geta.

This chapter first covers the four main centres along the Woldia–Addis Ababa road running from north to south – that is Woldia, Hayk, Dessie and Kombolcha – before covering more outlying excursions from these towns. Dessie and Kombolcha are connected by a fair asphalt road to Addis Ababa and Woldia (this should be extended north as far as Mekele during the lifespan of this edition), and by a good bus network in both directions. There is also plenty of local transport between Dessie, Kombolcha and Hayk. Details of transport possibilities to the other excursions mentioned above are given under the appropriate heading in the main body of this chapter. Ethiopian Airlines flies daily between Addis Ababa and Kombolcha (for Dessie).

WOLDIA

This medium-sized hillside town sees a solid trickle of traveller through-traffic, simply because it is the most popular springboard for road trips to Lalibela. Woldia lies amongst pretty rolling hills, but otherwise it might most favourably be described as humdrum and amorphous, and more accurately perhaps as a tedious and scruffy urban sprawl. It is most lively on the market days of Tuesday and Saturday. Within Ethiopia, Woldia is perhaps best known these days as the birthplace of the tycoon Al Amoudi, the owner and constructor of the Addis Ababa Sheraton.

Getting there and away

Woldia straddles the asphalt Adigrat road some 520km from Addis Ababa, 120km north of Dessie and 230km south of Mekele. Buses between Woldia and either Dessie or Mekele leave at around 06.00. If you don't feel like the early start, plenty of buses and trucks run along the main Addis Ababa–Mekele road, and they all stop at Woldia, so you shouldn't have any difficulty finding transport in either direction before noon.

Heading south from Woldia, there is plenty of transport to Dessie, which lies 120km and about two hours away along what is now a good tar road. From Dessie, you can easily bus through to Addis Ababa in a day. A recent introduction is the 'modern' buses that run directly from Woldia to Addis Ababa in a day (a 10–12-hour trip), though most older buses between these towns still overnight at Debre Birhan or somewhere nearby.

At least one bus daily, as well as the odd Land Rover, runs between Woldia and Lalibela in either direction. The trip takes five hours, and you are advised to show up at the bus station at 07.00, even though the bus generally only gets going at 09.00. For further details of transport between Woldia and Lalibela, see page 337.

When you arrive in Woldia, you might want to use a *gari* to get you and your luggage up the 1.5km climb between bus station and town centre.

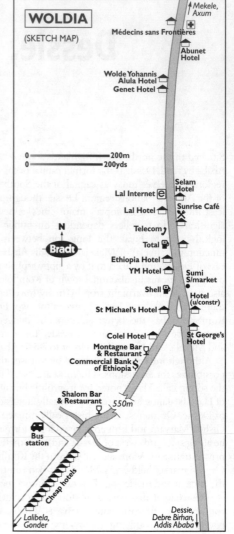

Where to stay
Moderate

Lal Hotel (54 rooms) ✆ 033 3310367/3310314 or 011 6623731; e lato@ethionet.et; www.lalhotelsandtour.com. The presence of the multi-storey Lal Hotel – country cousin to its smarter Lalibela namesake – in a town not otherwise distinguished by comely accommodation comes as a welcome surprise. It's undoubtedly the best lodging in town, but the rooms seem rather bare for the asking price and the hotel as a whole is poorly maintained, perhaps because recent improvements in the roads south to Dessie and west to Lalibela have turned it into something of a white elephant. Sgl/dbl/twin rooms with en-suite hot shower cost birr 84/105/126, while suites cost birr 156.

Budget
Selam Hotel ℡ 033 3311968; f 033 3310120. Situated more or less opposite the Lal, this smart new three-storey hotel is good value at birr 50 for a clean dbl with en-suite hot shower.

Shoestring
Wolde Yohannis Alula Hotel ℡ 033 3311080. Probably the best cheapie in town is this orange double-storey hotel on the Mekele road. It charges birr 25 for a clean room with a proper dbl bed and en-suite cold shower.

Genet Hotel Situated next door to the Wolde Yohannis Alula Hotel, this has similar en-suite rooms at the same price, as well as decent rooms using a common shower for birr 12.

Kidane Kihasi Hotel This green-and-yellow hotel seems about the best of the dozen sordid cheapies that line the road in front of the bus station like pouting finalists in a 'worst hotel in Ethiopia' competition. Rooms here cost birr 7–10 apiece, and there's plenty of choice, yours rather than mine!

Where to eat
The restaurant at the **Lal Hotel** is the best in town, and serves a variety of Western and local dishes in the birr 10–15 range. The **Sunny Café** next to the Selam Hotel serves juice, coffee, a few cakes, and fresh bread. The nearby **Sumi Supermarket** is quite well stocked.

HAYK
The small town of Hayk, which straddles the Woldia road about 20km north of Dessie, must surely be a contender for the most underrated and under-utilised accessible stopover anywhere along the northern circuit. True, the town itself is nothing to shout about, despite its pretty setting among rolling green hills, but – although you wouldn't know it approaching from Dessie – there is a beautiful 3,500ha lake situated only 2km from the town. Lying at an altitude of 2,030m, the lake is of great interest both for its birdlife and for the historical monastery that stands on its western shore (see box *Hayk Istafanos*, pages 314–15).

Curiously, the lake is generally referred to as Lake Hayk – Hayk being the Amharigna word for lake – and less frequently but with equal redundancy as Lake Lago. There are several bodies of water in Africa whose modern name derives from a local word meaning lake, generally as a result of an excited explorer mistakenly assuming that a bemused local muttering 'lake' was doing more than stating the obvious. More likely in this case, however, that Hayk's original name was forgotten centuries ago and it has come to be called after the monastery of Hayk Istafanos, which simply means 'Istafanos on the lake'.

Call it what you want – Hayk, Lake or Lago – this is a lovely, atmospheric spot. The deep turquoise water, ringed by verdant hills and fringed by lush reed-beds, is still plied by traditional fishermen on papyrus *tankwas*. Birders will be in their element: not only does the lake support a profusion of waterbirds (including large numbers of pink-backed pelican), but the shore and the surrounding fields and forest patches host a rich variety of colourful barbets, woodpeckers, kingfishers, bee-eaters, sunbirds and weavers. An early-morning stroll along the road between the lake and the wooded peninsula on which the monastery stands could easily yield between 50 and 100 species, with the monastery grounds in particular a good spot for flocks of the endemic black-headed lovebird and the lovely paradise flycatcher.

Getting there and away
Minibuses between Hayk and Dessie run throughout the day, and take less than one hour in either direction. It would also be easy enough to disembark at Hayk from any bus running between Woldia and Dessie, or – in a private vehicle – to stop off at the lake en route. Whether you are in a vehicle or on foot, you can get to the lake from the main roundabout in town by following the side road that runs almost parallel to the main road (with a mosque to your right). On the outskirts of town, the road forks: the right fork

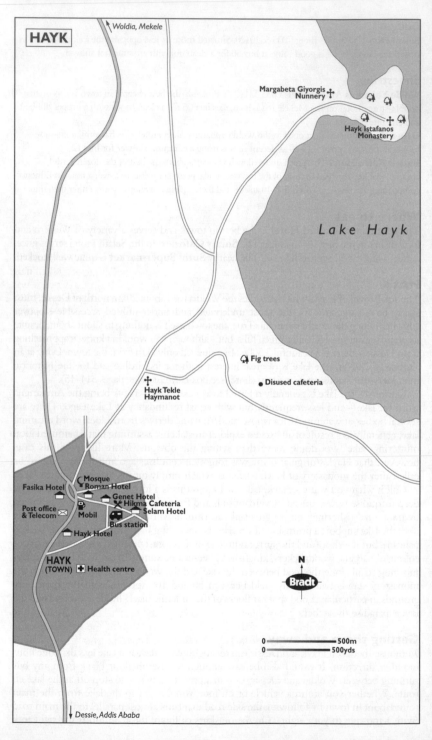

HAYK

↑ Woldia, Mekele

Margabeta Giyorgis Nunnery ✝

Hayk Istafanos Monastery

Lake Hayk

Fig trees

Disused cafeteria

✝ Hayk Tekle Haymanot

Mosque
Roman Hotel
Fasika Hotel
Genet Hotel
Hikma Cafeteria
Selam Hotel
Post office & Telecom ✉
Mobil
Bus station
Hayk Hotel

HAYK
(TOWN) ✚ Health centre

N

Bradt

0 —————— 500m
0 —————— 500yds

↓ Dessie, Addis Ababa

will bring you to an abandoned lakeshore cafeteria next to a trio of large, gnarled fig trees (seasonally laden with breeding cormorants and pelicans), while the left fork runs uphill and parallel to the western shore of the lake for about 2km before descending to Hayk Istafanos.

Where to stay and eat

Roman Hotel (60 rooms) ☎ 033 2220223. This new and very reasonably priced high-rise hotel on the east side of the main road charges birr 20 for a reasonably large and clean room with ³/₄ bed and en-suite cold shower, or birr 15 for a similar room using the common shower. There is a ground-floor bar and restaurant serving fish cutlets – something of a Hayk speciality.

Fasika Hotel (24 rooms) ☎ 033 2220390. Situated on the west side of the main road directly opposite the Roman Hotel, this is another new high-rise hotel, not quite so swanky as its exterior might suggest, but good value all the same at birr 20 for a smaller room with ³/₄ bed and en-suite cold shower, or birr 15 for a room using the common shower. There is a ground-floor restaurant, and the rooftop *tukul* bar offers a good view.

DESSIE

Large, modern and notably deficient in character, Dessie has few admirers, and its utilitarian aura is only partially offset by an attractive setting at an altitude of 2,600m near the base of Mount Tossa. The city was founded by Emperor Yohannis IV, who was struck by the apparition of 'a star with fringes of light' while encamped nearby in 1882. That an impressive comet was visible from the eastern highlands of Ethiopia in late 1882 is well documented, but the emperor, whether consciously or unconsciously echoing the actions of a distant predecessor at Debre Birhan centuries before, perceived the apparition to be a miracle. He immediately set about building a church on the site, which he christened Dessie ('My Joy'), a name whose misplaced ebullience has instigated a skyward arch in the eyebrows of more than one subsequent visitor!

In 1888, Dessie became the capital of Ras Mikael Ali of Wolo, an Oromo chief who had converted to Christianity under Yohannis IV ten years earlier. Ras Mikael was one of the major political players in late 19th-century Ethiopia, even before he integrated himself into the Showan imperial family by marrying Emperor Menelik II's daughter in 1893. The son of this union, Iyasu, was selected by Menelik II as his successor, and became Emperor of Ethiopia in 1913, only to be toppled three years later in an imperial coup masterminded by Ras Tefari (later Haile Selassie). Ras Mikael responded to this insult by leading 120,000 troops against the Showan monarchy in the Battle of Segale, probably the largest battle fought on Ethiopian soil between Adwa and Maychew. Mikael was defeated, and taken captive. He died two years later.

Ras Mikael oversaw Dessie's emergence as a trading centre of note. With its strategic location on the trade routes between Ankober and Tigrai, Mikael's young capital served a crucial role in the war with Italy in 1896. By the outbreak of World War I, the town had become the largest market centre in Wolo. As with Gonder to its west, Dessie's pleasant climate, fertile surrounds and convenient location ensured it became an important administrative centre under the Italian occupation. Much of the modern town centre dates to the occupation and subsequent decades, the period over which Dessie outgrew its rustic roots to become the capital of Wolo region and one of the largest cities in Ethiopia. In 1970, a population of 80,000 made it the third largest city in the empire after Addis Ababa and Asmara, the latter now part of Eritrea. Dessie lost out to Bahir Dar when the regional capital of Amhara was chosen in 1994, and it has been leapfrogged by the new regional capital and several other emergent cities to stand seventh on the national population list, with an estimated 131,000 residents in 2005.

Substantial as it is, the modern town, which sprawls along the main road for a good 5km, has a somewhat decrepit air. For most travellers, Dessie amounts to little more

HAYK ISTAFANOS

Hayk Istafanos, set on a thickly wooded peninsula within easy walking distance of the town of Hayk, is one of the most historically important and influential monasteries in Ethiopia. According to the local priests, the church's founder was one Saint Kala'e Selama, a monk from Jerusalem who arrived there in AD862. The story goes that Hayk formerly supported a pagan cult of python-worshippers, who were converted to Christianity when the Saint made the python disappear with his cross. Shortly after, Kala'e Selama persuaded Emperor D'il Nead to visit Hayk, and together they founded a church. While they were deciding which saint to dedicate the church to, a large animal descended from the sky with two *tabots*, one for Istafanos and one for Giyorgis. The church was named for Istafanos, and the second *tabot* stored within it for several centuries before a second church – today the nunnery of Margebeta Giyorgis – was established alongside Hayk Istafanos.

Although one tradition states that a monastic community called Debre Egziabher (Mountain of God) existed on the shores of Lake Hayk as early as AD627, it is probable that Hayk Istafanos remained an ordinary church for the first 400 years of its existence. Then, in the middle of the 13th century, during the reign of Nakuta La'ab, the Gonder-born monk Abba Iyasus Moa, having completed a seven-year apprenticeship at Debre Damo, was led to Hayk Istafanos by the Archangel Gabriel to found a monastery there. Iyasus Moa presided over the monastery for 52 years; he died in 1293 at the age of 89 and is buried within the church. Legend has it that he slept in a sitting position throughout his tenure, and that his waking hours were spent lugging around a heavy stone cross and kissing the ground – 10,000 times every day!

Hayk Istafanos was the most powerful monastery in Ethiopia from the late 13th to the early 15th centuries, largely as a result of the role played by Iyasus Moa in the 'restoration' of the Solomonic line circa 1270. It is said that the rightful Solomonic heir Tesfai Iyasus visited Iyasus Moa to ask for his help in usurping the throne from the Zagwe rulers. The monk prophesised that his noble visitor would one day have a son who would grow up to become king – and so the as-yet-unborn Yakuno Amlak did,

than a convenient overnight stopover point between Addis Ababa and Lalibela, or a base from which to explore Hayk or Makdala Hill. Of minor interest are a few fading occupation-era buildings, notably Bahil Amba, a once grand cinema built entirely with materials imported from Italy. Of slightly greater architectural value and antiquity is a large hilltop banquet hall known as Ayiteyef Palace, constructed by Ras Mikael in 1915. Nearby, and older still, is the church of Enda Medhane Alem, which is situated on a juniper-covered hill on the eastern outskirts of town, and was built by Ras Mikael on the site of a church reputedly destroyed centuries earlier by Ahmed Gragn. More ambitiously, you could walk to the peak of Mount Tossa, which offers views in all four directions almost as far as the Afar Depression. To get there, head to the west end of the town, drive part of the way up, and you can walk the remainder in about one hour.

These minor pickings aside, the list of tourist attractions within Dessie starts and ends with the regional museum, which opened in 1980 in the former residence of Dejasmach Josef. In addition to some interesting ethnographic displays and traditional musical instruments, the museum houses a cannon made in 1890 and used by Menelik II at the Battle of Adwa, a few 19th-century religious tracts, and some of the most lifeless stuffed animals you'll ever see. Nothing is labelled in English, but the guide is quite knowledgeable. The hill on which the museum stands – above the junction for the Kombolcha road – offers a good view over the city centre. The museum is open

after having first trained for several years at Hayk Istafanos. Ancient tradition claims that Yekuno Amlak transferred a third of the realm's property to Hayk Istafanos. During the 15th century, Hayk Istafanos faded in political significance due to the rise of Debre Libanos, the monastery founded in western Showa by Tekle Haymanot (who trained under Iyasus Moa), but it remained sufficiently important that Francisco Alvares was taken to see it in the 1520s. A few years later, Ahmed Gragn destroyed the original church.

In Alvares's day, Hayk Istafanos was set 'on a small island' which the monks went 'to and from… with a boat of reeds'. A more recent visitor, the German missionary Johan Krapf, who visited in 1841, was paddled to the monastery across a deep channel. Today, however, Hayk Istafanos lies on a peninsula and can be reached on foot – it is not clear whether this is because the water level has retreated, or the channel has simply been filled in. Either way, Hayk Istafanos is a fascinating and peaceful spot, set in lovely wooded grounds teeming with birds. The church itself appears to be quite modern, but the superb treasury houses several unusual artefacts, ranging from the heavy stone cross that belonged to Iyasus Moa, to a set of hollowed-out sacrificial stones formerly used by the pagans he converted. An entrance fee of birr 10 is charged. Women are not permitted to enter the monastery grounds, but may visit the adjacent nunnery of Margebeta Giyorgis, which was reputedly founded about 800 years ago.

Several of the most valuable treasures held at Hayk Istafanos were hidden from public view when I visited the monastery in 2001, but I was told they would be displayed in a new museum as of September that year. Most notable among these is an illustrated biography of Iyasus Moa written during his lifetime, making it one of the oldest books in Ethiopia. So far as I could ascertain upon revisiting the monastery in 2005, this museum had still not opened, or was not open to lay visitors, but we're talking serious 'how many priests does it take to answer a simple yes-or-no question?' territory here (and, for that matter, 'how many permits does a travel writer require to ask that simple bloody question?') – so who knows?

from 08.30 to 12.30 and 14.00 to 17.00 daily (mornings only at weekends). Entrance costs birr 7.

Getting there and away
Ethiopian Airlines flies between Addis Ababa and Dessie, but not between Dessie and Lalibela, which makes the service of limited interest to tourists. The airport is about 25km from Dessie on the outskirts of Kombolcha.

Dessie is 400km from Addis Ababa along a (mostly) well-maintained surfaced road, and 120km south of Woldia along a rather more pot-holed strip of asphalt. The drive from Addis Ababa normally takes five to six hours in a private vehicle, not allowing for breaks, while the drive to Woldia takes about two hours. From Woldia, it takes around four hours of solid driving to get to either Lalibela or Mekele, which means that either town takes the best part of 12 hours' non-stop driving to reach from Addis Ababa, for which reason an overnight stop at Dessie (or somewhere close by) is recommended.

Dessie is an important public transport hub. Buses to and from Mekele via Woldia leave every morning at around 06.00 and take at least seven hours. Buses between Addis Ababa and Dessie also leave in the early morning and take about eight hours. There is regular local transport from Dessie to Hayk and Kombolcha, and at least one bus runs daily in either direction between Dessie and Mille (on the Assaita road) via Kombolcha and Bati.

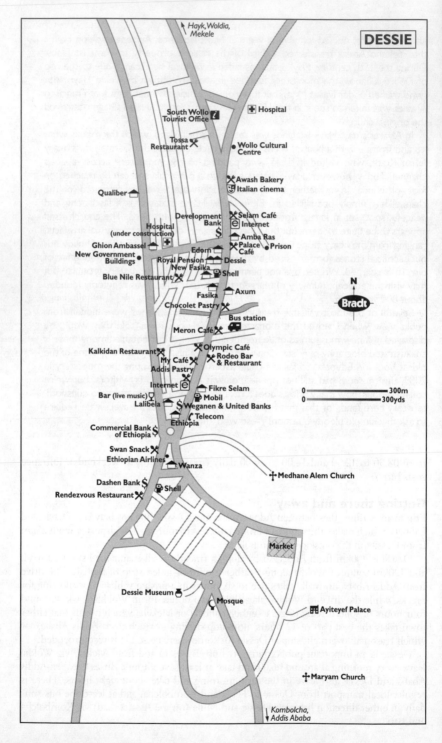

DESSIE

Hayk, Woldia, Mekele

Hospital

South Wollo Tourist Office

Tossa Restaurant

Wollo Cultural Centre

Awash Bakery
Italian cinema

Qualiber

Development Bank

Selam Café
Internet

Hospital (under construction)

Amba Ras Palace Café

Prison

Ghion Ambassel
New Government Buildings

Edom

Royal Pension
New Fasika

Dessie

Blue Nile Restaurant

Shell

Fasika

Axum

Chocolet Pastry

Meron Café

Bus station

Kalkidan Restaurant

Olympic Café

My Café

Rodeo Bar & Restaurant

Addis Pastry

Internet

Fikre Selam

Bar (live music)

Mobil

Lalibela

Weganen & United Banks

Telecom

Ethiopia

Commercial Bank of Ethiopia

Swan Snack

Ethiopian Airlines

Wanza

Medhane Alem Church

Dashen Bank

Rendezvous Restaurant

Shell

N

Bradt

0 ——————— 300m
0 ——————— 300yds

Market

Dessie Museum

Mosque

Ayiteyef Palace

Maryam Church

Kombolcha, Addis Ababa

There is now a direct bus between Dessie and Lalibela via Woldia, run by the Church Administration, and taking ten hours in either direction. This bus leaves Lalibela on Thursday and Sunday, and Dessie on Friday and Tuesday.

Where to stay
Moderate
Qualiber Hotel (18 rooms) ↘ 033 1111548. This new and rather oddly named hotel, set on a quiet back road a short distance northwest of the city centre, is currently the most commodious option in a city less than amply endowed with tourist-orientated lodgings. The clean, cosy and brightly decorated rooms with en-suite hot shower and TV are good value at birr 70/90 for a sgl/dbl. A good ground-floor bar and restaurant is attached.

Amba Ras Hotel (20 rooms) ↘ 033 1119118. Conveniently situated on the main road through Dessie, this is another decent set-up, albeit a bit more rundown, but good value at birr 72/88/110 for a sgl/dbl/ste with en-suite hot shower. The ground-floor restaurant and bar is acceptable.

New Fasika Hotel (18 rooms) ↘ 033 1117705. The relatively upmarket annexe of the Fasika Hotel, a long-serving budget favourite, charges birr 65/95 for a very clean sgl/dbl with en-suite hot shower and TV.

Lalibela Hotel (20 rooms) ↘ 033 1113093/1116908. Although it seems a bit dingy by comparison with the places listed above, this comfortable hotel isn't bad value at birr 60/90 for an en-suite sgl/dbl on the first floor or birr 70 for a ground-floor dbl.

Ghion Ambassel Hotel (32 rooms) ↘ 033 1111115. There's nothing wrong with this long-serving government hotel, which has a quiet location in green grounds just five minutes' walk from the main road, but it comes across as rather gloomy and overpriced by comparison with its competitors at birr 90/112 for a timeworn sgl/dbl with en-suite hot shower.

Budget
Fasika Hotel (33 rooms) ↘ 033 1112930. This has been the standout in its range for years, and the large, comfortable rooms with en-suite hot shower remain very popular and indisputably good value at birr 45/50 sgl/dbl.

Ethiopia Hotel Despite a convenient location, this scruffy hotel on the main roundabout feels overpriced at birr 44 for a sgl with cold shower only.

Shoestring
Royal Pension (12 rooms) ↘ 033 1114939. Savoury shoestring options are thin on the ground in Dessie, but this small lodging, around the corner from the Fasika, is a welcome exception, charging birr 25 for a bare but clean room with a genuine dbl bed and en-suite hot shower, or birr 15 for a similar room using a common shower. If it is full, the nearby Fikre Selam and Axum hotels, though seriously inferior, are about the best of the rest.

Where to eat
With the exception of the New Fasika, the hotels listed above in the moderate category all have good restaurants serving Western and local dishes in the birr 10–15 range – the **Qualiber** and **Lalibela** hotels are particularly recommended. The **Tossa Restaurant** comes highly recommended for Ethiopian dishes, while the **Kalkidan Restaurant** near the Lalibela Hotel specialises in cutlets and other dishes made with fish from Lake Hayk.

There must be a dozen pastry shops and cafés lining the main road through Dessie. The pick is probably the **Palace Café** (formerly Ras Pastry) next to the Amba Ras Hotel, which serves an excellent selection of cakes and pastries, as well as fresh orange juice, coffee, mini-pizzas and local meals. Also worth trying are **My Café**, **Meron Café** and **Chocolet Pastry**. For fresh bread, the Awash Bakery north of the Amba Ras Hotel is recommended.

Listings
Internet and email
Dessie is well endowed when it comes to internet facilities, remarkably so when you arrive there from further north. One of the largest internet cafés stands on the main road opposite the Fikre Selam Hotel, but there are several others dotted around town, charging around birr 0.30 per minute to browse.

Nightlife
For live music, the brightly coloured but anonymous hotel more or less opposite the Lalibela Hotel has a resident band that performs lively cover versions of current Amharigna hits. John Graham writes in one of his columns that: 'The nightclubs and Asmari bars at the western end of Dessie are renowned. Asmari singers, with their one-stringed instruments, are incredibly clever at creating lyrics. Once they know your name, you will be treated to an Amharigna praise song about your generosity, intelligence, sexual appetite or whatever other compliments they can think of. You are expected to give a generous tip.'

Tourist information
The South Wolo Tourist Office is situated on the main road north of the city centre, close to the hospital.

KOMBOLCHA
Overshadowed by the nearby metropolis of Dessie, from which it is divided by just 25km of madly scenic asphalt road, Kombolcha is the site of the main airport serving South Wolo and an industrial and commercial centre of some substance in its own right – indeed, with a population estimated at around 70,000, it comfortably stands among the 20 largest settlements in Ethiopia. The town centre, set at an altitude of 1,850m, is likeable enough and noticeably warmer than nearby Dessie, but otherwise unremarkable.

The Yegof Forest on the ridge overlooking Kombolcha still supports relic populations of Menelik's bushbuck, vervet monkey, leopard and various smaller mammals. In a short 1996 study, 62 bird species were recorded in this forest, including the endemic Abyssinian woodpecker and Abyssinian catbird, and tropical boubou, olive pigeon and blue-headed coucal.

There is no overwhelming reason to stay in Kombolcha over Dessie, but then nor is there any real reason not to. I thought Kombolcha the more attractive of the two towns, and it is also well placed for day trips to Bati and the Geta Lion. Both towns have good facilities and public transport connections – the better hotels in Dessie are far smarter than their counterparts in Kombolcha, but Dessie fares less well when it comes to decent budget accommodation. Assuming that you're just passing through, it probably makes sense to stay in the town closest to your next destination.

Getting there and away
Details are much the same as for Dessie, though it is worth noting that many long-distance buses (for instance between Dessie and Addis Ababa) generally stop to drop or pick up passengers outside the Hikma Pension, not at the bus station. Minibuses run between Kombolcha and Dessie throughout the day on a fill-up-and-go basis; the trip takes around 45 minutes. There is also at least one bus daily through to Mille (on the Assaita road), passing through Bati and sometimes continuing as far as the junction to Assaita itself.

It's a long steep walk from the bus station into the town centre, where most of the hotels are – a horse-drawn *gari* is the answer.

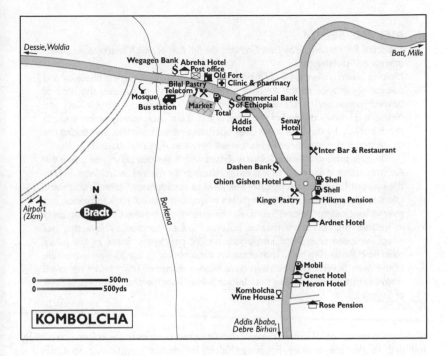

If you fly to Dessie, the airport – more accurately, the airstrip and customs shack – actually lies just 2km from Kombolcha. There are not normally any taxis to meet flights to Kombolcha, so you may have to hitch or walk into the town centre to pick up transport in to Dessie.

Where to stay
Budget
Meron Hotel (28 rooms) ☎ 033 5510134. Probably the smartest option in town, this charges a surprisingly steep birr 50/70 for a sgl/dbl room with en-suite hot shower.
Hikma Pension ☎ 033 5510015. This established hotel on the main traffic roundabout charges birr 25/40 for a large, clean room with dbl/twin bed and en-suite hot shower. It has a popular restaurant with a large veranda, and serves a selection of juices and pastries – it's a good place to pick up lifts on to Addis, and to take advantage of the clean public toilets.

Shoestring
Gishen Hotel ☎ 033 5510013. This seems fair value at birr 25 for a large dbl or twin using a clean common shower. The restaurant is recommended for roast lamb, which costs birr 10.
Abreha Hotel Not as good value, but more convenient for backpackers since it's only 100m from the bus station, this has clean rooms with a cold shower for birr 35, while rooms using a communal shower cost birr 30. The restaurant is worth a try: a substantial plate of roast lamb with bread and salad costs birr 10.

Excursions from Dessie and Kombolcha
Gishen Debre Kerbe
The monastery of Gishen Debre Kerbe – also often called Gishen Maryam after the oldest of its four churches – is one of the most revered in Ethiopia. It lies northwest of Dessie off the road to Wegel Tena, and is situated on a massive cross-shaped rock *amba*

MEKANE SELAM

Extracted from an article by John Graham, the full text of which is accessible online at www.addistribune.com

Mekane Selam is the capital of Debre Sina Woreda, an area of great historical and cultural significance to the Amhara people. Mekane Selam is also the back of beyond: connected to Dessie by 180km of very bad road (through Kabi and Aksta), it is literally the end of the road, one of the most westerly points you can reach in Wolo by car. The town does boast an airstrip, however, and during the dry season it receives three flights a week between Addis Ababa and Dessie.

The area around Mekane Selam is dotted with five-sided pillars not unlike the Axumite stelae in appearance and easily mistaken for manmade artefacts. In fact, the source of these pillars, possibly unknown to outsiders until John Graham was taken to see it a couple of years ago, is a magnificent natural rock formation in a river valley close to Mekane Selam. Reminiscent of the famous Giants' Causeway in Ireland, the rocks are basaltic columnar pillars, formed by lava that has effectively been crystallised into tightly packed pentagons. Some of the pillars must be close to 10m high. The formation stretches for about 30m on either side of the river. Several local buildings have been constructed using pillars removed from this formation, including the Mekane Selam branch of the Commercial Bank of Ethiopia.

(flat-topped mountain). Gishen is one of the oldest monasteries in the country, reputedly founded in the 5th century by King Kaleb. Its greater significance to Orthodox Christians, however, is the legend that it possesses the piece of the True Cross (the cross on which Jesus was crucified) that was brought to Ethiopia during the 14th-century reign of Emperor Dawit. Gishen Amba, with its cruciform shape, was chosen by Emperor Zara Yaqob as the best place to store this holy treasure. The True Cross is reputedly stashed Russian doll-style within four boxes (respectively made of iron, bronze, silver, and gold), which are suspended by chains within a closed subterranean chamber at the end of a tunnel 20m below the ground. In common with the Ark of the Covenant at Axum, it is off-limits to all but a select few. Whether or not there is any truth in the legend of the True Cross, the cruciform plateau and its four churches are very beautiful and sacred, and Gishen routinely attracts many thousands of pilgrims over Meskel (the Festival of the True Cross).

Gishen Amba has a second, more verifiable claim to fame, as the source of Dr Johnson's morality tale of Rasselas, the prince who was imprisoned in a valley encircled by mountains by the King of Abyssinia. During several periods in Ethiopian history, it has been customary for the emperor to protect his throne by imprisoning his potential successors – sons, brothers, uncles and other princes – on a near impregnable mountaintop. The Portuguese priest Alvares described this practice in his account of his lengthy sojourn in Ethiopia, providing the inspiration for Johnson's tale, as well – somewhat bizarrely – as the vision of an earthly paradise described in Milton's *Paradise Lost*. The tale of Rasselas in turn formed the driving obsession behind Thomas Pakenham's travels in Ethiopia in 1955, documented in his compulsively readable book *The Mountains of Rasselas* (see *Further Reading*, page 565). According to Pakenham, Gishen Amba is one of three mountains that have been used to imprison princes at different points in Ethiopia's history; it was preceded in this role by the monastery at Debre Damo, and succeeded by Mount Wehni near Gonder. Gishen first served as a royal prison in 1295, when Emperor Yakuno Amlak sent his five sons there, and it held a solid stream of similar captives until it was virtually razed by Ahmed Gragn in the 16th century.

In Pakenham's day, Gishen was accessible only by foot or by mule. Today, the monastery can be reached by road as a long day trip from Dessie, or as an overnight trip in conjunction with Makdala Hill (see page 340). In a private vehicle, you need to drive out of Dessie towards Wegel Tena, following a good gravel road that passes a 50m-high waterfall on the Kaskasa (literally 'Cold') River a few kilometres out of town, then runs through the small town of Kutaber. The turn-off to Gishen, signposted in Amharigna only, is roughly 70km out of Dessie, and entails a 17km ascent along a road that deteriorates badly over the last 5km. The final ascent to the top of the mountain must be done on foot and takes about 30 minutes. Reasonably regular buses run between Dessie and Wegel Tena, but there is no public transport to Gishen itself except over Meskel, when hundreds of buses head out there.

Makdala Hill

It was to Makdala that an embattled and embittered Emperor Tewodros retreated in 1867, as his dream of a unified Ethiopia crumbled under the strain of internal and external pressures, most significantly his own growing unpopularity with his subjects. His once all-conquering army reduced through desertion and rebellion to a tenth of its former size, and his pleas for British alliance unanswered, the emperor was forced to abandon his capital at Debre Tabor and to barricade himself in the hilltop castle at Makdala. In a final and rather desperate attempt to lever Britain into giving him military support, Tewodros took with him a group of European prisoners. In 1868, after Britain's attempt to negotiate for the release of the prisoners ended in the negotiator himself being jailed, a force of 32,000 troops was sent to Makdala, under the command of Lord Napier and with the support of the future Emperor Yohannis IV. Tewodros, rather than face capture, took his own life. He was buried in the church at Makdala at the request of his wife.

Makdala Hill lies about 100km northwest of Dessie as the crow flies, and about 18km cross-country from the remote town of Tenta. The recommended route to Tenta, about 130km in all, is to follow the Wegel Tena road, passing the junction to Gishen Amba, then after about 95km turning left on to the Tenta road shortly before you reach Wegel Tena. Tenta can also be reached by following the road south to Guguftu then turning northeast through Amba Maryam. The condition of both these routes is variable, so if you are driving yourself, you may want to ask the tourist office in Dessie for current advice. If you are dependent on public transport, you will probably have to use the route through Wegel Tena. Either way, you are looking at a four-to-six-hour drive, depending to some extent on the state of the road.

A certain degree of bureaucracy is involved in setting up a visit to Makdala. Before heading out, it is strongly advised that you obtain a letter of permission from the tourist office in Dessie or police station in Kombolcha. You will also need to visit the police station in Ajbar, which lies on the Amba Maryam road 12km south of Tenta, where you will be expected to pick up an all-but-obligatory police escort at a daily charge of birr 50. (The idea, as explained to Barry Austin, is to protect travellers against various real or imaginary dangers – 'lions'? – but the escort 'turned out to be a most worthwhile investment, as he knew all the short-cuts, where we could get *tella*, and where the famous guns are located'.) From Ajbar, you have to head back to Tenta, where mules or donkeys can be hired at birr 20–30 per day, and porters at birr 15 per day. From Tenta, the trek to Makdala takes half a day using a combination of mules and walking. The path initially drops some 700m in altitude before ascending to the top of the mountain, which lies at an altitude of around 3,000m. The scenery is wonderful, and the fortifications erected by Tewodros are still in place. So, too, is Sebastopol, Tewodros's pet name for the unmarked (and unfireable) bronze cannon built by the missionaries he took hostage at Gafat. You could, at a push, trek to Makdala and back as a long day trip out of Tenta, but most visitors

AWLIYAW: THE LARGEST AND OLDEST TREE IN ETHIOPIA?

Edited from an article by Dr Alula Pankhurst, the full text of which can be accessed online at www.addistribune.com

The protected Anabe Forest, one of the few areas of indigenous yellowwood forest to remain in southern Wolo, was 'discovered' as recently as 1978 by a forester looking for a nursery site. It is situated some 30km west of Gerba on the road from Kombolcha to Bati. Until recently, the rough road from Gerba to the forest was passable only as far as the market town of Adame, from where one had to walk for three hours. However, following the construction of a new road by local people through an Employment Generation Scheme organised by Concern with EU funding, the forest is now easily accessible by 4x4.

Tucked away near steep cliffs and surrounded by cultivated fields, Anabe Forest is practically invisible until you arrive within a couple of kilometres of its edge. It currently covers an area of about 50ha, but used to be considerably larger. In *An Illustrated Guide to the Trees and Shrubs in the Red Cross Project Areas in Wolo*, Professor Mesfin Tadesse mentions an Amharigna saying which translates as 'Anabe is said to be growing old and greying, a solitary individual could now cross it without fear'.

Sadly, exotic trees, notably pines, have been planted in peripheral parts of the forest. The heart of the forest is, however, still dominated by the indigenous yellowwood *Podocarpus falcatus*, known as *Zegba* in Amharigna. This gigantic tree, one of the most beautiful in Ethiopia, is an evergreen with a dense crown. It provides cool shade and nourishment for birds and small mammals, and shelter to guereza monkeys, which also eat its fruit. Indeed, we saw a few troops of this beautiful monkey, now rare in so much of the country, since its black-and-white coat is illegally sought for making carpets. Because yellowwood is classified as a 'high-class softwood', it is a prime source of timber, used for cupboards, shelves, panels, matchsticks etc. In the middle of the past century, it was the number one commercial species in Ethiopia,

carry a tent and camp on the hill, where local people can arrange firewood and water, but not food.

Tenta itself is a rather dreary place, lacking electricity or running water, and notable mostly for the surrounding scenery. Worth a look, and situated only a couple of kilometres north of Tenta, is the circular stone church of Tenta Mikael, built by Ras Mikael of Dessie at the turn of the 20th century. A three-tiered construction enclosed by a high wall supporting majestic towers and turrets, the church contains the domed tomb of Ras Mikael. Tenta boasts a couple of grotty local hotels. Slightly better accommodation is available at Ajbar. In a private vehicle, it is possible to continue northwest from Tenta to Lalibela, but be warned this short stretch of road is in very poor condition and may be impassable after heavy rain.

Bati

The small town of Bati is situated roughly 40km east of Kombolcha between the central highlands and the low-lying Rift Valley, where it forms an important cultural crossroads for the Amhara, Oromo and semi-nomadic desert-dwelling Afar people. For more than two centuries, Bati has hosted Ethiopia's largest cattle and camel market, attracting up to 20,000 people every Monday. If you're in the area at the right time of the week, the market is well worth the relatively minor diversion, not only for the sheer scale of the phenomenon, but also for the glimpse into a facet of Ethiopia very different to anything you'll encounter in the highlands. Coming from the highlands, the Afar seem to belong to another Africa

accounting for 60% of production. Less than 1% of Ethiopia's original *Podocarpus* forest is thought to survive intact today.

The most special tree in Anabe is known locally as *Awliyaw*, a term suggestive of its revered status (*Weliy* means prophet in the Islamic tradition and *Awliya* often refers to a Zar possession cult). Legend has it that it existed before all the other trees, when the land was barren and that it gave rise to all the other trees. There is a story that a man attempted to climb the tree to catch a queen bee, but retreated when a snake confronted him. The man is said to have died within three days, for having disrespected the sanctuary.

This sacred tree is estimated by Professor Mesfin to be about 12.5m in circumference and about 4m in diameter. True enough, when we measured the tree, we found it to be 12.7m in circumference. Is this the largest tree in Ethiopia? The tree is said to be 63m high. Is this figure correct? Has anyone seen a taller tree in this country? Forestry reports from the 1940s suggest a maximum height of 50m for *Zegba* trees, whereas reports in the 1990s suggest a maximum of 35m.

Awliyaw is said to be more than 700 years old, which may seem incredible, but studies of old trees in other parts of the world mention exceptional cases of trees that have surpassed a millennium and even cases of trees, notably yews, that may be up to 1,400 years old. In his beautiful book *Meetings with Remarkable Trees*, Thomas Pakenham depicts an oak that was standing at the time of William the Conqueror in 1066. If *Awliyaw* is as old as it is said to be, then it must have been planted before the restoration of the Solomonic dynasty in 1270!

It is sad that a tree as venerable as *Awliyaw* is so little known. I have only ever come across one photograph of it (showing a 'human chain' around its trunk, and published by Professor Mesfin), and it isn't described in any tourist guides. Is this because Anabe Forest has been fairly inaccessible in the past? If so, then perhaps the new road will generate greater interest in it. In a country where deforestation is such a pressing concern, this exceptional example of natural beauty surely deserves more celebration!

altogether: the bare-breasted women with their wild plaited hairstyles and elaborate ornate jewellery, the tall, proud men strutting around with Kalashnikovs slung over their shoulder, and lethal traditional dagger tucked away in a prominent hide sheath.

So far as travel practicalities go, a fair surfaced road connects Bati to Kombolcha, and several buses run between the two towns daily, with traffic being heaviest on a Monday. The trip takes about 60 minutes in a private vehicle and 90 minutes by bus, so it is possible to visit as a day trip out of Kombolcha or Dessie. It is worth noting that the road from Kombolcha to Bati continues on to Mille on the asphalt highway between Awash and Assaita/Assab. Off the road between Kombolcha and Bati lies the Anabe Forest (see box above).

A few cheap and basic hotels are dotted around the small town centre, while the best restaurant is painted blue and lies on the opposite side of town to (about 300m away from) the bus station. A more commodious option, though only barely so, is the Ghion Kersa Hotel (*seven rooms;* ☏ *033 5530007*), which lies in scenic grounds about 2km out of town on the northern verge of the Kombolcha road. The hotel charges birr 37.50 for a rundown little double room using a common shower and has an acceptable restaurant and bar. With only seven rooms available, it would be a good idea to ring through a booking for the night before or after market day.

The Geta Lion

One of the more intriguing of Ethiopia's lesser-known monuments is the monolithic sculpture of a lion at Geta, to the southeast of Kombolcha. Suspended about one metre from the edge of a small hill studded with euphorbia shrubs, the carving depicts the front part of a male lion, with bulging oriental-looking eyes, lines representing the mane, ferociously bared teeth, and feet stretched forwards. When the lion was sculpted, and by whom, is a matter of pure conjecture. Given the Ethiopian gift for manufacturing legend, the absence of a local tradition linking the lion to the Queen of Sheba, or Abreha and Atsbeha, or any other historical figure, is quite remarkable. The furthest that locals are prepared to commit themselves is that the sculpture has been there for as long as anybody can remember. In all probability, the Geta Lion dates to Axumite times or earlier. A Maltese Cross carved into the basal rock might be seen to indicate that the lion was sculpted after Christianity was introduced to Ethiopia. It could also be that, like the cruciform carving alongside the (otherwise very different) engraving of a lion a few kilometres outside Axum, this cross was added centuries after the original lion was sculpted. The enigmatic origin of the Geta Lion is compounded when one recognises that it exists in apparent isolation – no similar monument is known within a radius of hundreds of kilometres!

The Geta Lion can be reached by following the Addis Ababa road south of Kombolcha for 12km to Chekorti, from where one must turn on to an eastbound side road signposted for Geta Mosque. From the mosque, which lies less than 5km along the side road, it's roughly a 30-minute walk to the lion sculpture. Geta Mosque, founded in the mid 19th century by the renowned Islamic scholar Haji Bushra Mohammed, is also of some interest as a pilgrimage site attracting thousands of worshippers on Muslim holidays.

Harbu Hot Springs

About 15km from Kombolcha along the road to Addis Ababa, the small town of Harbu is noted for its hot springs, which lie about 3km west of the main road. The springs are believed to have curative properties, and have been used by locals for bathing and drinking for longer than five centuries. They feed a short stream that flows into the larger Borkena River.

Dessie to Addis Ababa

The 400km asphalt road that connects Dessie to Addis Ababa is one of many in Ethiopia that can as easily be whizzed along in a day as it can be explored more slowly over several. If you are looking at the former option, all you need really know is that it's roughly a six-hour drive in a private vehicle, and takes about eight hours on one of the many buses that depart in either direction between Dessie and Addis Ababa at around 06.00 daily. Aside from Kombolcha, just 25km from Dessie, the largest town along this stretch of road is Debre Birhan, which lies about 130km (two hours' drive) northeast of Addis Ababa, but there are several smaller towns along the way, notably Debre Sina at the base of the spectacular Mezezo Escarpment.

Should exploration be on your agenda, the most popular excursion – a scenic hour's drive east of Debre Birhan – is to Ankober, a small town that is of interest to historians as the site of the former Showan capital, and to naturalists for its endemic birds and gelada baboons. Even more worthwhile in terms of wildlife is the little-known Guassa Plateau near Mehal Meda, where large numbers of gelada can be observed about 90 minutes' drive east of Tarmabir, alongside the second-largest remaining population of the rare Ethiopian wolf. There are also several atmospheric but little-visited monasteries in the vicinity of Debre Sina, Tarmabir and Mehal Meda.

FROM KOMBOLCHA TO DEBRE SINA/TARMABIR

As with many such trips in northern Ethiopia, the roughly 250km run between Kombolcha (or Dessie) and Debre Birhan can be covered either as a straightforward non-stop drive or bus trip, or else broken up by hopping between towns. And, once again, which way you decide to go is largely dependent on time and temperament: a direct bus will be much quicker, but hopping between towns adds the element of chance that some travellers prefer. With an early start, you should easily get between Dessie and Debre Birhan in a day using local transport.

Kombolcha to Debre Sina

There is plenty of transport between Dessie and Kombolcha. At Kombolcha, you could wait near the Hikma Hotel, the best place to pick up long-distance buses or to try for a lift southwards in a private vehicle. Alternatively, head to the bus station and hop on one of the small buses that leave every couple of hours for Kemise, 50km south of Kombolcha. **Kemise** is a busy little Oromo town, and, apparently, a popular truck stop, so there are plenty of hotels and restaurants. The likelihood of spending a night here by chance is very small, as buses run on to Senbete and Ataye until as late as 16.00. If you do, there are several cheap hotels along the main road – the Arayaaredaa and Alemu hotels are adequate, and the former seems to serve the best food in town – though a better option is the relatively smart Oasis Hotel on the southern outskirts.

With an interest in birds, you may actually choose to spend the night in Kemise. About

10km south of town, the road skirts the **Borkana Wetlands** immediately after crossing the bridge over the eponymous river. Here, stretching along the western fringe of the road for about 2km, you'll find a combination of open water, mudflats, river, marsh and reed-beds, seasonally affected by the river's input, but perennially wet due to several hot springs which bubble out in the area. At the end of the rainy season, the ample birdlife may disperse to a smaller but wetter seasonal swamp about 3km north of Kemise. Either way, without leaving the road you stand a good chance of seeing marabou and saddle-billed stork, the endemic blue-winged goose, pelicans, ibises, and much more.

There's not a lot to be said about **Ataye** (marked on some maps as **Efeson**), but if you do get stuck, the Sai Hotel is a superior dollar-a-night place, with large rooms, a communal cold shower and friendly staff. It's not signposted, but all buses from the north stop right in front of it – anybody can show you where it is. Also recommended is the Roman Hotel on the Addis Ababa side of town. For eating, a couple of restaurants serve indifferent *yefigel wat* and fried eggs, and the snack bar with yellow umbrellas on the Dessie side of town does juice, coffee, eggs, bread and cakes. Definitely worth checking out, should you be around at the right time, is the market held every Sunday at **Senbete**, only 9km south of Ataye. This is the best market in the area after Bati's famous Monday market, attracting villagers for miles around, predominantly Oromo people, but also Afar, Amhara and Argeba. Should you want to spend the night, there are a couple of indifferent small hotels in Senbete.

South of Ataye, the next town of real substance is **Robit**, on the banks of the wide but normally dry Robit River. Except perhaps on Wednesdays, when the town is the site of a colourful market, there's no overwhelming reason why you'd want to stop in Robit, but equally there is no shortage of low-rent accommodation should you decide to. Best bet is the Birangete Hotel, which has en-suite rooms for birr 20, basic rooms for birr 8, and a decent but slow restaurant.

About halfway along the 32km road between Robit and Debre Sina, the small town of **Armaniya** is the base from which one can visit **Mercurios Monastery**, which is renowned for housing a very old painting of Saint Mercurios on horseback. The reason for this painting's fame, according to two local eyewitnesses, is that the horse miraculously starts to move on procession days, which are normally held on 5 August and 4 December. Frankly, your guess is as good as mine, but should you happen to be in the area at the right time, and be inspired to check it out, I'd be fascinated to hear more. The monastery stands one to two hours' walk from Armaniya. Should you need a room, the bright-green Armaniya Anbassa Hotel looks adequate.

Debre Sina

Situated along the main Addis Ababa road at the northern foot of the immense Mezezo Escarpment, Debre Sina is a significant – and significantly chilly – town boasting several hotels and restaurants. A scenic location and a bustling Monday and Thursday market aside, Debre Sina (Amharigna for 'Mount Sinai') holds little of inherent interest to travellers, but it does make a good springboard for visits to a number of little-known monasteries that lie along roads branching northwest from Tarmabir, a smaller – and even colder – town set at an altitude of around 3,250m on the escarpment on the main road 10km south of Debre Sina. The road between Debre Sina and Tarmabir passes through an impressive 587m-long, 8m-wide and 6.5m-high Italian-built tunnel, in an area regularly frequented by gelada baboons.

Getting there and away

Debre Sina straddles the main road between Dessie and Addis Ababa about 60km north of Debre Birhan. There is plenty of public transport along this road. Tarmabir is separated from Debre Sina by a stunning 10km road of surfaced switchbacks, passing through the

Mussolini Tunnel. The cliffs here are reputedly a good place to see the endemic gelada baboon (I've yet to have the pleasure), while a site along the main road about 4km before Tarmabir is one of two established areas where the localised Ankober serin (see *Ankober*, page 332) is regular. Reasonably regular local transport connects Debre Sina and Tarmabir.

Where to stay and eat

Tinsae Hotel This double-storey building on the Addis Ababa side of town about 100m from the bus stop is excellent value at around birr 25 for a small but well-maintained room with ¾ bed and en-suite hot shower (very welcome in this climate). The ground-floor restaurant serves reasonable Ethiopian food, coffee, and draught or bottled beer.

Addis Metraf Hotel A similar distance from the bus station, but in the opposite direction, this double-storey hotel also has en-suite rooms for birr 25 – it's not bad, but there is no hot water and rooms are a bit scruffy.

Degasmuch Teseme Hotel Situated right next to the bus station, this is as quiet and clean as you could reasonably expect at birr 10 for a room using common showers.

Adkanu Maryam and Adjana Mikael

These two monasteries both lie to the west of the main Addis Ababa road close to the small town of Sela Dingay. The more accessible of the two is Adkanu Maryam. This is an attractive and atmospheric partly hewn cave church, said to date to the 15th-century rule of Zara Yaqob, and is built up along a juniper-covered cliff face. It is open to lay worshippers, but also serves as a monastery, with several hermit cells carved into the rocks alongside the main courtyard, and a few nuns hanging around the outbuildings. During Lent, large numbers of pilgrims from Addis Ababa and elsewhere congregate around the church. A nearby spring produces holy water. Church treasures include a large silver cross of an unspecified date. Nearby Adjana Mikael, another cave church but reputedly much older than Adkanu Maryam, is set at the base of a cliff, and known for the holy water produced by a spring.

Neither monastery receives tourists regularly or seems to know quite what to do with them – entrance fees have not, as yet, caught on, though it would be fitting to leave a small donation. Their very remoteness is a big part of the churches' charm, but it also means that one should be especially conscious of the sensibilities of the priest and his congregation. Women should wear a skirt that reaches below their knees and cover their head in a scarf, cloth or even a towel, and all visitors should ask permission before pointing a camera at anything.

Getting there and away

To reach either monastery from Debre Sina, you first need to head to Tarmabir, 10km further south along the Addis Ababa road, then follow a side road west for 20km to Sela Dingay. The drive from Debre Sina to Sela Dingay takes about 45 minutes one-way in a private vehicle. Using public transport, there's a fair amount of traffic between Debre Sina and Tarmabir, while a daily bus and the odd light vehicle links Tarmabir to Sela Dingay; if you don't intend spending the night in Sela Dingay, the earliest possible start is recommended. Be aware that a modern church also called Adkanu Maryam lies unspectacularly alongside this road, about 3km before you enter Sela Dingay.

Once in Sela Dingay, the walk to the Adkanu Maryam monastery, which takes 20–30 minutes, is easy though a bit steep in parts, offering some great views across the Kaskasa River Gorge on the way – anybody will show you the footpath for a small tip. The monastery of Adjana Mikael is about three hours from Sela Dingay on foot, though a rough road there should be passable by 4x4 during the dry season only – either way, you will need a local guide. Note that some maps erroneously show the road towards Sela Dingay branching west from Debre Sina rather than Tarmabir.

Where to stay and eat

It would be easy enough to visit these monasteries as a day trip from Debre Sina or en route between Debre Sina and Debre Birhan, especially if you have a private vehicle. Should you elect to stay in Tarmabir, however, there is one acceptable shoestring hotel on the junction with the road to Sela Dingay. Alternatively, the Addis Hotel in Sela Dingay charges birr 5 for a very simple room with a ¾ bed; cold bucket showers are provided on request (not a request you're likely to make with any conviction at this altitude) and a restaurant serves local dishes, beers, sodas and coffee.

MENZ

Situated to the northwest of Debre Sina, the chilly highland region known as Menz was one of the few parts of Showa to survive the Muslim and Oromo incursions of the 16th and 17th centuries, and it is regarded to be the ancestral home of the Showan monarchy. Practically unknown to tourists, the region boasts two significant and very different attractions, namely the spooky monastery of Arbara Medhane Alem and the fantastically underrated and wildlife-rich Guassa Plateau, the latter being the most accessible site for Ethiopian wolf anywhere north of Bale National Park. Seldom visited as they are, both sites are readily accessible from the 100km road that links Mehal Meda, the rather low-key traditional capital of Menz, to Tarmabir on the asphalt road between Debre Birhan and Debre Sina.

Getting around

In a private vehicle, the road to Mehal Meda, which bisects the Guassa Plateau, can be covered in about two hours, not allowing for stops. It is thus perfectly possible to visit both Guassa and Arbara Medhane Alem as a day trip out of Debre Sina or Debre Birhan, or en route between the two towns. If you are driving yourself, a potentially confusing quirk of the road running northwest to Menz is that, contrary to expectations, it initially branches eastward from Tarmabir, more or less opposite the junction for the road to Sela Dingay, only to cut back in a westerly direction above the Italian-built tunnel that encloses (and renders invisible) the main road to Debre Sina!

After about 8km, the road from Tarmabir to Mehal Meda offers some amazing views over the escarpment to the Sharobe River, before passing through the small village of Mezezo at the 14km mark. Another 15km further, the road bisects a patch of eucalyptus forest whose dense undergrowth is frequented by Bohor reedbuck, Menelik's bushbuck and the very localised Erckell's francolin. The small town of Bash flanks the road some 50km from Tarmabir, then 10km further, at Malaya, there is a junction where you need to turn right. Another 7km past this is Yegam, the closest village to Arbara Medhane Alem. The road ascends to the Guassa Plateau 8km out of Yegam and bisects it for about 10km before descending slightly for the last 15km stretch to Mehal Meda.

For those dependent on public transport, two buses daily connect Addis Ababa to Mehal Meda via Debre Birhan, leaving at 06.00 and taking the best part of a full day in either direction. It would be easy enough to hop off the bus at Yegam or on the plateau, but there isn't too much other transport along this road, so you do risk being stranded overnight. If I were to take this risk, I would first bus all the way through to Mehal Meda, spend the night there, then use the bus towards Addis the next morning to get to Guassa, which would at least mean that I'd have the best part of a day to find transport out. Outside of Mehal Meda, the only accommodation I'm aware of in Menz is one small local hotel in Mezezo.

Arbara Medhane Alem

This small cave church and monastery has a magnificent cliff setting at an altitude of around 3,000m northeast of the Mehal Meda road near the village of Yegam, 67km from Tarmabir. It can be reached in ten to 15 minutes along a very steep footpath leading downhill from Yegam into a grove of eucalyptus trees. Initially, the church might seem anticlimactic – the modern building is just 20 years old – but for a small donation the priests will lead you downhill into the patch of indigenous bush that hides the old church. The most remarkable feature of the church is an ancient mausoleum piled high with mummified corpses, some of whose limbs stick out of the wrapping in macabre contortions. Oddly, nobody in Yegam seems to have a coherent theory about how old the mummies are, or how they got there – my local informant reckoned they belonged to a tribe of angel-like beings who descended from the sky at least 100 years ago!

Guassa Plateau

Set at a mean altitude of 3,200m, the Guassa Plateau extends over 110km², making it one of the largest extant Afro-alpine ecosystems in Ethiopia (or elsewhere in Africa for that matter). It is the highest plateau in Ethiopia's central highlands, and it forms an important catchment area, feeding some 26 streams that eventually flow into the Blue Nile. Uniquely in Ethiopia, where centralised conservation efforts have met with limited success in recent years, the local community near Guassa has been managing its natural resources in a sustainable way for at least 400 years.

Some local ambivalence to the Guassa Plateau is revealed by a local legend concerning a monk called Yohannis. A pregnant woman accused the highly respected monk, who was sworn to celibacy, of being the father of her soon-to-be-born child. The local people asked the woman to repeat this shocking claim in front of the disgraced Yohannis, and so she did, stating: 'Let me turn into stone if I tell a lie.' As she spoke, the woman was transformed into stone, and the betrayed monk abandoned the area with a curse: 'Let this land turn cold and bleak for evermore, and the rich agricultural land become scrub.' As the monk spoke, the plateau, formerly known for its fine *tef*, was transformed into a bleak and non-cultivatable landscape of windswept heather tussocks and grassy swamps. A commemorative day for Yohannis is observed throughout Menz on 26 January.

Seven of Ethiopia's endemic mammals are resident on the plateau (22.6% of the endemic mammalian fauna), including what ranks as one of the largest surviving populations of Ethiopian wolf, and several troops of the grass-eating gelada baboon. In addition, a total of 111 bird species have been recorded, including 14 endemics, among them an important population of the globally threatened Ankober serin (first recorded here in 1998) and spot-breasted plover, wattled ibis, thick-billed raven, blue-winged goose, Rouget's rail, Rüppell's black chat and Abyssinian longclaw. A good place to look for endemic birds (and the Ethiopian wolf for that matter) is the marshy area that lies to the right of the Mehal Meda road 84km from Tarmabir, and the moist valley fed by the Teter River to the left of the road about 1km further.

Estimates of the plateau's Ethiopian wolf population vary from 20 to 50 individuals, with the lower figure probably closest to the mark. General consensus among local communities is that the population has decreased over the last few years, due to a combination of habitat destruction, civil war, drought, disease and poisoning. Wolf densities on Guassa are strongly linked to densities of the four rodent species that account for almost 90% of their prey locally, and these were known to decline during a recent drought that also coincided with the death of at least six undernourished wolves on Guassa.

Practically speaking, Guassa is by far the easiest place to see the Ethiopian wolf after Bale National Park, and is the most accessible wolf habitat north of Addis Ababa. The wolves are regularly sighted from the main road across the plateau, and they are not at all shy of human observers. They are most active in the early morning and late afternoon, but might be seen at any time of the day – indeed I recently had two excellent wolf sightings crossing the plateau at midday, as well as seeing three gelada troops totalling some 200 individuals. Another carnivore likely to be seen on the plateau is the smaller, browner and less distinctly marked Eurasian jackal.

There is no reason why self-sufficient travellers (that means with tent, warm clothing and food) couldn't camp at the Guassa rangers' post, which lies on the roadside about 10km past Yegam, and explore the area on foot from there. The area close to the rangers' post is good for gelada and Ethiopian wolf, and the rangers will probably be happy to guide you for a small tip. There is some talk of a rest camp being built on the plateau, possibly in collaboration with local community leaders and the Ethiopian Wolf Conservation Project, but this is unlikely to happen soon.

Mehal Meda

The informal capital of Menz is an odd little place, far removed from the recognised tourist circuit, and very friendly – indeed the rare arrival of a *faranji* seems to induce an infectious communal mood of the giggles. That aside, it is of limited interest except a base from which to explore the Guassa Plateau 15km to its east. As for accommodation, the best bet is the Nyala Hotel (✆ *011 6813360*), 200m from the bus station, which charges birr 10 for a clean room using a common shower, or birr 15 for one with en-suite facilities. It's all rapidly downhill from there, but the best of the remaining half-dozen or so places (and proud possessor of what seems to be the town's only coffee machine) is the National Hotel, where a basic room costs birr 6. Both hotels serve a limited selection of local dishes.

DEBRE BIRHAN

This friendly highland town of 50,000 souls, set 130km northeast of Addis Ababa, though of some historical note is nothing out of the ordinary today. It is of logistical significance, particularly to birdwatching tours, as the closest large town to Ankober (described later in this chapter), and would make a good first stop on a relaxed itinerary northwards from the capital. Debre Birhan firmly fits into the sprawling category of Ethiopian towns. A church and open fields separate the old town centre, which lies towards Addis Ababa, from the bus station and the newer buildings on the Dessie road.

Debre Birhan – which translates as 'Mountain of Light' – was almost certainly founded in 1456 by Emperor Zara Yaqob. Legend has it that a miraculous nocturnal light (quite probably Halley's Comet) greeted the emperor when he was encamped here, prompting him to erect a church and use the site as his permanent capital until his death in 1468. The adolescent town was abandoned by Zara Yaqob's successor Ba'eda Maryam, only to rise to prominence again 50 years later when the imperial troops based at Debre Birhan were routed by the Muslim army of Ahmed Gragn. After capturing Debre Birhan, Gragn declared that 'Abyssinia is conquered' – presumptuous, as it transpired, but in the case of Debre Birhan not entirely incorrect. The area around Debre Birhan was Oromo territory for the next two centuries, to be reclaimed by the Showan monarchy only in the early 18th century. Long abandoned but never forgotten, Debre Birhan was soon rebuilt and it served as a kind of secondary capital for four successive Showan emperors throughout the 19th century.

Little indication of Debre Birhan's former importance survives today. The original church built by Zara Yaqob presumably fell victim to Gragn, and no obvious 19th-century relics remain. The church built by Emperor Menelik II in 1906, on the site first selected by Zara Yaqob, is nevertheless one of the most beautiful and spiritually affecting modern churches in the country. The inner walls are decorated with some marvellous paintings – including one of Zara Yaqob looking at a celestial body, reportedly modelled on Halley's Comet when it passed over at the beginning of the 20th century. Curio hunters might take note that the woollen carpets and blankets for which Debre Birhan is famous within Ethiopia can be bought directly from the co-operative that manufactures them at a shop close to the Telecommunications building.

Getting there and away
There are buses throughout the morning between Debre Birhan and Addis Ababa, and a few buses every day between Debre Birhan and Ankober. Early-morning buses leave Debre Birhan for Robit and Efeson, where you can pick up further transport to Dessie or Kombolcha. Direct buses from Addis to Dessie pass through Debre Birhan in the mid morning.

Where to stay
Moderate
Eva Hotel (19 rooms) ☎ 011 6813607. Situated on the left side of the main road as you enter town from Addis Ababa, this slick new hotel is easily the best in Debre Birhan, though not fantastic value at birr 100 for a modern carpeted dbl or twin with en-suite hot shower. A modern restaurant is attached.

Budget
Girma Hotel (30 rooms) ☎ 011 6811300. This likeable hotel, the pick of a cluster of decent cheapies on the Debre Sina side of town, charges birr 40 for a clean room with a genuine dbl bed and en-suite shower in the main block, or birr 30 for a significantly lesser room using a common shower. There is a bar with DSTV but no restaurant.
Akalu Hotel (10 rooms) ☎ 011 6811115. The established favourite with most tour operators who take ornithological tours to Ankober, this pleasant small hotel, set on a quiet back road, is good value at birr 40 for a clean and comfortable room with a ¾ bed and an en-suite hot shower. The attached restaurant has meat dishes even during fasting seasons.
Helen Hotel ☎ 011 6811204. Situated opposite the Girma, this is another good hotel, charging birr 30 for an en-suite room with cold shower and ¾ bed, or birr 16 for one using a common shower.

Shoestring
Etagegnehu Hotel This double-storey hotel near the main traffic roundabout doesn't have hot water, but is good value at birr 20 for an en-suite room or birr 10 for one using a common shower.
Tsigereda Hotel Adequate rooms using a common shower cost birr 12. There's a whole row of similarly priced lodges around the bus station, but they all look like dumps and none seems to have showers, common or otherwise.

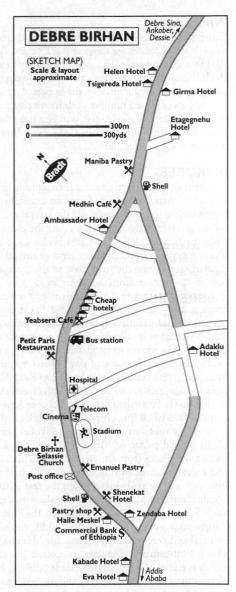

Where to eat

There are plenty of decent restaurants dotted around town, but the only ones that cater towards *faranji* palates are those at the **Eva** and **Akalu** hotels, both of which charge birr 10–15 for a main course. The most 'happening' place in Debre Birhan is undoubtedly **Petit Paris**, which lies on the main road roughly opposite the hospital, and doubles as a bar, pastry shop and restaurant, with the option of sitting indoors or out in the green garden.

The pick of quite a number of different pastry shops is the **Yeabsera Café**, which lies on the first floor of a high-rise building near the bus station, and serves great pastries, juices and coffee. The **Medhin Café**, **Namibia Pastry** and **Emanuel Pastry** are also good spots for a coffee and cake.

ANKOBER

This remote small town, situated at an altitude of around 3,000m on the escarpment that falls to the Afar Depression, forms an excellent goal for a day or overnight trip out of Debre Birhan. Both the town and the road there are fantastically scenic, passing through rolling green meadows with views over the escarpment and lush Wof Wusha Forest that clings to its sheer slopes. The area is also good for endemic birds such as wattled ibis, blue-winged goose and Ankober serin (more of which below), while gelada baboons are regularly seen along the road close to the escarpment, and Ethiopian wolves still occur, probably as vagrants from the Menz area.

Ankober, like nearby Debre Birhan, is a settlement of some antiquity, though almost certainly not – as has been suggested based on phonetic similarities – the site of the mysterious 10th-century capital of Kubar mentioned in Arab writings. In medieval times, Ankober acted as a tollgate along the trade route between the Afar Depression and the highlands. The town's name literally translates as the 'Gate of Anko', which, according to local tradition, was the name of a wife of an Oromo chief who ruled the town at some point. In the early 18th century, Ankober fell to King Abiye of Showa, and soon after it became capital of Abiye's son and successor Amha Iyesus, who is regarded to be the founder of the modern town. From then onwards, Ankober served as the capital or joint capital of Showa, up until 1878 when Emperor Menelik II relocated his capital to the Entoto Hills.

A steep road from the centre of Ankober leads downhill for about 2km to the site of the ruined palace of Menelik II, set atop a small, steep, juniper-covered hillock some ten minutes from the road on foot. All that's left of the palace is one long stone-and-mortar wall measuring some 1.5m high; difficult to say why this one wall should have survived virtually intact when the rest of the palace crumbled to virtual oblivion. Locals claim that Menelik built the palace on the site formerly used by his grandfather Sahle Selassie (who ruled from 1813 to 1847), the Showan king whose regular military campaigns co-opted modern-day Addis Ababa and Arsi into Showa, and laid the political and economic foundation for Menelik's eventual domination over Ethiopia. Three 19th-century churches are dotted around the base of this hill, the oldest of which is Kidus Mikael, built by Sahle Selassie. None of these churches is of any great architectural or aesthetic merit, and, in order to enter any of them, you will probably have to produce a letter of authority from the church administration office in Ankober.

Ankober's historical importance is today overshadowed by its status among ornithologists as the type locality of the Ankober serin (*Serinus ankoberensis*). First described in 1979, this rather nondescript seedeater was long thought to be restricted to a 20km stretch of escarpment running north from Ankober. In 1996, however, a flock was observed and photographed in the Simien Mountains, a vast extension to the serin's known range, and several other localities have subsequently been identified. Birders heading up this way will reliably observe seedeaters in abundance – streaky serin, brown-rumped serin and the endemic black-headed siskin are all common. But you will need to work the escarpment running immediately north of the road to stand any chance of locating the Ankober serin, which is brown with a pale streaked crown, and most easily identified by what appears to be a pale chin in flight. Non-birders, on sighting this rather nondescript seedeater, could be forgiven for wondering what all the fuss is about! Other interesting birds to look out for along this road include the endemic blue-winged goose and Abyssinian longclaw, as well as lammergeyer, moorland and Erckell's francolin, blue rock thrush, and the rare Somali chestnut-winged starling.

Dedicated birders are certain to want to follow the steep but fairly well maintained road that descends from Ankober for 15km to the small town of Aliyu Amba. Set at an altitude of about 1,500m near the base of the escarpment, Aliyu Amba is in itself remarkable only for boasting a venerable mosque. Of interest to birders, however, is the Melka Jebdu River, 3km out of town along the Dulecha road, and recently identified as a reliable site for the yellow-throated serin (*Serinus flavigula*). This distinctively marked bird is one of the most localised of Ethiopia's endemic birds – it is only otherwise recorded with any regularity on Fantelle Volcano in Awash National Park – but is quite easy to tick in the vestigial acacia woodland lining the Melka Jebdu River where it crosses the road.

Getting there and away

Ankober is situated 40km east of Debre Birhan along an unsurfaced but reasonably well-maintained road that branches right from the main Debre Sina road roughly 500m after you exit the outskirts of Debre Birhan. The drive from Debre Birhan takes about 45–60 minutes without stops. If you intend visiting Ankober as a day trip from Debre Birhan using public transport, then an early start is advisable, as the few buses that cover this road daily leave at 05.00 (in either direction).

Those with a private vehicle – preferably 4x4 – should probably expect to take 45 minutes to cover the steep road from Ankober east to Aliyu Amba. From Aliyu Amba, it is possible to continue southeast along a rough road to Dulecha (23km) and then to the main road near Awash National Park (90km). There is not, so far as I can establish, any public transport through to Aliyu Amba, but you should have no trouble finding a lift on Thursday, when the main market is held.

KOREMASH
Based on information in an article by John Graham, the full text of which is available online at www.addistribune.com

There are several places where you can drive off the road between Debre Birhan and Addis Ababa for viewpoints over the Awash Valley. One of the best is Koremash, which lies 12.5km along a 4x4, dry-season-only track from the main road, illegibly signposted 64km northwest of the Meganagna junction on Haile Gebre Selassie Road. Koremash is a small Amhara village perched above a cliff offering fantastic views over the Afar lowlands and the Awash River Valley. Negus Haile Melakot, the father of Menelik II, chose this site for his stronghold and ammunition dump, and Menelik used it as his armoury until the turn of the 20th century. A dozen stone buildings, about 15m long, 5m wide and 3m high, date from about 150 years ago, but undergo regular renovation, so are in good shape. In some of the buildings there are impressive juniper ceilings, on top of which the ammunition was reputedly stored. An active government centre today, the compound was used by the Italians as an administrative and military centre. In one building there is an Italian stone plaque inscribed Forttino Botteco, the name they gave Koremash, with the details of the Italian military brigade.

Where to stay
Moderate
Ankober Lodge ❧ 011 5510433 or 091 1653643; f 011 5515506; e ankoberlodge@yahoo.com. This new tourist lodge, which opened shortly before this edition went to print, has a commanding and historic location on Ankober Hill, with views over the Rift Escarpment. Comfortable accommodation in traditionally styled en-suite rooms with hot showers costs US$25/35 sgl/dbl, and the restaurant, rebuilt in the style of Emperor Menelik, serves a variety of European and national dishes.

There are two very basic hotels in Ankober, both of which are painted green and charge birr 6 for a single room. The **Ingadaso Tekle Memorial Hotel**, less than 100m from where the buses stop, is marginally the nicer. The **Getachew Tekle Selassie Hotel** lies about 100m further back towards Debre Birhan. A couple of restaurants serve local food.

Lalibela and Surrounds

The strange, isolated town of Lalibela, set high in the mountains of Lasta, is famed for its rock-hewn churches, and is arguably the one place in Ethiopia that no tourist should miss. Known as Roha until recent times, Lalibela was the capital of the Zagwe dynasty, which ruled over Ethiopia from the 10th century to the mid 13th century, and its modern name derives from that of the most famous of the Zagwe rulers, the 12th-century King Lalibela.

According to local legend, Lalibela was born the brother of the incumbent king. As a young child he was covered by a swarm of bees, which his mother took as a sign that he would one day be king himself. (One reported translation of Lalibela is 'the bees recognise his sovereignty', which isn't at all bad for four syllables; another more mundane and succinct translation is 'miracle'.) The king was none too pleased at this prophecy, and eventually tried to poison his younger brother, but instead of killing him he cast him into a deep sleep that endured for three days. While sleeping, Lalibela was transported to heaven by an angel and shown a city of rock-hewn churches, which he was ordered to replicate. Rather neatly, his elder brother had a simultaneous vision in which Christ instructed him to abdicate in favour of Lalibela. Another version of the legend is that Lalibela went into exile in Jerusalem, and was inspired by a vision to create a 'new' Jerusalem of rock at Roha.

As soon as he was crowned, Lalibela set about gathering the world's greatest craftsmen and artisans in order to carve the churches. Legend has it that at least one of the churches was built in a day with the help of angels – or, as Graham Hancock suggests in *The Sign and the Seal* (and not a great deal more plausibly) with the assistance of Freemasons! In fact, the excavation of the churches *is* something of a mystery – some sources estimate that in the order of 40,000 people would have been required to carve them – so it's not surprising that their origin has been clouded in legend. If anywhere I have visited would make me start contemplating supernatural intervention – or, for that matter, the timely arrival of a bunch of bearded grail-seekers – it would have to be Lalibela.

LALIBELA

Even before you visit the churches, Lalibela is a strikingly singular town. The setting alone is glorious. Perched at an altitude of 2,630m, among wild craggy mountains and vast rocky escarpments, there is a stark cathedral-like grandeur to Lalibela that recalls the Drakensberg Mountains of South Africa and Lesotho. The houses of Lalibela are of a design unlike anywhere else in Ethiopia, two-storey circular stone constructs that huddle in an amorphous mass over the steep slopes on which the town is built.

But people visit Lalibela for the churches. And, no matter if you have visited other rock-hewn churches in Ethiopia, nothing will prepare you for these. The Lalibela churches are *big* – several are in excess of 10m high – and, because they are carved below ground level, they are ringed by trenches and courtyards, the sides of which are cut into

LALIBELA AT ETHIOPIAN CHRISTMAS
Extracted from a letter from Raoul Boulakia

We saw the Christmas service, which was interesting, and not what I expected when people told me the monks would dance, as they really mournfully sway and march in procession. What I found most impressive was the devotion of the rural people, hiking for days and even weeks to get there, and sleeping on the ground outside the churches. The multitude of pilgrims is really amazing. However, I expect there would be far fewer lodging and transportation hassles coming at other times. Either way is a trade-off. If you go at Christmas or Timkat, you get to see the magnitude of how important a religious site it is. If you go at other times, it should be calmer and easier to arrange. Rates also go up for Christmas and Timkat, sometimes during the course of a day as hotel owners realise everything is sold out. Whatever, it's still one of the manmade wonders of the world.

with stone graves and hermit cells, and connected to each other by a tangled maze of tunnels and passages. In size and scope, the church complex feels like a subterranean village. Yet each individual church is unique in shape and size, precisely carved and minutely decorated. Lalibela is, in a word, awesome. When the Portuguese priest Francisco Alvares was taken to Lalibela in 1521, he doubted that his compatriots would believe what he had seen. In his narrative *A True Relation of the Lands of Prester John* he wrote: 'It wearied me to write more of these works, because it seemed to me that they will accuse me of untruth… there is much more than I have already written, and I have left it that they may not tax me with it being falsehood.'

Were it virtually anywhere but in Ethiopia, Lalibela would rightly be celebrated as one of the wonders of the world, as readily identified with Ethiopia as are the pyramids or the Sphinx with Egypt. As it is, Lalibela is barely known outside Ethiopia, and Ethiopia itself is associated first and foremost with desert and drought – not a little ironic, when you consider that the fertile Nile Basin, on which Egypt depends, receives 90% of its water from the Ethiopian Highlands.

Lalibela's obscurity is shameful but for those who visit the town it is part of the charm. These churches are not primarily tourist attractions, being prodded and poked away from their original context, nor are they the crumbling monuments of a dead civilisation. What they are, and what they have been for at least 800 years, is an active Christian shrine, the spiritual centre of a town's religious life. It is naïve, and perhaps a bit patronising, to think in terms of unchanging cultures. Nevertheless, if you wander between the churches in the thin light of morning, when white-robed hermits emerge Bible-in-hand from their cells to bask on the rocks, and the chill highland air is warmed by Eucharistic drumbeats and gentle swaying chants, you can't help but feel that you are witnessing a scene that is fundamentally little different to the one that has been enacted here every morning for century upon century. The joy of Lalibela, the thing that makes this curiously medieval town so special, is that it is not just the rock-hewn churches that have survived into the modern era, but also something more organic. The churches breathe.

More prosaically, many of the churches are being damaged by seepage, and, for the last few years, they have been protected by roofs and scaffolding. This will hopefully help preserve the churches for future generations, but it cannot be said to add much to their aesthetics as things stand. A plan to replace the scaffolding with less visually intrusive shelters has been talked about for some years now – possibly one large, high translucent roof covering each of the main clusters – but this is unlikely to reach fruition during the lifespan of this edition.

Getting there and away

Not so long ago, Lalibela was legendarily inaccessible. When Thomas Pakenham visited back in 1955, there was no road: it took him four days to reach Lalibela from Dessie by mule, and the town typically received fewer than five parties of foreign visitors annually. Even as recently as 1997, access by air restricted to the dry season, and the road to Lalibela was frequently impassable after heavy rain. All that has changed, however, with the recent opening of a surfaced airstrip and the construction of all-weather gravel roads south to Gashena and north to Sekota – today, Lalibela is accessible by road and by air throughout the year.

By air

Daily flights connect Lalibela to Addis Ababa, Gonder, Bahir Dar and Axum throughout the year. The new airport, with a surfaced airstrip, lies about 25km from the town centre along a surfaced road passing below the monastery at Nakuta La'ab. All flights are met by Habte Independent Tours and by other private operators, which generally charge birr 30 per person for a one-way transfer to town. As with all domestic flights, it is necessary to confirm your ticket out of Lalibela a day in advance; the new Ethiopian Airlines office is situated on the main square close to the Blue Lal Hotel.

By road

Lalibela is not connected to any other town by asphalt, but it can be approached by gravel road from several different directions, depending on how it slots in with your other travel plans. The direct drive from Addis Ababa takes two days, but Lalibela can normally be reached in one day from Bahir Dar, Gonder or Dessie, whether you use public or private transport. In a private vehicle, it is just about possible to reach Lalibela in one day from Mekele or Axum, but two days would make for a more relaxed trip – and it would be the minimum travel period on public transport.

The most popular and easiest access route coming from Mekele, Dessie or direct from Addis Ababa is the graded 175km road from Woldia. This route entails following the China Road west out of Woldia for 111km, first passing through the small town of Dilb (set in a river valley 25km from Woldia), and then tackling a spectacular 1,500m ascent to the breezy footslopes of Mount Abuna Yosef. You need to turn right at the junction town of Gashena, set at an altitude of around 3,000m some 64km from Lalibela. About 20km before you reach Lalibela, turn right onto the asphalt road connecting the town to the airport.

This road between Woldia and Lalibela can usually be covered in four hours in a private 4x4, depending on how recently it was graded and how much rain has fallen since, but it takes a couple of hours longer on public transport, which costs birr 12 one way. A daily bus service, which leaves at around 06.00 in either direction, is more comfortable and cheaper than the overcrowded Land Cruisers that cover the same road daily. There is also now a direct bus between Dessie and Lalibela via Woldia. This bus is owned by the Church Administration, takes ten hours in either direction, and leaves from Lalibela on Thursdays and Sundays or from Dessie on Fridays and Tuesdays. There is also now a direct bus service between Lalibela and Addis Ababa, leaving at 06.00 in either direction and taking two full days, with an overnight stop in Dessie.

Coming from the direction of Bahir Dar or Gonder, follow the asphalt road between these two towns to Werota, which lies about 1km south of the junction for the eastbound China Road to Woldia via Debre Tabor, Nefas Mewcha and Gashena. It is a long day's drive in a private vehicle, so leave early. Coming towards Lalibela on public transport, this route will entail catching a bus from Gonder or Bahir Dar to Woldia (birr 35–40), disembarking at Gashena, and then hitching or waiting for public transport north along the 64km road to Lalibela, which should cost birr 10, though *faranjis* are often

TO LALIBELA VIA SEKOTA

Oddly underutilised by tourists, the 380km gravel road that runs through the remote heartland of northern Ethiopia to connect Adwa and Lalibela via Abi Aday and Sekota forms a perfectly viable shortcut to the more popular route between Axum and Lalibela via Adigrat. The same road can also be used to drive between Mekele and Lalibela, cutting west from the main Adigrat road either at Mekele (for Abi Aday) or at Korem (for Sekota). Using public transport, buses and/or minibuses cover all stretches except for Sekota to Lalibela, where you may have to hitch or catch a lift with a truck.

With a private vehicle and a very early start, it should be possible, in all instances, to get through to Lalibela in one long day: allow two-and-a-half hours to cover the 115km from Axum to Abi Aday (via Adwa and Mai Kenetal) or 95km from Mekele to Abi Aday (via Hagare Selam), another three-and-a-half to four-and-a-half hours to cover the 155km between Abi Aday and Sekota, and then about three hours for the 130km from Sekota to Lalibela itself. Alternatively, you could overnight at Abi Aday or Sekota to break things up – the former has better facilities, the latter is the more inherently interesting town, and both lie close to some worthwhile churches. For further coverage of **Abi Aday** and the rock-hewn churches of the Tembien see page 293.

Heading southward from Abi Aday towards Sekota, you need to turn right after 15km, at the junction with the road to Mekele via Hagare Selam. Another 19km and an altitudinal plunge to around 1,500m brings you to **Yechilay**, set in an otherwise unexpectedly austere landscape of spindly acacia scrubland populated by the odd herdsman and his coterie of skinny goats and long-horned cattle. The double-storey Tekaze Hotel on the Abi Aday side of Yechilay is probably the smartest lodging between here and Lalibela; if nothing else, this probably says all you need to know about accommodation standards in Sekota!

Between here and **Tinarwa**, 25km further south, the road bisects an isolated enclave of relatively low-lying Sahelian savanna, whose parched appearance – thick red sand, foreboding black rock, dry riverbeds, scraggly trees – comes as a real contrast even to the relatively dry highlands of northern Tigrai. It comes as no surprise to learn that this searing semi-desert, so visually reminiscent of the arid badlands of the Ethiopian–Kenyan border region, lay at the epicentre of the dreadful famine of 1985 – indeed, the television footage that first drew global attention to this tragedy was of victims who had evacuated the area between here and Sekota to hike to the main road at Korem.

After passing through the village of **Abegele** about 8km further on, the road crosses a series of watercourses that form part of the Tekaze drainage basin, the most impressive of which is the **Tserari River**, set at around 1,200m close to the isolated and venerable monastery of Bar Kidane Mihret. A striking feature of this area is the immense baobabs that line the rocky slopes. Bare contorted branches reaching skyward from squat, bulbous trunks, these ancient and obese trees – some must surely be thousands of years old – come across as if they have sucked the last drop of life from what was already a cruelly parched landscape.

It comes as a relief when, after another 50km or so, the road ascends back into the highlands of **Wag**, an ancient Agaw principality that converted to Christianity as early as the 6th century, possibly under the influence of the Syrian saint Abba Yemata. Wag is

overcharged. Most travellers get through in one day, but this cannot be guaranteed, so you may need to bed down in Gashena, where the Adani Demisay Hotel charges birr 15 for basic but acceptable rooms. We've also heard reports of these buses stopping at Nefas Mewcha in the mid afternoon for no apparent reason and staying there overnight. In the opposite direction, a bus to Gashena leaves Lalibela at 06.00 daily, and arrives there in

thought by many historians to have been an important centre of political power during the little-documented era that followed the collapse of the Axumite Empire and preceded the rise of the Zagwe dynasty at Lalibela. It is probable that Wag will eventually turn out to be the site of the mysterious Kubar, referred to by the 10th-century Arab writer Al-Masudi as 'capital of Abyssinia... a great city [with] extensive territories stretching as far as the Abyssinian Sea [including] the coastal plain beyond Yemen'. More recently, Wag lay at the heart of the area affected by the terrible famine of 1985.

The principal town of Wag, situated 155km south of Abi Aday, **Sekota** is reminiscent of Lalibela, with its characteristic two-storey stone dwellings, and if anything it retains an even greater architectural integrity. The town's most noteworthy landmark, situated on the main traffic roundabout, is the Church of Webila Maryam, which is at least 200 years old and reputedly contains several interesting 19th-century paintings, though there was nobody around to open it up when I tried to check. There isn't a great deal of choice on the accommodation front: the best bet is the Tadesse Hotel on the main roundabout, which charges an inflated *faranji* price of birr 20 for a seriously basic room using common showers, and it serves adequate meals, decent coffee and the usual chilled drinks.

A worthwhile excursion from Sekota is to the near-monolithic rock-hewn church of **Wukro Meskel Kristos**, which lies about 6km south of town, just ten minutes' walk east of the Lalibela road. Tradition holds that Wukro Meskel Kristos predates the Lalibela churches (some say it was excavated during the medieval reign of Yemrehanna Kristos, others that it dates to the 6th-century rule of Kaleb), and was the inspiration for many of them, which – if it is true – could mean it is the oldest near-monolith in Ethiopia. The rock-hewn church expert David Buxton, who visited Wukro Meskel Kristos in the 1960s, was of the opinion that the church is more recent, probably excavated in the 14th century. Either way, it's an atmospheric little church, and the ornate façade and decorated interior make it well worth the small effort required to reach it from the main road. Entrance costs birr 50, women are forbidden, and the church has been covered in scaffolding since 1998.

Six ancient coffins are stowed in the main church, while another stash of perhaps 50 coffins containing ancient mummies lies in an adjacent cave **mausoleum**. As usual, how they got there is a matter for conjecture. According to the priest I spoke to, the six coffins in the church house the bodies of former governors of Wag, while the mummies in the cave were Kaleb-era administrators who were carried to the church by angels after their death. When David Buxton visited the church in the 1950s, he was told that the mummies were former Wagsuns – Kings of Wag – who were customarily exhumed from their original graves about 20 years after their death and reburied in smaller caskets. Another legend has it that these are the bodies of priests who committed an unspecified sin and were struck down violently by God – certainly the few mummies that have spilled out of their coffins don't look like they died a peaceful death!

About 20km south of Sekota, you reach the junction with the 65km road to Korem, where you need to turn right if you are heading for Lalibela. It is then a straight 110km drive to Lalibela, with the possibility of diverting to the churches around Bilbilla en route.

plenty of time to connect with the buses from Dessie to Gonder, which pass through Gashena at around midday. For more details of this route, see the box *Debre Tabor and the 'China Road'* on pages 340–1.

The final approach to Lalibela is from the north, along the recently upgraded 95km road that connects Adwa (22km from Axum) to Lalibela via Abi Aday and Sekota. This

DEBRE TABOR AND THE 'CHINA ROAD'

Based primarily on a series of articles written by John Graham for the Addis Tribune, with additional input from the staff of Four Seasons Travel Agency

Travellers who head directly between Lalibela and Bahir Dar or Gonder will follow the 'China Road', which connects the Lake Tana region and Woldia via Debre Tabor, Nefas Mewcha and Gashena (junction town for Lalibela). Built by the Chinese in the late 1970s and arguably the best gravel road in Ethiopia (despite traversing some very scenic but seriously mountainous terrain) it provides access to several infrequently visited churches and points of interest.

With an early start, it is possible to drive between the Lake Tana region and Lalibela in a day. Using **public transport**, the daily bus between Bahir Dar and Woldia can drop you at Gashena, where you might be able to bus directly on to Lalibela. Coming from Gonder, you may first have to bus as far as Debre Tabor or Nefas Mewcha, and sleep over there before travelling on to Gashena the next day. Travellers with sufficient time and interest may elect to take the trip in stages, a particularly appealing prospect with a private vehicle!

Should you want **accommodation** along the way, the best place in Debre Tabor is the two-storey Guna Hotel, which has good en-suite rooms. There are two other decent hotels in Debre Tabor, one in front of the Guna and the other adjacent to the bus station facing the police station. In Nefas Mewcha, the place of choice is the Hotel Mullu, but if it is full there is a number of other hotels around the bus station. Gashena, on the junction to Lalibela, also has several basic lodges.

Debre Tabor, the first substantial town along this road, is 42km east of Werota junction, with the possibility of making a short diversion en route to **Awramba** (see page 214). Emperor Seife Ara'ad founded Debre Tabor in the 13th century, but the town rose to prominence only in the early 17th century, when it was used as a base to contain the Oromo incursions. Debre Tabor effectively served as capital of Ethiopia for much of the turbulent 19th century: it emerged as the successor to Gonder in 1803 during the reign of a local nobleman called Ras Gugsa Mursa, briefly the most powerful political figure in Ethiopia, and it retained this status until 1889, when Menelik II was crowned emperor.

The only relics of Debre Tabor's heyday are two old churches. The first, **Tabor Iyasus**, lies on a forested hill 3km from the town centre. Although almost as old as the town itself, the present building – a magnificent circular construction enclosed by a large stone wall – was built by Ras Gugsa in the early 1800s. The interior has intricately carved pillars and fine 19th-century paintings. It also houses several treasures, including Ras Gugsa's ceremonial robe, and a throne-bed that belonged to Empress Taitu. The second less remarkable church is **Tabor Maryam**, constructed with the support of Tewodros II in the 1860s.

The hamlet of **Gafat** is associated with the most critical and bizarre episode in Tewodros's reign – the hostage taking of missionaries who were then forced to manufacture a cannon. Local people will point you towards the foundations and walls of the buildings used as foundries, and to the hill where the soldiers who guarded the missionaries were camped. The cannon built by the missionaries – which didn't work, despite their best efforts – now stands on Makdala Hill over 100km away. To get to Gafat, you must drive for 2km along the main road east of Debre Tabor, then follow a rough dirt turn-off heading north, then – when the road peters out – walk for another 1km or so.

The 75km road between Debre Tabor and Nefas Mewcha passes several little-visited points of interest, including the 4,231m **Mount Guna**. Its 40km² of Afro-alpine moorland above the 3,800m contour is home to a small, isolated and highly vulnerable population of around 20 Ethiopian wolves, one of only four viable populations of the race that occurs northwest of the Rift Valley. Although I've not heard of any traveller visiting this mountain, it lies a short distance south of the main road, and local shepherds might act as guides.

The spectacular rock-hewn church of **Wukro Medhane Alem** was reputedly excavated by King Lalibela and is sometimes referred to as Wukro Lalibela. Unusually, this church – which consists of several different parts – contains four *tabots*, as well as a treasury of old crosses, manuscripts and other relics. The workmanship is excellent, with several fine carvings on the ceiling and walls. Follow the Nefas Mewcha road for 20km out of Debre Tabor to a signposted turn-off at Kimer Dingay. Proceed for 300m, then turn left across a large ditch on to a sparkling white road that is reduced to rough rock after a few hundred metres. Although the road is scheduled for improvement, it is currently impassable after 4km, so you must walk the remaining 4km.

The most singular and perhaps the finest church that can be reached from this road is **Gaynt Bethlehem**, a seminary specialising in advanced studies on Saint Yared, who wrote most of the praise songs used by the Orthodox Church. Enclosed with an unflattering circular thatched *tukul*, Bethlehem is built-up in the ancient Axumite style with a rectangular 200m² floor plan. Notable features include three old juniper doorways, fantastic carvings in the wooden beams holding up the roof, two basilica domes with ornate designs, plenty of old Ge'ez Bibles, and several wonderful old paintings on deteriorating cloth depicting scenes from the life of Jesus. Outside the church lies a 7m-long fallen Axumite pillar. Not unpredictably, oral tradition dates Bethlehem to the rule of Abreha we Atsbeha, but Thomas Pakenham, the first outsider to see this church, felt that the combination of Axum and Constantinople styles indicated a construction date between the 9th and 11th centuries, while other sources date its construction to the late 14th century. Pakenham's wonderful book *The Mountains of Rasselas* (see *Further Reading* on page 265) contains a full chapter about the church, as well as some great photographs. Getting to Bethlehem today is less of a mission than it was in the 1950s, but is still a considerable side trip. It is reached along a rough road that heads southward from the China Road at the western edge of Nefas Mewcha. Follow this for 50km, passing through the small market town of Arb Gebeya after 23km.

Less concisely named, but more accessible, the church of **Zur Amba Abba Aragawi Sihar Aryam** is built into an *amba* which is visible from the China Road some 20km before Nefas Mewcha. Architecturally of minor interest, it has a fascinating history, and several old treasures. Tradition has it that the original church at Zur Amba was built in memory of Abba Aregawi in the 6th-century reign of Gebre Meskel, abandoned in the time of Ahmed Gragn, and resurrected by Libawi Christos about 200 years later. From Salli, a rough 3.5km track leads to the base of the *amba*, followed by a steep 30-minute hike.

At Checheho, 25km east of Nefas Mewcha alongside the Woldia road, **Abba Defar** is excavating two new rock-hewn churches called Gebriel and Bal-Egziabher. The larger measures about 10m deep by 5m wide, and has several large central pillars. The rock is unusually soft and chalky, giving the interior an attractive white appearance. Abba Defar started to excavate the church after receiving a holy vision; he works with a couple of assistants and lives in a small cave above the church.

road can also be reached from the northeast along the road connecting Mekele to Abi Aday, or on the recently improved road between Korem and Sekota. In all cases, an early start and strict no-sightseeing policy would allow you to get through in one day using a private vehicle – the actual driving time is nine to ten hours without breaks – but there would be a strong case for breaking up the trips at Abi Aday or Sekota. Using public transport, regular buses and minibuses connect Adwa or Mekele to Abi Aday and regular light vehicles run along the 155km stretch from Abi Aday to Sekota. Without a private vehicle you may struggle to find transport along the 130km stretch between Sekota and Lalibela, though several trucks use this route. For details of Abi Aday, see page 338. For details of Sekota, see the box *To Lalibela via Sekota* on pages 338–9.

At the time of writing, there is no direct all-weather road to Lalibela from Addis Ababa, so most people travel via Woldia (or Bahir Dar). This might well change during the lifespan of this edition. Construction on the vaunted 'new road' via Alem Katema started a few years ago and recent reports suggest it is just about doable over two days as things stand, assuming you have a 4x4 and that it hasn't rained for a couple of months. Whether the completion of this road – if and when it ever is completed – will usher in a direct bus service between Lalibela and Addis Ababa is anybody's guess.

Where to stay

Hotels in Lalibela are uniformly overpriced by comparison with anywhere else in Ethiopia, probably because this is one place where tourists rather than locals constitute the bulk of the custom at all levels. You might be asked double the price quoted below when large numbers of tourists are in town, and four- or five-times that price during any important festival such as Timkat or Meskel. By contrast, most hotels will negotiate downwards when things are quiet. Several hotels quote prices in US dollars but all will accept payment in local currency.

Upmarket

Roha Hotel (64 rooms) ☏ 033 3360156; e ghion@ethionet.et; www.ghionhotel.com.et. Situated about 2km from the town centre and the main cluster of churches, the Lalibela unit in the government Ghion chain is much as you'd expect if you've stayed at any of its sister hotels. It has a nice location and probably remains the smartest place in town, despite growing competition from the private sector and non-availability of hot water outside of specified hours. Rooms cost US$38/50/60 sgl/dbl/ste. Meals are good and cost birr 15 for the main course only or birr 25 for a set menu.

Lal Hotel (65 rooms) ☏ 033 3360008/3360044/3360183 or 011 6626586; e lato@ethionet.et. Situated about 200m from the Roha, back towards the town centre, this smart private hotel has dropped its rates and raised its standards greatly in recent years. Large, comfortable traditionally decorated rooms with en-suite hot shower cost US$24/30/36 sgl/dbl/twin from October to January, dropping to birr 21/25/30 at other times, with further discounts negotiable when things are quiet. It is a good place to arrange 4x4 transport to the outlying monasteries, and the *tukul*-style restaurant is far better than that at the Ghion.

Lasta Hotel (26 rooms) ☏ 033 3360040/7; e jghandts@ethionet.et. Formerly the New Jerusalem Guesthouse, this highly regarded three-storey hotel lies about 200m from the Lal, along a cul de sac from where there are stirring views over the rolling mountains of Lasta. Large tiled doubles with en-suite hot shower and a view cost US$30/40 sgl/dbl, while similar rooms without the view go for a negotiable US$20/25 sgl/dbl. The restaurant serves good traditional and Western dishes in the birr 20–25 price range, and the English-speaking management is very helpful.

Tukul Village Hotel (24 rooms) ☏ 033 3360564/3360565; e tours@timelessethiopia.com. Scheduled to open in December 2005, this promising joint Dutch–Ethiopian venture, situated opposite the Lal with a superb view over Bet Giyorgis, will aim to combine traditional architecture with international standards of service. Accommodation will be in stone-and-thatch double-storey

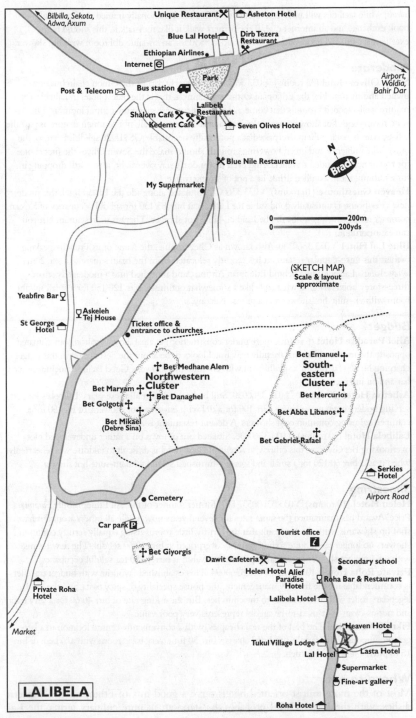

Bilbilla, Sekota,
Adwa, Axum

Unique Restaurant ✕   🏠 Asheton Hotel

Blue Lal Hotel 🏠   Dirb Tezera
                     Restaurant ✕

Ethiopian Airlines •

Internet ⓔ

Park   Airport,
        Woldia,
        Bahir Dar

Post & Telecom ✉   Bus station 🚐

Lalibela
Restaurant

Shalom Café ✕   🏠 Seven Olives Hotel
Kedemt Café ✕

✕ Blue Nile Restaurant

N

My Supermarket •   Bradt

0 ▭▭▭▭▭ 200m
0 ▭▭▭▭▭ 200yds

(SKETCH MAP)
Scale & layout
approximate

Yeabfire Bar ⵏ

Askeleh
ⵏ Tej House

St George 🏠
Hotel

Ticket office &
entrance to churches

Bet Emanuel ✝
South-
eastern
Cluster

✝ Bet Medhane Alem
Northwestern
Cluster   Bet Mercurios ✝

Bet Maryam ✝
      ✝ Bet Danaghel
Bet Golgota ✝
              Bet Abba Libanos ✝
Bet Mikael
(Debre Sina)
              ✝
              Bet Gebriel-Rafael

🏠 Serkies
   Hotel

Airport Road

Cemetery •

Car park 🅿   Tourist office ℹ

Secondary school •

✝ Bet Giyorgis

Dawit Cafeteria ✕   🏠 🏠
Helen Hotel Alief   Roha Bar & Restaurant ⵏ
             Paradise
             Hotel   Lalibela Hotel 🏠

Private Roha 🏠
Hotel

Heaven Hotel 🏠

Market   Tukul Village Lodge 🏠   Lasta Hotel
          Lal Hotel 🏠
                     Supermarket •
                     🗿 Fine-art gallery

LALIBELA

Roha Hotel 🏠

tukuls, while facilities will include a restaurant with an internationally trained chef, a multilingual book exchange and an internet café. If the owners walk it like they talk it, this should be an excellent set-up, and good value too at around US$30 for an en-suite dbl room with hot shower.

Moderate

Seven Olives Hotel (33 rooms) ➘ 033 3360020. Formerly part of the Ghion chain but now owned and managed by the Ethiopian Orthodox Church, this is the oldest hotel in Lalibela, set in mature well-wooded grounds that come as a pleasant surprise given the central location. The en-suite rooms with hot shower are also looking a little mature – well, not so much mature as past the sell-by date – making them overpriced at a potentially negotiable US$15/28 sgl/dbl. Even so, the old-world ambience and green flowering grounds should make the Seven Olives the first choice for romantically minded travellers. And even if you don't stay overnight, it is worth dropping in for a tranquil meal, a chilled drink, or a pot of strong coffee.

Heaven Guesthouse (10 rooms) ➘ 033 3360075. Situated alongside the Lasta Hotel, this modest new guesthouse is unusually good value for Lalibela at birr 85/130 for sgl/dbl occupancy of a clean, compact room with a genuine dbl bed and en-suite hot shower. There is no restaurant but you can eat next door.

Blue Lal Hotel ➘ 033 3360380. Also known as Chez Sophie, the name of its French-speaking owner, this once-popular restaurant has recently relocated from the main square to a site 20m away along an alley leading behind Ethiopian Airlines, and morphed into a moderately smart three-storey hotel charging what feels like a somewhat optimistic birr 120/150 for a small sgl/dbl room with en-suite hot shower and a private balcony.

Budget

Alief Paradise Hotel (6 rooms, more under construction) e alparahotel@yahoo.com. Situated opposite the tourist office, this friendly new hotel looks to be about the best option in this range, charging birr 60/80/100 for a sgl/dbl/twin with en-suite hot showers. Good facilities include a juice bar and an internet café.

Asheton Hotel (20 rooms) ➘ 033 3360030. Still bedraggled after all these years, Lalibela's longest-serving budget hotel now charges birr 100 for a dbl with en-suite hot showers, or birr 50 for a cramped sgl using common cold showers. A decent restaurant is attached.

Lalibela Hotel (20 rooms) ➘ 033 3360036. Situated out of town on a rather undeveloped plot overlooking Bet Giyorgis, this otherwise acceptable new hotel is difficult to endorse wholeheartedly when it asks birr 60/120 for a small and sparsely furnished sgl/dbl with en-suite hot shower.

Shoestring

Helen Hotel (10 rooms) ➘ 033 3360053. This former winner of the 'All Ethiopia Silly *Faranji* Price' Award has maintained the same rates for several years now, while all others around it have shot up skywards, with the net result that the scruffy little rooms using equally scruffy common showers no longer seem quite so outrageously overpriced at birr 30/60 sgl/dbl. The new rooms with en-suite hot shower are actually quite decent value at birr 40/80 for sgl/dbl occupancy.

Private Roha Hotel (10 rooms) ➘ 033 3360094. This established favourite with budget travellers is commendable for the friendly management, the house speciality of spicy pasta, and the legendary toilet with a view across to the churches. But the asking rate of birr 40/60 for a very basic and not-as-clean-as-it-used-to-be sgl/dbl represents very poor value.

Fikre Selam Hotel The best of the real cheapies, with a conveniently central location in a large green compound, this family-run hotel charges birr 30 for a very basic room with a ¾ bed, or birr 15 to pitch a tent in the garden.

Where to eat

Most of the more tourist-oriented hotels serve a good mix of Ethiopian and Western dishes, with the **Lasta Hotel** probably the standout in pure culinary terms, the **Lal**

Hotel running it a close (and more affordable) second, and the **Seven Olives Hotel** scoring top marks for *al fresco* ambience. Also recommended is the restaurant at the **Blue Lal Hotel**, which is owned and managed by an Ethiopian woman who lived in France for a decade, and who still transports many of her ingredients personally from Addis Ababa – spaghetti and fruit juice are the specialities.

Situated next to the Seven Olives, the **Blue Nile Restaurant**, owned by the former husband of the Blue Lal's Sophie, is popular with both locals and travellers alike for its good local food. Proceeds go towards the support of 13 AIDS orphans who are housed and cared for by the owner. Other good local eateries include the **Roha Café** next to the Lalibela Hotel, the traditionally decorated **Dirb Tezera** in the same building that used to house the Blue Lal, the **Lalibela Restaurant** opposite the Seven Olives, and the excellent **Unique Restaurant**, which serves tasty pizzas, local dishes and roast meat directly opposite the Asheton Hotel.

For those wanting to try the local tipple for which Lalibela is justly famed, the **Askelech Tej House** is strongly endorsed by local guides, while the *tej* at the **Helen Hotel** has been described as 'heavenly'. The identity parade of coffee shops that form a neat row along the south of the main square can collectively be relied upon to serve coffee, tea, fresh bread and possibly a pastry or two. If you want to stock up on dried food before trekking to one of the monasteries, **My Supermarket** opposite the Blue Nile Restaurant stocks a fair range of imported goods such as processed cheese, biscuits and chocolate.

Listings
Communications
The Telecommunications building is on the main square. Email and internet facilities were in the process of being introduced to Lalibela in early 2005 and are likely to become more widely available over the next year or so – internet cafés can be found at the Alief Paradise and Lasta hotels, as well as at a new office on the main square.

Crafts
The main clusters of craft stalls are on the main square and along the road between the Lal and Roha hotels. Also close to the Roha Hotel is the fine art shop run by the self-taught local artist Tegegne Yirdaw, who sells watercolours and monochrome sketches for around birr 150–200.

Foreign exchange
Please note that no reliable foreign-exchange facilities are available in Lalibela. It's advisable to bring as much local currency as you're likely to need. If you're stuck, speak to the receptionist at the Roha Hotel, who will generally change US dollar bills at a rate only marginally lower than the bank rate.

Tourist information
The newly opened tourist office (✆ 033 3360167) has a rather improbable suburban location opposite the Alief Paradise Hotel. The people who work there seem to be very helpful and they usually stock a few useful brochures and maps. The official Lalibela Guides Association (✆ 033 3360065; e syhlal@ethionet.et) has an office near the Roha Hotel, where registered guides can be arranged for birr 150 per day for groups of up to three or birr 200 per day for larger groups.

An ancient but nevertheless exceptionally informative 32-page free booklet on Lalibela was reprinted by the ETC in 2000 and may or may not be available at the ETC office on Meskel Square in Addis Ababa. Also worth looking out for is Tilahun Assefa's very useful booklet *Lalibela: World Wonder Heritage*, which used to be available for a small charge in Lalibela itself but appeared to be out of print in 2005.

Vehicle rental

Based in the Roha Hotel, Habte Independent Tours (↘ 033 3360090/3360406) can arrange vehicle rental and guided tours to churches outside Lalibela. As an example, a group of up to five people can expect to pay around birr 800–900 (excluding guide and church entrance fees) for a day trip to the Bilbilla churches and Yemrehanna Kristos. The usual rate for overnight vehicle rental is birr 750–800 per day.

Sightseeing

Lalibela's churches are divided into two clusters, separated by the Jordan River – one local legend has it that the river was given this name after King Lalibela returned from Jerusalem. The **northwest cluster** comprises seven churches: Bet Medhane Alem, Bet Maryam, Bet Meskel, Bet Danaghel, Bet Debre Sina, Bet Golgotha and the Selassie Chapel. The **southeast cluster** consists of five churches: Bet Emanuel, Bet Mercurios, Bet Abba Libanos, Bet Lehem and Bet Gebriel-Rafael. A thirteenth church, **Bet Giyorgis**, stands discrete from the two main clusters.

The various churches of Lalibela were constructed using one of two different methods. Bet Giyorgis and the churches in the northwest cluster are mostly excavated from below the ground, and are surrounded by courtyards and trenches, so that they mimic normal buildings. Several of these churches are monoliths or three-quarter monoliths – free from the surrounding rock on three or four sides – a style of excavation that is unique to Ethiopia. The churches of the southeast cluster are similar to many churches in Tigrai, in that most of them were excavated from a vertical rock face by exploiting existing caves or cracks in the rock.

Practicalities

Tours of Lalibela start at the northwest cluster of churches, which lies a short walk downhill from the Seven Olives Hotel. Here you must buy a ticket for birr 100 allowing access to all the churches in town (but not the monasteries outside town). Hang on to this ticket, because it's valid for as many days as you spend in Lalibela.

Although it is reasonably easy to find your own way around the church complex, especially with a copy of Tilahun Assefa's Lalibela booklet, there is a strong case for organising a guide. Firstly, the guides – the official ones anyway – are generally very knowledgeable and informative. They also know all the priests, and so you'll be spared the hassle of having to raise the priest who keeps the key for each church. No less compelling is that the moment you appoint a guide the others will leave you in peace (and the guides at Lalibela – or rather the non-official guides – are increasingly becoming an irritant in this respect).

One of the official guides registered by the Lalibela Guides Association can be contacted through any of the hotels. The official guides are more knowledgeable than their unofficial counterparts, and are held in greater respect by the priests. Rates are negotiable, starting at around birr 200 daily for a large group or birr 150 daily for up to three people. Off-season, the official guides are often happy to take around backpackers at a better rate, while rates generally escalate during busy periods. If you are happy with the service provided, by all means tip, but you are under no obligation – the guides association forbids its members from asking for tips.

Unofficial guides ask less than official guides, but they are unlikely to be as knowledgeable, and it is often impossible to get into the churches with them. Many, too, are masters of the manipulative sulk – they will as a matter of course look insulted and start muttering about tips when you pay them the agreed fee, and so, as a matter of course, will taint what was probably otherwise a fine day. Make it clear from the start that the rate you have agreed is final. If you are in town for a few days, make the guide aware of this, and that you will appoint him on a day-by-day basis.

THE LALIBELA CROSS

On 10 March 1997, the 800-year-old Lalibela Cross was discovered to have gone missing from the church of Medhane Alem. This cross, which is made of solid gold and reportedly weighs in at around 7kg, is said to have been the personal property of King Lalibela, and it is perhaps the most treasured artefact of the Ethiopian Church, more holy than anything in Jerusalem or Rome.

When the theft of the cross was discovered, the village responded with a mass outpouring of grief, according to one report 'beating their breasts, tearing out hair and calling on God to rescue them'. The head priest of the church was arrested and the church itself was closed and placed under a police cordon for several days. When I was in Lalibela two weeks later, the air was heavy with innuendo, and our guide spoke gleefully about how the truth would be extracted from the priest even if it meant torturing him to death.

Nothing was heard of the whereabouts of the missing cross until two years later, when it was noticed by customs officials in the luggage of an art dealer returning home to Brussels from Ethiopia. The Lalibela Cross was returned to its rightful place with due ceremony in May 1999, but the theft serves to highlight one of the more negative effects of increased tourism to Ethiopia's cultural and historical sites. Visiting Lalibela is not quite like visiting the pyramids, but it becomes increasingly difficult to spend more than five minutes in the town or church complex without bumping into another tourist. Whether tourism is 'good' or 'bad' for Lalibela is a matter of opinion, and one on which I refuse to be drawn, if only because there is something exceedingly annoying about glibly concerned Westerners who enjoy the luxuries of modern living themselves warbling on about the destruction of cultures elsewhere. All the same, the theft of the Lalibela Cross does serve as a reminder of how far-reaching the actions of one tourist can be.

Except when it comes to the subject of money, most guides (official or not) are genuinely helpful, and they'll sort out anything you want from a good local meal or a better hotel to helping you bargain for curios. Many people leave Lalibela very pleased with their guide, and quite a number have written to me commending a specific individual. I have, however, resisted the temptation to pass on names; that sort of licence can easily be abused, and there is always an element of personal chemistry in such matters.

Having appointed a guide, you'll also be latched on to by a shoe-bearer when you enter the church complex. This is a man who will take responsibility for your shoes while you are inside the churches, carry them between nearby churches, personally assist in putting them back on your feet at appropriate moments, and leer at you for good measure when the mood takes him. You won't regret taking the path of least resistance – the shoe-bearers evidently mean well, far better they carry shoes for a living than beg or starve, and once you've appointed one and agreed to give him birr 5 or 10 at the end of your tour, you can relax.

Assuming you've paid your entrance fee, you're free to walk where you like and photograph what you like anywhere in the complex (with the obvious exception of the Holy of Holies at the back of each church). It is, however, customary to slip a birr or two to any person you put centre frame – your guide will be able to advise you on this. Video photography is permitted only upon payment of a birr 150 filming fee.

The northwest cluster

The most easterly church in this cluster is **Bet Medhane Alem**. This is the largest monolithic rock-hewn church in the world, measuring 11.5m in height and covering an area of almost 800m². A plain building, supported by 36 pillars on the inside and another

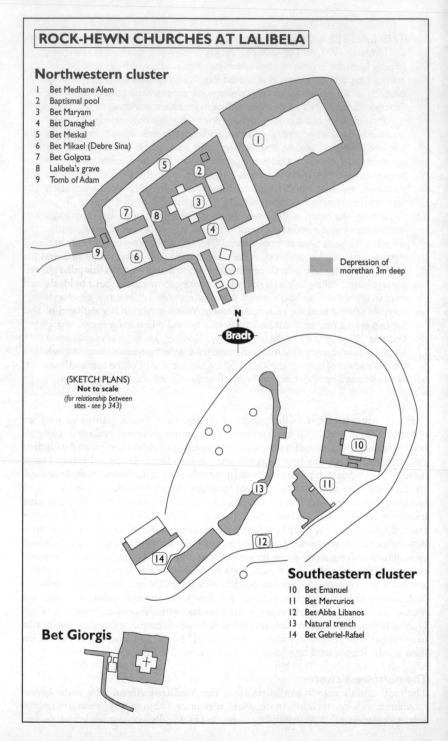

ROCK-HEWN CHURCHES AT LALIBELA

Northwestern cluster

1 Bet Medhane Alem
2 Baptismal pool
3 Bet Maryam
4 Bet Danaghel
5 Bet Meskal
6 Bet Mikael (Debre Sina)
7 Bet Golgota
8 Lalibela's grave
9 Tomb of Adam

Depression of morethan 3m deep

N

Bradt

(SKETCH PLANS)
Not to scale
*(for relationship between
sites - see p 343)*

Southeastern cluster

10 Bet Emanuel
11 Bet Mercurios
12 Bet Abba Libanos
13 Natural trench
14 Bet Gebriel-Rafael

Bet Giorgis

36 around the outside, Bet Medhane Alem has a classical nobility reminiscent of an Ancient Greek temple, a similarity that has led some experts to think it was modelled on the original St Mary Zion Church built by King Ezana at Axum. The interior of the church is also plain, and its vast size creates a cathedral-like austerity. Several graves have been carved into the rock floor; they are no longer permanently occupied, but when I visited a helpful priest leapt into one and played possum for my benefit. Bet Medhane Alem has its own wide courtyard whose walls are pockmarked with niches that originally served as graves or hermits' caves.

A short tunnel leads to a second courtyard enclosing three more churches. The largest of these, **Bet Maryam**, is thought to have been the first church built in Lalibela. Because of its association with the Virgin, it remains the most popular church in the complex among Ethiopians. Smaller and less imposing than Medhane Alem, but also a monolith, Bet Maryam has a more intimate and elaborately carved interior, with carvings of the original Lalibela Cross and of the Star of David, and dense paintings on parts of the roof. The church is 13m high and its upper floor has seven rooms used to store church treasures. Above the entrance is a relief of two riders fighting a dragon. Within the church, one veiled pillar is reputedly inscribed with the Ten Commandments in Greek and Ge'ez, as well as the story of how the churches of Lalibela were excavated, and the story of the beginning and end of the world. The local priests say that this pillar glowed brightly until the 16th century, and they claim it would be too dangerous to lift the veil and show it to researchers.

Carved into the northern wall of Bet Maryam's courtyard, the tiny chapel of **Bet Meskel** is barely 40m^2 in area. In the southern wall, and even smaller, the atmospheric chapel of **Bet Danaghel** (House of the Virgin Martyrs) was reputedly constructed in honour of 50 Christian maiden nuns murdered by the Roman ruler Julian the Apostate in the 4th century, a legend recorded in the Ethiopian Book of Martyrs. Also in the courtyard is a pool that is believed to cure any infertile woman who is dipped into the water three times on Ethiopian Christmas – the water is certainly green and slimy enough to suggest a favourable effect on procreativity. The water level is about 2m below the courtyard, so the women have to be lowered down on a harnessed rope – a rather comic sight!

The third courtyard in the northwest cluster contains the twin churches of **Bet Debre Sina** (also called **Bet Mikael**) and **Bet Golgotha**. These churches share an entrance and together they form a semi-monolith. I found these churches the most atmospheric in Lalibela, with a dank dungeon-like atmosphere and a pervasive air of sanctity. The historical relationship between the twin churches is confused by the presence of several *tabots*, but the structure suggests they have always functioned separately. The interior of Bet Golgotha (the one church in Lalibela that women are prohibited from entering) is remarkable in that it has seven life-size reliefs of saints carved around its walls. There is also a legend that King Lalibela is buried beneath a slab on the floor of this church, and that the soil of this supposed grave has healing powers. The **Selassie Chapel**, which lies within Bet Golgotha, is considered the holiest place in Lalibela. Few visitors have ever been permitted to enter it. The western exit from the courtyard lies at the base of the **Tomb of Adam**, a cruciform hermit's cell decorated by mutilated paintings of the kings of Lalibela. Some of the rock-hewn caves near this were recently converted into a church.

The southeast cluster

Whereas the northwest cluster of churches possesses a sense of cohesion that suggests it was conceived as a whole, quite possibly by King Lalibela as the legends suggest, the southeast cluster comes across as more hotchpotch in design. Several of the individual churches in this cluster are thought to have been secular in origin and some predate the reign of Lalibela by five centuries.

Bet Gebriel-Rafael is a strange church, surrounded by a rock trench of perhaps 5m in depth. In effect, this trench is rather like a dry moat, and it must be crossed on a rickety wooden walkway. This fortress-like appearance, combined with the unusual alignment of the church, has long led experts to think that it was originally built as the residence of King Lalibela. More recent architectural studies by the British archaeologist David Phillipson indicate that both it and the nearby Bet Mercurios were excavated as the core of a fortified palatial complex during the politically unstable 7th and 8th centuries, when the Axumite Empire was in the process of disintegrating. From the outside, Bet Gebriel-Rafael is a very imposing and memorable sight. The northern façade, its height greatly exaggerated by the trench below, is distinguished by a row of arched niches, which, although they show strong Axumite influences, give the building a somewhat Islamic appearance. Inside, the church is surprisingly small and plain, decorated only by three carved Latin crosses. The priest spun me an intriguing story about a secret tunnel that leads to a second set of rooms underneath the church. These rooms, if they exist, are presumably on a level with the floor of the surrounding trench. The priest also said that nobody knows where this tunnel is any longer!

According to the legends, **Bet Abba Libanos** was built overnight by Lalibela's wife Meskel Kebre, assisted by a group of angels. The church has been built around a cave in a vertical face, and although the roof is still connected to the original rock, the sides and back are separated from the rock by narrow tunnels. The pink-tinged façade, which once again shows strong Axumite influences in its arched and cruciform windows, lies under an overhang in a way that is reminiscent of some churches in Tigrai. The interior of the church is most notable for a small light in the altar wall which, according to the priests, shines of its own accord 24 hours a day. A tunnel of about 50m in length leads from the right aisle of this church to the chapel of **Bet Lehem**, a small and simple shrine that could well have been a monastic cell used for private prayers by King Lalibela.

Bet Emanuel is a 12m-high monolith – the only church of this type in the southeast cluster – and it is considered by art historians to be the finest and most precisely worked church in Lalibela, possibly because it was the private church of the royal family. The exterior of the church imitates the classical Axumite wood-and-stone built-up church typified by Yemrehanna Kristos outside Lalibela. An ornamental frieze of blind windows dominates the church's interior.

Bet Mercurios is a cave church. It was originally used for secular purposes, and may well be around 1,400 years old. The presence of iron shackles in a trench suggests it may have served as a jail or courtroom. The interior is partially collapsed – the entrance was rebuilt from scratch in the late 1980s – but it does boast a beautiful if rather faded 15th-century wall frieze of what looks like the three wise men or a group of saints. There is also a recently restored painting displayed in the church, in which a most beatific-looking Saint Mercurios is depicted amidst a group of dog-headed men, his sword trailing through the guts of the evil King Oleonus.

Bet Giyorgis

This isolated monolith – the only such church that was still free of scaffolding in early 2005 – is the most majestic of all Lalibela's churches. It must measure close to 15m in height and, like the churches of the northwestern group, it is excavated below ground level in a sunken courtyard enclosed by precipitous walls. The most remarkable feature of this church is that it is carved in the shape of a symmetrical cruciform tower. The story is that Giyorgis – St George as he is known to us – was so offended that none of Lalibela's churches was dedicated to him that he personally visited the king to set things straight. Lalibela responded by promising he would build the finest of all his churches for Giyorgis. So enthusiastic was the saint to see the result of Lalibela's promise that he rode his horse right over the wall into the entrance tunnel. The holes in the stone tunnel walls are the hoof prints of St George's horse – or so they tell you in Lalibela.

CHURCHES OUTSIDE LALIBELA

The mountains around Lalibela are studded with medieval monasteries and churches, many of which are very different to their Lalibela counterparts, and are infrequently visited by tourists. With the exception of the monasteries at Nakuta La'ab and Asheton Maryam, both of which can be visited as affordable and relatively straightforward day trips from Lalibela, access to many of these churches is not easy unless you are prepared to spend several days trekking in the mountains, or have access to – or can afford to hire – a 4x4 vehicle. For those who want to see a good selection of churches and monasteries in one go, the Bilbilla Circuit to the north of Lalibela forms the obvious first choice, affording access to four different churches over a day by vehicle. The churches to the south and east are more scattered: Nakuta La'ab is traditionally very popular with backpackers, since it can be reached on foot without a guide, while the mule ride to Asheton Maryam also forms a straightforward day trip out of Lalibela. The other churches to the south and east of Lalibela are more difficult to access, and there is no vehicular circuit comparable with the one around Bilbilla.

The entrance fee to these outlying churches is not included in the price of the ticket for the churches within Lalibela. Yemrehanna Kristos charges a fixed entrance fee of birr 50 per person. The other churches are widely quoted as charging birr 20 apiece, but based on our experiences all but Nakuta La'ab and Asheton Maryam now ask more, and the priests don't respond well to attempts at negotiation. Although no set fee is charged for video cameras, you can expect them to attract a payment at least equivalent to the entrance fee. Women are permitted to visit all of the churches and monasteries described below.

Churches near Bilbilla

This relatively compact and very varied circuit of churches comprises Yemrehanna Kristos, Arbuta Insesa, Bilbilla Chirkos and Bilbilla Giyorgis. These churches all stand within 10km of the village of Bilbilla, itself some 30km from Lalibela off the road northwards to Sekota and Adwa. To explore all four churches along this circuit by vehicle takes about eight hours, including walking times of five to 20 minutes each way to the various churches. The vehicle hire will cost upwards of birr 700 in Lalibela, and can be arranged through any of the more expensive hotels or through an official guide. Any one of these churches can be visited from Lalibela by mule as a ten-to-15-hour round day trip, for which you should expect to pay a guide fee of birr 150 as well as a mule-hire fee of birr 75. Yemrehanna Kristos qualifies as first choice for a day trip of this sort. To trek to all of the churches would require three to four days; official guides in Lalibela will be able to advise you about setting up a trip.

The turn-off to **Bilbilla Chirkos** branches left from the Sekota road 27km past the main square in Lalibela and about 2km before Bilbilla. The church, 6km from the main road, is covered in scaffolding which is clearly visible to the right before you reach the parking area, from where a gentle 500m footpath through a small forest patch and across a stream leads to the church. A tall semi-monolith encircled by deep trenches, Bilbilla Chirkos is architecturally reminiscent of Bet Gebriel-Rafael in Lalibela, with its intricately worked pink-tinged façade. Notable features of the interior include the 12 thick pillars, some very old paintings of Maryam and Giyorgis (with dragon) and various other saints, and the cross that is carved into the dome in front of the sanctuary. Several beehives lie within the church; the holy honey they produce is said to have curative powers. Treasures include several goatskin books including an illustrated 800-year-old Ge'ez history of Kidus Chirkos. The age of Bilbilla Chirkos is unknown. One tradition holds that it is the oldest rock-hewn church in Lasta, excavated during the 6th-century rule of Emperor Kaleb. Other sources suggest it is roughly contemporaneous with the Lalibela churches. Unlike many other outlying churches, no monastery is attached to Bilbilla Chirkos. An interesting site that can be reached by driving another 15km past Bilbilla Chirkos then hiking for another two hours into the hills is **Kiddist Arbuta Washa**, the cave in which Lalibela was reputedly born.

Back on the main Axum road, the turn-off to Bilbilla village lies to the right about 2km past the Bilbilla Chirkos turn-off. The village is about 1km from the Axum road and visible from it. The road to Bilbilla crosses a stream that can only be forded by a vehicle with good clearance, ideally a 4x4. Signposted from the village, a 15–20-minute walk leads through the marketplace and uphill to **Bilbilla Giyorgis**, also covered in scaffolding. Carved into the rock face, Bilbilla Giyorgis has an imposing façade decorated with a frieze said to represent the 12 vaults of heaven, and it is surrounded by a tunnel in a manner reminiscent of Bet Mercurios in Lalibela. As with Bilbilla Giyorgis, there are several holy beehives in this church.

Continuing for 6km east along the side road through Bilbilla, you will come to **Arbuta Insesa**, reached on foot in five minutes following a gently sloping path uphill through a patch of euphorbia and other trees. This small, sunken semi-monolith is neither as beautiful nor as imposing as similar churches in Lalibela town, though the absence of scaffolding in early 2001 made it easier to photograph than some. A small spring within the church produces holy water. This appears to be a very old church, with pillars and doors mimicking the Axumite design of some built-up churches, and it is dedicated to the four beasts, symbols of the four evangelists who followed Kidus Yohannis (Saint John). A lengthy walk from here leads to the little-visited monastery of **Gedamit Maryam**, where there is an interesting built-up church.

COMMUNITY TOURISM IN NORTH WOLO
By Mark Chapman

A local charity called TESFA is working with local communities in the North Wolo mountains near Lalibela, to develop simple facilities catering to tourists who wish to get off the beaten trail, trek in breathtaking scenery and see the real culture of the highlanders. As of now TESFA has assisted two communities in Meket Woreda to develop trekking camps, though more are likely to follow. These communities manage the enterprises and retain the proceeds from them.

The first site, located in the parish of Mequat Maryam, is set on a promontory of the plateau at around 2,800m, jutting out to the southwest with spectacular views across the rural landscape – a sundown drink here is an unforgettable experience. The second site, at Wajela, is set in gentler scenery with a beautiful wood of acacia trees, and numerous stands of eucalyptus in the surrounding village. The site itself stands on a cliff above the juniper forest and church of Weketa Maryam, with its intriguing cave complex.

Using local materials where possible, the communities have constructed *tukuls* (round thatched houses) with comfortable beds, clean sheets and blankets. Each site has four beds: two doubles and two singles, split in two rooms, though the plan is to increase this to six beds in the coming months. Each site has a restaurant and an eco-toilet – a seat with a view – allowing peaceful contemplation of the landscape! A shower is available in one site, and this will soon be extended to the second site.

The communities will prepare three meals a day, plus a snack on arrival after your hike. As a result, and to ensure that there are no double bookings, advance bookings are required. The price per person/per full day is birr 300 inclusive of food,

The indisputable gem among the churches around Bilbilla, not least because it is so fundamentally different to anything in town, is the **Monastery of Yemrehanna Kristos**. Situated at an altitude of around 2,700m and protected by an unflattering modern outer wall, Yemrehanna Kristos is an old built-up church within a large cavern. It is a particularly fine example of late-Axumite architecture, built with alternating layers of wood and granite faced with white gypsum that give it the appearance of a gigantic layered chocolate cream cake. Among many interesting architectural features are the cruciform carved windows, an etched wood-panel roof, a coffer ceiling with inlaid hexagons, and a large dome over the sanctuary. A reliable tradition has it this church was built by its namesake, Yemrehanna Kristos, the third Zagwe ruler and a predecessor of King Lalibela, recorded as ascending to the throne in AD1087 and ruling for about 40 years. Yemrehanna Kristos is credited with restoring links between Ethiopia and the Coptic Church (an unverified legend states that he visited Egypt during his reign, and the priests at the monastery claim that all the wood used in the church's construction was imported from Egypt, while the gypsum was brought from Jerusalem). The church and its curative holy water formed an important site of pilgrimage in medieval times. Behind the main building, adding an eerie quality to the already dingy cavern, lie the bones of some of the 10,740 Christian pilgrims who, it is claimed, travelled from as far afield as Egypt, Syria and Jerusalem to die at this monastery. In front of the church, a small opening reveals muddy soil, said to be part of a subterranean freshwater lake below the cave. By road, Yemrehanna Kristos can be reached by continuing 9km eastwards from Arbuta Insesa (ie: 15km from Bilbilla village) to a parking area on the right side of the road. From here, a rather steep 15-minute walk – watch out for loose rocks underfoot – leads uphill to the monastery through a lovely patch of juniper forest. Reasonably fit

accommodation, guide, and pack animals, but excluding bottled drinks (beer, water and more are available) and transport.

The plateau at Meket is set on a lava bed associated with the formation of the Rift Valley. This lava dried into hexagonally formed basalt rocks, which makes the cliffs both beautiful and intriguing. Some of the basalt in the area (Wegel Tena Basalt) was reputedly formed deeper in the earth's crust than any other rock in the world. Weketa Maryam is just one of the many cave structures in the area's escarpments. Some were evidently used as churches, a few still are. Some, like Weketa, show signs of being carefully excavated, while others are simply enlarged natural caves. The Weketa cave has also suffered partial collapse and appears to have lost the front section.

Trekking routes largely follow the escarpment edges and give a chance to see local farming techniques and other elements of local culture. With luck, visitors should also see some of the local wildlife (gelada, birds of prey, rock hyrax, klipspringer). For those interested in spending more time with the communities, to see how they cook and farm, this can easily be arranged.

Transport by 4x4 can be arranged from Lalibela and Bahir Dar through local operators. Habte Independent Tours in Lalibela charges birr 800 each way between Lalibela and Meket, and birr 2,400 from Meket to Bahir Dar. Alternatively local buses can be taken. Buses from Lalibela can drop you at the crossroads 'town' of Gashena, where you can meet your guide. Buses from Bahir Dar, Gonder, Woldia or Dessie can drop you at Filakit where the guides are based. For self-drive, vehicles can be parked in Filakit (on the Woldia–Werota road), and brought to meet you as required.

For up-to-date information, check the website www.community-tourism-ethiopia.com or contact Mark Chapman on ☏ 011 1140583/1233840 or 091 1416452; e chapman@ethionet.et or tesfacbt@ethionet.et

travellers unable or unwilling to hire a vehicle might think seriously about visiting this monastery on mule-back – a 10–12 hour round trip from Lalibela.

Between Lalibela and Bilbilla, a road leads westwards to **Sarsana Mikael**, a damaged and almost disused monolith reached by a tunnel, notable for the black stone on its door, which is said to kill immediately any sinner who touches it. The road to this church was impassable on last inspection, but may eventually be repaired. You can visit the church on foot or on the back of a donkey or mule.

Nakuta La'ab Monastery

The easiest of all the outlying churches to reach is the Monastery of Nakuta La'ab, named after its constructor, the nephew and successor of King Lalibela. One tradition has it that Nakuta La'ab ruled from this church, which he called Qoqhena, during an 18-month break in Lalibela's monarchy, another is that he took refuge here after he was deposed. Along with Lalibela, Nakuta La'ab is the only Zagwe ruler to be included under a recognisable name in all the available lists of Ethiopian kings. He ascended to the throne upon the death of Lalibela; some sources place his period of rule at 40–48 years, others indicate that he might have been forced from the throne within a few years of becoming king.

The monastery accredited to Nakuta La'ab consists of a relatively simple church built around a shallow cave in which several holy pools are fed by natural springs. The church has many treasures, some of which are claimed to have belonged to Nakuta La'ab himself. These include paintings, crosses and an illuminated leather Bible. There are also some great paintings in the church. One advantage over the churches in town is that the treasures are brought out into the open where they can be examined in decent light.

Nakuta La'ab is roughly 6km from Lalibela, and is seen from a distance along the road between the airport and the town. It can be reached on foot by following the surfaced airport road out of Lalibela, a straightforward walk that will take an hour to 90 minutes. About halfway out, you'll pass a small gorge where birders might want to stop for a short while – we saw the endemic white-winged and Rüppell's black chat here, as well as Ortolon and cinereous buntings, paradise flycatcher, northern wryneck and ten types of raptor along the way. When you reach a little village on the left side of the road, you must follow a clearly signposted track for about 500m to reach the monastery. Entrance costs birr 20. If you don't feel like the walk, you can arrange to see the monastery en route to or from the airport, or you can organise to go by mule, which costs birr 35–40 for mule and muleteer, plus a guide fee.

Asheton Maryam

Another monastery that's quite often visited by travellers is Asheton Maryam, which lies at an altitude of almost 4,000m on the high mountain overlooking Lalibela. This monastery is also associated with King Nakuta La'ab, who most probably founded it, and who may even be buried in the chapel. The church is carved out of a cleft into a cliff face, and the execution is rougher than at most other churches in and around Lalibela. Asheton Maryam houses some interesting crosses and other church treasures, but the excursion is just as remarkable for the church's setting and the views on the way up. Entrance costs the same as Nakuta La'ab, as does the hire of a mule and muleteer. Most people go up by mule, but it's only two hours' walk from Lalibela, albeit along a rather steep path strewn in parts with loose stones.

Genata Maryam and beyond

One of the most interesting outlying churches is **Genata Maryam**, a large monolith carved into a pink-tinged outcrop near the source of the Tekaze River. Supported by pillars, the church is very different from any of the excavations in Lalibela in that it is not hidden within a trench, but carved openly on a rocky hilltop – though the cover of scaffolding rather detracts from the impact of seeing it from afar. According to tradition, Genata Maryam was excavated during the reign of Yakuno Amlak, the king who 'restored' the Solomonic line in the early 13th century. A notable feature of the interior is the elaborate paintings said to date to the 13th century. Genata Maryam is about four hours' walk or mule ride from Lalibela, or 45 minutes' drive. You reach it by following the airport road for 9km out of town, and then taking a clearly signposted left turn onto the old Woldia road. About 13km past this junction (rather than the 17km indicated on the signpost) you will reach a small village, also known as Genata Maryam, where a left turn leads to the church after 700m. You can drive to within 50m of the church, which is reached by a short but steep footpath.

Inaccessible by road, **Mekina Medhane Alem** is a built-up cave church similar in style to Yemrehanna Kristos in its characteristically Axumite use of layered wood and stone. Although there is little historical evidence to back it up, tradition holds that the church dates to the 6th century AD. The decorated interior boasts intricate geometric patterns as well as many old paintings – notably one of roosters fighting next to the sun and the moon above the door. The monastic church lies on a spur of Mount Abuna Yosef, about three hours from Genata Maryam by foot or mule.

Hikes or mule treks to the above churches can be extended to form a four- to five-day circuit culminating with the ascent to the 4,190m peak of Mount Abuna Yosef. Several obscure churches can be visited on this circuit. The cliffs around Abuna Yosef are favoured by gelada troops and recent anecdotal evidence in the form of complaints from local shepherds suggests that the small Ethiopian wolf population associated with the mountain is on the increase. Although currently accessible only on foot or by mule, Abuna Yosef should eventually be connected to Lalibela by a road currently under construction.

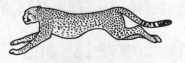

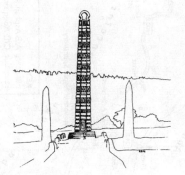

Stelae at Axum

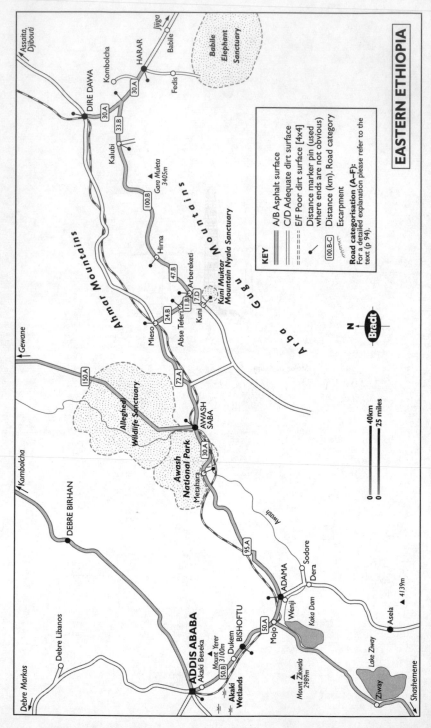

EASTERN ETHIOPIA

KEY

A/B Asphalt surface
C/D Adequate dirt surface
E/F Poor dirt surface [4x4]
Distance marker pin (used where ends are not obvious)
100.B-C Distance (km). Road category
Escarpment

Road categorisation (A–F):
For a detailed explanation please refer to the text (p 94).

Bradt

N

0 ——— 40km
0 ——— 25 miles

Assaita, Djibouti
Jijiga
HARAR
Babile
Babile Elephant Sanctuary
Kombolcha
30.A
DIRE DAWA
Fedis
30.A
33.B
Kalubi
100.B
Gara Muleta 3405m
Ahmar Mountains
Hirna
47.B
Arbereketi
24.B
11.B
7.D
Kuni
Mieso
Abse Teferi
Kuni Muktar Mountain Nyala Sanctuary
Gugu Mountains
Arba Gugu
72.A
150.A
Gewane
Alleghedi Wildlife Sanctuary
AWASH SABA
30.A
Awash National Park
Metahara
Kombolcha
DEBRE BIRHAN
95.A
Awash
ADAMA
Sodore
Dera
4139m
Wenji
Koka Dam
Asela
ADDIS ABABA
Akaki Beseka
Mount Yerer 3100m
BISHOFTU
Dukem
50.B
50.A
Mojo
Lake Ziway
Debre Markos
Debre Libanos
Akaki Wetlands
Mount Zikwala 2989m
Ziway
Shashemene

Part Four

Eastern Ethiopia

INTRODUCTION

This section covers parts of Ethiopia lying to the east of the capital over three chapters. The first of these chapters ambles along the surfaced road between Addis Ababa and the large but rather bland town of Adama (Nazret). This 100km stretch of asphalt can be covered in a couple of hours or over several days, with obvious highlights including the wetlands around the Akaki River, the airforce town of Bishoftu and its attendant crater lakes, and the atmospheric mountaintop monastery at Zikwala. All these places can easily form the goal of a self-standing day or overnight trip out of the capital. They can also be visited en route to southern Ethiopia – the junction for the main road south lies at Mojo, 75km from Addis Ababa, while Adama itself is the starting point for an important route south to the highlands of Arsi and Bale zones.

The second chapter in this section covers Awash National Park, which is the closest thing Ethiopia has to the savanna reserves of east Africa, and an excellent overnight trip from Addis Ababa. It also covers the arid section of the Rift Valley that follows the course of the Awash River north of Awash National Park to its delta in a series of desert lakes near the Djibouti border. Although little visited by travellers, this is a fascinating and very different part of Ethiopia, home to the pastoralist Afar people, and – somewhat unexpectedly – bisected by what is arguably the best surfaced road in the country.

The final chapter in this section concentrates on the alluring walled city of Harar, the spiritual home of Ethiopia's large Muslim community, as well as its altogether less inspiring modern twin city of Dire Dawa. Lying more than 500km east of Addis Ababa, Dire Dawa and Harar are accessible from the capital not only by road, but also by daily Ethiopian Airlines flights – not to mention the country's only passenger train service! The base from which Ahmed Gragn waged his 16th-century *jihad* against the Christian Highlands, Harar formed the most important trade centre in Ethiopia for much of the 19th century – when it was visited by the explorer Richard Burton and home to the French poet Arthur Rimbaud – and it is also the birthplace of the late Emperor Haile Selassie. Today, the old town is one of the most popular tourist sites in Ethiopia. Not only does its labyrinth of alleys and Muslim shrines provide a striking contrast to the Christian pre-eminence in northern Ethiopia, but it is also home to the renowned hyena man of Harar.

Addis Ababa to Adama by Road

The 100km of surfaced road that runs southeast from Addis Ababa towards the bustling town of Adama will be traversed by most travellers heading to any parts of Ethiopia that lie south or east of the capital. Adama itself has excellent facilities for visitors, but since it is of little inherent interest to travellers, and can be reached by bus or in a private vehicle in a couple of hours from Addis Ababa, few visitors to Ethiopia spend long in the town. The road between Addis Ababa and Adama does, however, provide access to several notable natural attractions including the Akaki Wetlands, Mount Zikwala and the crater lakes of Bishoftu, any of which makes for an easy goal for a day trip out of the capital.

Public transport is plentiful along the road covered in this chapter, with regular buses from the capital to Adama and other towns further east and south supplemented by light vehicles ferrying local passengers between small towns such as Akaki, Dukem, Bishoftu (Debre Zeyit), and Mojo. For self-drive travellers, or those hopping between towns in light vehicles, it's worth mentioning that Mojo, halfway between Bishoftu and Adama, forms the junction of the asphalt road that runs south through the Rift Valley to Moyale (Kenyan border) and Arba Minch (gateway to the Lower Omo Valley). Adama itself is also an important route focus, lying at the junction of the main road east towards Awash National Park, Harar and Assaita, and a dirt road heading south through the town of Asela towards Bale National Park.

AKAKI WETLANDS

The wetland complex fed by the Akaki River about 20km southeast of Addis is among the best in the country and of particular interest to birdwatchers. Its mix of habitats includes the open river, reedy marshes, a string of small natural lakes, the larger artificial Abba Samuel Dam, and a very attractive waterfall. The wetlands stretch for about 12km from the small town of Akaki Beseka on the Bishoftu road, and can readily be explored as a day trip from Addis Ababa. Bear in mind that, like any seasonal wetland, it may dry out completely in the dry season or in years of drought.

Getting there and away

Minibuses from Addis to Akaki Beseka leave regularly from in front of the railway station and take about half an hour. They can also be picked up at the Saris minibus stop, which lies about 5km from the city centre on the Bishoftu road. When you want to move on from Akaki Beseka, it is easy to find transport back to Addis or on to Bishoftu.

Where to stay

The obvious way to visit the Akaki wetlands is as a day trip from Addis. If, however, you intend travelling further east or south, it might make better sense to spend a night in Akaki Beseka before you visit the wetlands; they are very exposed and it would be worth

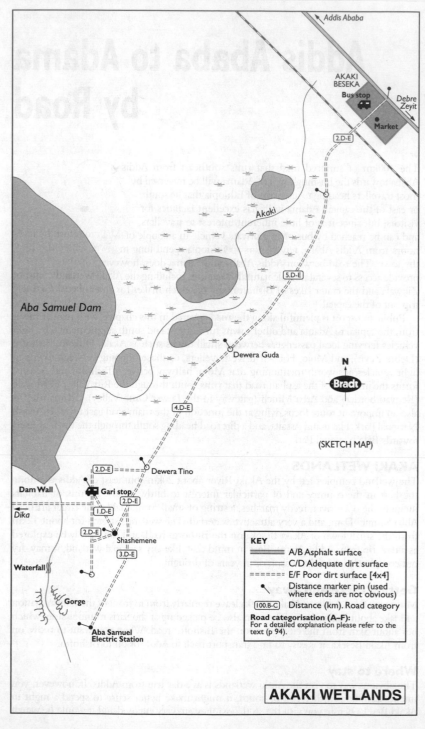

AKAKI
BESEKA
Bus stop

Debre
Zeyit

Market

2.D-E

Akaki

5.D-E

Aba Samuel Dam

Dewera Guda

N

Bradt

4.D-E

(SKETCH MAP)

2.D-E Dewera Tino

Dam Wall

Gari stop

Dika

2.D-E

1.D-E

2.D-E

Shashemene

3.D-E

Waterfall

Gorge

Aba Samuel
Electric Station

KEY

A/B Asphalt surface

C/D Adequate dirt surface

====== E/F Poor dirt surface [4x4]

● Distance marker pin (used
where ends are not obvious)

100.B-C Distance (km). Road category

Road categorisation (A–F):
For a detailed explanation please refer to the
text (p 94).

AKAKI WETLANDS

getting the earliest possible start. There are several cheap hotels in Akaki Beseka, nothing very special but a lot cheaper than their equivalent in Addis. Best of the bunch is the **Dessie Hotel**, which has decent dollar-a-night rooms and communal showers. The hotel is unsignposted on the side road where minibuses to and from Addis terminate; it has a red gate and a few shrubs in front.

Exploring the wetlands

The only form of public transport between Akaki Beseka and the villages around the wetlands is the horse-drawn *gari*. A *gari* out of Akaki Beseka can be picked up at the marketplace. *Garis* back to Akaki Beseka congregate about 500m from Abba Samuel Dam Wall, near a footbridge over the river that leads to the village of Dika. If you want to explore the wetlands reasonably thoroughly, the best plan would be to walk one way (about 13km and reasonably flat) and use a *gari* the other way. My feeling is that you would be best walking out provided you get an early start (you could set off at 06.00 if you spent the previous night in Akaki Beseka), as the area is very exposed and it becomes hot after around 10.00. You could then return by *gari* later in the day. With a later start, it might make more sense to take a *gari* out to get a feel for the terrain, and then to return by foot.

The interesting part of the wetlands starts about 3km out of town, where the river supports several small lakes, all of them visible from the road. During the rainy season, this whole area becomes a large, marshy floodplain. When I visited, towards the end of the rains, the marsh had receded, but I was still impressed by the numbers of greater flamingo and ducks on the open water and the variety of waders to be seen on the mudflats. This area is also noted for interesting European migrants such as European stork, yellow and grey wagtails, and a variety of wheatears. The most common terrestrial bird is the red-chested wheatear, a species that is virtually confined to Ethiopia, while the reeds and grass support large numbers of red bishop and various widows. Wattled ibis are common and vociferous.

About 7km out of town, you arrive at the nondescript hilltop village of Dewera Guda. Four kilometres further, at Dewera Tino, you come to a fork in the road. Take the right turn towards a village called Shashemene. The first sign of Shashemene is a small kiosk, where you might want to break for a soda and packet of dry biscuits. From the shop, a footpath leads for about 500m across boulder-strewn ground to the village proper and, a bit further on, the bank of the river. About 100m downstream from where you reach the river, it tumbles attractively over a cliff into a small gorge. Follow the edge of the gorge for 200m or so and there's an easy descent to the bottom, from where you can walk back over rocks to the base of the falls. The waterfall must be around 20m high and it is split into nine separate streams – it's very pretty, particularly after the rains when the water is high and the surrounding countryside is strewn with wild flowers. In the gorge, look out for the localised black duck and mountain wagtail, and the endemic white-winged cliff-chat.

From the waterfall, you can either return to the shop outside Shashemene, from where a clear footpath leads across a field to Abba Samuel Dam Wall, or else follow the river upstream to the same destination. The Italians built the dam in 1939 for the country's first hydro-electric plant, but this is no longer operative because of silt. Scenically, Abba Samuel is something of a disappointment as it is choked with water hyacinth, but the nearby bridge is the best place to pick up a *gari* back to Akaki Beseka.

Note that if you ask around in Akaki Beseka for transport to Shashemene, people are likely to think you mean the town of the same name in the Rift Valley.

BISHOFTU (DEBRE ZEYIT) AND SURROUNDS

Set at an altitude of 1,900m some 45 minutes' drive from Addis Ababa, Bishoftu is a substantial town – indeed, with a population exceeding 100,000, it is the tenth largest in the country – that sprawls rather untidily for several kilometres along the main Adama road. The surrounding area is remembered as the site of Ahmed Gragn's famous victory over Emperor Lebna Dengal in 1529, which resulted in the destruction of several towns and the looting of some important churches, and which also cleared the way for the region to be occupied by the Oromo who still inhabit it today. The town is also known as Debre Zeyit (Mountain of Olives), the official 'Christian' name imposed on it by Haile Selassie in the early 1960s, and is still marked as such on many maps despite having officially reverted to its more historically valid Oromo name of Bishoftu in the late 1990s.

Bishoftu has since 1945 been the site of the country's main airforce base and training centre (don't photograph anything from the airforce base gate on the Adama road or about 3km further east), and it is also the site of a well-known veterinary training institution, but otherwise it might easily be dismissed by visitors as a thoroughly uninteresting and scruffy little place on casual inspection. From the main road through town, there is not a hint of the fact that it lies at the epicentre of what is perhaps the most accessible crater-lake field in Africa. At least six such lakes are dotted around Bishoftu, two of which – Bishoftu and Hora – lie practically within the town centre – making it an excellent goal for a day trip out of the capital, or first stop before heading further east or south.

Getting there and away
Bishoftu straddles the surfaced Adama road roughly 50km east of Addis Ababa and can be reached from the capital in less than an hour in a private vehicle, bearing in mind that the traffic is probably the densest to be found along any open road in Ethiopia. Regular buses for Bishoftu leave from the Adama bus station in central Addis Ababa. The trip takes around one hour by bus, assuming the traffic out of Addis Ababa isn't too heavy. From Bishoftu, there is also plenty of transport on to Adama.

Bishoftu's bus station has recently been relocated about 1km from the town centre along the Addis Ababa road. A steady stream of minibuses runs between the town centre and bus station, charging a fare of less than birr 1.

Where to stay
Upmarket
No genuine tourist-class accommodation currently exists around Bishoftu, but one such hotel is earmarked for renovation and another is under construction at the time of writing.

Hora Ras Hotel This former government hotel, perched attractively on the rim of Lake Hora, was somewhat rundown when it was bought by a local businessman in 2000 and closed for renovation. There is no indication as yet as to when (or indeed whether) it will reopen, but assuming it happens during the lifespan of this edition, it's well worth walking the 2km from the town centre for a drink or meal – the view over the lake is superb.

Kiroftu Resort & Spa ✆ 091 1248213. Currently under construction on the rustic northern shore of Lake Kiroftu, this promising resort, built traditional-style in stone and thatch, is likely to open in early 2006.

Moderate
Ethiopian Airforce Officers Club ✆ 011 4338035/4330729. Until such time one of the above hotels opens, the best substitute is the unpromising sounding Ethiopian Air Force Officers' Club (ETAF to its friends, rather more cheerily), which lies along the road between the town centre and Lake Hora. The large rooms with en-suite hot shower and DSTV are pretty good, though not so smart as to entirely justify an inflated *faranji* rate of birr 200. The club also serves good Western and Ethiopian food, the bar has DSTV, and the pretty palm-lined grounds contain a swimming pool and a small playground for children.

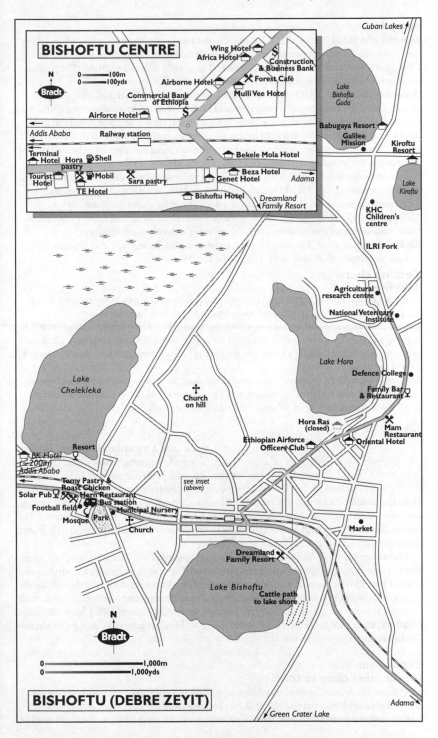

BISHOFTU CENTRE

Bradt

0 ——— 100m
0 ——— 100yds

N

Cuban Lakes

Wing Hotel
Africa Hotel
Construction
& Business Bank
Airborne Hotel
Forest Café
Commercial Bank
of Ethiopia
Mulli Vee Hotel
Airforce Hotel
Addis Ababa
Railway station
Terminal
Hotel
Hora
pastry
Shell
Bekele Mola Hotel
Tourist
Hotel
Mobil
Sara pastry
Beza Hotel
Adama
TE Hotel
Genet Hotel
Bishoftu Hotel
Dreamland
Family Resort

Lake
Bishoftu
Guda

Babugaya Resort
Galilee
Mission
Kiroftu
Resort

Lake
Kiroftu

KHC
Children's
centre

ILRI Fork

Agricultural
research centre

National Veterinary
Institute

Lake Hora

Defence College

Family Bar
& Restaurant

Lake
Chelekleka

Church
on hill

Hora Ras
(closed)

Mam
Restaurant

Ethiopian Airforce
Officers Club

Oriental Hotel

Resort

BK Hotel
(≈ 200m)
Addis Ababa

Tomy Pastry &
Roast Chicken

see inset
(above)

Solar Pub
Hern Restaurant
Football field
Bus station
Mosque
Park
Municipal Nursery
Church

Market

Dreamland
Family Resort

Lake Bishoftu

Cattle path
to lake shore

N

Bradt

0 ——— 1,000m
0 ——— 1,000yds

Adama

BISHOFTU (DEBRE ZEYIT)

Green Crater Lake

Budget

Bishoftu Afaf Hotel ℩ 011 4338299. The pick in this category for some years now, this well-run hotel lies in the town centre overlooking Lake Bishoftu, and is signposted from the main road. Clean rooms with en-suite hot showers cost birr 50 sgl (with ³/₄ bed) or birr 70 dbl. The pleasant and sensibly priced restaurant/bar offers a view over the lake.

Babugaya Hotel ℩ 011 4331155. Situated out of town on the rim of Lake Bishoftu Guda, this pleasant family-run lodge provides adequately comfortable accommodation in en-suite rooms with a ³/₄ bed and hot shower. The view is great and a footpath leads to the lakeshore. Food and drink are not always available, but you should be able to eat at the nearby Kiroftu Resort once that has opened. The hotel is not signposted: look out for the yellow metal gate adorned in brown with the letters AA on the left side of the road about 100m past the junction for the Kiroftu Resort.

Bekele Mola Hotel ℩ 011 4338005. Easy to pick out with its brightly painted blue exterior near the main roundabout, the Bishoftu branch of the Bekele Mola isn't the smartest in the chain, but it represents the usual good value at birr 35 for a small dbl with en-suite hot water.

Airforce Hotel ℩ 011 4330620. Situated on the opposite side of the railway tracks to the Bekele Mola, this also charges birr 35 for an acceptable sgl room with en-suite cold shower.

BK Hotel Situated about 2km from the town centre along the Addis Ababa road, this has clean en-suite sgl rooms with dbl bed and cold water for birr 35.

Shoestring

Terminal Hotel Situated near the old bus station, this long-serving pick of the cheapies charges birr 20 for an adequately clean and quiet room with ³/₄ bed and en-suite cold shower.

Tourist Hotel Also close to the old bus station, this charges birr 20 for a room with en-suite showers, and despite a superficial recent facelift the rooms are rather scruffy and the attached bar discouragingly riotous – ask for a room near the back of the compound and you should be spared most of the racket!

Airborne Hotel About the cleanest of several cheapies on the road towards Lake Hora, between the main roundabout and the Construction and Development Bank. Most cater primarily to the by-the-hour market, and charge around birr 10–15 for an overnight stay.

Where to eat

In the town centre, the obvious place to eat is the new **Dreamland Family Resort**, which serves a wide selection of local dishes, alongside burgers, sandwiches, pasta and grills in the birr 10–25 range, in green terraced grounds with a view over Lake Bishoftu. Also very good, close-by, but less attractive overall, is the restaurant at the **Bishoftu Afaf Hotel**, which serves a reasonable variety of local and *faranji* dishes in the birr 10–15 range, and has a view over the lake. Out along the Addis Ababa road, not far from the bus station, **Tomy Pastry and Roast Chicken** serves decent half chickens for birr 15. Pastry shops are thin on the ground in the town centre.

There are two good restaurants along the road towards Lake Hora. Quite close to the town centre is the airy and clean **Mam Restaurant** where chicken and fish dishes cost around birr 12–15. There is a good pastry and coffee shop next door. Further along the same road, the unexpectedly trendy **Family Bar and Restaurant** – décor complete with vintage car – serves spaghetti, burgers, tuna melt, BBQ chicken, BBQ beef rib chops (rated by one reader as the best cuts of meat you will find in Ethiopia), and on weekends chicken *fajitas*. Meals are in the birr 30–40 range.

Excursions
Crater lakes close to town

Any of the crater lakes around town can be visited as a short foot excursion or by *gari*. It is equally possible to visit the lot of them by foot over the course of a day. The most central goal is the alkaline **Lake Bishoftu**, which can be reached from the main road by turning uphill at the Shell petrol station and walking for about 100m. The best view over the lake is from the Dreamland Family Resort on the eastern rim. On the opposite side of the crater to the Hotel Bishoftu Afaf, a small waterfall plunges into the lake. A steep cattle path leads to the shore of the lake, which measures up to 90m in depth, and supports some interesting birds, notably a wintering population of ferruginous duck and breeding pairs of Rüppell's griffin vulture.

Far more visually appealing is **Lake Hora**, 2km from the town centre and which can easily be reached by following signposts to the closed Hora Ras Hotel. This saline body of water, almost 40m deep, is the largest crater lake in the Bishoftu area, and its thickly wooded slopes teem with birds. A footpath leads from the Hora Ras to the lakeshore, where a recreation resort sells drinks and basic meals, and has a few boats for rental. The footpath that circumnavigates most of the crater rim takes a few hours to walk – theft is a real risk, so leave your valuables behind or take a local guide. According to local tradition, an important and very colourful Oromo thanksgiving festival called the Irrecha has taken place on the shore of Lake Hora annually for more than 1,000 years. The Irrecha Festival takes place on 1 October, and celebrates the traditional Oromo notion of Waka (One God). Some believers carry a sheaf of leaves or yellow flowers to the water's edge to praise Waka for the bounty of nature, while others dance traditionally in circles, or walk around the lake in small groups. It's a fascinating affair, well worth seeing if you're in the area at the right time – outsiders are made to feel very welcome.

If you are keen to see more lakes after Hora, continue along the main road out of town towards the agricultural college. About 2km past the Hora Ras, you come to a fork in the road where there is a small black-and-white signpost marked 'ILRI'. Take the right fork, past the KHC Children's Centre till you reach the Catholic Galilee Mission. To your right, a side road leads to **Lake Kiroftu**, notable more perhaps for its excellent fishing than for any scenic qualities. Alternatively, continue straight on past the Galilee Centre for about 500m, where a road to your left leads down to the shore of **Lake Bishoftu Guda**, a large and very attractive lake with lushly vegetated shores.

Especially if you have an interest in birds, you can walk back from here to the ILRI fork, but instead of returning to town take the fork you bypassed on the way out. Follow this road for about 1km and you come to the floodplain of **Lake Chelekleka**, not a crater lake, but a shallow pan that shows marked seasonal fluctuations in water level and often dries up entirely towards the end of the dry season. You can follow the same road back to town with the floodplain and finally the lake to your left the whole way. Chelekleka is very pretty with Mount Yerer in the background, and also offers the best birdwatching in the area. The open water supports a variety of waterfowl. Knob-billed duck, pygmy goose and spur-winged goose might be present at any time of year, while migrants such as garganey, pintail, northern shoveler, ferruginous duck and European crane are likely during the European winter. The lake sometimes hosts large concentrations of lesser flamingo, and the shore is often dense with waders. You might want to stop in for a drink at the small resort on the southern shore – entry costs birr 1 and no food other than popcorn is available.

You can walk the above circuit in its entirety – you'll cover about 10–12km in all, most of it reasonably flat – but you might also think about hiring a *gari*, at least for part of the circuit. I would be inclined to get a *gari* as far as Kiroftu, then to meander back to town on foot via Chelekleka. With a private vehicle, you could also seek out the pair of Cuban-built dams known rather imaginatively as the **Cuban Lakes** – they lie about 15km north of Lake Bishoftu Guda and are of great interest to birdwatchers.

Green Crater Lake

If the above circuit doesn't quench your lake-viewing appetite, you could think about heading out to the Green Crater Lake (also known as Aranguade Bahir or Hora Hado), which lies about 10km south of town along a road that branches from the main Adama road near the airforce base. Measuring about 30m deep, the Green Crater Lake lies at the base of a very steep crater. The unusually alkaline water supports a high concentration of the algae *Spirulina*, which creates a green cast in the right light. The algae consumes all the oxygen it produces by day during the night, so that the water becomes anaerobic in the early hours of morning, for which reason fish – and birds that survive mainly by fishing – are entirely absent. The lake does, however, support a good variety of waders, and concentrations of more than 20,000 lesser flamingo gather in its shallows from time to time. Without private transport, the best way to reach the lake is by *gari*; expect to pay around birr 20 for the round trip.

Mount Zikwala

This 2,989m-high extinct volcano, relatively recent in geological origin, rises to more than 600m above the surrounding countryside some 30km south of Bishoftu, and dominates the skyline for miles around. The juniper forest on the crater rim supports a smattering of large mammals, most visibly troops of guereza monkey, but also common duiker and klipspringer. It is also rich in forest birds, including the endemic black-winged lovebird, Abyssinian catbird and Abyssinian woodpecker, and a variety of forest starlings. The beautiful lake in the middle of the 2km-wide crater is sacred to Orthodox Ethiopians, who claim that it glows at night, and it often hosts a variety of unusual migrant ducks during the European winter. Zikwala is almost certainly the source of the Abyssinian mountain marked as 'Xiquala' on Fra Mauro's world map of 1459.

The main attraction of Zikwala is the church and monastery of Zikwala Maryam, which according to one legend were founded in the 4th century by a pair of Egyptian monks. A more plausible tradition links the monastery's foundation to Gebre Manfus Kidus, also known as Abbo, an Egyptian priest who arrived in Ethiopia in the time of King Lalibela. The older of the two extant churches – constructed in the early 20th century – is covered in frescos of its patron saint, whose St Francis-like reputation for befriending animals extended to living with lions and hyenas. The monks will show you a crack between two rocks of which it is said only the pure of conscience will squeeze through, as well as the sacred stone that is said to mark Abbo's grave. Note, however, that another tradition has it that the saint's body was taken to Jerusalem by angels and buried next to the tomb of Jesus, while a third claims that he is buried at Gurage Zone at the ancient Abbo Medrikabd Monastery near Bui on the road between Tiya and Butajira.

It is especially worth visiting Zikwala on 5 Tekemt and 5 Megabit (normally 15 October and 14 March), when the monastery forms the scene of a large religious festival dedicated to Gebre Manfus Kidus. There is a mass pilgrimage to the mountain from Addis Ababa and other parts of Showa Province on these days.

Zikwala is an easy target for a day trip from Addis or Bishoftu, provided you have your own vehicle. The turn-off to the mountain is on the Addis Ababa road, next to the juice bar just outside Bishoftu. From there it is about 30km to the base of the mountain, where there is a small village called Wember Maryam. The steep 10km road that climbs from the base to the top of the mountain is normally motorable in a 4x4, but when the road hasn't been maintained for a while it becomes impassable.

Without a vehicle, you'll be dependent on the occasional 4x4s that run between Bishoftu and Wember Maryam at the base of the mountain. These normally leave from Bishoftu at around 06.00 and take two hours. You will almost certainly have to walk the 10km up the mountain. There is no formal accommodation in the area, but you should be allowed to pitch a tent on the crater rim. If you are in the area at the right time of year, there is plenty of transport from Addis Ababa directly to Zikwala Maryam on the festival days mentioned above.

Mount Yerer

The 3,100m-high Mount Yerer is a four-million-year-old extinct volcano set on the western Rift Valley wall, to the north of the village of Dukem on the Addis–Bishoftu road. The deep semi-collapsed caldera has a towering rock in its centre. The crater rim offers excellent views across to the crater lakes around Bishoftu, and is also notable for supporting large numbers of breeding raptors. Also of interest is an elusive hermit's cave, where the mummified body of a hermit can be seen in a glass coffin.

The caldera is about 10km from Dukem. You can get part way there via a motorable forestry track, which peters out at around the 2,500m mark. From the roadhead, you will have to find your own way to the summit, so it might be useful to ask around in Dukem for a guide. The Mapping Authority's 1:50,000 sheet number 0838 B2 shows Mount Yerer and Dukem. A huge selection of hotels catering to all sub-Sheraton tastes and budgets line the main road through Dukem.

ADAMA (NAZRET)

Adama is the third largest town in Ethiopia, with a population of around 190,000. Reaction to it tends to be determined by the direction from which one arrives: the town centre feels positively laidback, almost countrified, by comparison with Addis Ababa, but it comes across as unusually vibrant and modern in appearance coming from anywhere else in the country, with an excellent range of restaurants, hotels and internet cafés. The national government recently earmarked Adama to take over from Addis Ababa as capital of Oromia, in a controversial and unilateral ruling that sparked several political rallies (some pro, some con) in early 2004. The decision does now seem to be cast in stone – in all likelihood the vast complex of administrative buildings being constructed on the western outskirts of town will be operational within the lifespan of this edition.

Somewhat kinkily described in an out-of-print ETC brochure as 'a perfect combination of the practical and the gay', whatever that might mean, Adama is perched at an altitude of around 1,600m on the fertile plateau that divides the narrowest stretch of the Ethiopian Rift Valley from the central highlands. It forms an important urban focal point not only for local cattle farmers, but also for the nearby Wenji Sugar Plantation, the oldest agricultural concern of its sort in the country, and several fruit and vegetable farms. Although it is popular with Addis weekenders for the nearby Sodore Spa, and blessed with an above-par range of tourist facilities, Adama, when all's said and done, is a rather nondescript sort of town. Still, for eastbound travellers, it's as good a place as any to cast away the paranoia often induced by first exposure to Addis Ababa and slip into the pace of small-town Ethiopia.

As with nearby Bishoftu, Adama was renamed during the last years of the imperial era in accordance with a policy to replace secular Oromo place names with something a touch more ecclesiastical, in this instance Nazret, a corruption of Nazareth (Haile Selassie's birthplace of Ejerso Gworo near Harer was reputedly earmarked to be renamed Bethlehem to reinforce the traditional belief in the royal lineage's Solomonic roots). Although the name Adama is officially reinstated, the town is still marked as Nazret on most maps of Ethiopia, and popularly referred to as such by most non-Oromo-speaking Ethiopians – and with a little imagination, the back avenues of Adama, lined with palm trees and donkey carts, do just about evoke its pseudonymous biblical namesake.

Getting there and away

There is regular transport between Addis Ababa, Adama and points in between. Buses between Addis and Adama take around two hours, and the trip is a bit shorter in a private vehicle. If you are heading south from Adama, there is regular transport on to Asela; or to Mojo, where you can easily pick up traffic to Ziway and the Rift Valley. Heading east, there are a couple of buses daily to Awash. Note that buses from central Ethiopia to Harar and Dire Dawa leave in the early morning from Adama as opposed to Addis Ababa.

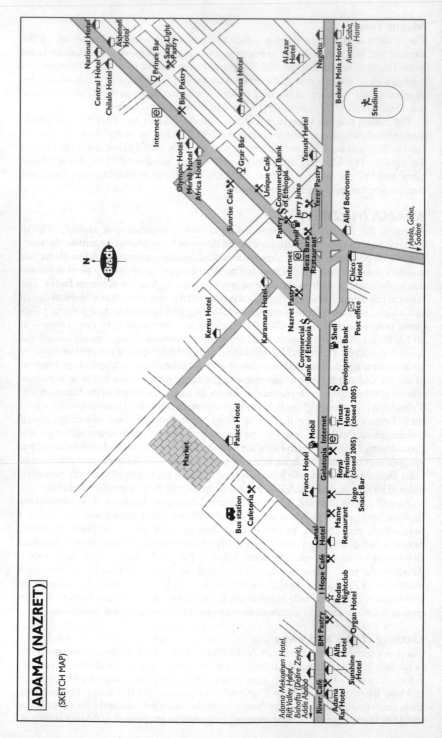

ADAMA (NAZRET)
(SKETCH MAP)

Where to stay
Upmarket
Adama Mekonnen Hotel (30 rooms) ☎ 022 1110888. The smartest place to overnight in Adama is this large, modern multi-storey hotel situated about 1km from the town centre along the Addis Ababa road. It's a bit bland, but very well maintained, and equally good value at birr 92/138 for a large standard dbl/twin or birr 198 for a suite, all with DTSV, carpets, and en-suite hot showers.

Moderate
Hotel Panafric (24 rooms) ☎ 022 1126888/1122720; e panafric@ethionet.et. Situated close to the Adama Mekonnen, this new hotel on the main road towards Addis Ababa is one of the best deals in its range, charging birr 65/75/95 for a clean en-suite sgl/dbl/twin with hot water and TV.
Palace Hotel (40 rooms) ☎ 022 1113800. With a central location opposite the bus station and market, the Palace Hotel also scores higher on amenities than it does on character. Still, the en-suite dbl rooms with hot water are good value at birr 75/115 without/with DSTV, or birr 150 for a suite.
Adama Ras Hotel ☎ 022 1112188. This stalwart government hotel looks a touch tired by comparison with the competition, but the wooded grounds do lend it considerably more character and aesthetic appeal than almost anything else on offer in Adama. The en-suite twin rooms are pretty good value at birr 80, while the suites, with two bedrooms sleeping four people as well as a lounge, might appeal to families or small groups at birr 188. The restaurant and rooms form a quadrangle around a swimming pool, which was actually filled with water – a first! – when I visited in 2005, and costs birr 3.50 for hotel residents or birr 7 for residents.

Budget
Bekele Mola Hotel (35 rooms) ☎ 022 1112312. A personal favourite, this typically likeable and recently renovated representative of the Bekele Mola chain is set in wooded, flowering grounds about five minutes' walk from the main roundabout along the Awash road. Large en-suite dbl bungalows with hot water and carpet cost birr 69/90 on wkday/wkend, while rooms in the smarter double-storey building at the back of the gardens are rather less of a bargain at a cost of birr 90/116–160, though they all have a balcony and DSTV. The grounds are teeming with birds, and dotted with chairs and tables. An outdoor bar serves snacks and drinks near the entrance.
Al Azar Hotel (20 rooms) ☎ 022 1113425. Situated around the corner from the Bekele Mola, this small hotel is pretty good value at birr 40–60 for a large en-suite dbl with hot water, depending on size.
Alief Bedrooms (18 rooms) ☎ 022 1110390. Centrally located on the main roundabout, this long-serving hotel remains good value – a large dbl using a separate (but private) hot shower costs birr 35 and an en-suite dbl with hot shower costs birr 50/60 without/with TV.
Chico Hotel (30 rooms) ☎ 022 1110155. This decent and centrally located hotel charges birr 30 for a small sgl room with en-suite cold shower (but common toilet) or birr 60 for a large en-suite dbl with hot showers.

Shoestring
Africa and Olympic hotels With so many good budget deals available, it's tempting to recommend that even the most impecunious of travellers splash out on a decent room in Adama. But if your budget doesn't allow for this, these two lodges, set close together on the main road north of the main roundabout, both charge around birr 10 for an adequate room with ¾ bed and common cold showers and are marginally preferable to the selection of dumps clustered around the bus station.

Where to eat
As with accommodation, travellers are spoilt for choice when it comes to eating out in Adama. Most of the hotels listed above serve a good range of local and *faranji* dishes at

OROMIA

The largest and most populous of the federal states defined when the central government redrew the regional map of Ethiopia in 1994, Oromia covers an area of 367,000 km² – more than 30% of Ethiopia's total surface area – and its population has risen from 18 to 21 million over the last decade. The irregular shape of the region has – somewhat fancifully – been compared to a lopsided and distended bow tie, with the self-governing city-state of Addis Ababa lying more or less where the knot would be. Nine of the 20 largest urban settlements in Ethiopia lie within Oromia (12 if you include the self-governing cities of Addis Ababa, Dire Dawa and Harar), the largest being Adama (Nazret), followed by Jimma, Awassa, Bishoftu (Debre Zeyit), Shashemene, Nekemte, Asela, Hosaina and Sodo, and another 15 towns within the region each support a population of 20,000 or more.

Until recently, Oromia had no capital as such, and it is still administered from the regional headquarters in Addis Ababa, but these will soon be relocated to the newly earmarked capital of Adama. Divided into 12 zones and 180 districts, Oromia is a region of vast geographic and climatic diversity. It encompasses not only the highland crags and meadows around Addis Ababa, but also the lush rainforest around Jimma and Nekemte in the west, much of the southern Rift Valley, and the arid acacia scrub towards the Kenyan border. The common factor throughout the region is cultural: Oromia, as its name implies, is the home of the Oromo people, Ethiopia's largest ethnic group.

Until recently more frequently referred to as the Galla, a name that was evidently used by their neighbours rather than by themselves, the Oromo originally came from the Kenyan border area currently occupied by the Borena, a subgroup of the Oromo. They migrated north from this homeland in the early 16th century, a movement

reasonable prices. Another good spot for a meal or snack (great burgers) is the **River Café** next to the Adama Ras Hotel. True, it might more accurately be named the Drainage Ditch Café, but it's still a pleasant place to eat outdoors, and wasn't at all whiffy on any of our recent visits.

Worthy of a special mention is the atmospheric restaurant at the (otherwise rather iffy) **Franco Hotel**, founded by its long-departed Italian namesake in the 1960s, but now locally owned. The atmosphere and décor still retain an Italian influence – like being transported to a rather down-at-heel European café – and most items on the extensive menu of Italian and local dishes cost less than birr 15. The bar serves fresh orange juice, pastries, draught beer, and is divided from the restaurant by what must be the largest – perhaps the only? – fish tank in Ethiopia.

Aficionados of *kitfo* might want to follow in the footsteps of Renate Kerkhofs, who reckons that the best *kitfo* in Ethiopia is served at an anonymous restaurant close to the main roundabout. To find it, head for Jerry Juice, walk past the restaurant next door, then turn left into an alley and it should be behind this block.

A genuine surprise for the sweet of tooth is the **Gelatopia** on the main street, which serves ice cream cones in half-a-dozen flavours for birr 3. The **Sunrise Café** is possibly the finest pastry shop in the country outside of the capital, serving excellent cakes, coffee and juice at prices that are mildly inflated by local standards but a bargain by any other. Several other pastry shops are dotted around town: the **Yerer Pastry**, **BM Pastry** and **I Hope Café** look to be the pick of a selection of worthy contenders. Next to the Yerer Pastry, **Jerry Juice** has been recommended for its orange juice. The **Negistu Hotel** opposite the Bekele Mola hotel has a pleasant beer garden with good music.

which, whether by chance or design, coincided with Ahmed Gragn's *jihad* against the Christian Empire. It could be argued that the Oromo migration effectively put an end to the war, as both Christian and Muslim Ethiopians found their territory under siege from a third source. Certainly, the Oromo were the main beneficiaries of the holy war, taking advantage of the weakened state of both parties to occupy much of what is now southern Ethiopia, including vast tracts of land that had formerly been part of, or paid tribute to, the Christian Empire.

Today, the Oromo are divided into six main groups and hundreds of subgroups, which share in common a well-documented and rigid male age-set system, called *Geda*. At the beginning of every eight-year cycle, marked by a spate of initiations and circumcisions, the age-sets all move up one rung. The dominant age-set consists of the 16–24-year-old group, which elects from within its ranks an administrative leader known as the *Abagada*, who serves until the next eight-year cycle begins. This is an unusually democratic social structure, firstly because no hereditary element is involved in political leadership, and secondly because it creates a built-in sell-by date not dissimilar to the limit of two presidential terms written into many modern national constitutions. Once an age-set enters its sixth cycle, its members are regarded to be elders, and will play an advisory role in governance.

The Oromo believe in one God, known as Waka: traditionalists hold that theirs is the oldest monotheistic religion in the world, and that Moses borrowed his ideas from them. Central to Oromo belief is the sacred staff or *Boku*, which symbolises the inviolable Law of God, and is handled only by the incumbent *Abagada*. The most important traditional festival in the Oromo calendar is the Irrecha, held on 1 October at several sites throughout the region – notably Lake Hora outside Bishoftu. These days, however, traditional Oromo beliefs are increasingly subservient to Christianity and Islam.

Excursions
Sodore
The hot springs resort of Sodore, situated at an altitude of 1,700m, stretches for about 1km on the banks of the Awash River about 25km south of Adama. The large, 3m-deep swimming pool, usually dry during the week, is a popular draw for Addis weekenders. For most tourists, however, the Awash River and fringing riparian forest will probably be of greater interest. Vervet monkeys and crocodiles are often encountered in the grounds, and the odd hippo still makes an appearance. The riverine forest also offers excellent birding. The resort is riddled with footpaths and makes for a diverting day or overnight trip from Adama.

The only proper accommodation, at the **Sodore Spa Wabe Shebelle Hotel** (`\ 011 1113400;` e *washo.et@ethionet.et; www.wabeshebellehotels.com.et*), is emphatically not for the budget conscious, and seems rather rundown for the asking price of birr 150–200 for an en-suite room. There is, however, an attractively rambling campsite, where you can pitch your own tent for birr 15 or rent a standing tent for birr 60. The campsite isn't guarded and I wouldn't recommend you leave anything valuable in your tent; lockers are available for hire in the pool enclosure.

Sodore lies 7km off the Adama–Asela road; the turn-off is clearly signposted. There are regular minibuses between Adama and the resort gates. A nominal entrance fee is charged on arrival.

Dera Delfekar Proposed Regional Park
This 25km² sanctuary protects a pair of wooded hills on the eastern bounds of the small town of Dera, which lies roughly 27km from Adama (9km past the Sodore junction)

along the main Asela road. Unfenced, and lacking any formal facilities, the park nevertheless supports more than 20 mammal species – notably greater and lesser kudu, klipspringer, common duiker, hippo, striped hyena, and various small predators. More than 100 birds, predominantly acacia-associated species, have been recorded. Access is straightforward, since any vehicle heading from Adama in the direction of Asela can drop you in Dera. The footpath into the reserve is signposted from the main road through town, and there are no fees or restrictions on walking, though it might be advisable to take a local guide to show you the way. Should you choose to spend the night in Dera – early morning and late afternoon being when wildlife and birds are most active – the Hotel Dodota and Yohannis Hotel look about the best of a dozen or so cheapies running along the main road.

Koka Dam and Hippo Pool

Damming the Awash River about 15km west of Adama as the crow flies, Koka was constructed in the late 1950s with war reparation payments from Italy. Since opening in 1960, it has been one of Ethiopia's most important sources of hydro-electric power. The lake formed behind the dam – called Koka or Gelila – is to the best of my knowledge the most expansive artificial body of water in Ethiopia, with a surface area of 180km^2. Situated close to the dam wall is the plush Gelila Palace, which Haile Selassie donated to charity in the 1960s. For several years after that, the Gelila Hotel had the reputation of being one of the plushest hotels in Ethiopia, managed by the Ghion Group, with all profits diverted to charity. Sadly, it is no longer functional.

Although it is an important site for water birds, Koka is of interest to tourists primarily for a hippo pool in the Awash River a short distance downstream from the dam, at the confluence with the river that rises from the nearby Garagadi Hot Springs. The pools here are a reliable place to see hippos, various birds and – with increasing frequency – crocodiles. The turn-off south towards the dam lies on the main Addis Ababa road about 15km west of Adama and 10km east of Mojo, at a big blue sign. Follow this road for 12km to a construction site, where you can park. A guide is bound to offer his services, but it's easy enough to make your own way to the river. The best time to visit is early morning or late afternoon, when it's still cool, and the birds and animals are most active. It's an easy side trip in a private vehicle, but public transport is limited.

Garagadi Hot Springs

This collection of 16 hot springs bubbles from a large field about 15km from Adama near the village of Wenji and the eponymous sugar plantation. The steaming pools formed by the hot springs are bathed in by local villagers, as well as by pilgrims from elsewhere in the country. Further away from the springs crocodiles are still resident in the river – which eventually leads to the hippo pool at the confluence with the Awash described above.

In theory, Garagadi could be visited in conjunction with Koka Dam, as the two sites are only 6km apart along a rough 4x4 track, but this would require crossing the dam wall (which doubles as a bridge) and this is not permitted without written permission! As a result, it's debatable whether the springs are worth the effort of visiting. But if you want to, you need to backtrack almost 30km from Koka to Adama, and then turn right immediately before the Awash Hotel as you enter town. Follow this gravel road for 10km, then turn right as you enter Wenji village, following the signpost for Wenji Feeding Lot. The track is rather indistinct from here, so keep asking directions, and you should reach the river after about 3km, below cliffs inhabited by baboons. Turn left at the river and you will get to the springs after another 2km. Occasional public transport connects Adama to Wenji, where you can walk or take a *gari* to the springs.

Awash National Park and the Assab Road

This chapter follows the Rift Valley northwest from Adama through to Assaita, former capital of the Federal State of Afar, and on to the border post for western Djibouti and the port of Assab in the far south of Eritrea. The region in question is generally low-lying and arid, though it is also studded with several imposing freestanding massifs associated with geologically recent volcanic activity.

The only established tourist attraction in this part of Ethiopia is Awash National Park, which is arguably the most rewarding savanna reserve in Ethiopia, and – bisected by the surfaced road to Dire Dawa some 200km east of Addis Ababa – certainly the most accessible. The wider stretch of the Rift Valley running northward from the national park – essentially an above-sea-level southerly extension of the Danakil – offers few readily accessible tourist attractions but is notable for its austere desert landscapes and nomadic Afar inhabitants.

The dominant aquatic feature of the region is the 1,200km Awash River, which rises at Fougnan Bote ('The Nostrils') in the Ethiopian Highlands about 50km west of Addis Ababa, then arcs southward past Melka Kunture and Mount Zikwala before changing direction to flow in a broad northeasterly direction through the artificial Lake Koka, past Nazret, and along the southern border of Awash National Park, eventually emptying into a series of saline lakes between Assaita and the Djibouti border. Ironically, the name Awash reputedly translates from Oromifa as 'the beast that consumes everything in its path' – given that it flows through desert or semi-desert for most of its length, 'the river that sustains everything alongside its path' might be a little fairer!

Aside from Awash National Park, part of which falls within Oromia region, the region covered in this chapter all falls within the boundaries of the vast but thinly populated Federal State of Afar. Unexpectedly, perhaps, an excellent surfaced road runs right through the region, branching from the Dire Dawa road a few kilometres east of the town of Awash Sabat, from where it heads north through the small towns of Awash Arba, Gewane and Mille to the Djibouti and Eritrean borders. The only other approach route is a good unsurfaced road that connects Kombolcha (near Dessie) to Mille via Bati, thereby allowing you to explore the region as an extension of the northern historical circuit. Public transport runs daily along both these major routes.

AWASH NATIONAL PARK

This scenic 756km² national park, established in 1966 and gazetted three years later, is situated in the dry acacia savanna of the Rift Valley some 200km east of Addis Ababa. The park is bisected by the Dire Dawa road for a distance of almost 20km between the small towns of Metahara and Awash Saba. A magnificent 150m-deep gorge, carved by the Awash River, forms the southern boundary of the park, and there is a substantial waterfall where the river spills into the gorge. To the north of the Dire Dawa road, the skyline is dominated by the ragged edges of the 2,007m-high Mount Fantelle, a dormant volcano

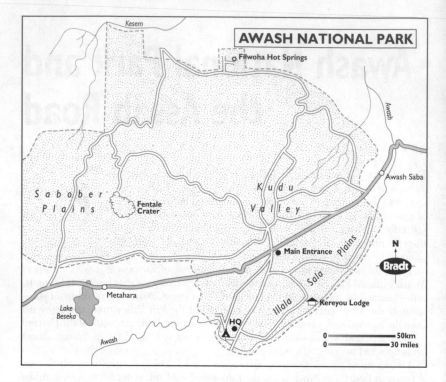

whose 350m-deep crater towers imperiously above the surrounding bush. Mount Fantelle is responsible for the bleak 200-year-old lava flows that cross the road immediately west of Metahara, and its steam vents can sometimes be seen displaying from the surrounding plains at night. The Filwoha Hot Springs, which feed a series of beautiful translucent blue pools, are situated in a grove of tall doum palms on the northern boundary of the park. Also of interest is the 35km² Lake Beseka, which lies just outside the park along the main road west of Metahara, nestled in a strange landscape of chunky black lava blocks where it has increased in area tenfold in the last three decades.

Although 80 mammal species have been recorded in Awash – the majority being various bats, rodents and elusive small predators – the game viewing is arguably less of an attraction than the scenery and birdlife. The dense acacia scrub that characterises much of the park makes it difficult to spot game, populations of which are in any case rather low and skittish due to ongoing poaching. The most visible large mammals are Beisa oryx, Soemmering's gazelle and Salt's dik-dik, all of which are as likely to be seen from the surfaced public road to Dire Dawa as they are along roads within the park. Elsewhere, the thick bush and low animal densities around the Awash River harbour lesser and greater kudu, Defassa waterbuck and warthog; while more developed riverine forest may hide parties of vervet monkeys and, less commonly, guereza. The most common primate, however, is the baboon: the national park lies at a point where the ranges of the Hamadryas and Anubis baboons converge, and hybrids are frequently observed along the river east of the waterfall. Klipspringer and mountain reedbuck are found on the slopes of Fantelle Volcano. Predators are seen only infrequently, but a good variety is present including lion, leopard, cheetah, spotted and striped hyena, and black-backed and golden jackal. Lions are most likely to be seen in the vicinity of Filwoha Hot Springs; their nocturnal roars are regularly heard at the nearby campsite. The endemic Swayne's hartebeest was introduced to Awash in 1974, and the localised Grevy's zebra used to be resident, but neither species has been observed for some years.

Whatever the national park's limitations when it comes to big game, it has to be regarded as one of Ethiopia's premier birding destinations, with a checklist of 450 species and growing. For dedicated tickers, the primary attraction is the presence of the endemic yellow-throated serin and near-endemic sombre rock chat on the slopes of Fantelle Volcano, as well as the endemic Ethiopian cliff swallow in the Awash Gorge. Raptors are generally well represented; many species breed in the gorge and on the slopes of the volcano. Water birds are abundant on Lake Beseka, and to a lesser extent around Filwoha, while the riparian forest around the park headquarters harbours species. The acacia-scattered plains support an excellent range of dry-country birds such as Abyssinian roller, various sandgrouse, larks, hornbills and waxbills, and seven species of bustard – notably the localised and uncommon Arabian bustard. The gorgeous carmine bee-eater, which breeds in sandbanks in the Awash Gorge, is very common.

Entrance to Awash costs the usual birr 50 per 48 hours.

Getting there and away
If you are driving yourself, simply head out of Addis along the surfaced Dire Dawa road for about three hours, passing through Adama halfway. The road from Adama to Awash passes through a striking landscape of crumbling black lava flows and small volcanic hills, with the Rift Valley wall a haze in the background. The entrance gate lies on the main road about halfway between the towns of Metahara and Awash Saba. Without your own vehicle, the most straightforward way to visit Awash is through an Addis-based tour operator.

Hitching into Awash isn't really on. It's not so much that the rangers at the gate would be likely to object as that the low tourist traffic would make it most unlikely you'd find a lift. If time isn't a factor, however, you can soak up much of the park's atmosphere by spending a night in Awash Saba or Metahara, both of which are easily reached from Adama (buses take around three hours and there appears to be a reasonably regular trundle of other traffic too). Another option would be the train from Addis Ababa to Djibouti, which – coming from Addis Ababa – arrives in Awash Saba before midnight.

Where to stay
The only accommodation within the national park is **Kereyou Lodge**, part of the Ras Hotel chain, and bookable through the head office in Addis Ababa or any tour operator (not that it's often overrun with clients!). The best thing about the lodge is the location above a spectacular stretch of the Awash Gorge. Accommodation, which costs birr 200/double, consists of 20 rundown and stuffy self-contained caravans clustered in an untidy garden behind the main lodge building. Meals and drinks are available.

There are two **campsites**, one near the park headquarters (a short walk from the waterfall) and the other at the hot springs. Camping costs birr 20 per person. The campsites both have great locations, but lack any facilities worth talking about, and are only suitable for those self-sufficient in food and drinking water.

It is also possible to stay outside the park, at the nearby towns of Awash Saba or Metahara, or at the new Bilen Lodge (see box, page 378).

Game drives and walks
The main game-viewing circuit runs south from the main Amareti entrance gate to the park headquarters, which lies less than 500m from the Awash Falls, then follows a rough road east through dense scrub to Kereyou Lodge. From Kereyou, a road crosses back to the main gate via the open Ilala Sala Plain, which is reliably studded with small herds of oryx and a good place to see bustards – back to the main gate. It's definitely worth stopping at the waterfall, which consists of several muddy streams frothing over a drop of

BILEN LODGE

This eco-friendly lodge, built under consultation with local Afar communities, opened in October 2001, and is situated 12km off the main Addis Ababa–Djibouti road, following a junction signposted to the left some 36km past Awash Arba. The lodge consists of 15 en-suite chalets designed in the style of Afar houses and covered in reed mats, as well as a restaurant and bar. It overlooks the Bilen Hot Spring, where Thesiger stopped on his Awash Expedition in the 1930s (there are photos of the area in his *Danakil Diaries*). The springs are big enough to swim in, so long as you don't mind sharing the water with camels, which are brought here to drink by Afar herders, and enjoy a hot soak. Cultural activities on offer include organised village visits and camel treks with local Afar herders.

The area around the lodge has a similar combination of habitats to the national park, including riverine forest, acacia woodland, savanna and wetlands, and it harbours a similar variety of birds. More than 460 bird species have been recorded in this area: particularly prominent around camp are Nile Valley and shining sunbirds, golden-breasted starling, white-headed sparrow weaver, Abyssinian roller, carmine bee-eater, yellow-throated spurfowl and Liechtenstein's sandgrouse. Wildlife seen in the vicinity of the lodge includes Beisa oryx, lesser kudu, Salt's dik-dik, warthog, spotted hyena, crocodile, hippo and Hamadryas and Anubis baboon. Lions are heard more often than they are seen, but they do pass through camp from time to time.

Accommodation costs US$30/40 single/double, and can be booked through Village Ethiopia (contact details, page 83). Lunch and dinner cost US$8 per meal.

---

perhaps 10m into the black volcanic rock of the gorge – a short footpath leads to the base, and the fringing woodland is good for birds. The small museum at the headquarters displays useful checklists of all the birds, mammals and reptiles recorded in the park, as well as the predictable selection of stuffed animals. This circuit, which covers about 30km in total, can normally be driven in any vehicle with reasonable clearance, and should take two to three hours allowing for game viewing, a stop at the waterfall and the lodge (cold drinks and superb viewpoint), longer if you are birding. Maps depict a road circuit east of Kereyou, but this was out of service in early 2001. Visitors are not normally required to take a game scout along the roads running to the south of the main gate.

The 30km road to the hot springs leaves from the main Dire Dawa road roughly opposite the main gate, passing through the dense scrub of Kudu Valley along the way. Don't expect to see much game on this road – warthog and Hamadryas baboon are both quite common, greater and lesser kudu less so – but the springs are worth the effort. The road is 4x4 only, but it's in fair condition and only takes about an hour in either direction. There is also a road to the top of Mount Fantelle, but it is in poor condition, and most visitors end up walking the last stretch – this is a steep two-hour hike on exposed slopes, and best done in the cool of the morning. For security reasons, it is mandatory to take an armed game scout on any excursion to areas north of the main Dire Dawa road. This costs birr 50 per excursion.

Aside from the trek up to Fantelle, and the short footpaths to the hot springs and waterfall, walking is not permitted within the national park. It is, however, possible to walk around Lake Beseka from Metahara, and to hike around the part of the Awash Gorge that lies east of the park boundary near Awash Saba.

Metahara

The small, scruffy town of Metahara, situated less than 5km from the national park as the crow flies, is known throughout Ethiopia for the large sugar plantation on its outskirts. Metahara is of interest to travellers for its attractive location near the base of Fantelle and proximity to the expanding Lake Beseka, which is five minutes from town on the Addis Ababa road. The town has a good selection of cheap local hotels. The pick is probably the **Hotel Ergosha** next to the Shell filling station, which charges birr 15 for a ground-floor room with common shower and birr 20 for a first-floor en-suite room – rooms are all large, clean, and have proper double beds. The **Kassaye Hotel** also seems decent value, though the lively garden bar looks like it would be more fun to drink in than to sleep next to! The **Axum**, **Hibret** and **Lidita** hotels also look decent enough – the last serves good fruit juice too. Any bus heading between Adama and Awash Saba will stop here on request.

The main reason for stopping in Metahara would be to walk in the vicinity of Lake Beseka. There is good access to the lake from the main Adama road, which crosses over it via a causeway that is divided into two sections by what amounts to an island of black chunky lava rocks. The birdlife on this shallow lake is profuse and the patches of acacia scrub on the far bank should also repay exploration. The scenery, too, is rather special, with the ragged edges of Fantelle Volcano looming a few kilometres to the north – the Metahara night sky is often lit with fireworks from the crater's vents.

A few words of warning: crocodiles are present in the lake and, although it's unlikely that any crocodile large enough to attack a person would survive so close to town, you should be cautious. I've been told that hippos are also present, but I'm inclined to think this is nonsense. Secondly, the lakeshore is hot and exposed, so it's best visited in the cool of the morning, and you should protect yourself from the sun at all times. Finally, Lake Beseka may not lie within the national park but Fantelle does – it would be illegal to try to walk there.

Awash Saba

This scruffy and nondescript little town, which appears to have mushroomed around Awash railway station, lies about 30km past Metahara and a short distance outside the park boundary. Arrive here with a pale skin, and you'll find that conversation is limited mainly to humourless variations on the words 'you', 'money' and 'give', an unwelcome reminder of how things used to be throughout much of Ethiopia a few years ago. As for the sights – aside from the railway station, there's a church, a neat mosque, and an odd pointy stone column thing next to the station, which serves no apparent purpose other than to provide the local goats with a sliver of afternoon shade. The Monday market attracts plenty of traditional Afar people from the surrounding plains.

Awash Saba is typical small-town Ethiopia, but with one substantial redeeming feature. About 500m behind the station the dusty plain is cut into by the precipitous Awash Gorge, the drama of which is accentuated by a row of low volcanic hills above the opposite cliff. There's some good raptor-scanning here – auger buzzard, vultures, kestrels and falcons – and a chance of seeing the elusive Ethiopian cliff swallow. A footpath leads to the base of the gorge and the Awash River and, although the immediate surrounds have suffered from vigorous goat chomping, there's some interesting-looking riverine woodland a kilometre or so back towards the park boundary. Be cautioned, however, that the park begins about 3km from Awash Saba, and there's no telling what official attitudes would be if you inadvertently crossed the line.

Often referred to simply as Awash and more occasionally Awash Station, Awash Saba (Awash Seven) is so-named to distinguish it from Awash Arba (Awash Forty), a town situated some 20km away on the Assab road. Nobody has ever been able to explain these numeric designations to me, and I can think of no obvious significance to them myself. All the same, it seems sensible to use the full names for these towns given that they share their first word not only with each other, but also with a nearby river, gorge and national park.

Getting there and away

In a private vehicle, Awash Saba can be reached in about three hours from Addis Ababa, and five to six hours from Dire Dawa. The junction for the surfaced road northwest through Afar lies about 5km east of town along the Dire Dawa road. Awash Saba is an important transport hub, and you're unlikely to wait long for a lift east or west. Plenty of buses pass through town en route between Addis Ababa and Dire Dawa, and local minibuses cover the road to Adama. Public transport along the road to Afar is rather less frequent, but at least one bus daily heads out to Gewane, where you should easily find transport on to Mille or Logiya. If public transport fails you, you could try for a lift with a truck – dozens daily head on through from Awash Saba to Djibouti.

Where to stay and eat

Buffet D'Aouache (7 rooms) 022 2240008. Built by the French to service the Djibouti railway ('Aouache' being the French spelling of Awash) and now under Greek management, this is an unexpected gem, with its recently renovated whitewashed colonial architecture draped in flowering creepers. Your first reaction might well be to wonder how this place has stumbled viably into the 21st century, a mystery that is explained the moment the train chugs into the adjoining station and the courtyard fills with hungry, thirsty passengers. The clean, comfortable rooms range from birr 50 for a twin using a common shower to birr 100 for a 'Head of State' suite – reputedly where Haile Selassie and Charles De Gaulle stayed in the hotel's glory days! Even if you don't stay here, it's worth popping in for a meal – well-prepared steak and shish kebab (or eminently avoidable roast chicken) at around birr 15 per portion – and to escape Awash Saba's persistent children.

Awash Meridian Hotel (20 rooms) ☎ 022 2240051. Formerly the St George Hotel, the renamed and renovated Awash Meridian is set in a large compound on the main road, and charges birr 57 for a spacious and spotless new room with a genuine dbl bed, mosquito netting, fan and en-suite hot shower. More basic rooms using a common shower are available for birr 25. A good rooftop bar is attached.

Genet Hotel ☎ 022 2240008. Popular with tour operators, this relatively overpriced but otherwise commendable hotel lies alongside the main Addis Ababa road on the western outskirts of town. It charges birr 50 for a small dbl with en-suite shower or birr 80 for a larger room, all with fan and running water. The restaurant is pretty good too – roast chicken seems to be the speciality.

THE ASSAB ROAD

The main route through Afar region, is – unexpectedly, perhaps, at least until you register its significance as a trucking route between the port of Djibouti and Addis Ababa – one of the best roads in Ethiopia, certainly the only one of comparable length where one could sustain a driving speed of 80–100km/h or greater without feeling too reckless. The road branches from the Dire Dawa road about 5km east of Awash Saba. It then runs in a broad northeasterly direction for about 500km, approximately following the course of the Awash River (but only occasionally coming within sight of it) until it reaches the borders with Djibouti and Eritrea – the former open and bustling with truck activity, the latter closed for some years now.

The largest town in the region is Assaita, which boasts a population of around 20,000 and a scenic location overlooking the Awash River some 50km south of the Assab road. Other relatively sizeable towns along the Assab road include Awash Arba, Gewane, Mille and Logiya, none of which supports significantly more than 10,000 souls. In the late 1990s, Assaita was superseded as capital of Afar by Semera, the latter not so much a town as a custom-built cluster of administrative buildings and high-rise apartment blocks set in bleakly surreal isolation just 7.5km east of Logiya.

Most of the region's Afar inhabitants remain semi-nomadic pastoralists, though some make a living from excavating or transporting salt blocks from the vast saline pans north of the Assab road – relics of a time not too distant when large parts of Afar region were submerged by a southern extension of the Red Sea. A limited range of crops is grown along the banks of the Awash River, but the rest of the region, despite its rich volcanic soil, receives too little rainfall for agricultural purposes.

Afar has not always been as arid – or as low-lying – as it is today. Five million years ago, this land lay at an altitude of greater than 1,000m above sea level, and its moist climate supported a lush cover of grassland and forest – not to mention a variety of early hominids. Several of the world's most significant hominid fossils have been unearthed in Afar. The best known of these is 'Lucy', which was discovered and nicknamed by Donald Johanson at Hadar in 1974 (see box *A Visit to Hadar*, page 384). More recently, an Ethiopian graduate student Yohannis Haile Selassie found 5.8-million-year-old fossils of a bipedal creature whose combination of ape-like and hominid features suggest it might well represent the so-called 'missing link' in the divergent evolutionary paths of modern chimpanzees and humans.

The surfaced road through Afar is an important trucking route, since it provides access to the seaports of Assab (Eritrea) and Djibouti. Passenger transport is relatively thin on the ground, however, and more or less confined to the main road, the side road to Assaita, and the road between Mille and Kombolcha (near Dessie). To see the region properly, you really need a private vehicle. It is not advisable to head seriously off-road without a back-up vehicle and knowledgeable guide or GPS. No organised tours head into this remote part of Ethiopia. For tailored itineraries, a useful contact with considerable experience in Afar region is Village Ethiopia (see page 83 for contact details).

THE AFAR

The Afar (or Danakil) regard themselves to be the oldest of Ethiopia's ethnic groups, having occupied their inhospitably arid homeland to the east of the Ethiopian Highlands for at least two thousand years. The Afar have a history of trade with the highlanders that stretches back to the early Axumite period, and possibly before that. Until modern times, Afar country effectively served as Ethiopia's mint, producing the *amoles* (salt-bars) that served as currency in the highlands – the Portuguese priest Alvarez recorded that in the early 16th century three or four *amoles* was enough to buy a good slave! Extracted from a number of salt pans scattered around the Afar Depression, the salt-bars still form a major item of trade for the Afar people, who transport them on camelback to Tigrai along the ancient caravan routes.

Arabic sources indicate that, despite Afar's ancient trade links with the Christian Highlands, Islam was widely practised in the region as early as the 13th century. In 1577, the Sultan of Harar relocated his capital to a town called Awassa, which was situated more or less where Assaita stands today. This move initially sparked some resistance among the surrounding Afar nomads, though it did much to consolidate the Islamic influence in the area, especially as the Sultan's army and the Afar were frequently united in battle against the invading Oromo. In the late 17th century, Awassa fell under the rule of an Afar Sultan called Kedafu, who founded a dynasty that survived into the late 20th century. The Sultan of Afar was forced into exile under the Derg, but he is still regarded as the King of Afar by his people, and his residence – about 5km outside Assaita – was restored in early 2001 in anticipation of his permanent return home.

Traditionally, the Afar are nomadic pastoralists, living in light, flimsy houses made of palm fronds and matting, which they transport from one location to the next on camelback. Recent decades have seen a trend towards urbanisation in Afar, as well as an increased dependence on agriculture in the fertile and well-watered area around Assaita. Nevertheless, the nomadic lifestyle is still widely practised away from the towns, and visitors to the region will often see Afar men driving their precious camel herds along the roadside. The Afar men have a reputation for ferocity and xenophobia – as recently as the 1930s, it was still customary to kill male intruders to the area, and lop off their testicles as a trophy.

By comparison with the highlanders, Afar people tend to be very tall and dark. The women have intricate frizzed and braided hairstyles, and wear long brown skirts, brightly coloured bead necklaces, heavy earrings, and brass anklets. The men often wear their hair in a thick Afro style similar to that described in an account by a 14th-century visitor from the highlands. They dress in a light cotton toga, which is draped over one shoulder. Traditionally, Afar men rarely venture far without the curved 40cm-long dagger they sling around their waist in a long, thin leather pouch. These days, the traditional knife may be supplemented or replaced by a rifle slung casually over the shoulder. Both weapons are frequently put to fatal use in disputes between rival clans.

The information below roughly follows the Assab road in a northerly direction from the junction 5km west of Awash Saba.

Awash Saba to Gewane

A few pot-holes notwithstanding, the 150km stretch of road connecting Awash Saba to Gewane is in tiptop condition. At least one bus daily runs between Awash Saba and Gewane, taking about four hours in either direction. Coming from Awash Saba in a private vehicle, you must first head along the Dire Dawa road, then after about 5km turn left at a prominent and clearly signposted junction, passing through the not insubstantial town of Awash Arba after another 14km. The road can be covered easily in two hours in a private vehicle, though there are a few places where you might want to stop or divert from the main road.

First up, roughly 36km past Awash Arba, a road to the left leads to Bilen Lodge, 10km from the main road (see box *Bilen Lodge*, page 378), and a good base from which to explore southern Afar. The road then passes through the austere and rather featureless Alleghedi Plain, which is afforded nominal protection in the eponymous wildlife reserve, and still harbours thin (and seldom observed) populations of game, notably Beisa oryx and Grevy's zebra.

The small town of Meteka, about 30km south of Gewane, is inherently unremarkable, but it does mark the beginning of the Meteka Wetlands. This marshy part of the Awash floodplain runs close to the western verge of the main road and offers excellent birding all year through. It is particularly rewarding in the European winter. The Awash River forms part of a flyway used by thousands of Palaearctic migrants; all sorts of unusual passage migrants have been recorded around Meteka in September/October and March/April. In a private vehicle, it is possible to leave the main road at Meteka and cut west for about 10km to Lake Erta Ale (also known as Hertali).

A somewhat unremarkable urban sprawl, **Gewane** is distinguished only by the imposing presence of Mount Ayelu, an isolated peak of volcanic origin which rises above the surrounding plains to an altitude of 2,145m on the east of the town. Facilities include three filling stations, a couple of bars with chilled drinks (welcome in this climate), and a few basic hotels. If you need to spend a night, the hotel behind the Shell garage looks about the best bet, charging birr 15 for a clean room with a common shower. Should you be thinking of exploring Yangudi Rassa National Park beyond the main road, the park office is in Gewane.

Yangudi Rassa National Park

Proposed in 1977, but never officially gazetted, this 5,000km² national park consists of a dormant 1,383m-high volcano called Mount Yangudi together with the surrounding Rassa Plains. It harbours the only extant population of the African wild ass, a critically endangered species ancestral to the domestic donkey, and is bisected by the Assab road for a distance of roughly 50km. However, the odds of actually seeing a wild ass in transit are extremely slim, especially as feral populations of domestic donkeys are also found in the area, and the two are difficult to tell apart. You'll improve your chances slightly – but not greatly – if you pick up a guide at the park office in Gewane, and leave the main road.

Several other large mammal species survive in Yangudi Rassa, notably Beisa oryx, Soemmering's and dorcas gazelle, gerenuk and possibly Grevy's zebra, but – like the ass – they are thinly distributed and unlikely to be observed by casual visitors. A good selection of dry-country birds is resident – the Arabian bustard is a 'special' and ostriches are frequently observed – and the park lies along an important migration passage.

Mille

This small town, set on the banks of the Mille River roughly 150km north of Gewane, is of note primarily as a minor route focus. About 10km south of town lies the junction of the main Assab road and the side road that runs west towards Bati, Kombolcha and Dessie, forming the only reliable road and public transport link between Afar and the northern historical circuit. At least one bus daily connects Mille to Dessie (via Bati and Kombolcha) and to Assaita. There is not currently any public transport between Mille and Gewane, but it's easy enough to pick up a lift with a truck. Direct buses between Addis Ababa and Assaita follow the route through Dessie rather than passing through Gewane.

A VISIT TO HADAR

The formerly obscure and otherwise unremarkable patch of Ethiopian soil known as Hadar leapt to prominence in 1974 when Donald Johanson unearthed what was then the oldest hominid fossil ever discovered: the 3–4 million-year-old remains of a female, nicknamed Lucy, and assigned to a new species *Australopithecus afarensis*. Hadar is the most famous of several similarly significant palaeontological sites in this part of Ethiopia, but – while the regional council does appear to have vague plans for future development – none is currently geared up for tourists. With a private vehicle, a guide, and a letter of authority, however, it is perfectly possible to visit Hadar, as the following edited extract from a letter by Iain Jackson demonstrates:

> To fulfil my ambition of seeing Hadar, I first had to get a permit from the office of the Afar Regional Council in Assaita. I stayed in Assaita for three nights, and eventually got my permit. I discovered there is some confusion about the location of Hadar, arising from a map published and given wide circulation in Ethiopia, which shows a representation of Lucy covering hundreds of square kilometres to the north of Serdo. In fact, the site lies 25–30km south of Eloha, a small village on the Kombolcha–Mille road.
>
> I went to Kombolcha, hired a 4x4 land vehicle for the day, and drove to Eloha. There, two men, one of whom claimed to have worked with the American team that discovered Lucy – for eight years – offered themselves as guide and shotgun rider. We set off in a generally southerly direction over stony scrub, through sand gullies, and eventually into more open countryside, where we saw a group of eight ostriches at fairly close quarters, an Abyssinian hare, and many diverse birds. After something like an hour, we halted in a small, dusty and barren valley and walked a few hundred metres to several small hills covered in thousands of fossilised bone fragments. It was here, declared our guide, that Lucy was found.
>
> I had been told in Addis Ababa that the site had no interpretative centre and no marker, but here, aside from the fossils, there was nothing! If the Americans had been here for eight years, surely they would have left behind a fence, and a few excavation pits and spoil heaps, but the ground looked absolutely undisturbed. It crossed my mind that I was the victim of a hoax, but the site did look like it does in the few pictures I've seen, so I guess I give it the benefit of the doubt. In any event, I enjoyed the excursion.

Note from PB: The village Iain refers to as Eloha is actually called Eli Wuha, which I'm told translates as Tortoise Water, and straddles the Kombolcha–Mille road exactly 50km east of Bati and 40km west of the junction with the Assab road. The village isn't much to look at architecturally, but it hosts a busy traditional Afar market daily, and has a few bars selling chilled drinks. Ask around, and you should have no difficulty locating a guide to take you to Hadar, which lies off the road towards Mille about an hour's drive away and remains totally undeveloped for tourism. It is not clear whether a permit is actually required to visit Hadar – either way, it is unlikely that there would be anybody present at the site to check.

In a private vehicle, you're unlikely to spend longer in Mille than is required to refuel the car and grab a cold drink. Using public transport, you may well have to spend a night here between bus trips. At least half-a-dozen local guesthouses, charging around birr 8–10 for a basic room, are dotted around the small town – recommend would be too strong a word, but the Central Hotel looks about the best of the bunch.

Logiya and Semera

North of Mille, the road passes through a hauntingly bleak landscape of bare volcanic boulders piled high between valleys of gravel and stunted grass, to emerge after roughly 50km at Logiya, one of the few places where the Assab road and Awash River briefly converge. Logiya feels larger and busier than either Gewane or Mille, with a good (or should that be bad?) dozen basic hotels and restaurants lining the main road. If you need a bed, the best bet is the National Hotel, which lies on the Assaita side of town and charges birr 8 for a cramped but adequate room (single bed only) and a few coins for use of the shower. Opposite the National Hotel, Redwam Snacks is about the only restaurant to serve anything other than *yefigel tibs* – fried eggs, fresh bread, tuna sandwiches, and fruit juice!

Exactly 7.5km east of Logiya, the Assab road cuts through Semera, the new regional capital of Afar. More of a concept than it is a town, Semera comes across as the brainchild of some vindictive soul who held a serious grudge against regional government officials and their families – basically it consists of a depressing cluster of modern offices and tall apartment blocks standing in the middle of the desert, in mad isolation from any existing settlement! So far as facilities go, there is one active filling station (complete with fridge) but that's about it – if you are looking for a meal or a place to crash, then do so in Logiya. If you are travelling on north to the Danakil (see page 303), then Semera is where you need to sort out your permits before continuing on to Serdo, which lies 40km further northeast at the junction for the track heading north to Lake Afrera.

Assaita

The former administrative capital of Afar and largest town in the region, Assaita is situated some 50km south of the Assab road on a rise overlooking a stretch of the Awash River lined with palms and cultivation. First impressions as you drive into this fantastically hot and rather dusty backwater, passing through a jumble of rundown administrative buildings and offices, are less than promising. Once settled in, however, Assaita is not without interest: overwhelmingly Muslim and defiantly rustic, the town centre has an atmosphere and architectural mood quite unlike any other town in Ethiopia, and it is an excellent place for contacts with Afar people. Ideally, try to be in town on Tuesday, when the main market is held.

For travellers dependent on public transport, Assaita is pretty much the end of the road, with limited possibilities for exploration, though the tourist office can arrange for you to visit an Afar village within walking distance of the town for around birr 60 per group. With a vehicle, Assaita forms a useful base from which to explore a number of nearby attractions, many of which can only be visited with written authority from the tourist office in Semera (see box *Lakes around Assaita* on page 386).

The turn-off to Assaita is no more than 10km east of Semera along the Assab road. It isn't overtly signposted, and could easily be missed – look out for the blue signpost with Amharic script and PO Box 50 written underneath at the junction. A more enduring landmark is a small lake, fringed by acacia trees and often surrounded by Afar camel herders, on the northern side of the Assab road a few kilometres east of the junction – if you pass this lake coming from Semera, then you know you've missed the junction. Immediately after the junction, the 50km dirt road to Assaita passes through a scrubby area dotted with several apparently permanent pools (plenty of birds and occasional troops of Hamadryas baboon), before opening out into a flat, thinly vegetated floodplain surrounded

LAKES AROUND ASSAITA

With thanks to Peile Thompson, who in 2001 trekked the length of the Awash River north of Awash Saba, the first person to do so unsupported since Wilfred Thesiger in 1934.

South of Assaita, the Awash River terminates into a chain of about six shallow saline and freshwater lakes, of which the largest (and last) is Lake Abbe on the border with Djibouti. The deep blue lakes, fringed by lush salt-tolerant vegetation and surrounded by high mountains, support dense populations of hippos and crocodiles. The lakes form one of the most important water bird sites in Ethiopia, and attract large numbers of Palaearctic migrants during the European winter. On the Djibouti side, Lake Abbe is a popular weekend destination. The Ethiopian side of the lakes, however, is totally undeveloped for tourism, and likely to remain so for some time. At the time of writing, the lakes are inaccessible in a vehicle, following the collapse of the bridge across a river at Ebobe, 10km south of Assaita. Until such time as this road is repaired, the only feasible way of reaching the lakes is by hiking or setting up a camel expedition.

Over May and June of 2001, Peile Thompson explored this area on foot, using routes that hadn't been walked by a *faranji* since Wilfred Thesiger in the 1930s. Peile travelled with six camels (to carry supplies and water), and many of the routes he followed would be suitable only to experienced and well-prepared adventurers carrying sufficient water to last several days. However, he has kindly passed on details of a relatively straightforward round hike between Assaita and Lakes Gummare and Afambo, which could be undertaken over two (or better three) days without inordinate preparation.

To do this hike, you'd need to carry two or three days' food, depending on how long you take over it. Drinking water is available at reasonably regular intervals, but it's always advisable to carry some water (and refill whenever possible) in case the pumps aren't working. It would be inviting problems to travel through this part of Afar country without a local Afar guide, and written authority from the regional authority. A permit can easily be arranged through the tourist office in Assaita. The tourist office can also arrange a local guide for birr 60 per day. Travelling in this area without a guide is foolhardy, not only because he will interact with local Afar people on your behalf, but also because there is a genuine risk of losing your way, with potentially fatal results.

The most accessible lakes are Gummare and Afambo, which are linked by a short stretch of river about 20km south of Assaita by road. To get to the lakes, you must first follow the main road south of town for about 10km to the river at Ebobe. If you want to cut down the walking time, a local bus service does run at least once daily between Assaita and Ebobe (timings are erratic), and there is plenty of transport along this road on Tuesdays (market day). You can normally cross the river on foot, but the banks are too steep for a vehicle, which is why the bus and all other transport terminates here. Shortly past the crossing is a police post, where you will be turned back if you don't have written authority. South of this, the track runs through fertile land dotted with rural Afar settlements and small papyrus-fringed lakes – the birdlife is incredible.

Another 10km or so along the track, you reach a deep 15m-wide river. Here, the local Afar people have made a raft out of fallen reeds and will pull you

by large dunes. Using public transport, three buses daily run between Assaita and Logiya.

There are two decent local hotels in Assaita, both situated within 200m of the bus station, and used to catering for travellers. The **Lem Hotel** (↘ *033 5550050*), which lies

and your kit across to the other side for birr 5 each. You could swim it, but there are a lot of crocodiles around! About 500m beyond this crossing, you reach the river linking Lake Afambo to Lake Gummare. There used to be a bridge over this 150m crossing, but it collapsed some time ago. This crossing has to be done with a raft as there are many crocs and hippos around in the lake. The border traders are all queuing up to get on the rafts, with camels laden with salt and goods. The animals swim across, but the goods are placed on a papyrus raft and ferried to the other side. The people who operate the rafts will charge you ridiculous sums to get across, knowing you have no option... but don't be tempted to swim it as we did, we nearly got scoffed, and the locals went crazy! This is real smuggler's country, so be a little careful, as things get heated and everyone is armed. For the few that make it here, the view of Lake Gummare is magnificent with the rich birdlife, the Afar hustle and bustle, and the high surrounding escarpment that drops down to the opposite lakeshore.

Having crossed the river, you pick up the track again as it winds up the high escarpment towards the Djibouti border. After about 3km, this climb of several hundred metres in elevation leads towards a point marked on several maps as Afambo. We expected there to be some form of settlement here... wrong, unless you count a derelict bunch of buildings and an observation post, remnants of the old Derg border post! From the abandoned camp, the views over the lakes and back west towards Assaita are awesome. Note, however, that the surrounding area is mined, so you should always stick to the path, and that no safe route other than the track you have climbed connects the camp to the lakes. The hike up from the crossing to Afambo takes about 90 minutes, but it's really worth the effort for the views.

There is no accommodation around the lakes, nor are there formal campsites. Travellers can camp rough anywhere they like, ideally slightly away from the villages to avoid masses of people (and ticks!). The area is very hot, even at night, so it's not necessary to carry a lot of camping gear – but you will need some protection from the prolific mosquitoes. Expect to be investigated by young Afar warriors asking questions (and sometimes a fee). This is when you need a local guide and piece of paper with the Afar Tourism Board stamp on it. I should stress that federal stamps and pieces of paper count for nothing in Afar, you must have something with an Afar government stamp or people will turn you back.

From the crossing point described above, Peile notes that, with adequate preparation, it is possible to continue south along a little-used track that follows the eastern shore of Lake Afambo to Lake Abbe, where you can cross into Djibouti. The hike from the crossing point to Lake Abbe will take four days, and Peile stresses that absolutely no drinking water is available until you reach Lake Abbe, where there are some freshwater springs. Lake Afambo's water was potable in Thesiger's day, but it is now very saline due to the decrease in water flow caused by the various irrigation schemes along the Awash River. In this hot and exposed terrain, you would need to carry at least 10 litres of water per person per day – in other words a total of 40 litres of drinking water per person for the full hike, which would have to be carried on camelback.

on the main road coming into the town centre, charges birr 20 for a large clean room with a proper double bed and fan. It also has a good common shower. The hotel often fills up early, so it's worth ringing ahead to book a room. The **Basha Amare Beyene Hotel**,

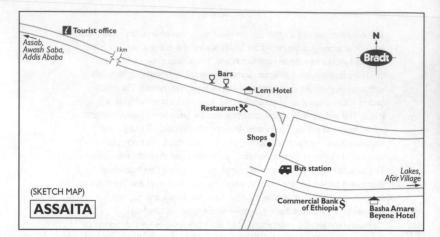

which lies just past the bus station next to the Commercial Bank of Ethiopia, has small rooms for birr 16, but it's far more pleasant to sleep outdoors (birr 10 per bed in the courtyard, birr 15 per bed on the breezy balcony overlooking the river). The food at the Basha Amare Beyene Hotel is the best in town – don't miss the local speciality called *hagabi*, a firm, spicy type of *wat* made from powdered peas. There are a few more basic hotels dotted around the town, but in this stinking-hot climate you really want to sleep securely outdoors, or to have a fan in your room.

Dichioto

Heading east from the junction to Assaita, the Assab road passes through some genuinely fascinating scenery, dominated by ancient lava flows and bizarre volcanic outcrops, before reaching the small town of Dichioto. Based on our experience, this is the one stretch of the Assab road where you're likely to see much wildlife – we encountered Soemmering's gazelle, Hamadryas baboon and ostrich – and it also passes a few small lakes where Afar pastoralists bring their camels to water. Dichioto is a rather odd settlement of brightly painted corrugated-iron buildings with large balconies. As the last Ethiopian town before the Djibouti border, it is a popular stopover with truck drivers, and has consequently acquired an unexpectedly shiftless, seedy atmosphere. Hotels there are in abundance, all charging birr 8–10 per bed whether you sleep in a small sweaty room or follow the local custom of kipping outdoors – for what it's worth, the Andinet Hotel looks more savoury than most.

Eli Dar Depression

East of Dichioto, the Assab road descends to the Eli Dar Depression, the most accessible of several salt lakes in Afar. The descent itself is pretty spectacular, passing over evocatively barren rocky slopes with the lake shimmering off-white below. You may also see salt caravans travelling up the pass. At the base of the depression lies Dobi – marked prominently on maps at the junction of the roads to Assab and Djibouti, but in reality little more than a collection of a dozen or so rickety shacks that provide shelter from the searing heat and sell lukewarm sodas and beers. In a private vehicle, Eli Dar makes for an easy and worthwhile diversion coming to or from Assaita. For backpackers, any bus or truck heading to Djibouti can drop you at Dobi. An early start is recommended – it shouldn't be too difficult to find a lift back out, but there is no formal accommodation should you get stuck in Dobi overnight.

Harar and Dire Dawa

East of Awash Saba, the southern Rift Valley Escarpment rises to
the Arba Gugu and Chercher mountain ranges, to form a long
narrow eastern extension of the southern highlands which
points towards the Djibouti border like a crooked finger.
Moist and fertile, the far eastern highlands are no less scenic
than their northern counterparts, but culturally the area is
strikingly different. The dominant ethnic group here (as in much
of the Rift Valley) is the Oromo, who speak a Nilotic language, are
generally less Semetic in appearance than the northern highlanders, and are relatively
recent converts to Judaic religions.

Historically, the most significant settlement in the far east is the walled city of Harar,
which more or less took its present shape in the 15th century, and subsequently served as
the launching pad for Ahmed Gragn's destructive assault on the Christian empire of the
central and northern highlands. Famed, too, as the birthplace of Ras Tefari Mekonnen
(later Emperor Haile Selassie), and the base for the French poet Rimbaud's African
adventures, Harar is regarded as the spiritual home of Ethiopia's large and ancient Muslim
community. For travellers, the walled city forms a fascinating and refreshing contrast to
the ubiquitous Christian monuments of northern Ethiopia. It is also renowned for its
hyena men, who earn their keep by feeding wild hyenas nightly on the city's fringes.

For all its historical importance, Harar is today overshadowed as an economic force by
Dire Dawa, which was founded 55km from Harar at the turn of the 20th century to
service the Addis Ababa–Djibouti railway line, and has subsequently prospered to
become Ethiopia's second largest city. Situated at the base of the Rift Valley Escarpment,
Dire Dawa is lower, hotter and drier than Harar, and of relatively little interest – though
as the main regional transport hub and the site of the airport servicing Harar, most
travellers will pass through the city at some point.

Most travellers who visit this area restrict their exploration to Harar itself and (by default)
Dire Dawa, either flying in directly from Addis Ababa, or else coming overland by rail or
express bus. There is, however, some interesting sightseeing outside of the two main towns.
The road to Dire Dawa from Awash Saba, passing through the Chercher and Arba Gugu
mountains, is splendidly scenic, and worth taking slowly. Also of interest, situated within
day-tripping distance of Harar, are the Babile Elephant Sanctuary, the Valley of Marvels, the
Somali regional capital of Jijiga, and the mysterious rock paintings near Kombolcha.

TO HARAR AND DIRE DAWA BY ROAD

Harar and Dire Dawa are both situated about 525km from Addis Ababa and 300km from
Awash National Park along a good asphalt road. In a private vehicle, one can drive from
Addis Ababa to either city over the course of a longish day, while those using public
transport can bus directly to Dire Dawa or Harar from Adama or Awash Saba.
Alternatively, the journey can be done in stages, using local buses, with potential stops en
route including Asbe Teferi, Kuni, Hirna and Kulubi.

Awash Saba to Asbe Teferi

Immediately east of Awash Saba, a bridge crosses the Awash River and the rocky, dusty land around town gives way to a bleakly monotonous cover of dry acacia scrub. Parties of colourfully dressed Oromo women appear from nowhere to board the bus in an excited gossipy clatter, the odd camel or donkey wanders blithely along the verge, and you may see the occasional Salt's dik-dik make a startled dash into the scrub. The most notable point of interest off this stretch of road is the monastery of **Asabot Selassie**, which stands on the prominent peak of Asabot Mountain (2,539m) and houses several ancient Ge'ez manuscripts describing the miracles performed by Abuna Samuel, the church's founder. The monastery lies 20km northeast of Asabot town, and can be reached by a rough track which branches off the main road about 60km from Awash Saba.

About 12km past Asabot, turn right at **Mieso**, at the junction of the new road and the (practically disused) old road to Dire Dawa. It's something of a relief to break the dusty tedium when, 24km past Mieso, you pull in to **Asbe Teferi**, the largest town along this stretch of road, with a population of around 29,000. Asbe Teferi is rescued from visual anonymity by the presence of a few balconied double-storey legacies of the Italian occupation and an attractive setting in the Chercher and Arba Gugu foothills, despite which it possesses a hot dusty feel more of the plains than of the highlands.

There's plenty of public transport heading out in all directions from Asbe Teferi, and little reason to linger on there. But if you're in need of nourishment or a bed for the night, a few options exist. The smartest lodging (and the best place to eat) is the Aschalew Hotel (✆ 022 5510276), which charges a rather inflated *faranji* price of birr 70 for a clean little en-suite room with ³/₄ bed and cold shower, or a preposterous birr 50 for a similar room using common showers. Not quite so nice, but more reasonably priced, is the Girum Hotel (✆ 022 5510273) opposite the Shell garage, which charges birr 35 for an en-suite room with ³/₄ bed and cold shower or birr 25 for one using the common showers.

An ambitious excursion from Asbe Teferi would be to the **Dindin Forest** and **Achare and Aynage Caves** near Machara, roughly 100km further east. The little-studied but extensive Dindin Forest is an Afro-montane assemblage set on the steep eastern slopes of the 3,574m-high Mount Arba Gugu. The Achare and Aynage complex of caves, which lies about 6km from Machara, is thought to be the most extensive subterranean network in Ethiopia after Sof Omar, yet it remained unexplored until 1995, when it was visited by a caving expedition from Britain's Huddersfield University.

Kuni Muktar Mountain Nyala Sanctuary

A particularly worthwhile diversion for wildlife enthusiasts who won't have the opportunity to visit the Bale Mountains is this defunct sanctuary flanking the village of Kuni 25km southeast of Asbe Teferi. Kuni Muktar was set aside in 1990 to protect the mountain nyala herds and other wildlife resident on the forested slopes of Mounts Jallo and Muktar, which rise to altitudes of above 3,000m immediately west and east of Kuni respectively. By the mid 1990s, the sanctuary had lost any formal protection it might once have enjoyed, following an intensive bout of poaching, and it was thought for some years after this that no wildlife remained there. But recent reports suggest that the mountain nyala population on Muktar is now largely recovered: one reputable researcher counted more than 30 head in a day in 2002, while local information indicates that at least 100 individuals are present, including a high proportion of youngsters. There are also large numbers of Menelik's bushbuck on Jallo, while the juniper and podocarpus forest on both mountains harbours Abyssinian catbird and other suitable endemic bird species.

The best time to seek out mountain nyala is in the early morning or late afternoon (ideally at around 07.00 or 17.00), when small herds leave the forest to drink at a stream situated about 30–45 minutes' walk along a rough track leading left from the central marketplace in Kuni. To get there from Asbe Teferi, follow the Dire Dawa road for 18km as far as Arbereketi, where a right turn leads to Kuni after 7km. You can reach Kuni on public transport (regular minibuses leave from the junction at Arbereketi) but there is no formal accommodation, which means you would need a really early start out of Asbe Teferi to be at the sanctuary in good time. There is no sanctuary office in Kuni, but it is easy enough to find a local guide to help you locate the mountain nyala.

Asbe Teferi to Dire Dawa/Harar

East of Asbe Teferi, the Dire Dawa road climbs into the cool, moist **Chercher Mountains**, a literal breath of fresh air after the hot, dusty plains. The views from the road, over row after row of verdant peaks, are fantastic; even better, I'm sure, if you join the bus driver, conductor and passengers in their frenzied consumption of *chat*. The hills are densely cultivated, mostly with sorghum, but patches of juniper and eucalyptus forest can still be seen, as well as impressive stands of euphorbia candelabra in the rockier areas.

After about 60km of this gorgeous scenery, you'll pull in to **Hirna**, a cheerful and colourful small town set among glistening green hills and fertile valleys. This is the sort of bountiful, beautiful setting that cannot help but bring a lightness to your step – simply strolling out of town along the main road is visual bliss, and footpaths lead from the town in all directions. This could be fantastic walking country... and there are plenty of basic hotels in town if you want to explore. When you are ready to move on, buses for Dire Dawa or Harar leave Hirna throughout the day and take about four hours. If you can't find a bus to the town you want to go to, then catch one to the other town and ask to be dropped at the T-junction with the road that connects Harar and Dire Dawa – there's plenty of transport from this junction in either direction.

On the way to the T-junction you pass the small town of **Kulubi**, which enjoys a degree of renown disproportionate to its size thanks to the presence of a church called **Kulubi Gebriel** on a hilltop 2.5km from the town centre. In 1896, Ras Mekonnen, father of Haile Selassie, stopped at what was then a rather modest shrine to Saint Gebriel on the hill outside Kulubi to pray for his assistance in the looming military confrontation with Italy. Ethiopia duly defeated Italy at Adwa, and when Ras Mekonnen returned to Harar he ordered a magnificent church to be built at Kulubi in honour of the inspirational saint.

Aesthetically, it's debatable whether the domed sandstone church built by Ras Mekonnen is of much inherent interest to anybody other than students of modern Ethiopian architecture. But, rather oddly, given its relative modernity in a country liberally dotted with ancient churches of mysterious origin, Kulubi Gebriel has become the target of a fantastic biannual pilgrimage, one regarded by Ethiopian Christians as equivalent to the Islamic call to Mecca. On 26 July and 28 December, the days dedicated to saint Gebriel, more than 100,000 Ethiopians from all over the country descend on the church, a festive occasion with few peers anywhere in Ethiopia. Aside from being a wonderful cultural spectacle, the pilgrimage can disrupt normal public transport patterns in the area for a few days, and bus seats are booked up weeks in advance.

DIRE DAWA

The modern city of Dire Dawa is the second largest in Ethiopia, with a population estimated at around 265,000. It was founded in 1902 under the name of Addis Harar (New Harar) to service the Franco-Ethiopian railway that connects Djibouti to Addis Ababa. Because of its strategic location, the upstart town soon came to outrank Harar in commercial and industrial significance, though even as recently as 1970 it supported a significantly smaller population. In recent years, Dire Dawa has experienced something of an economic boom as a result of the secession of Eritrea, which left Ethiopia without a seaport of its own. The recent border war with Eritrea has served to strengthen the importance of Dire Dawa, since it effectively made Djibouti Ethiopia's only reliable link with the Indian Ocean.

IN DEFENCE OF DIRE DAWA

From an email from Arthur Gerfers

The description of Dire Dawa as 'hot, sweaty and entirely without charm', I found to be out of touch with the reality. It doesn't take a city-planning expert to recognise that Dire Dawa represents a refreshing change from most other towns in Ethiopia or Africa, for that matter. The streets here, first of all, are paved and relatively clean. The pavements here are continuous and without holes. Streetside shop fronts and residences offer the eye a line of continuity, a pleasant sense of urban order so glaringly absent in African cities. This town is easy to manoeuvre on foot, with fountains and parks for rest stops. Graffiti-covered walls surrounding seemingly vacant lots are a far cry from the exposed open spaces of other towns, which usually resemble nothing more than rubbish heaps. The reckless misuse of space so prevalent in African town-building, from muddy corner lots to functionless green spaces to decaying military plazas, leads only to the concentration of unsightliness. Ultimately the visitor is left with a sense of placelessness. The opposite, however, is true of Dire Dawa; indeed here one always has the feeling of being someplace. Even oversized socialist-era eyesores are woven methodically into the human scale of the town. And most all of the streets are tree-lined, perhaps the strongest card in this town's suit. Their boughs keep the pavement shaded and the air somewhat cool, despite the dogged humidity. I know how circumstances can play into one's judgement of a town. Perhaps you were having a bad day when you visited, or maybe it was god-awful hot. But being so pleasantly surprised by Dire Dawa, a town to which I was exiled for one day, I felt obligated to counter your sweeping dismissal of it.

Set at an altitude of 1,150m, Dire Dawa is divided into two distinct parts by the wide arc created by the *wadi* (normally dry watercourse) carved by the Dachata River. Kezira, the French-designed city centre, lies to the west of the watercourse, and consists of a neat grid of avenues which emanate from the central square in front of the railway station, and which are flanked by shady trees and staid colonial-style buildings. The old Muslim quarter of Megala, by contrast, is more organic in shape and mood, with all alleys apparently leading to the colourful bustle of its vast and excellent central market. The two parts of town are connected by a bridge in the north and by a seasonal causeway in the south.

In the first edition of this guide I described Dire Dawa as 'hot, sweaty and charmless', to the ire of several readers. Subsequent visits to Dire Dawa have given me little cause to revise my original assessment, so rather than plead a cause to which I don't subscribe, let me instead refer you to Arthur Gerfers's passionate comments in the box *In Defence of Dire Dawa* (above). Whatever else, the pro-Dire Dawa contingent does concede that 'there isn't much to see' in the town. The large **market**, often attended by rural Oromo and Afar in traditional garb, is definitely worth a look, and busiest in the morning. A second **livestock market** is situated about 500m east of the main bridge across the *wadi*. The **railway station** building will be a must for students of colonial architecture. The large multi-storey **palace**, which served as Haile Selassie's residence whenever he visited Dire Dawa, might also be of interest, but casual visits are not permitted, and little of the building is visible from outside the palace grounds.

Once you've exhausted the sightseeing, one possibility would be to retire to the Ras Hotel, with the twin attractions of attractive green grounds and a welcoming swimming pool. Less passively, you might want to check your email at the Tele Centre opposite the railway station (birr 0.40 per minute), or pop into a bar or coffee shop to watch (or participate in) the locally popular game of bingo, or buy some packaged Harar coffee at the Green Gold Shop near the railway station, or create total chaos by entering into a prolonged French monologue with one of the locals who insist on greeting any passing *faranji* with their solitary Francophone phrase: a loud '*Bon jour*'. Then again, assuming that you're not waiting for a flight or train, you could, as advised in the first edition, bugger off to Harar!

Getting there and away

Ethiopian Airlines flies daily between Addis Ababa and Dire Dawa, with flights sometimes continuing on to Jijiga in the east. Onward tickets should always be confirmed a day in advance. The airport, situated about 5km from the city centre, is a large, modern, stinking-hot building with a bar (whew!), and roof fans that don't work because some unspeakable dolt erected supportive pillars in their line of rotation. A charter taxi to the city centre costs birr 40. Flights are also met by shared taxis, whose drivers routinely overcharge tourists and aren't very open to negotiation.

Daily buses to Addis Ababa leave from the new bus station from between 05.00 and 06.00, and take about 12 hours, stopping briefly at all towns of significance en route. Minibuses run back and forth to Harar every 10 minutes or so throughout the day, leaving from the old bus station near the market, and taking about one hour in either direction. For details of the rail service to Addis Ababa and Djibouti see the box *The Djibouti Railway* (pages 394–5).

Where to stay
Upmarket
Dire Dawa Ras Hotel (50 rooms) ☏ 025 1113255; e rashoteldiredawa@yahoo.com. One of the best government hotels in Ethiopia, this large high-rise is set in a pleasantly leafy garden, which has the unexpected bonus of a swimming pool, open to day visitors at a small fee. The large en-suite rooms with DSTV, fan and hot bath cost birr 118/255 sgl/dbl. Other facilities include a good restaurant and bar, and a business centre with pricey internet facilities (birr 1.35 per minute).

Moderate
Dil Hotel (18 rooms) ☏ 025 1114181. Situated just 1km from the airport along the main road towards the town centre, this new three-storey hotel has a rather isolated and uninspiring setting, though plenty of construction work appears to be taking place in the vicinity. The large carpeted dbl rooms with DSTV, fan and cold shower cost birr 200 – a *faranji* price that seems mildly delusional when you consider how inferior it is to the Ras.
Fasika Hotel (20 rooms) ☏ 025 1111260. Also situated some distance from the town centre, 500m along a quiet avenue running eastward from the airport road, this pleasant hotel charges birr 80 for a 'second class' dbl with fan, TV and en-suite hot shower, or birr 100 for a larger 'first class' room. A decent restaurant is attached.

Budget
Mekonnen Hotel (11 rooms) ☏ 025 1113348. This long-serving favourite has plenty of character and a convenient location on the central square facing the railway station, and charges birr 25 for a large, clean room with a genuine dbl bed and fan, using common showers. Unfortunately, it's often full.
Continental Hotel (16 rooms) One could make too much of the fact that Evelyn Waugh stayed at this central hotel in its distant 1930s' heyday, but still it's not a bad bet in its price range, charging birr 20/32 for an en-suite sgl/dbl with fan, cold shower and possibly quite a bit of noise drifting in from the pleasant courtyard bar.

THE DJIBOUTI RAILWAY

This box is based extensively on letters from Christine Wenaweser and Luca Zanetti, with input from Arthur Gerfers, Iain Jackson, Marie Hogervorst, and Kirk Melcher and Maren Stoltenberg.

Ethiopia's only railway service runs along the French-built line connecting Addis Ababa to Djibouti via Awash Saba and Dire Dawa. The Djibouti train is not exactly the *Orient Express*, and the trip is perhaps most sensibly viewed as an experience in its own right rather than public transport. In its favour, the train does offer a change of pace from the interminable bus trips that are normal elsewhere in the country. The relatively few travellers who do undertake this tough but fascinating trip invariably regard it as a highlight of their time in Ethiopia, if not at the time, then in hindsight. But, as one reader pointed out a couple of years back, 'first class is not our first class by Western standards, nor our second class, nor even our third class'. First-class carriages, take note, have subsequently been discontinued!

The train runs to a notoriously unreliable timetable and is given to inexplicable stops of several hours' duration, most of which seem to be linked to the huge amount of smuggling between Ethiopia and Djibouti. In theory, one train runs daily in either direction except on Sunday, leaving Addis Ababa at around 14.00 and Dire Dawa at 11.00. The trip from Addis Ababa to Dire Dawa takes up to 20 hours, and the leg from Dire Dawa to Djibouti is of similar duration. In practice, you are best heading to the train station on a daily basis to check out the current situation – the railway staff are helpful and speak good English and French. Delays are part of the routine, so you shouldn't think about boarding the train if arriving up to 12 hours late will affect your travel plans adversely.

A ticket between Addis and Dire Dawa costs the equivalent of US$8. Reader consensus up until a year or two ago was that first class, which used to cost about 50% more (and presumably will again, should the service ever be resumed), is the only sane way to travel. For now, in the words of a recent victim, 'you will have to sit, like it or not, for 20 hours at least'. Tickets can only be bought on the day of departure, when the booking office opens at 07.00 in an atmosphere of total chaos. Tickets often sell out within 30 minutes of the office opening, so get in the queue early or – better – see if you can persuade somebody to sell you a ticket a day in advance. You should also be at the station in good time before departure if you want to be

National Hotel \ 025 1113415. Situated next to the Commercial Bank near the bridge, the large but dingy en-suite rooms with fan and cold shower at this former government hotel seem overpriced at birr 50, but the rooms using common shower aren't bad value at birr 23.

Meseret Hotel \ 025 1113305. Set 50m from the Harar road close to the new bus station in an area liberally dotted with restaurants and bars, this quiet double-storey hotel, built around a green courtyard, charges birr 30 for a clean en-suite room with ³/₄ bed, cold shower and no fan.

Shoestring

Addis Ababa Hotel Situated in Megala opposite the bridge to Kezira, this popular budget haunt charges birr 10/20 for an adequate sgl/dbl using a common shower. Some rooms have a good view over the *wadi*.

Solomon Belede Hotel Another affordable central hotel, this charges birr 30 for a rather rundown but adequate en-suite room with a ³/₄ bed.

Wagda Hotel Situated just a block up from the main square, this grubby hotel charges birr 10 for a basic room – the common shower and toilet wouldn't win any hygiene awards, but it does look as if it sees the occasional mop.

certain of getting a seat; it's often the case that more tickets are sold than there are seats available. Christine reckons that cargo trains are more comfortable than passenger trains, and tend to get from A to B more quickly. You might need to improvise to make the most of the possibilities on the cargo train (she spent much of her time on the back of a pick-up truck being carried by the train).

Theft has long been something of a problem on the overnight train. Reports over the last couple of years have been consistently positive: the windows are fenced (which means they can safely be left open) and the security presence is high. Nevertheless, you shouldn't think about leaving your bags unguarded even for a moment. Be especially vigilant when the already overcrowded train stops at a station, as it will fill up with the usual chaotic crew of vendors, bored adults, and curious children. The train is well guarded, at least to start with. To quote one reader: 'The armed guards with rifles, who reminded us of old Western movies, were drinking beers the whole trip. After a few hours we heard some shooting noises, but everybody was laughing hard at the ducking *faranjis*, although the guards did lift their rifles.'

Soft drinks, beer and bread can normally be bought on the train. Local food is sold at several small stations, while more substantial meals are to be had when the train stops in Awash Saba. Drinking water is not available, and the train is often very hot and sweaty, so bring plenty with you. The toilets beggar polite description.

Christine and Luca travelled by train all the way to Djibouti (and back). This tiny Francophone country, named after its main port and capital, has assumed great strategic significance to Ethiopia following the recent closure of all borders with Eritrea. Unless you have plans to travel within Djibouti, it's debatable whether this leg of the trip is justifiable to anybody but serious rail buffs or passport-stamp collectors. Djibouti town reportedly has little to recommend it; the kindest epithet I've come across is 'likeable dump'. Also be warned that costs are high: accommodation starts at US$30 per room (the Djibouti Palace Hotel near the Assemblée Nationale has been recommended for offering reasonably priced rooms with air conditioning, TV and running water). In addition to buying a Djibouti visa in Addis Ababa you'll need to fork out another US$60 for a fresh Ethiopian visa once in Djibouti (assuming that you want to return to Ethiopia). Then again, it is such obscure, difficult journeys such as the Djibouti train that often result in the most memorable travel experiences (and the most amusing readers' letters!). If you decide to give it a go, let me know how it went.

Where to eat

The **Ras Hotel** does decent Western meals for around birr 20. Better, however, is the excellent **Paradiso Restaurant**, which is set in an atmospheric old house along the Harar road, and serves a selection of Italian and Ethiopian dishes, along with various roast meats, for birr 12–20. The **Harar Road Restaurant** opposite serves cheaper local dishes in a pleasant garden, while **Menelaos Roast Chicken** near the palace serves whole roast chickens for birr 20 and good tuna salad for birr 12. More centrally, just one block away from the railway station, the all-in-one **Burger and Chicken Mito** serves a varied and reasonably priced selection of meals, snack, pastries, juices, hot drinks and beers.

Dini Paradise next to the bridge serves a variety of snacks, pastries and juices in green surrounds. Also good for snacks and juices is the **Peacock Cafeteria** on the Harar road facing the stadium. The bar on the ground floor of the **Mekonnen Hotel**, cool and draped with lush bougainvillea, serves beer, coffee, pastries and snacks, and is a pleasant place to hang out, especially if you are waiting for the train. The garden bar at the **Wagda Hotel** is a good place to sip a draught beer or two.

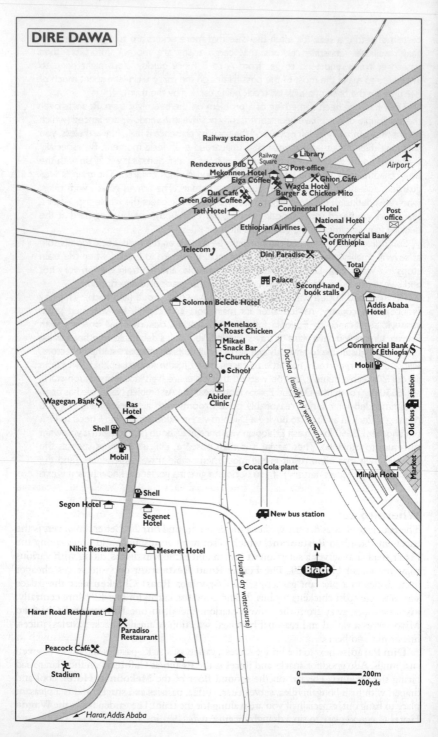

DIRE DAWA

Railway station

Railway Square

Library

Rendezvous Pub
Mekonnen Hotel
Elga Coffee
Dus Café
Green Gold Coffee
Tati Hotel

Post office

Ghion Café
Wagda Hotel
Burger & Chicken Mito

Continental Hotel

Ethiopian Airlines

National Hotel

Post office

Commercial Bank
of Ethiopia

Telecom

Dini Paradise

Total

Palace

Second-hand
book stalls

Solomon Belede Hotel

Addis Ababa
Hotel

Menelaos
Roast Chicken

Mikael
Snack Bar

Church

Commercial Bank
of Ethiopia

Mobil

School

Dachata (usually dry watercourse)

Wagegan Bank

Ras
Hotel

Shell

Abider
Clinic

Old bus station

Mobil

Coca Cola plant

Minjar Hotel

Market

Shell

Segon Hotel

Segenet
Hotel

New bus station

Nibit Restaurant

Meseret Hotel

N

Bradt

Harar Road Restaurant

Paradiso
Restaurant

Peacock Café

(Usually dry watercourse)

Stadium

0 ——— 200m
0 ——— 200yds

Harar, Addis Ababa

LAGA ODA ROCK PAINTINGS
In an earlier edition of this guide I wrote:

> These reputedly excellent prehistoric rock paintings have acquired
> something close to legendary status – 'only the old people know
> where they are' – and, given time, have the potential to create a
> virtual industry of misinformation. Various guides I spoke to put them
> between 2km and 30km out of town; the 'not in our region'
> assessment of the regional tourist office gives weight to the higher
> estimate, as does the claim of the only person I met who had seen
> them that they were three hours' walk from the main road. He
> reckoned you'd have to walk through an area bristling with frenzied
> spearmen. All very odd, but no doubt there's some enthusiastic
> traveller out there up to the challenge; if you aren't speared to death,
> let me know how it goes.

Toby Savage did just that:

> We travelled from Addis to Dire Dawa where I was part of a team
> studying the elusive rock art. The good news is that it does exist and
> is only about two hours' drive from Dire Dawa in a 4x4 with a guide.
> We had to obtain permission from the head of the tourist board in
> Dire Dawa (Sebsebe Gezahegne, PO Box 407, Dire Dawa), and
> Ahmed Mohamed Buh of the Trade, Transport Industry & Tourism
> Office (025 1112466; f 025 1112441). Both were very helpful in
> taking us to see Laga Oda Cave, though it took three days of
> 'negotiation'. Once there the art is not that special, and the distance
> and hard journey would disappoint most tourists. There are many
> other sites in the region, which we hope to find and document next
> November.

HARAR
The spiritual heart of Ethiopia's large Islamic community, Harar is considered by some
Muslims to be the fourth holiest city in the world after Mecca, Medina and Jerusalem,
while travel scribe John Graham rates it as 'the most pleasant city to visit in Ethiopia'.
Harar is indeed a lively, friendly and stimulating town, one whose aura of cultural
integrity and lived-in antiquity is complemented by a moderate highland climate that
comes as a positive relief after the festering claustrophobia of Dire Dawa.

Harar lies at the centre of a fertile agricultural area, renowned for its high-quality
coffee, though this crop has been increasingly replaced by *chat* in recent years. But the
main attraction of the region is Harar itself, or rather the walled city of Jugal that lies at
its ancient heart. Old Harar remains strongly Muslim in character – its 90-odd mosques,
many of them private, are said to form the largest concentration of such shrines in the
world. By contrast, the newer part of town, which runs along the Dire Dawa road, is
predominantly Christian, though the frizzy-headed traditional Oromo are also much in
evidence.

Considering the prominent role that Harar has played in Muslim–Christian–Galla
conflicts past, the modern town possesses a surprising mood of religious and cultural
tolerance, one that is doubly refreshing in the present global political climate. Indeed, for
a city of such devout pedigree, Harar has an undercurrent that is more than a little – dare
I say it – hedonistic. The compulsive chewing of *chat* dominates every aspect of public life

HARAR: A POTTED HISTORY

The early days of Harar are shrouded in legend. The city's foundation is often attributed to Sultan Abu Bekr Mohammed of the Walashma dynasty, who is known to have abandoned the established Walashma capital at Dakar in favour of Harar in 1520. But, while Abu Bekr's move was instrumental in pushing the city to prominence, Harar is certainly much older than this. The town is mentioned in an early 14th-century manuscript, and its oldest mosque was reputedly founded in the 12th century. One tradition is that Harar was originally a Christian city and went by a different name until its patron saint, an Arabian settler called Shakih Abadir, settled there in the 10th century, renamed it Harar, and organised its first Islamic administrative system. Others claim that Harar became Islamic as early as the 7th century, when it was settled by an Arabic community led by a contemporary and follower of the prophet Mohammed called Sheik Hussein. Yet another legend relating to the origin of Harar is that when Mohammed ascended to heaven he saw the hill on which it stands as a shining light, and an angel told him it was the Mountain of Saints.

Harar rose to significance in an atmosphere of turmoil and bloodshed. Within five years of settling in Harar, Abu Bekr Mohammed was killed by Ahmed Gragn, a popular and highly militant imam who assumed control of the city by installing Umar Din, another member of the Walashma dynasty, as a puppet sultan to be supervised by Gragn's brother. His hold on Harar secure, Gragn ordered all Muslims to stop paying tribute to the Christian Emperor Lebna Dengal, who had angered him a few years earlier by sending a pillaging raid to the Islamic region of Hubut. Lebna Dengal retaliated to Gragn's subversive instructions by sending a punitive military expedition to Harar, one that was soundly defeated by Gragn's army. Inspired by this victory, Gragn then used Harar as the base from which a succession of bloody and destructive raids was launched on the Christian empire. Gragn was killed in battle in 1543, but the *jihad* continued with diminishing effect for several years, under the direction of Gragn's widow Bati Del Wambara and nephew Nur Ibn al-Wazir. In 1559, the imperial army, led by Emperor Galawdewos, marched on Harar once again. And, once again, it was defeated – the emperor was killed and his head paraded around town on a stake.

The long years of war took their economic toll on Harar's resources. Following the battle of 1559, the *jihad* was more or less abandoned as the city faced a new threat in the form of the Galla (Oromo) tribes who had taken advantage of the Muslim–Christian conflict to occupy much of southern Ethiopia. It was during the 1560s that Sultan Nur erected the tall protective walls that have enclosed old Harar ever since. After Nur's death in 1567, however, Harar was ruled by two ineffective sultans in

and, to paraphrase the sentiments of one (Muslim) resident, you really do need something liquid to chill you out after a good chew. Any preconceptions about fundamentalist Harar can be washed down at the bars which, I suspect, come close to matching public mosques one for one within the old city walls. Harar is the sort of easygoing, cosmopolitan town where you could settle in for a week and do nothing more exerting than just soak up the atmosphere.

Getting there and away

Flights and trains from Addis Ababa mostly terminate at Dire Dawa rather than Harar, as do most direct buses to the area, though one direct bus runs between Harar and Addis Ababa daily, costing birr 56 and taking 13 hours. Dire Dawa and Harar are connected by a good 55km asphalt road, which is covered by a regular stream of minibuses taking about

succession, and became increasingly vulnerable to attacks by the Galla. In 1575, the sultan was evicted by Mansur Mohammed, who abandoned Harar in favour of a new capital at the oasis of Awsa in the Danakil Desert. For almost a century, Harar was politically subordinate to Awsa.

Harar's resurrection began in 1647, when Emir Ali ibn Daud took control of the city, and formed an autonomous ruling dynasty. Despite frequent fighting with the Galla, the walled city grew in stature over the next century to become the most populous and important trade centre in the region, issuing its own currency, and known by repute throughout the Islamic world. Only Muslims, however, were allowed to enter the city walls, and as a result its location was the source of more rumour than substance in the Christian world. The first European to visit Harar, in 1855, was the British explorer Richard Burton, who spent ten anxious days in what he referred to as 'the forbidden city', unsure whether he was a guest or prisoner of the Emir (see box *Richard Burton in Harar*, page 404). Another famous 19th-century visitor was the French poet Arthur Rimbaud, who abandoned poetry at the age of 19 and then, after seven footloose years in Europe, moved to Harar in 1880, where he set himself up as a trader and was based until his death in 1891.

Harar's almost 250-year-long era of autonomous rule came to an end in 1875, when Egypt captured the city and killed the Emir. The ensuing Egyptian occupation met strong internal resistance, and it collapsed in 1885, when Emir Abdullah was installed. Two years later, however, the walled city once again lost its autonomy, this time to the Prince of Showa, the future Emperor Menelik II, who defeated Emir Abdullah's forces at the Battle of Chelenko in 1887. Menelik warded off the danger of renewed religious sectarianism by including several members of the Emir's family in his new administration, which he headed with a Christian governor, Ras Mekonnen – the father of the future Emperor Haile Selassie.

Harar was regarded as the most important trading centre in Ethiopia in the late 19th century, but since 1902, when the Djibouti railway line was built, its commercial role has been secondary to that played by Dire Dawa. In some respects, modern Harar is destined always to play second fiddle to Dire Dawa, especially while Djibouti's significance as the closest Red Sea port to Addis Ababa is bolstered by the ongoing border closure with Eritrea. Nevertheless, Harar was still the third largest town in Ethiopia in 1968, and it remained the political capital of Hararge Province throughout the Haile Selassie and Derg eras. In the 1994 reshuffle of administrative regions, Harar, now the 11th largest city in Ethiopia, was accorded a disproportionate degree of autonomy when it was recognised as one of three federal city-states countrywide.

one hour in either direction. The bus and minibus station is outside the city walls, close to the Christian Market and the Harar Gate.

Where to stay
Moderate
Harar Ras Hotel (42 rooms) ☏ 025 6660027. Situated about 1km from the Harar Gate along the Dire Dawa road, this rather austere double-storey government hotel has no garden worth talking about and isn't up to the standard of its counterpart in Dire Dawa. Nevertheless, the recently renovated en-suite rooms are pretty good value at birr 125/162 sgl/dbl. Set menus in the restaurant cost birr 25.

Belayneh Hotel (22 rooms) ☏ 025 6663020. Consistently popular with both independent travellers and tour operators since it opened in 1995, this four-storey hotel has a superbly

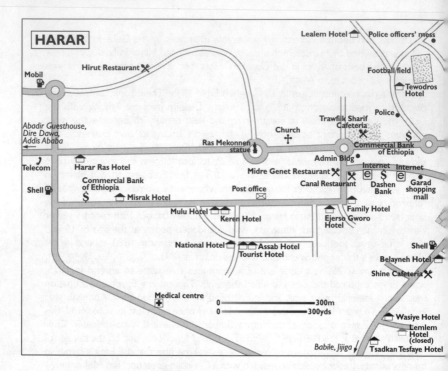

convenient location on the fringe of the walled city just 200m from the bus station, from where it is easily identified by the parasols on the roof. Unfortunately, it has capitalised on the steady custom generated by tour operators and guidebooks by repeatedly raising prices whilst letting services slide. The compact en-suite rooms with cold shower are among the cleanest in town, but at birr 115/138 for a dbl/twin, you'd think the management could splash out on a rooftop tank to counter the regular water cuts that afflict Harar – hot-water boilers would be a nice gesture too, come to think of it! The rooftop restaurant is no longer operational, but the ground-floor restaurant serves decent local and Western dishes.

Abadir Guesthouse (40 rooms) ☏ 025 6660721. This new hotel, which stands on the Dire Dawa road about 1km past the Ras, hasn't got the most ideal location for travellers dependent on public transport. But the large, slightly frayed-looking en-suite rooms do represent pretty good value at birr 60/80 sgl/dbl – what's more it's one of the few hotels in Harar with 24-hour running hot water.

Budget

Tewodros Hotel (23 rooms) ☏ 025 6660217. This long-standing backpackers' favourite is situated a short distance outside the Harar Gate, not far from the bus station, in a part of town regularly frequented by hyenas after dark. The rather dingy ground-floor rooms, using a common shower, seem overpriced for what they are at birr 25. Better value are the small but clean first-floor rooms with ¾ bed and en-suite cold shower at birr 50, and the similar rooms with hot shower at birr 70 (ask for rooms 15, 16, 117 or 118 and you are more than likely to see hyenas crossing the football pitch below from around 21.30 onwards). A good restaurant is attached, and the friendly resident guide is used to arranging excursions at affordable rates.

Tsadkan Tesfaye Hotel ☏ 025 6661546. Recommended in the previous edition, this double-storey hotel situated a few hundred metres from the bus station along the Jijiga road now seems poor value at birr 50 for a scruffy en-suite dbl!

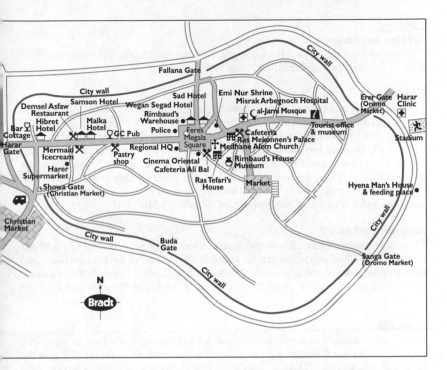

Shoestring

Lemlem Hotel This basic lodge situated out past the Tewodros Hotel has clean rooms using common shower for birr 15 as well as a few en-suite rooms with cold shower for birr 25–35 depending on size.

Ejerso Gworo Hotel The best of the sordid cluster of hotels in the new part of town within a few hundred metres of the post office. Huge en-suite rooms cost birr 25, and more basic rooms birr 10.

Misrak Hotel Also situated near the post office, this reasonably new hotel has clean rooms with a dbl bed at birr 15, common shower only.

Sad Hotel There are a few grotty and showerless hotels within the walled city – the Sad Hotel, situated on Feres Megala, may or may not be the pick of the bunch, but the location is ideal for those who want to soak up the nocturnal atmosphere of old Harar and the name is irresistibly to the point!

Where to eat

The restaurant at the **Tewodros Hotel** has been one of the best in Harar for some years now, and is popular with locals and travellers alike. The house speciality is roast chicken, which costs birr 15 per half bird and comes with an impressive array of condiments, but the menu is quite extensive. The **Ras Hotel** dishes up the usual government-hotel food at birr 25 for a set three-course menu. The restaurant at the **Belayneh Hotel** has a long varied menu, with most meals falling in the birr 10–15 range. The **Hirut Restaurant**, though not very central, serves good local meals at very reasonable prices.

Several pastry shops have sprung up in Harar in recent years. The pick is probably the **Canal Cafeteria**, which serves fresh fruit juice and pastries, and also stocks a fair range of imported sweets and biscuits. In the walled city, the **Cafeteria Ali Bal** is a great place to watch the passing show at Feres Megala over a pastry or coffee, and **Mermaid Ice Cream** for pastries and soft-serve ice cream cones.

Listings

Foreign exchange

The best option is the Dashen Bank out past the Christian Market, but the Commercial Bank of Ethiopia also has foreign-exchange facilities.

Guides

An official guide is not necessary to explore Harar, but most are very knowledgeable and you will get more from your initial foray into town if you go with a guide. This can be arranged through most of the hotels, or through the cultural centre/museum, and you will typically be asked birr 150 per day for their services. The young 'guides' who hang around Feres Megala and elsewhere accosting any passing *faranji* – or *faranjo* as they say locally – with an optimistic 'remember me?' are not generally very knowledgeable and they can be irritatingly banal conversationalists, but using the service of one such youngster will at least deflect the attention of the other children.

Internet and email

There are several internet cafés dotted around town, charging a uniform birr 0.40 per minute. A couple of good cafés can be found in the vicinity of the Dashen Bank, and there's another one on the Jijiga road past the Tsadkan Tesfaye Hotel. In the old town, the Harar Internet Café is situated just 20m from the Harar Museum and Cultural Centre.

Nightlife

Harar is well endowed with bars, several of which – rather unexpectedly – lie within the walled city. The **Bar Cottage**, with its organic banana-leaf walls, is almost as cosy as the name suggests, and the CD deck blares out a remarkably eclectic music selection. Also worth a try are the **GC Pub**, the bar at the **Samson Hotel,** and the line of bars on the main square. Outside of the walled city, the rowdy bar at the **Tourist Hotel** plays a mixture of reggae and Ethiopian music, and hosts live music on some nights. More reliable for live music is the nearby **National Hotel**, where a traditional band usually cranks into action at 22.00.

Tourist information

There is a tourist information office in the Harar Museum and Cultural Centre (*open wkdays only*). Anybody who arrives here in search of esoteric travel tips is likely to be disappointed, but it does sell a superb foldout colour map of Harar for birr 60.

Sightseeing

The prime attraction of Harar is the old walled city, which covers an area of about 60ha and supports an estimated population of 22,000 living in roughly 5,500 houses. Known locally as **Jugal**, the old town is enclosed by the 5m-high wall that effectively defined the full extent of Harar until the Italian occupation. Built in the 1560s by Sultan Nur, the wall hasn't changed shape significantly since that time, despite several renovations over the years. Five traditional gates lie along its 3.5km circumference, and two further gates were added during the rule of Menelik II and Haile Selassie, one of which was subsequently closed up during the Italian occupation.

On your first outing into the old town, it isn't a bad idea to take a guide to show you the major landmarks, but do negotiate a fee in advance. Once you have your bearings, it's more fun perhaps to wander around on your own and follow your nose. The old town is a fascinating place, far more than the sum of its landmarks – it boasts a rich sense of community, and every walk reveals new points of interest. You may also want to stop at the market, preferably in the afternoon when it's busiest, and perhaps look at a few of the curio shops in the area – they stock some interesting stuff and there's only the mildest pressure to do more than browse.

The normal first point of entry into the old town is the **Harar Gate**, also known as the Duke's Gate, a motor-friendly addition dating from the rule of Haile Selassie. This gate faces west and connects the Dire Dawa road through the new town to the main road through the old town. The other gate connecting the old and new towns is the **Showa Gate**, known in Harari as Asmaddin Beri, which adjoins the Christian Market opposite the bus station. The other four gates, running in anti-clockwise order from the Showa Gate are the **Buda Gate** (called Bedri Beri in Harari), the **Sanga Gate** (Sukutat Beri), **Erer Gate** (Argob Beri) and **Fallana Gate** (Assum Beri). In addition to the Amharigna and Harari names, every gate has a different name in Oromifa, Somali and Arabic. Although it is most convenient to enter the old town via the Harar or Showa gates, neither such approach has an impact comparable with arriving at the Buda Gate, from where a labyrinth of cobbled alleys flanked by traditional whitewashed stone houses winds uphill towards Feres Megala and Gidir Megala.

The walled city is roughly oblong in shape. The most important landmark within the walls, at least for orientation purposes, is the central square known as **Feres Megala** (literally 'Horse Market', though these days Peugeot Megala would be a more apt description), from which radiates a quintet of main (mostly motor-width) alleys leading to each of the gates. The main commercial road in the old town, lined with shops, bars and hotels, runs between Harar Gate and Feres Megala. Strung between these main thoroughfares is a web of atmospheric cobbled alleys, which are confusing to navigate at first, though the city is too small for you to go far without encountering a main road or obvious landmark.

Feres Megala is the obvious place to start any walking tour of Harar, and the best place to find a guide – assuming that one hasn't found you already. The square is lined with interesting old buildings. The hotel between the police station and the corner of the road to the Fallana Gate was formerly Gerazmatch House, built by the Egyptians and used as a warehouse by Rimbaud during the first year of his stay in Harar. Also on the main square lies the **Church of Medhane Alem**, built in 1890 on the site of a mosque constructed 15 years earlier by the unpopular Egyptian occupiers, and described by E Sylvia Pankhurst as 'a charming example of Ethiopian ecclesiastical architecture of the Menelik period'. The old town's main *chat* market lies on the southern verge of Feres Megala.

The road that runs east from the square next to the church leads to **Erer Gate**, which is where Richard Burton entered Harar. Erer Gate is the site of a colourful Oromo *chat* market, and it is also the closest gate to the site used by the hyena man. Outside the Erer Gate there stands an interesting Muslim cemetery comprising hundreds of graves, each of which is decorated by a unique and often very colorful painting. To get there from the gate, walk through the stadium, then after around 50m turn right where the road forks at a mosque, following an enclosed alley for about 300m until it terminates at the cemetery. One reader comments: 'This place is really amazing during sunsets and sunrises. We spent time there every evening just sitting in silence, listening to the prayers coming from the mosques and feeling this extraordinary spiritual atmosphere.'

Several points of interest lie along or off the road between the central square and Erer Gate, including the 16th-century domed **tomb of Emir Nur**, and a Catholic Mission that dates from the late 19th century. Also on this road is the **al-Jami Mosque**, which was founded in 1216 according to local tradition. The present-day building possesses at least one minaret dating to the 1760s, but otherwise it is architecturally undistinguished and looks to be no more than 50 years old. Further out towards the Erer Gate, the **Harar Museum and Cultural Centre** (*open wkdays only; entrance birr 10*) is worth visiting for its complete replica of an old Harari house.

RICHARD BURTON IN HARAR

The early European explorers of the African interior were, as a rule, prone to describing their 'discoveries' in somewhat hyperbolic terms – understandable, really, when you consider the risks and hardships they routinely endured en route. Perhaps the most noteworthy exception to this rule is the acerbic and unflattering description of Harar by Richard Burton, who, in 1855, became the first European to visit the most holy of Ethiopia's Islamic cities. Burton was not impressed, as the following edited extracts from his book *First Footsteps in Africa* make clear:

> An irregular wall, lately repaired, but ignorant of cannon, is pierced with five large gates, and supported by oval towers of artless construction. The only large building is the Jami or Cathedral, a long barn of poverty-stricken appearance, with broken down gates and two whitewashed minarets of truncated conoid shape. The streets are narrow lanes, up hill and down dale, strewed with gigantic rubbish heaps, upon which repose packs of mangy one-eyed dogs. There are no establishments for learning, no endowments, as generally in the east, and apparently no encouragement to students: books also are rare and costly.
>
> The Somali say of the city that it is a paradise inhabited by asses: certainly the exterior of the people is highly unprepossessing. Among the men, I did not see a handsome face: their features are course and debauched; many of them squint, others have lost an eye by smallpox, and they are disfigured by scrofula and other diseases. The bad expression of their countenances justifies the proverb 'Hard as the heart of Harar'.
>
> The government of Harar is the Amir. These petty princes have a habit of killing and imprisoning all those who are suspected of aspiring to the throne. The Amir Ahmed succeeded his father about three years ago. His rule is

Leading east from the main square, between the Cafeteria Ali Bal and Cinema Oriental, there is a narrow lane called **Mekina Girgir** (Machine Road) in reference to the sewing machines of the (exclusively male) street tailors who work there. Follow this lane for 150m and a left turn will bring you to **Ras Mekonnen's Palace**, said by some to date to the late 1890s and by others to 1910. Showing a clear Indian architectural influence, this house is said to be where Ras Tefari (the future Emperor Haile Selassie) spent much of his childhood, though I can find no outside confirmation of this local hearsay. Indeed, more reliable sources suggest that Ras Mekonnen built this palace for his close friend and ally Menelik II (who, as it transpired, never had occasion to visit Harar after its construction) and that Ras Tefari actually grew up in a double-storey house situated near Harar Mikael Church and the associated Tomb of Ras Mekonnen off the Jijiga road about 1.5km south of the walled town. Partially gutted during the Italian occupation, the former palace was restored as a museum and library in the early 1970s, and formally opened by Haile Selassie, but this venture evidently didn't survive the Derg – today, the house is occupied by a traditional herbal practitioner who, so the sign informs us, is able to cure anything from gastritis to cancer.

Next door to the former palace is the building referred to locally as Rambo's House – Rambo being Rimbaud, the house he is said to have rented when he lived in Harar. A vaguely Oriental double-storey building constructed by an Indian merchant, **Rimbaud's House** is architecturally notable for its frescoed ceiling (which locals say was painted by the poet) and offers great views over the town. But it's questionable whether Rimbaud ever rented the place. So far as I can ascertain, the house was built in 1908, a full 17 years

severe if not just. Ahmed's principal occupations are spying on his many stalwart cousins, indulging in vain fears of the English, the Turks and the Hajj Sharmarkay, and amassing treasure by commerce and escheats.

He judges civil and religious causes in person. The punishments, when money forms no part of them, are mostly according to Koranic code. The murderer is placed in the market street, blindfolded, and bound hand and foot: the nearest of kin to the deceased then strikes his neck with a sharp and heavy butcher's knife, and the corpse is given over to the relations for Muslim burial. When a citizen draws dagger upon another or commits any petty offence, he is bastinadoed in a peculiar manner: two men ply their horsewhips upon his back and breast, and the prince, in whose presence the punishment is carried out, gives order to stop. Theft is punished by amputation of the hand.

Harar is essentially a commercial town: its citizens live, like those of Zayla, by systematically defrauding the Galla Badawin, and the Amir has made it a penal offence to buy by weight and scale. The citizens seem to have a more than Asiatic apathy, even in pursuit of gain. When we entered, a caravan was set out for Zayla on the morrow, after ten days, hardly half of its number had mustered.

Harar is still, as of old, the great 'halfway house' for slaves from Zangaro, Gurage and the Galla tribes. Abyssinians and Amharas, the most valued, have become rare since the King of Showa prohibited the exportation. Women vary in value from 100 to 400 Ashfaris, boys from 9 to 150: the worst are kept for domestic purposes, the best are driven by the Western Arabs or the subjects of the Imam of Muskat, in exchange for rice and dates. I need scarcely say that commerce would thrive on the decline of slavery: whilst the Falateas or manrazzias are allowed to continue, it is vain to expect industry in the land.

after Rimbaud's untimely death in France, caused by complications resulting from the amputation of an infected leg. Even if the timing is flawed, it is conceivable that Rimbaud did once live in an older house on the same site, but more likely the association stems from the house having been featured in a movie about the poet's life.

Restored with the help of the Italian and French embassies and various other organisations, Rimbaud's House now functions as a museum. The ground-floor displays, dedicated to the poet, are arguably of marginal interest, with the exception of a couple of photographs taken during his stay in Harar. Far more compelling is the first-floor collection of turn-of-the-20th-century photographs of Harar. Providing a fascinating perspective on the modern development of the town, this collection disproves any talk of unchanging Harar. The plain, one-storey, flat-roofed mud dwellings of the period bear less resemblance to anything seen here today than they do to houses found in some parts of the west African Sahel (or for that matter to the Argobba houses at nearby Koremi). Likewise, the traditional 'ball' hairstyles and plain robes worn by the women of Harar a century ago have now all but vanished in favour of more generic Ethiopian braided hairstyles and bright, colourful dresses. Also of interest are photographs of Medhane Alem Church while it was under construction, and Erer and Fallana gates before they crumbled away. Excellent stuff – all the better if you're fortunate enough to be led around by the articulate and erudite curator Shakib Ahmed!

Heading back to Mekina Girgir, a short walk downhill leads you to the **Gidir Megala** (Grand Market), which is also sometimes referred to as the Muslim Market to distinguish it from its Christian and Oromo counterparts outside the city walls. One of the liveliest urban markets in Ethiopia, particularly on Saturdays, the market is today dominated by a rather monolithic Italian-era building. On the east side of the market, the whitewashed **Tomb of Sheik Said Ali Hamdogn**, an early leader of Harar, stands above a subterranean water source that can reputedly meet the needs of the whole town in time of drought. Immediately north of this stands the former Egyptian Bank.

Ask your guide to show you the inside of a **traditional Harar house**, about 100 of which still survive more or less intact, including one said to have been built for Emir Yusuf in the 18th century. As viewed from the outside, the houses of Harar are unremarkable rectangular blocks occasionally enlivened by an old carved door. But the design of the interiors is totally unique to the town. The ground floor has an open plan, and is dominated by a carpet-draped raised area where all social activity (ie: chewing *chat*) takes place. The walls are decorated with small niches and dangling items of crockery, including the famed Harar baskets, some of which are hundreds of years old. Above the main door are grilles from where carpets are hung to indicate there is a daughter of marriageable age in the family. When the carpets come down, newlyweds in Harar take residence in a tiny corner cell, where they spend their first week of wedlock in cramped, isolated revelry, all they might need being passed to them by relatives through a small service window.

Sprawling in a broadly westerly direction from the old city walls, the so-called **new town**, much of which dates to the Italian era, supports the majority of Harar's total population of around 100,000, but holds little of interest to tourists. The **Christian Market** outside Showa Gate is worth a look, bustling as it is with mostly Oromo vendors who've come in from the villages for the day. For students of colonial architecture, the Italian-built **town hall** a block away from the Harar Gate is a rather impressive example of the genre, while art enthusiasts might want to inspect the **Statue of Ras Mekonnen**, cast in bronze by the renowned local artist Afewerk Tekle, between the town centre and the Ras Hotel. Further out of town, about 5km along the Jijiga road and reached easily by shared taxi, the church and cemetery at Deker offer a good view over the walled city (best for photography in the afternoon).

Should the historical sightseeing start to wear you out, a worthwhile and somewhat more thirst-quenching excursion is to the **Harar Beer Factory**, which opened in 1984 and can be reached in ten minutes on foot from the Christian Market using a shortcut. The best time to go is in the morning (08.00–11.00), when the general manager is in his office and can arrange a half-hour tour of the factory and possibly free souvenirs such as a T-shirt and baseball cap. After that, you can retire to the factory club, which has DSTV, the cheapest beer in town, and reasonably priced hot meals.

The hyena man

One of Harar's most enduringly popular attractions is its resident hyena man. There are currently two hyena men, a pair of nutters who make their living by feeding wild hyenas, thereby providing proof (were any needed) that Ethiopians are capable of perversity far beyond the call of duty. Exactly how and when this bizarre practice arose is an open question. One story is that it started during the great famine of the 1890s, during which, it is said, the people of Harar fed the starving hyenas in an altogether less deliberate way. Most other sources indicate that it is a more modern phenomenon, probably no more than 50 years old. So far as I'm aware, the earliest written account of the hyena man was published in a 1958 edition of the *Ethiopian Observer*. I have also recently received a letter from long-time Ethiophile Harry Atkins, who says: 'I was in Harar in 1949 and there was no hyena man; on another visit in 1959 he was there.' This dating would appear to be confirmed by one of incumbent hyena men, Yusuf Pepe, who told me that he is the fifth in line, and that the practice was started by a man called Dozo in the 1950s.

In 1990, Ahmed Zekaria of the Institute of Ethiopian Studies wrote an essay indicating that the practice of feeding hyenas may be loosely rooted in a much older annual ceremony called Ashura, which takes place in Harar on 7 Muhharam (normally 9 July). According to the tradition related by Zekaria, the festival dates back to a famine many centuries ago, which forced the wild hyenas in the hills around Harar to attack livestock and even people. The people of Harar decided to feed the hyenas porridge to stave off their hunger, and after the famine ended they renewed their pact annually by leaving out a bowl of porridge covered in rich butter near Abobker shrine during the Ashura Festival. It is said that the hyenas' reaction to the porridge is a portent for the year ahead. If they eat more than half of the porridge, then the year ahead will be bountiful, but if they refuse to eat, or they eat the lot, then famine or pestilence is predicted. The practice of feeding meat to the hyenas on a daily basis is obviously quite a leap from an annual feeding ceremony involving porridge, but the Ashura Festival does indicate that the performance of the modern hyena man is rooted in a more ancient custom.

As something of a footnote to the above, Paul Clammer writes: 'Ashura commemorates the death of Hussein, grandson of the Prophet Mohammed, at the Battle of Kerbala in AD680. This battle created an ongoing schism between the two strands of Islam – those who thought the successor to Mohammed should be elected and those who favoured the hereditary claims of Hussein. The former won the battle and went on to form the majority Sunni branch of Islam, while the losers now form the numerically smaller Shia branch, which commemorates the martyrdom of Hussein at the Ashura Festival. All well and good, but Ethiopia's Muslims are exclusively Sunni and thus don't recognise Ashura, which means that whatever link exists between Ashura and the feeding of hyenas in Harar must be obscure and interesting indeed.'

However and whenever it started, a visit to the hyena man will rank as a highlight of any visit to Harar. Having seen plenty of hyenas in less contrived proximity, I must confess that I first went with a fair degree of scepticism. To my surprise, I ended up greatly enjoying the atmospheric spectacle, which starts at around 19.00, and takes place at one of two feeding sites outside the walled city: these are the shrine of Aw Anser Ahmed (between Erer and Sanga gates) and the Christian Slaughterhouse (outside Fallana Gate). The ritual is that the hyena man starts calling the hyenas by name, then, after ten minutes or so, the animals appear from the shadows. Timid at first, the hyenas are soon eating bones passed to them by hand, and the hyena man teases them and even passes them bones from his mouth (visitors are invited to do the same thing).

Some reservations should be voiced regarding the wisdom of feeding hyenas. Hyenas skulk around the fringes of many African towns. Under normal circumstances they are far too timid for there to be a serious likelihood of them attacking people, but nevertheless they are Africa's second largest predator and potentially very dangerous. Hand-feeding a hyena is, in essence, habituating it – or in plainer English, making it lose its fear of people. In *A Far Country*, a book based on a visit to Ethiopia in 1988, Philip Marsden-Smedley reports that, on the very day he was in Harar, a hyena mauled an Oromo woman close to town. The hyena was shot and Marsden-Smedley, at the time unwittingly, watched the hyena men feed its carcass to its companions.

Most people organise to see the hyena man through a guide. The rate is to some extent negotiable, but will generally be from birr 30–50 per person, depending on group size, with an additional charge for a taxi and the guide. The taxi isn't strictly necessary – the hyena man operates barely 100m outside of the city walls – but the headlights are useful for seeing the hyenas in the dark, and having seen a hyena's jaw in close-up action, you may be glad of the protection when you head back into town. If you prefer not to use a guide, you can make advance arrangements directly with the man himself for birr 30–50 per head. Head out of the walled city through Erer Gate and turn right along the road that runs along the outside of the city wall, passing the Harar Clinic, a mosque and a small stadium to your left. After about 300m, on the left side of the road, you'll see Aw Ansar Ahmed Shrine, a whitewashed edifice intertwined with the trunk and roots of a large fig tree. Yusuf Pepe, the hyena man, lives in the house right next to the shrine, and will set up a feeding session with a couple of hours' notice.

Excursions from Harar
Aweday and Alemaya
The small towns of Aweday and Alemaya are situated along the Dire Dawa road some 6km and 21km from Harar respectively. The former is renowned as the site of the country's largest *chat* market, where copious amounts of eastern Ethiopia's finest are sold for distribution to Addis Ababa and elsewhere. Alemaya, by contrast, is of interest mainly for the eponymous lake that flanks the Dire Dawa road on its northern outskirts – the most southerly and accessible of a chain of freshwater bodies that also includes Lakes Adele, Hora Jutu and Finkile. When full, Lake Alemaya often supports considerable concentrations of greater and lesser flamingo, as well as large numbers of white pelican, avocet, black-tailed godwit, and up to 10,000 red-knobbed coots. Until recent years, the lake was at its best during the European winter, when a profusion of migrant waterfowl and waders boosted the resident birds. Since the late 1990s, however, Alemaya has tended to drain completely during the dry season, the start of which more or less coincides with the arrival of Palaearctic migrants to east Africa. Any vehicle heading between Harar and Dire Dawa can drop you at Aweday or Alemaya.

Ejerso Gworo
Situated high in the mountains some 25km northeast of Harar as the crow flies, the village of Ejerso Gworo is known primarily as the birthplace of Ras Tefari Mekonnen on 23 July 1892. The future emperor's parents Ras Mekonnen and his wife Yeshimebet had been unfortunate with their previous children, so they deliberately chose Ejerso Gworo for the occasion, in accordance with an ancient Ethiopian belief that the chance of a problematic birth decreases at a higher altitude. Surprisingly, perhaps, there is no obvious shrine at Ejerso Gworo to commemorate the birth of Haile Selassie – the last emperor did at one point consider renaming the village Bethlehem, but eventually he settled on constructing a church dedicated to Kidane Mihret there. En route to Ejerso Gworo, the road from Harar passes through the somewhat larger town of Kombolcha, which is known for its bustling daily *chat* market, the surrounding green countryside studded with rustic Oromo villages, and an immense cavern in the surrounding farmland.

In a private vehicle, Ejerso Gworo can easily be visited as a day trip out of Harar – expect the drive to take up to 90 minutes in either direction. There is no shortage of public transport covering the 18km road between Harar and Kombolcha, and a few basic lodges to choose from should you want to overnight there. Transport on to Ejerso Gworo is rather more erratic, but you shouldn't have to wait for an indecently long time, and there is at least one basic hotel there should the need arise.

Koremi
The clifftop village of Koremi, situated some 17km southeast of Harar, is reputedly one of the oldest settlements in this part of Ethiopia – indeed, some locals claim that it actually predates Harar. Legend has it that Koremi's founder was a north African refugee and holy man named Amir Abu Bukkah, who led his followers to Ethiopia via Yemen and Somalia circa AD1130. Known locally as the Argobba (which translates more or less as 'Arrivals'), the refugees settled briefly at Deker, 5km from present-day Harar along the Jijiga road, but were made to feel unwelcome there and eventually moved further south to what is now Koremi. According to this legend, the antecedents of the Harari people later

migrated to the area from the vicinity of present-day Awash National Park and forged a good relationship with the Argobba, with whom they founded the city of Harar.

Today, the Argobba inhabit much of the hilly country immediately southeast of Harar, where they use sophisticated methods of terracing to grow cash crops such as coffee and *chat*. They share a common religion with their Harari neighbours, and they also speak the same language, albeit with an accent sufficiently different for any local to know the difference. Strongly traditional, with a general appearance similar to that of the Oromo, the Argobba are renowned for the beauty of their women, who certainly tend to be a striking apparition as they stroll through the countryside adorned by colourful robes, beaded jewellery and braided hair. They are also known for their 'double-faced' clothing, which can be worn either way around – the colourful side is reserved for weddings and other festive occasions, the black side for funerals.

Boasting an imperious clifftop setting chosen for its defensibility, Koremi is a labyrinthine conglomeration of a few dozen tightly packed stone houses, most if not all of which are many hundreds of years old. The interiors are similar to the traditional homesteads of Harar, with the main difference being that they remain unplastered and unpainted, while the rectangular stone exteriors, reminiscent of some Tigraian houses, collectively evoke what Harar itself must have looked like in Burton's day. The views from Koremi are stunning, stretching for miles across the plains to Mount Gendebure in the vicinity of Kombolcha.

Accessible only in a private vehicle or on foot, Koremi can be reached by following the Jijiga road out of Harar as far as Deker, where you need to turn right onto a rough and easily missed 4x4 track. After about 8.5km you pass through the tiny but delightfully named settlement called Hajifaj, in memory of an 18th-century holy man whose tomb stands in Harar. Hajifaj is the site of an important local market every Monday and Friday, when there may be some public transport there from Deker. Koremi lies another 4km past Hajifaj, passing a striking balancing rock formation immediately to your right about three-quarters of the way there. No formal facilities for tourism exist at Koremi, so it is advisable to take a guide from Harar to ensure all goes smoothly.

Babile and the Valley of Marvels

The small town of Babile, which straddles the Jijiga road about 30km east of Harar, gives its name not only to a popular brand of bottled sparkling water but also to Ethiopia's only elephant sanctuary. Ironically, however, the sparkling water is now bottled at a factory in Harar, which also forms the most logical base from which to visit the eponymous elephant sanctuary (see box *Babile Elephant Sanctuary*, pages 410–11). Babile does host a busy general market on Saturdays, as well as an important camel market on Mondays and Thursdays, but the main point of local interest is the so-called Valley of Marvels, which is traversed by the Jijiga road 5–10km east of town.

A desolate landscape of red earth, low acacia scrub, forbidding cacti and tall chimney-like termite mounds, the Valley of Marvels is renowned for its gravity-defying balancing rock formations, most especially Dakata Rock, which appears to be just one puff away from collapse. The rock lies close to the Jijiga road, about 7km past Babile, so the best idea is to catch a bus to Jijiga and ask to be dropped at Dakata (marked by a few stalls). A good trail starts at the telegraph pole with '36+600' written vertically down it. Inhabited by colourful Oromo pastoralists, the Dakata area also hosts a fair bit of wildlife, most visibly warthog and Hamadryas baboon, but various antelope and the occasional lion and hyena are also seen. The dry-country birdlife is terrific.

Coming from Harar, it is easy enough to get to the Valley of Marvels and back in a day using public transport, since minibuses between Harar and Babile only take an hour. You could also stop at the valley en route between Harar and Jijiga. Alternatively, a few basic hotels can be found in Babile, none of which charges more than birr 10 for a room – the Samson Hotel on the Harar side of town looks about the best.

BABILE ELEPHANT SANCTUARY

With thanks to Yirmed Demeke of the Institute of Biodiversity Conservation

The arid country to the south of Harar supports an isolated and somewhat vulnerable elephant population afforded nominal protection in the Babile Elephant Sanctuary, which extends over roughly 7,000km² between the Gobelle River about 30km south of Harar and the Fafen River southwest of Jijiga. Some authorities assign the elephants of Babile to a unique race *Loxodonta africana orleansi*, partially on the basis of their small tusks – though, given that reduced tusk size is a predictable feature of any elephant subpopulation that has suffered selective poaching for ivory, further molecular and morphological analysis will be required to determine the validity of this taxonomic distinction. Either way, following their probable extinction in Somalia, this is the last extant elephant population to occur in the eastern Horn of Africa, and it must thus be regarded as a high conservation priority. The sanctuary also provides refuge to the black-maned Abyssinian lion, various antelope including greater and lesser kudu, the striking Hamadryas baboon, and a spectacular selection of dry-country birds, including the endemic Salvadori's Serin.

Despite the establishment of the sanctuary in 1962, the range of this isolated elephant population is thought to have shrunk by about 65% in the last 20 years, with the part of the sanctuary east of the Dakata River having been abandoned some 15 years ago. Meanwhile, the population has halved from an estimated 300 individuals in the 1970s to a minimum of 148 elephants today. According to the rangers, however, the current tally does represent a significant increase on a mid 1990s estimate of around 75 individuals, a suggestion supported by the high proportion of calves (including a full 16 yearlings) counted in 2004–05. The elephants are sustained by seasonal movements between the Erer and Gobelle river valleys, and some travels were also noted to the west bank of the Dakata River during the transitional period of movement between these valleys. The elephants sometimes move outside the sanctuary, particularly to the western ridge of the Gobelle Valley for an average of 12 km, about 17km north of the sanctuary following the Gobelle and Hamaresa valleys, and to a part of the upper Erer Valley some 12km outside its northern boundary.

The best time of year to seek out the elephants is from mid November to early March, when they congregate in the part of the Upper Gobelle Gorge that runs through Fedis District, about an hour's drive south of Harar. To get there, from Harar town, follow the Dire Dawa road out of town for about 2km, and then turn onto the Fedis road, which branches to the left about 500m past the Abadir Guesthouse and immediately in front of a large green mosque opposite a Total garage. After about 24km, you pass through the small town of Boku, capital of Fedis District (and often just referred to as Fedis), from where you need to continue driving for another 6–22km, depending on where the elephants are currently hanging out. If you are fortunate, you might find a herd resting under the ficus sycamore trees on the close rim of the gorge. If not, you will need to trek to the valley floor. This is a steep hike that requires a fair level of agility and takes about 30 minutes in either direction, but it comes with a near certainty of spotting elephants between December and

JIJIGA

The self-styled capital of Somali region, Jijiga is a reasonably large town (population 40,000) situated 106km east of Harar along a decent gravel road. On first contact, the town must be classed a disappointment – despite its status as regional capital, Jijiga comes across as just another medium-sized lowland town with a less perceptible Somali feel

February, particularly at around 06.00–11.00 and 16.00–18.00 when the animals are most active. Security was a problem in this area a couple of years back; this no longer seems to be the case but you might want to ask around before heading this way.

The other good time of year to look for the elephants is between June and September, when they are concentrated in the Upper Erer Valley to the southeast of Harar. There are two motorable tracks to this area, one of which branches south from the Harar–Jijiga road at Bisidimo, 18km out of Harar, while the other branches south about 17km closer to Babile. Both tracks lead to the 'Menschen for Menschen' compound, from where you must drive another 6km south before you disembark. It can take up to 90 minutes to hike into the valley, but the walk is not difficult because there is no gorge. The vegetation in this area is very thick and the disturbance level by cattle herders is high, so the elephants tend to lurk in the densest acacia-cactus vegetation in the heat of the day, when they can be difficult to locate – and are prone to aggressive behaviour when surprised. The chance of seeing the elephants is highest in the evening and early morning, when they are most mobile (and it is also less likely you will startle them by stumbling on them at close quarters).

Assuming that you have access to a 4x4 (hireable through any guide in Harar), the biggest obstacle to visiting Babile Elephant Sanctuary at present is the daft bureaucratic logistics. In order to visit the sanctuary, you must first check in at the office to pick up the mandatory game scout (without whose assistance you would be unlikely to locate any elephants) and to pay the associated fee of birr 50 per party. Unfortunately, this office is situated in Babile, 30km east of Harar in the opposite direction to the Gobelle Gorge, which enforces quite a bit of unnecessary driving on prospective visitors, especially during the dry season. Furthermore, because the office is open from 08.30 to 17.00 only, and the best time to seek out the elephants is in the early morning, you will probably need to drive out to Babile the day before you want to visit the sanctuary to pick up the scout and take him with you to sleep in Harar (which can be arranged for an extra birr 50). The office doesn't have a phone, but another possibility would be to ask the Ethiopian Wildlife Department in Addis Ababa (❨ 011 5514183) to radio through to arrange for a scout to meet you in Harar. Either way, the well-hidden office in Babile lies about 200m along an unsignposted side road running north from the main Harar–Jijiga road almost directly opposite the 'Bank of Abyssinia 557km' signboard – if in doubt try asking for zihon bero (elephant keepers' office).

The good news is that there's serious talk of relocating the sanctuary office from Babile to Harar, or at least opening a sub-office and posting some scouts in Harar, and this will possibly happen as soon as 2006. It is also possible that old tracks leading right into the elephants' territory will be repaired, so that they can be sought by vehicle rather than on foot. There is no accommodation in the reserve and it can easily be visited as a day trip out of Harar, but camping in both valleys is possible provided you are careful and take guards from the sanctuary office and possibly militia. Unless you already have a vehicle or are prepared to rent one, the sanctuary is inaccessible on public transport – the closest you could get is Boku, which has a couple of basic lodges and is passed through by elephants once in a blue moon, but the odds of that happening during a one-off visit are as good as zero.

than you might expect or hope for. That perception might change, however, when you are confronted by the town's focal point: a vast sprawling market, of interest not so much for any traditional goods, but rather for secondhand and electronic goods that have fallen off the back of Somalia (more accurately, the yet-to-be-officially-recognised state of Somaliland, with which Jijiga has close trade links).

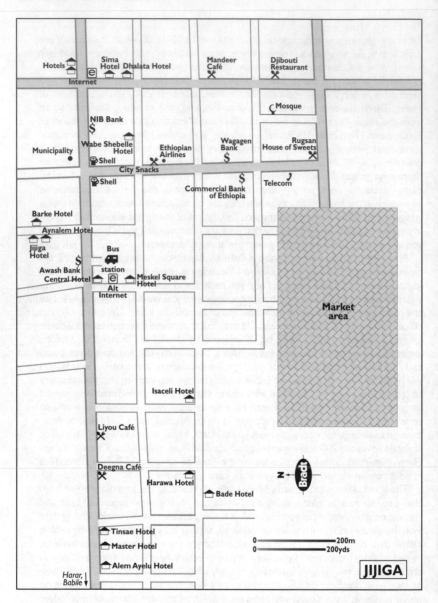

Further in its favour, Jijiga, prone as it is to periodic influxes of aid workers, boasts an unexpectedly cosmopolitan feel, as reflected in the high standard of hotels, restaurants and other facilities – all of which is worth knowing should you happen to be posted there by an aid organisation, but probably doesn't add up to a very convincing reason to visit out of choice. Indeed, the best thing about Jijiga is arguably the drive there from Harar, which passes through the spectacular Valley of Marvels outside Babile (see page 409) and the impressive and well-wooded Karamara Mountains (the latter reputedly unsafe to climb due to the presence of landmines, a relic of a clash between Ethiopian and Somali forces in the 1970s).

Getting there and away

The only realistic overland approach to Jijiga is the road from Harar, which takes two-and-a-bit hours to cover in a private vehicle. A few buses daily run between Harar and Jijiga, taking four to five hours in either direction. Ethiopian Airlines also flies to Jijiga regularly from Addis Ababa via Dire Dawa. Note that tensions between various Somali factions based around Jijiga occasionally run high, and spates of banditry are not unknown. Things had been quiet for some years when this edition was researched, and there's no reason why tourists should be at greater risk than the locals who bus back and forth from Harar daily. All the same, it would be advisable to ask local advice about the security situation before heading out this way.

Where to stay

Bade Hotel (30 rooms) ☎ 025 7752841. Situated on a back road about 500m from the bus station and two blocks from the main Harar road, this is the best hotel in Jijiga, offering comfortable accommodation in large clean rooms with a proper dbl bed, TV and en-suite hot shower for birr 75. A good restaurant is attached.

Alem Ayelu Hotel ☎ 025 7752814. Set alongside the Harar road 500m west of the bus station, this pleasant hotel seems fair value at birr 35 for a dbl with en-suite cold showers.

Master Hotel Set alongside the Alem Ayelu, this acceptable hotel seems relatively overpriced at birr 50 for an en-suite room with ³/₄ bed or birr 30 for a similar room using the common shower.

Meskel Square Hotel This looks about the best of a dozen or so budget hotels clustered within a block of the bus station, most of which have rooms for around birr 15.

Where to eat

The town centre is studded with local eateries, of which the **Djibouti Restaurant** and **City Snacks & Café** are both worth a try. For Western fare, the best option is the **Bade Hotel**. More noteworthy than all of these is the remarkable **Rugsan Café**, which wouldn't look out of place on the Piazza in Addis Ababa – it serves good cakes, sandwiches, burgers, juice and coffee, as well as stocking a bumper selection of imported crisps, biscuits and chocolates.

Part Five

Southern Ethiopia

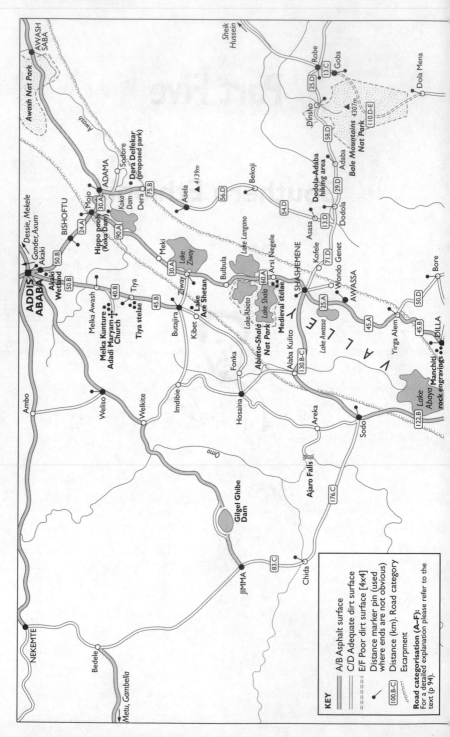

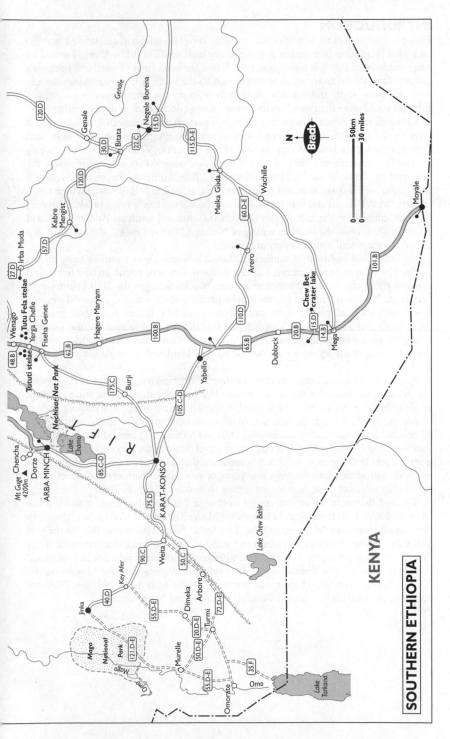

SOUTHERN ETHIOPIA

KENYA

N

Bradt

0   50km
0   30 miles

Genale

Bitata

Negele Borena

Genale

120.D

30.D

22.C

15.D

115.D-E

Wachille

60.D-E

Moyale

101.B

Kebre Mengist

Irba Muda

57.D

120.D

Melka Guda

Arero

Chew Bet crater lake

Mega

27.D

Wenago

Tutu Fela stelae

Yerga Chefie

Fiseha Genet

48.B

Tututi stelae

62.B

Hagere Maryam

100.B

110.D

65.B

Dublock

20.B

15.D

14.B

Burji

175.C

Yabello

105.C-D

Mt Guge
Chencha
4200m

Dorze

ARBA MINCH

Lake Chamo

Nechisas Nat Park

RIFT

85.C-D

KARAT-KONSO

75.D

Lake Chew Bahir

Key Afer

90.C

Weita

50.C

40.D

Jinka

55.D-E

Dimeka

20.D-E

Turmi

72.D-E

Arbore

121.D-E

Murelle

50.D-E

55.D-E

35.F

Omorate

Omo

Lake Turkana

Mago
Mago National Park

Omo

INTRODUCTION

Ethiopia is not one of the world's more crowded travel destinations, and while I have no idea what proportion of travellers to the country head south of Addis Ababa, I would be surprised to learn that it is more than 10%. Given the singularity of northern Ethiopia's cultural sites, the relatively scant attention paid to the south is understandable enough. And yet, were north and south to split into separate countries tomorrow, southern Ethiopia could more than stand on its feet as a tourist destination in its own right.

Although most African countries pale by comparison with southern Ethiopia when it comes to historical sightseeing – rock-hewn churches, mysterious medieval stelae and remote monasteries being among its underrated attractions – the region is of primary interest for its natural and cultural attractions. Bale National Park is unquestionably the best part of Ethiopia for viewing endemic wildlife, home to the country's largest populations of Ethopian wolf and mountain nyala, as well as half the birds whose range is restricted to Ethiopia and Eritrea. In addition, there is the lovely string of lakes that dots the Rift Valley floor, the lush forests of Wondo Genet and southern Bale, the vast arid plains south of Dilla, the majestic setting of Nechisar National Park... this, in short, is a region of exceptional natural beauty and variety.

Culturally, the highlight of southern Ethiopia is South Omo, a remote zone tucked against the Kenyan border where a dozen or more different ethnic groups live – and decorate themselves – in a manner that scarcely acknowledges the 20th century ever happened. No less interesting are the Konso people and their walled stone villages, the Dorze with their tall conical huts, and the semi-nomadic Borena with their precious cattle herds and singing wells. Tangled into this rich cultural mosaic are the Oromo, Ethiopia's largest ethno-linguistic group, with one foot in the modern world, and the other hoisting them up on to the saddle to ride blanketed through the frosty Bale Highlands.

Southern Ethiopia lacks for any clearly defined tourist circuit, and – unlike the regions covered in other sections in this book – it would be limiting rather than helpful to attempt to describe it in terms of a prescribed loop. The main regional transport hub is Shashemene, which lies at the junction of the roads north to Addis Ababa, west to Arba Minch and South Omo, south to Awassa, Dilla and Moyale, and east to Dodola and Bale. Passing through Shashemene, it is possible to travel between the area covered in any one given chapter in this section and that covered in another. For this reason, I have attempted to divide this section into chapters that more or less define themselves as travel units, rather than sequence them in terms of getting from one place to another.

The first chapter in this section covers an obscure but rewarding route running south from Addis Ababa to Butajira and Hosaina via Melka Kunture Prehistoric Site, the rock-hewn church of Adadi Maryam, and the Tiya Stelae Field. The second follows the Rift Valley and its lakes from Addis Ababa south to the junction town of Shashemene and city of Awassa. The third covers the wonderful trekking country and wildlife of Bale National Park and environs. The fourth covers the road from Awassa south to Moyale on the Kenyan Border. The fifth chapter concentrates on Arba Minch and Nechisar National Park, and the sixth on the cultural wonders of Konso and South Omo.

Addis Ababa to the Rift Valley via Butajira

The 125km road between Addis Ababa and Butajira provides access to a string of fascinating and very different archaeological and historical sites, as well as forming an attractive springboard for travel elsewhere in the southern Rift Valley. The main points of interest along this road are the archaeological site of Melka Kunture, the rock-hewn church of Adadi Maryam, and the stelae field at Tiya. South of Butajira, along the road towards Sodo, lie several more isolated stelae, as well as the crater lake of Areshetan and the remote Ajaro Falls. While these places are under-publicised and little visited by comparison with the more famous sites of northern Ethiopia, and admittedly less overwhelming, I would rate the time I spent exploring them as among the highlights of my Ethiopian travels.

Any of the low-key historical sites between Addis Ababa and Butajira would make for a straightforward day trip from the capital, especially since the new asphalt road between Addis Ababa and Butajira opened in 2004. The same road can also be covered as part of a slower and more scenic route between the capital and Lake Ziway in the Rift Valley. With an early start and a private vehicle, you could see all the key sites along the Butajira road and still reach Ziway in one day. An extra day would be required to do the same thing on public transport.

From Butajira, a 100km road continues southward to Hosaina, reaching Sodo on the main asphalt road between Addis Ababa and Arba Minch after another 96km. Seldom used by travellers, this road already forms a viable route between Addis Ababa and Sodo as things stand. It seems likely to gain popularity as a genuine shortcut between Addis Ababa and South Omo once the new asphalt road to Butajira is extended all the way to Hosaina and eventually to Sodo, an eagerly anticipated development locally, and one for which funding has already been secured.

ADDIS ABABA TO BUTAJIRA

To get to any of the places covered below, you must follow the Jimma road out of Addis Ababa for 20km to Alem Gena, where the unsignposted road south to Butajira branches to the left. The distance from Alem Gena to Butajira is roughly 105km: the road reaches Melka Awash after 30km, passes the turn-off to Adadi Maryam after another 5km, and runs through Tiya after a further 35km. Regular public transport connects Addis Ababa to Butajira, leaving from the main Autobus Terra. There is direct transport to Melka Awash and Tiya before 09.00, but later in the day you may have to pay full fare on a bus to Butajira and ask to be dropped. Once on the Butajira road, you may sometimes have to wait a while for transport, as passing buses will often be full, but this situation is likely to improve as the volume of traffic increases following the asphalting of the road.

Melka Awash and Melka Kunture

Also known as Awash Dilday, Melka Awash is a small town on the north bank of the Awash River, some 50km from Addis Ababa by road. It is a good base from which to explore the nearby sites, provided that you can live with very basic accommodation. The Awash River Gorge below the bridge adjoining Melka Awash is also worth exploring. Immediately east of the bridge, at the start of the gorge, the river forms a series of three low but powerful waterfalls, the last of which has a wild, swirling pool at its base and is best viewed from the footpath along the northern rim. Also on the north of the gorge are some substantial patches of acacia woodland, which together with the raptors and swallows circling above the cliffs promise rewarding birdwatching.

The main local attraction is the Melka Kunture Prehistoric Site, which is situated on the south face of the Awash River Gorge opposite Melka Awash. Regarded to be one of the most important Stone-Age sites in Ethiopia, Melka Kunture's potential was first recognised in 1963 by G Dekker, who realised that the layers of rock washed away by the river during the annual floods represented a fossil record covering more than a million years. The first major excavations at the site took place over the period 1965–81, and further excavations occurred over 1991–95. Until recently, the site was closed to casual visitors, but an informative site museum now charges an entrance fee of birr 10 per person, and the curator is usually delighted to welcome a few visitors to his lonely patch!

Melka Kunture is best known for the numerous Stone-Age artefacts that have been unearthed along the river, including a variety of cleavers, hand-axes and other tools made from basalt and other hard rocks. The site has also proved to be an important source of fossils of extinct mammal species, including hippo, giraffe, gelada and wildebeest, the latter long absent from Ethiopia. Although the site has not yet thrown up any hominid fossils as significant as those unearthed at Hadar or Turkana, several *Homo erectus* fossils have been found, dating back between 1.5 and 1.7 million years. Cranial fragments of early *Homo sapiens*, probably more than 500,000 years old, have also been uncovered.

Situated downstream of the bridge at a bend in the river referred to in Oromifa as Dubatu, a vast complex of artificial caves corresponds closely with a mysterious site visited by Francisco Alvares in 1523 but not identified again until the early 1970s, when Richard Pankhurst wrote an article about it for the *Ethiopia Observer* (Vol XVI, No 1). Alvares describes a 'very strong' town set in 'a very deep hollow... upon a great river, which made a great chasm' that consisted almost entirely of houses carved into the cliff face with an entrance the size of 'the mouth of a large vat' but 'so large inside that 20 or 30 persons could find room there with their baggage'. Alvares was told that the caves were originally carved by the Gurage, 'a people (as they say) who are very bad, and none of them are slaves, because they say that they let themselves die, or kill themselves, rather than serve Christians'. When he visited, however, the town had been taken over by Christians who had built 'small walled and thatched houses' in the hollow, as well as 'a very good church inside'. In addition, Alvares describes what is evidently a rock-hewn monastery on a cliff further upstream, built on a crag that 'faces the rising sun', and above which were carved 'fifteen cells for monks, all of which have windows over the water'. According to Pankhurst, the vast caves described by Alvares, though long abandoned, can still be entered today, while the disused monastery lies nearby at a place called Wagide.

To get to Melka Kunture, follow the Butajira road southwards from Addis Ababa for about 50km until you reach Melka Awash and a large bridge over the Awash River. About 100m after crossing the bridge towards Butajira, you'll see the signpost for Melka Kunture to your right. From here, it's about 1km to the fenced site, following a reasonably clear motorable track through the fields. If you can't find the way, anybody will be able to point you there. There are a few dollar-a-night hotels in Melka Awash, none of which has showers, but you can buy a jerry can of washing water for a nominal fee. A restaurant serves eggs and bread.

Previous page Dorze hut up to 5m high (AVZ)

Above Harari home with bowls, dishes and baskets on the walls (AVZ)

Below left Fisherman on Lake Tana, near Bahir Dar (JC)

Below right Afar man milking cow, Assaita (AVZ)

Adadi Maryam

The southernmost extant rock-hewn church in Ethiopia, Adadi Maryam lies to the west of the Butajira road on a small hill some five minutes' walk from the village of Adadi. Scholars date the church to some time between the 12th and 14th centuries, while local tradition associates it with King Lalibela's visit to nearby Mount Zikwala in AD1106. Adadi Maryam is far closer in style to its counterparts at Lalibela than to any rock-hewn church in Tigrai. Although smaller and more roughly hewn, it is, like several Lalibela churches, a subterranean semi-monolith encircled by a wide tunnel containing a few disused monastic cells. It measures 19m long and 16m wide, and has 24 windows and ten doors. The tunnel that leads from the back of the church to a nearby watercourse was carved later to prevent flooding.

It has been suggested that Adadi Maryam was the site of the first meeting, in 1523, between Emperor Lebna Dengal and the Portuguese expedition led by Rodrigo de Lima and documented by the priest Francisco Alvares. Whether or not this is true, it is known that Ahmed Gragn attacked the church a few years later. Although the excavation survived this raid more or less intact, the large cross above the entrance was severely damaged, and the priests were either killed or forced to flee. The church subsequently fell into disuse, and it remained so for several centuries while the Oromo occupied the surrounding area. Adadi Maryam was discovered by local hunters and reopened during the reign of Menelik II, and it remains in active use today, though its original name has evidently been forgotten – Adadi is the Oromifa name for a type of bush that grows in the vicinity. The Swiss Embassy funded extensive restoration work on the church over 1996–98. Entrance costs birr 30.

Travellers with sufficient time and interest might want to seek out the disused complex of rock-hewn caves that lies in a small gorge about 2km northwest of Adadi at Laga Degaga. It is thought that these caves housed a monastic community associated with the church prior to the 16th-century attack by Ahmed Gragn.

Getting there and away

The turn-off to Adadi, 5km past Melka Awash, is clearly signposted from the Butajira road. The 13km drive from the junction to the church takes less than 30 minutes in a private vehicle. The best days to visit Adadi using public transport are Thursday and Saturday (market days) when pick-up trucks head there from Melka Awash between 07.30 and 09.00 and a bus leaves from the Autobus Terra in Addis Ababa at about 06.00. Once you have viewed the church, you'll probably have to wait an hour or two for transport back to the main road. You might want to fill the time and your stomach with the excellent and inexpensive *shiro wat* served at the restaurant on the edge of the market. On non-market days, there is very little transport to Adadi. I saw no sign of accommodation in Adadi, but you could probably ask to pitch a tent somewhere in the village.

Tiya

Tiya marks the northern limit of a belt of mysterious engraved stelae that stretches across southern Ethiopia through Dilla (on the Moyale road) to Negele Borena (see box *The stelae of southern Ethiopia*, page 479). Remarkably little is known about the origin of these stelae, or of the meaning of the symbols that are carved upon them. Recent excavations at Tiya revealed that the stones mark the mass graves of males and females who died when they were between 18 and 30 years of age, and who were laid to rest in a foetal position about 700 years ago. The presence of several engraved swords on the stelae suggests that the people buried were soldiers, but this evidence is far from conclusive.

Listed as a UNESCO World Heritage Site, the stelae field at Tiya today comprises some 45 stones of up to 2m in height, several of which had collapsed prior to their careful re-erection in their original positions by a team of French archaeologists of the past decade. The largest stele in the field originally stood 5m high, but only the base remains *in situ* – the top part has been removed to the university in Addis Ababa. Nearly all the stones are engraved. Apart from the stylised swords, the number of which is thought to represent the number of people killed by the warrior it commemorates, two symbols predominate: plain circles, and what looks like a pair of podgy leaves rising on a stem from a rectangular base. I noticed that where all three symbols were present on one stone, the circles were generally near the top, the swords in the middle, and the twin leaves close to the base.

The plain circles appear on about one in ten stones, and seem to denote that a female is buried underneath. The pairs of leaves look like the *enset* (false bananas) plantain that is still widely grown in southern Ethiopia. Recent thinking is that they represent a traditional wooden headrest, and are a sort of visual RIP note. On some stones you'll see what looks like a Greek 'E', a symbol for which no plausible interpretation has been thought up. Despite the relative simplicity of the stelae and engravings, I found them very mysterious and haunting. The repetitive intent that apparently lies behind the symbols is no less impressive than the more finely honed and grandiose stelae of Axum.

Tiya invites speculation. Even to the untrained eye, it is clear that these stelae (along with those around Butajira) don't fall neatly into the phallic or anthropomorphic schools of decoration found elsewhere in southern Ethiopia, but represent a third, more ornate style of carving. Because of this, it seems likely that they were erected more recently than their more easterly counterparts, probably between the late 12th and early 14th centuries. I thought it significant that, like the stelae at Axum, the only comparable constructions that I'm aware of in sub-Saharan Africa, the Gragn Stones, appear to predate the arrival of Christianity to the area, and were definitely erected as grave markers. The Gragn Stone belt passes through the heart of the modern territory of the Gurage, whose language is closely affiliated to Tigrigna and who presumably moved to southern Ethiopia from Tigrai several centuries ago. Lying as it does some 30km south of the roughly contemporaneous rock-hewn church at Adadi, Tiya would appear to mark the medieval boundary between pagan and Christian Ethiopia. Could it also be that the Gragn Stones are remnants of an otherwise-forgotten offshoot of the pre-Christian stelae-building traditions of Axum?

Getting there and away

Tiya straddles the Butajira road almost 40km south of Melka Awash. The stelae field lies less than 1km out of town. Coming from the direction of Addis, the unsignposted turn-off to the stones is to your left, about 100m past the Tiya Stelae Hotel near the telecommunications office. About 200m further, upon reaching a red water-tank, turn right. After a minute or two's further walking, you will see the stelae enclosed in a fence on the rise ahead. Entrance costs birr 10. There are vague plans to set up a cultural tourism project at Tiya, which will involve training guides, visiting other sites in the area, and upgrading the presentation of the site.

Where to stay and eat

Should you need to overnight in Tiya, the recently opened **Sisay Mola Hotel** is the best bet, charging birr 15 for a clean en-suite room with cold shower only. The attached restaurant should be operating by the time you read this. There are also three or four showerless, dollar-a-night hotels along the main road – the **Tiya Stelae Hotel** has been recommended as friendly.

BUTAJIRA

Many travellers who explore the area between Melka Awash and Tiya will be likely to return directly to Addis Ababa. Should you be heading on to the Rift Valley, however,

GURAGE

Butajira lies at the heart of Gurage country, a mountainous area lying towards the southern end of the central highlands. The Gurage, the fifth largest ethno-linguistic group in Ethiopia, are historically affiliated to the Amhara of the northern highlands, and have long associations with its Christian traditions, as evidenced by the presence of the rock-hewn church of Adadi Maryam and numerous other abandoned troglodyte dwellings and shrines in their homeland. The Gurage evidently became isolated from Amhara during the time of Ahmed Gragn, and developed independently until they were re-integrated in the 19th century. Today, the area remains a Semetic-speaking enclave surrounded by Oromo and other unrelated peoples, and its people are split between ancient Orthodox Christians and more recent converts to Islam.

The Gurage social structure is unusual in that economic roles are not dictated by caste, by class, or by gender. The Gurage do, however, have a strange relationship with the Watta or Fuga people, who have adopted the Gurage language and customs, and serve the triple role of artisans, hunters and spiritual mediums within Gurage society. It is the Watta who are responsible for erecting the main beams of Gurage houses, which are attractive beehive structures similar to those seen around Sodo and elsewhere in Walaita. A guiding Gurage principle is that 'idleness is a sin, work is the key to success, failure to improve one's land is bad farming and cannot be blamed on the spirits'. Perhaps related to this dictum, perhaps simply because of Gurage's proximity to Addis, there are many Gurage in the city, and they have a reputation for industry, business acumen, and also academic success.

there is plenty of transport to Butajira, a pleasantly green if uninspiring small town boasting an unexpectedly good selection of good affordable accommodation. The green highlands around Butajira are very attractive, and there is much to explore in the surrounding area for those with the time and inclination, as covered under the heading *From Butajira to Hosaina* below.

Getting there and away

Regular public transport runs directly between Addis Ababa and Butajira, as well as along the 50km road between Butajira and Ziway in the Rift Valley. A third onward option, definitely worth thinking about if you intend to head directly towards Arba Minch and/or the Lower Omo Valley, would be to continue directly south via Hosaina to Sodo-Walaita. There are regular buses along this road, and it is likely to be surfaced in the near future.

Where to stay and eat

Fikado Asore Hotel ✆ 046 1150142/3. This multi-storey block is the smartest option, situated 50m from the main road behind the telecommunications centre. Large doubles with satellite television, carpeting, balcony and en-suite hot shower cost birr 50, while smaller ground-floor rooms, also with hot shower, cost birr 30. A decent restaurant is attached.

Tsegaye Hotel Situated behind the Mobil garage, this pleasant hotel charges birr 30 for a clean room with ¾ bed and en-suite hot shower.

Matiwos Baka Memorial Hotel Older and less central, this popular hotel near the church charges birr 30 for a clean but rather scruffy room with a proper dbl bed and en-suite hot shower, or birr 20 for a room with a smaller bed and cold shower only. It serves adequate food, and has a pleasant beer garden in the courtyard.

FROM BUTAJIRA TO HOSAINA

Due to be surfaced in its entirety in the near future, the 100km gravel road that runs southwest from Butajira to Hosaina via Kibet passes through some attractive highland scenery and can be covered in about two hours without stops. It also offers access to a few worthwhile off-the-beaten-track sites, of which Lake Ara Shetan and the stelae of Silté are the most accessible, while the more remote Boyo Wetlands are of great ornithological significance. There's plenty of public transport between Butajira and Hosaina, whether you want to bus directly through to Sodo or prefer to explore the area more slowly.

Lake Ara Shetan

Coming from the north, the first point of interest is Lake Ara Shetan, which stands alongside the Hosaina road at an elevation of 2,281m some 10km south of Butajira. Sometimes referred to by outsiders as Lake Butajira, this pretty emerald-green lake, nestled within the sheer 120m-high walls of an almost perfectly circular explosion crater, has a diameter of around 880m and a depth of at least 50m. It forms the most southerly link in a chain of craters, lava flows and other relics of geologically recent volcanic activity that runs for 80km northeast along the Rift Valley Escarpment as far as the Bishoftu Crater Lakes.

Scenic though it might be, Ara Shetan is viewed as a somewhat malignant presence by locals. Its name literally means 'Lake of Satan', and its creation is ascribed to an evil sorcerer who had fought the local peasants for years before finally he was mortally wounded at the site of the present-day lake. Legend has it that as the sorcerer drew his dying breath, he drove his spear hard into the ground, and bellowed out a curse 'let this be the devil's home', whereupon the earth below him imploded, swallowed him up, and filled with water. A taboo still exists on throwing any stone into the lake – legend has it that the devil would hurl it back even harder at the person who threw it, with fatal consequences.

Invisible from the Hosaina road, Ara Shetan nevertheless lies almost immediately east of it, and the rim is accessible via a 500m motorable track. Any public transport heading between Butajira and Kibet will be able to set you down at the start of this track. With a local guide, it would be possible to walk on from Ara Shetan to the nearby **Aynege Cave**, which is presided over by a Muslim holy man and supposedly connects to the Sof Omar Caves east of the Bale Mountains, as well as to a nearby lake known as Tinishu Abaya (Little Abaya).

Silté

Straddling the Hosaina road only 4km southwest of Lake Ara Shetan, **Kibet** is the principal town of the Silté people, whose attractive traditional homesteads with tall domed thatched roofs can be seen dotted around the surrounding countryside. The Silté area is also known for its many medieval stelae, which are similar in shape and decoration to those found around Tiya, though generally more ornately worked. Unfortunately, archaeologists have removed many of the best stelae to Addis Ababa, and I'm not aware of any stelae field numerically comparable with the one outside Tiya.

The most worthwhile stop in this area is probably the stele known locally as **Asano Dengai**, which ranks as the most intricately worked individual stele I've come across in southern Ethiopia, despite having been decapitated. Asano Dengai stands in isolation below a large fig tree next to a recently built mosque 500m east of the Hosaina road at Ketigora, which lies about 8km south of Kibet overlooking Lake Saida. There is also a cluster of six stelae, all of which are either decapitated or collapsed, at the village of **Wazira**, about 1km from the road between Kibet and Ketigora along a side road signposted for the Wolega Siddist Elementary School. Worth noting, for those using public transport, that at least one basic guesthouse is to be found in Kibet.

Boyo Wetlands

Two sites close to Hosaina are listed in the Important Bird Area inventory published by the Ethiopian Natural History and Wildlife Society. The more interesting and accessible of these sites is the Boyo Wetlands, which consists of an extensive seasonal swamp centred upon Lake Boyo, a shallow but perennial freshwater body also sometimes known as Lake Bilate after the river that flows through its eastern tip to eventually empty into Lake Abaya near Arba Minch. There are some interesting thatched Hadiya homesteads in the lake's hinterland, many painted in geometric designs, and you may also notice modern cemeteries marked with engraved stones reminiscent of (and presumably inspired by) their more ancient counterparts around Silté.

Set at an altitude of around 1,500m near the small town of Bonosha, Lake Boyo was formerly designated a Controlled Hunting Area to protect its heaving hippo population. According to local sources, these hippos were hunted to extinction in 1994, but a couple of refugee pods from Abiata-Shala recently re-colonised the area and are quite regularly seen in the open water. For birders, the wetlands are of greatest interest during the European winter, when thousands upon thousands of migrant waders and ducks converge on the area. Resident species include black-crowned crane and a variety of ibises, egrets and herons. The wetlands are also regarded to be possibly the most important northern hemisphere stronghold for the endangered wattled crane – 62 individuals were counted in a 1996 survey, while an expedition in 2004 encountered a flock of 108, the largest aggregation ever recorded in Ethiopia.

Lake Boyo is situated less than 20km east of Hosaina as the crow flies, and the wetlands extend to within 10km of town at the height of the rains. Yet by road you will need to cover 55km just to get to Bonosha, from where you need to walk for another hour or so to reach the lakeshore. The junction for Bonosha branches east from the Butajira road 31km from Hosaina, at the police checkpoint immediately north of Achamo. From here, it is exactly 24km along a rather poor road to Bonosha, passing through Shashago after 9km, where you need to turn left at the main intersection. It should be possible to make your way to the lake unaccompanied – it lies in a depression about 4km west of town – but it would certainly simplify matters to find a local guide. If you are dependent on public transport, at least one bus daily runs between Hosaina and Bonosha, where very basic accommodation can be found near the market square.

HOSAINA

The capital of Hadiya zone, Hosaina combines a bustling commercial atmosphere with a feel of dusty parochialism, possibly because it is one of the few Ethiopian towns of comparable size (population 60,000) whose roads remain entirely unsurfaced and whose hotels are so seldom troubled by the tourist trade. Set at an altitude of above 2,300m in a mountainous region, Hosaina lies at the core of an important centre of *enset* cultivation, though the region's fertile volcanic soils can grow practically any crop during the rainy season. The town must also be regarded as a route focus of sorts, one whose importance is likely to increase following the completion of a surfaced road connecting it to Addis Ababa and Sodo.

Hosaina (a local variation on Hosanna) is the main town of the Hadiya, cultural affiliates to the Gurage who speak a vastly different Cushitic language called Hadinya and are traditionally Muslim, though recent years have seen a strong swing towards Protestantism. Hadiya has proved to be a hotbed of anti-government feeling in the post-Derg era. In the build-up to the May 2000 election, five people were killed in the area when security forces threw a live grenade at protesters, and two more died of gun wounds in similar circumstances. Despite central government's attempts both to coerce and to cajole votes in the eventual polling, which was postponed to June in Hadiya, a full 75% of the vote went to two local opposition parties, each of which won one seat in the Council of People's Representatives.

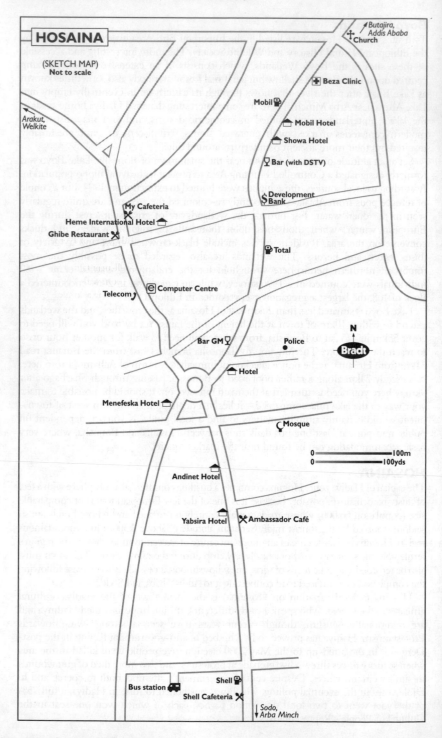

Getting there and away

Although visited by very few travellers, Hosaina is a route focus of sorts, situated at the junction of a 100km road running northeast to Butajira, a 95km road south to Sodo-Walaita, and a 115km road northwest to Welkite – in all cases you are looking at around two hours' drive in a private vehicle. Hosaina is serviced by regular public transport in all directions, including a daily bus service running directly between Addis Ababa and Sodo.

Where to stay

Heme International Hotel (32 rooms) ✆ 046 5552264. This prominent central multi-storey block is comfortably the smartest town, though the slightly shabby rooms don't quite live up to the promise of the pretentiously shiny exterior. Still, it's difficult to quibble at the asking price of birr 66 for a large carpeted dbl with a private balcony and en-suite hot showers, or birr 83 for a similar room with TV. The restaurant is pretty good too.

Mobil Hotel (20 rooms) ✆ 046 5552742. This adequate hotel opposite the eponymous garage on the Butajira road is poor value at the *faranji* price of birr 50 for a compact room with ¾ bed and en-suite shower, since this pushes it into the same price league as the vastly superior Heme International.

Yabsera Hotel (18 rooms) ✆ 046 5550518. The friendly lodge set in a well-maintained old building close to the bus station charges birr 35 for a large, clean upstairs room with a proper dbl bed, en-suite hot shower and TV, or birr 12 for a clean ground-floor room using a common shower.

Where to eat

The only place that serves Western-style food is the **Heme International Hotel**, which charges around birr 15 for a main course. A decent **cafeteria** selling meals, snacks and pastries is tucked behind the Shell garage around the corner from the bus station on the Sodo road. Good local food can be had at the **Ghibe Restaurant** on the Welkite road, while the brightly painted double-storey **My Cafeteria** on the opposite side of the same road serves excellent snacks, pastries, juices and coffee, as does the inferior **Ambassador Café** opposite the Yabsera Hotel.

Excursions
Ajaro Falls

A worthwhile diversion for those driving between Hosaina and Sodo are the scenic Ajaro Falls, which lie to the west of the main road. The falls actually consist of two separate but parallel waterfalls on the Soke and Ajacho rivers, set perhaps 100m apart and plunging in tandem over a cliff about 100m high into the thickly wooded gorge formed by the Soke River, a tributary of the Omo. The waterfall can be reached along a 25km turn-off west from the Sodo road about 65km south of Hosaina, and a few kilometres north of the town of Areka.

The viewpoint, easily accessible from the main road, is at the top of a steep cliff facing the waterfalls. A very steep and slippery footpath runs to the base of the gorge, and is used by locals, but be warned that stories abound of people falling to their death – even the sure-footed local livestock sometimes plunges off. At the top, an easy walk leads to the forest-fringed bank of the Ajacho River. There's a friendly traditional Walaita village of beehive huts here too. The distance from Areka to Sodo is only 28km, so the falls could be visited as a round trip from there.

Arakit

Situated along the Welkite road about 55km north of Hosaina and 35km south of Imbidir, Arakit is an attractively sprawling small town characterised by the traditional

Gurage homesteads and neatly fenced compounds that are so typical of these fertile highlands. Boasting a couple of small local lodgings, Arakit is potentially an excellent base for anybody wishing to immerse themselves in Gurage culture. Also of interest is the eponymous lake immediately north of the town centre, which sometimes hosts large flocks of pelican, ibis and migrant waterfowl such as the striking northern pintail.

SODO

Sodo, the bustling capital of Walaita district, lies at the crossroads where the main surfaced road between Shashemene and Arba Minch intersects with the dirt road north from Addis Ababa (or Welkite) via Hosaina as well as to a newly upgraded road to Jimma in western Ethiopia. Often referred to by the district name of Walaita rather than Sodo, this town of around 55,000 people lies at an altitude of around 2,100m on a green and hilly part of the Rift Valley Escarpment notable for its maize cultivation.

Most tourists pass straight through Sodo, but if you are travelling on public transport the town makes for a pleasant if unremarkable break en route between Shashemene or Hosaina and Arba Minch – if nothing else, the cool, moist highland air comes as pleasant relief after the dry heat of the Rift Valley. The mountain behind the town looks eminently climbable, and the town itself – despite having grown immeasurably since I first visited it in 1994 – is small enough that you need only walk 1km in any direction to find yourself on quiet, lush country roads with fantastic views to Lake Abaya, perhaps 30km distant and several hundred metres lower in the Rift Valley.

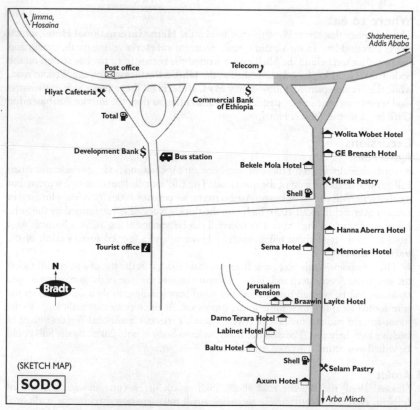

THE 'NEW' SODO–JIMMA ROAD

Completed in 1999, the reconstructed and upgraded road connecting Sodo to Jimma should, in theory, make it far easier than it has been in the past to cross between the Rift Valley and western Ethiopia without having to go through Addis Ababa. The road can be driven in five to six hours in a private vehicle, and is very scenic throughout, but especially the descent into the Omo River Gorge.

For backpackers, the potential significance of this road is immense. But, so far as I can ascertain, it is limited at present by an absence of public transport. I am assured that this is likely to change in the near future.

If you are driving along this road yourself, head out of Sodo, past the post office for 7km, then turn left at the first junction following the signpost for Chida. Look out here for the characteristic Walaita huts, which are similar in design, although less over-the-top, than the famous Dorze huts of Chencha. About 50km out of Sodo, you'll cross the modern bridge that spans the Omo River. On climbing the gorge on the west side of the river, you'll notice some large stone ruins to your right, reputedly the remains of a large fort built by King Kawo Halalo of the medieval Dawaro Empire. At the 140km mark is a small bridge, where we noticed an unusual swallow overhead (I suspect it could be the undescribed cliff swallow recorded in several other parts of Ethiopia). At the 176km mark, you reach Chida, the largest town on the road (which isn't saying much), perched high on a grassy escarpment. Here, you need to turn right at a T-junction, before the final descent to Jimma.

Getting there and away

Sodo stands 96km south of Hosaina along a good dirt road that's scheduled to be upgraded to asphalt in the not-too-distant future. The drive takes two hours in a private vehicle, though you need to double that if you are thinking of diverting to the Ajaro Falls. A couple of buses daily run northwards from Sodo to Hosaina, from where it is easy to pick up public transport towards Butajira (for Addis Ababa) and to a lesser extent Welkite. In addition, one direct bus in either direction runs daily between Addis Ababa and Sodo via Hosaina and Butajira, leaving at around 06.30.

Sodo lies 130km from Shashemene and 120km from Arba Minch on an asphalt road that is becoming somewhat riddled with pot-holes in parts, particularly towards Shashemene. Once again, you are looking at a two-hour drive at most in either direction, assuming you make no stops or diversions. Buses between Sodo and Shashemene fill up and leave throughout the morning and take about three hours for each leg. There is no public transport along the road west to Jimma, and the drive takes at least three hours in a private vehicle.

Where to stay
Moderate

Bekele Mola (7 rooms) ☏ 046 5512382–6. Ostensibly the smartest hotel in Sodo, the Bekele Mola is pleasant enough and has a convenient central location in a green compound, but the en-suite doubles with hot shower feel rather basic for the asking price of birr 66/112 sgl/dbl occupancy. The reasonably priced restaurant is a justifiably popular lunchtime target for tours headed between Shashemene and Arba Minch.

Hanna Aberra Hotel (12 rooms) ☏ 046 5512418. There are perhaps half-a-dozen hotels in Sodo charging a uniform birr 25 to Ethiopians for a room with a ³⁄₄ bed and en-suite hot shower and there is not much to choose between them except the extent to which they elevate the *faranji* price. This new hotel is the current pick, charging birr 30 for a clean en-suite room (avoid the ones facing the main road) or birr 20 for a room using common showers.

Jerusalem Pension (17 rooms) ☎ 046 5512922. The historical favourite in this price range, the pleasant multi-storey pension now charges birr 35 for a clean en-suite room or birr 20 for a similar room using common showers.

Axum Hotel (20 rooms) ☎ 046 5510139. Standards have dipped and prices been raised up at this former favourite – it's seriously overpriced at birr 45 for a rundown room with en-suite cold shower.

Baltu Hotel (19 rooms) ☎ 046 5512469. This also feels a bit scruffy and overpriced at birr 50 for an en-suite dbl, but it has one clear asset in that the bed is king-size rather than ³/₄ size.

Where to eat

For meals, the **Bekele Mola Hotel** serves fair Western food, while the **Birhanu Hotel** opposite is one of the best spots for local dishes. Between meals, the **Misrak Pastry** opposite the Shell garage is excellent for pastries, coffee and juice, while the **Selam Pastry** near the Axum Hotel also looks very good. The **Hiyat Cafeteria** next to the Total garage is a pleasant place for an outdoor coffee or snack.

The Rift Valley South to Awassa

After the historical circuit in the north, the stretch of the Rift Valley between Addis Ababa and Awassa via the junction town of Shashemene is probably the part of Ethiopia most regularly travelled by visitors to the country. A great many such travellers are merely passing through the region en route to the Omo Valley, the Kenyan border, or Bale National Park, but that doesn't mean it is bereft of interest. The main attraction of the region is a string of six lakes, every one of which lies close to the main Awassa road, and makes for a rewarding excursion.

The most northerly of these is Lake Koka, the only artificial body of water in the chain, and probably the least memorable. South of Koka, Lake Ziway, which lies alongside the eponymous town, is well worth a look for its prolific birdlife, with the possibility of exploring its ancient island monastery. Farther south again is a cluster of three lakes, Langano, Abiata and Shala, the first a popular swimming and watersport resort, the others protected in a national park renowned for its prolific birds and therapeutic hot springs. Finally, there is Lake Awassa, situated on the outskirts of the eponymous town.

Direct access to Awassa and the Rift Valley lakes is along a good asphalt road, which branches south from the Adama road at Mojo, 75km east of Addis Ababa, and is covered by all manner of public transport. More adventurous travellers might, however, elect to drive or bus along a little-used dirt road that passes through Tiya and Butajira before connecting with the asphalt at Ziway (described in *Chapter 21*). This 'scenic route' offers access to a trio of very different cultural and archaeological sites: the rock-hewn church of Adadi Maryam, the ancient stelae field at Tiya, and the prehistoric diggings at Melka Kunture.

There would be a strong case for terminating this chapter at Shashemene, the most important junction town in southern Ethiopia. Shashemene stands at the crossroads of the asphalt road south to Moyale (see *Chapter 24*), the dirt road east via Dodola to Bale National Park (see *Chapter 23*), the asphalt road southwest towards Arba Minch (see *Chapter 25*) and the normal gateway to the Lower Omo Valley (see *Chapter 26*). It might be worth noting here that Shashemene, strategic importance notwithstanding, is one of the least appealing towns in Ethiopia. The nearby resort of Wondo Genet is a far more appealing place to spend a night or two.

Situated only 25km south of Shashemene along the road towards Moyale, the city of Awassa is the springboard for onward travel into the arid but attractively untrammelled badlands that stretch down to the Kenyan border at Moyale. It is also a worthwhile excursion in its own right, even if you have no intention of heading further south. By refreshing contrast to the jumble that is Shashemene, Awassa is one of the few Ethiopian cities to show clear evidence of town planning. The city's orderly, shady avenues lead down to the lushly vegetated shore of Lake Awassa, notable for its prolific birdlife, and the semi-habituated monkeys that clamber around the forested grounds of what, for those who place atmosphere before facilities, must rank close to being Ethiopia's finest budget hotel.

THE GREAT RIFT VALLEY

The Great Rift Valley is the single largest geographical feature on the African continent, and was the only such feature visible to the first astronauts to reach the moon. The process of rifting started some 20 million years ago along a 4,000km-long fault line that stretches from the Red Sea south to Mozambique's Zambezi Valley. The gradual expansion of the valley has been accompanied by a large amount of volcanic activity: the floor is studded with dormant and extinct volcanoes such as Fantelle in Ethiopia and Longonot in Kenya. Africa's two highest peaks, Mount Kilimanjaro and Mount Kenya, are also volcanic products of the rifting process, even though they lie outside of the Rift Valley. Millions of years from now, the Rift Valley will fill with ocean water, to split what is now Africa into two discrete landmasses, much as happened millions of years ago when Madagascar was separated from the African mainland.

The Ethiopian portion of the Rift Valley runs from the Red Sea to Lake Turkana on the Kenyan border. In northern Ethiopia, it forms the Danakil Depression, an inaccessible and inhospitable desert that dips to an altitude of 116m below sea level, one of the lowest points on the earth's surface. South of the Danakil Depression, due east of Addis Ababa, the Rift narrows around Awash National Park to bisect the Ethiopian Highlands into the northwestern and southeastern massifs. In Ethiopia, as elsewhere along its length, the Rift Valley has formed an important barrier to animal movement and plant dispersal. For this reason, several animals are restricted to one or other side of the Rift, while populations of many animals that occur on both sides of the Great Rift, for instance Ethiopian wolves, form genetically distinct races.

The southern part of the Ethiopian Rift Valley is lower, warmer and drier than other densely populated parts of the country. Covered in acacia woodland and studded with lakes, it is also one of the few parts of Ethiopia that feels unequivocally African – in many respects the region is reminiscent of the Rift Valley lakes region of central Kenya. The six main lakes of the Ethiopian Rift formed during the last Ice Age, originally as two large lakes, one of which embraced what are now Lakes Ziway, Abiata, Shala and Langano, the other Lakes Abaya and Chamo.

South of Lake Chamo, the Rift Valley expands into the hot, barren scrublands of the Kenyan border region. The Rift here becomes less clearly defined, but it supports two further lakes, Chew Bahir and Turkana, both of which are practically inaccessible from the Ethiopian side (the vast bulk of Turkana's surface area lies in Kenya). The Kenyan border area is most notable for two of Ethiopia's most important national parks, Omo and Mago, which are among the most undeveloped game reserves in Africa, and noted not so much for their abundance of game (though most major plains animals are present) but for their wilderness atmosphere.

Although the Rift Valley is everywhere lower and hotter than the highlands, most of the lake region between Ziway and Arba Minch lies at an elevation of between 1,000m and 1,500m and temperatures are rarely uncomfortably hot. Rainfall figures are lower than in the highlands, but the pattern is broadly similar, with one long rainy season generally starting in April and finishing in July or August.

The region covered in this chapter is readily accessible by public transport. The road between Addis Ababa and Awassa is surfaced in its entirety, and can be covered in a private vehicle within five hours. Regular buses run directly between Addis Ababa and Shashemene, 25km from Awassa, typically taking around six hours in either direction. For backpackers wishing to hop between various points of interest, there is also plenty of light transport connecting most towns en route, for instance Bishoftu, Mojo, Meki, Ziway and Arsi Negele.

ADDIS TO ZIWAY

The surfaced road to Ziway follows the Adama road (covered in the chapter *Addis Ababa to Adama by Road*) for about 75km as far as Mojo, passing through Akaki and Bishoftu en route. At Mojo, a right turn to the south, at a large intersection opposite a cluster of hotels and a filling station, marks the beginning of the descent into the Rift Valley towards Ziway. In a private vehicle, this is a straightforward run, at least once you've dodged the heavy traffic for the first 20km or so out of Addis Ababa, and you can expect to reach Mojo junction in about 90 minutes and Ziway after another hour or so.

Using public transport, you can easily pick up a direct bus from Addis Ababa to Ziway, or on to Shashemene or Awassa, but it is also possible to hop southwards using the light vehicles that connect all major towns en route. If you choose, or need, to stop over along the way, **Mojo** is an inconsequential but pretty small town halfway, set on the banks of the Mojo River between Bishoftu and Adama. There are several decent hotels, including a good **Bekele Mola** (✆ *011 4160006*) where en-suite rooms cost birr 20. For details of points of interest between Addis Ababa and Mojo – including the Akaki Wetlands and Bishoftu – see the chapter *Addis Ababa to Adama by Road*.

The first major settlement along the Moyale road is **Meki**, some 60km south of Mojo. Meki is of no great interest in itself, but it's a well-equipped little town with several restaurants, pastry shops and dollar-a-night hotels, and there is a **Bekele Mola Hotel** behind the Shell garage on the Ziway side of town, with en-suite rooms for birr 20. Meki is also a possible base for exploring **Lake Koka**, which fringes the main road about 20km back towards Mojo. Koka is artificial, and it is generally overlooked by tourists, but, ringed by hills and covered in flowering hyacinth, it is just as scenic as many of the natural Rift Valley lakes and it offers excellent birdwatching, particularly around the marshy area at the inlet of the Awash River. There are a couple of villages closer to Koka but neither is situated near the inlet, nor do they appear to have any accommodation, so it would be simpler to overnight in Meki and ask a minibus heading towards Mojo to drop you at the bridge over the Awash River. There are regular minibuses from Meki to Ziway when you are ready to move on.

ZIWAY

Lake Ziway, also known as Lake Dambal, is the northernmost of Ethiopia's natural Rift Valley lakes and the largest of the four covered in this chapter, with a surface area of roughly 430km². Lake Ziway lies about 160km south of the capital as the crow flies, and the well-equipped small town of the same name on its western shore lies about three hours' drive away along a good surfaced road, making it an ideal first stop on a trip through the Rift Valley. Lying at an altitude of 1,636m and ringed by steep volcanic hills, this shallow lake is fed by two major rivers, the Maki and Katar, and is drained at its southwestern tip by the Bulbula River, which in turn flows into Lake Abiata. The lake supports an abundant population of *Tilapia nilotica*, a medium-sized flat fish that can weigh up to 1.5kg and makes for fine eating (the restaurants in Ziway have a justified reputation for great *asa wat* and *kutilet*).

Although Ziway is less heralded in this respect than Lakes Abiata and Shala, it arguably offers the best birdwatching of any Rift Valley lake, including large aggregations of water-associated species attracted to the reed-lined fringes by the thriving *tilapia* population. Excellent birdwatching is to be had by turning off the main road through Ziway on to the side road heading east immediately before the Shell garage and Bekele Mola Hotel. After about 2km, this road leads to a raised causeway and jetty fringed by papyrus marsh and teeming with birds, most visibly marabou stork and white pelican. You could easily identify 50-plus species here in a couple of

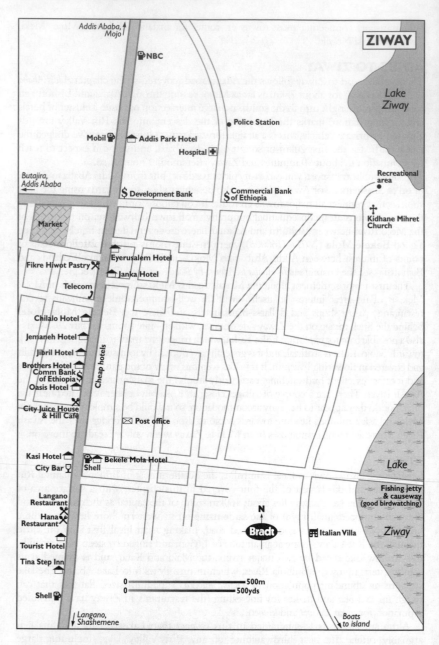

hours – look out for greater and lesser jacana, white pelican, yellow-billed stork, black crake, lesser moorhen, lesser jacana, black-tailed godwit, garganey, European marsh harrier, Rüppell's griffin vulture and red-breasted pipit. This is one of the best places in Africa to see the localised black egret (also known as the black heron), whose unusual habit of fishing with its wings raised to form a canopy gives rise to its colloquial name of 'umbrella bird'.

MARYAM TSION MONASTERY

The largest of the five islands on Lake Ziway, clearly visible from the mainland, is known to the local Oromo as Tullo Guddo ('Large Mountain') and to the Amhara as Debre Tsion (Mount Zion). On the highest peak, the church of Maryam Tsion is quite possibly the oldest active monastery in southern Ethiopia. A church has stood on this peak since at least the 12th century, and perhaps even earlier. Tradition has it that the Ziway area was settled by refugee priests from Axum in the 9th century, during the time of Queen Yodit, and that they brought with them the Ark of the Covenant for safe-keeping. According to this legend, Tullo Guddo was the sanctuary for the Ark of the Covenant for 70 years, before it was considered safe to return it to Axum. This tradition is backed up by the fact that the Zay people of Ziway speak a Tigrigna-like tongue quite distinct from the Oromifa spoken in the surrounding area, and also by the large number of ancient Ge'ez manuscripts stored among the church's treasures, most famously a 14th-century *Sinkesar* containing vivid and beautiful illustrations of 19 popular saints.

During the 16th and 17th centuries, the Zay Christians led an isolated island-bound existence. They retreated to the islands in the time of Ahmed Gragn, when Christians were driven out of the Rift Valley by the Galla people, and became entirely cut off from the mainstream of Ethiopian Christianity. How the Zay survived these years of isolation with their traditions intact is something of a mystery, one most probably explained by the fact that the Galla were inept sailors and unable to build boats (indeed, the Oromo name for the Zay is Laki, which translates as rower, in reference to this distinguishing feature). As Christian–Muslim tensions eased, the islanders occasionally sailed to shore to trade, and became known to the Galla as skilful weavers, but basically they remained an isolated community, dependent on their densely terraced cultivation and on the lake's abundant fish for survival. Rumours of their isolated brethren had always filtered through to the Christians of the highlands, where it was believed, correctly, that the churches on Ziway held a wealth of ancient *tabots* and illuminated religious manuscripts. It was only in 1886 that Emperor Menelik conquered the Ziway area and the liberated islanders were able to move back to the lakeshore. Today, just three of Ziway's islands are occupied, and most Zay people visit them only for religious ceremonies. But Maryam Tsion remains an active monastery.

It's possible to take what amounts to public transport to the island. In the slightly paraphrased words of Armand Gauthier and Angela Eaton: 'Taking a boat to the village and monastery on Tullo Guddo Island was a highlight of our trip, though a pain in the ass to organise. The only boat that runs there is moored inside a locked Fisherman's Union compound a bit south of the main lake access. It is owned by a man named Gaetun and leaves very early in the morning. Just getting past the guards into the compound was quite difficult. Gaetun seems quite trustworthy, but he will ask a higher fee of tourists – birr 50 or more as opposed to the birr 5 asked of locals. We bargained him down to about half of this, and he was good-natured about it. You must bring food and water with you to the island. The village is tiny with no tourist amenities, and so beautiful that I'm still amazed by it. A nice gift for the monastery would make you a hero or heroine – they were very proud of some Catholic gift-shop pictures and icons that they had been given.' Armand and Angela indicate that there is no accommodation on the island, but it would be difficult to imagine any problem related to pitching a tent.

The lake is also noted for hippos, which are occasionally visible from the jetty, but are more likely to be seen by hiring a boat to visit one of their more regular haunts. It is possible to extend such an excursion to visit one of Ziway's five islands, which are of ancient volcanic origin, and have supported isolated Christian communities for many centuries, as suggested by names such as Galila and Debre Sina, which are Amharigna for 'Galilee' and 'Mount Sinai' respectively. Of particular interest is the ancient Monastery of Maryam Tsion (see box, page 435) on the 6km² island of Tullo Guddo, whose terraced slopes ascend to a 1,889m peak some 10km east of Ziway town.

Getting there and away
The best access point to the lake is Ziway town, which lies on the main Moyale road about 160km from Addis and 90km from Mojo. There are two possible routes between Addis Ababa and Ziway. The first is described above, the second in meandering detail in the chapter *Addis Ababa to the Rift Valley via Butajira*. If it's speed you're after, any bus leaving Addis Ababa for Shashemene can drop you at Ziway – it's a three- to four-hour trip.

Where to stay
Moderate
Tourist Hotel (34 rooms) ✆ 046 4412615. The closest thing to a tourist-class hotel in Ziway is the aptly named Tourist Hotel, situated a few hundred metres past the town centre along the road towards Shashemene. The en-suite rooms with hot shower are definitely the best in town, and are reasonably priced at birr 50 sgl (with dbl bed) or birr 60 twin. Sgl rooms using the common shower cost birr 25. The restaurant is excellent.

Budget
Bekele Mola Hotel (27 rooms) ✆ 046 4412571. The best value in town thanks to Bekele Mola's ongoing adherence to a non-discriminatory pricing policy, this pleasant hotel is set in small but attractive flowering grounds immediately behind the Shell garage. It charges birr 35 for a large chalet with en-suite hot shower and a king-sized bed, or birr 29 for a smaller room with en-suite hot shower and a ³/₄ bed.

Addis Park Hotel ✆ 046 4410611. Also recommended is this price bracket, this has en-suite rooms with dbl bed and hot water for birr 33 without television or birr 44 with television.

Shoestring
Kasi Hotel Unsignposted opposite the Shell garage, but easily identified by the surrounding bougainvillea creepers, this long-serving local hotel has clean rooms for birr 10 using the common shower, or birr 15 with private cold shower.

Brothers Hotel This popular hotel on the main road near the bus station charges birr 15 for a clean room with en-suite cold shower.

Where to eat
The restaurant at the **Tourist Hotel** serves excellent food indoors or in the courtyard. The fish cutlet, made from local *tilapia*, is particularly recommended at birr 8 inclusive of a small salad, but everything is good, including the vegetarian dishes, and nothing is more expensive than birr 10. Also recommended for *faranji* food are the restaurants in the **Bekele Mola** and **Park** hotels. The **Hana** and **Langano** restaurants next to the Tourist Hotel serve good local meals. The best place for pastries, juices and breakfast snacks is the **Hill Café** above **City Snacks**.

LAKE LANGANO
Lake Langano, with a surface area of 305km² and depth of up to 45m, is more developed for tourism than any other lake in the Ethiopian Rift Valley, and the recently opened

Bishangari Lodge on its southern shore ranks as the only upmarket eco-tourism venture in Ethiopia that could stand comparison with its peers elsewhere in Africa. In addition, two well-established but rather more rundown resorts lie on Langano's western shore, the government Wabe Shebelle Hotel and private Bekele Mola Hotel, while the newer Abule Bassuma Lodge opened on the northern tip of the lake in 2000. Bishangari aside, all of these places are very popular at weekends when they take on a manic sub-Club Med atmosphere that's unlikely to appeal greatly to foreign tourists. During the week, the resorts all have a more restful air, and they will be far more appealing to anybody seeking a bit of natural tranquillity.

For many, the main attraction of Lake Langano is that it is safe for swimming, though frankly the murky brown water has little going for it other than a reported absence of bilharzia. The resorts all offer a variety of water sports at a price, while boat trips can be made to an island noted for its hot springs or in search of hippos and crocodiles. The wooded shore is of great interest to bird enthusiasts: not only does it support an excellent variety of water- and acacia-associated species, but two undescribed birds (a cliff swallow and a serin with a white rump) have recently been reported from the vicinity of the Bekele Mola Hotel. The resorts on the western side of Langano, in particular the Bekele Mola, offer good access to the scenic and decidedly hiker-friendly Abiata-Shala National Park.

Getting there and away

Lake Langano lies to the south of Ziway, a few kilometres east of the main Moyale road. Coming from the north, you will first pass the turn-off for the 13km dirt road to the new Abule Bassuma Lodge, which is signposted out of the village of Bulbula, about 30km past Ziway. About 10km further south, the Wabe Shebelle Hotel lies about 3km east of the main road along a signposted dirt track. Another 10km or so south of this junction, the turn-off to the Bekele Mola Hotel is clearly signposted opposite the main entrance to Abiata-Shala National Park.

Without a vehicle, the best hotel to head for is the Bekele Mola, which lies only 3km from the main Moyale road and is thus within easy walking distance of the entrance to Abiata-Shala National Park. Any vehicle heading between Ziway and Shashemene will drop you at the turn-off to the hotel, though you may be asked to pay full fare to the next town (this isn't *faranji* discrimination, as locals are asked to do the same). It's easy to hitch from the turn-off to the Bekele Mola Hotel at the weekend, but during the week you'll probably have to walk, which takes about 30 minutes.

To reach Wenney Lodge, follow the asphalt Awassa road south of the turn-off to the Bekele Mola Hotel for 2km, and then turn left onto a clearly signposted dirt road and follow it for 16km to the lakeshore. For Bishangari, stick on the surfaced Awassa road for another 1km, and then turn left along a rough but soon-to-be-upgraded gravel road running east towards Asela in the Arsi Highlands. Turn left after 10km, along a road signposted for a health centre. After 6km, you pass the health centre, from where it is another 4km to the lodge.

Where to stay
Upmarket
Bishangari Lodge (16 rooms) ✆ 011 5517533/091 1201317; e reservations@bishangari.com; www.bishangari.com. Situated on the remote southwestern shore of Langano, this superb lodge was originally established in 1997 to raise funds for conservation projects in East Langano Nature Reserve, and it reopened in its present fully restored and upgraded incarnation in 2002. Accommodation is in smart wooden chalets, each of which contains two dbl beds and an en-suite solar-heated shower and toilet, as well as a private balcony. The lodge as a whole possesses an organic feel and blends into the environment in a manner that contrasts strikingly with the harsh

angularity typical of pretty much every other tourist lodge in Ethiopia. The lodge is set in a stand of riparian ficus woodland that attracts small mammals such as guereza and grivet monkey, warthog, bushbuck and genet, as well as forest birds such as the exquisite Narina trogon, which is sometimes seen from the bar. More than 400 bird species have been recorded within walking distance of the camp, and guided walks frequently result in a tally of 70 species in the space of a few hours. Among the more conspicuous birds are the great white and pink-backed pelican, African fish eagle, bare-faced go-away bird, silvery-cheeked hornbill, banded barbet, beautiful sunbird and little weaver. Other activities on offer include hiking (US$11 per person per party), horseback excursions (US$14 per person plus US$14 guide fee per group), mountain biking (US$4 per person per hour) and boat rides in search of hippos (US$35 per hour for up to four people). Accommodation in the wooden chalets costs US$65/120 sgl/dbl wkday, US$93/163 wkend, or US$150/250 over the peak season of mid December to mid January. Accommodation in more primitive *tukuls* costs US$47/88 sgl/dbl wkday, US$64/113 wkend, or US$90/132 over the peak season of mid December to mid January. All rates are full board.

Moderate

Wenney Lodge ❩ 091 8766249 or 091 8766248; e reservations@wenneylodge.com; www.wenneyecolodge.com. Due to open as this edition went to print, this new lodge owned by Greenland Tours bridges the gulf in price and quality that separates Bishangari from the more down-at-heel lodges elsewhere on the lakeshore. The en-suite accommodation has an attractive organic feel, is very bright and clean, and costs US$58/68 sgl/twin bed only. There is a restaurant at the site, while activities offered include horseriding, swimming, boating, mountain biking and birdwatching.

Abule Bassuma Lodge ❩ 011 6615593; e iacona.eng.plc@ethionet.et. Originally built by Mengistu as a weekend retreat for his army officers, this is the most attractive of the more affordable established Langano resorts, with the rather tacky overuse of garish paint compensated for by the spacious layout and pretty location on a densely vegetated peninsula on the northern lakeshore. Now privatised, the lodge consists of 15 bungalows spread out on a hillside, each of which has two or three dbl bedrooms and a lounge. Rates for a three-bedroom bungalow are birr 517/690 wkday/wkend, while a two-bedroom bungalow costs birr 345/460 and a twin room with a dedicated toilet and shower close by costs birr 173/230. There is a restaurant and bar overlooking the lake. Down the steps by the lakeside, there is a large warm-water pool (birr 10 per day) and a jetty from where boats can take you to a nearby island with hot spring and bird colony. Camping costs birr 50 per person on a stony site, with its own toilets, amongst bungalows.

Bekele Mola Hotel Popular with locals, less so with tourists, the lakeshore Bekele Mola charges birr 150 for a large bungalow. All rooms are en suite with hot water, but some rooms are more rundown than others, and this is not reflected in the prices – so do ask to see a room before you take it. Alternatively, you can pitch a tent in the grounds for a hefty birr 35 per person. The restaurant serves adequate grub at highly inflated rates (birr 15 for soup, birr 30 for mains, exclusive of taxes) and the most unpalatable coffee in Ethiopia. The tap water is not safe to drink. Bookings are best made through the head office in Addis Ababa.

Wabe Shebelle Hotel ❩ 011 5517187; f 011 5518477; e washo.et@ethionet.et; www.wabeshebellehotels.com.et. Signposted from the main road a few kilometres south of Bulbula, this beautifully situated hotel offers slightly shabby chalet accommodation in the birr 250–400 range, depending on the size of the chalet and whether you pitch up during the week or at the weekend (when rates are higher). The restaurant is acceptable, and the overall atmosphere less hectic than at the Bekele Mola. Bookings can be made through the Wabe Shebelle Hotel in Addis Ababa.

ABIATA-SHALA NATIONAL PARK

The 887km² Abiata-Shala National Park, bordered to the east by the main Moyale road, is dominated by the two Rift Valley lakes for which it is named, and which together account for more than half of its area. Although the two lakes are separated by a mere

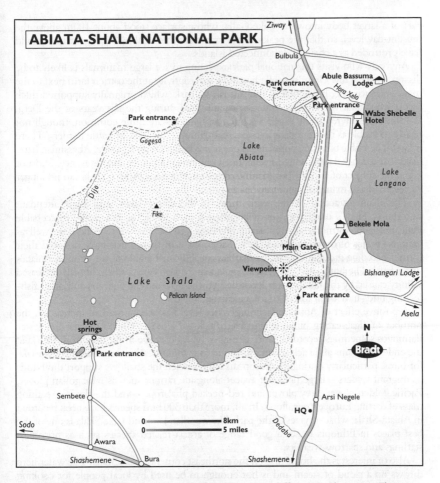

3km-wide sliver of hilly land, they could not be more different in character. The more southerly Lake Shala is nestled within a truly immense volcanic caldera that collapsed 3.5 million years ago, and its surface is studded with a collection of small volcanically formed islands. Despite its relatively modest surface area of 410km², Shala extends to an incredible depth of 266m, and has been calculated to hold a greater volume of water than any other Ethiopian lake, including Lake Tana, which covers an area almost ten times larger. By contrast, the northerly Lake Abiata consists of a 200km² brackish pan, nowhere more than 14m deep, and surrounded by tightly cropped grass flats exposed over the last couple of decades by a steady drop in its water level.

Little more than 1km south of Lake Shala, accessible only along a 20km track leading northwest from the Shashemene–Sodo road at Burra, a small but beautiful crater lake called Chitu Hora is nestled within a tuff ring that formed as a result of volcanic activity perhaps 10,000 years ago. The lake surface stands a full 80m below the rim, and harbours a semi-resident flock of up to 10,000 flamingos. An Oromifa name, Chitu Hora translates as 'Broken Lake' in reference to a local tradition that it was once connected with Shala. There is no geological evidence to suggest that the two lakes have been connected at any point in the 500 years since the Galla settled this part of the Rift Valley. But oddly enough, this would have been the case some 5,000 years ago, when Abiata and Shala both formed part of a larger body known as Lake Galla, whose surface stood about 100m above the present-day level, so that the peaks of the crater in which Lake Shala is situated would have protruded as a chain of disconnected islands.

Anybody who visits this national park expecting to see large mammals is likely to be disappointed. A few Grant's gazelle live in virtual captivity at the ostrich farm next to the main entrance gate, but much of the rest of the park, which originally supported thick acacia woodland, was heavily settled and cultivated during the last years of the Derg. Wildlife has suffered badly as a consequence. Baboons are quite common, though not nearly so visible as the abundant livestock brought into the park by cattle herders. There may still be viable breeding populations of greater kudu, Grant's gazelle, Abyssinian hare, black-backed jackal and spotted hyena, but I saw no evidence of their presence. Short of being the subject of a major programme of re-introductions, Abiata-Shala can no longer be regarded as a mammal sanctuary of any note.

The main attraction of the park today is the scenic lakes, and their attendant waterbirds. Shala's main point of avian interest used to be the practically inaccessible Pelican Island, formerly an important breeding ground for white pelican as well as various species of cormorant and stork. Sadly, most of these birds have deserted their former breeding ground, an exodus that is probably attributable to the drop in Abiata's water level. The birds used to breed at Shala and feed on Abiata's fish, but the increased salinity caused by the fall in water has killed off the fish, and the pelicans and other fish-feeding birds have been forced to forage further afield.

A positive effect of Abiata's declining water level has been a marked increase in the number of algae-eating birds, with mixed flocks of almost 300,000 greater and lesser flamingos sometimes recorded. The flamingos typically arrive in the area from Kenya at the end of the rains and stick around for up to four months. Abiata is now the better lake for birds, particularly during the European winter when the shallows support thousands of migrant waders – large flocks of avocet alongside rarities such as Mongolian plover, Pacific golden plover, grey plover and red-necked phalarope – and the sky is a seething mass of darting European swallows. In all, more than 300 bird species have been recorded in Abiata-Shala; what survives of the park-like woodland around Lake Shala is one of the best places in Ethiopia to see a good range of acacia-related species such as hornbills, starlings and sparrow-weavers.

Also of interest is the hot spring on the northeast corner of Lake Shala. The water here throws up a cloud of steam and is hot enough to be used by local people for cooking maize cobs. It's also a popular bathing spot: the sight of the naked or white-robed bathers stumbling through the swirling steam gives the place a curiously Biblical quality, rather spoiled by heaps of discarded maize cobs and the kids who accumulate around you asking for money and photos.

More than anything, Abiata-Shala is of interest because it highlights some of the central issues facing African conservationists. It is the most heavily encroached park that I have seen in Africa, and in many respects its status as a conservation area seems a bit of a joke. But easy as it is to laugh, Ethiopia's conservation authority is desperately under-funded and the government of such a poor country cannot place conservation at the top of its priorities. My first reaction on seeing the hot springs overrun by bathers and littered with their waste was annoyance. On balance, I wonder if it is realistic, or even right, to want to preserve a pristine quality purely to satisfy the aesthetic sensibility of tourists. Local people are using the springs for heat and water, and are using the reserve's land for grazing and cultivation. Surely that is their prerogative?

Putting aside the rights and wrongs of the situation, the fact is that Abiata-Shala is not the most impressive of national parks, except perhaps for dedicated birders. If you have your own vehicle or are operating to time restrictions, it's debatable whether the park is worth visiting at all, especially when far more alluring national parks beckon further south. For backpackers, however, the park is definitely worth devoting a day to. Walking is permitted, though it is advisable to take an armed guard for security, and an excellent 12km round trip from the main entrance gate will allow you to see most places of interest, including a well-positioned viewpoint over the two lakes, the hot springs, and the shore of Lake Shala. An entrance fee of birr 50 per person per 48 hours is charged, while vehicle entrance costs birr 10 – multiple entries within the 48-hour period are permitted. An optional guide will cost around birr 50 extra per party.

Getting there and away
The main entrance gate is boldly signposted on the Moyale road directly opposite the turn-off to the Langano Bekele Mola Hotel; any vehicle passing between Ziway and Shashemene can drop you there. If you plan on hiking to the lakes, it's advisable to get an early start, as the area becomes very hot around midday. The most sensible approach would be to speak to the rangers at the gate when you first arrive and organise to leave early the next day, then to head to the Bekele Mola for the night and walk back up to the gate in the morning.

Where to stay and eat
In a private vehicle, the park can easily be visited as a day trip from any hotel in the Langano region, or for that matter en route between Addis Ababa and points further south. For backpackers on a reasonably generous budget, the obvious place to stay is at the Bekele Mola Hotel at Lake Langano just 3km from the entrance gate (see page 436). A far cheaper option, however, would be to spend the night at Arsi Negele (see below). Self-sufficient travellers in a private vehicle could also think about staying at the little-known and inexpensive self-catering hut that lies on the southern shore of Lake Shala close to Chitu Hora, and can be reached along a 20km track from Burra or Awara on the Shashemene–Sodo road – ask at the gate or at the park headquarters in Arsi Negele for further details.

ARSI NEGELE
This small town on the Shashemene road about 30km south of the Abiata-Shala entrance gate is the site of the national park headquarters. With an early start, Arsi Negele could easily be used as a base from which to visit the national park as a day trip – there's plenty of traffic between the two. There is no shortage of accommodation either, though the smart new **Awash Park Hotel** is the only place to transcend shoestring status.

Situated next to the Kura Evangelical Church only 2km from Arsi Negele in the direction of Addis Ababa, there is a circle of five stones, each with a ring engraved on the top and what could be a symbol of grass or wheat nearer the base. When I asked locally, nobody could tell me much about these stones, but the degree of weathering makes it difficult to accept that they were carved, as one local suggested, a mere 40 years ago. My guess, recently confirmed by the tourist office in Dilla, is that they are so-called **Gragn Stones**, of similar vintage and origin to the ones at Tiya and Silté.

SHASHEMENE
Best known for the Rastafarian community called Jamaica that lies on its northern outskirts, the sprawling town of Shashemene is the major transport hub in southern Ethiopia, connecting the main road between Addis Ababa and Moyale to routes east to Dodola and Bale National Park, west towards Sodo-Walaita, Arba Minch and the Omo River, and southeast to Kebre Mengist and Negele Borena. Unfortunately, Shashemene has little going for it other than its logistical convenience. It is the archetypal junction town: a mushrooming amorphous clutter of ugly buildings and leering, loutish youths with a population that has reputedly risen by more than 2,000% to a total of 86,000 in the last decade or so.

Shashemene is the one town in Ethiopia that receives consistently negative reports from travellers. The main reason for this is a decided element of hostility towards

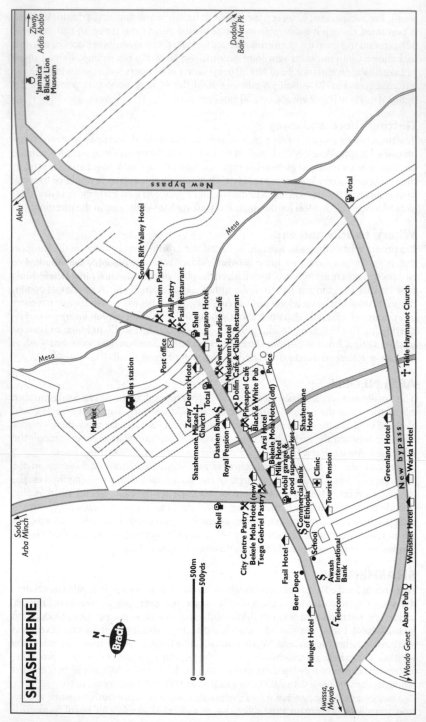

SHASHEMENE

N

Bradt

0   500m
0   500yds

Ziway,
Addis Ababa

Dodola,
Bale Nat Pk

'Jamaica'
& Black Lion
Museum

Alelu

New bypass

Mesa

Total

South Rift Valley Hotel

Mesa

Lemlem Pastry
Alfa Pastry
Fasil Restaurant
Shell
Langano Hotel
Sweet Paradise Café
Meskerem Hotel
Dolfin Café & Cilalo Restaurant
Pineappel Café
Black & White Pub
Police
Tekle Haymanot Church
Shashemene Hotel

Post office

Bus station

Market

Zeray Derass Hotel
Shashemene Mikael
Church   Total
Dashen Bank
Royal Pension
Arsi Hotel
Bekele Mola Hotel (old)
Mile Hotel
Mobil garage &
good supermarket
Commercial Bank
of Ethiopia
Clinic
Tourist Pension

Sodo,
Arba Minch

Shell

City Centre Pastry
Bekele Mola Hotel (new)
Tsega Gebriel Pastry

Fasil Hotel

Beer Depot
School
Awash
International
Bank
Telecom

Muluget Hotel

New bypass

Greenland Hotel
Warka Hotel
Wubishet Hotel
Abaro Pub

Wondo Genet

Awassa,
Moyale

foreigners – one reader awards Shashemene the all Ethiopia 'Fuck You' prize in reference to a popular local manner of addressing visitors. Theft, too, appears to be an increasingly serious concern. Leaving a car unlocked in Shashemene is inviting trouble, and one should be circumspect about trusting any teacher, civil servant, or other professional who becomes overly concerned about your welfare. If you need an escort to the bus station or whatever, arrange it through your hotel – a few travellers have been mugged and stripped of their possessions by seemingly trustworthy people who befriended them in a bar or restaurant.

Unless you are visiting Jamaica, Shashemene is probably the last place you'd want to stay the night by choice. But junction town it is, and if you spend a while in the south you may well need to bed down in Shashemene at some point. Otherwise, your first reaction on arriving there will almost certainly be to try to move on as soon as possible. If you decide to follow this impulse, it's worth knowing that there is no shortage of public transport to the infinitely more appealing town of Awassa, or to the popular hot-springs resort at Wondo Genet, both of which are covered later in this chapter and lie around 20–25km from Shashemene.

Getting there and away

Shashemene lies slightly more than 250km from Addis Ababa, a roughly four-hour drive along a good asphalt road. Regular buses leave throughout the morning to and from Addis Ababa, and take about six hours in either direction. Direct buses to and from Mojo or Ziway to the north leave regularly throughout the day.

Heading on from Shashemene, your options are wide open. Minibuses ply between Shashemene and Awassa throughout the day, leaving every 15–30 minutes and taking a similar time to get to their destination. There is also reasonably regular transport throughout the day to Sodo-Walaita in the west, Dodola in the east and Dilla in the south. Direct buses to or from destinations further afield such as Yabello or Moyale (south), Arba Minch (southwest) Goba or Dinsho (east) and Kebre Mengist or Negele Borena (southeast) generally leave in the morning only. For such routings, you are advised to check departure times and book a seat the evening before you plan to travel.

Where to stay
Moderate

South Rift Valley Hotel (67 rooms) ↘ 046 1103725. Situated north of the town centre along a side road connecting the old main road to the new bypass (it's signposted, if you look closely) this perennially popular hotel set in attractive green grounds has recently been upgraded to a smart five-storey block and it's also the only place in town with a 24-hour water supply. The spacious rooms in the new block all have DSTV and en-suite hot shower, and cost birr 80–120 during the week and birr 100–130 at weekends depending on size. The perfectly acceptable dbl rooms in the old block cost birr 50 and also come with DSTV and en-suite hot shower. A good restaurant is attached.

Budget

New Bekele Mola Hotel ↘ 046 1103348. Situated along the main road opposite its older namesake, this three-storey hotel seems very good value at birr 35 for a clean en-suite room with hot water and a genuine dbl bed. It often fills up early, so it's worth ringing ahead to make a booking.
Shashemene Pension This new hotel on the back roads behind the Old Bekele Mola has very clean, comfortable rooms, but they seem like poor value at an inflated *faranji* price of birr 50, especially as the showers are common.

Shoestring

Old Bekele Mola Hotel ↘ 046 1103344. Predictably, the original Bekele Mola is looking a little tired these days, but it really isn't bad value at birr 17 for a clean tiled dbl using common showers.

Tourist Pension This is the best deal in this range, charging birr 15 for a very clean room with a ¾ bed and en-suite cold shower. But there are literally dozens of other cheapies to be found along the main road, most of which charge birr 10–15 for a basic room using common showers.

Where to eat
The Western dishes served at the **Bekele Mola** and **Rift Valley** hotels are good value at birr 10–15 for a large main course. Several hotels along the main road serve Ethiopian dishes. **Fasika Pastry** is the best pastry shop in town, with good fruit juice and cakes, and excellent crusty bread – worth stocking up on if you plan on camping at Langano or Wondo Genet. There are plenty of bars along the main road – the wildly decorated bar in the **Zeray Derass Hotel** is among the liveliest. Excellent fruit juice is served at the **Fasil Hotel** opposite the Commercial Bank of Ethiopia.

Excursions
In addition to the places mentioned below, Shashemene lies only 25km north of the far more pleasant town of Awassa, described below, and it would serve as a good base for a day visit to the Senkele Game Reserve on the Arba Minch road (see *Chapter 25*).

Wondo Genet
This popular hot-springs resort lies among forested hills near the village of **Wosha**, about 20km south of Shashemene. The nominal attraction is the swimming pool fed by the springs just outside the entrance of the government hotel. The springs are said to have curative properties, which encouraged Emperor Haile Selassie to build a private lodge that has subsequently been integrated into the hotel. The road up to the hotel peters out about 500m past the swimming pool, but not before you can check out the boiling, bubbling vents where the hot water rises. Beyond this, there are several footpaths up the hill, and the open view behind you means there is little danger of getting lost.

The Wondo Genet area is of great interest to hikers and nature lovers. The hotel gardens support Anubis baboon, guereza and grivet monkey, as well as raucous flocks of comical silvery-cheeked hornbill and the beautiful white-cheeked turaco. The juniper-covered hills behind the hotel support a large variety of forest birds, including mountain buzzard, spotted creeper, Abyssinian woodpecker, yellow-fronted parrot, banded barbet, double-toothed barbet, Ethiopian oriole, Ethiopian slaty flycatcher, tree pipit and black saw-wing. Knowledgeable freelance bird guides can be located at the entrance to the hotel and charge birr 30 to take a guided walk in the surrounding forest – they are excellent at locating the elusive Narina trogon. Regularly seen forest mammals include bushbuck. Also of interest is swampy **Lake Dabashi**, about 4km west of Wosha. The swamps are reputedly home to hippos and crocodiles, and they support a wide range of water and forest birds. There is a road between Wosha and the lake.

Getting there and away
In a private vehicle, Wondo Genet can be reached by driving south through Shashemene to the Telecommunications Tower, from where a clearly signposted road branches east to the resort. There are a few buses daily between Shashemene and the village of Wondo Genet, but take note that the turn-off to the springs and Wabe Shebelle hotel is 5km *before* Wondo Genet, at Wosha. From Wosha it is 3km to the hot springs and hotel; the turn-off is clearly signposted.

Where to stay
Wabe Shebelle Hotel (39 rooms) ☎ 046 2203763; e washo.et@ethionet.et; www.wabeshebellehotels.com.et. Constructed as an imperial holiday residence during the Haile Selassie era, this pleasantly faded government hotel lies in wooded grounds right next to the hot

springs. The large, clean en-suite dbl rooms seem pretty good value at birr 146 wkday, which is the quietest time to visit, or birr 184 over weekends (the wkend rate includes a lamentable buffet breakfast). The angular 1970s-style restaurant makes an eloquent case for the introduction of architectural crimes against humanity as a hanging offence, though this particular offender might just be spared the noose for having had the good sense to face the patio towards the spectacular sunsets over Lake Awassa!

Abyssinia Hotel ⟩ 091 1231948. The best of a few inexpensive hotels situated in Wosha, 3km from the hot springs, this charges birr 35 for a clean tiled room with a ³/₄ bed and en-suite shower. More basic rooms are available for birr 15.

'Jamaica' Rastafarian Community

Many travellers who visit Shashemene do so to spend time at the nearby Rastafarian commune, which is known informally as 'Jamaica' and was formed (as the name suggests) by a group of Jamaican devotees of Haile Selassie during the later years of the emperor's reign. Until recently, unsolicited visitors to the commune were not made to feel particularly comfortable, though travellers who were invited by individual Rastafarians they had met in Shashemene or elsewhere were welcomed warmly. These days, however, tourists are welcome to pop into the recently opened Black Lion Museum, which celebrates the community's Rastafarian roots, and formal house-stays can also be arranged at a fixed rate. The popularity of 'Jamaica' is likely to rocket if there is any truth to persistent rumours that the late great Bob Marley is to be reburied outside Shashemene. The commune and museum is clearly signposted along the Addis Ababa road about 2km from the town centre, near to the junction with the Dodola road.

Senkele Game Sanctuary

This 58km² reserve lies to the south of the Shashemene–Arba Minch road near the small centre of Aje. The reserve was set aside to protect the country's largest concentration of the endemic Swayne's hartebeest, though the original herd of 3,000 has diminished to a few hundred because of poaching both during and after the civil war. Despite this reduction in numbers, the small size of the reserve and open terrain make it the one place in Ethiopia where Swayne's hartebeest sightings are practically guaranteed. Other mammal species to be seen in the light acacia woodland that covers the reserve include greater kudu, oribi, waterbuck, warthog and common jackal. More than 100 bird species have been recorded.

The turn-off to the sanctuary is 5km past Aje; it's a further 10km between the turn-off and the entrance gate. There are 65km of roads in the sanctuary. Walking within the reserve is permitted, but access is a problem without your own vehicle. There is no campsite or accommodation in the reserve, but you could visit Senkele as a day excursion from Shashemene or en route to Arba Minch. There are also a few basic hotels in Aje.

AWASSA

The lakeside city of Awassa is situated at an altitude of 1,685m in the Rift Valley 275km south of Addis Ababa and 25km south of Shashemene. It was formerly the capital of Sidamo region, and is today the capital of the snappily entitled Southern Nations, Nationalities and Peoples' region, an ethnically and linguistically diverse region formed in 1994 when five of the Derg-era regions of Ethiopia, Sidamo included, were amalgamated into one administrative unit. Awassa is the largest city in the Ethiopian Rift Valley, supporting a population of around 116,000, and the compact, attractively laid-out centre has an unusually bright and modern character. In addition to being a convenient staging post for journeys south towards Moyale, Awassa is an amiable and comfortable place to spend a night or two, with the added bonus of lying on the easterly shore of the pretty Rift Valley lake also called Awassa.

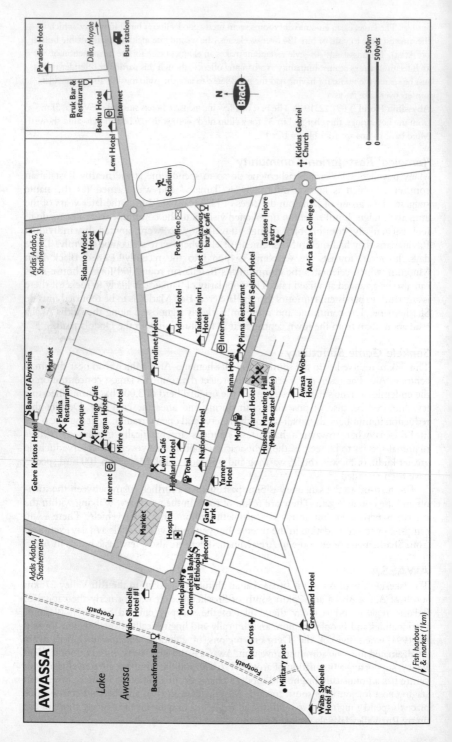

The main attraction of Awassa is undoubtedly its lake, which is the smallest in the Ethiopian Rift Valley, covering an area of around 9,000ha. Set in an ancient volcanic caldera, Lake Awassa has no outlets, yet the water remains fresh, and the lake supports a rich variety of plankton and an abundance of fish. The mountainous backdrop of the lake, together with the lush fringing vegetation, matches any of the Kenyan Rift Valley lakes for scenery. The dense scrub and fig woodland along the lake's shore is well preserved and teeming with birds. Guereza and grivet monkeys are practically resident in the grounds of the second Wabe Shebelle Hotel, and very habituated to people. Hippos are also present in the lake, but generally only seen from a boat – these can be hired at the small beach at the end of the main road near the Unique Park Hotel.

Built to prevent flooding when the lake rises, a dyke runs along the shore of Awassa close to the town. It starts about 1km north of the first Wabe Shebelle Hotel, and then runs southward almost to the second Wabe Shebelle Hotel (you have to cut back to the road just before the second hotel, as a military camp prevents direct access). The dyke doubles as a good walking trail, and is of special interest to birdwatchers. Fish eagle, silvery-cheeked hornbill, grey kestrel, several types of weaver, and the endemic black-winged lovebird, yellow-fronted parrot, banded barbet and Ethiopian oriole are common in patches of forest. Blue-headed coucal, Bruce's green pigeon and white-rumped babbler are regular in the marshy scrub east of the footpath. A variety of herons, storks, terns, plovers and waders are to be seen in the water or along the shore, and there is perhaps no better place in Africa to see the colourful and localised pygmy goose.

In the city centre, there is a worthwhile open market, which draws colourful villagers from all around on the main market days of Monday and Thursday. There is a daily fishing market on the lakeshore, about 1km south of the second Wabe Shebelle Hotel. For a good view over the lake, climb the small but steep Tabor Hill, also behind the second Wabe Shebelle Hotel. The Commercial Bank of Ethiopia changes US dollars cash and travellers' cheques, as well as other major currencies.

Getting there and away

Awassa lies on the surfaced road from Addis Ababa to Moyale. The 275km drive from Addis Ababa takes four to five hours. The 25km stretch between Shashemene and Awassa can normally be covered in less than half an hour. Coming to Awassa, note that a high proportion of public transport from destinations to the north, east and west will terminate at Shashemene. This isn't a major inconvenience, as a steady stream of minibuses covers the 25km road between Shashemene and Awassa, so you'd be unlucky to wait more than 15 minutes for onward transport. Buses from destinations to the south, such as Moyale and Negele Borena, will normally stop at Awassa before continuing on to Shashemene. The new bus station in Awassa is 15 minutes' walk from the main road and around half-an-hour by foot from the Wabe Shebelle hotels, so you might want to catch a horse-drawn *gari* into town. Most transport coming from the direction of Shashemene does follow the lakeside road into town, before turning into the main road at the roundabout between the Unique Park Hotel and the bank, so you can ask to be dropped somewhere more convenient before reaching the bus station.

When you're ready to move on from Awassa, its subservience to Shashemene as a transport hub should be taken into account. There are at least two buses daily running directly from Awassa to Addis Ababa via Ziway, as well as from Awassa to Arba Minch via Sodo. Buses from Shashemene to destinations along the Moyale road must pass through Awassa, but there is no guarantee that you will get a seat if you wait for them there. For other destinations, you will generally have to catch a minibus through to Shashemene first. For relatively nearby towns, such as Sodo or Dodola, this isn't a major concern, as transport leaves from Shashemene throughout the morning. For longer hauls, for instance to Goba or Moyale, buses tend to leave Shashemene in the early morning only, so you might need to spend the night in Shashemene before heading on.

Where to stay
Upmarket

Hotel Pinna (32 rooms) ⚲ 046 2202343/2210335. The only hotel in Awassa to be placed in the upmarket category on pure merit (as opposed to an inflated *faranji* price), the Pinna scores well on pretty much every account except for the uninspired location. The rooms range in price from birr 160 for a dbl (with king-size bed) or birr 192 for a twin to birr 225–275 for a large suite – all with en-suite hot showers, mosquito netting and DSTV.

Awassa Wabe Shebelle Hotel #1 (36 rooms) ⚲ 046 2205393/5/6; e washo.et@ethionet.et; www.wabeshebellehotels.com.et. Were it not for the fence that divides it from the lake, this stalwart government hotel would have a superb location, but even as things stand the grounds are very attractive, and the service and food – at one time a source of regular complaints – have improved immeasurably in recent years. Unfortunately, things are let down by the en-suite rooms, which range in price from birr 127–167 but would be poor value at half – nay, a third – of that price.

Awassa Wabe Shebelle Hotel #2 (28 rooms) ⚲ 046 2205397; e washo.et@ethionet.et; www.wabeshebellehotels.com.et. If it's location you are after, this has to be your first choice, even though the scruffy en-suite rooms are radically overpriced at birr 94/157 for an en-suite sgl/dbl with hot shower. For most visitors, however, the relaxed atmosphere and well-wooded lakeshore grounds will more than compensate. Indeed, the hotel virtually functions as a wildlife sanctuary: fish eagles nest in the fig trees, guereza and vervet monkeys and silvery-cheeked hornbills are regular visitors, woodland and water birds are everywhere, and even the odd hippo makes an appearance. The restaurant is pretty good, too.

Lewi Hotel (20 rooms) ⚲ 046 2206310. Formerly one of the better deals in town, this comfortable high-rise hotel has subsequently *faranji*-priced itself out of contention, with rates that have tripled in the space of three years to stand at birr 160/180 for a mediocre sgl/dbl with en-suite hot shower and DSTV. The location close to the bus station makes it very convenient for an overnight stopover, rather less so should you intend to spend time at the lake. A restaurant, pastry shop and bar are attached.

Moderate

Paradise Hotel (24 rooms) ⚲ 046 2204336/68. Situated close to the bus station, this pleasantly modest new hotel offers genuine value for money at birr 52 for a clean, tiled room with en-suite hot shower or birr 58 for a similar room with 32-channel DTSV. Recommended!

Beshu Hotel (20 rooms) ⚲ 046 8824634. Situated around the corner from the Paradise, this new hotel is also good value at birr 56 for a bright tiled dbl with en-suite hot showers and TV.

Gebre Kristos Hotel (30 rooms) ⚲ 046 2202780/1. This reasonably central and reasonably priced high rise has a variety of rooms ranging in price from birr 52 for a sgl with ¾ bed to birr 80 for a large twin. It is a little more rundown than the hotels above, but still good value, and all rooms are en suite with hot water and mosquito nets.

Yamere Hotel This long-serving hotel on the main street charges birr 95 for compact but good-quality en-suite rooms with a proper dbl bed, birr 150 for larger rooms, and birr 25 for rooms using the shower.

Budget

Midre Genet Hotel (22 rooms) ⚲ 046 2203810/2200185. This central hotel lies about ten minutes' walk from the lakeshore and charges birr 40 for a large, clean tiled room with a genuine dbl bed and en-suite hot showers, or birr 10–12 for an adequate room without a shower. Good value!

Kifre Selam Hotel (16 rooms) This conveniently central hotel has clean, carpeted rooms with an en-suite cold shower and dbl bed for birr 36, as well as more basic rooms for birr 10. Also good value!

Shoestring

Admas Hotel Rising head and shoulders above the usual herd of sordid cheapies, this clean and quiet hotel set in the back roads halfway between the bus station and the lakeshore charges birr 20 for a room with ¾ bed and en-suite cold shower or birr 10 for a room using the common shower.

Medruth Pension Tucked away in an alley off the main road, this quiet guesthouse charges birr 20 for a clean little room with a sgl bed and en-suite cold shower.

Where to eat

Both government (**Wabe Shebelle**) hotels do decent Western dishes at very reasonable prices. The second wins out on service and atmosphere – in fact, you could happily spend the afternoon relaxing here before or after a meal. In the town centre, adjacent to the eponymous hotel, the **Pinna Restaurant** consists of a ground-floor pastry and coffee shop and first-floor restaurant, both of which are excellent and inexpensive. The **Lewi Hotel** near the bus station serves good local and foreign dishes, with the roast lamb recommended. The **Post Rendezvous** next to the post office is recommended for fish cutlets and fruit juices. Heading right from the junction at the church at the top of the main road, the **Logitta Restaurant**, **Tirufat Hotel** and **Alte Hotel** are all recommended for local dishes by a volunteer working in Awassa, while the new **Kai Wat Restaurant** opposite the Pinna is a slightly more upmarket version of the same thing. Several other juice and pastry shops lie along the main road and in the **Hussein Marketing Centre**.

23

The Bale and Arsi Highlands

This chapter covers the former administrative regions of Bale and Arsi, both of which still retain a distinct identity in the minds of most Ethiopians, despite having been incorporated into the Federal State of Oromia in 1995. Bale and Arsi lie in the moist green highlands southeast of the Rift Valley, and are generally quite cool by day and often very cold at night. The highlands support several substantial towns, most notably the former regional capitals of Goba (Bale) and Asela (Arsi). More easterly parts of Bale are low-lying, dry and hot, giving way to the Somali desert. So, too, are the plains to the south of Bale, around Dola Mena and Negele Borena, an area covered at the end of this chapter.

The regional travel focus is Bale Mountains National Park, which protects Ethiopia's second highest mountain range and is the best place for viewing a cross section of the country's unique vertebrates, including Ethiopian wolf, mountain nyala, Menelik's bushbuck, giant molerat and 16 endemic bird species. The national park offers good facilities to hikers, but can also be crossed by vehicle or on horseback. A new hiking and trekking circuit outside of the national park, developed with German funding near the small town of Dodola, easily ranks as the most organised eco-tourism project in Ethiopia.

The northern gateway town to the Arsi–Bale region is Dodola, which is situated close to the junction of the two most widely used road routes to Goba from Addis Ababa. The more direct of these routes, as followed in this chapter, runs via Adama, Asela and Dodola, and was in very poor condition in early 2005, when it took nine bumpy hours to get between Adama and Goba. Bale can also be approached from the Rift Valley, using a road that connects Goba and Shashemene via Dodola. Whichever way you approach Dodola, the road to Goba runs right past the park headquarters at Dinsho, so it is advisable to stop there rather than go on to Goba.

A more obscure route into or out from Bale runs south from Goba to Dola Mena and Negele Borena, from where you can cut west to the main Moyale road via Kebre Mengist (emerging north of Dilla) or via Arero (emerging at Yabello). The road south of Goba runs across the Sanetti Plateau – the highest point in the park and the best place to see Ethiopian wolves – and through the Harenna Forest before arriving at Dola Mena. This route is certainly not on if you are in a rush – it will take at least three days to complete on public transport – but if you have the time it is well worth using, both for scenery and for wildlife.

It is possible to drive from Addis Ababa to Bale National Park or Goba over one long day. The better route is via the Rift Valley, since it is surfaced as far as Shashemene and (if you're not in a rush) offers access to the lovely Rift Valley lakes. The route via Asela is more scenic, so there is a strong case for heading down to Goba on one road and returning on the other. For those using public transport, direct buses run between Goba, Shashemene and Addis. Alternatively, the trip can be done in hops, using a combination of light vehicles, local buses and trucks. There is no normal public transport between Goba and Negele Borena, but light vehicles cover the route.

The area covered in this chapter is of singular interest to birdwatchers and the loop through Bale Mountains National Park to Yabello via Negele Borena is likely to form the core of any serious ornithological tour of Ethiopia. The Bale park headquarters at Dinsho is an excellent spot for montane forest endemics, while the Sanetti Plateau is the best place in Ethiopia to see highland endemics and unusual migrant raptors, and the Harenna Forest hosts an interesting selection of forest birds. Genale, on the road to Negele Borena, is the most reliable site for the eagerly sought Ruspoli's turaco, while the dry badlands around Negele Borena host two very localised endemic larks. The run from Negele Borena to Yabello offers a chance to see two species known only from southeast Ethiopia and Somalia, while Yabello itself lies at the epicentre of the small territory of the endemic Streseman's bush crow and white-tailed swallow.

ASELA

Asela is the nondescript administrative capital of Arsi zone, which, according to the Asela Ras Hotel's publicity pamphlet, is 'famous for its wild animals'. Hmmm... while it's true that relict populations of mountain nyala do still persist in the region's more remote forests, Arsi as a whole strikes me as more notable for its decidedly domesticated hillsides, where orderly green fields of millet, maize, barley and rapeseed are bounded by neat rows of eucalyptus trees to form a series of unspectacular but eye-pleasing vistas vaguely reminiscent of the English countryside. As for Asela itself, it's difficult to think of anything remotely interesting to say about this neat little highland town, which lies at an elevation of around 2,300m and makes for a reasonably attractive overnight stop between Addis and Bale. There's nothing much to do in Asela, but the town is small enough that you could wander out to explore the surrounding country lanes, which on a clear day offer great views eastward towards the 4,021m peak of Mount Chilalo – a gently ascending climbable goal if you have a couple of days to spare!

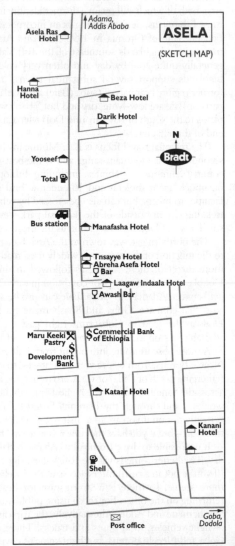

Getting there and away

Coming from Addis Ababa, you need to follow the 100km surfaced road to Adama, where a right turn at the main central junction leads after another 75km of graded dirt road to Asela. In a private vehicle, the trip should take about four hours, with the possibility of stopping at Sodore or Dera Delfekar Reserve along the way (see *Excursions*, page 373). On public transport, the most straightforward option is to hop on a bus to Adama, where you can easily pick up another bus to Asela. Transport between Asela and Dodola, to the south, generally leaves in the early morning.

Where to stay
Moderate
Asela Ras Hotel ❧ 022 3311089. Built in the 1970s, this pleasant and fairly well maintained government hotel charges birr 50 for a second-class room (one ³/₄ bed, hot shower) and birr 87 for a larger first-class room (two sgl beds, hot bath). There's a pleasant bar attached, and the cavernous restaurant serves decent meals at around birr 10–15.

Budget
Beza Hotel The pick of a cluster of private hotels close to the Asela Ras, this stands on a short side road, is signposted in Amharigna only, and charges birr 25 for a clean dbl with en-suite hot water.
Kanani Hotel This small hotel in the back roads is good value at birr 30 for a large en-suite room with a dbl bed and hot shower.
Laagaw Indaala Hotel This is arguably the best private hotel in Asela, but it seems relatively poor value at the inflated *faranji* price of birr 20 for a small room with ³/₄ bed using common shower, or birr 40 for a better room with en-suite hot shower.
Hanna Hotel Recommended in previous editions of this guide, this place has capitalised on the traveller custom by inventing a silly *faranji* price of birr 30 for a basic room with a cold shower.

Shoestring
Tensae Hotel The best of the cluster of shoestring hotels set around the bus station, this friendly place charges birr 10 for a room using common showers.

Where to eat
The best place to eat is the **Asela Ras Hotel**, where decent Western meals cost birr 10–15. **Maru Keekii** opposite the Commercial Bank of Ethiopia is the best place for pastries, while the patio bar at the **Kataar Hotel** serves snacks and fruit juices. The garden bar next door to the Kataar looks to be a good spot for a drink.

ASELA TO DODOLA
The gateway town to the Bale region is Dodola, which lies at the junction of the Asela, Goba and Shashemene roads. If you're coming from Shashemene, you'll find no difficulty getting a bus through to Dodola, but things are less straightforward coming from Asela. There are rumoured to be direct buses, but I never located one and instead ended up hopping from town to town.

The first town to head for is **Bekoji**, which lies some 56km past Asela at a crisp altitude of 2,700m. At least one bus covers this route, leaving at 06.30, and there may sometimes be another bus later in the day. This is a lovely drive, through evocative frosty moorland covered in heath-like plants. Bird enthusiasts should keep an eye open for wattled ibis and Abyssinian longclaw. The local horsemen, swathed in warm shawls and blankets, put me in mind of the Basotho of Lesotho. Certainly if you felt like exploring the area, you'd have no difficulty finding a horse or mule to hire.

Bekoji itself is a large, sprawling country town, and the surrounding countryside has enormous walking potential. Running potential, too, come to think of it! This unassuming town and its immediate environs can lay claim to being the birthplace of a rash of top international long-distance runners, including an incredible five Olympic medallists: the legendary 5,000 and 10,000m world-record holder Haile Gebre Selassie, the two-time women's gold winner Derartu Tulu, the 2004 gold and silver medallist Kenenisa Bekele, the 1996 women's marathon champion Fatuma Robe, and recent bronze medallist Tirunesh Dibala. Athletics talent spotters are pointed to Bekoji's finest, the **Hotel Ibsaa**, which stands 50m from the bus station and asks birr 20 for an en-suite room with ³/₄ bed and cold shower.

From Bekoji, there is supposedly the odd bus on to **Asasa**, but I found it more productive to wait outside the bus station for a private truck or pick-up – you'll have to pay the same as you would for a bus but you should get away more quickly. In the vicinity of Meraro, about 30km south of Bekoji, the 2,960m Kara Pass is flanked by the 4,190m Mount Kasa to the west and the 3,806m Mount Enkolo to the east. From here on, you'll start to see the yellow and orange aloes that are so characteristic of the Bale area, and also large rural homesteads ringed by neat mud or euphorbia enclosures. Asasa itself is similar in size and feel to Bekoji, and there are several small hotels. It's only 14km on to Dodola, and the towns are connected by a regular minibus service, but arriving late in the day you may choose to stay put.

DODOLA AND ADABA

Dodola, although it is situated a few kilometres past the junctions of the roads from Asela and Shashemene, was until recently a workaday highland town – altitude 2,400m – with little to offer tourists. That all changed, however, with the recent opening of an elaborate network of mountain huts and hiking and trekking trails through the forested mountains to the south of Dodola and Adaba (a small town 29km east of Dodola on the Bale road). Part of an Integrated Forest Management Project (IFMP), and backed with German funding and expertise, this professional and well-organised set-up is of considerable significance to the conservation of the fauna and flora of some of Ethiopia's most extensive remaining montane forest and moorland. It is also fantastic news for keen hikers and trekkers, who can spend anything from a couple of days to a week exploring the scenic trails and seeking out Ethiopia's endemic wildlife. For those without time to undertake extensive hikes, the attractive Lensho Waterfall, about 30 minutes' walk from Dodola town centre, forms a good goal for a short walk – the IFMP office can supply detailed directions.

Getting there and away

Coming direct from Addis Ababa, a bus service via Asela leaves the main Autobus Terra at 07.00 and arrives in Dodola at about 15.30. Another direct bus service via Shashemene leaves Addis Ababa at 08.00. Details of travelling from Asela to Dodola are covered under the heading *Asela to Dodola* earlier in the chapter. Several buses daily run between Shashemene and Dodola, taking two to three hours in either direction. There appears to be a regular bus service between Dodola and Adaba, and the trip takes around one hour. The bus may not run in the afternoon.

A village near the small town of **Kofele**, which lies 50km from Shashemene along the Dodola road, was for some years known in birding circles as *the* place to see the rare Abyssinian long-eared owl, which was reliably to be found roosting in a group of eucalyptus trees. Recent reports suggest the bird has moved on or passed away, but if you want to check it out, the local children will know whether it's around and where to find it.

Heading eastward from Adaba, it's 58km to the Bale National Park Headquarters near Dinsho. At least one bus heading towards Bale will pass through Dodola and Adaba in the mid morning, but you may struggle to find a seat. I had no problem finding a lift on a truck between Adaba and Dinsho. Once you've got a lift, you'll be treated to some of the most sensational landscapes in southern Ethiopia: craggy peaks interspersed with streams and waterfalls and, between August and November, fields of blue and yellow wild flowers and stands of red-hot poker. A few kilometres before entering Dinsho, the road passes briefly through the Gaysay sector of Bale National Park, where you are almost certain to see mountain nyala and may well catch a glimpse of a member of the Ethiopian wolf pack that is resident in the area.

Where to stay and eat

Bale Mountain Hotel 〵 046 6600016. The best place to stay in Dodola, this hotel opened in 1998 as a starting base for hikers, and it is clearly signposted about 1km out of town along the Asela–Shashemene road, behind a Mobil filling station and a short walk from the IFMP headquarters. Two types of room are available, all with one dbl bed. Rooms using a common hot shower cost birr 20, while en-suite rooms with hot shower cost birr 30/40 for sgl/dbl occupancy. The hotel is set in green grounds surrounded by hedges, and the restaurant serves beers, sodas and coffee, and Western and local meals by advance order.

Kabale Hotel This more central government-run hotel on the main road about 100m from the bus station is the next-best option in Dodola, with acceptable dollar-a-night rooms and clean communal toilets and showers.

Asefa Hailu Hotel Adaba's finest, this pleasant lodge lies opposite the post office and has clean rooms with private hot showers for birr 20. Also in Adaba, there is an excellent little coffee shop behind the Shell garage, and the Hotel Abiya serves decent local meals and drinks.

ADABA–DODOLA INTEGRATED FOREST MANAGEMENT PLAN

The recently established IFMP circuit of guided trails and huts through the mountains south of Dodola and Adaba forms an excellent and inexpensive goal for keen hikers and trekkers. Implemented by the German aid organisation GTZ, the project is a non-profit activity aimed at conserving the remnants of the area's Afro-montane forest by creating employment and generating community earnings from tourism. The main attraction of the trail is the mountain scenery and high-altitude vegetation, which comprises some 50,000ha of natural forest as well as areas of Afro-alpine moorland. Birdlife is prolific and large mammals are present in small numbers. The mountains covered by the trails are effectively a western extension of the Bale range, and there are plans to link the IFMP trails and huts with two new huts that are due to be constructed in Bale's Web Valley.

The dominant tree types in the forest zone are the African juniper, the coniferous *Podocarpus falcatus* and the fragrant *Hagenia abyssinica*. Above 3,200m, forest gives way to open moorland of Saint John's wort and heather, dotted with giant thistle shrubs with ball-shaped red flowers and giant lobelias. The juniper and hagenia forests protect a similar composition of birds to that found at Dinsho. Among the more visible species are wattled ibis, Rouget's rail, black-winged lovebird, yellow-fronted parrot, banded barbet, Abyssinian woodpecker, Abyssinian longclaw, Abyssinian catbird, white-backed black tit, Ethiopian oriole, white-cheeked turaco, black kite, augur buzzard and lammergeyer. The most visible large mammals are vervet and guereza monkeys, but Ethiopian wolf, mountain nyala and Menelik's bushbuck inhabit the mountains, and although they are not as common as in Bale, they are sometimes seen by trekkers.

The circuit of trails connects five simple but fully equipped mountain huts. Running from west to east, these are Wahoro (3,300m), Angafu (3,460m), Adele (3,300m), Mololicho (3,080m) and Duro (3,350m). The full circuit can be covered over five nights and six days, but any one of the huts can be reached from the trailhead within four hours, so it is possible to visit one or two huts only. IFMP encourages visitors to trek on horseback, for which no prior riding experience is necessary. Hiking is also permitted, but ascending to an altitude of 3,500m can be very tiring, particularly if you are not acclimatised to high altitudes. A guide must accompany all visitors. The best time for

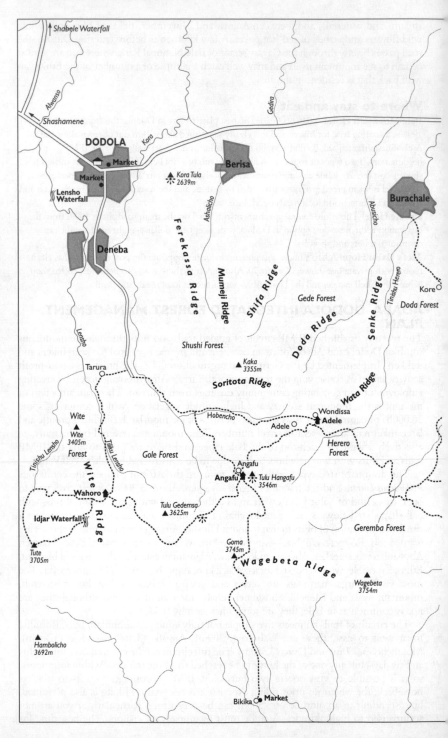

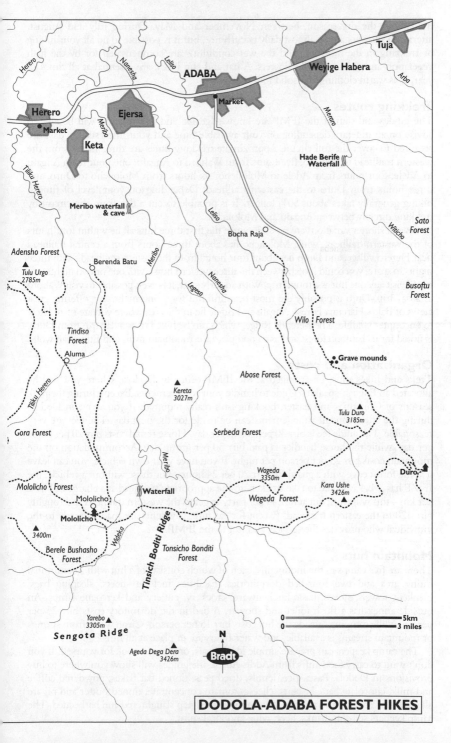

DODOLA-ADABA FOREST HIKES

trekking is the dry season, between November and May. During July and August, afternoon showers are an almost daily occurrence, but it is possible to do all your hiking or trekking in the morning, and the wet conditions are compensated for by the lush vegetation and abundant wild flowers. A hat and sun block are essential at all times of year, as is warm clothing and solid footwear.

Trekking routes

The guides and staff at the IFMP are knowledgeable and helpful, and will be able to advise on an itinerary depending on your available time and your interests. Six days are required to cover the full circuit. Approximate trekking times are three hours from the western trailhead to Wahoro, five hours from Wahoro to Angafu, one hour from Angafu to Adele, four hours from Adele to Mololicho, six hours from Mololicho to Duro, and three hours from Duro to the eastern trailhead. Depending on your level of fitness, hiking generally takes about 50% longer. It is possible to cut a day from the circuit by trekking directly between Angafu and Mololicho.

Several shorter variations are possible, since the first three huts all lie within four hours of the western trailhead, while Mololicho lies about three hours from a central trailhead near Herero village, and Duro lies about four hours from the eastern trailhead. With three nights to spare, you could loop between the three western huts; with one or two nights you could visit any one hut as a round trip. With an early start, it is even possible to visit Wahoro as a day trip. Duro is possibly the most beautiful hut for a one-night stay, offering great views of Bale's Harenna Forest. Angafu and Adele lie in the area where you are most likely to encounter wildlife. The Berenda Ridge, which can be hiked to as a day trip from Duro, is noted for its bamboo forest and as a good place for mountain nyala and Ethiopian wolf.

Organisation and costs

Treks and hikes must be arranged at the IFMP office in Dodola, where you will be allocated an English-speaking guide to handle your requirements. Except during the peak seasons of Christmas and Easter, booking isn't really required. If you arrive in Dodola during the afternoon, all arrangements can be made for the next day. The fees are very reasonable. The guide fee is birr 30 per group per day. Horse rental costs birr 20 per horse per day, while the horse handler is paid birr 30 per group day. Accommodation on the mountain costs birr 25 per person per night. If you have your own vehicle, you can leave it at the forest edge with a guard for birr 20 per 24 hours. For those without a vehicle, the IFMP has a 4x4 available to take trekkers to the appropriate trailhead at a charge of birr 2 per km – this will work out at birr 44 per party to get to the western trailhead and roughly birr 120 to the eastern trailhead. Except for car hire, payments are made directly to the individual who provides the service, and not to the IFMP.

Mountain huts

There are five camps in the mountains, each of which consists of a hut with a communal eating area and two four-bed dormitories. Facilities include sheets, sleeping bags, blankets, towels, stoves, basic kitchenware, crockery, cutlery and kerosene lamps. An outside annex has a flush toilet and shower. A bed in the dormitory costs birr 25 per person, while camping outside the hut costs birr 15 per person. Clean water from springs or mountain streams is available, and water filters are in place at all huts.

The camp keepers can prepare simple local meals, or you can cook for yourself. If you don't want to carry foodstuffs from Addis Ababa, the guides will show you where to buy provisions in Dodola. Pasta, rice, lentils, dried peas, tinned oat flakes, powdered coffee and milk, chocolate bars, biscuits, cheese, tomato concentrate, tinned butter and oil are all available. You can also arrange to have a goat or sheep slaughtered and barbecued. The camp keepers sell soft drinks, beer, wine and local spirit.

Further information
The project has an informative website www.baletrek.com, and information sheets and an excellent colour map are available at the office in Dodola. Although trekking arrangements can usually be made on the spot, queries and advance bookings can be directed to the Dodola office at the head office in Addis Ababa ($\searrow$ *011 6610083;* f *011 6621738;* e *tds@ethionet.et*).

BALE MOUNTAINS NATIONAL PARK
This scenic 2,200km² national park, set aside in the 1960s but never officially gazetted, protects the higher reaches of the Bale range, including Mount Tullo Deemtu, which at 4,377m is the second highest peak in Ethiopia. The main attractions of the park are the wild alpine scenery, particularly on the 4,000m-high Sanetti Plateau, and the relative ease with which one can see up to a dozen endemic birds as well as Ethiopian wolves and mountain nyala. Bale is very accessible on public transport, and can be explored on foot, or on horseback, or by vehicle – the road across the Sanetti Plateau, built by the Derg to provide an alternative emergency access route to the south, is reportedly the highest all-weather road in Africa.

The Bale Mountains are of relatively ancient volcanic origin, having formed from solidified lava more than 10 million years ago. The slopes above 3,500m supported glacial activity until as recently as 2,000 years ago, and still receive the occasional snowfall, most often in the dry season between November and February. More than 40 streams including the Web, Genale and Welmel rise in the Bale Watershed, most of which eventually flow into the mighty Juba or Wabe Shebelle rivers after they cross the border into Somalia.

The main habitats protected by Bale are juniper and hagenia woodland, Afro-montane forest, and Afro-alpine moorland. The juniper-hagenia woodland lies at elevations of between 2,500m and 3,300m, and is mostly found on the northern slopes, such as around the park headquarters at Dinsho. At similar elevations on the southern slopes, the vast and little-studied Harenna Forest is the park's main stand of Afro-montane forest. Afro-alpine moorland is characteristic of altitudes above 3,500m, with the most extensive patches to be found on the Sanetti Plateau and in the Web River Valley. The moorland, as well as the open vegetation below the forest zone, is characterised by wonderful wild-flower displays, particularly between August and November. One of the most common and distinctive plants throughout the Bale region is the red-hot poker, an aloe that grows to shrub height and can be identified by its orange spear-shaped flowers.

The characteristic large mammals of Bale's juniper woodland are the mountain nyala and Menelik's bushbuck (a species and race endemic to Ethiopia) as well as warthog and bohor reedbuck. Moorland is the favoured habitat of the Ethiopian wolf. Commonly seen mammals of the extensive Harenna Forest, which lies south of the Sanetti Plateau, include guereza, vervet monkey, the localised bamboo-dwelling Bale monkey, olive baboon, Menelik's bushbuck and bushpig. Large predators such as lion, leopard and African wild dog are resident but rarely seen by visitors. Bale National Park region is undoubtedly the best part of Ethiopia for endemic birds.

Accessible as it is today, Bale was one of the last parts of Africa to attract serious scientific exploration, and it remains sufficiently out of the way even today that very few travellers make it there by comparison with, say, the Simiens. The earliest-recorded visitor to the Sanetti Plateau was the German naturalist Carl van Erlanger, who traversed it in 1899, discovering the giant molerat in the process. Bizarrely, no further expedition to the upper slopes of Bale was documented between then and the late 1950s, when the Finnish geographer Helmer Smels made several visits to the area, discovering – among other things – that the mountains hosted a previously unsuspected population of the rare Ethiopian wolf. It was the British naturalist Leslie Brown, upon visiting the mountains in

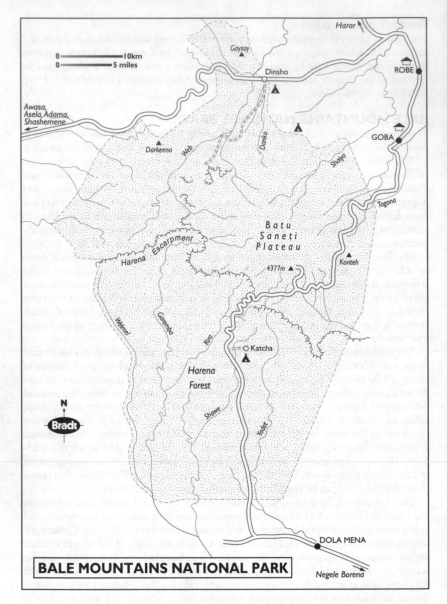

BALE MOUNTAINS NATIONAL PARK

1963, who first recognised that Bale might actually be the wolf's main stronghold, and it was he who proposed that the area be set aside as a national park. Only in 1974 did James Malcolm collect the first wolf census data to confirm Brown's belief.

An entrance fee of birr 50 is levied per 48 hours. No fee is charged simply for driving or using public transport on the public roads through the park. Written by Ethiopian wolf expert Stuart Williams, the excellent 52-page booklet *Bale Mountains: A Guidebook* was published in 2002 by the Ethiopian Wolf Conservation Programme in conjunction with various other international conservation bodies, and can be bought at a few bookshops in Addis Ababa as well as at the park headquarters at Dinsho.

Orientation and access

The park headquarters and resthouse are situated off the Dodola–Goba road, about 2km east of the village of Dinsho. The forest immediately around the headquarters is the best place to look for the park's endemic antelope and forest birds. It is also where all hikes and treks must be set up and paid for. Coming from the direction of Dodola in a private vehicle, you need to drive through Dinsho and continue uphill in the direction of Goba, then take the signposted turn-off to your right and follow it for about 1km. Any bus or truck heading between Dodola and Goba will stop at Dinsho, from where it takes about 30 minutes to walk to the headquarters following the same route. When you decide to move on from Dinsho, note that most buses passing through Dinsho in either direction will be full. Get an early start, and ask any trucks that pass through for a lift.

By road, the Sanetti Plateau lies about 60km from Dinsho, following the main road through Robe and Goba, then continuing south from Goba towards Dola Mena. The Harenna Forest lies further south along the same road. This is an all-weather road, and it can be driven along in a private 4x4, or else by using the limited public transport that runs between Goba and Dola Mena (see page 467). To visit the plateau by road, it is best to base yourself in Goba. To visit it by foot or horseback, you will have to make arrangements at Dinsho.

Where to stay

There is an excellent **resthouse** tucked away in the juniper forest at the park headquarters. A variety of rooms are available and cost from birr 20–50 per person depending on facilities. Bedding can be provided on request. The resthouse has a communal kitchen, toilets and showers, and a large lounge with a log fire. The small museum displays a selection of stuffed animals, including several endemics. Mountain nyala and Menelik's bushbuck often walk past the resthouse gardens, as do warthog. If you are staying here, you'll probably want to take advantage of the kitchen and cook for yourself. Basic foodstuffs such as eggs, potatoes and macaroni can be bought in Dinsho, but it's advisable to bring most of what you need along with you. A couple of restaurants in Dinsho offer scrambled eggs, *injera* and *shai*.

The facility-free **campsite** on a hill behind the resthouse offers panoramic views over Dinsho village and across to several peaks, including Batu Tiko. The hill is covered in heath-like vegetation and juniper forest and there is plenty of wildlife to be seen in the area. Camping costs birr 20 per person.

Dinsho itself is an attractive montane village: chilly, wet, and recently uplifted by the arrival of electricity. There are a few dollar-a-night hotels from where you could explore the national park as a day trip. The **Hoteela Tsehai** and **Hoteela Genet**, which lie opposite each other on the main road through town, have basic dollar-a-night rooms and acceptable local restaurants. The unexpectedly smart appearance of the **Wolf's Den Café** might raise expectations – no food was available on last inspection, however, only a leaflet offering organised treks and hikes in the national park.

The only option at present for overnight trekkers and hikers is to camp at one of several designated sites. However, plans are in place for a network of **mountain huts** to be constructed; the first two huts should be situated within the Web River Valley and at the top of the valley. Although primarily aimed towards hikes and treks based out of Dinsho, these huts will be linked by a footpath to the most easterly of the IFMP huts north of Adaba, with the long-term goal of creating an extended network of trails and huts running from Dodola to the Sanetti Plateau.

In addition to the limited accommodation in and around Dinsho, a far better selection of hotels is to be found in **Goba** and **Robe** towns, both of which lie outside the national park but are close enough to Dinsho to serve as a base for motorised visitors. If you intend heading to the Sanetti Plateau and Harenna Forest, or continuing south towards Dola

Mena, it's best to spend a night in Goba beforehand. Robe and Goba are covered under separate headings on pages 465 and 467 respectively.

Activities and excursions
Dinsho Walking Trail
The walking trail which leads through the juniper forest around the park headquarters demands a few hours' exploration as it protects the main concentration of Bale's mountain nyala. This exceptionally handsome antelope is abundant in the area – estimated population is about 1,000 and it's not unusual to come across four or five herds – as is the superficially similar but much smaller and more solitary Menelik's bushbuck. Other mammals you can expect to see here are warthog, bohor reedbuck and possibly guereza monkeys. Birdwatching around the headquarters is good (see box *Bale's birds*), though, as is often the case, you will probably see fewer birds in the forest proper than you will in the broken woodland fringing the road that leads from the turn-off to the headquarters. The forest is characterised by light undergrowth, which allows for good game viewing, and also by the herby aroma of fallen hagenia leaves. An unusual plant of the Dinsho area is the white-flowered Abyssinian rose, the only flowering rose that is indigenous to Africa.

The Gaysay Extension
This northerly extension of Bale National Park protects the 3,543m Mount Gaysay, as well as the eponymous river and small Lake Bassasso. Gaysay is of particular interest to travellers with limited time and without transport, since it is transected for several kilometres by the Dodola road, starting about 3km west of Dinsho. Some indigenous forest remains here, with both mountain nyala and Menelik's bushbuck commonly seen in forest clearings, but otherwise the area is covered in moist grassland that becomes quite marshy near the lake and river. At least one pack of Ethiopian wolf has a territory centred on the Gaysay extension, and I've twice now seen a wolf from the main road. The marshy

---

BALE'S BIRDS
Bale National Park is rightly regarded to be the best place to see a good range of those birds that are endemic to Ethiopia and Eritrea. At least 16 such endemics have been recorded in the park, including the Bale parisoma, which is unique to Bale, and a casual visitor could hope to spot most of them over the course of a few hours each at Dinsho and on the Sanetti Plateau. In addition to its endemics, Bale is a good site to pick up several localised highland birds and migrant waterfowl and raptors, and the park supports isolated breeding populations of several other noteworthy species.

Even before arriving at Dinsho, it is worth stopping a few times as you pass through the Gaysay extension of the park, a reliable site for the endemic Rouget's rail and Abyssinian longclaw, as well as several other water and grassland birds. Dinsho itself is an excellent spot for endemics – black-winged lovebird, white-backed black tit, Abyssinian catbird, Abyssinian slaty flycatcher, thick-billed raven and white-collared pigeon – while other forest birds include white-cheeked turaco, Abyssinian ground thrush, olive thrush and Cape eagle owl.

The most alluring birdwatching spot is of course the Sanetti Plateau. The ascent there from Bale is not without interest. Forest patches along this road hold similar species to Dinsho, notably the nondescript but endemic Bale parisoma. Ascending above the forest zone, the alpine chat and endemic black-headed siskin are abundant, and moorland and chestnut francolin often dart across the road. A few pairs of very confiding Rouget's rail are resident along the artificial drainage stream that runs to the left of the road for about 1km.

areas also support birds more normally associated with the Sanetti Plateau, most visibly Rouget's rail, which is very common here. Guide walks to Gaysay can be arranged at the park headquarters about an hour away on foot. It is also possible to hike to the top of Mount Gaysay.

Web River Valley

Set at an elevation of roughly 3,500m, about 10km southwest of Dinsho, the Web Valley supports a moorland cover similar in appearance to the Sanetti Plateau, though with a markedly different floral composition, dominated by various Alchemilla species. Abundant small rodents make the Web Valley ideal Ethiopian wolf territory: several packs are resident, and as easily seen as they are on the Sanetti Plateau, despite large numbers having perished as a result of a (rapidly contained) rabies outbreak in 2003. The rough 11km track between Dinsho and the Web Valley takes about an hour to drive – 4x4 only – and involves crossing a natural rock bridge over the Danka River where rock hyrax are frequently observed. There is an attractive waterfall at the confluence of the Web and Wolla rivers. With an early start, it is possible to hike or trek to the Web Valley as a day trip out of Dinsho. Camping is permitted in the area.

Sanetti Plateau

The Sanetti Plateau is cited as the world's largest expanse of Afro-alpine moorland, a montane habitat confined to altitudes of 3,500m to 4,500m on east Africa's tallest mountains. Because such habitats are isolated from similar ones on other mountains, they tend to display a very high degree of endemism, and Sanetti is no exception. Among other things, the plateau is renowned for supporting the most substantial extant population of Ethiopian wolf, which is far more numerous and more easily seen here than in the Simien Mountains. It is some measure of how little explored Bale was until recent times that this wolf population was first made known to science in 1959. Other characteristic

At one or other of the tarns on the Sanetti Plateau, you can be confident of sighting the endemic blue-winged goose, wattled ibis and spot-throated plover, as well as a representative of sub-Saharan Africa's only breeding population of ruddy shelduck and, in season, a number of migrant waterfowl. An isolated population of the localised wattled crane is present seasonally, and usually easy to observe when it is around. The variety of smaller birds is somewhat limited. Red-throated pipit, Thekla lark, Abyssinian longclaw and (seasonally) yellow wagtail are the common ground birds, while the lovely tacazze sunbird is often seen feeding on flowering aloes.

The commonest raptor is the auger buzzard, sometimes seen in its localised melanistic phase. Kestrels and buzzards are quite common too: the rare saker falcon has been recorded three times on the plateau, though be aware that the more common lanner falcon here often has an unusually pale crown. Sanetti is a great place for large eagles. The tawny eagle is the most common of these, supplemented by the European imperial and steppe eagle. In 1993, it was discovered that Bale hosts sub-Saharan Africa's only recorded breeding population of golden eagle. The plateau also supports the most southerly breeding population of the crow-like chough.

The Harenna Forest, though less well known scientifically, supports a greater variety of forest birds, with new records likely as more birders explore the area. Endemics include white-backed black tit, Abyssinian catbird, Abyssinian woodpecker, Ethiopian oriole, yellow-fronted parrot and the taxonomically uncertain brown saw-wing swallow. Other specials include the African cuckoo hawk, and brown-backed honeyguide.

mammals of the plateau are golden jackal and klipspringer, neither of which is seen with great frequency, and Abyssinian hare, the endemic giant molerat, and a number of other endemic small burrowing rodents.

The Sanetti Plateau can be driven to from Goba town in about 45 minutes. The road starts with a 1,300m hike in altitude, through tangled thickets and woodland where francolins sprint across the road and, in summer, fields of red-hot poker point ever skywards. Look back, and the plains around Goba stretch to an indistinct horizon. About 13km past Goba, the road levels out and you are surrounded by typical Afro-alpine vegetation: clumped grey heather interspersed with lichen-covered rocks and stands of giant lobelia, strange other-worldly plants that can grow up to 3m high and whose corky bark and waxen leaves readily withstand extreme sub-zero temperatures. Ethiopian wolf are unexpectedly common, most often seen singly or in pairs sniffing out small rodents before they can scurry to the safety of their burrows. About halfway across the plateau the road skirts a series of crystal-clear tarns, where you can expect to see several endemic birds as well as migrant waterfowl. Somewhat desolate in appearance when it is overcast, the plateau is uniquely beautiful under blue skies, particularly in the soft light of early morning and late afternoon.

In a private vehicle, a round trip to the plateau from Goba should take about four hours, depending of course on how long you choose to spend up there. Travellers without a private vehicle can visit the plateau on a three- or four-night trek out of Dinsho, or by catching a lift with one of the trucks that serve as public transport between Goba and Dola Mena. It is possible to hire a 4x4 for the day through one of the hotels in Goba, but this will cost at least US$100.

Harenna Forest

At the southern end of the Sanetti Plateau, the Harenna Escarpment affords an astounding view over the forest almost 2,000m below. The road then switchbacks exhilaratingly to the base of the escarpment, where the green heather suddenly transforms to a Grimm-Brothers' forest of low gnarled trees laden with moss and swathed in old-man's beard. The forest clears as you hit a collection of mud huts known as Rira, where, with a bit of luck hot tea and dry biscuits are available. After Rira, the road south towards Dola Mena continues through the Harenna Forest for a further 40km or so.

Before 1983, when the road under discussion was cut, the Harenna Forest was virtually unknown to science and, although a pioneering expedition has since collected several new amphibian and reptile species, the bulk of the Harenna Forest has never been explored and there are doubtless countless species awaiting discovery. The forest is far denser than the juniper woodland around Dinsho, and it comprises a more varied selection of trees, with a similar appearance and composition to the forests found on other east African mountains. A wealth of birds is resident, while mammals likely to be seen from the main road include olive baboon, guereza monkey, bushbuck and bushpig. Leopard are still around, a pride of four lions is resident in the area around the campsite, and African wild dogs are seen from time to time – most recently that I'm aware of in 1999.

As with the Sanetti Plateau, the Harenna Forest can be visited as a day trip out of Goba in a private vehicle. Allocate a full day to the trip, and leave as early as you can. With camping equipment and a private vehicle, you could pitch a tent at the small campsite a few kilometres from Rira. Hiking or trekking to Harenna from Dinsho isn't a realistic proposition, unless you have a lot of time to spare. All transport between Goba and Dola Mena passes through the forest.

Overnight treks and hikes

The staff at the park headquarters can arrange hikes and pony/horse treks deeper into the park. These range from one to five days in duration. The most popular option is a three-day horse or pony trek to the Sanetti Plateau, which allows you plenty of time to explore the alpine moorland and all but guarantees a sighting of Ethiopian wolf. The park can organise horse hire from Dinsho for birr 14 per animal per day, and a guide will cost birr 40. You must organise your own food. Several day hikes to nearby peaks are also possible. Arrangements are flexible and the warden and rangers can advise you according to your time restrictions and interests. There is excellent trout fishing in the rivers around Dinsho – the guides at the resthouse can provide information. Also worth checking out is the Tuesday market in Dinsho town.

ROBE

The town of Robe lies on the main Goba road 25km past Dinsho and 13km before Goba itself. It is a large town with adequate facilities, but strangely subdued and nondescript, straggling for a couple of kilometres along a eucalyptus-lined main road. There are few compelling reasons to stay in Robe, unless perhaps you are heading to Sof Omar (see page 466) on public transport, or else you are motorised and want to use the pleasant and sensibly priced Bekele Mola Hotel as a base to explore the region. The hectic Thursday market is worth a look. A possible 4x4 day excursion from Robe is to Gasera, which offers a magnificent viewpoint over the Wabe Shebelle Gorge, home to Ethiopia's most southerly gelada population. Gasera lies about 65km out of Robe, branching northward from the Dinsho road after 6km, then turning right at the small market town of Ali after another 20km or so.

Getting there and away

Coming from Dinsho, any vehicle heading towards Goba can drop you at Robe. The new bus station stands in isolation some distance from the town centre along the Goba road, so unless you are heading for the Bekele Mola, ask to be dropped off more centrally. There is regular light transport between Robe and Goba.

It is worth noting that finding transport out of Robe towards Dodola can be difficult as most buses come from Goba and will be full when they pass through Robe at around 11.00. More sensible, perhaps, is to get up

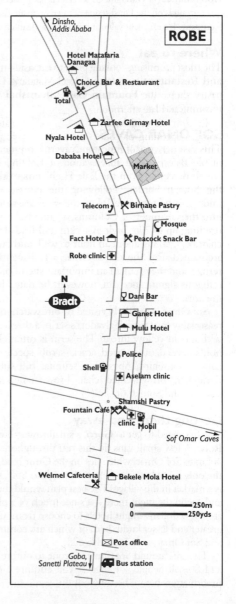

ROBE

Dinsho, Addis Ababa

Hotel Matafaria Danagaa

Choice Bar & Restaurant

Total

Zarfee Girmay Hotel

Nyala Hotel

Dababa Hotel

Market

Telecom — Birhane Pastry

Mosque

Fact Hotel — Peacock Snack Bar

Robe clinic

N

Bradt

Dani Bar

Ganet Hotel

Mulu Hotel

Police

Shell

Aselam clinic

Shamshi Pastry

Fountain Café

clinic Mobil

Sof Omar Caves

Welmel Cafeteria — Bekele Mola Hotel

0 ——— 250m
0 ——— 250yds

Post office

Goba, Sanetti Plateau ↓ Bus station

early and wait for a lift in a truck or private vehicle at the police roadblock at the Dinsho end of town, or else catch a local bus to Goba, where long-haul buses start.

Where to stay

Bekele Mola Hotel Clearly signposted on the Goba side of town between the bus station and main traffic roundabout, this hotel is far better value than anything in Goba. The semi-detached rooms are large and airy, with en-suite hot showers, and cost birr 35/45 for a dbl/twin. The restaurant serves unmemorable but affordable Western dishes.

Hotel Matafaria Danagaa Of several cheaper places, the best is this simple lodge set in large quiet grounds on the Dinsho side of town opposite the signpost for the Ethiopian Insurance Company. It's excellent value at birr 15 for a clean en-suite room with cold shower and dbl bed.

Where to eat

The most promising-looking place to eat, aside from the Bekele Mola, is the **Choice Bar and Restaurant** next to the Hotel Matafaria Danagaa. Robe is well served with good pastry shops: the **Fountain Café**, **Shamshai Pastry** and **Welmel Cafeteria** are all recommended.

SOF OMAR CAVES

This vast network of limestone caverns, reputedly the largest in Africa, lies 100km east of the Bale range at an elevation of 1,300m. It has been carved by the Web River, which descends from the Bale Highlands to the flat, arid plains that stretch towards the Somali border. Following the course of the clear aquamarine Web River underground for some 16km, the caves are reached through a vast portal, which leads into the Chamber of Columns, a cathedralesque hall studded with limestone pillars reaching up to 20m high. A 1.7km trail leads from the entrance through several other chambers, taking about an hour to walk and crossing the river seven times. The caves are named after Sheikh Sof Omar, a 12th-century Muslim leader who used them as a refuge, and they remain an important site of pilgrimage for Ethiopian Muslims. Their religious significance can, however, be dated back to the earliest animist religions of the area.

Sof Omar is regularly visited by birdwatchers because it is one of two sites where it's reasonably easy to see Salvadori's serin, a threatened and localised dry-country endemic with a bold yellow throat. The serin is often elusive, but even if you miss it, the area holds several other good acacia-scrub species, notably orange-bellied parrot, blue-naped mousebird, Abyssinian scimitar-bill sulphur-breasted bush shrike, small grey flycatcher, brown-tailed chat, brown-tailed apalis, bristle-crowned and Fischer's starling, and Somali tit.

Getting there and away

You first need to get to **Goro**, a small town about 60km east and two hours' drive from Robe. A few small vans do this run throughout the morning. From Goro, it is roughly 40km to Sof Omar, which lies on the Ginir road. If you are restricted to public transport, the only day when you can get through to Sof Omar from Goro is Saturday, when there is a market in the village. The best plan would therefore be to head out to Goro on Friday and spend the night there – it's not much of a place and there is no electricity, but there are a few dollar-a-night hotels to choose from. On the way out to the caves, look out for greater and lesser kudu, both of which are common in the dry acacia scrub around Goro and Sof Omar, as is Salt's dik-dik.

The area around Sof Omar is prone to outbreaks of fighting between the local Oromo and Somali people – I suggest you enquire about security at the Bale National Park headquarters before heading out this way.

GOBA

The capital of Bale region lies at an altitude of around 2,500m in the cool, breezy foothills below the Sanetti Plateau. It's an open, spacious and rather unfocused town – the main residential areas sprawl outwards from a disused airstrip that is gradually being built over, while the government buildings and churches are perched discretely on a nearby hill. Like Robe, Goba has a subdued, almost rural atmosphere, which makes it seem cut off from the mainstream of Ethiopian life.

Getting there and away

Buses from Shashemene to Bale terminate at Goba, and there is also a steady stream of local transport from nearby Robe. Buses returning to Shashemene leave Goba between 08.00 and 09.30. Details of the route southwards to Dola Mena are below.

Where to stay

Goba Wabe Shebelle Hotel ❧ 011 5517187; f 011 5518477; e washo.et@ethionet.et; www.wabeshebellehotels.com.et. At the top of the range, this adequate government hotel lies in overgrown grounds about 2km out of town along the Robe road. The en-suite rooms with hot water cost birr 125/155 dbl/twin. The restaurant is head and shoulders above anything else in Goba.

Yilma Amossa Hotel Situated opposite the new bus station, this comfortable old hotel used to be a real gem, but standards have slid and *faranji* prices risen in recent years. The large en-suite rooms cost birr 40 and have a dbl bed, built-in cupboards, old wooden floor, basin, cold shower and private veranda covered in creepers. There are also more basic rooms using communal showers for birr 25. The rooms are the best of any private hotel in Goba, even if they do seem a touch overpriced, but a bigger turn-off is the noisy bar, which sometimes keeps throbbing until dawn. The once-excellent restaurant seems to have shut up shop.

Lama Hotel This nearby hotel is more reasonably priced, at birr 15 for a small en-suite room with three-quarter bed and cold shower, but before taking a room do check whether there's live music that night – or once again you're unlikely to get much sleep until the wee hours.

Genet Hotel Facing the bus station, this is about the best shoestring option, though the rooms are small and there is no running water. On the plus side, it is quiet, the people seem friendly, the grounds are large and rustic, the dbl beds are quite large, and they'll provide hot water by the bucket on request.

Where to eat

The best option, despite being some distance from the town centre, is the Wabe Shebelle Hotel. In town, the **Bartena Restaurant** is the best of a sorry bunch. On the plus side, several good pastry shops run along the main road – the **City Café** and **Sami Café** are recommended, as is the **Nyala Pastry** next to the Yilma Amossa Hotel. If you're heading out to Dola Mena and you fancy a breakfast or you want to stock up on eatables, the Nyala opens, with freshly baked bread on sale and coffee machine whirring, at the unusually early hour of 06.00.

GOBA TO NEGELE BORENA VIA DOLA MENA

The trip from Goba south to Negele Borena is one of the most exciting off-the-beaten-track routes in Ethiopia. Normally, it can be driven in a day in a private vehicle, or covered over two or three days using the hit-and-miss public transport. The road may be impassable in parts after heavy rain (one traveller wrote to say it took him six days to cover in the flooding of 1997). Before heading down this way in a private vehicle, you might want to check that the bridge over the Genale River has been rebuilt, or that the river itself is low enough to be fordable.

The best part of the journey is the initial 110km, where the road leads across the **Sanetti Plateau** and through the **Harenna Forest** (covered in detail under *Bale*

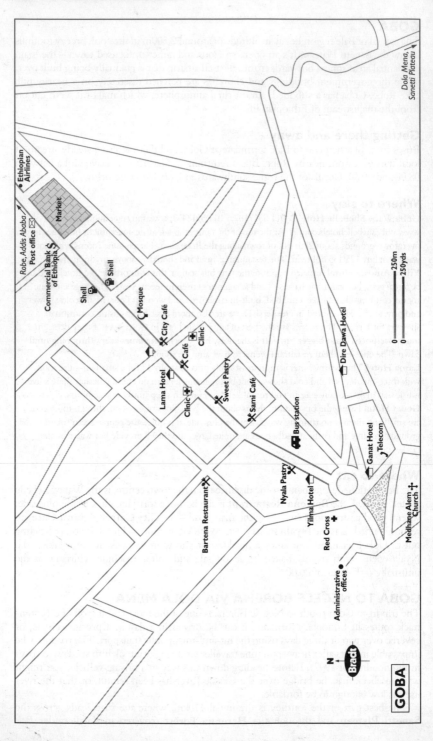

GOBA

N

Bradt

0   250m
0   250yds

Dola Mena,
Sanetti Plateau

Ethiopian
Airlines

Robe, Addis Ababa
Post office

Market

Commercial Bank
of Ethiopia

Shell

Shell

Mosque

City Café

Café   Clinic

Lama Hotel

Clinic

Sweet Pastry

Sami Café

Bus station

Dire Dawa Hotel

Ganat Hotel

Telecom

Nyala Pastry

Yilma Hotel

Bartena Restaurant

Red Cross

Administrative
offices

Medhane Alem
Church

Above Narga Selassie monastery, Lake Tana (AVZ)

Right Bet Emanuel rock-hewn church, 12m-high monolith, Lalibela (AVZ)

Below Royal compound, Gonder (AVZ)

Next page Boy sitting in cliff-entrance to Abuna Yemata Guh rock-hewn church (AVZ)

Mountains National Park on page 459) to Dola Mena. There are no buses between Goba and Dola Mena (a source of some relief when you tackle the steep descent to Harenna) and transport isn't prolific, but one pick-up truck runs in each direction on most days, leaving Goba from in front of the bus station between 06.00 and 07.00. It's worth asking about transport at the Yilma Hotel a day in advance, especially if you want a front seat. The going rate is about birr 25 for a perch in the back, double that for a seat up front. It's worth paying the extra, not only as protection from the elements, but also because it gives you the best vantage point for spotting birds and mammals and for taking photos. With binoculars, camera and field guides on my lap, in a vehicle moving slowly enough for game-viewing, and with a driver who seemed delighted to point out animals and several times offered to stop, I viewed it not as an expensive ride but a very cheap safari. For the combination of scenery, animal viewing and comfort, I would rate this as the best public transport ride I've done in Africa.

After the Sanetti Plateau and Harenna Forest, dusty little **Dola Mena** could hardly fail to be an anti-climax. I suspect, though, that under any circumstances it would be a bit of a dump. Nevertheless, whether you intend to retreat to Goba or advance to Negele Borena, you will almost certainly have to spend the night here. The whole tone of Dola Mena takes some adjustment after a few days in the Bale Highlands: dusty acacia scrub replaces lush cultivated fields; camels throng the marketplace (main market on Wednesday) and their skimpily dressed Somali owners replace the blanketed horsemen of the highlands. Most of all, those cold showers you flirted with in the Goba evening chill seem suddenly the stuff of dreams. There is electricity in Dola Mena; it seems so out of place as to be remarkable. The only hotels I could find in Dola Mena rub shoulders with each other on the Negele road. Neither has a name, and there's nothing much to choose between them: rooms cost less than a dollar and there are no showers. The precarious long drop at the hotel I chose made every toilet excursion feel like walking the plank (you really don't want to think about what's underneath). As for eating, you have the choice of *yefigel wat* or scrambled eggs, though careful perusal of the main road will reveal a restaurant with a coffee machine and fresh crusty bread. For amusement, you could wander down to the river outside town or the market, or glue yourself to the screen of the video cinema opposite the hotels.

I was told there is 'a lot' of transport between Dola Mena and Negele Borena, which, if my experience was representative, is something of an exaggeration. It does seem that at least one vehicle does the run daily, pretty much when it feels like it – I arose at 06.00 as instructed, only to find the vehicle was still cruising for passengers at 09.30. As with the Goba–Dola Mena run, fares are high (I paid birr 30 for a seat in the back of an open pick-up) and not particularly negotiable. When you finally hit the road, the first 20km out of Dola Mena are unpromising – dense acacia woodland and potentially good kudu country – but this is Ethiopia, and pretty soon you are climbing through broad-leaved woodland with sweeping views across rugged mountains in all directions. As the journey progresses, you'll notice some wonderful termite sculptures, many of which must top 5m in height. The 178km ride through this thinly populated countryside takes six to eight hours, and is broken by meal stops at **Midre** and **Genale** (see box *Genale and Prince Ruspoli's turaco*, page 470).

NEGELE BORENA

Negele is something of a frontier town, a cultural boiling pot that is predominantly Oromo but also has strong Somali, Borena and Muslim influences making it quite unlike anywhere else I visited in Ethiopia. Despite its size – Negele is unexpectedly substantial – there is a dusty impermanence about the place that I found quite appealing. The only really solid looking building in the town centre is the bank, otherwise the streets are lined with shanty-like homesteads and small private businesses. Negele's distinctive character and cultural blend are personified in one of the most lively and absorbing markets in east

GENALE AND PRINCE RUSPOLI'S TURACO

While it may be of limited interest to most people, the small town of Genale is a veritable Mecca for birdwatchers. The riverine forest along this stretch of the Genale River is a prime locality for sighting one of Africa's rarest birds, the beautiful Prince Ruspoli's turaco. This large and colourful frugivore is named after the Italian explorer who first collected a specimen in 1892, but died without making a record of where the turaco had been found. For a full 50 years after this, the locality and habitat favoured by the prince's enigmatic turaco was a mystery to scientists.

In the early 1940s, the first live specimen was recorded in the Arero Forest east of Yabello. It would be another 30 years before a second population was found at Genale. A couple of other sites have subsequently been discovered, and although the nest, eggs and habitat requirements of Prince Ruspoli's turaco remain a complete mystery, it is now thought that the bird is commoner than was previously supposed. Nevertheless, its remarkable appearance – large, bright green, with red eyelids and a floppy white crest – has combined with its unusual history and endangered status on the IUCN red list to ensure it ranks as among the most prized of Ethiopian endemics.

Prince Ruspoli's turaco is quite easy to locate in the riparian forest along the banks of the Genale River near the eponymous town, but you do need to know where to look. A local guide called Adem Dube has been recommended by several ornithologists, who would probably not have found the turaco without his expertise. It usually takes an hour or two to reach the right spot and locate the bird. There is a good chance of encountering several other interesting species along the way – black sparrowhawk, Narina trogon, Bruce's green pigeon, Levaillant's cuckoo, rufous chatterer and the highly localised white-winged dove and Juba weaver are all around. If you need to spend the night in Genale, it is a pleasant enough town, with a very attractive setting, and there are a few local restaurants and hotels to choose from. There is regular transport south to Negele Borena.

Africa – especially on Saturdays when the camel market is held. True enough, most people wouldn't go out of their way to visit Negele – birdwatchers once again being the exception – but it is a friendly and interesting place, and after two days of bump-and-grind in pick-up trucks, I was more than happy to settle in for a couple of nights.

Getting there and away

Transport from Goba and Dola Mena is described in the preceding section, and transport on to Kebre Mengist and Shashemene is described in the one that follows. In both cases, the route can be reversed without any significant changes, though it is worth noting that light vehicles out of Negele (for instance to Dola Mena) leave not from the bus station but from the marketplace.

A less obvious route to or from Negele, but one of particular interest to travellers who are tying in a trip to Bale with other parts of the far south, or who are coming to or from Kenya, would be to hop on a truck for Yabello or Mega. These leave from the market at around 06.00 on most days, and the 300km ride takes a full day. Mega lies on the main highway between Addis Ababa and the Moyale border, about 100km from the border post and 100km from Yabello. All transport along the Yabello–Moyale road stops at Mega. From Yabello, much transport continues north to Awassa and there should be a pick-up truck most days heading east to Konso, from where you can get transport on to Jinka or

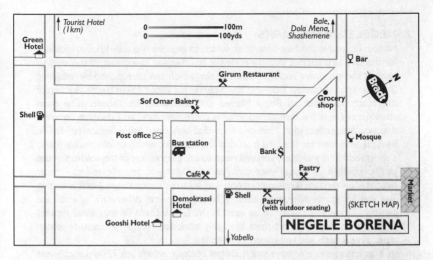

Arba Minch. This route is covered under the heading *From Negele to Yabello* later in this chapter.

Where to stay

Green Hotel The best accommodation is at this central hotel, where comfortable en-suite rooms cost birr 30 and rooms using a common shower birr 20. A good local restaurant is attached.

Tourist Hotel Also recommended, even if it is rather optimistically named, this hotel is perched on a small jacaranda-covered hill about 1km from the town centre. The comfortable old rooms have private toilets and showers, and cost birr 25. There are cheaper rooms using communal showers. The hotel has a bar but no restaurant.

Manashiree Liban Hotel Of the cheaper places, this recent recommendation, just five minutes' walk from the bus station, is run by an obliging English-speaking family, and charges birr 10 for a clean room using communal showers.

Where to eat

If you don't eat at your hotel, try the **Girum Restaurant**, especially if they are serving *espestino*, a deliciously spicy stew of beef, potatoes and carrots that I encountered nowhere else in Ethiopia (probably a Somali dish). They also do *wat* and pasta. For breakfast and snacks, the **coffee shop** with outdoor seating around the corner from the bank does good juices, coffee, cakes, bread and light meals such as eggs and pasta.

FROM NEGELE TO SHASHEMENE

The 320km drive westward from Negele Borena to the main Moyale road takes the best part of a day. One bus to Shashemene leaves Negele Borena every morning at around 06.00, taking about ten to 12 hours to reach its destination. The trip can also be covered in hops using the local buses and light vehicles that connect the small towns along the way.

A couple of buses leave Negele Borena for **Kebre Mengist** daily before 09.00. This is a 120km ride and it takes three to four hours, gently rising from the thorny, termite-sculpted landscapes around Negele to the dense forest and pine plantations of the southern highlands. Kebre Mengist is not the most intrinsically prepossessing place – the first serious *faranji* hysteria I had hit since Dodola, though not anywhere near as bad – but the forested surrounds offer some compensation. If you are staying over, the **Natsaanatti Hotel** next to the bank has very acceptable rooms with private shower and

NEGELE'S RARE LARKS

Negele Borena is the best base from which to explore the only known localities for the two lark species that are endemic to Ethiopia. The closer of the sites to town is the extensive and arid **Liben Plain**, which can be reached by following the main road southeast from the town centre for about 15km to the junction of the roads southeast to Bogol Manyo and southwest to Yabello. The main attraction here is the threatened Sidamo short-toed lark, an Ethiopian endemic that was first collected in 1968 and recorded only once again before 1994. The best place to look for this bird is around the junction, which unfortunately is also a sensitive military area, so you will need to ask permission of the soldiers at the junction before you leave your car. Assuming that you are allowed to – most people are – the lark is not uncommon within its restricted range, but it is elusive and can be quite difficult to identify because several other lark species are present. Other birds likely to be seen in the area include various small raptors and vultures, Somali short-toed lark, tiny cisticola, Heuglin's bustard, golden pipit, pygmy batis and red-naped bush-shrike.

The other, more remote site is **Bogol Manyo**, which lies 270km southwest of Negele along a rough dirt road that takes the best part of a day to drive. The only reason why you'd be likely to make this tedious excursion is to see the Degodi lark, a little-known and threatened species that was described as recently as 1975 and has only been seen by a handful of truly dedicated birdwatchers. Assuming that you fit in this category, the lark is easy to locate, and the long dusty drive there offers some more than acceptable birding in its own right. The stretch of road 50–60km east of Filtu has recently produced a few sightings of the endemic Salvadori's serin, and Ethiopian saw-wing swallow is also found in the area. Other birds that have been recorded along the road include grasshopper buzzard, imperial and martial eagle, buff-crested and white-bellied bustard, Somali bee-eater, black-throated barbet, red-naped bush-shrike, rufous-tailed rock-thrush, Shelley's starling, short-billed crombec, Somali tit, straw-tailed whydah and Somali bunting. There is no accommodation in Bogol Manyo, but visitors are normally permitted to sleep in the village hall for a negotiated fee. Bogol Manyo lies in a relatively sensitive border area, and it would be sensible to seek current advice before heading out this way.

toilet for birr 12, while the **Tegist Firee Hotel** opposite the Shell garage is the most attractive of the dollar-a-night jobs. The best place to eat, the **Betasab Restaurant**, is hidden away in the back streets, but anybody will be able to direct you there.

I was told I shouldn't miss the mushrooming mining settlement of **Shikaro**, which lies about 20km south of Kebre Mengist and the main road. It's an easy afternoon trip from Kebre Mengist as buses in both directions leave every half-hour or so, but the road out is a lot more interesting than the town itself. Shikaro is the quintessential mining town – ugly, loud and sprawling – and whatever charms it may have were entirely wasted on me. I was rather more interested in the forested ridge immediately south of the town; at least until I was informed it was crawling with armed policemen who are instructed to shoot suspected gold-collectors on sight. A more alluring prospect than Shikaro would be to disembark from the bus at **Abake Forest Station**, halfway between Kebre Mengist and Shikaro, where the road passes through some excellent forest. There are guereza monkeys and other large mammals to be seen in the area, and the birdwatching should be excellent (this is one of the few areas where the endemic Prince Ruspoli's turaco has been recorded). The least encroached-upon patch of forest starts about 1km past the forest station towards Shikaro.

Getting out of Kebre Mengist is fairly straightforward before mid morning. Buses to Shashemene leave at around 06.00 and 08.00, depending on how quickly they fill up. You could also wait for the bus from Negele, though that runs the risk of there being no seats available. The trip from Kebre Mengist to Shashemene takes a good eight hours.

From Kebre Mengist, the road climbs through light forest into a hilly area reminiscent of western Uganda, where small wood-and-thatch huts are lit by smoky fires, and surrounded by thickets of a plantain-like plant that is used to make porridge. The road then switchbacks into much denser forest, crawling with guereza monkeys and birds, and interspersed with thickly grassed meadows. This is a lovely area – if you're tempted to explore, the village of **Irba Muda**, 57km past Kebre Mengist, looks a suitable base, and there is at least one basic hotel (painted yellow). Irba Muda is ringed by cultivation, but it's all pristine forest and lush highland meadow beyond a radius of 1km or so.

The next town along the road, **Bore**, is about 27km past Irba Muda. Although it is just a dot on most maps, Bore seems a more substantial settlement than Kebre Mengist, and it's a popular lunch stop with bus and truck drivers. There is no forest close enough to Bore to warrant a special stop, but, in hindsight, it's probably a more attractive overnight option than Kebre Mengist. If you were coming from Negele and got to Kebre Mengist after all transport to Shashemene had departed, it might be worth looking for a lift as far as Bore – there's also far more onward transport from here. If you end up spending a night, the nameless hotel with a yellow façade, blue concrete veranda and a red gate serves good food and coffee, and the rooms look fine.

The scenery immediately after Bore, though a little dull, is enlivened in the rainy season by red-hot pokers. Then, rather suddenly, you hit the Rift Valley Escarpment, from where the road snakes downhill through eucalyptus plantations with occasional glimpses of Lake Awes in the distance. The descent is interrupted by a brief stop at the singularly ramshackle and charmless town of **Wendo**. There are a few basic hotels, but there's little reason to make use of them, especially when half an hour out of town you connect with the tarred Moyale road, from where it's a straightforward 60km cruise through the Rift Valley northwards to Shashemene via Awassa, or southwards to Dilla.

FROM NEGELE TO YABELLO

The rough and rutted 300km road directly connecting Negele Borena to Yabello is unlikely to do any favours to anybody with a susceptible back, nor will it hold much of interest to the average tourist, but it is travelled by almost all serious birdwatching tours through Ethiopia. The primary reason for this is that the road connects two towns known as the best place to spot particular endemics, but it also passes through an area of genuine ornithological interest in its own right. The road can be covered in a day with an early start, assuming you are in a private vehicle, but there is some basic accommodation in Arero, some 180km from Negele Borena, should you want to break up the trip. Public transport is as good as non-existent, though the occasional pick-up trucks that traverse the road will take passengers for a negotiable fee.

Coming from Negele, you need to follow the Bogol Manyo road southeast of town for about 15km, where a right turn to the southwest takes you on to the Yabello road. The junction lies at the north end of the ornithologically important **Liben Plain** (see box *Negele's rare larks*, page 472). About 10km southwest of the junction, the road skirts the **Mankubsa-Welenso Forest**, an unusually low-lying patch of open-canopy juniper woodland where the endemic Prince Ruspoli's turaco and Salvadori's serin both occur sparsely along with several other interesting forest species. The forest and surrounds are also home to a variety of mammals, including warthog, giant forest hog, leopard, spotted hyena, guereza and vervet monkey, and olive baboon.

Roughly 120km out of Negele, the road enters the small town of **Melka Guda**. Almost immediately after passing through this town, the bridge across the Dawa River is an obligatory stop for birders, since it is a reasonably reliable place to pick up white-winged turtle dove and Juba weaver, species whose range is restricted to southeast Ethiopia and neighbouring Somalia. Even if you miss these jackpots, a host of good birds – smaller black-bellied sunbird, golden pipit, Pringle's puffback, red-naped bush shrike and bare-eyed thrush – are common in the area.

Another excellent place to stop, and possibly spend a night, is **Arero**, which lies about 60km past Melka Guda near to the most southerly forest in Ethiopia. Local specials are headed by two endemics, the beautiful Prince Ruspoli's turaco and rare Salvadori's seedeater, both of which are fairly common in this area. More than 160 birds have been recorded in all, as has a fair variety of large mammals, notably bushbuck, bushpig, guereza monkey – even the occasional lion and leopard. Passing through Arero, a wide variety of dry-country species includes the endemic Streseman's bush crow and white-tailed swallow (see *Yabello for Birders,* page 483), along with black-capped social weaver, grey-headed silverbill, Archer's greywing and little spotted woodpecker.

The Moyale Road

The 500km road that runs southward from Awassa to the border town of Moyale is likely to be travelled in its entirety only by people heading to or from Kenya. Nevertheless, far from being just a feeder road, this long stretch of mostly well-maintained asphalt does boast several worthwhile and untrammelled cultural, archaeological and ornithological attractions. The largest town it passes through is Dilla, a relaxed agricultural hub set at the heart of an area of considerable archaeological interest for its ancient rock engravings and medieval stelae fields. Continuing south from here, green highland eventually gives way to low-lying acacia scrub, populated by colourful Borena pastoralists and their prized herds of cattle. Yabello, the largest town between Dilla and the border, is renowned among ornithologists for lying at the heart of the territory occupied by two of Ethiopia's most localised endemics: the white-tailed swallow and peculiar Streseman's bush crow.

Past Yabello, the Moyale road passes through the heart of Borena country towards the somewhat underwhelming small town of Mega. Wild mammals still persist here, albeit in low concentrations. Pairs of Guenther's dik-dik are regularly sighted on the side of the main road, while ground squirrels and mongooses scamper across it – and with luck one might come across larger antelope such as Grant's gazelle, gerenuk and lesser kudu. For a better chance of encountering large mammals – Burchell's zebra, warthog and the endemic Swayne's hartebeest – a side trip to the remote Yabello Game Sanctuary Park is a possibility for motorised travellers. Interesting stops towards Mega include the Borena village of Dublock, known for its so-called singing wells, as well as the bizarre apparition that is Lake Chew Bet, a small saline body of water at the base of an immense volcanic crater.

Remote it might be, but the Moyale road, surfaced in its entirety, is one of the best in Ethiopia, and serviced by reliable if relatively infrequent public transport. Accommodation south of Dilla and north of Moyale tends to be rudimentary, even by Ethiopian standards, but it can be found in Yabello, Mega and even Dublock. One practicality worth noting is that foreign-exchange facilities are lacking entirely south of Awassa, at least before Moyale itself, where there is an equipped bank. For those crossing between the two countries, visas for Kenya can be obtained upon arrival at the border, but there is no chance of crossing from Kenya into Ethiopia without a visa bought in advance in Nairobi or elsewhere.

There are a few routes by which one might connect with, or depart from, the main 500km of road between Awassa and Moyale. Coming from Negele Borena, a reasonable dirt road, covered by regular buses, leads westward via Kebre Mengist to the junction of Wendo 60km south of Awassa (see *Chapter 23*). The far rougher road that connects Negele Borena directly to Yabello is of little interest to most travellers, but is popularly followed on ornithological tours. Two further routes connect this road to Konso, the gateway for South Omo. The first, a recently upgraded 105km road from Yabello, is covered by a few pick-up trucks weekly, and frequently used by travellers heading between Kenya and South Omo. A newer and better road runs to Konso from Fiseha Genet, about 30–40km south of Dilla. Both routes are covered in *Chapter 25*.

DILLA

The bustling, breezy town of Dilla, administrative capital of Gedea zone, and since 1996 site of the most important college in southern Ethiopia, lies in the fertile green mountains of the eastern Rift Valley Escarpment. It is an important agricultural business centre, known particularly for the excellent coffee grown in the vicinity, and the surrounding hills are covered in patches of indigenous forest interspersed with rustic homesteads and small *enset* plantations. Dilla is a pleasant if unremarkable town, not unattractive from whichever direction you approach it, but coming from the dusty badlands of Ethiopia's far south and the north of Kenya, it must – both literally and figuratively – come as a breath of fresh air. The town is mostly of interest to travellers as the best base from which to visit a number of important archaeological sites, including two major stelae fields and some fine prehistoric rock carvings.

Getting there and away

Dilla is situated roughly 90km south of Awassa along a good surfaced road. En route, close to the junction for Kebre Mengist and Negele Borena (see *Bale and Arsi Highlands*, page 451), the road passes through Yirga Alem, an undistinguished semi-urban sprawl which – somewhat incredibly – served as the capital of Sidamo before this role was usurped by Awassa. A short distance before entering Dilla, you'll see plenty of vendors selling locally grown pineapples along the roadside. The drive takes about two hours in one of the regular minibuses and buses that connect Dilla to Awassa, and is quicker in a private vehicle.

For travellers trying to get between Addis Ababa and Moyale as quickly as possible, Dilla is the place to break up the two-day trip. A few buses daily connect Addis Ababa to Dilla, leaving Addis from the main Autobus Terra at around 06.00 and taking about ten hours with stops at Ziway, Shashemene and Awassa. A few buses daily run along the 420km road between Dilla and Moyale. They used to leave at around 06.00 in either direction, but recent information is that Moyale-bound buses leave at the unusual hour of 02.00 – 'to avoid something or other' – and take around 12 hours, stopping at Yabello and Mega. See also the box *Dilla to Yabello by road* on page 480.

AREGASH LODGE

➲ 046 2251136 or 011 5514254/82/90; f 011 5514221; e alltour@ethionet.et
Situated in Yirga Alem off the Awassa road some 30km north of Dilla, Aregash Lodge is the smartest place to stay in this part of Ethiopia, with a lovely rustic highland location complemented by accommodation in bamboo thatched *tukuls* built in the style of a traditional Sidamo village. It is particularly popular with birdwatchers, with more than 100 species recorded in the nearby forest. Other activities include guided treks to the nearby forest, horseback and mountain-bike riding, and visits to historical caves, sacred sites and natural hot- and cold-water springs. En-suite rooms cost birr 300 single or double occupancy, while four-bed units cost birr 400. The Italian-style meals are extra – breakfast costs birr 25, lunch birr 50 and dinner birr 60. Yirga Alem is located 8km northeast of Aposto Junction on the Awassa–Dilla road – drive through town until the asphalt road ends, then keep going for another kilometre and the first turn on the left will bring you to the lodge after 400m.

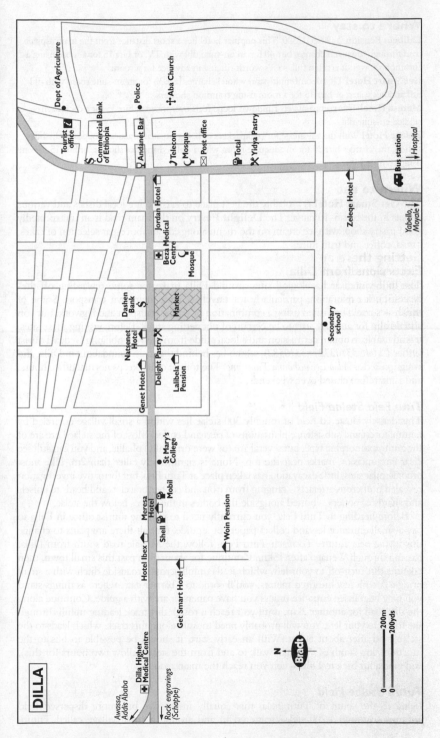

DILLA

Awassa,
Addis Ababa

Dilla Higher
Medical Centre

Rock engravings
(Schoppe)

Hotel Ibex

Get Smart Hotel

Shell

Meresa
Hotel

Mobil

Woin Pension

St Mary's
College

Genet Hotel

Natsenet
Hotel

Delight Pastry

Lalibela
Pension

Dashen
Bank

Market

Secondary
school

Jordan Hotel

Beza Medical
Centre

Mosque

Tourist
office

Commercial Bank
of Ethiopia

Dept of Agriculture

Police

Andanet Bar

Aba Church

Telecom

Mosque

Post office

Total

Yidya Pastry

Zeleqe Hotel

Bus station

Hospital

Yabello,
Moyale

N

Bradt

0   200m
0   200yds

Where to stay

Lalibela Pension ☎ 046 3312300. This popular hotel lies a short distance from the main asphalt road through town and charges birr 40 for an en-suite dbl with TV, or birr 15 for a room using a common shower. It is often full, so it's worth ringing in advance for a room.

Get Smart Hotel This decent multi-storey hotel charges birr 30 for an en-suite room with dbl bed and hot water, or birr 15 for a room using common showers.

Meresa Hotel This comparatively rundown lodge feels overpriced at birr 35 for a cockroach-riddled en-suite dbl.

Zeleqe Hotel With the advantage for backpackers of being situated practically opposite the bus station, this charges birr 30 for an adequate room with a dbl bed and hot shower, or birr 15 for one using common showers.

Where to eat

The **Get Smart Hotel** is probably the best place to eat, serving local dishes and various cutlets in the birr 6–10 range. The **Delight Pastry** on the main road is an unexpectedly good pastry shop, with ice cream on the menu alongside an above-par selection of cakes, bread, coffee and fruit juice.

Excursions from Dilla

The little-visited archaeological sites around Dilla make for some rewarding off-the-beaten-track exploration, particularly for travellers with their own transport. Some of these sites could be visited using a combination of public transport and legwork, but you should aim for an early start to be certain of not getting stuck. Before visiting these sites, it is advisable to obtain permission and a local guide from the very obliging Gedea Tourist Office (☎ 046 3310272 or 3310582), which lies behind the main roundabout in Dilla, and is signposted as *Adaa Ege'nishanna Tuurizme*. The tourist office keeps normal office hours, and is therefore closed over weekends.

Tutu Fela Stelae Field

This densely clustered field of roughly 300 stelae lies within a small village encircled by natural forest and subsistence plantations of *enset* and coffee. Most of the stelae here are of the anthropomorphic type, but several are (or were originally) phallic, and you can still see clear circumcision marks near the top. None is significantly taller than 2m. Like most other similar sites, little excavation has taken place at Tutu Fela, but formative investigation revealed numerous artefacts – ranging from iron and copper bracelets and beads to chisels and shards of pottery – buried alongside the bodies in the graves below the stelae.

Before heading to Tutu Fela, you currently need to visit the tourist office in Dilla to pay a small entrance fee and collect papers or a guide, though there are plans to change this in the near future. To reach Tutu Fela, follow the Moyale road south from Dilla, passing through Wenago after 15km. Continue for about 3km past this small town, then take the dirt turn-off to your left, which leads uphill across a roadside ditch with a small bridge. After a few hundred metres, you'll come to a barrier gate, where as things stand you may be refused entrance unless you have papers or are with a guide. Continue along the dirt road for another 2km, until you reach a rough dirt track leading uphill through the forest to your left. You will probably need to walk along this track, which leads to the stelae field after about 500m. With an early start, it should be possible to bus to the junction 3km south of Wenago, walk to and from the stelae (allow two hours for this), and grab a lift back to Dilla when you reach the main road.

Tututi Stelae Field

Lying to the south of Tutu Fela, this equally impressive but more dispersed field comprises around 1,200 stelae scattered in and around a small village called Tututi.

THE STELAE OF SOUTHERN ETHIOPIA

An estimated 10,000 stelae (obelisks) are scattered across the south of Ethiopia, extending in a rough belt from Tiya southeast to the vicinity of Negele Borena. Little concrete is known about the origin of these stelae or the societies that erected them. Local tradition attributes the stelae to the 15th-century Muslim leader Ahmed Gragn, but the formative findings of Professor Roger Joussaume, the only archaeologist to have worked the sites, indicates that they were erected centuries before Gragn was born, over a 400–500-year period starting in the 9th century.

Approximately 50 stelae fields are known in Gedea zone, and two broad styles of stelae are recognised. The older of these, probably dating to the 9th century, are the phallic stelae, which are typically cylindrical in shape, and rounded at the top, with incisions that leave little room for ambiguity about what they are meant to represent. The stelae appear to have marked graves, and the bodies beneath them were buried in a foetal position. The later anthropomorphic stelae, thought to date to the 12th century, are attributed to a different society to their precursors. These stelae are generally flattened, and are marked with symbolic human features, though in several instances they have a cylindrical shape, and were clearly modified from existing phallic stelae. Although they, too, marked graves, the society which erected them evidently buried their dead lying flat rather than in a foetal position.

The two largest stelae fields in Gedea are Tutu Fela and Tututi, both of which lie within 45 minutes' drive of Dilla and are described on pages 478–9. The Tututi field is made up almost exclusively of phallic stelae, whereas anthropomorphic stelae dominate at Tutu Fela. It is thought that the relatively well-known stelae at Tiya and Silté, which are flattened like anthropomorphic stelae, but carved with far greater sophistication and more abstract symbols, were erected and carved at a later date than those further south. It is not known to what extent these mysterious medieval stelae influenced the decorated gravestones still erected today by the Oromo, who are relatively recent arrivals to the area and might well have displaced the original stelae-erecting society. There are also some parallels between the later stelae found around Dilla and the anthropomorphic wooden grave markers of the Konso – who, interestingly, retain an oral tradition suggesting that they might have migrated to their present homeland from the eastern Rift Valley Escarpment.

Almost all of the stelae here are phallic, and one measuring 7.55m from base to top is probably the tallest stele ever erected in southern Ethiopia. About 90% of the stelae at Tututi have toppled over, the tallest one among them. Some stelae have been incorporated into the base of the local huts, or are used as seats or to sharpen knives (one large stele rather ignominiously props up a rustic latrine). Despite this, there are still several stelae of up to 6m high standing where they were originally erected more than 1,000 years ago. So far as I can establish, no excavation has taken place at Tututi.

As with Tutu Fela, tourists are required to obtain permission and pay a fee at the tourist office in Dilla before visiting Tututi. Having done this, follow the Moyale road through Wenago, past the turn-off for Tutu Fela, and then for another 8.5km to the tiny village of Chelba. At Chelba, take a right turn on to a dirt road, which will bring you to Tututi after 1.5km. It would be possible to visit this site by using public transport as far as Chelba, then walking to the stelae.

Manchiti rock engravings

The area around Dilla, although better known for its wealth of medieval stelae, is also rich in rock engraving sites, moving and mysterious relics of an otherwise-forgotten prehistoric society, adding yet another layer to one's perception of Ethiopia's enigmatically complex past. The most accessible and probably finest of these sites is Manchiti (also called Shappe), situated at an altitude of 1,300m roughly 8km from the town centre. The site consists of a partially collapsed frieze of at least 50 cattle, which move herd-like along the vertical rock face at the top of a narrow river gully. The individual engravings, ranging in length from 40–70cm, are nearly identical in their highly stylised form, with unnaturally small heads, large decorated horns and grossly engorged udders. The identity of the carvers, like so much about Ethiopia's past, remains a mystery, but the engravings show affinities with those at sites in the vicinity of Harar and parts of Eritrea. It is thought that the engravings at Manchiti are at least 3,000 years old. Roger Joussaume, the first Westerner to visit the site back in 1967, noted that the triangular objects that decorate the engraved horns resemble the buffalo-hair 'acorns' hung from the horns of the cattle of present-day Ethiopian pastoralists such as the Nuer and Dinka.

Manchiti is difficult to find without local guidance. From the main roundabout in Dilla, you need to follow the Awassa road for roughly 2km, forking left (away from Awassa) on the outskirts of town opposite the Dilla Higher Medical Centre. Follow this road for another 2km, passing the Teacher Education and Medical University, then after another 100m turn left into a side road. After another 3km, you will cross a bridge over a stream. Having crossed the stream, the road diffuses into several indistinct but motorable tracks, one of which, after another 2–3km, will bring you to the top of the valley in which the engravings lie (if you don't have a guide, you'll need to keep asking directions). The rutted track to the bottom of the valley was impassable when we visited,

DILLA TO YABELLO BY ROAD

The 210km asphalt road from Dilla south to Yabello marks a dramatic shift in landscape from cool, fertile highlands to the barren acacia scrub of the southern Rift Valley. The drive should take about four hours in a private vehicle, while buses take around six hours. All the larger towns between Dilla and Yabello are connected by local minibus services, which backpackers can use to cover the journey in stages. The opportunities for sightseeing along this road are, to put it bluntly, somewhat limited.

The first town of substance along the way is **Yerga Chefie**, which literally means cool grass, and is famous within Ethiopia for its high-quality coffee. The only reason you'd be likely to want to sleep here, or at **Fiseha Genet** 10km further south along the Moyale road, is if you are thinking of using the new all-weather road that connects Fiseha Genet to Konso (see *Approach roads to Konso* on page 497). The Lewison Hotel in Yerga Chefie is a decent budget hotel, where rooms with hot showers cost birr 20–30, while several shoestring hotels can be found in Fiseha Genet.

The largest town between Dilla and Yabello, lying roughly halfway between them, is **Hagere Maryam**, where several budget hotels and restaurants are clustered around the minibus station. South of this unremarkable town, the road passes through one last patch of juniper forest before finally descending to the dry plains – home to the colourful Borena people (see box *The Borena*, page 482) and renowned by ornithologists for two highly localised endemics (see box *Yabello for birders*, page 483).

but the engravings lay no more than five minutes on foot from where we parked. Travellers without private transport can grab a minibus as far as the university, but they will have to walk the last 5–6km, and should employ the services of a local guide and carry plenty of drinking water.

Three similar sites lie within 2–3km of each other to the southeast of Dilla, around the border of Bule and Wenago districts. None of these sites is as impressive as Manchiti, and access will be difficult unless a bridge that collapsed circa 2000 along the main road to Bule has been repaired. The most important site here is **Gelma** (or Ili Malcho Kinjo), situated in the village of Odola near Wechema. Ten stylised cows, very similar to those at Manchiti, are engraved here in two clusters. About 2km north of this, the **Soka Dibicha** consists of two sets of three relatively roughly engraved cattle lying on facing banks of the Bulla River. At the third site, **Godena Kinjo**, 'discovered' as recently as 1993, are three engraved cows. All three sites can be reached by following the Moyale road south for about 5km from the main roundabout, then turning left on to the Bule road shortly after you pass the church of Gebriel Chichu. After about 12km, you need to turn right at the village of Kuda until you reach the collapsed bridge. A local guide would be close to essential to find the actual sites, which lie between 3km and 5km from the bridge.

Gidicho Island

The old Amhara name for Lake Abaya, whose eastern shore is situated some 30km due east of Dilla as the crow flies, is Yegidicho Hayk – the Lake of the Gidicho, a people whose territory is confined to the northern lake hinterland and islands. Their main stronghold is the remote island also known as Gidicho, which extends over about 20km² off the northeastern shore of Lake Abaya, about 30km south of the mouth of the Bilate River. The eponymous inhabitants of Gidicho, who speak a Cushitic language with affiliations to Somali, are known for the unusual two-storey houses they build, and for their impressive wooden boats, which can measure up to 8m long. The island also supports a small community of Gatami people, who are hippo hunters and potters by tradition, though most now subsist from a combination of fishing and cultivation. The water around Gidicho Island is home to a profusion of crocodiles, hippos and birds. The small settlement of Gidicho Market on the facing mainland can be reached along a rough 4x4 50km trail through the near-uninhabited plains that descend to the lakeshore, ideally in the company of a local guide. From there you will have to take a boat across the channel to the island, which lies about 1.5km offshore.

YABELLO

Yabello can lay fair claim to being a minor route focus, since it effectively lies at the junction of the asphalt road between Dilla and Moyale, the recently upgraded eastern route towards Konso and the Lower Omo Valley, and a rougher road running northeast to Negele Borena. Yabello is likely to form an overnight stop on any serious birding tour of Ethiopia, or for anybody who is driving from the Kenyan border directly to Konso or the Omo Valley. Unfortunately, Yabello has little other than its location and birding to recommend it, except perhaps on Saturday when it is the site of a big market attended by Borena pastoralists from miles around. Travellers thinking of heading this way using public transport might take on board the experiences of one couple we met: five long nights in Yabello waiting for a lift to Konso!

Assuming that you have wheels, Yabello forms a useful base for a few day trips, for instance to one of the **Borena cultural sites** described under the heading *From Yabello to Moyale*. Also within easy day-tripping distance of the town is the **Yabello Game Sanctuary**, which protects 2,500 km² of dry acacia savanna a short distance east of the main Moyale road. A small number of Swayne's hartebeest are present in the sanctuary, as are other savanna species such as Burchell's zebra, greater and lesser kudu, Grant's

THE BORENA

Perhaps the most rigid pastoralists of all southern Ethiopia's people, the Borena occupy a vast territory of arid land stretching from the escarpment north of Dilla all the way south to the Uaso Ngiro River near the foot of Mount Kenya. Linguistically and ethnically, the Borena are regarded to be a southern branch of the Oromo nation, but their adherence to a semi-nomadic lifestyle has more in common culturally with the other desert nomads of northern Kenya than with any modern Ethiopian ethnic groups.

Characteristically tall and lean, the Borena acquired a reputation as fearsome warriors among early European visitors to their inhospitable homeland, based on their regional supremacy at the time. In later years, as the Abyssinian highlanders made inroads into the northern part of their territory, many Borena families were forced to migrate southwards, where they subsisted by cattle-raiding and attacking agriculturist settlements in northern Kenya. Within Ethiopia, however, the Borena have a reputation as a peace-loving and gracious people. Between themselves, the Borena hold strong taboos against raising one's voice in anger, and unprovoked violence.

Staunchly traditional in both custom and dress, the Borena add a definite splash of colour to the harsh, monotonous country they inhabit. The women, decorated similarly to some of the people of South Omo, drape colourful shawls and dresses from their shoulders, while the men walk around bare-chested with a sarong wrapped around their waist, and a spear or gun slung over their shoulder. In common with many other African pastoralists, Borena society is based on a rigid age-set system, with each set moving though stages of life and responsibility together. The Borena measure their wealth and worth in terms of the size of their herd. It is said that two Borena men will enquire about the state of each other's cattle long before they enquire about the health of wives, children and other such trivialities. I'm not sure whether to believe a related story, which is that a married Borena woman may sleep with any man she chooses – the man drives his spear into the ground in front of her hut, and the husband is not permitted to intrude while the spear is in place.

A remarkable feature of Borena culture is the 'singing well'. Many such wells are dotted around Borenaland, both in Ethiopia and in Kenya, each one supporting many thousands of head of cattle living for miles around. Water is retrieved from these wells communally, by a row of up to 50 men who sing and chant as they pass buckets from one to the other – an inspiring sight. The most accessible singing well in Ethiopia lies immediately outside Dublock, on the main road between Yabello and Mega. This well can be visited in conjunction with the crater lake Chew Bet – a major source of the salt-bars that have long formed an important export item in the Borena barter economy.

In the rainy season of 1999–2000, Borenaland was denied its usual measly quota of precipitation, resulting in a serious drought with drastic consequences for the region's inhabitants. In some areas, up to 90% of the cattle died, and crops grown to supplement the staple diet of milk and meat were completely destroyed. An unfortunate result of the drought was increased tension over water and grazing areas between the Borena and their Somali neighbours to the east. This drought has subsequently ended, and the area – or at least the part covered in this chapter – is perfectly safe for travel.

gazelle and a variety of small predators. The sanctuary is best known, however, for its endemic birds (see box *Yabello for birders* below). The road from Yabello to Negele Borena via the Yabello Game Sanctuary and Arero is also of great ornithological interest (see heading *From Negele to Yabello,* page 473).

Getting there and away

Yabello lies roughly halfway between Dilla and Moyale, and 5km west of the asphalt road along the dirt road to Konso. In a private vehicle, the direct drive from either Dilla or Moyale should take no longer than four hours. The drive to Konso now takes about two to three hours. The 300km road between Negele Borena and Yabello takes a full day, allowing for stops at the main birding locations en route.

Public transport to Dilla or Moyale is reasonably reliable. In addition to local minibuses between various small towns along these roads, a daily bus service connects Yabello and Dilla, taking around six hours in either direction. The daily bus between Dilla and Moyale stops in Yabello. No formal public transport runs along the roads

YABELLO FOR BIRDERS

Whatever else the area may lack in terms of tourist attractions, Yabello and its immediate surrounds form an essential fixture on any birding itinerary through Ethiopia. The reason for this, quite simply, is the exclusive presence of two of the most range-restricted of African bird species. These are Streseman's bush crow and the white-tailed swallow, respectively described in 1938 and 1942, and restricted to the arid acacia scrub that lies within a radius of 100km or so of Yabello. Quite why these two birds occupy such a small territory is a mystery that has so far eluded ornithologists – the arid acacia scrub around Yabello is practically indistinguishable from that which covers much of southern Ethiopia and northern Kenya. But whatever the explanation, few self-respecting birders would visit Ethiopia and not come in search of this pair of localised endemics, both of which are common within their restricted range, and often seen along the main asphalt road.

Streseman's bush crow is by far the more interesting of the two birds. Placed in the monospecific genus *Zavattarionis*, its nearest genetic ally is thought to be the European chough, a small, lightly built crow whose range extends into the Ethiopian Highlands. However, with its white head and belly, grey back, black wings, narrow pointed beak, and bare blue facemask, Streseman's bush crow bears little outward resemblance to any other African crow. Usually seen hanging about in small family parties that hop along the ground like overgrown sparrow-weavers, it is roughly the size of a roller, but holds itself like a starling. Although little studied, this fascinating bird is totally unmistakable even at a distant glance – you'd be extraordinarily unlucky to drive along the main road north or south of Yabello and not encounter a flock.

Fortunately, Yabello's interest to birders is not limited to the two endemics. The route to Yabello from Negele is known for hosting several localised specials, while the acacia bush immediately around Yabello, arid though it may be, supports a rich proliferation of colourful birds, several of which are more or less endemic to the dry scrub of northern Kenya and southern Ethiopia. Vulturine guinea fowl, golden-bellied starling, Abyssinian ground hornbill, white-headed buffalo weaver, golden pipit, bare-faced go-away bird and the ubiquitous but aptly named superb starling are just a few of the more striking species you can expect to see in the area, along with a good selection of small raptors.

following the east–west axis to Konso and Negele Borena, but the occasional trucks that run along them will take paying passengers.

Where to stay and eat

Hotella Waagaa Haraa The best of a rather poor bunch, this basic lodge lies along the main road as you enter Yabello from either Dilla or Moyale. Clean rooms with a dbl bed cost around birr 12, and there is a reliable communal shower.

Green Hotel This place charges birr 10 for slightly scruffier rooms.

Hotel Guuyaa Dhaiootaa This has adequate rooms for birr 19 and the restaurant two doors up has the reputation of being the best in town, which isn't saying much. It also stocks a limited range of tinned provisions and biscuits, should you need to stock up before heading west.

FROM YABELLO TO MOYALE

The 200km stretch of asphalt connecting Yabello to Moyale runs through dry red earth plains covered in light acacia scrub, punctuated by towering termite sculptures, and thinly populated by the Borena pastoralists whose bright traditional attire lends a welcome splash of colour to an otherwise harsh landscape. There is some game to be seen in this area, with the diminutive dik-dik and long-necked gerenuk being the most visible large mammals. Birders who have missed out on Streseman's bush crow still stand a good chance of encountering it as far south as Meta, the only town of substance along the route. Look out, too, for the proliferation of more widespread but equally colourful birds (see box *Yabello for birders,* page 483), which do their best to outdo the human population in the gaudiness stakes.

Not allowing for stops, the drive from Yabello to Moyale should take no longer than three hours in a private vehicle. It will take closer to five hours using the daily bus between Yabello and Moyale. If you want to head straight between Dilla and Moyale, there is at least one bus daily in either direction. A low volume of local transport runs between Yabello and Mega, and Mega and Moyale.

The most interesting stop along the asphalt is **Dublock**, an overgrown Borena village straddling the main Moyale road about 65km south of Yabello. Two so-called '**singing wells**' are situated on the edge of Dublock, in a small evergreen grove no more than 500m east of the main road. The name 'singing wells' refers to the Borena tradition of forming a chanting human chain to haul buckets of water from the well to its lip roughly 50m away. This communal activity generally takes place only in the dry season, when herdsmen who live two hours' distant will congregate at the edge of Dublock between around 09.00 and 14.00 to collect water for their livestock (the water isn't considered fit for human consumption). For travellers dependent on public transport, it might be optimistic to stop off at Dublock unless you intend staying the night, in which case the choice lies between the Hotel Bifftun Baree and the Hotel Nayaayaa, both of which are functional shoestring set-ups unlikely ever to attract superlatives.

Roughly 20km south of Dublock, a good gravel road heads eastward for 15km to come out at a small village on the rim of a **saline crater lake** known to Amharigna speakers as **Chew Bet** (Salt House) and to Orominga speakers as Ili Sod. The inky-black lake, which lies at the base of a 200m-deep crater, is at once starkly beautiful and rather menacing, and the detour is justified by the view from the rim alone. Looking, as they say, costs nothing, but should you want to take photographs, or to follow the steep footpath leading to the crater floor – the latter advisable only in the cool of the early morning or late afternoon – then you'll be asked a fee of birr 50 at the village. The lake is an important regional centre of salt extraction, worked by the villagers on a 15-days-on, 15-days-off basis so as to keep the levels sustainable. There's no accommodation in the village, but the raw salt is collected by regular pick-up trucks from Mega, which should make it easy enough for backpackers to get a lift to the lake – just make sure that the driver is willing to give you a lift back when his truck is full!

From the turn-off to the lake, the asphalt road continues south for 14km to **Mega**. Nestled in a pretty valley, this one-street town offers little in the way of sightseeing, but it has a fair selection of shoestring hotels. Students of Italian military history might want to check out the impressive ruined Mussolini-era fort that stands on a hill alongside the Dilla road about 1km from Mega. The section of road immediately north of this fort passes through a somehow unnatural-looking plain of cropped grass hemmed in by barren hills – barren and remarkably even, it looks almost like a floodplain, but is presumably the result of a recent (in geological terms) fall of volcanic ash. The old British

MOYALE TO NAIROBI

Crossing through to Kenya, border formalities are relaxed, though the border does close from time to time, so check the situation in advance. Visas for Kenya can be obtained on the spot (as they can these days at all Kenyan borders). Coming in the opposite direction, do note that Ethiopian visas must be bought in advance – this, among almost all borders in this part of Africa, would be about the most depressing to be turned back at. One minor note of caution: it could be a freak incident, but one reader reports that his entrance permit was accidentally stamped to expire on the day he entered Ethiopia. This error was picked up when he passed through the roadblock outside Moyale, and when he went back to the immigration office to have the error corrected, the official who stamped his passport wasn't around and he was forced to leave Ethiopia immediately! As I say, probably a one-off error, but sufficient justification to check the dates stamped in your passport on the spot.

On the Kenyan side of Moyale, the **Hotel Medina** is about the best bet, though it really can't be recommended by comparison with what is available on the Ethiopian side (the most favourable report calls it 'tolerable') and water is often unavailable. The quick and expensive way of getting from Moyale to Nairobi is by air; a couple of companies run regular but unscheduled charter flights between the border and the capital. Visit the Yetu Agency, or just ask around, to find out when the next plane arrives. Tickets generally sell to travellers for the equivalent of around US$100. Locals pay half the price, but based on recent first-hand reports there is surprisingly little room for negotiation.

There is no formal road transport between Moyale and **Isiolo**, but truck convoys cover the route roughly three times a week. It's easy to find a lift on a truck, so the best thing is to check on the Ethiopian side of the border when the next convoy leaves or else you might be stranded on the Kenyan side of the border for a couple of days. A truck ride to Isiolo should cost in the region of birr 80, and it will take two hot, dusty, bumpy days, passing through some stunning desert scenery where the occasional large mammal and traditional Samburu village break the tedium.

You'll probably stop overnight at the montane oasis of **Marsabit**, where there are several decent budget hotels. This is a stop that you might want to prolong, since the town lies adjacent to the forested **Marsabit National Park**, home to many elephants, antelope and birds. An excellent campsite lies on the edge of town, close to the park entrance gate, and you can also camp at the little-used lodge which lies about 5km into the park on the edge of a stunning crater lake. Once in Isiolo there are several budget hotels (the new **Madina Classic Lodge** is the current pick), and plenty of transport runs on to Nairobi along a blissfully surfaced road – you'll get through in a day.

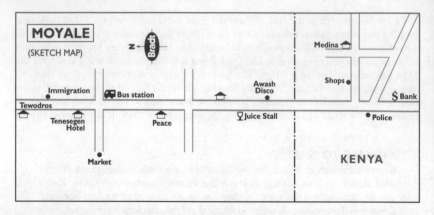

MOYALE (SKETCH MAP)

Consulate also lies on a hill outside town; you may even bump into the Consul's ex-chauffeur!

MOYALE

Lying 100km south of Mega, **Moyale** is in effect two different but economically interdependent towns that share a name but are divided by an international border. The Ethiopian town is marginally larger than its Kenyan namesake, but there's not much to choose between the two in terms of facilities – as a rule, most travellers prefer the town in the country in which they are arriving, or at least find it more exotic than the one in the country they are leaving behind.

At the **Boran Moyale Hotel**, well signposted about five minutes' walk uphill from the bus station, a clean and spacious self-contained bungalow sleeping four costs birr 70. Not quite as nice, the **Bekele Mola Hotel** has rooms with private showers but no running water for birr 20. Similar in standard and price, the **Tewodros Hotel** has received consistently good reports for several years, and the **Tropical Hotel** is also worth a try. Also recommended is the **Tenesegen Hotel**, which has clean rooms for birr 10, showers with running water, and attractively flowering grounds. Food isn't a problem in Moyale. Buses to Yabello depart at between 05.00 and 06.00 daily, and take about seven hours. On the Kenyan side of the border, the Sharif Hotel above the bank has been recommended.

Arba Minch and the Konso Highlands

The principal town of southwest Ethiopia, Arba Minch is seldom visited by travellers in its own right, but it does see quite a bit of tourist traffic as a result of forming the most convenient overnight stop between Addis Ababa and South Omo. It is nevertheless a rather attractive town, situated about 500km south of Addis Ababa among green hills that offer grand views over the Rift Valley lakes of Chamo and Abaya. It also serves as the base for several worthwhile day or overnight trips, most notably to the underrated Nechisar National Park, which protects part of the two lakes mentioned above as well as the forest-fringed hot springs for which Arba Minch is named.

Also within easy striking distance of Arba Minch is the highland town of Chencha, noted for its unusual traditional architecture. Of further cultural interest, situated on a southerly extension of the Ethiopian Highlands some 90km along the route to South Omo, is the small town of Karat, capital of Konso, a district named after its skilled agriculturist inhabitants, who are noted for their fortified hilltop villages and eerie grave statues.

ARBA MINCH

Arba Minch, the former capital of the defunct Gamo-Gofa Province, consists of two discrete settlements separated by 4km of tar road and an altitude climb of almost 200m. Downtown Sikela is the larger, more bustling commercial and residential centre, while uptown Shecha is a vaguely posher settlement of unimposing government buildings, hotels, and the homes of government employees. Despite its former status as provincial capital and a population estimated at around 75,000, Arba Minch retains a small-town character – perhaps because it really is two small towns as opposed to one large one.

If Arba Minch is inherently just another humdrum medium-sized Ethiopian town, it does boast a setting that is far from the ordinary. The town lies at an elevation of around 1,300m in the foothills of the Rift Valley wall, above a cliff overlooking the mountainous sliver that separates the lakes of Chamo and Abaya. With mountains rising to almost 4,000m to the west, it is difficult to think of a more perfectly sited town anywhere in east Africa. Moshi, on the footslopes of Kilimanjaro, comes close – the difference is that in Arba Minch, wherever you walk, and at whatever time of day, there are stunning views in all directions, and the longer you spend in the town the more impressive it all becomes.

Once you have tired of the town itself, there is plenty to do in the vicinity. Immediately east of town lies Nechisar National Park, which protects large parts of Lakes Chamo and Abaya, as well as fair-sized herds of game. Even without a vehicle, parts of the park and the lakes' shores can be explored either on foot or by boat. Also of interest is the highland town of Chencha, an easy day trip using public transport from Arba Minch.

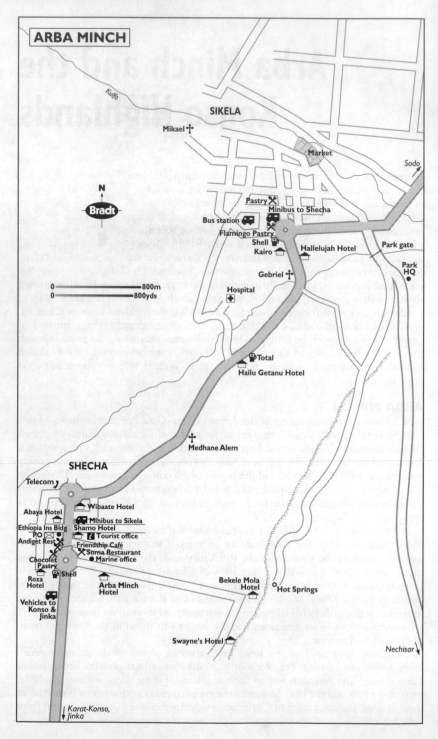

ARBA MINCH

Kulfo

SIKELA

Mikael ✝

Market

Sodo

N

Bradt

Pastry ✗

Minibus to Shecha

Bus station 🚐

Flamingo Pastry

Shell

Kairo

Hallelujah Hotel

Park gate

Gebriel ✝

Park HQ

0 ▭▭▭▭ 800m
0 ▭▭▭▭ 800yds

Hospital

Total

Hailu Getanu Hotel

Medhane Alem ✝

SHECHA

Telecom

Wibaate Hotel

Abaya Hotel

Minibus to Sikela

Ethiopia Ins Bldg

Shamo Hotel

PO

Tourist office

Andiget Rest ✗

Friendship Café

Soma Restaurant

Chocolet Pastry

Marine office

Roza Hotel

Shell

Bekele Mola Hotel

Arba Minch Hotel

Hot Springs

Vehicles to Konso & Jinka

Swayne's Hotel

Karat-Konso, Jinka

Nechisar

Getting there and away

Ethiopian Airlines flies to Arba Minch two or three times weekly, continuing on to Jinka except when the airstrip there is too wet. The new airport lies about 7km from Sikela, off the Sodo road. There are no taxis to meet flights, so you will have to hitch or walk into town.

By road, the most popular access route from the north or east is via the surfaced (but in parts badly pot-holed) 250km road that branches westward from the Moyale road at Shashemene. Coming from Addis Ababa, it is easy to cover this route in one day, whether by bus or in a private vehicle, though most people choose to break the journey with an overnight stop at Langano, Awassa or Wondo Genet (see *Chapter 22*). An alternative route via Butajira and Hosaina, connecting with the main road at Sodo, is actually shorter than the road through Shashemene and seems likely to gain in popularity once it is fully surfaced (see *Chapter 21*). Coming from the west, Arba Minch can be reached in a day along a good gravel road connecting Sodo to Jimma, while the best route from the south is via Yabello and Karat-Konso.

There are plenty of buses between Arba Minch and Shashemene, and at least one daily directly to or from Awassa. These leave from the main bus station in Sikela, but morning buses normally stop in Shecha, outside the Abaya Hotel, to pick up passengers before they head to the bus station. If you are travelling on to Konso, Jinka or Yabello, there is a bus to Jinka once or twice a week, though the timetable is rather erratic. If you don't connect with the bus, then you'll be reliant on lifts with the pick-up trucks that cluster in front of the Shell garage in Shecha at around 06.00. Regular minibuses ply between Sikela and Shecha, starting up at around 06.30.

Where to stay
Moderate

Swayne's Hotel ✆ 046 8811895 or 011 6632595/7/8; tel/f 046 8812200; e reservations@swayneshotel.com or swayneshotel@yahoo.com; www.swayneshotel.com. Owned and managed by Greenland Tours, this new clifftop hotel, which lies about 2km outside Shecha, is perched on the edge of a rocky scarp inhabited by semi-tame olive baboons and boasting a great view over Lakes Chamo and Abaya to the eastern Rift Valley wall. The smartest option in Arba Minch, it provides accommodation in comfortable en-suite rooms with hot shower, a traditional reed exterior, and a more conventional interior at birr 200/250 for sgl/dbl occupancy. A good restaurant is attached.

Bekele Mola Hotel ✆ 046 8810046. Situated close to Swayne's Hotel and offering a similarly spectacular view, the rather timeworn Bekele Mola charges birr 162 for a dbl bungalow with en-suite hot shower. Camping is permitted at birr 20 per person, with access to a shower. Decent meals are available at birr 15, with the choice of eating in the rather moribund dining room or on the pretty veranda overlooking the lakes (if you do eat outdoors, keep an eye open for the semi-tame olive baboons that come past most days).

Budget

Arba Minch Hotel The pick of a clutch of decent budget hotels in Shecha, this relatively new family-run hotel is situated a couple of hundred metres along the road towards the Bekele Mola. Quiet and clean, it charges birr 40/60 for a spacious sgl/dbl bed with en-suite cold shower.

Abaya Hotel Set in attractive grounds on the main road through Shecha, this place is good value at birr 40 for a decent en-suite room with a ³/₄ bed, with the bonus that most long-haul buses stop immediately outside to pick up passengers before heading down to the main bus station in Sikela. Be warned, however, that the bus drivers who crash here are partial to revving their engines at antisocial hours, the noisy bar stays open very late, and the resident bevy of bar girls has a reputation for hassling male travellers and making female travellers feel unwelcome.

Hallelujah Hotel Sikela's finest, this pleasant little hotel is situated a couple of hundred metres along the Shecha road and charges birr 40 for a clean en-suite dbl. A larger and probably smarter hotel was under construction next door in mid 2005.

Shoestring

Hailu Getanu Hotel Situated next to the Total garage along the main road between Sikela and Shecha, this charges birr 15 for a small but clean room with ¾ bed and common showers. The location is relatively quiet, but it is also a little inconvenient, as it's a 10–15-minute walk from most of the restaurants and bars.

Roza Hotel Although it is better known for its food, this unpretentious hotel in Sikela has a few basic rooms using a common shower for birr 15.

Kairo Hotel Situated next to the Shell garage, this is probably the pick of the numerous budget cheap dives in Sikela, but overpriced at birr 30 for a small room with ¾ bed and access to clean common showers. Although there are a few hotels situated closer to the bus station, they are mostly very rundown and seedy.

Where to eat

The local speciality in Arba Minch is *asa kutilet* (fish cutlet), which normally consists of a mound of fried battered *tilapia*, a spicy green dip, a couple of crusty bread rolls, and a plate of salad, and costs around birr 6–8 at most places. Good fish cutlet is to be had at the **Abaya Hotel**, **Andiget Restaurant**, **Soma Restaurant** and **Roza Hotel**. The **Bekele Mola Hotel** serves fish cutlet at twice the price (arguably worth it just for the view), and is definitely the place to head for if you want to eat something other than fish. For good *asa wat*, the **Teruye Restaurant** opposite the post office has been recommended. Good pastry shops include the **Chocolet Pastry** in Shecha and **Flamingo Pastry** in Sikela.

Listings
Car rental

A local driver/guide called Tsehai Bogale (❞ *046 8811278*) has been recommended for arranging guided 4x4 trips to South Omo and Nechisar.

Swimming pool

A tempting goal on a hot day is the swimming pool at the university on the road to Shashemene. You can take a bus to the campus, also known as the Institute of Water Technology, which is rundown and laid out with lots of gaping empty green spaces. The pool, located at the rear of the campus, is big and refreshing, though over-chlorinated. A half-hearted lifeguard will charge you a nominal fee to leap in. Beverages are available at the small cafeteria in the next block of buildings.

Tourist information

The helpful tourist office, which lies outside Shecha about 750m towards the Bekele Mola Hotel, is worth visiting for current advice before you head out to the places listed below.

NECHISAR NATIONAL PARK

Designated and demarcated in 1974 but never formally gazetted, the 514km² Nechisar National Park protects an untrammelled landscape of mountains and lakes as thrillingly beautiful as that of any African game reserve. Set in the Rift Valley at an altitude of 1,100–1,650m, within walking distance of Arba Minch, the park protects not only the easterly Nechisar ('White Grass') Plains for which it is named, but also significant portions of Lakes Chamo and Abaya, and the mountainous Egzer Dilday ('Bridge of God') that divides the two lakes. Habitats range from the knotted acacia scrub of Egzer

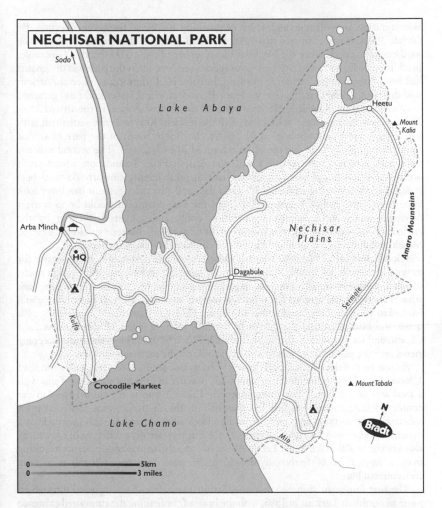

Dilday to the wide-open grasslands of the Nechisar Plain, or from the open water of Lakes Abaya and Chamo to the dense groundwater forest that divides the lakes from Arba Minch.

This high level of habitat diversity is reflected in a checklist of 70 mammal and 342 bird species, though many of the larger mammals on that list have been exterminated. Scientific exploration of the park is far from complete: a 1991 Cambridge expedition to Nechisar discovered 15 endemic butterflies and eight endemic dragonfly species. The same expedition also returned home with the wing of a previously undescribed bird, which was described and named the Nechisar nightjar, *Caprimulgus solala*, in 1995. Thought to be endemic to Ethiopia, this nightjar might well be regarded as the most elusive of all African birds – a live individual has yet to be identified. Nechisar is also the only known Ethiopian locality for the white-tailed lark and it also protects an exceptionally isolated population of white-fronted black chat.

The practically uninhabited plains of Nechisar fared reasonably well as a sanctuary until 1991, but its conservation infrastructure collapsed along with the Derg, leading to an influx of settlement by the agriculturalist Kori and the pastoralist Guji Oromo, as well as overgrazing, over-fishing, high levels of poaching and illegal firewood collection. By the late 1990s, it was estimated that 1,800 Kori had settled in the Sermille Valley in the southeast of the park, while the Nechisar Plains sustained some 3,000 head of Guji cattle. In addition, at least a dozen large mammal species resident when the park was designated had been exterminated, including elephant, buffalo, black rhinoceros, cheetah, African wild dog, Rothschild's giraffe, Grevy's zebra, Beisa oryx, eland, lesser kudu and gerenuk.

After long years of neglect, Nechisar received two welcome shots in the arm in 2004. The first was the negotiated relocation of all the resident Kori to a new settlement with boreholes, a clinic and a school at Abulo Alfecho, 15km south of the park (a similar agreement with the Guji Oromo is far advanced in early 2005). The second was the signing of a management contract with the African Parks Foundation, a non-profit organisation that has played a significant role in rehabilitating similarly down-at-heel game reserves elsewhere in Africa. It's early days still (the management handover took place only at the end of February 2005), but the long-term goal would be to convert Nechisar into a viable tourist conservation entity and tourist destination by the eradication of poaching, the fencing off of those parts of the reserve closest to Arba Minch, and the reintroduction of the likes of elephant, buffalo and cheetah.

For the time being, Nechisar remains a low-key wildlife destination, most notable for its wild scenery. It has an untrammelled atmosphere, in part because of the rough roads, which force its closure after rain, and in part because of the low tourist volume (the park attracts an average of around 1,500 foreign tourists annually, so in all probability you'll have it to yourself). The road across the Egzer Dilday is particularly exhilarating as it twists and bumps around the curves of the hills offering splendid views across Lake Chamo and its volcanically formed islands. Once across the bridge, there are sweeping views over the plains to the majestic volcanic hills on the eastern boundary.

A great part of the park's appeal derives from its two scenic lakes. Set at an altitude of 1,268m, Lake Abaya is the most extensive body of water in Ethiopia after Lake Tana, with a total area of 1,160km². The more southerly Lake Chamo is the third largest in the country, despite covering slightly less than half of Abaya's surface area, and it supports substantial numbers of hippo and crocodile. Both lakes are rather shallow, reaching a maximum depth of 13m and 10m respectively, but they are very different in coloration: also known as Kai Hayk ('Red Lake') Abaya has an unusual rusty appearance resulting from a suspension of ferrous hydroxide in its water, whereas Chamo is a more conventional blue.

The first European visitor to this area, Arthur Donaldson-Smith, passed through en route to northeast Turkana in 1895, with the hope of confirming the rumoured existence of one 'Lake Aballa'. He discovered that the locals actually called it Abaya, and was led not to the lake we know today as Abaya but rather to the one we now know as Chamo. A year later, the Italian explorer Vittorio Bottego became the first European to reach the shores of the larger lake, which he christened Regina Margherita, the name by which it was most widely known through the remainder of the imperial era. Unlike the name Chamo, which was used by the Burji people on its southern shore, the name Abaya has little historical validity. This lake is traditionally known by at least half a dozen names locally, among them Gumaraki, Yegidicho, Begade, Beki, Kai and Dambala, but not Abaya, which literally means 'Big Water' and was applied generically to any substantial freshwater body (part of the reason for Donaldson-Smith's apparent misidentification).

The best area for game viewing is the open Nechisar Plain. The most common large mammal here is Burchell's zebra, which is regularly seen in herds of 100 or more. You should also see Grant's gazelle and, with a bit of luck, one of the 100-odd resident Swayne's hartebeest. Cheetah and African wild dog are probably extinct, and lions are heard more often than they are seen – though a large maned male was reported lounging around on Egzer Dilday in early 2005. The acacia and combretum woodland of Egzer

Dilday is home to Guenther's dik-dik and greater kudu, while crocodile, hippo and waterbuck are frequently seen from the viewpoint over Lake Chamo. Acacia birds such as rollers, sparrow-weavers and starlings are well represented, and Nechisar seems to be particularly good for raptors.

Entirely different in its faunal composition is the lush groundwater forest close to the park entrance, which is dominated by sycamore figs reaching up to 30m high. Guereza and vervet monkeys are common here, as are troops of olive baboon. Other forest animals include bushbuck, bushpig and warthog. The forest is a very rewarding area for birds, but it is also predictably frustrating in the dense cover – you can at least be certain of encountering the large and raucous silvery-cheeked hornbill. Also on the Arba Minch side of the park is the famous and misleadingly named crocodile market, where hundreds of these large reptiles accumulate to sun themselves on the shore of Lake Chamo. The turn-off for the rough 9km track to the crocodile market lies about 3km past the park headquarters and immediately after the bridge across the Kulfo River.

A visitation fee of birr 70 per person per is levied, valid for 48 hours but allowing one entry only. In addition, a vehicle fee of birr 20 is payable for a private vehicle, with an additional birr 60 charged to vehicles registered with a tour company. For further information about the rehabilitation of the park, visit the website www.africanparks-conservation.com, which among other things contains a monthly progress report for Nechisar listing interesting sightings and other notable events.

Getting there and away

The park headquarters lie about 2km from Arba Minch. To reach them, follow the Sodo road out of Sikela for about 1km, and then turn right into the side road next to the training college. You need a 4x4 vehicle to enter the park itself, but you can walk to the headquarters or to the hot springs and surrounding forest below the Bekele Mola Hotel.

The crocodile market can be visited in a six-seat motorboat owned by the Marine Authority in Shecha. The price is evidently somewhat negotiable, but expect to pay around birr 250 for one or two people, or birr 300 for larger parties.

Where to stay

Most people visit Nechisar as a day trip from Arba Minch. There are, however, two little-used campsites about 5km from the headquarters on the forested banks of the Kulfo River. Neither site has anything in the way of facilities, but if you're properly equipped they are blissfully peaceful and wonderfully sited for seeing forest animals. Watch out for crocodiles in the river.

It is permitted to camp elsewhere in the park, provided that you are self-sufficient when it comes to food and water, and remove all your rubbish when you leave.

The Hot Springs

Arba Minch translates as 'Forty Springs', and the field of hot springs after which the town is named lies at the base of the cliff below the Bekele Mola Hotel. Although these springs are within Nechisar National Park, the road to them is considered a public road by the park authorities, so walking is permitted and no park fees are charged. The area around the springs is covered in dense forest, which gives you an excellent opportunity to explore this habitat on foot, and you can swim in a pool at the springs. Even if the springs are closed to the public, as seems to have been the case recently, the walk out is arguably of greater interest than the destination.

The springs can be reached in one of two ways. The shortest route from Shecha is via a steep footpath that starts next to the Bekele Mola Hotel. Be warned, however, that this path is not at all clear, and a wrong turn could leave you stranded in the acacia scrub south of the springs and cut off from the cliff by an uncrossable gully. If you do decide to risk it, take a local guide, put on decent walking shoes, and bear in mind that the springs are almost directly below the hotel, so you will know you're going the wrong way if you start veering to the right.

Without a local guide, a more certain option is the public road from Sikela. Walk out from Sikela as if heading to the national park entrance (follow the Sodo road for about 1km then turn right into the road next to the training college). Just before the park headquarters there is a fork in the road. The left fork is signposted for the park headquarters; you want the right fork, which follows the base of the cliff for about 3km, passing first through low dense scrub then through a wonderful patch of forest before reaching the springs. This road offers excellent birdwatching, while vervet and guereza monkeys and olive baboons are abundant, and the odd dik-dik and bushbuck might be heard or seen crashing into the undergrowth.

Arba Minch Crocodile Farm

The Arba Minch Crocodile Farm, run by the Department of National Resources, lies about 6km out of town near Lake Abaya. About 8,000 animals are kept on the farm, with an age range of one to six years. The crocodiles are hatched from eggs taken from the lake but a number have been reintroduced to keep the natural population in balance. The farm consists of a dozen or so cages, each of which contains several hundred bored-looking crocodiles of a similar age. A guided tour costs birr 10.

To get to the farm, follow the Sodo road out of Sikela for about 4km till you reach the clearly signposted turn-off. On the way you will cross a bridge over a river and later detour round the town's airstrip to your right. If you don't feel like the walk, vehicles heading towards the lakeside town of Lante will be able to drop you at the turn-off. The 2km of road between the turn-off and the farm passes through forest and thick scrub, excellent for birds and monkeys, and worth exploring in its own right even if you are not particularly interested in visiting the crocodile farm. The road continues past the farm for about 500m to a landing stage on the shore of Lake Abaya, where there is good birdwatching and a chance of seeing hippos and crocodiles in their natural state.

CHENCHA

Mention the small highland town of Chencha to anybody in Arba Minch and they give an involuntary shiver. Set at an altitude of 2,900m in the Guge hills, 37km north of Arba Minch by road, Chencha is best known locally for its cold, misty weather and year-round moist climate culminating in an average monthly precipitation of 200mm in each of March, April, May and October. Chencha today is something of a backwater – the dramatic series of switchbacks that climbs 1,600m to the town over a mere 22km is often impassable after heavy rain – but incredibly it once served as the capital of Gamo-Gofa before this role was usurped by Arba Minch.

Aside from the dramatic views back to the Rift Valley lakes near Arba Minch, Chencha is of interest to travellers as the home of the Dorze people, renowned cotton weavers whose tall beehive-shaped dwellings are among the most distinctive traditional structures to be seen anywhere in Africa. The Dorze speak an Omotic tongue, similar to several languages of the Lower Omo Valley, and are thought to have occupied their present highland enclave of less than 30km² for at least 500 years. The main occupations of the region are subsistence farming and weaving: every Dorze compound is surrounded by a smallholding of tobacco, *enset* and other crops, and contains at least one loom which is constantly worked by one or other member of the family. The *shama* cloth produced around Chencha is regarded to be the finest in Ethiopia: plain white *gabbi* robes and brightly coloured scarf-like *netalas* are sold along the roadside.

It is, above all, the unique Dorze houses that make Chencha worth a diversion. These remarkable extended domes measure up to 6m tall (roughly the height of a two-storey building), and are constructed entirely from organic material. A scaffold of bamboo sticks is first set in place, and then a combination of grass and *enset* (false banana) leaves is woven around the scaffold used to create solid insulating walls and a roof. Most Dorze houses also have a low frontal extension, used as a reception area. The spacious interior of the huts is centred on a large fireplace, used for cooking and to generate heat, and different areas are set apart for sleeping and for smaller livestock. Dorze dwellings are enduring structures, and one hut will generally serve a married couple for a lifetime – when the base of a hut becomes infested by termites or starts to rot, the entire structure can be lifted up and relocated to a close-by site.

Coming from Arba Minch, the main concentration of traditional houses is reached before you arrive in Chencha, at the small town known as **Dorze**. Within Dorze town, it appears to be normal for only one hut to be enclosed within a compound. Along the road between Dorze and Chencha, there are several compounds containing two or more huts. It is possible to stop at any compound and ask to look around, but you should expect to pay something to go inside or to take photographs. It is advisable to agree on a fee upfront: we stopped to photograph several compounds, and were generally asked for birr 30, but found it easy to negotiate this down to something more sensible. Also of interest in the Chencha area is the impressive 30m-high **Toro Waterfall**, which can be reached from the village along a pretty 30-minute walking path – any local will be able to guide you.

The drive from Arba Minch to Chencha takes about an hour in a private vehicle. The route involves following the surfaced Addis Ababa road back for 14km, then turning left onto a dirt road which reaches Dorze after 15km and Chencha after another 8km. There is no normal transport to Chencha, but several 4x4 vehicles make the journey each morning, except after heavy rain when the road becomes impassable. Vehicles for Chencha leave from Sikela near the bus station. The trip takes around two hours in each direction, so a day trip is perfectly feasible, especially on the market days of Monday and Saturday. Should you want to spend a night in the area, the basic but friendly **Chencha Hotel** on the main road through Chencha asks a princely birr 5 for a room with a double bed, and has a common cold shower (not a madly appealing prospect at this altitude!). A couple of basic restaurants can be found in Chencha, and there is even a pastry shop. If you are in the area at the right time, the Dorze celebration of Meskel (1 October) is reputedly very colourful.

KARAT-KONSO

Situated on the banks of the seasonal Segen River at an altitude of 1,650m, Karat-Konso is the capital town of Konso Special Woreda, and the junction town through which passes all road traffic into South Omo. Physically dominated by that road junction, this town of roughly 3,000 inhabitants might prosaically be described as a traffic roundabout of comically vast dimensions surrounded by a solitary petrol station, a scattering of local hotels, and a sprawl of dusty lanes lined with scruffy, low-rise buildings. Certainly, Karat-Konso could hardly offer a less auspicious first impression of what is actually a fascinating part of Ethiopia.

First impressions of Karat-Konso can be deceptive. It is undeniably the case that the town boasts little (apart from an unusually high hassle factor) to distinguish it from a hundred other small Ethiopian settlements of its ilk. Equally true, however, is that the Konso people of the surrounding hills adhere to a unique and complex culture every bit as absorbing as that of the more renowned lowland peoples of the Omo region. On most days, you'll see few signs of this in the town itself, the exception being Mondays and Thursdays, when a large traditional market is held about 2km from the town centre along the Jinka road. Also worth a look, especially if you will not be heading out to one of the traditional villages, is the collection of wooden totems housed in the tourist office behind Karat-Konso's main traffic roundabout.

Karat-Konso forms an excellent base from which to explore the surrounding hills, and the traditional villages that dot them. For travellers dependent on public transport or on their own two feet, the obvious first point of call is Dekatu, a walled Konso village situated close to the market and only 3km from the centre of Karat-Konso. Further afield, and with access to a vehicle, the magnificent hilltop settlement of Mecheke is the region's established 'tourist village', though several other similar villages can be visited in the company of a good local guide. Other local points of interest include the sculpted sand formation outside Gesergiyo village, and the house of the traditional chief Walda Dawit Kalla.

Note that the town of Karat-Konso is generally referred to as Konso, but its official (and more correct) name is Karat. In order to preclude confusion between the Konso people, the region of Konso, and the town that governs them both, I have referred to the town throughout as Karat-Konso, and reserved the use of the term Konso for the people and their territory.

Getting there and away

Karat-Konso is the gateway town to South Omo, and all travellers who visit the region by road will have to pass through it. Whether you travel in a rented or private vehicle, or use public transport, the road trip from Addis Ababa to Karat-Konso takes at least two days in either direction. Using public transport, three days is probably more realistic, unless you have an unusually high tolerance of sitting on buses. Although many travellers visit the region covered in this chapter as a self-standing trip out of Addis Ababa, it is equally possible to tag it on to broader travels in southern Ethiopia, or en route between Kenya and central Ethiopia. Details of reaching the various springboards for Konso – Arba Minch, Yabello and Fiseha Genet – are given in the relevant sections elsewhere in this guide.

The most popular access road to Konso goes via Arba Minch, which is where most people break up the trip for a night or two. A second established access road, one that has seen great recent improvements, cuts across eastwards from the main Dilla–Moyale road at Yabello. A third and newer road to Konso leads southwest from the small town of Fiseha Genet on the Dilla–Moyale road.

To/from Arba Minch

The 85km dirt road between Karat-Konso and Arba Minch is regularly graded, and is currently the best of the access roads. The drive generally takes up to three hours in a private vehicle, with little to distract you along the way. A bus runs daily from Arba Minch to Konso, continuing on to Jinka, throughout the year, though the service may be suspended after unusually heavy rain, in which case you can assume that roads from Konso into South Omo will be firmly out of commission. Various light vehicles also cover the road between Arba Minch and Jinka – all going well, the run shouldn't take longer than four hours.

A direct bus reputedly runs between Addis Ababa and Jinka, taking up to 36 hours including an overnight stop, but it evidently does the run no more than twice a week, and departure details – or the departure time itself – are somewhat vague.

To/from Yabello

The 105km road between Yabello and Karat-Konso now takes about three hours to drive in a private vehicle, ideally one with high clearance and 4x4. Leaving from Yabello, the road is in fair condition passing through the small Borena town of Leloi after 26km, and it remains so until **Brindal** 40km further. Brindal is a lovely and unaffected Borena village, dominated by circular reed-and-grass houses with flat or rounded roofs. It's a rewarding place for photography – assuming that you're prepared to pay the going rate of birr 2 per person – and a small roadside bar serves tea, coffee, beer and biscuits. There is no accommodation here, but camping is safe, provided that you ask permission before pitching a tent.

Upon leaving Brindal, you need to turn right at the first junction (the southerly fork leads to Tenta). The hilly semi-desert scenery from here on in is fantastic, with further compensation in the form of remote Borena settlements, and a surprising amount of wildlife – olive baboon, Guenther's dik-dik, and flocks of vulturine guinea fowl, iridescent cobalt chests to the fore as they scurry dementedly across the track. After 35km, the road connects with the new Fiseha Genet road about 5km out of Karat-Konso.

There is no public transport along the road between Yabello and Karat-Konso, but occasional trucks will take passengers for a fee. It's easy enough to find out about suitable transport; in theory the best days to travel by truck are Saturday (market day in Yabello) and to a lesser extent Monday or Thursday (market day in Karat-Konso). In practice, it's all rather hit-and-miss – I recently met travellers who had been stuck in Yabello for five days before they found transport on to Karat-Konso!

To/from Fiseha Genet

The new 175km all-weather dirt road connecting Fiseha Genet to Karat-Konso opened in 2002. The significance of this new route for locals, as well as for travellers heading to or from Kenya, is that it allows for direct access between the Dilla–Moyale road and Konso all year through. For travellers coming from Addis Ababa, it forms an easy alternative to the Arba Minch route, allowing one to visit South Omo as a loop, coming along one route and returning via the other.

Fiseha Genet straddles the surfaced Moyale road about 55km south of Dilla. Several local hotels are dotted around the small town, though better accommodation is available at nearby Yerga Chefie on the Dilla road (see box *Dilla to Yabello by road* on page 480). In a private vehicle, the drive from Fiseha Genet to Karat-Konso takes about five hours, which means that it would be possible to cover this route in a day starting at Dilla or Awassa. There is no public transport along this road, nor is it in regular use by trucks.

Where to stay and eat

The lodgings in Konso won't seem very special coming from Arba Minch, Jinka or Murelle, but they are positively luxurious by comparison with anything in Yabello, or elsewhere in South Omo.

Saint Mary Hotel Situated on the main traffic roundabout, this recently expanded three-storey hotel is probably the best in town, charging birr 50 for a clean en-suite room with a ³/₄ bed. The attached

THE KONSO

With thanks to Dinote Kusia Shenkere of the Konso Tourist Office

Although less celebrated than the colourful ethnic groups of South Omo, Konso must rank as among the most singular of African nations. Now governed as a Special Woreda within the Southern Nations, Nationalities and Peoples' region, the people of Konso had little contact with the rest of Ethiopia until recent times, and the area remains staunchly traditionalist in character.

The Konso inhabit an isolated region of basalt hills – essentially an extension of the southern highlands – lying at an altitude range of roughly 1,500m to 2,000m, and flanked to the east by the semi-desert Borena lowlands and to the west by the equally harsh Lower Omo Valley. Oddly, the Konso have no strong tradition relating to their origins, other than that they came to their present homeland from somewhere further east 500–1,000 years ago. They speak an east Cushitic language, and have few apparent cultural links with the people of the surrounding lowlands or the Ethiopian Highlands.

Mixed agriculturists, the Konso make the most of the hard, rocky slopes that characterise their relatively dry and infertile homeland through a combination of extensive rock terracing, the use of animal dung as fertiliser, crop rotation, and hard work. The most important crop in the region is sorghum, which is harvested twice annually: after the short rains in June and July, and after the long rains in February and March. Sorghum is used to make a thick local beer, while the finely ground flour forms the base of the Konso staple dish of *korkorfa* or *dama*, a sort of doughball that is cooked like a dumpling in a stew or soup. Other important crops include maize, beans and coffee. Oddly, the Konso shun coffee beans in favour of the leaves, which are sun-dried, ground to a fine powder, and mixed with sunflower seeds and various spices, to form an easily stored local equivalent to instant coffee!

The most outwardly distinctive feature of Konso country is the aesthetically pleasing towns and villages, which in some respects bear an unexpected (though purely coincidental) resemblance to the Dogon villages of Mali. Unusually for this part of Africa, the Konso traditionally live in congested centralised settlements, typically situated on the top of a hill and enclosed by stone walls measuring up to 2m high. These walled hilltop settlements usually have no more than three or four entrance gates, and can be reached only via a limited number of steep footpaths. This made the villages easily defensible, an important consideration for an isolated people whose territory was, in the past, under constant threat of cattle raids and military attacks from the flanking lowlands.

Within the defensive town walls, low stick-and-stone walls and leafy *Moringa stenopetelai* (shiferaw) trees enclose every individual compound, to create a labyrinth of narrow, shady alleys. Each family compound typically consists of between three and five circular thatched stone huts, as well as an elevated granary or *kosa* used to store sorghum and maize, and a taller but smaller platform where freshly cooked food is stowed away too high for children to reach it. The compounds are entered via gateways, which are supported and covered by thick wooden struts, a defensive design that forces any aspirant attackers to crawl into the compound one by one.

Every village consists of a number of sub-communities, each of which is centred upon a *mora* or communal house. This is a tall building with an open-sided ground floor supported by juniper trunks, and a sharply angled thatched roof covering a wooden

restaurant is said to be better than the one at the Konso Edget, but the subtlety was wasted on me.
Konso Edget Hotel Set in large but rather barren gardens on the main traffic roundabout, this pleasant hotel charges birr 30/50 for a clean and brightly painted sgl/twin with en-suite showers. A restaurant-cum-bar serves refrigerated drinks, fruit juice, and decent local meals.

ceiling. The ground floor serves as a shady place where villagers – men, boys and girls, but not grown women – can relax, gossip, play and make important communal decisions. Customarily, all boys from the age of 12 upwards are required to sleep in the ceiling of the *mora* until they get married, and even married men are expected to spend part of the night there. This custom, though still enforced, derives from more beleaguered days, when the elder boys and men often needed to be mobilised quickly when a village was attacked. The *mora* also serves as a guesthouse for male visitors from other villages. Girls and women are not generally allowed to sleep in the *mora*, though these days some villages will make an exception for *faranji* tourists!

Konso society is structured around the *Kata* generation set, a system not dissimilar to the *Gada* of the neighbouring Borena people, or that practised by the Maasai and Samburu of east Africa. Although the exact cycle differs from one village to the next, any given village will initiate a new generation – consisting of boys of between eight and 25 years old – every 18 years. Traditionally, young men who had not yet been initiated into a generation were usually permitted to marry, but any offspring that their wives produced would be killed at birth – a custom that is no longer practised. Should you happen to be in Konso country during December, January or September, this is when *Kata* induction ceremonies take place, so it's worth asking about them locally. The highlight of the ceremony is the erection of an *Olahita* (generation pole) in the village's ceremonial square – it is easy to tell roughly how old any given village is by counting the number of poles and multiplying the total by 18!

The erection of poles and stones form an important part of Konso ritual. In any village square, you'll see a number of so-called Victory Stones standing to mark important events – generally victories over attempted raiders or conquerors – in the village's history. More famous are the Konso *waga*, carved wooden grave markers that are often (and rather misleadingly) referred to as totems. Traditionally, a *waga* will be erected above the grave of any important Konso man or warrior, surrounded by smaller statues of his wives and defeated foes. The sombre facial features of the dead warrior are carved onto the *waga*, complete with enlarged and bucked teeth made from animal bones – creating a rather leery impression that is only reinforced by the impressively proportioned penis the deceased typically has clasped in his hand! Intriguingly, these grave markers and victory stones have an obvious precursor in the stelae that mark medieval graves around modern-day Dilla, and oral tradition indicates that the proto-Konso migrated from about the right place at about the right time for there to be some link between these customs.

Although the Konso are animists by custom, the last 50 years have seen many youngsters convert to Protestant denominations. Traditional attire is gradually giving way to the ubiquitous trousers or skirt and T-shirt – one could actually be forgiven for thinking that the traditional Konso costume consists of blue T-shirts with an angled white stripe, a huge consignment of which must have been imported from China a few years back! On a more serious note, the practice of erecting engraved grave markers has largely disappeared in recent decades, and many of the finest remaining examples were recently collected by the regional tourist office before they could be damaged or sold to foreign collectors. In most other senses, however, modern Konso society remains strikingly informed by, and in touch with, a unique and ancient cultural heritage. The area is well worth exploring.

Green Hotel Similar in standard to the above, this new hotel on the Arba Minch road charges birr 50 for an en-suite room with ¾ bed.
Mago Park Hotel It's a dump, but the price is right at birr 5–10 for small room with a single bed. There is no shower, common or otherwise.

Konso campsite The official campsite lies behind the tourist office and charges birr 10 per person.

Excursions from Karat-Konso

The main attractions of the Konso region are the traditional Konso villages described in the box *The Konso* on page 498. Several such villages, notably Dekatu and Mecheke, can be visited using Karat-Konso as a base. Before visiting any villages, it is mandatory to pop into the tourist office in Karat-Konso, pay a birr 30 fee allowing you to visit as many villages as you like, and collect a receipt and permit for each village you intend to visit. You can check out their collection of *waga* statues at the same time. It is normal, though not necessary, to pick up an official guide from the tourist office. The official guides are very knowledgeable and helpful, but will expect a fair tip. If you choose not to take a guide, make sure you are given a letter of introduction to carry with you.

Aside from Dekatu, none of the attractions listed below is easily visited without a private vehicle. If you arrive in Karat-Konso using public transport, the tourist office can arrange rental of a 4x4 vehicle for half a day – sufficient time to visit at least two villages. This will cost around birr 250–300, but do make sure that the driver, the guide and yourself are clear about which places you will be visiting. Although the blanket fee covers entry to any village of your choice, and in theory photography, you should expect to tip any individual you specifically photograph. The going rate in the Konso area is birr 1–2.

Every village in Konso now has a caretaker whose job it is to collect and keep your permit for that specific village, and also to check that a receipt was issued by the tourist office in Karat-Konso. The caretaker will most likely refuse entry to any traveller who doesn't have this paperwork in their possession. Be warned that the tourist office in Konso may be unable to issue a receipt on a Sunday or a public holiday, which means that you may be forbidden from entering some of the villages you have a permit for!

Dekatu

Although it practically borders on Karat-Konso, the town of Dekatu is rightly regarded to be a separate entity, since it still functions as a self-standing traditional community. Contained within Dekatu's town walls are 21 sub-communities, each of which has its own *mora* (community house), making this one of the largest traditional towns anywhere in Konso. Dekatu is known for hosting one of the region's best *waga* makers; should you want to meet him, or to have a statue commissioned, you will need to go with a guide. Otherwise, assuming that you have the requisite paperwork from the tourist office, Dekatu is easy enough to reach independently on foot. Follow the Jinka road out of Karat-Konso for about 2km until you reach the large Monday and Thursday market on the left side of the road. From here, Dekatu is visible to your right, a walled town perched on a hill below and about 1km from the market. It is easily reached by a number of footpaths.

Mecheke

The best known and most regularly visited of the traditional Konso towns (among other things, this is where Angela Fisher did much of her exquisite Konso photography), Mecheke lies on a tall hill some 13km from Karat-Konso. Judging by the number of generation poles, the town is at least 400 years old, and today it supports about 3,000 people split into about ten sub-communities. People here are very used to tourists – your presence is likely to be greeted by youngsters playing the *kehaita* (a local musical instrument) and weaving in the hope of being photographed – but the atmosphere is pretty relaxed and friendly. There are four groups of *waga* statues left in Mecheke, some of them estimated to be more than 150 years old.

To reach Mecheke from the main roundabout in Karat-Konso, follow the Jinka road for 5.5km, turn left on to a side road which you need to follow for 5km, then turn left again on to a motorable track and follow it for 3km to a parking spot below the town walls. No public transport runs along this road. Should you be interested in spending the night, a payment of birr 10 allows you to camp in the grounds of the local school or – more authentically – to crash with the local lads in one of the community houses (women as well as men are permitted to do this).

Gesergiyo

Smaller and less atmospheric than the two towns listed above, Gesergiyo is of interest primarily for the adjacent formation of sand pinnacles sculpted by occasional water flow in a normally dry gorge. It is a magnificent and very unusual natural phenomenon – I've seen similar rock formations, but nothing comparable made entirely of sand. The superficial resemblance to a row of 'skyscrapers' led some local wag to christen the formation 'New York', a nickname that has stuck.

Oral tradition has it that 'New York' is of supernatural origin. The story is that a local chief awoke one day to find his ceremonial drums had been stolen during the night. He enlisted the help of God, who swept away the earth from where the thieves had buried the drums, creating the sand formation in the process. It is said that the thieves, realising that God knows all, immediately confessed to their sins – their fate goes unrecorded! To this day, light-fingered Konso youngsters are taken to Gesergiyo as a reminder that God doesn't like thieves, and will see what they get up to.

Gesergiyo lies 17km from Karat-Konso by road, and is easily visited in combination with Mecheke. Coming from Mecheke, drive back 3km to the last intersection, where – instead of heading right towards Karat-Konso – you need to turn left. After 2.5km, the road passes through **Fasha**, known for holding what is regarded to be one of the four most important Konso markets every Saturday, and as the site of a century-old Orthodox church that is reputedly the oldest in the Konso territory. Driving on through Fasha, the road reaches Gesergiyo after another 4km.

Chief Gezahegne Woldu's Compound

Isolated on a hill and surrounded by juniper forest, the compound of Chief Gezahegne Woldu is situated some 7km from Karat-Konso off the road towards Mecheke. It's a fascinating and atmospheric place, cluttered with venerable chiefly artefacts ranging from beer vats to furniture, and the chief himself speaks good English and makes for a gracious and welcoming host – provided that visitors arrive in the company of an official guide. In the forest outside the compound stand several *waga* statues, marking the graves of earlier chiefs and their wives. By arrangement with the tourist office, it is permitted to camp outside the compound, or to sleep within it, upon payment of a nominal fee.

Chief Gezahegne is the paramount leader of the Kertita clan. The clan is an important patrilineal unit of Konso society – members of the same clan, for instance, are forbidden from marrying – and each of the nine clans is represented by its own elected local headman in any given Konso village. The paramount chief of any given clan acts as a spiritual guru as well as in a judicial role; he and his immediate family live in total isolation, in order that he has no involvement in the day-to-day life of a community. The idea is that this will ensure his impartiality when settling intra-clan disputes and crimes, which are still often dealt with by the chief rather than national government. The title of clan chief is strictly hereditary, and Gezahegne is 20th in a line that has lived in the same compound for about 500 years. Sadly, the Kertita lineage is one of only three of the original nine chieftaincies to survive into the present day.

It is customary in Konso for the death of a paramount clan chief to be denied after the event. Instead, an official embalmer tends (for which read mummifies) the chief, and word is given out that he is very ill. Only after nine years and nine months is it finally announced that the chief is dead, with full blame falling on the embalmer, who – poor sod – is heavily fined for his predetermined failure. How and why this unusual custom arose is unknown. It has been suggested that a delayed announcement will allow time for a relative of the chief to remedy the problem should he have died without male issue. A more plausible explanation, given that it is tacitly realised that any chief being attended by an embalmer is unlikely to make a full recovery, is that the charade softens the blow of the departure of a popular and respected leader.

This custom was followed in 1990, when Kalla Koyote, Gezahegne's grandfather, died at an age of more than 100 years. The chief was duly embalmed, and confined to his compound with influenza. This, however, was a difficult time in Konso, due to a severe local drought and the ongoing civil war, and it was felt that a living chief was better equipped to navigate any crises than a terminally ill one. Kalla's death was announced seven months after he had died, his embalmed body was buried in a ceremony that lasted for eight days, and his son (and Gezahegne's father) Walda Dawit Kalla was installed as chief. The events surrounding Chief Kalla Koyote's death form the subject of a fascinating article in an old issue of the *Social Ethnology Bulletin of Addis Ababa University*, a copy of which is kept in the chief's compound. Sadly, the amiable Chief Walda Dawit Kalla passed away in 2004 – his body was held in state for just nine days before it was buried and his son Gezahegne was made the new chief.

South Omo

Nothing in highland Ethiopia prepares one for South Omo. Nor, for that matter, does much else in modern Africa. Apocryphal, perhaps, but easy enough to believe when confronted by the region's extraordinary cultural integrity, that there is more than a smattering of truth in the assertion that as recently as 50 years ago the people of South Omo were scarcely aware that such an entity as Ethiopia existed.

South Omo is literally fantastic. Descending from the green, urbane highlands into the low-lying plains of South Omo feels like a journey not merely through space, but also through time, as one enters the vast and thinly populated badlands that divide the mountainous centre of Ethiopia from its counterpart in Kenya. Like much of neighbouring northern Kenya, South Omo is as close as one can come to an Africa untouched by outside influences. The culturally diverse, immaculately colourful and defiantly traditionalist agro-pastoralists who inhabit the region seem to occupy a physical and psychic landscape little different to that of their nomadic ancestors. This is Africa as it once was, or as some might still imagine it to be, and its mere existence is at once wonderful and scarcely credible. That this surreal oasis of Afro-traditionalism lies within the boundaries of Ethiopia – the least stereotypically African of the continent's sub-Saharan nations – borders on the outrageous.

It seems facile to label South Omo as a living museum. Yet in many senses, that is exactly what it is. Four of Africa's major linguistic groups are represented in the region, including the so-called Omotic-speakers, a language group as endemic to South Omo as the Ethiopian wolf is to the Abyssinian Highlands. All in all, depending on where one draws the lines, as many as two-dozen different tribes occupy South Omo, some numbering tens of thousands, others no more than 500, each one of them culturally unique. The most renowned of the Omotic-speakers are the Mursi, famed for their practice of inserting large clay plates behind the lower lips of their women. Other important groups of South Omo include the Hamer-Bena, the Karo and the Ari, whose cultures and quirks of adornment – body scarring, body painting and the like – are treated more fully in tint boxes scattered throughout this chapter.

South Omo is often portrayed as some sort of cultural Garden of Eden. This notion is unduly romantic. The Mursi disfigure their women monstrously. Ritualised wife beating is an integral part of Hamer society. Every year without fail, outbreaks of intertribal fighting – usually provoked by cattle disputes – result in numerous fatalities. In South Omo, such killers are not normally apprehended; on the contrary, they wear whatever mark of Cain is customary within their specific tribe with a warrior's pride. But, while one cannot gloss over the harsh realities of life in South Omo, there is much that is genuinely uplifting about the sheer tenacity of this incredibly rich cultural mosaic, comprising some 30 distinct ethno-linguistic groupings, several of which number fewer than 1,000 people. Romanticise or condemn it, South Omo is there, it is fascinating, and it is utterly unique.

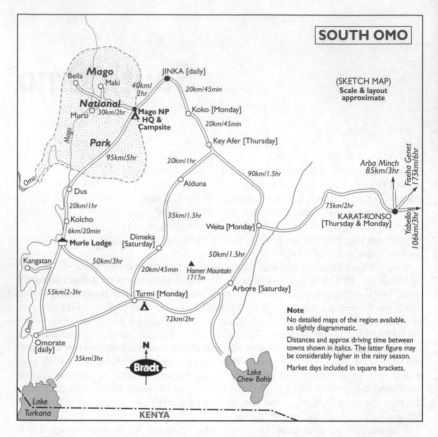

Tourism to South Omo, while hardly large scale, is catching on in a substantial way, and it does seem to have stimulated a vociferous and often grasping spirit of commercialism that can detract from what would otherwise be a fascinating experience – indeed, as one traveller recently pointed out, South Omo may be an interesting place to visit, but it is not much fun to travel there. A related, and more serious, concern is the extent to which tourism could undermine the area's traditional cultures. My personal feeling is that a variety of factors – the increasing influence of central government, the infiltration of exotic religions, the steady population growth – will conspire to make it difficult for South Omo to remain as it is today indefinitely. Tourism, doubtless, is one such factor, though possibly as reinforcing of traditional culture as it is destructive. Whatever else one might say about tourism, it does attract a brand of outsider who is generally positive about local traditions. The same cannot always be said for the Bible-wielding meddlers who arrive in the area seeking to replace indigenous systems of belief with their own.

In keeping with its traditionalist mood, South Omo does not lend itself to efficient casual exploration. Jinka, the administrative centre, is accessible enough on public transport or by air. Elsewhere, one must either explore the region on what amounts to a private safari, using a car and driver hired in Addis Ababa, or else surrender oneself to the vagaries of local transport and elasticity of South Omo time. Either way, as a self-standing trip, or an extension to a journey through the historical northern highlands of Ethiopia, South Omo is a once-in-a-lifetime experience.

PLANNING YOUR TRIP
When to visit
Unlike other tourist areas in Ethiopia, travel in South Omo is strongly limited by seasonal factors. C J Carr describes the region as 'highly unstable… in terms of precipitation and winds throughout the year, with great fluctuations often erratic in occurrence'. Add to this the poor roads that characterise the region, and the black cotton soil around Mago National Park (treacherously sticky and often impassable after any significant rainfall), and it will be evident that travelling through South Omo during the rainy season is a serious no-no!

The rainy season in the far southwest is significantly different from that in the rest of Ethiopia, and although rainfall figures are low – typically no more than 400mm per annum – the unpredictable timing and quantity of rain regularly leads to local flooding or drought. Bearing the above in mind, Ethiopian Rift Valley Safaris, which owns Murelle Lodge and has 20 years' experience in the region to its credit, advises strongly against travelling during April and May, when the big rains usually fall. If the rains are early or late, or unusually heavy, March or June might be just as bad. The rest of the year is normally fine, though the short rains, which generally fall in October, sometimes put a temporary stop on travel.

The above warnings apply mainly to places south of the main Konso–Jinka road. Karat-Konso itself is normally accessible throughout the year, as are villages along the main road towards Jinka. Depending on how heavy the rains have been, it may also be possible to reach Turmi and Omorate during the rainy season.

Access and itinerary planning
The most normal – and best – way to explore the region covered by this chapter is on a road safari out of Addis Ababa. A minimum of eight days, but ideally longer, should be allocated for such a journey (see *Itineraries* below). Because there are few organised tours to the region, the normal procedure is to pre-book a vehicle with a recognised tour operator in Addis Ababa (see *Tour operators*, page 82–3). This will generally work out at US$150–200 per day, inclusive of camping gear, guide and cook. The advantage of dealing with an acknowledged tour operator is that the vehicle will generally be in good shape, and the guide will have experience of the region, both of which are important considerations in this remote and unpredictable area. It is possible to arrange a private vehicle more cheaply upon arrival in Addis Ababa. The Wutma and Baro hotels can arrange vehicles at rates as low as US$100 per day, depending on season and your negotiating skills. Be warned, however, that while privately arranged safaris generally run smoothly, there are no guarantees about the state of the vehicle or experience of the guide, and there will be little accountability should things go wrong.

Two other options exist. The first is an organised fly-in safari, and the second is the DIY approach. Most fly-in safaris use one of Ethiopian Airlines' thrice-weekly flights from Addis Ababa to Jinka via Arba Minch. This will generally be more costly than driving down, since the vehicle will need to drive from Addis Ababa whether or not you are on board. The main advantage of flying down, aside from the added comfort, is that it cuts two days of travel either side off exploring South Omo. Once again any recognised tour operator can arrange a package of this sort. It should be noted that, even if you fly in to Jinka and work with the best operator, the rough roads that characterise the region cannot be avoided and are a great equaliser – streamlined, air-conditioned luxury is not an option.

The final option, and by far the cheapest, is the DIY approach. This involves bussing down to Karat-Konso, and exploring the region using a limited network of internal public transport. The villages along the Jinka road, such as Key Afer, are readily accessible on public transport, while Turmi and several other more remote villages can be reached on the sporadic trickle of passenger-carrying trucks. Realistically, Mago National Park and its Mursi inhabitants can be visited only in a private vehicle. In Jinka, it is possible to hire a 4x4 at a similar daily rate to those offered in Addis Ababa, with the obvious financial advantage that you'll be paying this rate for one or two days only, as opposed to longer than a week. If you intend travelling independently in South Omo, be warned that this is as tough as it gets in Ethiopia – erratic and bumpy transport, lousy accommodation and indifferent food are to be expected. Assuming that this doesn't put you off, a realistic minimum of eight days should be allocated to explore the region as a round trip out of Addis Ababa on public transport, though this would entail spending a high proportion of your waking hours on buses and trucks. Ten days or two weeks, inclusive of a few stops en route, would be far more relaxed. If time is a limiting factor, it might be worth considering flying one-way or return between Addis Ababa and Jinka.

Itineraries

This section is best studied in conjunction with the map on page 504, which shows all roads through the region, as well as distances, approximate dry-season driving times, and important market days. Essentially, the road network through the region consists of the 205km trunk route running northwest from Karat-Konso to Jinka, and three rougher roads that run south from this trunk road to connect at the town of Turmi. The most easterly of the southbound roads – in other words, the one closest to Konso – runs directly south from Weita through Arbore to Turmi. The central road leaves the main road a few kilometres east of Key Afer, and runs through Alduna and Dimeka to Turmi. The most westerly road runs from Jinka south through Mago National Park and Murelle, from where two roads lead to Turmi, one direct, the other via Omorate.

The relatively limited number of halfway-decent roads through South Omo means that the tourist circuit is fairly well defined. Assuming that you have a private vehicle, and sufficient time – realistically, an absolute minimum of four days (three nights) to get between Konso and Jinka – there is little reason to deviate from the established circuit. This circuit entails driving from Konso to Turmi via Weita on the first day, from Turmi to Murelle (with a possible side trip to Omorate or Dimeka) on the second day, from Murelle to Mago National Park on the third day, then heading up to Jinka on the fourth day. For those travelling out of Addis Ababa, this loop will form the core of a trip of at least eight days' (seven nights) duration, allowing for overnight stops at Arba Minch and Karat-Konso on the way down, and at Jinka and Arba Minch on the way up. An additional two days would allow you to explore Nechisar National Park outside Arba Minch, and to stop over for a full day somewhere in South Omo – Turmi, Mago National Park, or Murelle are the obvious contenders. Two full weeks would make for a very relaxed trip, with little need to pre-plan your itinerary in detail, and plenty of opportunity to explore places of interest on the way to or from Addis Ababa.

For travellers without private transport, the above circuit is unrealistic because of a lack of public transport through Murelle and Mago National Park. A more realistic circuit, malleable dependent on market days, would be to spend a day exploring the villages outside Jinka, then head southwards to Turmi on a truck, and after a night or two there return back to the main Jinka–Konso road, to stop over at Weita or Key Afer. Short of catching an extraordinarily lucky hitch, the only way to get to Mago National Park and the Mursi villages is in a private vehicle rented in Jinka.

One factor that will come into play with any itinerary through South Omo is market days, which are generally held to be the best days to arrive in any given town. I must confess that I think the importance of markets is sometimes overstated – I found it far more rewarding to visit smaller villages on non-market days – but certainly you should aim to tailor your itinerary to coincide with at least one big market. The best markets are probably the Saturday market at Dimeka, the Monday market at Turmi, and the

Thursday market at Key Afer. Other market days are given under individual town entries, and on the map on page 504.

As a final planning factor, it is probably worth noting that there is no bridge across this part of the Omo or Mago rivers. The bridge in Mago National Park was torn down in the flooding of 1997, and although it is partially rebuilt, construction work had ceased in early 2001, with no indication that it will be resumed. Local opinion is that the partially constructed bridge is unlikely to survive the rainy season. The main implication of this is that Omo National Park cannot realistically be visited from the Jinka side; the only route – tough and little used – leads south from Jimma in western Ethiopia.

Other practicalities
Permits
Visitors to Omorate and more occasionally Turmi are often asked by the police to produce their passport and a written letter of authority. For travellers on an organised tour, the latter essentially amounts to a letter from the tour operator. Independent travellers, however, will be expected to have a letter from the tourist office in Addis Ababa, Jinka or Karat-Konso. Without such a letter, you could hit quite serious problems – the protocol in Omorate is that you will be 'jailed' in a hotel and shoved on to the next vehicle out of town. Things are unlikely to come to that in Turmi, but a letter will save you a lot of hassle. I've not heard of written authority being asked for elsewhere in the region, but that doesn't mean it couldn't happen.

Accommodation and camping
Full details of accommodation are given under individual town and village entries, but the following overview might help in planning your trip.

The only remotely upmarket bases from which one can explore the region are Murelle Lodge, which is owned by Ethiopia Rift Valley Safaris and overlooks the Omo River at Murelle, and Greenland Tours' newer Evangadi Lodge at Turmi. Basing yourself at either of these lodges is somewhat restrictive insofar as all other villages and towns must be visited as a day trip, but there is no alternative that doesn't entail staying in very basic lodges or camping.

Reasonable local hotels with en-suite rooms are available in Jinka. Otherwise, the only settlements in the region to offer any form of accommodation are Turmi, Dimeka, Omorate and Key Afer. On a scale that admittedly runs from the truly sordid to the merely basic, the hotels in Omorate plumb depths of awfulness rarely equalled even in Ethiopia. The hotels in Turmi and Dimeka are only marginally better, and there is a comparatively good hotel in Key Afer.

A more appealing option, assuming that you have a tent, is to camp. Proper campsites exist at Jinka, Turmi, Key Afer and Murelle Lodge, while in Weita, Omorate and Arbore it is established practice to camp at the police station for a small fee.

Food and drink
Culinary delights are few and far between in South Omo. The hotel restaurants in Jinka serve reasonable Ethiopian fare and a very limited selection of Western meals. Elsewhere, you'll always find at least one local restaurant that serves the standard Ethiopian diet of *injera* and *wat*, occasionally supplemented by (normally cold) spaghetti. If you are camping, it's probably preferable to cook for yourself – speak to your tour operator about this, or (if travelling independently) try to stock up on dry food before you reach South Omo. Jinka has a few decent supermarkets, but the selection available in Arba Minch, Shashemene, Awassa or Addis Ababa is infinitely better.

The usual bottled soft drinks and beer are widely available, along with tea and fizzy *Ambo* mineral water. Bottled still mineral water is thin on the ground, and generally vastly overpriced where it is available, so it's worth bringing a stash with you, assuming that you are in a private vehicle. The water in South Omo is generally not safe to drink.

South Omo is the one part of Ethiopia where the practice of charging inflated *faranji* prices now extends to food and drink as well as hotel rooms.

Photography

You can assume that anybody you want to photograph in South Omo will expect to be paid. The going rate varies from one person and one village to the next. For straight portraits, a fee of birr 1 is pretty standard, though the Mursi in particular will generally expect more, and it is increasingly the case that the subject will count how many times you click the shutter and increment the fee accordingly – in other words, somebody who asks for birr 1 will demand birr 5 if you click the shutter five times. If you really want to spend some time photographing one particular person, it's best to explain this and agree a higher rate in advance. Once the finances have been agreed, people are generally relaxed about being photographed, though it is also not uncommon for arguments to break out.

Unfortunately, the 'pay to snap' mentality in South Omo has recently mutated into the rather presumptuous expectation that tourists should be willing to photograph (and pay) any local who wants them to. This can sometimes create an unpleasant atmosphere: every person you walk past seems to yell 'faranji', 'photo', 'birr' or a variation thereof, and some become quite hostile if you don't accede to their demand. Certainly, photography has come to dominate relations between travellers and the people of South Omo to the extent that any less voyeuristic form of interaction seems to be all but impossible. One way around this is to simply pack away your camera while you are in South Omo, and buy a few postcards instead.

THE KONSO–JINKA ROAD: WEITA, KEY AFER AND KOKO

The scenic road between Karat-Konso and Jinka covers 205km and takes about five hours to drive, longer on public transport. The villages of Weita, Key Afer and Koko all lie along this road, and any one of them is worth stopping at, particularly on the local market days of Sunday in Weita, Monday in Koko, and Thursday in Key Afer.

Heading west from Karat-Konso, it should take about two hours to cover the 80km road westward to Weita in a private vehicle. From Weita it takes another three hours to reach either Jinka or Turmi. The only formal public transport heading westward is the daily bus from Arba Minch to Jinka, which may or may not have seats available by the time it passes through Karat-Konso. Most locals depend on pick-up trucks and other transport that informally carries paying passengers; any of the hotels in Karat-Konso will be able to put you in touch with truck drivers heading west. As a rule, it is easy enough to find transport on any given day to Jinka, or to villages along the main road between Karat-Konso and Jinka. Trucks heading southwest to Turmi or Omorate are rather less frequent, but run as far as Turmi on most days.

Weita

Situated some 75km from Karat-Konso along the Jinka road, about 5km west of the bridge across the Weita River, the tiny settlement of Weita lies within Tsemai territory (see box, page 509), though the busy Sunday market is also attended by Ari and Bana people. Weita has a rather impermanent feel, one that suggests it probably owes its existence to its location at the junction of the side road to Turmi via Arbore. Market days excepted, Weita isn't a terribly interesting place, dominated as it is by a large outdoor cafeteria and restaurant complex that attracts more passing truck traffic than it does colourful locals. There is no accommodation, but it is permitted to camp in the police compound.

THE TSEMAI

The Tsemai, the dominant people of Weita village on the Konso–Jinka road, are among the least-known ethnic groups of Ethiopia. Estimated to total some 5,000 people, their territory extends along the western bank of the Weita River, known in Tsemai as the Dulaika River. They are mixed subsistence farmers who practise flood cultivation, with the major crops being sorghum and maize. They also rear livestock, especially cattle, and keep beehives for honey. The Tsemai speak an east Cushitic language that is closely related to the one spoken in Konso, which, according to oral tradition, is from where their founding chief, Asasa, originated. The present chief, who lives at the long-standing Tsemai capital of Ganda Bogolkila, is claimed to be the ninth in line after Asasa, suggesting that this migration might have happened between 150 and 250 years ago.

Although their appearance and dress style is similar to that of the Omotic Ari people, the Tsemai share closer political and spiritual affiliations with the Arbore, who speak a similar language, and whose territory lies adjacent to the Tsemai chief's village. The Tsemai also frequently and openly intermarry with the Hamer, whose territory lies immediately west of theirs. In common with many other people of southern Ethiopia, society is structured around an age-set system. Four fixed age sets are recognised, with every set graduating in seniority once a decade, when a new generation of boys between the ages of about 11 and 22 is initiated.

Key Afer

The relatively large and cosmopolitan town of Key Afer is situated at a refreshing altitude of around 1,800m on the Konso–Jinka road, 80km northwest of Weita, and a few kilometres west of the junction with the side road south to Turmi via Dimeka. For travellers dependent on public transport, Key Afer is by far the most accessible town of interest in the Omo region – any vehicle heading between Konso and Jinka can drop you there – and well worth dedicating a night to.

The dominant people of Key Afer are the Ari (see box, page 510), but Bana and Hamer people also live in and around town. The best day to visit is Thursday, when the town hosts a multi-cultural market that is as colourful as any in the region. On other days, the town centre is relatively modern in feel, but the back streets east of the market square are lined with traditional homes. Local boys will offer to take you to a small traditional village about 15 minutes' walk from town.

The **Abebe Hotel** in Key Afer is a cut above most village hotels in the region. Adequately clean rooms with concrete floors and a three-quarter bed cost birr 15, and the restaurant serves decent local meals, cold beers, and soft drinks. Be reassured, however, that the bucket showers and common toilet are in line with usual Omo Valley fleapit standards. Camping is permitted in the police compound, though the new **Shaba Tourist Campsite**, which lies about 500m along the Konso road is a more appealing prospect.

Koko

Lying roughly halfway along the 40km stretch of road between Key Afer and Jinka, and sharing these towns' temperate highland climate, Koko is a small but attractive Ari village noted for its busy Monday market. For independent travellers, this market would make for a straightforward day excursion out of Jinka, as a fair number of vehicles trot back and forth from Jinka to the market. On other days of the week, Koko is of marginal interest. There is no accommodation in the village.

THE ARI

The Ari occupy perhaps the largest territory of any of the ethno-linguistic groups of South Omo, extending from the northern border of Mago National Park into the highlands around Jinka and Key Afer, and further north. The Ari numbered 100,000 souls according to the 1984 census, and the population is considerably larger today. In common with the Hamer, the Ari speak a south Omotic language, which is divided into ten distinct regional dialects. The Ari of the highlands and lowlands have quite different subsistence economies, but both are mixed farmers who grow various grains (as well as coffee and *enset* at higher altitudes), keep livestock, and produce excellent honey. In urban centres such as Jinka and Key Afer, the Ari now mostly wear Western costumes. In more rural areas, you will still see Ari women draped in the traditional *gori* (a dress made with leaves from the *enset* and *koisha* plants), and decorated around the waist and arms with colourful beads and bracelets.

WEITA TO TURMI VIA ARBORE AND LAKE CHEW BAHIR

The 120km road running southwest from Weita to Turmi passes, for the most part, through flat arid acacia scrub populated by the Tsemai in the north and the closely related Arbore people in the south. This harsh landscape, thinly populated by pairs of Guenther's dik-dik and home to a variety of colourful dry-country birds, is dominated by the austere Hamer Mountains, which rise to a height of 1,707m on the western horizon. The full drive takes the best part of four hours without stops.

The only urban punctuation en route, and well worth the minor diversion, is the small town of Arbore, which lies a few hundred metres east of the road, close to the boundary of Tsemai and Arbore territory some 50km south of Weita. A kilometre or two south of Arbore, a rough and little-used track veers southeast from the main road to reach the alluringly remote Lake Chew Bahir after three or four hours of virtual bushwhacking – a side trip best undertaken in the company of a police escort from Arbore town.

Perhaps 40km south of Arbore, the road veers westwards to climb into the Hamer Mountains, offering sweeping views back to the open Arbore plains, before descending again into the wild expanses of Hamer country, covered under the next heading.

Arbore

Although relatively large, Arbore is far more rustic and unaffected than many similarly sized towns in South Omo, with the police station on its outskirts more or less the only building that isn't constructed along traditional lines. In common with their linguistically and culturally affiliated Tsemai neighbours, the Arbore migrated to their present homeland from Konso perhaps two centuries ago. Because they have ancestral and cultural links to Konso and the pastoralists of the surrounding lowlands, the Arbore traditionally played an important role as middlemen in trade between the Omo River and the Konso Highlands. The town of Arbore lies in an area where several tribal boundaries converge, and because the Arbore people routinely intermarry with other ethnic groups, it is also inhabited by a substantial number of Hamer and even Borena women – adding a cosmopolitan feel to the worthwhile Saturday market. There is no accommodation in Arbore, but camping is permitted in the police compound.

Lake Chew Bahir

The territory of the Arbore people runs as far south as Lake Chew Bahir, a vast but little-visited expanse of salt water abutting the Kenyan border. It comes at no surprise to learn that this saline sump, still remote and inhospitable today, was perhaps the last African lake of comparable size to remain unknown to Europeans: its existence was little more than a rumour until Count Teleki arrived on its shore, fresh from having been the first European to set eyes on Lake Turkana, in April 1888. Teleki christened the lake in honour of Princess Stefanie, the consort of his Hungarian sponsor Prince Rudolf. The name Lake Stefanie is still sometimes used today, but the older local name of Chew Bahir – literally 'Ocean of Salt' – seems more apt.

Lying at an altitude of 520m, Lake Chew Bahir is a curious body of water, noted for its substantial fluctuations in water level and expanse. In the 1960s, the lake consisted of some 2,000km² of open water, nowhere more than 8m deep, but for much of the rest of the 20th century it was reduced to a rank swamp in an otherwise dry basin. The key to Chew Bahir's fluctuating water level is thought to be the level of Lake Chamo, which feeds it via the Segen and Gelana Delai rivers. Lake Chew Bahir has no outlet – it lies in an area where evaporation outstrips rainfall fourfold – and as a consequence it quickly shrinks in area without sufficient inflow, and the water is too saline to be drunk by man or beast.

Nominally protected within the vast **Chew Bahir Wildlife Reserve**, the lake and its hinterland of dry acacia woodland still support low volumes of ungulates such as Grevy's zebra, greater and lesser kudu, gerenuk and Grant's gazelle, as well as lion, spotted hyena and various small carnivores. More reliable is the birdlife in the permanent swamp that lies at the mouth of the Gelana Delai River, the closest part of the lake basin to Arbore. Lesser flamingos are usually present in concentrations ranging from a couple of thousand to hundreds of thousands, along with a variety of storks, waterfowl and waders. The surrounding acacia woodland is an important site for dry-country birds characteristic of the badlands that separate the highlands of central Kenya from those of southern Ethiopia: vulturine guinea fowl, Shelley's and golden-bellied starling, pink-breasted lark, scaly chatterer and grey-headed silverbill are just a few of the more interesting species present.

Lake Chew Bahir can be reached in three or four hours from Arbore, following a track that heads southeast from the Turmi road immediately south of town. The track is difficult to follow unless you know the way, and the lake's location on the sporadically

REFLECTIONS ON KEY AFER MARKET

Edited from a letter from Arthur Gerfers

At last, my first real live pagan African market. The lovely Bena woman with red clay braids who was seated before me has moved on over into the main marketplace. Her husband has stayed behind and keeps watch over ornately bound gourds containing butter and vegetables. Many of the men have shaven heads from the forehead to the middle of the skull, lending them a proud, regal appearance. Their earlobes are pierced three, sometimes four times, with large rings and strings of beads hanging down. They are usually bare-chested and wear a tight cloth wrap around the waist reaching about mid thigh; the calves are large and muscular. They wear jewellery round the neck consisting of red and blue or black and orange beads. I can only guess at the significance. The gold or silver bands and bracelets they wear may have some meaning too. The bright colours and lustrous metals against black skin are striking. These people smell intensely of wood smoke. Their variety and exotic appearance defies written description. Photography has also proven disappointing, as the beautiful or striking views of these people cannot be captured by the tourist's camera, before which their exquisitely handsome features seem to turn to stone.

sensitive Kenyan border makes it inadvisable to visit without an armed escort. This can be arranged at the police station in Arbore, where you can also ensure that somebody in authority knows to send out a search party in the event of a breakdown or any other mishap – weeks may pass without a vehicle heading down this way! A full day must be allocated to the excursion – better still, take camping gear and spend the night at the lake – and it would be advisable to carry sufficient water and food to last a couple of days longer than you intend to spend at the lake.

HAMER COUNTRY: TURMI AND DIMEKA

The Hamer, with their characteristic high cheekbones, elaborate costumes of beads, cowries and leather, and thick copper necklaces, are among the most readily identifiable of the South Omo peoples (see box *The Hamer*, opposite). The main towns of the Hamer are Turmi and Dimeka, both of which host compelling and colourful weekly markets – on Monday and Saturday respectively – and will reward anybody who settles into them for a few days. Turmi and Dimeka alike boast a fair selection of (admittedly somewhat unwholesome) hotels and restaurants, and can be reached with relative ease either in a private vehicle or on the back of a truck. Turmi in particular will form an undoubted highlight of any trip through South Omo, and it is particularly accessible, since all roads lead there eventually.

Turmi

Despite its small size, Turmi is an important transport hub, lying at the pivot of the three main roads that run southwards from the Konso–Jinka road. Best known for its Monday market, possibly the most important in Hamer country, Turmi is a strikingly traditional small town, and well worth a couple of days whether or not they happen to coincide with the market. A couple of small traditional Hamer villages lie within a 2km radius of Turmi town; any local kid will take you to one of them for a small fee.

Reaching Turmi is reasonably straightforward. If you are driving through the region, you could scarcely avoid the place, since all roads pretty much lead to it. On most days, at least one passenger truck will travel to Turmi from Konso via Weita and Arbore, as will one truck from Key Afer via Dimeka. This is not, however, written in stone – it is perfectly possible that you'll have to wait around for a day before finding transport to or from Turmi. Visitors to Turmi used to be required to report to the police upon arrival. Evidently, this is no longer the case, but a visitation fee of birr 50 is levied on all tourists – the guy who collects this fee will find you.

Where to stay and eat
Moderate
Evangadi Lodge 〄 011 6632595/7/8; e reservations@evangadilodge.com; www.evangadilodge.com. Owned and managed by Greenland Tours, this newly opened tented camp verges the normally dry Little Kaske River, about 1km out of town along the Konso road. At present, accommodation consists of spacious standing tents using common showers, which cost birr 250 sgl or dbl occupancy, but a proper lodge is likely to be up and running by the end of 2005, with rooms costing around birr 400. Camping is permitted, and facilities include a cooking hut for self-sufficient visitors, but no restaurant or bar at the time of writing.

Shoestring
Buska Restaurant This long-serving hotel, which lies along the main road through Turmi, now charges an extortionate birr 25/50 for a very basic but clean sgl/twin using a common shower.
Nagaya Hotel Also situated in the town centre, this seems better overall value at birr 15–20 for a sgl. No shower is available, but you can use the community shower opposite the government buildings about 200m along the Dimeka road for the princely sum of birr 2.

THE HAMER

The Hamer, who number about 35,000 and occupy a large territory that stretches east from the Omo River to Lake Chew Bahir, stand out as perhaps the archetypal people of South Omo. Not only do they speak one of the Omotic tongues unique to this small area of southern Ethiopia, but they also display an elaborate and eclectic selection of body decorations that embraces the full gamut of Omo specialities, with the notable exception of lip plates.

The women are particularly striking, adorned with thick plaits of ochre-coloured hair hanging down in a heavy fringe, leather skirts decorated with cowries, a dozen or more copper bracelets fixed tightly around their arms, thick welts on their body created by cutting themselves and treating the wound with ash and charcoal, and colourful beaded bands hanging from around their waists. Married women wear one or more thick copper necklaces, often with a circular wedge perhaps 10cm long projecting out of the front. The men, though also given to body scarring, are more plainly adorned except when they paint themselves with white chalk paste before a dance or ceremony. The clay hair buns fashioned on some men's heads indicate that they have killed a person or a dangerous animal within the last year.

In common with most other people of South Omo, the Hamer are pastoralists by custom, and take great pride in the size of their cattle herd, though in reality agriculture now plays a far greater role in their subsistence. They are closely allied to the Bena people, whose territory lies to the north of theirs, and who speak a similar language and freely intermarry with the Hamer. The well-documented cultural links between Ancient Egypt and highland Ethiopia may also extend to the Hamer and other people of South Omo. Professor Ivo Strecker, who has studied Hamer culture for three decades, and lived among them for long periods, notes that the environment and agro-pastoralist lifestyle of the Hamer is close to that of the early period of Egyptian civilisation. Furthermore, he has documented striking similarities between current day utensils and decorations of the Hamer and identical items depicted on early Egyptian paintings, notably the *woko*, a type of hooked forked herding stick, and the headrests used by Hamer men.

Although most visitors to South Omo visit a Hamer market, it is also very rewarding to visit one of the smaller villages that lie outside the Hamer towns of Turmi and Dimeka. Incredibly neat, and constructed entirely from mud, wood and thatch, one of the most striking aspects of these small villages – which typically consist of a few extended families across perhaps 10–15 huts – is the total absence of non-organic or Western artefacts. It might seem banal when put into words, but it is nevertheless rather sobering to encounter such simplicity and evident lack of material want, and to contrast it against our own restless need for distraction and accumulation of useless paraphernalia.

The most important event in Hamer society is the Bull Jumping Ceremony, the culmination of a three-day long initiation rite that is normally held before the long rains, between late February and early April. On the afternoon of the third day, up to 30 bulls are lined up in a row. The initiate, stark naked and sporting a demented unkempt Afro hairstyle, has to leap on to the back of the first bull, then from one bull to the next, until he reaches the end of the row. He must then turn around and repeat the performance in the opposite direction, then a third and fourth time, before he has proved his worth to everybody's satisfaction. This rite of passage out of the way, the initiates then embark on a frenzied spree of institutionalised violence, repeatedly beating the backs of all their female relatives with sticks until the screaming women are left battered, bleeding and scarred for life.

Tourist Hotel Situated along the Weita road, on the outskirts of town about 500m from the main junction, this charges birr 25 for a clean sgl room. It has an acceptable local restaurant, but the Kaske Bar & Restaurant next door is better, and has the bonus of a fridge.

Camping

Kaske River Campsite More appealing than the hotels in Turmi is this attractively situated community-run campsite, which lies about 3km out of town along the Weita road. The campsite has an unexpectedly lush and shady setting in the riparian fig woodland along the western bank of the normally dry Kaske River, and is passed through most days by guereza monkeys and baboons. It is also rattling with birdlife, with Bruce's green pigeon, black-headed oriole and grey-headed bush shrike among the more prominent and colourful species. The dry acacia scrub behind the site is a good place to seek out dry-country birds such as the gorgeous golden-bellied starling. Alongside the campsite is a water pump that produces potable water and attracts a steady stream of local Hamer villagers. Recently added facilities include two toilets, two showers, and a cooking hut. Camping costs birr 20 per tent. It is recommended that you pay for a guard, which costs birr 40 per party. **Kaina Lodge** e omotour@ethionet.et. Run by a company called Budget Ethiopia Tours, this new campsite lies 3km out of town along an easily missed track that branches from the Konso road between the clinic and the primary school. It has an attractive, isolated location, and facilities amount to two showers and toilets, and a generator (with a fridge on its way). Camping costs birr 25 per tent. A restaurant, bar and rooms are all likely to be completed within the lifespan of this edition.

Dimeka

The principal town of Hamer country, Dimeka is larger and more built-up than Turmi, and correspondingly less traditional in overall mood. Assuming that you've already spent some time in and around Turmi, however, my feeling is that making a specific side trip to Dimeka is worth the effort only on Saturdays, when the market positively vibrates with Hamer villagers who have walked into town from miles around. Dimeka lies on the southern verge of Bena territory, and its market attracts a fair number of Bena people, agriculturists who are similar in appearance to the Hamer, with whom they share strong cultural affinities and freely intermarry.

Dimeka lies about 20km north of Turmi and 55km south of Key Afer along the road connecting these two towns. You will therefore pass through Dimeka – with the option of stopping over – if you travel directly between Key Afer and Turmi, a drive of roughly four hours in a private vehicle. At least one passenger-carrying truck runs along this road on most days, though this cannot be relied upon fully. There is normally regular transport between Turmi and Dimeka on market days in either town.

The pick of the accommodation in Dimeka – all things being relative – is probably the **Ashebir Hotel**, where a simple room with a single bed costs birr 20. Similar rooms cost birr 15 at the **Buska Bar**, which also has the only fridge in town, while the **Tourist Cafeteria** charges the same price for a small cell with a mattress on the floor. The best place to eat, according to locals, is the **Amsel Bar** next door to the Ashebir. As in Turmi, none of the hotels has a shower, but you can use the one at the secondary school for a small fee.

OMORATE

Marked on some maps as Kalem, Omorate lies on the sweltering eastern bank of the Omo River at the terminus of a 72km road running west from Turmi. The town itself is the archetypal tropical backwater: unexpectedly large, not at all traditional in mood, yet almost totally isolated from the rest of Ethiopia. There is, it has to be said, something rather depressing about Omorate, epitomised by the relics of the agricultural scheme that was initiated with North Korean funds in the Mengistu era and faltered to a standstill more than a decade back. The entrenched victims of this aborted master plan still haunt the bars of Omorate, willing to talk the ear off any stranger about their misfortune. The seedy, end-of-the-road atmosphere that hovers over Omorate isn't helped by its climatic shortfalls – temperatures upwards of 40°C combine with fine clay dust and a paucity of shade to make life pretty uncomfortable.

In its favour, Omorate is a very friendly place, and wholly free of *faranji* hysteria. It is also – bizarrely – the only place in South Omo where travellers without a private vehicle can actually *see* the river for which the region is named. And, in the absence of a shower anywhere in town, the Omo River, muddy though it may be, provides nigh irresistible, if not necessarily bilharzia-free, relief from the merciless heat. The river aside, the main attraction of Omorate is the Dasanech villages that lie outside of the town; see *Excursions*, below.

Omorate, though it lies some distance from Kenya, functions by default as a minor border town. Improbable as it might sound, pick-up trucks from goodness-knows-where in Kenya regularly appear on the opposite bank of the river to unload mysterious parcels of goods on to the small ferry. The police, for reasons best known to themselves, insist that all *faranjis* arrive with a letter of authority from the tourist office in Addis Ababa, Jinka or Konso – when pressed for an explanation, they knowingly explain 'we are close to Kenya'. For the same reason, a police escort – who will demand a hefty tip for his unwanted and almost certainly unnecessary services – is a prerequisite for the, um, expedition across the river to the Dasanech village on the facing bank.

Getting there and away

The 72km road from Turmi to Omorate passes through flat and relatively open grassy savanna country. Pairs of Guenther's dik-dik are to be seen in relative profusion, and we also encountered a few gerenuk, a lovely long-necked antelope related to gazelles. On the avian front, flocks of white-throated and northern carmine bee-eaters hog the limelight, dazzlingly colourful and acrobatic as they swoop and hawk from their roadside perches. The road is usually in pretty good shape except after rain, and the drive should take well under two hours. There is no public transport, but ask around in Turmi and you'll more often than not locate a truck heading to Omorate on any given day. Precisely 59km from the central junction, you pass a junction south towards Lake Turkana, a little-used route that should emphatically not be attempted except with a local escort who knows the way. Four kilometres further towards Omorate lies the junction with the road north towards Murelle and Mago National Park (covered under *Murelle and surrounds*, page 516).

Where to stay and eat

The highly coveted accolade of 'best hotel in Omorate' is a tough call. Put it this way, should you have a tent, then you are heartily recommended not to get involved; rather pitch camp in the patch of shade overlooking the river at the back of the police compound. Of the three contending hotels, all clustered iniquitously opposite the police station, the **Adama Hotel** seems the least off-putting, if only because the rooms have larger beds than their competitors. Rooms here cost birr 10, as they do at the neighbouring and lamentably mistitled **Tourist Hotel**. Whether the marginally cheaper and even more sordid **National Hotel** represents better value for money is the sort of burning question that will help see you through the night should counting cockroaches fail to cure any insomnia brought on by the heat and dirt! All of these hotels have bars, and restaurants of a sort, but the fish restaurant opposite the Adama Hotel is a better bet.

Excursions
Dasanech villages

The Dasanech, alternatively known as the Galeb or Reshiat, range across a large territory following the western banks of the Omo River south to Lake Turkana. Local oral tradition, reinforced by that of the Turkana, recounts that the Dasanech migrated to their current homeland from a region called Nyupe, to the west of Turkana, after being forced out by the expansionist wars of the Turkana in the late 18th century. Like the Turkana, Samburu and Gabbra of northern Kenya, the Dasanech were originally pure pastoralists, living an almost totally nomadic lifestyle. The abundant water frontage and fertile soil of their present territory has subsequently pushed them towards a more diverse subsistence economy, based around fishing and agriculture as well as herding livestock.

The nomadic roots of the Dasanech are most clearly seen today in their traditional villages, comprising small, flimsy, domed huts strongly reminiscent of the impermanent structures built by other African desert pastoralists, from the Tuareg of the Sahara to the Nama of the Kalahari. One such village lies on the west bank of the Omo, practically opposite Omorate, and can be reached for a few birr and in a few minutes by utilising the flat-bottomed boat that serves as a ferry across the river (police escort mandatory). Another similar village lies about 20 minutes' walk south of the town centre on the east bank of the river – so far as I know, you can walk or drive here without a police escort, though we might simply have been lucky!

MURELLE AND SURROUNDS

Situated on the eastern bank of the Omo River, some 55km north of Omorate and a similar distance northwest of Turmi, Murelle Lodge is the one set-up in South Omo to which the term upmarket could conceivably be applied. It thus forms the normal base for fly-in tours of the region, and for any other visitors who don't fancy camping or sampling the rustic delights of South Omo's local hostelries. The lodge is conveniently situated along the road from Turmi or Omorate to Mago National Park and Jinka, for which reason the adjoining campsite is a popular overnight stop with camping trips. For visitors on an extended tour of South Omo, the main local attractions are the Karo villages of Kolcho and Dus, and the Bumi village of Kangatan, all of which lie within an hour's drive of Murelle. For visitors basing themselves out of Murelle, the towns of Turmi, Dimeka and Omorate form feasible day trips, while Mago National Park and its Mursi villages can be visited as an overnight camping trip from the lodge, or en route to or from Jinka.

Getting there and away

Coming from the south, two routes can be used to reach Murelle. I haven't personally covered the direct road from Turmi, but it is about 70km long and generally takes two to three hours, with a fair amount of game to be seen along the way.

We travelled along the 55km road that branches northwards from the Turmi–Omorate road about 9km east of Omorate. The dry, red earth savanna this road passes through offers some of the best game viewing in the region. Guenther's dik-dik is as common as ever, and there is a good chance of seeing gerenuk, Grant's gazelle, and the localised tiang (a race of topi associated with the most easterly extent of its range). With an early start, you might well encounter the delightful bat-eared fox, easily distinguished by its oversized ears and black 'bank-robber' eye-mask as it trots through the grass or dozes under a shady shrub. As for birds, colourful swooping bee-eaters do their best to steal the show, but look out too for raptors – we saw at least a dozen species including the handsome black-breasted snake eagle – and colourful red-and-yellow barbets performing their risible clockwork duets from the top of the prolific termite hills.

The road north from Murelle to Mago National Park is covered under the section on that park. No public transport runs close to Murelle from any direction, nor do trucks head there with any regularity – a private vehicle, or lucky hitch, are the only options.

MURELLE AND THE MURLE

The origin of the name Murelle – also transliterated as Murle and pronounced with a rolling 'r' – is somewhat enigmatic. It has always been a place where wild and domesticated animals come to drink, because of the gentle decline of the land towards the river. Aside from the modern lodge, however, Murelle has not supported a settlement in living memory, yet Murle is depicted on several maps, dating right back to the one produced by Count Teleki on his pioneering 1888 Turkana expedition. Stranger still, there actually is a Murle tribe living in this part of Ethiopia, mentioned in several accounts of European explorers, but based for as long as anybody can remember to the west of the Omo River near the Sudanese border.

Why the Karo now refer to this part of the riverbank as Murelle, or Murle, is anybody's guess: it could be that some Murle people settled in the area at some point, or that it was the site of a fight between the Karo and Murle, or something equally significant. Call me a sceptic, but given the inaccuracies that exist on practically every existing map of South Omo, I would not be surprised to learn that the name stems from generations of cartographers having copied a misunderstanding on the part of Teleki regarding the placement of the Murle territory!

Where to stay and eat

Murelle Lodge Bookings through Ethiopian Rift Valley Safaris (ERVS), PO Box 3658, Addis Ababa; ↘ 011 1552128/8591/1127; f 011 1550298; e ervs@ethionet.et; www.ethiopianriftvalleysafaris.com. Set in a shady riverine grove fringing the Omo River, this attractive and comfortable lodge consists of ten cool, airy bungalows with shady verandas and en-suite showers and toilet. The lodge lies in the heart of the Murelle Hunting Concession, an area where wildlife, though hardly prolific, is far more visible than in any other unprotected part of South Omo. The grounds are a delight: guereza monkeys swing by on a daily basis, and birds are everywhere – notably the colourful and vociferous black-headed bush shrike. A certain authenticity is added to the atmosphere by the nocturnal roaring of the Abyssinian lions (refugees from a zoo in Addis Ababa) that live in a cage next to the camp!

Originally built as a hunting camp, Murelle Lodge now primarily caters to the eco-tourism market, and is used by ERVS as the base for a variety of all-inclusive, exclusive and costly packages, ranging from fly-in charters that land right at the nearby airstrip, to drive-down trips out of Addis Ababa. Activities include game drives and nature walks with a tracker, seasonal boat trips on the Omo River, and of course visits to nearby and more remote traditional villages. The food is good, with a strong Italian flavour, and refrigerated soft drinks and beers are available to lodge guests. Accommodation is available to visitors who are not on an ERVS package, but it *must* be pre-booked in Addis Ababa.

Murelle Campsite A leafy campsite, also owned by ERVS, lies right alongside the lodge. It is by far the nicest place to camp in South Omo, and well worth the charge of US$8 per person per night. Unlike the lodge, no advance booking is necessary, but it is important that campers are self-sufficient in terms of food and drinks. Due to the difficult logistics of obtaining food and drink supplies in this remote corner of Ethiopia, meals and drinks are not for sale to campers.

Excursions

Kangatan

Kangatan is the only accessible habitation of the Bumi, a tribe of some 6,000 pastoralists who live on the western side of the Omo River. They normally inhabit the land south of Omo National Park, but will move into the park's southern plains when water or grazing is scarce. The Bumi speak an eastern Nilotic language, and share close affiliations with the Turkana people of northern Kenya, immediately evident in the tentacle-like tangle of leather necklaces and side-cropped hairstyles worn by the women. Like the Turkana, the Bumi are semi-nomadic hunters and cattle-herders by custom, measuring their wealth in terms of the size of their herd, though flood agriculture now plays an increasingly important role in their subsistence. They also share with the Turkana a reputation for aggression and ferocity in battle: even today, they are often involved in fatal altercations related to cattle raiding and inter-tribal rivalry with their Surma, Karo and Hamer neighbours.

Kangatan lies above the western bank of the Omo, perhaps 10km southwest of Murelle as the crow flies. The drive from Murelle takes 30–45 minutes, following the Omorate road south for about 10km, then turning right on to a track leading to a police compound on the eastern bank of the river facing Kangatan. You can park safely in the compound, from where a small local boat will take you across the river for a small fee. It is advisable to visit in the company of a guide from Murelle, who will know the villagers and ensure you are welcomed.

Kolcho and Dus

Murelle Lodge lies within the territory of the Karo, a small tribe – some estimates place the population as no more than 1,000 – which speaks an Omotic language close to that of the neighbouring Hamer. Pastoralists by tradition, their cattle herds were exterminated by disease some years back, and they now subsist primarily by growing sorghum, maize and other crops along the river. In common with the Hamer, scarification plays an important role in Karo body decoration, and the men plaster their hair into tight buns after killing a human enemy or a dangerous animal. The hairstyle favoured by Karo women is rather striking: tightly cropped at the side, and tied into bulbous knots and dyed ochre on top, it makes them look as if they have rushed out of the bathroom without removing their shower cap.

The Karo are best known for the elaborate body painting they indulge in before important ceremonies. They dab their torsos with white chalk paint, reputedly in imitation of the plumage of a guinea fowl. Colourful facemasks are painstakingly prepared with a combination of pastes made by mixing water with chalk, charcoal, powdered yellow rock, and iron ore. You'd have to be unusually lucky to arrive at Murelle when a genuine celebration is about to take place, but colourful dances can be arranged through the lodge (or directly) at one of the nearby Karo villages for around birr 300 per party.

Discounting the staff village, the closest Karo settlement to Murelle is Kolcho, a compact settlement of perhaps 30 simple huts set on a magnificent sand cliff overlooking a large sweep in the Omo River. Kolcho is about 6km – no more than 20 minutes' drive – from Murelle. Further afield, about 20km from Murelle and a good hour by road, the Karo village of Dus is much larger and has a less spectacular setting, but is worth a visit if you are heading on north towards Omo National Park.

MAGO NATIONAL PARK

Proclaimed in the 1960s, the 2,162km² Mago National Park is bisected by the Mago River, which flows into the Omo on the park's southern boundary. Although Mago National Park shares some 5km of its southwestern boundary with Omo National Park, and the protected areas effectively form one ecological unit, crossing between the two was never easy, and it has become practically impossible since the region's bridges were swept away in the flooding of 1997.

Along with Omo National Park, Mago is the closest thing in Ethiopia to the renowned savanna reserves of east Africa, and its potential as a tourist attraction – marketed in combination with the fascinating cultures of South Omo – is immense. For the time being, however, the access roads to the park remain poor (and sometimes impassable after rain), internal roads are little better, and tourist development is limited to a few basic camping sites along the Mago River. Despite the financial impetus that tourism might give to preserving what wildlife remains in this beleaguered sanctuary, it seems that this situation is unlikely to change in the foreseeable future.

Mago National Park is dominated by dense acacia woodland, which is interspersed with small areas of open savanna, the pristine riparian forest that lines the Mago River, and the extensive Neri Swamp. Most of the park lies on the Rift Valley floor at an altitude below 500m, and is correspondingly hot and sweaty, but the northern sector rises sharply to the rift escarpment and the 2,528m-high Mount Mago.

The extensive checklist mentions close to 100 mammal species, though populations of many large mammals are now severely depleted through years of poaching and inadequate conservation measures. According to the park rangers, the thousand-strong buffalo herds for which the park was once renowned are today reduced to about 400 head. Only 200 elephants remain, generally concentrating in the area around the park headquarters and campsites during the dry season, particularly in August. As for other large herbivores, the density of the bush makes it difficult to get much of a feel for numbers, especially as the wildlife here is generally quite skittish. Based on our observations, however, Defassa waterbuck is by far the most visible antelope, though gerenuk, tiang, bushbuck, Lelwel hartebeest, greater and lesser kudu and the ubiquitous Guenther's dik-dik are also present in significant numbers.

Most tourists who visit the park do so not for the wildlife, but to see the Mursi villages along the Mago River (see box *The Mursi*, page 520), and Mago is emphatically not suited to a first-time safari-goer hoping for a few quick snaps of lions and elephants. On the other hand, should you be seeking a more holistic picture of the African wilderness as it was before mass tourism, Mago is pretty much that – tsetse flies and mosquitoes included! With that frame of mind, whatever animals you do come across will be a bonus. And you never know your luck – the only predator we encountered was a solitary black-backed jackal, but leopard are around (though secretive as ever), cheetah may be seen in more open areas, and the lion population is estimated at a healthy 200. You might also look out for two unusually marked dry-country variations on more familiar creatures: the beautiful and highly photogenic reticulated giraffe, and the striking Grevy's zebra, which is larger and has much narrower stripes than the more widespread plains zebra (also found in Mago). Olive baboon are frequently seen, while the common savanna-dwelling patas and vervet monkeys are supplemented along the river by guereza, blue and De Brazza's monkey – the last an isolated population of a species associated with the west African rainforest. More than 300 bird species have been recorded, with typical dry-country specials boosted by more localised birds such as the Egyptian plover, Pel's fishing owl, black-rumped waxbill and dusky babbler.

Entrance costs birr 70 per person and birr 80 per vehicle. A fee of birr 40 per day or birr 60 overnight must be paid directly to the armed scout (mandatory).

Getting there and away

Mago National Park headquarters can be approached by road from Murelle in the south or from Jinka in the north. The 115km drive from Murelle takes about six hours, and there is a genuine risk of getting lost without a driver or guide who knows the route. The road is in reasonable shape as far as Dus, 20km north of the lodge, but after that it deteriorates to a very rough and frequently indiscernible track. It is impassable after rain.

The steep dirt road between Jinka and Mago National Park headquarters is only 40km long, but it generally takes two hours to cover in the dry season. After light rain, the black cotton soil becomes very slippery, and the drive might take three to four hours. After heavy rain, this road is also impassable.

THE MURSI

The most celebrated residents of South Omo are undoubtedly the Mursi, a distinctive group of pastoralists who number about 5,000, and whose territory is more or less bounded by the Omo River to the west and the Mago River to the east. The subject of several television documentaries, as well as Leslie Woodhead's book *A Box Full of Spirits* (Heinemann), the Mursi are best known for one admittedly very quirky item of decoration: the famous lip plates.

The custom is that when a Mursi woman reaches the age of about 20, a slit is cut between her lower lip and mouth. Over the next year, the gap is progressively stretched until it is large enough for a small circular clay plate, indented like a pulley, to be inserted between the lip and the mouth. As the lip stretches, so the plate is replaced with a larger one, a process that is repeated until eventually the gap is large enough to hold a clay plate of perhaps 15cm in diameter, and the woman can ideally pull her distended lip over her head. The larger the lip plate a woman can wear, the greater her value when she is married – a real whopper might fetch a price of 50 head of cattle.

An alternative and probably false explanation – that the idea is to make a married woman as unattractive as possible to potential adulterers and slave raiders – does take on a grim ring of truth when you actually visit a Mursi village. Contrary to what the publicity shots might have you believe, Mursi women don't actually wear their lip plate all that much – it's far too heavy and uncomfortable. Instead, the wretched ladies wander about in what appears to be a monumental sulk, with their distended lip hanging limply below the jaws. Call me a culture-bound git, but a Mursi woman *sans*

Mago National Park can be reached only in a private vehicle. If you are travelling independently on public transport, the only realistic way to visit Mago is as a day or overnight trip out of Jinka. The NTO office in Jinka, 2.5km from the town centre along the Konso road, rents out 4x4 vehicles at a daily rate of around US$150. Cheaper rates are generally offered by private individuals through the various hotels in Jinka – just ask around! It will obviously cut the individual cost if you can hook up with like-minded travellers in Jinka to form a group.

Where to stay and eat

There is no accommodation in or near Mago National Park. Unless you intend to visit the park on a day trip out of Jinka, which is perfectly possible, you will have to camp at one of the sites that line the Mago River a few kilometres from the park headquarters. Although basic – facilities are more or less limited to a water pump – the sites are very beautiful, tucked away in the riverine fig forest. Forest birds and monkeys are likely to be seen from the campsite, and elephant occasionally come through during the dry season. All food and drinks should be brought with you, as nothing is available in the park. The camping fee is birr 30 per tent, and you must also pay birr 60 to have an armed scout stay with you overnight.

JINKA

As the administrative capital of South Omo zone, Jinka is often perceived to be the obvious gateway into the region. In reality, while Jinka is serviced by the only scheduled flights to South Omo, and is the best place for independent travellers to rent a vehicle into Mago National Park, it is pretty much the end of the line insofar as road travel is concerned. Backpackers could easily explore the more accessible villages of South Omo without ever coming within spitting distance of Jinka, while those travelling in a private

lip plate is not, by any standards, a pretty sight – one can't help but feel for the teenage girls who will soon be mutilated in a similar fashion!

Mind you, the path to matrimony is no smoother for Mursi men. Traditionally, no Mursi man can marry unless he has won a *Donga*, a stick fight in which two contestants painted in white chalk paste pummel each other violently with heavy 2m-long poles. In past times, fights to the death were commonplace, but these days it is more normal for one fighter to submit before things go that far. The victorious fighter is carried off by a group of eligible girls, who then decide which one of them will marry him.

Ever since the bridge over the Mago River was washed away a few years back, the only accessible Mursi villages have been situated on the east side of the river within Mago National Park. The easiest village to visit, some two hours' drive from the park headquarters, is Bella, which can be reached by following the Jinka road north for 8km, then turning left onto a track that leads to a ranger outpost some 15km further, then continuing straight ahead for another 17km, ignoring the track for Maki to your right, and climbing the escarpment as you approach the village itself.

Bella is situated just outside the northwestern park boundary, on a beautiful plateau that is encircled by mountains and lies near the source of the Usno River. A fee of birr 30 per vehicle must be paid to the elders, and a further fee must be paid to any person who you photograph. The starting rate is birr 2 per picture, and they count every click of the shutter. Lip plates can be bought from the girls and women, should you fancy a souvenir. Further relevant details are included under the heading *Mago National Park* above.

vehicle are likely to pass through Jinka only because it happens to lie along the main road in or out of Mago National Park. A 'road tax' of birr 50 per vehicle is levied upon entering town from the Kondo side.

Existing in virtual isolation from the rest of Ethiopia, Jinka has a rather quaint atmosphere that combines urban and rural attributes in equal proportion. Which of these comes to the fore will depend largely on whether you've bussed or flown in directly from Addis Ababa or Arba Minch, or bumped and skidded uphill from the sultry backwaters of South Omo. Either way, the town seems to straddle two worlds. High, cool and damp, Jinka stands far apart from the rest of South Omo, with such typical small-town facilities as petrol stations, a bank, and a clutch of acceptable hotels. Equally, elements such as the grassy airstrip at the centre of town undermine any pretensions Jinka might have to be much more than a small, half-forgotten administrative centre in the back of beyond. Whatever else, this is a likeable enough town, and the large Saturday market is certainly worth a look, attracting traders from all over South Omo, in particular Ari, Bana, Besheda and Besketo people.

The one formal tourist attraction in Jinka is the recently opened **South Omo Research Centre & Museum** (✆ 046 7750149; *www.uni-mainz.de/Organisationen/SORC*), which is perched on a hill overlooking the town centre and offers an attractive view over it. The excellent anthropological museum (*open Tue–Sat 09.00–12.00 and 15.00–19.00*) provides a useful overview of the various cultures of South Omo, and is well worth the birr 10 entrance fee. Film programmes and anthropological lectures can be set up for groups with advance notice.

Getting there and away

Jinka is situated 205km northwest of Konso, and can be reached via a reasonable dirt road in about five hours, except after heavy rain. A daily bus now connects Arba Minch and

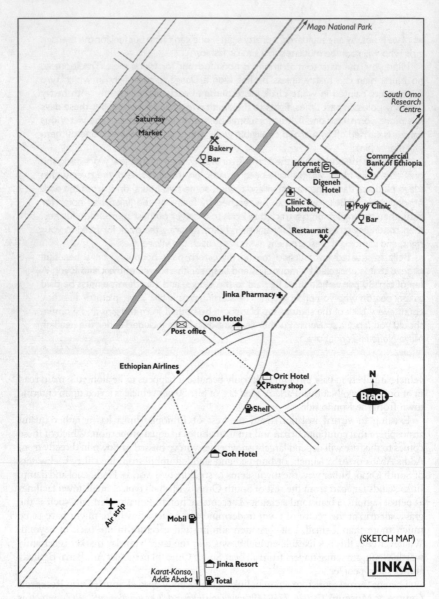

Jinka via Konso, as do various light vehicles and trucks. Ethiopian Airlines flies between Addis Ababa and Jinka via Arba Minch three times a week. For details of driving between Jinka and Mago National Park, see the section on *Mago National Park*, page 518.

Where to stay
Moderate
Jinka Resort ☎ 046 7751043 or 011 6189240; f 046 7750144; e afiatwe@ethionet.et. The recently opened lodge, by far the smartest option in Jinka, lies in large green grounds a short distance from the town centre next to a Total garage on the Konso road. The comfortable rooms cost birr

RAFTING THE OMO

The most adventurous way to reach South Omo is along the river for which the region is named which, during September and October, is high enough to be navigable for most of its length. Ten- and 20-day rafting trips on the Omo River have been run by Remote River Expeditions during these months almost since 1984. The trips start near Weliso, passing through the 1,500m-deep Serenity Canyon, as well as otherwise inaccessible Walaita villages, waterfalls, swimming holes, and hot springs. Hippos, crocodiles, monkeys and various antelope, – sometimes even lions – are often encountered on the way. The ten-day trip ends at the bridge on the Sodo–Jimma road, while the 20-day version continues into South Omo, offering contacts with the Bumi, Bodi and Mursi people. Although the majority of the journey is on flat water, and no experience is required, both sections include challenging rapids. For more information contact Remote River Expeditions, USA; ⊐ 1 303 810 6524; toll free: 1 800 558 1083; e gary@remoterivers.com; www.remoterivers.com.

149/172 for a sgl with en-suite cold/hot shower, or birr 230 for a twin with hot shower. A pleasant campsite with clean toilets and showers charges birr 35 per tent. A good restaurant is attached.

Budget

Goh Hotel ⊐ 046 7751033. The pick of the second stringers is this modern hotel centred on a pleasant courtyard bar and restaurant on the edge of the central airstrip. It's a nice enough place, but the urine-extracting *faranji* rates have escalated threefold since the last edition of this guide was researched, and it really is astonishingly poor value at a (negotiable) birr 80/120 for an en-suite sgl/dbl or birr 40 for a sgl using the common showers.

Orit Hotel ⊐ 046 7751045. Set in flowering green gardens no more than 200m from the Goh, this long-serving and reliable hotel but wildly overpriced is shabbier than the Goh, but charges identical – and equally negotiable – *faranji* rates. And here endeth the search for this edition's winner of the 'All Ethiopia Silly Faranji Price' award…

Omo Hotel ⊐ 046 7751067. Shabbier still, but a lot cheaper, the Omo Hotel charges birr 40/50 for a sgl/dbl with en-suite cold shower.

Shoestring

Digeneh Hotel This looks about the best bet of the cheaper dives, charging birr 20 for a basic room with dbl bed and access to a common cold shower. The attached internet café costs birr 0.75 per minute.

Camping

Rocky Campsite This beautiful green site, set some 3km along the Konso road, combines an attractive setting with good facilities, including flat terraced campsites, clean toilets and showers, three kitchen houses, and a bar selling beers and sodas. You must bring your own food, but a cook is available if you don't feel like preparing it yourself.

Where to eat

The best place to eat is the **Jinka Resort**, which serves a good selection of Western and local dishes at reasonable prices. Adequate restaurants can also be found at the **Goh**, **Orit** and **Omo** hotels, all of which serve a selection of cheap local and Western dishes. An anonymous café next to the Orit Hotel sells fresh juice, while the **Mehbub Café** on the other side of the same hotel also has tasty pastries and coffee. Overlooking the market square is a good bakery, as well as a bar serving decent coffee and occasional pastries.

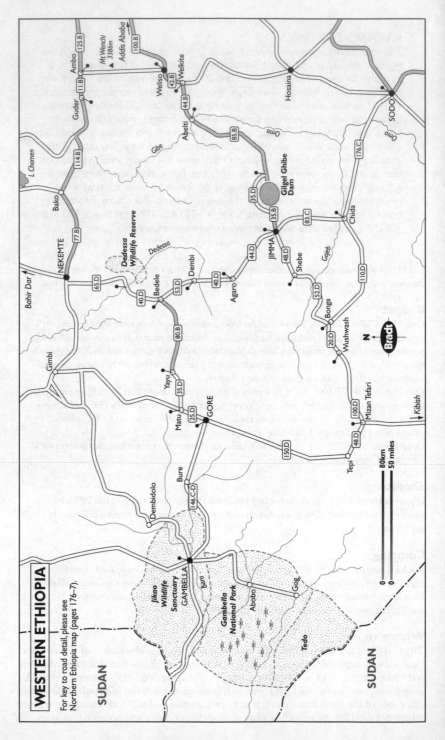

WESTERN ETHIOPIA

For key to road detail, please see
Northern Ethiopia map (pages 176–7).

SUDAN

SUDAN

Addis Ababa
Mt Wenchi ▲ 3386m
100.B
Ambo 125.B
Guder 11.B
Weliso
Welkite 42.B
44.B
85.B
Abelti
Hosaina
SODO
176.C
Omo
Omo
Gibe
L Chomen
114.B
35.D
Gilgel Ghibe Dam
35.B
35.B
83.C
Chida
Bako
NEKEMTE 77.B
65.D
Dedessa Wildlife Reserve
Dedessa
Bedele 53.D
40.D
Dembi
40.D
44.D
JIMMA
48.D
Shebe
Gojeb
110.D
Bahir Dar
Agaro
52.D
Bonga
Wushwash
20.D
Gimbi
80.B
Yayu 35.D
N
Bradt
Matu 25.D
GORE
Mizan Tefari
100.D
Kibish
150.D
48.D
Tepi
80km
50 miles
Dembidolo
Bure
146.C-D
Jikao Wildlife Sanctuary
GAMBELLA
Baro
Abobo
Gog
Gambella National Park
Tedo
SUDAN
0
0

Part Six

Western Ethiopia

INTRODUCTION

More than any other part of the country, it is the lush western highlands, all rolling hills, neat cultivation and dense montane forest, that subvert preconceptions about Ethiopia being a land of desert and famine. Despite its great natural beauty, however, the western highlands lack for a well-defined sightseeing route and boast few organised tourist attractions, for which reason the region is ignored by both the tourist industry and more than 99% of independent travellers to Ethiopia. And this, really, is half of the charm of western Ethiopia: the chapters that follow describe one of Africa's great off-the-beaten-track loops, an area of intimate and lush green scenery broken into convenient day-sized travel bites by a series of well-equipped towns.

The ultimate goal for any traveller heading west of Addis Ababa is the steamy riverport of Gambella, reached via a dramatic descent from the breezy highlands into the sweltering Sudanese border region. Set on the northern bank of the Baro River, part of the Nile drainage system, Gambella is both an atmospheric and fascinating destination in its own right, and more or less the end of the road insofar as public transport is concerned. The region can be explored as a loop between Addis Ababa and Gambella, which entails heading out to Gambella via Ambo and Nekemte, and returning to Addis Ababa via Jimma and Weliso, but it could as easily be done in reverse. Equally, those with limited time could restrict themselves to a short overnight loop through Ambo and Weliso via Lake Wenchi, as described in *Chapter 27*, or travel more extensively in the highlands described in *Chapter 28* without actually going as far as Gambella.

There is regular public transport connecting the towns on both legs of the loop. During the wet season, the direct road between Nekemte and Gambella on the northern leg may be out of service; when this happens, you can get there via a road connecting Nekemte to Bedele on the southern leg. The loop described in the following chapters is all but self-contained, in that there are few decent roads connecting it to other parts of Ethiopia. An exception is the recently upgraded road between Sodo and Jimma, which would allow travellers to cross between the Rift Valley and western Ethiopia without returning to Addis Ababa.

Most of the places described in this section lie at an elevation of 2,000m or greater, and are thus relatively cool and moist. Gambella, which lies below the escarpment, has a hot, humid climate reminiscent of the east African coast and Lake Victoria hinterland.

The Wenchi Loop

An inviting taster for the western highlands and worthwhile excursion out of Addis Ababa in its own right is provided by the road loop that runs west for 125km from the capital to the bustling town of Ambo, then cuts southward for about 65km to the resort town of Weliso, 100km from Addis Ababa on the Jimma road. The focal point of this road loop is the spectacular Wenchi Crater Lake, which lies to the east of the road connecting Ambo to Wenchi, and also offers some worthwhile indigenous forest reserves, a trio of attractive waterfalls in the vicinity of Ambo, and a recently privatised and refurbished hot springs resort at Weliso.

In a private vehicle, you could complete this loop in one long day, especially once the new surfaced road between Addis Ababa and Ambo, under construction in 2005, has been completed in its entirety, though this wouldn't leave a great deal of time for sightseeing. A more realistic and relaxed approach would be to dedicate two or three days to the exercise, planning on overnight stops at Menegasha State Forest, Ambo or Weliso, depending on your budget and interests. There is plenty of public transport along the main roads connecting Addis Ababa to Ambo or to Weliso, the respective springboards for travel on to Nekemte/Gambella or Jimma/Mizan Tefari, but transport between Ambo and Weliso is rather more limited.

FROM ADDIS ABABA TO AMBO

The hot springs resort of Ambo makes an obvious goal for a first overnight stop on any trip to western Ethiopia, but there are a couple of interesting diversions along the way, all of which – like Ambo itself – can easily be visited as a day trip from the capital. Foremost among these is the underrated and under-utilised Menegasha National Forest, where a network of foot trails and excellent budget accommodation can be found in one of the largest remaining montane forests in Ethiopia. Of interest solely to birdwatchers is the Gefersa Reservoir, while further west the road to Ambo cuts through the historical small town of Addis Alem. Another point of interest is the Chilimo Forest near Ginchi, the site of a newly established community tourism project.

Gefersa Reservoir

This large reservoir, set at an altitude of 2,600m in the Akaki catchment area some 18km west of Addis Ababa, was dammed in 1938 as a source of water for the expanding capital, and its carrying capacity was boosted by a second dam built further upstream in 1966. The lack of fringing vegetation makes the reservoir rather bland visually, but it is popular with birdwatchers, as much as anything for its proximity to the capital. Gefersa probably can't be recommended to travellers who will be heading to the prime birdwatching spots of southern Ethiopia, but it is a good place to observe some endemic species not easily seen at the main stops along the northern historical circuit. The ubiquitous wattled ibis and more localised blue-winged goose are virtually guaranteed at Gefersa, while

Abyssinian longclaw, Rouget's rail and black-headed siskin are also regular, along with a few interesting non-endemics such as red-breasted sparrowhawk and (during the European winter) a variety of migrant waterfowl.

Menegasha National Forest

The magnificent Menegasha National Forest incorporates some 2,500ha of natural forest along with 1,300ha of exotic plantation forest, at altitudes ranging from 2,300m to 3,000m on the southern and western slopes of Mount Wechecha. Dominated by tall juniper, hagenia and podocarpus trees, Menegasha protects the most substantial remaining patch of indigenous forest in the Addis Ababa region. Above the forest line, the 3,385m-high Mount Wechecha, an extinct volcano, supports a cover of Afro-alpine moorland dominated by *erica* and *helichrysum* species. The forest is inhabited by various large mammals, and offers birders with limited time in Ethiopia the opportunity to see several key species more often associated with the forests around Wondo Genet and at Dinsho in Bale National Park. It is worth noting that a mountain called Menegasha lies between Addis Ababa and Mount Wechecha.

Menegasha Forest has an unusual place in east African history, providing the earliest-known instance anywhere in the region of an official conservation policy being adopted. In the mid 15th century, Emperor Zara Yaqob became concerned at the high level of deforestation on Mount Wechecha, and he arranged for a large tract of juniper forest to be replanted with seedlings from the Ankober area. The forest was protected by imperial decree over the subsequent centuries, until eventually Emperor Menelik II set it aside as the Menegasha State Forest in the late 1890s.

Menegasha is well organised for day visits and for extended stays. Emanating from the forestry headquarters is a 6km motorable track deep into the forest, as well as a network of ten walking trails, ranging in length from 0.3km to 9km, and variously taking in a lovely waterfall as well as the 3,385m Damocha Peak. The most frequently seen large mammals along these trails are the guereza monkey and endemic Menelik's bushbuck, but baboon and common duiker are also encountered on occasion, and leopard and serval are both present. The forest birding is superb. The endemic Ethiopian oriole and yellow-fronted parrot are regular around the headquarters. Several other endemics are likely to be encountered – black-winged lovebird, banded barbet, Abyssinian woodpecker and Abyssinian catbird among them – alongside other good forest birds such as crowned eagle, Narina trogon, white-cheeked turaco and Abyssinian ground thrush. The entrance fee is birr 20 for non-residents and birr 10 for residents.

Accommodation at the forestry headquarters consists of a large homely cottage containing one double room, two twin rooms, a lounge, a toilet and shower, and a kitchen with a fridge and gas cooker. The bedrooms are rented out individually at around birr 30 per person. There is also an eight-bed dormitory, with common shower and kitchen attached, at a charge of birr 12 per person. Camping is permitted at the headquarters for between birr 10 and birr 30 per tent (depending on the tent size), as well as at designated spots along the walking trails. Visitors should bring all their own food and drink. Booking is not normally necessary, though the cottage does occasionally fill up over weekends, so you might want to ring the forest manager (❨ 011 5154975) in advance to be on the safe side.

Coming along the Ambo road from Addis Ababa, the approach road to the forest lies a few kilometres past the small town of Menegasha, and it is signposted for 'Tseday Farm Horticulture Development Enterprises'. The approach road isn't well maintained, and particularly during the rainy season it is suitable for 4x4 vehicles only. After 16km, the approach road crosses a small bridge, and immediately after that passes through the small village of Suba, where a left turn leads for 2km to the forestry headquarters.

The forest can also be approached from the Jimma road, turning right along the road to the Meta Brewery after you pass through the small town of Sebeta roughly

30km from Addis Ababa. The approach road from Sebeta to Suba, also 16km long, is generally in a fair state of repair and, except after heavy rain, it should be passable in a saloon car. There is no public transport to Suba, and hitching might involve a very long wait at the junction. If you decide to give it a go, the route from Sebeta probably carries the greater volume of traffic. Should you fail to find a lift, Sebeta does boast a few basic hotels.

Addis Alem

Situated roughly halfway between Addis Ababa and Ambo, the small town of **Addis Alem** was founded in 1900 as the projected capital of Menelik II, who gave it its name, which means 'New World'. Addis Alem would probably be the capital of Ethiopia today were it not for the introduction of the fast-growing Australian eucalyptus tree at a time when Addis Ababa's wood resources were looking decidedly finite. The hilltop palace constructed for Menelik under the supervision of American and Indian engineers prior to 1902, when the planned relocation to Addis Alem was abandoned, became the Church of Ejare Debre Tsion Maryam which today pokes above the forest 1km from the main road to dominate the town's skyline. The circular church, decorated with paintings of lions and cheetahs, is of interest primarily for the Menelik-era treasures in its keep. These historical connections aside, Addis Alem is otherwise a rather dull little town. If you need to spend the night, the **Alemu Selassie Hotel** at the Mobil garage has adequate rooms with double beds and access to a common shower.

Chilimo Forest

Chilimo Forest is a small area of indigenous forest extending over about 50km² some 7km north of the town of Ginchi, which lies 87km west of Addis Ababa on the Ambo road. An isolated relic of the dry evergreen montane forest that once covered much of this part of Ethiopia, it offers the opportunity to experience Ethiopia's natural environment relatively close to the capital. Chilimo offers numerous natural features, from stunning views to dense closed-canopy forest teeming with monkeys, birds and other forest creatures. The Royal Lodge in the centre of the forest was a gift from Haile Selassie to the Empress Menen to celebrate the birth of their son.

Community-based management groups in various local villages have been assigned to control adjacent forest patches under signed forest management plans and agreements. These communities will currently offer informal hospitality to self-sufficient campers (at their own risk) and will also act as local forest guides. Fees for all services are negotiable. It is hoped in the near future that the communities will be providing formal camping services, as well as guided walks, rides and local activities. For news of progress, contact the Participatory Forest Management Programme on ℣ 011 1550511/1550154 or ℮ cfwcp@ethionet.et.

AMBO

This scruffy small town of around 40,000 inhabitants stands at an altitude of around 2,100m on the Huluka River some 125km west of Addis Ababa by road. It was temporarily renamed Hagare Hiwot (Healthy Country), and is still referred to as such on some maps. Haile Selassie was rather partial to bathing in the therapeutic hot springs that lie in the town centre and which still form the centrepiece of a low-key resort and accompanying swimming pool. Entrance to the hot springs complex costs birr 4, and is worthwhile whether you want to take a dip in the pool (which despite the dirty appearance of the mineral-rich water is refilled regularly) or just enjoy the birdlife attracted to the surrounding fig trees. Ambo is also the home of Ethiopia's most popular brand of mineral water, and visits to the bottling factory, about 5km out of town on the Nekemte road, are encouraged.

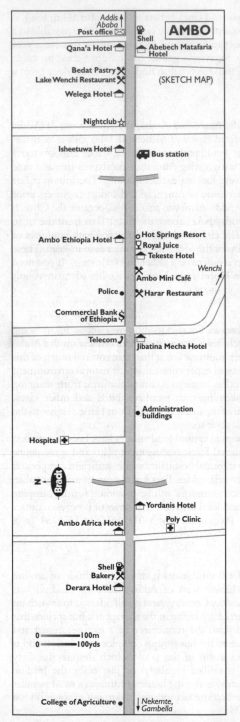

Addis
Ababa
Post office ⊠

Qana'a Hotel 🏠

Bedat Pastry ✕
Lake Wenchi Restaurant ✕

Welega Hotel 🏠

Nightclub ☆

Isheetuwa Hotel 🏠

Ambo Ethiopia Hotel 🏠

Police ●

Commercial Bank
of Ethiopia $

Telecom ☏

Hospital ✚

z → Bradt

Ambo Africa Hotel 🏠

Shell 🅿
Bakery ✕
Derara Hotel 🏠

0 ▬▬▬ 100m
0 ▬▬▬ 100yds

College of Agriculture ●

🅿
Shell
Abebech Matafaria
Hotel

AMBO

(SKETCH MAP)

🚍 Bus station

○ Hot Springs Resort
Q Royal Juice
🏠 Tekeste Hotel

✕
Ambo Mini Café

✕ Harar Restaurant

Wenchi
↗

Jibatina Mecha Hotel

● Administration
buildings

🏠 Yordanis Hotel

Poly Clinic
✚

| Nekemte,
▼ Gambella

Getting there and away

The 125km drive from Addis Ababa takes about 2.5 hours, passing through a pretty but less than dramatic highland area of green cultivated fields set below distant mountains, though the number of diversions linked to the construction of the new asphalt road can push this up to three hours. This is likely to change for the better when the superior and marginally shorter asphalt road is completed in 2006. Public transport to Ambo leaves the main Autobus Terra in Addis Ababa throughout the day. Direct buses between Addis Ababa and Nekemte, the next main town along the western loop, pass through Ambo but are usually full. There is no direct transport between Nekemte and Ambo; you will probably need to change buses at Bako (see *Getting there and away* under *Nekemte*, page 545).

Where to stay and eat
Moderate

Abebech Matafaria Hotel (50 rooms) ☏ 011 2362365/6. This smart new five-storey hotel lies in compact but shady grounds close to the bus station on the Addis Ababa side of town. The clean and unusually modern rooms are excellent value at birr 50/60 for a dbl/twin with en-suite hot shower and private balcony, while suites with a king-size bed and bath cost birr 100. A good restaurant serves local and international cuisine in the birr 15–30 range.

Ambo Ethiopia Hotel (46 rooms) ☏ 011 2362002/7; e amboethhotel@ethionet.et. Built as an elementary school in 1949 and converted to a hotel six years later, this former government hotel, set in a leafy riverfront garden opposite the hot springs resort, had become rather rundown prior to being privatised in 2003. An attractive stone building with wooden floors and high ceilings, it is currently in the process of being renovated and already looks a far more tempting prospect than it did a few years back. The rooms don't quite match the standard set by the Abebech Matafaria, but the place has a lot more character and ranks as very good value at birr 34 for a dbl using common showers, birr 46/52 for a sgl/dbl with en-suite hot shower, or birr 100 for a suite with DSTV. The restaurant serves good food indoors or al fresco at birr 10–20 for a main course.

Budget
Ambo Africa Hotel (12 rooms) ❧ 011 2362288. The only other place in town with hot showers, but otherwise a pretty standard budget lodging, this place is vastly inferior to the two hotels listed above, but more expensive than either thanks to a wildly exaggerated *faranji* price of birr 55 for an en-suite dbl.

Shoestring
Derara Hotel (28 rooms) ❧ 011 2360459. The pick of several cheap hotels studded around town, this friendly local lodging also seems rather optimistic in asking *faranjis* to pay an inflated rate of birr 36 for an adequate dbl with en-suite cold shower or birr 24 for a room using the common showers.
Jibatina Mecha Hotel ❧ 011 2362253. A long-serving cheapie, this place has clean en-suite rooms for birr 25, as well as cheaper rooms using a common shower. The flowering grounds boast a bar and restaurant, but the rooms are set far enough away that noise isn't a discouraging factor.

Excursions
Teltele Valley Park
A worthwhile excursion from Ambo is this small park that opened recently as a joint venture between the newly privatised Ambo Ethiopia Hotel and the Ambo Agricultural College. The park lies below the 2,200m-high Senkele Mountain and consists of a steep wooded gorge carved by the Teltele and Huluka rivers prior to their confluence about 4km west of Ambo (following the Guder road for 2km then turning right onto a dirt track). There are three waterfalls in the park, the tallest of which measures 25m high, while a range of low-key wildlife includes Anubis baboon, guereza, bushbuck, porcupine, monitor lizard and a great many birds. Still under development, facilities already include a campsite and a selection of steep walking trails ranging from 500m to 4.5km in length, and standing tents with superb views of the river were under construction when we visited in 2005. Entrance costs birr 30 per person inclusive of a two-hour guided walk and a coffee ceremony, a horseriding excursion costs an additional birr 20 per person, while an overnight stay costs birr 100 per person, inclusive of entrance fee, a guided tour, coffee ceremonies, and a solar-heated shower – goat or sheep barbecues can be arranged at an extra charge. Further enquiries and bookings should be directed to the Ambo Ethiopia Hotel, which is also where you must pay your fees, collect a guide, and pick up a map.

Guder Falls
This waterfall, which lies on the Nekemte road about 1km past the small town of Guder, doesn't really warrant the prominent posting it receives on most maps of Ethiopia, but it does carry an impressive volume of water in the rainy season, and the surrounding riverine forest is rattling with monkeys and birds. It's supposed to be best on Sundays, when the sluice gates are opened for Ethiopian weekenders. To get to the waterfall from Ambo, catch one of the regular minibuses that cover the 13km road to Guder, and then walk out of Guder along the Nekemte road. The road crosses a large bridge, and then climbs a gentle rise, at the top of which there is a gate to your left. You may have to bang at the gate for a while to get somebody to open it, but once you are in the enclosure there is a clear footpath to the base of the waterfall. Given that public transport to Nekemte starts in Ambo rather than Guder, Ambo is the more attractive place to overnight for westbound travellers. There is, however, plenty of inexpensive accommodation in Guder. Best bet is the **Guder Falls Hotel**, which lies above the waterfall in green

grounds inhabited by guereza and a variety of birds, charges birr 15 for an adequate single room in a chalet, and serves acceptable meals and drinks.

MOUNT WENCHI

This massive extinct volcano, which reaches an elevation of 3,386m, is situated to the south of Ambo along the dirt road that connects to Weliso on the Jimma road. The main attraction is the picturesque caldera, which is settled and quite densely cultivated, and also encloses a 560ha lake dotted with small islands. On one of these islands stands the venerable monastery of **Wenchi Chirkos**, the foundation of which is attributed by some to the 15th-century Emperor Zara Yaqob and by others to the 13th-century Saint Tekle Haymanot. An extensive plateau covered in Afro-alpine heather and moorland surrounds the crater, and a few relic patches of natural forest remain in the area. Although the lake is currently accessible only as a day trip (whether out of Ambo or Weliso, or en route between the two), the same people who own the Abebech Matafaria Hotel in Ambo are in the process of building a new hotel on the crater rim.

In a private vehicle, the 27km drive from Ambo to the market village of Wenchi takes about one hour. Wenchi can also be approached from Weliso on the Addis Ababa–Jimma road, by turning on to the dirt road that heads roughly northwards from opposite the Reffeera Hotel. After 24km, this road passes through the small town of Daryun, from where it is another 13km to Wenchi village. Whichever way you come, you might want to ask about the condition of the road in advance, particularly if you are not in a 4x4 vehicle. It was excellent in the dry season of 2005, with the exception of a 2km stretch north of Wenchi village, which was split by rivulets but still passable slowly in any vehicle.

Once at Wenchi village, a rough 2km road leads eastwards to the crater rim. When we last visited, this side road was just about motorable in a 4x4 to within about 500m of the crater rim, after which it became impassable. Until this road has been improved, you'll need to follow a steep footpath from the rim to the lake, a walk of about one hour in either direction. Alternatively, you can hire a horse in Wenchi village. This was once a time-consuming process that involved lots of bargaining and some occasional hassle, but the local administration now have an excellently organised rota system for local horse owners, fronted courteously and efficiently by a former English teacher whose office lies next to the hotel currently under construction. Horses come at the fixed price of birr 15 per person each way, using a different horse to go up and to go down, and a guide fee of birr 60 per party is also charged. Expect the round trip to take up to seven hours.

Once at the lakeshore, boats are available for the five-to-ten-minute ride to the monastery. The official price of the boat crossing is birr 40 per person, which seems a bit steep for ten minutes as compared to the cost of the long hours spent on horseback. However, Frank Riskin reports that in early 2005: 'we eventually reached the lake at the end of a hot three-to-four-hour trip down the magic green valley on horse and foot, but there was no boat. Much shouting across the water by locals ensued, and we enjoyed an hour's rest, but still no boat. We were then walked round the lakeside and offered an old wooden boat with 10cm of water slopping about its floor plus three plastic bowls for bailing the water out! Half of our party declined, the other half risked it and survived. Meanwhile our doubters entrusted their lives to a slightly drier dug-out canoe. Once across the lake, there sitting idle were the new horses – the problem, we were told, is that the investor is perceived to be exploiting the local labour with very low payments, so they refuse to use the new boat!'

A second viewpoint over the crater is situated 2km from Wenchi, practically alongside the Ambo road. From this viewpoint, you can also see **Lake Dundi** in the distance. According to one very excited local we encountered, the people who dwell near Lake Dundi live in mortal fear of a solitary but gigantic man-eating crocodile, for which reason they refuse to take boats on to the water. True or not, you could check this out for yourself by hiring a horse in Wenchi for around birr 30 – the trip reportedly takes about three hours in each direction on horseback.

Without private transport, reaching Wenchi is problematic. The occasional 4x4 vehicle does serve as public transport between Ambo and Weliso. These reportedly run most mornings in the dry season and will drop passengers at Wenchi village, from where it is easy enough to walk to the crater. So far, so good – the problem is how to get back, since no accommodation is to be found in Wenchi, and what little transport there is in the afternoon is likely to be fully loaded by the time it passes through Wenchi. One way to get around this would be to visit on a Sunday: this is the main market day in Wenchi, and plenty of trucks head to and from the village throughout the day. On other days, one possibility would be to use public transport from Weliso as far as Daryun, where the basic, clean and inexpensive Hotel Beeteli serves as a fallback. Finally, it is perfectly possible to camp near the lake: this is said to be safe, though as always when camping wild it would be advisable to ask somebody's permission before you pitch your tent.

WELISO

This small town on the Jimma road about 100km southwest of Addis Ababa is sometimes referred as Ghion in reference to its hot spring, the water of which is regarded to be holy by Ethiopian Christians. The holy water flows into the church of Weliso Maryam, 15 minutes' walk from the main road, which attracts many sick and disabled pilgrims. It is customary for those cured by the water to leave behind artefacts associated with their illness. A museum-cum-barn in the church grounds holds dozens of crutches and walking sticks, as well as chains left behind by the mentally ill, and charms and talismans by those possessed by evil spirits. No fee is charged to visit the church, but a donation is expected.

The best place to stay in Weliso, indeed one of Ethiopia's most underrated hostelries, is the excellent **Negash Lodge** (↘ *011 3410002/410147*), a recently privatised and renovated former government hostel situated about 1km south of the main street past the church. The hotel is centred on an excellent warm outdoor pool with a shallow end (full Friday to Monday) and it also contains Ethiopia's only indoor pool. The six en-suite double rooms in the main building have been beautifully refurbished and cost birr 137 each. There are also some old square garden *tukuls*, which seem very good value at birr 62.50 for a twin. An excellent base for visiting Wenchi, this hotel also hosts plenty of monkeys in the garden, not to mention a prolific birdlife.

There is plenty of transport out of Weliso in either direction throughout the day. Heading to or from Addis Ababa, you could take a break at the small town of Debre Genet, where a church dedicated to St Gebriel is notable for its large golden dome and some excellent paintings inside. The wooded grounds have been known to throw up interesting birds, such as white-cheeked turaco and Gambaga flycatcher. A short distance from the church, there are some hot springs in a small valley.

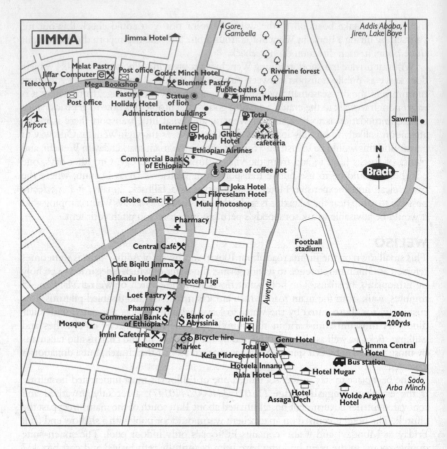

The Western Highlands

Disadvantaged when it comes to both prescribed sightseeing and tourist amenities of any merit, the undulating highlands of Ethiopia's 'Wild West' do nevertheless boast a distinct sense of place, one that stands in bountiful contrast to the stark landscapes associated with the dry eastern borderlands. Indeed, this little-visited highland region, with its rich loamy soils and plentiful year-through rainfall nourishing an uninterrupted swathe of lush cultivation, dank natural forest and feral coffee, could easily deceive the unprepared visitor into thinking he had taken a wrong turn and ended up somewhere on the verdant slopes that characterise the Uganda-Congolese border.

Despite this natural abundance, the region is difficult to recommend wholeheartedly to first-time visitors to Ethiopia, at least not unless they have plenty of time on their hands or nurse a penchant for wilful off-the-beaten-track exploration. The towns of the southwestern highlands, with the arguable exception of Jimma, are uniformly unmemorable, while road conditions and public transport tends to be ropey even by Ethiopian standards, acceptable accommodation and restaurant options are few and far between, and the range of tourist attractions is as limited as it is low-key. All things considered, the most likely reason why you'd choose to travel through the western highlands is by way of transit to the dormant riverboat terminus of Gambella, a travel cul-de-sac that might well be resuscitated as an international trade route following recent moves towards renewed political stability in southern Sudan.

JIMMA

Jimma is comfortably the largest settlement in western Ethiopia, with a population estimated at around 125,000 in 2005. Until 1994, it served as the administrative capital of Kaffa, a region whose Oromo and non-Oromo components were subsequently split between the new administrative regions of Oromia (of which Jimma is a part) and the Southern Nations, Nationalities and Peoples' Region. The fertile hills of what was formerly Kaffa are probably where the coffee plant was first cultivated, and the area remains one of Ethiopia's main coffee-growing centres, with cultivated strains often growing metres away from their wild counterparts in the forest undergrowth. Essentially a 20th-century creation, Jimma saw a great deal of development during the Italian occupation, but its name derives from that of a much older kingdom whose former capital Jiren lies on the outskirts of the modern city.

Although Jimma lacks for any major tourist attractions, there is some interesting sightseeing to be had around town, and you couldn't hope for a friendlier, greener, or better-equipped place to rest up between bus trips. In fact, after a couple of weeks travelling in the west, Jimma – with its cropped green lawns and neat well-tended grid of roads – comes across as quite shockingly modern and cosmopolitan, a reminder of just how poky most western Ethiopian towns really are. The park alongside the river wouldn't look out of place in a European village, nor would the hand-holding couples you see walking through it. There are even public baths, for goodness sake – though the absence of water helps to bring perceptions crashing back to earth!

The only organised tourist attraction within the city centre is the **Jimma Museum**, close to the public baths, where a selection of the personal effects of Abba Jiffar, the last independent king of Jimma, are housed alongside some worthwhile ethnographic displays relating to the Oromo and other local cultures. Entrance costs birr 10, and a knowledgeable English-speaking guide will show you around. Also worth a look is the patch of riverine woodland behind the museum, which appears to support a resident troop of guereza monkeys as well as the outlandish silvery-cheeked hornbill. At the other side of the city centre, the bustling market is worth a look, particularly if you are eager to buy some of the excellent local basketwork. Of interest to wealthier curio hunters (and evidence of Jimma's relative prosperity), are the numerous jewellery shops that line the main road, selling locally crafted silver and gold products. Somewhat more bizarrely, this road also houses what might well be the world's largest concentration of **barbershops**. Also worth a mention is **Jiffar Computers** next to the Mega Book Shop and the anonymous **internet café** next to the Mobil garage, both of which charge birr 0.40 per minute to browse.

Getting there and away

Ethiopian Airlines flies between Addis Ababa, Jimma and Gambella a few times weekly. Jimma's airport lies about 3km from the town centre. There are daily buses in both directions between Jimma and Nekemte, and Jimma and Matu, all of which leave at

---

THE JIMMA KINGDOM

Although the modern town of Jimma served as the capital of an administrative region called Kaffa until 1994, it is – rather confusingly – situated to the northeast of the ancient kingdom of Kaffa, within the discrete kingdom of Jimma, which unlike Kaffa had its roots in the Oromo incursion of the 16th century and was predominantly Muslim rather than Christian. Blessed with richly fertile soils and noted for its fine coffee, Jimma served as an important centre of commerce at the convergence of several trade routes. By the 19th century, Jimma was the most powerful political entity in western Ethiopia, covering an area of 13,000km^2, and with an economy based on the sale and trade of coffee and other agricultural produce, precious metals, ivory and slaves captured in the far west. The market at Hirmata, the largest in western Ethiopia, was attended by up to 30,000 people every Thursday.

The last autonomous ruler of Jimma was King Abba Jiffar, who ascended to the throne in 1878 and made his capital at Jiren, only 7km from the modern town of Jimma. Abba Jiffar took power at a time when the autonomy of kingdoms such as Jimma and Kaffa was severely threatened by the expansionist policies and military prowess of Showa under the future Emperor Menelik II. Six years into his reign, Abba Jiffar, rather than resisting the inevitable, decided to throw his lot in with Showa, and to pay tribute to Menelik.

After that, Jimma effectively became a semi-autonomous vassal state to Showa, still under the rule of Abba Jiffar, but overseen by a governor appointed by Menelik. Alexander Bulatovich, who travelled through western Ethiopia in 1897, described Jimma as one of the three 'richest and most industrial settlements' in the region and 'very densely populated'. Bulatovich also wrote that: 'The best iron items and cloth are fashioned there. Merchants from Jimma conduct trade with the southern regions and with Kaffa. All the residents of Jimma, as well as King Abba Jiffar, are Mohammedan.'

around 06.00 and stop in Bedele between 10.00 and midday. Direct buses to and from Addis leave before 07.00; buses that cover this route later in the day will generally stop overnight somewhere along the way. For details of the new road connecting Jimma to Sodo, see box The 'new' Sodo-Jimma road on page 429.

Where to stay
Moderate

Central Jimma Hotel (40 rooms) ☎ 047 1118283. Currently the best option in the town centre, this new multi-storey hotel, situated opposite the bus station, charges a *faranji* price of birr 75 for a large, clean dbl or twin with tiled floor, private balcony, strong en-suite hot shower and birr 50 for a smaller room using the common shower. There is also an excellent coffee bar and restaurant on the ground floor, extending onto a large area of pavement with a view of the bus station! One minor quibble (actually, it seriously pissed me off at the time) is that the only room rates posted up at reception are the (50% cheaper) local prices – unless you ask in advance, you'll only find out when you come to pay, that as a *faranji* you are expected to hand over twice as much without query (and it's considered poor form to interrupt the receptionist's mantra of '*faranji* pay double, *faranji* rich'!)

Godet Minch Hotel (10 rooms) Built in the 1930s, this time-warped hotel has a wonderfully creaky character, epitomised by the wood-panelled public area consisting of a ground floor bar and internal balcony complete with cosy compartmentalised salons. The recently refurnished en-suite doubles are probably the smartest rooms in Jimma, albeit not the quietest, and cost birr 120 for sgl or dbl occupancy.

Wolde Argaw Hotel (57 rooms) ☎ 047 1112731/2, f 047 1116434. Although the rooms are starting to look in need of a little TLC by comparison with their sparkling new counterparts at the upstart Central Jimma Hotel, this popular three-storey hotel, situated on the opposite side of the bus station, remains one of the best deals in Jimma (and it also advertises its separate local and *faranji* rates clearly). Spotless en-suite doubles with a balcony and hot water cost birr 92, while rooms using the common shower cost birr 50 and suites cost birr 184. The bar and restaurant are also good.

Ghibe Hotel (27 rooms) ☎ 047 1110073. This stalwart hostelry in the old town centre may have passed into private hands a couple of years back, but it retains the rather moribund atmosphere typical of former government hotels, redeemed only by its compact but green grounds and occasional visits by a troop of guereza monkeys. Forking out the *faranji* price of birr 87.50 for one of the dingy little rooms would be an act so charitable as to render one eligible for sainthood.

Jimma Degita Hotel (40 rooms) ☎ 047 1110646. This is another recently privatised government hotel, and wildly overpriced for *faranjis* at birr 70 for a small dbl, birr 92 for standard dbl and birr 150 for a suite.

Budget

Aramaic Hotel (8 rooms) ☎ 047 1114359. Situated along the Addis Ababa road about 1km past the turn-off to Jiren, this excellent new hotel must rank as the overall best value in Jimma, though its location is less than ideal for travellers using public transport. Accommodation is in spacious dbl rooms with a clean tiled floor and an en-suite hot shower. The restaurant serves a selection of local and international dishes in the birr 10–12 range, and there is also a pleasant garden bar, which closes at around 22.30, early enough so as not to interfere with one's sleep.

Genu Hotel (13 rooms) ☎ 047 1116065. Conveniently located around the corner from the bus station, this slightly rundown but comfortable, friendly and very reasonably priced hotel charges birr 30 for an en-suite room with one dbl bed and birr 50 for a larger room with two dbl beds.

Shoestring

Hotel Enanu/Innanu The pick of a cluster of about a dozen cheap hotels on the back roads around the bus station, this quiet hotel charges birr 15 for a clean en-suite room with a dbl bed and cold shower.

FROM JIMMA TO ADDIS

The 350km road between Jimma and Addis Ababa is now surfaced in its entirety, with the exception of a roughly 30km dirt detour around the Agelgil Ghibe Dam, which opened in 2004 as a fresh source of hydro-electric power for Addis Ababa, Gonder and Mekele. The drive generally takes around six to seven hours in a private vehicle, while the early morning buses that cover the route typically arrive at their destination up to ten hours later, and buses that leave later in the day may stop overnight at either Welkite or Weliso.

The main point of scenic interest en route is the **Omo River Gorge** between Jimma and Welkite. The descent to the base of the gorge follows a spectacular stretch of road with wild granite outcrops in the distance and dense acacia woodland clinging to the hills. At the bottom of the gorge, the small village of **Ghibe** (marked on some maps as Abelti) straddles the Omo River. There is nothing that is obviously a hotel in Gibe, but the women who run the coffee shop claim that rooms are available – with plenty of dense riverine scrub to explore, and wild scenery in every direction, you may well be tempted. The 'real' **Abelti**, incidentally, lies on a tall mountain which you pass a bit further north – you can walk up to the hilltop town, which boasts stunning panoramic views, a couple of OK cheap hotels, and great roast chicken at the Zeray Deres Restaurant!

You're more likely to spend a night at the busy little roadside town of **Welkite** by accident rather than design, since buses between Jimma and Addis Ababa sometimes stop there overnight. Welkite isn't somewhere you'd make an effort to visit, but if you are stranded it's a friendly little place with plenty of shoestring hotels and bars lining the main strip. The **Teffera Hotel** has self-contained rooms for birr 16, and slightly cheaper rooms using communal facilities – the manager speaks good English and the restaurant serves excellent *kai wat*. From Welkite, unless you arrive too late in the day, there is plenty of local transport on to Addis Ababa, passing through the resort town of Weliso, covered as part of the Wenchi Loop in *Chapter 27*.

Where to eat

The **Sennait Restaurant** on the ground floor of the Central Jimma Hotel is excellent, charging birr 10-14 for a varied selection of local and exotic dishes – pastries, juice, coffee and cheap draft beer are all available too. The two former government hotels serve good Western and local meals for around birr 10–12, as does the Wolde Argaw Hotel. Several juice and pastry shops and local restaurants line the main roads through the town centre. The bar at the **GM Hotel** is an atmospheric spot for a drink.

Excursions from Jimma

Abba Jiffar's Palace

Abba Jiffar was the charismatic, powerful – and exceptionally tall – king who ruled over Jimma from 1878 until his death in 1932. He is remembered today for his canny decision in 1884 to pay tribute to Menelik's then-expanding empire of Showa in exchange for a degree of autonomy not conceded to fiefdoms that were co-opted into Showa by force. The impressive palace built by Abba Jiffar during the early years of his rule still stands on a low hill at the former royal compound of Jiren, 8km from the city centre by road. Constructed at a cost of 400kg of gold and 65,000 Maria Theresa dollars – money gained largely through the ruler's active involvement in the slave trade – the palace is a fine example of an admittedly no more than diverting style of early colonial architecture. The largest of the four buildings in the palace compound, which served as the king's

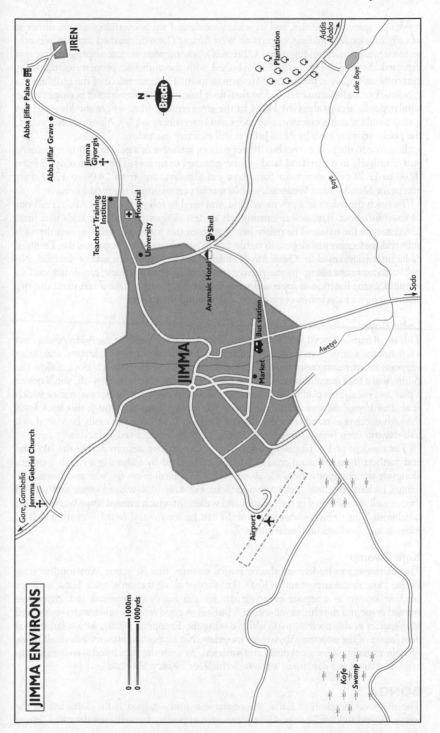

JIMMA ENVIRONS

JIREN

Abba Jiffar Palace

Abba Jiffar Grave

Jimma Giyorgis

Teachers' Training Institute

Hospital

University

Shell

Aramaic Hotel

Bus station

Market

JIMMA

Plantation

Addis Ababa

Lake Boye

Boye

Sodo

Awetu

Jemma Gebriel Church

Gore, Gambella

Airport

Kofe Swamp

N

Bradt

0   1000m
0   1000yds

residence, spans two storeys, and its wide veranda and shady overhangs are reminiscent of early missionary buildings in parts of West Africa. The whitewashed interior, recently restored with partial funding from UNESCO, is somewhat austere at present, but it is expected that it will eventually be furbished with the authentic property of the king, currently on display at the Jimma Museum in town. The centrepiece of the building is a ground-floor auditorium enclosed by first-floor balconies (the inspiration perhaps for the similar public area of the GM Hotel in the city centre?), from where the king and his guests would watch musicians, gladiators and entertainers at play. Alongside the palace, the public mosque built by Abba Jiffar is still in active use today.

Entrance to the palace costs birr 10 per person, inclusive of a guided tour in a language you're unlikely to understand (and will be expected to tip for). The palace is open from 09.00 to 12.30 daily except for Saturdays and Sundays, and from 14.00 to 17.30 daily except for Mondays and Wednesdays. No special permission is required to visit it.

To reach the palace in a private vehicle, you need to follow the Addis Ababa road out of town for about 3km, before turning left along a signposted road that leads past Jiren University to the palace. The palace lies 5km from this junction, climbing first through suburbia then cultivated slopes. Roughly 1.5km before reaching the palace, the Tomb of Abba Jiffar (signposted for *Qabrii Mootii Abbaa Jifaar*) lies on the left side of the road. No public transport heads up to the palace: travellers without a vehicle can either catch a minibus to the junction at Jiren and walk the last 5km, or else take a taxi from the city centre or hire a bicycle from one of the stalls around the market.

Lake Boye

This small marsh-fringed lake, situated no more than 200m south of the Addis Ababa road a few minute's drive from Jimma, is a reliable and accessible spot to see hippos, and it also supports an interesting selection of water and woodland birds. To reach Boye, follow the Addis Ababa road out of Jimma for about 8km. As you approach the turn-off, you'll notice a pine and eucalyptus plantation to your left, as well as two white signposts, one of which reads *Bon Voyage*. Almost immediately after the second signpost, a rough dirt track leads through eucalyptus trees to within 50m of the lake. Lake Boye can easily be visited as a half-day trip from Jimma using public transport, or by hiring a taxi or bicycle.

The resident pod of hippos seems to favour the shallow western part of the lake, the end furthest from the main road – this can be reached by following a rough footpath alongside the eucalyptus trees for about 500m. The birdlife on the lake and its marshy fringes includes the little grebe, white pelican, endemic blue-winged goose and wattled ibis, as well as a variety of herons, ducks and waders, of which painted snipe was our most notable sighting. Silvery-cheeked hornbills can be seen – and heard – in the patch of indigenous woodland on the far shore.

Kofe Swamp

Also of interest to birders are the perennial swamps that lie about 3km southwest of Jimma close to the airport and at Kofe 4km further along the same road. These swamps are best known as a regular breeding site for the highly endangered and impressive wattled crane and the elusive red-chested flufftail. A good range of other water-associated bird species is also present, particularly during the European winter, as is a substantial population of the endemic Abyssinian longclaw. No hippos are present, but small herds of Bohor reedbuck are sometimes encountered. As with the sites listed above, Kofe can easily be visited as a day trip in a private vehicle, or by bicycle or taxi.

BONGA

The medieval kingdom of Kaffa, whose name is immortalised as the derivative of the words 'coffee' and 'café' (see box *Ethiopian Coffee*, opposite), lay to the southwest of Jimma in what is now the Kaffa-Sheka zone of the Southern Nations, Nationalities and Peoples' Region. The people of Kaffa are part of the Ghibe ethno-linguistic group, and speak their own Kaficho language. A credible oral tradition states that Kaffa was founded in the late 14th century by the Minjo dynasty, and was originally ruled from a town called Shada, of which little is known except for its name. In the early 16th-century reign of King Bonkatato, the royal capital shifted to the extant town of Bonga, which retained its importance into the 1880s, when Paul Soleillet, the first European visitor to Kaffa, regarded it to be the largest settlement in the region, and reported that a palace was still maintained there.

Kaffa, though it lay outside the Christian empire of the highlands, appears to have fallen under its sporadic influence. Oral traditions indicating that Emperor Sarsa Dengal's 16th-century expedition to western Ethiopia resulted in the limited introduction of Christianity to Kaffa are backed up by the presence of a monastery dating to around 1550 only 12km from Bonga town. Kaffa was too remote to be affected by the *jihad* of Ahmed Gragn, and it withstood the subsequent Oromo incursion into the western highlands by digging deep protective trenches around the major settlements. Kaffa remained an autonomous state from its inception until Emperor Menelik II conquered it in the late 19th century, and imprisoned its last king at Ankober.

Although Bonga remains the administrative centre of Kaffa-Sheka zone, there is little about Bonga today that hints at any great antiquity or former significance. Situated some 3km south of the Mizan Tefari road, it's an attractive enough town, sprawling along a high ridge that offers some stirring views over the surrounding forested slopes, and

ETHIOPIAN COFFEE

Kaffa is generally regarded to be the region from where the Arabica strain of coffee originated, and it is also where this plant was first cultivated. A popular legend, said variously to date to between the 3rd and 10th centuries, claims that a young herdsman called Kaldi first observed the stimulating properties of wild coffee. When his goats became hyperactive after eating the leaves and berries, Kaldi swallowed some of the berries himself, found that he too became abnormally excited, and ran to a nearby monastery to share his discovery.

Initially, the monks didn't share the young goatherd's enthusiasm, but instead chastised him for bringing evil stimulants to their monastery and threw the offending berries into a fire. But then, seduced by the aromatic smell of the roasting berries, the monks decided to give them a go and found that they were unusually alert during their nocturnal prayers. Soon, it became accepted practice throughout Christian Ethiopia to chew coffee beans before lengthy prayer sessions, a custom that still persists in some parts of the country today. Later, it was discovered that the roasted berry could be ground to powder to produce a tasty and energising hot drink – one that still goes by a name derived from the Kaffa region in most places where it is drunk.

The drink of coffee probably remained an Ethiopian secret until the 16th century, when it was traded along the Indian Ocean spice route and cultivated in Yemen and other hilly parts of Arabia. The bean first arrived in Europe via Turkey in the 17th century, and it rapidly took off – more than 200 coffee shops reputedly traded in Venice alone by the early 18th century. Today, coffee exports typically account for up to 70% of Ethiopia's annual foreign revenue. Of Ethiopia's annual coffee crop of four million bags, 90% or more is grown on subsistence farms and smallholdings, and about 40% remains within this coffee-mad country.

studded with a few buildings that must date to before the Italian occupation. Surprisingly, perhaps, the town does boast a small local history museum, but this was closed when I last visited (on a Sunday) and nobody I spoke to seemed at all clear about what if any displays may or may not lurk within its prefabricated walls.

A more convincing reason to visit Bonga perhaps is the opportunity to explore the Bonga Forest Reserve, which sprawls over some 500km^2 of the surrounding hillsides. These are among the last remaining subtropical moist forests of any significant size to be found in Ethiopia, and are renowned for their abundance of sustainable non-timber forest products – coffee, forest cardamom, forest pepper and honey. Relatively unexplored by outsiders, and managed by community-based committees, these closed-canopy forests also host large numbers of monkey, a rich and largely undocumented avifauna, and numerous interesting natural features including hot springs and waterfalls. At the time of writing, the local Forest Management Groups will informally host self-sufficient campers at their own risk, and act as guides for a negotiable fee. It is hoped in the near future that the communities will be providing formal camping services, guided walks, horseback excursions and other activities. For further information contact the Participatory Forest Management Programme (✆ 011 1550511/1550154; email cfwcp@ethionet.et).

There's plenty of public transport connecting Jimma to Bonga, and a fair selection of accommodation to choose from once you are there. The centrally situated National Hotel (✆ 047 3310051) situated 50m uphill from the Telecom tower looks the best bet in the town centre, or you could try the slightly smarter Yemanu Egsabir Hotel, which lies alongside the 3km feeder road to the town centre from the main road between Jimma and Mizan Tefari.

MIZAN TEFARI AND SOUTHWEST OMO

Whether you drive there from Jimma in the east or Matu in the north, the road to the muddy, misty highland town of Mizan Tefari traverses some of the most lush of Ethiopian landscapes, climbing hill after verdant hill swathed in indigenous montane forest. Unlike the surrounding scenery, however, the town itself doesn't impress greatly. True enough, it's a friendly little place, set below an attractive backdrop of forested hills, but it is primarily of interest to travellers as a springboard for visits to the nearby Bebeka and Tepi coffee plantations, or the descent to the small Surma village of Kibish on the southwestern frontier of Southwest Omo.

Getting there and away

Most visitors to Mizan Tefari approach from the northeast, along a relatively rough 250km gravel road passing through Shebe, Bonga and Wushwush. This drive takes around six hours in a private vehicle, not allowing for stops, and the best part of a full day by bus. A worthwhile stop a few kilometres east of Wushwush, at least for aficionados of *tej*, is at Arat Silsa (literally 460, after a prominent signpost showing the distance from Addis Ababa in kilometres), where an isolated roadside shop sells a high-quality brew for a bargain birr 3 per litre.

Mizan Tefari can also be approached in a southerly direction from Matu. This drive takes at least six hours in a private vehicle and a full day using public transport, most probably swapping vehicles at Gore (25km south of Matu at the junction with the Gambella road, try the Tewodros Hotel should you get stuck there overnight) and at Tepi (50km before Mizan Tefari).

Where to stay and eat

Aden Hotel ✆ 047 3350542. Situated in a green compound on the southeastern outskirts of town, this small but comfortable hotel is unquestionably the best in town, but sometimes full on account of its justifiable popularity with tour groups bound for Kibish. Compact but clean rooms with dbl bed and en-suite hot shower cost birr 40, while rooms using the common shower cost birr 15.

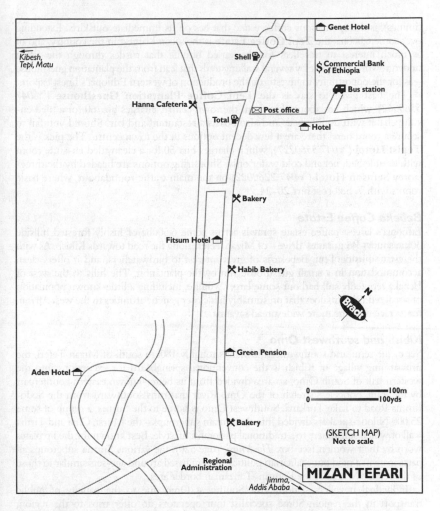

The restaurant is about the best in town, and a bar is attached, but it is advisable to check out food and drink prices before you order – the billing system seems to be rather elastic!

Fitsum Hotel More central and less likely to be full than the Aden, this otherwise significantly inferior hotel charges birr 40 for a cramped en-suite dbl without running hot water, or birr 20 for a room using the common shower. The food is pretty good and very inexpensive, but the ground floor bar generates a lot of noise and the staff routinely try to overcharge tourists for beers and food.

Green Pension ⟩ 047 3350538. This adequate hotel charges birr 40 for a first-floor room with a dbl bed or birr 30 for a similar ground-floor room. It is cleaner and quieter than the Fitsum, but poor value by comparison to the Aden given that the rooms are not en suite.

Hanan Cafeteria Decent eateries are in short supply in Mizan Tefari, but this small café serving pastries, snacks, coffee and juice is well worth a try.

Around Mizan Tefari
Tepi

The main attraction of this small town 50km northwest of Mizan Tefari, and the only reason you'd be likely to overnight there (unless you misjudged your public transport timings), is the eponymous coffee estate that lies on its immediate outskirts. Extending over some 6,000ha, the **Tepi Coffee Estate** is the second largest in the country, and of as much interest to travellers for the varied birdlife that rustles through the forest undergrowth – accessible by several walking trails that lead from the plantation guesthouse – as for the opportunity to investigate the production of western Ethiopia's finest export.

The best place to stay is the **Tepi Coffee Plantation Guesthouse** (↘ *047 5560062*), which lies about 1km from the town centre, charges birr 60 for a tiled en-suite chalet with double bed, and also boasts a restaurant and bar. Should you fail to secure a room here, there are a few decent options in the town centre. The pick is the **Tegist Hotel** (↘ *047 5560227*), which charges birr 50 for a clean tiled en-suite room with double bed, net and cold water only. Shoestring options are headed by the three-storey **Samson Hotel** (↘ *047 2260022*) on the main traffic roundabout, where basic rooms with ¾ bed cost birr 20–24.

Bebeka Coffee Estate

Ethiopia's largest coffee estate sprawls across some 6,500ha of lushly forested hillside 30km south – 45 minutes' drive – of Mizan Teferi along the road towards Kibish. As with the estate outside Tepi, Bebeka is of great interest to birdwatchers, and it offers clean accommodation in a small guesthouse run by the plantation. The hills to the west of Bebeka reputedly still harbour some larger wildlife, including a little-known population of small reddish buffaloes that presumably has closer genetic affinities to the west African forest race than the more widespread savanna.

Kibish and southwest Omo

Set in the semi-arid southwestern lowlands roughly 180km south of Mizan Teferi, the unassuming village of Kibish is the conventional springboard for excursions into the western half of South Omo, an area divided from its better-known eastern counterpart by the long, bridgeless stretch of the Omo River that runs southward from the Sodo-Jimma Road to Lake Turkana. Southwest Omo is home to the Surma, a group of some 25,000 Nilotic-speakers divided into three main subgroups – the Mursi, Chai and Tirma – all of which still adhere to a traditional pastoralist lifestyle. Best known for the lip plates worn by their women (see box *The Mursi*, page 520), the various Surma subgroups all participate in a rigid but egalitarian political system based around age-sets similar to those of the related Maasai of the Kenyan–Tanzanian border area.

Individual travellers seldom visit Southwest Omo due to the paucity of public transport in the region. Some specialist tour operators do offer trips to the region, however, catering to hardy walkers who want to explore a part of South Omo as yet largely unaffected by tourism. A popular option is to spend five or six days hiking from Kibish to the Omo River, overnighting at various traditional villages on the way, then crossing by boat and having a support vehicle to meet you on the other side.

Kibish may be a good starting point for treks, but the village itself highlights the ugly side of cultural tourism, with its Surma residents affecting all manner of quirks associated with the region's other tribes to come across as a sort of South Omo one-stop shop. When I visited, the absence of any market or other focal point other than myself meant that I was trailed around by a mob of several dozen adults and children pleading for razors, sweets, pens and medical care and trying to sell everything from lip plates to spears – all uncomfortably inauthentic and voyeuristic, even if it is difficult to say whether it was myself or the villagers who were guilty of voyeurism!

There is no public transport to Kibish and the drive from Mizan Tefari takes a good five to six hours in a private 4x4. The first semi-urban punctuation comes 30km south of Mizan Tefari in the form of Bebeka and its fantastically verdant coffee plantation. From here the road descends into more open savanna, studded with tall acacias and bands of riparian woodland that support a rich birdlife. After 70km of this rough road and thinly inhabited countryside the road emerges at Dima, a small market town set on the north bank of the Akabu River. Its town centre gutted by fire in early 2005, Dima normally offers the choice of a few hotels, but the only one currently operational is the Mahari Hotel, which offers basic rooms, local meals and cold drinks to passing travellers.

After crossing the Akabu, the road runs southeast for another 67km to Tulgit, a small traditional village centred on an American missionary outpost. On the way, you should see the occasional Surma cattle-herder wandering stark naked through the empty countryside, generally armed with a spear or gun as protection. It's another 15km to Kibish, a giddy descent that will probably take at least 45 minutes – hopefully you'll have better luck than I did trying to convince the driver to drop down to first gear rather than sticking in second and relying solely on an overheating brake to control his speed!

The first thing you need to do upon arriving in Kibish is pop into the police station to part with as much money as the officers on duty can extract from you. Simply to visit the marketplace 100m down the road you may be asked to hand over birr 50 per person for the village entrance fee, birr 50 for a police escort, and birr 35 apiece for two local 'militia'. Raise one eyebrow and they may drop the requirement to one policeman and one militia, raise two and the police escort may be waived, after which you'll probably find you've no eyebrows left to raise and need to fork out birr 85 for the excursion. An additional fee is charged to camp in the police station – no other accommodation options exist.

NEKEMTE

Formerly known as Lekemti, Nekemte, which lies about 200km west of Ambo by road, was until 1994 the capital of Wolega Region, and today it serves as the administrative centre for the East Wolega zone of Oromia region. The lushly forested area around Nekemte is one of the most agriculturally productive in Ethiopia, and it boasts considerable mineral wealth in the form of gold, platinum, copper, iron and lead. Nekemte itself is a leafy, pretty and (during the rainy season) very muddy small town, centred on a pair of traffic roundabouts set some 200m apart. Its likeable tropical ambience is undermined by an unusually poor selection of hotels and the inordinate degree of pointing, yelling and giggling directed at any passing *faranji* – nothing hostile, but rather exhausting!

High on the list of Nekemte's redeeming features is the excellent **Wolega Museum**, which was established in 1989 on the northern traffic roundabout, and is definitely one of the best ethnographic museums in the country. Displays include a vast collection of Oromo artefacts such as leatherware, basketwork, woodcarvings and musical instruments, as well as the first Bible translated into the local Oromo dialect. The guide speaks little English but his imaginatively mimed demonstrations of how the various artefacts are made or used are almost as entertaining as the exhibits themselves.

South of Nekemte, the recently delineated **Dedessa Wildlife Reserve** protects a 1,300km^2 tract of mid altitude deciduous woodland bisected by the Dedessa River as it runs eastward from the main road towards Bedele. A watershed from which flows 15 streams and rivers, this area of relatively pristine bush is known to support 30 mammal species, including lion, elephant, buffalo, hippo, bushbuck and guereza monkey, as well as a rich variety of birds. Access is currently restricted to the main Bedele road, which crosses the Dedessa River some 65km south of Nekemte – look out for hippos in the river and baboons and birds in the riparian woodland – but there is serious talk of cutting a game viewing road through the reserve in late 2005, so it might be worth asking around about new developments in Nekemte.

Getting there and away

The roughly 30km drive from Addis Ababa to Nekemte via Ambo takes around five to six hours in a private vehicle, not allowing for stops. The scenery between Ambo and

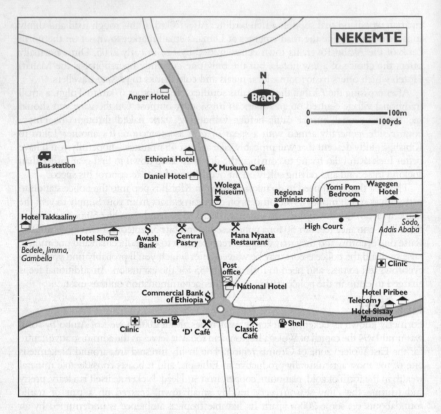

Nekemte is wonderful. Past Guder, the road climbs into a highland area with panoramic views across the surrounding valleys and mountains. The whole area is well-watered: the road crosses several fast-flowing streams and, after Bako, the cultivation and moorland give way to thick woodland and patches of forest. Vervet monkeys and a variety of widow birds can be seen from the road.

There are direct buses between Addis Ababa and Nekemte. If you are leaving from Ambo, you may be better off catching a bus from Ambo to Bako, where you can pick up another bus to Nekemte. With a reasonably early start – 09.00 at the latest – you should make it through to Nekemte in a day, but transport out of Bako peters out at around 13.00. There are several hotels in Bako if you do get stuck.

A little-used but reasonably good 250km dirt road also connects Nekemte to Bure on the surfaced road between Addis Ababa and Bahir Dar. Using private transport, it is perfectly possibly to travel between Nekemte and Bahir Dar in one (long) day using this road, but travellers dependent on public transport will probably need to break up the trip at Kosober, which straddles the road between Bure and Bahir Dar.

For details of travelling on to Gambella via Dembidolo, see the *Getting there and away* section under that town. If you are doing your own navigating, note that there are two towns called Arjo in this area – one is on the road to Gimbi and the other on the road to Bedele.

Where to stay and eat

Anger Hotel ✆ 057 6613767. Emphatically the best bet in a town that boasts few if any truly attractive accommodation options is this clean little private hotel situated a couple of hundred metres north of the northern traffic roundabout. It's fair value at birr 25 for a dbl with en-suite showers or birr 15 for a room using common showers. The food is pretty good too.

Ethiopia Hotel ↘ 057 6611088. This chronically rundown former government hotel is a serious contender for this edition's 'All Ethiopia Silly *Faranji* Price' award at birr 60/80 for a gloomy sgl/dbl with en-suite rising damp and cold trickle – a deal that looks particularly unattractive coming straight from Ambo. In its favour, the restaurant serves good, inexpensive meals.

Wegegan Hotel (43 rooms) ↘ 057 6615001. The rooms at Nekemte's other former government hotel are a little brighter than those at the Ethiopia, but the combination of dodgy electrics, leaky taps, knackered toilets and erratic cold-water supply adds up to pretty poor value at the *faranji* price of birr 48 for a ground-floor en-suite twin or birr 60 for a similar room on the first floor. The food is pretty good and reasonably priced.

Daniel Hotel ↘ 057 6615165. Despite the noisy location and slightly disreputable ground-floor bar, this feels like better value than either government hotel should the Anger be full, though it is still a touch overpriced at birr 30/40 for a scruffy en-suite sgl/dbl with occasional hot water.

Classic Café Situated to the east of the southern traffic roundabout, this unexpected gem serves a good selection of snacks, pastries, juices and meals – an excellent spot for breakfast. Also worth a look-in is the **Central Pastry** to the west of the northern roundabout.

BEDELE

This small nondescript town is something of a route focus, lying at the junction of the roads to Matu, Jimma and Nekemte. Bedele's main claim to fame is that it is the home of Ethiopia's newest and best beer factory, which lies about 2km out of town. Tourists are welcome to look around, provided they have a passport to hand. Also worth a look might be the forested hill a kilometre or so past the market. According to a local kid, this hill is crawling with lions and tigers; the odd yeti too, no doubt, had I asked. Guereza monkeys and forest birds seem more likely.

In my experience, the most memorable aspect of Bedele is the thoroughly unpleasant children, who yell non-stop wherever you go, and are not averse to the odd bit of stone-throwing. Only very mildly in their favour, the youth of Bedele are at least original, with the standard cries of 'you' and 'money' being enlivened by the odd 'ahoy' (a greeting acquired from the Czechs who built the Bedele beer factory) and, just a teeny bit offensively, 'Ali Baba', which means thief (perhaps the Czechs bounced?).

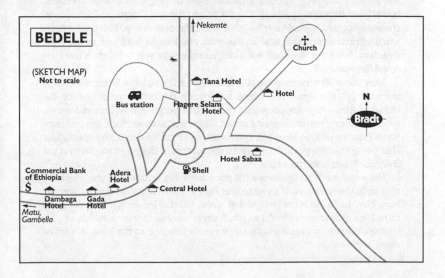

The road west from Bedele towards Matu is among the most densely forested in western Ethiopia, crossing several large rivers and bypassing some attractive waterfalls. Guereza monkeys are abundant, vervet monkeys and olive baboons are reasonably common, and birdwatching should be excellent. A good base would be the village of Yayu, about 40km from Matu along the Bedele road, which boasts a couple of very basic hotels serving reasonable food. The area immediately around Yayu is quite cultivated, but there are some lovely forested hills about 2km along the main road to Bedele.

Getting there and away
Bedele is situated at a crossroads roughly 105km south of Nekemte, 115km east of Matu and 135km north of Jimma. In all cases, expect the drive there to take around two hours in a private vehicle and three to four hours by bus. There are direct buses between Jimma and Nekemte and between Jimma and Matu, so on either of these routes you will pass straight through Bedele. There is, however, no direct transport between Matu and Nekemte, so on this route you will have to take a Jimma-bound bus as far as Bedele, then try to find a bus coming *from* Jimma to take you where you want to go. This shouldn't normally be a problem, but you may have to overnight in Bedele. If you do stay over in Bedele, you can skip the 06.00 start for once and enjoy a bit of a lie-in and breakfast. Buses pass through Bedele between 10.00 and midday.

Where to stay and eat
Hotel Hagare Selam ✆ 057 4450123/59. Formerly the Menasha Hotel, the Hagare Selam is far and away the best lodging in Bedele, and has been for at least a decade. Clean rooms with private

---

SOR WATERFALL
The main attraction in the vicinity of Matu is the Sor Waterfall, which can be reached by following the Gore road west out of town for 7km, then turning left at the sign for the Gore Water Treatment Plant to follow a rough and muddy track that passes the water treatment plant after 7.5km and arrives at the village of Becho after another 5.5km. From Becho, you can drive or walk along an even rougher track for about 4km, before heading on to an indistinct and slippery footpath through a patch of dense jungle alive with creepers, butterflies, baboons, guereza monkeys and birds – most visibly silvery-cheeked hornbill, Heuglin's robin-chat and Ethiopian oriole. More than likely you'll attract an entourage of enthusiastic children to lead you in the right direction, but if not, anybody will point you the right way – *fafuati* is the local word for waterfall!

After about 30 minutes of slipping and tripping through the forest, you'll hear the waterfall, the signal for a steep ten-minute descent – watch out for the vicious nettles – to a viewpoint near the top of a gorge. It is an impressive sight even in the dry season, plunging about 20m over a sheer rock amphitheatre surrounded by tall tree ferns and mist forest, and must be thoroughly spectacular after heavy rain. It is possible to walk to the bottom of the gorge and swim in the chilly pool at its waterfall's base.

The excursion is straightforward if you have a 4x4 vehicle, and you should be able to do the round trip in three to four hours. There is limited public transport from Matu to Becho in the form of 4x4 'taxis', but it all leaves in the morning and turns back almost immediately, so you'll either have to charter a vehicle or plan on staying in one of the very basic birr 6 rooms attached to the *buna bet* (coffee shop) in Bechu.

hot showers and bowl toilets cost birr 30, while rooms using common showers fall in the birr 12–20 range. The restaurant is also probably the best in town, serving a good selection of local meat and vegetarian dishes. If the rooms here are full, several generic shoestring dives are dotted around town, but none merit individual mention.

MATU

This attractive highland town, the former capital of the defunct Illubador Province, is of interest to travellers primarily as the springboard for the descent into the steamy tropical lowlands that flank the Baro River and the port of Gambella. Despite its well-wooded hilly surrounds, it is an unremarkable sort of place: a typically sprawling highland town, founded in 1913 at an altitude of 1,600m near the western escarpment of the Ethiopian Highlands, and today dotted with a few smart but rather unconvincing administrative buildings. The central market is lively and welcoming, or you could stretch your legs by taking a short walk to the forest-fringed Sor River, which crosses the Bedele Road some 2km northeast of the town centre (a good spot for guereza monkeys). Further afield, an excellent goal for a day trip is the impressive Sor Waterfall (see box *Sor Waterfall* opposite).

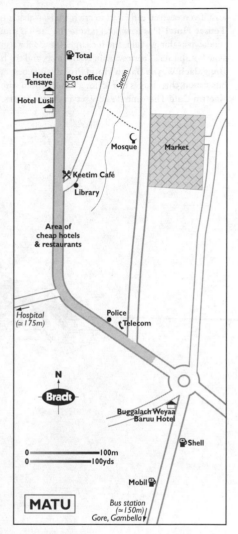

Getting there and away

Coming from Jimma or Nekemte, Matu lies about 115km from Bedele along a (mostly) surfaced road. The drive between Bedele to Matu takes about two to three hours in a private vehicle or four to five hours by bus. Direct buses run between Jimma and Matu but coming from Nekemte you will probably have to change buses (and possibly spend the night) at Bedele. Coming from Mizan Tefari, a reasonably maintained 220km dirt road runs northward to Matu via Tepi and Gore, a journey that should take the up to six hours in a private vehicle and the best part of a full day by bus. Heading west from Matu, a daily bus service to Gambella leaves in either direction at around 06.00; the 170km journey takes around seven hours.

Where to stay and eat

Lusii Hotel Situated on the left side of the main road as you enter town from the Bedele side, this long-serving establishment is not as clean as it used to be, but it remains fair value at birr 15 for a large room with a ¾ bed using the common shower, or birr 30 for a similar room with en-suite hot shower. It has a good restaurant and a busy bar with a veranda. The only drawback, at least if you need an early start to catch a bus, is that it is a ten-minute walk from the bus station.

Tensae Hotel This new hotel next to the Lusii is similar in standard, perhaps a little less rundown as things stand, and it charges birr 33 for a small but clean room with a ¾ bed and en-suite hot shower. The restaurant is adequate, and the bar can be quite lively.

Buggalach Weyaa Baruu Hotel Probably the best of a clutch of basic hotels dotted around the bus station, this charges birr 15 for a scruffy room with ¾ bed and common shower.

Keetim Café This central eatery serves decent snacks, pastries and coffee.

Gambella

The small westerly state of Gambella, boasting a population of below 250,000, is something of an anomaly within Ethiopia, displaying stronger historical, ethnic and climatic links to neighbouring Sudan than to the highlands to its east. Hot, humid, low-lying and swampy, Gambella is dominated geographically by the sluggish Baro River and its various tributaries, all of which eventually flow across the border into the Blue Nile – navigable from the port of Gambella on the northern bank of the Baro all the way to its confluence with the White Nile at Khartoum.

The only real tourist attraction in the region is the remote Gambella National Park, which hosts several rare antelope and bird species, but requires considerable effort – as well as a reliable 4x4 and experienced driver – to visit. Unless you are planning to explore the national park, when the dry season has obvious advantages, the best time to visit Gambella is during the rainy season of May to October, when the scenery is lush and green, and temperatures seldom hit the peaks of 40°C or more that are regally recorded during February and March.

Two main ethnic groups live in Gambella. The Anuwak, who speak a language closely related to that of the Luo in Kenya, are fishermen and mixed agriculturists by tradition. They are strikingly tall people, and very dark-skinned for Ethiopians. Their elegantly enclosed homesteads give the region much of its character, and the name Gambella derives from the Anuwak name for the *Gardenia lutea* tree that grows widely in the surrounding area. The smaller but even more dark-skinned Nuer originated in Nilotic-speaking parts of Sudan and, although they are relatively recent arrivals in this area, they are now the numerically dominant group in Gambella.

There is a long history of tension between Anuwak and Nuer, fuelled in part by SPLA incursions from Sudan, and parts of the region have been unsafe for travel since the end of 2003, when an attack on a UN truck sparked a series of riots that left more than 150 people dead, destroyed hundreds of homes, and caused several thousand villagers to flee across the border into Sudan. This tension spilt over into Gambella town itself in early 2004, when local militants led a series of fatal attacks on highlanders resident in the town, causing Ethiopian Airlines to suspend all flights to Gambella for several months. Things seemed fairly harmonious when we revisited the area in early 2005, but it would certainly be advisable to seek current advice before heading this way.

GAMBELLA

Gambella is an oddity among Ethiopian towns, and a most appealing one. Lying at an altitude of 450m in the swampy, mosquito-ridden lowlands west of the Ethiopian plateau, the port exudes an atmosphere of tropical languor, dictated as much by its lush riverine vegetation and almost unbearable humidity as by its remoteness from just about everywhere else. This powerful sense of place is underscored by the presence of the Baro River, whose brown waters roll lazily past town to create an almost absurdly accurate

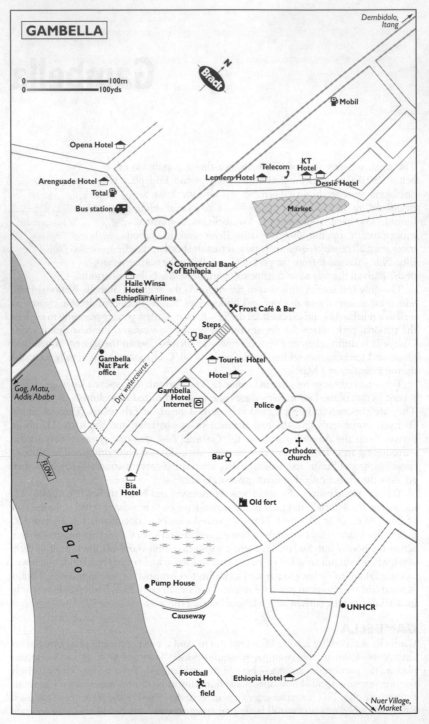

GAMBELLA

0 ——————— 100m
0 ——————— 100yds

Dembidolo, Itang

Mobil

Opena Hotel

Telecom KT Hotel

Arenguade Hotel Lemlem Hotel Dessie Hotel

Total

Bus station

Market

Commercial Bank of Ethiopia

Haile Winsa Hotel

Ethiopian Airlines

Frost Café & Bar

Steps

Bar

Gambella Nat Park office

Tourist Hotel

Hotel

Gog, Matu, Addis Ababa

Dry watercourse

Gambella Hotel Internet

Police

Bar

Orthodox church

FLOW

B a r o

Bia Hotel

Old fort

Pump House

Causeway

UNHCR

Football field

Ethiopia Hotel

Nuer Village, Market

fulfilment of every Western archetype of a tropical river port – particularly during the rainy season, nowhere else in Ethiopia is quite so overwhelmingly Conradian, so cinematically African!

Part of Gambella's charm lies in its spacious, amorphous layout. Years ago, when I first entered the town via the large, impressive concrete bridge over the Baro, I expected something equally grand. Instead, I found myself deposited at the nominal bus station (a bare patch of ground in front of a Total garage) with a large roundabout to my right and no obvious evidence of a town anywhere in sight. After a slightly panicky walkabout, I established that what passes for the town centre lies hidden in a well-wooded dip between the main road and the river. Gambella, as it transpired, isn't really a town, but two wide avenues spasmodically lined with government buildings, and a scattering of small village-like hut clusters kept discrete by patches of forest, swamp and streams.

Whatever the climate between locals, as far as *faranji* need be concerned Gambella couldn't be a friendlier town. I found it rather sad that, en route to Gambella, I was repeatedly warned by highlanders of the backwardness of the people ('it is not good place for you'). In my opinion, the Nuer and Anuwak could teach many highlanders a thing or two about civility to foreigners. Wherever I went I was greeted in Anuwak or Nuer (*mali* and *derichot* are the respective greetings); several times English-speakers came up to exchange greetings and shake hands with no hint of a motive other than friendliness, and the children were bashfully playful rather than loud and demanding. On the few occasions I was yelled at in Gambella, I invariably turned around to see the distinctive features of a highlander. Don't be put off by advance notices – Gambella is a lovely place and the people are utterly charming.

Among its other singularities, Gambella has a rather curious modern history. In the late 19th century Sudan fell under British rule, and the Baro, which is navigable as far as Khartoum, was seen by both Britain and Ethiopia as an excellent highway for exporting coffee and other produce from the fertile western highlands to Sudan and Egypt. The Ethiopian emperor granted Britain use of part of Ethiopia as a free port in 1902 and, after an unsuccessful attempt to establish a port elsewhere, Gambella was established in 1907. This tiny British territory, a few hundred hectares in size, was bounded by the Baro River to the south, the tributary which now bisects the town to the west, the patch of forest to the east of the modern town, and the small conical hill to its north. Gambella became a prosperous trade centre as ships from Khartoum sailed in regularly during the rainy season when the water was high, taking seven days downriver and 11 days upriver. The Italians captured Gambella in 1936, when the now-ruined fort near the Gambella Hotel was built, but it was returned to Britain after a bloody battle in 1941. Gambella then became part of Sudan in 1951, but it was re-incorporated into Ethiopia five years later. The port ceased functioning under the Mengistu regime and it remains closed because of ongoing tension between the SPLA and the Ethiopian government.

Gambella offers little in the way of organised sightseeing, and its remoteness hardly makes it a prime target for mass tourism. The area is, however, rich in wildlife, and the layout of the town is such that just strolling around you can see plenty of birds and monkeys. It is worth devoting some time to the bridge over the Baro, which only one vehicle is permitted to cross at a time. Photographing the bridge, or from the bridge, may or may not be forbidden, dependent most probably on the attitude of the guard on duty, so do ask permission before you pull out a camera. To the west of the bridge is a shady avenue that follows the river's course – one of Gambella's few apparent British relics, along with a group of old grave stones near the port.

Local people wash and swim here without apparent concern, but every now and again somebody is taken by a crocodile, so it would definitely be chancy to leap into the water in areas not used by locals. The people of Gambella will still caution travellers with the sad story of Bill Olsen, the Peace Corps Volunteer who took a holiday in Gambella in 1966, ignored local advice about a large crocodile known to live in a certain part of the river, and was never seen alive again. On the whole, better to stick to your hotel shower than to tempt a similar fate by leaping into the muddy Baro!

Gambella's main attraction is its singular and absorbing sense of place, and wonderfully evocative atmosphere. Specific points of interest are the ruined Italian fort close to the river, the swamp between the river and the fort, the isolated hill about 1km north of the town centre, and the village of traditional homesteads running down towards the river from the small market about 100m east of the Ethiopia Hotel. In the market, you can buy the woven baskets and bubble pipes that are characteristic of the area, while birders might want to head down to the river's edge immediately downriver of the bridge in search of the rare Egyptian plover, a regular visitor.

There no longer seems to be a tourist office worth talking about in Gambella, but the people at the national park office (*near Ethiopian Airlines;* ✆ *047 5510912*) seem to be very knowledgeable and helpful when it comes to information about exploring outlying parts of Gambella State.

Getting there and away

Ethiopian Airlines flies from Addis Ababa to Gambella three times per week. The airport lies about 15km out of town, and there are no taxis, so you will need to hitch a ride in with a fellow passenger or ask the people at the Ethiopian Airlines town office to help you out.

If you are looping through the west, the most obvious route between Nekemte and Gambella (though emphatically neither the best nor the shortest) runs through Gimbi and Dembidolo (see *Dembidolo*, page 556). If this route is impossible, which is generally the case during the rains, or you are coming from Jimma, then the only alternative is the far better road through Bedele, Matu and Bure. The drive from Matu to Gambella should take about five hours, so it will take a full day to reach Gambella from either Nekemte or Jimma in a private vehicle. Using public transport, you will have to catch the 06.00 bus from Nekemte or Jimma to Bedele, which takes three to four hours. At Bedele, you should be able to find transport on to Matu the same day. You will, however, have to overnight in Matu before heading on to Gambella. Matu and Bedele, and transport to these towns, is described later in the chapter, as part of the return leg to Addis.

The small highland village of Bure, on the road between Matu and Gambella, is a popular lunch stop for bus drivers, There isn't much to see at Bure today, but Alexander Bulatovich, who passed through the village in 1897, mentioned that it lay at the junction of several trade routes and formed 'an important point of barter with tribes on this side of the Baro … and market for coffee'. Bulatovich described how people from the lowlands 'bring for sale elephant tusks and sometimes their livestock, and in exchange for that they buy ornaments, beads and cloth'. From Bure, you descend almost one kilometre in altitude to the Baro Valley, a spectacular switchback drive through tall elephant grass, passing several troops of olive baboon along the way.

The road follows the course of the Baro River for a while before crossing one of its tributaries on a rather rickety wooden bridge, then about 30km before Gambella, there's a police roadblock, near to the substantial Sudanese refugee village of Bonga, which now grows enough maize to be self-sufficient. Approaching Gambella, the road passes through a thinly populated and primal savanna of acacias and tall clumped grass interspersed with bald granite hills – the atmosphere is such that I found myself half expecting to see an elephant cross the road at any minute, even though I know there is no longer much wildlife in the area.

Where to stay and eat
Moderate
Ethiopia Hotel (20 rooms) ℡ 047 5512042/4. Set in potentially very attractive but poorly maintained grounds overlooking the northern bank of the Baro River about 1km east of the town centre, this government hotel is the only thing to distantly approach tourist class accommodation in Gambella, and as such it is where all but the most cash-strapped or masochistic of travellers will end up. That said, the timeworn dbl/twin rooms with (sporadically working) fans and en-suite shower are lousy value at birr 150. On the plus side, the hotel has a steamily decrepit charm in keeping with the overall mood of Gambella, there is DSTV in the bar, plenty of monkeys and birds roam the gardens, the food is pretty good, and the staff do an impressive job of keeping ready a supply of cold beers and sodas in the face of regular power cuts and intense natural heat.

Bia Hotel (10 rooms) ℡ 047 5511611. This new hotel overlooking the river 100m upriver of the bridge has a perfect location and attractive green grounds, but the en-suite rooms with ¾ bed are rather rundown, cramped and depressing, with bucket showers only. Still as the only non-government hotel with fans, it has to be classed as a tempting option at birr 26 sgl or dbl occupancy. The attached bar is a good place for a riverside drink, but (like most other hotels in Gambella) has some potential to disrupt attempts at an early night.

Budget
Tourist Hotel ℡ 047 5511584. The pick of a less than tempting batch of budget dives scattered around Gambella, this adequate hotel charges birr 15 for a moderately grubby room with ¾ bed and access to the common hot shower. The attached bar seems more sedate than most.

Arenguade Hotel Exploiting its proximity to the bus station, this overpriced dump charges birr 20 for a grotty room with a mosquito net and pervasive smell of urine thrown into the deal.

Opena Hotel Situated opposite the bus station, this once popular cheapie has dropped standards of late, and now seems to function primarily as a very noisy bar. If you have earplugs, the grubby little rooms are adequate value at birr 20 with en-suite shower and net.

Haile Wensa Hotel Regarded by many locals as serving the best food in Gambella, this hotel looks slightly less tempting as a place to stay – the rooms aren't bad value at birr 15 but they are centred on a very noisy bar.

GAMBELLA NATIONAL PARK AND SURROUNDS
This remote and swampy park was established primarily to protect its populations of two endangered wetland antelope whose range is restricted to this part of Ethiopia and adjacent regions in southern Sudan: the white-eared kob and Nile lechwe. The park has never been fully protected, and the wildlife today has to compete with cotton plantations and Sudanese refugee or resettlement camps. Nevertheless, the area does support significant – though rapidly shrinking – populations of elephant, buffalo and lion, as well as roan antelope, tiang, Lelwel hartebeest, olive baboon and guereza monkey.

Several interesting birds inhabit the Gambella National Park, notably Ethiopia's only population of the elusive and weird looking shoebill stork, a papyrus dweller that has been recorded in the area just once since the 1960s, more likely due to a paucity of observers than any serious decline in numbers. Other interesting and unusual species found in the park include the country's only population of the localised Uelle paradise whydah, the lovely red-throated and little green bee-eaters, as well as black-faced firefinch, red-necked buzzard, Egyptian plover, African skimmer and several localised but drab cistocolas and other warblers.

According to the helpful warden, who can be contacted at the national park office in town (℡ 047 5510912), the best part of the park for game viewing is called Matara and lies about 185km west of Gambella town along a road running through the village of Inwany on the southern bank of the Baro. White-eared kob and Nile lechwe are both likely to seen in the Matara area, but its distance from town and the poor condition of the road means that you would need a reliable 4x4 to get there, and should plan on camping for at least one night. You'd also need to bring all your own food and drink, and arrange a game scout and possibly an armed guard through the national park office.

Less challenging would be to head south to the small towns of Abobo and Agenga, which lie on the recently redrawn eastern boundary of the national park, 42km and 105km respectively from Gambella town. Although animals might be seen anywhere in this area (or, for that matter, nowhere), one worthwhile stop just a few kilometres from Abobo is at Lake Alwara. Abobo itself is a good place for traditional Anuwak contacts, has a few basic lodgings, and can be reached by public transport (currently only on Mondays and Fridays, where there is a convoy to tie in with the local market). Further south, Agenga can be reached in about three hours in a private 4x4, and has been ear-marked as the site of the new national park headquarters, but is currently of limited interest in terms of wildlife viewing possibilities. Also of interest is the very scenic Lake Tata, which lies off the road between Abobo and Gog. Occasional buses from Gambella to Gog via Abobo can drop you at the gravel junction to Lake Tata, from where it's less than an hour on foot to the shore. There is no accommodation, but an Anuwak village lies alongside the lake – with the permission of the local chief, you should be welcome to pitch a tent and to swim.

Another possibility would be to follow the good dirt road that runs parallel to the Baro River (and the northern boundary of Gambella National Park) from Gambella to the Sudanese border at Jikawa. This takes you through an area inhabited by Anuwak fishermen and Nuer pastoralists whose lifestyles are virtually untouched by Western influences. This is best seen at the sprawling village of Itang, which stands on the northern bank of the Baro some 7km south of the Jikawa Road along an unsignposted feeder road 50km from Gambella. At least one bus connects Gambella and Itang daily, taking about two hours in either direction, and a couple of shops around the busy traditional market serve tea and basic food. So far as I can ascertain there is no accommodation so you would need to ask around for a bed in a local dwelling or to arrange to camp at the police station. The area is rich in birds not easily seen elsewhere in Ethiopia, and there is some wildlife around (most visibly bushbuck, oribi and baboon). It is also potentially volatile, due to its location on the Sudanese border, so do make enquiries before heading off – especially if you intend to continue onward to the equally traditional border village of Jikawa.

DEMBIDOLO

Founded in the 19th century on the western edge of the Ethiopian highlands, Dembidolo peaked in importance in the early 20th century, when it formed an important stop along the trade route to Sudan via Gambella and the Baro River. Dembidolo served for some decades as the major commercial centre and administrative capital of Wolega province, but it has subsequently become something of a backwater, serviced by erratic public transport and often totally inaccessible during the rainy season. For those who wish to loop through the west without retracing their steps, however, Dembidolo does have the distinction of being the largest town along the 340km northern route between Nekemte and Gambella.

Getting there and away

Public transport through Dembidolo is of the hit-and-miss variety. There is, in theory, a daily bus between Nekemte and Dembidolo. This leaves in either direction at any time between 05.30 and 07.00, costs an unusually steep birr 60, and takes anything from ten to 15 hours, depending on the state of the – normally horrendous – road, and the number of breakdowns. If this bus isn't running, then you'll probably have to change vehicles at Gimbi, 113km from Nekemte and 100km from Dembidolo. In the opposite direction, a

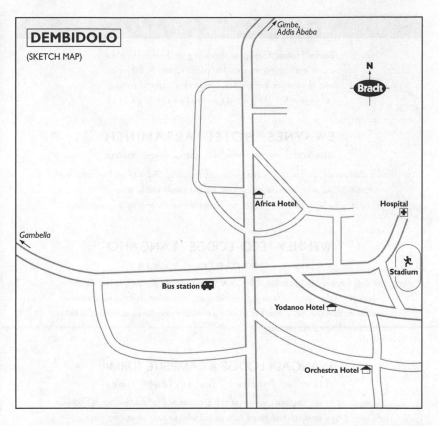

daily minibus sometimes runs between Dembidolo and Gambella, leaving Gambella at 06.00, reaching Dembidolo at midday or so, before turning around back to Gambella. And sometimes it doesn't – one reader spent three days stranded in Dembidolo (during the dry season) until he found a lift with a truck on to Gambella. He also points out that if the truck had broken down, he could have been in for a long wait ('bring plenty of Ambo' is his advice). After rain, no vehicles at all run along this road.

Where to stay

There are a few hotels in Dembidolo, of which the best is probably the **Birhan Hotel**, reached by walking from the bus station to the main roundabout, taking a right turn, and walking for less than five minutes – it's on the right side of the road. Clean rooms here cost birr 12, and the friendly bar has a satellite television. The **Orchestra**, **Africa** and **Yadanoo** hotels have been mentioned, though not exactly recommended, in recent readers' letters.

558

Appendix 1

ETHIOPIAN SWING

Practically unknown to the rest of the world, the music of Ethiopia, in common with so many other aspects of this insular highland country, sounds like nothing you've ever heard before. True enough, many outsiders find the trademark lurching three-four signature, twitchy cross-rhythms, brassy instrumentation, taut pentatonic melodies and nail-on-blackboard vocal affectations somewhat impenetrable on initial contact, I daresay even a little irritating. But, while repeated exposure won't make converts of us all, Ethiopia's diverse blend of the traditional and the contemporary, of exotic and indigenous styles must rank as one of Africa's greatest undiscovered musical legacies, reaching its apex with the ceaselessly inventive and hypnotically funky horn-splattered sides of 'Ethiopian swing' recorded for a handful of independent labels in Addis Ababa between 1969 and 1978.

The roots of the music scene that blossomed in Addis Ababa during the dying years of the imperial era are predictably peculiar. It all started in April 1924, when Ras Tefari, then acting as regent for the Empress Zawditu, made a state visit to Jerusalem and was received by a brass band consisting of Armenian orphans. Who knows whether it was the actual music that caught the future emperor's attention, or simply the plight of his fellow Orthodox Christians, who had fled their homeland to escape the genocide perpetrated by their Islamic Turkish neighbours in 1915? Either way, the Arba Lijotch (Forty Children), as they came to be known affectionately by their hosts, arrived in Addis Ababa in September of that year to form the first imperial brass band under the tutelage of the long-time Armenian-born Ethiopian-resident music professor Kevork Nalbandian.

The underpaid Arba Lijotch disbanded of its own accord in July 1928. But the foundation stone had been laid for the permanent Imperial Bodyguard Band formed in 1929 under the leadership of the Swiss orchestra leader Andre Nicod. Comprising a few dozen arbitrarily chosen slaves from Wolega, the original Imperial Bodyguard Band was by all accounts more notable for its noisiness than its aptitude, but its limited repertoire of stuffy marches nevertheless became something of a fixture at important imperial occasions, and some genuine talent soon started to emerge from the ranks prior to the Italian occupation of 1935. The occupation formed something of a low watermark for the fortunes of Ethiopian musicians, many of whom were imprisoned, in particular the traditional *azmari* minstrels whose subversive lyrics used the time-honoured *sem ena werk* (wax over gold) technique of using love songs as a vehicle for stinging political innuendo.

The reinstatement of Haile Selassie after six years in exile was soon followed by the creation of a new Imperial Bodyguard Band under Kevork Nalbandian, who handed over the reins to his equally influential nephew Nerses in 1949. From the mid 1940s to late 1950s, a succession of foreign music teachers such as Alexander Kontorowicz and Franz Zelwecker were hired to run academies whose graduates went on to play in an ever-growing number of brass-oriented orchestras, all of which – oddly enough – were effectively on the payroll of one or other imperial institution, be it the police, or the military, or even Addis Ababa municipality. Despite this, the musical vocabulary of these brass bands gradually expanded by exposure to exotic new styles such as jazz, rhythm-and-blues, and soul, which were broadcast around the country from the American military radio station in Asmara.

So the scene was set for the explosion of musical fecundity that peaked during the edgy, uncertain, exciting years that separated the failed coup of 1960 from its more consequential 1974 sequel. As was the case elsewhere in the world, the 1960s witnessed immense social changes in Addis

ETHIOPIQUES

Compiled by Ethiopian music expert Francis Falceto, the ever-expanding series of **Ethiopiques** CDs released by the French label Buda is of particular significance for making available a vast number of old vinyl recordings that had been out of print since the 1970s. Available in specialist CD shops, the full series can also be ordered online through the label's website www.budamusique.com or other online retailers such as www.amazon.com or www.amazon.co.uk. Better still, the full series can be downloaded cheaply and legally from www.emusic.com, a superb site that charges as little as US$0.22 per track if you take out a contract.

Highlights of the series – there aren't really any lowlights – include **Ethiopiques 1** and **3**, which anthologise some of the most popular tracks released by Amha between 1969 and 1975, providing an excellent overall introduction to the era's leading artists such as Mahmoud Ahmed, Girma Beyene, Muluqen Mellesse, Hirut Bekele, Alemayehu Eshete and Tlahoun Gessesse. Either set is a great starting point.

Better still in my opinion, not least for its greater focus on female artists such as the sublime Bizunesh Bekele (the uncrowned 'First Lady' of Swinging Addis) and her unrelated namesake Hirut Bekele, is **Ethiopiques 13: Ethiopian Groove**. As noted above, this is a re-release of an early 1990s' collection of Kaifa's 1976–78 output, also compiled by Francis Falceto, and its present format is marred only by the criminal absence of the trio of early Aster Aweke recordings that ranked as highlights of the original.

Ethiopiques 5 performs a similar round-up of some of the best Tigrigna recordings made by prominent Eritrean artists of the same era, such as Tewelde Redda, Tekli Tesfa-Ezghi, and the irresistibly nicknamed Tebereh 'Doris Day' Tesfa-Hunegn. Aside from the linguistic difference, much of this music has a more traditional, drum-based sound than its Amharigna equivalent, and the melodies, based on the same pentatonic scale, are often punctuated by yelps, chants and the wild ululation characteristic of African tribal music from the Cape to the Horn.

The 1970s' recordings of **Mahmoud Ahmed** feature exclusively on **Ethiopiques 6** and **7**. The latter disc, subtitled *Ere Mela Mela*, is an expanded version of the eponymous release by the Belgian label Crammed Disc in 1986 and include one full KLP as well as several 45s recorded in 1975. **Ere Mela Mela** is something of a legend as the first Western release by any Ethiopian artist, and it earned rave reviews in the likes of the *NME* and the *New York Times*. Other dedicated single-artist releases in the series include **Ethiopiques 9** (funky 'Abyssinian Elvis' **Alemayehu Eshete**) and **Ethiopiques 14** (the revered jazz-influenced saxophonist **Getachew Mekurya**).

For those with an ear for the more traditional forms, a highly recommended starting point is **Ethiopiques 2**, an anthology of *azmari* and *bolel* singers working the *tej* bets and bars of Addis Ababa. Very different but equally engaging is **Ethiopiques 18: The Lady With The Krar**, a collection of beautiful traditional *azmari* renditions on a lyre-like instrument called a *krar* by former actress Asnaqech Werku – as a bonus, English and French translations of the pithy lyrics are provided with the CD.

If you're looking to cherry pick a few *Ethiopiques* tracks to **download** from www.emusic.com, here's my selection: 'Ete Endenesh Gedawo' by Muluqen Mellesse (Vol 1), 'Yeqer Memekatesh' (Vol 1), 'Tezeta' by Seyfu Yohannis (Vol 1), 'Bolel' by Zawditu & Yohannis (Vol 2), 'Temeles' by Alemayehu Eshete & Hirut Bekele (Vol 3), 'Ab Teqay Qerebi' by Tewelde Redda (Vol 5), the rocksteady-tinged 'Ewnetegna Feger' by Hirut Bekele (Vol 13), the wonderfully haunting 'Ateqegn' by Bizunesh Bekele (Vol 13), 'Yegenet Muziqa' by Getachew Mekurya (Vol 14) and 'Fegrie Denna Hun' by Asnaqech Werku (Vol 17).

Ababa, underlain by the growing sense of the imperial regime as an illiberal, outmoded and ultimately doomed institution. This realisation, initially confined to the educated classes in major urban centres such as Addis Ababa, Asmara and Dire Dawa, though it would spread into rural areas by the early 1970s, stemmed partly from the challenge that the failed coup of 1960 had presented to the notion of imperial immortality. But it was also doubtless associated with the increased exposure to an outside world that was itself changing rapidly, as more and more outsiders affiliated to broadly left-of-centre institutions such as the Organisation of African Unity, Non-Alignment Pact, and American Peace Corps made Ethiopia their temporary home.

Sadly, the evocative monochrome photographs collected in Francis Falceto's recently published book *Abyssinie Swing* are practically all that remains of the wild R 'n' B-influenced sounds and hedonistic nightclubs that partied until the early morning during the heady early years of the so-called Golden Age of Ethiopian Music. In 1948, the emperor had passed legislation that effectively granted the state-run Hagere Fiker Maheber an exclusive license to import and produce gramophone records, and this no doubt worthy institution (literally, 'The Love of Country Association') concentrated its best efforts on recording dull state events and the like for posterity. As a result, those of us who weren't there can only guess what the music of this era actually sounded like, but mid-60s' photographs of rows of future recording stars such as Mahmoud Ahmed and Tlahoun Gessesse harmonising in finger-clicking unison suggest a greater dependence on vocal harmonies than is evident on the recorded material that would eventually emerge from 'Swinging Addis'.

For the modern audiophile, Ethiopia's musical Golden Age effectively began in 1969, when Amha Eshete, manager of the country's first non-institutional band the Soul Echoes, decided to risk imperial wrath and form his own independent label Amha Records. Despite some initial rumblings from Hagere Fiker Maheber, Amha Records was allowed to operate freely and it positively thrived, releasing an average of 20 45rpm singles and two LPs annually, and launching the recording careers of the likes of Mahmoud Ahmed, Muluqen Mellesse, Hirut Bekele, Alemayehu Eshete, Getachew Kassa and Tlahoun Gessesse prior to its closure in 1975. By that time, however, two other labels inspired by Amha were also thriving, Philips Ethiopia and Kaifa Records, the latter formed by the highly influential and long-serving Ali Abdullah Kaifa, better known as Ali Tango. The 500-odd two-track recordings produced by these independent labels collectively forms practically the only aural record of the Ethiopian music scene during the last two decades of the imperial era, and it also constitutes the bulk of the music re-released on the *Ethiopiques* CDs since the late 1990s by the French label Buda.

So what did it sound like? Well, on one level, strongly derivative of contemporary Western music, as hinted at by the nicknames of popular artists such as the Asmara-based singers Tebereh 'Doris Day' Tesfa-Hunegn and Tukabo 'Mario Lanza' Welde-Maryam. Even the most cursory listen to a few tracks by Alemayehu Eshete, the so-called 'Abyssinian Elvis', suggests a more than passing familiarity with the extended funk workouts beloved of James Brown's backing band, while jazz buffs liken the blazing saxophone work of Getachew Mekurya to Albert Ayler and Ornette Coleman. Elsewhere, you'll hear hints of Stax, Motown, early rock 'n' roll, pop, fusion jazz, blues-rock bands such as Santana and Chicken Shack, and even – in the late 1970s – ska and reggae. But such influences are superficial, as almost every track recorded during this period also displays that distinctively Ethiopic combination of a lopsided rat-a-tat shuffle, uneasy Arabic-sounding pentatonic shifts, and strained, quavering, rather nasal vocals. The result, in most instances, is at once edgy and hypnotic, mournful yet danceable, propulsive yet jerky – above all, perhaps, very, very strange. The recordings of Alemayehu Eshete, for instance, don't really sound like James Brown so much as they evoke the improbable notion of the Godfather of Soul in his funky late-60s' pomp being asked to perform an Islamic prayer call!

Over 1974–75, the imperial era came to its final, bloody conclusion, and Swinging Addis collapsed with it, to be replaced by the joyless socialist dictates of the Derg. The live music scene in particular was muted, thanks to an overnight curfew that endured for a full 16 years. The pioneering Amha Records closed in 1975, and its owner left Addis Ababa for the USA. All the same, Ethiopia

ASTER AND GIGI

The most consistently popular Ethiopian recording artist since she first appeared on the scene in the late 1970s is Gonder-born, California-based Aster Aweke, who still enjoys such a high profile among her compatriots that it would be remarkable to go a full day in any Ethiopian city without hearing what the *Rough Guide to World Music* describes as 'a voice that kills'. It is certainly one of the most thrilling and vocal instruments ever to have emerged from Africa, pitched somewhere between Aretha Franklin (a stated influence), Kate Bush and Björk, with a fractured but raunchy quality that can be utterly heartbreaking.

The closest thing Ethiopia has thus far produced to a genuine crossover artist, Aster has 20 albums to her credit, though her earliest – and some say best – material for Kaifa is available only on hard-to-track-down cassettes in Addis Ababa (and long overdue the attention of those nice people at *Ethiopiques*). Seven albums are available on CD, of which **Aster** is frequently recommended as the best starting point, for reasons that elude me – aside from the standout acoustic rendition of the chestnut 'Tizita', one of her most compelling recordings ever, it is typified by bland mid tempo backings and unusually muted vocal performances. My first choice would be the 1993 CD **Ebo**, which is distinguished by the propulsive growling opening blast of 'Minu Tenekana', the twitchy, wide-eyed 'Esti Inurbet', and a trio of fine ballads, the wracked 'Yene Konjo', the hauntingly melodic 'Yale Sime' and pretty but overlong 'Yewah Libane'.

Heir apparent to Aster's long-standing international status as Ethiopia's best-known singer is the 31-year-old Ejigayehu Shibabaw, who embarked on a solo career under her more concise nickname of **Gigi** after stints singing and performing in Kenya, France and South Africa. Gigi is an acknowledged disciple of Aster (in a 2004 interview with *Afripop*, she states: 'If it wasn't for [Aster] I wouldn't be a singer. I was so much in love with her music and I still love her'), and possesses a similarly haunting voice, though admittedly it's not quite so strung out or fractured.

Gigi's first album **One Ethiopia** (downloadable from www.emusic.com) is likeable enough without being hugely distinguished, but her second eponymous CD, which features contributions from the likes of jazz musicians Herbie Hancock, Wayne Shorter, Bill Laswell, Pharaoh Sanders and various traditional Ethiopian musicians, is a stunner. Released in 2001, Gigi's appeal lies in its organic, eclectic sound, which sets typical Amharigna vocal infections against a rich fusion of jazz, reggae and other African styles – had I heard standout track 'Bale Washintu' blind, for instance, I would have assumed it originated from Mali rather than Ethiopia. The follow up **Zion Roots**, released in 2004, is reputedly just as good.

The release of Gigi inspired *Afripop* to proclaim its namesake as 'the most important new African singer on the scene today', while *New York Times* critic Jon Pareles rated it number one in a year-end round up of the Best Obscure Albums of 2001. Meanwhile, its bold experimentation across genres and the use of a song traditionally reserved for male singers has drawn some criticism from more conservative elements in Ethiopian society. But one person who evidently listened favourably is Aster, whose sublime 2004 release **Aster's Ballads** (re-recordings of 12 self-penned classics, many otherwise unavailable except on cassette) has a strikingly fresh and intimate sound, with the tinny keyboard fills that characterise her other CD releases replaced by an altogether warmer, earthier ambience.

in the late 1970s wasn't quite the musical wasteland it is sometimes portrayed to have been. Kaifa Records thrived on the demand for fresh recordings to accompany the surreptitious lock-in parties that replaced the nightclub scene of years earlier. Indeed, some of the label's finest vinyl releases date to 1976–78, as anthologised on the out-of-print 16-track CD *Ethiopian Groove: The Golden 70s* (recently reissued with an altered track listing as *Ethiopiques 13*). Furthermore, from 1978 onwards,

Kaifa switched its attention from vinyl to the cheaper medium of cassettes, resulting in sales of greater than 10,000 copies for a popular release, as opposed to around 3,000 vinyl copies. It was in 1978, too, that a Gonderine teenage prodigy named Aster Aweke – destined to become arguably the greatest recorded female vocalist ever produced by Africa – cut a pair of debut 45rpm singles for Kaifa, followed by five full-length cassettes, before relocating to the USA in 1981.

All the same, the dawn of the cassette era does seem to have coincided with a slump in innovative musicianship. Music was still recorded prolifically under the Derg, it still sold well, and the likes of Aster Aweke and Mahmoud Ahmed produced some superb vocal performances. But, linked perhaps to the demise of the live music scene and emigration of many of the country's finest musicians, the punch and elasticity that characterised the backing bands captured on Amha and Kaifa's vinyl releases gradually gave way to a more stodgy and synthetic will-that-do style of backing that detracted from even the most evocative singing. All-plodding mid tempo dreariness punctuated by pointless tinkling frills, this genre of musical backing still persists on some recordings made in the post-Derg era, many of which also drag on for far too bloody long – if the greats could say it in three minutes, why do mediocre modern session musicians require six, seven or eight minutes to plink-plonk their way to a tepid conclusion? More encouragingly, the potential breakthrough artist Gigi has reverted to a warmer, more organic live sound on her recent recordings, and other newcomers such as the female duo Abro Adeg (literally 'Two Friends') and American-based warbler Hana Shenkute do at least attempt to use synthesised backings creatively. Recent years have also seen a resurgence of traditional music in the form of Addis Ababa's *bolel* singers, who mix the pithy sarcasm and grumbling bluesiness of the ancient *azmari* minstrels with more contemporary cultural and political observations.

In addition to the CDs mentioned in the boxes *Ethiopiques* and *Aster & Gigi*, a good entry-level compilation of Ethiopian sounds is the **Rough Guide to Ethiopian Music**, which was released in 2004 and includes tracks by artists including Aster Aweke, Mahmoud Ahmed and Alemayehu Eshete.

Gelada baboon

Appendix 2

FURTHER READING

Books about Ethiopia aren't quite so thin on the ground as they were a few years back, though many more interesting titles remain difficult to locate or are dauntingly expensive. Within Ethiopia, the best places to buy local-interest books are **Bookworld** and the **Africans Bookshop** in Addis Ababa. The curio shop next to the ETC tourist office and shops in Bole Airport stock a good range too.

Few European or American bookshops stock much in the way of books about Ethiopia, but you can order most of the volumes listed below through online sellers such as amazon.com or amazon.co.uk. The **Red Sea Press**, one of the most prolific publishers about Ethiopia and the Horn of Africa, has an online catalogue and ordering facilities at www.africanworld.com. **Shama Publishers**, an Ethiopian company with a tantalising and ever-expanding selection of titles, should soon have similar facilities at www.shamabooks.com.

Eastern Books in London specialises in rare and out-of-print books on Ethiopia. For a full stock list with prices, contact 128 Ashtonville Street, London SW18 5AQ; ℣f 020 8871 0880.

General and coffee-table books

Amin, M, Matheson, A and Willetts, D *Journey Through Ethiopia* Camerapix, 1997. This is one of the best general coffee-table books about Ethiopia, combining strong photography and quality reproduction with readable introductory text. The publisher Camerapix was founded by the late Muhammad Amin, who won an award for the documentary coverage that indirectly prompted the international response to the 1985 famine.

Amin, M, Balletto, B and Willetts, D *Spectrum Guide to Ethiopia* Camerapix, 1995. This is the Ethiopian title in a series of travel guides, which – despite a uniformly high standard – feel more appropriate on the coffee table or in the tour coach than in the backpack.

Batistoni, M and Chiara, P C *Old Tracks in the New Flower: A Historical Guide to Addis Ababa* Arada Books, 2004. This is a fascinating record of the early days of Ethiopia's capital, with illustrations and descriptions of about 100 of the most interesting old buildings scattered around the city.

Beckworth, C and Fisher, A *Africa Ark* Harry N Abrams, 1990. It seems almost dismissive to describe this visually superlative, lavish – and very expensive – tome as a coffee-table book. Carol Beckworth and Angela Fisher are regarded to be the finest photographic documenters of African culture in the business, and this book – ranging from South Omo to Tigrai – leaves one in no doubt as to why! Supplemented by Graham Hancock's informative text, this is simply one of the finest photographic books ever produced about Africa.

Di Salvo, Mario *Churches of Ethiopia: The Monastery of Narga Selassie* Skira, 1999. A fascinating and visually impressive photographic document of the beautiful church built by the Empress Mentewab on a remote island in Lake Tana, with text that ties the specific church into a broader overview of the monastic tradition on Lake Tana – not nearly as dull as it sounds!

Golzábez, J and Cebrián, D *Touching Ethiopia* Shama Books, 2004 This sumptuous new 400-page tome can't quite decide whether it wants to be a coffee-table book or something more authoritative, but it succeeds remarkably well on both counts. Probably the best overall visual introduction to Ethiopia in print, it is particularly strong on the oft-neglected south, west and east.

Hancock, G, Pankhurst, R and Willetts, D *Under Ethiopian Skies* H&L Communications, 1983. A bit dated and compromised somewhat by its apologist stance on the Mengistu government, the text of this coffee-table book is nevertheless very well written. The photography fails to reflect the beauty of the country, possibly because of poor reproduction, more likely an indication of the difficult situation under which the photos must have been taken – in the midst of a civil war.

Hancock, Graham *The Sign and the Seal* Heinemann, 1992. This lively account of the Ark of the Covenant's alleged arrival in Ethiopia is as popular with tourists as it is reviled by academics (the respected historical writer Paul Henze describes it as 'fiction masquerading as historical research'). It is, for all that, an entertaining work, one that captures the imagination, and as the only popular book of a historical (or quasi-historical) nature published about Ethiopia in decades, it must qualify as almost essential reading.

Munro-Hay, Stuart *Ethiopia: The Unknown Land* IB Tauris, 2002. This authoritative site-by-site historical overview of Ethiopia's most popular antiquities would make for a superb companion to a more conventional travel guide for readers seeking more scholarly and detailed background information.

Munro-Hay, Stuart *The Quest for the Ark of the Covenant: The True Story of the Tablets of Moses* IB Tauris, 2005. Inspired by the more outlandish postulations in Hancock's *Sign and the Seal*, this readable albeit rather dry tome provides a scholarly assessment of the probable fate of the Ark – inevitably concluding that it is almost certainly not (and never was) stashed away anywhere in Ethiopia.

Nomachi, Kazyoshi *Bless Ethiopia* Odyssey Publications, 1998. Photographically, this is by far the most creative document of Ethiopia I've come across, capturing typical ecclesiastical scenes from unusual and striking angles. Highly recommended.

Pankhurst, Richard and Gerard, Denis *Ethiopia Photographed* Kegan Paul, 1997. A follow-up to *Ethiopia Engraved*, this lovely and absorbing book is a must for old-photograph junkies, consisting of a wealth of photographs taken from 1867 to 1936, placed in context through accompanying text by Richard Pankhurst.

Pankhurst, Richard and Ingrams, Leila *Ethiopia Engraved* Kegan Paul, 1988. This book is a fascinating visual document of 17th- to 19th-century Ethiopia as seen through the engravings of contemporary European visitors.

Travel accounts

Alvares, Francisco *Prester John of the Indies* Cambridge, 1961. The oldest Ethiopian travelogue in existence, written by a Portuguese priest almost 500 years ago, remains a fascinating and often astonishingly insightful read, but it is out of print and very difficult to locate.

Avrahamís, Amhuel *Treacherous Journey* Shapolsky Books, New York, 1986. A different type of travelogue, described by one reader as a 'tremendous adventure story' of a Falasha's escape from persecution under the Derg. It also includes a lot of information about the Bet Israel or Falasha, and the beliefs and values of the people who shelter the author along the way.

Buxton, David *Travels in Ethiopia* London, 1967. Short but interesting document of Ethiopian travels in the immediate post-World War II era, has some interesting black-and-white photos, out of print but often available at a price at secondhand bookstalls in Addis Ababa.

Graham, John *Ethiopia off the Beaten Trail* Shama Books, 2001. John Graham is the popular travel correspondent for the *Addis Tribune*, and a contributor to the fourth edition of this Bradt Travel Guide. This first collection of his informative and occasionally irreverent travel essays reflects the author's delight in exploring Ethiopia's less travelled corners.

Henze, Paul *Ethiopian Journeys* Shama Books, 2001. Paul Henze's classic travel account of Ethiopia during the last years of the imperial era, out of print for two decades, is another alluring title in the new Shama Books catalogue.

Kaplan, Robert *Surrender or Starve: Travels in Ethiopia, Sudan, Somalia and Eritrea* Vintage, 2003. This excellent and often rather chilling journalistic travelogue details the political factors that hugely exacerbated drought-related famines in the Horn of Africa during the 1980s.

Marsden-Smedley, Philip *A Far Country* Century, 1990. This is a readable and interesting account of a 1988 trip through Mengistu-era Ethiopia. I can't say that I noticed the author exploring, as the jacket blurb suggests, 'the way that individuals – and whole races – idealise far places and how this prompts dreams of returning'. But the simple fact that he explores Ethiopia, and was the first person to write about doing so in several decades, is good enough reason to read this entertaining book.

Murphy, Dervla *In Ethiopia with a Mule* John Murray, 1969. Recommended travelogue that describes an Ethiopia way away from any tourist trail.

Pakenham, Thomas *The Mountains of Rasselas* Seven Dials, 1999. This is a vivid and well-written account of the author's failed attempt to reach the remote Ethiopian mountaintop where princes were imprisoned in the Gonderine period. Originally published in 1959, it was reissued in a glossy coffee-table format four decades later, complete with photographs taken in 1955 as well as more recent ones.

Rushby, Kevin *Eating the Flowers of Paradise* Flamingo, 1999. A fascinating book about the culture of *chat* consumption, half of which is set in Ethiopia, between Addis and Harar, before crossing the Red Sea from Djibouti to Yemen – as one reader notes 'the book reads a lot better than *chat* tastes!'

Shah, Tahir *In Search of King Solomon's Mines* Arcade Publishing, 2003. Set mainly in Ethiopia, this compulsively readable and highly entertaining book follows the misadventures of a London-based member of the Afghan aristocracy who is led a wild goose chase by – of all things – a map, bought in a Jerusalem market, that purportedly shows the route to King Solomon's mines!

Stewart, Julia *Eccentric Graces: Eritrea and Ethiopia through the Eyes of a Traveller* Red Sea Press, 1998. The most modern travelogue about Ethiopia, based on travels shortly before the two countries declared war on each other, this readable book seems to fall into the 'love it or hate it' category, but is nevertheless a good introduction to travelling through Ethiopia today.

Thesiger, Wilfred *The Life of my Choice*, 1987. This includes childhood reminiscences of growing up in Abyssinia, Haile Selassie's coronation, the liberation campaign in 1941, treks in the south of the country, plus a vivid account of a six-month journey through the Danakil in 1933 – recommended, along with the same author's *Danakil Diaries*, particularly if you are heading into the eastern deserts.

Waugh, Evelyn *Remote People* Penguin, 1931. Witty travelogue detailing parts of Haile Selassie's coronation, plus travels in Djibouti and an account of the railway to Awash.

Waugh, Evelyn *When the Going was Good*. One of several Waugh books that refer to his Abyssinian sojourn, this is recommended by Dr Ann Waters-Bayer for 'including some interesting accounts of his travels in Ethiopia'.

History and background

Beyene, T, Pankhurst, R and Bekele, S *Kasa and Kasa: Papers on the Lives, Times and Images of Tewodros II and Yohannis IV (1855-1889)* Institute of Ethiopian Studies, 1990. Exactly why Ethiopia survived into the 20th century as an independent state is a question open to some debate. It is certainly linked to the mid- to late-19th-century rise of three successive emperors of unifying vision, two of whose careers are covered in this excellent collection of essays.

Bredin, Niles *The Pale Abyssinian* Flamingo, 2001. This recent biography of the explorer James Bruce is highly readable and a good accompaniment on any trip in the north of the country.

Buxton, David *The Abyssinians* Thames and Hudson, 1970. A number of people have recommended this as a good general introduction to just about every aspect of Ethiopian history and culture. It's a bit dated, but well worth reading if you can locate a copy.

Getachew, Indrias *Beyond the Throne: The Enduring Legacy of Emperor Haile Selassie I* Shama Books, 2001. Edited by Richard Pankhurst, with a foreword by Harold Marcus, and endorsed by the royal family, this well written and lavishly illustrated overview of Ethiopia's last emperor, with several never-before-seen photographs, is the first in a series of three related titles about Haile Selassie.

Giday, Belai *Ethiopian Civilisation* Giday, 1991. Cheap and widely available in Ethiopia, this book essentially consists of unqualified legend posing as history. I have no problem with the legendary aspect, but the author should clarify that modern historians dismiss much of it as myth. (In fact, instead of merely recounting legends dressed as fact, it would be rather nice to see an Ethiopian who apparently knows his stuff convince us of the truth behind the legends.)

Hailemelekot, Abebe *The Victory of Adowa* Self-published, 1998. This is a workmanlike overview of the proudest moment in modern Ethiopian history, well worth the birr 30 it costs in shops in Addis Ababa.

Henze, Paul *Eritrea's War* Shama Books, 2001. Written by a former diplomat and recognised expert on Ethiopian politics, this should be of great interest to travellers wishing to get to grips with the circumstances surrounding the recently ended border war between Ethiopia and Eritrea.

Henze, Paul *Layers of Time: A History of Ethiopia* Hurst, 2000. Probably the most approachable one-volume introductory history in print, this includes a useful overview of ancient and medieval Ethiopia, but is particularly good on modern history up to the fall of the Derg. Described by the noted Axumite historian Dr Stuart Munro-Hay as offering 'a well-balanced overview of Ethiopian history from the remotest past to modern times'.

Hibbert, Christopher *Africa Explored: Europeans in the Dark Continent* Penguin, 1982. This readable and interesting overview of the age of European exploration of Africa includes good accounts of Bruce's expedition, as well as Richard Burton's trip to Harar.

Johanson, D & Edey, M *Lucy: The Beginning of Humankind* Simon & Schuster, 1990. The definitive account of the discovery of the legendary hominid fossil dubbed Lucy, as written by the acclaimed palaeontologist who led the digs.

Kapuscinski, Richard *The Emperor* Random House, 1983. This impressionistic and strangely compelling account of the last days of Haile Selassie is transcribed from interviews with his servants and confidants, and offers valuable insights into Ethiopia immediately before the 1974 revolution.

Marcus, Harold *A History of Ethiopia* University of California Press, 1994. In this very readable general history, Marcus summarises all the initiate needs to know over a flowing and erudite 220 pages – a recommended starting point.

Ministry of Education and Fine Arts *Ethiopia: A Short Illustrated History* Ministry of Education and Fine Arts. Another cheap local book, this is not authoritative but does offer a fair overview and perspective to travellers who don't want to buy an expensive imported title.

Moorehead, Alan *The Blue Nile*, 1962. This compulsive introduction to the exploits of James Bruce and the Napier expedition is one of the few books about that little chunk of Africa between Egypt and South Africa that can be relied upon to be sitting in the shelves of most libraries.

Munro-Hay, Stuart *Aksum: An African Civilisation of Late Antiquity* Edinburgh University Press, 1991. This very readable book by a well-known authority on the subject offers a good overview of all aspects of Axumite civilisation. It is available online at www.users.vnet.net/alight/aksum.

Pakenham, Thomas *The Scramble For Africa* Jonathan Ball, 1991. Recommended as much because it is one of the most crisp, unsentimental and informative books ever written about African history as because it puts Ethiopia's independence in a continental context. It was the winner of the WH Smith Literary Award and South Africa's Alan Paton Award, and is, in the words of Simon Roberts (*The Natal Witness*) 'Conrad's *Heart of Darkness* with the floodlights switched on'. If 700-page tomes switch you off, Chapter 27 is as good an account as you'll find of the pivotal events in Ethiopia circa 1895–97.

Pankhurst, Richard *The Ethiopians (People of Africa)* Blackwell Publishers, 2001. This reissued title by the doyen of modern Ethiopian historical writing provides an excellent introduction to Ethiopia's varied cultures and social history.

Pankhurst, Richard *The Ethiopian Borderlands* Red Sea Press, 1997. Subtitled *Essays in Regional History from Ancient Times to the End of the 18th Century*, this fascinating book sees Pankhurst, the most prolific writer on Ethiopian historical matters, provide a historical overview to those parts of Ethiopia that are generally ignored in mainstream texts.

Pankhurst, Richard *History of Ethiopian Towns from the Middle Ages to the early 19th Century* Wiesbaden, 1982. This is the first in a two-volume series covering the origin and history of most large towns – and many small ones – in Ethiopia (the second deals with the mid 19th century onwards). It's an invaluable resource that deserves wider circulation.

Pankhurst, Richard *Social History of Ethiopia* Institute of Ethiopian Studies, 1990. This detailed tome covers Ethiopian society between the late medieval period and the rise of Tewodros in the 19th century. Thorough and insightful, it is probably too academic and esoteric for the general reader.

Phillipson, David *The Monuments of Aksum* Addis Ababa University Press, 1997. The book is essentially an annotated and translated transcript of the original findings of the DAE Axum Expedition of 1906. It remains an excellent introduction to Axum's archaeological wealth, and also contains some great pictures of early 20th-century Axum.

Phillipson, David *Archaeology at Aksum 1993–7* Society of Antiquities of London, 2001. This mighty and long-awaited two-volume tome will be the first to place in perspective the results of the extensive excavations around Axum that have taken place since the fall of the Derg in 1991. At US$150 for the two volumes, however, it is clearly aimed at the truly dedicated rather than casual readers.

Reader, John *Africa: A Biography of the Continent* Hamish Hamilton, 1997. This award-winning book, available as a Penguin paperback, provides a compulsively readable introduction to Africa's past, from the formation of the continent to post-independence politics – the ideal starting point for anybody seeking to place their Ethiopian experience in a broader African context.

Tibebu, Teshale *The Making of Modern Ethiopia 1896–1974* Red Sea Press, 1995. This book provides an excellent and original overview of modern Ethiopia and its ancient cultural roots. In a sense, it possibly provides a more meaningful and comprehensible introduction to Ethiopia than the straight general histories. Recommended.

Zewde, Bahru *A History of Modern Ethiopia 1855–1974* James Currey, 1991. Pitched at the general reader as much as the historian, this book is accurate, well written, affordable and generously illustrated – an essential purchase. It is available in most bookshops in Addis Ababa for around US$5.

Art and music

Falceto, Francis *Abyssinie Swing: A Pictorial History of Modern Ethiopian Music* Shama Books, 2001. This monochrome document of the emergence of the (now almost forgotten) jazz-tinged music scene that blossomed in the dying years of the imperial era is utterly irresistible. The photographs, which span the years 1868 to 1973, are consistently evocative, while the text, though more concise than might be hoped for, is as authoritative as one would expect of a book compiled by the editor of the acclaimed *Ethiopiques* CD compilation series. All in all, it's an essential purchase for anybody with more than a passing interest in Ethiopia's rich musical heritage.

Gerster, Georg *Churches in Rock* Phaidon Press, 1970. Superb but long-out-of-print visual document of the Tigraian rock churches, as well as lesser-known architectural gems such as Bethlehem Gaynt south of Lalibela.

Heldman, Marilyn et al *African Zion: The sacred art of Ethiopia* Yale University Press, 1994. Expensive (£40) but beautiful, and written by leading scholars of Ethiopian and Byzantine art, this lavishly illustrated book covers the art of highland Ethiopia from the 4th to the 18th centuries.

Natural history
Mammals

Dorst, J and Dandelot, P *Field Guide to the larger mammals of Africa* Collins, 1983.

Estes, Richard *The Safari Companion* Green Books (UK), Russell Friedman Books (SA), Chelsea Green (USA). This unconventional book might succinctly be described as a field guide to mammal behaviour. It's probably a bit esoteric for most one-off visitors to Africa, but a must for anybody with a serious interest in wildlife.

Haltenorth, T and Diller, H *Field guide to the Mammals of Africa including Madagascar* Collins, 1984. Formerly the standard field guides to the region, these books are still recommended in many travel guides and other resources. In my opinion, they have largely been superseded by subsequent publications, and now come across as very dated and badly structured – with mediocre illustrations to boot.

Kingdon, Jonathan *The Kingdon Field Guide to African Mammals* Academic Press, 1997. The most detailed, thorough and up to date of several titles covering the mammals of the region, this superb book transcends all expectations of a standard field guide. The author, a highly respected biologist, supplements detailed descriptions and good illustrations of all the continent's large mammals with an ecological overview of each species. An essential purchase for anybody with a serious interest in mammal identification – or their natural history.

Last, Jill *Endemic Mammals of Ethiopia* Ethiopian Tourist Commission, 1982. This lightweight, slightly dated and very inexpensive booklet includes detailed descriptions of appearance and behaviour for Ethiopia's seven endemic mammal species and races. A worthwhile purchase!

Sillero-Zuburi, C and Macdonald, D *The Ethopian wolf: Status Survey and Conservation Action Plan* IUCN, 1997. Although primarily what it claims to be, this important work of reference also includes detailed information about most aspects of Ethopian wolf ecology.

Stuart, Chris and Tilde *The Larger Mammals of Africa* Struik, 1997. This useful field guide doesn't quite match up to Kingdon's, but it's definitely the best of the rest, and arguably more appropriate to readers with a relatively casual interest in African wildlife. It's also a lot cheaper and lighter!

Stuart, Chris and Tilde *Southern, Central and East African Mammals* Struik, 1995. This excellent mini-guide, compact enough to slip into a pocket, is remarkably thorough within its inherent space restrictions, though Ethiopia's wildlife is less well covered than that of more popular safari destinations.

Birds

Frances, J and Shirihai *Ethiopia: In Search of Endemic Birds* Julian Frances, 1999. This self-published booklet describing the authors' sightings on a field trip in 1997 is a useful companion for anybody on a self-guided birding trip through Ethiopia. Contact address is 65 Fleet Street, London, EC4Y 1HS.

Sinclair, I and Ryan, P *Birds of Africa South of the Sahara* Struik Publishers, 2003. The first field guide to this vast region covers all 2,100-plus species recorded there in a remarkably compact 700-odd pages, and is one of only two titles to illustrate every bird you are likely to encounter in Ethiopia. The accurate illustrations are supported by reliable text and good distribution maps. The one book any self-respecting birdwatcher needs to take to Ethiopia!

Smith, Steve *Bird Calls of Ethiopia*. This self-published tape of common Ethiopian birdcalls can be ordered from the author at 42 Lower Buckland Rd, Lymington, Hampshire, SO41 9DL.

Tilahun, S, Edwards, S and Egziabher, T *Important Bird Areas of Ethiopia* EW&NHS, 1998. This detailed booklet provides a very detailed overview of Ethiopia's most important birding locales, and is of interest to ecologists and birders alike.

Urban, E and Brown, L *Checklist of the Birds of Ethiopia* University Press, 1971. The best general survey of Ethiopia's avifauna in print, this is a must for serious birders, with excellent detail on habitats and distribution. It is no substitute for a proper field guide (no illustrations for a start), and is obviously dated with respect to recently described endemics and other newly recorded birds. A revision is reputedly in the pipeline. It can be bought through the University Book Shop *(PO Box 1176 Addis Ababa;* ☏ *011 5518896)*. UK readers can get it at Subbuteo Natural History Books in Treuddyn, near Mold, Denbighshire, CH7 4LN (☏ *01352 770581;* f *01352 771591)*.

Urban, E and Poole, J *Endemic Birds of Ethiopia* Ethiopian Tourist Commission, 1980. Similar to the 'endemic mammals' title, this is a useful and inexpensive booklet describing and illustrating the 23 Ethiopian and Eritrean endemics that had been described prior to 1980.

Van Perlo, Ber *Illustrated Checklist to the Birds of Eastern Africa* Collins, 1995. Van Perlo's guide was until recently the only book to illustrate and show distribution details of all Ethiopian species. It has since been superseded by Sinclair & Ryan's tome, which has more detailed text, better illustrations, and a more user-friendly layout, but – weight-conscious and casual birdwatchers take note – is also a lot bulkier.

Vivero, Jose *The Endemic Birds of Ethiopia and Eritrea* Shama Books, 2001. This recently published pocketbook provides the most detailed and up-to-date coverage yet of the 30-plus bird species endemic to Ethiopia and Eritrea, making it an excellent supplement to a standard field guide – though note that several recently recognised species, such as the Ethiopian cisticola, are excluded.

Williams, J and Arlott, N *Field Guide to the Birds of East Africa* Collins, 1980. As with the older Collins mammal field guides, Williams's was for years the standard field guide to the region, and is still widely mentioned in travel literature. Unfortunately, it feels rather dated today: fewer than half the birds in the region are illustrated, several are not even described, and the bias is strongly towards common Kenyan birds.

Zimmerman, D et al *Birds of Kenya and Northern Tanzania* Russell Friedman Books, 1996. This monumentally handsome hardback tome is arguably the finest field guide to any African territory in print. The geographical limitations with regard to Ethiopia barely need pointing out, but while this book cannot be recommended as a primary field guide outside of the region it specifically covers, its wealth of descriptive and ecological detail and superb illustrations make it an excellent secondary source within Ethiopia. A lighter and cheaper but less detailed paperback version was published in 1999.

Others

Kingdon, Jonathan *Island Africa* Collins, 1990. This highly readable and award-winning tome about evolution in ecological 'islands' such as deserts and montane forests is recommended to anybody who wants to place the high level of endemism noted in the Ethiopian Highlands in a broader continental context.

Nievergelt, B, Good, T and Guttinger, R *A Survey on the Flora and Fauna of the Simien Mountains National Park* Walia, 1998. This massively detailed and attractively illustrated 100-page book will be of great interest to any wildlife or plant lover visiting the Simien Mountains.

Stuart, Chris & Tilde *Africa's Vanishing Wildlife* Southern Books, 1996. An informative and pictorially strong introduction to the endangered and vulnerable mammals of Africa, this book combines coffee-table production with an impassioned and erudite text.

Health

Wilson-Howarth, Dr Jane *Healthy Travel: Bugs, Bites and Bowels* Cadogan, 1995

Wilson-Howarth, Dr Jane and Ellis, Dr Matthew *Your Child's Health Abroad: A manual for travelling parents* Bradt, 2004 (2nd edition).

Internet sites

www.abyssiniacybergateway.net Good search engine and plenty of historical links.

www.addistribune.com The *Addis Tribune* has an excellent website for news, views and other background and travel detail – with searchable archives dating back five years.

www.afripop.org Several features about Ethiopian music including a full-length interview with rising star Gigi.

www.birdtours.co.uk\trireports\ethiopia Excellent and detailed trip report from Jan Vermeulen. Comprehensive report by Giles Mulholland of interest to people driving around Ethiopia, or to Ethiopia from South Africa.

www.ethiopiatoday.com Good search engine linked to thousands of sites specialised with a high Ethiopia interest.

www.ethio.com News, chat lines, and useful links.

www.ethioembassy.org.uk Informative not only regarding pre-visit paperwork, but also current affairs. Online articles by the likes of Paul Henze.

www.flyethiopian.com Booking site for Ethiopian Airlines.

www.geocities.com\~dagmawu Probably the best site pertaining to the recent war between Ethiopia and Eritrea, with links to articles covering all aspects of the war in quality international newspapers.

www.tour.ethiopiaonline.com Useful tourist information and current travel tips.

www.safarilink.com Safari link is an impartial African information resource which can be useful when planning holidays to Africa.

Appendix

LANGUAGE
With thanks to Yared Belete of Grant Express Travel and Tours Services (GETTS)

Amharigna (pronounced Amharinya and more often known outside the country as Amharic) is a Semetic language that derives from Ge'ez, the language of the Axumites and the Ethiopian Orthodox Church to this day. Amharigna is the first language of the Amhara people who live in north–central Ethiopia. Along with English, Amharigna is still the official language of Ethiopia and is thus the language most often used between Ethiopians of different linguistic backgrounds, performing a similar role to that of Swahili in the rest of east Africa.

In practical terms, you will find that most Ethiopians who have been to high school speak passable, if idiosyncratic, English, though in many cases they get little opportunity to use it, and so are rather rusty. Except in Tigrai and remote rural areas, almost everyone speaks some Amharigna, and – unless you stay exclusively in tourist hotels – you will find it difficult to get by without a few basic phrases. People are often very surprised and responsive if you can speak a few words of the language. If you spend a while in Tigrai, and in Oromifa-speaking parts of southern Ethiopia (which includes the Rift Valley and most points east of it), it can be helpful to know a few words of the local tongue. In Tigrai, the response to a tourist who can say even one Tigrigna phrase is less that of surprise than of total astonishment. It really is worth making the effort.

Amharigna

The section that follows is not meant to be a comprehensive introduction to Amharigna. A cheap and light grammar and mini-dictionary, *Amharic for Foreigners* by Semere Woldegabir, is readily available in Addis Ababa and recommended to natural linguists who want to get to grips with the complex grammar and sentence construction of Amharigna, or the intricacies of pronunciation. My experience, however, suggests that most visitors will find this book more daunting than helpful and that the few basic phrases they need to know are buried beneath reams of detail that are of little use to somebody with no long-term interest in becoming fluent in the language. Better to carry Lonely Planet's *Amharic* phrasebook.

What follows is essentially the Pidgin-Amharigna I picked up over four months in the country. Most of this came not from books, which invariably confused me, but from English-speaking Ethiopians with a natural sympathy to the difficulties of learning a language from scratch. It could be argued that I should be getting a fluent Amharigna-speaker to write this. I would disagree: it is not difficult to get by in Amharigna, but only if you ignore its grammatical complications. I simply don't speak enough Amharigna to be able to complicate it, and what little I do speak was learnt the hard way. It is difficult to imagine that many tourists to Ethiopia will need more Amharigna than the simplified version that follows. If, after a couple of weeks, you exhaust what I learnt in four months, it only strengthens the case for keeping things simple.

But... I do apologise to Amharigna speakers for any liberties that I might have taken with their language; my only excuse is that whatever errors might follow stood me in good stead during my time in Ethiopia; my only rejoinder is that you do some utterly bemusing things to my home language, and I would never let 'correctness' override the will to communicate.

It is worth noting that there is often no simple and correct English transcription of Amharigna words, as evidenced by such extremes of spelling as Woldio/Weldiya, Mekele/Maqale, Zikwala/Zouqala and even Addis Ababa/Adees Abeba. Generally, I have spelt Amharigna words as they sound to me. People who are unfamiliar with African languages should be aware that Amharigna, like most other African languages, is pronounced phonetically – the town name Bore is not pronounced like boar, but *Bor-ay*.

The magic word

The one word that every visitor to Ethiopia should know is *ishee*. This is the sort of word that illustrates the gap between 'proper' grammar/dictionaries, and the realities of being in a new country and trying to assimilate the language quickly. *Ishee,* more or less, means OK, but (not unlike the English equivalent) it can be used in a variety of circumstances: as an alternative to the myriad ways of saying hello or goodbye, to signal agreement, to reassure people, etc. This is not just a foreigners' short cut – *ishee* is the single most spoken word in Ethiopia, and I have often heard entire conversations that apparently consist of nothing more than two Ethiopians bouncing *ishees* backwards and forwards. Of course *ishee* is a colloquial word – but most people aren't out to take offence and they understand the problems facing foreigners who can't speak the local language; a foreigner smiling and saying the word *ishee* is as acceptable a signal of goodwill or friendliness as would be a foreigner smiling and saying 'OK' in Britain. Another useful catchphrase in some situations is *chigger yellem* – no problem. And, incidentally, the word 'OK' is also widely used in Ethiopia.

Greetings and farewells

Useful all-purpose greetings are *tadias* and *tenayistillign*, which basically mean hello, how are you? These are common greetings that can be used with anyone and on all occasions. In many parts of the country, the Arabic greeting *selam* – literally 'peace' – is in common use. To ask how somebody is, ask *dehnaneh?* to a male and *dehnanesh?* to a female. The correct response, always, is *dehena*, pronounced more like '*dena*' or *dehnanegn* – I am well. There are tens of other greetings, depending on the time of day and the sex and number of people you are speaking to. There is little need for visitors to learn these greetings. If you want to anticipate them being used on you, all you need know is that they invariably start with the phrase *indemin-* and the correct response is invariably *dehena*. There are just as many ways of saying goodbye or farewell – *dehnahunu* or *chau* (adopted from and pronounced like the Italian *ciao*) is fine in most circumstances. Ethiopians often precede their *chau* with an *ishee*!

Some essentials

The first barrier to be crossed when you travel in linguistically unfamiliar surroundings is to learn how to ask a few basic questions and to understand the answers. The answers first: *awo* means yes and *aydelem* means no. In casual use, these are often shortened to *aw* (pronounced like the 'ou' in our) and *ay* (pronounced like eye). Some Ethiopians replace their *aw* with a rather startling inhalation of breath.

In general travel-type queries, you'll often use and hear the words *aleh* (there is) and *yellem* (there is not). To find out if a place serves coffee (*buna*), you would ask *buna aleh?* The response should be *aleh* or *yellem*.

Once you have established that what you want is in the *aleh* state, you can ask for it by saying *ifelegalehu* (I want). More often, Ethiopians will just say what they want and how many – *and buna* (one coffee) or *hulet birra* (two beers). It is not customary to accompany your request with an *ibakih* or *ibakesh* (please, to a male and female respectively), but you should always say *ameseghinalehu* (thank you) when you get what you asked for. The response to thank you is *minimaydelem* (you're welcome).

If you don't want something – like, say, the green comb that a street hawker is thrusting in your face – then say *alfelagem* or simply shake your head. If this makes little impression, you can say *hid* (go) to children, or anyone who is obviously much younger than you, but you shouldn't really say something that overtly offish to an adult.

In Amharigna, the word *no* (pronounced like the English know) means something roughly equivalent to 'is'. In Amharigna conversations, Ethiopians often interject a *no* much as we might say 'true' or 'really'. Needless to say, this can cause a certain amount of confusion if you say 'no' to somebody who isn't familiar with English – they may well assume you are saying 'yes'.

The word for 'where' is *yet*, from which derive the questions *yetno?* (where is?), *wedetno?* (to where?) and *keyetno?* (from where?). The word for 'what' is *min*, which gives you *mindeno?* (what is it?), *lemin?* (why?), *minaleh?* (what is there?) and *indet?* (how?). *Meche?* means 'when?', which gives you *mecheno?* (when is it?), *man?* means 'who?' and *sintno?* means 'how much?'.

Simple questions can be formed by prefixing the above phrases with a subject. Some examples:

Awtobus yemihedow?	Where is this bus going?
Migib minaleh?	What food is there?
Alga aleh?	Is there a room? (*alga* literally means bed)
Postabet yetno?	Where is the post office?
Wagaw sintno?	How much does it cost?
Sa'at sintno?	What (literally 'how much') is the time?
Simih mano?	What is your name? (male)
Simish mano?	What is your name? (female)
Hisap sintno?	How much is the bill?

Some useful Amharigna words

after/later	*behuwala*	dirty	*koshasha*
afternoon	*kesa'at behuwala*	donkey	*ahiya*
again	*indegena*	egg	*inkulal*
and	*na*	enough	*beki*
at	*be*	(enough!)	*(beka)*
bad	*metfo*	Ethiopian	*Habesha* or *Ityopyawi*
banana	*muz*	excuse (me)	*yikirta*
beautiful	*konjo*	far	*ruk*
bed	*alga*	fast	*fetan*
beef	*yebere siga*	first	*andegna* or
beer	*birra*		*mejemerya*
before	*befit*	fish	*asa*
bicycle	*bisikleet*	food	*migib*
big	*tilik*	foreigner	*faranji*
bus	*awtobus*	glass	*birchiko*
but	*gin*	go	*hid*
car (or any motor		good	*tiru*
vehicle)	*mekeena*	he	*issu*
cart	*gari*	help	*irdugn*
cent (or just money)	*santeem*	here	*izih*
chicken	*doro*	horse	*feres*
church	*bet kristyan*	hospital	*hakim bet*
clean	*nitsuh*	hour	*sa'at*
coffee	*buna*	house (or any	
cold	*kezkaza*	building)	*bet*
come (female)	*ney*	I	*ine*
come (male)	*na*	in	*wust*
correct	*lik*	insect	*tebay*
cost	*waga*	island	*desiet*
(make a discount)	*(waga kenis)*	key	*kulf*
country (or region)	*ager*	lake	*hayk*
cow	*lam*	little	*tinish*

luggage	*gwaz* or *shanta*	room	*kifil*
me	*inay*	salt	*chew*
meat	*siga*	sea	*bahir*
milk	*wotet*	she	*iswa*
money	*genzeb*	shop	*suk*
morning	*tiwat*	short	*achir*
mountain	*terara*	shower	*showa* or
Mr	*Ato*		*metatebia bet*
Mrs	*Weyzero*	sleep	*inkilf*
Miss	*Weyzerit*	slowly	*kes*
much	*bizu*	small	*tinish*
mutton	*yebeg siga*	sorry	*aznallehu*
near	*atageb* or *kirb*	stop	*akum*
newspaper	*gazeta*	sugar	*sukwar*
nice	*tiru*	tall	*rejim*
night	*lelit*	tea	*shai*
now	*ahun*	there	*iza*
of	*ye*	they	*innessu*
or	*weyim*	ticket	*karnee* or *ticket*
orange	*birtukan*	today	*zare*
peace	*selam*	toilet	*shintbet*
petrol	*benzeen*	tomorrow	*nege*
pig	*asama*	very	*betam*
problem	*chigger*	warm	*muk*
quickly	*tolo*	water	*wuha*
region	*bota*	yesterday	*tilant*
restaurant	*migib bet*	you (female)	*anchee*
river	*wenz*	you (male)	*ante*
road	*menged*		

Numbers

1	*and*		20	*haya*
2	*hulet*		25	*haya amist (hamist)*
3	*sost*		30	*selasa*
4	*arat*		40	*arba*
5	*amist*		50	*hamsa*
6	*sidist*		60	*silsa*
7	*sabat*		70	*seba*
8	*simint*		80	*semagnya*
9	*zetegn*		90	*zetena*
10	*asir*		100	*meto*
11	*asra and*		200	*hulet meto*
12	*asra hulet*		1,000	*shee*
			1,000,000	*meelyon*

Days of the week

Sunday	*Ihud*	Thursday	*Hamus*
Monday	*Segno*	Friday	*Arb*
Tuesday	*Maksegno*	Saturday	*Kidame*
Wednesday	*Irob*		

Festivals

New Year   *Inkutatash*
Christmas   *Gena*
Easter   *Fasika*

Time

(see box *Ethiopian time*, page 12)

Tigrigna

Many people in Tigrai speak no Amharigna, so a few words of the local language – which shares many words with Amharigna as the two are both derived from Ge'ez – might be useful:

bad	*himek*	milk	*tsaba*
banana	*mu-uz*	nice	*dehan*
beautiful	*gondjo*	no	*nanai*
black	*tselim*	No	*yechone*
border	*dob*	OK	*hirai*
bus	*shishento*	rain	*zenab*
chicken	*dorho*	red	*kaje*
coffee	*buna*	room (in hotel)	*madakasi*
come (female)	*ne'e*	sick	*houmoum*
come (male)	*na'a*	tea	*shai*
egg	*unkulale*	thank you	*yekanyelay*
excuse me	*yikerta*	The coffee tastes good	*oo-oum buna*
fine	*tsebuk*	This way	*uzi*
food	*migbi*	today	*lomo anti*
go	*kid*	toilet	*shintebet*
good	*tsbuk*	tomorrow	*naga*
goodbye	*selamat* or *daahankun*	water	*mai*
hello	*selam*	What is your name?	*shimka men yoe?*
here	*hausi*	where?	*lave?*
How are you? (female)	*Kemayla-hee*	white	*tsada*
How are you? (male)	*Kemayla-ha*	yes	*ouwa*
How much?	*Kendai*	yesterday	*tsbah*
is there...?	*alo...?*		

Numbers

1	*hada*	6	*shidista*
2	*kilita*	7	*showata*
3	*salista*	8	*shimwunta*
4	*arbata*	9	*tishiata*
5	*hamishte*	10	*aseta*

Oromifa

Oromifa is the main language of southern Ethiopia, spoken throughout the Federal State of Oromia. Unlike Amharigna, it is transcribed using familiar Roman numerals, though with little consistency in spelling. In theory, the consonants are doubled to denote a stress (with *manna*, for instance, you would stress the 'n') while doubled vowels denote that the sound of that vowel should be longer than a single vowel. In practice, the application of the doubled letter seems rather more arbitrary – one signpost in any given town might read 'hotela' (hotel), another 'hootteellaa', and others different variants thereof. There is no overwhelming need to speak any Oromifa – everybody in this area speaks some Amharigna – other than the delight that it will give Oromifa speakers to hear a *faranji* speak their language.

Some Oromifa words and phrases

again	*ammas, lammaffaa*	man	*dira*
bar	*manna buna*	market	*gabaaya/gabaa*
black	*guracha*	mineral water	*bishaan amo*
brown	*magala*	money	*qarshi*
bus	*awtobisii*	mosquito	*bookee busaa*
business	*daldala*	mother	*haadha*
buy	*bituu*	mountain	*tullu*
child	*muca*	no (I do not)	*wawu/laki*
church building	*mana kadhataa*	no problem	*rakkon hin jiru*
coffee	*buna*	now	*amma*
cost	*gati*	office	*wajira*
Did you understand?	*Isini galeeraa?*	please	*maaloo*
Do you speak	*Afaan faranji ni*	police	*polisii*
English?	*beektaa?*	post office	*mana posta*
drink	*dhugi*	quantity	*baay'ina*
early	*dafee*	red	*dima*
eat	*nyaadhu*	restaurant	*mana nyaataa*
enter	*deenaa*	road	*daandii, karaa*
far	*fagoo*	room	*kutaa*
father	*abba*	shop	*sukii*
fire	*ibidda*	sister	*obboleettii*
friend	*michu*	tea	*shaayii*
go	*deemuu*	thank you	*galatoomi/ galatoomaa*
goodbye	*nagaan turi*	there	*achi*
green	*magarisa*	today	*har'a*
grey	*dalacha*	toilet	*mana fincaanii*
hello	*ashamaa/akkam/attam*	tomorrow	*booru*
here	*as*	traveller	*kara-adeemtuu*
hotel	*hoteela/*	village	*ganda*
	mana keessummaa	water	*bishaan*
house	*mana/manna*	We are visitors	*Nuyi duwwattoota*
How are you?	*Attam jirta/jirtu?*	What is your name?	*Maqaan kee eenyu?*
How much? (price)	*Mega?*	when	*yoom*
I am fine	*Nagaa/Fayyaa*	Where is it?	*Eessa?/Eessa dha?*
lady	*gifti*	white	*adi*
lake	*garba*	woman	*dubartii*
late	*yeroo dabarsuu*	yellow	*kelloo*
light	*ibsaa*	yes (I do)	*eeyyee*

Days of the week

Sunday	*Dilbata*	Thursday	*Kamsa*
Monday	*Wiixata*	Friday	*Jimata*
Tuesday	*Kibxata*	Saturday	*Sanbata*
Wednesday	*Roobii*		

Numbers

1	*toko*	6	*jaha*
2	*lama*	7	*torba*
3	*sadi*	8	*saddet*
4	*afur*	9	*sagal*
5	*shan*	10	*kudha*

11	kudha-tokko	60	jaatama
12	kudha-lama	70	torbatama
20	digdama	80	saddeettama
30	sodoma	90	sagaltama
40	afurtama	100	dhiba
50	shantama	1,000	kuma

Speaking English to Ethiopians

As you learn to speak a bit of Amharigna, you will generally find your skill at communicating in the language is largely dependent on the imagination and empathy of the person you are speaking to. The moment some people realise you know a few words, they will speak to you as if you are fluent and make you feel thoroughly hopeless. Other people will take care to speak slowly and to stick to common words, and as a result you feel as if you're making real progress. The same principle applies in reverse and, as a result, many Ethiopians find it easier to communicate in English with native French or Italian speakers than they do with native English speakers.

Communicating with Ethiopians is not just about learning Amharigna, but also about pitching your use of English to reflect Ethiopian idiosyncrasies of pronunciation, grammar and vocabulary. In other words, the English-language communication skills of any Ethiopian you meet will partly be dependent on *your* empathy and imagination.

The first and most obvious rule is to speak slowly and clearly. If you are not understood at first, don't simply repeat the same phrase but look for different, less complex ways of conveying the same idea.

A good way of getting a feel for pronunciation is to look at the English transcription of Amharigna words that were initially borrowed from English – *meelyon* (million), *giroseri* (grocery) or *keelometer* (kilometre). A common tendency is to make more emphatic vowel sounds. Another tendency, presumably because few Ethiopian words have consonants without a vowel in between, is to drop things like the 'r' in import (so it sounds like *im-pot*), or else to insert a vowel sound – often an 'ee' or 'i' – between consonants (I pointed one Ethiopian girl to the market when she asked for a *pinipal*; it was only when she took out a pen and paper I realised it was a penpal and not a pineapple she was after).

Remember, too, that there is always a tendency to use the grammatical phrasing of your home tongue when you speak a second language. For instance, an Ethiopian might ask you 'time how much?', which is a direct translation of *sa'at sintno?*. They are more likely to understand *you* if you say 'time how much?' – or at least keep your question as straightforward as possible, for instance 'what is the time?' – than if you ask something more embroidered like 'do you happen to have the time on you?' Many English-speakers are inclined to fluff straightforward queries to strangers with apologetic phrasing like 'I'm terribly sorry' or 'could you tell me'. In an Ethiopian context, this sort of thing just obstructs communication.

You will find that certain common English words are readily understood by Ethiopians, while other equally common words draw a complete blank. The Amharigna word *bet* literally means house, but it is used to describe any building or even a room, so that a *postabet* is a post office, a *bunabet* is a coffee shop, and a *shintabet* is a toilet. You will thus find that Ethiopians often use the English word 'house' in a much looser context that we would. Another example of this is the phrase 'it is possible', which for some reason has caught on almost everywhere in Africa. 'It is possible to find a bus?' is more likely to be understood than 'do you know if there is a bus?'. Likewise, 'is not possible' is a more commonly used phrase than 'it is impossible'.

This sort of thing occurs on an individual level as well as a general one. One Ethiopian friend used the word 'disturb' to cover every imaginable simile of the word. If a phrase like 'I am angry about this' or 'this is really noisy' didn't click, then 'I am much disturb over this' certainly would. Another middle-aged friend kept referring to a girl in her late teens as his parent – presumably he meant cousin. One decided 'plonker' who befriended me kept talking about my family (he must have said 'I think you have good family' 50 times); it took me some time to realise that the family to which he was referring was in fact the hotel where I was staying. The point being not only to attune yourself to the nuances of English as it is spoken in Ethiopia, but also to pick up on the words favoured by individuals, and to try to stick to words you have heard them use.

Finally, you should be aware that when Ethiopians ask you to play with them, they only want to talk. This one has all sorts of potential for misunderstandings. I was thrown a little on my first night in Addis when a bar girl (local euphemism for prostitute) sat down at my table and suggested 'we play?'. A woman travelling on her own might – understandably to us, but not to the enquirer – respond rather curtly to such a suggestion. This is because the Amharigna phrase used in the same situation – *techawat* (say something) – is the imperative of both *mechewawot* (talk) and *mechawot* (play)!

Appendix 4

GLOSSARY

Abba	Father (priest)
Abuna	Metropolitan of Ethiopia Church of Suffragan Bishop
Amba	Hill or mountain with flat top, often the site of a monastery or church
Ambo	Fizzy bottled mineral water, named after the town from where it is sourced
Amharigna	Amharic, language of the Amhara people and national language of Ethiopia
Animist	Religion worshipping ancestors and/or animate objects (plants, animals)
Ato	Mister
Autobus (terra)	Bus (station)
Bet	Literally 'house', often used to denote a shop (eg: *buna bet* = coffee shop)
Bet Israel	see *Falasha*
Bet Kristian	Church
Buna	Coffee
Chat	Mildly narcotic leaf chewed in vast quantities in Muslim areas
Coptic Church	Alexandria-based Church affiliated to but not synonymous with Ethiopian Orthodox Church
Derg	Military socialist dictatorship 1974–91
Endemic	Bird or mammal found only in one country
Enset	Type of plantain (false-banana) grown widely in southern Ethiopia
Falasha	Ethiopian group who practise an archaic form of Judaism
Ful	Popular vegetarian breakfast dish, often very garlicky
Gabbi	Plain off-white cotton cloth worn toga-like by rural Ethiopian men, particularly in the north
Galla	Obsolete term for people now known as the Oromo
Gari	Horse-drawn cart used for carrying goods and passengers
Ge'ez	Archaic language, used in Ethiopian Church, root of Amharigna
Ghebbi	Palace or large house
Injera	Vast pancake made from fermented *tef*, the staple diet of Ethiopians
Itegue	Empress/Princess
Kidus	Saint
Kitfo	Local delicacy made with minced meat, often raw or very lightly cooked
Maize	Corn
Mana/Manna	Oromifa equivalent of Amharigna 'bet' (eg: *manna buna* = coffee house/shop)
Mercato	Market
Meskel	Cross; also the name of a religious ceremony and yellow flower
Monolithic church	Rock-hewn church standing free from the surrounding rock on all four sides
Monotheistic	One God; used to describe the Judaic faiths: Christianity, Islam and Judaism
Negus	King

Netela	Cotton cloth similar to *gabbi*, but with embroidered edge, worn by women
Nine Saints	5th–6th-century saints who are largely responsible for spread of Christianity beyond Axum
Oromifa	Language spoken by the Oromo people
Ras	Prince
Selassie	Trinity
Semi-monolithic church	Rock-hewn church standing free from the rock on three sides
Shai	Tea
Shama	White cloth worn toga-like by Ethiopian women
Shifta	Bandit
Stele (pl: stelae)	A standing stone or obelisk, usually marking a grave in Ethiopia
Tabot	Replica of the Ark of the Covenant that sanctifies an Ethiopian church
Tankwa	Papyrus boat
Tef	Grain endemic to the Ethiopian Highlands
Tej	Mead-like alcoholic drink made from honey or sugar
Tella	Thick low-alcohol 'beer' made from millet or barley
Tholoh	Tigraian dish of barley balls dunked fondue-style in a spicy sauce
Tukul	Round thatched house
Wat	Sauce, often spicy, eaten with *injera*
Waziro	Mrs

Appendix 5

KEY HISTORICAL AND LEGENDARY FIGURES IN ETHIOPIA

Following the Ethiopian custom, Ethiopian figures are listed by their name, not by their father's name.

Abadir Umar Arrida	13th-century sheikh regarded to be the holiest saint of Harar
Abba Jiffar II	Powerful late 19th-century ruler of Jimma
Abreha we Atsbeha	4th-century twin emperors of Axum who adopted these names after converting to Christianity
Afewerk Tekle	Ethiopia's leading post-World War II artist with noted works in St George Cathedral and Africa Hall in Addis Ababa
Afse, Abba	5th–6th century, one of the Nine Saints, founded church in Yeha
Ahmed Gragn	16th-century Muslim leader who waged *jihad* against Christian empire
Alvares, Francisco	16th-century Portuguese priest who spent a decade in Ethiopia, visiting Lalibela and other important sites
Aregawi, Abba	5th–6th century, one of the Nine Saints, founded Debre Damo monastery
Arwe	Legendary serpent king of pre-Judaic cult of Axum area, killed by a royal ancestor of the Queen of Sheba
Aster Aweke	Popular modern Ethiopian female singer, now based in USA
Athanasius	4th-century Patriarch of Egyptian Coptic Church who baptised Frumentius and died a refugee in Ethiopia
Bani al-Hamuya	10th-century queen, led attack on Axum, often identified with Yodit, more likely from pagan Damot Empire
Basen	Important Axumite king, ruled at about the time of Christ
Bruce, James	18th-century Scottish explorer who travelled widely in Ethiopia, credited as finding source of Blue Nile
Burton, Sir Richard	19th-century explorer, first European to visit Harar
Cosmos Indicopleustes	Alexandrian merchant who visited Ethiopia in 6th century and wrote detailed account of trip
Da Gama, Christopher	Leader of 16th-century Portuguese expedition to find Prester John, died in battle in Muslim war
De Covilhão, Pero	Spanish Jesuit 'spy' sent by King John of Portugal to the Kingdom of Prester John during rule of Susneyos
Eleni	Influential wife of Zara Yaqob, who she outlived by 50 years; regent during the early rule of Lebna Dengal
Ethiopic	Legendary great-grandson of Noah, said to have founded Ethiopia
Ezana	Pre-Christian name of Axumite emperor later known as Abreha, regarded to be greatest of Axumite rulers
Fasilidas	Emperor of Ethiopia 1632–67, son of Susneyos, restored Orthodox Church and civil order, founded Gonder
Frumentius	4th-century priest, converted Axumite rulers and became first Patriarch of Ethiopian Church

Gadarat	2nd-century Axumite king credited with expanding the empire into modern Yemen
Galawdewos	Ethiopian emperor who defeated Ahmed Gragn in battle (with Portuguese assistance) in 1543
Garima, Abba	5th–6th century, one of the Nine Saints, founded eponymous monastery south of Adwa
Gebre Meskel	6th-century Axumite king, son of Kaleb, associated with foundation of several monasteries
Gebriel	Archangel Gabriel
Giyorgis	Ethiopian name for St George
Graziani, Rudolfo	Viceroy of Ethiopia during Italian occupation
Gudit	Synonym for Yodit (Judith)
Habbuba, Emir	Legendary 10th-century founder of Harar
Haile Selassie	Last Emperor of Ethiopia, murdered 1974
Ilg, Alfred	Swiss advisor to Menelik II, played a major role in development of Ethiopia during Menelik's rule
Iskinder	Emperor of Ethiopia 1478–94, ascended to throne aged eight, died in battle aged 24
Iyasu	Emperor of Ethiopia 1682–1706, strongest of Gonderine rulers
Iyasu II	Emperor of Ethiopia 1913–16, ousted in conspiracy led by Ras Tefari
Iyasus	Ethiopian name for Jesus, several variants of spelling in use
Iyasus Moa	Eminent monk trained at Debre Damo, founded Hayk Istafanos monastery, helped 'restore' Solomonic rule
Jafar Taleb	6th–7th-century cousin and follower of prophet Mohammed, founder of Islamic community in Ethiopia
Kaleb	6th-century Axumite king, successful military expansionist, built large palace outside modern Axum
Lalibela	12th-century emperor and saint, excavated the complex of churches in the town that is now named for him
Lebna Dengal	Emperor of Ethiopia 1508–40, name translates as 'Incense of the Virgin', died during war with Ahmed Gragn
Libanos, Abba	5th–6th century, one of Nine Saints, eminent monastery of Debre Libanos named for him
Lij Iyasu	see Iyasu II
Lucy	Name given to 3.5-million-year-old human skull found in Hadar in 1974
Makeda	Ethiopian name for Queen of Sheba
Maryam	Ethiopian name for Mary, mother of Jesus Christ
Meles Zenawi	Prime Minister of Ethiopia 1991–present
Menelik I	Legendary Axumite king, credited by tradition as founding Axum circa 1000BC
Menelik II	Emperor of Ethiopia 1889–1913, defeated Italy at Battle of Adwa; founded Addis Ababa
Mengistu Haile Maryam	Dictatorial leader of Ethiopia 1974–91
Mentewab	Queen Consort 1730–55 after death of husband Bakafa, end of reign signalled end of Gonderine strength
Nakuta La'ab	Nephew and successor to Emperor Lalibela, founded eponymous monastery outside Lalibela town
Napier, Sir Robert	Led 1869 British military expedition that led to defeat and suicide of Tewodros II
Nur Ibn al-Wazir	Nephew and successor to Ahmed Gragn as leader of Harar, continued Gragn's *jihad*

Pais, Pero	Priest whose conversion of Susneyos to Catholicism sparked a civil war and led to expulsion of Portuguese
Pantaleon, Abba	5th–6th century, one of Nine Saints, founded eponymous monastery near modern Axum
Prester John	Legendary medieval figure, ruled rich Christian empire in Indies, possibly based on emperor of Ethiopia
Queen of Sheba	Legendary queen, claimed by Ethiopians as Axumite mother of Menelik I, more probably Yemeni
Ramhai	3rd-century Axumite ruler associated with the largest stele (33m high) ever erected in ancient times
Ras Desta Demtew	Son-in-law of Haile Selassie, led unsuccessful military campaign against Italian invasion in 1936
Ras Mekonnen	Nobleman appointed as governor of Harar by Menelik II, father of future Emperor Haile Selassie
Ras Mikael Ali	Powerful late 19th-century ruler of Wolo, ally of Menelik II, grandfather of Emperor Iyasu II
Ras Tefari	Pre-coronation name of Emperor Haile Selassie
Rimbaud, Arthur	Prodigal French poet who abandoned poetry aged 19 to end up dealing arms in Harar
Sahle Selassie	Expansionist ruler of Showa 1813–47, paved way for grandson Menelik II's eventual rise to emperor
Salama, Abba	Pseudonymous with Frumentius
Solomon	King of Israel, legendarily said to have sired Menelik I
Susneyos	Early 17th-century emperor, converted by Portuguese Jesuits causing civil war, abdicated 1632
Taitu	Wife of Menelik II, co-founder of Addis Ababa
Tekle Haymanot	Priest who spread Christianity through Showa in the 13th century, and founded Debre Libanos monastery
Tekle Haymanot	10th-century emperor credited as founding Zagwe dynasty and effectively ending Axumite era
Tewodros II	Emperor of Ethiopia 1855–69, first emperor in a century to unify fiefdoms of various princes
Yakuno Amlak	13th-century emperor who founded (or restored) Solomonic dynasty
Yared	6th-century priest, patronised by King Gebre Meskel, credited with writing most Ethiopian church music
Yemrehanna Kristos	Medieval emperor, predecessor of Lalibela. Best known for the eponymous church he built near Bilbilla
Yodit	Legendarily militant 9th-century Falasha queen, razed Axum and many churches in northern Ethiopia
Yohannis IV	Emperor of Ethiopia 1872–89, played a major role uniting Ethiopia
Zara Yaqob	15th-century emperor, founded several churches and monasteries, as well as town of Debre Birhan
Zawditu	Empress of Ethiopia 1921–30, daughter of Menelik II

Note The titles 'Emperor' and 'King' are occasionally used interchangeably in the text, in reference to particular heads of state.

Appendix 6

SOME ETHIOPIC TRANSCRIPTIONS OF PLACE NAMES
By Yared Belete of Grant Express Travel and Tours Services (GETTS)

Abi Aday	አቢአዳ	Dinsho	ዲንሾ
Adadi	አዳዲ	Dire Dawa	ድሬዳዋ
Adama / Nazret	አዳማ/ናዝሬት/	Djibouti	ጆቡቲ
Addis Ababa / Finfine	አዲስ አበባ/ፍንፍኔ/ .	Dodola	ዶዶላ
Addis Alem	አዲስ አለም	Dola Mena	ዶሎ መና
Adi Arkay	አዲ አርቃዬ	Entoto	እንጦጦ
Adigrat	አዲግራት	Fiche	ፍቼ
Adwa	አድዋ	Gambella	ጋምቤላ
Akaki Beseka	አቃቂ በስቃ	Gefersa	ገፈርሳ
Alem Katema	አለም ከተማ	Goba	ጎባ
Aliyu Amba	አልዩ አምባ	Gonder	ጎንደር
Ambo	አምቦ	Gorgora	ጎርጎራ
Ankober	አንኮበር	Harar	ሐረር
Arba Minch	አርባ ምንጭ	Hawzien	ሐውዜን
Arero	አረሮ	Hayk	ሃይቅ
Arsi Negele	አርሲ ነገሌ	Hosaina	ሆሳእና
Asbe Teferi	አሰበ ተፈሪ	Inda Selassie / Shire	እንዳስላሴ/ሽሬ
Asela	አሰላ	Jijiga	ጅጅጋ
Assaita	አሳይታ	Jimma	ጅማ
Atsbi	አጽቢ	Jinka	ጅንካ
Awash	አዋሽ	Karat / Konso	ካራት/ኮንሶ
Awassa	አዋሳ	Kebre Mengist	ክብረመንግሥት
Axum	አክሱም	Kombolcha	ኮምቦልቻ
Babile	ባቢሌ	Kosober / Injibara	ኮሶበር/እንጅብራ
Bahir Dar	ባህር ዳር	Lalibela	ላሊበላ
Bati	ባቲ	Matu	መቱ
Bedele	በደሌ	Maychew	ማይጨው
Bilbilla	ቢልቢላ	Mega	መሐል ሜዳ
Bishoftu / Debre Zeyit	ቢሾፍቱ/ደብረዘይት/	Mehal Meda	መቀሌ
Butajira	ቡታጀራ	Mekele	ሜታ
Chencha	ጨንቻ	Metahara	መተሐራ
Debark	ደባርቅ	Mille	ሚሌ
Debre Birhan	ደብረብርሃን	Mizan Tefari	ሚዛን ተፈሪ
Debre Markos	ደብረማርቆስ	Mojo	ሞጆ
Debre Sina	ደብረሲና	Nechisar	ነጭሳር
Debre Tabor	ደብረታቦር	Negash	ነጋሽ
Dembidolo	ደምቢዶሎ	Negele	ነገሌ
Dessie	ደሴ	Nekemte	ነቀምቲ
Dilla	ዲላ	Robe	ሮቢ

585

Sekota	ሰቆጣ	Tiya	ጢያ
Sela Dingay	ሰላድንጋይ	Weliso	ወሊሶ
Senkele	ሰንቀሌ	Welkite	ወልቂጤ
Shashemene	ሻሸሙኔ	Woldia	ወልድያ
Silté	ስልጤ	Wondo Genet	ወንዶገነት
Simien	ሰሜን	Wukro	ውቅሮ
Sinkata	ሰንቃጣ	Yabello	ያቤሎ
Sodo / Walaita	ሶዶ/ወላይታ	Yeha	የሃ
Sodore	ሶደሬ	Zege	ዘጌ
Sof Omar	ሶፍኡመር	Zikwala	ዝቋላ
Tarmabir	ጣርማበር	Ziway	ዝዋይ

E-moil   joseaba12@yohoo.com.

YOSEPh. Abony

Bradt Travel Guides

Africa Overland	£15.99	Kenya	£14.95
Albania	£13.95	Kiev City Guide	£7.95
Amazon	£14.95	Latvia	£13.99
Antarctica: A Guide to the Wildlife	£14.95	Lille City Guide	£6.99
The Arctic: A Guide to Coastal		Lithuania	£13.99
Wildlife	£14.95	Ljubljana City Guide	£6.99
Armenia with Nagorno Karabagh	£13.95	London: In the Footsteps of	
Azores	£12.95	the Famous	£10.95
Baghdad City Guide	£9.95	Macedonia	£13.95
Baltic Capitals: Tallinn, Riga,		Madagascar	£14.95
Vilnius, Kaliningrad	£11.95	Madagascar Wildlife	£14.95
Bosnia & Herzegovina	£13.95	Malawi	£12.95
Botswana: Okavango Delta,		Maldives	£13.99
Chobe, Northern Kalahari	£14.95	Mali	£13.95
British Isles: Wildlife of Coastal		Mauritius	£12.95
Waters	£14.95	Mongolia	£14.95
Budapest City Guide	£7.95	Montenegro	£13.99
Cambodia	£11.95	Mozambique	£12.95
Cameroon	£13.95	Namibia	£14.95
Canada: North – Yukon, Northwest Territories		Nigeria	£15.99
£13.95		North Cyprus	£12.95
Canary Islands	£13.95	North Korea	£13.95
Cape Verde Islands	£12.95	Palestine with Jerusalem	£12.95
Cayman Islands	£12.95	Panama	£13.95
Chile	£16.95	Paris, Lille & Brussels: Eurostar Cities	£11.95
Chile & Argentina: Trekking Guide	£12.95	Peru & Bolivia: Backpacking &	
China: Yunnan Province	£13.95	Trekking	£12.95
Cork City Guide	£6.95	Riga City Guide	£6.95
Costa Rica	£13.99	River Thames: In the	
Croatia	£12.95	Footsteps of the Famous	£10.95
Dubrovnik City Guide	£6.95	Rwanda	£13.95
East & Southern Africa:		St Helena, Ascension,	
Backpacker's Manual	£14.95	Tristan da Cunha	£14.95
Eccentric America	£13.95	Serbia	£13.99
Eccentric Britain	£13.99	Seychelles	£13.99
Eccentric California	£13.99	Singapore	£11.95
Eccentric Edinburgh	£5.95	Slovenia	£12.99
Eccentric France	£12.95	South Africa: Budget Travel Guide	£11.95
Eccentric London	£12.95	Southern African Wildlife	£18.95
Eccentric Oxford	£5.95	Spitsbergen	£14.99
Ecuador, Peru & Bolivia:		Sri Lanka	£12.95
Backpacker's Manual	£13.95	Sudan	£13.95
Ecuador: Climbing & Hiking	£13.95	Switzerland: Rail, Road, Lake	£12.99
Eritrea	£12.95	Tallinn City Guide	£6.95
Estonia	£12.95	Tanzania	£14.95
Ethiopia	£13.95	Tasmania	£12.95
Falkland Islands	£13.95	Turkmenistan	£14.99
Faroe Islands	£13.95	Tibet	£12.95
Gabon, São Tomé & Príncipe	£13.95	Uganda	£13.95
Galápagos Wildlife	£15.99	Ukraine	£14.95
Gambia, The	£12.95	USA by Rail	£13.99
Georgia with Armenia	£13.95	Venezuela	£14.95
Ghana	£13.95	Vilnius City Guide	£6.99
Hungary	£14.99	Your Child Abroad: A Travel	
Iran	£14.99	Health Guide	£9.95
Iraq	£14.95	Zambia	£15.95
Kabul Mini Guide	£9.95	Zanzibar	£12.95

WIN £100 CASH!

READER QUESTIONNAIRE

**Send in your completed questionnaire for the chance to win
£100 cash in our regular draw**

All respondents may order a Bradt guide at half the UK retail price – please
complete the order form overleaf.

(Entries may be posted or faxed to us, or scanned and emailed.)

We are interested in getting feedback from our readers to help us plan future Bradt
guides. Please complete this quick questionnaire and return it to us to enter into
our draw.

Have you used any other Bradt guides? If so, which titles? . . . .
. . . .

What other publishers' travel guides do you use regularly? . . . .
. . . .

Where did you buy this guidebook? . . . .

What was the main purpose of your trip to Ethiopia (or for what other reason did
you read our guide)? eg: holiday/business/charity etc.. . . . .
. . . .

What other destinations would you like to see covered by a Bradt guide?
. . . .

Would you like to receive our catalogue/newsletters?

YES / NO (If yes, please complete details on reverse)

If yes – by post or email? . . . .

Age (circle relevant category) 16–25   26–45   46–60   60+

Male/Female (delete as appropriate)

Home country . . . .

Please send us any comments about our guide to Ethiopia or other Bradt Travel
Guides. . . . .
. . . .
. . . .
. . . .

Bradt Travel Guides
23 High Street, Chalfont St Peter, Bucks SL9 9QE, UK
Telephone: +44 (0)1753 893444 Fax: +44 (0)1753 892333
Email: info@bradtguides.com
www.bradtguides.com

CLAIM YOUR HALF-PRICE BRADT GUIDE!

Order Form

To order your half-price copy of a Bradt guide, and to enter our prize draw to win £100 (see overleaf), please fill in the order form below, complete the questionnaire overleaf, and send it to Bradt Travel Guides by post, fax or email.

Please send me one copy of the following guide at half the UK retail price

Title   *Retail price*   *Half price*

... .

Please send the following additional guides at full UK retail price

No   *Title*   *Retail price*   *Total*

...   .

...   .

...   .

                                         Sub total ....

                              Post & packing ....

(£1 per book UK; £2 per book Europe; £3 per book rest of world)

                                           Total ....

Name ....

Address ....

Tel .... Email ....

☐ I enclose a cheque for £ .... made payable to Bradt Travel Guides Ltd

☐ I would like to pay by credit card. Number: ....

    Expiry date: ... / ...   3-digit security code (on reverse of card) .....

☐ Please add my name to your catalogue mailing list.

☐ I would be happy for you to use my name and comments in Bradt marketing material.

Send your order on this form, with the completed questionnaire, to:

Bradt Travel Guides/ETH
23 High Street, Chalfont St Peter, Bucks SL9 9QE
Tel: +44 (0)1753 893444 Fax: +44 (0)1753 892333
Email: info@bradtguides.com   www.bradtguides.com

Index

Page references in italics indicate maps

∂ 242
2 2136